ALMANAC

Contributing Writers

Marty Strasen
Mike Sheridan
Nick Rousso
Michael Bradley
Pete Palmer
Bruce Herman
Murray Rubenfeld
Vince Vittore
Bob Bellotti

Marty Strasen is a sports writer for the *Waterloo Courier* in Iowa and has also written for several major newspapers, including the *Detroit Free Press*. He is a former assistant editor of *Basketball Weekly*.

Mike Sheridan is managing editor of *Basketball Times* and *Eastern Basketball*.

Nick Rousso is editor of *Ultimate Sports Basketball*. He is the former editor of *Dick Vitale's Basketball* and *Don Heinrich's College Football* and was an associate editor for *Bill Mazeroski's Baseball, The Show,* and *Don Heinrich's Pro Preview*.

Michael Bradley is a freelance writer whose work has appeared in *The Sporting News, The Philadelphia Inquirer,* and a variety of national sports publications.

Pete Palmer edited both *Total Baseball* and *The Hidden Game of Baseball* with John Thorn. He was the statistician for *1996 Baseball Almanac* and *1992 Fantasy League Baseball*. Palmer is a member of the Society for American Baseball Research (SABR).

Bruce Herman is a sports writer and consultant who's contributed to The Topps Company, ESPN, Tribune Media Services, Dunfey Publishing, several major-league baseball teams, *Sports Illustrated, USA Today Baseball Weekly,* and *Inside Sports*.

Murray Rubenfeld is executive producer of "The Sports Card Report Radio Show" and has written extensively on basketball for several hobby publications. He is a basketball card price-guide analyst for *The Sports Card News* and *The Confident Collectors Basketball Card Price Guide*.

Vince Vittore is an editor at *Cable World* and a freelance writer.

Bob Bellotti is the author of five books on the NBA, including *The Points Created Pro Basketball Book*. Since 1989, he has worked as a statistical consultant to NBA teams. He also has been a correspondent for *The Sporting News* since 1993.

Statistics in the College Basketball Review section were provided by the National Collegiate Athletic Association.

Front cover photo: Jonathan Daniel/Allsport USA.
Back cover photo: Doug Pensinger/Allsport USA.

CONTENTS

4 CONTENTS

CONTENTS

6   CONTENTS

NBA Veterans and Rookies

In this section, you'll find scouting reports on 300 NBA veterans and 60 NBA rookies (plus a recap of the 1996 college draft on page 308). The NBA will tip off the 1996-97 season with 348 players, so this section is sure to include most every player on each NBA roster.

Each player's scouting report begins with his vital stats: team, position, height, weight, etc. Next comes a four-part evaluation of the player. "Background" reviews the player's career, starting with college and continuing up through the 1995-96 season. "Strengths" examines his best assets, including such traits as character and leadership. "Weaknesses" assesses the player's significant flaws, including things like attitude and off-court behavior. And "analysis" tries to put the player's game into perspective.

For a quick run-down on each player, you'll find a "player summary" box. The box also includes a "fantasy value" figure, which suggests a draft price for any of the fantasy basketball games that have mushroomed throughout the country. The price range is a guide based on $260 for a 15-player roster. Some players are valued at $0, meaning they are not worth drafting. Finally, the box contains a "card value" figure, which is a suggested buying price for a mint 1995-96 basketball card of that player. The values do not reflect cards from premium sets.

The scouting reports of the NBA veterans include their college and NBA statistics. The college stats include games (G), field-goal percentage (FGP), free-throw percentage (FTP), rebounds per game (RPG) or assists per game (APG), and points per game (PPG). The veterans' NBA stats include the following:

- games (G)
- minutes (MIN)
- field goals made (FGs/FG)
- field-goal percentage (FGs/PCT)
- 3-point field goals made (3-PT FGs/FG)
- 3-point field-goal percentage (3-PT FGs/PCT)
- free throws made (FTs/FT)
- free-throw percentage (FTs/PCT)
- offensive rebounds (Rebounds/OFF)
- total rebounds (Rebounds/TOT)
- assists (AST)
- steals (STL)
- blocked shots (BLK)
- points (PTS)
- points per game (PPG)

The 60 NBA rookies receive half-page write-ups with abbreviated statistics.

MAHMOUD ABDUL-RAUF

Team: Sacramento Kings
Position: Guard
Height: 6'1" **Weight:** 162
Birthdate: March 9, 1969
NBA Experience: 6 years

College: Louisiana St.
Acquired: Traded from Nuggets for Sarunas Marciulionis and a 1996 second-round pick, 6/96

Background: In two seasons at LSU, the former Chris Jackson broke NCAA freshman records for points in a game against a Division I opponent (55), points in a season (965), and scoring average (30.2 PPG). He spent six years with Denver, winning the 1992-93 Most Improved Player Award before converting to Islam in 1993. He established several career highs during the 1995-96 season and was dealt to the Kings in the off-season.

Strengths: Abdul-Rauf is one of the sweetest shooters in the game. He missed only ten of his 229 free throws in 1993-94, and he again led the league in that category last season (.930). He sticks the 3-pointer with ease. The ball seems to be attached to the hand of Abdul-Rauf, who is one of the quickest men in basketball. He averaged a career-best 19.2 PPG in 1995-96.

Weaknesses: Abdul-Rauf has been called a shooting guard trapped in a point guard's body. He generally looks for the shot before the pass. Nuggets coach Bernie Bickerstaff preferred to call him a "quasi-guard," meaning Abdul-Rauf can do it all. However, he does play defense like many great shooters. A foot injury hampered him late last year.

Analysis: Abdul-Rauf, who has overcome Tourette's Syndrome (a neurological disorder), made more headlines for a pre-game move than for any of his on-court accomplishments last year. Citing religious reasons, he refused to stand for the national anthem and was promptly suspended by the NBA. After much criticism, he opted to stand and pray, and was reinstated for the remainder of the season.

PLAYER SUMMARY

Will........................score from all over
Can't ....dominate on defense
Expect ....automatic free throws
Don't Expect ....patriotism
Fantasy Value $10-12
Card Value ....8-15¢

COLLEGE STATISTICS

		G	FGP	FTP	APG	PPG
88-89	LSU	32	.486	.815	4.1	30.2
89-90	LSU	32	.461	.910	3.2	27.8
Totals		64	.474	.863	3.6	29.0

NBA REGULAR-SEASON STATISTICS

				FGs		3-PT FGs		FTs		Rebounds						
		G	MIN	FG	PCT	FG	PCT	FT	PCT	OFF	TOT	AST	STL	BLK	PTS	PPG
90-91	DEN	67	1505	417	.413	24	.240	84	.857	34	121	206	55	4	942	14.1
91-92	DEN	81	1538	356	.421	31	.330	94	.870	22	114	192	44	4	837	10.3
92-93	DEN	81	2710	633	.450	70	.355	217	.935	51	225	344	84	8	1553	19.2
93-94	DEN	80	2617	588	.460	42	.316	219	.956	27	168	362	82	10	1437	18.0
94-95	DEN	73	2082	472	.470	83	.386	138	.885	32	137	263	77	9	1165	16.0
95-96	DEN	57	2029	414	.434	121	.392	146	.930	26	138	389	64	3	1095	19.2
Totals		439	12481	2880	.443	371	.354	898	.916	192	903	1756	406	38	7029	16.0

RAFAEL ADDISON

Team: Charlotte Hornets
Position: Forward/Guard
Height: 6'8" **Weight:** 250
Birthdate: July 22, 1964

NBA Experience: 5 years
College: Syracuse
Acquired: Signed as a free agent, 9/95

Background: Addison was named first-team All-Big East as a junior at Syracuse, where his career scoring average was nearly 15 PPG. After a mediocre senior year, he was drafted in the second round of the NBA draft, spent his rookie year with Phoenix, and played four years in Italy. After a two-year stay with the Nets, he returned to Italy for one more season and has since played single years in Detroit and Charlotte.

Strengths: Addison is a solid defender with a great attitude. He is more than willing to come off the bench and blanket his man, whether it is a guard or a forward. He has a knack for getting his hands on the basketball and possesses above-average spring. He runs the floor and has shown signs of being a good shooter.

Weaknesses: Addison, a marginal offensive player, is not in the league to score. He does very little off the dribble and gets most of his offense on open jumpers and in transition. His shooting range is limited to about 18 feet, and his jump shot is a streaky proposition. Addison has never been a very aware passer.

Analysis: Addison played his best NBA ball with the Pistons for 79 games in 1994-95, but they released him before the end of that season. He did not crack Charlotte's regular rotation last season, when he averaged fewer than ten minutes per game and posted career lows in most categories. He will stick with it, but he needs to hit the jumper to earn a chance.

PLAYER SUMMARY

Will	run, defend
Can't	take over on offense
Expect	a role-player
Don't Expect	starts
Fantasy Value	$0
Card Value	5-8¢

COLLEGE STATISTICS

		G	FGP	FTP	RPG	PPG
82-83	SYR	31	.521	.651	3.2	8.4
83-84	SYR	32	.559	.836	6.0	17.7
84-85	SYR	31	.520	.727	5.8	18.4
85-86	SYR	32	.532	.793	5.6	15.0
Totals		126	.534	.763	5.2	14.9

NBA REGULAR-SEASON STATISTICS

				FGs		3-PT FGs		FTs		Rebounds						
		G	MIN	FG	PCT	FG	PCT	FT	PCT	OFF	TOT	AST	STL	BLK	PTS	PPG
86-87	PHO	62	711	146	.441	16	.320	51	.797	41	106	45	27	7	359	5.8
91-92	NJ	76	1175	187	.433	14	.286	56	.737	65	165	68	28	28	444	5.8
92-93	NJ	68	1164	182	.443	7	.206	57	.814	45	132	53	23	11	428	6.3
94-95	DET	79	1776	279	.476	24	.289	74	.747	67	242	109	53	25	656	8.3
95-96	CHA	53	516	77	.467	0	.000	17	.773	25	90	30	9	9	171	3.2
Totals		338	5342	871	.452	61	.271	255	.770	243	735	305	140	80	2058	6.1

CORY ALEXANDER

Team: San Antonio Spurs
Position: Guard
Height: 6'1" **Weight:** 190
Birthdate: June 22, 1973

NBA Experience: 1 year
College: Virginia
Acquired: First-round pick in 1995 draft (29th overall)

Background: Alexander began his career at Virginia with much promise, but he suffered ankle injuries in each of his last two seasons. He averaged 4.7 APG for his career, second in school history, and was tops among ACC guards with 4.2 RPG in his final season. The last pick in the first round of the 1995 draft, Alexander averaged just 9.3 minutes over 60 games with San Antonio during his rookie campaign.

Strengths: Alexander brings exceptional quickness to the point guard position. He is a true point guard who handles the ball well and knows where to deliver it. He has 3-point range and is expected to be a capable shooter when given the chance. Alexander is not afraid to attack the boards or take the ball into traffic. His quickness also makes him a promising full-court defensive player.

Weaknesses: Alexander has much to prove. His assist-to-turnover ratio was less than 2-to-1 as a rookie, an indication that he was somewhat overwhelmed. He tries to do too much at times and will learn to make better decisions as he sees more minutes. His jump shot and his defense were far from consistent during his debut season. Alexander made less than 70 percent from the line in college and was no better as a pro.

Analysis: Thought to be brittle after two broken ankles at Virginia, Alexander fell to the Spurs despite the fact that some considered him a higher first-round talent. With Avery Johnson and Doc Rivers carrying the Spurs' point guard duties, Alexander earned 17 DNP-CDs (did not play-coach's decision) and sat on the bench for nine of the season's final 31 games. It's hard to evaluate a player based on "garbage" minutes.

PLAYER SUMMARY	
Will	set up the offense
Can't	waste his chances
Expect	good quickness
Don't Expect	heady plays
Fantasy Value	$0
Card Value	12-20¢

COLLEGE STATISTICS

		G	FGP	FTP	APG	PPG
91-92	VIRG	33	.376	.686	4.4	11.2
92-93	VIRG	31	.453	.705	4.6	18.8
93-94	VIRG	1	—	—	2.0	—
94-95	VIRG	20	.452	.701	5.5	16.7
Totals		85	.427	.698	4.7	15.1

NBA REGULAR-SEASON STATISTICS

			FGs		3-PT FGs		FTs		Rebounds						
	G	MIN	FG	PCT	FG	PCT	FT	PCT	OFF	TOT	AST	STL	BLK	PTS	PPG
95-96 SA	60	560	63	.406	26	.394	16	.640	9	42	121	27	2	168	2.8
Totals	60	560	63	.406	26	.394	16	.640	9	42	121	27	2	168	2.8

KENNY ANDERSON

Team: Portland Trail Blazers
Position: Guard
Height: 6'1" **Weight:** 168
Birthdate: October 9, 1970

NBA Experience: 5 years
College: Georgia Tech
Acquired: Signed as a free agent, 7/96

Background: A legend at New York City's Archbishop Malloy High, Anderson was an instant hit at Georgia Tech. He led the ACC in assists as a freshman. He remained at Georgia Tech only through his sophomore season, then joined former teammates Dennis Scott and Brian Oliver in the NBA. After a disappointing rookie season, Anderson emerged and played in the 1994 All-Star Game. He was traded to Charlotte in January, once again finished among league assist leaders, then departed for Portland in the off-season.

Strengths: Anderson is a classic point guard with a scorer's mentality. He is a terrific ball-handler, passer, and penetrator with a special ability to see the floor. He can create plays and finish them and has 3-point range with his awkward-looking jumper. He can operate any offense. Quick hands and superior anticipation work to Anderson's advantage on defense.

Weaknesses: Anderson's slight build did not limit him in college as it does in the NBA. He is a tempting post-up target. His shooting is inconsistent, his best mark from the field being a .435 campaign in 1992-93. Last year he hit at just a .418 rate. He has yet to help a team contend.

Analysis: Anderson certainly produced in New Jersey, but even more was expected of him—a testament to his phenomenal talent as a youngster. Few guards in the game have the ability to see their options and execute them like Anderson. Fans as well as critics are waiting to see better leadership. The trade to the Hornets helped turn down the spotlight and seemed to have aided Anderson. He promises to be a good fit in Portland.

PLAYER SUMMARY	
Will	set up teammates
Can't	live on jump shots
Expect	creative offense
Don't Expect	physical play
Fantasy Value	$20-25
Card Value	10-25¢

COLLEGE STATISTICS

		G	FGP	FTP	APG	PPG
89-90	GT	35	.515	.733	5.3	20.6
90-91	GT	30	.437	.829	5.6	25.9
Totals		65	.473	.787	5.4	23.0

NBA REGULAR-SEASON STATISTICS

		G	MIN	FGs		3-PT FGs		FTs		Rebounds		AST	STL	BLK	PTS	PPG
				FG	PCT	FG	PCT	FT	PCT	OFF	TOT					
91-92	NJ	64	1086	187	.390	3	.231	73	.745	38	127	203	67	9	450	7.0
92-93	NJ	55	2010	370	.435	7	.280	180	.776	51	226	449	96	11	927	16.9
93-94	NJ	82	3135	576	.417	40	.303	346	.818	89	322	784	158	15	1538	18.8
94-95	NJ	72	2689	411	.399	97	.330	348	.841	73	250	680	103	14	1267	17.6
95-96	NJ/CHA	69	2344	349	.418	92	.359	260	.769	63	203	575	111	14	1050	15.2
Totals		342	11264	1893	.414	239	.332	1207	.802	314	1128	2691	535	63	5232	15.3

NICK ANDERSON

Team: Orlando Magic
Position: Guard/Forward
Height: 6'6" **Weight:** 220
Birthdate: January 20, 1968

NBA Experience: 7 years
College: Illinois
Acquired: First-round pick in 1989 draft (11th overall)

Background: Anderson was a unanimous All-Big Ten selection on the "Flying Illini" Final Four team of 1988-89. He was an instant starter and double-figure scorer for Orlando, where he's played all seven of his NBA seasons. He led the Magic in scoring in 1991-92, the year before Shaquille O'Neal joined the team. He has averaged at least 14 PPG every year except his rookie season.

Strengths: Anderson can score in any number of ways. He can get to the hoop with his tremendous quickness and leaping ability, he is a dangerous 3-point shooter, and he is tough for opposing guards to stop in the post. He can also play small forward. He is often asked to guard the other team's top player, and he makes them work for their points.

Weaknesses: Anderson is not the most gifted ball-handler or passer. Most starting two guards have the edge on him there. He has worked to improve his shooting, but his free-throw accuracy still lags behind. Anderson's overall shooting percentage and scoring average dropped last season.

Analysis: Anderson will never attain the NBA stardom he seemed destined for before O'Neal and Anfernee Hardaway joined the Magic. To his credit, he has accepted a lesser role and learned to be a team player for one of the league's top contenders. Anderson is a complete player who works at his game and is capable of huge nights. The Magic will need some huge nights from him now that Shaq's gone.

PLAYER SUMMARY	
Will	bury clutch shots
Can't	handle the ball
Expect	3-pointers
Don't Expect	All-Star honors
Fantasy Value	$19-22
Card Value	8-15¢

COLLEGE STATISTICS

		G	FGP	FTP	RPG	PPG
87-88	ILL	33	.572	.642	6.6	15.9
88-89	ILL	36	.538	.669	7.9	18.0
Totals		69	.553	.657	7.3	17.0

NBA REGULAR-SEASON STATISTICS

				FGs		3-PT FGs		FTs		Rebounds						
		G	MIN	FG	PCT	FG	PCT	FT	PCT	OFF	TOT	AST	STL	BLK	PTS	PPG
89-90	ORL	81	1785	372	.494	1	.059	186	.705	107	316	124	69	34	931	11.5
90-91	ORL	70	1971	400	.467	17	.293	173	.668	92	386	106	74	44	990	14.1
91-92	ORL	60	2203	482	.463	30	.353	202	.667	98	384	163	97	33	1196	19.9
92-93	ORL	79	2920	594	.449	88	.353	298	.741	122	477	265	128	56	1574	19.9
93-94	ORL	81	2811	504	.478	101	.322	168	.672	113	476	294	134	33	1277	15.8
94-95	ORL	76	2588	439	.476	179	.415	143	.708	85	335	314	125	22	1200	15.8
95-96	ORL	77	2717	400	.442	168	.391	166	.692	92	415	279	121	46	1134	14.7
Totals		524	16995	3191	.465	584	.369	1336	.696	709	2789	1545	748	268	8302	15.8

WILLIE ANDERSON

Unrestricted Free Agent
Last Team: New York Knicks
Position: Guard/Forward
Height: 6'8" **Weight:** 200
Birthdate: January 8, 1967

NBA Experience: 8 years
College: Georgia
Acquired: Traded from Raptors with Victor Alexander for Doug Christie and Herb Williams, 2/96

Background: Anderson finished eighth on Georgia's all-time scoring list and played on the United States Olympic team in 1988. After he averaged 18.6 PPG and finished second in Rookie of the Year voting with San Antonio, his scoring average declined for four straight years while leg injuries limited him. He began last season in Toronto before a February trade sent him to New York.

Strengths: Anderson, who was at one time compared to former Spurs great George Gervin, is a versatile veteran. He plays both the two and three spots regularly and can even fill in at the point. He has the agility and moves to drive for dishes or points, and he also shoots with range. Anderson is a quiet leader.

Weaknesses: Anderson will never match his first-year statistical totals. Leg injuries have slowed him, and he no longer shows the offensive confidence he once had. He is not a pure shooter, and he does not possess the explosiveness to the bucket that was his trademark before rods were inserted in both legs. He too often settles for long jumpers.

Analysis: Anderson averaged 12.4 PPG in Toronto, where he started 44 of his 49 games. The trade to New York, however, robbed him of minutes and saw his role reduced. While he is not the player he was in his first few pro seasons, Anderson's ability to play multiple positions will keep him in someone's rotation.

PLAYER SUMMARY	
Will	find a role
Can't	match rookie numbers
Expect	versatility
Don't Expect	explosiveness
Fantasy Value	$1
Card Value	5-8¢

COLLEGE STATISTICS

		G	FGP	FTP	RPG	PPG
84-85	GEOR	13	.487	.625	1.5	3.3
85-86	GEOR	29	.503	.787	3.4	8.5
86-87	GEOR	30	.500	.794	4.1	15.9
87-88	GEOR	35	.500	.784	5.1	16.7
Totals		107	.500	.784	3.9	12.6

NBA REGULAR-SEASON STATISTICS

				FGs		3-PT FGs		FTs		Rebounds						
		G	MIN	FG	PCT	FG	PCT	FT	PCT	OFF	TOT	AST	STL	BLK	PTS	PPG
88-89	SA	81	2738	640	.498	4	.190	224	.775	152	417	372	150	62	1508	18.6
89-90	SA	82	2788	532	.492	7	.269	217	.748	115	372	364	111	58	1288	15.7
90-91	SA	75	2592	453	.457	7	.200	170	.798	68	351	358	79	46	1083	14.4
91-92	SA	57	1889	312	.455	13	.232	107	.775	62	300	302	54	51	744	13.1
92-93	SA	38	560	80	.430	1	.125	22	.786	7	57	79	14	6	183	4.8
93-94	SA	80	2488	394	.471	22	.324	145	.848	68	242	347	71	46	955	11.9
94-95	SA	38	556	76	.469	3	.158	30	.732	15	55	52	26	10	185	4.9
95-96	TOR/NY	76	2060	288	.436	34	.283	132	.810	48	246	197	75	59	742	9.8
Totals		527	15671	2775	.471	91	.258	1047	.785	535	2040	2071	580	338	6688	12.7

GREG ANTHONY

Team: Vancouver Grizzlies
Position: Guard
Height: 6'1" **Weight:** 176
Birthdate: November 15, 1967

NBA Experience: 5 years
College: Portland; Nevada-Las Vegas
Acquired: Selected from Knicks in
1995 expansion draft

Background: Anthony spent his first college season at Portland, where he played shooting guard. Jerry Tarkanian moved him to the point at UNLV, where Anthony directed the Rebels to the national title in 1990 and to the Final Four in 1991. He spent four disappointing years in New York before blossoming in Vancouver last season as the team's top pick in the expansion draft.

Strengths: Anthony is a take-charge type who jumped on his chance to start and led the Grizzlies in scoring (14.0 PPG) and assists (6.9 APG). He has good quickness to the bucket and can thread the needle with his passes. Anthony can finish his own drives and has become a better perimeter threat. He expends energy on both ends.

Weaknesses: There's a reason Anthony was considered a bust in New York, and it starts with the even .400 he shot from the field in his first four years. He improved his rate with the Grizzlies, but his matchups still tend to play for the drive rather than the shot. Defensively, Anthony tends to gamble and is an easy mark for post-up guards.

Analysis: Anthony has enjoyed a rebirth in western Canada, where he ran the controls of the most futile team in basketball. With little pressure to win and much less scrutiny than he had in the Big Apple, he became Vancouver's best offensive weapon both as a passer and a scorer. Anthony has always been able to talk a big game. Now he's getting his chance to play one.

PLAYER SUMMARY	
Will	drive and dish
Can't	shoot 50 percent
Expect	confidence, energy
Don't Expect	a timid style
Fantasy Value	$6-8
Card Value	7-10¢

COLLEGE STATISTICS

		G	FGP	FTP	APG	PPG
86-87	PORT	28	.398	.694	4.0	15.3
88-89	UNLV	36	.443	.699	6.6	12.9
89-90	UNLV	39	.457	.682	7.4	11.2
90-91	UNLV	35	.456	.775	8.9	11.6
Totals		138	.437	.707	6.9	12.6

NBA REGULAR-SEASON STATISTICS

		G	MIN	FGs FG	PCT	3-PT FGs FG	PCT	FTs FT	PCT	Rebounds OFF	TOT	AST	STL	BLK	PTS	PPG
91-92	NY	82	1510	161	.370	8	.145	117	.741	33	136	314	59	9	447	5.5
92-93	NY	70	1699	174	.415	4	.133	107	.673	42	170	398	113	12	459	6.6
93-94	NY	80	1994	225	.394	48	.300	130	.774	43	189	365	114	13	628	7.8
94-95	NY	61	943	128	.437	56	.361	60	.789	7	64	160	50	7	372	6.1
95-96	VAN	69	2096	324	.415	90	.332	229	.771	29	174	476	116	11	967	14.0
Totals		362	8242	1012	.405	206	.307	643	.749	154	733	1713	452	52	2873	7.9

B.J. ARMSTRONG

Team: Golden State Warriors
Position: Guard
Height: 6'2" **Weight:** 185
Birthdate: September 9, 1967
NBA Experience: 7 years

College: Iowa
Acquired: Traded from Raptors for Victor Alexander, Carlos Rogers, and draft rights to Dwayne Whitfield, Martin Lewis, and Michael McDonald, 9/95

Background: After becoming Iowa's all-time leader in assists, Armstrong was Chicago's top bench player during the team's 1991 and 1992 NBA championship seasons. The baby-faced guard led the league in 3-point accuracy in 1992-93 (another title year) and started in the 1994 All-Star Game. Toronto picked him up in the 1995 expansion draft, then traded him to Golden State.

Strengths: Armstrong is one of the most dangerous jump-shooters in the game. Leave him open and he'll kill you from behind the 3-point arc. He has converted better than 40 percent from long distance every season and is annually among NBA leaders. He rarely misses a free throw. Armstrong is durable, plays solid defense, and can fill either guard spot.

Weaknesses: Armstrong does not possess the natural playmaking ability of other point guards in the NBA. He's better at spotting up than creating in traffic, and he does not rack up huge assist or steal totals. Armstrong is more of a complementary player than a star.

Analysis: Armstrong won three championships and became an All-Star in Chicago, where he was surrounded by great players and did not have to be a leading man. On a less talented team, his sure-handed, steady approach to playing point guard draws far less notice. His string of 528 consecutive games played ranks Armstrong third in the league, behind only A.C. Green and Michael Cage.

PLAYER SUMMARY	
Will	drain the 3
Can't	dominate games
Expect	durability
Don't Expect	flashy playmaking
Fantasy Value	$7-9
Card Value	8-15¢

COLLEGE STATISTICS

		G	FGP	FTP	APG	PPG
85-86	IOWA	29	.485	.905	1.4	2.9
86-87	IOWA	35	.519	.794	4.2	12.4
87-88	IOWA	34	.482	.849	4.6	17.4
88-89	IOWA	32	.484	.833	5.4	18.6
Totals		130	.492	.831	4.0	13.1

NBA REGULAR-SEASON STATISTICS

				FGs		3-PT FGs		FTs		Rebounds						
		G	MIN	FG	PCT	FG	PCT	FT	PCT	OFF	TOT	AST	STL	BLK	PTS	PPG
89-90	CHI	81	1291	190	.485	3	.500	69	.885	19	102	199	46	6	452	5.6
90-91	CHI	82	1731	304	.481	15	.500	97	.874	25	149	301	70	4	720	8.8
91-92	CHI	82	1875	335	.481	35	.402	104	.806	19	145	266	46	5	809	9.9
92-93	CHI	82	2492	408	.499	63	.453	130	.861	27	149	330	66	6	1009	12.3
93-94	CHI	82	2770	479	.476	60	.444	194	.855	28	170	323	80	9	1212	14.8
94-95	CHI	82	2577	418	.468	108	.427	206	.884	25	186	244	84	8	1150	14.0
95-96	GS	82	2262	340	.468	98	.473	234	.839	22	184	401	68	6	1012	12.3
Totals		573	14998	2474	.479	382	.446	1034	.856	165	1085	2064	460	44	6364	11.1

VINCENT ASKEW

Team: New Jersey Nets
Position: Guard/Forward
Height: 6'6" **Weight:** 235
Birthdate: February 28, 1966

NBA Experience: 7 years
College: Memphis St.
Acquired: Traded from SuperSonics for Greg Graham, 7/96

Background: After a three-year career at Memphis State, Askew entered the NBA draft early, was selected 39th overall by Philadelphia in 1987, and was waived after 14 games. He played in Italy and in the World Basketball League and was twice named MVP of the Continental Basketball Association. He has since played for Golden State, Sacramento, and Seattle, mostly in a reserve role. He joins the Nets for 1996-97.

Strengths: Askew provides defensive versatility. He matches up with players at three positions and uses his strength to his advantage. His offense has come a long way in recent years. While he has worked on his jumper and has 3-point range, his best offensive work comes on the blocks. Askew finds a way to get his shots against bigger players. He also passes well.

Weaknesses: Considering his post-up game and his defensive intensity, it is somewhat surprising that Askew is not a better rebounder. On offense, he is best used as a complementary player rather than as a go-to guy. While he offers versatility, he has not achieved greatness at any particular position.

Analysis: Askew, who once set a single-season scoring record in the CBA, emerged during three seasons as a prominent reserve with the SuperSonics, providing a mix of offense and defense. His best attribute is his ability to stand tall at either forward spot as well as big guard, and he can even bring the ball up in a pinch.

PLAYER SUMMARY

Will ....guard his man
Can't ....dominate the glass
Expect ....versatility, defense
Don't Expect ....a scoring machine
Fantasy Value $2-4
Card Value ....5-8¢

COLLEGE STATISTICS

		G	FGP	FTP	RPG	PPG
84-85	MSU	35	.511	.634	3.3	8.3
85-86	MSU	34	.490	.814	6.7	10.9
86-87	MSU	34	.483	.787	5.0	15.1
Totals		103	.492	.751	5.0	11.4

NBA REGULAR-SEASON STATISTICS

		G	MIN	FGs FG	FGs PCT	3-PT FGs FG	3-PT FGs PCT	FTs FT	FTs PCT	Rebounds OFF	Rebounds TOT	AST	STL	BLK	PTS	PPG
87-88	PHI	14	234	22	.297	0	.000	8	.727	6	22	33	10	6	52	3.7
90-91	GS	7	85	12	.480	0	.000	9	.818	7	11	13	2	0	33	4.7
91-92	GS	80	1496	193	.509	1	.100	111	.694	89	233	188	47	23	498	6.2
92-93	SAC/SEA	73	1129	152	.492	2	.333	105	.705	62	161	122	40	19	411	5.6
93-94	SEA	80	1690	273	.481	6	.194	175	.829	60	184	194	73	19	727	9.1
94-95	SEA	71	1721	248	.492	31	.330	176	.739	65	181	176	49	13	703	9.9
95-96	SEA	69	1725	215	.493	29	.337	125	.767	65	218	163	47	15	584	8.5
Totals		394	8080	1115	.486	69	.304	709	.752	354	1010	889	268	95	3008	7.6

KEITH ASKINS

Team: Miami Heat
Position: Guard/Forward
Height: 6'8" **Weight:** 224
Birthdate: December 15, 1967

NBA Experience: 6 years
College: Alabama
Acquired: Signed as a free agent, 9/90

Background: Askins, an Alabama native, stayed home to play for the Crimson Tide. He averaged 9.9 points and 5.1 rebounds per game as a senior, not enough to draw any team's attention in the 1990 NBA draft. Miami gave him a chance as a free agent, and Askins has fared well enough to last six seasons. He averaged a career-high 6.1 PPG during the 1995-96 season.

Strengths: Defense is the name of the game with Askins. Quick and gritty, he is able to match up well with players at three positions and has done well against some of the game's top scorers. He's more physical than his size would indicate. Askins also rebounds and runs well, and he has become a dangerous long-range threat. He made 41.8 percent of his 3-pointers last season.

Weaknesses: Askins is not a scorer. In his first five seasons, he never averaged more than 4.6 PPG. He does not take the ball to the basket, create shots off the dribble, or post up with any frequency. He's catch-and-shoot all the way. Askins also falls below the norm when it comes to ball-handling and passing.

Analysis: Give Askins credit. A defensive specialist for most of his career, he has worked on his jumper and now must be considered a legitimate 3-point threat. His calling card remains his defense, though. In fact, the most attention-getting play Askins made last year was delivering a blow that caused Michael Jordan some back pain in the playoffs.

PLAYER SUMMARY	
Will	stick like glue
Can't	set up the offense
Expect	a 3-point threat
Don't Expect	10 PPG
Fantasy Value	$0
Card Value	7-10¢

COLLEGE STATISTICS

		G	FGP	FTP	RPG	PPG
86-87	ALAB	32	.475	.552	3.0	2.9
87-88	ALAB	30	.417	.694	4.9	5.7
88-89	ALAB	31	.497	.686	4.2	7.8
89-90	ALAB	35	.437	.656	5.1	9.9
Totals		128	.453	.658	4.3	6.7

NBA REGULAR-SEASON STATISTICS

		G	MIN	FGs FG	FGs PCT	3-PT FGs FG	3-PT FGs PCT	FTs FT	FTs PCT	Rebounds OFF	Rebounds TOT	AST	STL	BLK	PTS	PPG
90-91	MIA	39	266	34	.420	6	.240	12	.480	30	68	19	16	13	86	2.2
91-92	MIA	59	843	84	.410	25	.342	26	.703	65	142	38	40	15	219	3.7
92-93	MIA	69	935	88	.413	22	.338	29	.725	74	198	31	31	29	227	3.3
93-94	MIA	37	319	36	.409	4	.190	9	.900	33	82	13	11	1	85	2.3
94-95	MIA	50	854	81	.391	21	.269	46	.807	86	198	39	35	17	229	4.6
95-96	MIA	75	1897	157	.402	99	.418	45	.789	113	324	121	48	61	458	6.1
Totals		329	5114	480	.405	177	.355	167	.739	401	1012	261	181	136	1304	4.0

STACEY AUGMON

Team: Detroit Pistons
Position: Guard/Forward
Height: 6'8" **Weight:** 205
Birthdate: August 1, 1968
NBA Experience: 5 years

College: Nevada-Las Vegas
Acquired: Traded from Hawks with Grant Long for future considerations, 7/96

Background: Augmon, who played four positions for UNLV, established a reputation as the nation's finest college defensive player. He played on the 1988 United States Olympic team and was a key player in UNLV's run to the national championship in 1990. He was drafted No. 9 by Atlanta and made the NBA All-Rookie first team. He has averaged from 12 to 15 PPG in each of his five pro seasons. Detroit traded for him last summer.

Strengths: Nicknamed "Plastic Man," Augmon has the wingspan and athletic ability to make an impact at both ends of the floor. He gets to the basket, runs the court, and is considered one of the best finishers in the league. His post-up game is strong. His instincts for the ball and ability to beat opponents to the boards help him on the defensive side.

Weaknesses: Augmon is a much better slasher than shooter, and the 3-point shot does not fall within his range. In fact, opponents can leave him open from 18-20 feet. Augmon is not an especially gifted passer or dribbler, and his build is slight. He's less effective when the pace slows.

Analysis: Augmon can make the steal or grab the defensive board, then beat his man down the court for a jam. At his best, he's an energetic mix of offense and defense. If he could develop a respectable jump shot, Augmon would make it hard for a coach to keep him off the floor. Although his play seems to have leveled off, the Pistons are hoping he'll step it up again.

PLAYER SUMMARY	
Will	slash to the hoop
Can't	rely on 3-pointers
Expect	fastbreak points
Don't Expect	power moves
Fantasy Value	$11-14
Card Value	10-20¢

COLLEGE STATISTICS

		G	FGP	FTP	RPG	PPG
87-88	UNLV	34	.574	.647	6.1	9.2
88-89	UNLV	37	.519	.663	7.4	15.3
89-90	UNLV	39	.553	.671	6.9	14.2
90-91	UNLV	35	.587	.727	7.3	16.5
Totals		145	.555	.677	6.9	13.7

NBA REGULAR-SEASON STATISTICS

		G	MIN	FGs FG	FGs PCT	3-PT FGs FG	3-PT FGs PCT	FTs FT	FTs PCT	Rebounds OFF	Rebounds TOT	AST	STL	BLK	PTS	PPG
91-92	ATL	82	2505	440	.489	1	.167	213	.666	191	420	201	124	27	1094	13.3
92-93	ATL	73	2112	397	.501	0	.000	227	.739	141	287	170	91	18	1021	14.0
93-94	ATL	82	2605	439	.510	1	.143	333	.764	178	394	187	149	45	1212	14.8
94-95	ATL	76	2362	397	.453	7	.269	252	.728	157	368	197	100	47	1053	13.9
95-96	ATL	77	2294	362	.491	1	.250	251	.792	137	304	137	106	31	976	12.7
Totals		390	11878	2035	.488	10	.213	1276	.739	804	1773	892	570	168	5356	13.7

VIN BAKER

Team: Milwaukee Bucks
Position: Forward
Height: 6'11" **Weight:** 250
Birthdate: November 23, 1971

NBA Experience: 3 years
College: Hartford
Acquired: First-round pick in 1993 draft (eighth overall)

Background: Baker caught the eye of NBA scouts when he finished second in scoring in Division I as a junior. At Hartford, he broke school records for career scoring, field goals, free throws, and blocked shots. Drafted eighth overall by Milwaukee, Baker made the 1994 All-Rookie Team and has played in each of the last two All-Star Games. He averaged 21.1 PPG and 9.9 RPG in 1995-96.

Strengths: Baker's star is rising. He combines power and finesse and has a vast array of moves around the basket. His quickness and leaping ability have helped him become a leading scorer and rebounder who has averaged a double-double over the past two years. He handles the ball very well for his size, defends big forwards adequately, and can fill in at center. Baker works at his game and comes to play.

Weaknesses: His free-throw shooting has come a long way through much repetition, but it remains the most obvious weakness in Baker's game. He lacks consistency with his perimeter jump shot, but it also has improved. It remains to be seen what Baker can do to help his team become a winner. He sometimes tries to do too much.

Analysis: The Bucks had very few reasons to smile in 1995-96, but Baker was clearly one of them. He solidified his status as an All-Star and improved his scoring by about four points a night. Consider, too, that the durable Baker continues to log more minutes than almost anyone in the league. Baker is giving the Bucks their money's worth. In fact, they could use four more of him.

PLAYER SUMMARY

Will	score, rebound
Can't	carry Bucks alone
Expect	double-doubles
Don't Expect	high free-throw pct.
Fantasy Value	$45-50
Card Value	20-40¢

COLLEGE STATISTICS

		G	FGP	FTP	RPG	PPG
89-90	HART	28	.617	.390	2.9	4.7
90-91	HART	29	.491	.678	10.4	19.6
91-92	HART	27	.440	.657	9.9	27.6
92-93	HART	28	.477	.625	10.7	28.3
Totals		112	.475	.637	8.5	20.0

NBA REGULAR-SEASON STATISTICS

			FGs		3-PT FGs		FTs		Rebounds						
		G	MIN	FG	PCT	FG	PCT	FT	PCT	OFF	TOT	AST	STL	BLK	PTS	PPG
93-94	MIL	82	2560	435	.501	1	.200	234	.569	277	621	163	60	114	1105	13.5
94-95	MIL	82	3361	594	.483	7	.292	256	.593	289	846	296	86	116	1451	17.7
95-96	MIL	82	3319	699	.489	10	.208	321	.670	263	808	212	68	91	1729	21.1
Totals		246	9240	1728	.490	18	.234	811	.613	829	2275	671	214	321	4285	17.4

CHARLES BARKLEY

Team: Houston Rockets
Position: Forward
Height: 6'6" **Weight:** 252
Birthdate: February 20, 1963
NBA Experience: 12 years

College: Auburn
Acquired: Traded from Suns for Robert Horry, Sam Cassell, Chucky Brown, and Mark Bryant, 8/96

Background: Barkley was known as the "Round Mound of Rebound" at Auburn, where he was named SEC Player of the Year as a junior. He won Olympic gold in 1992 and 1996 and was named league MVP in 1992-93, his first year with Phoenix. He was dealt to Houston after demanding that the Suns trade him. He's a perennial All-Star.

Strengths: Barkley's game features the complete package. He is always among the top few rebounders and scorers in the league. He shoots with range, muscles inside against seven-footers, and gets to the line. His strength and demeanor make him intimidating. He is a dominant force and a leader who plays to win.

Weaknesses: Barkley's controversial past includes late-night bar fights, courtside spitting, and countless controversial quotes. He has paid numerous league fines. He has battled various injuries, although he said he never felt better than he did last season.

Analysis: Barkley, one of the league's most talented players and captivating personalities over the last decade, grabbed his 10,000th rebound in February. He became only the tenth player in NBA history to amass 10,000 boards and 20,000 points. Barkley was at the top of his game in 1995-96.

PLAYER SUMMARY	
Will	intimidate, dominate
Can't	withhold his opinion
Expect	20 PPG, 12 RPG
Don't Expect	many off nights
Fantasy Value	$55-60
Card Value	35-75¢

COLLEGE STATISTICS

		G	FGP	FTP	RPG	PPG
81-82	AUB	28	.595	.636	9.8	12.7
82-83	AUB	28	.644	.631	9.5	14.4
83-84	AUB	28	.638	.683	9.5	15.1
Totals		84	.626	.652	9.6	14.1

NBA REGULAR-SEASON STATISTICS

		G	MIN	FGs		3-PT FGs		FTs		Rebounds		AST	STL	BLK	PTS	PPG
				FG	PCT	FG	PCT	FT	PCT	OFF	TOT					
84-85	PHI	82	2347	427	.545	1	.167	293	.733	266	703	155	95	80	1148	14.0
85-86	PHI	80	2952	595	.572	17	.227	396	.685	354	1026	312	173	125	1603	20.0
86-87	PHI	68	2740	557	.594	21	.202	429	.761	390	994	331	119	104	1564	23.0
87-88	PHI	80	3170	753	.587	44	.280	714	.751	385	951	254	100	103	2264	28.3
88-89	PHI	79	3088	700	.579	35	.216	602	.753	403	986	325	126	67	2037	25.8
89-90	PHI	70	3085	706	.600	20	.217	557	.749	361	909	307	148	50	1989	28.4
90-91	PHI	67	2498	665	.570	44	.284	475	.722	258	680	284	110	33	1849	27.6
91-92	PHI	75	2881	622	.552	32	.234	454	.695	271	830	308	136	44	1730	23.1
92-93	PHO	76	2859	716	.520	67	.305	445	.765	237	928	385	119	74	1944	25.6
93-94	PHO	65	2298	518	.495	48	.270	318	.704	198	727	296	101	37	1402	21.6
94-95	PHO	68	2382	554	.486	74	.338	379	.748	203	756	276	110	45	1561	23.0
95-96	PHO	71	2632	580	.500	49	.280	440	.777	243	821	262	114	56	1649	23.2
Totals		881	32932	7393	.550	452	.269	5502	.738	3569	10311	3495	1451	818	20740	23.5

DANA BARROS

Team: Boston Celtics
Position: Guard
Height: 5'11" **Weight:** 163
Birthdate: April 13, 1967

NBA Experience: 7 years
College: Boston College
Acquired: Signed as a free agent, 9/95

Background: Barros, who finished his career as the all-time scoring leader at Boston College, served mostly as a reserve in four years in Seattle, and his .446 3-point shooting in 1991-92 was tops in the NBA. A trade to Philadelphia made him a starter in 1993-94. The next year, he played in the All-Star Game and was named the NBA's Most Improved Player. He spent most of last season as a Celtic sub.

Strengths: Barros is blessed with a beautiful stroke and is not shy about showing it. His NBA-record string of 89 consecutive games with at least one 3-point basket was snapped in January. Small but extremely quick, he is also adept at getting to the hole. Barros has become a better team player.

Weaknesses: Barros is not as polished a playmaker as most point guards, possessing the mentality of a two guard. His assist-to-turnover ratio will not lead the league, and he is sometimes too content to settle for the long-range jumper. He is suspect on defense because of his size.

Analysis: When it comes to converting 3-pointers, free throws, and outside shots of any kind, Barros is one of the best. His career has been a roller-coaster ride, sending him from bench-warmer to All-Star to prominent reserve. There was a time when coming off the bench bothered Barros, but he thrived as the Celtics' "super-sub" last season.

PLAYER SUMMARY

Will ....ripple the nets
Can't ....block shots
Expect ....supreme confidence
Don't Expect................assist records
Fantasy Value $9-11
Card Value ....8-15¢

COLLEGE STATISTICS

		G	FGP	FTP	APG	PPG
85-86	BC	28	.479	.791	3.5	13.7
86-87	BC	29	.458	.850	3.8	18.7
87-88	BC	33	.480	.850	4.1	21.9
88-89	BC	29	.475	.857	3.3	23.9
Totals		119	.473	.841	3.7	19.7

NBA REGULAR-SEASON STATISTICS

			FGs		3-PT FGs		FTs		Rebounds						
		G	MIN	FG	PCT	FG	PCT	FT	PCT	OFF	TOT	AST	STL	BLK	PTS	PPG
89-90	SEA	81	1630	299	.405	95	.399	89	.809	35	132	205	53	1	782	9.7
90-91	SEA	66	750	154	.495	32	.395	78	.918	17	71	111	23	1	418	6.3
91-92	SEA	75	1331	238	.483	83	.446	60	.759	17	81	125	51	4	619	8.3
92-93	SEA	69	1243	214	.451	64	.379	49	.831	18	107	151	63	3	541	7.8
93-94	PHI	81	2519	412	.469	135	.381	116	.800	28	196	424	107	5	1075	13.3
94-95	PHI	82	3318	571	.490	197	.464	347	.899	27	274	619	149	4	1686	20.6
95-96	BOS	80	2328	379	.470	150	.408	130	.884	21	192	306	58	3	1038	13.0
Totals		534	13119	2267	.466	756	.415	869	.860	163	1053	1941	504	21	6159	11.5

BRENT BARRY

Team: Los Angeles Clippers
Position: Guard
Height: 6'6" **Weight:** 185
Birthdate: December 31, 1971
NBA Experience: 1 year

College: Oregon St.
Acquired: Draft rights traded from Nuggets with Rodney Rogers for Randy Woods and draft rights to Antonio McDyess, 6/95

Background: Brent is the son of Hall of Famer Rick Barry and brother of Jon, Drew, and Scooter. Barry progressed slowly at Oregon State and didn't move into first-round draft consideration until his senior season, when he ranked second in the Pac-10 in scoring and steals. Denver drafted him 15th overall and traded him to the Clippers in the Antonio McDyess deal. Barry averaged 10.1 PPG and cracked the starting lineup as a rookie.

Strengths: Brent is more athletic than his father ever was, as he demonstrated when he took off from the free-throw line to win the NBA's Slam Dunk Contest on All-Star Weekend. He also has some of his dad's feel for the game. He displays terrific court vision and passing skills to go along with his size and quickness. He plays defense and finished among league leaders with 41.6 percent from 3-point range.

Weaknesses: Barry is not a classic shooting guard in that he looks to set up teammates more often than he looks to score. His biggest trouble area is creating his own shot. He is much more effective spotting up or coming off screens, and about half of his field-goal tries come from behind the arc. Barry could stand some extra muscle, though he is a surprisingly tough defender.

Analysis: Much like his dad, Barry has a knack for getting the ball to the right place at the right time and for making his teammates look better. With the Clippers, that's no small feat. He enjoyed a better rookie season than many of those drafted ahead of him, and his Jordanesque jam at the San Antonio All-Star showcase will be on highlight films for years to come.

PLAYER SUMMARY	
Will	deliver the ball
Can't	be left open
Expect	comparisons to Dad
Don't Expect	a stopper
Fantasy Value	$10-12
Card Value	25-75¢

COLLEGE STATISTICS

		G	FGP	FTP	RPG	PPG
91-92	OSU	31	.419	.667	1.5	5.2
92-93	OSU	23	.411	.851	2.1	7.2
93-94	OSU	27	.498	.759	5.2	15.2
94-95	OSU	27	.514	.823	5.9	21.0
Totals		108	.480	.794	3.7	12.1

NBA REGULAR-SEASON STATISTICS

		G	MIN	FGs FG	FGs PCT	3-PT FGs FG	3-PT FGs PCT	FTs FT	FTs PCT	Rebounds OFF	Rebounds TOT	AST	STL	BLK	PTS	PPG
95-96	LAC	79	1898	283	.474	123	.416	111	.810	38	168	230	95	22	800	10.1
Totals		79	1898	283	.474	123	.416	111	.810	38	168	230	95	22	800	10.1

JON BARRY

Team: Atlanta Hawks
Position: Guard
Height: 6'4" **Weight:** 194
Birthdate: July 25, 1969

NBA Experience: 4 years
College: Pacific; Paris; Georgia Tech
Acquired: Signed as a free agent, 8/96

Background: One of four sons of Hall of Famer Rick Barry to play Division I basketball, Barry played at Pacific and Paris (Texas) Junior College before leading Georgia Tech in 3-point field goals as a senior. He was drafted by Boston in 1992 and, after not being able to agree on a contract, was traded to Milwaukee. After three years with the Bucks and one with the Warriors, he signed with Atlanta during the off-season.

Strengths: Barry has court sense that runs in the family, and it's something that can't be coached. He sees plays before they happen, he hustles, and he is a splendid passer. He works relentlessly at both ends. Barry also inherited a nice shooting stroke. He hit close to half of his 3-point shots last season and makes his free throws.

Weaknesses: Barry has struggled to find consistency as a pro. He's the type of player who needs steady floor time to make his mark, as he does little that stands out on a one-night basis. Barry is not quick enough to cause problems as an on-the-ball defender, nor is he enough of an athlete to have an impact on the boards. He could help his cause on offense by improving his dribble.

Analysis: Rick and Jon became the first father-son duo in Warriors history when Jon signed with his dad's former team last season. Jon has some of his dad's intangibles. However, he does not possess the scoring ability you see in starting two guards, and he is not the man you want at the point. He's a team player who is still struggling to find a happy home.

PLAYER SUMMARY	
Will	make 3-pointers
Can't	crack starting lineup
Expect	neat passes
Don't Expect	a nifty dribble
Fantasy Value	$1
Card Value	7-10¢

COLLEGE STATISTICS

	G	FGP	FTP	RPG	PPG
87-88 PAC	29	.372	.746	2.6	9.5
90-91 GT	30	.444	.732	3.7	15.9
91-92 GT	35	.429	.697	4.3	17.2
Totals	94	.421	.717	3.6	14.4

NBA REGULAR-SEASON STATISTICS

			FGs		3-PT FGs		FTs		Rebounds						
	G	MIN	FG	PCT	FG	PCT	FT	PCT	OFF	TOT	AST	STL	BLK	PTS	PPG
92-93 MIL	47	552	76	.369	21	.333	33	.673	10	43	68	35	3	206	4.4
93-94 MIL	72	1242	158	.414	32	.278	97	.795	36	146	168	102	17	445	6.2
94-95 MIL	52	602	57	.425	16	.333	61	.762	15	49	85	30	4	191	3.7
95-96 GS	68	712	91	.492	44	.473	31	.838	17	63	85	33	11	257	3.8
Totals	239	3108	382	.421	113	.354	222	.771	78	301	406	200	35	1099	4.6

BENOIT BENJAMIN

Unrestricted Free Agent
Last Team: Milwaukee Bucks
Position: Center
Height: 7'0" **Weight:** 264
Birthdate: November 22, 1964

NBA Experience: 11 years
College: Creighton
Acquired: Traded from Grizzlies for
Eric Murdock and Eric Mobley, 11/95

Background: Benjamin played for Creighton and led the nation in blocked shots (5.1 BPG) as a junior. He gave up his final year of college eligibility to enter the NBA draft and played five-plus years with the Clippers. Benjamin has played with six different teams over the last six years, including Vancouver and Milwaukee last season.

Strengths: Benjamin has a soft touch from 15 feet and is also capable of scoring with hook shots in the paint. He is good for about one blocked shot per game and has enjoyed some big seasons on the defensive glass. He does have size.

Weaknesses: The word "enigma" should be stitched on the back of Benjamin's extra-large jersey. He has never displayed the desire or consistency to compete at a high level. Benjamin is a regular in a coach's doghouse for his tendency to disappear. He almost never sets up a teammate for a bucket.

Analysis: Benjamin, when he retires, will be remembered as someone who never reached his potential. He has certainly had his chances, but even the expansion Grizzlies decided to unload him after just 13 games north of the border. Teams have learned to expect the worst from him.

PLAYER SUMMARY	
Will	score on hooks
Can't	sustain decent effort
Expect	inconsistency
Don't Expect	passes
Fantasy Value	$4-6
Card Value	5-8¢

COLLEGE STATISTICS

		G	FGP	FTP	RPG	PPG
82-83	CREI	27	.555	.655	9.6	14.8
83-84	CREI	30	.543	.743	9.8	16.2
84-85	CREI	32	.582	.738	14.1	21.5
Totals		89	.562	.720	11.3	17.7

NBA REGULAR-SEASON STATISTICS

				FGs		3-PT FGs		FTs		Rebounds						
		G	MIN	FG	PCT	FG	PCT	FT	PCT	OFF	TOT	AST	STL	BLK	PTS	PPG
85-86	LAC	79	2088	324	.490	1	.333	229	.746	161	600	79	64	206	878	11.1
86-87	LAC	72	2230	320	.449	0	.000	188	.715	134	586	135	60	187	828	11.5
87-88	LAC	66	2171	340	.491	0	.000	180	.706	112	530	172	50	225	860	13.0
88-89	LAC	79	2585	491	.541	0	.000	317	.744	164	696	157	57	221	1299	16.4
89-90	LAC	71	2313	362	.526	0	.000	235	.732	156	657	159	59	187	959	13.5
90-91	LAC/SEA	70	2236	386	.496	0	.000	210	.712	157	723	119	54	145	982	14.0
91-92	SEA	63	1941	354	.478	0	.000	171	.687	130	513	76	39	118	879	14.0
92-93	SEA/LAL	59	754	133	.491	0	.000	69	.663	51	209	22	31	48	335	5.7
93-94	NJ	77	1817	283	.480	0	.000	152	.710	135	499	44	35	90	718	9.3
94-95	NJ	61	1598	271	.510	0	.000	133	.760	94	440	38	23	64	675	11.1
95-96	VAN/MIL	83	1896	294	.498	0	.000	140	.722	141	539	64	45	85	728	8.8
Totals		780	21629	3558	.497	1	.048	2024	.722	1435	5992	1065	517	1576	9141	11.7

MARIO BENNETT

Team: Phoenix Suns
Position: Forward
Height: 6'9" **Weight:** 235
Birthdate: August 1, 1973

NBA Experience: 1 year
College: Arizona St.
Acquired: First-round pick in 1995 draft (27th overall)

Background: Though he played just three seasons at Arizona State and sat out a year because of a knee injury, Bennett became the school's all-time leading shot-blocker and set the Sun Devil mark for career field-goal accuracy. He averaged 18.7 points and 8.2 rebounds per game before becoming a late first-round draft choice of the Suns in 1995. Preseason knee surgery kept him from making his NBA debut until March.

Strengths: Bennett could become a very effective rebounder and shot-blocker at the NBA level. He has good size to handle the power forward position, and his quickness and timing help him challenge shots. He runs the floor well for a big man and fills a lane on the break. He is especially dangerous on the offensive glass. Bennett knows his way around the basket.

Weaknesses: Bennett had two anterior cruciate tears in his left knee before ever joining the NBA, and more knee troubles limited his rookie season to 19 games. Bennett is more of a finesse player around the basket than a forceful one, yet he does not handle the ball or pass well enough to survive as a three. He needs to get stronger and learn that there's more to defense than blocking shots. Bennett is a poor free-throw shooter.

Analysis: What an initiation! After missing the first three-quarters of his rookie season while recovering from knee surgery, Bennett wound up starting 14 of the last 19 games. He averaged 4.5 points and 2.6 rebounds per game, numbers that will climb if he stays off the injured list. His talent far exceeds his draft status, but there are serious questions about whether his legs will allow him to enjoy a long career.

PLAYER SUMMARY

Will ....swat shots
Can't ....shake knee troubles
Expect.....................dunks, putbacks
Don't Expect.......................a shooter
Fantasy Value $0
Card Value ....10-20¢

COLLEGE STATISTICS

		G	FGP	FTP	RPG	PPG
91-92	ASU	33	.574	.614	6.8	12.5
93-94	ASU	21	.593	.508	8.6	16.2
94-95	ASU	33	.592	.491	8.2	18.7
Totals		87	.587	.530	7.8	15.7

NBA REGULAR-SEASON STATISTICS

		MIN	FGs		3-PT FGs		FTs		Rebounds						
	G		FG	PCT	FG	PCT	FT	PCT	OFF	TOT	AST	STL	BLK	PTS	PPG
95-96 PHO	19	230	29	.453	0	.000	27	.643	21	49	6	11	11	85	4.5
Totals	19	230	29	.453	0	.000	27	.643	21	49	6	11	11	85	4.5

DAVID BENOIT

Team: New Jersey Nets
Position: Forward
Height: 6'8" **Weight:** 220
Birthdate: May 9, 1968

NBA Experience: 5 years
College: Tyler; Alabama
Acquired: Signed as a free agent, 8/96

Background: Benoit started playing basketball in high school and began his college career at Tyler Junior College before transferring to Alabama. He averaged ten-plus PPG in both of his years there. Benoit was the Rookie of the Year in the Spanish League in 1990-91. He has spent all five of his NBA seasons with the Utah Jazz—as a reserve the first three years and as a starter for most of the last two. He joins the Nets for 1996-97.

Strengths: Benoit is a fine athlete and a relentless worker who plays his best ball in transition. He hustles down the floor, ignites his team with fantastic finishes, and rarely gets tired. He is also a good defensive rebounder, a capable shot-blocker, and a willing defender. He has worked on his jumper, having hit a career-best .486 from the field two years ago.

Weaknesses: Benoit is more athlete than basketball player. His shooting is sporadic, and his entire offensive repertoire is raw. He does not create for himself or others. His field-goal accuracy dipped to .439 last season after peaking the year before, and he hits only about one-third of his 3-point bombs. Benoit does not handle the ball or pass well.

Analysis: Benoit has overcome his share of obstacles. He was never drafted by an NBA team, and before the 1994-95 season he checked into an alcohol treatment program. Since then, he has posted his best season and an average one back-to-back. He needs to add to his offensive game to be an effective half-court player.

PLAYER SUMMARY	
Will	finish the break
Can't	live off jump shots
Expect	full-court hustle
Don't Expect	many assists
Fantasy Value	$4-6
Card Value	5-8¢

COLLEGE STATISTICS

		G	FGP	FTP	RPG	PPG
88-89	ALAB	31	.507	.738	8.0	10.8
89-90	ALAB	35	.515	.767	6.1	10.5
Totals		66	.511	.752	7.0	10.6

NBA REGULAR-SEASON STATISTICS

			FGs		3-PT FGs		FTs		Rebounds						
	G	MIN	FG	PCT	FG	PCT	FT	PCT	OFF	TOT	AST	STL	BLK	PTS	PPG
91-92 UTA	77	1161	175	.467	3	.214	81	.810	105	296	34	19	44	434	5.6
92-93 UTA	82	1712	258	.436	34	.347	114	.750	116	392	43	45	43	664	8.1
93-94 UTA	55	1070	139	.385	12	.203	68	.773	89	260	23	23	37	358	6.5
94-95 UTA	71	1841	285	.486	38	.330	132	.841	96	368	58	45	47	740	10.4
95-96 UTA	81	1961	255	.439	64	.333	87	.777	90	383	82	43	49	661	8.2
Totals	366	7745	1112	.446	151	.316	482	.791	496	1699	240	175	220	2857	7.8

TRAVIS BEST

Team: Indiana Pacers
Position: Guard
Height: 5'11" **Weight:** 182
Birthdate: July 12, 1972

NBA Experience: 1 year
College: Georgia Tech
Acquired: First-round pick in 1995 draft (23rd overall)

Background: One of the top high school recruits in his class and a three-time All-ACC choice as a collegian, Best finished his Georgia Tech career among the school's top five in points, assists, steals, and 3-pointers. He joined Phil Ford as the only players in ACC history to compile 2,000 points and 600 assists. Best was drafted 23rd by Indiana in 1995 and averaged less than ten minutes per contest as a rookie.

Strengths: Best is a fine shooter. He was one of the top free-throw shooters in college basketball over his final two seasons, and he made 83 percent as a rookie. He also has an accurate eye from 3-point range to complement his darting drives toward the basket. Best handles the ball well and has enough quickness to trouble opponents on both offense and defense. He plays tougher than he looks.

Weaknesses: Best's scoring bent might not be an asset as his career progresses. He is not considered a "pure" point guard, mostly because he is accustomed to taking the shot as often as he sets up teammates. Assist-to-turnover ratio is a good indicator of success for a lead guard, and Best's was well under 2-to-1 in limited first-year time. There are concerns about his defense.

Analysis: Best has a big upside, but he was never able to crack an Indiana rotation that had Mark Jackson (81 games) and Haywoode Workman (77) sharing the point guard duties last season. Best has the look of a high-scoring reserve who could make things happen at both ends of the floor. This year, he'll be stuck behind Jalen Rose. While he's waiting, he should work on the drive-and-dish.

PLAYER SUMMARY	
Will	sink his free throws
Can't	see over the defense
Expect	reserve minutes
Don't Expect	assist records
Fantasy Value	$3-5
Card Value	10-20¢

COLLEGE STATISTICS

		G	FGP	FTP	RPG	PPG
91-92	GT	35	.449	.735	2.5	12.3
92-93	GT	30	.472	.752	3.1	16.3
93-94	GT	29	.462	.866	3.6	18.3
94-95	GT	30	.446	.847	3.2	20.2
Totals		124	.456	.809	3.1	16.6

NBA REGULAR-SEASON STATISTICS

			FGs		3-PT FGs		FTs		Rebounds						
	G	MIN	FG	PCT	FG	PCT	FT	PCT	OFF	TOT	AST	STL	BLK	PTS	PPG
95-96 IND	59	571	69	.423	8	.320	75	.833	11	44	97	20	3	221	3.7
Totals	59	571	69	.423	8	.320	75	.833	11	44	97	20	3	221	3.7

MOOKIE BLAYLOCK

Team: Atlanta Hawks
Position: Guard
Height: 6'1" **Weight:** 185
Birthdate: March 20, 1967

NBA Experience: 7 years
College: Midland; Oklahoma
Acquired: Traded from Nets with Roy Hinson for Rumeal Robinson, 11/92

Background: Born Daron Oshay Blaylock, Mookie earned All-America recognition at Oklahoma and was the first NCAA player to collect 200 assists and 100 steals in back-to-back seasons. Drafted 12th overall by New Jersey in 1989, he was traded to Atlanta in 1992 and has enjoyed his four best years as a Hawk. He played in the 1994 All-Star Game and is a regular on the All-Defensive Team.

Strengths: Blaylock is the complete package at the point. His quickness and instincts help him rank among league leaders in steals annually. He is also an above-average rebounder for his position. On offense, he can score off drives and shoot with 3-point range. Blaylock is creative off the dribble.

Weaknesses: Too often in the last few years, Blaylock has abandoned his playmaking for 3-point bombs. He does not shoot for a high percentage and is prone to ice-cold nights. On those nights, the Hawks usually lose. Blaylock is no better than an average shooter who sometimes tries to do too much.

Analysis: Blaylock is clearly one of the best defensive point guards in basketball, if not the best. He is capable of shutting down almost anyone, and his knack for steals is extraordinary. His last two years have been his best in the scoring column, but the extra offense has come at the expense of assists. More discretion would serve Blaylock and his team well.

PLAYER SUMMARY	
Will	pick your pocket
Can't	hoist his FG pct.
Expect	200-plus steals
Don't Expect	sweet shooting
Fantasy Value	$20-25
Card Value	8-15¢

COLLEGE STATISTICS

		G	FGP	FTP	APG	PPG
85-86	MIDL	34	.566	.738	—	16.8
86-87	MIDL	33	.516	.723	—	19.6
87-88	OKLA	39	.460	.684	5.9	16.4
88-89	OKLA	35	.455	.650	6.7	20.0
Totals		141	.495	.696	6.3	18.1

NBA REGULAR-SEASON STATISTICS

				FGs		3-PT FGs		FTs		Rebounds						
		G	MIN	FG	PCT	FG	PCT	FT	PCT	OFF	TOT	AST	STL	BLK	PTS	PPG
89-90	NJ	50	1267	212	.371	18	.225	63	.778	42	140	210	82	14	505	10.1
90-91	NJ	72	2585	432	.416	14	.154	139	.790	67	249	441	169	40	1017	14.1
91-92	NJ	72	2548	429	.432	12	.222	126	.712	101	269	492	170	40	996	13.8
92-93	ATL	80	2820	414	.429	118	.375	123	.728	89	280	671	203	23	1069	13.4
93-94	ATL	81	2915	444	.411	114	.334	116	.730	117	424	789	212	44	1118	13.8
94-95	ATL	80	3069	509	.425	199	.359	156	.729	117	393	616	200	26	1373	17.2
95-96	ATL	81	2893	455	.405	231	.371	127	.747	110	332	478	212	17	1268	15.7
Totals		516	18097	2895	.416	706	.343	850	.742	643	2087	3697	1248	204	7346	14.2

MUGGSY BOGUES

Team: Charlotte Hornets
Position: Guard
Height: 5'3" **Weight:** 144
Birthdate: January 9, 1965

NBA Experience: 9 years
College: Wake Forest
Acquired: Selected from Bullets in 1988 expansion draft

Background: At famed Dunbar High in Baltimore, Bogues teamed with Reggie Williams and the late Reggie Lewis. At Wake Forest, Bogues set ACC career records for assists and steals. His pro career took off after Charlotte plucked him from the Bullets in the 1988 expansion draft. The league's all-time leader in assist-to-turnover ratio (nearly 5-to-1) missed most of 1995-96 after knee surgery.

Strengths: Bogues makes even the so-called quick playmakers look as though they're standing still. He's a pest on both ends of the court. Few can stop him from driving and dishing off, and he is always a threat to swipe your dribble. He almost never loses the ball or misses a free throw.

Weaknesses: The obvious drawback is his size. Bogues can't shoot over anyone, and even Spud Webb can post him up. His jumper has improved, but he is not a big scorer and is no threat to beat you from 3-point range.

Analysis: Bogues had never been on the NBA's injured list before the 1995-96 season, but arthroscopic knee surgery last August forced him to miss the first 46 games and most of the season's second half as well. He had led the league in assist-to-turnover ratio in six of the previous seven seasons while raising his scoring average for four straight years.

PLAYER SUMMARY

Will .... cause havoc
Can't .... be pressured
Expect .... pinpoint passes
Don't Expect .... turnovers
Fantasy Value $2-4
Card Value .... 5-10¢

COLLEGE STATISTICS

		G	FGP	FTP	APG	PPG
83-84	WF	32	.304	.692	1.7	1.2
84-85	WF	29	.500	.682	7.1	6.6
85-86	WF	29	.455	.730	8.4	11.3
86-87	WF	29	.500	.806	9.5	14.8
Totals		119	.473	.749	6.6	8.3

NBA REGULAR-SEASON STATISTICS

			FGs		3-PT FGs		FTs		Rebounds						
		G	MIN	FG	PCT	FG	PCT	FT	PCT	OFF	TOT	AST	STL	BLK	PTS	PPG
87-88	WAS	79	1628	166	.390	3	.188	58	.784	35	136	404	127	3	393	5.0
88-89	CHA	79	1755	178	.426	1	.077	66	.750	53	165	620	111	7	423	5.4
89-90	CHA	81	2743	326	.491	5	.192	106	.791	48	207	867	166	3	763	9.4
90-91	CHA	81	2299	241	.460	0	.000	86	.796	58	216	669	137	3	568	7.0
91-92	CHA	82	2790	317	.472	2	.074	94	.783	58	235	743	170	6	730	8.9
92-93	CHA	81	2833	331	.453	6	.231	140	.833	51	298	711	161	5	808	10.0
93-94	CHA	77	2746	354	.471	2	.167	125	.806	78	313	780	133	2	835	10.8
94-95	CHA	78	2629	348	.477	6	.200	160	.889	51	257	675	103	0	862	11.1
95-96	CHA	6	77	6	.375	0	.000	2	1.000	6	7	19	2	0	14	2.3
Totals		644	19500	2267	.460	25	.153	837	.813	438	1834	5488	1110	29	5396	8.4

ANTHONY BOWIE

Team: Orlando Magic
Position: Guard
Height: 6'6" **Weight:** 200
Birthdate: November 9, 1963

NBA Experience: 7 years
College: Oklahoma
Acquired: Signed as a free agent, 12/91

Background: Bowie played college ball at Oklahoma and was drafted by Houston in 1986, but he played his first NBA ball with San Antonio in 1988-89. He was signed by the Rockets in 1989 but was let go the following year. Bowie played his best ball in his first two years after joining Orlando from the CBA. He has spent the last five years with the Magic.

Strengths: Bowie is an energetic and versatile player who can shoot well in streaks. He is dangerous spotting up on the break, he has 3-point range, and he nails a high percentage of his free throws. Bowie can also be a disruptive on-the-ball defender. He plays with fire.

Weaknesses: Bowie often goes too fast for his own good and does not make wise decisions. His ball-handling and passing are suspect. He is better at finishing than starting plays. Bowie is at his best in transition and coming off screens rather than creating on his own. If you live with his streaks, you die with his cold spells.

Analysis: Bowie made big news for the first time last season when he notched his first triple-double. He grabbed his tenth rebound, called a late timeout in a game the Magic already had well in hand, and designed his own play to gain a tenth assist. The opposing Pistons, in protest, refused to defend. Other than this incident, Bowie's career has been quiet of late.

PLAYER SUMMARY	
Will	hit free throws
Can't	create for others
Expect	loads of energy
Don't Expect	more triple-doubles
Fantasy Value	$0
Card Value	5-10¢

COLLEGE STATISTICS

		G	FGP	FTP	RPG	PPG
84-85	OKLA	37	.515	.773	5.8	13.4
85-86	OKLA	35	.502	.808	4.6	13.3
Totals		72	.509	.787	5.2	13.4

NBA REGULAR-SEASON STATISTICS

				FGs		3-PT FGs		FTs		Rebounds						
		G	MIN	FG	PCT	FG	PCT	FT	PCT	OFF	TOT	AST	STL	BLK	PTS	PPG
88-89	SA	18	438	72	.500	1	.200	10	.667	25	56	29	18	4	155	8.6
89-90	HOU	66	918	119	.406	6	.286	40	.741	36	118	96	42	5	284	4.3
91-92	ORL	52	1721	312	.493	17	.386	117	.860	70	245	163	55	38	758	14.6
92-93	ORL	77	1761	268	.471	15	.313	67	.798	36	194	175	54	14	618	8.0
93-94	ORL	70	948	139	.481	1	.056	41	.837	29	120	102	32	12	320	4.6
94-95	ORL	77	1261	177	.480	12	.300	61	.824	54	139	159	47	21	427	5.5
95-96	ORL	74	1078	128	.471	12	.387	40	.870	40	123	105	34	10	308	4.2
Totals		434	8125	1215	.473	64	.309	376	.821	290	995	829	282	104	2870	6.6

SHAWN BRADLEY

Team: New Jersey Nets
Position: Center
Height: 7'6" **Weight:** 248
Birthdate: March 22, 1972
NBA Experience: 3 years

College: Brigham Young
Acquired: Traded from 76ers with Tim Perry and Greg Graham for Derrick Coleman, Rex Walters, and Sean Higgins, 11/95

Background: From tiny Castle Dale, Utah, Bradley played just one season at Brigham Young and blocked 177 shots as a freshman. He once swatted 14 in a game. He spent two years in Australia on a Mormon mission, then entered the NBA draft and was taken second overall by the 76ers. After two-plus years of criticism in Philly, Bradley was traded to the Nets during 1995-96 and enjoyed his best season.

Strengths: Everything Bradley contributes stems from his height. He is at his best when the other team has the ball, rating among the leading shot-swatters in the league. He has a wide wingspan to cover a lot of ground in the lane, and he has improved his rebounding. A star baseball player in high school, Bradley is a good athlete. He has worked on his offense, improving to 11.9 PPG last year.

Weaknesses: Built like a toothpick, Bradley apparently is unable to pack on much-needed pounds. The Nets have settled for helping him get stronger, if not bigger. Bradley's offensive moves remain mechanical, though he has developed a promising hook shot. His field-goal percentage is horrible for a big man, and he does not handle double-teams well. He gets very few assists and loads of fouls.

Analysis: Philadelphia's failed experiment may turn out to be New Jersey's gain. Bradley began to emerge near the end of the 1994-95 season, and his improved play in 1995-96 raised hopes that one day he will rank among the league's more productive pivot men. Bradley might never live down the fact he was chosen before Anfernee Hardaway, but at least he's trying.

PLAYER SUMMARY	
Will	block shots
Can't	bulk up
Expect	more improvement
Don't Expect	slick moves
Fantasy Value	$8-10
Card Value	10-20¢

COLLEGE STATISTICS

		G	FGP	FTP	RPG	PPG
90-91	BYU	34	.518	.692	7.7	14.8
Totals		34	.518	.692	7.7	14.8

NBA REGULAR-SEASON STATISTICS

			FGs		3-PT FGs		FTs		Rebounds						
	G	MIN	FG	PCT	FG	PCT	FT	PCT	OFF	TOT	AST	STL	BLK	PTS	PPG
93-94 PHI	49	1385	201	.409	0	.000	102	.607	98	306	98	45	147	504	10.3
94-95 PHI	82	2365	315	.455	0	.000	148	.638	243	659	53	54	274	778	9.5
95-96 PHI/NJ	79	2329	387	.443	1	.250	169	.687	221	638	63	49	288	944	11.9
Totals	210	6079	903	.439	1	.100	419	.649	562	1603	214	148	709	2226	10.6

TERRELL BRANDON

Team: Cleveland Cavaliers
Position: Guard
Height: 5'11" **Weight:** 180
Birthdate: May 20, 1970

NBA Experience: 5 years
College: Oregon
Acquired: First-round pick in 1991 draft (11th overall)

Background: Brandon played only two seasons at Oregon, but he led the Pac-10 in scoring and steals as a junior. Chosen 11th in the NBA draft, he served a four-year apprenticeship under Mark Price as backup point guard for the Cavaliers. Brandon earned the starting job in 1995-96 and enjoyed an All-Star season, leading the team in scoring, assists, and steals.

Strengths: Brandon is an offensive-minded point guard possessing explosive speed with the basketball. He has good vision and court sense, is an excellent leaper, and has become a fine leader. He has a quick release and 3-point range, and when opponents play in his face he can blow past for a layup. Brandon is one of the league's top free-throw shooters.

Weaknesses: Brandon has quickness and desire on his side, but his defense still lags behind his offense. The biggest problem is his size. He is simply too small to muscle up against his man or keep from being posted up by taller point guards like Penny Hardaway. Brandon will occasionally try to do too much by himself.

Analysis: Brandon has made the Cavaliers his team, and the league has taken notice. In 1996, he became only the eighth player in NBA history under six feet tall to play in the All-Star Game. He recorded career highs in most categories, surpassing his career total for 3-point field goals in one season as a starter. The fact that the Cavs parted with Price says a lot about Brandon.

PLAYER SUMMARY

Will ....create shots
Can't ....post up for points
Expect ....explosive drives
Don't Expect ......missed free throws
Fantasy Value $30-35
Card Value ....7-12¢

COLLEGE STATISTICS

		G	FGP	FTP	APG	PPG
89-90	OREG	29	.474	.752	6.0	17.9
90-91	OREG	28	.491	.850	5.0	26.6
Totals		57	.484	.810	5.5	22.2

NBA REGULAR-SEASON STATISTICS

				FGs		3-PT FGs		FTs		Rebounds						
		G	MIN	FG	PCT	FG	PCT	FT	PCT	OFF	TOT	AST	STL	BLK	PTS	PPG
91-92	CLE	82	1605	252	.419	1	.043	100	.806	49	162	316	81	22	605	7.4
92-93	CLE	82	1622	297	.478	13	.310	118	.825	37	179	302	79	27	725	8.8
93-94	CLE	73	1548	230	.420	7	.219	139	.858	38	159	277	84	16	606	8.3
94-95	CLE	67	1961	341	.448	48	.397	159	.855	35	186	363	107	14	889	13.3
95-96	CLE	75	2570	510	.465	91	.387	338	.887	47	248	487	132	33	1449	19.3
Totals		379	9306	1630	.449	160	.353	854	.857	206	934	1745	483	112	4274	11.3

FRANK BRICKOWSKI

Team: Boston Celtics
Position: Forward/Center
Height: 6'9" **Weight:** 248
Birthdate: August 14, 1959

NBA Experience: 11 years
College: Penn St.
Acquired: Signed as a free agent, 8/96

Background: Brickowski led Penn State in scoring his junior and senior years. After being drafted in the third round by the Knicks, he played overseas for three years in Italy, France, and Israel. He has played for the Sonics (twice), Lakers, Spurs, Bucks, and Hornets, in 11 NBA seasons, and sat out one entire year with the Kings (1994-95) because of a shoulder injury. He joins the Celtics for 1996-97.

Strengths: Brickowski has good size and footwork, and he knows his way around the basket. He has been an effective low-post scorer during his career and has become a surprisingly accurate 3-point shooter. He uses his muscle on defense.

Weaknesses: Injuries have limited what Brickowski can do. His knees are bad, and his right shoulder cost him a season. He no longer takes his man off the dribble like he once could, nor is he dominant in the post. Brickowski is not a strong rebounder or passer, and he picks up a lot of fouls.

Analysis: Brickowski, wearing down and unable to burn defenders with quickness, developed another weapon last season. After hitting just 16 treys over his first ten seasons, he doubled his output by drilling 32 of his 79 tries (.405). It's not a role that will make him a starter, however.

PLAYER SUMMARY

Will	pull his man outside
Can't	pound on his knees
Expect	aggressive defense
Don't Expect	long stretches
Fantasy Value	$1-3
Card Value	5-7¢

COLLEGE STATISTICS

		G	FGP	FTP	RPG	PPG
77-78	PSU	25	.457	.840	2.6	3.8
78-79	PSU	24	.495	.792	4.5	5.7
79-80	PSU	27	.521	.781	7.5	11.3
80-81	PSU	24	.601	.778	6.3	13.0
Totals		100	.537	.788	5.3	8.5

NBA REGULAR-SEASON STATISTICS

		G	MIN	FGs FG	FGs PCT	3-PT FGs FG	3-PT FGs PCT	FTs FT	FTs PCT	Rebounds OFF	Rebounds TOT	AST	STL	BLK	PTS	PPG
84-85	SEA	78	1115	150	.492	0	.000	85	.669	76	260	100	34	15	385	4.9
85-86	SEA	40	311	30	.517	0	.000	18	.667	16	54	21	11	7	78	2.0
86-87	LA/SA	44	487	63	.508	0	.000	50	.714	48	116	17	20	6	176	4.0
87-88	SA	70	2227	425	.528	1	.200	268	.768	167	483	266	74	36	1119	16.0
88-89	SA	64	1822	337	.515	0	.000	201	.715	148	406	131	102	35	875	13.7
89-90	SA	78	1438	211	.545	0	.000	95	.674	89	327	105	66	37	517	6.6
90-91	MIL	75	1912	372	.527	0	.000	198	.798	129	426	131	86	43	942	12.6
91-92	MIL	65	1556	306	.524	3	.500	125	.767	97	344	122	60	23	740	11.4
92-93	MIL	66	2075	456	.545	8	.308	195	.728	120	405	196	80	44	1115	16.9
93-94	MIL/CHA	71	2094	368	.488	4	.200	195	.768	85	404	222	80	27	935	13.2
95-96	SEA	63	986	123	.488	32	.405	61	.709	26	151	58	26	8	339	5.4
Totals		714	16023	2841	.520	48	.320	1491	.740	1001	3376	1369	639	281	7221	10.1

SCOTT BROOKS

Unrestricted Free Agent
Last Team: Dallas Mavericks
Position: Guard
Height: 5'11" **Weight:** 165
Birthdate: July 31, 1965
NBA Experience: 8 years

College: Texas Christian; San Joaquin Delta; Cal.-Irvine
Acquired: Traded from Rockets for Morlon Wiley and a 1995 second-round pick, 2/95

Background: Brooks divided his college career between Texas Christian, San Joaquin Delta Junior College, and finally Cal.-Irvine, where he led the Pacific Coast Athletic Association in scoring, steals, and free-throw percentage. Despite being bypassed in the NBA draft, he emerged from the CBA to play for Philadelphia, Minnesota, Houston, and Dallas over the last eight seasons.

Strengths: Brooks is a tireless worker who loves to pressure the ball. His quickness, hands, and ability to handle the ball make him a nice spark plug off the bench. He's a good penetrator, hits the 3, and rarely misses a free throw. He plays hard, makes few mistakes, and understands his role.

Weaknesses: Most of his offense comes when nothing else is available for Brooks, who is a passer first and scorer second. His size puts him at a huge disadvantage on defense, where he has trouble matching up against the bigger and better guards in the league. Brooks can't keep his man off the boards.

Analysis: This California surfer type loves playing basketball. Problem is, he has been stuck playing it behind the likes of Sam Cassell and Kenny Smith in Houston and Jason Kidd in Dallas. Brooks is a true setup man. He comes off the bench, runs the offense, and gets the ball to the right people. Scoring is not his game.

PLAYER SUMMARY	
Will	drive and dish
Can't	challenge shots
Expect	ball pressure
Don't Expect	a scoring bent
Fantasy Value	$0
Card Value	5-8¢

COLLEGE STATISTICS

		G	FGP	FTP	APG	PPG
83-84	TCU	27	.529	.714	1.4	3.8
84-85	SJD	31	.525	.882	—	13.1
85-86	UCI	30	.448	.886	3.2	10.3
86-87	UCI	28	.478	.845	3.8	23.8
Totals		116	.489	.860	2.8	12.8

NBA REGULAR-SEASON STATISTICS

			FGs		3-PT FGs		FTs		Rebounds						
	G	MIN	FG	PCT	FG	PCT	FT	PCT	OFF	TOT	AST	STL	BLK	PTS	PPG
88-89 PHI	82	1372	156	.420	55	.359	61	.884	19	94	306	69	3	428	5.2
89-90 PHI	72	975	119	.431	31	.392	50	.877	15	64	207	47	0	319	4.4
90-91 MIN	80	980	159	.430	45	.333	61	.847	28	72	204	53	5	424	5.3
91-92 MIN	82	1082	167	.447	32	.356	51	.810	27	99	205	66	7	417	5.1
92-93 HOU	82	1516	183	.475	41	.414	112	.830	22	99	243	79	3	519	6.3
93-94 HOU	73	1225	142	.491	23	.377	74	.871	10	102	149	51	2	381	5.2
94-95 HOU/DAL	59	808	126	.458	25	.362	64	.810	14	66	116	34	4	341	5.8
95-96 DAL	69	716	134	.457	25	.403	59	.855	11	41	100	42	3	352	5.1
Totals	599	8674	1186	.450	277	.370	532	.846	146	637	1530	441	27	3181	5.3

CHUCKY BROWN

Team: Phoenix Suns
Position: Forward
Height: 6'8" **Weight:** 215
Birthdate: February 29, 1968
NBA Experience: 7 years

College: North Carolina St.
Acquired: Traded from Rockets with Robert Horry, Sam Cassell, and Mark Bryant for Charles Barkley, 8/96

Background: Brown was selected to the All-ACC first team after his senior year at N.C. State, and he finished his career second on the school's career field-goal percentage list. Drafted 43rd in 1989, he has played all or parts of seven seasons with the Cavaliers, Lakers, Nets, Mavericks, and Rockets. The former CBA player became a full-time starter for Houston last year. He was part of the Charles Barkley deal in the off-season and joins the Suns for 1996-97.

Strengths: Brown's biggest asset is his team-first approach to the game. He has a variety of offensive weapons, including a jump hook with either hand and a decent jumper to about 16 feet. He runs the floor and battles on defense. He shoots a high percentage from the floor and can play both forward spots.

Weaknesses: Brown is a complementary player, not a main attraction. He is not as strong as most starting power forwards and not nearly as quick as most threes. He does not boast a dangerous post-up game, nor will he create anything off the dribble. Brown struggles from the free-throw line.

Analysis: One of many ex-CBA players to latch on with Houston in recent years, Brown helped the Rockets to their 1995 title as a valuable role-player. He earned a starting job last year and sustained the same hustle and desire that helped him escape from the minor leagues. Brown's career year is evidence that hard workers can make it in the NBA.

PLAYER SUMMARY

Will ....outwork his opponent
Can't ....create off the dribble
Expect ....high FG pct.
Don't Expect ....flashy moves
Fantasy Value $0
Card Value ....5-8¢

COLLEGE STATISTICS

		G	FGP	FTP	RPG	PPG
85-86	NCST	31	.475	.618	2.2	3.1
86-87	NCST	34	.587	.762	4.3	6.6
87-88	NCST	32	.572	.636	6.0	16.6
88-89	NCST	31	.548	.648	8.8	16.4
Totals		128	.557	.667	5.3	10.6

NBA REGULAR-SEASON STATISTICS

				FGs		3-PT FGs		FTs		Rebounds						
		G	MIN	FG	PCT	FG	PCT	FT	PCT	OFF	TOT	AST	STL	BLK	PTS	PPG
89-90	CLE	75	1339	210	.470	0	.000	125	.762	83	231	50	33	26	545	7.3
90-91	CLE	74	1485	263	.524	0	.000	101	.701	78	213	80	26	24	627	8.5
91-92	CLE/LAL	42	431	60	.469	0	.000	30	.612	31	82	26	12	7	150	3.6
92-93	NJ	77	1186	160	.483	0	.000	71	.724	88	232	51	20	24	391	5.1
93-94	DAL	1	10	1	1.000	0	.000	1	1.000	0	1	0	0	0	3	3.0
94-95	HOU	41	814	105	.603	1	.333	38	.613	64	189	30	11	14	249	6.1
95-96	HOU	82	2019	300	.541	1	.125	104	.693	134	441	89	47	38	705	8.6
Totals		392	7284	1099	.514	2	.067	470	.704	478	1389	326	149	133	2670	6.8

DEE BROWN

Team: Boston Celtics
Position: Guard
Height: 6'1" **Weight:** 175
Birthdate: November 29, 1968

NBA Experience: 6 years
College: Jacksonville
Acquired: First-round pick in 1990 draft (19th overall)

Background: Brown was Jacksonville's main man as a junior, leading the Dolphins in scoring, rebounding, and steals while splitting time between big guard and small forward. He was a first-team All-Rookie guard in Boston, then missed more than half of the 1991-92 season after knee surgery. He has started for most of his six seasons, but last year he was hampered by injuries and was often used as a reserve.

Strengths: Brown has a tremendous vertical leap that helped him win the NBA's 1991 Slam Dunk Contest. He plays both guard spots. Brown has lightning-quick speed and is especially dangerous on the break, where he can dish off or finish the play. He sinks his free throws and can drop 3-pointers. He comes up with his share of steals.

Weaknesses: Brown has been inconsistent throughout his career. While he plays both backcourt positions, he has not starred at either one. Since he's slight in build, there is not much he can do defensively when his man posts him up or runs him off a solid screen. He is not one of the better playmakers you'll see, especially in a half-court game.

Analysis: Knee and toe injuries contributed to Brown's poor 1995-96 season, and his upcoming seventh year in the league could be a telling one. Will Brown find his comfort zone, or will he continue to show flashes of stardom but fail to provide consistency? He has the athletic ability and skills to be a steady performer.

PLAYER SUMMARY

Will ....get off his feet
Can't..................shake inconsistency
Expect......................a versatile guard
Don't Expect ....physical strength
Fantasy Value $7-9
Card Value ....8-15¢

COLLEGE STATISTICS

		G	FGP	FTP	APG	PPG
86-87	JACK	21	.431	.591	0.8	3.4
87-88	JACK	28	.452	.818	2.0	10.1
88-89	JACK	30	.490	.824	3.7	19.6
89-90	JACK	29	.496	.683	5.2	19.3
Totals		108	.482	.762	3.1	13.9

NBA REGULAR-SEASON STATISTICS

				FGs		3-PT FGs		FTs		Rebounds						
		G	MIN	FG	PCT	FG	PCT	FT	PCT	OFF	TOT	AST	STL	BLK	PTS	PPG
90-91	BOS	82	1945	284	.464	7	.206	137	.873	41	182	344	83	14	712	8.7
91-92	BOS	31	883	149	.426	5	.227	60	.769	15	79	164	33	7	363	11.7
92-93	BOS	80	2254	328	.468	26	.317	192	.793	45	246	461	138	32	874	10.9
93-94	BOS	77	2867	490	.480	30	.313	182	.831	63	300	347	156	47	1192	15.5
94-95	BOS	79	2792	437	.447	126	.385	236	.852	63	249	301	110	49	1236	15.6
95-96	BOS	65	1591	246	.399	68	.309	135	.854	36	136	146	80	12	695	10.7
Totals		414	12332	1934	.452	262	.335	942	.833	263	1192	1763	600	161	5072	12.3

P.J. BROWN

Team: Miami Heat
Position: Forward
Height: 6'11" **Weight:** 240
Birthdate: October 14, 1968

NBA Experience: 3 years
College: Louisiana Tech
Acquired: Signed as a free agent, 7/96

Background: Brown, drafted by New Jersey in 1992, spent his first professional season in Greece after making contract demands the Nets were not prepared to meet. He averaged 17.0 PPG and 13.7 RPG overseas. New Jersey signed the former Louisiana Tech shot-blocking standout and first-team All-Sun Belt player before the 1993-94 season. He improved his scoring in each of his three NBA seasons and signed a huge free-agent deal with Miami in July 1996.

Strengths: Brown loves to play defense and is often asked to guard the opposition's best player, whether he's a two, three, or four. He has long arms and good timing to block shots and is also a solid rebounder. He creates contact and makes sure his matchup has to work for his points. Brown has gradually improved his offensive contributions to become a double-figure scorer.

Weaknesses: Putting the ball in the basket is not Brown's specialty, and it likely never will be. He does not have much to offer on the perimeter, and his shooting percentage is poor for a man who gets most of his touches close to the lane. You don't want Brown handling the ball on the perimeter. His physical style of play also leads to frequent foul trouble.

Analysis: Brown is a durable player who puts in a full workday. He has become a starter not for his scoring, but rather for his willingness to make the "hustle plays" while playing tough defense. You can count on him to block a shot, grab a half-dozen rebounds, and score ten-plus points on most nights. You can also count on him doing so without the need for much fanfare or pats on the back.

PLAYER SUMMARY	
Will	defend the stars
Can't	avoid fouls
Expect	constant hustle
Don't Expect	3-pointers
Fantasy Value	$4-6
Card Value	5-8¢

COLLEGE STATISTICS

		G	FGP	FTP	RPG	PPG
88-89	LT	32	.415	.568	5.6	4.7
89-90	LT	27	.461	.593	8.5	8.9
90-91	LT	31	.540	.653	9.7	14.4
91-92	LT	31	.489	.730	9.9	12.7
Totals		121	.488	.654	8.4	10.1

NBA REGULAR-SEASON STATISTICS

				FGs		3-PT FGs		FTs		Rebounds						
		G	MIN	FG	PCT	FG	PCT	FT	PCT	OFF	TOT	AST	STL	BLK	PTS	PPG
93-94	NJ	79	1950	167	.415	1	.167	115	.757	188	493	93	71	93	450	5.7
94-95	NJ	80	2466	254	.446	4	.167	139	.671	178	487	135	69	135	651	8.1
95-96	NJ	81	2942	354	.444	3	.200	204	.770	215	560	165	79	100	915	11.3
Totals		240	7358	775	.438	8	.178	458	.734	581	1540	393	219	328	2016	8.4

RANDY BROWN

Team: Chicago Bulls
Position: Guard
Height: 6'2" **Weight:** 191
Birthdate: May 22, 1968

NBA Experience: 5 years
College: Houston; New Mexico St.
Acquired: Signed as a free agent, 10/95

Background: Brown started his college career at Houston, transferred to New Mexico State after his sophomore year, and set school records for assists and steals while twice earning first-team All-Big West honors. Sacramento made him a second-round draft choice in 1991 and used him as a reserve for four years. Brown signed as a free agent with the Bulls before last season.

Strengths: Brown's best attribute is his defense. He's quick and tough, has good hands, and is not afraid to challenge opponents. If he played even 20 minutes per game, he'd probably rank among the top thieves in the NBA. He also rebounds from the backcourt and makes hustle plays.

Weaknesses: Brown's offensive skills border on CBA-level. He is not a good enough ball-handler or passer to thrive at the point, yet his jump shot will not earn him a living as a starting two. He shoots a very low percentage from the field, he struggles from the free-throw line, and the 3-pointer is not his shot, either. Brown has seen his playing time shrink.

Analysis: Brown wears a zero on the back of his jersey, and that's about as much scoring as you'll get from him. On the other hand, it's also the number of points to which he tries to hold each opponent. Brown is a one-dimensional player who can inspire a team with his defense and hurt it on the other end of the floor. He averaged less than ten minutes per game last season.

PLAYER SUMMARY

Will ....pick your pocket
Can't ....shoot straight
Expect........................limited minutes
Don't Expect ....much offense
Fantasy Value $0
Card Value ....7-12¢

COLLEGE STATISTICS

		G	FGP	FTP	APG	PPG
86-87	HOUS	28	.506	.583	2.9	3.8
87-88	HOUS	29	.451	.750	5.6	7.0
89-90	NMST	31	.446	.712	3.5	13.2
90-91	NMST	29	.399	.691	6.4	12.1
Totals		117	.436	.703	4.6	9.1

NBA REGULAR-SEASON STATISTICS

				FGs		3-PT FGs		FTs		Rebounds						
		G	MIN	FG	PCT	FG	PCT	FT	PCT	OFF	TOT	AST	STL	BLK	PTS	PPG
91-92	SAC	56	535	77	.456	0	.000	38	.655	26	69	59	35	12	192	3.4
92-93	SAC	75	1726	225	.463	2	.333	115	.732	75	212	196	108	34	567	7.6
93-94	SAC	61	1041	110	.438	0	.000	53	.609	40	112	133	63	14	273	4.5
94-95	SAC	67	1086	124	.432	14	.298	55	.671	24	108	133	99	19	317	4.7
95-96	CHI	68	671	78	.406	1	.091	28	.609	17	66	73	57	12	185	2.7
Totals		327	5059	614	.443	17	.230	289	.672	182	567	594	362	91	1534	4.7

MARK BRYANT

Team: Phoenix Suns
Position: Forward
Height: 6'9" **Weight:** 245
Birthdate: April 25, 1965
NBA Experience: 8 years

College: Seton Hall
Acquired: Traded from Rockets with Robert Horry, Sam Cassell, and Chucky Brown for Charles Barkley, 8/96

Background: As a senior, Bryant helped take Seton Hall to its first NCAA Tournament and was an All-Big East selection. A late first-round draft pick, he spent seven years in Portland as a reserve forward before being picked up by Houston, where he averaged career highs in scoring and rebounding last season. He was part of a package sent to the Suns in the off-season for Charles Barkley.

Strengths: Bryant is a hard-working player who knows how to help a team. He plays tough interior defense and is willing to throw his weight around. He rebounds, runs the floor, and owns a decent short-range jump shot. He shoots for a high percentage because he knows his limitations.

Weaknesses: Bryant is a limited offensive player who will never score a lot of points. He possesses neither great range nor sleek moves to the hoop. He is not a good ball-handler or passer, either. In short, he is easy to overlook in a box score. Bryant has battled foul trouble throughout his career. Quicker players can give him trouble.

Analysis: The move to Houston was a good one for the unspectacular but hard-working Bryant. Surrounded by talented teammates, he was able to spend his energy coming off the bench and igniting the team with his all-out effort, rebounding, and defense. A veteran reserve who can still contribute at both ends, Bryant is a nice fit as a complementary player.

PLAYER SUMMARY	
Will	make half his shots
Can't	take over a game
Expect	a hard-working reserve
Don't Expect	10 PPG
Fantasy Value	$1
Card Value	5-8¢

COLLEGE STATISTICS

		G	FGP	FTP	RPG	PPG
84-85	SH	26	.475	.649	6.8	12.2
85-86	SH	30	.523	.678	7.5	14.0
86-87	SH	28	.496	.706	7.1	16.8
87-88	SH	34	.564	.748	9.1	20.5
Totals		118	.521	.705	7.7	16.2

NBA REGULAR-SEASON STATISTICS

		G	MIN	FGs		3-PT FGs		FTs		Rebounds		AST	STL	BLK	PTS	PPG
				FG	PCT	FG	PCT	FT	PCT	OFF	TOT					
88-89	POR	56	803	120	.486	0	.000	40	.580	65	179	33	20	7	280	5.0
89-90	POR	58	562	70	.458	0	.000	28	.560	54	146	13	18	9	168	2.9
90-91	POR	53	781	99	.488	0	.000	74	.733	65	190	27	15	12	272	5.1
91-92	POR	56	800	95	.480	0	.000	40	.667	87	201	41	26	8	230	4.1
92-93	POR	80	1396	186	.503	0	.000	104	.703	132	324	41	37	23	476	5.9
93-94	POR	79	1441	185	.482	0	.000	72	.692	117	315	37	32	29	442	5.6
94-95	POR	49	658	101	.526	1	.500	41	.651	55	161	28	19	16	244	5.0
95-96	HOU	71	1587	242	.543	0	.000	127	.718	131	351	52	31	19	611	8.6
Totals		502	8028	1098	.501	1	.100	526	.681	706	1867	272	198	123	2723	5.4

JUD BUECHLER

Team: Chicago Bulls
Position: Guard/Forward
Height: 6'6" **Weight:** 228
Birthdate: June 19, 1968

NBA Experience: 6 years
College: Arizona
Acquired: Signed as a free agent, 9/94

Background: Buechler was Arizona's top scorer and rebounder as a senior, and he finished his career with a blazing 54.7 shooting percentage. He was All-Pac-10 his senior year and has spent six NBA seasons with four different teams. After stints with the Nets, Spurs, and Warriors, Buechler has been a Chicago reserve in each of the last two seasons.

Strengths: Buechler is a coach's player. He knows his NBA career depends on doing the dirty work, so that's what he does. He rebounds, sets picks, and gets after his man on defense. He sacrifices his body for the good of the team. Buechler can play big guard or either forward spot. He is dangerous from the 3-point arc.

Weaknesses: Buechler is not among the most physically gifted players in the NBA. He defers to others on the offensive end, as he is unable to create off the bounce. He lacks the quickness to keep up with speedy players for more than spot minutes. Surprisingly, Buechler has never been accurate from the free-throw line.

Analysis: If you judge a player by the number of scratches and bruises he takes for the team, Buechler is a success. He makes few mistakes and earns playing time because of his hustle and his willingness to bang on defense. He's the definition of a team player who gets the most out of his talents.

PLAYER SUMMARY	
Will	bang on defense
Can't	direct the offense
Expect	all-out hustle
Don't Expect	windmill jams
Fantasy Value	$0
Card Value	5-8¢

COLLEGE STATISTICS

		G	FGP	FTP	RPG	PPG
86-87	ARIZ	30	.486	.571	2.3	4.5
87-88	ARIZ	36	.516	.655	2.4	4.7
88-89	ARIZ	33	.607	.816	6.6	11.0
89-90	ARIZ	32	.538	.765	8.3	14.9
Totals		131	.547	.743	4.9	8.7

NBA REGULAR-SEASON STATISTICS

		G	MIN	FGs FG	PCT	3-PT FGs FG	PCT	FTs FT	PCT	Rebounds OFF	TOT	AST	STL	BLK	PTS	PPG
90-91	NJ	74	859	94	.416	1	.250	43	.652	61	141	51	33	15	232	3.1
91-92	NJ/SA/GS	28	290	29	.408	0	.000	12	.571	18	52	23	19	7	70	2.5
92-93	GS	70	1287	176	.437	20	.339	65	.747	81	195	94	47	19	437	6.2
93-94	GS	36	218	42	.500	12	.414	10	.500	13	32	16	8	1	106	2.9
94-95	CHI	57	605	90	.492	15	.313	22	.564	36	98	50	24	12	217	3.8
95-96	CHI	74	740	112	.463	40	.444	14	.636	45	111	56	34	7	278	3.8
Totals		339	3999	543	.449	88	.381	166	.651	254	629	290	165	61	1340	4.0

SCOTT BURRELL

Team: Charlotte Hornets
Position: Forward
Height: 6'7" **Weight:** 218
Birthdate: January 12, 1971

NBA Experience: 3 years
College: Connecticut
Acquired: First-round pick in 1993 draft (20th overall)

Background: A defensive star at Connecticut, Burrell became the only player in NCAA Division I history to amass 1,500 points, 750 rebounds, 300 steals, and 275 assists. He doubled as a baseball pitcher in the Blue Jays' farm system for three seasons. Burrell was drafted 20th by Charlotte and became a starter in his second year. He raised his scoring average to 13.2 PPG in 1995-96, but shoulder surgery ended his season after just 20 games.

Strengths: Everyone knew Burrell could play defense, but his accuracy from the 3-point arc (about 40 percent) and penchant for scoring were shocks to almost everyone. He made only two 3-pointers as a rookie before breaking loose. On defense, he uses his wingspan and quick hands to anticipate passes and get steals. A great athlete, Burrell hustles and loves to run.

Weaknesses: Burrell is a spot-up shooter. He has trouble creating his own shot (except in transition) and is less effective off the dribble. He is also not the best passer or ball-handler among NBA starting small forwards. The greatest concern is his recent history of injuries. A dislocated right shoulder cut last season short, and a ruptured Achilles did the same the year before.

Analysis: If he can stay healthy for a full season, Burrell has the look of an emerging young player with vast potential. He has lived up to his lofty defensive reputation while demonstrating a surprising knack for putting the ball in the hole. He complements his natural athletic ability with a great attitude and work ethic, and he wants nothing more than a full 1996-97 season to shine.

PLAYER SUMMARY

Will	play the passing lanes
Can't	avoid injuries
Expect	defense, 3-pointers
Don't Expect	many open looks
Fantasy Value	$10-13
Card Value	10-20¢

COLLEGE STATISTICS

		G	FGP	FTP	RPG	PPG
89-90	CONN	32	.386	.623	5.5	8.2
90-91	CONN	31	.440	.592	7.5	12.7
91-92	CONN	30	.453	.611	6.1	16.3
92-93	CONN	26	.411	.760	6.0	16.1
Totals		119	.426	.640	6.3	13.1

NBA REGULAR-SEASON STATISTICS

			FGs		3-PT FGs		FTs		Rebounds						
	G	MIN	FG	PCT	FG	PCT	FT	PCT	OFF	TOT	AST	STL	BLK	PTS	PPG
93-94 CHA	51	767	98	.419	2	.333	46	.657	46	132	62	37	16	244	4.8
94-95 CHA	65	2014	277	.467	96	.409	100	.694	96	368	161	75	40	750	11.5
95-96 CHA	20	693	92	.447	37	.378	42	.750	26	98	47	27	13	263	13.2
Totals	136	3474	467	.452	135	.398	188	.696	168	598	270	139	69	1257	9.2

MITCHELL BUTLER

Team: Portland Trail Blazers
Position: Guard/Forward
Height: 6'5" **Weight:** 210
Birthdate: December 15, 1970
NBA Experience: 3 years

College: UCLA
Acquired: Traded from Bullets with
Rasheed Wallace for Harvey Grant
and Rod Strickland, 7/96

Background: Butler was a standout on a UCLA team that also included current NBA players Don MacLean and Tracy Murray. Though he helped the Bruins back to national prominence while playing as many as four different positions, Butler was bypassed in the 1993 NBA draft. He played his way onto Washington's roster and enjoyed two surprising years before seeing limited duty in 1995-96. A July 1996 trade sent him to Portland.

Strengths: Butler is blessed with athletic ability and versatility. He can play both guard and forward, posting up smaller players and driving past bigger ones. He has a quick first step and fares well in an up-tempo game, where he can pull up for jumpers, finish with jams, or find open men. Butler is capable of playing in-your-face defense.

Weaknesses: Butler showed some 3-point promise during his second season, but he has struggled with his shot. He converts at a low rate from both the field and the free-throw line and often finds his man leaving him to double-team another player. Butler has never been a big scorer.

Analysis: Once considered a marginal talent coming out of college, Butler was a pleasant surprise for two years before spending most of the 1995-96 season on the end of the Bullets' bench. He simply did not do enough on offense to justify a spot in the regular rotation, although his defense and athletic ability remain promising. He needs to work on his jumper and develop consistency in all phases of the game.

PLAYER SUMMARY	
Will	run the floor
Can't	light it up
Expect	reserve minutes
Don't Expect	consistency
Fantasy Value	$0
Card Value	5-7¢

COLLEGE STATISTICS

		G	FGP	FTP	RPG	PPG
89-90	UCLA	33	.538	.625	2.8	6.2
90-91	UCLA	32	.548	.513	4.2	7.9
91-92	UCLA	33	.489	.451	4.2	8.0
92-93	UCLA	32	.512	.526	5.3	9.5
Totals		130	.519	.528	4.1	7.9

NBA REGULAR-SEASON STATISTICS

		G	MIN	FGs FG	FGs PCT	3-PT FGs FG	3-PT FGs PCT	FTs FT	FTs PCT	Rebounds OFF	Rebounds TOT	AST	STL	BLK	PTS	PPG
93-94	WAS	75	1321	207	.495	0	.000	104	.578	106	225	77	54	20	518	6.9
94-95	WAS	76	1554	214	.421	46	.326	123	.665	43	170	91	61	10	597	7.9
95-96	WAS	61	858	88	.384	13	.217	48	.578	29	118	67	41	12	237	3.9
Totals		212	3733	509	.441	59	.286	275	.614	178	513	235	156	42	1352	6.4

JASON CAFFEY

Team: Chicago Bulls
Position: Forward
Height: 6'8" **Weight:** 256
Birthdate: June 12, 1973

NBA Experience: 1 year
College: Alabama
Acquired: First-round pick in 1995
draft (20th overall)

Background: Caffey averaged a modest 10.4 points per game at Alabama, earning second-team All-SEC accolades as a senior. He also contributed 8.0 RPG in his senior year for the Crimson Tide and shot better than 50 percent in each of his last three seasons. Caffey was chosen 20th by the Bulls in the 1995 draft, and the rookie spent most of Chicago's 72-win season on the Bulls' bench and the injured list.

Strengths: Caffey is an athletic player who seems taller because of his long arms and explosive leaping ability. He can be a force on the offensive boards, and he can also beat his man to the basket off the dribble. Some pundits feel Caffey will eventually become comfortable at the three spot in addition to the four. He gets out on the break, has good hands, and is willing to work hard on defense.

Weaknesses: One has to wonder whether Caffey will ever be an adequate shooter. His free-throw percentage is terrible and his range quite limited. He made only four 3-pointers in college and is not a threat to spot-up from the NBA arc. Caffey is not strong enough to push the bigger power forwards around in the paint, so something has to give. His history includes various injuries, and he was nagged by a few last season.

Analysis: As expected, Caffey did not see much floor time in his first pro season. Instead, the Bulls turned to forwards named Rodman, Pippen, and Kukoc. Caffey has a long way to go before earning a spot in the regular rotation. He could help his chances by working on his jump shot and mastering a few post moves. Knee injuries have troubled him in the past.

PLAYER SUMMARY

Will .... soar after rebounds
Can't .... shoot free throws
Expect .... much coaching
Don't Expect .... creative moves
Fantasy Value $0
Card Value .... 12-20¢

COLLEGE STATISTICS

		G	FGP	FTP	RPG	PPG
91-92	ALAB	30	.425	.333	2.2	2.4
92-93	ALAB	29	.518	.615	8.7	14.5
93-94	ALAB	29	.520	.629	6.3	12.8
94-95	ALAB	31	.509	.545	8.0	12.1
Totals		119	.509	.578	6.3	10.4

NBA REGULAR-SEASON STATISTICS

			FGs		3-PT FGs		FTs		Rebounds						
	G	MIN	FG	PCT	FG	PCT	FT	PCT	OFF	TOT	AST	STL	BLK	PTS	PPG
95-96 CHI	57	545	71	.438	0	.000	40	.588	51	111	24	12	7	182	3.2
Totals	57	545	71	.438	0	.000	40	.588	51	111	24	12	7	182	3.2

MICHAEL CAGE

Team: Philadelphia 76ers
Position: Forward/Center
Height: 6'9" **Weight:** 248
Birthdate: January 28, 1962

NBA Experience: 12 years
College: San Diego St.
Acquired: Signed as a free agent, 8/96

Background: Cage was voted Western Athletic Conference Player of the Year as a senior at San Diego State. He finished as the school's career leader in scoring, rebounding, and games played. He won the NBA rebounding title in 1987-88 and has played every game over the last seven seasons. He spent the last two seasons with Cleveland but has also played with the Clippers and Sonics. He joins the 76ers for 1996-97.

Strengths: The tough, muscular Cage has made his living off the backboard and still rates among the better board men in the league. He can block shots, and he plays tough interior defense. Cage can fill in at center and shoots a high percentage. He makes steals, and his durability has been remarkable.

Weaknesses: Offense does not come easily for Cage. His low-post moves are predictable, and he has no range to speak of. He's not a reliable ball-handler or passer and is a lousy free-throw shooter.

Analysis: Cage is a consummate pro who knows what he can and can't do. He shows up to rebound and play defense and leaves the brunt of the offense to those more qualified. And does he ever show up! His current streak of 574 consecutive games played is second only to A.C. Green's 812.

PLAYER SUMMARY	
Will	...................come to work
Can't	.....................shoot free throws
Expect	....................defense, rebounds
Don't Expect	............missed games
Fantasy Value	.....................................$1
Card Value	.....................................5-7¢

COLLEGE STATISTICS

		G	FGP	FTP	RPG	PPG
80-81	SDST	27	.558	.756	13.1	10.9
81-82	SDST	29	.488	.661	8.8	11.0
82-83	SDST	28	.570	.747	12.6	19.5
83-84	SDST	28	.562	.741	12.6	24.5
Totals		112	.548	.732	11.8	16.5

NBA REGULAR-SEASON STATISTICS

				FGs		3-PT FGs		FTs		Rebounds						
		G	MIN	FG	PCT	FG	PCT	FT	PCT	OFF	TOT	AST	STL	BLK	PTS	PPG
84-85	LAC	75	1610	216	.543	0	.000	101	.737	126	392	51	41	32	533	7.1
85-86	LAC	78	1566	204	.479	0	.000	113	.649	168	417	81	62	34	521	6.7
86-87	LAC	80	2922	457	.521	0	.000	341	.730	354	922	131	99	67	1255	15.7
87-88	LAC	72	2660	360	.470	0	.000	326	.688	371	938	110	91	58	1046	14.5
88-89	SEA	80	2536	314	.498	0	.000	197	.743	276	765	126	92	52	825	10.3
89-90	SEA	82	2595	325	.504	0	.000	148	.698	306	821	70	79	45	798	9.7
90-91	SEA	82	2141	226	.508	0	.000	70	.625	177	558	89	85	58	522	6.4
91-92	SEA	82	2461	307	.566	0	.000	106	.620	266	728	92	99	55	720	8.8
92-93	SEA	82	2156	219	.526	0	.000	61	.469	268	659	69	76	46	499	6.1
93-94	SEA	82	1708	171	.545	0	.000	36	.486	164	444	45	77	38	378	4.6
94-95	CLE	82	2040	177	.521	0	.000	53	.602	203	564	56	61	67	407	5.0
95-96	CLE	82	2631	220	.556	0	.000	50	.543	288	729	53	87	79	490	6.0
Totals		959	27026	3196	.516	0	.000	1602	.669	2967	7937	973	949	631	7994	8.3

ELDEN CAMPBELL

Team: Los Angeles Lakers
Position: Forward/Center
Height: 6'11" **Weight:** 250
Birthdate: July 23, 1968

NBA Experience: 6 years
College: Clemson
Acquired: First-round pick in 1990 draft (27th overall)

Background: Campbell led the Atlantic Coast Conference in blocked shots three straight years and became Clemson's all-time scoring leader. He scored 21 points in an NBA Finals game as a rookie and has rated among the league's top 15 shot-blockers four times since. A starting power forward over the last three years, Campbell averaged a career-high 13.9 PPG during the 1995-96 season.

Strengths: Best known for his shot-blocking and defensive intimidation, Campbell displays great instincts for the ball, has a huge wingspan, and is a superb athlete and leaper. He swatted about 2.6 shots per game last season, a career best, and his on-the-ball defense is also reliable. He has made himself a more active offensive player and shot 50 percent for the first time.

Weaknesses: Labeled inconsistent over his first few seasons, Campbell is beginning to shake that reputation. He is still guilty at times of not looking for his shots inside, and his face-up game is merely adequate. Campbell has improved his touch from the free-throw line but remains subpar. With his physical tools, he can still become a more effective rebounder.

Analysis: Campbell's detractors are becoming fewer as he continues to approach his potential. He raised his level of play in virtually every aspect of the game last season, from scoring to shot-blocking to accuracy from the field and the free-throw line. He may not be the Lakers' main attraction, but Campbell is on the right track.

PLAYER SUMMARY

Will ....swat shots
Can't ....live off jumpers
Expect ....disruptive defense
Don't Expect ....3-point range
Fantasy Value $16-19
Card Value ....7-10¢

COLLEGE STATISTICS

		G	FGP	FTP	RPG	PPG
86-87	CLEM	31	.554	.702	4.1	8.8
87-88	CLEM	28	.629	.619	7.4	18.8
88-89	CLEM	29	.550	.688	7.7	17.5
89-90	CLEM	35	.522	.599	8.0	16.4
Totals		123	.562	.641	6.8	15.3

NBA REGULAR-SEASON STATISTICS

		G	MIN	FGs		3-PT FGs		FTs		Rebounds		AST	STL	BLK	PTS	PPG
				FG	PCT	FG	PCT	FT	PCT	OFF	TOT					
90-91	LAL	52	380	56	.455	0	.000	32	.653	40	96	10	11	38	144	2.8
91-92	LAL	81	1876	220	.448	0	.000	138	.619	159	423	59	53	159	578	7.1
92-93	LAL	79	1551	238	.458	0	.000	130	.637	127	332	48	59	100	606	7.7
93-94	LAL	76	2253	373	.462	0	.000	188	.689	167	519	86	64	146	934	12.3
94-95	LAL	73	2076	360	.459	0	.000	193	.666	168	445	92	69	132	913	12.5
95-96	LAL	82	2699	447	.503	0	.000	249	.713	162	623	181	88	212	1143	13.9
Totals		443	10835	1694	.469	0	.000	930	.670	819	2438	476	344	787	4318	9.7

ANTOINE CARR

Team: Utah Jazz
Position: Forward/Center
Height: 6'9" **Weight:** 225
Birthdate: July 23, 1961

NBA Experience: 12 years
College: Wichita St.
Acquired: Signed as a free agent, 10/94

Background: Carr played with Cliff Levingston and Xavier McDaniel at Wichita State, where his No. 35 was retired after an All-America career. He played five-plus years in Atlanta before becoming a big scorer in Sacramento. He spent three years in San Antonio and has been a Utah reserve over the last two seasons.

Strengths: The powerful Carr can play both power forward and center because of his strong low-post game at both ends of the floor. He holds his position in the lane, loves to put his body on opposing players, and has a vast array of scoring moves. He can also step outside and stick jumpers.

Weaknesses: Though strong enough to shatter a backboard (he once did so during warmups), Carr has never been a great rebounder. This notorious bruiser has always picked up a lot of fouls. His passing and ball-handling are subpar.

Analysis: After a dozen years in the league, Carr is still able to play a prominent role off the bench. He is a skilled offensive player, particularly in the post, and he knows how to deliver bruising defense against opposing big men. The versatile veteran can contribute for a couple more years.

PLAYER SUMMARY

Will ....play two positions
Can't ....hide from officials
Expect ....a veteran reserve
Don't Expect ....loads of boards
Fantasy Value $0
Card Value ....5-8¢

COLLEGE STATISTICS

		G	FGP	FTP	RPG	PPG
79-80	WSU	29	.501	.667	5.9	15.2
80-81	WSU	33	.586	.765	7.3	15.8
81-82	WSU	28	.566	.791	7.0	16.0
82-83	WSU	22	.575	.765	7.6	22.6
Totals		112	.557	.746	6.9	17.1

NBA REGULAR-SEASON STATISTICS

				FGs		3-PT FGs		FTs		Rebounds						
		G	MIN	FG	PCT	FG	PCT	FT	PCT	OFF	TOT	AST	STL	BLK	PTS	PPG
84-85	ATL	62	1195	198	.528	2	.333	101	.789	79	232	80	29	78	499	8.0
85-86	ATL	17	258	49	.527	0	.000	18	.667	16	52	14	7	15	116	6.8
86-87	ATL	65	695	134	.506	1	.333	73	.709	60	156	34	14	48	342	5.3
87-88	ATL	80	1483	281	.544	1	.250	142	.780	94	289	103	38	83	705	8.8
88-89	ATL	78	1488	226	.480	0	.000	130	.855	106	274	91	31	62	582	7.5
89-90	ATL/SAC	77	1727	356	.494	0	.000	237	.795	115	322	119	30	68	949	12.3
90-91	SAC	77	2527	628	.511	0	.000	295	.758	163	420	191	45	101	1551	20.1
91-92	SA	81	1867	359	.490	1	.200	162	.764	128	346	63	32	96	881	10.9
92-93	SA	71	1947	379	.538	0	.000	174	.777	107	388	97	35	87	932	13.1
93-94	SA	34	465	78	.488	0	.000	42	.724	12	51	15	9	22	198	5.8
94-95	UTA	78	1677	290	.531	1	.250	165	.821	81	265	67	24	68	746	9.6
95-96	UTA	80	1532	233	.457	0	.000	114	.792	71	200	74	28	65	580	7.3
Totals		800	16861	3211	.508	6	.143	1653	.780	1032	2995	948	322	793	8081	10.1

CHRIS CARR

Team: Minnesota Timberwolves
Position: Guard
Height: 6'5" **Weight:** 207
Birthdate: March 12, 1974

NBA Experience: 1 year
College: Southern Illinois
Acquired: Signed as a free agent, 7/96

Background: Carr improved his scoring average considerably each year at Southern Illinois before leaving school after his junior season. He was named Missouri Valley Conference Player of the Year in 1994-95. One of the final three picks in the 1995 draft, he spent much of his rookie year on the Phoenix bench but did make ten starts. He joins the Timberwolves for 1996-97.

Strengths: Carr possesses good size for a guard and is able to get off his feet. He is capable of scoring in the post, in transition, and from 3-point distance. Carr can easily get his shot off the dribble and is a threat to nail several in a row. He races down the court and can trigger the break. He made better than eight of every ten free throws as a rookie. His best asset may be his youth. He's still developing.

Weaknesses: Carr is a streaky player. His jump shot comes and goes, and his cold spells can relegate him to the bench quicker than you can say "airball." He has a lot to learn about NBA defense. He's not quick enough to handle starting two guards, or at least he hasn't yet proven to be. Carr has been perceived by some as a selfish player with a below-average feel for the game and marginal skills.

Analysis: Critics were everywhere when Carr signed with an agent and came out of school early. He first surprised them when he made the Suns' roster, and then again when he showed an ability to get his shot off. He averaged less than ten minutes per game and struggled, but Carr finished his rookie year with a stunning 17-point playoff performance against San Antonio that could bode well for his future.

PLAYER SUMMARY	
Will	score in spurts
Can't	shut down his man
Expect	further strides
Don't Expect	stardom
Fantasy Value	$0
Card Value	7-12¢

COLLEGE STATISTICS

		G	FGP	FTP	RPG	PPG
92-93	SIU	31	.591	.545	3.5	3.9
93-94	SIU	30	.518	.807	6.6	14.1
94-95	SIU	32	.480	.771	7.3	22.0
Totals		93	.503	.757	5.8	13.5

NBA REGULAR-SEASON STATISTICS

			FGs		3-PT FGs		FTs		Rebounds						
	G	MIN	FG	PCT	FG	PCT	FT	PCT	OFF	TOT	AST	STL	BLK	PTS	PPG
95-96 PHO	60	590	90	.415	11	.262	49	.817	27	102	43	10	5	240	4.0
Totals	60	590	90	.415	11	.262	49	.817	27	102	43	10	5	240	4.0

SAM CASSELL

Team: Phoenix Suns
Position: Guard
Height: 6'3" **Weight:** 185
Birthdate: November 18, 1969
NBA Experience: 3 years

College: San Jacinto; Florida St.
Acquired: Traded from Rockets with Robert Horry, Chucky Brown, and Mark Bryant for Charles Barkley, 8/96

Background: From legendary Dunbar High in Baltimore, Cassell had two sensational seasons at San Jacinto J.C. in Texas before transferring to Florida State. He prospered on a talented Seminole unit, leading the Atlantic Coast Conference in steals. Drafted 24th by Houston in 1993, he came up big off the bench on back-to-back championship teams, then upped his scoring to 14.5 PPG last season. He was dealt to the Suns as part of the Charles Barkley deal last August.

Strengths: Many consider Cassell the best backup point guard in the NBA because of his scoring and playmaking ability. He uses his superb quickness and agility to get to the basket almost anytime he pleases. Cassell is a very good free-throw shooter, and he also has 3-point range. He gets after it on defense and seems to be at his best when he's under big-game pressure.

Weaknesses: Taking better care of the ball and becoming a better outside shooter should be the top two tasks on Cassell's list of goals. He will turn the ball over while trying to make the spectacular play, and he does not shoot a high percentage from the field or 3-point arc. Cassell tends to take risks on both ends of the court, and they don't always pan out.

Analysis: Cassell, destined to be a starter soon, is capable of igniting his team with scoring and playmaking. He did so as a reserve with the Rockets, while developing a reputation for making clutch plays late in games. He has also made several 40- to 50-footers to beat buzzers in his young career. He underwent arthroscopic surgery on his right elbow in March.

PLAYER SUMMARY	
Will	get past his man
Can't	rely on his jumper
Expect	clutch plays
Don't Expect	conservative play
Fantasy Value	$6-8
Card Value	10-20¢

COLLEGE STATISTICS

		G	FGP	FTP	APG	PPG
91-92	FSU	31	.454	.704	3.8	18.4
92-93	FSU	35	.502	.759	4.9	18.3
Totals		66	.478	.733	4.4	18.3

NBA REGULAR-SEASON STATISTICS

				FGs		3-PT FGs		FTs		Rebounds						
		G	MIN	FG	PCT	FG	PCT	FT	PCT	OFF	TOT	AST	STL	BLK	PTS	PPG
93-94	HOU	66	1122	162	.418	26	.295	90	.841	25	134	192	59	7	440	6.7
94-95	HOU	82	1882	253	.427	63	.330	214	.843	38	211	405	94	14	783	9.5
95-96	HOU	61	1682	289	.439	73	.348	235	.825	51	188	278	53	4	886	14.5
Totals		209	4686	704	.430	162	.331	539	.834	114	533	875	206	25	2109	10.1

CEDRIC CEBALLOS

Team: Los Angeles Lakers
Position: Forward
Height: 6'7" **Weight:** 225
Birthdate: August 2, 1969

NBA Experience: 6 years
College: Cal. St. Fullerton
Acquired: Traded from Suns for a future first-round pick, 9/94

Background: Ceballos, a Hawaii native, played just one year of varsity basketball in high school before going on to lead the Big West in scoring as a junior and senior at Cal. State Fullerton. A No. 48 pick, he surprised many by becoming a starter in Phoenix and was the NBA's most accurate field-goal shooter in 1992-93. After a trade, he played in the 1995 All-Star Game as a Laker and has led the team in scoring the last two years.

Strengths: Ceballos is an energetic, athletic player who can flat-out score. He plays above the rim, gets to the basket, and shoots a high percentage. He runs the floor and has great hands. Ceballos is a spirited performer who won the NBA's Slam Dunk Contest in 1992 with a blindfolded jam. He also rebounds well and has improved his perimeter shot and free-throw accuracy.

Weaknesses: Defense has been the main question regarding Ceballos. Although Laker coach Del Harris has insisted on improvement, Ceballos sometimes has to be pushed in that area. He is not an accurate 3-point shooter but continues to launch treys nonetheless. He could also stand to be more aware of open teammates.

Analysis: Ceballos can put a team on his shoulders and carry it offensively. However, in March, the league saw a less attractive side of him when he disappeared for two games without notifying anyone of his decision to "take care of family issues." Although Ceballos denied it, many speculated he was upset with Magic Johnson's increased minutes.

PLAYER SUMMARY	
Will	light up the nets
Can't	dominate on defense
Expect	20-plus PPG
Don't Expect	a distributor
Fantasy Value	$35-40
Card Value	8-12¢

COLLEGE STATISTICS

		G	FGP	FTP	RPG	PPG
88-89	CSF	29	.442	.672	8.8	21.2
89-90	CSF	29	.485	.670	12.5	23.1
Totals		58	.463	.671	10.7	22.1

NBA REGULAR-SEASON STATISTICS

		G	MIN	FGs FG	FGs PCT	3-PT FGs FG	3-PT FGs PCT	FTs FT	FTs PCT	Rebounds OFF	Rebounds TOT	AST	STL	BLK	PTS	PPG
90-91	PHO	63	730	204	.487	1	.167	110	.663	77	150	35	22	5	519	8.2
91-92	PHO	64	725	176	.482	1	.167	109	.736	60	152	50	16	11	462	7.2
92-93	PHO	74	1607	381	.576	0	.000	187	.725	172	408	77	54	28	949	12.8
93-94	PHO	53	1602	425	.535	0	.000	160	.724	153	344	91	59	23	1010	19.1
94-95	LAL	58	2029	497	.509	58	.397	209	.716	169	464	105	60	19	1261	21.7
95-96	LAL	78	2628	638	.530	51	.277	329	.804	215	536	119	94	22	1656	21.2
Totals		390	9321	2321	.525	111	.314	1104	.739	846	2054	477	305	108	5857	15.0

REX CHAPMAN

Unrestricted Free Agent
Last Team: Miami Heat
Position: Guard
Height: 6'4" **Weight:** 188
Birthdate: October 5, 1967

NBA Experience: 8 years
College: Kentucky
Acquired: Traded from Bullets with rights to Terrence Rencher for Jeff Webster and Ed Stokes, 6/95

Background: Chapman became the first freshman to lead Kentucky in scoring. He left after his sophomore season and was a 15-plus PPG scorer for Charlotte in his first three pro years. Chapman averaged a career-high 18.2 PPG for Washington in 1993-94 but has been limited by injuries for two straight years, including the 1995-96 season in Miami.

Strengths: Chapman has always been regarded as a fine athlete with springs in his legs. He can drive past his man or beat defenses with his 3-point shooting. Chapman has also been accurate from the free-throw line while maintaining a career scoring average of better than 15 PPG. Chapman can also handle the point guard spot in a pinch.

Weaknesses: Chapman has favored the 3-pointer too much in the last few years, cutting down his number of drives and his trips to the free-throw line. Shaky shot selection has been the knock on him throughout his career. Chapman is a below-average defensive player, and he has been prone to injuries.

Analysis: Chapman missed almost half the 1995-96 season (his first in Miami) after November surgery to repair an inflamed Achilles tendon. He did play some fabulous minutes for the Heat, once making nine of ten 3-point shots against Chicago for a career-high 39 points. If anyone can convince Chapman to play defense, it's Heat coach Pat Riley.

PLAYER SUMMARY	
Will	look for treys
Can't	stay off injured list
Expect	15 PPG
Don't Expect	a stopper
Fantasy Value	$2-4
Card Value	5-10¢

COLLEGE STATISTICS

		G	FGP	FTP	RPG	PPG
86-87	KENT	29	.444	.735	2.3	16.0
87-88	KENT	32	.501	.794	2.9	19.0
Totals		61	.475	.771	2.6	17.6

NBA REGULAR-SEASON STATISTICS

		G	MIN	FGs FG	FGs PCT	3-PT FGs FG	3-PT FGs PCT	FTs FT	FTs PCT	Rebounds OFF	Rebounds TOT	AST	STL	BLK	PTS	PPG
88-89	CHA	75	2219	526	.414	60	.314	155	.795	74	187	176	70	25	1267	16.9
89-90	CHA	54	1762	377	.408	47	.331	144	.750	52	179	132	46	6	945	17.5
90-91	CHA	70	2100	410	.445	48	.324	234	.830	45	191	250	73	16	1102	15.7
91-92	CHA/WAS	22	567	113	.448	8	.276	36	.679	10	58	89	15	8	270	12.3
92-93	WAS	60	1300	287	.477	43	.371	132	.810	19	88	116	38	10	749	12.5
93-94	WAS	60	2025	431	.498	64	.388	168	.816	57	146	185	59	8	1094	18.2
94-95	WAS	45	1468	254	.397	86	.314	137	.862	23	113	128	67	15	731	16.2
95-96	MIA	56	1865	289	.426	125	.371	83	.735	22	145	166	45	10	786	14.0
Totals		442	13306	2687	.437	481	.343	1089	.799	302	1107	1242	413	98	6944	15.7

CALBERT CHEANEY

Team: Washington Bullets
Position: Guard/Forward
Height: 6'7" **Weight:** 215
Birthdate: July 17, 1971

NBA Experience: 3 years
College: Indiana
Acquired: First-round pick in 1993 draft (sixth overall)

Background: Though not highly recruited out of high school, Cheaney received a scholarship from Indiana and developed into one of the top players in Hoosier history. He set a Big Ten record for total points and won the John Wooden and James Naismith Player of the Year awards. Drafted sixth overall by Washington in 1993, he has been a two-year starter and 14-plus PPG scorer.

Strengths: Cheaney is a graceful athlete with smooth moves and the ability to get his own shot. Some called him the best pure shooter in the 1993 draft, and his form suggests his accuracy will rise from the field as well as the 3-point arc. Cheaney is an effective transition player and a capable ball-handler and passer. He can play big guard and small forward.

Weaknesses: Once adept at taking college games into his own hands, Cheaney has not displayed the confidence to do the same in NBA arenas. He has all the skills to be a big-time scorer, but seems content to get his points as they come. He averages only about three trips to the line per game. He'll follow up a great effort with an ordinary one. Cheaney is a below-average rebounder.

Analysis: The next year or two will tell whether Cheaney can become a go-to player. He has enjoyed rather quiet success in the starting five of a sub-.500 Washington team as a good shooter with some slick moves. He is also valuable for his ability to defend both threes and fours. His feet are wet. Now's the time for a more assertive Cheaney to emerge as a force.

PLAYER SUMMARY	
Will	get his shot
Can't	control the boards
Expect	agile moves
Don't Expect	a one-man show
Fantasy Value	$10-13
Card Value	8-15¢

COLLEGE STATISTICS

		G	FGP	FTP	RPG	PPG
89-90	IND	29	.572	.750	4.6	17.1
90-91	IND	34	.596	.801	5.5	21.6
91-92	IND	34	.522	.800	4.9	17.6
92-93	IND	35	.549	.795	6.4	22.4
Totals		132	.559	.790	5.4	19.8

NBA REGULAR-SEASON STATISTICS

		G	MIN	FGs FG	FGs PCT	3-PT FGs FG	3-PT FGs PCT	FTs FT	FTs PCT	Rebounds OFF	Rebounds TOT	AST	STL	BLK	PTS	PPG
93-94	WAS	65	1604	327	.470	1	.043	124	.770	88	190	126	63	10	779	12.0
94-95	WAS	78	2651	512	.453	96	.339	173	.812	105	321	177	80	21	1293	16.6
95-96	WAS	70	2324	426	.471	52	.338	151	.706	67	239	154	67	18	1055	15.1
Totals		213	6579	1265	.463	149	.324	448	.762	260	750	457	210	49	3127	14.7

PETE CHILCUTT

Team: Vancouver Grizzlies
Position: Forward
Height: 6'11" **Weight:** 235
Birthdate: September 14, 1968
NBA Experience: 5 years
College: North Carolina

Acquired: Traded from Rockets with Tim Breaux, 1996 first- and second-round picks, and a 1997 second-round pick for two 1996 second-round picks, 6/96

Background: A solid complementary player for coach Dean Smith at North Carolina, Chilcutt was never named All-ACC, but he played every game during his four years with the Tar Heels. He was drafted 27th by Sacramento in 1991 and has played for the Kings, Pistons, and Rockets in his five seasons. He played a career-low 651 minutes last season before being unloaded to the Grizzlies in the off-season.

Strengths: Chilcutt has a soft shooting touch with good range for a big man. He poses matchup problems for power forwards and centers who like to stay near the bucket because he can hit the 3-pointer. He works hard, rebounds, and swats a few shots. Chilcutt is a team player who knows the game.

Weaknesses: Chilcutt doesn't possess exceptional speed, quickness, jumping ability, or any other athletic skill. In fact, nothing about his game is awe-inspiring. He does not create off the dribble and is out of his element in the post. He needs open jumpers to score. Chilcutt possesses neither the strength nor the speed to be an above-average defensive player.

Analysis: Chilcutt has an NBA championship ring to show for his two years with the Rockets, but he can hardly be called a key contributor. He did play in 74 games last season, but his scoring average of 2.7 PPG was a career worst. Chilcutt offers little besides hard work and the ability to score from long range. He will probably never be more than a sound, complementary player off the bench.

PLAYER SUMMARY	
Will	...........................make 3-pointers
Can't	...................pose scoring threat
Expect	.............sound fundamentals
Don't Expect	...........first-rate ability
Fantasy Value	.................................$0
Card Value	...................................5-7¢

COLLEGE STATISTICS

		G	FGP	FTP	RPG	PPG
87-88	NC	34	.564	.706	3.2	4.9
88-89	NC	37	.537	.623	5.4	6.9
89-90	NC	34	.514	.714	6.6	9.0
90-91	NC	35	.538	.765	6.6	12.0
Totals		140	.536	.710	5.5	8.2

NBA REGULAR-SEASON STATISTICS

				FGs		3-PT FGs		FTs		Rebounds						
		G	MIN	FG	PCT	FG	PCT	FT	PCT	OFF	TOT	AST	STL	BLK	PTS	PPG
91-92	SAC	69	817	113	.452	2	1.000	23	.821	78	187	38	32	17	251	3.6
92-93	SAC	59	834	165	.485	0	.000	32	.696	80	194	64	22	21	362	6.1
93-94	SAC/DET	76	1365	203	.453	3	.200	41	.631	129	371	86	53	39	450	5.9
94-95	HOU	68	1347	146	.445	35	.407	31	.738	106	317	66	25	43	358	5.3
95-96	HOU	74	651	73	.408	37	.378	17	.654	51	156	26	19	14	200	2.7
Totals		346	5014	700	.453	77	.383	144	.696	444	1225	280	151	134	1621	4.7

RANDOLPH CHILDRESS

Team: Portland Trail Blazers
Position: Guard
Height: 6'2" **Weight:** 188
Birthdate: September 21, 1972

NBA Experience: 1 year
College: Wake Forest
Acquired: Traded from Pistons with Bill Curley for Otis Thorpe, 9/95

Background: Childress finished his collegiate career No. 2 on Wake Forest's all-time scoring list and was the second-most prolific 3-point shooter in ACC history despite missing the 1991-92 season because of a knee injury. He finished his career with 40, 30, and 37 points in consecutive games in the 1995 ACC Tournament. A first-round draftee of Detroit, he was traded to Portland and had his rookie year interrupted by January shoulder surgery.

Strengths: Childress has the potential to become a decent-scoring point guard. He has a smooth shooting stroke and deep range. He's capable of driving past his man for buckets, assists, or trips to the free-throw line, where he'll convert at a clip of 80 percent or better. Childress is a good ball-handler and an adequate playmaker. He'll expend energy on defense and came into the NBA with tons of confidence.

Weaknesses: Bigger guards will get the best of Childress, who is not among the quickest point men in the league. He was a much better scorer than distributor during his amateur career, so he still has to prove he can get the ball to the right place at the right time. Childress struggled to get his shots in limited rookie playing time, and his percentage (.316) reflected his troubles.

Analysis: Don't jump to quick conclusions about Childress, who injured his shoulder in a game at Cleveland last December after just 28 games. Before that, he was seeing fewer than nine minutes per game and struggling to prove himself in a minimal role with the Blazers. Childress will probably continue to play the waiting game while learning to run the offense with a steadier hand. He will eventually contribute.

PLAYER SUMMARY	
Will	look for shots
Can't	win starting job
Expect	deep range
Don't Expect	pinpoint passing
Fantasy Value	$0
Card Value	20-40¢

COLLEGE STATISTICS

		G	FGP	FTP	RPG	PPG
90-91	WF	29	.449	.772	2.1	14.0
92-93	WF	30	.484	.810	2.8	19.7
93-94	WF	29	.415	.789	3.4	19.6
94-95	WF	32	.438	.833	3.6	20.1
Totals		120	.446	.804	3.0	18.4

NBA REGULAR-SEASON STATISTICS

			FGs		3-PT FGs		FTs		Rebounds						
	G	MIN	FG	PCT	FG	PCT	FT	PCT	OFF	TOT	AST	STL	BLK	PTS	PPG
95-96 POR	28	250	25	.316	13	.277	22	.815	1	19	32	8	1	85	3.0
Totals	28	250	25	.316	13	.277	22	.815	1	19	32	8	1	85	3.0

CHRIS CHILDS

Team: New York Knicks
Position: Guard
Height: 6'3" **Weight:** 195
Birthdate: November 20, 1967

NBA Experience: 2 years
College: Boise St.
Acquired: Signed as a free agent, 7/96

Background: Childs was an unheralded college player at Boise State who went undrafted. He spent his first five pro seasons playing with six different CBA teams. A recovering alcoholic, he spent time in the Lucas Center in Houston and, after a relapse, checked into a similar center in Miami in 1993. Childs finally broke into the NBA with New Jersey in 1994-95 and—surprisingly—became the Nets' starting point guard in 1995-96. He signed on with the Knicks last summer.

Strengths: Childs shows leadership and tenacity on both ends of the floor. He looks to set up his teammates and can also score on his own, with a pretty nice shot from the 3-point arc and free-throw line. He'll make better than eight in ten from the stripe. Childs is an unselfish player who remembers where his career started. He works his tail off and truly enjoys playing defense.

Weaknesses: Childs does not rate among the top playmakers in the game, although he is clearly advancing. Most of his points come from the outside, as he has not completely mastered finishing his drives and would rather dish off anyway. His shooting percentage improved from .380 as a rookie but could stand a further boost. Childs also must learn to preserve his fouls to stay on the floor.

Analysis: Who would have thought that Childs, the MVP of the CBA Finals as recently as 1994, would make the heralded Kenny Anderson expendable to the Nets? Anyone with a hand raised is not telling the truth. Childs is a heady point guard who specializes in ball pressure on defense and ball movement on offense. He carried the Nets at times last season, and he only stands to get better. Look for him to step it up even more with New York.

PLAYER SUMMARY	
Will	distribute
Can't	be left open
Expect	continued emergence
Don't Expect	more CBA days
Fantasy Value	$10-13
Card Value	5-8¢

COLLEGE STATISTICS

		G	FGP	FTP	APG	PPG
85-86	BSU	28	.413	.791	3.0	10.7
86-87	BSU	30	.448	.826	2.9	15.4
87-88	BSU	30	.476	.853	3.3	14.3
88-89	BSU	30	.444	.801	4.2	13.7
Totals		118	.443	.818	3.3	13.6

NBA REGULAR-SEASON STATISTICS

				FGs		3-PT FGs		FTs		Rebounds						
		G	MIN	FG	PCT	FG	PCT	FT	PCT	OFF	TOT	AST	STL	BLK	PTS	PPG
94-95	NJ	53	1021	106	.380	41	.328	55	.753	14	69	219	42	3	308	5.8
95-96	NJ	78	2408	324	.416	95	.367	259	.852	51	245	548	111	8	1002	12.8
Totals		131	3429	430	.407	136	.354	314	.833	65	314	767	153	11	1310	10.0

DOUG CHRISTIE

Team: Toronto Raptors
Position: Guard/Forward
Height: 6'6" **Weight:** 205
Birthdate: May 9, 1970
NBA Experience: 4 years

College: Pepperdine
Acquired: Traded from Knicks with Herb Williams for Willie Anderson and Victor Alexander, 2/96

Background: Christie became Pepperdine's best player since Dennis Johnson, leading the Waves to the NCAA Tournament in 1991 and 1992. He was drafted 17th by Seattle in 1992, but was not able to settle on a contract and was traded to the Lakers. In L.A., Christie became a starter in his second season but spent most of his third on the bench in New York. He played for New York and Toronto in 1995-96.

Strengths: Christie is a splendid athlete who stays in great shape and can play big guard as well as small forward. He runs the floor, makes a good percentage of his 3-pointers (43.4 last season), and is a gifted passer who never averaged less than four APG as a collegian. Christie puts forth his best effort on defense and comes up with a lot of steals.

Weaknesses: What is he? As a guard, Christie had not been a consistent shooter until finding the mark from 3-point land last season. As a forward, he gives away too much size to stay competitive at either end of the floor. Christie's biggest flaw has been his out-of-control play. Some feel he tries too hard. NBA officials seem to concur, whistling him for fouls at every turn. He makes poor decisions.

Analysis: Christie enjoyed his second-best NBA season in 1995-96. He made at least one steal in all but two of his 32 games with the expansion Raptors, for whom he started 17 times after his brief stint far down the Knicks' bench. Still, one has to doubt whether Christie will ever approach his 1993-94 scoring average of 10.3 PPG. For a four-year vet, he's very raw.

PLAYER SUMMARY	
Will	pick your pocket
Can't	stay out of foul trouble
Expect	plenty of hustle
Don't Expect	sound decisions
Fantasy Value	$3-5
Card Value	8-12¢

COLLEGE STATISTICS

		G	FGP	FTP	RPG	PPG
89-90	PEPP	28	.503	.714	4.1	8.9
90-91	PEPP	28	.469	.765	5.2	19.1
91-92	PEPP	31	.466	.746	5.9	19.5
Totals		87	.473	.747	5.1	16.0

NBA REGULAR-SEASON STATISTICS

			FGs		3-PT FGs		FTs		Rebounds						
	G	MIN	FG	PCT	FG	PCT	FT	PCT	OFF	TOT	AST	STL	BLK	PTS	PPG
92-93 LAL	23	332	45	.425	2	.167	50	.758	24	51	53	22	5	142	6.2
93-94 LAL	65	1515	244	.434	39	.328	145	.697	93	235	136	89	28	672	10.3
94-95 NY	12	79	5	.227	1	.143	4	.800	3	13	8	2	1	15	1.3
95-96 NY/TOR	55	1036	150	.445	46	.434	69	.742	34	154	117	70	19	415	7.5
Totals	155	2962	444	.432	88	.361	268	.720	154	453	314	183	53	1244	8.0

DERRICK COLEMAN

Team: Philadelphia 76ers
Position: Forward
Height: 6'10" **Weight:** 260
Birthdate: June 21, 1967
NBA Experience: 6 years

College: Syracuse
Acquired: Traded from Nets with Rex Walters and Sean Higgins for Shawn Bradley, Tim Perry, and Greg Graham, 11/95

Background: Teamed with Billy Owens and Sherman Douglas, Coleman played on one of Syracuse's most talented teams ever. He won several college Player of the Year awards as a senior. New Jersey selected him as the No. 1 pick in 1990, and he went on to win Rookie of the Year honors. The former All-Star and Dream Team II member was traded to the 76ers during an injury-ravaged 1995-96 season.

Strengths: Coleman is capable of scoring 20-plus points and pulling down ten-plus boards every night. His power moves to the basket are often unstoppable, and he also scores on jump shots and transition slams. He's supremely confident, having learned the game on the playgrounds of Detroit. Coleman is one of the top rebounding forwards in the league, and he is a gifted defender.

Weaknesses: All of the above are contingent on Coleman showing up to play. He is known as a prima donna who does not work hard enough to reach his vast potential or earn his gigantic salary. Players on his own team have said as much. His shooting percentage is subpar, and he is not the 3-point shooter he thinks he is. When things don't go his way, he complains.

Analysis: Coleman's attitude was dragging the Nets even further down, so they sent him to nearby Philly in a deal involving Shawn Bradley. The 76ers' gamble cannot be evaluated yet, because injuries to Coleman's right ankle cost him most of the 1995-96 season. He started last year on the injured list with an irregular heartbeat.

PLAYER SUMMARY	
Will	put up big numbers
Can't	keep his mouth shut
Expect	20-plus PPG
Don't Expect	consistent hustle
Fantasy Value	$20-25
Card Value	12-20¢

COLLEGE STATISTICS

		G	FGP	FTP	RPG	PPG
86-87	SYR	38	.560	.686	8.8	11.9
87-88	SYR	35	.587	.630	11.0	13.5
88-89	SYR	37	.575	.692	11.4	16.9
89-90	SYR	33	.551	.715	12.1	17.9
Totals		143	.568	.684	10.7	15.0

NBA REGULAR-SEASON STATISTICS

		G	MIN	FGs FG	FGs PCT	3-PT FGs FG	3-PT FGs PCT	FTs FT	FTs PCT	Rebounds OFF	Rebounds TOT	AST	STL	BLK	PTS	PPG
90-91	NJ	74	2602	514	.467	13	.342	323	.731	269	759	163	71	99	1364	18.4
91-92	NJ	65	2207	483	.504	23	.303	300	.763	203	618	205	54	98	1289	19.8
92-93	NJ	76	2759	564	.460	23	.232	421	.808	247	852	276	92	126	1572	20.7
93-94	NJ	77	2778	541	.447	38	.314	439	.774	262	870	262	68	142	1559	20.2
94-95	NJ	56	2103	371	.425	28	.233	376	.767	167	591	187	35	94	1146	20.5
95-96	PHI	11	294	48	.407	7	.333	20	.625	13	72	31	4	10	123	11.2
Totals		359	12743	2521	.460	132	.278	1879	.769	1161	3762	1124	324	569	7053	19.6

BIMBO COLES

Team: Golden State Warriors
Position: Guard
Height: 6'2" **Weight:** 185
Birthdate: April 22, 1968
NBA Experience: 6 years

College: Virginia Tech
Acquired: Traded from Heat with Kevin Willis for Tim Hardaway and Chris Gatling, 2/96

Background: Coles left Virginia Tech as the all-time Metro Conference scoring leader. He also set a school record for assists and was a member of the 1988 United States Olympic team. Drafted in the second round in 1990, Coles played five-plus seasons in Miami before a February trade sent him to Golden State last year. He left the Heat as the team's all-time assists leader with 1,946.

Strengths: Coles brings a little bit of everything to the point guard position. He uses his quickness to penetrate and is willing to deliver the ball. He also can be dangerous from long range. Coles is a fine transition player who tries to get the break going. He gets after his man on defense and has been willing to spend much of his time as a reserve.

Weaknesses: Here, a little bit of everything also enters the picture. Coles is not a consistent outside shooter, nor does he rate with the better playmakers. He has trouble finishing after hauling the ball in among the big fellas, and his offense in general has not been steady. The same can be said of his defense, although the effort is there.

Analysis: Coles was on his way to perhaps his best statistical season with Miami before he headed west with Kevin Willis in a trade that brought Tim Hardaway and Chris Gatling to the Heat. Miami was not convinced Coles could lead the team deep into the playoffs, and indeed he does seem better-suited as a third guard.

PLAYER SUMMARY	
Will	look for teammates
Can't	rely on jump shots
Expect	hustle on defense
Don't Expect	great consistency
Fantasy Value	$4-6
Card Value	5-8¢

COLLEGE STATISTICS

		G	FGP	FTP	APG	PPG
86-87	VT	28	.412	.716	4.0	10.0
87-88	VT	29	.443	.741	5.9	24.2
88-89	VT	27	.455	.785	5.2	26.6
89-90	VT	31	.404	.738	3.9	25.3
Totals		115	.429	.748	4.8	21.6

NBA REGULAR-SEASON STATISTICS

		G	MIN	FGs FG	FGs PCT	3-PT FGs FG	3-PT FGs PCT	FTs FT	FTs PCT	Rebounds OFF	Rebounds TOT	AST	STL	BLK	PTS	PPG
90-91	MIA	82	1355	162	.412	6	.176	71	.747	56	153	232	65	12	401	4.9
91-92	MIA	81	1976	295	.455	10	.192	216	.824	69	189	366	73	13	816	10.1
92-93	MIA	81	2232	318	.464	42	.307	177	.805	58	166	373	80	11	855	10.6
93-94	MIA	76	1726	233	.449	20	.202	102	.779	50	159	263	75	12	588	7.7
94-95	MIA	68	2207	261	.430	16	.211	141	.810	46	191	416	99	13	679	10.0
95-96	MIA/GS	81	2615	318	.409	88	.346	168	.796	49	260	422	94	17	892	11.0
Totals		469	12111	1587	.437	182	.279	875	.801	328	1118	2072	486	78	4231	9.0

MARTY CONLON

Team: Milwaukee Bucks
Position: Forward
Height: 6'11" **Weight:** 245
Birthdate: January 19, 1968

NBA Experience: 5 years
College: Providence
Acquired: Signed as a free agent,
8/94

Background: After a steady career at Providence College, Conlon played with four different NBA teams in his first three pro seasons and also spent some time in the CBA. He played all 82 games for the Bucks in 1994-95, averaging a career-high 9.9 PPG. He finally played two years for the same team when the Bucks re-signed him before Conlon's modest 1995-96 season.

Strengths: Conlon can be a dangerous face-up shooter with range extending to 18-20 feet, and he also knows how to score with some crafty moves in the lane. He can create matchup problems with his touch. Conlon is an unselfish player who knows the game, works hard at it, and understands his role.

Weaknesses: Conlon's athletic ability is ordinary at best. He is not a physical specimen, he does not own any speed or quickness to speak of, and he is overmatched when trying to defend opponents on the perimeter or in the paint. You don't want him touching the ball for much longer than it takes to shoot an open jumper. His ball-handling, passing, and shot-blocking are all below average.

Analysis: Conlon is a marginal talent who not only has stuck around in the NBA, but who has been able to make clutch jumpers and score double figures when given the opportunity. On a better team, opportunities would be few and far between for Conlon. He stands a chance because of his outside shot, his sound fundamentals, and his work habits. He'll never be a standout.

PLAYER SUMMARY	
Will	shoot jumpers
Can't	keep up on defense
Expect	a dedicated worker
Don't Expect	starts
Fantasy Value	$0
Card Value	7-10¢

COLLEGE STATISTICS

		G	FGP	FTP	RPG	PPG
86-87	PROV	34	.448	.831	2.9	4.4
87-88	PROV	11	.511	.833	5.6	13.2
88-89	PROV	29	.524	.728	7.0	14.3
89-90	PROV	29	.502	.738	7.6	14.7
Totals		103	.505	.765	5.7	11.0

NBA REGULAR-SEASON STATISTICS

			FGs		3-PT FGs		FTs		Rebounds						
	G	MIN	FG	PCT	FG	PCT	FT	PCT	OFF	TOT	AST	STL	BLK	PTS	PPG
91-92 SEA	45	381	48	.475	0	.000	24	.750	33	69	12	9	7	120	2.7
92-93 SAC	46	467	81	.474	0	.000	57	.704	48	123	37	13	5	219	4.8
93-94 CHI/WAS	30	579	95	.576	0	.000	43	.811	53	139	34	9	8	233	7.8
94-95 MIL	82	2064	344	.532	8	.276	119	.613	160	426	110	42	18	815	9.9
95-96 MIL	74	958	153	.468	5	.167	84	.764	58	177	68	20	11	395	5.3
Totals	277	4449	721	.511	13	.200	327	.696	352	934	261	93	49	1782	6.4

TYRONE CORBIN

Unrestricted Free Agent
Last Team: Miami Heat
Position: Forward
Height: 6'6" **Weight:** 225
Birthdate: December 31, 1962

NBA Experience: 11 years
College: DePaul
Acquired: Traded from Kings with Walt Williams for Billy Owens and Kevin Gamble, 2/96

Background: After leading DePaul in both scoring and rebounding as a junior and senior, Corbin made his NBA debut with San Antonio. He has played for eight teams in 11 NBA seasons, including Atlanta, Sacramento, and Miami over the last two years. He has been a reserve at most of his stops.

Strengths: Corbin has earned a reputation as a hard worker and physical player. He fights for rebounds, gets good inside position, comes up with steals and loose balls, and plays strong defense on men his size or bigger. Corbin can stick the medium-range jumper and is known as a workaholic.

Weaknesses: The bumping and grinding inside are necessary because Corbin does not own the silky-smooth game that many of the NBA's small forwards possess. He does not create much off the dribble for either himself or his teammates. His overall effectiveness is on the decline.

Analysis: Corbin has made a nice NBA living largely because of his mental and physical toughness. His actual skills, to be truthful, are quite ordinary by big-league standards. He simply works for all the points and rebounds he gets. These days, those points and boards are getting harder to come by.

PLAYER SUMMARY

Will ....make hustle plays
Can't ....unpack his bags
Expect ....coachability
Don't Expect....................many starts
Fantasy Value $1
Card Value ....5-8¢

COLLEGE STATISTICS

		G	FGP	FTP	RPG	PPG
81-82	DeP	28	.417	.718	6.1	5.1
82-83	DeP	33	.471	.773	7.9	10.6
83-84	DeP	30	.525	.744	7.4	14.2
84-85	DeP	29	.534	.814	8.1	15.9
Totals		120	.504	.764	7.4	11.5

NBA REGULAR-SEASON STATISTICS

		G	MIN	FGs		3-PT FGs		FTs		Rebounds		AST	STL	BLK	PTS	PPG
				FG	PCT	FG	PCT	FT	PCT	OFF	TOT					
85-86	SA	16	174	27	.422	0	.000	10	.714	11	25	11	11	2	64	4.0
86-87	SA/CLE	63	1170	156	.409	1	.250	91	.734	88	215	97	55	5	404	6.4
87-88	CLE/PHO	84	1739	257	.490	1	.167	110	.797	127	350	115	72	18	625	7.4
88-89	PHO	77	1655	245	.540	0	.000	141	.788	176	398	118	82	13	631	8.2
89-90	MIN	82	3011	521	.481	0	.000	161	.770	219	604	216	175	41	1203	14.7
90-91	MIN	82	3196	587	.448	2	.200	296	.798	185	589	347	162	53	1472	18.0
91-92	MIN/UTA	80	2207	303	.481	0	.000	174	.866	163	472	140	82	20	780	9.8
92-93	UTA	82	2555	385	.503	0	.000	180	.826	194	519	173	108	32	950	11.6
93-94	UTA	82	2149	268	.456	6	.207	117	.813	150	389	122	99	24	659	8.0
94-95	ATL	81	1389	205	.442	14	.250	78	.684	98	262	67	55	16	502	6.2
95-96	SAC/MIA	71	1284	155	.442	3	.167	100	.833	81	244	84	63	20	413	5.8
Totals		800	20529	3109	.470	27	.185	1458	.796	1492	4067	1490	964	244	7703	9.6

TERRY CUMMINGS

Team: Milwaukee Bucks
Position: Forward
Height: 6'9" **Weight:** 250
Birthdate: March 15, 1961

NBA Experience: 14 years
College: DePaul
Acquired: Signed as a free agent, 9/95

Background: Cummings led DePaul in rebounding in each of his three seasons, was drafted second overall by San Diego in 1982, and won Rookie of the Year honors. Cummings starred with Milwaukee and San Antonio before undergoing major knee surgery in 1992. He returned to the Bucks for his 14th NBA season in 1995-96.

Strengths: Cummings is a two-time All-Star who was once one of the top scoring and rebounding forwards in basketball. He can still get his shot off, and he's capable of providing solid minutes either inside or outside. He's no slouch on defense.

Weaknesses: Cummings cannot approach some of the things he used to do. He is no longer a primary option in the offense because his jumper is inconsistent and he has lost a step. He struggles from the free-throw line.

Analysis: Always a warrior, Cummings played his 30,000th NBA minute in 1995-96, starting 13 of 81 games in his return to the Bucks. He ranks among Milwaukee's top ten all-time in several categories, including rebounds and points. His best days are long gone, but Cummings does have something left.

PLAYER SUMMARY

Will ....come to battle
Can't ....regain lost step
Expect ....toughness, know-how
Don't Expect ....three more years
Fantasy Value $0
Card Value ....7-12¢

COLLEGE STATISTICS

		G	FGP	FTP	RPG	PPG
79-80	DeP	28	.508	.832	9.4	14.2
80-81	DeP	29	.498	.750	9.0	13.0
81-82	DeP	28	.567	.756	11.9	22.3
Totals		85	.530	.775	10.1	16.4

NBA REGULAR-SEASON STATISTICS

				FGs		3-PT FGs		FTs		Rebounds						
		G	MIN	FG	PCT	FG	PCT	FT	PCT	OFF	TOT	AST	STL	BLK	PTS	PPG
82-83	SD	70	2531	684	.523	0	.000	292	.709	303	744	177	129	62	1660	23.7
83-84	SD	81	2907	737	.494	0	.000	380	.720	323	777	139	92	57	1854	22.9
84-85	MIL	79	2722	759	.495	0	.000	343	.741	244	716	228	117	67	1861	23.6
85-86	MIL	82	2669	681	.474	0	.000	265	.656	222	694	193	121	51	1627	19.8
86-87	MIL	82	2770	729	.511	0	.000	249	.662	214	700	229	129	81	1707	20.8
87-88	MIL	76	2629	675	.485	1	.333	270	.665	184	553	181	78	46	1621	21.3
88-89	MIL	80	2824	730	.467	7	.467	362	.787	281	650	198	106	72	1829	22.9
89-90	SA	81	2821	728	.475	19	.322	343	.780	226	677	219	110	52	1818	22.4
90-91	SA	67	2195	503	.484	7	.212	164	.683	194	521	157	61	30	1177	17.6
91-92	SA	70	2149	514	.488	5	.385	177	.711	247	631	102	58	34	1210	17.3
92-93	SA	8	76	11	.379	0	.000	5	.500	6	19	4	1	1	27	3.4
93-94	SA	59	1133	183	.428	0	.000	63	.589	132	297	50	31	13	429	7.3
94-95	SA	76	1273	224	.483	0	.000	72	.585	138	378	59	36	19	520	6.8
95-96	MIL	81	1777	270	.462	1	.143	104	.650	162	445	89	56	30	645	8.0
Totals		992	30476	7428	.486	40	.282	3089	.706	2876	7802	2025	1125	615	17985	18.1

DELL CURRY

Team: Charlotte Hornets
Position: Guard
Height: 6'5" **Weight:** 208
Birthdate: June 25, 1964

NBA Experience: 10 years
College: Virginia Tech
Acquired: Selected from Cavaliers in
1988 expansion draft

Background: Curry, the Metro Conference Player of the Year as a Virginia Tech senior, was drafted by the Baltimore Orioles as a pitcher and the Utah Jazz for basketball. He was traded to Cleveland and picked up by Charlotte in the expansion draft. He has averaged double figures in the last nine of his ten seasons and won the Sixth Man Award in 1993-94. He made 27 starts in 1995-96.

Strengths: Curry has the ability to light up the scoreboard in a hurry with a dangerous shot, particularly from 3-point range. He ranks among the most accurate 3-point and free-throw shooters in the game. A durable veteran, he remains one of the best pure shooters in basketball.

Weaknesses: Perhaps too congenial in his approach, Curry is neither a willing nor an able defender. He's not physical with players his size or larger and lacks the quickness to keep up with smaller ones. Curry is not a gifted passer. In short, his jump shot carries him.

Analysis: Curry's stroke is a thing of beauty. When he is hot, you want the ball to touch his hands every time down the floor. He also offers a willingness to do his job in a reserve role, although he saw his string of 357 consecutive backup gigs snapped in January when injuries to Charlotte's starters pressed him into starting duty.

PLAYER SUMMARY	
Will	make treys, free throws
Can't	shut down his man
Expect	instant offense
Don't Expect	physical play
Fantasy Value	$9-11
Card Value	7-10¢

COLLEGE STATISTICS

		G	FGP	FTP	RPG	PPG
82-83	VT	32	.475	.850	3.0	14.5
83-84	VT	35	.522	.759	4.1	19.3
84-85	VT	29	.482	.758	5.8	18.2
85-86	VT	30	.529	.789	6.8	24.1
Totals		126	.505	.785	4.8	19.0

NBA REGULAR-SEASON STATISTICS

		G	MIN	FGs FG	FGs PCT	3-PT FGs FG	3-PT FGs PCT	FTs FT	FTs PCT	Rebounds OFF	Rebounds TOT	AST	STL	BLK	PTS	PPG
86-87	UTA	67	636	139	.426	17	.283	30	.789	30	78	58	27	4	325	4.9
87-88	CLE	79	1499	340	.458	28	.346	79	.782	43	166	149	94	22	787	10.0
88-89	CHA	48	813	256	.491	19	.345	40	.870	26	104	50	42	4	571	11.9
89-90	CHA	67	1860	461	.466	52	.354	96	.923	31	168	159	98	26	1070	16.0
90-91	CHA	76	1515	337	.471	32	.372	96	.842	47	199	166	75	25	802	10.6
91-92	CHA	77	2020	504	.486	74	.404	127	.836	57	259	177	93	20	1209	15.7
92-93	CHA	80	2094	498	.452	95	.401	136	.866	51	286	180	87	23	1227	15.3
93-94	CHA	82	2173	533	.455	152	.402	117	.873	71	262	221	98	27	1335	16.3
94-95	CHA	69	1718	343	.441	154	.427	95	.856	41	168	113	55	18	935	13.6
95-96	CHA	82	2371	441	.453	164	.404	146	.854	68	264	176	108	25	1192	14.5
Totals		727	16699	3852	.461	787	.395	962	.853	465	1954	1449	777	194	9453	13.0

PREDRAG DANILOVIC

Team: Miami Heat
Position: Guard
Height: 6'6" **Weight:** 200
Birthdate: February 26, 1970

College: None
NBA Experience: 1 year
Acquired: Traded from Warriors with Billy Owens for Rony Seikaly, 11/94

Background: A native of Yugoslavia, Danilovic played professional ball in Belgrade and in Bologna, Italy, earning European Player of the Year honors in 1994. He led the Yugoslavian national team to its berth in the 1996 Olympics. Selected by Golden State in the second round (43rd overall) of the 1992 draft, "Sasha" was acquired by Miami in the 1994 Billy Owens-Rony Seikaly trade. His first season in the NBA was cut short by a wrist injury.

Strengths: Danilovic owns a beautiful shooting stroke and has the size and strength to get his shot almost anytime he wants it. The NBA 3-pointer looks like a layup for a man who drilled the longer European trey with regularity. He can hit it with hands in his face. Danilovic is also an adept passer, a fine transition player, and a promising backcourt rebounder.

Weaknesses: Like many European stars who migrate to the NBA, Danilovic has much work to do on the defensive end. He does not have the raw quickness to shut down the top shooting guards, a fact that will not be lost on opposing coaches. Having Pat Riley as a coach should help. Danilovic also needs to improve his ball-handling and his ability to shoot off the dribble.

Analysis: That Danilovic earned a starting job in his first NBA season did not come as too great a surprise to those who saw him play in Europe. He was on his way to an All-Rookie campaign before an injury to his right wrist required early-January surgery and ended his debut after 18 games, although he came back for one more game late in the season and participated in Miami's playoff loss to Chicago. In one December week, he averaged 19.5 PPG and made 13 of his 22 long-range shots. He's more than a gunner.

PLAYER SUMMARY	
Will	burn you with treys
Can't	dominate on defense
Expect	good court sense
Don't Expect	dribble-drives
Fantasy	$9-11
Card Value	12-20¢

COLLEGE STATISTICS

—DID NOT PLAY—

NBA REGULAR-SEASON STATISTICS

			FGs		3-PT FGs		FTs		Rebounds						
	G	MIN	FG	PCT	FG	PCT	FT	PCT	OFF	TOT	AST	STL	BLK	PTS	PPG
95-96 MIA	19	542	83	.451	34	.436	55	.764	12	46	47	15	3	255	13.4
Totals	19	542	83	.451	34	.436	55	.764	12	46	47	15	3	255	13.4

YINKA DARE

Team: New Jersey Nets
Position: Center
Height: 7'0" **Weight:** 265
Birthdate: October 10, 1972

NBA Experience: 2 years
College: George Washington
Acquired: First-round pick in 1994
draft (14th overall)

Background: The Nigerian-born Dare did not begin playing organized basketball until 1991-92 at Milford Academy, and he spent only two seasons at George Washington. He led the Colonials to two NCAA Tournament bids and led the Atlantic 10 in rebounds and blocked shots as a freshman. After skipping his final two college seasons, Dare was drafted 14th overall by New Jersey in 1994 but spent all but one game of his rookie year on the injured list. He started 23 of 58 games in 1995-96.

Strengths: Dare combines size, agility, speed, quickness, and strength. He gets off the floor and can play an intimidating role on defense. His per-minute shot-blocking rate suggests he could swat two per game if given 30 minutes of action instead of the ten minutes he usually sees. Dare would also pull down about nine RPG in that same span. He does not try to exceed his limits.

Weaknesses: Dare has very few offensive skills. He does not own a jump shot, and he knows little about scoring in the post. He's also an awful free-throw shooter. Dare needs a lot of work on the very basic elements of the game. He holds one dubious distinction: After two seasons, he has never been credited with an assist. Dare does pick up a lot of fouls, and he can't dribble the ball.

Analysis: Dare showed great improvement in 1995-96 after a rookie season that featured only one shot—an airball—in three minutes of floor time. He is the definition of a project, and so far the Nets' work with him has yet to pay large dividends. Dare has potential as a shot-blocker and rebounder. His offensive skills are so weak, though, that he's bound to have a tough go of it.

PLAYER SUMMARY	
Will	challenge shots
Can't	score, pass
Expect	offensive struggles
Don't Expect	assists
Fantasy Value	$0
Card Value	7-12¢

COLLEGE STATISTICS

		G	FGP	FTP	RPG	PPG
92-93	GW	30	.551	.473	10.3	12.2
93-94	GW	30	.538	.585	10.3	15.4
Totals		60	.544	.529	10.3	13.8

NBA REGULAR-SEASON STATISTICS

			FGs		3-PT FGs		FTs		Rebounds						
	G	MIN	FG	PCT	FG	PCT	FT	PCT	OFF	TOT	AST	STL	BLK	PTS	PPG
94-95 NJ	1	3	0	.000	0	.000	0	.000	0	1	0	0	0	0	0.0
95-96 NJ	58	626	63	.438	0	.000	38	.613	56	181	0	8	40	164	2.8
Totals	59	629	63	.434	0	.000	38	.613	56	182	0	8	40	164	2.8

ANTONIO DAVIS

Team: Indiana Pacers
Position: Forward
Height: 6'9" **Weight:** 230
Birthdate: October 31, 1968

NBA Experience: 3 years
College: Texas-El Paso
Acquired: Second-round pick in 1990 draft (45th overall)

Background: Davis finished his career at Texas-El Paso fifth on the all-time rebounding chart and was named to the WAC All-Defensive Team as a senior. Indiana's second-round draft choice in 1990, he spent his first two pro seasons in Greece and his third in the Italian League. His sophomore season in Indiana was limited by a back injury, but he averaged a career-high 8.8 PPG while playing all 82 games in 1995-96.

Strengths: Davis is an exceptional leaper who is capable of controlling the glass. He is especially strong on the offensive boards, and also gets a lot of his points with an effective face-up jump shot to 16 feet. Davis puts forth a strong defensive effort against players his size and bigger. When at his tenacious best, he comes off the bench and gives his matchup fits.

Weaknesses: While Davis has been surprising in his ability to stick the mid-range jumper, his low-post offense is nothing to boast about. He seems content to pick up his points off the offensive glass, which is not all bad on a talented Pacer team. Davis is a poor free-throw shooter, and passing is perhaps the weakest aspect of his game. He won't dole out many assists.

Analysis: The sophomore jinx Davis struggled through in 1994-95 was more the result of a nagging back injury than a lack of effort on his behalf. He returned to play some outstanding ball during much of last season, mainly giving the Pacers a boost off the bench with his defense and rebounding. If he ever becomes more assertive on offense, Davis would be a handful.

PLAYER SUMMARY	
Will	defend, rebound
Can't	set up teammates
Expect	offensive boards
Don't Expect	slick moves
Fantasy Value	$1-3
Card Value	7-10¢

COLLEGE STATISTICS

		G	FGP	FTP	RPG	PPG
86-87	UTEP	28	.344	.433	1.8	1.3
87-88	UTEP	30	.590	.548	6.5	9.3
88-89	UTEP	32	.544	.619	8.0	14.3
89-90	UTEP	32	.522	.642	7.6	10.8
Totals		122	.540	.600	6.1	9.2

NBA REGULAR-SEASON STATISTICS

				FGs		3-PT FGs		FTs		Rebounds						
		G	MIN	FG	PCT	FG	PCT	FT	PCT	OFF	TOT	AST	STL	BLK	PTS	PPG
93-94	IND	81	1732	216	.508	0	.000	194	.642	190	505	55	45	84	626	7.7
94-95	IND	44	1030	109	.445	0	.000	117	.672	105	280	25	19	29	335	7.6
95-96	IND	82	2092	236	.490	1	.500	246	.713	188	501	43	33	66	719	8.8
Totals		207	4854	561	.487	1	.333	557	.678	483	1286	123	97	179	1680	8.1

DALE DAVIS

Team: Indiana Pacers
Position: Forward
Height: 6'11" **Weight:** 230
Birthdate: March 25, 1969

NBA Experience: 5 years
College: Clemson
Acquired: First-round pick in 1991 draft (13th overall)

Background: At Clemson, Davis teamed with Elden Campbell for three seasons to form the "Duo of Doom." Davis led the ACC in rebounding three straight years. The 13th pick in the 1991 draft, he has started at power forward for the Pacers in the last four of his five seasons and has amassed almost as many rebounds as points (more than 3,000 each) during his pro career.

Strengths: Davis is an aggressive, hard-working player who loves a challenge. He is physically strong, with fine athletic ability and long arms that make him a force as a rebounder and shot-blocker. He rarely takes a shot he won't make, and he does not mind taking a secondary role on offense. Davis annually ranks among the top in the league in field-goal accuracy.

Weaknesses: That Davis shoots a high percentage from the field despite his woeful touch says much about the types of shots he takes—dunks, putbacks, and gimmies. His range is limited, his low-post moves are too often predictable, and he is one of the worst free-throw shooters in basketball. Passing is not his forte, either.

Analysis: A self-proclaimed rebounding and defensive force, Davis has to be considered one of the top power forwards in the game despite his glaring offensive weaknesses. What he lacks on offense, he makes up for with defense, rebounding, and intimidation. His attacking style has played a large role in Indiana's rise to annual Eastern Conference contention.

PLAYER SUMMARY	
Will	block shots, rebound
Can't	make free throws
Expect	double-doubles
Don't Expect	ill-advised shots
Fantasy Value	$9-11
Card Value	8-15¢

COLLEGE STATISTICS

		G	FGP	FTP	RPG	PPG
87-88	CLEM	29	.532	.506	7.7	7.8
88-89	CLEM	29	.670	.646	8.9	13.3
89-90	CLEM	35	.625	.596	11.3	15.3
90-91	CLEM	28	.532	.580	12.1	17.9
Totals		121	.588	.589	10.0	13.6

NBA REGULAR-SEASON STATISTICS

				FGs		3-PT FGs		FTs		Rebounds						
		G	MIN	FG	PCT	FG	PCT	FT	PCT	OFF	TOT	AST	STL	BLK	PTS	PPG
91-92	IND	64	1301	154	.552	0	.000	87	.572	158	410	30	27	74	395	6.2
92-93	IND	82	2264	304	.568	0	.000	119	.529	291	723	69	63	148	727	8.9
93-94	IND	66	2292	308	.529	0	.000	155	.527	280	718	100	48	106	771	11.7
94-95	IND	74	2346	324	.563	0	.000	138	.533	259	696	58	72	116	786	10.6
95-96	IND	78	2617	334	.558	0	.000	135	.467	252	709	76	56	112	803	10.3
Totals		364	10820	1424	.554	0	.000	634	.520	1240	3256	333	266	556	3482	9.6

HUBERT DAVIS

Team: Toronto Raptors
Position: Guard
Height: 6'5" **Weight:** 183
Birthdate: May 17, 1970

NBA Experience: 4 years
College: North Carolina
Acquired: Traded from Knicks for a
1997 first-round pick, 7/96

Background: A nephew of former North Carolina and NBA great Walter Davis, Hubert Davis gradually developed into a Tar Heel star, leading the ACC in 3-point field-goal percentage as a junior and his team in scoring as a senior. He was drafted 20th overall by the Knicks in 1992 and averaged double figures in scoring in the last three of his four seasons. He was traded to the Raptors in July 1996.

Strengths: Walter Davis was one of the greatest shooters in NBA history, and his nephew has that sweet stroke as well. Hubert will drill better than 40 percent from 3-point distance, boasts an accurate pull-up jumper, and is deadly when he squares up. He has become more aggressive in looking for shots. Davis takes to coaching and rarely misses a free throw.

Weaknesses: Davis is slight in build and also lacks the great quickness that would allow him to get shots more easily. Make him put it on the floor and he becomes a less effective scorer. Like a lot of great shooters, Davis does not specialize in defense. He does work at it, but he gets posted up by bigger guards and taken by quicker ones. His ball-handling and passing need work, too.

Analysis: Over the last three seasons, Davis has converted his long-range shots at a rate that puts him among the NBA's elite bombers. With a little prodding, he has also become more assertive in his all-around game. Only John Starks and Trent Tucker have made more 3-pointers in Knicks uniforms. Tight defense can take Davis out of his game, but give him another year or two.

PLAYER SUMMARY	
Will	pump in 3-pointers
Can't	star on defense
Expect	a sweet stroke
Don't Expect	rebounds
Fantasy Value	$6-8
Card Value	7-12¢

COLLEGE STATISTICS

		G	FGP	FTP	RPG	PPG
88-89	NC	35	.512	.774	0.8	3.3
89-90	NC	34	.446	.797	1.8	9.6
90-91	NC	35	.521	.835	2.4	13.3
91-92	NC	33	.508	.828	2.3	21.4
Totals		137	.498	.819	1.8	11.8

NBA REGULAR-SEASON STATISTICS

		G	MIN	FGs		3-PT FGs		FTs		Rebounds		AST	STL	BLK	PTS	PPG
				FG	PCT	FG	PCT	FT	PCT	OFF	TOT					
92-93	NY	50	815	110	.438	6	.316	43	.796	13	56	83	22	4	269	5.4
93-94	NY	56	1333	238	.471	53	.402	85	.825	23	67	165	40	4	614	11.0
94-95	NY	82	1697	296	.480	131	.455	97	.808	30	110	150	35	11	820	10.0
95-96	NY	74	1773	275	.486	127	.476	112	.868	35	123	103	31	8	789	10.7
Totals		262	5618	919	.474	317	.449	337	.830	101	356	501	128	27	2492	9.5

TERRY DAVIS

Team: Dallas Mavericks
Position: Forward/Center
Height: 6'10" **Weight:** 250
Birthdate: June 17, 1967

NBA Experience: 7 years
College: Virginia Union
Acquired: Signed as a free agent, 8/91

Background: From tiny Virginia Union, Davis made headlines as a two-time Central Intercollegiate Athletic Association Player of the Year. Though he wasn't drafted, he signed with Miami in 1989 and spent two years there. He enjoyed his two most productive years in Dallas before shattering his left elbow in a gruesome car accident in the spring of 1993. He has not been the same player since.

Strengths: Davis specializes in rebounds and interior defense. He presents a good combination of strength and agility, and he plays with fire in his eyes. Davis is capable of handling the power forward and center positions. He gets after his man and can score with his back to the basket.

Weaknesses: Davis is not a well-versed offensive player. His range is limited to the paint area, and he's a dismal free-throw shooter. He simply does not have good touch, and his elbow injury has been a further setback. Davis is not the player you want making decisions with the ball. He's a weak passer and dribbler.

Analysis: In his defense, Davis has been slowed by injuries. He underwent arthroscopic surgery last season to remove torn cartilage from his left knee, causing him to miss the final two months. His problems run deeper than the knife, however. In addition to his offensive limits, Davis has not been the defensive and rebounding force he was a few years ago.

PLAYER SUMMARY

Will ....hit the boards
Can't.........................make jump shots
Expect.............................physical play
Don't Expect ....starts
Fantasy Value $0
Card Value ....5-8¢

COLLEGE STATISTICS

		G	FGP	FTP	RPG	PPG
85-86	VU	27	.462	.605	4.3	4.1
86-87	VU	32	.521	.690	11.3	11.5
87-88	VU	31	.566	.715	10.9	22.7
88-89	VU	31	.615	.682	11.9	22.3
Totals		121	.567	.692	9.8	15.5

NBA REGULAR-SEASON STATISTICS

				FGs		3-PT FGs		FTs		Rebounds						
		G	MIN	FG	PCT	FG	PCT	FT	PCT	OFF	TOT	AST	STL	BLK	PTS	PPG
89-90	MIA	63	884	122	.466	0	.000	54	.621	93	229	25	25	28	298	4.7
90-91	MIA	55	996	115	.487	1	.500	69	.556	107	266	39	18	28	300	5.5
91-92	DAL	68	2149	256	.482	0	.000	181	.635	228	672	57	26	29	693	10.2
92-93	DAL	75	2462	393	.455	2	.250	167	.594	259	701	68	36	28	955	12.7
93-94	DAL	15	286	24	.407	0	.000	8	.667	30	74	6	9	1	56	3.7
94-95	DAL	46	580	49	.434	0	.000	42	.636	63	156	10	6	3	140	3.0
95-96	DAL	28	501	55	.509	0	.000	27	.574	43	117	21	10	4	137	4.9
Totals		350	7858	1014	.467	3	.167	548	.608	823	2215	226	130	121	2579	7.4

TODD DAY

Team: Boston Celtics
Position: Guard/Forward
Height: 6'6" **Weight:** 185
Birthdate: January 7, 1970
NBA Experience: 4 years

College: Arkansas
Acquired: Traded from Bucks with Alton Lister for Sherman Douglas, 11/95

Background: The 1988 prep Player of the Year in Memphis, Day signed with Arkansas and teamed in the backcourt with Lee Mayberry. Day led Arkansas to a 115-24 record in four seasons and earned several All-America honors as a junior and senior. He was drafted eighth overall by Milwaukee. After averaging a career-high 16.0 PPG in 1994-95, Day was traded to the Celtics early last season.

Strengths: The explosive Day can score from inside and out. He has been a prolific 3-point shooter since the arc was shortened two years ago, and he is also capable of driving to the bucket with either hand. He is a fine finisher who gets up and down the floor quickly. He has quick feet, long arms, and the ability to leap out of the gym. Day can play both the big guard and small forward positions.

Weaknesses: Day is a streaky player. That goes for his shooting, his control of the basketball, and his defense. After converting 39 percent of his 3-pointers in his final full season in Milwaukee, he did not even shoot that well from the field last season. He has yet to show the dedication to defense his coaches would like to see. He makes poor decisions that have cut into his playing time.

Analysis: Coming off his best season in 1994-95, Day spent much of the 1995-96 campaign taking a giant step backward. Despite scoring 41 points in a game against Minnesota, he never gained a level of comfort with the Celtics. He came off the bench for most of the season, struggled to his worst shooting season, and was horribly inconsistent.

PLAYER SUMMARY	
Will	shoot the trey
Can't	hit half his shots
Expect	athletic ability
Don't Expect	consistency
Fantasy Value	$5-7
Card Value	10-15¢

COLLEGE STATISTICS

		G	FGP	FTP	RPG	PPG
88-89	ARK	32	.451	.715	4.0	13.3
89-90	ARK	35	.491	.760	5.4	19.5
90-91	ARK	38	.473	.747	5.3	20.7
91-92	ARK	22	.499	.764	7.0	22.7
Totals		127	.479	.747	5.3	18.9

NBA REGULAR-SEASON STATISTICS

				FGs		3-PT FGs		FTs		Rebounds						
		G	MIN	FG	PCT	FG	PCT	FT	PCT	OFF	TOT	AST	STL	BLK	PTS	PPG
92-93	MIL	71	1931	358	.432	54	.293	213	.717	144	291	117	75	48	983	13.8
93-94	MIL	76	2127	351	.415	33	.223	231	.698	115	310	138	103	52	966	12.7
94-95	MIL	82	2717	445	.424	163	.390	257	.754	95	322	134	104	63	1310	16.0
95-96	MIL/BOS	79	1807	299	.366	100	.331	224	.780	70	224	107	81	51	922	11.7
Totals		308	8582	1453	.411	350	.333	925	.736	424	1147	496	363	214	4181	13.6

TERRY DEHERE

Team: Los Angeles Clippers
Position: Guard
Height: 6'4" **Weight:** 190
Birthdate: September 12, 1971

NBA Experience: 3 years
College: Seton Hall
Acquired: First-round pick in 1993 draft (13th overall)

Background: A prep teammate of Bobby Hurley, Dehere was slow to develop in high school but became a star at Seton Hall. He was the Pirates' main offensive weapon for four years, during which he became the Big East's all-time leading scorer. Dehere was named league Player of the Year as a senior. After a slow rookie season, the No. 13 pick in the 1993 draft has improved his scoring average in each of two years since.

Strengths: Dehere has a dangerous shooting stroke. He ranked eighth in the league in 3-point percentage last year, hitting .440 from the arc. His release is as quick as his feet, which give him the ability to drive past almost any defender. Dehere has the ability to play both guard positions, and he racks up his share of assists. His quickness also serves him well in defending the ball.

Weaknesses: Dehere has struggled with his offensive consistency, although he certainly found his shooting touch last season. When the outside shot is taken away, his game diminishes. He can beat his man off the drive but is not one of the better finishers. Slight in build, Dehere gives way to big guards on the blocks. He is prone to playing out of control.

Analysis: Dehere, who struggled for most of his first two seasons, was used as a third guard in 1995-96 and responded with his best campaign. He averaged a career-high 12.4 PPG and gave the Clippers a steady long-range threat off the bench. His ability to play both guard spots makes Dehere a perfect fit for that role, and his overall game has benefitted.

PLAYER SUMMARY	
Will	stick the trey
Can't	slow the pace
Expect	quickness
Don't Expect	rebounds
Fantasy Value	$8-10
Card Value	7-12¢

COLLEGE STATISTICS

		G	FGP	FTP	RPG	PPG
89-90	SH	28	.402	.797	3.4	16.1
90-91	SH	34	.463	.839	3.0	19.8
91-92	SH	31	.427	.830	3.7	19.4
92-93	SH	35	.461	.818	3.0	22.0
Totals		128	.442	.822	3.2	19.5

NBA REGULAR-SEASON STATISTICS

				FGs		3-PT FGs		FTs		Rebounds						
		G	MIN	FG	PCT	FG	PCT	FT	PCT	OFF	TOT	AST	STL	BLK	PTS	PPG
93-94	LAC	64	759	129	.377	23	.404	61	.753	25	68	78	28	3	342	5.3
94-95	LAC	80	1774	279	.407	48	.294	229	.784	35	152	225	45	7	835	10.4
95-96	LAC	82	2018	315	.459	139	.440	247	.755	41	143	350	54	16	1016	12.4
Totals		226	4551	723	.422	210	.392	537	.767	101	363	653	127	26	2193	9.7

VINNY DEL NEGRO

Team: San Antonio Spurs
Position: Guard
Height: 6'4" **Weight:** 200
Birthdate: August 9, 1966

NBA Experience: 6 years
College: North Carolina St.
Acquired: Signed as a free agent, 7/92

Background: After sinking nearly 45 percent of his 3-point shots at North Carolina State, Del Negro was an All-ACC pick as a senior. He played two pro seasons with Sacramento before putting in a two-year stint in Italy. Del Negro was selected Italian A League MVP after averaging 26.0 PPG in 1992. He has spent the last four seasons with San Antonio, raising his scoring average in each of the last three.

Strengths: Del Negro is an outstanding outside shooter with 3-point range. He is a heady player who handles the ball well, rarely makes a mistake, delivers the right passes, and has a keen knowledge of the game. He can play point guard in addition to his more natural two position. Del Negro is an 84-percent career free-throw shooter. He is a solid defensive rebounder.

Weaknesses: What Del Negro offers in fundamentals he lacks in sheer explosiveness. He is not quick enough to create havoc off the dribble or to enjoy much success defensively against the speed burners, although he is a better athlete than his body indicates. He would have more trouble if asked to be a first or second offensive option night after night.

Analysis: Del Negro will never be an All-Star, but he has been invaluable to the Spurs since they made him the starting shooting guard. He has worked exceptionally well with David Robinson, taking full advantage of his opportunities when defenses key on the star center. Del Negro scored a career-high 14.5 PPG last year while contributing to a true team concept.

PLAYER SUMMARY

Will ....find open men
Can't..............................carry a team
Expect ....accurate shooting
Don't Expect ....monster jams
Fantasy Value $7-9
Card Value ....5-8¢

COLLEGE STATISTICS

		G	FGP	FTP	RPG	PPG
84-85	NCST	19	.571	.652	0.7	2.1
85-86	NCST	17	.367	.636	0.8	1.7
86-87	NCST	35	.494	.887	3.3	10.4
87-88	NCST	32	.515	.839	4.9	15.9
Totals		103	.502	.825	2.9	9.1

NBA REGULAR-SEASON STATISTICS

				FGs		3-PT FGs		FTs		Rebounds						
		G	MIN	FG	PCT	FG	PCT	FT	PCT	OFF	TOT	AST	STL	BLK	PTS	PPG
88-89	SAC	80	1556	239	.475	6	.300	85	.850	48	123	206	65	14	569	7.1
89-90	SAC	76	1858	643	.462	10	.313	135	.871	39	198	250	64	10	739	9.7
92-93	SA	73	1526	218	.507	6	.250	101	.863	19	163	291	44	1	543	7.4
93-94	SA	77	1949	309	.487	15	.349	140	.824	27	161	320	64	1	773	10.0
94-95	SA	75	2360	372	.486	66	.407	128	.790	28	192	226	61	14	938	12.5
95-96	SA	82	2766	478	.497	57	.380	178	.832	36	272	315	85	6	1191	14.5
Totals		463	12015	1913	.486	160	.371	767	.836	197	1157	1608	383	46	4753	10.3

VLADE DIVAC

Team: Charlotte Hornets
Position: Center
Height: 7'1" **Weight:** 250
Birthdate: February 3, 1968

NBA Experience: 7 years
College: None
Acquired: Traded from Lakers for draft rights to Kobe Bryant, 7/96

Background: Divac was a national hero in the former Yugoslavia before being drafted by the Lakers in 1989. He led Partizan to the European club championship in 1988 and averaged 20 PPG and 11 RPG in his three years there. He was named to the 1990 NBA All-Rookie Team and has emerged as one of the top centers in the league. After playing all seven of his NBA seasons in L.A., he reluctantly okayed a trade to the Hornets before the 1996-97 season.

Strengths: Divac is a very skilled center in most respects. He is a gifted passer and ball-handler for a center and has a polished offensive arsenal. He has always been a deft shooter with range. Divac provides shot-blocking and rebounding and runs the floor well for a big man. His low-post game has evolved.

Weaknesses: The biggest knock on Divac is simply that he is not Shaq, Hakeem, or Mr. Robinson. He is not capable of dominating games with sheer power and athletic ability. He is still prone to nights when he lets others carry the load. He led the Lakers in turnovers last season and is not a reliable free-throw shooter.

Analysis: Divac became a force in 1994-95, but last season his numbers slipped in several categories. Much of that had to do with the emergence of teammates as scoring threats, but certainly Laker fans would have liked to see Divac take a more assertive stance nightly. Hornets fans will look to Divac to step in as a leader and a force.

PLAYER SUMMARY	
Will	find open men
Can't	overpower Shaq
Expect	double-doubles
Don't Expect	20 PPG
Fantasy Value	$25-30
Card Value	8-12¢

COLLEGE STATISTICS

—DID NOT PLAY—

NBA REGULAR-SEASON STATISTICS

			FGs		3-PT FGs		FTs		Rebounds						
	G	MIN	FG	PCT	FG	PCT	FT	PCT	OFF	TOT	AST	STL	BLK	PTS	PPG
89-90 LAL	82	1611	274	.499	0	.000	153	.708	167	512	75	79	114	701	8.5
90-91 LAL	82	2310	360	.565	5	.357	196	.703	205	666	92	106	127	921	11.2
91-92 LAL	36	979	157	.495	5	.263	86	.768	87	247	60	55	35	405	11.3
92-93 LAL	82	2525	397	.485	21	.280	235	.689	220	729	232	128	140	1050	12.8
93-94 LAL	79	2685	453	.506	9	.191	208	.686	282	851	307	92	112	1123	14.2
94-95 LAL	80	2807	485	.507	10	.189	297	.777	261	829	329	109	174	1277	16.0
95-96 LAL	79	2470	414	.513	3	.167	189	.641	198	679	261	76	131	1020	12.9
Totals	520	15387	2540	.510	53	.229	1364	.707	1420	4513	1356	645	833	6497	12.5

SHERMAN DOUGLAS

Team: Milwaukee Bucks
Position: Guard
Height: 6'1" **Weight:** 198
Birthdate: September 15, 1966

NBA Experience: 7 years
College: Syracuse
Acquired: Traded from Celtics for
Todd Day and Alton Lister, 11/95

Background: Douglas was the catalyst on a Syracuse team that included Billy
Owens and Derrick Coleman. As a senior, he became the NCAA career assists
leader and a first-team All-American. Despite being drafted in the second round,
he made the NBA All-Rookie Team with Miami in 1989-90. He spent parts of five
seasons with Boston before being traded to Milwaukee last November.

Strengths: Douglas has a knack for penetrating despite average quickness at
best. He is a nifty ball-handler with deceptive moves to the hoop. He can dish the
ball to teammates or toss in off-balance shots in traffic. He once led the Heat in
scoring and can sink jumpers if his defender overplays the drive.

Weaknesses: Douglas has been inconsistent through much of his career. He is
not a pure shooter, and he sometimes fashions himself as more of a scorer than
a distributor. Douglas also does not rate among the better backcourt defenders.
He does not have great lateral quickness and does not come up with many steals
or rebounds.

Analysis: A scorer some nights and a distributor others, Douglas has been a
very productive player at times in his career. He has his share of critics, however,
who point to his tendency toward erratic play. The fact is, Douglas is a point
guard who has never guided a team to great success. Some would say that's no
coincidence.

PLAYER SUMMARY	
Will	penetrate
Can't	start for a contender
Expect	deceptive moves
Don't Expect	clamp-down defense
Fantasy Value	$7-9
Card Value	7-12¢

COLLEGE STATISTICS

		G	FGP	FTP	APG	PPG
85-86	SYR	27	.613	.727	2.1	5.4
86-87	SYR	38	.531	.744	7.6	17.3
87-88	SYR	35	.519	.693	8.2	16.1
88-89	SYR	38	.546	.632	8.6	18.2
Totals		138	.538	.695	7.0	14.9

NBA REGULAR-SEASON STATISTICS

		G	MIN	FGs FG	FGs PCT	3-PT FGs FG	3-PT FGs PCT	FTs FT	FTs PCT	Rebounds OFF	Rebounds TOT	AST	STL	BLK	PTS	PPG
89-90	MIA	81	2470	463	.494	5	.161	224	.687	70	206	619	145	10	1155	14.3
90-91	MIA	73	2562	532	.504	4	.129	284	.686	78	209	624	121	5	1352	18.5
91-92	MIA/BOS	42	752	117	.462	1	.100	73	.682	13	63	172	25	9	308	7.3
92-93	BOS	79	1932	264	.498	6	.207	84	.560	65	162	508	49	10	618	7.8
93-94	BOS	78	2789	425	.462	13	.232	177	.641	70	193	683	89	11	1040	13.3
94-95	BOS	65	2048	365	.475	20	.244	204	.689	48	170	446	80	2	954	14.7
95-96	BOS/MIL	79	2335	345	.504	40	.364	160	.731	55	180	436	63	5	890	11.3
Totals		497	14888	2511	.488	89	.255	1206	.674	399	1183	3488	572	52	6317	12.7

CLYDE DREXLER

Team: Houston Rockets
Position: Guard
Height: 6'7" **Weight:** 222
Birthdate: June 22, 1962
NBA Experience: 13 years

College: Houston
Acquired: Traded from Trail Blazers with Tracy Murray for Otis Thorpe, draft rights to Marcelo Nicola, and a conditional first-round pick, 2/95

Background: Drexler gained notoriety for his breathtaking dunks at the University of Houston, where he played in two Final Fours. He has maintained that reputation as a pro, playing his first 11-plus years in Portland and taking the Blazers' all-time lead in several categories. The nine-time All-Star helped Houston to the 1995 NBA championship.

Strengths: "Clyde the Glide" is still a superstar with great leaping and scoring ability. He makes things happen and has produced reels of fabulous finishes. Drexler owns 3-point range, and his post-up moves give small guards fits. His passing and rebounding are splendid.

Weaknesses: Injuries have hampered Drexler in recent seasons. He underwent arthroscopic surgery on his right knee in February and missed most of the second half of the 1995-96 season. His shooting accuracy has slipped.

Analysis: Drexler was playing as if his legs had found a fountain of youth last season. He averaged 19.3 PPG, 7.2 RPG, 5.8 APG, and 2.0 SPG before his knee surgery, adding yet another All-Star start to his resume. He won't be able to do it forever, but the man can still energize a team in countless ways.

PLAYER SUMMARY	
Will	thrill the crowd
Can't	be left open
Expect	veteran leadership
Don't Expect	82 games
Fantasy Value	$20-25
Card Value	12-25¢

COLLEGE STATISTICS

		G	FGP	FTP	RPG	PPG
80-81	HOUS	30	.505	.588	10.5	11.9
81-82	HOUS	32	.569	.608	10.5	15.2
82-83	HOUS	34	.536	.737	8.8	15.9
Totals		96	.538	.643	9.9	14.4

NBA REGULAR-SEASON STATISTICS

				FGs		3-PT FGs		FTs		Rebounds						
		G	MIN	FG	PCT	FG	PCT	FT	PCT	OFF	TOT	AST	STL	BLK	PTS	PPG
83-84	POR	82	1408	252	.451	1	.250	123	.728	112	235	153	107	29	628	7.7
84-85	POR	80	2555	573	.494	8	.216	223	.759	217	476	441	177	68	1377	17.2
85-86	POR	75	2576	542	.475	12	.200	293	.769	171	421	600	197	46	1389	18.5
86-87	POR	82	3114	707	.502	11	.234	357	.760	227	518	566	204	71	1782	21.7
87-88	POR	81	3060	849	.506	11	.212	476	.811	261	533	467	203	52	2185	27.0
88-89	POR	78	3064	829	.496	27	.260	438	.799	289	615	450	213	54	2123	27.2
89-90	POR	73	2683	670	.494	30	.283	333	.774	208	507	432	145	51	1703	23.3
90-91	POR	82	2852	645	.482	61	.319	416	.794	212	546	493	144	60	1767	21.5
91-92	POR	76	2751	694	.470	114	.337	401	.794	166	500	512	138	70	1903	25.0
92-93	POR	49	1671	350	.429	31	.233	245	.839	126	309	278	95	37	976	19.9
93-94	POR	68	2334	473	.428	71	.324	286	.777	154	445	333	98	34	1303	19.2
94-95	POR/HOU	76	2728	571	.461	147	.360	364	.824	152	480	362	136	45	1653	21.8
95-96	HOU	52	1997	331	.433	78	.332	265	.784	97	373	302	105	24	1005	19.3
Totals		954	32793	7486	.476	602	.311	4220	.789	2392	5958	5389	1962	641	19794	20.7

CHRIS DUDLEY

Team: Portland Trail Blazers
Position: Center
Height: 6'11" **Weight:** 240
Birthdate: February 22, 1965

NBA Experience: 9 years
College: Yale
Acquired: Signed as a free agent, 8/93

Background: A Yale graduate, Dudley was second in the nation in rebounding as a senior. Cleveland drafted him in 1987 but sent him to New Jersey during the 1989-90 season. Dudley turned down a $21-million, seven-year offer from the Nets for an $11-million, seven-year deal in Portland before the 1993-94 season. His defense and rebounding have made him a starter.

Strengths: Dudley attacks the glass and opposing players with equal abandon. He knows how to use his large frame to wall off opponents from the backboards. He has an aggressive, forceful approach to just about everything he does. Dudley is a smart, tough defender who blocks shots. He is well aware of his offensive deficiencies.

Weaknesses: Dudley has proved that brains have nothing to do with shooting. He is one of the most pathetic free-throw shooters in the league. In fact, his offensive game in general, including his passing and dribbling, is very weak. He commits a lot of fouls and scores very few points.

Analysis: Last season, Dudley ended a string of six consecutive years shooting worse than 42 percent from the floor. Still, he's hardly an offensive force. Not many pro players are content to pound the daylights out of people and chase every rebound without scoring, but that's how Dudley makes his living. No NBA starter has a worse shooting touch.

PLAYER SUMMARY	
Will	inflict pain
Can't	sink a pair
Expect	defense, rebounds
Don't Expect	offense
Fantasy Value	$1-3
Card Value	5-8¢

COLLEGE STATISTICS

		G	FGP	FTP	RPG	PPG
83-84	YALE	26	.464	.467	5.1	4.5
84-85	YALE	26	.446	.533	10.2	12.6
85-86	YALE	26	.539	.482	9.8	16.2
86-87	YALE	24	.569	.542	13.3	17.8
Totals		102	.513	.512	9.5	12.7

NBA REGULAR-SEASON STATISTICS

				FGs		3-PT FGs		FTs		Rebounds						
		G	MIN	FG	PCT	FG	PCT	FT	PCT	OFF	TOT	AST	STL	BLK	PTS	PPG
87-88	CLE	55	513	65	.474	0	.000	40	.563	74	144	23	13	19	170	3.1
88-89	CLE	61	544	73	.435	0	.000	39	.364	72	157	21	9	23	185	3.0
89-90	CLE/NJ	64	1356	146	.411	0	.000	58	.319	174	423	39	41	72	350	5.5
90-91	NJ	61	1560	170	.408	0	.000	94	.534	229	511	37	39	153	434	7.1
91-92	NJ	82	1902	190	.403	0	.000	80	.468	343	739	58	38	179	460	5.6
92-93	NJ	71	1398	94	.353	0	.000	57	.518	215	513	16	17	103	245	3.5
93-94	POR	6	86	6	.240	0	.000	2	.500	16	24	5	4	3	14	2.3
94-95	POR	82	2245	181	.406	0	.000	85	.464	325	764	34	43	126	447	5.5
95-96	POR	80	1924	162	.453	0	.000	80	.510	239	720	37	41	100	404	5.1
Totals		562	11528	1087	.411	0	.000	535	.461	1687	3995	270	245	778	2709	4.8

JOE DUMARS

Team: Detroit Pistons
Position: Guard
Height: 6'3" **Weight:** 195
Birthdate: May 23, 1963

NBA Experience: 11 years
College: McNeese St.
Acquired: First-round pick in 1985 draft (18th overall)

Background: Dumars led the Southland Conference in scoring three times at McNeese State. He got pegged early as a defensive specialist in the NBA but has surpassed 13,000 career points over 11 years in Detroit. Dumars was named MVP of the 1989 Finals, played for Dream Team II, and is a five-time All-Star.

Strengths: Dumars was once a regular on the NBA All-Defensive Team and was once known as Michael Jordan's greatest defensive nemesis. He is an unassuming leader and a deadly shooter with great range. Free throws are close to automatic. Dumars has loads of experience at both guard slots.

Weaknesses: Not the player he once was, Dumars has seen his shooting percentage plunge in recent years. He has played through nagging injuries and does not drive to the hole as frequently as he once did. He has been used mostly as a reserve of late, though he was pressed into starting duty late last season.

Analysis: Dumars, who last year was the lone holdover from Detroit's 1989 and 1990 NBA title teams, remains a class act and a veteran presence. His shooting, penetrating, and defense, however, have seen their best days. His No. 4 will belong in the Palace of Auburn Hills rafters once he retires.

PLAYER SUMMARY	
Will	take clutch shots
Can't	shake leg injuries
Expect	leadership, class
Don't Expect	another title
Fantasy Value	$2-4
Card Value	10-20¢

COLLEGE STATISTICS

		G	FGP	FTP	RPG	PPG
81-82	MSU	29	.444	.719	2.2	18.2
82-83	MSU	29	.435	.711	4.4	19.6
83-84	MSU	31	.471	.824	5.3	26.4
84-85	MSU	27	.495	.852	4.9	25.8
Totals		116	.462	.788	4.2	22.5

NBA REGULAR-SEASON STATISTICS

		G	MIN	FGs FG	FGs PCT	3-PT FGs FG	3-PT FGs PCT	FTs FT	FTs PCT	Rebounds OFF	Rebounds TOT	AST	STL	BLK	PTS	PPG
85-86	DET	82	1957	287	.481	5	.313	190	.798	60	119	390	66	11	769	9.4
86-87	DET	79	2439	369	.493	9	.409	184	.748	50	167	352	83	5	931	11.8
87-88	DET	82	2732	453	.472	4	.211	251	.815	63	200	387	87	15	1161	14.2
88-89	DET	69	2408	456	.505	14	.483	260	.850	57	172	390	63	5	1186	17.2
89-90	DET	75	2578	508	.480	22	.400	297	.900	60	212	368	63	2	1335	17.8
90-91	DET	80	3046	622	.481	14	.311	371	.890	62	187	443	89	7	1629	20.4
91-92	DET	82	3192	587	.448	49	.408	188	.867	82	188	375	71	12	1635	19.9
92-93	DET	77	3094	677	.466	112	.375	343	.864	63	148	308	78	7	1809	23.5
93-94	DET	69	2591	505	.452	124	.387	276	.836	35	151	261	63	4	1410	20.4
94-95	DET	67	2544	417	.430	103	.305	277	.805	47	158	368	72	7	1214	18.1
95-96	DET	67	2193	255	.426	121	.406	162	.822	28	138	265	43	3	793	11.8
Totals		829	28774	5136	.466	577	.370	3023	.843	607	1840	3907	778	78	13872	16.7

RICHARD DUMAS

Unrestricted Free Agent
Last Team: Philadelphia 76ers
Position: Forward
Height: 6'7" **Weight:** 225
Birthdate: May 19, 1969

NBA Experience: 3 years
College: Oklahoma St.
Acquired: Signed as a free agent, 8/95

Background: Dumas was a two-year standout at Oklahoma State before he was forced to take his career to Israel because of academic and alcohol troubles. He was drafted in the second round by the Suns in 1991 but was suspended before his rookie season for failing a drug test. After a strong debut in 1992-93, he missed the 1993-94 season because of a relapse. He has played just 54 games since the second suspension.

Strengths: Dumas is a slasher with a quick first step who knows how to put the ball in the hole. Mentor John Lucas once compared Dumas's natural ability to that of Julius Erving. Dumas thrives in the open court and has a good jump shot, which he can get off the dribble. He handles the ball well. He can be an exciting, exuberant player who ignites his team.

Weaknesses: Obviously, Dumas is a high-risk player because of his battle with substance abuse. Since his breakthrough season three years ago, he has spent more games on the NBA's suspended list than he has on the floor. When he has played, Dumas has not approached his first-year level of play in any aspect of the game. He has lost a great deal of confidence.

Analysis: No one is sure what to expect of Dumas these days, other than this: He will probably never enjoy another year like his 1992-93 season. No one is predicting All-Star status anymore, and some would be surprised if he becomes a regular contributor. Dumas does have athletic ability and raw talent on his side. The biggest thing working against him, at times, is Dumas himself.

PLAYER SUMMARY	
Will	slash to the hoop
Can't	afford another slip-up
Expect	a close watch
Don't Expect	another 1992-93
Fantasy Value	$1
Card Value	7-10¢

COLLEGE STATISTICS

		G	FGP	FTP	RPG	PPG
87-88	OSU	30	.546	.747	6.4	17.4
88-89	OSU	28	.448	.617	7.0	15.7
89-90	OSU	12	.549	.636	5.4	12.7
Totals		70	.501	.685	6.5	15.9

NBA REGULAR-SEASON STATISTICS

				FGs		3-PT FGs		FTs		Rebounds						
		G	MIN	FG	PCT	FG	PCT	FT	PCT	OFF	TOT	AST	STL	BLK	PTS	PPG
92-93	PHO	48	1320	302	.524	1	.333	152	.707	100	223	60	85	39	757	15.8
94-95	PHO	15	167	37	.507	0	.000	8	.500	18	29	7	10	2	82	5.5
95-96	PHI	39	739	95	.468	2	.222	49	.700	42	99	44	42	6	241	6.2
Totals		102	2226	434	.509	3	.231	209	.694	160	351	111	137	47	1080	10.6

TONY DUMAS

Team: Dallas Mavericks
Position: Guard
Height: 6'5" **Weight:** 190
Birthdate: August 25, 1972

NBA Experience: 2 years
College: Missouri-Kansas City
Acquired: First-round pick in 1994 draft (19th overall)

Background: Dumas put up huge college numbers at Missouri-Kansas City, leading the Kangaroos in scoring in each of his last three years and setting career records for points and rebounds. He was ranked eighth nationally in scoring as a senior with 26.0 PPG, and he once tallied 44 and 43 points on back-to-back nights. The 19th overall pick in 1994, Dumas saw limited action as a Dallas rookie but upped his contribution to 11.6 PPG last season.

Strengths: Dumas looks to score and knows how to do it. He possesses great quickness and leaping ability and is not afraid to challenge. He'll drive to the hole, can finish his own plays, and knows how to draw fouls. In short, he's a natural scorer. Dumas proved last season he is capable of burning a team with the 3-pointer if you don't take it away from him. He is supremely confident.

Weaknesses: Dumas needs to fine-tune his game. He plays recklessly at times, meaning he'll launch bad shots, fail to find open teammates, or allow his man to get a layup. Dumas is not a defensive ace (and never has been), though he has the necessary athletic prowess. His passing, rebounding, ball-handling, and free-throw shooting all lag a bit behind his scoring.

Analysis: When given the opportunity in his young career, Dumas played some impressive minutes. In 33 minutes off the bench against Phoenix last season, he scored 39 points on 15-of-19 shooting, hitting six of his nine 3-point shots (the most points in the NBA last season off the bench). He was given a chance to start late last season and further demonstrated his scoring bent. There are other parts of the game to master, but this small-school standout shows some promise.

PLAYER SUMMARY	
Will	attack the basket
Can't	shut down his man
Expect	a scoring bent
Don't Expect	rebounds
Fantasy Value	$2-4
Card Value	10-15¢

COLLEGE STATISTICS

		G	FGP	FTP	RPG	PPG
90-91	MKC	29	.499	.754	4.6	15.9
91-92	MKC	28	.521	.775	4.6	21.5
92-93	MKC	27	.489	.718	5.5	23.8
93-94	MKC	29	.421	.757	5.7	26.0
Totals		113	.477	.753	5.1	21.8

NBA REGULAR-SEASON STATISTICS

				FGs		3-PT FGs		FTs		Rebounds						
		G	MIN	FG	PCT	FG	PCT	FT	PCT	OFF	TOT	AST	STL	BLK	PTS	PPG
94-95	DAL	58	613	96	.384	22	.301	50	.649	32	62	57	13	4	264	4.6
95-96	DAL	67	1284	274	.418	74	.357	154	.599	58	115	99	42	13	776	11.6
Totals		125	1897	370	.409	96	.343	204	.611	90	177	156	55	17	1040	8.3

LEDELL EACKLES

Unrestricted Free Agent
Last Team: Washington Bullets
Position: Guard
Height: 6'5" **Weight:** 230
Birthdate: November 24, 1966

NBA Experience: 6 years
College: San Jacinto; New Orleans
Acquired: Signed as a free agent, 12/95

Background: Eackles led the American South Conference in scoring with 23.4 PPG as a senior at New Orleans and was named league Player of the Year. Drafted in the second round by Washington, he played his first four pro seasons with the Bullets. After a stint on Indiana's suspended list and a brief CBA tour, he returned to the NBA with Miami in 1994-95 and rejoined the Bullets last year.

Strengths: Eackles is a true scorer. He can hit jumpers with 3-point range or bull his way through the lane for buckets or trips to the free-throw line. He has been compared to a fullback for his head-down style. He is a sound passer with a good feel for the game and a nice touch from the free-throw line.

Weaknesses: Consistency has never been a strong suit for Eackles, whose weight has ballooned at times in his career. He's not known as a hard worker. He is not a strong defensive player, giving away quickness to most of his matchups. Eackles is not a great ball-handler, he contributes little on the boards, and he's spent a lot of time on the hardwood.

Analysis: Eackles did not play organized basketball before he was signed by the Bullets last season, nor did he play during the 1992-93 or 1993-94 seasons. With just six seasons under his belt, he will play the 1996-97 campaign at age 30. Eackles hit 42 percent of his 3-pointers last season and is capable of playing an "instant offense" role off the bench.

PLAYER SUMMARY

Will ....bull to the hoop
Can't ....defend quickness
Expect ....instant offense
Don't Expect ....a physical specimen
Fantasy Value...................................$0
Card Value ....7-10¢

COLLEGE STATISTICS

		G	FGP	FTP	RPG	PPG
84-85	SJ	29	.550	.730	5.4	19.0
85-86	SJ	37	.583	.755	6.4	27.2
86-87	NO	28	.456	.724	4.1	22.6
87-88	NO	31	.508	.802	4.9	23.4
Totals		125	.523	.768	5.3	23.3

NBA REGULAR-SEASON STATISTICS

| | | | MIN | FGs | | 3-PT FGs | | FTs | | Rebounds | | | | | | |
		G	MIN	FG	PCT	FG	PCT	FT	PCT	OFF	TOT	AST	STL	BLK	PTS	PPG
88-89	WAS	80	1459	318	.434	9	.225	272	.786	100	180	123	41	5	917	11.5
89-90	WAS	78	1696	413	.439	19	.322	210	.750	74	175	182	50	4	1055	13.5
90-91	WAS	67	1616	345	.453	14	.237	164	.739	47	128	136	47	10	868	13.0
91-92	WAS	65	1463	355	.468	7	.200	139	.743	39	178	125	47	7	856	13.2
94-95	MIA	54	898	143	.439	18	.439	91	.722	33	95	72	19	2	395	7.3
95-96	WAS	55	1238	161	.427	54	.422	98	.831	44	148	86	28	3	474	8.6
Totals		399	8370	1735	.445	121	.334	974	.762	337	904	724	232	31	4565	11.4

ACIE EARL

Team: Toronto Raptors
Position: Center/Forward
Height: 6'10" **Weight:** 240
Birthdate: June 23, 1970

NBA Experience: 3 years
College: Iowa
Acquired: Selected from Celtics in 1995 expansion draft

Background: Earl led the Big Ten in blocked shots as a freshman at Iowa and finished his college career with 365 swats—seventh in NCAA history at the time. He moved into Iowa's all-time top five in scoring, rebounding, and blocks. A first-round choice of the Celtics in 1993, Earl was a disappointing reserve for two years. His first season in Toronto was quiet until he broke loose in the last two weeks.

Strengths: Though he gives away a couple of inches to most NBA centers, Earl has the ability to block shots and score with his back to the basket. He has worked hard to develop his low-post game and is able to make hook shots, turnaround jumpers, and short face-ups. He hits the offensive glass and torched his old team for 40 points last season.

Weaknesses: Earl is not a good athlete. He's a step slow, he stays pretty close to the floor, and he moves methodically. His marginal athletic ability accounts for most of his troubles over three seasons. Earl takes some bad shots, and often his good ones get swatted. He converts a poor percentage from the field, and he does not get to the line enough. His defensive skills are below average.

Analysis: How do you explain Earl's finish to the 1995-96 season? After playing about half of the season's first 75 games and averaging 4.3 PPG during that span, he scored at a 22.4-PPG pace over the final seven games and was also a rebounding and shot-blocking presence. Toronto fans were left scratching their heads and hoping that Earl's strong finish bodes well for his future.

PLAYER SUMMARY	
Will	post up
Can't	out-quick his man
Expect	blocked shots
Don't Expect	consistency
Fantasy Value	$3-5
Card Value	8-12¢

COLLEGE STATISTICS

		G	FGP	FTP	RPG	PPG
89-90	IOWA	22	.440	.739	3.5	6.0
90-91	IOWA	32	.503	.665	6.7	16.3
91-92	IOWA	30	.533	.667	7.8	19.5
92-93	IOWA	32	.505	.701	8.9	16.9
Totals		116	.508	.680	7.0	15.3

NBA REGULAR-SEASON STATISTICS

		G	MIN	FGs		3-PT FGs		FTs		Rebounds		AST	STL	BLK	PTS	PPG
				FG	PCT	FG	PCT	FT	PCT	OFF	TOT					
93-94	BOS	74	1149	151	.406	0	.000	108	.675	85	247	12	24	53	410	5.5
94-95	BOS	30	208	26	.382	0	.000	14	.483	19	45	2	6	8	66	2.2
95-96	TOR	42	655	117	.424	0	.000	82	.719	51	129	27	18	37	316	7.5
Totals		146	2012	294	.411	0	.000	204	.673	155	421	41	48	98	792	5.4

TYUS EDNEY

Team: Sacramento Kings   **NBA Experience:** 1 year
Position: Guard   **College:** UCLA
Height: 5'10" **Weight:** 152   **Acquired:** Second-round pick in 1995
Birthdate: February 14, 1973   draft (47th overall)

Background: A hero of the 1995 NCAA Tournament, Edney lifted UCLA past Missouri with a last-second basket in the second round, and the Bruins went on to win the national championship. Edney won the 1995 Frances Pomeroy Naismith Award as the top college senior under six feet. He was a late second-round draft choice of Sacramento but spent most of his rookie season as a starter, averaging 10.8 PPG and 6.1 APG.

Strengths: Edney's lightning-quick feet are the key to his game. He can knife into the lane for assists or points and has a variety of crafty moves. A gritty player, he is not afraid to challenge despite the fact that he is usually the smallest man on the floor. He's what some call a "gamer." The Kings expect Edney to become a disruptive on-the-ball defender because of his quick hands.

Weaknesses: It's a good thing Edney has quickness on his side, because he certainly doesn't have size. His slight build makes him a tantalizing post-up target and makes it difficult for Edney to wear anyone out. He is an inconsistent outside shooter (.412 from the field last year) and will make his share of mistakes with the ball, too. Edney has a brief history of injuries.

Analysis: Some have called Edney the steal of the 1995 draft. After all, it is rare to find a 47th choice who steps in to start as a rookie. Indeed, Edney's ability to handle the rigors of the NBA schedule as a first-team point guard did come as a surprise to many. Keep in mind, however, that he was considered to be exploitable on defense on a sub-.500 Kings team. He'll be expected to raise his level of play.

PLAYER SUMMARY	
Will	pick up the pace
Can't	block shots
Expect	aggressive drives
Don't Expect	steady shooting
Fantasy Value	$3-5
Card Value	50¢-$1.00

COLLEGE STATISTICS

		G	FGP	FTP	RPG	PPG
91-92	UCLA	32	.472	.797	2.1	5.6
92-93	UCLA	33	.483	.841	3.5	13.6
93-94	UCLA	28	.466	.820	3.4	15.4
94-95	UCLA	32	.497	.764	3.1	14.3
Totals		125	.481	.805	3.0	12.1

NBA REGULAR-SEASON STATISTICS

				FGs		3-PT FGs		FTs		Rebounds						
		G	MIN	FG	PCT	FG	PCT	FT	PCT	OFF	TOT	AST	STL	BLK	PTS	PPG
95-96	SAC	80	2481	305	.412	53	.368	197	.782	63	201	491	89	3	860	10.8
Totals		80	2481	305	.412	53	.368	197	.782	63	201	491	89	3	860	10.8

BLUE EDWARDS

Team: Vancouver Grizzlies
Position: Guard/Forward
Height: 6'4" **Weight:** 229
Birthdate: October 31, 1965

NBA Experience: 7 years
College: Louisburg; East Carolina
Acquired: Selected from Jazz in 1995 expansion draft

Background: Edwards was a junior college All-American before his two-year career at East Carolina. As a senior, he led the Pirates in seven statistical categories. He spent his first three years with Utah, but he has changed address four times in the last four years. He served a second stint with the Jazz two years ago before averaging 12.7 PPG with the expansion Grizzlies in 1995-96.

Strengths: Edwards combines speed and strength and comes custom-made for transition basketball. He's a fine athlete who finishes well and can bring a crowd to its feet. He's a tremendous leaper, he can post up, and he's capable of big nights from the 3-point arc. Edwards is foremost a scorer, but he also rebounds.

Weaknesses: Edwards is a streaky shooter, and his ball-handling and passing skills are below average for a player who has spent most of his career at shooting guard. He has never displayed the consistency to stick around as a prominent player on a winning team. Quicker guards give Edwards fits.

Analysis: Edwards does a little bit of everything. He can score from the outside, on the blocks, or in transition. He can play two positions, and he holds his own on the boards. He played perhaps his best minutes as a sixth man for Utah. Edwards's move to Canada did wonders for his playing time, but he could not carry the Grizzlies.

PLAYER SUMMARY

Will........................finish on the break
Can't ....make Grizzlies win
Expect ....versatility
Don't Expect ....fancy dribbling
Fantasy Value $2-4
Card Value ....7-10¢

COLLEGE STATISTICS

		G	FGP	FTP	RPG	PPG
84-85	LOU	29	.636	.645	6.1	17.8
85-86	LOU	31	.700	.658	6.0	22.3
86-87	EC	28	.561	.739	5.6	14.4
88-89	EC	29	.551	.755	6.9	26.7
Totals		117	.612	.701	6.2	20.4

NBA REGULAR-SEASON STATISTICS

				FGs		3-PT FGs		FTs		Rebounds						
		G	MIN	FG	PCT	FG	PCT	FT	PCT	OFF	TOT	AST	STL	BLK	PTS	PPG
89-90	UTA	82	1889	286	.507	9	.300	146	.719	69	251	145	76	36	727	8.9
90-91	UTA	62	1611	244	.526	6	.250	82	.701	51	201	108	57	29	576	9.3
91-92	UTA	81	2283	433	.522	39	.379	113	.774	86	298	137	81	46	1018	12.6
92-93	MIL	82	2729	554	.512	37	.349	237	.790	123	382	214	129	45	1382	16.9
93-94	MIL	82	2322	382	.477	38	.358	151	.799	104	329	171	83	27	953	11.6
94-95	BOS/UTA	67	1112	181	.461	22	.293	75	.833	50	130	77	43	16	459	6.9
95-96	VAN	82	2773	401	.419	84	.343	157	.755	98	346	212	118	46	1043	12.7
Totals		538	14719	2481	.487	235	.341	961	.767	581	1937	1064	587	245	6159	11.4

KEVIN EDWARDS

Team: New Jersey Nets
Position: Guard
Height: 6'3" **Weight:** 210
Birthdate: October 30, 1965

NBA Experience: 8 years
College: Lakewood; DePaul
Acquired: Signed as a free agent, 7/93

Background: Edwards finished his college career with the best shooting percentage (53.3) ever by a DePaul guard and was known for his high-flying dunks. He spent his first five pro seasons in Miami and the past three in New Jersey. A torn Achilles tendon limited Edwards to 14 games in 1994-95, and knee tendinitis reduced his 1995-96 campaign to just 34 outings.

Strengths: When at full strength, Edwards can flat-out score. He has a quick first step to the basket, the ability to finish his drives or pull up for short jumpers, and 3-point range. He gets to the line and is a career 80-percent free-throw shooter. Edwards is also no slouch on defense. He takes pride in his efforts on both ends of the floor.

Weaknesses: Despite scoring in double figures in each of his eight NBA seasons, Edwards has never converted a high percentage from the floor. He is the definition of a streaky player. He has also been turnover-prone during his career. Injuries have now made Edwards a question mark. He shot just .364 from the field last season.

Analysis: Including the injury-shortened 1994-95 season, Edwards had averaged about 14 PPG for three consecutive seasons and seemed to have found his niche with the Nets. Edwards struggled badly in his return last season, however, and a knee injury then further tested his patience. The 1996-97 season looks to be an important one for his confidence.

PLAYER SUMMARY	
Will	score, defend
Can't	shake recent injuries
Expect	streak shooting
Don't Expect	15 PPG
Fantasy Value	$3-5
Card Value	7-10¢

COLLEGE STATISTICS

		G	FGP	FTP	RPG	PPG
84-85	LAKE	33	.589	.715	5.4	18.6
85-86	LAKE	32	.626	.761	7.5	24.1
86-87	DeP	31	.536	.808	5.0	14.4
87-88	DeP	30	.533	.783	5.3	18.3
Totals		126	.576	.760	5.8	18.9

NBA REGULAR-SEASON STATISTICS

				FGs		3-PT FGs		FTs		Rebounds						
		G	MIN	FG	PCT	FG	PCT	FT	PCT	OFF	TOT	AST	STL	BLK	PTS	PPG
88-89	MIA	79	2349	470	.425	10	.270	144	.746	85	262	349	139	27	1094	13.8
89-90	MIA	78	2211	395	.412	9	.300	139	.760	77	282	252	125	33	938	12.0
90-91	MIA	79	2000	380	.410	24	.286	171	.803	80	205	240	130	46	955	12.1
91-92	MIA	81	1840	325	.454	7	.219	162	.848	56	211	170	99	20	819	10.1
92-93	MIA	40	1134	216	.468	5	.294	119	.844	48	121	120	68	12	556	13.9
93-94	NJ	82	2727	471	.458	35	.354	167	.770	94	281	232	120	34	1144	14.0
94-95	NJ	14	466	69	.448	18	.400	40	.952	10	37	27	19	5	196	14.0
95-96	NJ	34	1007	142	.364	42	.404	68	.810	14	75	71	54	7	394	11.6
Totals		487	13734	2468	.430	150	.335	1010	.799	464	1474	1461	754	184	6096	12.5

CRAIG EHLO

Team: Seattle SuperSonics
Position: Guard/Forward
Height: 6'7" **Weight:** 205
Birthdate: August 11, 1961

NBA Experience: 13 years
College: Odessa; Washington St.
Acquired: Signed as a free agent, 7/96

Background: As a senior, Ehlo set a Pac-10 record for assists at Washington State. He was a Houston reserve before a CBA stint, then spent seven years with Cleveland. Ehlo signed with Atlanta before the 1993-94 season and came back from knee surgery in 1995-96. He joins the Sonics for 1996-1997.

Strengths: Ehlo is an accurate 3-point shooter who has made almost 600 career treys. He always seems to find a way to get open. He's also a tough defender who throws his body around for the team. A 13-year veteran, Ehlo is an outstanding presence in the locker room.

Weaknesses: Ehlo does not possess the quickness or athletic ability to stick with faster players one-on-one, nor does he create much offense on his own. He is a complementary player who gets little fanfare.

Analysis: Ehlo is the type of player who can shoot holes in a game plan if you're not careful, but who is most valuable for his leadership and team-first example. He rarely does anything to hurt his own team. That he could be productive for this long—especially when few would have expected it—is testament to his work habits.

PLAYER SUMMARY

Will.........................play a team game
Can't ....create off the dribble
Expect ....range, leadership
Don't Expect..............two more years
Fantasy Value $1
Card Value ....5-8¢

COLLEGE STATISTICS

		G	FGP	FTP	RPG	PPG
79-80	ODES	28	.487	.714	5.1	12.6
80-81	ODES	30	.500	.772	6.8	20.7
81-82	WSU	30	.479	.600	2.2	5.1
82-83	WSU	30	.547	.633	3.2	12.0
Totals		118	.505	.701	4.3	12.6

NBA REGULAR-SEASON STATISTICS

			MIN	FGs FG	FGs PCT	3-PT FGs FG	3-PT FGs PCT	FTs FT	FTs PCT	Rebounds OFF	Rebounds TOT	AST	STL	BLK	PTS	PPG
83-84	HOU	7	63	11	.407	0	.000	1	1.000	4	9	6	3	0	23	3.3
84-85	HOU	45	189	34	.493	0	.000	19	.633	8	25	26	11	3	87	1.9
85-86	HOU	36	199	36	.429	3	.333	23	.793	17	46	29	11	4	98	2.7
86-87	CLE	44	890	99	.414	5	.172	70	.707	55	161	92	40	30	273	6.2
87-88	CLE	79	1709	226	.466	22	.344	89	.674	86	274	206	82	30	563	7.1
88-89	CLE	82	1867	249	.475	39	.390	71	.607	100	295	266	110	19	608	7.4
89-90	CLE	81	2894	436	.464	104	.419	126	.681	147	439	371	126	23	1102	13.6
90-91	CLE	82	2766	344	.445	49	.329	95	.679	142	388	376	121	34	832	10.1
91-92	CLE	63	2016	310	.453	69	.413	87	.707	94	307	238	78	22	776	12.3
92-93	CLE	82	2559	385	.490	93	.381	86	.717	113	403	254	104	22	949	11.6
93-94	ATL	82	2147	316	.446	77	.348	112	.727	71	279	273	136	26	821	10.0
94-95	ATL	49	1166	191	.453	51	.381	44	.620	55	147	113	46	6	477	9.7
95-96	ATL	79	1758	253	.428	82	.371	81	.786	65	256	138	85	9	669	8.5
Totals		811	20223	2890	.456	594	.374	904	.693	957	3029	2388	953	228	7278	9.0

MARIO ELIE

Team: Houston Rockets
Position: Guard/Forward
Height: 6'5" **Weight:** 210
Birthdate: November 26, 1963

NBA Experience: 6 years
College: American International
Acquired: Traded from Trail Blazers
for a 1995 second-round pick, 8/93

Background: A world traveler, Elie played in Portugal, Argentina, Ireland, and Miami (of the USBL) after his college career at American International. He was drafted by Milwaukee in 1985 but was released before the season. Elie played in the CBA during 1989-90 and saw his first NBA action in 1990-91 with Philadelphia (three games). His three-year stay in Houston has been his longest since college, and the Rockets inked him to a new deal over the off-season.

Strengths: Elie, who speaks four languages, is also a whiz when it comes to defense. He holds his own against big scorers, whether they're guards or forwards. He has also become a steady offensive threat, canning his unorthodox jump shot with 3-point range and making a living off transition pull-ups. He gets to the hole, is a good passer, and very rarely misses a free throw.

Weaknesses: This category grows shorter by the season. Elie is not a dominant athlete, nor is he overpowering on the offensive end. Without the presence of superstar teammates Olajuwon and Drexler to open things up, it's a safe bet Elie's game would suffer. Wrist surgery cut short his 1995-96 season.

Analysis: A former seventh-round draft choice, Elie is the perfect example of a late bloomer. He played a vital role in helping the Rockets to their 1994 and 1995 championships, and his confidence has soared because of it. A former journeyman, he is now respected league-wide for his defense, shooting, and work ethic. Elie is a team player, a workhorse, and a class act.

PLAYER SUMMARY

Will ....hound his man
Can't ....get used to one town
Expect ....a reserve spark plug
Don't Expect ....a superstar
Fantasy Value $5-7
Card Value ....5-8¢

COLLEGE STATISTICS

		G	FGP	FTP	RPG	PPG
81-82	AI	25	.586	.742	8.3	15.4
82-83	AI	31	.527	.739	7.7	15.9
83-84	AI	31	.565	.794	8.6	18.9
84-85	AI	33	.549	.777	9.0	20.1
Totals		120	.555	.767	8.4	17.7

NBA REGULAR-SEASON STATISTICS

		G	MIN	FGs		3-PT FGs		FTs		Rebounds		AST	STL	BLK	PTS	PPG
				FG	PCT	FG	PCT	FT	PCT	OFF	TOT					
90-91	PHI/GS	33	644	79	.497	4	.400	75	.843	46	110	45	19	10	237	7.2
91-92	GS	79	1677	221	.521	23	.329	155	.852	69	227	174	68	15	620	7.8
92-93	POR	82	1757	240	.458	45	.349	183	.855	59	216	177	74	20	708	8.6
93-94	HOU	67	1606	208	.446	56	.335	154	.860	28	181	208	50	8	626	9.3
94-95	HOU	81	1896	243	.499	80	.398	144	.842	50	196	189	65	12	710	8.8
95-96	HOU	45	1385	180	.504	41	.323	98	.852	47	155	138	45	11	499	11.1
Totals		387	8965	1171	.484	249	.354	809	.852	299	1085	931	321	76	3400	8.8

SEAN ELLIOTT

Team: San Antonio Spurs
Position: Forward
Height: 6'8" **Weight:** 220
Birthdate: February 2, 1968
NBA Experience: 7 years

College: Arizona
Acquired: Traded from Pistons for draft rights to Bill Curley and a 1997 second-round pick, 7/94

Background: Elliott was college basketball's 1989 Player of the Year at Arizona, where he broke Lew Alcindor's Pac-10 record with 2,555 career points. He enjoyed four fine years in San Antonio before a trade involving Dennis Rodman sent him to Detroit and a substandard 1993-94 season. He was dealt back to the Spurs in July 1994 and was named to the All-Star Team last season.

Strengths: Elliott has a diverse offensive arsenal. He can drive past almost any defender, and he also owns a nice perimeter touch with range. Combining those skills, Elliott is an explosive scorer who can take over games. Despite his lack of bulk, his quick hands and feet help him stay in front of his man on defense. He's a clutch player who loves to win and knows how.

Weaknesses: About the only area Elliott seems incapable of dominating is the glass, but he's also had teammates like Rodman and David Robinson who take care of that. As mentioned, he lacks bulk and will not push many forwards around. He's neither a great post-up threat nor a snazzy dribbler.

Analysis: Comfortable with his surroundings and happy with his new contract, Elliott enjoyed the best season of his seven-year career last year. He averaged 20.0 PPG, played in the All-Star Game on his home floor, and helped the Spurs to another fine season. He and Robinson form one of the better one-two punches in basketball.

PLAYER SUMMARY	
Will	star at both ends
Can't	outrebound Mr. Robinson
Expect	explosive scoring
Don't Expect	another 1993-94
Fantasy Value	$30-35
Card Value	10-20¢

COLLEGE STATISTICS

		G	FGP	FTP	RPG	PPG
85-86	ARIZ	32	.486	.749	5.3	15.6
86-87	ARIZ	30	.510	.770	6.0	19.3
87-88	ARIZ	38	.570	.793	5.8	19.6
88-89	ARIZ	33	.480	.841	7.2	22.3
Totals		133	.512	.793	6.1	19.2

NBA REGULAR-SEASON STATISTICS

				FGs		3-PT FGs		FTs		Rebounds						
		G	MIN	FG	PCT	FG	PCT	FT	PCT	OFF	TOT	AST	STL	BLK	PTS	PPG
89-90	SA	81	2032	311	.481	1	.111	187	.866	127	297	154	45	14	810	10.0
90-91	SA	82	3044	478	.490	20	.313	325	.808	142	456	238	69	33	1301	15.9
91-92	SA	82	3120	514	.494	25	.305	285	.861	143	439	214	84	29	1338	16.3
92-93	SA	70	2604	451	.491	37	.356	268	.795	85	322	265	68	28	1207	17.2
93-94	DET	73	2409	360	.455	26	.299	139	.803	68	263	197	54	27	885	12.1
94-95	SA	81	2858	502	.468	136	.408	326	.807	63	287	206	78	38	1466	18.1
95-96	SA	77	2901	525	.466	161	.411	326	.771	69	396	211	69	33	1537	20.0
Totals		546	18968	3141	.478	406	.379	1856	.812	697	2460	1485	467	202	8544	15.6

DALE ELLIS

Team: Denver Nuggets
Position: Guard/Forward
Height: 6'7" **Weight:** 215
Birthdate: August 6, 1960

NBA Experience: 13 years
College: Tennessee
Acquired: Signed as a free agent, 10/94

Background: Ellis was an All-American at Tennessee, where he averaged 22.6 PPG his senior year. He was a faceless reserve with Dallas for three years, but an infamous trade for Al Wood brought him to Seattle and stardom. Ellis has spent the last two of his 13 seasons in Denver. He holds the NBA's career record for 3-point buckets.

Strengths: Ellis still has a picture-book jumper, and few players in history have been as accurate from deep (40-plus percent career). He shot .412 from the arc last season. Ellis has made at least 100 long ones in each of the last five seasons.

Weaknesses: Other than the 3-point shot, Ellis has a game filled with holes. He is not a great defensive player, rebounder, or ball-handler. He creates virtually none of his offense with the bounce, instead working off screens or spotting up.

Analysis: Ellis continues to stockpile 3-point buckets at a clip no one in league history has matched. His second year in Denver was better than his first, as he finished second on the team with 14.9 PPG and scored his 16,000th career point. He's a true specialist.

PLAYER SUMMARY	
Will	add to 3-point record
Can't	star in other areas
Expect	100-plus treys
Don't Expect	multiyear deals
Fantasy Value	$3-5
Card Value	7-10¢

COLLEGE STATISTICS

		G	FGP	FTP	RPG	PPG
79-80	TENN	27	.445	.775	3.6	7.1
80-81	TENN	29	.597	.748	6.4	17.7
81-82	TENN	30	.654	.796	6.3	21.2
82-83	TENN	21	.601	.751	10.0	22.6
Totals		107	.595	.765	6.3	19.3

NBA REGULAR-SEASON STATISTICS

			FGs		3-PT FGs		FTs		Rebounds						
	G	MIN	FG	PCT	FG	PCT	FT	PCT	OFF	TOT	AST	STL	BLK	PTS	PPG
83-84 DAL	67	1059	225	.456	12	.414	87	.719	106	250	56	41	9	549	8.2
84-85 DAL	72	1314	274	.454	42	.385	77	.740	100	238	56	46	7	667	9.3
85-86 DAL	72	1086	193	.411	63	.364	59	.720	86	168	37	40	9	508	7.1
86-87 SEA	82	3073	785	.516	86	.358	385	.787	187	447	238	104	32	2041	24.9
87-88 SEA	75	2790	764	.503	107	.413	303	.767	167	340	197	74	11	1938	25.8
88-89 SEA	82	3190	857	.501	162	.478	377	.816	156	342	164	108	22	2253	27.5
89-90 SEA	55	2033	502	.497	96	.375	193	.818	90	238	110	59	7	1293	23.5
90-91 SEA/MIL	51	1424	340	.474	57	.363	120	.723	66	173	95	49	8	857	16.8
91-92 MIL	81	2191	485	.469	138	.419	164	.774	92	253	104	57	18	1272	15.7
92-93 SA	82	2731	545	.499	119	.401	157	.797	81	312	107	78	18	1366	16.7
93-94 SA	77	2590	478	.494	131	.395	83	.776	70	255	80	66	11	1170	15.2
94-95 DEN	81	1996	351	.453	106	.403	110	.866	56	222	57	37	9	918	11.3
95-96 DEN	81	2626	459	.479	150	.412	136	.760	88	315	139	57	7	1204	14.9
Totals	958	28103	6258	.486	1269	.403	2251	.782	1345	3553	1440	816	168	16036	16.7

LaPHONSO ELLIS

Team: Denver Nuggets
Position: Forward
Height: 6'8" **Weight:** 240
Birthdate: May 5, 1970

NBA Experience: 4 years
College: Notre Dame
Acquired: First-round pick in 1992 draft (fifth overall)

Background: Ellis finished his college career as one of only four Notre Dame players to score 1,000 points and grab 1,000 rebounds. He became the all-time Irish leader in blocked shots despite missing parts of two seasons due to academics. He was drafted fifth overall by Denver in 1992 and was a first-team All-Rookie choice. He has been sidelined by knee injuries for most of the last two years.

Strengths: When healthy, Ellis has been a highly productive scorer, rebounder, and shot-blocker. He averaged 15.4 PPG, 8.6 RPG, and 1.0 BPG in his second season. He has great natural instincts on both ends of the floor. He can play both forward slots, scoring on post-up moves or facing the basket.

Weaknesses: Ellis found a cyst on his right kneecap in November 1994, and another on his left kneecap in April 1995. Bone graft surgery repaired both, but there is no guarantee Ellis will ever have the legs he once did. In the past, he has not been as comfortable with his face-up game as he has been inside. He has never been a reliable free-throw shooter.

Analysis: Ellis seemed to be on the path to stardom before his first knee surgery. Through January 1996, Ellis had missed 107 of 113 games. Since his comeback, he has not approached his second-year level of play. He lost weight and was thrust into a small forward role for which he was not fully prepared. He said he plans to locate a comfortable weight before the 1996-97 season and regain his old form, no matter where he's asked to play.

PLAYER SUMMARY	
Will	score inside and out
Can't	shake knee troubles
Expect	blocks, boards
Don't Expect	an easy road back
Fantasy Value	$5-7
Card Value	10-20¢

COLLEGE STATISTICS

		G	FGP	FTP	RPG	PPG
88-89	ND	27	.563	.684	9.4	13.5
89-90	ND	22	.511	.675	12.6	14.0
90-91	ND	15	.573	.716	10.5	16.4
91-92	ND	33	.631	.655	11.7	17.7
Totals		97	.577	.675	11.1	15.5

NBA REGULAR-SEASON STATISTICS

				FGs		3-PT FGs		FTs		Rebounds						
		G	MIN	FG	PCT	FG	PCT	FT	PCT	OFF	TOT	AST	STL	BLK	PTS	PPG
92-93	DEN	82	2749	483	.504	2	.154	237	.748	274	744	151	72	111	1205	14.7
93-94	DEN	79	2699	483	.502	7	.304	242	.674	220	682	167	63	80	1215	15.4
94-95	DEN	6	58	9	.360	0	.000	6	1.000	7	17	4	1	5	24	4.0
95-96	DEN	45	1269	189	.438	4	.182	89	.601	93	322	74	36	33	471	10.5
Totals		212	6775	1164	.489	13	.224	574	.692	594	1765	396	172	229	2915	13.8

PERVIS ELLISON

Team: Boston Celtics
Position: Forward/Center
Height: 6'10" **Weight:** 225
Birthdate: April 3, 1967

NBA Experience: 7 years
College: Louisville
Acquired: Signed as a free agent, 7/94

Background: As a freshman, Ellison was the MVP of the 1986 NCAA Tournament after lifting Louisville to the title. He recorded 2,000 points and 1,000 rebounds in college and finished his career among the NCAA's all-time leaders in blocked shots. The top pick in the 1989 draft, he won the Most Improved Player Award with Washington in 1991-92. He's played the last two years for Boston.

Strengths: Ellison is a shot-blocking presence in the middle. He has long arms and good timing. He can be an effective rebounder and defensive player. Ellison scores in the post using either hand. He has averaged as many as 20 PPG, and he is an above-average passer.

Weaknesses: Ellison plays on a bad set of knees. He has undergone multiple operations that have robbed him of quickness and kept him on the bench. He has played 70 games in only one of his seven seasons. Ellison has never been much of a power player. He does not shoot well from the perimeter or the free-throw line.

Analysis: Injuries played a key role in Ellison's slow NBA start, and they continue to plague him. His 69 games last season were the most he played since his second year in the league, and he did haul down 6.5 RPG. He is nowhere near the offensive or defensive player he once was, however, and even that player was something of a disappointment.

PLAYER SUMMARY	
Will	block shots
Can't	regain lost step
Expect	stints on injured list
Don't Expect	10 PPG
Fantasy Value	$1
Card Value	7-10¢

COLLEGE STATISTICS

		G	FGP	FTP	RPG	PPG
85-86	LOUI	39	.554	.682	8.2	13.1
86-87	LOUI	31	.533	.719	8.7	15.2
87-88	LOUI	35	.601	.692	8.3	17.6
88-89	LOUI	31	.615	.652	8.7	17.6
Totals		136	.577	.687	8.4	15.8

NBA REGULAR-SEASON STATISTICS

			FGs		3-PT FGs		FTs		Rebounds					
	G	MIN	FG	PCT	FG	PCT	FT	PCT	OFF	TOT	AST	STL	BLK	PTS	PPG
89-90 SAC	34	866	111	.442	0	.000	49	.628	64	196	65	16	57	271	8.0
90-91 WAS	76	1942	326	.513	0	.000	139	.650	224	585	102	49	157	791	10.4
91-92 WAS	66	2511	547	.539	1	.333	227	.728	217	740	190	62	177	1322	20.0
92-93 WAS	49	1701	341	.521	0	.000	170	.702	138	433	117	45	108	852	17.4
93-94 WAS	47	1178	137	.469	0	.000	70	.722	77	242	70	25	50	344	7.3
94-95 BOS	55	1083	152	.507	0	.000	71	.717	124	309	34	22	54	375	6.8
95-96 BOS	69	1431	145	.492	0	.000	75	.641	151	451	62	39	99	365	5.3
Totals	396	10712	1759	.511	1	.050	801	.691	995	2956	640	258	702	4320	10.9

PATRICK EWING

Team: New York Knicks
Position: Center
Height: 7'0" **Weight:** 240
Birthdate: August 5, 1962

NBA Experience: 11 years
College: Georgetown
Acquired: First-round pick in 1985 draft (first overall)

Background: Ewing led Georgetown to three NCAA title games, prevailing in 1984, and was the consensus Player of the Year as a senior while setting records across the board. He won Olympic gold in 1984 and 1992. Ewing earned NBA Rookie of the Year honors in 1986 with the Knicks and has been a perennial All-Star. He enjoyed another great season in 1995-96.

Strengths: A franchise player, Ewing is the complete package in the pivot. He intimidates on defense, swats shots, hoards rebounds, and is virtually unstoppable one-on-one when he gets the ball in the post. He has a dangerous jump shot that no one can challenge.

Weaknesses: There is very little Ewing can't do outside of shooting a lot of 3-pointers or trying his hand at guard. He has played in the Finals but has yet to win a championship ring. It's about the only thing missing in his career.

Analysis: Ewing has been considered one of the premier centers in the league for several years and has earned serious MVP consideration along the way. He is New York's all-time leader in games, points, rebounds, blocks, steals, and minutes. He is annually among NBA leaders in scoring, rebounding, and shot-blocking.

PLAYER SUMMARY	
Will	carry his team
Can't	be single-teamed
Expect	points, rebounds, blocks
Don't Expect	All-Star absences
Fantasy Value	$45-50
Card Value	25-40¢

COLLEGE STATISTICS

		G	FGP	FTP	RPG	PPG
81-82	GEOR	37	.631	.617	7.5	12.7
82-83	GEOR	32	.570	.629	10.2	17.7
83-84	GEOR	37	.658	.656	10.0	16.4
84-85	GEOR	37	.625	.637	9.2	14.6
Totals		143	.620	.635	9.2	15.3

NBA REGULAR-SEASON STATISTICS

		G	MIN	FGs FG	FGs PCT	3-PT FGs FG	3-PT FGs PCT	FTs FT	FTs PCT	Rebounds OFF	Rebounds TOT	AST	STL	BLK	PTS	PPG
85-86	NY	50	1771	386	.474	0	.000	226	.739	124	451	102	54	103	998	20.0
86-87	NY	63	2206	530	.503	0	.000	296	.713	157	555	104	89	147	1356	21.5
87-88	NY	82	2546	656	.555	0	.000	341	.716	245	676	125	104	245	1653	20.2
88-89	NY	80	2896	727	.567	0	.000	361	.746	213	740	188	117	281	1815	22.7
89-90	NY	82	3165	922	.551	1	.250	502	.775	235	893	182	78	327	2347	28.6
90-91	NY	81	3104	845	.514	0	.000	464	.745	194	905	244	80	258	2154	26.6
91-92	NY	82	3150	796	.522	1	.167	377	.738	228	921	156	88	245	1970	24.0
92-93	NY	81	3003	779	.503	1	.143	400	.719	191	980	151	74	161	1959	24.2
93-94	NY	79	2972	745	.496	4	.286	445	.765	219	885	179	90	217	1939	24.5
94-95	NY	79	2920	730	.503	6	.286	420	.750	157	867	212	68	159	1886	23.9
95-96	NY	76	2783	678	.466	4	.143	351	.761	157	806	160	68	184	1711	22.5
Totals		835	30516	7794	.515	17	.159	4183	.744	2120	8679	1803	910	2327	19788	23.7

DANNY FERRY

Team: Cleveland Cavaliers
Position: Forward
Height: 6'10" **Weight:** 235
Birthdate: October 17, 1966
NBA Experience: 6 years
College: Duke

Acquired: Draft rights traded from Clippers with Reggie Williams for Ron Harper, 1990 and 1992 first-round picks, and a 1991 second-round pick, 11/89

Background: After an illustrious career at Duke, in which he was named the nation's Player of the Year as a senior, Ferry snubbed the NBA and spent a year in Italy to avoid playing with the Clippers. When his rights were traded to Cleveland for Ron Harper, he made his disappointing NBA debut. Ferry finally broke through in his sixth season, averaging a career-high 13.3 PPG in 1995-96.

Strengths: Ferry is at his best on the perimeter despite his 6'10" size. He knows where to spot up and will hit from 3-point land when given an open look. The son of former NBA player Bob Ferry, Danny is a team player with a good sense of where and when to deliver the ball. He has regained some of the confidence he once had in college.

Weaknesses: Ferry is mainly a shooter. He feeds off others instead of making things happen himself, and his slow feet make it impossible for him to be a stalwart on defense. He does not use the dribble well, nor does he dominate the glass. Ferry is a limited athlete who will never be a star.

Analysis: Ferry had to be considered one of the most improved players in the NBA in 1995-96. After letting everyone down for most of his first five seasons, it was a long time coming. Ferry shot the ball with confidence, put forth a better effort on defense and the boards, and helped the Cavaliers to a surprisingly solid season. It was a refreshing change.

PLAYER SUMMARY	
Will	knock down shots
Can't	fulfill expectations
Expect	team play
Don't Expect	a huge fan club
Fantasy Value	$3-5
Card Value	5-8¢

COLLEGE STATISTICS

		G	FGP	FTP	RPG	PPG
85-86	DUKE	40	.460	.628	5.5	5.9
86-87	DUKE	33	.449	.844	7.8	14.0
87-88	DUKE	35	.476	.828	7.6	19.1
88-89	DUKE	35	.522	.756	7.4	22.6
Totals		143	.484	.775	7.0	15.1

NBA REGULAR-SEASON STATISTICS

				FGs		3-PT FGs		FTs		Rebounds						
		G	MIN	FG	PCT	FG	PCT	FT	PCT	OFF	TOT	AST	STL	BLK	PTS	PPG
90-91	CLE	81	1661	275	.428	23	.299	124	.816	99	286	142	43	25	697	8.6
91-92	CLE	68	937	134	.409	17	.354	61	.836	53	213	75	22	15	346	5.1
92-93	CLE	76	1461	220	.479	34	.415	99	.876	81	279	137	29	49	573	7.5
93-94	CLE	70	965	149	.446	14	.275	38	.884	47	141	74	28	22	350	5.0
94-95	CLE	82	1290	223	.446	94	.403	74	.881	30	143	96	27	22	614	7.5
95-96	CLE	82	2680	422	.459	143	.394	103	.769	71	309	191	57	37	1090	13.3
Totals		459	8994	1423	.447	325	.381	499	.833	381	1371	715	206	170	3670	8.0

MICHAEL FINLEY

Team: Phoenix Suns
Position: Guard/Forward
Height: 6'7" **Weight:** 215
Birthdate: March 6, 1973

NBA Experience: 1 year
College: Wisconsin
Acquired: First-round pick in 1995 draft (21st overall)

Background: Finley, who left Wisconsin as the school's all-time leading scorer, was never an Associated Press All-American but earned honorable-mention honors after each of his final three seasons. He slipped to 21st overall in the 1995 NBA draft after what was considered a subpar senior year. Finley burst onto the Suns' scene during his rookie season, averaging 15.0 PPG and starting all but ten of 82 games.

Strengths: Finley is an explosive leaper with athletic ability to spare. Quickness runs through everything he does, including scoring, offensive rebounding, and defense. Finley is a much better shooter than anyone anticipated. His field-goal percentage of 47.6 was remarkable for a rookie, and he has 3-point range. Finley is a scrappy player who loves an up-tempo game and expends loads of energy.

Weaknesses: At times, Finley falls too in love with the long-range jumper. He made less than a third of his 3-pointers as a rookie, and should probably forsake the well-defended bombs for quick drives to the bucket or passes to open teammates. He does not stack up to other forwards as well on the defensive glass as he does on the offensive boards. Finley sometimes plays too hard for his own good.

Analysis: Explain this: Finley made less than 38 percent of his shots as a college senior, then lit up NBA defenders at about a ten-percent-better clip. If you're at a loss, you're in good company. No one knew Finley would be the player he is, especially on offense. His shooting was the biggest stunner, but his overall confidence and poise all over the court came as pleasant surprises for the Suns. Charles Barkley is predicting stardom for this young player.

PLAYER SUMMARY

Will ....outjump his man
Can't ....slow down
Expect......................scoring, defense
Don't Expect ....jitters
Fantasy Value $14-17
Card Value ....75¢-$2.00

COLLEGE STATISTICS

		G	FGP	FTP	RPG	PPG
91-92	WISC	31	.453	.742	4.9	12.3
92-93	WISC	28	.467	.771	5.8	22.1
93-94	WISC	29	.466	.786	6.7	20.4
94-95	WISC	27	.379	.773	5.2	20.5
Totals		115	.440	.769	5.6	18.7

NBA REGULAR-SEASON STATISTICS

				FGs		3-PT FGs		FTs		Rebounds						
		G	MIN	FG	PCT	FG	PCT	FT	PCT	OFF	TOT	AST	STL	BLK	PTS	PPG
95-96	PHO	82	3212	465	.476	61	.328	242	.749	139	374	289	85	31	1233	15.0
Totals		82	3212	465	.476	61	.328	242	.749	139	374	289	85	31	1233	15.0

VERN FLEMING

Unrestricted Free Agent
Last Team: New Jersey Nets
Position: Guard
Height: 6'5" **Weight:** 185
Birthdate: February 4, 1962

NBA Experience: 12 years
College: Georgia
Acquired: Signed as a free agent, 9/95

Background: Fleming teamed with Dominique Wilkins at Georgia and, as a senior, led the SEC in scoring. He played on the 1984 Olympic team and was credited by Michael Jordan as providing his toughest defense in practices. He spent 11 productive seasons in Indiana before donning a Nets jersey last year.

Strengths: Fleming is the Pacers' all-time assists leader. This savvy player knows how to run an offense and can also play the two spot. He has a height advantage over most playmakers and has always been able to rebound. He also plays smart defense and makes few mistakes.

Weaknesses: Fleming is no longer an explosive scorer, and he has never been a great outside shooter. He has made just three 3-pointers in the last three years. He is not among the more creative point guards in the game and is no speedster. Age has caught up with Fleming.

Analysis: Fleming will probably give coaching a try after he retires in a year or two. He is widely regarded as one of the more knowledgeable players in the NBA. These days, Fleming's smarts carry him as far as his skill level does. He surpassed the 10,000-point and 3,000-rebound plateaus last season.

PLAYER SUMMARY	
Will	play solid minutes
Can't	blow past defenders
Expect	heady play
Don't Expect	three more years
Fantasy Value	$0
Card Value	5-8¢

COLLEGE STATISTICS

		G	FGP	FTP	RPG	PPG
80-81	GEOR	30	.480	.697	2.7	10.0
81-82	GEOR	31	.496	.640	3.9	9.9
82-83	GEOR	34	.535	.716	4.6	16.9
83-84	GEOR	30	.503	.754	4.0	19.8
Totals		125	.508	.705	3.8	14.2

NBA REGULAR-SEASON STATISTICS

				FGs		3-PT FGs		FTs		Rebounds						
		G	MIN	FG	PCT	FG	PCT	FT	PCT	OFF	TOT	AST	STL	BLK	PTS	PPG
84-85	IND	80	2486	433	.470	0	.000	260	.767	148	323	247	99	8	1126	14.1
85-86	IND	80	2870	436	.506	1	.167	263	.745	102	386	505	131	5	1136	14.2
86-87	IND	82	2549	370	.509	2	.200	238	.788	109	334	473	109	18	980	12.0
87-88	IND	80	2733	442	.523	0	.000	227	.802	106	364	568	115	11	1111	13.9
88-89	IND	76	2552	419	.515	3	.130	243	.799	85	310	494	77	12	1084	14.3
89-90	IND	82	2876	467	.508	12	.353	230	.782	118	322	610	92	10	1176	14.3
90-91	IND	69	1929	356	.531	4	.222	161	.729	83	214	369	76	13	877	12.7
91-92	IND	82	1737	294	.482	6	.222	132	.737	69	209	266	56	7	726	8.9
92-93	IND	75	1503	280	.505	7	.194	143	.726	63	169	224	63	9	710	9.5
93-94	IND	55	1053	147	.462	0	.000	64	.736	27	123	173	40	6	358	6.5
94-95	IND	55	686	93	.495	0	.000	65	.722	20	88	109	27	1	251	4.6
95-96	NJ	77	1747	227	.433	3	.107	133	.751	49	170	255	41	5	590	7.7
Totals		893	24721	3964	.498	38	.181	2159	.764	979	3012	4293	926	105	10125	11.3

GREG FOSTER

Team: Utah Jazz
Position: Center/Forward
Height: 6'11" **Weight:** 240
Birthdate: October 3, 1968

NBA Experience: 6 years
College: UCLA; Texas-El Paso
Acquired: Signed as a free agent, 10/95

Background: Foster led Texas-El Paso to two consecutive NCAA Tournament appearances and was named MVP of the Western Athletic Conference Tournament as a senior. A 1990 second-rounder, he won a job with the Bullets and has since played with Atlanta, Milwaukee, Chicago, Minnesota, and Utah over six seasons. He has seen action in 70-plus games in each of the last two seasons.

Strengths: Foster stands 6'11" and weighs 240 pounds, and that's his biggest plus. He has a soft touch and good range for a big man, which helps him pull opposing frontcourt players away from the basket. Foster can contribute on the boards, and he shot 84.7 percent from the free-throw line last year.

Weaknesses: Foster is soft—plain and simple. He's slow, he does not have low-post scoring moves, and he is not a force on the boards or on defense. Foster seems content to shoot jumpers instead of asserting himself in the middle, and he's a streaky shooter at that. He won't block many shots, nor will his passes lead to baskets. He's inconsistent in all aspects of the game.

Analysis: Foster was considered a project coming into the league, and it's apparent he will never develop into a top-notch player. The one thing he does well is find work. Despite his not playing well for any of his six teams, there always seems to be another NBA job waiting. Unless Foster decides to assert himself in the paint, don't expect the trend to continue.

PLAYER SUMMARY	
Will	shoot jumpers
Can't	unpack his suitcase
Expect	limited minutes
Don't Expect	forceful moves
Fantasy Value	$0
Card Value	5-8¢

COLLEGE STATISTICS

		G	FGP	FTP	RPG	PPG
86-87	UCLA	31	.500	.500	2.5	3.3
87-88	UCLA	11	.527	.432	5.5	8.5
88-89	UTEP	26	.483	.651	7.3	11.1
89-90	UTEP	32	.465	.811	6.2	10.6
Totals		100	.483	.661	5.2	8.2

NBA REGULAR-SEASON STATISTICS

		G	MIN	FGs FG	FGs PCT	3-PT FGs FG	3-PT FGs PCT	FTs FT	FTs PCT	Rebounds OFF	Rebounds TOT	AST	STL	BLK	PTS	PPG
90-91	WAS	54	606	97	.460	0	.000	42	.689	52	151	37	12	22	236	4.4
91-92	WAS	49	548	89	.461	0	.000	35	.714	43	145	35	6	12	213	4.3
92-93	WAS/ATL	43	298	55	.458	0	.000	15	.714	32	83	21	3	14	125	2.9
93-94	MIL	3	19	4	.571	0	.000	2	1.000	0	3	0	0	1	10	3.3
94-95	CHI/MIN	78	1144	150	.472	7	.304	78	.703	85	259	39	15	28	385	4.9
95-96	UTA	73	803	107	.439	1	.125	61	.847	53	178	25	7	22	276	3.8
Totals		300	3418	502	.459	8	.195	233	.737	265	819	157	43	99	1245	4.2

RICK FOX

Team: Boston Celtics
Position: Guard/Forward
Height: 6'7" **Weight:** 250
Birthdate: July 24, 1969

NBA Experience: 5 years
College: North Carolina
Acquired: First-round pick in 1991 draft (24th overall)

Background: Born in Canada, Fox moved to the Bahamas when he was two years old. He had a limited basketball background before playing high school ball in Warsaw, Indiana. Though never a marquee player at North Carolina, Fox was drafted in the first round by the Celtics in 1991. He spent most of his first four seasons as a reserve before starting 81 games in 1995-96.

Strengths: Few players hustle like Fox. He's a hard-working player with a strong body who is not afraid to challenge. His drives to the hoop produce points, free throws, and assists, and he can also fill the nets from the outside. He averaged a career-high 14.0 PPG last season. He works hard on defense and will mix it up with larger players. He can play big guard in addition to forward.

Weaknesses: Fox has been an inconsistent shooter during his career. Opponents are best advised to cut off his drive. He does not have great ball-handling skills and is thus better suited to forward than guard. Much of what Fox produces on the floor is a direct result of his exceptional work ethic, rather than due to his extraordinary basketball skills. He led Boston last year in fouls and turnovers.

Analysis: When Dominique Wilkins opted to play in Greece, the door opened for Fox to become Boston's starting small forward. It's the better of his two positions, and he responded in 1995-96 with career highs in several statistical categories. He was among the team leaders in scoring, rebounds, assists, and steals.

PLAYER SUMMARY	
Will	sacrifice his body
Can't	avoid fouling
Expect	drives, defense
Don't Expect	20 PPG
Fantasy Value	$10-13
Card Value	7-10¢

COLLEGE STATISTICS

		G	FGP	FTP	RPG	PPG
87-88	NC	34	.628	.500	1.9	4.0
88-89	NC	37	.583	.790	3.8	11.5
89-90	NC	34	.522	.735	4.6	16.2
90-91	NC	35	.453	.804	6.6	16.9
Totals		140	.518	.757	4.2	12.2

NBA REGULAR-SEASON STATISTICS

		G	MIN	FGs FG	FGs PCT	3-PT FGs FG	3-PT FGs PCT	FTs FT	FTs PCT	Rebounds OFF	Rebounds TOT	AST	STL	BLK	PTS	PPG
91-92	BOS	81	1535	241	.459	23	.329	139	.755	73	220	126	78	30	644	8.0
92-93	BOS	71	1082	184	.484	4	.174	81	.802	55	159	113	61	21	453	6.4
93-94	BOS	82	2096	340	.467	33	.330	174	.757	105	355	217	81	52	887	10.8
94-95	BOS	53	1039	169	.481	31	.413	95	.772	61	155	139	52	19	464	8.8
95-96	BOS	81	2588	421	.454	99	.364	196	.772	158	450	369	113	41	1137	14.0
Totals		368	8340	1355	.465	190	.352	685	.768	452	1339	964	385	163	3585	9.7

KEVIN GAMBLE

Team: Sacramento Kings
Position: Guard/Forward
Height: 6'5" **Weight:** 225
Birthdate: November 13, 1965
NBA Experience: 9 years

College: Lincoln; Iowa
Acquired: Traded from Heat with Billy Owens for Walt Williams and Tyrone Corbin, 2/96

Background: After an unspectacular college career at Lincoln College and Iowa, Gamble was drafted by Portland in the third round of the 1987 draft. He wound up playing in the CBA and the Philippines. He got another NBA chance in 1988-89 with the rebuilding Celtics and made the most of it over six years. He has since played with the Heat and Kings, mostly as a reserve.

Strengths: Gamble is a reliable outside shooter who connected at better than 50 percent from the field in four of his six Celtic years. He is accurate from 3-point range and can get his shot on spot-ups or off the dribble. Gamble plays both small forward and shooting guard and does not make a lot of mistakes.

Weaknesses: Besides shooting, Gamble does not contribute much. He has never been a standout defender or rebounder. He does not possess the great lateral quickness to thwart the slashers, nor is he strong enough to muscle the big guys. His offensive production has slipped drastically over the last three seasons.

Analysis: Gamble was once Boston's best offensive player, but he has since watched his shooting and scoring numbers take a dive in a backup role with Miami and Sacramento. He converted just 40 percent from the field last year after entering the season at 51.5 percent for his career. Gamble seems to be at a crossroads.

PLAYER SUMMARY	
Will	get his shots
Can't	regain consistency
Expect	a 3-point marksman
Don't Expect	great variety
Fantasy Value	$0
Card Value	5-8¢

COLLEGE STATISTICS

		G	FGP	FTP	RPG	PPG
83-84	LINC	30	.559	.777	9.2	21.3
84-85	LINC	31	.579	.817	9.7	20.5
85-86	IOWA	30	.474	.700	1.7	2.6
86-87	IOWA	35	.544	.697	4.5	11.9
Totals		126	.558	.768	6.2	14.1

NBA REGULAR-SEASON STATISTICS

		G	MIN	FGs FG	FGs PCT	3-PT FGs FG	3-PT FGs PCT	FTs FT	FTs PCT	Rebounds OFF	Rebounds TOT	AST	STL	BLK	PTS	PPG
87-88	POR	9	19	0	.000	0	.000	0	.000	2	3	1	2	0	0	0.0
88-89	BOS	44	375	75	.551	2	.182	35	.636	11	42	34	14	3	187	4.3
89-90	BOS	71	990	137	.455	3	.167	85	.794	42	112	119	28	8	362	5.1
90-91	BOS	82	2706	548	.587	0	.000	185	.815	85	267	256	100	34	1281	15.6
91-92	BOS	82	2496	480	.529	9	.290	139	.885	80	286	219	75	37	1108	13.5
92-93	BOS	82	2541	459	.507	52	.374	123	.826	46	246	226	86	37	1093	13.3
93-94	BOS	75	1880	368	.458	25	.243	103	.817	41	159	149	57	22	864	11.5
94-95	MIA	77	1223	220	.489	39	.398	87	.784	29	122	119	52	10	566	7.4
95-96	MIA/SAC	65	1325	152	.401	44	.386	38	.792	21	113	100	35	8	386	5.9
Totals		587	13555	2439	.506	174	.333	795	.811	357	1350	1223	449	159	5847	10.0

KEVIN GARNETT

Team: Minnesota Timberwolves
Position: Forward
Height: 6'11" **Weight:** 220
Birthdate: May 19, 1976

NBA Experience: 1 year
College: None
Acquired: First-round pick in 1995 draft (fifth overall)

Background: Garnett, who starred at Mauldin (South Carolina) High School and Chicago's Farragut Academy and wowed scouts with an MVP performance at the 1995 McDonald's All-America Game, became the first NBA player in more than 20 years to be drafted directly from the prep ranks. Chosen fifth overall by Minnesota, he became a starter in the second half of the 1995-96 season and came on strong.

Strengths: Garnett has all the raw skill in the world. He jumps out of the gym, runs the floor like a greyhound, has good range with the jumper, and can explode to the basket. He rebounds, comes up with steals, makes good passes, and blocks shots. There is very little Garnett is unable to do on a basketball floor. He has been called a cross between Danny Manning and Ralph Sampson. He can handle both forward spots.

Weaknesses: You walk before you run, and some of Garnett's first NBA steps were a little wobbly. He does not yet have the physical strength to match up with the bigger forwards in the league, and his defense in particular needs some work. He tends to go for the swat after allowing his man to gain position. Garnett was not the most consistent player last year, but he was just 19 years old.

Analysis: There was little doubt by the end of last season that Garnett will one day be a star. Just a teenager and obviously out of his element socially among NBA veterans, he still managed to work his way into the starting lineup by January and was Minnesota's best player down the stretch. Playing on such a bad team helped his minutes, but it kept him from showing his complete feel for the game.

```
          PLAYER SUMMARY
Will ........................play above the rim
Can't .................pick on Karl Malone
Expect ............................a future star
Don't Expect ....................a quick title
Fantasy Value .........................$16-19
Card Value .........................$1.25-2.50
```

COLLEGE STATISTICS

—DID NOT PLAY—

NBA REGULAR-SEASON STATISTICS

			FGs		3-PT FGs		FTs		Rebounds						
	G	MIN	FG	PCT	FG	PCT	FT	PCT	OFF	TOT	AST	STL	BLK	PTS	PPG
95-96 MIN	80	2293	361	.491	8	.286	105	.705	175	501	145	86	131	835	10.4
Totals	80	2293	361	.491	8	.286	105	.705	175	501	145	86	131	835	10.4

CHRIS GATLING

Team: Dallas Mavericks
Position: Forward/Center
Height: 6'10" **Weight:** 230
Birthdate: September 3, 1967

NBA Experience: 5 years
College: Old Dominion
Acquired: Signed as a free agent, 7/96

Background: Gatling did not play during his first two years in college, once under Prop 48 restrictions and once because of a transfer from Pittsburgh to Old Dominion. He was a two-time Sun Belt Player of the Year, scoring more than 20 PPG all three seasons. He spent his first four-and-a-half NBA seasons with Golden State before being traded to the Heat during the 1995-96 campaign. He signed a free-agent deal with the Mavs in July 1996.

Strengths: Gatling is among the most accurate field-goal shooters in the NBA. He led the league at a .633 clip two years ago, and in his worst season to date was still .539. "The Energizer" is an athletic, emotional player with springs in his legs. He's quick to the basket and owns a soft touch, a nice jump hook, and good hands. Gatling challenges shots on defense and has become a double-figure scorer.

Weaknesses: Gatling, a post player in college, is not at his best while facing the basket. He does not dominate physically but rather with his leaping ability and long arms. Despite a lofty percentage, he is no shooter. His range is limited, and he has trouble from the line. He rarely gets an assist.

Analysis: If he continues at his current pace, Gatling will rate among the top five field-goal shooters of all time when he gets the 2,000 buckets needed to qualify. He was not the most prominent player in a 1996 trade involving Tim Hardaway and Kevin Willis, but Miami was glad to have him. Gatling's numbers soared in a Heat uniform, and his future with the Mavs is bright.

PLAYER SUMMARY

Will ....energize
Can't ....distribute
Expect ....high shooting pct.
Don't Expect ....3-point range
Fantasy Value $10-13
Card Value ....5-8¢

COLLEGE STATISTICS

		G	FGP	FTP	RPG	PPG
88-89	OD	27	.616	.704	9.0	22.4
89-90	OD	26	.580	.670	10.0	20.5
90-91	OD	32	.620	.692	11.1	21.0
Totals		85	.606	.689	10.1	21.3

NBA REGULAR-SEASON STATISTICS

				FGs		3-PT FGs		FTs		Rebounds						
		G	MIN	FG	PCT	FG	PCT	FT	PCT	OFF	TOT	AST	STL	BLK	PTS	PPG
91-92	GS	54	612	117	.568	0	.000	72	.661	75	182	16	31	36	306	5.7
92-93	GS	70	1248	249	.539	0	.000	150	.725	129	320	40	44	53	648	9.3
93-94	GS	82	1296	271	.588	0	.000	129	.620	143	397	41	40	63	671	8.2
94-95	GS	58	1470	324	.633	0	.000	148	.592	144	443	51	39	52	796	13.7
95-96	GS/MIA	71	1427	326	.575	0	.000	139	.671	129	417	43	36	40	791	11.1
Totals		335	6053	1287	.583	0	.000	638	.650	620	1759	191	190	244	3212	9.6

KENNY GATTISON

Team: Utah Jazz
Position: Forward/Center
Height: 6'8" **Weight:** 257
Birthdate: May 23, 1964
NBA Experience: 9 years

College: Old Dominion
Acquired: Traded from Magic with
Brooks Thompson and a future first-
round pick for Felton Spencer, 8/96

Background: The Sun Belt Player of the Year at Old Dominion in 1986, Gattison finished his career as the league's career rebounding leader. He was third nationally in field-goal percentage as a senior. He started his NBA career with Phoenix before playing in Italy and serving six years with Charlotte. Back and neck injuries kept him on the Vancouver and Orlando benches for most of 1995-96. He was traded to Utah in August 1996.

Strengths: Gattison will do whatever is asked, no matter the consequences. He sets screens, blocks out, and bangs the boards. He is versatile, having played both center and power forward. He goes hard on defense.

Weaknesses: Gattison briefly lost the feeling in his hands after suffering a cervical injury six games into the 1994-95 season, and he has played only 40 regular-season games since. Even at full speed, he has virtually no touch, as his poor free-throw shooting indicates. His reckless, physical style of play gets him into foul trouble and has shortened his career.

Analysis: A healthy Gattison is the kind of player a coach loves. Though he is not especially skilled, he rebounds, battles bigger men, and makes his fouls count. He does the proverbial "dirty work" that can spell the difference between winning and losing. He did not play for Orlando at all before they dealt him.

PLAYER SUMMARY

Will ....answer the call
Can't ....handle the ball
Expect ....a physical style
Don't Expect ....82 games
Fantasy Value $0
Card Value ....5-8¢

COLLEGE STATISTICS

		G	FGP	FTP	RPG	PPG
82-83	OD	29	.503	.705	7.5	8.4
83-84	OD	31	.494	.650	7.1	11.1
84-85	OD	31	.538	.610	9.2	16.1
85-86	OD	31	.637	.673	7.8	17.4
Totals		122	.552	.650	7.9	13.3

NBA REGULAR-SEASON STATISTICS

		G	MIN	FGs FG	FGs PCT	3-PT FGs FG	3-PT FGs PCT	FTs FT	FTs PCT	Rebounds OFF	Rebounds TOT	AST	STL	BLK	PTS	PPG
86-87	PHO	77	1104	148	.476	0	.000	108	.632	87	270	36	24	33	404	5.2
88-89	PHO	2	9	0	.000	0	.000	1	.500	0	1	0	0	0	1	0.5
89-90	CHA	63	941	148	.550	1	1.000	75	.682	75	197	39	35	31	372	5.9
90-91	CHA	72	1552	243	.532	0	.000	164	.661	136	379	44	48	67	650	9.0
91-92	CHA	82	2223	423	.529	0	.000	196	.688	177	580	131	59	69	1042	12.7
92-93	CHA	75	1475	203	.529	0	.000	102	.604	108	353	68	48	55	508	6.8
93-94	CHA	77	1644	233	.524	0	.000	126	.646	105	358	95	46	59	592	7.7
94-95	CHA	21	409	47	.470	0	.000	31	.608	21	75	17	7	15	125	6.0
95-96	VAN/ORL	25	570	91	.479	0	.000	47	.603	35	114	14	10	11	229	9.2
Totals		494	9927	1536	.520	1	.083	850	.649	744	2327	444	290	327	3923	7.9

MATT GEIGER

Team: Charlotte Hornets
Position: Center
Height: 7'0" **Weight:** 260
Birthdate: September 10, 1969
NBA Experience: 4 years

College: Auburn; Georgia Tech
Acquired: Traded from Heat with Glen Rice, Khalid Reeves, and a 1996 first-round pick for Alonzo Mourning, Pete Myers, and LeRon Ellis, 11/95

Background: Geiger made the SEC All-Freshman team and started all 28 games as an Auburn sophomore. He transferred to Georgia Tech, where his 65 blocks as a senior rated second in school history. Once considered a lottery-type talent, he slipped to 42nd in the 1992 draft. He spent his first three years in Miami before being traded to Charlotte in the Alonzo Mourning deal at the start of the 1995-96 season.

Strengths: Geiger is one of the quicker and more mobile seven-footers in the league. He gets up and down the court like a smaller man and, unlike many centers, has the ability to put the ball on the floor. Geiger works on defense and has improved his low-post offense substantially. He enjoyed his most productive season in 1995-96, scoring a career-high 11.2 PPG and pulling in 8.4 RPG.

Weaknesses: Geiger will not threaten the upper-echelon centers of the NBA. He still has work to do on his low-post game, and his defense remains primitive despite his efforts. He was among the most frequent foulers in basketball last season, and he blocks less than one shot per game. Geiger racks up more than twice as many turnovers as assists. He does not have a great feel for the game.

Analysis: A project coming into the league, Geiger wound up starting most of last season as Charlotte's center, ahead of veteran Robert Parish and rookie George Zidek. He has worked as hard as anyone to become a contributor. His high field-goal percentage, aptitude for running, and willingness to bang are his main strengths. If he can build on last season, watch out.

PLAYER SUMMARY	
Will	use his dribble
Can't	avoid foul trouble
Expect	transition buckets
Don't Expect	assists
Fantasy Value	$1-3
Card Value	5-8¢

COLLEGE STATISTICS

		G	FGP	FTP	RPG	PPG
87-88	AUB	30	.513	.660	4.1	6.4
88-89	AUB	28	.504	.688	6.6	15.9
90-91	GT	27	.549	.671	6.4	11.4
91-92	GT	35	.611	.706	7.3	11.8
Totals		120	.545	.687	6.1	11.4

NBA REGULAR-SEASON STATISTICS

		G	MIN	FGs		3-PT FGs		FTs		Rebounds		AST	STL	BLK	PTS	PPG
				FG	PCT	FG	PCT	FT	PCT	OFF	TOT					
92-93	MIA	48	554	76	.524	0	.000	62	.674	46	120	14	15	18	214	4.5
93-94	MIA	72	1199	202	.574	1	.200	116	.779	119	303	32	36	29	521	7.2
94-95	MIA	74	1712	260	.536	4	.400	93	.650	146	413	55	41	51	617	8.3
95-96	CHA	77	2349	357	.536	3	.375	149	.727	201	649	60	46	63	866	11.2
Totals		271	5814	895	.543	8	.296	420	.713	512	1485	161	138	161	2218	8.2

KENDALL GILL

Team: New Jersey Nets
Position: Guard
Height: 6'5" **Weight:** 210
Birthdate: May 25, 1968
NBA Experience: 6 years

College: Illinois
Acquired: Traded from Hornets with Khalid Reeves for Kenny Anderson and Gerald Glass, 1/96

Background: Gill helped Illinois to the Final Four as a junior and the following year was named a first-team All-Big Ten selection and a UPI first-team All-American. Gill spent his first three NBA seasons in Charlotte and led the Hornets in scoring at 20.5 PPG during his second season. After a rocky 1994-95 campaign in Seattle, he rejoined the Hornets but was then traded to New Jersey.

Strengths: Gill is a great leaper who plays bigger than his 6'5" height. He is a fine open-court player who finishes with slams and handles the ball well for a shooting guard. He has played the point. He is not afraid to take clutch shots or challenge his man off the dribble. Gill is one of the better rebounding guards, and he uses his quickness on defense.

Weaknesses: Gill has turned off coaches, teammates, media members, and the public with complaints about his playing time. His problems reached the boiling point in Seattle two seasons ago, when he took a leave to deal with depression. He has failed to find comfort with any of his roles and has been inconsistent. He is not a pure shooter.

Analysis: Gill has been accused of paying more attention to his individual numbers than to team concepts. If that's the case, he can't be very happy about where his career has taken him. He has yet to become a consistent force on the perimeter, and unless he does so, it is unlikely he will approach his second-year numbers again.

PLAYER SUMMARY	
Will	use his quickness
Can't	accept bench time
Expect	big scoring nights
Don't Expect	steady shooting
Fantasy Value	$13-16
Card Value	8-12¢

COLLEGE STATISTICS

		G	FGP	FTP	RPG	PPG
86-87	ILL	31	.482	.642	1.4	3.7
87-88	ILL	33	.471	.753	2.2	10.4
88-89	ILL	24	.542	.793	2.9	15.4
89-90	ILL	29	.500	.777	4.9	20.0
Totals		117	.501	.755	2.8	12.0

NBA REGULAR-SEASON STATISTICS

		G	MIN	FGs FG	FGs PCT	3-PT FGs FG	3-PT FGs PCT	FTs FT	FTs PCT	Rebounds OFF	Rebounds TOT	AST	STL	BLK	PTS	PPG
90-91	CHA	82	1944	376	.450	2	.143	152	.835	105	263	303	104	39	906	11.0
91-92	CHA	79	2906	666	.467	6	.240	284	.745	165	402	329	154	46	1622	20.5
92-93	CHA	69	2430	463	.449	17	.274	224	.772	120	340	268	98	36	1167	16.9
93-94	SEA	79	2435	429	.443	38	.317	215	.782	91	268	275	151	32	1111	14.1
94-95	SEA	73	2125	392	.457	63	.368	155	.742	99	290	192	117	28	1002	13.7
95-96	CHA/NJ	47	1683	246	.469	26	.329	138	.784	72	232	260	64	24	656	14.0
Totals		429	13523	2572	.456	152	.323	1168	.772	652	1795	1627	688	205	6464	15.1

ARMON GILLIAM

Team: Milwaukee Bucks
Position: Forward/Center
Height: 6'9" **Weight:** 250
Birthdate: May 28, 1964

NBA Experience: 9 years
College: Independence; UNLV
Acquired: Signed as a free agent, 8/96

Background: As a college senior, Gilliam was a consensus second-team All-American while leading UNLV to the Final Four and averaging 23.2 points and 9.3 rebounds per game. Phoenix selected him second in the 1987 draft, and he was an All-Rookie pick. The nine-year veteran has since played in Charlotte, Philadelphia, and New Jersey. The Bucks picked him up in the off-season.

Strengths: Nicknamed "The Hammer" for his physical style, Gilliam has played both power forward and center throughout his career. He can be unstoppable when he gets the ball in the post, where he tosses in hooks with both hands, and he also sports a deft one-handed jumper. He's a consummate pro.

Weaknesses: Despite his size and strength, Gilliam is not known for his defense. He rarely blocks a shot, and he has never rebounded as well as he did last season. He's a poor ball-handler and not much better as a passer. He has never made a 3-pointer in his NBA career.

Analysis: Gilliam's play as a sixth man in 1994-95 helped convince the Nets that Derrick Coleman was expendable. Gilliam became the starting power forward when D.C. was traded to the 76ers, and Armon responded by leading the team in scoring and rebounding. He scored a career-high 18.3 PPG last season. He reads as much Christian literature as he can get his hands on.

PLAYER SUMMARY	
Will	come to play
Can't	dominate on "D"
Expect	scoring inside and out
Don't Expect	a 3-pointer
Fantasy Value	$9-11
Card Value	7-10¢

COLLEGE STATISTICS

		G	FGP	FTP	RPG	PPG
82-83	IND	38	.621	.632	8.3	16.9
84-85	UNLV	31	.621	.653	6.8	11.9
85-86	UNLV	37	.529	.737	8.5	15.7
86-87	UNLV	39	.600	.728	9.3	23.2
Totals		145	.590	.693	8.3	17.2

NBA REGULAR-SEASON STATISTICS

			MIN	FGs		3-PT FGs		FTs		Rebounds						
		G		FG	PCT	FG	PCT	FT	PCT	OFF	TOT	AST	STL	BLK	PTS	PPG
87-88	PHO	55	1807	342	.475	0	.000	131	.679	134	434	72	58	29	815	14.8
88-89	PHO	74	2120	468	.503	0	.000	240	.743	165	541	52	54	27	1176	15.9
89-90	PHO/CHA	76	2426	484	.515	0	.000	303	.723	211	599	99	69	51	1271	16.7
90-91	CHA/PHI	75	2644	487	.487	0	.000	268	.815	220	598	105	69	53	1242	16.6
91-92	PHI	81	2771	512	.511	0	.000	343	.807	234	660	118	51	85	1367	16.9
92-93	PHI	80	1742	359	.464	0	.000	274	.843	136	472	116	37	54	992	12.4
93-94	NJ	82	1969	348	.510	0	.000	274	.759	197	500	69	38	61	970	11.8
94-95	NJ	82	2472	455	.502	0	.000	302	.770	192	613	99	67	49	1212	14.8
95-96	NJ	78	2856	576	.474	0	.000	277	.791	241	713	140	73	53	1429	18.3
Totals		683	20807	4031	.493	0	.000	2412	.774	1730	5130	870	516	502	10474	15.3

BRIAN GRANT

Team: Sacramento Kings
Position: Forward
Height: 6'9" **Weight:** 254
Birthdate: March 5, 1972

NBA Experience: 2 years
College: Xavier (Ohio)
Acquired: First-round pick in 1994 draft (eighth overall)

Background: Despite coming out of high school with little fanfare, Grant made an early impact at Xavier. He finished second in the nation in field-goal accuracy as a junior (.654), led the Musketeers in rebounding all four years, and was a two-time MCC Player of the Year. Drafted eighth overall by Sacramento, Grant was an All-Rookie first-teamer and enjoyed an even better second season in 1995-96.

Strengths: The long-armed Grant is an exceptional athlete with loads of talent. He knows how to score in the post and has an improving jump shot to boot. Grant jumps well and is dangerous on the offensive glass, and it was his defense and rebounding that enticed the Kings in the first place. He led the team in blocked shots and was second in rebounding in each of his first two seasons.

Weaknesses: There is little not to like about Grant's game, with the exception of his frequent foul trouble. He is simply too aggressive at the defensive end of the floor, often hacking his man when trying for steals or going over the back for rebounds. Once he learns to cut out the senseless fouls, he'll likely become a stopper. His ball-handling and passing also need work.

Analysis: It's too bad Grant doesn't play in a more visible market, because his star would be rising fast. NBA insiders certainly know what he can do. He makes better than half his shots, and he does it despite drawing loads of defensive attention. He may be an inch or two short, but he stacks up as a top-notch power forward because of his effort and athletic ability.

PLAYER SUMMARY

Will..go all-out
Can't ....avoid whistles
Expect ....points, boards, blocks
Don't Expect.......................obscurity
Fantasy Value $15-18
Card Value ....15-30¢

COLLEGE STATISTICS

		G	FGP	FTP	RPG	PPG
90-91	XAV	32	.572	.694	8.5	11.6
91-92	XAV	26	.576	.583	9.1	11.8
92-93	XAV	30	.654	.692	9.4	18.5
93-94	XAV	29	.559	.713	9.9	16.7
Totals		117	.594	.676	9.2	14.7

NBA REGULAR-SEASON STATISTICS

		G	MIN	FGs FG	FGs PCT	3-PT FGs FG	FGs PCT	FTs FT	FTs PCT	Rebounds OFF	Rebounds TOT	AST	STL	BLK	PTS	PPG
94-95	SAC	80	2289	413	.511	1	.250	231	.636	207	598	99	49	116	1058	13.2
95-96	SAC	78	2398	427	.507	4	.235	262	.732	175	545	127	40	103	1120	14.4
Totals		158	4687	840	.509	5	.238	493	.684	382	1143	226	89	219	2178	13.8

GARY GRANT

Team: Miami Heat
Position: Guard
Height: 6'3" **Weight:** 185
Birthdate: April 21, 1965

NBA Experience: 8 years
College: Michigan
Acquired: Signed as a free agent, 8/96

Background: A consensus All-American at Michigan, Grant concluded his career as the school's all-time leader in assists and earned Big Ten Defensive Player of the Year honors as a junior. He led all NBA rookies in steals and assists but had an up-and-down seven-year stay with the Clippers. Grant signed with the Knicks before the 1995-96 season but saw action in only 47 games. He joins Miami for 1996-97.

Strengths: Grant has always been able to do one thing well—defend. He combines good quickness and instincts and loves to hound his man. Grant has good size, handles the ball well, works hard, and has matured after starting his career as a mistake-prone player. He hit better than 80 percent of his free throws over the past three seasons.

Weaknesses: Injuries have become the primary concern. His final season with the Clippers was spoiled by knee and back ailments, and he has also undergone ankle surgery. He is not a stopper when he can't go all-out. Grant does not penetrate often, and his outside shooting is streaky. His offensive skills are modest.

Analysis: Grant spent most of the 1994-95 season on the bench because of injuries, then sat for most of his first year with the Knicks because he was not good enough to crack the rotation. If you're looking for an offensive-minded point guard, Grant is not your man. His calling card is defense, and he can still play it.

PLAYER SUMMARY	
Will	hound his man
Can't	rely on jump shots
Expect	backup minutes
Don't Expect	creativity
Fantasy Value	$1
Card Value	7-10¢

COLLEGE STATISTICS

		G	FGP	FTP	APG	PPG
84-85	MICH	30	.550	.817	4.7	12.9
85-86	MICH	33	.494	.744	5.6	12.2
86-87	MICH	32	.537	.782	5.4	22.4
87-88	MICH	34	.530	.808	6.9	21.1
Totals		129	.528	.790	5.7	17.2

NBA REGULAR-SEASON STATISTICS

				FGs		3-PT FGs		FTs		Rebounds						
		G	MIN	FG	PCT	FG	PCT	FT	PCT	OFF	TOT	AST	STL	BLK	PTS	PPG
88-89	LAC	71	1924	361	.435	5	.227	119	.735	80	238	506	144	9	846	11.9
89-90	LAC	44	1529	241	.466	5	.238	88	.779	59	195	442	108	5	575	13.1
90-91	LAC	68	2105	265	.451	9	.231	51	.689	69	209	587	103	12	590	8.7
91-92	LAC	78	2049	275	.462	15	.294	44	.815	34	184	538	138	14	609	7.8
92-93	LAC	74	1624	210	.441	11	.262	55	.743	27	139	353	106	9	486	6.6
93-94	LAC	78	1533	253	.449	17	.274	65	.855	42	142	291	119	12	588	7.5
94-95	LAC	33	470	78	.470	4	.250	45	.818	8	35	93	29	3	205	6.2
95-96	NY	47	596	88	.486	8	.333	48	.828	12	52	69	39	3	232	4.9
Totals		493	11830	1771	.452	74	.267	515	.773	331	1194	2879	786	67	4131	8.4

HARVEY GRANT

Team: Washington Bullets
Position: Forward
Height: 6'9" **Weight:** 235
Birthdate: July 4, 1965
NBA Experience: 8 years

College: Clemson; Independence;
Oklahoma
Acquired: Traded from Trail Blazers
with Rod Strickland for Rasheed
Wallace and Mitchell Butler, 7/96

Background: Harvey is the identical twin of the Magic's Horace Grant. The two enrolled together at Clemson, but they were competing for the same spot and Harvey transferred to Oklahoma, where he led the Sooners to the NCAA title game in 1988. Grant was dealt to Portland in 1993 and then traded back to the Bullets last summer.

Strengths: Grant possesses good athletic ability, runs the floor, and is very unselfish (some say too unselfish). He uses his lean, wiry body to the best of his ability on defense, and he has a decent jump shot from 18 feet and in. A natural forward, he also filled in at shooting guard for the Blazers.

Weaknesses: Harvey is not as muscular as Horace and not as effective in the paint. Especially in the last two years, he has not been aggressive on the offensive end. Grant seems to prefer being a role-player. He has been accused of playing soft and staying away from the boards. His ball-handling skills are below average.

Analysis: The Blazers had hoped Grant would be more assertive in 1995-96, but he failed to average double figures in scoring for the second straight season and the fourth time in eight years. This is a man who consistently netted 18-20 PPG with the Bullets. Hopefully, the trade back to Washington will do him some good.

PLAYER SUMMARY

Will ....score in transition
Can't ....outperform his brother
Expect ....versatility
Don't Expect ....20 PPG
Fantasy Value $1-3
Card Value ....7-10¢

COLLEGE STATISTICS

		G	FGP	FTP	RPG	PPG
84-85	CLEM	28	.496	.585	4.5	5.1
85-86	IND	33	.586	.707	11.8	22.4
86-87	OKLA	34	.534	.730	9.9	16.9
87-88	OKLA	39	.547	.729	9.4	20.9
Totals		134	.553	.712	9.1	17.0

NBA REGULAR-SEASON STATISTICS

				FGs		3-PT FGs		FTs		Rebounds						
		G	MIN	FG	PCT	FG	PCT	FT	PCT	OFF	TOT	AST	STL	BLK	PTS	PPG
88-89	WAS	71	1193	181	.464	0	.000	34	.596	75	163	79	35	29	396	5.6
89-90	WAS	81	1846	284	.473	0	.000	96	.701	138	342	131	52	43	664	8.2
90-91	WAS	77	2842	609	.498	2	.133	185	.743	179	557	204	91	61	1405	18.2
91-92	WAS	64	2388	489	.478	1	.125	176	.800	157	432	170	74	27	1155	18.0
92-93	WAS	72	2667	560	.487	1	.100	218	.727	133	412	205	72	44	1339	18.6
93-94	POR	77	2112	356	.460	2	.286	84	.641	109	351	107	70	49	798	10.4
94-95	POR	75	1771	286	.461	8	.308	103	.705	103	284	82	56	53	683	9.1
95-96	POR	76	2394	314	.462	21	.313	60	.545	117	361	111	60	43	709	9.3
Totals		593	17213	3079	.477	35	.246	956	.708	1011	2902	1089	510	349	7149	12.1

HORACE GRANT

Team: Orlando Magic
Position: Forward
Height: 6'10" **Weight:** 235
Birthdate: July 4, 1965

NBA Experience: 9 years
College: Clemson
Acquired: Signed as a free agent, 7/94

Background: In his senior season at Clemson, Grant was named ACC Player of the Year after averaging 21.0 PPG. Drafted tenth overall in 1987, he played a key role on Chicago's three straight championship teams, annually ranking among NBA leaders in field-goal percentage. He was an All-Star in his seventh and final year with the Bulls, then joined Orlando before the 1994-95 season.

Strengths: Grant stands among the most talented and athletic power forwards in the game. He's an All-Defensive performer who blocks shots, rebounds, and guards players at multiple positions. He's a quick leaper who can both outrun and outmuscle most of his matchups. He sticks the 18-foot jumper with regularity.

Weaknesses: Grant is not as dangerous in post-up or dribble-drive situations as he is spotting up or scoring in transition. Many of his points last year came directly because of double-teams on Shaquille O'Neal and Anfernee Hardaway. Nagging injuries the last three seasons have kept him from a full slate.

Analysis: Grant, one of the hardest-working players in basketball, has helped Orlando reach a new level. He continues to earn his big money, both for what he does on the court and for his workmanlike approach to the game. Now that Shaq is gone, Horace will have to step up his game to the next level if the Magic are to stay competitive.

PLAYER SUMMARY	
Will	rebound, defend
Can't	post up like Shaq
Expect	high field-goal pct.
Don't Expect	selfish play
Fantasy Value	$18-21
Card Value	10-15¢

COLLEGE STATISTICS

		G	FGP	FTP	RPG	PPG
83-84	CLEM	28	.533	.744	4.6	5.7
84-85	CLEM	29	.555	.637	6.8	11.3
85-86	CLEM	34	.584	.725	10.5	16.4
86-87	CLEM	31	.656	.708	9.6	21.0
Totals		122	.598	.704	8.0	13.9

NBA REGULAR-SEASON STATISTICS

		G	MIN	FGs FG	FGs PCT	3-PT FGs FG	3-PT FGs PCT	FT	FTs PCT	Rebounds OFF	Rebounds TOT	AST	STL	BLK	PTS	PPG
87-88	CHI	81	1827	254	.501	0	.000	114	.626	155	447	89	51	53	622	7.7
88-89	CHI	79	2809	405	.519	0	.000	140	.704	240	681	168	86	62	950	12.0
89-90	CHI	80	2753	446	.523	0	.000	179	.699	236	629	227	92	84	1071	13.4
90-91	CHI	78	2641	401	.547	1	.167	197	.711	266	659	178	95	69	1000	12.8
91-92	CHI	81	2859	457	.578	0	.000	235	.741	344	807	217	100	131	1149	14.2
92-93	CHI	77	2745	421	.508	1	.200	174	.619	341	729	201	89	96	1017	13.2
93-94	CHI	70	2570	460	.524	0	.000	137	.596	306	769	236	74	84	1057	15.1
94-95	ORL	74	2693	401	.567	0	.000	146	.692	223	715	173	76	88	948	12.8
95-96	ORL	63	2286	347	.513	1	.167	152	.734	178	580	170	62	74	847	13.4
Totals		683	23183	3592	.532	3	.075	1474	.682	2289	6016	1659	725	741	8661	12.7

A.C. GREEN

Team: Phoenix Suns
Position: Forward
Height: 6'9" **Weight:** 225
Birthdate: October 4, 1963

NBA Experience: 11 years
College: Oregon St.
Acquired: Signed as a free agent, 9/93

Background: Green was named Pac-10 Player of the Year as a junior at Oregon State and wound up his career as the school's second-leading rebounder and third-leading scorer. He led the Lakers in rebounding for four straight years and started in the 1990 All-Star Game. He has served the last three of his 11 seasons with Phoenix.

Strengths: A hard-working player, Green is most valuable these days for his rebounding and defense. He also runs the floor, knows how to finish, and gets to the line. He never stops hustling. Green is the most durable player in basketball. He has played all 82 games in ten of his 11 seasons.

Weaknesses: Green is not a dominant low-post player, nor is he a steady long-range shooter. He gets a lot of his points on putbacks and "garbage" buckets in addition to his face-up jumpers. Green won't block many shots.

Analysis: Green is pro basketball's iron man. He stands third on the all-time consecutive-games-played list at 813 and counting. Last season, he overcame a hard blow to the jaw to keep the streak alive. His numbers are declining, but he remains a valuable leader and a class act.

PLAYER SUMMARY	
Will	lead by example
Can't	pour in points
Expect	defense, rebounds
Don't Expect	days off
Fantasy Value	$2-4
Card Value	7-10¢

COLLEGE STATISTICS

		G	FGP	FTP	RPG	PPG
81-82	OSU	30	.615	.610	5.3	8.6
82-83	OSU	31	.559	.689	7.6	14.0
83-84	OSU	23	.657	.770	8.7	17.8
84-85	OSU	31	.599	.680	9.2	19.1
Totals		115	.602	.696	7.7	14.7

NBA REGULAR-SEASON STATISTICS

				FGs		3-PT FGs		FTs		Rebounds						
		G	MIN	FG	PCT	FG	PCT	FT	PCT	OFF	TOT	AST	STL	BLK	PTS	PPG
85-86	LAL	82	1542	209	.539	1	.167	102	.611	160	381	54	49	49	521	6.4
86-87	LAL	79	2240	316	.538	0	.000	220	.780	210	615	84	70	80	852	10.8
87-88	LAL	82	2636	322	.503	0	.000	245	.773	245	710	93	87	45	937	11.4
88-89	LAL	82	2510	401	.529	4	.235	282	.786	258	739	103	94	55	1088	13.3
89-90	LAL	82	2709	385	.478	13	.283	278	.751	262	712	90	66	50	1061	12.9
90-91	LAL	82	2164	258	.476	11	.200	223	.738	201	516	71	59	23	750	9.1
91-92	LAL	82	2902	382	.476	12	.214	340	.744	306	762	117	91	36	1116	13.6
92-93	LAL	82	2819	379	.537	16	.348	277	.739	287	711	116	88	39	1051	12.8
93-94	PHO	82	2825	465	.502	8	.229	266	.735	275	753	137	70	38	1204	14.7
94-95	PHO	82	2687	311	.504	43	.339	251	.732	194	669	127	55	31	916	11.2
95-96	PHO	82	2113	215	.484	14	.269	168	.709	166	554	72	45	23	612	7.5
Totals		899	27147	3643	.505	122	.273	2700	.743	2564	7122	1064	774	469	10108	11.2

TOM GUGLIOTTA

Team: Minnesota Timberwolves
Position: Forward
Height: 6'10" **Weight:** 240
Birthdate: December 19, 1969

NBA Experience: 4 years
College: North Carolina St.
Acquired: Traded from Warriors for Donyell Marshall, 2/95

Background: "Googs" became the third North Carolina State player to record 1,500 points and 800 rebounds in a career. He led the ACC in rebounding and 3-pointers per game as a senior. His father was a high school coach, and two of his brothers played professionally in Europe. The No. 6 draft choice of Washington in 1992, Gugliotta has played on three teams in his four NBA seasons.

Strengths: Though not dominant in any one area, Gugliotta does a little bit of everything. He has been compared to Larry Bird by none other than Michael Jordan and Pat Riley. He shoots with range, finds open men, rebounds, handles the ball, runs the floor, and plays tough defense. He has started at guard, forward, and center during his short career. He became a shot-blocking force last season.

Weaknesses: As noted, Gugliotta is not known for dominant ability in any one area. He does not have a great arsenal of inside moves. His one true weak area has been free-throw shooting, but he raised his rate significantly last year. He has trouble guarding quick forwards on the perimeter. Despite good effort, he has not been able to awaken the slumbering Timberwolves.

Analysis: Gugliotta has been involved in separate, high-profile deals for Chris Webber and Donyell Marshall during his short career. The Minnesota front office, however, now sees him as a cornerstone of the franchise. Gugliotta is a true team player who would fare even better if surrounded by better talent, as he is at his home. His wife, Nikki, has won a women's national duathlon championship (running and cycling).

PLAYER SUMMARY	
Will	do it all
Can't	save T'Wolves alone
Expect	great versatility
Don't Expect	selfish play
Fantasy Value	$40-45
Card Value	10-20¢

COLLEGE STATISTICS

		G	FGP	FTP	RPG	PPG
88-89	NCST	21	.429	.655	1.7	2.7
89-90	NCST	30	.504	.672	7.0	11.1
90-91	NCST	31	.500	.644	9.1	15.2
91-92	NCST	30	.449	.685	9.8	22.5
Totals		112	.476	.668	7.3	13.7

NBA REGULAR-SEASON STATISTICS

				FGs		3-PT FGs		FTs		Rebounds						
		G	MIN	FG	PCT	FG	PCT	FT	PCT	OFF	TOT	AST	STL	BLK	PTS	PPG
92-93	WAS	81	2795	484	.426	38	.281	181	.644	219	781	306	134	35	1187	14.7
93-94	WAS	78	2795	540	.466	40	.270	213	.685	189	728	276	172	51	1333	17.1
94-95	WAS/GS/MIN															
		77	2568	371	.443	60	.323	174	.690	165	572	279	132	62	976	12.7
95-96	MIN	78	2835	473	.471	26	.302	289	.773	176	690	238	139	96	1261	16.2
Totals		314	10993	1868	.452	164	.295	857	.704	749	2771	1099	577	244	4757	15.1

TOM HAMMONDS

Team: Denver Nuggets
Position: Forward
Height: 6'9" **Weight:** 225
Birthdate: March 27, 1967

NBA Experience: 7 years
College: Georgia Tech
Acquired: Signed as a free agent, 2/93

Background: Hammonds was a third-team All-American as a senior at Georgia Tech. Though drafted ninth overall by Washington in 1989, Hammonds has played sparingly in his seven NBA seasons. His best numbers came with the Bullets and Hornets in 1991-92, when he averaged 11.9 PPG. He has spent the last three-plus seasons coming off the Denver bench.

Strengths: Hammonds uses his weight room-sculpted body to play tough defense and set hard picks. He can cause defensive problems at both the three and four spots. Hammonds can post up, he hits the offensive glass, and he gets up and down the floor with ease. He is a team player.

Weaknesses: Hammonds is a classic 'tweener. He is not wide or strong enough to thrive at power forward, yet his skills facing the basket are not where they need to be for the three spot. He has not shown an ability to put the ball on the floor, nor does he pass the ball well. Most of the big forwards give him problems on defense.

Analysis: It's clear that Hammonds is not the talent he was projected to be coming out of college. As a lottery pick, he has to be considered a major disappointment, although his work ethic is admirable. Hammonds has helped the Nuggets as a role-player, and his versatility stands to keep him in the league for at least a couple more years.

PLAYER SUMMARY

Will ....run the floor
Can't ....dribble, pass
Expect ....a role-player
Don't Expect ....30-minute games
Fantasy Value $0
Card Value ....5-7¢

COLLEGE STATISTICS

		G	FGP	FTP	RPG	PPG
85-86	GT	34	.609	.816	6.4	12.2
86-87	GT	29	.569	.797	7.2	16.2
87-88	GT	30	.568	.826	7.2	18.9
88-89	GT	30	.538	.773	8.1	20.9
Totals		123	.566	.801	7.2	16.9

NBA REGULAR-SEASON STATISTICS

		G	MIN	FGs FG	FGs PCT	3-PT FGs FG	3-PT FGs PCT	FTs FT	FTs PCT	Rebounds OFF	Rebounds TOT	AST	STL	BLK	PTS	PPG
89-90	WAS	61	805	129	.437	0	.000	63	.643	61	168	51	11	14	321	5.3
90-91	WAS	70	1023	155	.461	0	.000	57	.722	58	206	43	15	7	367	5.2
91-92	WAS/CHA	37	984	195	.488	0	.000	50	.610	49	185	36	22	13	440	11.9
92-93	CHA/DEN	54	713	105	.475	0	.000	38	.613	38	127	24	18	12	248	4.6
93-94	DEN	74	877	115	.500	0	.000	71	.683	62	199	34	20	12	301	4.1
94-95	DEN	70	956	139	.535	0	.000	132	.746	55	222	36	11	14	410	5.9
95-96	DEN	71	1045	127	.474	0	.000	88	.765	85	223	23	23	13	342	4.8
Totals		437	6403	965	.480	0	.000	499	.696	408	1330	247	120	85	2429	5.6

ANFERNEE HARDAWAY

Team: Orlando Magic
Position: Guard
Height: 6'7" **Weight:** 207
Birthdate: July 18, 1972
NBA Experience: 3 years

College: Memphis St.
Acquired: Draft rights traded from Warriors with 1996, 1998, and 2000 first-round picks for draft rights to Chris Webber, 6/93

Background: Hardaway was *Parade's* 1989-90 national High School Player of the Year. He sat out his freshman year at Memphis State under Prop 48, then suffered a gunshot wound in his right foot in 1991. He recovered and twice became his conference's Player of the Year. He was drafted No. 3 by Golden State but was immediately dealt to Orlando. He has quickly become an NBA superstar.

Strengths: "Penny" has been compared to Magic Johnson. He has great size for a point guard, which allows him to see the floor and spot open men. He ignites the fastbreak, handles the ball deftly, and knows how to get off his shot in traffic. He can take over games. Hardaway is a 20-plus PPG scorer and also provides quick, aggressive defense. "Pennies for Penny's Pals" raises money for charity.

Weaknesses: Hardaway is a better scorer than shooter. Although he has hoisted his field-goal percentage over the 50-percent mark, he makes fewer than one-third of his 3-pointers. The opposition is best advised to keep him on the perimeter. He commits a lot of turnovers, but he also handles the ball a lot. The lightning-quick guards give him some trouble.

Analysis: It has not taken Hardaway long to emerge as the best point guard in the NBA. "I've only coached one guy with a game like his," said Heat head coach Pat Riley, referring, of course, to Magic. Penny will start All-Star Games for years to come. Now that Shaq is gone, the Magic is basically Penny's team. A member of the 1996 Dream Team, his endorsement appeal is soaring.

PLAYER SUMMARY	
Will	...make things go
Can't	...be easily contained
Expect	...points, assists, steals
Don't Expect	...All-Star absences
Fantasy Value	...$70-75
Card Value	...50¢-$2.00

COLLEGE STATISTICS

		G	FGP	FTP	APG	PPG
91-92	MSU	34	.433	.652	5.5	17.4
92-93	MSU	32	.477	.767	6.4	22.8
Totals		66	.456	.717	5.9	20.0

NBA REGULAR-SEASON STATISTICS

				FGs		3-PT FGs		FTs		Rebounds						
		G	MIN	FG	PCT	FG	PCT	FT	PCT	OFF	TOT	AST	STL	BLK	PTS	PPG
93-94	ORL	82	3015	509	.466	50	.267	245	.742	192	439	544	190	51	1313	16.0
94-95	ORL	77	2901	585	.512	87	.349	356	.769	139	336	551	130	26	1613	20.9
95-96	ORL	82	3015	623	.513	89	.314	445	.767	129	354	582	166	41	1780	21.7
Totals		241	8931	1717	.498	226	.314	1046	.762	460	1129	1677	486	118	4706	19.5

TIM HARDAWAY

Team: Miami Heat
Position: Guard
Height: 6'0" **Weight:** 195
Birthdate: September 12, 1966
NBA Experience: 6 years

College: Texas-El Paso
Acquired: Traded from Warriors with Chris Gatling for Bimbo Coles and Kevin Willis, 2/96

Background: Hardaway surpassed Nate Archibald as the all-time scoring leader at the University of Texas-El Paso. In 1989-90, he led all rookies in assists and steals while directing the Golden State offense. Hardaway has played in three All-Star Games and for Dream Team II. He underwent knee and wrist surgery in the last three years, prior to his 1996 trade to Miami.

Strengths: Few can handle the ball like Hardaway. His between-the-legs crossover dribble, dubbed the "UTEP two-step," mesmerizes even the best of defenders and usually opens a clear lane to the basket. Hardaway combines speed and strength, and he can ignite a team's offense as both a distributor and scorer. His long-range shot is unorthodox, but he shoots it with 3-point range.

Weaknesses: Hardaway shoots a poor percentage from the field, yet he keeps gunning. It's hard to argue with his assist totals, but some feel he could be an even better playmaker if he put his scoring second. Injuries have limited him, but he has come back strong. Hardaway's biggest problem in Golden State was his tendency to air his gripes in public.

Analysis: Hardaway was not comfortable with the way things wound up in Oakland, where he was benched in favor of B.J. Armstrong last season. His trade was Miami's gain. With the Heat, the king of the crossover dribble regained his confidence and the form that earned him recognition as one of the best point guards in basketball.

PLAYER SUMMARY	
Will	run the show
Can't	shoot 50 percent
Expect	double-doubles
Don't Expect	sloppy dribbling
Fantasy Value	$17-20
Card Value	10-15¢

COLLEGE STATISTICS

		G	FGP	FTP	APG	PPG
85-86	UTEP	28	.521	.651	1.9	4.1
86-87	UTEP	31	.490	.663	4.8	10.0
87-88	UTEP	32	.449	.754	5.7	13.6
88-89	UTEP	33	.501	.741	5.4	22.0
Totals		124	.484	.718	4.5	12.8

NBA REGULAR-SEASON STATISTICS

				FGs		3-PT FGs		FTs		Rebounds						
		G	MIN	FG	PCT	FG	PCT	FT	PCT	OFF	TOT	AST	STL	BLK	PTS	PPG
89-90	GS	79	2663	464	.471	23	.274	211	.764	57	310	689	165	12	1162	14.7
90-91	GS	82	3215	739	.476	97	.385	306	.803	87	332	793	214	12	1881	22.9
91-92	GS	81	3332	734	.461	127	.338	298	.766	81	310	807	164	13	1893	23.4
92-93	GS	66	2609	522	.447	102	.330	273	.744	60	263	699	116	12	1419	21.5
94-95	GS	62	2321	430	.427	168	.378	219	.760	46	190	578	88	12	1247	20.1
95-96	GS/MIA	80	2534	419	.422	138	.364	241	.790	35	229	640	132	17	1217	15.2
Totals		450	16674	3308	.453	655	.355	1548	.772	366	1634	4206	879	78	8819	19.6

DEREK HARPER

Team: Dallas Mavericks
Position: Guard
Height: 6'4" **Weight:** 206
Birthdate: October 13, 1961

NBA Experience: 13 years
College: Illinois
Acquired: Signed as a free agent, 7/96

Background: Harper led the Big Ten in steals for two years, then declared for the NBA draft after his junior season. He was the first player in league history to improve his scoring average in each of his first eight years. After ten-plus years in Dallas, he was traded to New York, where he spent two-plus years before returning to Dallas via free agency last summer.

Strengths: A respected all-around talent, Harper is respected league-wide for his willingness to play belly-up defense. He is also one of the league's premier 3-point marksman, a reliable ball-handler and passer, and a veteran leader who gives all he's got.

Weaknesses: Harper is not the most creative playmaker, and he has lost a little of the quickness that has ranked him among the all-time NBA top ten in steals. He is no longer an explosive scoring machine.

Analysis: The Knicks freed up Harper to become their No. 2 offensive option last season by giving some of the ball-handling duties to forward Anthony Mason. After 13 seasons, Harper can still put the ball in the hole. He is a first-rate person and player who continues to get the job done.

PLAYER SUMMARY

Will ....work on defense
Can't ....score like he used to
Expect......................3-point accuracy
Don't Expect ....less than 10 PPG
Fantasy Value $2-4
Card Value ....7-10¢

COLLEGE STATISTICS

		G	FGP	FTP	APG	PPG
80-81	ILL	29	.413	.717	5.4	8.3
81-82	ILL	29	.457	.756	5.0	8.4
82-83	ILL	32	.537	.675	3.7	15.4
Totals		90	.478	.701	4.7	10.9

NBA REGULAR-SEASON STATISTICS

		G	MIN	FGs FG	PCT	3-PT FGs FG	PCT	FTs FT	PCT	Rebounds OFF	TOT	AST	STL	BLK	PTS	PPG
83-84	DAL	82	1712	200	.443	3	.115	66	.673	53	172	239	95	21	469	5.7
84-85	DAL	82	2218	329	.520	21	.344	111	.721	47	199	360	144	37	790	9.6
85-86	DAL	79	2150	390	.534	12	.235	171	.747	75	226	416	153	23	963	12.2
86-87	DAL	77	2556	497	.501	76	.358	160	.684	51	199	609	167	25	1230	16.0
87-88	DAL	82	3032	536	.459	60	.313	261	.759	71	246	634	168	35	1393	17.0
88-89	DAL	81	2968	538	.477	99	.356	229	.806	46	228	570	172	41	1404	17.3
89-90	DAL	82	3007	567	.488	89	.371	250	.794	54	244	609	187	26	1473	18.0
90-91	DAL	77	2879	572	.467	89	.362	286	.731	59	233	548	147	14	1519	19.7
91-92	DAL	65	2252	448	.443	58	.312	198	.759	49	170	373	101	17	1152	17.7
92-93	DAL	62	2108	393	.419	101	.393	239	.756	42	123	334	80	16	1126	18.2
93-94	DAL/NY	82	2204	303	.407	73	.687	112	.687	20	141	334	125	8	791	9.6
94-95	NY	80	2716	337	.446	106	.363	139	.724	31	194	458	79	10	919	11.5
95-96	NY	82	2893	436	.464	121	.372	156	.757	32	202	352	131	5	1149	14.0
Totals		1013	32695	5546	.467	908	.353	2378	.746	630	2577	5836	1749	278	14378	14.2

RON HARPER

Team: Chicago Bulls
Position: Guard
Height: 6'6" **Weight:** 216
Birthdate: January 20, 1964

NBA Experience: 10 years
College: Miami (OH)
Acquired: Signed as a free agent, 9/94

Background: Harper left Miami of Ohio with the all-time Mid-American Conference scoring record and was second in Rookie of the Year voting with Cleveland. He was traded to the Clippers in November 1989, tore the anterior cruciate ligament in his right knee in 1990, and in 1994 signed a free-agent contract with the Bulls. After a disappointing 1994-95 season, Harper became a starter in 1995-96.

Strengths: Harper thrives in the open court and has been a tremendous finisher in transition. He first made a name for himself as a high-scoring slasher, and he has scored more than 11,000 career points. He has also been a willing passer and rebounder, and he's become a strong defensive force for the Bulls.

Weaknesses: Harper is not a shooter, and he no longer possesses the explosive legs that made him a prime-time scorer. He used to be able to outscore his matchup routinely, but not anymore. He's not a reliable free-throw shooter or ball-handler.

Analysis: Once a marquee player who averaged at least 18 PPG in seven of his eight seasons before coming to Chicago, Harper is now a role-playing starter. He shed some of the doubts last year when he started all season for the first NBA team to win at least 70 regular-season games.

PLAYER SUMMARY

Will ....finish the break
Can't ....outshine his teammates
Expect ....scoring spurts
Don't Expect ....15 PPG
Fantasy Value $2-4
Card Value ....8-12¢

COLLEGE STATISTICS

		G	FGP	FTP	RPG	PPG
82-83	MIAM	28	.497	.674	7.0	12.9
83-84	MIAM	30	.537	.570	7.6	14.9
84-85	MIAM	31	.541	.661	10.7	24.9
85-86	MIAM	31	.545	.665	11.7	24.4
Totals		120	.534	.642	9.3	19.5

NBA REGULAR-SEASON STATISTICS

				FGs		3-PT FGs		FTs		Rebounds						
		G	MIN	FG	PCT	FG	PCT	FT	PCT	OFF	TOT	AST	STL	BLK	PTS	PPG
86-87	CLE	82	3064	734	.455	20	.213	386	.684	169	392	394	209	84	1874	22.9
87-88	CLE	57	1830	340	.464	3	.150	196	.705	64	223	281	122	52	879	15.4
88-89	CLE	82	2851	587	.511	29	.250	323	.751	122	409	434	185	74	1526	18.6
89-90	CLE/LAC	35	1367	301	.473	14	.275	182	.788	74	206	182	81	41	798	22.8
90-91	LAC	39	1383	285	.391	48	.324	145	.668	58	188	209	66	35	763	19.6
91-92	LAC	82	3144	569	.440	64	.303	293	.736	120	447	417	152	72	1495	18.2
92-93	LAC	80	2970	542	.451	52	.280	307	.769	117	425	360	177	73	1443	18.0
93-94	LAC	75	2856	569	.426	71	.301	299	.715	129	460	344	144	54	1508	20.1
94-95	CHI	77	1536	209	.426	31	.282	81	.618	51	180	157	97	27	530	6.9
95-96	CHI	80	1886	234	.467	28	.269	98	.705	74	213	208	105	32	594	7.4
Totals		689	22887	4370	.451	360	.282	2310	.721	978	3143	2986	1338	544	11410	16.6

LUCIOUS HARRIS

Team: Philadelphia 76ers
Position: Guard
Height: 6'5" **Weight:** 205
Birthdate: December 18, 1970

NBA Experience: 3 years
College: Long Beach St.
Acquired: Signed as a free agent, 7/96

Background: Harris completed his four years at Long Beach State as the leading scorer in Big West history. He averaged 23.1 PPG as a senior and earned all-conference first-team honors in each of his last two years. He was the first pick in the second round of the 1993 draft. Harris averaged 9.5 points per game in his second NBA season before dropping to 7.9 PPG during the 1995-96 campaign. He joins Philadelphia for 1996-97.

Strengths: Harris has been a valuable player for his ability to fill either the one or two spot. He presents a good combination of size and quickness, can get his own shot, and is capable of knocking down 3-pointers. Harris is dangerous in transition, where he can pull up for jumpers or take it all the way. He is a steady dribbler and passer who does not make many mistakes.

Weaknesses: Though he was often used as a fill-in for Jason Kidd, Harris is not a creative playmaker. He averaged one assist every 12.9 minutes last year, running the offense in a no-frills style. He is not the kind of guard who makes those around him better. Harris has good size but is not a particularly strong player. His defense and rebounding have not been selling points.

Analysis: It's not surprising that Harris played his best ball when big guard Jim Jackson was injured two years ago. He's better off when someone else runs the offense and leaves him free to shoot from the 3-point arc. Harris can handle the offense, however, and he has the look of a player who might someday thrive as a high-scoring third guard.

PLAYER SUMMARY

Will	play one and two
Can't	make dazzling plays
Expect	a third guard
Don't Expect	3 APG
Fantasy Value	$4-6
Card Value	7-10¢

COLLEGE STATISTICS

		G	FGP	FTP	RPG	PPG
89-90	LBS	32	.430	.694	4.8	14.3
90-91	LBS	28	.396	.700	4.7	19.7
91-92	LBS	30	.471	.734	4.3	18.8
92-93	LBS	32	.525	.774	5.3	23.1
Totals		122	.458	.727	4.8	19.0

NBA REGULAR-SEASON STATISTICS

				FGs		3-PT FGs		FTs		Rebounds						
		G	MIN	FG	PCT	FG	PCT	FT	PCT	OFF	TOT	AST	STL	BLK	PTS	PPG
93-94	DAL	77	1165	162	.421	7	.212	87	.731	45	157	106	49	10	418	5.4
94-95	DAL	79	1695	280	.459	55	.387	136	.800	85	220	132	58	14	751	9.5
95-96	DAL	61	1016	183	.461	47	.376	68	.782	41	122	79	35	3	481	7.9
Totals		217	3876	625	.449	109	.363	291	.774	171	499	317	142	27	1650	7.6

HERSEY HAWKINS

Team: Seattle SuperSonics
Position: Guard
Height: 6'3" **Weight:** 190
Birthdate: September 29, 1966

NBA Experience: 8 years
College: Bradley
Acquired: Traded from Hornets with
David Wingate for Kendall Gill, 6/95

Background: Hawkins went from being a 6'3", all-city center at Westinghouse High School in Chicago to an outside gunner at Bradley. As a senior, he led the nation in scoring and was named the nation's Player of the Year. He left college as the fourth-leading scorer in NCAA history. He started his career as a high-scoring 76er before trades to Charlotte and Seattle.

Strengths: Hawkins remains one of the more respected shooters in basketball. He is dangerous from the 3-point arc, and he misses very few free throws. Though not especially quick, Hawkins can get to the hoop and is accurate with both hands. He brings a contagious work ethic to the job, whether it's practice or a game.

Weaknesses: Though he has been an All-Star, Hawkins seems to prefer a supporting role to high-scoring duties. It's rare for him to put a team on his back. Hawkins is not among the top passing and ball-handling guards in the league, and his defense against the upper-echelon guards is suspect.

Analysis: Unlike in Charlotte, Hawkins exceeded expectations during his first year with Seattle. That's not just because his scoring average was back up over 15 PPG. He was most valuable for his locker room presence, his hard-working example, and his team-first approach. The durable Hawkins has played in 297 consecutive games.

PLAYER SUMMARY

Will ....hit treys, free throws
Can't ....defend the big guys
Expect ....a team leader
Don't Expect ....missed starts
Fantasy Value $20-25
Card Value ....8-12¢

COLLEGE STATISTICS

		G	FGP	FTP	RPG	PPG
84-85	BRAD	30	.581	.771	6.1	14.6
85-86	BRAD	35	.542	.768	5.7	18.7
86-87	BRAD	29	.533	.793	6.7	27.2
87-88	BRAD	31	.524	.848	7.8	36.3
Totals		125	.539	.806	6.5	24.1

NBA REGULAR-SEASON STATISTICS

				FGs		3-PT FGs		FTs		Rebounds							
		G	MIN	FG	PCT	FG	PCT	FT	PCT	OFF	TOT	AST	STL	BLK	PTS	PPG
88-89	PHI	79	2577	442	.455	71	.428	241	.831	51	225	239	120	37	1196	15.1
89-90	PHI	82	2856	522	.460	84	.420	387	.888	85	304	261	130	28	1515	18.5
90-91	PHI	80	3110	590	.472	108	.400	479	.871	48	310	299	178	39	1767	22.1
91-92	PHI	81	3013	521	.462	91	.397	403	.874	53	271	248	157	43	1536	19.0
92-93	PHI	81	2977	551	.470	122	.397	419	.860	91	346	317	137	30	1643	20.3
93-94	CHA	82	2648	395	.460	78	.332	312	.862	89	377	216	135	22	1180	14.4
94-95	CHA	82	2731	390	.482	131	.440	261	.867	60	314	262	122	18	1172	14.3
95-96	SEA	82	2823	443	.473	146	.384	247	.873	86	297	218	149	14	1279	15.6
Totals		649	22735	3854	.467	831	.399	2749	.867	563	2444	2060	1128	231	11288	17.4

ALAN HENDERSON

Team: Atlanta Hawks
Position: Forward
Height: 6'9" **Weight:** 235
Birthdate: December 12, 1972

NBA Experience: 1 year
College: Indiana
Acquired: First-round pick in 1995 draft (16th overall)

Background: A four-year starter at Indiana, Henderson finished his career as the Hoosiers' all-time leading rebounder and shot-blocker and was fifth all-time in scoring. He was the top rebounder on the U.S. Goodwill Games team in 1994 and registered 48 double-doubles in his college career. The 16th pick in the 1995 draft, Henderson came off the Atlanta bench as a rookie and averaged 6.4 PPG and 4.5 RPG.

Strengths: Henderson has the look of a productive rebounder and shot-blocker who can play either forward position. He posted some double-figure rebound games as a rookie despite averaging about 18 minutes per outing, and he is not afraid to challenge bulkier big men. He's a smooth athlete with decent court sense and good timing. Some feel Henderson is also a promising scorer. He takes to coaching and wants to emerge.

Weaknesses: Henderson has some work to do on the offensive end. Though he is capable of scoring on mid-range jumpers or with his back to the basket, he is neither consistent enough with the former nor strong enough for the latter. Henderson's lack of bulk also works against him on defense, where NBA forwards have to do more than challenge shots. He did not enter the league with supreme confidence.

Analysis: Not expected to be an impact player in his first season, Henderson is just about on schedule. He played quite well at times, just not consistently enough to deserve heavy minutes on a regular basis. He will continue to work on his low-post moves, his jumper, and his strength. His rebounding and shot-blocking are a given. Expect to see more of Henderson in the coming years.

PLAYER SUMMARY	
Will	rebound, block shots
Can't	shove around big guys
Expect	a versatile athlete
Don't Expect	stardom
Fantasy Value	$1-3
Card Value	20-40¢

COLLEGE STATISTICS

		G	FGP	FTP	RPG	PPG
91-92	IND	33	.508	.661	7.2	11.6
92-93	IND	30	.487	.637	8.1	11.1
93-94	IND	30	.531	.657	10.3	17.8
94-95	IND	31	.597	.634	9.7	23.5
Totals		124	.540	.646	8.8	16.0

NBA REGULAR-SEASON STATISTICS

			FGs		3-PT FGs		FTs		Rebounds						
	G	MIN	FG	PCT	FG	PCT	FT	PCT	OFF	TOT	AST	STL	BLK	PTS	PPG
95-96 ATL	79	1416	192	.442	0	.000	119	.595	164	356	51	44	43	503	6.4
Totals	79	1416	192	.442	0	.000	119	.595	164	356	51	44	43	503	6.4

CARL HERRERA

Team: San Antonio Spurs
Position: Forward
Height: 6'9" **Weight:** 225
Birthdate: December 14, 1966

NBA Experience: 5 years
College: Jacksonville; Houston
Acquired: Signed as a free agent, 9/95

Background: Born in Trinidad and raised in Venezuela, Herrera did not play ball until age 13. He was noticed by colleges for his play as a 16-year-old point guard on the Venezuelan national team in the Pan-Am Games. He played two years of junior college ball and one at the University of Houston, then started his pro career in Spain. He has spent four years with the Rockets and one with the Spurs.

Strengths: Herrera is a magnificent athlete with a great pair of hands. He was a volleyball star as a teenager, and it's easy to understand why when you watch him get off his feet on the hardwood. He's a power forward who can run the floor like a guard. He has been a forceful defensive presence who can score in the post.

Weaknesses: Herrera is not a consistent offensive player. His jumper is a funny-looking affair that finds the mark only in streaks. He is not a steady force from the low post, and his free-throw shooting is nothing short of atrocious. Herrera does not have good court sense. He does not pass or dribble well, and he does not control the glass.

Analysis: Herrera played on two NBA championship teams in Houston, and he was a valuable contributor at times. He signed with San Antonio before the 1995-96 season and averaged just nine minutes per game in 44 outings, his worst season. He has been slowed by injuries, but also holding him back has been his inability to accept a reserve role.

PLAYER SUMMARY	
Will	....................................run the floor
Can't	......................set up teammates
Expect	................a decent hook shot
Don't Expect	............double-doubles
Fantasy Value	....................................$0
Card Value	....................................7-10¢

COLLEGE STATISTICS

		G	FGP	FTP	RPG	PPG
89-90	HOUS	33	.565	.804	9.2	16.7
Totals		33	.565	.804	9.2	16.7

NBA REGULAR-SEASON STATISTICS

		G	MIN	FGs FG	PCT	3-PT FGs FG	PCT	FTs FT	PCT	Rebounds OFF	TOT	AST	STL	BLK	PTS	PPG
91-92	HOU	43	566	83	.516	0	.000	25	.568	33	99	27	16	25	191	4.4
92-93	HOU	81	1800	240	.541	0	.000	125	.710	148	454	61	47	35	605	7.5
93-94	HOU	75	1292	142	.458	0	.000	69	.711	101	285	37	32	26	353	4.7
94-95	HOU	61	1331	171	.523	0	.000	73	.624	98	278	44	40	38	415	6.8
95-96	SA	44	393	40	.412	0	.000	5	.294	30	81	16	9	8	85	1.9
Totals		304	5382	676	.505	0	.000	297	.659	410	1197	185	144	132	1649	5.4

GRANT HILL

Team: Detroit Pistons
Position: Forward
Height: 6'8" **Weight:** 225
Birthdate: October 5, 1972

NBA Experience: 2 years
College: Duke
Acquired: First-round pick in 1994 draft (third overall)

Background: Hill, along with Bobby Hurley and Christian Laettner, formed the core of back-to-back national championship teams at Duke in 1991 and 1992. Hill was a consensus All-American in 1993-94 and was the first ACC player to amass 1,900 points, 700 rebounds, 400 assists, 200 steals, and 100 blocks. The third pick in the 1994 draft, he shared 1995 Rookie of the Year honors with Jason Kidd and enjoyed an even better second season.

Strengths: Hill quite literally does it all. He was the only player in 1995-96 to rank among the NBA's top 20 in scoring, rebounding, and assists. Hill is a tremendous slasher who has the ability to get to the bucket from anywhere on the court. He owns a great crossover dribble, can finish his own plays or find open teammates, and is also a potent post-up scorer. Hill has great defensive anticipation, crashes the boards, plays a team game, and is a first-rate citizen off the floor.

Weaknesses: About the only significant flaw in Hill's game is his shooting range. He is not a great threat from behind the 3-point line, nor is he a pure shooter in general. Hill needs to hone his jumper and hoist his free-throw percentage in the years to come.

Analysis: The son of former NFL star Calvin Hill has quickly become one of the NBA's hottest attractions and one of its best all-around players. A 1996 Dream Team member and spokesman for the game, Hill has received more All-Star votes than anyone in the league in each of his first two seasons. No player in the NBA leads his team in as many important categories. Hill is a truly dominant player who has the Pistons on the rise.

PLAYER SUMMARY

Will......................score, pass, rebound
Can't ....pour in 3-pointers
Expect ....an NBA spokesman
Don't Expect ....a disappointment
Fantasy Value $55-60
Card Value ....75¢-$1.75

COLLEGE STATISTICS

		G	FGP	FTP	RPG	PPG
90-91	DUKE	36	.516	.609	5.1	11.2
91-92	DUKE	33	.611	.733	5.7	14.0
92-93	DUKE	26	.578	.746	6.4	18.0
93-94	DUKE	34	.462	.703	6.9	17.4
Totals		129	.532	.698	6.0	14.9

NBA REGULAR-SEASON STATISTICS

		G	MIN	FGs FG	FGs PCT	3-PT FGs FG	3-PT FGs PCT	FTs FT	FTs PCT	Rebounds OFF	Rebounds TOT	AST	STL	BLK	PTS	PPG
94-95	DET	70	2678	508	.477	4	.148	374	.732	125	445	353	124	62	1394	19.9
95-96	DET	80	3260	564	.462	5	.192	485	.751	127	783	548	100	48	1618	20.2
Totals		150	5938	1072	.469	9	.170	859	.742	252	1228	901	224	110	3012	20.1

TYRONE HILL

Team: Cleveland Cavaliers
Position: Forward
Height: 6'9" **Weight:** 245
Birthdate: March 17, 1968

NBA Experience: 6 years
College: Xavier (OH)
Acquired: Signed as a free agent, 7/93

Background: Hill joined an exclusive group of college players to score 2,000 points and grab 1,000 rebounds in a career. He was among the top three nationally in rebounding as a junior and senior at Xavier. He spent his first three NBA years banging the boards for Golden State and was a 1995 All-Star in his second year with Cleveland. He missed 38 games last season after being injured in a hit-and-run automobile accident.

Strengths: Before suffering a bruise of the spinal cord in the accident last November, Hill had emerged as one of the best rebounding forwards in the NBA. He has a muscular body and uses it to get inside position. He snares boards with great instincts and desire. Hill has also been a hard-working defensive player and a capable low-post scorer.

Weaknesses: Hill is a poor outside shooter, and you don't want him at the free-throw line in a close game. He has no feel for where and when to pass the ball. Hill does not have great lateral quickness, and he picks up a lot of fouls trying to chase speedsters on the perimeter.

Analysis: Two games into the 1995-96 season, as Hill was trying to establish himself as a perennial rebounding force and All-Star performer, he almost lost his life in a car accident. Residual weakness in his right arm and leg cast doubt on his future as a player, but Hill came back after missing just 38 games and showed signs of returning to peak form.

PLAYER SUMMARY	
Will	box out
Can't	swish free throws
Expect	rebounds, interior defense
Don't Expect	shooting touch
Fantasy Value	$9-11
Card Value	8-12¢

COLLEGE STATISTICS

		G	FGP	FTP	RPG	PPG
86-87	XAV	31	.552	.672	8.4	8.8
87-88	XAV	30	.557	.745	10.5	15.3
88-89	XAV	33	.606	.701	12.2	18.9
89-90	XAV	32	.581	.658	12.6	20.2
Totals		126	.579	.692	11.0	15.9

NBA REGULAR-SEASON STATISTICS

		G	MIN	FGs FG	FGs PCT	3-PT FGs FG	3-PT FGs PCT	FTs FT	FTs PCT	Rebounds OFF	Rebounds TOT	AST	STL	BLK	PTS	PPG
90-91	GS	74	1192	147	.492	0	.000	96	.632	157	383	19	33	30	390	5.3
91-92	GS	82	1886	254	.522	0	.000	163	.694	182	593	47	73	43	671	8.2
92-93	GS	74	2070	251	.508	0	.000	138	.624	255	754	68	41	40	640	8.6
93-94	CLE	57	1447	216	.543	0	.000	171	.668	184	499	46	53	35	603	10.6
94-95	CLE	70	2397	350	.504	0	.000	263	.662	269	765	55	55	41	963	13.8
95-96	CLE	44	929	130	.512	0	.000	81	.600	94	244	33	31	20	341	7.8
Totals		401	9921	1348	.513	0	.000	912	.653	1141	3238	268	286	209	3608	9.0

JEFF HORNACEK

Team: Utah Jazz
Position: Guard
Height: 6'4" **Weight:** 190
Birthdate: May 3, 1963
NBA Experience: 10 years

College: Iowa St.
Acquired: Traded from 76ers with Sean Green and a conditional second-round pick for Jeff Malone and a conditional first-round pick, 2/94

Background: Hornacek walked on at Iowa State, earned a scholarship, and wound up setting a Big Eight career assist record with 665. His ten-year NBA career has evolved in a similar pattern—from unheralded to highly respected. He led the Suns in 1991-92 with 20.1 PPG and played in the 1992 All-Star Game. Hornacek has been a perfect fit in two-plus years with Utah.

Strengths: A dead-eye gunner, Hornacek can kill you from anywhere on the court—inside or outside the 3-point line. He annually rates among NBA leaders in free-throw and 3-point accuracy. He makes few mistakes, is good with both hands, and approaches the game with a great work ethic. He can handle both guard positions.

Weaknesses: The fact that Hornacek is not a great athlete has not stopped him from achieving at every level. His size (or lack of it) works against him on defense, but he makes up for it with savvy play.

Analysis: A coach's son, Hornacek has a thorough understanding of the game and plays it at a high level. He spent half of last season as a sixth man, a role he may find himself playing more often in years to come. It suits him well because of his smarts and his ability to spark a team from two positions.

PLAYER SUMMARY

Will ....drill treys, free throws
Can't ....physically dominate
Expect ....skills, smarts, savvy
Don't Expect ....mistakes
Fantasy Value $18-21
Card Value ....8-12¢

COLLEGE STATISTICS

		G	FGP	FTP	RPG	PPG
82-83	ISU	27	.422	.711	2.3	5.4
83-84	ISU	29	.500	.790	3.5	10.0
84-85	ISU	34	.521	.844	3.6	12.5
85-86	ISU	33	.478	.776	3.8	13.7
Totals		123	.489	.790	3.3	10.7

NBA REGULAR-SEASON STATISTICS

			MIN	FGs		3-PT FGs		FTs		Rebounds		AST	STL	BLK	PTS	PPG
		G		FG	PCT	FG	PCT	FT	PCT	OFF	TOT					
86-87	PHO	80	1561	159	.454	12	.279	94	.777	41	184	361	70	5	424	5.3
87-88	PHO	82	2243	306	.506	17	.293	152	.822	71	262	540	107	10	781	9.5
88-89	PHO	78	2487	440	.495	27	.333	147	.826	75	266	465	129	8	1054	13.5
89-90	PHO	67	2278	483	.536	40	.408	173	.856	86	313	337	117	14	1179	17.6
90-91	PHO	80	2733	544	.518	61	.418	201	.897	74	321	409	111	16	1350	16.9
91-92	PHO	81	3078	635	.512	83	.439	279	.886	106	407	411	158	31	1632	20.1
92-93	PHI	79	2860	582	.470	97	.390	250	.865	84	342	548	131	21	1511	19.1
93-94	PHI/UTA	80	2820	472	.470	70	.337	260	.878	60	279	419	127	13	1274	15.9
94-95	UTA	81	2696	482	.514	89	.406	284	.882	53	210	347	129	17	1337	16.5
95-96	UTA	82	2588	442	.502	104	.466	259	.893	62	209	340	106	20	1247	15.2
Totals		790	25344	4545	.500	600	.396	2099	.867	712	2793	4177	1185	155	11789	14.9

ROBERT HORRY

Team: Phoenix Suns
Position: Forward
Height: 6'10" **Weight:** 220
Birthdate: August 25, 1970
NBA Experience: 4 years

College: Alabama
Acquired: Traded from Rockets with Sam Cassell, Chucky Brown, and Mark Bryant for Charles Barkley, 8/96

Background: Named Alabama prep Player of the Year at Andalusia High, Horry stayed at home and twice helped the Crimson Tide to the Sweet 16 of the NCAA Tournament. He finished his career as the all-time school leader in blocked shots. Drafted 11th in 1992, Horry was a four-year starter in Houston before being dealt to the Suns as part of the Charles Barkley deal.

Strengths: Horry is a splendid athlete who stands out on defense and in transition. The former SEC All-Defensive player has a nose for the ball and rejects a lot of shots for a small forward. He can stop threes and fours equally well. Horry will also score, getting most of his points on the break or with an accurate 3-point jumper. He sets up teammates with smart passes and gets a lot of steals.

Weaknesses: Ball-handling is probably the weakest aspect of Horry's game. He does not take full advantage of his quickness and long physique by burning opponents off the dribble, preferring to take his chances from the perimeter. More than half his shots are 3-point attempts. Horry is not the scoring machine many starting small forwards are, but Houston hasn't needed him to be.

Analysis: Horry seems to play his best ball when it counts. He raised his game to its highest level while helping the Rockets to their second championship. He then enjoyed his best regular season in 1995-96, shaking off back injuries that had nagged him the year before and averaging a career-high 12.0 PPG. Horry does need to expand his offensive repertoire.

PLAYER SUMMARY	
Will	run the floor
Can't	use the dribble
Expect	defense, 3-pointers
Don't Expect	power moves
Fantasy Value	$10-13
Card Value	10-20¢

COLLEGE STATISTICS

		G	FGP	FTP	RPG	PPG
88-89	ALAB	31	.427	.644	5.0	6.5
89-90	ALAB	35	.467	.760	6.2	13.1
90-91	ALAB	32	.449	.804	8.1	11.9
91-92	ALAB	35	.470	.727	8.5	15.8
Totals		133	.458	.742	7.0	12.0

NBA REGULAR-SEASON STATISTICS

				FGs		3-PT FGs		FTs		Rebounds						
		G	MIN	FG	PCT	FG	PCT	FT	PCT	OFF	TOT	AST	STL	BLK	PTS	PPG
92-93	HOU	79	2330	323	.474	12	.255	143	.715	113	392	191	80	83	801	10.1
93-94	HOU	81	2370	322	.459	44	.324	115	.732	128	440	231	119	75	803	9.9
94-95	HOU	64	2074	240	.447	86	.379	86	.761	81	324	216	94	76	652	10.2
95-96	HOU	71	2634	300	.410	142	.366	111	.776	97	412	281	116	109	853	12.0
Totals		295	9408	1185	.447	284	.255	455	.742	419	1568	919	409	343	3109	10.5

ALLAN HOUSTON

Team: New York Knicks
Position: Guard
Height: 6'6" **Weight:** 210
Birthdate: April 4, 1971

NBA Experience: 3 years
College: Tennessee
Acquired: Signed as a free agent, 7/96

Background: Kentucky's Mr. Basketball as a prep, Houston was headed to the University of Louisville, where his father Wade was an assistant. Plans changed when the elder Houston took the head-coaching job at Tennessee. Allan enjoyed a bang-up career with the Vols, finishing second in SEC history to Pete Maravich in career points. The 11th pick in the 1993 draft bolstered his scoring average each season before signing on with the Knicks last July.

Strengths: Houston is a combination shooter and scorer. He has excellent mechanics on his jump shot, is one of the more prolific and accurate 3-point shooters in basketball, and can get his shot either off designed plays or off the dribble. Houston is also quick to the hoop, and he'll cash in when sent to shoot free throws. Like most coaches' sons, he knows the game well, and he shows up ready to work.

Weaknesses: There's a reason Houston has spent much of his practice time on defense. He was not ready to guard NBA players when he came into the league, and he still lacks the footwork, instincts, and toughness that made ex-teammate Joe Dumars a stopper for years. The Pistons experimented with Houston at the point, but he's a two all the way.

Analysis: Houston raised his scoring average by six points in his second season and another five in his third, landing at 19.7 PPG in 1995-96. No less dramatic has been his improved defense, which he has really concentrated on while letting the offensive game come to him. After grooming him to fill Dumars's shoes, the Pistons watched Houston go to New York during the off-season.

PLAYER SUMMARY	
Will	shoot, score
Can't	defend like Joe D.
Expect	good court sense
Don't Expect	much bench time
Fantasy Value	$19-22
Card Value	10-15¢

COLLEGE STATISTICS

		G	FGP	FTP	RPG	PPG
89-90	TENN	30	.437	.805	2.9	20.3
90-91	TENN	34	.482	.863	3.1	23.7
91-92	TENN	34	.453	.840	5.3	21.1
92-93	TENN	30	.465	.878	4.8	22.3
Totals		128	.460	.849	4.0	21.9

NBA REGULAR-SEASON STATISTICS

			FGs		3-PT FGs		FTs		Rebounds						
	G	MIN	FG	PCT	FG	PCT	FT	PCT	OFF	TOT	AST	STL	BLK	PTS	PPG
93-94 DET	79	1519	272	.405	35	.299	89	.824	19	120	100	34	13	668	8.5
94-95 DET	76	1996	398	.463	158	.424	147	.860	29	167	164	61	14	1101	14.5
95-96 DET	82	3072	564	.453	191	.427	298	.823	54	300	250	61	16	1617	19.7
Totals	237	6587	1234	.445	384	.410	534	.833	102	587	514	156	43	3386	14.3

JUWAN HOWARD

Team: Washington Bullets
Position: Forward
Height: 6'9" **Weight:** 250
Birthdate: February 7, 1973

NBA Experience: 2 years
College: Michigan
Acquired: First-round pick in 1994 draft (fifth overall)

Background: Howard was the first of Michigan's heralded Fab Five recruiting class to sign with the Wolverines; the others followed. Together, they played in two national championship games before the early exit of Chris Webber allowed Howard to grab more of the spotlight. He went pro after his junior year (he still graduated on time) and was drafted fifth by Washington. Howard made the All-Star Game in his second season. A coveted free agent last summer, he signed a huge deal with Miami but returned to Washington after the NBA voided the deal.

Strengths: Howard is a schooled low-post player who can also step out and knock down the 18-footer. The result of this lethal combination: He can score against almost anyone. Howard, who also runs the floor and attacks the glass, averaged 22.1 PPG last season. He also racked up a large number of assists and is considered one of the best passing forwards in basketball. Howard is capable of becoming a double-figure rebounder down the road. On top of that, he is a willing and able defender, a team leader, and a civic-minded role model.

Weaknesses: Howard does not have the best springs in his legs and, though he plays solid defense, is not a threat to block many shots. Quick players are capable of causing him problems on the perimeter and putting him in foul trouble.

Analysis: Expectations were high when Howard entered the NBA, and he has done nothing but exceed them. A hard-working player and natural leader, he has proved to be even more valuable to the Bullets than his more-heralded college teammate, Webber. In addition to his all-around talent and desire to win, Howard is one of the most charitable players in professional sports. He has funded three learning centers for inner-city children needing help in their studies.

PLAYER SUMMARY	
Will	lead by example
Can't	block many shots
Expect	20 PPG
Don't Expect	passive defense
Fantasy Value	$30-35
Card Value	25-75¢

COLLEGE STATISTICS

		G	FGP	FTP	RPG	PPG
91-92	MICH	34	.450	.688	6.2	11.1
92-93	MICH	36	.506	.700	7.4	14.6
93-94	MICH	30	.557	.675	8.9	20.8
Totals		100	.510	.688	7.5	15.3

NBA REGULAR-SEASON STATISTICS

				FGs		3-PT FGs		FTs		Rebounds						
		G	MIN	FG	PCT	FG	PCT	FT	PCT	OFF	TOT	AST	STL	BLK	PTS	PPG
94-95	WAS	65	2348	455	.489	0	.000	194	.664	184	545	165	52	15	1104	17.0
95-96	WAS	81	3294	733	.489	4	.308	319	.749	188	660	360	67	39	1789	22.1
Totals		146	5642	1188	.489	4	.200	513	.714	372	1205	525	119	54	2893	19.8

LINDSEY HUNTER

Team: Detroit Pistons
Position: Guard
Height: 6'2" **Weight:** 195
Birthdate: December 3, 1970

NBA Experience: 3 years
College: Alcorn St.; Jackson St.
Acquired: First-round pick in 1993 draft (tenth overall)

Background: After playing high school ball in Jackson, Mississippi, Hunter spent a year at Alcorn State but transferred to Jackson State for the 1990-91 season. There, he averaged 26.7 PPG as a senior, fifth highest in the nation. The No. 10 draft choice in 1993, Hunter was a second-team All-Rookie selection. The three-year Piston missed half of his second season with a broken foot.

Strengths: Hunter is a lightning-quick point guard who can get his shot off despite tight defense. He has a quick release and outstanding range, and he improved his 3-point accuracy to .405 in 1995-96 after making just .333 in his first two years combined. A great athlete, Hunter is at his best in the open court and can be explosive.

Weaknesses: Hunter has been terribly inconsistent and shoots a woeful percentage from the floor. The fact is, he does not finish plays well enough to thrive as a two guard (where he played in college), and he is not the playmaker, decision-maker, or ball-handler he needs to be to stand out at the point. Hunter's assist-to-turnover ratio is less than exemplary, and he takes too many chances on defense.

Analysis: Hunter is still learning the nuances of being a point guard, and he has had the luxury of playing with good passers and ball-handlers like Grant Hill and Allan Houston. It's a good thing, too, because he has had his share of troubles running the offense and making the right decisions. Though Hunter started for most of last season, Joe Dumars was brought in to start late in the season to provide veteran leadership.

PLAYER SUMMARY	
Will	shoot with range
Can't	finish his drives
Expect	further development
Don't Expect	great decisions
Fantasy Value	$1
Card Value	8-12¢

COLLEGE STATISTICS

		G	FGP	FTP	APG	PPG
88-89	ASU	28	.393	.719	3.5	6.0
90-91	JSU	30	.409	.695	3.5	20.9
91-92	JSU	28	.412	.637	4.3	24.8
92-93	JSU	34	.412	.771	3.4	26.7
Totals		120	.409	.709	3.7	19.9

NBA REGULAR-SEASON STATISTICS

			FGs		3-PT FGs		FTs		Rebounds						
	G	MIN	FG	PCT	FG	PCT	FT	PCT	OFF	TOT	AST	STL	BLK	PTS	PPG
93-94 DET	82	2172	335	.375	69	.333	104	.732	47	189	390	121	10	843	10.3
94-95 DET	42	944	119	.374	36	.333	40	.727	24	75	159	51	7	314	7.5
95-96 DET	80	2138	239	.381	117	.405	84	.700	44	194	188	84	18	679	8.5
Totals	204	5254	693	.377	222	.368	228	.719	115	458	737	256	35	1836	9.0

BOBBY HURLEY

Team: Sacramento Kings
Position: Guard
Height: 6'0" **Weight:** 165
Birthdate: June 28, 1971

NBA Experience: 3 years
College: Duke
Acquired: First-round pick in 1993 draft (seventh overall)

Background: One of many quality players from St. Anthony's, a prep powerhouse in New Jersey, Hurley went to Duke and did nothing but win. The Blue Devils went to three Final Fours and won two national crowns (1991 and 1992) with Hurley, who set the NCAA career assists record. His rookie year ended in December 1993 when he suffered serious injuries in an auto accident. He has rejoined the Kings in a reserve role.

Strengths: Hurley has drawn comparisons to the likes of Bob Cousy and John Stockton for his instincts as a point guard. He makes wise decisions with the ball, steers the fastbreak beautifully, and can set up teammates with pinpoint passes. Hurley has stood up to countless pressure situations in his life and career. He's a lifelong gym rat whose return to the NBA was uplifting.

Weaknesses: Since suffering injuries to his knee, ribs, shoulder, and back (among others) in the accident, Hurley has not duplicated the promising level of play he attained as a rookie. He never was a great shooter, and he converted a woeful .283 from the field last season. He has been tentative in taking the ball to the hole, and he does not have the size to cause problems on defense.

Analysis: It appears we will never know how good Hurley would have been had he not suffered injuries that were once considered life-threatening. The comeback kid has become a frustrated young man who is unhappy with his playing time, but unable to do anything to warrant more. He needs a serious confidence boost and a respectable jump shot if he hopes to stick around.

PLAYER SUMMARY	
Will	handle the ball
Can't	regain his confidence
Expect	much off-season work
Don't Expect	respectable shooting
Fantasy Value	$0
Card Value	12-20¢

COLLEGE STATISTICS

		G	FGP	FTP	APG	PPG
89-90	DUKE	38	.351	.769	7.6	8.8
90-91	DUKE	39	.423	.728	7.4	11.3
91-92	DUKE	31	.433	.789	7.6	13.2
92-93	DUKE	32	.421	.803	8.2	17.0
Totals		140	.410	.776	7.7	12.4

NBA REGULAR-SEASON STATISTICS

				FGs		3-PT FGs		FTs		Rebounds						
		G	MIN	FG	PCT	FG	PCT	FT	PCT	OFF	TOT	AST	STL	BLK	PTS	PPG
93-94	SAC	19	499	54	.370	2	.125	24	.800	6	34	115	13	1	134	7.1
94-95	SAC	68	1105	103	.363	21	.276	58	.763	14	70	226	29	0	285	4.2
95-96	SAC	72	1059	65	.283	22	.289	68	.800	12	75	216	28	3	220	3.1
Totals		159	2663	222	.336	45	.268	150	.785	32	179	557	70	4	639	4.0

JIM JACKSON

Team: Dallas Mavericks
Position: Guard
Height: 6'6" **Weight:** 215
Birthdate: October 14, 1970

NBA Experience: 4 years
College: Ohio St.
Acquired: First-round pick in 1992 draft (fourth overall)

Background: A rare two-time Mr. Basketball in Ohio, Jackson led Toledo Macomber to a state championship as a senior. He started all 93 games in his three years at Ohio State. Jackson was named Big Ten Freshman of the Year and was a consensus All-American as a junior. The fourth pick in the 1992 draft has emerged as a high-scoring guard in four seasons with Dallas.

Strengths: Jackson is a tremendous talent and a big-time scorer. He is blessed with the ability to post up, drive to the hoop, or hit from the perimeter. He has improved his long-range shooting. He is also the kind of player who can make those around him look better. His passing skills are advanced, he gets to the boards, and he hits better than 80 percent of his free throws. He plays with desire.

Weaknesses: Jackson is a scorer first and a shooter second. He is far from automatic when he gets an open shot from 18 feet, preferring to drive and draw contact. Jackson has made a habit of trying to do too much at times, but that's understandable considering that he plays for the Mavericks. He is not one of the best ball-handling guards.

Analysis: Jackson, whose 1994-95 season was cut short because of an ankle injury, did not score as many points last season but improved in other areas. He had falling-outs with teammates Jason Kidd and Jamal Mashburn. Dallas can't go on losing forever, and Jackson is expected to play a major role in the team's climb back to contention.

PLAYER SUMMARY	
Will	score, pass
Can't	take Mavs to title
Expect	about 20 PPG
Don't Expect	slick dribbling
Fantasy Value	$25-30
Card Value	20-50¢

COLLEGE STATISTICS

		G	FGP	FTP	RPG	PPG
89-90	OSU	30	.499	.785	5.5	16.1
90-91	OSU	31	.517	.752	5.5	18.9
91-92	OSU	32	.493	.811	6.8	22.4
Totals		93	.503	.784	5.9	19.2

NBA REGULAR-SEASON STATISTICS

				FGs		3-PT FGs		FTs		Rebounds						
		G	MIN	FG	PCT	FG	PCT	FT	PCT	OFF	TOT	AST	STL	BLK	PTS	PPG
92-93	DAL	28	938	184	.395	21	.288	68	.739	42	122	131	40	11	457	16.3
93-94	DAL	82	3066	637	.445	17	.283	285	.821	169	388	374	87	25	1576	19.2
94-95	DAL	51	1982	484	.472	35	.318	306	.805	120	260	191	28	12	1309	25.7
95-96	DAL	82	2820	569	.435	121	.363	345	.825	173	410	235	47	22	1604	19.6
Totals		243	8806	1874	.443	194	.337	1004	.812	504	1180	931	202	70	4946	20.4

MARK JACKSON

Team: Denver Nuggets
Position: Guard
Height: 6'1" **Weight:** 192
Birthdate: April 1, 1965
NBA Experience: 9 years

College: St. John's
Acquired: Traded from Pacers with Ricky Pierce and a 1996 first-round pick for Jalen Rose, Reggie Williams, and a 1996 first-round pick, 6/96

Background: Jackson was a second-team All-American as a senior at St. John's and finished his career with the school's all-time assist record. With the Knicks, he was the unanimous choice for NBA Rookie of the Year in 1988 and won a trip to the 1989 All-Star Game. After five seasons in New York, two with the Clippers, and two with the Pacers, he was dealt to the Nuggets in the off-season.

Strengths: When Jackson drives toward the bucket, he has the ability to either find the open man or make acrobatic shots. His court vision is superb, and he remains one of the leading assist men in the game. He has been a double-figure scorer for most of his career and has always hit the boards.

Weaknesses: Jackson is not regarded as a great outside shooter, although he has improved his 3-point accuracy. Opponents are still best off keeping him on the perimeter. Jackson is not among the quicker guards around, and defense is not his forte.

Analysis: Jackson got off to somewhat of a shaky start with the Pacers in 1994-95, but he learned how to handle the controls of the talented team. Now he will have to do the same for the Nuggets. This combination scorer and distributor gets teammates involved in the offense. He is approaching 6,000 career assists.

PLAYER SUMMARY	
Will	create
Can't	stop high scorers
Expect	drives and dishes
Don't Expect	15 PPG
Fantasy Value	$5-7
Card Value	7-10¢

COLLEGE STATISTICS

		G	FGP	FTP	APG	PPG
83-84	STJ	30	.575	.688	3.6	5.8
84-85	STJ	35	.564	.725	3.1	5.1
85-86	STJ	36	.478	.739	9.1	11.3
86-87	STJ	30	.504	.806	6.4	18.9
Totals		131	.510	.751	5.6	10.1

NBA REGULAR-SEASON STATISTICS

		G	MIN	FGs FG	FGs PCT	3-PT FGs FG	3-PT FGs PCT	FTs FT	FTs PCT	Rebounds OFF	Rebounds TOT	AST	STL	BLK	PTS	PPG
87-88	NY	82	3249	438	.432	32	.254	206	.774	120	396	868	205	6	1114	13.6
88-89	NY	72	2477	479	.467	81	.338	180	.698	106	341	619	139	7	1219	16.9
89-90	NY	82	2428	327	.437	35	.267	120	.727	106	318	604	109	4	809	9.9
90-91	NY	72	1595	250	.492	13	.255	117	.731	62	197	452	60	9	630	8.8
91-92	NY	81	2461	367	.491	11	.256	171	.770	95	305	694	112	13	916	11.3
92-93	LAC	82	3117	459	.486	22	.268	241	.803	129	388	724	136	12	1181	14.4
93-94	LAC	79	2711	331	.452	36	.283	167	.791	107	348	678	120	6	865	10.9
94-95	IND	82	2402	239	.422	27	.310	119	.778	73	306	616	105	16	624	7.6
95-96	IND	81	2643	296	.473	64	.430	150	.785	66	307	635	100	5	806	10.0
Totals		713	23083	3186	.461	321	.310	1471	.764	864	2906	5890	1086	78	8164	11.5

AVERY JOHNSON

Team: San Antonio Spurs
Position: Guard
Height: 5'11" **Weight:** 180
Birthdate: March 25, 1965

NBA Experience: 8 years
College: Cameron; Southern
Acquired: Signed as a free agent, 7/94

Background: Johnson led the nation in assists as a junior and senior at Southern University, where he was a two-time Southwestern Athletic Conference Player of the Year. Undrafted, he latched on in Seattle and has also played for Denver, San Antonio, Houston, and Golden State. His third stint with the Spurs began in 1994-95 and has seen him emerge as one of the NBA's best lead guards.

Strengths: A pure point guard, Johnson covers the court like a pinball. His quickness allows him to penetrate and show off his crafty passing skills. He sees the court better than most, and his 9.6 APG last season ranked him third in the league. He has also become a 13-plus PPG scorer. Johnson is a tough customer who makes those around him better.

Weaknesses: The younger brother of former NBA guard Vinnie Johnson is not the shooting machine his brother once was, although defenders have to respect him to about 18 feet. His range does not extend to the 3-point line, and he is a subpar free-throw shooter.

Analysis: The devoutly religious and highly personable Johnson has the heart of a lion and a game to match. He has spent most of his career as a hard-working player who set up the offense, passed to open men, and hustled on defense. Now, he's also scoring in addition to serving as an inspirational leader on a contending team.

PLAYER SUMMARY	
Will	distribute
Can't	burn you from deep
Expect	leadership, toughness
Don't Expect	foul language
Fantasy Value	$11-14
Card Value	5-8¢

COLLEGE STATISTICS

		G	FGP	FTP	APG	PPG
84-85	CAM	33	.509	.618	3.2	4.3
86-87	SOUT	31	.439	.615	10.7	7.1
87-88	SOUT	30	.537	.688	13.3	11.4
Totals		94	.497	.641	8.9	7.5

NBA REGULAR-SEASON STATISTICS

				FGs		3-PT FGs		FTs		Rebounds						
		G	MIN	FG	PCT	FG	PCT	FT	PCT	OFF	TOT	AST	STL	BLK	PTS	PPG
88-89	SEA	43	291	29	.349	1	.111	9	.563	11	24	73	21	3	68	1.6
89-90	SEA	53	575	55	.387	1	.250	29	.725	21	43	162	26	1	140	2.6
90-91	DEN/SA	68	959	130	.469	1	.111	59	.678	22	77	230	47	4	320	4.7
91-92	SA/HOU	69	1235	158	.479	4	.267	66	.653	13	80	266	61	9	386	5.6
92-93	SA	75	2030	256	.502	0	.000	144	.791	20	146	561	85	16	656	8.7
93-94	GS	82	2332	356	.492	0	.000	178	.704	41	176	433	113	8	890	10.9
94-95	SA	82	3011	448	.519	3	.136	202	.685	49	208	670	114	13	1101	13.4
95-96	SA	82	3084	438	.494	6	.194	189	.721	37	206	789	119	21	1071	13.1
Totals		554	13517	1870	.490	16	.145	876	.709	214	960	3184	586	75	4632	8.4

EDDIE JOHNSON

Team: Indiana Pacers
Position: Forward
Height: 6'7" **Weight:** 215
Birthdate: May 1, 1959

NBA Experience: 14 years
College: Illinois
Acquired: Signed as a free agent, 9/95

Background: Johnson set Illinois career records for scoring, rebounding, and field goals. He starred for the Kings before winning the NBA's 1989 Sixth Man Award with Phoenix. The 14-year NBA veteran has also played for Seattle, Charlotte, and Indiana, and he spent the 1994-95 season in Greece.

Strengths: The 37-year-old Johnson can still shoot the basketball. He always could. He's dangerous when spotting up from 3-point range and is well over 80 percent from the free-throw line in his career. Johnson is a heady professional.

Weaknesses: Take away his jump shot, and Johnson struggles. He does not go to the hole much, he's not a good ball-handler, and passing the ball is not his calling. Johnson also has a tough time on defense. He lacks the lateral quickness to keep his man from scoring.

Analysis: Johnson has lost at least a step, but he can still knock down strings of jumpers. He has enjoyed a longer career than most players can aspire to. He still loves playing the game, and he does not mind playing it in short stretches. His contract runs through the end of 1996-97.

PLAYER SUMMARY

Will.............................heat up quickly
Can't ....score like he used to
Expect ....reserve minutes
Don't Expect ......two strong seasons
Fantasy Value $0
Card Value ....7-10¢

COLLEGE STATISTICS

		G	FGP	FTP	RPG	PPG
77-78	ILL	27	.427	.741	3.1	8.1
78-79	ILL	30	.415	.531	5.7	12.1
79-80	ILL	35	.462	.655	8.9	17.4
80-81	ILL	29	.494	.756	9.2	17.2
Totals		121	.454	.671	6.9	14.0

NBA REGULAR-SEASON STATISTICS

			FGs		3-PT FGs		FTs		Rebounds						
	G	MIN	FG	PCT	FG	PCT	FT	PCT	OFF	TOT	AST	STL	BLK	PTS	PPG
81-82 KC	74	1517	295	.459	1	.091	99	.664	128	322	109	50	14	690	9.3
82-83 KC	82	2933	677	.494	20	.282	247	.779	191	501	216	70	20	1621	19.8
83-84 KC	82	2920	753	.485	20	.313	268	.810	165	455	296	76	21	1794	21.9
84-85 KC	82	3029	769	.491	13	.241	325	.871	151	407	273	83	22	1876	22.9
85-86 SAC	82	2514	623	.475	4	.200	280	.816	173	419	214	54	17	1530	18.7
86-87 SAC	81	2457	606	.463	37	.314	267	.829	146	353	251	42	19	1516	18.7
87-88 PHO	73	2177	533	.480	24	.255	204	.850	121	318	180	33	9	1294	17.7
88-89 PHO	70	2043	608	.497	71	.413	217	.868	91	306	162	47	7	1504	21.5
89-90 PHO	64	1811	411	.453	70	.380	188	.917	69	246	107	32	10	1080	16.9
90-91 PHO/SEA	81	2085	543	.484	39	.325	229	.891	107	271	111	58	9	1354	16.7
91-92 SEA	81	2366	534	.459	27	.252	291	.861	118	292	161	55	11	1386	17.1
92-93 SEA	82	1869	463	.467	17	.304	234	.911	124	272	135	36	4	1177	14.4
93-94 CHA	73	1460	339	.459	59	.393	99	.780	80	224	125	36	8	836	11.5
95-96 IND	62	1002	180	.413	45	.352	70	.886	45	153	69	20	4	475	7.7
Totals	1069	30183	7334	.475	447	.331	3018	.841	1709	4539	2409	692	175	18133	17.0

ERVIN JOHNSON

Team: Denver Nuggets
Position: Center
Height: 6'11" **Weight:** 245
Birthdate: December 21, 1967

NBA Experience: 3 years
College: New Orleans
Acquired: Signed as a free agent, 7/96

Background: Johnson didn't play high school ball and nearly passed on college, too. He bagged groceries in a Baton Rouge, Louisiana, store for almost three years before soliciting a scholarship from New Orleans, where he set several school records. A late first-round choice, Johnson saw increased minutes in each of his three pro seasons in Seattle, starting for most of 1995-96. He joins the Nuggets for 1996-97.

Strengths: Johnson hails from Block High School, and blocks are what he does best. He averaged about a block-and-a-half per game last season, finishing among the top 20 in the league. E.J. was a defensive specialist in college who has done a decent job in the pros as well. He is a capable rebounder at both ends, he runs the floor well for a big man, and he plays within himself.

Weaknesses: For offense, Johnson is not your man. He is very limited with the ball in his hands, scoring most of his points off the glass and in transition. "Garbage points" are his offensive specialty. Johnson's hands are small and stiff, and he racks up far more turnovers than assists. He has no range to speak of, very little touch, and a questionable feel for the game. He misses far too many free throws.

Analysis: Johnson has worked on his low-post moves, but he will not become a first-rate offensive player at this level. What he provides is defense. He does an admirable job of battling big men in the post, and he also has the ability to defend forwards on the perimeter. He was quite effective in Seattle's aggressive, trapping style.

PLAYER SUMMARY	
Will	run, defend
Can't	shoot, score
Expect	blocked shots
Don't Expect	deft touch
Fantasy Value	$6-8
Card Value	8-12¢

COLLEGE STATISTICS

		G	FGP	FTP	RPG	PPG
89-90	NO	32	.579	.561	6.8	6.3
90-91	NO	30	.572	.537	12.2	12.7
91-92	NO	32	.584	.714	11.1	15.4
92-93	NO	29	.619	.674	11.9	18.4
Totals		123	.591	.646	10.5	13.1

NBA REGULAR-SEASON STATISTICS

			FGs		3-PT FGs		FTs		Rebounds						
	G	MIN	FG	PCT	FG	PCT	FT	PCT	OFF	TOT	AST	STL	BLK	PTS	PPG
93-94 SEA	45	280	44	.415	0	.000	29	.630	48	118	7	10	22	117	2.6
94-95 SEA	64	907	85	.443	0	.000	29	.630	101	289	16	17	67	199	3.1
95-96 SEA	81	1519	180	.511	1	.333	85	.669	129	433	48	40	129	446	5.5
Totals	190	2706	309	.475	1	.250	143	.653	278	840	71	67	218	762	4.0

KEVIN JOHNSON

Team: Phoenix Suns
Position: Guard
Height: 6'1" **Weight:** 190
Birthdate: March 4, 1966
NBA Experience: 9 years
College: California

Acquired: Traded from Cavaliers with Mark West, Tyrone Corbin, 1988 first- and second-round picks, and a 1989 second-round pick for Larry Nance, Mike Sanders, and a 1988 first-round pick, 2/88

Background: Johnson concluded his college career as California's all-time leader in scoring, assists, and steals. He averaged more than 21 points and 11 assists per game in his first four full seasons in Phoenix. Johnson won the Most Improved Player Award in 1988-89. A three-time NBA All-Star and Dream Team II member, he has been held back by groin, hamstring, and knee injuries.

Strengths: When Johnson is at full speed, there is virtually no one capable of stopping his one-on-one penetration. Leave him open from outside and he will bury 20-foot jumpers. His passing skills are made more devastating because he draws multiple defenders when he goes to the hoop. Johnson is approaching 1,000 career steals.

Weaknesses: Injuries are the primary concern, and a big one. Johnson's body has not allowed him to play more than 67 games in any of the last four seasons. Without him in the lineup, Phoenix is simply not the same team.

Analysis: When playing at 100 percent, Johnson is still one of the dominant lead guards in the NBA. Too often over the last several seasons, however, his teammates have not been able to count on him to be 100 percent, or even to be in uniform. He has been both a source of great hope and a cause of great frustration.

PLAYER SUMMARY	
Will	drive, dish, score
Can't	stay off injured list
Expect	classy leadership
Don't Expect	82 games
Fantasy Value	$25-30
Card Value	10-15¢

COLLEGE STATISTICS

		G	FGP	FTP	APG	PPG
83-84	CAL	28	.510	.721	2.3	9.7
84-85	CAL	27	.450	.662	4.1	12.9
85-86	CAL	29	.490	.815	6.0	15.6
86-87	CAL	34	.471	.819	5.0	17.2
Totals		118	.477	.757	4.4	14.0

NBA REGULAR-SEASON STATISTICS

		G	MIN	FGs FG	FGs PCT	3-PT FGs FG	3-PT FGs PCT	FTs FT	FTs PCT	Rebounds OFF	Rebounds TOT	AST	STL	BLK	PTS	PPG
87-88	CLE/PHO	80	1917	275	.461	5	.208	177	.839	36	191	437	103	24	732	9.1
88-89	PHO	81	3179	570	.505	2	.091	508	.882	46	340	991	135	24	1650	20.4
89-90	PHO	74	2782	578	.499	8	.195	501	.838	42	270	846	95	14	1665	22.5
90-91	PHO	77	2772	591	.516	9	.205	519	.843	54	271	781	163	11	1710	22.2
91-92	PHO	78	2899	539	.479	10	.217	448	.807	61	292	836	116	23	1536	19.7
92-93	PHO	49	1643	282	.499	1	.125	226	.819	30	104	384	85	20	791	16.1
93-94	PHO	67	2449	477	.487	6	.222	380	.819	55	167	637	125	10	1340	20.0
94-95	PHO	47	1352	246	.470	4	.154	234	.810	32	115	360	47	18	730	15.5
95-96	PHO	56	2007	342	.507	21	.368	342	.859	42	221	517	82	13	1047	18.7
Totals		609	21000	3900	.494	66	.224	3335	.837	398	1971	5789	951	157	11201	18.4

LARRY JOHNSON

Team: New York Knicks
Position: Forward
Height: 6'7" **Weight:** 250
Birthdate: March 14, 1969

NBA Experience: 5 years
College: Odessa; Nevada-Las Vegas
Acquired: Traded from Hornets for Anthony Mason and Brad Lohaus, 7/96

Background: L.J. originally signed with Southern Methodist, but he ended up at Odessa (Texas) Junior College after SMU officials questioned his retake of the SAT. UNLV won the national title in Johnson's first season there, and he was the nation's consensus Player of the Year in 1990-91. He was drafted No. 1 overall by Charlotte and won 1991-92 Rookie of the Year honors. He has since played in two All-Star Games and for Dream Team II.

Strengths: Johnson possesses incredible strength that carries over into virtually every aspect of the game. He can't be moved once he gets position on the low blocks. He scores in the post, on pull-ups, and from the 3-point arc. Johnson is one of the premier passing forwards in basketball, and he also rebounds and defends with tenacity. His career average approaches 20 PPG.

Weaknesses: A bad back that kept Johnson on the injured list for much of the 1993-94 season has been the only significant trouble spot for Johnson. He was a little more timid upon his return, although last season erased most of those doubts. Johnson plays aggressive defense, but he's not much of a shot-blocker.

Analysis: Some doubted whether Johnson would ever regain his All-Star form after his back troubles. Those critics, however, were awfully quiet during the 1995-96 season while Johnson scored 20-plus PPG for the second time in his career, regained his standing among the NBA's rebounding leaders, and put to rest any questions about his confidence. The Knicks can't wait for him to do it in New York.

PLAYER SUMMARY

Will......................score, pass, rebound
Can't ....sky for blocks
Expect...20 PPG
Don't Expect ....passive play
Fantasy Value $40-45
Card Value ....20-40¢

COLLEGE STATISTICS

		G	FGP	FTP	RPG	PPG
87-88	ODES	35	.649	.794	12.3	22.3
88-89	ODES	35	.653	.760	10.9	29.8
89-90	UNLV	40	.624	.767	11.4	20.6
90-91	UNLV	35	.662	.818	10.9	22.7
Totals		145	.648	.780	11.4	23.7

NBA REGULAR-SEASON STATISTICS

		G	MIN	FGs FG	FGs PCT	3-PT FGs FG	3-PT FGs PCT	FTs FT	FTs PCT	Rebounds OFF	Rebounds TOT	AST	STL	BLK	PTS	PPG
91-92	CHA	82	3047	616	.490	5	.227	339	.829	323	899	292	81	51	1576	19.2
92-93	CHA	82	3323	728	.526	18	.254	336	.767	281	864	353	53	27	1810	22.1
93-94	CHA	51	1757	346	.515	5	.238	137	.695	143	448	184	29	14	834	16.4
94-95	CHA	81	3234	585	.480	81	.386	274	.774	190	585	369	78	28	1525	18.8
95-96	CHA	81	3274	583	.476	67	.366	427	.757	249	683	355	55	43	1660	20.5
Totals		377	14635	2858	.496	176	.347	1513	.771	1186	3479	1553	296	163	7405	19.6

EDDIE JONES

Team: Los Angeles Lakers
Position: Guard/Forward
Height: 6'6" **Weight:** 190
Birthdate: October 20, 1971

NBA Experience: 2 years
College: Temple
Acquired: First-round pick in 1994 draft (tenth overall)

Background: Jones sat out his freshman year at Temple for academic reasons before easing into his college career. A two-year starter, he became the Atlantic 10 Conference's best player and finished his career as the first player in Temple history with 100 assists and 100 blocked shots. Jones, drafted tenth overall in 1994, was the highest-scoring Laker rookie since Magic Johnson and an All-Rookie first-teamer. His scoring dropped slightly in 1995-96.

Strengths: Jones is extraordinarily quick and loves to run. He flies up-court and is often rewarded with crowd-pleasing slams. He is a splendid leaper who is able to get past his man in a half-court set. He is able to get his own shot and has 3-point range. Jones, who led all rookies in steals (2.05 per game) two years ago, uses his quickness and wide wingspan on the defensive end. He is an explosive, energetic player in most areas.

Weaknesses: Jones is also a streaky player in most regards. He is capable of hitting for 30 points one night and dropping off to single digits the next. His 3-point shots were surprising as a rookie, but he's no longer taking anyone by surprise. Like a lot of disruptive defensive players, Jones is not afraid to take chances. He doesn't always get away with them.

Analysis: A starter in his first NBA game, Jones has been impressive for most of his first two seasons. That's not to say his game is complete. He will learn when to force the action and when to let the game come to him. Says teammate Cedric Ceballos, "He has the ability to be the best player in the West at the two-guard position." Jones is off to a flying start.

PLAYER SUMMARY	
Will	finish the break
Can't	handle the point
Expect	hustle plays
Don't Expect	lead feet
Fantasy Value	$18-21
Card Value	30-60¢

COLLEGE STATISTICS

		G	FGP	FTP	RPG	PPG
91-92	TEMP	29	.437	.547	4.2	11.4
92-93	TEMP	32	.458	.604	7.0	17.0
93-94	TEMP	31	.470	.662	6.8	19.2
Totals		92	.458	.614	6.1	16.0

NBA REGULAR-SEASON STATISTICS

				FGs		3-PT FGs		FTs		Rebounds						
		G	MIN	FG	PCT	FG	PCT	FT	PCT	OFF	TOT	AST	STL	BLK	PTS	PPG
94-95	LAL	64	1981	342	.460	91	.370	122	.722	79	249	128	131	41	897	14.0
95-96	LAL	70	2184	337	.492	83	.366	136	.739	45	233	246	129	45	893	12.8
Totals		134	4165	679	.475	174	.368	258	.731	124	482	374	260	86	1790	13.4

POPEYE JONES

Team: Toronto Raptors
Position: Forward
Height: 6'8" **Weight:** 265
Birthdate: June 17, 1970
NBA Experience: 3 years

College: Murray St.
Acquired: Traded from Mavericks with a 1997 first-round pick for Jimmy King and 1997 and 1998 first-round picks, 7/96

Background: A two-time Ohio Valley Conference Player of the Year and an NCAA Tournament regular at Murray State, Jones was drafted by Houston in the second round in 1992. He made his pro debut in the Italian A2 League. His rights were traded to Dallas, and he set a Mavs rookie record for rebounding. He has rated among the NBA leaders in that category each of the last two seasons. The Raptors traded for him in the off-season.

Strengths: He's Popeye the rebounding man. Jones has a massive frame and knows how to get to the boards on both ends of the floor. He really works at it and is quick off his feet for a big man. Jones has a great set of hands, is an outstanding passer, and has upped his scoring average. He hits hook shots and has made himself a reliable free-throw shooter.

Weaknesses: Jones is still not an offensive force, other than being one of the best offensive rebounders in the game. His range is 16 feet, his jumper is inconsistent, and he simply does not look to score much. His field-goal percentage is atrocious for an inside player. Jones has bettered his defense, but it does not come naturally.

Analysis: It's no secret where Jones will carve his niche in the NBA. On the backboards, there are few better. He amassed a team-record 28 rebounds against Indiana last season en route to a second consecutive year with a double-figure board average. Jones needs to fine-tune his game in other areas, but he's willing to work. Tendinitis in his knee slowed him late last season.

PLAYER SUMMARY

Will	control the glass
Can't	sky for blocks
Expect	double-doubles
Don't Expect	18 PPG
Fantasy Value	$1-3
Card Value	7-10¢

COLLEGE STATISTICS

		G	FGP	FTP	RPG	PPG
88-89	MSU	30	.489	.754	4.6	5.8
89-90	MSU	30	.500	.757	11.2	19.5
90-91	MSU	33	.493	.711	14.2	20.2
91-92	MSU	30	.488	.778	14.4	21.1
Totals		123	.493	.751	11.2	16.7

NBA REGULAR-SEASON STATISTICS

			FGs		3-PT FGs		FTs		Rebounds						
	G	MIN	FG	PCT	FG	PCT	FT	PCT	OFF	TOT	AST	STL	BLK	PTS	PPG
93-94 DAL	81	1773	195	.479	0	.000	78	.729	299	605	99	61	31	468	5.8
94-95 DAL	80	2385	372	.443	1	.083	80	.645	329	844	163	35	27	825	10.3
95-96 DAL	68	2322	327	.446	14	.359	102	.767	260	737	132	54	27	770	11.3
Totals	229	6480	894	.452	15	.288	260	.714	888	2186	394	150	85	2063	9.0

MICHAEL JORDAN

Team: Chicago Bulls
Position: Guard
Height: 6'6" **Weight:** 198
Birthdate: February 17, 1963

NBA Experience: 11 years
College: North Carolina
Acquired: First-round pick in 1984 draft (third overall)

Background: Jordan hit the winning basket in the 1982 NCAA championship game and went on to earn consensus All-America recognition. He earned NBA Rookie of the Year honors, was an All-Star in his first nine seasons and again last year, and has won four NBA championships, four league MVP Awards, four Finals MVP honors, and two Olympic golds. He retired before the 1993-94 season but returned in March 1995.

Strengths: Jordan is considered by many to be the greatest basketball player in history. He plays virtually every aspect of the game at its highest level, and he is one of the most intense competitors in sport. Sometimes Jordan's outstanding defensive skills, uncanny playmaking, and aggressive rebounding are overshadowed by his unparalleled shot-making.

Weaknesses: About the only thing Jordan cannot do is play major-league baseball. He tried as an outfielder, but he stalled in Double-A with a batting average just over .200. His stamina is not what it once was.

Analysis: Jordan's career scoring average is the highest in NBA/ABA annals, he was the NBA's Defensive Player of the Year in 1988, and he won his eighth league scoring crown in his first full year after chasing his baseball dream. He also led the Bulls to an unprecedented 72-win regular season.

PLAYER SUMMARY	
Will	take over games
Can't	accept losing
Expect	Hall of Fame honors
Don't Expect	a run at the PGA
Fantasy Value	$80-85
Card Value	$1.50-5.00

COLLEGE STATISTICS

		G	FGP	FTP	RPG	PPG
81-82	NC	34	.534	.722	4.4	13.5
82-83	NC	36	.535	.737	5.5	20.0
83-84	NC	31	.551	.779	5.3	19.6
Totals		101	.465	.748	5.0	17.7

NBA REGULAR-SEASON STATISTICS

		G	MIN	FGs FG	FGs PCT	3-PT FGs FG	3-PT FGs PCT	FTs FT	FTs PCT	Rebounds OFF	Rebounds TOT	AST	STL	BLK	PTS	PPG
84-85	CHI	82	3144	837	.515	9	.173	630	.845	167	534	481	196	69	2313	28.2
85-86	CHI	18	451	150	.457	3	.167	105	.840	23	64	53	37	21	408	22.7
86-87	CHI	82	3281	1098	.482	12	.182	833	.857	166	430	377	236	125	3041	37.1
87-88	CHI	82	3311	1069	.535	7	.132	723	.841	139	449	485	259	131	2868	35.0
88-89	CHI	81	3255	966	.538	27	.276	674	.850	149	652	650	234	65	2633	32.5
89-90	CHI	82	3197	1034	.526	92	.376	593	.848	143	565	519	227	54	2753	33.6
90-91	CHI	82	3034	990	.539	29	.312	571	.851	118	492	453	223	83	2580	31.5
91-92	CHI	80	3102	943	.519	27	.270	491	.832	91	511	489	182	75	2404	30.0
92-93	CHI	78	3067	992	.495	81	.352	476	.837	135	522	428	221	61	2541	32.6
94-95	CHI	17	668	166	.411	16	.500	109	.801	25	117	90	30	13	457	26.9
95-96	CHI	82	3090	916	.495	111	.427	548	.834	148	543	352	180	42	2491	30.4
Totals		766	29600	9161	.512	414	.332	5753	.844	1304	4879	4377	2025	739	24489	32.0

ADAM KEEFE

Team: Utah Jazz
Position: Forward
Height: 6'9" **Weight:** 241
Birthdate: February 22, 1970
NBA Experience: 4 years

College: Stanford
Acquired: Traded from Hawks for Tyrone Corbin and a 1995 second-round pick, 9/94

Background: Keefe was Stanford's rock in the middle, a three-time Pac-10 rebounding champion. The MVP of the NIT as a junior, he was also a world-class volleyball player. The tenth choice in the 1992 draft, Keefe played in 82 games as an Atlanta rookie before struggling the next season. His trade to Utah before the 1994-95 season put Keefe back into the rotation and helped his career.

Strengths: Keefe is big, strong, and smart. He plays within himself and thus has maintained a great field-goal percentage. He bangs the boards aggressively and is especially productive on the offensive glass. He is not afraid of contact. Keefe is also a pretty good face-up shooter within his limited range. He is a team player who makes the most of what he has.

Weaknesses: Keefe is not a good low-post player, which the Hawks learned the hard way, and he is a step slow when he goes to the hoop. He gets most of his points by crashing the boards and running the floor. Keefe does not intimidate defensively. Quicker forwards give him the most trouble; he can battle the bigger ones.

Analysis: The big redhead is clearly not one of the ten best players in his draft class. With Utah, however, he has been able to maximize his ability by coming off the bench as a role-player who does not need to score to make an impact. He was second on the Jazz in rebounding last season at 5.5 per game despite playing only slightly more than 20 minutes per contest. Keefe is a complementary player all the way.

PLAYER SUMMARY

Will.................................run, rebound
Can't ....light up the nets
Expect ....putbacks
Don't Expect ....10 PPG
Fantasy Value $1
Card Value ....5-8¢

COLLEGE STATISTICS

		G	FGP	FTP	RPG	PPG
88-89	STAN	33	.633	.689	5.4	8.4
89-90	STAN	30	.627	.725	9.1	20.0
90-91	STAN	33	.609	.760	9.5	21.5
91-92	STAN	29	.564	.746	12.2	25.3
Totals		125	.600	.736	9.0	18.6

NBA REGULAR-SEASON STATISTICS

				FGs		3-PT FGs		FTs		Rebounds						
		G	MIN	FG	PCT	FG	PCT	FT	PCT	OFF	TOT	AST	STL	BLK	PTS	PPG
92-93	ATL	82	1549	188	.500	0	.000	166	.700	171	432	80	57	16	542	6.6
93-94	ATL	63	763	96	.451	0	.000	81	.730	77	201	34	20	9	273	4.3
94-95	UTA	75	1270	172	.577	0	.000	117	.676	135	327	30	36	25	461	6.1
95-96	UTA	82	1708	180	.520	0	.000	139	.692	176	455	64	51	41	499	6.1
Totals		302	5290	636	.516	0	.000	503	.697	559	1415	208	164	91	1775	5.9

SHAWN KEMP

Team: Seattle SuperSonics
Position: Forward
Height: 6'10" **Weight:** 245
Birthdate: November 26, 1969

NBA Experience: 7 years
College: None
Acquired: First-round pick in 1989 draft (17th overall)

Background: Kemp never played a minute of college basketball. He was a Prop 48 casualty at Kentucky, transferred to Trinity Junior College amid scrutiny, then opted for the draft. He became a starter for the Sonics in his second season and has played in the last four All-Star Games. A Dream Team II member, Kemp enjoyed his best all-around season in 1995-96.

Strengths: Kemp's dunks made him famous, and he now has a well-rounded game to match. He is blessed with great quickness and dominating physical tools. He's strong and has a great vertical leap. Kemp is one of the best rebounding forwards in the league, and it is almost impossible to stop him one-on-one without fouling him. He also plays physical defense, blocks shots, and shoots a great percentage.

Weaknesses: Kemp stayed in more games last season than in the past, but he still picks up a lot of fouls because of his physical style. He also commits an inordinate number of turnovers. His ball-handling isn't the stuff of a guard.

Analysis: Kemp, a crowd-pleaser from the moment he stepped onto the NBA hardwood, is the main reason for Seattle's rise to prominence. He is a franchise player who has started the last two All-Star Games, and he put up numbers last season that had some people thinking MVP. He is certainly one of the very best power forwards in basketball.

PLAYER SUMMARY	
Will	dominate games
Can't	be stopped by one
Expect	20 PPG, 10 RPG
Don't Expect	All-Star snubs
Fantasy Value	$50-55
Card Value	30-75¢

COLLEGE STATISTICS

—DID NOT PLAY—

NBA REGULAR-SEASON STATISTICS

			FGs		3-PT FGs		FTs		Rebounds						
		G	MIN	FG	PCT	FG	PCT	FT	PCT	OFF	TOT	AST	STL	BLK	PTS	PPG
89-90	SEA	81	1120	203	.479	2	.167	117	.736	146	346	26	47	70	525	6.5
90-91	SEA	81	2442	462	.508	2	.167	288	.661	267	679	144	77	123	1214	15.0
91-92	SEA	64	1808	362	.504	0	.000	270	.748	264	665	86	70	124	994	15.5
92-93	SEA	78	2582	515	.492	0	.000	358	.712	287	833	155	119	146	1388	17.8
93-94	SEA	79	2597	533	.538	1	.250	364	.741	312	851	207	142	166	1431	18.1
94-95	SEA	82	2679	545	.547	2	.286	438	.749	318	893	149	102	122	1530	18.7
95-96	SEA	79	2631	526	.561	5	.417	276	.742	276	940	173	93	127	1550	19.6
Totals		544	15859	3146	.522	12	.222	2328	.728	1870	5171	940	650	878	8632	15.9

STEVE KERR

Team: Chicago Bulls
Position: Guard
Height: 6'3" **Weight:** 181
Birthdate: September 27, 1965

NBA Experience: 8 years
College: Arizona
Acquired: Signed as a free agent, 9/93

Background: Kerr was a second-team All-American as a senior at Arizona, where he set a Pac-10 record in 1987-88 by shooting an incredible .573 from 3-point range. He is the NBA's career leader in 3-point field-goal accuracy, although he has served mostly in a reserve role with Phoenix, Cleveland, Orlando, and Chicago. Kerr led the league in 3-point percentage two years ago and narrowly missed the title this past season, finishing second to Tim Legler.

Strengths: Kerr can shoot from anywhere. He hit better than 50 percent of his 3-point shots when the arc was deeper in 1989-90. The shorter distance adopted two years ago is a layup for him. Kerr is also a dead-eye free-throw shooter who makes smart passes. He is the definition of a team player.

Weaknesses: Kerr is not the most creative player, largely because he is a step slower than the average NBA guard. Take away his open looks and he has a hard time. Kerr gives away size, speed, or both to almost every one of his matchups. He has never been quite good enough to start.

Analysis: Kerr set an NBA record in 1994-95 when he connected on 52.4 percent of his 3-pointers, and he is liable to break it. No one has hit the trey at a better rate during his career. A coach's dream for his willingness to do whatever he is asked to do, Kerr played a significant role last year in helping the Bulls to the best record in NBA history.

PLAYER SUMMARY	
Will	drill 25-footers
Can't	crack starting lineup
Expect	remarkable accuracy
Don't Expect	complaints
Fantasy Value	$1
Card Value	7-10¢

COLLEGE STATISTICS

		G	FGP	FTP	RPG	PPG
83-84	ARIZ	28	.516	.692	1.2	7.1
84-85	ARIZ	31	.568	.803	2.4	10.0
85-86	ARIZ	32	.540	.899	3.2	14.4
87-88	ARIZ	38	.559	.824	2.0	12.6
Totals		129	.548	.815	2.2	11.2

NBA REGULAR-SEASON STATISTICS

				FGs		3-PT FGs		FTs		Rebounds						
		G	MIN	FG	PCT	FG	PCT	FT	PCT	OFF	TOT	AST	STL	BLK	PTS	PPG
88-89	PHO	26	157	20	.435	8	.471	6	.667	3	17	24	7	0	54	2.1
89-90	CLE	78	1664	192	.444	73	.507	63	.863	12	98	248	45	7	520	6.7
90-91	CLE	57	905	99	.444	28	.452	45	.849	5	37	131	29	4	271	4.8
91-92	CLE	48	847	121	.511	32	.432	45	.833	14	78	110	27	10	319	6.6
92-93	CLE/ORL	52	481	53	.434	6	.231	22	.917	5	45	70	10	1	134	2.6
93-94	CHI	82	2036	287	.497	52	.419	83	.856	26	131	210	75	3	709	8.6
94-95	CHI	82	1839	261	.527	89	.524	63	.778	20	119	151	44	3	674	8.2
95-96	CHI	82	1919	244	.506	122	.515	78	.929	25	110	192	63	2	688	8.4
Totals		507	9848	1277	.489	410	.480	405	.853	110	635	1136	300	30	3369	6.6

JEROME KERSEY

Team: Los Angeles Lakers
Position: Forward
Height: 6'7" **Weight:** 225
Birthdate: June 26, 1962

NBA Experience: 12 years
College: Longwood
Acquired: Signed as a free agent, 8/96

Background: Kersey rewrote the record books at NAIA Longwood College, where he became the all-time leader in points, rebounds, steals, and blocks. He started his pro career modestly before gaining consideration for the Most Improved Player Award in 1987-88, when he tallied 19.2 PPG. His scoring then dipped for six straight years. After 11 years in Portland, he played for Golden State in 1995-96 and joins the Lakers for 1996-97.

Strengths: Kersey hustles, rebounds, and comes up with a good share of steals for a forward. He's an exciting player in the open court, punctuating the fastbreak and chasing down opponents to block their layup attempts. He has enjoyed some high-scoring days.

Weaknesses: Kersey has struggled with shot selection, and his field-goal percentage reflects it. His conversion rate continues to decline (.410 last season). He's not a consistent jump-shooter or a good free-throw shooter. He is not the explosive scorer or solid defensive player he once was.

Analysis: Kersey was taken by Toronto in the 1995 expansion draft, but the Raptors let him go to the Warriors. He wound up starting 58 of 76 games and enjoyed a better season than most people anticipated he would have. He's at a point in his career, however, where he's getting by mainly on hustle.

PLAYER SUMMARY

Will ....chase down foes
Can't.............avoid shooting slumps
Expect ....full-court hustle
Don't Expect........................a stopper
Fantasy Value $0
Card Value ....7-10¢

COLLEGE STATISTICS

		G	FGP	FTP	RPG	PPG
80-81	LONG	28	.629	.586	8.9	16.9
81-82	LONG	23	.585	.633	11.3	17.0
82-83	LONG	25	.560	.608	10.8	14.6
83-84	LONG	27	.521	.606	14.2	19.6
Totals		103	.570	.607	11.3	17.0

NBA REGULAR-SEASON STATISTICS

		G	MIN	FGs		3-PT FGs		FTs		Rebounds		AST	STL	BLK	PTS	PPG
				FG	PCT	FG	PCT	FT	PCT	OFF	TOT					
84-85	POR	77	958	178	.478	0	.000	117	.646	95	206	63	49	29	473	6.1
85-86	POR	79	1217	258	.549	0	.000	156	.681	137	293	83	85	32	672	8.5
86-87	POR	82	2088	373	.509	1	.043	262	.720	201	496	194	122	77	1009	12.3
87-88	POR	79	2888	611	.499	3	.200	291	.735	211	657	243	127	65	1516	19.2
88-89	POR	76	2716	533	.469	6	.286	258	.694	246	629	243	137	84	1330	17.5
89-90	POR	82	2843	519	.478	3	.150	269	.690	251	690	188	121	63	1310	16.0
90-91	POR	73	2359	424	.478	4	.308	232	.720	169	481	227	101	76	1084	14.8
91-92	POR	77	2553	398	.467	1	.125	174	.664	241	633	243	114	71	971	12.6
92-93	POR	65	1719	281	.438	8	.286	116	.634	126	406	121	80	41	686	10.6
93-94	POR	78	1276	203	.433	1	.125	101	.748	130	331	75	71	49	508	6.5
94-95	POR	63	1143	203	.415	7	.259	95	.766	93	256	82	52	35	508	8.1
95-96	GS	76	1620	205	.410	3	.176	97	.660	154	363	114	91	45	510	6.7
Totals		907	23380	4186	.472	37	.196	2168	.697	2054	5441	1876	1150	667	10577	11.7

JASON KIDD

Team: Dallas Mavericks
Position: Guard
Height: 6'4" **Weight:** 208
Birthdate: March 23, 1973

NBA Experience: 2 years
College: California
Acquired: First-round pick in 1994 draft (second overall)

Background: A hotly recruited prep star in Oakland, California, Kidd stayed close to home with the Cal Bears and led the nation in steals per game as a freshman. He was the country's top assist man as a sophomore, earning All-America and Pac-10 Player of the Year honors. He left school two years early to join Dallas as the second overall draft pick in 1994. Kidd shared 1995 Rookie of the Year accolades with Grant Hill and started in the 1996 All-Star Game.

Strengths: Kidd is the best pure point guard to enter the NBA in years. He can get to the basket whenever he wants with his great quickness and strength. He owns uncanny playmaking skills and a knack for delivering the ball to the right place at the right time. Kidd's passes make highlight films as often as other players' dunks. No point guard in basketball hoards as many rebounds as Kidd, and few play harder on defense.

Weaknesses: The most glaring deficiency in this All-Star's game is his perimeter shooting. He is not reliable from the outside, which begs defenders to sag. Though he has 3-point range, Kidd connected on only one-third of his attempts last season and shot less than 40 percent from the field.

Analysis: Is Kidd the next Magic Johnson? While it's too early to draw that conclusion, you've got to like his chances. Recall, the 1996-97 season should be his rookie year. Kidd posted a triple-double in his first NBA game and now records them almost routinely. He is one of the top five in the league in assists and steals, and he can score in bunches, too. He'll be unstoppable when he develops a better jumper.

PLAYER SUMMARY	
Will	score, pass, rebound
Can't	make living with treys
Expect	triple-doubles
Don't Expect	soft defense
Fantasy Value	$25-30
Card Value	60¢-$1.25

COLLEGE STATISTICS

		G	FGP	FTP	APG	PPG
92-93	CAL	29	.463	.657	7.7	13.0
93-94	CAL	30	.472	.692	9.1	16.7
Totals		59	.468	.677	8.4	14.9

NBA REGULAR-SEASON STATISTICS

				FGs		3-PT FGs		FTs		Rebounds						
		G	MIN	FG	PCT	FG	PCT	FT	PCT	OFF	TOT	AST	STL	BLK	PTS	PPG
94-95	DAL	79	2668	330	.385	70	.272	192	.698	152	430	607	151	24	922	11.7
95-96	DAL	81	3034	493	.381	133	.336	229	.692	203	553	783	175	26	1348	16.6
Totals		160	5702	823	.383	203	.311	421	.695	355	983	1390	326	50	2270	14.2

CHRIS KING

Unrestricted Free Agent
Last Team: Vancouver Grizzlies
Position: Forward
Height: 6'8" **Weight:** 215
Birthdate: July 24, 1969

NBA Experience: 2 years
College: Wake Forest
Acquired: Signed as a free agent, 10/95

Background: King enjoyed a solid but unspectacular career at Wake Forest, averaging 15.3 points and 5.1 rebounds per game as a senior and making 52 percent of his career field-goal attempts. King was drafted 45th overall by Seattle in 1992 but played his first pro ball in Spain. He played 15 games for the Sonics in 1993-94, then spent the 1994-95 season in Greece. His NBA breakthrough came last season with the expansion Grizzlies.

Strengths: For starters, King is a fine athlete. He loves to run and is capable of grabbing a defensive rebound, making the outlet pass, and beating the opposition down the court for a jam. He works hard at both ends of the floor and possesses a promising face-up game with range to the 3-point arc. He looks for his teammates, plays hard on defense, and is a capable rebounder.

Weaknesses: King is not a big-time scoring threat. He can knock down jumpers, but his ball-handling is weak and he does little off the dribble. He got to the line less than twice a game despite starting for most of last season, and when he did get there he converted a low percentage. He is not a threat to burn you from the post, either. He lacks the strength to be a defensive stopper.

Analysis: King holds the distinction of having scored Vancouver's first-ever points. He made a layup in the team's opening game at Portland last year. King enjoyed some nice efforts in his first full NBA season after averaging 16.9 points and 9.2 rebounds per game in Greece during the 1994-95 campaign. His extensive experience overseas helped him, but so did playing on the worst team in the league. He needs to sharpen his offensive skills.

PLAYER SUMMARY	
Will	hustle on defense
Can't	dribble like a guard
Expect	transition scoring
Don't Expect	10 PPG
Fantasy Value	$0
Card Value	12-25¢

COLLEGE STATISTICS

		G	FGP	FTP	RPG	PPG
88-89	WF	28	.540	.654	6.1	14.4
89-90	WF	28	.546	.589	7.4	16.1
90-91	WF	30	.489	.636	5.7	15.1
91-92	WF	27	.505	.693	5.1	15.3
Totals		113	.519	.640	6.1	15.2

NBA REGULAR-SEASON STATISTICS

				FGs		3-PT FGs		FTs		Rebounds						
		G	MIN	FG	PCT	FG	PCT	FT	PCT	OFF	TOT	AST	STL	BLK	PTS	PPG
93-94	SEA	15	86	19	.396	2	.286	15	.577	5	15	11	4	0	55	3.7
95-96	VAN	80	1930	250	.427	44	.389	90	.662	102	285	104	68	33	634	7.9
Totals		95	2016	269	.425	46	.383	105	.648	107	300	115	72	33	689	7.3

JOE KLEINE

Team: Phoenix Suns
Position: Center
Height: 7'0" **Weight:** 271
Birthdate: January 4, 1962

NBA Experience: 11 years
College: Notre Dame; Arkansas
Acquired: Signed as a free agent, 8/93

Background: Kleine, who transferred to Arkansas after a year at Notre Dame, led the Razorbacks in scoring as a junior and senior and was a member of the 1984 U.S. Olympic team. He averaged 9.8 PPG with Sacramento in 1987-88, his best statistical season. He has served as a reserve for the better part of five-plus years with Boston and three with Phoenix.

Strengths: Opponents cringe when Kleine checks in to the game. He uses his huge body to put the hurt on people. He rebounds, sets hard picks, and makes his fouls count. Kleine is a pretty good shooter with decent range, and he hits his free throws.

Weaknesses: Finesse has no place in Kleine's game. He possesses poor hands and should be forbidden to dribble the ball. Foul trouble would be a problem if he saw more than about 12 minutes per game.

Analysis: Kleine knows his job and performs it with an exemplary work ethic. He has been a favorite of teammates, fans, and coaches because he does whatever is asked of him. He is hardly the center you want in your starting lineup, but off the bench he can be a nice fit. A fainting incident late last season will not keep him from playing.

PLAYER SUMMARY

Will ....cause pain
Can't...........................grab headlines
Expect ....a decent shooter
Don't Expect............................finesse
Fantasy Value $0
Card Value ....5-7¢

COLLEGE STATISTICS

		G	FGP	FTP	RPG	PPG
80-81	ND	29	.640	.750	2.4	2.6
82-83	ARK	30	.537	.633	7.3	13.3
83-84	ARK	32	.595	.773	9.2	18.2
84-85	ARK	35	.607	.720	8.4	22.1
Totals		126	.587	.723	7.0	14.5

NBA REGULAR-SEASON STATISTICS

		G	MIN	FGs FG	FGs PCT	3-PT FGs FG	3-PT FGs PCT	FT	FTs PCT	Rebounds OFF	Rebounds TOT	AST	STL	BLK	PTS	PPG
85-86	SAC	80	1180	160	.465	0	.000	94	.723	113	373	46	24	34	414	5.2
86-87	SAC	79	1658	256	.471	0	.000	110	.786	173	483	71	35	30	622	7.9
87-88	SAC	82	1999	324	.472	0	.000	153	.814	179	579	93	28	59	801	9.8
88-89	SAC/BOS	75	1411	175	.405	0	.000	134	.882	124	378	67	33	23	484	6.5
89-90	BOS	81	1365	176	.480	0	.000	83	.830	117	355	46	15	27	435	5.4
90-91	BOS	72	850	102	.468	0	.000	54	.783	71	244	21	15	14	258	3.6
91-92	BOS	70	991	144	.491	4	.500	34	.708	94	296	32	23	14	326	4.7
92-93	BOS	78	1129	108	.404	0	.000	41	.707	113	346	39	17	17	257	3.3
93-94	PHO	74	848	125	.488	5	.455	30	.769	50	193	45	14	19	285	3.9
94-95	PHO	75	968	119	.449	0	.000	42	.857	82	259	39	14	18	280	3.7
95-96	PHO	56	663	71	.420	2	.286	20	.800	36	132	44	13	6	164	2.9
Totals		822	13062	1760	.458	11	.256	795	.797	1152	3638	543	231	261	4326	5.3

JON KONCAK

Team: Orlando Magic
Position: Center
Height: 7'0" **Weight:** 250
Birthdate: May 17, 1963

NBA Experience: 11 years
College: Southern Methodist
Acquired: Signed as a free agent, 10/95

Background: Koncak concluded his career at Southern Methodist as the school's all-time leader in rebounds, blocked shots, and field-goal accuracy. He won a gold medal with the 1984 Olympic team. Koncak spent his first ten NBA seasons with Atlanta before signing a free-agent deal with Orlando before the 1995-96 campaign.

Strengths: Koncak is a solid defensive player. He understands the concept of position defense and is willing to fight for his spot. He brings good size to the middle. He almost never turns the ball over. Koncak knows his role and accepts it. He is a team player.

Weaknesses: Koncak offers next to nothing offensively, which is why Atlanta fans viewed him as an overpaid bust. He has not averaged even 6.0 PPG since his rookie year, and even his once-accurate jumper has failed him. Koncak's low-post game is weak, and ball-handling is out of the question.

Analysis: Koncak sounds like contract, and he first became famous for signing a six-year, $13.2 million deal in 1989 that had fans in Atlanta scratching their heads. Once it expired, the Hawks were happy to see him go. He filled in admirably for the Magic last season when Shaquille O'Neal was injured, but now that Shaq's gone, Koncak is likely to see more playing time.

PLAYER SUMMARY	
Will	play defense
Can't	do much else
Expect	backup minutes
Don't Expect	even 5 PPG
Fantasy Value	$0
Card Value	5-7¢

COLLEGE STATISTICS

		G	FGP	FTP	RPG	PPG
81-82	SMU	27	.461	.620	5.7	10.0
82-83	SMU	30	.527	.691	9.4	14.6
83-84	SMU	33	.621	.607	11.5	15.5
84-85	SMU	33	.592	.667	10.7	17.2
Totals		123	.559	.649	9.5	14.5

NBA REGULAR-SEASON STATISTICS

		G	MIN	FGs FG	FGs PCT	3-PT FGs FG	3-PT FGs PCT	FTs FT	FTs PCT	Rebounds OFF	Rebounds TOT	AST	STL	BLK	PTS	PPG
85-86	ATL	82	1695	263	.507	0	.000	156	.607	171	467	55	37	69	682	8.3
86-87	ATL	82	1684	169	.480	0	.000	125	.654	153	493	31	52	76	463	5.6
87-88	ATL	49	1073	98	.483	0	.000	83	.610	103	333	19	36	56	279	5.7
88-89	ATL	74	1531	141	.524	0	.000	63	.553	147	453	56	54	98	345	4.7
89-90	ATL	54	977	78	.614	0	.000	42	.532	58	226	23	38	34	198	3.7
90-91	ATL	77	1931	140	.436	1	.125	32	.593	101	375	124	74	76	313	4.1
91-92	ATL	77	1489	111	.391	0	.000	19	.655	62	261	132	50	67	241	3.1
92-93	ATL	78	1975	124	.464	3	.375	24	.480	100	427	140	75	100	275	3.5
93-94	ATL	82	1823	159	.431	0	.000	24	.667	83	365	102	63	125	342	4.2
94-95	ATL	62	943	77	.412	12	.333	13	.542	23	184	52	36	45	179	2.9
95-96	ORL	67	1288	84	.480	3	.333	32	.561	63	272	51	27	44	203	3.0
Totals		784	16409	1444	.470	19	.226	613	.597	1064	3856	785	542	790	3520	4.5

TONI KUKOC

Team: Chicago Bulls
Position: Forward/Guard
Height: 6'10" **Weight:** 230
Birthdate: September 18, 1968

NBA Experience: 3 years
College: None
Acquired: Second-round pick in 1990 draft (29th overall)

Background: Kukoc was considered one of the greatest players ever in Europe, starring in the Italian 1A League and earning several Player of the Year honors. He averaged 19 points, six rebounds, and five assists a game in his final year overseas. The Bulls drafted him in the second round in 1990 and finally lured him to the NBA in 1993-94. The 1995-96 Sixth Man Award winner has played both forward positions in his three years with Chicago.

Strengths: Kukoc does a little bit of everything, including shooting with 3-point range, handling the ball, rebounding, and finding the open man. In many ways, he's a lead guard in the body of a forward. The left-hander is most dangerous when he drives to the bucket, as he can score with a number of deceptive moves or create easy shots for teammates. When Kukoc gets on a roll, he is lethal.

Weaknesses: Kukoc, who was accustomed to playing zone defense in Europe, still has some trouble guarding NBA players man-to-man. He lacks the lateral quickness to stop speedy small forwards and can be overpowered by power forwards. A streaky player, he is prone to disappearing acts from time to time.

Analysis: Kukoc, who was first seen by many American basketball fans on Croatia's silver medal-winning Olympic team in 1992, has had his ups and downs in three NBA seasons. His second year saw the return of Michael Jordan to the Bulls, and last season he wound up sharing time at power forward with the eccentric Dennis Rodman. Kukoc has handled himself well through it all, and he finds ways to contribute with a wide variety of abilities.

PLAYER SUMMARY	
Will	handle the ball
Can't	outscore Jordan, Pippen
Expect	creative drives
Don't Expect	a stopper
Fantasy Value	$19-22
Card Value	15-30¢

COLLEGE STATISTICS

—DID NOT PLAY—

NBA REGULAR-SEASON STATISTICS

			FGs		3-PT FGs		FTs		Rebounds						
	G	MIN	FG	PCT	FG	PCT	FT	PCT	OFF	TOT	AST	STL	BLK	PTS	PPG
93-94 CHI	75	1808	313	.431	32	.271	156	.743	98	297	252	81	33	814	10.9
94-95 CHI	81	2584	487	.504	62	.313	235	.748	155	440	372	102	16	1271	15.7
95-96 CHI	81	2103	386	.490	87	.403	206	.772	115	323	287	64	28	1065	13.1
Totals	237	6495	1186	.478	181	.340	597	.755	368	1060	911	247	77	3150	13.3

CHRISTIAN LAETTNER

Team: Atlanta Hawks
Position: Forward/Center
Height: 6'11" **Weight:** 245
Birthdate: August 17, 1969
NBA Experience: 4 years

College: Duke
Acquired: Traded from Timberwolves with Sean Rooks for Andrew Lang and Spud Webb, 2/96

Background: The only college player on the 1992 Olympic Dream Team, Laettner was named national Player of the Year as a senior and was the catalyst behind Duke's back-to-back NCAA titles in 1991 and 1992. He is the only player in history to start in four Final Fours. The third selection in the 1992 draft, he spent three-plus seasons in Minnesota before his February trade to Atlanta last year.

Strengths: Laettner poses matchup problems because of his ability to score on the perimeter. He has good range with his jumper, yet is strong enough to get inside for short bank shots, dunks, and trips to the line. He is solid fundamentally and mentally tough, and he can fill in at center in addition to his natural power forward position. Laettner is an unselfish player who handles the ball and is able to spot the open man.

Weaknesses: Abrasive. Annoying. Cocky. All have been used to describe Laettner, who was not popular with the Minneapolis media and had turned off several teammates as well. Laettner has not lived up to his lofty expectations. His low-post game lags well behind his perimeter skills, and he shows few signs of being a dominant scorer or rebounder. His defense has been suspect.

Analysis: Laettner is a tough man to solve. He keeps pretty much to himself away from basketball, and on the court he has seemingly never progressed since his rookie season. In fact, until last season, his scoring had been in a slow decline. To his credit, some players would love to put up numbers like 16 points, seven boards, and three assists per game. The Hawks are hoping for more.

PLAYER SUMMARY

Will ....find open men
Can't ....shake his critics
Expect ....matchup troubles
Don't Expect ....an easy read
Fantasy Value $35-40
Card Value ....10-15¢

COLLEGE STATISTICS

		G	FGP	FTP	RPG	PPG
88-89	DUKE	36	.723	.717	4.7	8.9
89-90	DUKE	38	.511	.836	9.6	16.3
90-91	DUKE	39	.575	.802	8.7	19.8
91-92	DUKE	35	.575	.815	7.9	21.5
Totals		148	.574	.806	7.8	16.6

NBA REGULAR-SEASON STATISTICS

		G	MIN	FGs FG	FGs PCT	3-PT FGs FG	3-PT FGs PCT	FTs FT	FTs PCT	Rebounds OFF	Rebounds TOT	AST	STL	BLK	PTS	PPG
92-93	MIN	81	2823	503	.474	4	.100	462	.835	171	708	223	105	83	1472	18.2
93-94	MIN	70	2428	396	.448	6	.240	375	.783	160	602	307	87	86	1173	16.8
94-95	MIN	81	2770	450	.489	13	.325	409	.818	164	613	234	101	87	1322	16.3
95-96	MIN/ATL	74	2495	442	.487	9	.231	324	.818	184	538	197	71	71	1217	16.4
Totals		306	10516	1791	.475	32	.222	1570	.814	679	2461	961	364	327	5184	16.9

ANDREW LANG

Team: Milwaukee Bucks
Position: Center
Height: 6'11" **Weight:** 250
Birthdate: June 28, 1966

NBA Experience: 8 years
College: Arkansas
Acquired: Traded from Timberwolves for a future first-round pick, 7/96

Background: Lang completed his collegiate career at Arkansas as the school's all-time leader in blocked shots. A second-rounder in 1988, he blocked a career-high 201 shots with Phoenix in 1991-92. Lang went to Philadelphia in the 1992 trade that sent Charles Barkley to Phoenix, then played just over two years in Atlanta and part of last season with the T'wolves before being dealt to the Bucks in the off-season.

Strengths: Lang is a hard worker who stands tall on defense. He has blocked more than 1,000 shots in his eight seasons and has rated among the league's top 15 in each of the last two years. He is blessed with lateral quickness and good instincts. Lang has dramatically improved his low-post offense and his free-throw shooting.

Weaknesses: Lang has never been a scorer. Most of his points come from within a few feet of the hoop. His field-goal accuracy over the last four seasons has been dismal. Lang does not handle the ball or pass particularly well, he picks up a lot of fouls, and he is a below-average rebounder for a starting center.

Analysis: Lang averaged double figures in the scoring column for the first time last season. It's a direct result of his off-season work. "There comes a time when you want more," Lang said last year, after spending his early years as little more than a defensive specialist. Lang is the perfect example that sometimes you have to be patient with big men.

PLAYER SUMMARY	
Will	challenge shots
Can't	average 20 PPG
Expect	100-plus blocks
Don't Expect	dominant rebounding
Fantasy Value	$3-5
Card Value	7-10¢

COLLEGE STATISTICS

		G	FGP	FTP	RPG	PPG
84-85	ARK	33	.405	.563	2.0	2.6
85-86	ARK	26	.466	.607	6.5	8.2
86-87	ARK	32	.500	.644	7.5	8.1
87-88	ARK	30	.527	.450	7.3	9.3
Totals		121	.489	.575	5.7	6.9

NBA REGULAR-SEASON STATISTICS

		G	MIN	FGs		3-PT FGs		FTs		Rebounds		AST	STL	BLK	PTS	PPG
				FG	PCT	FG	PCT	FT	PCT	OFF	TOT					
88-89	PHO	62	526	60	.513	0	.000	39	.650	54	147	9	17	48	159	2.6
89-90	PHO	74	1011	97	.557	0	.000	64	.653	83	271	21	22	133	258	3.5
90-91	PHO	63	1152	109	.577	0	.000	93	.715	113	303	27	17	127	311	4.9
91-92	PHO	81	1965	248	.522	0	.000	126	.768	170	546	43	48	201	622	7.7
92-93	PHI	73	1861	149	.425	1	.200	87	.763	136	436	79	46	141	386	5.3
93-94	ATL	82	1608	215	.469	1	.250	73	.689	126	313	51	38	87	504	6.1
94-95	ATL	82	2340	320	.473	2	.667	152	.809	154	456	72	45	144	794	9.7
95-96	ATL/MIN	71	2365	353	.447	1	.200	125	.801	153	455	65	42	126	832	11.7
Totals		588	12828	1551	.480	5	.263	759	.747	989	2927	367	275	1007	3866	6.6

TIM LEGLER

Team: Washington Bullets
Position: Guard
Height: 6'4" **Weight:** 200
Birthdate: December 26, 1966

NBA Experience: 6 years
College: La Salle
Acquired: Signed as a free agent, 9/95

Background: Legler shot .456 from 3-point range in four years at La Salle, where he was a teammate of Lionel Simmons. Though undrafted, he has played six NBA seasons with six different teams. He is also a veteran of the USBL and WBL and has played in four CBA All-Star Games. Legler posted his best NBA season in 1995-96 after being spared from another CBA campaign by the Bullets.

Strengths: Legler is a pure shooter, possessing a beautiful long-range stroke that every guard in the NBA should admire. He led the league in 3-point percentage last season, draining better than half his shots from that distance. He also won the NBA's Long Distance Shootout with a record 65 points. He makes his free throws and works his tail off.

Weaknesses: Legler's deficiencies start with his lack of speed and quickness. He's not among the better athletes in the NBA. Most of his matchups have a step on him, which hurts Legler on defense. Offensively, he rarely uses his dribble to create shots for himself or teammates. He is a complementary player.

Analysis: At a time when the art of shooting has been lost on a lot of players, Legler is something of a throwback. His jumper is a sight to behold, and it's hard to imagine him returning to the CBA anytime soon. Legler is the definition of a man who has paid his dues. He's a likable guy who takes his job seriously and provides instant offense.

PLAYER SUMMARY	
Will	hit treys, free throws
Can't	unpack his bags
Expect	instant offense
Don't Expect	a CBA return
Fantasy Value	$1
Card Value	5-7¢

COLLEGE STATISTICS

		G	FGP	FTP	RPG	PPG
84-85	LaS	26	.469	.708	2.8	6.0
85-86	LaS	28	.502	.833	3.9	12.9
86-87	LaS	33	.478	.782	4.5	18.7
87-88	LaS	34	.502	.803	4.1	16.7
Totals		121	.490	.791	3.9	14.0

NBA REGULAR-SEASON STATISTICS

				FGs		3-PT FGs		FTs		Rebounds						
		G	MIN	FG	PCT	FG	PCT	FT	PCT	OFF	TOT	AST	STL	BLK	PTS	PPG
89-90	PHO	11	83	11	.379	0	.000	6	1.000	4	8	6	2	0	28	2.5
90-91	DEN	10	148	25	.347	3	.250	5	.833	8	18	12	2	0	58	5.8
92-93	UTA/DAL	33	635	105	.436	22	.338	57	.803	25	59	46	24	6	289	8.8
93-94	DAL	79	1322	231	.438	52	.374	142	.840	36	128	120	52	13	656	8.3
94-95	GS	24	371	60	.522	26	.520	30	.882	12	40	27	12	1	176	7.3
95-96	WAS	77	1775	233	.507	128	.522	132	.863	29	140	136	45	12	726	9.4
Totals		234	4334	665	.460	231	.451	372	.847	114	393	347	137	32	1933	8.3

ALTON LISTER

Team: Boston Celtics
Position: Center
Height: 7'0" **Weight:** 248
Birthdate: October 1, 1958
NBA Experience: 14 years

College: San Jacinto; Arizona St.
Acquired: Traded from Milwaukee with Todd Day for Sherman Douglas, 11/95

Background: Lister completed his three-year career at Arizona State ranked first in career blocks. He blocked more than 100 shots in each of his first eight NBA seasons before injuries and age began to catch up with him. He played with his fourth pro team—not counting his time spent in the Italian League—in 1995-96 after a trade sent him from Milwaukee to Boston.

Strengths: Lister has always been known for defense, and he still plays it relatively well. He knows where to position himself, uses his body well, and still gets up to challenge shots. Lister leaves the shooting to others.

Weaknesses: Offense has never been high on Lister's priority list. Only once in his 14-year career has he averaged double figures. He is a poor shooter, ball-handler, and passer with a weak low-post game. Enough said.

Analysis: Lister started 14 of 57 games in Boston last season, a sure sign of Celtic troubles in the middle. Lister is someone you want on the floor for perhaps eight or ten minutes to spell your regular big men. His best asset these days is his know-how.

PLAYER SUMMARY	
Will	get defensive position
Can't	dribble, pass, score
Expect	spot minutes
Don't Expect	a long-term deal
Fantasy Value	$0
Card Value	5-7¢

COLLEGE STATISTICS

		G	FGP	FTP	RPG	PPG
76-77	SJ	40	—	—	16.0	17.0
78-79	ASU	29	.498	.560	6.7	8.8
79-80	ASU	27	.504	.558	8.6	12.0
80-81	ASU	26	.560	.691	9.7	15.4
Totals		122	.523	.611	10.8	13.6

NBA REGULAR-SEASON STATISTICS

		G	MIN	FGs FG	FGs PCT	3-PT FGs FG	3-PT FGs PCT	FTs FT	FTs PCT	Rebounds OFF	Rebounds TOT	AST	STL	BLK	PTS	PPG
81-82	MIL	80	1186	149	.519	0	.000	64	.520	108	387	84	18	118	362	4.5
82-83	MIL	80	1885	272	.529	0	.000	130	.537	168	568	111	50	177	674	8.4
83-84	MIL	82	1955	256	.500	0	.000	114	.626	156	603	110	41	140	626	7.6
84-85	MIL	81	2091	322	.538	0	.000	154	.588	219	647	127	49	167	798	9.9
85-86	MIL	81	1812	318	.551	0	.000	160	.602	199	592	101	49	142	796	9.8
86-87	SEA	75	2288	346	.504	0	.000	179	.675	223	705	110	32	180	871	11.6
87-88	SEA	82	1812	173	.504	1	.500	114	.606	200	627	58	27	140	461	5.6
88-89	SEA	82	1806	271	.499	0	.000	115	.646	207	545	54	28	180	657	8.0
89-90	GS	3	40	4	.500	0	.000	4	.571	5	8	2	1	0	12	4.0
90-91	GS	77	1552	188	.478	0	.000	115	.569	121	483	93	20	90	491	6.4
91-92	GS	26	293	44	.557	0	.000	14	.424	21	92	14	5	16	102	3.9
92-93	GS	20	174	19	.452	0	.000	7	.538	15	44	5	0	9	45	2.3
94-95	MIL	60	776	66	.493	0	.000	35	.500	67	236	12	16	57	167	2.8
95-96	MIL/BOS	64	735	51	.486	0	.000	41	.641	67	280	19	6	42	143	2.2
Totals		893	18405	2479	.514	1	.111	1246	.595	1776	5817	900	342	1458	6205	6.9

GRANT LONG

Team: Detroit Pistons
Position: Forward
Height: 6'9" **Weight:** 248
Birthdate: March 12, 1966
NBA Experience: 8 years

College: Eastern Michigan
Acquired: Traded from Hawks with Stacey Augmon for future considerations, 7/96

Background: As a senior at Eastern Michigan, Long was named Mid-American Conference Player of the Year and MVP of the MAC Tournament. He was one of the NBA's most improved players during the 1991-92 campaign. He was traded from Miami to Atlanta two games into the 1994-95 season. Long enjoyed his best statistical season in 1995-96 before being swapped to Detroit.

Strengths: Long is one of the hardest-working players in basketball. He attacks the boards, runs the floor, plays go-get-'em defense, and can also score. Coaches love his attitude and his willingness to give 100 percent. He is a fine medium-range jump-shooter who excels in transition. He also gets several steals and is an alert passer.

Weaknesses: Long used to be an annual contender for the league lead in fouls, and he still picks up his share. He is an undersized power forward who runs into a little trouble against the better players with three or four inches on him. Long is not much of a low-post scorer, where again his size comes into play.

Analysis: Long is not the most gifted player you'll find, but there are few who work harder. You know what you're going to get from him, and he seems to squeeze a little more out of his ability every year. Long scored a career-high 13.1 PPG last season and came close to averaging a double-double with 9.6 RPG, also a personal best.

PLAYER SUMMARY

Will	maximize his talents
Can't	rely on post moves
Expect	double-doubles
Don't Expect	slack defense
Fantasy Value	$7-9
Card Value	7-10¢

COLLEGE STATISTICS

		G	FGP	FTP	RPG	PPG
84-85	EMU	28	.564	.609	4.0	4.1
85-86	EMU	27	.526	.644	6.6	8.6
86-87	EMU	29	.549	.725	9.0	14.9
87-88	EMU	30	.555	.765	10.4	23.0
Totals		114	.549	.725	7.6	12.9

NBA REGULAR-SEASON STATISTICS

				FGs		3-PT FGs		FTs		Rebounds						
		G	MIN	FG	PCT	FG	PCT	FT	PCT	OFF	TOT	AST	STL	BLK	PTS	PPG
88-89	MIA	82	2435	336	.486	0	.000	304	.749	240	546	149	122	48	976	11.9
89-90	MIA	81	1856	257	.483	0	.000	172	.714	156	402	96	91	38	686	8.5
90-91	MIA	80	2514	276	.492	1	.167	181	.787	225	568	176	119	43	734	9.2
91-92	MIA	82	3063	440	.494	6	.273	326	.807	259	691	225	139	40	1212	14.8
92-93	MIA	76	2728	397	.469	6	.231	261	.765	197	568	182	104	31	1061	14.0
93-94	MIA	69	2201	300	.446	1	.167	187	.786	190	495	170	89	26	788	11.4
94-95	MIA/ATL	81	2641	342	.478	11	.355	244	.751	191	606	131	109	34	939	11.6
95-96	ATL	82	3008	395	.471	31	.360	257	.763	248	788	183	108	34	1078	13.1
Totals		633	20446	2743	.477	56	.303	1932	.766	1706	4664	1312	881	294	7474	11.8

LUC LONGLEY

Team: Chicago Bulls
Position: Center
Height: 7'2" **Weight:** 292
Birthdate: January 19, 1969

NBA Experience: 5 years
College: New Mexico
Acquired: Traded from Timberwolves for Stacey King, 2/94

Background: Originally from Perth, Australia, Longley was coveted by pro scouts from the day he set foot on New Mexico's campus. He never emerged as a consistent force in college despite becoming the school's top career scorer and rebounder. After struggling with Minnesota, he was traded to Chicago in 1994 and has started in the pivot.

Strengths: The soft-handed Longley has refined skills for a seven-footer. He is a very good passer, and he can score in the post or with the face-up jumper. He is an unselfish player with a good sense of where and when to deliver the ball. Longley also uses his big body on the defensive end and blocks more than a shot per game.

Weaknesses: The big Aussie has been inconsistent for as long as anyone can recall. His intensity, desire, and ability to take the game seriously have been questioned. The fact that he is not an aggressive offensive player has not been a problem for the talented Bulls. Longley does not possess good foot speed, and knee and leg injuries have hampered him.

Analysis: In many ways, Longley has been the perfect fit for Chicago. The Bulls have enough scorers, and Longley's passing ability is custom-made for the famed triangle offense. Not many No. 7 picks would be content to be a role-player after five years, but Longley seems to have little desire to become a standout. He did average a career-high 9.1 PPG in 1995-96. He's a hard player to figure.

PLAYER SUMMARY	
Will	keep the ball moving
Can't	take over on offense
Expect	soft hands
Don't Expect	quickness
Fantasy Value	$3-5
Card Value	5-8¢

COLLEGE STATISTICS

		G	FGP	FTP	RPG	PPG
87-88	NM	35	.500	.392	2.7	4.0
88-89	NM	33	.578	.769	6.8	13.0
89-90	NM	34	.559	.821	9.7	18.4
90-91	NM	30	.656	.716	9.2	19.1
Totals		132	.586	.735	7.0	13.4

NBA REGULAR-SEASON STATISTICS

			FGs		3-PT FGs		FTs		Rebounds						
	G	MIN	FG	PCT	FG	PCT	FT	PCT	OFF	TOT	AST	STL	BLK	PTS	PPG
91-92 MIN	66	991	114	.458	0	.000	53	.663	67	257	53	35	64	281	4.3
92-93 MIN	55	1045	133	.455	0	.000	53	.716	71	240	51	47	77	319	5.8
93-94 MIN/CHI	76	1502	219	.471	0	.000	90	.720	129	433	109	45	79	528	6.9
94-95 CHI	55	1001	135	.447	0	.000	88	.822	82	263	73	24	45	358	6.5
95-96 CHI	62	1641	242	.482	0	.000	80	.777	104	318	119	22	84	564	9.1
Totals	314	6180	843	.466	0	.000	364	.744	453	1511	405	173	349	2050	6.5

GEORGE LYNCH

Team: Vancouver Grizzlies
Position: Forward
Height: 6'8" **Weight:** 223
Birthdate: September 3, 1970
NBA Experience: 3 years

College: North Carolina
Acquired: Traded from Lakers with Anthony Peeler for 1997 and 1998 second-round picks, 7/96

Background: Lynch never became the college superstar some thought he would be, but he found a niche and flourished in Dean Smith's North Carolina system. He set a school record with 241 career steals and was No. 2 all-time in rebounds. After winning a national title as a senior, he was drafted 12th by the Lakers. Lynch, a reserve for most of his first three seasons, joins the Grizzlies for 1996-97.

Strengths: Lynch runs the floor and attacks the offensive glass for what points he does score. However, the best thing Lynch has going for him is his defense. He goes after every loose ball, plays his man aggressively, and is not afraid to throw his athletic body around. He can chase players at three different positions. Lynch is also a promising rebounder.

Weaknesses: Poor ball-handling and perimeter-shooting skills could keep Lynch from making a big impact. His jumper is inconsistent, and he plays the perimeter like a power forward. Problem is, his body has small forward written all over it. He has limited range on his jumper and does not own a great variety of post-up moves. Without transition points and putbacks, the well is pretty dry.

Analysis: The Lakers' draft record in recent years has been exemplary, but Lynch was the exception. His playing time decreased in each of his pro seasons, bottoming out at just over 13 minutes per game in 1995-96. Since Lynch still has much work to do on his offensive skills, the lesser role could not have come at a worse time. He has much to prove in Vancouver.

PLAYER SUMMARY	
Will	hound his man
Can't	crack starting five
Expect	transition points
Don't Expect	sweet shooting
Fantasy Value	$1
Card Value	8-15¢

COLLEGE STATISTICS

		G	FGP	FTP	RPG	PPG
89-90	NC	34	.521	.663	5.4	8.6
90-91	NC	35	.523	.630	7.4	12.5
91-92	NC	33	.539	.649	8.8	13.9
92-93	NC	38	.501	.667	9.6	14.7
Totals		140	.519	.651	7.8	12.5

NBA REGULAR-SEASON STATISTICS

				FGs		3-PT FGs		FTs		Rebounds						
		G	MIN	FG	PCT	FG	PCT	FT	PCT	OFF	TOT	AST	STL	BLK	PTS	PPG
93-94	LAL	71	1762	291	.508	0	.000	99	.596	220	410	96	102	27	681	9.6
94-95	LAL	56	953	138	.468	3	.143	62	.721	75	184	62	51	10	341	6.1
95-96	LAL	76	1012	117	.430	4	.308	53	.663	82	209	51	47	10	291	3.8
Totals		203	3727	546	.479	7	.179	214	.645	377	803	209	200	47	1313	6.5

SAM MACK

Team: Houston Rockets
Position: Forward
Height: 6'7" **Weight:** 220
Birthdate: May 26, 1970

NBA Experience: 2 years
College: Iowa St.; Tyler; Houston
Acquired: Signed as a free agent, 2/96

Background: Mack was a second-team All-Southwest Conference performer as a senior at Houston after finishing sixth in the league in scoring. He was not drafted by an NBA team but earned a spot on San Antonio's 1992-93 roster and averaged 3.6 PPG in 40 contests. Mack served the next two-plus seasons for four different CBA teams before Houston gave him his second chance in the NBA last season. He started 20 of his 31 games with the Rockets.

Strengths: Mack is a smooth player with a sweet shooting stroke. He made exactly 40 percent (54 of 135) of his 3-point shots with the Rockets last year. He also converts a high rate from the free-throw line. He moves well without the ball and is especially dangerous pulling up for transition jumpers. Mack is a talented and aware passer and a hard worker who has paid his dues.

Weaknesses: The CBA is loaded with 'tweeners, and Mack was there for that reason. He does not handle the ball well enough to survive as a guard, but he's clearly a perimeter player. While he poses matchup problems with his shooting, he also falls victim to them on defense. Forwards can push him around inside, and guards are too quick. Almost half of Mack's shots are 3-pointers. He needs to do more inside the arc.

Analysis: Houston has made a recent habit of finding hard-working CBA players and turning them into NBA contributors. Mack was no exception. He took advantage of his call-up (because of Rockets injuries) and averaged 10.8 PPG. He will never match his CBA numbers in the big leagues (he was averaging 20.7 PPG and 4.3 RPG for Rockford), but Mack has a stroke that could keep him around.

PLAYER SUMMARY

Will ....spot up for 3s
Can't ....muscle inside
Expect ....instant offense
Don't Expect.................a CBA return
Fantasy Value $0
Card Value ....5-8¢

COLLEGE STATISTICS

		G	FGP	FTP	RPG	PPG
88-89	ISU	29	.462	.718	6.1	11.8
90-91	TYL	24	.553	.694	9.4	24.6
91-92	HOUS	31	.482	.775	5.8	17.5
Totals		84	.503	.730	7.0	17.6

NBA REGULAR-SEASON STATISTICS

		G	MIN	FGs FG	FGs PCT	3-PT FGs FG	3-PT FGs PCT	FT	FTs PCT	Rebounds OFF	Rebounds TOT	AST	STL	BLK	PTS	PPG
92-93	SA	40	267	47	.398	3	.136	45	.776	18	48	15	14	5	142	3.6
95-96	HOU	31	868	121	.422	54	.400	39	.848	18	98	79	22	9	335	10.8
Totals		71	1135	168	.415	57	.363	84	.808	36	146	94	36	14	477	6.7

DON MacLEAN

Team: Philadelphia 76ers
Position: Forward
Height: 6'10" **Weight:** 225
Birthdate: January 16, 1970

NBA Experience: 4 years
College: UCLA
Acquired: Signed as a free agent, 7/96

Background: MacLean finished his UCLA career as the leading scorer in school and Pac-10 history. He led Division I in free-throw percentage as a senior and was a first-team all-conference selection three years in a row. Detroit drafted MacLean, but trades have sent him to the Clippers, Bullets, and Nuggets. The 1994 Most Improved Player signed a free-agent deal with Philly in July 1996.

Strengths: MacLean has a quick release and is capable of scoring points by the bushel. He has been a deadly perimeter marksman, hitting better than 50 percent from the field in his second pro season. He knows how to get open and can also score off the drive. MacLean is capable of solid efforts on the defensive glass and from the free-throw line.

Weaknesses: MacLean's game has suffered because of various injuries, which have in turn taken some of his confidence. His knees, ankles, and a broken thumb have been the culprits during the last two years. With less playing time, he has not maintained any consistency. He is not a great 3-point threat, his ball-handling and passing are subpar, and defense is the worst part of his game.

Analysis: MacLean has gone from the most improved player in basketball to one with the most to prove. He has posted seven 30-point games in his four-year pro career, including a 38-point burst in 1995-96, but the Nuggets were not finding minutes for the offensive-minded forward as his first season in Denver progressed. A healthy 82-game schedule in Philadelphia might do wonders, as would a commitment to defense.

PLAYER SUMMARY	
Will	look to score
Can't	shut down his man
Expect	better shooting
Don't Expect	82 games
Fantasy Value	$4-6
Card Value	8-12¢

COLLEGE STATISTICS

		G	FGP	FTP	RPG	PPG
88-89	UCLA	31	.555	.816	7.5	18.6
89-90	UCLA	33	.516	.848	8.7	19.9
90-91	UCLA	31	.551	.846	7.3	23.0
91-92	UCLA	32	.504	.921	7.8	20.7
Totals		127	.531	.860	7.8	20.5

NBA REGULAR-SEASON STATISTICS

				FGs		3-PT FGs		FTs		Rebounds						
		G	MIN	FG	PCT	FG	PCT	FT	PCT	OFF	TOT	AST	STL	BLK	PTS	PPG
92-93	WAS	62	674	157	.435	3	.500	90	.811	33	122	39	11	4	407	6.6
93-94	WAS	75	2487	517	.502	3	.143	328	.824	140	467	160	47	22	1365	18.2
94-95	WAS	39	1052	158	.438	10	.250	104	.765	46	165	51	15	3	430	11.0
95-96	DEN	56	1107	233	.426	14	.286	145	.732	62	205	89	21	5	625	11.2
Totals		232	5320	1065	.463	30	.259	667	.791	281	959	339	94	34	2827	12.2

DAN MAJERLE

Team: Miami Heat
Position: Guard/Forward
Height: 6'6" **Weight:** 220
Birthdate: September 9, 1965

NBA Experience: 8 years
College: Central Michigan
Acquired: Signed as a free agent, 8/96

Background: Majerle was a three-time All-Mid-American Conference selection at Central Michigan, where he ranked second on the all-time scoring, steals, and field-goal percentage lists. He emerged as one of the NBA's best all-around talents with Phoenix, playing for Dream Team II and in three All-Star Games. He twice led the league in 3-pointers made and attempted before a trade to the Cavs. He signed a free-agent deal with the Heat in the off-season.

Strengths: Majerle has worn several hats during his eight-year career. Early on with the Suns, "Thunder Dan" gained recognition for his fearless drives and athletic dunks. In recent years, the trey has become his main offensive weapon. Majerle can also run the floor, pile up rebounds, pass, and play tough defense.

Weaknesses: Not everything in Majerle's game has changed for the better. When the Suns started relying on him as a shooter, his slashing moves to the bucket became much less frequent. He made only about a third of his bombs last season with the Cavs, and his field-goal percentage has plunged. He's not the athletic force he was just a few years ago.

Analysis: Majerle has started his last All-Star Game and will not be a candidate for upcoming Dream Teams. That's not to say he's no longer effective. The Cavaliers used him wisely as a sixth man last season, and he came up with some heroic efforts when called upon. He played all 58 minutes of a double-OT game against Seattle.

PLAYER SUMMARY

Will	pull up for treys
Can't	shoot 50 percent
Expect	big scoring nights
Don't Expect	an All-Star return
Fantasy Value	$5-7
Card Value	8-15¢

COLLEGE STATISTICS

		G	FGP	FTP	RPG	PPG
84-85	CMU	12	.568	.582	6.7	18.6
85-86	CMU	27	.527	.718	7.9	21.4
86-87	CMU	23	.555	.552	8.5	21.1
87-88	CMU	32	.521	.645	10.8	23.7
Totals		94	.536	.631	8.9	21.8

NBA REGULAR-SEASON STATISTICS

		G	MIN	FGs FG	PCT	3-PT FGs FG	PCT	FTs FT	PCT	Rebounds OFF	TOT	AST	STL	BLK	PTS	PPG
88-89	PHO	54	1354	181	.419	27	.329	78	.614	62	209	130	63	14	467	8.6
89-90	PHO	73	2244	296	.424	19	.237	198	.762	144	430	188	100	32	809	11.1
90-91	PHO	77	2281	397	.484	30	.349	227	.762	168	418	216	106	40	1051	13.6
91-92	PHO	82	2853	551	.478	87	.382	229	.756	148	483	274	131	43	1418	17.3
92-93	PHO	82	3199	509	.464	167	.381	203	.778	120	383	311	138	33	1388	16.9
93-94	PHO	80	3207	476	.418	192	.382	176	.739	120	349	275	129	43	1320	16.5
94-95	PHO	82	3091	438	.425	199	.363	206	.730	104	375	340	96	38	1281	15.6
95-96	CLE	82	2367	303	.405	146	.353	120	.710	70	305	214	81	34	872	10.6
Totals		612	20596	3151	.443	867	.364	1437	.741	936	2952	1948	844	277	8606	14.1

JEFF MALONE

Team: Miami Heat
Position: Guard
Height: 6'4" **Weight:** 205
Birthdate: June 28, 1961

NBA Experience: 13 years
College: Mississippi St.
Acquired: Signed as a free agent, 2/96

Background: Malone broke Bailey Howell's career scoring record as a four-year starter at Mississippi State. He spent his first seven pro seasons with Washington and played in two All-Star Games. He also enjoyed high-scoring days with Utah and Philadelphia before joining Miami late last season.

Strengths: Malone has been one of the purest perimeter shooters of his time, hovering around the 50-percent mark from the field for most of his career while scoring more than 17,000 points. He's hit off-balance shots from all over the floor. He's an 87-percent career free-throw shooter.

Weaknesses: Malone has been limited by injuries and age over the last two seasons. When he's not scoring, there's no reason to have him on the floor. He will not provide assists, defense, rebounds, or ball-handling. His legs are not what they used to be.

Analysis: As long as Malone can get his shots off, there's a place for him on someone's bench. Last year, however, he was released by the 76ers and played just seven games after landing in Miami. Another year like the last one will have him thinking about retirement.

PLAYER SUMMARY	
Will	drill leaning jumpers
Can't	rebound, defend
Expect	a reserve role
Don't Expect	1,000 more points
Fantasy Value	$0
Card Value	5-8¢

COLLEGE STATISTICS

		G	FGP	FTP	RPG	PPG
79-80	MSU	27	.459	.824	3.3	11.9
80-81	MSU	27	.490	.820	4.2	20.1
81-82	MSU	27	.549	.743	4.1	18.6
82-83	MSU	29	.531	.824	3.7	26.8
Totals		110	.512	.809	3.8	19.5

NBA REGULAR-SEASON STATISTICS

		G	MIN	FGs FG	FGs PCT	3-PT FGs FG	3-PT FGs PCT	FTs FT	FTs PCT	Rebounds OFF	Rebounds TOT	AST	STL	BLK	PTS	PPG
83-84	WAS	81	1976	408	.444	24	.324	142	.826	57	155	151	23	13	982	12.1
84-85	WAS	76	2613	605	.499	15	.208	211	.844	60	206	184	52	9	1436	18.9
85-86	WAS	80	2992	735	.483	3	.176	322	.868	66	288	191	70	12	1795	22.4
86-87	WAS	80	2763	689	.457	4	.154	376	.885	50	218	298	75	13	1758	22.0
87-88	WAS	80	2655	648	.476	10	.417	335	.882	44	206	237	51	13	1641	20.5
88-89	WAS	76	2418	677	.480	1	.053	296	.871	55	179	219	39	14	1651	21.7
89-90	WAS	75	2567	781	.491	1	.167	257	.877	54	206	243	48	6	1820	24.3
90-91	UTA	69	2466	525	.508	1	.167	231	.917	36	206	143	50	6	1282	18.6
91-92	UTA	81	2922	691	.511	1	.083	256	.898	49	233	180	56	5	1639	20.2
92-93	UTA	79	2558	595	.494	3	.333	236	.852	31	173	128	42	4	1429	18.1
93-94	UTA/PHI	77	2560	525	.486	7	.583	205	.830	51	199	125	40	5	1262	16.4
94-95	PHI	19	660	144	.507	11	.393	51	.864	11	55	29	15	0	350	18.4
95-96	PHI/MIA	32	510	76	.394	5	.313	29	.906	8	40	26	16	0	186	5.8
Totals		905	29660	7099	.484	86	.268	2947	.871	572	2364	2154	577	100	17231	19.0

KARL MALONE

Team: Utah Jazz
Position: Forward
Height: 6'9" **Weight:** 256
Birthdate: July 24, 1963

NBA Experience: 11 years
College: Louisiana Tech
Acquired: First-round pick in 1985 draft (13th overall)

Background: Malone finished third on the all-time scoring list at Louisiana Tech despite playing just three years. In 11 years with Utah, he has missed only four games. He has played in nine All-Star Games, winning MVP honors in 1989 and 1993, and has played for two Olympic Dream Teams. He has finished second to Michael Jordan in scoring four times and is annually in the top five.

Strengths: Nicknamed "The Mailman" because he delivers, Malone is virtually impossible for one man to stop. He's big, quick, and incredibly strong. If he fails to score, he almost always draws a foul. He will finish his career among the all-time leaders in free-throw attempts. He plays tough defense and is one of the best rebounding forwards in basketball.

Weaknesses: Malone has to work at his free-throw shooting. He does most of his board work at the defensive end rather than on the offensive glass.

Analysis: The Mailman keeps coming through, year after year. You can always count on him to deliver 20-plus points, ten rebounds, and several trips to the line per game. It's hard to believe it took so long, but he recorded his first triple-double last season. The unstoppable Malone stands at 23,000-plus points and counting.

PLAYER SUMMARY

Will.............................score, rebound
Can't.....................be single-covered
Expect ....Hall of Fame status
Don't Expect ....missed starts
Fantasy Value $75-80
Card Value ....20-40¢

COLLEGE STATISTICS

		G	FGP	FTP	RPG	PPG
82-83	LT	28	.582	.623	10.3	20.9
83-84	LT	32	.576	.682	8.8	18.8
84-85	LT	32	.541	.571	9.0	16.5
Totals		92	.566	.631	9.3	18.7

NBA REGULAR-SEASON STATISTICS

		G	MIN	FGs FG	FGs PCT	3-PT FGs FG	3-PT FGs PCT	FTs FT	FTs PCT	Rebounds OFF	Rebounds TOT	AST	STL	BLK	PTS	PPG
85-86	UTA	81	2475	504	.496	0	.000	195	.481	174	718	236	105	44	1203	14.9
86-87	UTA	82	2857	728	.512	0	.000	323	.598	278	855	158	104	60	1779	21.7
87-88	UTA	82	3198	858	.520	0	.000	552	.700	277	986	199	117	50	2268	27.7
88-89	UTA	80	3126	809	.519	5	.313	703	.766	259	853	219	144	70	2326	29.1
89-90	UTA	82	3122	914	.562	16	.372	696	.762	232	911	226	121	50	2540	31.0
90-91	UTA	82	3302	847	.527	4	.286	684	.770	236	967	270	89	79	2382	29.0
91-92	UTA	81	3054	798	.526	3	.176	673	.778	225	909	241	108	51	2272	28.0
92-93	UTA	82	3099	797	.552	4	.200	619	.740	227	919	308	124	85	2217	27.0
93-94	UTA	82	3329	772	.497	8	.250	511	.694	235	940	328	125	126	2063	25.2
94-95	UTA	82	3126	830	.536	11	.268	516	.742	156	871	285	129	85	2187	26.7
95-96	UTA	82	3113	789	.519	16	.400	512	.723	175	804	345	138	56	2106	25.7
Totals		898	33801	8646	.525	67	.283	5984	.722	2474	9733	2815	1304	756	23343	26.0

DANNY MANNING

Team: Phoenix Suns
Position: Forward/Center
Height: 6'10" **Weight:** 234
Birthdate: May 17, 1966

NBA Experience: 8 years
College: Kansas
Acquired: Signed as a free agent, 9/94

Background: Manning was voted college Player of the Year in 1988, when he led Kansas to the national title. He ended his college career with more than three dozen school, conference, and NCAA records. He has played in two All-Star Games in eight pro seasons, but surgeries to repair anterior cruciate ligaments in both knees have kept Manning from reaching his vast potential.

Strengths: Manning presents a unique blend of playmaking and big-time scoring. He drills his quick-release jumper and owns a deadly half-hook that he throws in from all angles. He moves well without the ball and has been called a point guard in the body of a forward. He makes teammates better. Manning's career scoring average is 18.4 PPG.

Weaknesses: For the downside of Manning, look at his knees. More and more players are making strong comebacks from ACL injuries, but from one to each knee? Manning returned in February 1996 after a one-year layoff, and the last time he played close to a full schedule was in 1992-93. He is not known for his defense.

Analysis: Manning was on his way to one of his best seasons in 1994-95, his debut with the Suns, when he injured his left knee. He was averaging 17.9 points and six rebounds per game and hitting a career-high 54.7 percent of his shots. His return last season was modestly encouraging, but the 1996-97 season will provide the real test.

PLAYER SUMMARY

Will	make others better
Can't	trade his knees
Expect	versatility
Don't Expect	82 games
Fantasy Value	$18-21
Card Value	12-20¢

COLLEGE STATISTICS

		G	FGP	FTP	RPG	PPG
84-85	KANS	34	.566	.765	7.6	14.6
85-86	KANS	39	.600	.748	6.3	16.7
86-87	KANS	36	.617	.730	9.5	23.9
87-88	KANS	38	.583	.734	9.0	24.8
Totals		147	.593	.740	8.1	20.1

NBA REGULAR-SEASON STATISTICS

		G	MIN	FGs FG	FGs PCT	3-PT FGs FG	3-PT FGs PCT	FTs FT	FTs PCT	Rebounds OFF	Rebounds TOT	AST	STL	BLK	PTS	PPG
88-89	LAC	26	950	177	.494	1	.200	79	.767	70	171	81	44	25	434	16.7
89-90	LAC	71	2269	440	.533	0	.000	274	.741	142	422	187	91	39	1154	16.3
90-91	LAC	73	2197	470	.519	0	.000	219	.716	169	426	196	117	62	1159	15.9
91-92	LAC	82	2904	650	.542	0	.000	279	.725	229	564	285	135	122	1579	19.3
92-93	LAC	79	2761	702	.509	8	.267	388	.802	198	520	207	108	101	1800	22.8
93-94	LAC/ATL	68	2520	586	.488	3	.176	228	.669	131	465	261	99	82	1403	20.6
94-95	PHO	46	1510	340	.547	6	.286	136	.673	97	276	154	41	57	822	17.9
95-96	PHO	33	816	178	.459	3	.214	82	.752	30	143	65	38	24	441	13.4
Totals		478	15927	3543	.515	21	.210	1685	.733	1066	2987	1436	673	512	8792	18.4

SARUNAS MARCIULIONIS

Team: Denver Nuggets
Position: Guard
Height: 6'5" **Weight:** 215
Birthdate: June 13, 1964
NBA Experience: 6 years

College: Vilnius St.
Acquired: Traded from Kings with a 1996 second-round pick for Mahmoud Abdul-Rauf, 6/96

Background: The Lithuanian Marciulionis was the leading scorer on the Soviet Union's 1988 Olympic gold medal-winning team and played for Lithuania in the 1992 Games as well. The first Soviet player in the NBA, he led all reserves in scoring (18.9 PPG) in 1991-92 with Golden State. Knee surgery wiped out his entire 1993-94 season. He has since spent one year apiece in Seattle and Sacramento, and he will see action this season with Denver.

Strengths: Although he plays left-handed, Marciulionis is ambidextrous. He makes strong drives to the basket from either side, can finish in traffic, and has made himself a 40-percent shooter from the 3-point arc. Marciulionis is also aware of teammates and is capable of creating good shots for others after penetrating. He works hard at the game and has rehabbed admirably.

Weaknesses: His inability to play Seattle's aggressive, trapping defense was the biggest reason Marciulionis was traded to Sacramento. He is not among the better ball-handling or rebounding guards in the NBA and also commits too many turnovers. Injuries continue to plague him.

Analysis: When healthy, Marciulionis can still be a high-scoring sixth man who eats second-line players alive with his driving, shooting, and passing. He experienced a rebirth of sorts in Sacramento until knee and quadricep injuries surfaced after the All-Star break. He has played more than 66 games in a season only once since his rookie year, and his defense remains sub-standard.

PLAYER SUMMARY	
Will	attack the basket
Can't	shut down his man
Expect	points off the bench
Don't Expect	a full season
Fantasy Value	$5-7
Card Value	7-10¢

COLLEGE STATISTICS

—DID NOT PLAY—

NBA REGULAR-SEASON STATISTICS

			FGs		3-PT FGs		FTs		Rebounds						
	G	MIN	FG	PCT	FG	PCT	FT	PCT	OFF	TOT	AST	STL	BLK	PTS	PPG
89-90 GS	75	1695	289	.519	10	.256	317	.787	84	221	121	94	7	905	12.1
90-91 GS	50	987	183	.501	1	.167	178	.724	51	118	85	62	4	545	10.9
91-92 GS	72	2117	491	.538	3	.300	376	.788	68	208	243	116	10	1361	18.9
92-93 GS	30	836	178	.543	3	.200	162	.761	40	97	105	51	2	521	17.4
94-95 SEA	66	1194	216	.473	35	.402	145	.732	17	68	110	72	3	612	9.3
95-96 SAC	53	1039	176	.452	64	.408	155	.775	20	77	118	52	4	571	10.8
Totals	346	7868	1533	.510	116	.369	1333	.767	280	789	782	447	30	4515	13.0

DONYELL MARSHALL

Team: Golden State Warriors
Position: Forward
Height: 6'9" **Weight:** 230
Birthdate: May 18, 1973

NBA Experience: 2 years
College: Connecticut
Acquired: Traded from Timberwolves for Tom Gugliotta, 2/95

Background: Out of Reading, Pennsylvania, Marshall was the most heralded recruit in UConn history. He did not disappoint, leading the Huskies to two NCAA Tournament bids and the 1994 Big East title. He set a school record for career blocked shots and a league scoring mark as a senior. The fourth pick in the 1994 draft, he was traded from Minnesota to Golden State midway through his rookie year. He spent most of the 1995-96 campaign on the Warrior bench.

Strengths: Marshall is an athlete. His quickness off the floor, wide wingspan, and great timing make him a potential force as a shot-blocker and rebounder. He also runs the floor like a guard, and he has shown glimpses of great finishing ability. He dunks a lot. Some feel he will develop into a big scorer who can post up or knock down jump shots with 3-point range.

Weaknesses: There are enough flaws in Marshall's game to make one wonder what Minnesota had in mind when it selected him fourth overall in 1994. His outside shot is nowhere close to reliable, and he has not shown a proficiency for working closer to the hoop for points. The fastbreak produces his best scoring chances. NBA defense requires more than challenging shots, and Marshall is not a banger. He has much work to do.

Analysis: Marshall came off the bench in his first NBA game to score 26 points (including five 3-pointers) and grab four rebounds, but he has gone nowhere but down since then. He never fit in with the T'Wolves, and he did not contribute much with Golden State last season. It looks like Minnesota was the winner in the Tom Gugliotta trade, although Marshall has enough athlete in him to turn it around.

PLAYER SUMMARY	
Will	run the floor
Can't	crack starting lineup
Expect	athletic ability
Don't Expect	steady shooting
Fantasy Value	$4-6
Card Value	15-30¢

COLLEGE STATISTICS

		G	FGP	FTP	RPG	PPG
91-92	CONN	30	.424	.742	6.1	11.1
92-93	CONN	27	.500	.829	7.8	17.0
93-94	CONN	34	.511	.752	8.9	25.1
Totals		91	.487	.770	7.6	18.1

NBA REGULAR-SEASON STATISTICS

		G	MIN	FGs FG	FGs PCT	3-PT FGs FG	3-PT FGs PCT	FTs FT	FTs PCT	Rebounds OFF	Rebounds TOT	AST	STL	BLK	PTS	PPG
94-95	MIN/GS	72	2086	345	.394	69	.284	147	.662	137	405	105	45	88	906	12.6
95-96	GS	62	934	125	.398	28	.298	64	.771	65	213	49	22	31	342	5.5
Totals		134	3020	470	.395	97	.288	211	.692	202	618	154	67	119	1248	9.3

DARRICK MARTIN

Unrestricted Free Agent
Last Team: Minnesota Timberwolves
Position: Guard
Height: 5'11" **Weight:** 170
Birthdate: March 6, 1971

NBA Experience: 2 years
College: UCLA
Acquired: Traded from Grizzlies for a second-round pick, 2/96

Background: Martin was the point guard on a UCLA team that included fellow NBA players Don MacLean and Tracy Murray. He was not drafted after his senior season, which ended with a stunning first-round NCAA loss to Tulsa. Martin came to the Timberwolves from the CBA as a rookie in 1994-95 and averaged 7.5 PPG. He played 24 games with Vancouver last season before rejoining Minnesota in a trade.

Strengths: Martin possesses great quickness and uses it to create havoc on defense. He averaged almost one steal per game last season in less than 20 minutes per contest. He also has the ability to push the ball in transition or blow by his man in a halfcourt set. He showed a better sense for where and when to pass the ball last season. Martin is a very good free-throw shooter.

Weaknesses: Sound decisions have not come naturally since Martin made the jump to the NBA. His assist-to-turnover ratio is only slightly better than 2-to-1, not a good figure for a small lead guard. And speaking of size, Martin's hurts him at both ends. He's an easy post-up target on defense, and he has not been able to finish on offense. Combined with inconsistent shooting, that's troublesome.

Analysis: Martin has quickness on his side, but there are many reasons to believe he will continue to struggle in the NBA ranks. Foremost, he does not own a reliable jump shot. Cut off his passing lanes, and Martin often throws up a shot he can't make or commits a turnover. He can make things happen in transition and with his quick hands on defense, but Martin is not yet where he needs to be.

PLAYER SUMMARY	
Will	swipe the ball
Can't	pump in treys
Expect	great wheels
Don't Expect	50-percent shooting
Fantasy Value	$0
Card Value	12-20¢

COLLEGE STATISTICS

		G	FGP	FTP	RPG	PPG
88-89	UCLA	31	.453	.747	1.9	8.5
89-90	UCLA	33	.466	.714	2.2	11.3
90-91	UCLA	32	.464	.750	2.4	11.6
91-92	UCLA	33	.433	.829	1.3	5.6
Totals		129	.458	.754	1.9	9.3

NBA REGULAR-SEASON STATISTICS

				FGs		3-PT FGs		FTs		Rebounds						
		G	MIN	FG	PCT	FG	PCT	FT	PCT	OFF	TOT	AST	STL	BLK	PTS	PPG
94-95	MIN	34	803	95	.408	7	.184	57	.877	14	64	133	34	0	254	7.5
95-96	VAN/MIN	59	1149	147	.406	20	.290	101	.842	16	82	217	53	3	415	7.0
Totals		93	1952	242	.407	27	.252	158	.854	30	146	350	87	3	669	7.2

JAMAL MASHBURN

Team: Dallas Mavericks
Position: Forward
Height: 6'8" **Weight:** 250
Birthdate: November 29, 1972

NBA Experience: 3 years
College: Kentucky
Acquired: First-round pick in 1993 draft (fourth overall)

Background: Dan Issel, Kenny Walker, and Jack Givens were the only players ahead of Mashburn on the Kentucky scoring list when he left after starting every game in his three years in Lexington. He was runner-up for the Wooden Award in his final season. Selected fourth by Dallas in 1993, Mashburn led all rookies in scoring and was fifth in the NBA in 1994-95. Knee surgery ended his 1995-96 season after just 18 games.

Strengths: Mashburn is a big-time scorer who can muscle in the paint, drive to the hoop, or stretch a defense with his 3-point shooting. His athletic, "Monster Mash" dunks and fluid style make him a fan favorite. He runs the floor, finds open men, handles the ball, and is tough for one man to defend because of his inside-outside combination. He can play both forward spots at a high level.

Weaknesses: Mashburn cannot be called an accomplished defender. He hardly ever blocks a shot and sometimes feels good defense means outscoring your man. Mashburn is better on the offensive boards than he is on the defensive glass, which is likely a symptom of his scoring mentality. His dismal field-goal percentage is the direct result of too many 3-point bombs.

Analysis: Mashburn has All-Star potential. The two biggest holes in his game are his love for the 3-point shot and his sporadic defense. Aside from that, he brings to the floor an inside-outside scoring combination that few players in the game possess. He was averaging 23.4 PPG when his left knee required arthroscopic surgery in February, and the Mavericks sorely missed him. Look for a strong comeback.

PLAYER SUMMARY

Will	wear out the nets
Can't	shoot 50 percent
Expect	20-plus PPG
Don't Expect	blocked shots
Fantasy Value	$17-20
Card Value	20-40¢

COLLEGE STATISTICS

		G	FGP	FTP	RPG	PPG
90-91	KENT	28	.474	.727	7.0	12.9
91-92	KENT	36	.567	.709	7.8	21.3
92-93	KENT	34	.492	.670	8.4	21.0
Totals		98	.516	.697	7.8	18.8

NBA REGULAR-SEASON STATISTICS

				FGs		3-PT FGs		FTs		Rebounds						
		G	MIN	FG	PCT	FG	PCT	FT	PCT	OFF	TOT	AST	STL	BLK	PTS	PPG
93-94	DAL	79	2896	561	.406	85	.284	306	.699	107	353	266	89	14	1513	19.2
94-95	DAL	80	2980	683	.436	113	.328	447	.739	116	331	298	82	8	1926	24.1
95-96	DAL	18	669	145	.379	35	.343	97	.729	37	97	50	14	3	422	23.4
Totals		177	6545	1389	.417	233	.313	850	.723	260	781	614	185	25	3861	21.8

ANTHONY MASON

Team: Charlotte Hornets
Position: Forward
Height: 6'7" **Weight:** 250
Birthdate: December 14, 1966

NBA Experience: 7 years
College: Tennessee St.
Acquired: Traded from Knicks with
Brad Lohaus for Larry Johnson, 7/96

Background: Mason finished his career at Tennessee State with more than 2,000 career points. He was drafted by Portland in the third round in 1988 but spent his first pro season in Turkey. He played for the Nets in 1989-90, spent most of the 1990-91 campaign in the CBA, and was a four-year reserve standout with the Knicks before starting in 1995-96. A July trade sent him to Charlotte.

Strengths: The 1995 Sixth Man Award winner is a menace to opponents who have the misfortune of running into him. He has a bruising body and uses it to establish a physical presence. Mason bangs, plays ferocious defense, is a dominant rebounder, runs the court, and makes most of his shots. He handles the rock and passes better than many guards.

Weaknesses: The downside with Mason has come off the court. He was suspended for ten days by the Knicks in 1994-95 for actions detrimental to the team. Mason is not a good shooter, and that goes for his free throws as well. He has never made a 3-pointer in his career.

Analysis: The 1995-96 season was Mason's first as a full-time starter, yet he led all NBA players in minutes by a wide margin, averaging a staggering 42 per game. In addition to his physical presence, he also helps set up the offense as an extraordinary "point forward." The Hornets are hoping Mason will be as valuable to them as he was to the Knicks franchise.

PLAYER SUMMARY

Will	bring it up the floor
Can't	make a 3-pointer
Expect	defense, rebounds
Don't Expect	much pine time
Fantasy Value	$10-13
Card Value	7-12¢

COLLEGE STATISTICS

		G	FGP	FTP	RPG	PPG
84-85	TSU	28	.469	.648	5.3	10.0
85-86	TSU	28	.482	.715	6.9	18.0
86-87	TSU	27	.448	.659	9.7	18.8
87-88	TSU	28	.454	.773	10.4	28.0
Totals		111	.461	.713	8.1	18.7

NBA REGULAR-SEASON STATISTICS

				FGs		3-PT FGs		FTs		Rebounds						
		G	MIN	FG	PCT	FG	PCT	FT	PCT	OFF	TOT	AST	STL	BLK	PTS	PPG
89-90	NJ	21	108	14	.350	0	.000	9	.600	11	34	7	2	2	37	1.8
90-91	DEN	3	21	2	.500	0	.000	6	.750	3	5	0	1	0	10	3.3
91-92	NY	82	2198	203	.509	0	.000	167	.642	216	573	106	46	20	573	7.0
92-93	NY	81	2482	316	.502	0	.000	199	.682	231	640	170	43	19	831	10.3
93-94	NY	73	1903	206	.476	0	.000	116	.720	158	427	151	31	9	528	7.2
94-95	NY	77	2496	287	.566	0	.000	191	.641	182	650	240	69	21	765	9.9
95-96	NY	82	3457	449	.563	0	.000	298	.720	220	764	363	69	34	1196	14.6
Totals		419	12665	1477	.526	0	.000	986	.681	1021	3093	1037	261	105	3940	9.4

TONY MASSENBURG

Unrestricted Free Agent
Last Team: Philadelphia 76ers
Position: Forward
Height: 6'9" **Weight:** 245
Birthdate: July 31, 1967

NBA Experience: 4 years
College: Maryland
Acquired: Traded from Raptors with Ed Pinckney for Sharone Wright, 2/96

Background: Massenburg played on a Maryland team that featured Walt Williams and Jerrod Mustaf and was a two-time All-ACC player. He averaged 18.0 PPG and 10.1 RPG as a senior. He played with four NBA teams in his first two seasons before spending two years in Spain. He has since played for three more NBA squads, including Toronto and Philadelphia in 1995-96.

Strengths: Massenburg is a combative defensive player who has spent a lot of time battling centers during his NBA career. He loves to bang the boards and does a fine job of it, having averaged 6.5 RPG last season. Massenburg is a fine athlete who hustles up and down the floor and fares well in a transition game. He has improved his low-post offensive skills and his face-up jumper.

Weaknesses: Massenburg does not have good perimeter skills. He is a poor ball-handler, and he rarely gets credit for an assist. He either shoots or the offense stalls. Massenburg is not a consistent force on offense. He'll put up big numbers one night and disappear the next. He has trouble defending quick forwards. Massenburg has played his best ball on bad teams.

Analysis: Massenburg is an example of a player who needed some seasoning overseas to realize what he could do in the NBA. Since working for two years in the Spanish League, he has enjoyed two promising NBA seasons, averaging 9.3 PPG in 1994-95 and 10.0 PPG in 1995-96 while improving his rebounding and defense. Now if he could just find a place to call home for more than a year!

PLAYER SUMMARY	
Will	bang on defense
Can't	spot open men
Expect	aggressive rebounding
Don't Expect	consistency
Fantasy Value	$1-3
Card Value	5-7¢

COLLEGE STATISTICS

		G	FGP	FTP	RPG	PPG
85-86	MARY	29	.500	.563	2.1	2.9
87-88	MARY	23	.520	.573	5.3	10.1
88-89	MARY	29	.550	.600	7.8	16.6
89-90	MARY	31	.505	.721	10.1	18.0
Totals		112	.523	.643	6.4	12.1

NBA REGULAR-SEASON STATISTICS

				FGs		3-PT FGs		FTs		Rebounds						
		G	MIN	FG	PCT	FG	PCT	FT	PCT	OFF	TOT	AST	STL	BLK	PTS	PPG
90-91	SA	35	161	27	.450	0	.000	28	.622	23	58	4	4	9	82	2.3
91-92	SA/CHA/BOS/GS															
		18	90	10	.400	0	.000	9	.600	7	25	0	1	1	29	1.6
94-95	LAC	80	2127	282	.469	0	.000	177	.753	160	455	67	48	58	741	9.3
95-96	TOR/PHI	54	1463	214	.495	0	.000	111	.707	127	352	30	28	20	539	10.0
Totals		187	3841	533	.477	0	.000	325	.719	317	890	101	81	88	1391	7.4

VERNON MAXWELL

Team: San Antonio Spurs
Position: Guard
Height: 6'4" **Weight:** 190
Birthdate: September 12, 1965

NBA Experience: 8 years
College: Florida
Acquired: Signed as a free agent, 8/96

Background: Maxwell broke Florida's all-time scoring record but later admitted to using cocaine and accepting cash payments. He has been in and out of trouble as a pro as well. He helped the Rockets to the 1994 NBA title but was suspended for ten games the next season after punching a Portland fan. He was released by Houston and spent the 1995-96 season with the 76ers. He rejoins the Spurs for 1996-97.

Strengths: Maxwell is known as a tough defender. He throws his weight around and backs down from no one. He can match up effectively with big guards and point men. Maxwell is an explosive 3-point shooter, capable of catching fire at any time, and he uses his quickness to get to the basket. He passes well and hits clutch shots.

Weaknesses: Though "Mad Max" is annually among the most frequent 3-point bombers in the league, he has never been among the most accurate. Maxwell is a loose cannon who was excluded by the Rockets from their 1995 championship run. His past includes an arrest on a weapons charge, along with substance abuse.

Analysis: Leave it to John Lucas to take a chance on Maxwell. An expert in dealing with trouble cases, Lucas handed Maxwell the ball and let him run the show. When he's hot, Maxwell is capable of giving any team a chance to win. The Spurs decided to take a chance on him and hope he can stay out of trouble.

PLAYER SUMMARY	
Will	...............................get on a roll
Can't	...............shoot for percentage
Expect	...........................tough defense
Don't Expect	........citizenship awards
Fantasy Value	...........................$8-10
Card Value	...................................7-10¢

COLLEGE STATISTICS

		G	FGP	FTP	RPG	PPG
84-85	FLOR	30	.445	.686	2.4	13.3
85-86	FLOR	33	.463	.701	4.5	19.6
86-87	FLOR	34	.485	.742	3.7	21.7
87-88	FLOR	33	.447	.715	4.2	20.2
Totals		130	.462	.715	3.7	18.8

NBA REGULAR-SEASON STATISTICS

		G	MIN	FGs		3-PT FGs		FTs		Rebounds		AST	STL	BLK	PTS	PPG
				FG	PCT	FG	PCT	FT	PCT	OFF	TOT					
88-89	SA	79	2065	357	.432	32	.248	181	.745	49	202	301	86	8	927	11.7
89-90	SA/HOU	79	1987	275	.439	28	.267	136	.645	50	228	296	84	10	714	9.0
90-91	HOU	82	2870	504	.404	172	.337	217	.733	41	238	303	127	15	1397	17.0
91-92	HOU	80	2700	502	.413	162	.342	206	.772	37	243	326	104	28	1372	17.1
92-93	HOU	71	2251	349	.407	120	.332	164	.719	29	221	297	86	8	982	13.8
93-94	HOU	75	2571	380	.389	120	.298	143	.749	42	229	380	125	20	1023	13.6
94-95	HOU	64	2038	306	.394	143	.324	99	.688	18	164	274	75	13	854	13.3
95-96	PHI	75	2467	410	.390	146	.317	251	.756	39	229	330	96	12	1217	16.2
Totals		605	18949	3083	.407	923	.320	1397	.731	305	1754	2507	783	114	8486	14.0

LEE MAYBERRY

Team: Vancouver Grizzlies
Position: Guard
Height: 6'1" **Weight:** 172
Birthdate: June 12, 1970

NBA Experience: 4 years
College: Arkansas
Acquired: Signed as a free agent, 7/96

Background: Mayberry led Arkansas to nine NCAA Tournament wins in four years and finished as the school's career leader in assists, steals, and 3-point field-goal percentage. A first-round draft choice of the Bucks, did not miss a game in his four seasons in Milwaukee, playing as both a starter and a reserve. Mayberry has ranked among NBA leaders in 3-point field-goal accuracy.

Strengths: Mayberry specializes in defense. Though he does not come up with a lot of steals, his on-the-ball defense has been very reliable. He is a fine 3-point shooter who gets his shot off in spite of his size. He is durable, he takes care of the ball, and he runs the offense. He loves the transition game and does not commit a lot of turnovers.

Weaknesses: Mayberry's offensive deficiencies are the main reason he came off the bench for most of last season. He runs a steady ship, but he is not aggressive in looking for his own scoring chances nor does he make much happen with creative playmaking. He does not contribute much on the backboards. Mayberry offers little from the free-throw line or from inside the 3-point arc.

Analysis: The Bucks felt they needed someone better at the point guard position, so they traded for Sherman Douglas and brought Mayberry off the bench. Earlier in his career, Mayberry lost the starting chores to Eric Murdock. There's nothing wrong with the way Mayberry plays defense, runs the offense, or shoots the trey. He has not been assertive offensively, however, and the Bucks let him go to Vancouver as a free agent.

PLAYER SUMMARY	
Will	set up the offense
Can't	trigger a turnaround
Expect	3-point accuracy
Don't Expect	10 PPG
Fantasy Value	$0
Card Value	8-15¢

COLLEGE STATISTICS

		G	FGP	FTP	APG	PPG
88-89	ARK	32	.500	.736	4.2	12.9
89-90	ARK	35	.507	.792	5.2	14.5
90-91	ARK	38	.484	.634	5.5	13.2
91-92	ARK	34	.492	.744	5.9	15.2
Totals		139	.495	.724	5.2	14.0

NBA REGULAR-SEASON STATISTICS

			FGs		3-PT FGs		FTs		Rebounds						
	G	MIN	FG	PCT	FG	PCT	FT	PCT	OFF	TOT	AST	STL	BLK	PTS	PPG
92-93 MIL	82	1503	171	.456	43	.391	39	.574	26	118	273	59	7	424	5.2
93-94 MIL	82	1472	167	.415	41	.345	58	.690	26	101	215	46	4	433	5.3
94-95 MIL	82	1744	172	.422	72	.407	58	.699	21	82	276	51	4	474	5.8
95-96 MIL	82	1705	153	.420	75	.397	41	.603	21	90	302	64	10	422	5.1
Totals	328	6424	663	.428	231	.388	196	.647	94	391	1066	220	25	1753	5.3

GEORGE McCLOUD

Team: Dallas Mavericks
Position: Forward/Guard
Height: 6'8" **Weight:** 225
Birthdate: May 27, 1967

NBA Experience: 6 years
College: Florida St.
Acquired: Signed as a free agent, 1/95

Background: McCloud was named Metro Conference Player of the Year as a senior at Florida State, where he finished his career ranked third on the career scoring list. Chosen seventh overall by Indiana in the 1989 draft, he spent his first four seasons with the Pacers before serving time in the CBA after being released. He returned to the NBA with Dallas in 1994-95 and enjoyed a career year last year.

Strengths: McCloud is an accomplished shooter with fantastic range. No one in the NBA attempted more 3-pointers than he did last season (678), and only Orlando's Dennis Scott made more. McCloud is also an accurate free-throw shooter, a decent rebounder, a capable passer, and a tough defender. He has overcome injuries and adversity through hard work and resiliency.

Weaknesses: McCloud is a streaky player, and his inconsistency was the main reason he struggled to make his mark in the NBA. Three different surgeries in his first three pro seasons did not help him, either. Ball-handling is not his strong suit, and he has not shown much of a game from inside the 3-point arc. More than half his shots are treys.

Analysis: McCloud was one of the most improved players in the NBA in 1995-96. After four disappointing years with the Pacers and some humbling games in the CBA, the No. 7 pick has finally made his mark. He started in place of the injured Jamal Mashburn for most of last season, averaged 18.9 PPG, and tied a single-game NBA record for 3-pointers attempted (20), making ten of them.

PLAYER SUMMARY	
Will	shoot with range
Can't	live up to draft status
Expect	instant offense
Don't Expect	a dazzling dribble
Fantasy Value	$6-8
Card Value	5-8¢

COLLEGE STATISTICS

		G	FGP	FTP	RPG	PPG
85-86	FSU	27	.483	.633	1.8	4.3
86-87	FSU	30	.442	.618	4.2	7.7
87-88	FSU	30	.479	.786	3.7	18.2
88-89	FSU	30	.448	.875	3.6	22.8
Totals		117	.460	.778	3.4	13.5

NBA REGULAR-SEASON STATISTICS

			FGs		3-PT FGs		FTs		Rebounds						
	G	MIN	FG	PCT	FG	PCT	FT	PCT	OFF	TOT	AST	STL	BLK	PTS	PPG
89-90 IND	44	413	45	.313	13	.325	15	.789	12	42	45	19	3	118	2.7
90-91 IND	74	1070	131	.373	43	.347	38	.776	35	118	150	40	11	343	4.6
91-92 IND	51	892	128	.409	32	.340	50	.781	45	132	116	26	11	338	6.6
92-93 IND	78	1500	216	.411	58	.320	75	.735	60	205	192	53	11	565	7.2
94-95 DAL	42	802	144	.439	34	.382	82	.833	82	147	53	23	9	402	9.6
95-96 DAL	79	2846	530	.414	257	.379	180	.804	116	379	212	113	38	1497	18.9
Totals	368	7523	1194	.406	437	.362	438	.791	350	1023	768	274	83	3263	8.9

ANTONIO McDYESS

Team: Denver Nuggets
Position: Forward
Height: 6'9" **Weight:** 220
Birthdate: September 7, 1974
NBA Experience: 1 year

College: Alabama
Acquired: Draft rights traded from Clippers with Randy Woods for Rodney Rogers and draft rights to Brent Barry, 6/95

Background: Before leaving school after his sophomore season, McDyess averaged 30.5 points and 18 rebounds per game for Alabama in two NCAA Tournament contests. He led the Crimson Tide in both scoring and rebounding in his final season. The No. 2 overall draft choice, his rights were sent to the Nuggets from the Clippers in a 1995 draft-day trade. McDyess finished among 1995-96 rookie leaders in rebounding and averaged 13.4 PPG.

Strengths: McDyess has prototypical size for a power forward, and he gets off the floor like few big men can. He's a great athlete who combines strength, speed, and leaping ability. He is well on his way to becoming a big-time NBA rebounder. McDyess owns a pretty nice touch close to the basket and the ability to battle inside against anyone. He blocks shots and hustles on defense.

Weaknesses: The finesse aspects of the game might take some time for McDyess to develop. Recall, he played only two years of college ball. His ball-handling and passing are sub-standard, he converts a poor percentage from the free-throw line, and he has very limited range. McDyess was called for a lot of first-year fouls. He needs to become a more consistent offensive threat by sharpening his post moves.

Analysis: McDyess has drawn early comparisons to the likes of Karl Malone and Charles Barkley. These comparisons are no doubt premature, but there is no question this physically blessed youngster has enormous potential to emerge as an NBA star. McDyess was shocked when his name appeared on the All-Star ballot during his rookie season. He should not be surprised when it remains there over the next several years. He's quite capable of averaging a double-double.

PLAYER SUMMARY	
Will ....rebound, block shots	
Can't............................handle the ball	
Expect ....double-doubles	
Don't Expect 3-pointers	
Fantasy Value $15-18	
Card Value $1.00-2.00	

COLLEGE STATISTICS

		G	FGP	FTP	RPG	PPG
93-94	ALAB	26	.564	.533	8.1	11.4
94-95	ALAB	33	.512	.667	10.2	13.9
Totals		59	.533	.625	9.3	12.8

NBA REGULAR-SEASON STATISTICS

			FGs		3-PT FGs		FTs		Rebounds						
	G	MIN	FG	PCT	FG	PCT	FT	PCT	OFF	TOT	AST	STL	BLK	PTS	PPG
95-96 DEN	76	2280	427	.485	0	.000	166	.683	229	572	75	54	114	1020	13.4
Totals	76	2280	427	.485	0	.000	166	.683	229	572	75	54	114	1020	13.4

JIM McILVAINE

Team: Seattle SuperSonics
Position: Center
Height: 7'1" **Weight:** 260
Birthdate: July 30, 1972

NBA Experience: 2 years
College: Marquette
Acquired: Signed as a free agent, 7/96

Background: McIlvaine led the nation as a senior by blocking 4.3 shots per game at Marquette. He finished his career with nearly as many blocks (399) as field goals (467). His draft stock dipped when he chose to miss the NBA's postseason camps, and Washington selected him 32nd overall in 1994. McIlvaine sat on the bench for most of his rookie season, then finished tenth in the league in blocks in 1995-96. He joins the Sonics for 1996-97.

Strengths: Great extension and timing make McIlvaine a threat to block just about any shot his man puts up. He was the only reserve in the NBA to block more than two shots per game last season. Per minute, his rate is extraordinary. He's not a top-flight athlete, but he moves pretty well for a seven-footer. McIlvaine's good hands make him a potentially solid rebounder. He knows his limits.

Weaknesses: Yes, McIlvaine is one of the best shot-blockers in the NBA. He is also one of its worst offensive players. This comes as no surprise, as he averaged less than 11 PPG in his college career despite towering over most of his defenders. McIlvaine is not a threat in the post or with the jumper. He has added 10-20 pounds of bulk but still gives away strength on defense and the boards.

Analysis: McIlvaine played well as a starter late last season when Gheorghe Muresan blew out his knee. If you like high-scoring centers, the big guy from Marquette is not your man. He'd struggle to hit double figures in an empty gym. He's tough on defense, however. His 48-minute average of 6.7 blocks last season led the league by a landslide, and his position defense is also improving.

PLAYER SUMMARY	
Will	block shots
Can't	shoot, score
Expect	2-plus BPG
Don't Expect	versatility
Fantasy Value	$3-5
Card Value	15-25¢

COLLEGE STATISTICS

		G	FGP	FTP	RPG	PPG
90-91	MARQ	28	.579	.598	4.7	8.0
91-92	MARQ	29	.545	.754	4.6	10.3
92-93	MARQ	28	.578	.714	4.8	11.0
93-94	MARQ	33	.528	.665	8.3	13.6
Totals		118	.552	.687	5.7	10.8

NBA REGULAR-SEASON STATISTICS

				FGs		3-PT FGs		FTs	Rebounds					
		G	MIN	FG	PCT	FG	PCT	FT	PCT	OFF	TOT	AST	STL	BLK	PTS	PPG
94-95	WAS	55	534	34	.479	0	.000	28	.683	40	105	10	10	60	96	1.7
95-96	WAS	80	1195	62	.428	0	.000	58	.552	66	230	11	21	166	182	2.3
Totals		135	1729	96	.444	0	.000	86	.589	106	335	21	31	226	278	2.1

DERRICK McKEY

Team: Indiana Pacers
Position: Forward
Height: 6'10" **Weight:** 225
Birthdate: October 10, 1966
NBA Experience: 9 years

College: Alabama
Acquired: Traded from SuperSonics with Gerald Paddio for Detlef Schrempf, 11/93

Background: McKey earned Southeastern Conference Player of the Year accolades after leading Alabama to a conference title as a junior. He entered the draft one year early and made the 1988 All-Rookie Team in his first of six seasons with Seattle. McKey has spent the last three of his nine pro years with Indiana.

Strengths: McKey is a versatile athlete who is considered one of the best passing forwards in basketball. He plays rock-solid defense against some of the league's best, comes up with at least a steal per game, and handles the ball better than most forwards. He can be a potent scorer, but he prefers to set up teammates.

Weaknesses: Some expected McKey to be a star. Thus, he's been labeled inconsistent because he has never averaged as much as 16 PPG. The feeling is he could be a more dominant offensive player if he ever put his mind to it. He's not a pure shooter, and he picks up a lot of fouls.

Analysis: Indiana fans were upset when the Pacers traded high-scoring Detlef Schrempf for McKey, a player capable of scoring 25 one night and taking three shots the next. McKey has won some fans, however. You can't accuse him of not playing defense or of putting statistics above team goals.

PLAYER SUMMARY	
Will	swipe the ball
Can't	score 20 a night
Expect	defense, passing
Don't Expect	stardom
Fantasy Value	$15-18
Card Value	8-12¢

COLLEGE STATISTICS

		G	FGP	FTP	RPG	PPG
84-85	ALAB	33	.477	.606	4.1	5.1
85-86	ALAB	33	.636	.786	7.9	13.6
86-87	ALAB	33	.581	.862	7.5	18.6
Totals		99	.580	.797	6.5	12.4

NBA REGULAR-SEASON STATISTICS

		G	MIN	FGs FG	FGs PCT	3-PT FGs FG	3-PT FGs PCT	FTs FT	FTs PCT	Rebounds OFF	Rebounds TOT	AST	STL	BLK	PTS	PPG
87-88	SEA	82	1706	255	.491	11	.367	173	.772	115	328	107	70	63	694	8.5
88-89	SEA	82	2804	487	.502	30	.337	301	.803	167	464	219	105	70	1305	15.9
89-90	SEA	80	2748	468	.493	3	.130	315	.782	170	489	187	87	81	1254	15.7
90-91	SEA	73	2503	438	.517	4	.211	235	.845	172	423	169	91	56	1115	15.3
91-92	SEA	52	1757	285	.472	19	.380	188	.847	95	268	120	61	47	777	14.9
92-93	SEA	77	2439	387	.496	40	.357	220	.741	121	327	197	105	58	1034	13.4
93-94	IND	76	2613	355	.500	9	.290	192	.756	129	402	327	111	49	911	12.0
94-95	IND	81	2805	411	.493	32	.360	221	.744	125	394	276	125	49	1075	13.3
95-96	IND	75	2440	346	.486	17	.250	170	.769	123	361	262	83	44	879	11.7
Totals		678	21815	3432	.496	165	.323	2015	.784	1217	3456	1864	838	517	9044	13.3

AARON McKIE

Team: Portland Trail Blazers
Position: Guard
Height: 6'5" **Weight:** 209
Birthdate: October 2, 1972

NBA Experience: 2 years
College: Temple
Acquired: First-round pick in 1994 draft (17th overall)

Background: McKie, a product of Philadelphia's Simon Gratz High, stayed home to attend Temple and enjoyed a fine career after sitting out his freshman year because of academics. He started all 92 of his college games. He and Temple teammate Eddie Jones were both drafted in the first round in 1994. McKie came on in the latter half of his rookie season and bumped his scoring contribution to 10.7 PPG as a starter in 1995-96.

Strengths: McKie brings good size and a great work ethic to the Blazer backcourt. He is not the quickest player in the NBA, but that does not stop him from driving to the basket or getting his shot off. McKie is not afraid to get physical on defense, and he takes pride in that aspect of the game. He's a threat to post 100 steals. McKie is also an above-average rebounder for a guard. He is a team-oriented player.

Weaknesses: McKie does not look smooth shooting the rock, and opponents are best advised to keep him from driving. He's capable of making 3-pointers, but not at a rate that can be compared with the top shooting guards in the game. McKie does not have the look of a prolific scorer. While he is aware of his teammates, he takes advantage of what's there rather than creating plays.

Analysis: Portland's trade of Clyde Drexler two years ago opened the door for McKie, and he stepped in and silenced some of those who were critical of his first-round selection. He overcame a broken facial bone below his left eye during the 1995 preseason to emerge as a starter for most of his sophomore pro season. He does have some offensive deficiencies.

PLAYER SUMMARY	
Will	rebound
Can't	stick to jump shots
Expect	aggressive defense
Don't Expect	15 PPG
Fantasy Value	$4-6
Card Value	8-15¢

COLLEGE STATISTICS

		G	FGP	FTP	RPG	PPG
91-92	TEMP	28	.433	.754	6.0	13.9
92-93	TEMP	33	.432	.789	5.9	20.6
93-94	TEMP	31	.401	.815	7.2	18.8
Totals		92	.421	.790	6.4	17.9

NBA REGULAR-SEASON STATISTICS

			FGs		3-PT FGs		FTs		Rebounds						
	G	MIN	FG	PCT	FG	PCT	FT	PCT	OFF	TOT	AST	STL	BLK	PTS	PPG
94-95 POR	45	827	116	.444	11	.393	50	.685	35	129	89	36	16	293	6.5
95-96 POR	81	2259	337	.467	38	.325	152	.764	86	304	205	92	21	864	10.7
Totals	126	3086	453	.461	49	.338	202	.743	121	433	294	128	37	1157	9.2

NATE McMILLAN

Team: Seattle SuperSonics
Position: Guard/Forward
Height: 6'5" **Weight:** 200
Birthdate: August 3, 1964

NBA Experience: 10 years
College: Chowan; North Carolina St.
Acquired: Second-round pick in 1986 draft (30th overall)

Background: McMillan was a junior college All-American before transferring to North Carolina State and averaging nearly seven assists per game as a senior. He has spent each of his ten pro seasons with Seattle and is the team's career assists leader. He is also closing in on 1,500 career steals, though he has never averaged more than 7.6 PPG.

Strengths: The sure-handed McMillan is known for his defense, rebounding, and passing. His good size, deceiving quickness, and relentless effort have helped him contain ones, twos, and threes over the past decade. He has raised the steal to an art form. McMillan is a reliable ball-handler and an unselfish leader who can hit the 3-pointer.

Weaknesses: McMillan has never been much of a scorer. The last time he averaged double figures in scoring was his second year of junior college. McMillan is a poor free-throw shooter who rarely gets to the line. He has lost some of the quickness that made him a stopper.

Analysis: McMillan led the NBA in steals as recently as 1993-94, and he is still good for close to two per game. Even some of the younger, quicker defenders would love to put up those numbers. Ankle surgery following the 1994-95 season and assorted knee and leg injuries have slowed the Sonics' versatile sixth man.

PLAYER SUMMARY	
Will	defend, rebound
Can't	regain young legs
Expect	1,500 career steals
Don't Expect	instant offense
Fantasy Value	$2-4
Card Value	5-8¢

COLLEGE STATISTICS

		G	FGP	FTP	RPG	PPG
82-83	CHOW	27	.580	.696	5.0	9.9
83-84	CHOW	35	.544	.769	9.8	13.1
84-85	NCST	33	.454	.674	5.7	7.6
85-86	NCST	34	.485	.733	4.6	9.4
Totals		129	.515	.722	6.4	10.1

NBA REGULAR-SEASON STATISTICS

		G	MIN	FGs FG	FGs PCT	3-PT FGs FG	3-PT FGs PCT	FTs FT	FTs PCT	Rebounds OFF	Rebounds TOT	AST	STL	BLK	PTS	PPG
86-87	SEA	71	1972	143	.475	0	.000	87	.617	101	331	583	125	45	373	5.3
87-88	SEA	82	2453	235	.474	9	.375	145	.707	117	338	702	169	47	624	7.6
88-89	SEA	75	2341	199	.410	15	.214	119	.630	143	388	696	156	42	532	7.1
89-90	SEA	82	2338	207	.473	11	.355	98	.641	127	403	598	140	37	523	6.4
90-91	SEA	78	1434	132	.433	17	.354	57	.613	71	251	371	104	20	338	4.3
91-92	SEA	72	1652	177	.437	27	.276	54	.643	92	252	359	129	29	435	6.0
92-93	SEA	73	1977	213	.464	25	.385	95	.709	84	306	384	173	33	546	7.5
93-94	SEA	73	1887	177	.447	52	.391	31	.564	50	283	387	216	22	437	6.0
94-95	SEA	80	2070	166	.418	53	.342	34	.586	65	302	421	165	53	419	5.2
95-96	SEA	55	1261	100	.420	46	.380	29	.707	41	210	197	95	18	275	5.0
Totals		741	19385	1749	.446	255	.339	749	.650	891	3064	4698	1472	346	4502	6.1

LOREN MEYER

Team: Dallas Mavericks
Position: Center
Height: 6'10" **Weight:** 260
Birthdate: December 30, 1972

NBA Experience: 1 year
College: Iowa St.
Acquired: First-round pick in 1995 draft (24th overall)

Background: Meyer missed 15 games at Iowa State in 1993-94 because of injuries sustained in a truck/train collision. His scoring average dipped by 6.5 PPG in his senior season, but he averaged 12 rebounds over the final seven games of the year and was drafted in the first round by Dallas. He saw more playing time as his rookie season progressed and wound up starting 21 of his 72 games.

Strengths: Meyer is a smart player who moves pretty well for a big man and can score facing the basket or with his back to it. His range extends to near the 3-point line. Meyer is a smart player who will hold his ground on defense and set picks. He gets up and down the floor and makes smart passes. His first-year work ethic has helped overcome some doubts about his desire.

Weaknesses: Meyer was not a consistent performer in college, and the same trend threatens to hurt him as a pro. He does not have the natural ability to get by on less than full speed. He is not capable of dominating the boards against NBA centers. He does not have a great vertical leap, nor is he a rock of strength in the middle. Meyer's rookie year was plagued by fouls. He managed to foul out in just six minutes against Miami.

Analysis: A happy-go-lucky guy from a small town in Iowa, Meyer stepped into a good situation in Dallas. He needed some early playing time to establish some confidence, and he was able to get that opportunity in Dallas. Meyer is not starting-center material, but with a little more seasoning he could get there. He'll have to avoid the hacking.

PLAYER SUMMARY	
Will	stand his ground
Can't	keep from fouling
Expect	improved scoring
Don't Expect	loads of blocks
Fantasy Value	$0
Card Value	15-25¢

COLLEGE STATISTICS

		G	FGP	FTP	RPG	PPG
91-92	ISU	34	.514	.596	3.1	5.1
92-93	ISU	31	.542	.710	4.9	9.8
93-94	ISU	12	.610	.737	9.5	22.2
94-95	ISU	34	.556	.732	8.9	15.7
Totals		111	.556	.713	6.1	11.5

NBA REGULAR-SEASON STATISTICS

			FGs		3-PT FGs		FTs		Rebounds						
	G	MIN	FG	PCT	FG	PCT	FT	PCT	OFF	TOT	AST	STL	BLK	PTS	PPG
95-96 DAL	72	1266	145	.439	3	.273	70	.686	114	319	57	20	32	363	5.0
Totals	72	1266	145	.439	3	.273	70	.686	114	319	57	20	32	363	5.0

OLIVER MILLER

Unrestricted Free Agent
Last Team: Toronto Raptors
Position: Center
Height: 6'9" **Weight:** 280
Birthdate: April 6, 1970

NBA Experience: 4 years
College: Arkansas
Acquired: Selected from Pistons in 1995 expansion draft

Background: Miller never gained as much attention as teammates Todd Day and Lee Mayberry at Arkansas, yet he became the school's career leader in blocked shots and field-goal percentage and was second in rebounds. Miller spent two years with the Suns and one with the Pistons before the Raptors selected him in the 1995 expansion draft. Miller ranked among NBA leaders in field-goal percentage and blocks last season.

Strengths: When he stays near his listed 280 pounds, Miller is a tremendous all-around talent. He is a good face-up shooter and an even better passer. He owns soft hands and is very agile for his size. His touch with the basketball is extraordinary. Miller can lift his big body off the floor to block shots and rebound. He converts a high percentage from the field because he won't take bad shots.

Weaknesses: Miller's weight has ballooned over the 300-pound mark, and it has caused him problems with his back, legs, and feet. There are also questions about Miller's dedication to the game. Those are the main reasons he was not taken until Toronto's last pick in the expansion draft. He's a poor free-throw shooter, and his post-up game is primitive.

Analysis: Toronto saw better commitment from Miller, but he has not arrived yet. Though he started all but a few games and proved that his reputation as a fine passer, instinctive shot-blocker, and good rebounder is well-deserved, Miller cannot be considered among the upper half of starting centers until he becomes a better threat in the post.

PLAYER SUMMARY

Will.....................................block shots
Can't ....make free throws
Expect ....superb touch
Don't Expect ....muscle definition
Fantasy Value $11-14
Card Value ....8-12¢

COLLEGE STATISTICS

		G	FGP	FTP	RPG	PPG
88-89	ARK	30	.547	.641	3.7	7.7
89-90	ARK	35	.639	.652	6.3	11.1
90-91	ARK	38	.704	.644	7.7	15.7
91-92	ARK	34	.602	.647	7.7	13.5
Totals		137	.636	.646	6.5	12.2

NBA REGULAR-SEASON STATISTICS

		G	MIN	FGs FG	FGs PCT	3-PT FGs FG	3-PT FGs PCT	FTs FT	FTs PCT	Rebounds OFF	Rebounds TOT	AST	STL	BLK	PTS	PPG
92-93	PHO	56	1069	121	.475	0	.000	71	.710	70	275	118	38	100	313	5.6
93-94	PHO	69	1786	277	.609	2	.222	80	.584	140	476	244	83	156	636	9.2
94-95	DET	64	1558	232	.555	3	.231	78	.629	162	475	93	60	116	545	8.5
95-96	TOR	76	2516	418	.526	0	.000	146	.661	177	562	219	108	143	982	12.9
Totals		265	6929	1048	.545	5	.139	375	.644	549	1788	674	289	515	2476	9.3

REGGIE MILLER

Team: Indiana Pacers
Position: Guard
Height: 6'7" **Weight:** 185
Birthdate: August 24, 1965

NBA Experience: 9 years
College: UCLA
Acquired: First-round pick in 1987 draft (11th overall)

Background: Miller was an All-Pac-10 selection as a senior and left UCLA ranked second to Lew Alcindor on the school's career scoring chart. He has spent all nine of his NBA seasons with Indiana, where he has become an All-Star regular and a member of the last two Dream Teams. He has led the league in free-throw accuracy and is annually near the top in scoring and 3-pointers.

Strengths: The combative Miller is not only one of the best shooters in basketball, but also one of the best offensive players. He is capable of outscoring entire teams for a quarter or more. Few players have his knack for drilling the off-balance shot while drawing the foul. Miller raises his team's level of play.

Weaknesses: Though he plays better defense than his thin frame looks capable of, Miller tends to keep away from the boards in favor of easy scoring chances on the break. And his best method of defense remains his ability to outscore almost anyone.

Analysis: Miller, the Pacers' career scoring leader, was one of the biggest names in the 1996 free-agent market. He commands a high price for his competitive nature, his explosive scoring skills, and his history of clutch performances. A broken eye socket in the final week of the 1995-96 season ended a remarkable run of durability.

PLAYER SUMMARY

Will ....hit clutch shots
Can't ....block shots
Expect....................explosive scoring
Don't Expect ......missed free throws
Fantasy Value $30-35
Card Value ....20-40¢

COLLEGE STATISTICS

		G	FGP	FTP	RPG	PPG
83-84	UCLA	28	.509	.643	1.5	4.6
84-85	UCLA	33	.553	.804	4.3	15.2
85-86	UCLA	29	.556	.882	5.3	25.9
86-87	UCLA	32	.543	.832	5.4	22.3
Totals		122	.547	.836	4.2	17.2

NBA REGULAR-SEASON STATISTICS

				FGs		3-PT FGs		FTs		Rebounds						
		G	MIN	FG	PCT	FG	PCT	FT	PCT	OFF	TOT	AST	STL	BLK	PTS	PPG
87-88	IND	82	1840	306	.488	61	.355	149	.801	95	190	132	53	19	822	10.0
88-89	IND	74	2536	398	.479	98	.402	287	.844	73	292	227	93	29	1181	16.0
89-90	IND	82	3192	661	.514	150	.414	544	.868	95	295	311	110	18	2016	24.6
90-91	IND	82	2972	596	.512	112	.348	551	.918	81	281	331	109	13	1855	22.6
91-92	IND	82	3120	562	.501	129	.378	442	.858	82	318	314	105	26	1695	20.7
92-93	IND	82	2954	571	.479	167	.399	427	.880	67	258	262	120	26	1736	21.2
93-94	IND	79	2638	524	.503	123	.421	403	.908	30	212	248	119	24	1574	19.9
94-95	IND	81	2665	505	.462	195	.415	383	.897	30	210	242	98	16	1588	19.6
95-96	IND	76	2621	504	.473	168	.410	430	.863	38	214	253	77	13	1606	21.1
Totals		720	24538	4627	.491	1203	.397	3616	.877	591	2270	2320	884	184	14073	19.5

CHRIS MILLS

Team: Cleveland Cavaliers
Position: Forward
Height: 6'6" **Weight:** 216
Birthdate: January 25, 1970

NBA Experience: 3 years
College: Kentucky; Arizona
Acquired: First-round pick in 1993 draft (22nd overall)

Background: Though he started every college game he played and won Pac-10 Player of the Year honors at Arizona, Mills had a star-crossed college career. He was forced to leave Kentucky after one year because of an illegal-payments scandal. Drafted 22nd in 1993, Mills has increased his role with Cleveland in each of his three pro seasons. He has led the Cavaliers in minutes played the past two seasons.

Strengths: Mills is a talented combination of shooter and scorer. He can finish his own drives and ignite a team on the fastbreak. Mills shoots better than 80 percent from the line and has 3-point range. He also rebounds well at both ends and has been a fine defensive player, capable of blocking shots and anticipating passes.

Weaknesses: Mills is not the quickest swingman in basketball, nor does he have size on his side. He's plenty aggressive, however, and that makes up for it. Mills has come a long way in shedding his "inconsistent" label, but he still falls in love with the jumper from time to time. He would shoot a better percentage from the floor and draw more fouls with better dedication to the drive.

Analysis: Mills has been a workhorse. He played all 58 minutes of a double-overtime game against Seattle last season and played 223 consecutive minutes at one stage. It's obvious the Cavaliers need Mills on the floor for his shooting, scoring, rebounding, defense, and enthusiasm for the game. He continues to improve in almost every aspect of the game.

PLAYER SUMMARY	
Will	score, rebound, defend
Can't	shoot 50 percent
Expect	durability, coachability
Don't Expect	much bench time
Fantasy Value	$11-14
Card Value	8-15¢

COLLEGE STATISTICS

		G	FGP	FTP	RPG	PPG
88-89	KENT	32	.484	.713	8.7	14.3
90-91	ARIZ	35	.519	.746	6.2	15.6
91-92	ARIZ	31	.506	.777	7.9	16.3
92-93	ARIZ	28	.520	.836	7.9	20.4
Totals		126	.508	.767	7.6	16.5

NBA REGULAR-SEASON STATISTICS

			FGs		3-PT FGs		FTs		Rebounds						
	G	MIN	FG	PCT	FG	PCT	FT	PCT	OFF	TOT	AST	STL	BLK	PTS	PPG
93-94 CLE	79	2022	284	.419	38	.311	137	.778	134	401	128	54	50	743	9.4
94-95 CLE	80	2814	359	.420	94	.392	174	.817	99	366	154	59	35	986	12.3
95-96 CLE	80	3060	454	.468	79	.376	218	.829	112	443	188	73	52	1205	15.1
Totals	239	7896	1097	.438	211	.369	529	.811	345	1210	470	186	137	2934	12.3

TERRY MILLS

Team: Detroit Pistons
Position: Forward
Height: 6'10" **Weight:** 250
Birthdate: December 21, 1967

NBA Experience: 6 years
College: Michigan
Acquired: Signed as a free agent, 10/92

Background: Mills helped lead Michigan to the 1989 NCAA championship as a junior, then earned honorable-mention All-America status as a senior. He was drafted by Milwaukee, traded, and spent his rookie year with Denver and New Jersey. Mills has spent the last four seasons in Detroit, twice leading the team in rebounds before coming off the bench in 1995-96.

Strengths: Mills is that rare power forward who can shoot with great range. He converted 109 treys the year the arc was shortened, and he continues to hoist them. He also uses his backside effectively in the post, where he is capable of using his soft touch to score. Mills has the size to be a force on the boards, yet he also boasts some finesse.

Weaknesses: Mills, who will never be a fitness spokesman, would rather play guard than power forward. He does most of his damage from the perimeter and very little near the basket. He has been neither an interested nor an adept defensive player during his six-year career. His focus and desire have been questioned. Basically, Mills is a power forward who doesn't play with much power.

Analysis: Mills seemed to have found his niche in his hometown, but the Pistons opted for more power from the four spot and brought in Otis Thorpe last season. That cut Mills's playing time from 35 minutes per game in 1994-95 to about 20 minutes a night last season. It also helped Detroit post a winning record for the first time in four years.

PLAYER SUMMARY

Will ....pull big men outside
Can't ....provide power
Expect ....matchup problems
Don't Expect ....consistency
Fantasy Value $4-6
Card Value ....5-8¢

COLLEGE STATISTICS

		G	FGP	FTP	RPG	PPG
87-88	MICH	34	.531	.729	6.4	12.1
88-89	MICH	37	.564	.769	5.9	11.6
89-90	MICH	31	.585	.759	8.0	18.1
Totals		102	.562	.755	6.7	13.8

NBA REGULAR-SEASON STATISTICS

				FGs		3-PT FGs		FTs		Rebounds						
		G	MIN	FG	PCT	FG	PCT	FT	PCT	OFF	TOT	AST	STL	BLK	PTS	PPG
90-91	DEN/NJ	55	819	134	.465	0	.000	47	.712	82	229	33	35	29	315	5.7
91-92	NJ	82	1714	310	.463	8	.348	114	.750	187	453	84	48	41	742	9.0
92-93	DET	81	2183	494	.461	10	.278	201	.791	176	472	111	44	50	1199	14.8
93-94	DET	80	2773	588	.511	24	.329	181	.797	193	672	177	64	62	1381	17.3
94-95	DET	72	2514	417	.447	109	.382	175	.799	124	558	160	68	33	1118	15.5
95-96	DET	82	1656	283	.419	82	.396	121	.771	108	352	98	42	20	769	9.4
Totals		452	11659	2226	.465	233	.371	839	.780	870	2736	663	301	235	5524	12.2

GREG MINOR

Team: Boston Celtics
Position: Guard/Forward
Height: 6'6" **Weight:** 210
Birthdate: September 18, 1971

NBA Experience: 2 years
College: Louisville
Acquired: Signed as a free agent, 10/94

Background: Minor was an All-Metro Conference performer at Louisville despite playing in the shadow of Dwayne Morton and Clifford Rozier. Minor led the Cardinals in rebounding as a sophomore, in minutes as a junior, and in steals as a senior. He was drafted in the first round by Indiana in 1994, but the Pacers' contract offer did not meet NBA requirements. That left him free to sign with Boston, where he averaged 9.6 PPG in his second season.

Strengths: Minor has been a pleasant surprise, shooting 50 percent or better in each of his first two years. This is especially encouraging since he does most of his damage from the perimeter. A swingman with first-rate athletic ability, Minor gets up and down the floor quickly and has shown signs of being a reliable defensive player. He gets to the boards. Minor finished third in the 1996 Slam Dunk contest.

Weaknesses: He has played mostly guard, so we must note that Minor is not a steady ball-handler when pressured. He is not a good 3-point shooter, and he has been too willing to settle for the jumper when perhaps a drive is the better play. He has not attained the consistency required to be called a top-notch defender. He's neither a thief nor a shot-blocker.

Analysis: Both Minor and Boston caught a break when, before his rookie season, the Pacers made him a qualifying offer that was $50,000 below the minimum required for first-round picks. The Celtics not only made the right offer, but were also able to provide the minutes Minor needed to gain some confidence at the NBA level. He started 47 of 78 games last season, mostly in the backcourt.

PLAYER SUMMARY	
Will	run and shoot
Can't	run the show
Expect	an athletic swingman
Don't Expect	long range
Fantasy Value	$1-3
Card Value	7-10¢

COLLEGE STATISTICS

		G	FGP	FTP	RPG	PPG
91-92	LOUI	30	.473	.733	5.1	9.7
92-93	LOUI	31	.527	.750	5.5	14.1
93-94	LOUI	34	.513	.729	6.1	13.8
Totals		95	.507	.739	5.6	12.6

NBA REGULAR-SEASON STATISTICS

				FGs		3-PT FGs		FTs		Rebounds						
		G	MIN	FG	PCT	FG	PCT	FT	PCT	OFF	TOT	AST	STL	BLK	PTS	PPG
94-95	BOS	63	945	155	.515	2	.167	65	.833	49	137	66	32	16	377	6.0
95-96	BOS	78	1761	320	.500	7	.259	99	.762	93	257	146	36	11	746	9.6
Totals		141	2706	475	.505	9	.231	164	.788	142	394	212	68	27	1123	8.0

SAM MITCHELL

Team: Minnesota Timberwolves
Position: Forward
Height: 6'7" **Weight:** 215
Birthdate: September 2, 1963

NBA Experience: 7 years
College: Mercer
Acquired: Signed as a free agent, 9/95

Background: Mitchell finished his career as Mercer's all-time leading scorer, but he got a late start as a pro. After being drafted and cut by Houston in 1985, he began a teaching career. He then played in the USBL, the CBA, and France before becoming the NBA's oldest rookie (26) in 1989-90. After three years in Minnesota and three in Indiana, he returned to the Timberwolves as a free agent in 1995-96.

Strengths: Mitchell overcomes his athletic deficiencies with a work ethic coaches respect. He is a versatile forward who plays with intensity and smarts. Mitchell runs the floor and dives for loose balls. He loves the baseline and is not afraid to drive. Mitchell plays tough defense, makes his free throws, and is a team player.

Weaknesses: Mitchell does nothing spectacular. His shooting range is limited, and he is not much of a scorer. He led the league with 338 fouls during his second season, although he has become a better and smarter defender. Mitchell is a below-average ball-handler and passer and lacks great size and quickness.

Analysis: It seems the only team for which Mitchell can average double figures is Minnesota, but scoring is not an important number with him. Mitchell cares more about making his man work for his points and doing the dirty work. He started during the first half of last season while talented rookie Kevin Garnett was being groomed for the job.

PLAYER SUMMARY	
Will	do the dirty work
Can't	make 3-pointers
Expect	hard-nosed defense
Don't Expect	stardom
Fantasy Value	$0
Card Value	5-8¢

COLLEGE STATISTICS

		G	FGP	FTP	RPG	PPG
81-82	MERC	27	.497	.717	3.7	7.1
82-83	MERC	28	.519	.784	5.9	16.5
83-84	MERC	26	.507	.781	7.1	21.5
84-85	MERC	31	.516	.750	8.2	25.0
Totals		112	.512	.763	6.3	17.7

NBA REGULAR-SEASON STATISTICS

			FGs		3-PT FGs		FTs		Rebounds						
	G	MIN	FG	PCT	FG	PCT	FT	PCT	OFF	TOT	AST	STL	BLK	PTS	PPG
89-90 MIN	80	2414	372	.446	0	.000	268	.768	180	462	89	66	54	1012	12.6
90-91 MIN	82	3121	445	.441	0	.000	307	.775	188	520	133	66	57	1197	14.6
91-92 MIN	82	2151	307	.423	2	.182	209	.786	158	473	94	53	39	825	10.1
92-93 IND	81	1402	215	.445	4	.174	150	.811	93	248	76	23	10	584	7.2
93-94 IND	75	1084	140	.458	0	.000	82	.745	71	190	65	33	9	362	4.8
94-95 IND	81	1377	201	.487	1	.100	126	.724	95	243	61	43	20	529	6.5
95-96 MIN	82	2145	303	.490	1	.056	237	.814	107	339	74	49	26	844	10.8
Totals	559	13694	1983	.452	8	.094	1379	.779	892	2475	592	333	215	5353	9.6

ERIC MOBLEY

Team: Vancouver Grizzlies
Position: Center
Height: 6'11" **Weight:** 257
Birthdate: February 1, 1970
NBA Experience: 2 years

College: Allegany; Pittsburgh
Acquired: Traded from Bucks with
Eric Murdock for Benoit Benjamin,
11/95

Background: Mobley, a top recruit out of New Rochelle, New York, was diverted to a community college in Maryland before transferring to Pittsburgh. He developed slowly but averaged almost three blocks per game as a senior. Selected 18th by Milwaukee in the 1994 draft, Mobley made 26 starts as a rookie. He was traded to Vancouver early last season, when his role became that of a spectator.

Strengths: There's a fine athlete in Mobley's big body. He's strong and agile and runs well for a big man. He has the potential to be a defensive intimidator who blocks shots and battles his opponent for position. Mobley shoots for a high percentage because he will not take many bad shots. He prefers slam dunks. He works hard at the game, has good hands, and wants to become a respected player.

Weaknesses: Mobley remains a substandard offensive player. He gets his points on jams and garbage buckets. His low-post moves will not scare many defenders, and his touch from the perimeter is poor. He has continued an embarrassing college trend by hitting a higher percentage of his field goals than his free throws. He has to bust his tail, because nothing comes easily to him.

Analysis: Mobley, who started his first NBA game, alternated between the injured list and the Vancouver bench for much of last season after earning quality minutes as a Bucks rookie. Such is life in the NBA for a player who often appears lost on offense. Mobley may have a future as a defensive specialist, but he's not there yet. His best bet would be developing a scoring move for year No. 3.

PLAYER SUMMARY	
Will	get off his feet
Can't	hit two free throws
Expect	size, athleticism
Don't Expect	smooth moves
Fantasy Value	$0
Card Value	15-25¢

COLLEGE STATISTICS

		G	FGP	FTP	RPG	PPG
91-92	PITT	33	.559	.410	4.6	7.2
92-93	PITT	28	.542	.553	7.5	10.4
93-94	PITT	27	.568	.492	8.8	13.7
Totals		88	.557	.486	6.8	10.2

NBA REGULAR-SEASON STATISTICS

				FGs		3-PT FGs		FTs		Rebounds						
		G	MIN	FG	PCT	FG	PCT	FT	PCT	OFF	TOT	AST	STL	BLK	PTS	PPG
94-95	MIL	46	587	78	.591	2	1.000	22	.489	55	153	21	8	27	180	3.9
95-96	MIL/VAN	39	676	74	.536	1	.500	39	.448	54	140	22	14	24	188	4.8
Totals		85	1263	152	.563	3	.750	61	.462	109	293	43	22	51	368	4.3

ERIC MONTROSS

Team: Dallas Mavericks
Position: Center
Height: 7'0" **Weight:** 270
Birthdate: September 23, 1971
NBA Experience: 2 years

College: North Carolina
Acquired: Traded from Celtics with a 1996 first-round pick for 1996 and 1997 first-round picks, 6/96

Background: Montross, an Indianapolis prep star, disappointed Hoosier fans by choosing to play his college ball at North Carolina. He helped the Tar Heels to a national championship as a junior and shot .585 from the field as a collegian. Drafted ninth by Boston in 1994, Montross made the All-Rookie second team. His play dropped off in 1995-96, and he was dealt to Dallas in the off-season.

Strengths: Montross uses his big frame to do the kinds of things centers are supposed to do. He takes up space in the middle, provides a physical presence, and scores on the interior. He can be a force on the boards. Montross has always hit a high percentage from the field, and his .566 was among the best in the NBA last season, although he did not have enough attempts to qualify among the league leaders. He hustles up and down the floor and wants to improve.

Weaknesses: Montross is not among the more athletic centers in the league, but his biggest weaknesses have been his face-up game and his passing. He has not been able to make the jumper with regularity, and he struggles even worse from the free-throw line. Montross is not a threat to block many shots, and he is overmatched by the game's premier centers.

Analysis: The 1996-97 season could be a pivotal one for Montross, who was a pleasant surprise to many as a rookie but took a step backward last year. His upside includes good strength, nice hands, and a proven ability to score and rebound on the inside. Montross is not Shaq, however, which is to say he had better learn to make his free throws and sharpen his offensive skills. Injuries also contributed to last year's slide.

PLAYER SUMMARY	
Will	battle inside
Can't	connect at the line
Expect	good hands, strength
Don't Expect	slick passes
Fantasy Value	$4-6
Card Value	12-20¢

COLLEGE STATISTICS

		G	FGP	FTP	RPG	PPG
90-91	NC	35	.587	.612	4.2	5.8
91-92	NC	31	.574	.624	7.0	11.2
92-93	NC	38	.615	.684	7.6	15.8
93-94	NC	35	.560	.558	8.1	13.6
Totals		139	.585	.624	6.8	11.7

NBA REGULAR-SEASON STATISTICS

				FGs		3-PT FGs		FTs		Rebounds						
		G	MIN	FG	PCT	FG	PCT	FT	PCT	OFF	TOT	AST	STL	BLK	PTS	PPG
94-95	BOS	78	2315	307	.534	0	.000	167	.635	196	566	36	29	61	781	10.0
95-96	BOS	61	1432	196	.566	0	.000	50	.376	119	352	43	19	29	442	7.2
Totals		139	3747	503	.546	0	.000	217	.548	315	918	79	48	90	1223	8.8

CHRIS MORRIS

Team: Utah Jazz
Position: Forward
Height: 6'8" **Weight:** 220
Birthdate: January 20, 1966

NBA Experience: 8 years
College: Auburn
Acquired: Signed as a free agent, 10/95

Background: Following in the footsteps of past Auburn greats Charles Barkley and Chuck Person, Morris was the fourth player selected in the 1988 NBA draft. The Nets looked like geniuses after two seasons, but Morris leveled off. His seven years in New Jersey were highlighted by turbulence. The Jazz signed him before the 1995-96 season and used him as both a starter and reserve.

Strengths: Athletic ability has never been a question with Morris. He runs the floor, drives to the hoop, and has 3-point range. He has been an explosive scorer throughout his career, capable of throwing a 25-point night at you. Morris is an exciting finisher who loves to dunk, and his defense has come a long way since his rookie year.

Weaknesses: Morris has been plagued by inconsistency, poor shot selection, and an attitude that has gotten him in trouble with some of his coaches. He wanted to be a star in New Jersey, and he never agreed with his role with the Nets. Morris is not the shooter he thinks he is, nor is he the scorer he once was.

Analysis: The embattled Morris needed a change, and Utah certainly provided it. By now, it's obvious he will never be the star some expected him to be after his first two years in the league. Younger fans who don't remember would never peg him as a former No. 4 pick. However, the athletic Morris can do enough to contribute.

PLAYER SUMMARY

Will	score in spurts
Can't	live up to draft status
Expect	slam dunks
Don't Expect	15 PPG
Fantasy Value	$3-5
Card Value	5-8¢

COLLEGE STATISTICS

		G	FGP	FTP	RPG	PPG
84-85	AUB	34	.477	.620	5.0	10.4
85-86	AUB	33	.500	.670	5.2	9.8
86-87	AUB	31	.559	.711	7.3	13.5
87-88	AUB	30	.481	.795	9.8	20.7
Totals		128	.501	.712	6.7	13.4

NBA REGULAR-SEASON STATISTICS

			FGs		3-PT FGs		FTs		Rebounds						
		G	MIN	FG	PCT	FG	PCT	FT	PCT	OFF	TOT	AST	STL	BLK	PTS	PPG
88-89	NJ	76	2096	414	.457	64	.366	182	.717	188	397	119	102	60	1074	14.1
89-90	NJ	80	2449	449	.422	61	.316	228	.722	194	422	143	130	79	1187	14.8
90-91	NJ	79	2553	409	.425	45	.251	179	.734	210	521	220	138	96	1042	13.2
91-92	NJ	77	2394	346	.477	22	.200	165	.714	199	494	197	129	81	879	11.4
92-93	NJ	77	2302	436	.481	17	.224	197	.794	227	454	106	144	52	1086	14.1
93-94	NJ	50	1349	203	.447	53	.361	85	.720	91	228	83	55	49	544	10.9
94-95	NJ	71	2131	351	.410	106	.334	142	.728	181	402	147	86	51	950	13.4
95-96	UTA	66	1424	265	.437	63	.320	98	.772	100	229	77	63	20	691	10.5
Totals		576	16698	2873	.443	431	.309	1276	.736	1390	3147	1092	847	488	7453	12.9

ALONZO MOURNING

Team: Miami Heat
Position: Center
Height: 6'10" **Weight:** 261
Birthdate: February 8, 1970
NBA Experience: 4 years

College: Georgetown
Acquired: Traded from Hornets with Pete Myers and LeRon Ellis for Glen Rice, Khalid Reeves, Matt Geiger, and a 1996 first-round pick, 11/95

Background: From Chesapeake, Virginia, Mourning was a coveted prep star, rating ahead of Shawn Kemp, Chris Jackson, and Billy Owens in the class of 1988. He set an NCAA record for career blocks (453) at Georgetown and became the first player to be selected Big East Player of the Year and Defensive Player of the Year in the same season. The No. 2 pick in 1992, Mourning is a two-time All-Star and was a Dream Team II member. A trade sent him from Charlotte to Miami for 1995-96.

Strengths: Mourning is an upper-echelon center in most phases of the game. Capable of dominating games on offense and defense, he ranks among the league leaders in scoring, rebounding, and shot-blocking. He can score on powerful post moves, hook shots, or jump shots with range to 20 feet. You almost have to foul him to stop him down low. Mourning is a ferocious competitor who loves contact and hates to lose.

Weaknesses: Mourning has improved his assist total each season, but he still racks up nearly twice as many turnovers. He prefers shooting to passing, even when it means fighting off a double-team. Mourning plays with a combative style that leads to a lot of fouls. His free-throw percentage needs boosting.

Analysis: While not considered along with Olajuwon, Ewing, Robinson, and O'Neal as one of the game's "big four" big men, Mourning is on the verge of expanding the club to five. You can't get much more consistent than the 20-plus points, ten rebounds, and three blocked shots per night he has provided during his first four seasons. Miami got a franchise player in Mourning.

PLAYER SUMMARY	
Will	score, rebound, defend
Can't	limit his fouls
Expect	a dominant career
Don't Expect	All-Star snubs
Fantasy Value	$70-75
Card Value	20-40¢

COLLEGE STATISTICS

		G	FGP	FTP	RPG	PPG
88-89	GEOR	34	.603	.667	7.3	13.1
89-90	GEOR	31	.525	.783	8.5	16.5
90-91	GEOR	23	.522	.793	7.7	15.8
91-92	GEOR	32	.595	.758	10.7	21.3
Totals		120	.566	.754	8.6	16.7

NBA REGULAR-SEASON STATISTICS

		G	MIN	FGs		3-PT FGs		FTs		Rebounds		AST	STL	BLK	PTS	PPG
				FG	PCT	FG	PCT	FT	PCT	OFF	TOT					
92-93	CHA	78	2644	572	.511	0	.000	495	.781	263	805	76	27	271	1639	21.0
93-94	CHA	60	2018	427	.505	0	.000	433	.762	177	610	86	27	188	1287	21.5
94-95	CHA	77	2941	571	.519	11	.324	490	.761	200	761	111	49	225	1643	21.3
95-96	MIA	70	2671	563	.523	9	.300	488	.685	218	727	159	70	189	1623	23.2
Totals		285	10274	2133	.515	20	.290	1906	.745	858	2903	432	173	873	6192	21.7

CHRIS MULLIN

Team: Golden State Warriors
Position: Forward
Height: 6'7" **Weight:** 215
Birthdate: July 30, 1963

NBA Experience: 11 years
College: St. John's
Acquired: First-round pick in 1985 draft (seventh overall)

Background: Mullin made every All-America team as a senior at St. John's. He graduated as the Big East's all-time scoring leader. Mullin's pro career hit a peak after he voluntarily entered alcohol rehab in 1987-88. The four-time All-Star and 1992 U.S. Olympian has spent much of the last four seasons on the injured list.

Strengths: Mullin shoots with great touch and 3-point range, and he can kill you even with a hand in his face. He is a superb passer, plays heady defense, and rarely misses a free throw. Mullin is a leader with an uncanny feel for the game and a desire to return to work full-time.

Weaknesses: Mullin has never been a great athlete, and injuries have taken their toll. The list includes finger, thumb, knee, and ankle ailments. Surgery to repair a torn ligament in his right hand ended his 1995-96 season after 55 games.

Analysis: Likened to Larry Bird for much of his career because of his shooting, his scoring, and his craftiness, Mullin is among Warrior all-time leaders in 17 categories. How much longer he can sustain a high level, however, depends on how well his body holds up. Jerome Kersey started ahead of him last season.

PLAYER SUMMARY

Will ....be a leader
Can't ....dunk over his man
Expect........................sweet shooting
Don't Expect.......................82 games
Fantasy Value $15-18
Card Value ....12-20¢

COLLEGE STATISTICS

		G	FGP	FTP	RPG	PPG
81-82	STJ	30	.534	.791	3.2	16.6
82-83	STJ	33	.577	.878	3.7	19.1
83-84	STJ	27	.571	.904	4.4	22.9
84-85	STJ	35	.521	.824	4.8	19.8
Totals		125	.550	.848	4.1	19.5

NBA REGULAR-SEASON STATISTICS

				FGs		3-PT FGs		FTs		Rebounds						
		G	MIN	FG	PCT	FG	PCT	FT	PCT	OFF	TOT	AST	STL	BLK	PTS	PPG
85-86	GS	55	1391	287	.463	5	.185	189	.896	42	115	105	70	23	768	14.0
86-87	GS	82	2377	477	.514	19	.302	269	.825	39	181	261	98	36	1242	15.1
87-88	GS	60	2033	470	.508	34	.351	239	.885	58	205	290	113	32	1213	20.2
88-89	GS	82	3093	830	.509	23	.230	493	.892	152	483	415	176	39	2176	26.5
89-90	GS	78	2830	682	.536	87	.372	505	.889	130	463	319	123	45	1956	25.1
90-91	GS	82	3315	777	.536	40	.301	513	.884	141	463	329	173	63	2107	25.7
91-92	GS	81	3346	830	.524	64	.366	350	.833	127	450	286	173	62	2074	25.6
92-93	GS	46	1902	474	.510	60	.451	183	.810	42	232	166	68	41	1191	25.9
93-94	GS	62	2324	410	.472	55	.364	165	.753	64	345	315	107	53	1040	16.8
94-95	GS	25	890	170	.489	42	.452	94	.879	25	115	125	38	19	476	19.0
95-96	GS	55	1617	269	.499	59	.393	137	.856	44	159	194	75	32	734	13.3
Totals		708	25118	5676	.512	488	.360	3137	.862	864	3191	2805	1214	445	14977	21.2

ERIC MURDOCK

Unrestricted Free Agent
Last Team: Vancouver Grizzlies
Position: Guard
Height: 6'1" **Weight:** 200
Birthdate: June 14, 1968

NBA Experience: 5 years
College: Providence
Acquired: Traded from Bucks with
Eric Mobley for Benoit Benjamin, 11/95

Background: As a junior at Providence, Murdock suffered a stress fracture in his leg and was hospitalized with an irregular heartbeat. He followed it up with a terrific senior year, however, and set an NCAA record with 376 career steals. After a slow start with Utah, Murdock came on in three-plus years with Milwaukee. The Bucks traded him to Vancouver early in the 1995-96 season.

Strengths: Murdock has quick hands that make him an expert thief. Despite coming off the bench for most of last season, he ranked seventh in the NBA in steals with 1.85 per game. Murdock brings scoring ability to the point guard spot, and he is also able to fill in at two guard. He is quick to the hoop, shoots with 3-point range, and plays with energy.

Weaknesses: Murdock continues to struggle with his role. His questionable decision-making limits him as a point guard, yet he is not a consistent enough shooter to be a two. Murdock posts a horrible percentage from the field. He does not set up teammates as well as most lead guards, and his defense involves too much gambling.

Analysis: Unless Murdock hoists his shooting percentage and learns to make better decisions with the ball, his days as a starter might be finished. Actually, he has the making of a dangerous sixth man who can take matters into his own hands on both offense and defense. His abilities to swipe the ball, shoot the 3-pointer, and beat his man will keep him on the floor.

PLAYER SUMMARY

Will ....pick your pocket
Can't ....shoot 50 percent
Expect ....defensive energy
Don't Expect ....consistency
Fantasy Value $3-5
Card Value ....7-10¢

COLLEGE STATISTICS

		G	FGP	FTP	APG	PPG
87-88	PROV	28	.413	.738	3.8	10.7
88-89	PROV	29	.457	.762	4.9	16.2
89-90	PROV	28	.419	.762	3.3	15.4
90-91	PROV	32	.445	.812	4.6	25.6
Totals		117	.436	.783	4.2	17.3

NBA REGULAR-SEASON STATISTICS

			FGs		3-PT FGs		FTs		Rebounds						
	G	MIN	FG	PCT	FG	PCT	FT	PCT	OFF	TOT	AST	STL	BLK	PTS	PPG
91-92 UTA	50	478	76	.415	5	.192	46	.754	21	54	92	30	7	203	4.1
92-93 MIL	79	2437	438	.468	31	.261	231	.780	95	284	603	174	7	1138	14.4
93-94 MIL	82	2533	477	.468	69	.411	234	.813	91	261	546	197	12	1257	15.3
94-95 MIL	75	2158	338	.415	90	.375	211	.790	48	214	482	113	12	977	13.0
95-96 MIL/VAN	73	1673	244	.416	45	.310	114	.797	26	169	327	135	9	647	8.9
Totals	359	9279	1573	.444	240	.344	836	.792	281	982	2050	649	47	4222	11.8

GHEORGHE MURESAN

Team: Washington Bullets
Position: Center
Height: 7'7" **Weight:** 303
Birthdate: February 14, 1971

NBA Experience: 3 years
College: Cluj
Acquired: Second-round pick in 1993 draft (30th overall)

Background: Muresan is the tallest player in the history of the NBA. He starred for a professional team in France, averaging 18.7 points and 10.3 rebounds per game, before Washington chose him in the second round of the 1993 draft. Muresan has made tremendous strides in three NBA seasons, leading the league with a .584 field-goal percentage during the 1995-96 campaign and earning the Most Improved Player Award.

Strengths: Muresan is a mountain of a man. His massive bulk is his most obvious and clearly his greatest attribute. He takes up space on defense, rates among the top ten in blocks, and has become a dangerous scorer in the paint. He has an accurate hook and a decent turnaround. Muresan has soft hands and can rebound without leaving the floor. His work ethic and heart are also big.

Weaknesses: Athletic ability does not show up on Muresan's resume. He is slow on his feet and cannot get far off the floor. He has a history of ankle and knee injuries, including one that cut short his 1995-96 season. Muresan commits far too many fouls, he is one of the game's least aware passers, and you never want him bouncing the ball or shooting clutch free throws.

Analysis: The most improved player in the NBA last season before a torn knee ligament sidelined him in April, Muresan has become a much better talent than most envisioned. His slow feet have not kept him from making an impact as a shot-blocker, rebounder, and able low-post scorer who makes even Shaquille O'Neal look small. He does have his limitations, but size is not one of them.

PLAYER SUMMARY	
Will	intimidate
Can't	elevate
Expect	rebounds, blocks
Don't Expect	many misses
Fantasy Value	$13-16
Card Value	8-15¢

COLLEGE STATISTICS

— DID NOT PLAY—

NBA REGULAR-SEASON STATISTICS

			FGs		3-PT FGs		FTs		Rebounds						
	G	MIN	FG	PCT	FG	PCT	FT	PCT	OFF	TOT	AST	STL	BLK	PTS	PPG
93-94 WAS	54	650	128	.545	0	.000	48	.676	66	192	18	28	48	304	5.6
94-95 WAS	73	1720	303	.560	0	.000	124	.709	179	488	38	48	127	730	10.0
95-96 WAS	76	2242	466	.584	0	.000	172	.619	248	728	56	52	172	1104	14.5
Totals	203	4612	897	.570	0	.000	344	.656	493	1408	112	128	347	2138	10.5

LAMOND MURRAY

Team: Los Angeles Clippers
Position: Forward
Height: 6'7"　**Weight:** 236
Birthdate: April 20, 1973

NBA Experience: 2 years
College: California
Acquired: First-round pick in 1994 draft (seventh overall)

Background: Murray and fellow 1994 lottery pick Jason Kidd played together at California. Murray led the Pac-10 in scoring as a senior and needed just three seasons to shatter Kevin Johnson's all-time school scoring record. The cousin of NBA forward Tracy Murray, the Clippers' Lamond ranked among rookie scoring leaders at 14.1 PPG, but saw his numbers and playing time decrease in 1995-96.

Strengths: Murray's best asset is his ability to do a little bit of everything. He combines shooting and scoring prowess with the ability to work for his own shots or find an opening and hit the 3-pointer. He runs the floor and has the size and skill to burn his man in the post. He's a high riser who knows his way around the offensive end of the floor and has untapped potential on defense.

Weaknesses: Start with the "C" words: consistency and commitment. His intensity and willingness to play hard on a consistent basis have been questioned. This is especially true on defense. There's no excuse for some of the shots Murray will give up. He has not been the hot shooter the Clippers were expecting, nor does he do anything to make life easier on his teammates. He needs to play harder and smarter.

Analysis: Nothing comes easy in the NBA, as Murray discovered last season. After a promising rookie campaign, some felt Murray put his game on cruise control as a sophomore. The result was a reserve role for most of the season, a job description he would rather not fill. Better commitment to defense and better value of the basketball would help Murray make a better impression on his Clipper coaches. They know all about his scoring.

PLAYER SUMMARY	
Will	run the court
Can't	star on defense
Expect	versatile scoring
Don't Expect	a captain
Fantasy Value	$3-5
Card Value	7-12¢

COLLEGE STATISTICS

		G	FGP	FTP	RPG	PPG
91-92	CAL	28	.474	.710	6.1	13.8
92-93	CAL	30	.517	.628	6.3	19.1
93-94	CAL	30	.476	.764	7.9	24.3
Totals		88	.489	.713	6.8	19.2

NBA REGULAR-SEASON STATISTICS

				FGs		3-PT FGs		FTs		Rebounds						
		G	MIN	FG	PCT	FG	PCT	FT	PCT	OFF	TOT	AST	STL	BLK	PTS	PPG
94-95	LAC	81	2556	439	.402	65	.298	199	.754	132	354	133	72	55	1142	14.1
95-96	LAC	77	1816	257	.447	37	.319	99	.750	89	246	84	61	25	650	8.4
Totals		158	4372	696	.417	102	.305	298	.753	221	600	217	133	80	1792	11.3

TRACY MURRAY

Team: Washington Bullets
Position: Forward
Height: 6'7" **Weight:** 228
Birthdate: July 25, 1971

NBA Experience: 4 years
College: UCLA
Acquired: Signed as a free agent, 7/96

Background: Murray was the highest-scoring player in California prep history when he signed to play at UCLA. While sharing the ball with Don MacLean, Murray finished his college career No. 2 in Pac-10 history in 3-point goals (197) and hit them at a 50-percent clip as a junior. He led the NBA in 3-point percentage (.459) in 1993-94 but has played with three different teams in his four seasons. The Bullets are his fourth team.

Strengths: Murray can flat-out shoot the ball from deep. There was no better 3-point shooter in the NBA in its final season with the long arc, and he has buried more than 40 percent from the shorter distance in each of the past two years. He creates matchup problems because big men are forced to play him outside the arc. Murray also nails his free throws and has become a better scorer.

Weaknesses: Murray lacks the quickness and strength to be a solid NBA defensive player. His body is not made for physical play. For a player with his height and touch, Murray is not much of a threat near the basket. He's a very poor rebounder, and his turnover total comes close to matching his assists. He's a specialist, to be sure.

Analysis: Murray, a throw-in for the Rockets in the Clyde Drexler deal two years ago, did not make Houston's playoff roster for the team's 1995 title run and was signed by expansion Toronto before the 1995-96 season. The Raptors got a fine shooter who served as a sixth man for much of the year and averaged a career-high 16.2 PPG. A unique player, Murray defines "instant offense."

PLAYER SUMMARY

Will ....shoot from deep
Can't........provide physical presence
Expect ....matchup problems
Don't Expect ....low-post points
Fantasy Value $5-7
Card Value ....7-12¢

COLLEGE STATISTICS

		G	FGP	FTP	RPG	PPG
89-90	UCLA	33	.442	.767	5.5	12.3
90-91	UCLA	32	.503	.794	6.7	21.2
91-92	UCLA	33	.538	.800	7.0	21.4
Totals		98	.500	.791	6.4	18.3

NBA REGULAR-SEASON STATISTICS

				FGs		3-PT FGs		FTs		Rebounds						
		G	MIN	FG	PCT	FG	PCT	FT	PCT	OFF	TOT	AST	STL	BLK	PTS	PPG
92-93	POR	48	495	108	.415	21	.300	35	.875	40	83	11	8	5	272	5.7
93-94	POR	66	820	167	.470	50	.459	50	.694	43	111	31	21	20	434	6.6
94-95	POR/HOU	54	516	95	.408	35	.407	33	.786	20	59	19	14	4	258	4.8
95-96	TOR	82	2458	496	.454	151	.422	182	.831	114	352	131	87	40	1325	16.2
Totals		250	4289	866	.446	257	.413	300	.804	217	605	192	130	69	2289	9.2

DIKEMBE MUTOMBO

Team: Atlanta Hawks
Position: Center
Height: 7'2" **Weight:** 250
Birthdate: June 25, 1966

NBA Experience: 5 years
College: Georgetown
Acquired: Signed as a free agent, 7/96

Background: Mutombo was raised in Zaire, a French-speaking African nation, and was forced to sit out his freshman season at Georgetown because the SAT was not offered in French. He earned Big East Defensive Player of the Year honors in 1990 and 1991. The fourth overall pick in the 1991 draft, Mutombo was the only rookie to play in the 1992 All-Star Game. He led the NBA in blocked shots the last three of his five seasons and signed on with Atlanta last summer.

Strengths: The NBA's Defensive Player of the Year in 1995, Mutombo is a force to be reckoned with. His great size, giant wingspan, and anticipation make him the best shot-blocker in the league. He is also one of the premier rebounders in basketball, and he never stops battling for position. Mutombo has developed an accurate hook and can score on the inside. He also runs well.

Weaknesses: Though his offense came as a pleasant surprise after modest college scoring days, Mutombo is not a Patrick Ewing, David Robinson, or Hakeem Olajuwon. He also lags behind when it comes to passing, ball-handling, and feel for the game. He has seen his scoring average drop in each of the past four years.

Analysis: Mutombo, an international spokesman for CARE and one of the most kind-hearted citizens in the game, shows no such compassion to the men he guards. He does not score much, but he has been the NBA's dominant defensive big man over the last few seasons. He continues to provide a dozen boards and four swats per game.

PLAYER SUMMARY	
Will	dominate on defense
Can't	score like Hakeem
Expect	12 RPG, 4 BPG
Don't Expect	ball-handling
Fantasy Value	$25-30
Card Value	15-25¢

COLLEGE STATISTICS

		G	FGP	FTP	RPG	PPG
88-89	GEOR	33	.707	.479	3.3	3.9
89-90	GEOR	31	.709	.598	10.5	10.7
90-91	GEOR	32	.586	.703	12.2	15.2
Totals		96	.644	.641	8.6	9.9

NBA REGULAR-SEASON STATISTICS

				FGs		3-PT FGs		FTs		Rebounds						
		G	MIN	FG	PCT	FG	PCT	FT	PCT	OFF	TOT	AST	STL	BLK	PTS	PPG
91-92	DEN	71	2716	428	.493	0	.000	321	.642	316	870	156	43	210	1177	16.6
92-93	DEN	82	3029	398	.510	0	.000	335	.681	344	1070	147	43	287	1131	13.8
93-94	DEN	82	2853	365	.569	0	.000	256	.583	286	971	127	59	336	986	12.0
94-95	DEN	82	3100	349	.556	0	.000	248	.654	319	1029	113	40	321	946	11.5
95-96	DEN	74	2713	284	.499	0	.000	246	.695	249	871	108	38	332	814	11.0
Totals		391	14411	1824	.523	0	.000	1406	.650	1514	4811	651	223	1486	5054	12.9

PETE MYERS

Team: Charlotte Hornets
Position: Guard/Forward
Height: 6'6″ **Weight:** 192
Birthdate: September 15, 1963
NBA Experience: 8 years

College: Faulkner St.; Arkansas-Little Rock
Acquired: Signed as a free agent, 2/96

Background: Myers, who played in relative obscurity at Arkansas-Little Rock, has been the definition of a journeyman. He has seen action with seven different teams in eight NBA seasons, including two stints with the Spurs and Bulls, and has also played in the CBA and Europe. Myers was traded from Charlotte to Miami last year, then re-signed with the Hornets after the Heat released him.

Strengths: Myers is a valuable defensive player. He brings good size to the backcourt and will not back down from anyone, including the big scorers. He has pretty good quickness and gets out on the break. Myers comes off the bench and plays hard, keeping within his offensive capabilities.

Weaknesses: The main reason Myers has bounced around for so long is his lack of an offensive strength. He's the kind of shooter teams leave open, knowing he's not going to kill them. He won't do much off the drive, either. His accuracy from the field and the free-throw line are troubling. His ball skills are marginal.

Analysis: Myers has two claims to fame. Foremost, he was the lucky Bull who had the unenviable task of taking over Michael Jordan's starting spot when M.J. retired. Earning him far less notoriety but a good share of NBA jobs has been his willingness to get all over his man. It's a good thing he knows how to play defense.

PLAYER SUMMARY	
Will	blanket his man
Can't	shoot, score
Expect	a specialist
Don't Expect	10 PPG
Fantasy Value	$0
Card Value	5-7¢

COLLEGE STATISTICS

		G	FGP	FTP	RPG	PPG
81-82	FAUL	26	.548	.743	5.1	12.4
82-83	FAUL	26	.578	.627	7.5	15.2
84-85	ALR	30	.451	.719	7.1	14.8
85-86	ALR	34	.534	.747	7.9	19.2
Totals		116	.521	.712	7.0	15.6

NBA REGULAR-SEASON STATISTICS

				FGs		3-PT FGs		FTs		Rebounds						
		G	MIN	FG	PCT	FG	PCT	FT	PCT	OFF	TOT	AST	STL	BLK	PTS	PPG
86-87	CHI	29	155	19	.365	0	.000	28	.651	8	17	21	14	2	66	2.3
87-88	SA	22	328	43	.453	0	.000	26	.667	11	37	48	17	6	112	5.1
88-89	PHI/NY	33	270	31	.425	0	.000	33	.688	15	33	48	20	2	95	2.9
89-90	NY/NJ	52	751	89	.396	0	.000	66	.660	33	96	135	35	11	244	4.7
90-91	SA	8	103	10	.435	0	.000	9	.818	2	18	14	3	3	29	3.6
93-94	CHI	82	2030	253	.455	8	.276	136	.701	54	181	245	78	20	650	7.9
94-95	CHI	71	1270	119	.415	10	.256	70	.614	57	139	148	58	15	318	4.5
95-96	MIA/CHA	71	1092	91	.368	14	.241	80	.656	35	140	145	34	17	276	3.9
Totals		368	5999	655	.420	32	.219	448	.668	215	661	804	259	76	1790	4.9

JOHNNY NEWMAN

Team: Milwaukee Bucks
Position: Forward/Guard
Height: 6'7" **Weight:** 205
Birthdate: November 28, 1963

NBA Experience: 10 years
College: Richmond
Acquired: Signed as a free agent, 10/94

Background: Newman, who set a career scoring record at Richmond, spent one year with Cleveland before being waived. He has since played for New York, Charlotte, New Jersey, and Milwaukee in his ten-year NBA career. He started all 82 games for the Bucks in 1995-96 and averaged 10.8 PPG after falling into single digits the year before.

Strengths: Newman is an impressive athlete who has always had a scoring bent. A slasher who also runs and shoots with 3-point range, he is capable of scoring in bunches. Newman can play both small forward and big guard and has become something of a stopper in the last few years.

Weaknesses: Newman is not the consistent offensive force he was earlier in his career. He is not among the best ball-handling or passing swingmen, and he does not drive to the bucket as readily as he once did. Newman's commitment to playing physical defense often lands him in foul trouble.

Analysis: Newman was Milwaukee's second-most reliable player last season, behind Vin Baker and Glenn Robinson. Several years back, no one would have believed that Newman's value would be as a defensive stalwart and not as a scorer. He is still capable of big offensive nights, but his know-how and versatility are now his best assets.

PLAYER SUMMARY

Will ....hound his man
Can't ....set up the offense
Expect ....veteran know-how
Don't Expect ....15 PPG
Fantasy Value......................................$1
Card Value......................................5-7¢

COLLEGE STATISTICS

		G	FGP	FTP	RPG	PPG
82-83	RICH	28	.529	.719	3.1	12.3
83-84	RICH	32	.528	.787	6.1	21.9
84-85	RICH	32	.551	.773	5.2	21.3
85-86	RICH	30	.517	.890	7.3	22.0
Totals		122	.532	.800	5.5	19.5

NBA REGULAR-SEASON STATISTICS

			FGs		3-PT FGs		FTs		Rebounds						
		G	MIN	FG	PCT	FG	PCT	FT	PCT	OFF	TOT	AST	STL	BLK	PTS	PPG
86-87	CLE	59	630	113	.411	1	.045	66	.868	36	70	27	20	7	293	5.0
87-88	NY	77	1589	270	.435	26	.280	207	.841	87	159	62	72	11	773	10.0
88-89	NY	81	2336	455	.475	97	.338	286	.815	93	206	162	111	23	1293	16.0
89-90	NY	80	2277	374	.476	45	.317	239	.799	60	191	180	95	22	1032	12.9
90-91	CHA	81	2477	478	.470	30	.357	385	.809	94	254	188	100	17	1371	16.9
91-92	CHA	55	1651	295	.477	13	.283	236	.766	71	179	146	70	14	839	15.3
92-93	CHA	64	1471	279	.522	12	.267	194	.808	72	143	117	45	19	764	11.9
93-94	CHA/NJ	81	1697	313	.471	24	.267	182	.809	86	180	72	69	27	832	10.3
94-95	MIL	82	1896	226	.463	45	.352	137	.801	72	173	91	69	13	634	7.7
95-96	MIL	82	2690	321	.495	61	.377	186	.802	66	200	154	90	15	889	10.8
Totals		742	18714	3124	.473	354	.322	2118	.807	737	1755	1199	741	168	8720	11.8

KEN NORMAN

Team: Atlanta Hawks
Position: Forward
Height: 6'8" **Weight:** 228
Birthdate: September 5, 1964

NBA Experience: 9 years
College: Wabash Valley; Illinois
Acquired: Traded from Bucks for Roy Hinson, 6/94

Background: Norman was a two-time All-Big Ten selection at Illinois, where he set a school record for field-goal percentage. He became a starter for the Clippers as a rookie and averaged a career-high 18.1 PPG in his second season. After six years in L.A., he has not enjoyed as much success in Milwaukee or Atlanta.

Strengths: Nicknamed "Snake" for his slithering moves around the basket, Norman thrives in an open-court game. He also makes some nifty shots in the paint and has added the 3-point shot to his arsenal in the last few seasons. Norman is capable of controlling the boards and playing strong "D."

Weaknesses: The glaring weakness in Norman's game is his horrendous free-throw shooting, which stands at less than 60 percent for his career and was only about 35 percent last season. It's perplexing, because he hit a better percentage from 3-point range last year. Norman is inconsistent, and some contend it's due to a lack of effort.

Analysis: Norman spent most of the 1995-96 season on the Atlanta bench, often earning a DNP-CD (did not play, coach's decision) in the final box score. For some reason, he has abandoned the rugged style of play that gained him notice in L.A. Norman now seems content to get his points from long range and on the break.

PLAYER SUMMARY	
Will	shoot 3-pointers
Can't	make free throws
Expect	reserve minutes
Don't Expect	a physical force
Fantasy Value	$1-3
Card Value	7-10¢

COLLEGE STATISTICS

		G	FGP	FTP	RPG	PPG
82-83	WAB	35	.605	.673	10.3	20.4
84-85	ILL	29	.632	.663	3.7	7.8
85-86	ILL	32	.641	.802	7.1	16.4
86-87	ILL	31	.578	.727	9.8	20.7
Totals		127	.608	.717	7.9	16.6

NBA REGULAR-SEASON STATISTICS

				FGs		3-PT FGs		FTs		Rebounds						
		G	MIN	FG	PCT	FG	PCT	FT	PCT	OFF	TOT	AST	STL	BLK	PTS	PPG
87-88	LAC	66	1435	241	.482	0	.000	87	.512	100	263	78	44	34	569	8.6
88-89	LAC	80	3020	638	.502	4	.190	170	.630	245	667	277	106	66	1450	18.1
89-90	LAC	70	2334	484	.510	7	.438	153	.632	143	470	160	78	59	1128	16.1
90-91	LAC	70	2309	520	.501	6	.188	173	.629	177	497	159	63	63	1219	17.4
91-92	LAC	77	2009	402	.490	4	.143	121	.535	158	448	125	53	66	929	12.1
92-93	LAC	76	2477	498	.511	10	.263	131	.595	209	571	165	59	58	1137	15.0
93-94	MIL	82	2539	412	.448	63	.333	92	.503	169	500	222	58	46	979	11.9
94-95	ATL	74	1879	388	.453	98	.344	64	.457	103	362	94	34	20	938	12.7
95-96	ATL	34	770	127	.465	33	.393	17	.354	40	132	63	15	16	304	8.9
Totals		629	18772	3710	.488	225	.320	1008	.568	1344	3910	1343	510	428	8653	13.8

CHARLES OAKLEY

Team: New York Knicks
Position: Forward
Height: 6'9" **Weight:** 245
Birthdate: December 18, 1963
NBA Experience: 11 years

College: Virginia Union
Acquired: Traded from Bulls with 1988 first- and third-round picks for Bill Cartwright and 1988 first- and third-round picks, 6/88

Background: The top Division II rebounder in the country in 1984-85, Oakley grabbed more than 17 per game at Virginia Union. He made the NBA All-Rookie Team and became one of the league's best rebounders with Chicago, then was traded to New York for Bill Cartwright in 1988. The 1994 All-Star and former All-Defensive player has fought off a recent run of injuries.

Strengths: Once the NBA's "Chairman of the Boards," Oakley uses his muscular body to get to the glass and still plays bruising defense. He contributes nearly ten boards per night, and it requires great courage to drive toward him. He is a reliable shooter from 20 feet, and he hits his free throws.

Weaknesses: Oakley does not jump well, relying more on strength and positioning. He commits a lot of fouls and blocks few shots. He has not been a popular player during his career, sometimes alienating teammates as much as opponents.

Analysis: Oakley played in 268 consecutive games before undergoing toe surgery two years ago. A broken right thumb sidelined him last season, and a fractured eye socket late in the year was his third broken bone in two years. It's ironic, because Oakley has made a successful career out of punishing his foes.

PLAYER SUMMARY

Will ....drop jumpers
Can't ....alter shots
Expect......................10,000 rebounds
Don't Expect ....low-post offense
Fantasy Value $9-11
Card Value ....7-12¢

COLLEGE STATISTICS

		G	FGP	FTP	RPG	PPG
81-82	VU	28	.620	.610	12.5	15.9
82-83	VU	28	.582	.588	13.0	19.3
83-84	VU	30	.612	.621	13.1	21.7
84-85	VU	31	.625	.669	17.3	24.0
Totals		117	.611	.626	14.0	20.3

NBA REGULAR-SEASON STATISTICS

		G	MIN	FGs FG	FGs PCT	3-PT FGs FG	3-PT FGs PCT	FTs FT	FTs PCT	Rebounds OFF	Rebounds TOT	AST	STL	BLK	PTS	PPG
85-86	CHI	77	1772	281	.519	0	.000	178	.662	255	664	133	68	30	740	9.6
86-87	CHI	82	2980	468	.445	11	.367	245	.686	299	1074	296	85	36	1192	14.5
87-88	CHI	82	2816	375	.483	3	.250	261	.727	326	1066	248	68	28	1014	12.4
88-89	NY	82	2604	426	.510	12	.250	197	.773	343	861	187	104	14	1061	12.9
89-90	NY	61	2196	336	.524	0	.000	217	.761	258	727	146	64	16	889	14.6
90-91	NY	76	2739	307	.516	0	.000	239	.784	305	920	204	62	17	853	11.2
91-92	NY	82	2309	210	.522	0	.000	86	.735	256	700	133	67	15	506	6.2
92-93	NY	82	2230	219	.508	0	.000	127	.722	288	708	126	85	15	565	6.9
93-94	NY	82	2932	363	.478	0	.000	243	.776	349	965	218	110	18	969	11.8
94-95	NY	50	1567	192	.489	3	.250	119	.793	155	445	126	60	7	506	10.1
95-96	NY	53	1775	211	.471	7	.269	175	.833	162	460	137	58	14	604	11.4
Totals		809	25920	3388	.493	36	.252	2087	.746	2996	8590	1954	831	210	8899	11.0

ED O'BANNON

Team: New Jersey Nets
Position: Forward
Height: 6'8" **Weight:** 222
Birthdate: August 14, 1972

NBA Experience: 1 year
College: UCLA
Acquired: First-round pick in 1995 draft (ninth overall)

Background: Several sources named O'Bannon national Player of the Year in 1994-95, when he led UCLA to the national championship. Despite a 1990 injury to his left knee that sidelined him for more than a year, O'Bannon finished his college career as the fourth-leading scorer in UCLA history. New Jersey selected him ninth overall and used him primarily off the bench during his rookie campaign.

Strengths: The left-handed O'Bannon is an athletic player who can beat his man off the dribble and ignite the fastbreak. He loves to run and is a great finisher who plays above the rim. He rebounds, passes, and displays a nice feel for the game. Everyone was sold on his leadership skills even before he carried UCLA to the 1995 national title. He's smart, team-oriented, and willing to work toward becoming an NBA standout.

Weaknesses: The two main concerns about O'Bannon are his shooting stroke and his knees, although his first NBA season was a healthy one. The same can't be said for his jumper. O'Bannon is a scorer, not a shooter. He was not a consistent perimeter threat in college, and he struggled badly against NBA defenders for most of last season. O'Bannon also needs to develop his own "D." The quicker and stronger forwards give him fits.

Analysis: O'Bannon was a mild disappointment last season. Nets fans wanted the superstar they watched tear up UCLA's Final Four foes in 1995, but instead they saw a 20-minutes-per-night athlete who failed to provide a consistent scoring threat. O'Bannon did show promise, and he could develop into a 15-point, seven-rebound contributor. If his jumper never comes around, it won't be for a lack of effort.

PLAYER SUMMARY	
Will	get to the hoop
Can't	provide leadership
Expect	further strides
Don't Expect	a 3-point gunner
Fantasy Value	$1
Card Value	40-80¢

COLLEGE STATISTICS

		G	FGP	FTP	RPG	PPG
91-92	UCLA	23	.416	.630	3.0	3.6
92-93	UCLA	33	.539	.707	7.0	16.7
93-94	UCLA	28	.484	.745	8.8	18.2
94-95	UCLA	33	.533	.785	8.3	20.4
Totals		117	.513	.739	7.0	15.5

NBA REGULAR-SEASON STATISTICS

			FGs		3-PT FGs		FTs		Rebounds						
	G	MIN	FG	PCT	FG	PCT	FT	PCT	OFF	TOT	AST	STL	BLK	PTS	PPG
95-96 NJ	64	1253	156	.390	10	.179	77	.713	65	168	63	44	11	399	6.2
Totals	64	1253	156	.390	10	.179	77	.713	65	168	63	44	11	399	6.2

HAKEEM OLAJUWON

Team: Houston Rockets
Position: Center
Height: 7'0" **Weight:** 255
Birthdate: January 21, 1963

NBA Experience: 12 years
College: Houston
Acquired: First-round pick in 1984 draft (first overall)

Background: Olajuwon led Houston to the Final Four three straight years, and he led the nation in rebounding and field-goal accuracy as a senior. He was named Southwest Conference Player of the 1980s. The former soccer goalie in Nigeria has made 11 All-Star trips in 12 years. He led Houston to the 1994 and 1995 NBA titles, earning Finals MVP honors each time. He was also named league MVP in 1993-94.

Strengths: Olajuwon is one of the most talented and versatile centers ever. Year after year, he is one of the best scorers, rebounders, and shot-blockers in the game. His baseline turnaround might be the most unstoppable shot in basketball. He has an amazing touch, passes well, and has earned two Defensive Player of the Year awards.

Weaknesses: Olajuwon piles up turnovers, but that's because he's sometimes triple-teamed. He is no longer a great force on the offensive boards.

Analysis: An American citizen, "The Dream" earned a special honor last season when he was selected to play with Dream Team III in the Atlanta Olympics. Having already secured his spot as one of the all-time greats, Olajuwon continues to play at a level that no center in basketball can surpass. He is the NBA's career leader in blocks.

PLAYER SUMMARY	
Will	lead his team
Can't	be guarded by one
Expect	Hall of Fame induction
Don't Expect	off nights
Fantasy Value	$85-90
Card Value	40-80¢

COLLEGE STATISTICS

		G	FGP	FTP	RPG	PPG
81-82	HOUS	29	.607	.563	6.2	8.3
82-83	HOUS	34	.611	.595	11.4	13.9
83-84	HOUS	37	.675	.526	13.5	16.8
Totals		100	.639	.555	10.7	13.3

NBA REGULAR-SEASON STATISTICS

				FGs		3-PT FGs		FTs		Rebounds						
		G	MIN	FG	PCT	FG	PCT	FT	PCT	OFF	TOT	AST	STL	BLK	PTS	PPG
84-85	HOU	82	2914	677	.538	0	.000	338	.613	440	974	111	99	220	1692	20.6
85-86	HOU	68	2467	625	.526	0	.000	347	.645	333	781	137	134	231	1597	23.5
86-87	HOU	75	2760	677	.508	1	.200	400	.702	315	858	220	140	254	1755	23.4
87-88	HOU	79	2825	712	.514	0	.000	381	.695	302	959	163	162	214	1805	22.8
88-89	HOU	82	3024	790	.508	0	.000	454	.696	338	1105	149	213	282	2034	24.8
89-90	HOU	82	3124	806	.501	1	.167	382	.713	299	1149	234	174	376	1995	24.3
90-91	HOU	56	2062	487	.508	0	.000	213	.769	219	770	131	121	221	1187	21.2
91-92	HOU	70	2636	591	.502	0	.000	328	.766	246	845	157	127	304	1510	21.6
92-93	HOU	82	3242	848	.529	0	.000	444	.779	283	1068	291	150	342	2140	26.1
93-94	HOU	80	3277	894	.528	8	.421	388	.716	229	955	287	128	297	2184	27.3
94-95	HOU	72	2853	798	.517	3	.188	406	.756	172	775	255	133	242	2005	27.8
95-96	HOU	72	2797	768	.514	3	.214	397	.724	176	784	257	113	207	1936	26.9
Totals		900	33981	8673	.516	16	.184	4478	.711	3352	11023	2392	1694	3190	21840	24.3

SHAQUILLE O'NEAL

Team: Los Angeles Lakers
Position: Center
Height: 7'1" **Weight:** 303
Birthdate: March 6, 1972

NBA Experience: 4 years
College: Louisiana St.
Acquired: Signed as a free agent, 7/96

Background: Shaq was a two-time All-American in his three years at Louisiana State and earned a handful of Player of the Year honors after his sophomore campaign. Few Rookie of the Year winners have ever made as big an impact as Shaq did. The first overall pick in the 1992 draft was the first rookie since Michael Jordan to start in the All-Star Game, and he has started each year since. He won the 1995 NBA scoring title. He bolted Orlando in July 1996 for a seven-year, $121-million free-agent deal with the Lakers.

Strengths: O'Neal is as powerful as any player in the game. He has torn down two backboards on slam dunks and is virtually unstoppable when he gets the ball in the paint. He scores, rebounds, and swats shots with the best of them. His field-goal percentage is among the best in the league, and he adds new moves every year. He's a fan favorite who has cut a rap album and starred in major motion pictures.

Weaknesses: The biggest struggles for this mega-star come from the free-throw line, which is too bad since he spends a lot of time there. He gets worse instead of better, having hit just .487 of his attempts in 1995-96. His stroke needs even more practice than his acting.

Analysis: O'Neal has played on each of the last two Dream Teams while solidifying his status as the most physically dominant player in the NBA. He sat out the first six weeks of the 1995-96 season with a broken thumb, but nothing can slow him from storming near the top of the league in scoring, rebounding, shot-blocking, and field-goal percentage. Shaq is a worldwide celebrity.

PLAYER SUMMARY	
Will	dominate
Can't	hit two free throws
Expect	mega-bucks
Don't Expect	single-teams
Fantasy Value	$70-75
Card Value	$1.25-2.75

COLLEGE STATISTICS

		G	FGP	FTP	RPG	PPG
89-90	LSU	32	.573	.556	12.0	13.9
90-91	LSU	28	.628	.638	14.7	27.6
91-92	LSU	30	.615	.528	14.0	24.1
Totals		90	.610	.575	13.5	21.6

NBA REGULAR-SEASON STATISTICS

		G	MIN	FGs FG	FGs PCT	3-PT FGs FG	3-PT FGs PCT	FTs FT	FTs PCT	Rebounds OFF	Rebounds TOT	AST	STL	BLK	PTS	PPG
92-93	ORL	81	3071	733	.562	0	.000	427	.592	342	1122	152	60	286	1893	23.4
93-94	ORL	81	3224	953	.599	0	.000	471	.554	384	1072	195	76	231	2377	29.3
94-95	ORL	79	2923	930	.583	0	.000	455	.533	328	901	214	73	192	2315	29.3
95-96	ORL	54	1946	592	.573	1	.500	249	.487	182	596	155	34	115	1434	26.6
Totals		295	11164	3208	.581	1	.091	1602	.546	1236	3691	716	243	824	8019	27.2

GREG OSTERTAG

Team: Utah Jazz
Position: Center
Height: 7'2" **Weight:** 280
Birthdate: March 6, 1973

NBA Experience: 1 year
College: Kansas
Acquired: First-round pick in 1995 draft (28th overall)

Background: Ostertag never averaged more than 10.3 PPG in any season at Kansas, but he finished his career as the leading shot-blocker in Big Eight history with 258 rejections. He did not become a regular starter until his junior season, and he led the Jayhawks in field-goal accuracy as a senior. Ostertag was a first-round draft choice of Utah, and he blocked 63 shots in 57 rookie games.

Strengths: Ostertag stands 7'2", and that's something you can't teach. He uses his big body to bang around in the post, box his opponents out, play physical defense, and block shots. He averaged one swat every 10.5 minutes last season and led the Jazz in blocks per game. Size alone makes Ostertag a potential rebounding force, and he has good hands. He has shown signs of an inside shooting touch.

Weaknesses: Ostertag is a poor offensive player. He does not have a go-to move in the post and is not going to beat teams with his jump shot. His range is limited to about 12 feet, he does not run well, and he rarely passes the ball. He tallied an embarrassing five assists in 661 minutes last year. Ostertag can be out-quicked by virtually everyone he guards. He'd be in frequent foul trouble if he saw more floor time.

Analysis: Ostertag, the latest in a long line of Utah mountain men, will stick around because of his size and shot-blocking ability. He can make an impact at the defensive end without having to do a lot, simply by taking up space. Make no mistake; Ostertag does have some skills. He needs to assert himself on defense and the boards to make up for his considerable offensive deficiencies.

PLAYER SUMMARY

Will	take up space
Can't	burn his man
Expect	blocked shots
Don't Expect	good passes
Fantasy Value	$1-3
Card Value	7-10¢

COLLEGE STATISTICS

		G	FGP	FTP	RPG	PPG
91-92	KANS	32	.545	.653	3.5	4.8
92-93	KANS	29	.517	.600	4.1	5.3
93-94	KANS	35	.533	.631	8.8	10.3
94-95	KANS	31	.596	.553	7.5	9.6
Totals		127	.550	.604	6.1	7.6

NBA REGULAR-SEASON STATISTICS

			FGs		3-PT FGs		FTs		Rebounds						
	G	MIN	FG	PCT	FG	PCT	FT	PCT	OFF	TOT	AST	STL	BLK	PTS	PPG
95-96 UTA	57	661	86	.473	0	.000	36	.667	57	175	5	5	63	208	3.6
Totals	57	661	86	.473	0	.000	36	.667	57	175	5	5	63	208	3.6

BO OUTLAW

Team: Los Angeles Clippers
Position: Center/Forward
Height: 6'8" **Weight:** 210
Birthdate: April 13, 1971

NBA Experience: 3 years
College: South Plains; Houston
Acquired: Signed as a free agent, 2/94

Background: Charles "Bo" Outlaw led the nation in field-goal percentage in 1992 and 1993 at the University of Houston, but he was bypassed in the 1993 NBA draft. He was tearing up the CBA when the Clippers signed him in February 1994. Outlaw stuck with the Clippers and finished ninth in the league with 1.86 blocks per game in 1994-95. He led the Clippers in blocks and field-goal accuracy last year.

Strengths: Outlaw is probably the best 6'8" shot-blocker in the NBA. What he gives up in size he makes up for in leaping ability, hustle, and heart. He has been asked to match up with centers much of the time, and he does an admirable job. He can also guard threes and fours. Outlaw is a well-conditioned athlete who runs like the wind and does not try to play over his head.

Weaknesses: Outlaw has horrible mechanics and a poor touch on his jump shot, and he is one of the worst free-throw shooters you'll find. Aside from "garbage" buckets, putbacks, and layups, he simply can't fill the nets. His field-goal accuracy is borne of slam dunks. Though he's built like a swingman, Outlaw does not handle the ball or pass well.

Analysis: Outlaw is a well-liked, charitable player who knows what he has to do to make it in the NBA. His job is defense, and he plays it pretty well. He's enough athlete to chase perimeter players all night, and he's got the energy to battle big men effectively. He blocks shots better than anyone else his size. One or two offensive moves might gain him more minutes.

PLAYER SUMMARY

Will ....tangle with centers
Can't ....buy a free throw
Expect ....1-plus BPG
Don't Expect ....a pretty stroke
Fantasy Value.................................$0
Card Value......................................5-8¢

COLLEGE STATISTICS

		G	FGP	FTP	RPG	PPG
89-90	SP	30	.563	.507	9.6	12.1
90-91	SP	30	.661	.574	10.9	13.2
91-92	HOUS	31	.684	.442	8.2	11.9
92-93	HOUS	30	.658	.495	10.0	16.2
Totals		121	.640	.503	9.7	13.3

NBA REGULAR-SEASON STATISTICS

				FGs		3-PT FGs		FTs		Rebounds						
		G	MIN	FG	PCT	FG	PCT	FT	PCT	OFF	TOT	AST	STL	BLK	PTS	PPG
93-94	LAC	37	871	98	.587	0	.000	61	.592	81	212	36	36	37	257	6.9
94-95	LAC	81	1655	170	.523	0	.000	82	.441	121	313	84	90	151	422	5.2
95-96	LAC	80	985	107	.575	0	.000	72	.444	87	200	50	44	91	286	3.6
Totals		198	3511	375	.553	0	.000	215	.477	289	725	170	170	279	965	4.9

BILLY OWENS

Team: Sacramento Kings
Position: Forward/Guard
Height: 6'9" **Weight:** 225
Birthdate: May 1, 1969
NBA Experience: 5 years

College: Syracuse
Acquired: Traded from Heat with
Kevin Gamble for Tyrone Corbin and
Walt Williams, 2/96

Background: Owens, the 1988 A.P. High School Player of the Year at Carlisle (Pennsylvania) High, finished his three-year career at Syracuse near the top of the school charts in several categories. He was one of the top NBA rookies with Golden State but has since had surgery on both knees. He has also played with Miami and Sacramento, averaging about 14 PPG.

Strengths: Owens has always been known as a talented and versatile player. He can play three positions, though he's most comfortable at small forward. Owens is at his best in an up-tempo game, where he can trigger the break like a point guard or finish with jams. He is an exceptional offensive rebounder, has a keen passing eye, and is capable of big scoring nights.

Weaknesses: Owens has not added much to his game since joining the pro ranks. He is not a consistent outside shooter, and his range is limited. He still misses almost four of every ten free-throw attempts. Owens has not improved much on the defensive end, either. His decision-making and his work ethic have been questioned by those in the know.

Analysis: Owens got off to a great start in 1995-96, becoming the triple-double threat many expected him to be five years ago. After being traded to Sacramento, however, his level of play dropped off to a point at which he has spent most of his career. He's a talented player whose numbers are good; it's just that much more had been expected of him.

PLAYER SUMMARY

Will	ignite the break
Can't	attain stardom
Expect	offensive boards
Don't Expect	tough defense
Fantasy Value	$13-16
Card Value	10-15¢

COLLEGE STATISTICS

		G	FGP	FTP	RPG	PPG
88-89	SYR	38	.521	.648	6.9	13.0
89-90	SYR	33	.486	.722	8.4	18.2
90-91	SYR	32	.509	.674	11.6	23.3
Totals		103	.505	.682	8.8	17.7

NBA REGULAR-SEASON STATISTICS

				FGs		3-PT FGs		FTs		Rebounds						
		G	MIN	FG	PCT	FG	PCT	FT	PCT	OFF	TOT	AST	STL	BLK	PTS	PPG
91-92	GS	80	2510	468	.525	1	.111	204	.654	243	639	188	90	65	1141	14.3
92-93	GS	37	1201	247	.501	1	.091	117	.639	108	264	144	35	28	612	16.5
93-94	GS	79	2738	492	.507	3	.200	199	.610	230	640	326	83	60	1186	15.0
94-95	MIA	70	2296	403	.491	2	.091	194	.620	203	502	246	80	30	1002	14.3
95-96	MIA/SAC	62	1982	323	.480	5	.278	157	.636	143	411	204	49	38	808	13.0
Totals		328	10727	1933	.502	12	.160	871	.631	927	2456	1108	337	221	4749	14.5

ROBERT PACK

Team: New Jersey Nets
Position: Guard
Height: 6'2" **Weight:** 190
Birthdate: February 3, 1969

NBA Experience: 5 years
College: Tyler; Southern California
Acquired: Signed as a free agent, 7/96

Background: Pack totaled 319 assists in just two years at Southern Cal. He joined former USC stars Gus Williams, Jacque Hill, and Larry Friend when he recorded back-to-back years of 100 or more assists. He was not drafted but earned a rookie contract with Portland and spent three years in Denver before being traded to Washington before 1995-96. Injuries have cut short his last two seasons. The Nets picked him up in the off-season.

Strengths: Most of what Pack does starts with his lightning quickness. He also has good strength, and he is able to drive past just about anyone either in a half-court game or in transition. He's capable of racking up points and assists. He shoots with 3-point range and hits his free throws consistently. Pack is as tough as nails on defense. The feisty sort, he is able to come up with steals and welcomes a challenge.

Weaknesses: Shooting is not Pack's specialty. He hits a poor percentage of his 3-pointers and takes some shots he should pass up. Pack's offense in general is hot and cold, though he feels the need to score. Better decision-making would improve his assist-to-turnover ratio, an important gauge of a point guard's effectiveness. Injuries have become a concern.

Analysis: Pack was beginning to emerge before a tear of the anterior cruciate ligament near the end of the 1994-95 season. He missed more than half of last season due to nerve damage in his right leg. When he's on the floor, Pack is a penetrating, productive point guard.

PLAYER SUMMARY	
Will	penetrate
Can't	pass up 3-pointers
Expect	supreme quickness
Don't Expect	error-free ball
Fantasy Value	$11-14
Card Value	5-8¢

COLLEGE STATISTICS

		G	FGP	FTP	APG	PPG
89-90	USC	28	.472	.677	5.9	12.1
90-91	USC	29	.480	.794	5.3	14.7
Totals		57	.476	.742	5.6	13.4

NBA REGULAR-SEASON STATISTICS

			FGs		3-PT FGs		FTs		Rebounds						
	G	MIN	FG	PCT	FG	PCT	FT	PCT	OFF	TOT	AST	STL	BLK	PTS	PPG
91-92 POR	72	894	115	.423	0	.000	102	.803	32	97	140	40	4	332	4.6
92-93 DEN	77	1579	285	.470	1	.125	239	.768	52	160	335	81	10	810	10.5
93-94 DEN	66	1382	223	.443	6	.207	179	.758	25	123	356	81	9	631	9.6
94-95 DEN	42	1144	170	.430	30	.417	137	.783	19	113	290	61	6	507	12.1
95-96 WAS	31	1084	190	.428	26	.265	154	.846	29	132	242	62	1	560	18.1
Totals	288	6083	983	.443	63	.290	811	.787	157	625	1363	325	30	2840	9.9

ROBERT PARISH

Unrestricted Free Agent
Last Team: Charlotte Hornets
Position: Center
Height: 7'0" **Weight:** 240
Birthdate: August 30, 1953

NBA Experience: 20 years
College: Centenary
Acquired: Signed as a free agent, 7/94

Background: The best player in Centenary history, "Chief" enjoyed four solid years with Golden State before his career blossomed in Boston. He helped the Celtics to championships in 1981, '84, and '86.

Strengths: Parish still rebounds and blocks shots, though his high-arching jumpers are less frequent. He will finish his career among the all-time leaders in scoring, rebounding, and blocks. He stays in great shape.

Weaknesses: Parish is no longer effective for long stretches, nor does he score. He is but a shadow of his former self in all phases of the game.

Analysis: Parish is headed for the Hall of Fame the first year he's eligible. At age 42, he broke Kareem Abdul-Jabbar's record of 1,560 games last season, and he even made 34 starts. Remarkable.

PLAYER SUMMARY	
Will	stay in shape
Can't	regain top form
Expect	the Hall to call
Don't Expect	two more years
Fantasy Value	$0
Card Value	8-15¢

COLLEGE STATISTICS

		G	FGP	FTP	RPG	PPG
72-73	CENT	27	.579	.610	18.7	23.0
73-74	CENT	25	.523	.628	15.3	19.9
74-75	CENT	29	.560	.661	15.4	18.9
75-76	CENT	27	.589	.694	18.0	24.8
Totals		108	.564	.655	16.9	21.6

NBA REGULAR-SEASON STATISTICS

				FGs		3-PT FGs		FTs		Rebounds						
		G	MIN	FG	PCT	FG	PCT	FT	PCT	OFF	TOT	AST	STL	BLK	PTS	PPG
76-77	GS	77	1384	288	.503	0	.000	121	.708	201	543	74	55	94	697	9.1
77-78	GS	82	1969	430	.472	0	.000	165	.625	211	679	95	79	123	1025	12.5
78-79	GS	76	2411	554	.499	0	.000	196	.698	265	916	115	100	217	1304	17.2
79-80	GS	72	2119	510	.507	0	.000	203	.715	257	793	122	58	115	1223	17.0
80-81	BOS	82	2298	635	.545	0	.000	282	.710	245	777	144	81	214	1552	18.9
81-82	BOS	80	2534	669	.542	0	.000	252	.710	288	866	140	68	192	1590	19.9
82-83	BOS	78	2459	619	.550	0	.000	271	.698	260	827	141	79	148	1509	19.3
83-84	BOS	80	2867	623	.542	0	.000	274	.745	243	857	139	55	116	1520	19.0
84-85	BOS	79	2850	551	.542	0	.000	292	.743	263	840	125	56	101	1394	17.6
85-86	BOS	81	2567	530	.549	0	.000	245	.731	246	770	145	65	116	1305	16.1
86-87	BOS	80	2995	588	.556	0	.000	227	.735	254	851	173	64	144	1403	17.5
87-88	BOS	74	2312	442	.589	0	.000	177	.734	173	628	115	55	84	1061	14.3
88-89	BOS	80	2840	596	.570	0	.000	294	.719	342	996	175	79	116	1486	18.6
89-90	BOS	79	2396	505	.580	0	.000	233	.747	259	796	103	38	69	1243	15.7
90-91	BOS	81	2441	485	.598	0	.000	237	.767	271	856	66	66	103	1207	14.9
91-92	BOS	79	2285	468	.535	0	.000	179	.772	219	705	70	68	97	1115	14.1
92-93	BOS	79	2146	416	.535	0	.000	162	.689	246	740	61	57	107	994	12.6
93-94	BOS	74	1987	356	.491	0	.000	154	.740	141	542	82	42	96	866	11.7
94-95	CHA	81	1352	159	.427	0	.000	71	.703	93	350	44	27	36	389	4.8
95-96	CHA	74	1086	120	.498	0	.000	50	.704	89	303	29	21	54	290	3.9
Totals		1568	45298	9544	.537	0	.000	4085	.721	4566	14635	2158	1213	2342	23173	14.8

CHEROKEE PARKS

Team: Minnesota Timberwolves
Position: Center
Height: 6'11" **Weight:** 275
Birthdate: October 11, 1972

NBA Experience: 1 year
College: Duke
Acquired: Traded from Mavericks for future considerations, 7/96

Background: Parks was a reserve on Duke's 1992 national championship team before moving into the starting five as a sophomore. He improved his production in points, rebounds, and assists in each of his four seasons. He finished his career second in school history in blocked shots and was taken 12th overall by Dallas in the 1995 draft. Parks saw limited action in 64 games during his rookie campaign. He joins the T'Wolves for 1996-97.

Strengths: Parks has the ability to pull opposing big men away from the paint with his long-range shooting. He also handles the ball well for a big man, furthering the matchup problems he can pose. Parks is a sound fundamental player who passes well from the high post and understands defensive concepts. He blocks a few shots.

Weaknesses: Parks gives away both strength and quickness to his opponents—not a healthy combination. He needs to add muscle to his finesse skills in order to stand up to the rigors of defending big men. His foot speed is not going to change for the better. Parks also has a slow trigger on his shot, and his low-post game needs a tune-up. He struggled from the field, the 3-point arc, and the free-throw line as a little-used rookie.

Analysis: Dallas drafted Parks 12 spots ahead of another big man, Loren Meyer, in 1995. The lesser-known player from Iowa State, however, wound up playing about 400 more minutes than the former prep All-American and high-profile "Dookie." Parks needs to continue working on his strength, as well as asserting himself on defense and the boards. His jump shot, in time, should take care of itself.

PLAYER SUMMARY	
Will	shoot with range
Can't	set speed records
Expect	finesse plays
Don't Expect	pure power
Fantasy Value	$0
Card Value	25-50¢

COLLEGE STATISTICS

		G	FGP	FTP	RPG	PPG
91-92	DUKE	34	.571	.725	2.4	5.0
92-93	DUKE	32	.652	.720	6.9	12.3
93-94	DUKE	34	.536	.772	8.4	14.4
94-95	DUKE	31	.501	.776	9.3	19.0
Totals		131	.551	.755	6.7	12.5

NBA REGULAR-SEASON STATISTICS

			FGs		3-PT FGs		FTs		Rebounds						
	G	MIN	FG	PCT	FG	PCT	FT	PCT	OFF	TOT	AST	STL	BLK	PTS	PPG
95-96 DAL	64	869	101	.409	7	.269	41	.661	66	216	29	25	32	250	3.9
Totals	64	869	101	.409	7	.269	41	.661	66	216	29	25	32	250	3.9

GARY PAYTON

Team: Seattle SuperSonics
Position: Guard
Height: 6'4" **Weight:** 190
Birthdate: July 23, 1968

NBA Experience: 6 years
College: Oregon St.
Acquired: First-round pick in 1990 draft (second overall)

Background: Payton was an All-American as a senior at Oregon State, where he set a school scoring record, ended his career second on the NCAA assists list, and set a Pac-10 record with 100 steals in his final season. Payton has been a six-year starter for Seattle and has played in the last three All-Star Games, and he led the league in steals for the first time last season. He was named Defensive Player of the Year last year and played on Dream Team III.

Strengths: Payton does everything a classic point guard should, and then some. He beats his man off the dribble and sets up his teammates, and he can score off spot-ups, fadeaway jumpers, and post-up moves. Most impressive is Payton's defense. He hounds the ball, makes his opponent work for everything he gets, and has been one of the NBA's best thieves.

Weaknesses: Although Payton has made great strides, some have wondered if he has the ability to be a great leader. A noted trash talker, he often makes opponents (and sometimes teammates) want to cram the ball down his throat. Payton is not one of the top 3-point or free-throw shooters at his position.

Analysis: Payton, generally regarded as the best defensive point guard in basketball, knows a thing or two about offense, too. He is among the leading assist men in the league, yet he also improved his scoring over his first five seasons and is now good for about 20 a night. Payton is clearly one of the best all-around lead guards in the NBA.

PLAYER SUMMARY	
Will	cause havoc on "D"
Can't	back down
Expect	points, assists, steals
Don't Expect	All-Star absences
Fantasy Value	$50-55
Card Value	15-25¢

COLLEGE STATISTICS

		G	FGP	FTP	APG	PPG
86-87	OSU	30	.459	.671	7.6	12.5
87-88	OSU	31	.489	.699	7.4	14.5
88-89	OSU	30	.475	.677	8.1	20.1
89-90	OSU	29	.504	.690	8.1	25.7
Totals		120	.485	.684	7.8	18.1

NBA REGULAR-SEASON STATISTICS

				FGs		3-PT FGs		FTs		Rebounds						
		G	MIN	FG	PCT	FG	PCT	FT	PCT	OFF	TOT	AST	STL	BLK	PTS	PPG
90-91	SEA	82	2244	259	.450	1	.077	69	.711	108	243	528	165	15	588	7.2
91-92	SEA	81	2549	331	.451	3	.130	99	.669	123	295	506	147	21	764	9.4
92-93	SEA	82	2548	476	.494	7	.206	151	.770	95	281	399	177	21	1110	13.5
93-94	SEA	82	2881	584	.504	15	.278	166	.595	105	269	494	188	19	1349	16.5
94-95	SEA	82	3015	685	.509	70	.302	249	.716	108	281	583	204	13	1689	20.6
95-96	SEA	81	3162	618	.484	98	.328	229	.748	104	339	608	231	19	1563	19.3
Totals		490	16399	2953	.488	194	.296	963	.701	643	1708	3118	1112	108	7063	14.4

ANTHONY PEELER

Team: Vancouver Grizzlies
Position: Guard
Height: 6'4" **Weight:** 212
Birthdate: November 25, 1969
NBA Experience: 4 years

College: Missouri
Acquired: Traded from Lakers with George Lynch for 1997 and 1998 second-round picks, 7/96

Background: The hotly recruited Peeler lived up to expectations at Missouri despite an inability to stay out of trouble. He was named Big Eight Player of the Year after averaging 23.4 PPG, 5.5 RPG, and 3.9 APG as a senior. Peeler slipped to 15th in the 1992 draft but enjoyed a fine rookie season. He overcame second-year leg injuries to help the Lakers as both a starter and a reserve, but he was sent to Vancouver in a July 1996 trade.

Strengths: Peeler, who was drafted by the Texas Rangers in 1988 as a left-handed pitcher and outfielder, is a tremendous athlete. He has a sweet perimeter stroke, makes a high percentage of his 3-pointers, and is also capable of beating his man off the dribble. Peeler handles the ball and passes so well that the Lakers once tried him as a point guard. His defense has improved.

Weaknesses: Peeler seems to have overcome a troubled past that includes a conviction on a weapons charge along with some other foul-ups. Some still wonder whether he has the commitment and work ethic required to become a standout. On the floor, Peeler is an ineffective rebounder, and he's prone to defensive lapses. He has not been a potent scorer when brought off the bench.

Analysis: In L.A., Eddie Jones was the main reason Peeler spent most of his first four seasons as a prominent reserve rather than a starter. He has not been able to step off the bench and score in droves, despite the fact that his 3-point stroke gives him the potential to be a force. Peeler needs to be more aggressive in his drives and his defense.

PLAYER SUMMARY	
Will	toss in 3-pointers
Can't	own the boards
Expect	10 PPG
Don't Expect	a stopper
Fantasy Value	$8-10
Card Value	10-15¢

COLLEGE STATISTICS

		G	FGP	FTP	RPG	PPG
88-89	MISS	36	.504	.754	3.7	10.1
89-90	MISS	31	.446	.769	5.4	16.8
90-91	MISS	21	.475	.768	6.2	19.4
91-92	MISS	29	.459	.806	5.5	23.4
Totals		117	.466	.779	5.1	16.8

NBA REGULAR-SEASON STATISTICS

		G	MIN	FGs FG	FGs PCT	3-PT FGs FG	3-PT FGs PCT	FTs FT	FTs PCT	Rebounds OFF	Rebounds TOT	AST	STL	BLK	PTS	PPG
92-93	LAL	77	1656	297	.468	46	.390	162	.786	64	179	166	60	14	802	10.4
93-94	LAL	30	923	176	.430	14	.222	57	.803	48	109	94	43	8	423	14.1
94-95	LAL	73	1559	285	.432	84	.389	102	.797	62	168	122	52	13	756	10.4
95-96	LAL	73	1608	272	.452	105	.413	61	.709	45	137	118	59	10	710	9.7
Totals		253	5746	1030	.447	249	.382	382	.778	219	593	500	214	45	2691	10.6

WILL PERDUE

Team: San Antonio Spurs
Position: Center
Height: 7'0"　**Weight:** 240
Birthdate: August 29, 1965

NBA Experience: 8 years
College: Vanderbilt
Acquired: Traded from Bulls for Dennis Rodman, 10/95

Background: As a senior at Vanderbilt, Perdue led the SEC in rebounding and was named SEC Player of the Year. A 1988 draftee of the Bulls, he played less than any other first-round choice as a rookie. He was a reserve for most of his seven years with the Bulls, finally starting in 1994-95. A trade for Dennis Rodman sent him to San Antonio before the 1995-96 season.

Strengths: Perdue plays hard, goes after rebounds, and is a pretty steady face-up shooter. He knows his limitations and plays within them. He is capable of giving some of the league's better centers a strong effort on the defensive end. He seems to fit in well on talented teams.

Weaknesses: A gifted athlete Perdue is not. He doesn't jump well at all, and he is slow on his feet. His high-scoring days ended in college, as he does not have a reliable low-post game. His free-throw shooting is even worse. Perdue is a poor passer and dribbler, even for a big man.

Analysis: Perdue, who owns three NBA championship rings but contributed little to those Chicago teams, enjoyed his best pro season in 1994-95. The Bulls, however, thought Luc Longley was better-suited to be the starter, and Perdue wound up as David Robinson's backup. He does an admirable job with what he has, but there's no mistaking Perdue for the Admiral.

PLAYER SUMMARY

Will.................................tackle his role
Can't ....beat out Mr. Robinson
Expect ....6 RPG
Don't Expect ....double-doubles
Fantasy Value...................................$0
Card Value ....5-7¢

COLLEGE STATISTICS

		G	FGP	FTP	RPG	PPG
83-84	VAND	17	.467	.444	2.2	2.7
85-86	VAND	22	.585	.438	2.8	3.5
86-87	VAND	34	.599	.618	8.7	17.4
87-88	VAND	31	.634	.673	10.1	18.3
Totals		104	.606	.620	6.8	12.3

NBA REGULAR-SEASON STATISTICS

				FGs		3-PT FGs		FTs		Rebounds						
		G	MIN	FG	PCT	FG	PCT	FT	PCT	OFF	TOT	AST	STL	BLK	PTS	PPG
88-89	CHI	30	190	29	.403	0	.000	8	.571	18	45	11	4	6	66	2.2
89-90	CHI	77	884	111	.414	0	.000	72	.692	88	214	46	19	26	294	3.8
90-91	CHI	74	972	116	.494	0	.000	75	.670	122	336	47	23	57	307	4.1
91-92	CHI	77	1007	152	.547	1	.500	45	.495	108	312	80	16	43	350	4.5
92-93	CHI	72	998	137	.557	0	.000	67	.604	103	287	74	22	47	341	4.7
93-94	CHI	43	397	47	.420	0	.000	23	.719	40	126	34	8	11	117	2.7
94-95	CHI	78	1592	254	.553	0	.000	113	.582	211	522	90	26	56	621	8.0
95-96	SA	80	1396	173	.523	0	.000	67	.536	175	485	33	28	75	413	5.2
Totals		531	7436	1019	.509	1	.071	470	.600	865	2327	415	146	321	2509	4.7

SAM PERKINS

Team: Seattle SuperSonics
Position: Forward/Center
Height: 6'9" **Weight:** 255
Birthdate: June 14, 1961
NBA Experience: 12 years

College: North Carolina
Acquired: Traded from Lakers for Benoit Benjamin and draft rights to Doug Christie, 2/93

Background: Perkins was a three-time All-American at North Carolina, where he earned an NCAA title in 1982 and won the Lapchick Award as the nation's outstanding senior in 1984. In six years with Dallas, he became the club's all-time leader in rebounds. He has spent his last six years with the Lakers and Sonics.

Strengths: Few players his size hit 3-pointers as well as Perkins, who can also score on drives and in the post. He is an 80-percent career free-throw shooter. Perkins is a smart defender who has blocked close to 800 career shots. He has a veteran's understanding of the game, and he comes to work.

Weaknesses: After 12 years and more than 900 regular-season games, Perkins is not the defensive force or rebounder he used to be. His offense has moved to the perimeter and away from the paint in the last few years. He is now used mainly in reserve stints.

Analysis: Perkins is most valuable for his professional demeanor and for the matchup problems he poses. He still draws starting assignments and has never averaged fewer than 11 PPG over his dozen years in the NBA. He surpassed 12,000 career points last season and has more than 6,000 career rebounds.

PLAYER SUMMARY

Will ....pull defenders outside
Can't ....regain young legs
Expect ....100 treys
Don't Expect ....35-minute stints
Fantasy Value $4-6
Card Value ....7-10¢

COLLEGE STATISTICS

		G	FGP	FTP	RPG	PPG
80-81	NC	37	.626	.741	7.8	14.9
81-82	NC	32	.578	.768	7.8	14.3
82-83	NC	35	.527	.819	9.4	16.9
83-84	NC	31	.589	.856	9.6	17.6
Totals		135	.576	.796	8.6	15.9

NBA REGULAR-SEASON STATISTICS

				FGs		3-PT FGs		FTs		Rebounds							
		G	MIN	FG	PCT	FG	PCT	FT	PCT	OFF	TOT	AST	STL	BLK	PTS	PPG
84-85	DAL	82	2317	347	.471	9	.250	200	.820	189	605	135	63	63	903	11.0
85-86	DAL	80	2626	458	.503	11	.333	307	.814	195	685	153	75	94	1234	15.4
86-87	DAL	80	2687	461	.482	19	.352	245	.828	197	616	146	109	77	1186	14.8
87-88	DAL	75	2499	394	.450	5	.167	273	.822	201	601	118	74	54	1066	14.2
88-89	DAL	78	2860	445	.464	7	.184	274	.833	235	688	127	76	92	1171	15.0
89-90	DAL	76	2668	435	.493	6	.214	330	.778	209	572	175	88	64	1206	15.9
90-91	LAL	73	2504	368	.495	18	.281	229	.821	167	538	108	64	78	983	13.5
91-92	LAL	63	2332	361	.450	15	.217	304	.817	192	556	141	64	62	1041	16.5
92-93	LAL/SEA	79	2351	381	.477	24	.338	250	.820	163	524	156	60	82	1036	13.1
93-94	SEA	81	2170	341	.438	99	.367	218	.801	120	366	111	67	31	999	12.3
94-95	SEA	82	2356	346	.466	136	.397	215	.799	96	398	135	72	45	1043	12.7
95-96	SEA	82	2169	325	.408	129	.355	191	.793	101	367	120	83	48	970	11.8
Totals		931	29539	4662	.467	478	.342	3036	.812	2065	6516	1625	895	790	12838	13.8

ELLIOT PERRY

Team: Phoenix Suns
Position: Guard
Height: 6'0" **Weight:** 160
Birthdate: March 28, 1969

NBA Experience: 4 years
College: Memphis St.
Acquired: Signed as a free agent, 1/94

Background: A product of the fertile Memphis prep ranks, Perry was a four-year standout at Memphis State who finished his college career with more than 2,200 points and 500 assists. He was a second-round draftee of the Clippers in 1991 but saw more action with Charlotte as a rookie. He was a CBA standout when the Suns signed him in 1993-94. Perry has made 77 starts over the last two years.

Strengths: Perry is a defensive menace who works his knee-high socks off. He uses his considerable energy to hound ball-handlers, and he was eighth in the league in steals with 1.9 per game in 1994-95. He gets points as well as assists off his effective penetration, and he's also capable of hitting 3-pointers when left open. He has played well as both a starter and reserve.

Weaknesses: Perry is neither as steady nor as creative as the man he has backed up, Kevin Johnson. His jump shot is also a work in progress, although he converted better than 50 percent from the floor when he started 51 games two years ago. Perry is no factor on the boards, and his assist-to-turnover ratio does not rival those of the NBA's top lead guards.

Analysis: If one good thing has come from K.J.'s continuous spell of injuries, it has been the play of Perry. He took his game to new levels while starting most of the 1994-95 season, and he returned to his spot-playing role when the main man had his health. Perry has the leadership and the abilities to be a starter for someone. His time is coming.

PLAYER SUMMARY	
Will	harass the ball
Can't	beat out K.J.
Expect	steals, assists
Don't Expect	rebounds
Fantasy Value	$6-8
Card Value	8-15¢

COLLEGE STATISTICS

		G	FGP	FTP	APG	PPG
87-88	MSU	32	.417	.806	4.1	13.1
88-89	MSU	32	.462	.821	3.7	19.4
89-90	MSU	30	.418	.753	5.0	16.8
90-91	MSU	32	.464	.793	4.6	20.8
Totals		126	.443	.794	4.3	17.5

NBA REGULAR-SEASON STATISTICS

				FGs		3-PT FGs		FTs		Rebounds						
		G	MIN	FG	PCT	FG	PCT	FT	PCT	OFF	TOT	AST	STL	BLK	PTS	PPG
91-92	LAC/CHA	50	437	49	.380	1	.143	27	.659	14	39	78	34	3	126	2.5
93-94	PHO	27	432	42	.372	0	.000	21	.750	12	39	125	25	1	105	3.9
94-95	PHO	82	1977	306	.520	25	.417	158	.810	51	151	394	156	4	795	9.7
95-96	PHO	81	1668	261	.475	24	.407	151	.778	34	136	353	87	5	697	8.6
Totals		240	4514	658	.477	50	.388	357	.779	111	365	950	302	13	1723	7.2

CHUCK PERSON

Team: San Antonio Spurs
Position: Forward
Height: 6'8" **Weight:** 235
Birthdate: June 27, 1964

NBA Experience: 10 years
College: Auburn
Acquired: Signed as a free agent, 8/94

Background: Auburn's all-time leading scorer when he graduated, Person won NBA Rookie of the Year honors in 1986-87. He spent six high-scoring years with Indiana and two with Minnesota before signing with San Antonio. Person has been a potent sixth man in his two seasons with the Spurs.

Strengths: Person has a quick release and great range. He has made countless clutch shots in his career, and he drilled more than 40 percent of his 3-pointers last season. "The Rifleman" makes smart passes, works hard on his game, and is capable of heating up in a hurry. He loves to compete.

Weaknesses: Although he's an accomplished shooter, Person has never knocked down a high percentage of his free throws. His mouth has talked him into trouble in the past, but those days seem to be behind him. He is frequently overmatched on defense, and his scoring peaked years ago.

Analysis: Person, who last season became the fourth player in NBA history to make 1,000 treys, has found the perfect job for this stage in his career—sweet-shooting sixth man on a contending team. He has never averaged single digits in scoring, and Person's 3-point accuracy in 1995-96 was a career high.

PLAYER SUMMARY	
Will	heat up quickly
Can't	be left open
Expect	instant offense
Don't Expect	high-flying slams
Fantasy Value	$2-4
Card Value	7-12¢

COLLEGE STATISTICS

		G	FGP	FTP	RPG	PPG
82-83	AUB	28	.541	.758	4.6	9.3
83-84	AUB	31	.543	.728	8.0	19.1
84-85	AUB	34	.544	.738	8.9	22.0
85-86	AUB	33	.519	.804	7.9	21.5
Totals		126	.536	.757	7.5	18.3

NBA REGULAR-SEASON STATISTICS

		G	MIN	FGs FG	FGs PCT	3-PT FGs FG	3-PT FGs PCT	FTs FT	FTs PCT	Rebounds OFF	Rebounds TOT	AST	STL	BLK	PTS	PPG
86-87	IND	82	2956	635	.468	49	.355	222	.747	168	677	295	90	16	1541	18.8
87-88	IND	79	2807	575	.459	59	.333	132	.670	171	536	309	73	8	1341	17.0
88-89	IND	80	3012	711	.489	63	.307	243	.792	144	516	289	83	18	1728	21.6
89-90	IND	77	2714	605	.487	94	.372	211	.781	126	445	230	53	20	1515	19.7
90-91	IND	80	2566	620	.504	69	.340	133	.675	114	426	382	68	18	1497	18.5
91-92	IND	81	2923	616	.480	132	.373	133	.675	114	426	382	68	18	1497	18.5
92-93	MIN	78	2985	541	.433	118	.355	109	.649	98	433	343	67	30	1309	16.8
93-94	MIN	77	2029	356	.422	100	.368	82	.759	55	253	185	45	12	894	11.6
94-95	SA	81	2033	317	.423	172	.387	66	.647	49	258	106	45	12	872	10.8
95-96	SA	80	2131	308	.437	190	.410	67	.644	76	413	100	49	26	873	10.9
Totals		795	26156	5284	.465	1046	.368	1430	.723	1122	4374	2477	629	177	13044	16.4

WESLEY PERSON

Team: Phoenix Suns
Position: Guard
Height: 6'6" **Weight:** 195
Birthdate: March 28, 1971

NBA Experience: 2 years
College: Auburn
Acquired: First-round pick in 1994 draft (23rd overall)

Background: The younger brother of San Antonio's Chuck Person, Wesley kept up the family tradition by attending Auburn. Playing on some bad teams, he finished third on the school's career scoring list behind his brother and former NBA player Mike Mitchell. Wesley broke every Auburn 3-point record. He fell to 23rd in the 1994 draft but led all rookies in 3-point percentage. He has started more than half of his pro games.

Strengths: Not unlike his big brother, Person is a dead-eye marksman. He is at his best when he gets the ball in rhythm, but he can also create his own shots off the dribble. Person is a better ball-handler and a more complete player than most analysts expected when he came out of college. He makes a good percentage of his free throws, helps out on the boards, and handles his role well.

Weaknesses: Defense is the main concern with Person, who is far too slight to pose problems for the guards who post up. He could use a few more pounds, and he does not possess blinding speed or quickness. Person's field-goal percentage was better during his rookie season than it was in 1995-96, which is not a good sign. He needs to do more from inside the arc to make defenders back off.

Analysis: Person's earlier-than-expected development made Dan Majerle expendable to the Suns. Person was the starting two guard for most of last season, although Phoenix also used him in a sixth-man role with some success. Bringing him off the bench is one way around some of his deficiencies on defense. Person's shooting stroke will ensure that he gets his minutes one way or another.

PLAYER SUMMARY	
Will	deliver from deep
Can't	play clamp-down "D"
Expect	finesse
Don't Expect	power
Fantasy Value	$3-5
Card Value	8-15¢

COLLEGE STATISTICS

		G	FGP	FTP	RPG	PPG
90-91	AUB	26	.471	.765	5.7	15.4
91-92	AUB	27	.506	.726	6.8	19.9
92-93	AUB	27	.556	.772	7.1	18.8
93-94	AUB	28	.484	.734	6.4	22.2
Totals		108	.504	.747	6.5	19.1

NBA REGULAR-SEASON STATISTICS

			FGs		3-PT FGs		FTs		Rebounds						
	G	MIN	FG	PCT	FG	PCT	FT	PCT	OFF	TOT	AST	STL	BLK	PTS	PPG
94-95 PHO	78	1800	309	.484	116	.436	80	.792	67	201	105	48	24	814	10.4
95-96 PHO	82	2609	390	.445	117	.374	148	.771	56	321	138	55	22	1045	12.7
Totals	160	4409	699	.461	233	.402	228	.778	123	522	243	103	46	1859	11.6

BOBBY PHILLS

Team: Cleveland Cavaliers   **NBA Experience:** 5 years
Position: Guard   **College:** Southern
Height: 6'5" **Weight:** 220   **Acquired:** Signed as a free agent,
Birthdate: December 20, 1969   3/92

Background: Phills, the son of a college dean, stayed home in Baton Rouge, Louisiana, to play at Southern U. He wound up launching 788 3-point shots in his career, making 4.4 a game as a senior. Milwaukee took him in the 1991 draft, but Phills was released and the Cavaliers signed him after a CBA stint. He established career highs in virtually every statistical category during 1995-96.

Strengths: An example that practice pays off, Phills entered the 1995-96 season as a suspect shooter and emerged as one of the top 3-point threats in the NBA. He made 44.1 percent of his treys last year after making less than 30 percent (22 total) over his first four years. Phills is a fine athlete who runs like the wind and loves to dunk. He hits his free throws and is a quick, physical defender.

Weaknesses: Among starting two guards, Phills does not stand out for his ball-handling or his creative moves. In fact, his half-court offense was very inconsistent before he spent long hours honing his long-distance stroke. He's better on the run. Phills has the athletic ability to make bigger contributions on the boards.

Analysis: Phills, who became a full-time starter in 1994-95, enjoyed a breakthrough season in 1995-96. He came close to doubling his previous career scoring average of 8.3 PPG while maintaining his solid defensive play. He has become an offensive force. Although Phills was hampered by injuries to his left knee late last season, he has made himself a player the Cavaliers cannot afford to be without.

PLAYER SUMMARY

Will ....defend his man
Can't ....be left open
Expect ....3-pointers, dunks
Don't Expect ....dribbling exhibitions
Fantasy Value $11-14
Card Value ....5-7¢

COLLEGE STATISTICS

		G	FGP	FTP	RPG	PPG
87-88	SOUT	23	.491	.714	1.8	3.7
88-89	SOUT	31	.431	.733	4.6	13.5
89-90	SOUT	31	.451	.657	4.3	20.1
90-91	SOUT	28	.407	.720	4.7	28.4
Totals		113	.413	.710	4.0	17.0

NBA REGULAR-SEASON STATISTICS

				FGs		3-PT FGs		FTs		Rebounds						
		G	MIN	FG	PCT	FG	PCT	FT	PCT	OFF	TOT	AST	STL	BLK	PTS	PPG
91-92	CLE	10	65	12	.429	0	.000	7	.636	4	8	4	3	1	31	3.1
92-93	CLE	31	139	38	.463	2	.400	15	.600	6	17	10	10	2	93	3.0
93-94	CLE	72	1531	242	.471	1	.083	113	.720	71	212	133	67	12	598	8.3
94-95	CLE	80	2500	338	.414	19	.345	183	.779	90	265	180	115	25	878	11.0
95-96	CLE	72	2530	386	.467	93	.441	186	.775	62	261	271	102	27	1051	14.6
Totals		265	6765	1016	.448	115	.404	504	.754	233	763	598	297	67	2651	10.0

RICKY PIERCE

Team: Denver Nuggets
Position: Guard
Height: 6'4" **Weight:** 215
Birthdate: August 19, 1959
NBA Experience: 14 years

College: Rice
Acquired: Traded from Pacers with Mark Jackson and a 1996 first-round pick for Jalen Rose, Reggie Williams, and a 1996 first-round pick, 6/96

Background: Pierce led Rice in scoring and rebounding for three straight years. The 14-year veteran played single seasons in Detroit and San Diego, then became a celebrated reserve in Milwaukee, winning two Sixth Man Awards. A 1991 All-Star with Seattle, he came off the Indiana bench last season and was traded to the Nuggets over the summer.

Strengths: Pierce has been one of the NBA's best pure shooters during his career, yet he also can use his strong upper body to get to the hoop and draw fouls. He still nails close to 85 percent of his free throws. He's a veteran who knows how to win in the clutch.

Weaknesses: Declining physical skills are bringing Pierce near the end of his career. Ball-handling, passing, and defense have never been his strong points, even in his younger days. Pierce is not the scoring machine he once was.

Analysis: Pierce will be remembered as one of the top free-throw shooters in NBA history, and one of its first prominent sixth men. The Nuggets hope his leadership and professionalism will help them in 1996-97. Pierce did raise his career total to more than 13,000 points.

PLAYER SUMMARY

Will	drill his free throws
Can't	regain scoring punch
Expect	professionalism
Don't Expect	starts
Fantasy Value	$0
Card Value	5-8¢

COLLEGE STATISTICS

		G	FGP	FTP	RPG	PPG
79-80	RICE	26	.480	.718	8.2	19.2
80-81	RICE	26	.518	.706	7.0	20.9
81-82	RICE	30	.511	.794	7.5	26.8
Totals		82	.504	.751	7.6	22.5

NBA REGULAR-SEASON STATISTICS

		G	MIN	FGs FG	FGs PCT	3-PT FGs FG	3-PT FGs PCT	FTs FT	FTs PCT	Rebounds OFF	Rebounds TOT	AST	STL	BLK	PTS	PPG
82-83	DET	39	265	33	.375	1	.143	18	.563	15	35	14	8	4	85	2.2
83-84	SD	69	1280	268	.470	0	.000	149	.861	59	135	60	27	13	685	9.9
84-85	MIL	44	882	165	.537	1	.250	102	.823	49	117	94	34	5	433	9.8
85-86	MIL	81	2147	429	.533	3	.130	266	.858	94	231	177	83	6	1127	13.9
86-87	MIL	79	2505	575	.534	3	.107	387	.880	117	266	144	64	24	1540	19.5
87-88	MIL	37	965	248	.510	3	.214	107	.877	30	83	73	21	7	606	16.4
88-89	MIL	75	2078	527	.518	8	.222	255	.859	82	197	156	77	19	1317	17.6
89-90	MIL	59	1709	503	.510	46	.346	307	.839	64	167	133	50	7	1359	23.0
90-91	MIL/SEA	78	2167	561	.485	46	.397	430	.913	67	191	168	60	13	1598	20.5
91-92	SEA	78	2658	620	.475	33	.268	417	.916	93	233	241	86	20	1690	21.7
92-93	SEA	77	2218	524	.489	42	.372	313	.889	58	192	220	100	7	1403	18.2
93-94	SEA	51	1022	272	.471	6	.188	189	.896	29	83	91	42	5	739	14.5
94-95	GS	27	673	111	.437	23	.329	93	.877	12	64	40	22	2	338	12.5
95-96	IND	76	1404	264	.447	35	.337	174	.849	40	136	101	57	6	737	9.7
Totals		870	21973	5100	.496	250	.308	3207	.875	809	2130	1712	731	138	13657	15.7

ED PINCKNEY

Unrestricted Free Agent
Last Team: Philadelphia 76ers
Position: Forward/Center
Height: 6'9" **Weight:** 240
Birthdate: March 27, 1963
NBA Experience: 11 years

College: Villanova
Acquired: Traded from Raptors with Tony Massenburg and future considerations for Sharone Wright, 2/96

Background: The highlight of Pinckney's career was leading Villanova to a national title in 1985 and being named tournament MVP. His 11-year NBA career started in Phoenix and has included stops in Sacramento, Boston, Milwaukee, Toronto, and Philadelphia. He has averaged double figures in scoring just twice.

Strengths: Pinckney can provide solid minutes at the four and five spots. He is capable of rebounding on both ends, playing good defense, and blocking a few shots. Pinckney hits for a high percentage from the field because he does not take bad shots. He's a 76-percent career free-throw shooter.

Weaknesses: "Easy Ed" has never been a productive pro scorer. His range is limited, and his low-post repertoire will not cause defenders to shudder. He's not much of a passer or ball-handler, either. At this stage in his career, Pinckney is not a consistent contributor in any single area.

Analysis: Pinckney has managed to carve out a long pro career despite the fact that he has never become a scorer, a dominant rebounding force, or a defensive whiz. What he has done is show up to work every day. His value is as a versatile reserve who can spell players at two positions.

PLAYER SUMMARY

Will ....fill in at center
Can't ....dominate the lane
Expect...........................a professional
Don't Expect ....10 PPG
Fantasy Value.................................$0
Card Value ....5-8¢

COLLEGE STATISTICS

		G	FGP	FTP	RPG	PPG
81-82	VILL	32	.640	.714	7.8	14.2
82-83	VILL	31	.568	.760	9.7	12.5
83-84	VILL	31	.604	.694	7.9	15.4
84-85	VILL	35	.600	.730	8.9	15.6
Totals		129	.604	.723	8.6	14.5

NBA REGULAR-SEASON STATISTICS

		G	MIN	FGs FG	PCT	3-PT FGs FG	PCT	FTs FT	PCT	Rebounds OFF	TOT	AST	STL	BLK	PTS	PPG
85-86	PHO	80	1602	255	.558	0	.000	171	.673	95	308	90	71	37	681	8.5
86-87	PHO	80	2250	290	.584	0	.000	257	.739	179	580	116	86	54	837	10.5
87-88	SAC	79	1177	179	.522	0	.000	133	.747	94	230	66	39	32	491	6.2
88-89	SAC/BOS	80	2012	319	.513	0	.000	280	.800	166	449	118	83	66	918	11.5
89-90	BOS	77	1082	135	.542	0	.000	92	.773	93	225	68	34	42	362	4.7
90-91	BOS	70	1165	131	.539	0	.000	104	.897	155	341	45	61	43	366	5.2
91-92	BOS	81	1917	203	.537	0	.000	207	.812	252	564	62	70	56	613	7.6
92-93	BOS	7	151	10	.417	0	.000	12	.923	14	43	1	4	7	32	4.6
93-94	BOS	76	1524	151	.522	0	.000	92	.736	160	478	62	58	44	394	5.2
94-95	MIL	62	835	48	.495	0	.000	44	.710	65	211	21	34	17	140	2.3
95-96	TOR/PHI	74	1710	171	.510	0	.000	136	.760	189	458	72	64	28	478	6.5
Totals		766	15425	1892	.535	0	.000	1528	.764	1462	3887	721	604	426	5312	6.9

SCOTTIE PIPPEN

Team: Chicago Bulls
Position: Forward
Height: 6'7" **Weight:** 228
Birthdate: September 25, 1965
NBA Experience: 9 years
College: Central Arkansas

Acquired: Draft rights traded from SuperSonics for draft rights to Olden Polynice, a 1989 second-round pick, and the option to exchange 1989 first-round picks, 6/87

Background: An NAIA All-American as a senior at Central Arkansas, Pippen improved rapidly with Chicago while helping the Bulls to four NBA titles in six years. He starred on the '95-96 team that has been called the best ever, ranking among NBA leaders in scoring, assists, and steals. He has played in six All-Star Games (MVP in 1994) and on the last two U.S. Olympic teams.

Strengths: Pippen's all-around contributions are matched by no one in basketball. He is the best passing forward in the NBA and one of the best defensive players at any position. He led the league in steals in 1994-95. The acrobatic Pippen has countless moves to the basket, is an electrifying transition player, and hits 3-pointers. He rebounds and takes it coast-to-coast.

Weaknesses: Pippen is a poor free-throw shooter and occasionally handles the ball loosely. He has received attention for playoff episodes like refusing to re-enter a game and his infamous migraine headache.

Analysis: Pippen has now been named to the All-NBA first team three consecutive seasons. When Michael Jordan was out of the NBA, Pippen led the Bulls in most significant statistical categories. With M.J., the explosive and versatile forward has led Chicago to the top. He's on the verge of MVP consideration.

PLAYER SUMMARY

Will ....star in most areas
Can't ....overshadow Jordan
Expect...................MVP consideration
Don't Expect .....single-digit games
Fantasy Value $65-70
Card Value ....30-75¢

COLLEGE STATISTICS

		G	FGP	FTP	RPG	PPG
83-84	CA	20	.456	.684	3.0	4.3
84-85	CA	19	.564	.676	9.2	18.5
85-86	CA	29	.556	.686	9.2	19.8
86-87	CA	25	.592	.719	10.0	23.6
Totals		93	.563	.695	8.1	17.2

NBA REGULAR-SEASON STATISTICS

				FGs		3-PT FGs		FTs		Rebounds						
		G	MIN	FG	PCT	FG	PCT	FT	PCT	OFF	TOT	AST	STL	BLK	PTS	PPG
87-88	CHI	79	1650	261	.463	4	.174	99	.576	115	298	169	91	52	625	7.9
88-89	CHI	73	2413	413	.476	21	.273	201	.668	138	445	256	139	61	1048	14.4
89-90	CHI	82	3148	562	.489	28	.250	199	.675	150	547	444	211	101	1351	16.5
90-91	CHI	82	3014	600	.520	21	.309	240	.706	163	595	511	193	93	1461	17.8
91-92	CHI	82	3164	687	.506	16	.200	330	.760	185	630	572	155	93	1720	21.0
92-93	CHI	81	3123	628	.473	22	.237	232	.663	203	621	507	173	73	1510	18.6
93-94	CHI	72	2759	627	.491	63	.320	270	.660	173	629	403	211	58	1587	22.0
94-95	CHI	79	3014	634	.480	109	.345	315	.716	175	639	409	232	89	1692	21.4
95-96	CHI	77	2825	563	.463	150	.374	220	.679	152	496	452	133	57	1496	19.4
Totals		707	25110	4975	.486	434	.317	2106	.687	1454	4900	3723	1538	677	12490	17.7

OLDEN POLYNICE

Team: Sacramento Kings
Position: Center
Height: 7'0" **Weight:** 250
Birthdate: November 21, 1964
NBA Experience: 9 years

College: Virginia
Acquired: Traded from Pistons for Pete Chilcutt, a 1994 second-round pick, and a conditional first-round pick, 2/94

Background: Polynice led Virginia in scoring and rebounding for two seasons and was a three-year leader in field-goal accuracy. He began his nine-year NBA career as a backup center with Seattle and has started for the L.A. Clippers, Detroit, and Sacramento. He averaged a double-double in 1993-94 and has come close to matching the feat in each of the last two years.

Strengths: Polynice has been Sacramento's leading rebounder since joining the Kings, and he also works hard on defense. He can bang with big men, yet is quick enough to get out and harass smaller players on the perimeter. He shoots for a high percentage, especially with his low-post hook shot.

Weaknesses: Polynice has a limited offensive arsenal. He is a poor ball-handler and perimeter shooter, and his free-throw shooting is atrocious. He is one of the worst passing centers in the league. Polynice has had some troubles with coaches and teammates because he speaks his mind.

Analysis: Polynice, who once went on a brief hunger strike for starving people in his native Haiti, averages close to ten boards per game and has been a double-figure scorer in each of the last three seasons. Although he is reliable, some question how far a team can go with O.P. in the middle.

PLAYER SUMMARY	
Will	toss in hooks
Can't	set up teammates
Expect	double-doubles
Don't Expect	jumpers
Fantasy Value	$7-9
Card Value	5-8¢

COLLEGE STATISTICS

		G	FGP	FTP	RPG	PPG
83-84	VIRG	33	.551	.588	5.6	7.7
84-85	VIRG	32	.603	.599	7.6	13.0
85-86	VIRG	30	.572	.637	8.0	16.1
Totals		95	.578	.612	7.0	12.1

NBA REGULAR-SEASON STATISTICS

		G	MIN	FGs FG	FGs PCT	3-PT FGs FG	3-PT FGs PCT	FTs FT	FTs PCT	Rebounds OFF	Rebounds TOT	AST	STL	BLK	PTS	PPG
87-88	SEA	82	1080	118	.465	0	.000	101	.639	122	330	33	32	26	337	4.1
88-89	SEA	80	835	91	.506	0	.000	51	.593	98	206	21	37	30	233	2.9
89-90	SEA	79	1085	156	.540	1	.500	47	.475	128	300	15	25	21	360	4.6
90-91	SEA/LAC	79	2092	316	.560	0	.000	146	.579	220	553	42	43	32	778	9.8
91-92	LAC	76	1834	244	.519	0	.000	125	.622	195	536	46	45	20	613	8.1
92-93	DET	67	1299	210	.490	0	.000	66	.465	181	418	29	31	21	486	7.3
93-94	DET/SAC	68	2402	346	.523	0	.000	97	.508	299	809	41	42	67	789	11.6
94-95	SAC	81	2534	376	.544	1	1.000	124	.639	277	725	62	48	52	877	10.8
95-96	SAC	81	2441	431	.527	1	.333	122	.601	257	764	58	52	66	985	12.2
Totals		693	15602	2288	.525	3	.200	879	.576	1777	4641	347	355	335	5458	7.9

TERRY PORTER

Team: Minnesota Timberwolves
Position: Guard
Height: 6'3" **Weight:** 195
Birthdate: April 8, 1963

NBA Experience: 11 years
College: Wisconsin-Stevens Point
Acquired: Signed as a free agent, 10/95

Background: Porter was an NAIA All-American as a junior and senior at Wisconsin-Stevens Point, where his shooting accuracy was remarkable for a guard. He spent the first ten of his 11 pro seasons in Portland, where he played in the NBA Finals and was a two-time All-Star. He started half the season for Minnesota in 1995-96.

Strengths: Porter has made more than 800 3-pointers during his career. He can play both guard positions, though he is a natural point man. He is good with both hands and uses his strength well on defense. Porter has earned respect for clutch performances and leadership.

Weaknesses: Age and injuries have slowed Porter, who did not possess blinding speed in the first place. He was never among the most creative guards in the league, even when his legs were young. His ability to score and his shooting accuracy are in decline.

Analysis: Porter, considered one of the better scoring point guards in the NBA for much of his career, has perhaps a year or two left as a third guard. He has failed to average ten points per game and shoot his usual 80 percent from the line over the last two seasons.

PLAYER SUMMARY	
Will	use his strength
Can't	maintain his stroke
Expect	reserve minutes
Don't Expect	quick drives
Fantasy Value	$1
Card Value	7-10¢

COLLEGE STATISTICS

		G	FGP	FTP	APG	PPG
81-82	WSP	25	.368	.692	0.8	2.0
82-83	WSP	30	.611	.697	5.2	11.4
83-84	WSP	32	.622	.830	4.2	18.8
84-85	WSP	30	.575	.834	4.3	19.7
Totals		117	.589	.796	3.8	13.5

NBA REGULAR-SEASON STATISTICS

		G	MIN	FGs FG	FGs PCT	3-PT FGs FG	3-PT FGs PCT	FTs FT	FTs PCT	Rebounds OFF	Rebounds TOT	AST	STL	BLK	PTS	PPG
85-86	POR	79	1214	212	.474	13	.310	125	.806	35	117	198	81	1	562	7.1
86-87	POR	80	2714	376	.488	13	.217	280	.838	70	337	715	159	9	1045	13.1
87-88	POR	82	2991	462	.519	24	.348	274	.846	65	378	831	150	16	1222	14.9
88-89	POR	81	3102	540	.471	79	.361	272	.840	85	367	770	146	8	1431	17.7
89-90	POR	80	2781	448	.462	89	.374	421	.892	59	272	726	151	4	1406	17.6
90-91	POR	81	2665	486	.515	130	.415	279	.823	52	282	649	158	12	1381	17.0
91-92	POR	82	2784	521	.461	128	.395	315	.856	51	255	477	127	12	1485	18.1
92-93	POR	81	2883	503	.454	143	.414	327	.843	58	316	419	101	10	1476	18.2
93-94	POR	77	2074	348	.416	110	.390	204	.872	45	215	401	79	18	1010	13.1
94-95	POR	35	770	105	.393	44	.386	58	.707	18	81	133	30	2	312	8.9
95-96	MIN	82	2072	269	.442	71	.314	164	.785	36	212	452	89	15	773	9.4
Totals		840	26050	4270	.469	844	.378	2719	.842	574	2832	5771	1271	107	12103	14.4

BRENT PRICE

Team: Houston Rockets
Position: Guard
Height: 6'1" **Weight:** 185
Birthdate: December 9, 1968

NBA Experience: 3 years
College: South Carolina; Oklahoma
Acquired: Signed as a free agent, 7/96

Background: The younger brother of Mark Price, Brent became a first-team All-Big Eight selection as a senior at Oklahoma after starting his college career at South Carolina. He led the Sooners in steals, assists, and 3-pointers in his final season. Washington drafted Price in the second round in 1992. He missed the 1994-95 season with a knee injury but returned last season and started 50 of 81 games. He joins the Rockets for the 1996-97 season.

Strengths: Like his big brother, Price can shoot the basketball with great range. He ranked sixth in the NBA in 3-point percentage (.462) last season and set a league record by making 13 in a row over three games. He also drills his free throws. Price runs the offense with a steady hand and led the Bullets in total assists in 1995-96. He knows the game, competes hard, and plays with savvy.

Weaknesses: Price, who tore the anterior cruciate ligament in his knee in the summer of 1994, does not have the quickness to be a standout defender. He does hustle, but he's forced to reach when the speedsters take it past him. Price does not penetrate as readily as the top lead guards. He shoots better coming off screens and spotting up than he does off the bounce.

Analysis: Brent finally got a chance to overshadow his big brother after the two became teammates in Washington last season. While Mark was injured, Brent took over as the Bullets' starter and enjoyed a career season. He remains more of a pure shooter than a set-up man, but his play in most areas solidified his standing as a legitimate NBA player with a future.

PLAYER SUMMARY	
Will	swish open jumpers
Can't	drive and dunk
Expect	great touch
Don't Expect	dumb mistakes
Fantasy Value	$7-9
Card Value	8-12¢

COLLEGE STATISTICS

		G	FGP	FTP	APG	PPG
87-88	SC	29	.460	.857	2.7	10.7
88-89	SC	30	.490	.844	4.3	14.4
90-91	OKLA	35	.416	.838	5.5	17.5
91-92	OKLA	30	.465	.789	6.2	18.7
Totals		124	.454	.828	4.7	15.5

NBA REGULAR-SEASON STATISTICS

				FGs		3-PT FGs		FTs		Rebounds						
		G	MIN	FG	PCT	FG	PCT	FT	PCT	OFF	TOT	AST	STL	BLK	PTS	PPG
92-93	WAS	68	859	100	.358	8	.167	54	.794	28	103	154	56	3	262	3.9
93-94	WAS	65	1035	141	.433	50	.333	68	.782	31	90	213	55	2	400	6.2
95-96	WAS	81	2042	252	.472	139	.462	167	.874	38	228	416	78	4	810	10.0
Totals		214	3936	493	.433	197	.395	289	.835	97	421	783	189	9	1472	6.9

MARK PRICE

Team: Golden State Warriors
Position: Guard
Height: 6'0" **Weight:** 180
Birthdate: February 16, 1964

NBA Experience: 10 years
College: Georgia Tech
Acquired: Signed as a free agent, 7/96

Background: Price, Georgia Tech's second all-time leading scorer when he graduated in 1986, was drafted by Dallas and immediately traded to the Cavaliers. Despite an appendectomy as a rookie, a tear of the anterior cruciate ligament in 1990, and wrist and foot surgery over the last two years, he has played in four All-Star Games and was a Dream Team II member.

Strengths: A healthy Price is one of the most dangerous shooters in the game. He is the NBA's all-time leader in free-throw percentage and among the all-time leaders in 3-point accuracy as well. Price is deceivingly quick, a splendid passer, and an underrated defender.

Weaknesses: Price played 48 games two years ago and just seven last season. One has to wonder how long he can hold up. He no longer has the lateral quickness to be a standout defender, and he's not going to beat the speedsters to the hoop on offense, either.

Analysis: Price has been a star for much of his ten-year career, with a perimeter jumper few can match. He underwent surgery to release a tendon in his left foot last November, but after returning for seven games he fractured a bone in the same foot. He has also had knee and wrist operations. His All-Star days look to be behind him. Golden State hopes he stays healthy this year.

PLAYER SUMMARY	
Will	shoot the lights out
Can't	keep off the injured list
Expect	automatic free throws
Don't Expect	82 games
Fantasy Value	$8-10
Card Value	12-15¢

COLLEGE STATISTICS

		G	FGP	FTP	APG	PPG
82-83	GT	28	.435	.877	3.3	20.3
83-84	GT	29	.509	.824	4.2	15.6
84-85	GT	35	.483	.840	4.3	16.7
85-86	GT	34	.528	.855	4.4	17.4
Totals		126	.487	.850	4.0	17.4

NBA REGULAR-SEASON STATISTICS

				FGs		3-PT FGs		FTs		Rebounds						
		G	MIN	FG	PCT	FG	PCT	FT	PCT	OFF	TOT	AST	STL	BLK	PTS	PPG
86-87	CLE	67	1217	173	.408	23	.329	95	.833	33	117	202	43	4	464	6.9
87-88	CLE	80	2626	493	.506	72	.486	221	.877	54	180	480	99	12	1279	16.0
88-89	CLE	75	2728	529	.526	93	.441	263	.901	48	226	631	115	7	1414	18.9
89-90	CLE	73	2706	489	.459	152	.406	300	.888	66	251	666	114	5	1430	19.6
90-91	CLE	16	571	97	.497	18	.340	59	.952	8	45	166	42	2	271	16.9
91-92	CLE	72	2138	438	.488	101	.387	270	.947	38	173	535	94	12	1247	17.3
92-93	CLE	75	2380	477	.484	122	.416	289	.948	37	201	602	89	11	1365	18.2
93-94	CLE	76	2386	480	.478	118	.397	238	.888	39	228	589	103	11	1316	17.3
94-95	CLE	48	1375	253	.413	103	.407	148	.914	25	112	335	35	4	757	15.8
95-96	WAS	7	127	18	.300	10	.333	10	1.000	1	7	18	6	0	56	8.0
Totals		589	18254	3447	.477	812	.408	1893	.907	349	1540	4224	740	68	9599	16.3

DINO RADJA

Team: Boston Celtics
Position: Forward
Height: 6'11" **Weight:** 263
Birthdate: April 24, 1967

NBA Experience: 3 years
College: None
Acquired: Second-round pick in 1989 draft (40th overall)

Background: The Celtics had to wait four years for Radja, who continued playing in Europe despite being drafted in 1989. He won a silver medal with Croatia in the 1992 Olympics, then averaged 21.5 points and 10.2 rebounds per game in the Italian 1A League. He was a second-team All-Rookie performer in 1993-94 and has improved his scoring average in each of his two years since.

Strengths: Radja knows how to score. He brings a fine set of offensive skills to the power forward position. He owns a good touch from the perimeter and has some aggressive moves with his back to the basket. He shoots well off the dribble. The big guy can also get out in transition. Radja blocks shots, grabs close to ten rebounds per game, and has continued to improve in just about all areas.

Weaknesses: The one flaw that stands out is common to many European imports—defense. Radja has ample size and quickness, but too often he simply does not get it done. He does alter shots, but he needs to do a better job of denying his man position. Improved upper-body strength would be a start. Radja has not learned to turn double-teams into scoring opportunities for his teammates.

Analysis: An ironic thing happened in Boston last season. American standout Dominique Wilkins took his high-scoring act overseas, leaving the player once considered the second best in Europe (behind Toni Kukoc) to become Boston's leading scorer. Radja is a well-versed scorer whom the Celtics have missed for multiple games in the last two seasons because of hand (1994-95) and ankle (1995-96) injuries.

PLAYER SUMMARY	
Will	get his shots
Can't	stop his man
Expect	20 PPG, 10 RPG
Don't Expect	assists
Fantasy Value	$25-30
Card Value	10-20¢

COLLEGE STATISTICS

—DID NOT PLAY—

NBA REGULAR-SEASON STATISTICS

			FGs		3-PT FGs		FTs		Rebounds						
		G	MIN	FG	PCT	FG	PCT	FT	PCT	OFF	TOT	AST	STL	BLK	PTS	PPG
93-94	BOS	80	2303	491	.521	0	.000	226	.751	191	577	114	70	67	1208	15.1
94-95	BOS	66	2147	450	.490	0	.000	233	.759	149	573	111	60	86	1133	17.2
95-96	BOS	53	1984	426	.500	0	.000	191	.695	113	522	83	48	81	1043	19.7
Totals		199	6434	1367	.504	0	.000	650	.736	453	1672	308	178	234	3384	17.0

THEO RATLIFF

Team: Detroit Pistons
Position: Forward/Center
Height: 6'10" **Weight:** 225
Birthdate: April 17, 1973

NBA Experience: 1 year
College: Wyoming
Acquired: First-round pick in 1995 draft (18th overall)

Background: Ratliff contributed almost nothing as a freshman at Wyoming. A year later, he led the nation in blocked shots, averaging 4.4 per game. He finished his career as the second-leading shot-blocker in NCAA history with 425 swats and was selected by Detroit with the 18th pick of the 1995 NBA draft. Despite limited playing time as a rookie, Ratliff led the Pistons in blocks and was among the league's top 20.

Strengths: Ratliff is a great athlete and an explosive leaper who will make his mark as a shot-blocker. His long reach, combined with great instincts and supreme effort, allow him to get his hands on shots just as they leave a shooter's fingertips. Ratliff also has a nose for the ball as it comes off the rim and the desire to be a big rebounder. He runs the floor and can play both the four and five positions.

Weaknesses: Most everything about offense is a trouble spot for Ratliff. He is neither a post nor perimeter scoring threat. He played with his back to the basket in college but is too slight to have his way with pro centers. For that matter, almost every power forward in the league has an edge in muscle, which could also keep Ratliff from reaching his rebounding goals. He rarely makes a good pass to his teammates.

Analysis: Mark Eaton made a nice living in the NBA on shot-blocking alone, but Eaton was a mountain. Ratliff has no such luck. The athletic youngster needs to become a more forceful defensive player, a more consistent rebounder, and at least a mild threat to score if he hopes to make bigger contributions down the road. His future looks to be as a defensive specialist.

PLAYER SUMMARY

Will ....swat shots, run
Can't ....find offensive comfort
Expect ....athletic defense
Don't Expect ....10 PPG
Fantasy Value.................................$0
Card Value ....20-40¢

COLLEGE STATISTICS

		G	FGP	FTP	RPG	PPG
91-92	WYOM	27	.438	.583	2.0	1.8
92-93	WYOM	28	.538	.517	6.2	9.2
93-94	WYOM	28	.569	.649	7.8	15.4
94-95	WYOM	28	.544	.633	7.5	14.4
Totals		111	.547	.608	5.9	10.3

NBA REGULAR-SEASON STATISTICS

			FGs		3-PT FGs		FTs		Rebounds						
	G	MIN	FG	PCT	FG	PCT	FT	PCT	OFF	TOT	AST	STL	BLK	PTS	PPG
95-96 DET	75	1305	128	.557	0	.000	85	.708	110	297	13	16	116	341	4.5
Totals	75	1305	128	.557	0	.000	85	.708	110	297	13	16	116	341	4.5

ELDRIDGE RECASNER

Unrestricted Free Agent
Last Team: Houston Rockets
Position: Guard
Height: 6'3" **Weight:** 190
Birthdate: December 14, 1967

NBA Experience: 2 years
College: Washington
Acquired: Signed as a free agent, 9/95

Background: In his four-year career at Washington, Recasner averaged 14.5 PPG in 117 contests. Never drafted by an NBA team, he began a professional basketball tour that began in Germany, then included stops in the Global Basketball Association, Turkey, and the CBA. He played three NBA games with Denver in 1994-95, then caught a break with Houston in 1995-96.

Strengths: Recasner's shooting touch is NBA material all the way. He is deadly from behind the arc, where he nailed 42.4 percent of his attempts last season and was third on the Rockets with 81 treys. He made 86.4 percent of his free throws. Recasner plays the point with a notion to score. He was a big scorer in college and the "minor leagues," and he can get his own shot off the dribble.

Weaknesses: Is he a point guard or a shooting guard? That's the question Recasner will have to answer. He's been used as the former, though he has not demonstrated the natural playmaking skills to help a team reach its potential. His slight build is also a setback, especially on defense. He lacks the strength to handle the rigors of NBA defense. His decision-making and ball-handling are also concerns.

Analysis: All in all, the 1995-96 season has to be considered a rousing success for Recasner, a journeyman guard who has seen it all in his pro career. If anyone has paid his dues, he has. He was the CBA's Most Valuable Player in 1994-95, when he averaged 20.4 PPG, 5.1 APG, and 3.8 RPG. He started 27 of 63 contests for Houston last year and is gaining confidence in the big leagues. Recasner should be around for a while.

PLAYER SUMMARY	
Will	create his shots
Can't	set assist records
Expect	an accurate stroke
Don't Expect	a dazzling dribble
Fantasy Value	$0
Card Value	12-20¢

COLLEGE STATISTICS

		G	FGP	FTP	RPG	PPG
86-87	WASH	35	.474	.697	3.7	8.4
87-88	WASH	28	.512	.820	3.8	17.0
88-89	WASH	28	.497	.828	3.4	18.1
89-90	WASH	26	.436	.884	3.9	16.2
Totals		117	.481	.812	3.7	14.5

NBA REGULAR-SEASON STATISTICS

			FGs		3-PT FGs		FTs		Rebounds						
	G	MIN	FG	PCT	FG	PCT	FT	PCT	OFF	TOT	AST	STL	BLK	PTS	PPG
94-95 DEN	3	13	1	.167	0	.000	4	1.000	0	2	1	3	0	6	2.0
95-96 HOU	63	1275	149	.415	81	.424	57	.864	31	144	170	23	5	436	6.9
Totals	66	1288	150	.411	81	.422	61	.871	31	146	171	26	5	442	6.7

BRYANT REEVES

Team: Vancouver Grizzlies
Position: Center
Height: 7'0" **Weight:** 295
Birthdate: June 8, 1973

NBA Experience: 1 year
College: Oklahoma St.
Acquired: First-round pick in 1995 draft (sixth overall)

Background: Reeves was a big nobody when he arrived on Oklahoma State's campus from tiny Gans, Oklahoma, in 1991, but he quickly became a dominating player. He earned Big Eight Player of the Year honors in 1993 and 1995, led Oklahoma State to the 1995 Final Four, and was named an All-American. Reeves was drafted sixth in 1995 by Vancouver and finished among rookie leaders in scoring and rebounding.

Strengths: "Big Country" is just that—big. Big enough to bang inside with just about anyone, in fact. Reeves is a highly skilled inside player. He knows how to seal his man off to get rebounds or work free for shots close to the basket. He also has soft hands and a deft shooting touch. He can step outside and hit 15-footers. Reeves is a hard worker and one of the most unassuming sorts you'll come across.

Weaknesses: Reeves is no David Robinson or Hakeem Olajuwon when it comes to quickness and athletic ability. He is not an explosive player in any respect. Reeves owns neither a sculpted body nor a vertical leap worth measuring. His passing needs work, and you don't want him dribbling the ball. Reeves was not a consistent offensive player during his rookie campaign. His lack of conditioning was a factor, especially early on.

Analysis: Reeves became a wildly popular college player for his "yes sir," small-town charm. Vancouver also warmed to the big guy, and his flat-top haircut became all the rage north of the border. He moved into the starting lineup when the Grizzlies traded Benoit Benjamin early last season, and he came along quite well. Reeves will never be quick, but he has the size, strength, and know-how to prosper in the paint.

PLAYER SUMMARY	
Will	seal off his man
Can't	get airborne
Expect	15 PPG, 10 RPG
Don't Expect	a big ego
Fantasy Value	$9-11
Card Value	60¢-$1.00

COLLEGE STATISTICS

		G	FGP	FTP	RPG	PPG
91-92	OSU	36	.521	.633	5.1	8.1
92-93	OSU	29	.621	.650	10.0	19.5
93-94	OSU	34	.585	.595	9.7	21.0
94-95	OSU	37	.586	.706	9.5	21.5
Totals		136	.585	.648	8.5	17.4

NBA REGULAR-SEASON STATISTICS

			FGs		3-PT FGs		FTs		Rebounds						
	G	MIN	FG	PCT	FG	PCT	FT	PCT	OFF	TOT	AST	STL	BLK	PTS	PPG
95-96 VAN	77	2460	401	.457	0	.000	219	.732	178	570	109	43	55	1021	13.3
Totals	77	2460	401	.457	0	.000	219	.732	178	570	109	43	55	1021	13.3

KHALID REEVES

Team: New Jersey Nets
Position: Guard
Height: 6'3" **Weight:** 201
Birthdate: July 15, 1972
NBA Experience: 2 years

College: Arizona
Acquired: Traded from Hornets with Kendall Gill for Kenny Anderson and Gerald Glass, 1/96

Background: A high-profile recruit from New York City, Reeves was considered a disappointment during his first three years at Arizona. As a senior, however, he nearly doubled his scoring average to 24.2 PPG and finished his career third on the all-time school scoring list. Drafted 12th by Miami in 1994, Reeves was fourth among rookies with 4.3 APG. He was traded twice last season and was unable to match his first-year accomplishments.

Strengths: Reeves is capable of playing both guard positions. He can create off the dribble and get teammates involved in his natural point guard role, yet he has also demonstrated the scoring aptitude and 3-point range you like in a shooting guard. He's not a speed-burner, but he knows how to take his man off the bounce. Reeves also rebounds and sticks with his matchups on defense.

Weaknesses: Not everyone is convinced Reeves is a point guard. His first NBA coach, Kevin Loughery, was one of the doubters. While his versatility is a plus, Reeves does seem to be trapped between the two backcourt positions. He's not a great shooter, and his scoring has been inconsistent at best. Reeves needs to take better care of the ball, make better decisions, and sharpen his overall skills.

Analysis: Reeves was involved in two prominent trades during the 1995-96 season. First, he was dealt from Miami to Charlotte in the deal that sent Alonzo Mourning to the Heat. He then went to New Jersey in a trade involving Kenny Anderson and Kendall Gill. Needless to say, Reeves was not the prominent player in either deal. His change of scenery and ankle troubles held back his progress after a promising rookie year.

PLAYER SUMMARY

Will ....find a role
Can't ....star at two guard
Expect..............adequate playmaking
Don't Expect......50-percent shooting
Fantasy Value $2-4
Card Value ....12-20¢

COLLEGE STATISTICS

		G	FGP	FTP	APG	PPG
90-91	ARIZ	35	.454	.690	2.9	9.1
91-92	ARIZ	30	.476	.788	3.7	13.9
92-93	ARIZ	28	.498	.727	2.9	12.2
93-94	ARIZ	35	.483	.799	2.9	24.2
Totals		128	.479	.763	3.1	15.0

NBA REGULAR-SEASON STATISTICS

				FGs		3-PT FGs		FTs		Rebounds						
		G	MIN	FG	PCT	FG	PCT	FT	PCT	OFF	TOT	AST	STL	BLK	PTS	PPG
94-95	MIA	67	1462	206	.443	67	.392	140	.714	52	186	288	77	10	619	9.2
95-96	CHA/NJ	51	833	95	.419	28	.308	61	.744	18	79	118	37	3	279	5.5
Totals		118	2295	301	.435	95	.363	201	.723	70	265	406	114	13	898	7.6

DON REID

Team: Detroit Pistons
Position: Forward/Center
Height: 6'8" **Weight:** 250
Birthdate: December 30, 1973

NBA Experience: 1 year
College: Georgetown
Acquired: Second-round pick in 1995 draft (58th overall)

Background: A role-playing defender and rebounder, Reid averaged just 15.9 minutes per game during his career at Georgetown. The Hoyas' captain as a senior, he blocked 60 shots in 31 games and recorded four double-doubles. Detroit took a chance on him with the 58th and final pick of the 1995 draft, and Reid wound up starting 46 of 69 games during his rookie season with the Pistons in 1995-96.

Strengths: Reid's biggest asset at this early stage is his work ethic and attitude. He does not shy away from contact, and he knows offense is not his job. He avoids launching bad shots, and his field-goal percentage reflects it. Reid moves well and could develop into a defensive specialist. He can block shots, rebound, and hold his man off the blocks. He averaged one block every 25 minutes.

Weaknesses: Reid averaged 4.5 PPG in college and will probably not do much better as a pro. He stands an inch or so short for a power forward, and about three inches short for a center. His post-up offense is almost as harmless as his jump shot, and that's saying something. Reid's range does not extend as far as the free-throw line. He needs to master some of the subtleties of NBA defense to keep from frequent foul trouble.

Analysis: No one envisioned Reid as a first-year starter, especially at center, but the Pistons were out of options. It did not turn out to be an overly costly move, as the team had enough veteran power in Otis Thorpe and plenty of scoring from its perimeter players. Reid is really a project who will be tutored heavily in the off-season. His work habits and defensive potential are a nice upside.

PLAYER SUMMARY	
Will	bring his hard hat
Can't	operate outside
Expect	interior defense
Don't Expect	prominence
Fantasy Value	$0
Card Value	12-20¢

COLLEGE STATISTICS

		G	FGP	FTP	RPG	PPG
91-92	GEOR	28	.433	.600	2.1	1.6
92-93	GEOR	32	.419	.452	2.1	1.6
93-94	GEOR	31	.643	.630	5.9	7.7
94-95	GEOR	31	.595	.516	5.7	7.2
Totals		122	.579	.561	4.0	4.5

NBA REGULAR-SEASON STATISTICS

			FGs		3-PT FGs		FTs		Rebounds						
	G	MIN	FG	PCT	FG	PCT	FT	PCT	OFF	TOT	AST	STL	BLK	PTS	PPG
95-96 DET	69	997	106	.567	0	.000	51	.662	78	203	11	47	40	263	3.8
Totals	69	997	106	.567	0	.000	51	.662	78	203	11	47	40	263	3.8

J.R. REID

Unrestricted Free Agent
Last Team: New York Knicks
Position: Forward/Center
Height: 6'9" **Weight:** 250
Birthdate: March 31, 1968

NBA Experience: 7 years
College: North Carolina
Acquired: Traded from Spurs with Brad Lohaus for Charles Smith and Monty Williams, 2/96

Background: Coming out of high school in 1986, Reid was the No. 1-ranked player in America. He was a consensus All-American as a North Carolina sophomore and played on the 1988 U.S. Olympic team. A second-team All-Rookie pick with Charlotte, he averaged 11-plus PPG during his first three seasons. He has been in single digits over the past four years with San Antonio and New York.

Strengths: Reid is a scorer. He has a nice all-around offensive game, including several dangerous moves in the post and a decent 15-foot jump shot. He also has the size, strength, and speed to beat opposing forwards. San Antonio used Reid quite effectively in its full-court defensive scheme. He's a good athlete.

Weaknesses: Reid has never contributed enough on the boards, and his level of play has been inconsistent on both offense and defense. He'll score 20 points one night and three the next. Reid is a below-average passer whose awareness of teammates and intensity have been questioned.

Analysis: Here's the problem: Reid fashions himself a scorer, yet he has failed to average even ten PPG in each of the last four seasons. To his credit, he has enjoyed some fine games while coming off the bench for both the Spurs and Knicks. However, Reid was once projected as a superstar. No one is making those predictions for him anymore.

PLAYER SUMMARY	
Will	make hook shots
Can't	set up teammates
Expect	reserve punch
Don't Expect	consistency
Fantasy Value	$1
Card Value	5-8¢

COLLEGE STATISTICS

		G	FGP	FTP	RPG	PPG
86-87	NC	36	.584	.653	7.4	14.7
87-88	NC	33	.607	.680	8.9	18.0
88-89	NC	27	.614	.669	6.3	15.9
Totals		96	.601	.668	7.6	16.2

NBA REGULAR-SEASON STATISTICS

			FGs		3-PT FGs		FTs		Rebounds						
		G	MIN	FG	PCT	FG	PCT	FT	PCT	OFF	TOT	AST	STL	BLK	PTS	PPG
89-90	CHA	82	2757	358	.440	0	.000	192	.664	199	691	101	92	54	908	11.1
90-91	CHA	80	2467	360	.466	0	.000	182	.703	154	502	89	87	47	902	11.3
91-92	CHA	51	1257	213	.490	0	.000	134	.705	96	317	81	49	23	560	11.0
92-93	CHA/SA	83	1887	283	.476	0	.000	214	.764	120	456	80	47	31	780	9.4
93-94	SA	70	1344	260	.491	0	.000	107	.699	91	220	73	43	25	627	9.0
94-95	SA	81	1566	201	.508	1	.500	160	.687	120	393	55	60	32	563	7.0
95-96	SA/NY	65	1313	160	.494	0	.000	107	.754	73	255	42	43	17	427	6.6
Totals		512	12591	1835	.475	1	.048	1096	.709	853	2834	521	421	229	4767	9.3

SHAWN RESPERT

Team: Milwaukee Bucks
Position: Guard
Height: 6'2" **Weight:** 195
Birthdate: February 6, 1972
NBA Experience: 1 year

College: Michigan St.
Acquired: Draft rights traded from Trail Blazers for draft rights to Gary Trent and a 1996 first-round pick, 6/95

Background: Respert missed the entire 1990-91 basketball season at Michigan State because of a knee injury, but he returned to spark the Spartans for four years. He averaged more than 21 PPG for his collegiate career, was eighth nationally in scoring as a senior, and left MSU as the No. 2 scorer in Big Ten history. He spent most of his rookie season on the Milwaukee bench despite being drafted eighth overall (by Portland).

Strengths: Respert, a 46-percent shooter from college 3-point range, was considered by many to be the best pure shooter in the 1995 draft. As do many rookies, Respert struggled to convert his jumpers in limited NBA minutes. He is comfortable shooting even from a few feet beyond the arc, and he'll make better than 80 percent of his free throws. Respert is an energetic player waiting to cut loose.

Weaknesses: Respert might be too small to excel as an NBA shooting guard, and his ball-handling and passing are not at the level of a pro point guard. His size is particularly troubling on defense, and Respert is not exceptionally quick, either. He's basically a shooter—not a scorer, passer, rebounder, or potential defensive whiz. As mentioned, Respert has struggled for both minutes and buckets.

Analysis: So far, Respert has been one of the big disappointments of the 1995 draft. Each of the seven players drafted ahead of him made a significant first-year impact on his team, as did several of those selected after Respert. In his defense, he was hardly given a chance until the last few weeks of the season. Don't write him off just yet. With some off-season work, he has the makings of a sweet-shooting third guard.

PLAYER SUMMARY	
Will	hit from deep
Can't	crack starting lineup
Expect	a future third guard
Don't Expect	physical defense
Fantasy Value	$1
Card Value	20-50¢

COLLEGE STATISTICS

		G	FGP	FTP	RPG	PPG
90-91	MSU	1	—	—	—	—
91-92	MSU	30	.503	.872	2.1	15.8
92-93	MSU	28	.481	.856	4.0	20.1
93-94	MSU	32	.484	.840	4.0	24.3
94-95	MSU	28	.473	.869	4.0	25.6
Totals		119	.483	.857	3.5	21.3

NBA REGULAR-SEASON STATISTICS

			FGs		3-PT FGs		FTs		Rebounds						
	G	MIN	FG	PCT	FG	PCT	FT	PCT	OFF	TOT	AST	STL	BLK	PTS	PPG
95-96 MIL	62	845	113	.387	42	.344	35	.833	28	74	68	32	4	303	4.9
Totals	62	845	113	.387	42	.344	35	.833	28	74	68	32	4	303	4.9

GLEN RICE

Team: Charlotte Hornets
Position: Forward/Guard
Height: 6'8" **Weight:** 220
Birthdate: May 28, 1967
NBA Experience: 7 years
College: Michigan

Acquired: Traded from Heat with Khalid Reeves, Matt Geiger, and a 1996 first-round pick for Alonzo Mourning, Pete Myers, and LeRon Ellis, 11/95

Background: Rice led Michigan to a national title in 1989 while averaging nearly 31 PPG in NCAA Tournament play. He finished his college career as the leading scorer in Big Ten history. Taken fourth overall in the 1989 draft, Rice became one of the NBA's top ten scorers during six seasons in Miami. He was traded to Charlotte before the 1995-96 season, when he made his All-Star debut.

Strengths: Count Rice among the prime-time scorers. He rarely misses a free throw and has his nights when he rarely misses anything. He has captured the league's Long Distance Shootout and is among the ten most prolific 3-point shooters of all time. Rice has learned to complement his perimeter punch with potent drives to the basket. He's an unselfish and motivated leader.

Weaknesses: Rice works hard on defense, but he lacks the great lateral quickness required to be a stopper. He does, however, generally outscore his matchup. The speed-burners give him the most trouble. Rice offers little on the offensive boards, a fact mainly attributable to his great range.

Analysis: Rice has finally achieved his long-time goal of becoming an All-Star. No one in the NBA worked harder for it. Actually, Rice has been playing at an All-Star level for the last several seasons, and he's not likely to slow down in the next few years. His size, stroke, and scoring make him a nightly force.

PLAYER SUMMARY	
Will	torch the nets
Can't	stick with speedsters
Expect	20-plus PPG
Don't Expect	complacency
Fantasy Value	$40-45
Card Value	7-12¢

COLLEGE STATISTICS

		G	FGP	FTP	RPG	PPG
85-86	MICH	32	.550	.600	3.0	7.0
86-87	MICH	32	.562	.787	9.2	16.9
87-88	MICH	33	.571	.806	7.2	22.1
88-89	MICH	37	.577	.832	6.3	25.6
Totals		134	.569	.797	6.4	18.2

NBA REGULAR-SEASON STATISTICS

		G	MIN	FGs FG	FGs PCT	3-PT FGs FG	3-PT FGs PCT	FTs FT	FTs PCT	Rebounds OFF	Rebounds TOT	AST	STL	BLK	PTS	PPG
89-90	MIA	77	2311	470	.439	17	.246	91	.734	100	352	138	67	27	1048	13.6
90-91	MIA	77	2646	550	.461	71	.386	171	.818	85	381	189	101	26	1342	17.4
91-92	MIA	79	3007	672	.469	155	.391	266	.836	84	394	184	90	35	1765	22.3
92-93	MIA	82	3082	582	.440	148	.383	242	.820	92	424	180	92	25	1554	19.0
93-94	MIA	81	2999	663	.467	132	.382	250	.880	76	404	184	110	32	1708	21.1
94-95	MIA	82	3014	667	.475	185	.410	312	.855	99	378	192	112	14	1831	22.3
95-96	CHA	79	3142	610	.471	171	.424	319	.837	86	378	232	91	19	1710	21.6
Totals		557	20201	4214	.461	879	.393	1651	.836	622	2741	1299	663	178	10958	19.7

POOH RICHARDSON

Team: Los Angeles Clippers
Position: Guard
Height: 6'1" **Weight:** 180
Birthdate: May 14, 1966
NBA Experience: 7 years

College: UCLA
Acquired: Traded from Pacers with Malik Sealy and draft rights to Eric Piatkowski for Mark Jackson and draft rights to Greg Minor, 6/94

Background: Richardson was a four-year starter and three-time All-Pac-10 star at UCLA, where he set a conference record for assists. He spent his first three pro seasons in Minnesota and a pair with Indiana before a second trade brought him to the Clippers two years ago. Richardson has never averaged less than ten PPG in his seven pro seasons.

Strengths: Richardson is a combination scorer and playmaker at the point. He shoots with 3-point range, has good moves to the basket, and has been in and out of the top ten in assists per game. He handles the ball well, and at times he has handled the brunt of the Clippers' offense.

Weaknesses: As a leader, Richardson falls short. He earned a reputation as a chronic complainer in Minnesota, and he failed to gain the respect of teammates and coaches in Indiana, too. Richardson converts a poor percentage from the field and from the line, and he does not attack the basket as often as his coaches would like. His defense is also subpar.

Analysis: The inconsistent Richardson has most of the tools of a quality point guard. His performance, however, has not always stood up to those skills. He has labored on bad teams for most of his career, but Richardson also bears some of the blame for all the losses. Injuries have contributed, too, including a stress fracture in his foot early last year.

PLAYER SUMMARY	
Will	run the offense
Can't	steer a winner
Expect	10 PPG
Don't Expect	star quality
Fantasy Value	$4-6
Card Value	5-8¢

COLLEGE STATISTICS

		G	FGP	FTP	APG	PPG
85-86	UCLA	29	.492	.689	6.2	10.6
86-87	UCLA	32	.527	.582	6.5	10.5
87-88	UCLA	30	.470	.667	7.0	11.6
88-89	UCLA	31	.555	.562	7.6	15.2
Totals		122	.513	.624	6.8	12.0

NBA REGULAR-SEASON STATISTICS

		G	MIN	FGs FG	FGs PCT	3-PT FGs FG	3-PT FGs PCT	FTs FT	FTs PCT	Rebounds OFF	Rebounds TOT	AST	STL	BLK	PTS	PPG
89-90	MIN	82	2581	426	.461	23	.277	63	.589	55	217	554	133	25	938	11.4
90-91	MIN	82	3154	635	.470	42	.328	89	.539	82	286	734	131	13	1401	17.1
91-92	MIN	82	2922	587	.466	53	.342	123	.691	91	301	685	119	25	1350	16.5
92-93	IND	74	2396	337	.479	3	.103	92	.742	63	573	573	94	12	769	10.4
93-94	IND	37	1022	160	.452	3	.250	47	.610	28	110	237	32	3	370	10.0
94-95	LAC	80	2864	353	.394	87	.357	81	.648	38	261	632	129	12	874	10.9
95-96	LAC	63	2013	281	.423	94	.384	78	.743	35	158	340	77	13	734	11.7
Totals		500	16952	2779	.452	305	.340	573	.650	392	1600	3755	715	103	6436	12.9

MITCH RICHMOND

Team: Sacramento Kings
Position: Guard
Height: 6'5" **Weight:** 215
Birthdate: June 30, 1965
NBA Experience: 8 years

College: Moberly Area; Kansas St.
Acquired: Traded from Warriors with Les Jepsen and a 1995 second-round pick for draft rights to Billy Owens, 11/91

Background: Richmond was a junior college All-American before he spent two years at Kansas State, where he set a single-season record for points. He was a near-unanimous choice for Rookie of the Year with Golden State in 1989 and has never averaged less than 21.9 PPG in eight seasons, including five with Sacramento. He is a three-time All-Star and a 1996 U.S. Olympian.

Strengths: Look up "pure scorer" in the dictionary, and Richmond might be pictured. He nails jumpers with men all over him, hits 3-pointers, and drives through traffic without fear. Opposing guards are at his mercy when he sets his muscular frame in the post. He runs the floor, rebounds, and gets his teammates involved. Richmond has also garnered All-Defensive consideration.

Weaknesses: Richmond is not one of the better ball-handling guards in the game, nor does he possess great speed or quickness. He commits a fair number of fouls and turnovers, but that's understandable when you consider all he does for his team.

Analysis: Richmond was paid the ultimate compliment last season when he was chosen for one of the final two positions on Dream Team III. The NBA as a whole celebrated, for no one has an unkind word to say about this classy veteran. A leader in every sense, he was named MVP of the 1995 All-Star Game and is the league's highest-scoring guard not named Michael Jordan.

PLAYER SUMMARY	
Will	provide leadership
Can't	dazzle with the dribble
Expect	at least 22 PPG
Don't Expect	off nights
Fantasy Value	$40-45
Card Value	12-20¢

COLLEGE STATISTICS

		G	FGP	FTP	RPG	PPG
84-85	MA	40	.480	.647	4.6	10.4
85-86	MA	38	.478	.689	6.6	16.0
86-87	KSU	30	.447	.761	5.7	18.6
87-88	KSU	34	.514	.775	6.3	22.6
Totals		142	.481	.732	5.8	16.5

NBA REGULAR-SEASON STATISTICS

		G	MIN	FGs FG	FG PCT	3-PT FGs FG	FG PCT	FTs FT	FT PCT	Rebounds OFF	TOT	AST	STL	BLK	PTS	PPG
88-89	GS	79	2717	649	.468	33	.367	410	.810	158	468	334	82	13	1741	22.0
89-90	GS	78	2799	640	.497	34	.358	406	.866	98	360	223	98	24	1720	22.1
90-91	GS	77	3027	703	.494	40	.348	394	.847	147	452	238	126	34	1840	23.9
91-92	SAC	80	3095	685	.468	103	.384	330	.813	62	319	411	92	34	1803	22.5
92-93	SAC	45	1728	371	.474	48	.369	197	.845	18	154	221	53	9	987	21.9
93-94	SAC	78	2897	635	.445	127	.407	426	.834	70	286	313	103	17	1823	23.4
94-95	SAC	82	3172	668	.446	156	.368	375	.843	69	357	311	91	29	1867	22.8
95-96	SAC	81	2946	611	.447	225	.437	425	.866	54	269	255	125	19	1872	23.1
Totals		600	22381	4962	.466	766	.393	2963	.840	676	2665	2306	770	179	13653	22.8

ISAIAH RIDER

Team: Portland Trail Blazers
Position: Guard
Height: 6'5" **Weight:** 222
Birthdate: March 12, 1971
NBA Experience: 3 years

College: Nevada-Las Vegas
Acquired: Traded from Timberwolves for Bill Curley, James Robinson, and a future first-round pick, 7/96

Background: Rider committed to Kansas State after graduating from high school in Alameda, California, but failed to qualify academically. He transferred to a junior college in Kansas, then to another in California, and finally to UNLV. He was second nationally in scoring in 1992-93. Called J.R. in college, he announced his preference for Isaiah before his All-Rookie 1993-94 season. Rider has been a 20-PPG scorer. The T'Wolves unloaded him to Portland in the off-season.

Strengths: Rider is an offensive force and an explosive athlete who plays with great intensity and confidence. He shoots with 3-point range, posts up, and finishes his drives with crowd-pleasing jams. He has won two Slam Dunk titles. The energetic Rider gets to the line and is a reliable free-throw shooter. He is capable of playing athletic defense and contributing on the boards.

Weaknesses: Rider's biggest downside has been his brushes with the law as well as failure to follow team rules. Tardiness to practice and general contempt for his superiors have landed him in trouble. On the court, no one has convinced Rider that defense is as important as scoring. He takes nights off without notice. Rider is not among the better ball-handling guards, and his turnovers are almost as frequent as his assists.

Analysis: Want a high-powered scorer with boundless confidence and the skills to match? Rider is your man. Looking for a leader and potential cornerstone of a franchise? In that regard, Rider has yet to prove himself. His individual play has been, more often than not, highly impressive. But his grasp of team basketball has not matched his gaudy scoring numbers, and Minnesota's record showed it.

PLAYER SUMMARY	
Will	slam with style
Can't	avoid controversy
Expect	20 PPG
Don't Expect	leadership
Fantasy Value	$12-15
Card Value	12-20¢

COLLEGE STATISTICS

		G	FGP	FTP	RPG	PPG
91-92	UNLV	27	.490	.747	5.2	20.7
92-93	UNLV	28	.515	.826	8.9	29.1
Totals		55	.505	.805	7.1	24.9

NBA REGULAR-SEASON STATISTICS

				FGs		3-PT FGs		FTs		Rebounds						
		G	MIN	FG	PCT	FG	PCT	FT	PCT	OFF	TOT	AST	STL	BLK	PTS	PPG
93-94	MIN	79	2415	522	.468	54	.360	215	.811	118	315	202	54	28	1313	16.6
94-95	MIN	75	2645	558	.447	139	.351	277	.817	90	249	245	69	23	1532	20.4
95-96	MIN	75	2594	560	.464	102	.371	248	.838	99	309	213	48	23	1470	19.6
Totals		229	7654	1640	.459	295	.359	740	.822	307	873	660	171	74	4315	18.8

STANLEY ROBERTS

Team: Los Angeles Clippers
Position: Center
Height: 7'0" **Weight:** 290
Birthdate: February 7, 1970

NBA Experience: 4 years
College: Louisiana St.
Acquired: Traded from Magic in three-team, multi-player deal, 9/92

Background: Roberts teamed with Shaquille O'Neal at LSU, but academic problems plagued him and he signed with a pro team in Spain. Though his rookie season began with jokes about his weight, he averaged 10.4 PPG with Orlando. He was traded to the Clippers before the 1992-93 campaign, but two Achilles tendon injuries sidelined Roberts for almost two full years until the 1995-96 season.

Strengths: Roberts can be an offensive force around the basket. Underneath that girth is a quick man with a killer spin move and some inside touch. Roberts is virtually impossible to budge once he gains position on the interior, and he has surprisingly good hands and footwork. Roberts has been a shot-blocking force at times during his career, and he is capable of big games on the boards.

Weaknesses: Roberts has reported to camp as large as 320 pounds and once ballooned close to 340 while on the injured list. It's no wonder he's had trouble with his heels. He led the league in personal fouls (332) and disqualifications (15) during the 1992-93 season and continues to hear whistles in his sleep. Roberts is a poor passer and runner, and his free-throw shooting is embarrassing. His dedication has to be questioned.

Analysis: Roberts will probably never fully shake his injury woes until he makes a commitment to staying below the 300-pound mark. Commitment, however, has been as big a problem for Roberts as his two Achilles injuries (both right and left). After a layoff of nearly two years, he played 51 games for the Clippers last season. Most of his missed games were due to more ankle and heel troubles.

PLAYER SUMMARY	
Will	score inside
Can't	skip a meal
Expect	more foot troubles
Don't Expect	commitment
Fantasy Value	$3-5
Card Value	5-8¢

COLLEGE STATISTICS

		G	FGP	FTP	RPG	PPG
89-90	LSU	32	.576	.460	9.8	14.1
Totals		32	.576	.460	9.8	14.1

NBA REGULAR-SEASON STATISTICS

				FGs		3-PT FGs		FTs		Rebounds						
		G	MIN	FG	PCT	FG	PCT	FT	PCT	OFF	TOT	AST	STL	BLK	PTS	PPG
91-92	ORL	55	1118	236	.529	0	.000	101	.515	113	336	39	22	83	573	10.4
92-93	LAC	77	1816	375	.527	0	.000	120	.488	181	478	59	34	141	870	11.3
93-94	LAC	14	350	43	.430	0	.000	18	.409	27	93	11	6	25	104	7.4
95-96	LAC	51	795	141	.464	0	.000	74	.556	42	162	41	15	39	356	7.0
Totals		197	4079	795	.509	0	.000	313	.506	363	1069	150	77	288	1903	9.7

ALVIN ROBERTSON

Unrestricted Free Agent
Last Team: Toronto Raptors
Position: Guard
Height: 6'4" **Weight:** 208
Birthdate: July 22, 1962

NBA Experience: 10 years
College: Crowder; Arkansas
Acquired: Signed as a free agent, 9/95

Background: Robertson was a junior college star and enjoyed a fine three-year career at Arkansas before playing on the 1984 U.S. Olympic team. A four-time All-Star and Defensive Player of the Year in 1986, he spent five years in San Antonio and three-plus in Milwaukee. Robertson returned from a two-year layoff to start for expansion Toronto in 1995-96.

Strengths: Robertson is and always has been a defensive nuisance. He plays solid on-the-ball defense and uses his quick hands to come up with steals. He is also strong enough to battle with the bigger guards. Robertson rebounds, keeps the ball moving, and provides veteran leadership.

Weaknesses: Age and injuries have taken a step from Robertson, who used to slash past defenders for a lot more points. Shooting has never been his forte, and he remains inconsistent from the outside. Robertson has made less than 70 percent of his free throws in his last two seasons.

Analysis: One of the comeback stories of the 1995-96 season was Robertson. After missing two full seasons because of injuries, he started alongside rookie Damon Stoudamire in the Toronto backcourt and ranked fifth in the league in steals with 2.16 per game. Robertson has more than 2,000 steals in his career.

PLAYER SUMMARY

Will ....pick your pocket
Can't ....regain lost step
Expect ....veteran leadership
Don't Expect ....three more years
Fantasy Value $3-5
Card Value ....5-8¢

COLLEGE STATISTICS

		G	FGP	FTP	RPG	PPG
80-81	CROW	34	.572	.652	8.4	18.0
81-82	ARK	28	.528	.603	2.2	7.3
82-83	ARK	28	.548	.661	4.9	14.2
83-84	ARK	32	.499	.670	5.5	15.5
Totals		122	.540	.655	5.4	14.0

NBA REGULAR-SEASON STATISTICS

				FGs		3-PT FGs		FTs		Rebounds						
		G	MIN	FG	PCT	FG	PCT	FT	PCT	OFF	TOT	AST	STL	BLK	PTS	PPG
84-85	SA	79	1685	299	.498	4	.364	116	.734	116	265	275	127	24	726	9.2
85-86	SA	82	2878	562	.514	8	.276	260	.795	184	516	448	301	40	1392	17.0
86-87	SA	81	2697	589	.466	13	.271	244	.753	186	424	421	260	35	1435	17.7
87-88	SA	82	2978	655	.465	27	.284	273	.748	165	498	557	243	69	1610	19.6
88-89	SA	65	2287	465	.483	9	.200	183	.723	157	384	393	197	36	1122	17.3
89-90	MIL	81	2599	476	.503	4	.154	197	.741	230	559	445	207	17	1153	14.2
90-91	MIL	81	2598	438	.485	23	.365	199	.757	191	459	444	246	16	1098	13.6
91-92	MIL	82	2463	396	.430	67	.319	151	.763	175	350	360	210	32	1010	12.3
92-93	MIL/DET	69	2006	247	.458	40	.328	84	.656	107	269	263	155	18	618	9.0
95-96	TOR	77	2478	285	.470	41	.272	107	.677	110	342	323	166	36	718	9.3
Totals		779	24669	4412	.477	236	.295	1822	.743	1621	4066	3929	2112	323	10882	14.0

CLIFFORD ROBINSON

Team: Portland Trail Blazers
Position: Forward
Height: 6'10" **Weight:** 225
Birthdate: December 16, 1966

NBA Experience: 7 years
College: Connecticut
Acquired: Second-round pick in 1989 draft (36th overall)

Background: Robinson led Connecticut in scoring for three consecutive years. Bypassed until the second round of the 1989 draft, the seven-year Portland pro did not miss a game in his first five years and improved his scoring in each of his first six. He won the NBA's 1993 Sixth Man Award. He has averaged at least 20 PPG in each of his three seasons as a Blazer starter.

Strengths: Robinson is an explosive and versatile scorer. He is capable of burning his opponent on athletic drives, from behind the 3-point arc, in the post, or on the break. Few players in basketball light it up from as many places on the floor, or as frequently as Robinson. He also blocks shots, rebounds, and gets to the free-throw line.

Weaknesses: Robinson has had some off-court incidents, including speeding tickets for driving 110 and 89 mph. He has also had some personality conflicts with teammates, and he's developed a reputation for coming up short in big games. He's a below-average free-throw shooter.

Analysis: Robinson has enjoyed two remarkable runs in his career. He played every game for five-plus seasons, and his six-year string of improving his scoring average thrust him into the top echelon of NBA scorers. A 1994 All-Star, Robinson can still make strides in the area of team play.

PLAYER SUMMARY

Will ....score inside and out
Can't ....drive 55 mph
Expect...............................20 PPG
Don't Expect......free-throw accuracy
Fantasy Value $30-35
Card Value ....7-12¢

COLLEGE STATISTICS

		G	FGP	FTP	RPG	PPG
85-86	CONN	28	.366	.610	3.1	5.6
86-87	CONN	16	.420	.570	7.4	18.1
87-88	CONN	34	.479	.655	6.9	17.6
88-89	CONN	31	.470	.684	7.4	20.0
Totals		109	.452	.644	6.1	15.3

NBA REGULAR-SEASON STATISTICS

			FGs		3-PT FGs		FTs		Rebounds						
		G	MIN	FG	PCT	FG	PCT	FT	PCT	OFF	TOT	AST	STL	BLK	PTS	PPG
89-90	POR	82	1565	298	.397	12	.273	138	.550	110	308	72	53	53	746	9.1
90-91	POR	82	1940	373	.463	6	.316	205	.653	123	349	151	78	76	957	11.7
91-92	POR	82	2124	398	.466	1	.091	219	.664	140	416	137	85	107	1016	12.4
92-93	POR	82	2575	632	.473	19	.247	287	.690	165	542	182	98	163	1570	19.1
93-94	POR	82	2853	641	.457	13	.245	352	.765	164	550	159	118	111	1647	20.1
94-95	POR	75	2725	597	.452	142	.371	265	.694	152	423	198	79	82	1601	21.3
95-96	POR	78	2980	553	.423	178	.378	360	.664	123	443	190	86	68	1644	21.1
Totals		563	16762	3492	.449	371	.351	1826	.678	977	3031	1089	597	660	9181	16.3

DAVID ROBINSON

Team: San Antonio Spurs
Position: Center
Height: 7'1" **Weight:** 250
Birthdate: August 6, 1965

NBA Experience: 7 years
College: Navy
Acquired: First-round pick in 1987 draft (first overall)

Background: As a senior at Navy, Robinson was college basketball's consensus Player of the Year. He set NCAA records for blocks in a game and a season. After a two-year stint in the Navy, he burst onto the NBA scene in 1989-90, winning unanimous Rookie of the Year honors. Robinson has since played on two Olympic teams and in the last six All-Star Games. He was named 1994-95 league MVP.

Strengths: Robinson's quickness allows him to explode to the hoop with unstoppable low-post spin moves, and his face-up jumper might be his best weapon. He is also one of the best passing centers in the game. He clears the boards, runs the floor, blocks shots, and comes up with steals. Robinson has both a Defensive Player of the Year Award and a league scoring title to his credit.

Weaknesses: It's a knock you can hang on several great players, but Robinson has not been able to rise up and carry his team to an NBA title, as Hakeem Olajuwon has.

Analysis: Mr. Robinson, who clinched the 1993-94 scoring crown with a 71-point game on the last day of the season, has been even better in the two years since. He has never averaged below 23 points per game, and he is annually among the league's top three in rebounds and blocks. A ring is the one thing he has yet to attain.

PLAYER SUMMARY

Will....................dominate most areas
Can't..........................be single-teamed
Expect ....Hall of Fame numbers
Don't Expect.................bad decisions
Fantasy Value $85-90
Card Value.................................30-60¢

COLLEGE STATISTICS

		G	FGP	FTP	RPG	PPG
83-84	NAVY	28	.623	.575	4.0	7.6
84-85	NAVY	32	.644	.762	11.6	23.6
85-86	NAVY	35	.607	.628	13.0	22.7
86-87	NAVY	32	.591	.637	11.8	28.2
Totals		127	.613	.627	10.3	21.0

NBA REGULAR-SEASON STATISTICS

				FGs		3-PT FGs		FTs		Rebounds							
		G	MIN	FG	PCT	FG	PCT	FT	PCT	OFF	TOT	AST	STL	BLK	PTS	PPG
89-90	SA	82	3002	690	.531	0	.000	613	.732	303	983	164	138	319	1993	24.3
90-91	SA	82	3095	754	.552	1	.143	592	.762	335	1063	208	127	320	2101	25.6
91-92	SA	68	2564	592	.551	1	.125	393	.701	261	829	181	158	305	1578	23.2
92-93	SA	82	3211	676	.501	3	.176	561	.732	229	956	301	127	264	1916	23.4
93-94	SA	80	3241	840	.507	10	.345	693	.749	241	855	381	139	265	2383	29.8
94-95	SA	81	3074	788	.530	6	.300	656	.774	234	877	236	134	262	2238	27.6
95-96	SA	82	3019	711	.516	3	.333	626	.761	319	1000	247	111	271	2051	25.0
Totals		557	21206	5051	.526	24	.261	4134	.747	1922	6563	1718	934	2006	14260	25.6

GLENN ROBINSON

Team: Milwaukee Bucks
Position: Forward
Height: 6'7" **Weight:** 240
Birthdate: January 10, 1973

NBA Experience: 2 years
College: Purdue
Acquired: First-round pick in 1994 draft (first overall)

Background: A former prep phenom from Gary, Indiana, Robinson sat out his freshman year at Purdue because of academics before becoming a star. His 30.3 PPG in 1993-94 led the NCAA, and he was the first player to lead the Big Ten in both scoring and rebounding since Mychal Thompson in 1978. The consensus Player of the Year and No. 1 NBA draft choice in 1994, Robinson led all rookies in scoring and made the 1996 Olympic team after his second season.

Strengths: "Big Dog" will probably average 20-plus PPG for the rest of his NBA life, thanks to an offensive game that features a soft jumper with 3-point range, an equally solid post-up game, and the ability to get his shot whenever he wants it. Few players his size can do the things he does with the ball. Robinson also rebounds, passes, gets to the line, and hits his free throws. Robinson is truly a multi-talented standout.

Weaknesses: Robinson led the NBA in turnovers as a rookie and came close to matching the feat in his second year. He constantly faces double-teams, and he has to learn not to force the action. He also needs to continue improving his defense, hoisting his field-goal percentage, and becoming a leader.

Analysis: Robinson learned in his second season that NBA stardom has its drawbacks. While he put up more big numbers, some were critical of his premature selection to Dream Team III (consider that Shawn Kemp was left off) and of the fact he has not turned the Bucks into a winner. The only non-All-Star on the 1996 Olympic team, Robinson shouldn't worry about the naysayers. He's a franchise talent who will dominate over the next decade.

PLAYER SUMMARY	
Will	score from anywhere
Can't	eliminate turnovers
Expect	All-Star showings
Don't Expect	less than 20 PPG
Fantasy Value	$30-35
Card Value	50-80¢

COLLEGE STATISTICS

		G	FGP	FTP	RPG	PPG
92-93	PURD	28	.474	.741	9.2	24.1
93-94	PURD	34	.483	.796	10.1	30.3
Totals		62	.479	.773	9.7	27.5

NBA REGULAR-SEASON STATISTICS

				FGs		3-PT FGs		FTs		Rebounds						
		G	MIN	FG	PCT	FG	PCT	FT	PCT	OFF	TOT	AST	STL	BLK	PTS	PPG
94-95	MIL	80	2958	636	.451	86	.321	397	.796	169	513	197	115	22	1755	21.9
95-96	MIL	82	3249	627	.454	90	.342	316	.812	136	504	293	95	42	1660	20.2
Totals		162	6207	1263	.452	176	.331	713	.803	305	1017	490	210	64	3415	21.1

JAMES ROBINSON

Team: Minnesota Timberwolves
Position: Guard
Height: 6'2" **Weight:** 180
Birthdate: August 31, 1970
NBA Experience: 3 years

College: Alabama
Acquired: Traded from Trail Blazers
with Bill Curley and a future first-round
pick for Isaiah Rider, 7/96

Background: Robinson scored 40 PPG as a senior at Murrah High School in Mississippi. He was a marquee recruit for Alabama and became the first freshman to lead the Crimson Tide in scoring since 1953. A late first-round choice of Portland in 1993, Robinson spent most of his first three NBA seasons backing up Rod Strickland at point guard. He has yet to average double digits in scoring. He joins the T'Wolves for 1996-97.

Strengths: Robinson, who once set a Mississippi high school record in the 300-meter hurdles and won the slam-dunk competition at a McDonald's All-America Game, has explosive athletic ability and a scoring bent. He is a dangerous 3-point shooter who also has the quickness to drive past his man. He plays length-of-the-floor defense and thrives at a fast pace.

Weaknesses: Robinson is a classic 'tweener. His questionable decision-making keeps him from being a pure point guard, yet he is too small to be a standout at the two spot. He plays out of control at times and tends to look for his own shot instead of setting the table for teammates. He shoots a poor percentage from the field and the free-throw line. Half of his attempts are 3-pointers.

Analysis: Robinson is a streaky player. He fared well at times in Portland when Strickland was out of the lineup, but he has never demonstrated the leadership or consistency that would earn him regular front-line minutes. There's no questioning his quickness, and he does step off the bench to provide perimeter points.

PLAYER SUMMARY	
Will	run the floor
Can't	shoot 50 percent
Expect	scoring binges
Don't Expect	a steady hand
Fantasy Value	$1
Card Value	7-10¢

COLLEGE STATISTICS

		G	FGP	FTP	APG	PPG
90-91	ALAB	33	.470	.699	1.2	16.8
91-92	ALAB	34	.445	.712	2.2	19.4
92-93	ALAB	29	.420	.682	2.3	20.6
Totals		96	.444	.695	1.9	18.9

NBA REGULAR-SEASON STATISTICS

				FGs		3-PT FGs		FTs		Rebounds						
		G	MIN	FG	PCT	FG	PCT	FT	PCT	OFF	TOT	AST	STL	BLK	PTS	PPG
93-94	POR	58	673	104	.365	23	.315	45	.672	34	78	68	30	15	276	4.8
94-95	POR	71	1539	255	.409	76	.341	65	.591	42	132	180	48	13	651	9.2
95-96	POR	76	1627	229	.399	102	.359	89	.659	44	157	150	34	16	649	8.5
Totals		205	3839	588	.396	201	.347	199	.638	120	367	398	112	44	1576	7.7

RUMEAL ROBINSON

Team: Los Angeles Lakers
Position: Guard
Height: 6'2" **Weight:** 195
Birthdate: November 13, 1966

NBA Experience: 5 years
College: Michigan
Acquired: Signed as a free agent, 8/96

Background: The hero of Michigan's 1989 national championship team as a junior, Robinson had a forgettable rookie year with Atlanta. He played his first four pro seasons with the Hawks, New Jersey, and Charlotte. He missed more than half the 1993-94 season with a foot injury and labored the next two years in the CBA. He signed with Portland in January 1996 and started 14 of 43 games with the Blazers. He joins the Lakers for 1996-97.

Strengths: Robinson has a strong, physical body sculpted for the wear of the NBA. He is not averse to using it at the defensive end, where he can check both ones and twos. He is a point guard with a scoring bent. Robinson can take the ball strong to the hoop, can create shooting space, and has 3-point range.

Weaknesses: Playmaking (more accurately, the lack of it) was the main reason Robinson wound up in the CBA for two seasons. He has never been able to set up teammates as well as he works for his own shot. His ego has played a part. A move to shooting guard is a stretch because Robinson does not drill jumpers consistently.

Analysis: Robinson was pegged by some to be an NBA standout after a college career in which he could do little wrong. He's a scorer who plays point guard, and therein lies the problem for teams that want to see a better grasp of team concepts. He can play defense, but it does not appear he will match his CBA scoring average of 20.2 PPG.

PLAYER SUMMARY	
Will	look to score
Can't	make teammates better
Expect	an NBA body
Don't Expect	5 APG
Fantasy Value	$0
Card Value	5-8¢

COLLEGE STATISTICS

		G	FGP	FTP	RPG	PPG
87-88	MICH	33	.553	.667	3.1	9.7
88-89	MICH	37	.557	.656	3.4	14.9
89-90	MICH	30	.490	.676	4.2	19.2
Totals		100	.528	.666	3.5	14.5

NBA REGULAR-SEASON STATISTICS

				FGs		3-PT FGs		FTs		Rebounds						
		G	MIN	FG	PCT	FG	PCT	FT	PCT	OFF	TOT	AST	STL	BLK	PTS	PPG
90-91	ATL	47	674	108	.446	2	.182	47	.587	20	71	132	32	8	265	5.6
91-92	ATL	81	2220	423	.456	34	.327	175	.636	64	219	446	105	24	1055	13.0
92-93	NJ	80	1585	270	.423	20	.357	112	.574	49	159	323	96	12	672	8.4
93-94	NJ/CHA	31	396	55	.362	8	.400	13	.448	6	32	63	18	3	131	4.2
95-96	POR	43	715	92	.416	30	.380	33	.647	19	78	142	26	5	247	5.7
Totals		282	5590	948	.435	94	.348	380	.603	158	559	1106	277	52	2370	8.4

DENNIS RODMAN

Team: Chicago Bulls
Position: Forward
Height: 6'8" **Weight:** 220
Birthdate: May 13, 1961
NBA Experience: 10 years

College: Cooke County; S.E. Oklahoma St.
Acquired: Traded from Spurs for Will Perdue, 10/95

Background: Only 5'11" as a high school senior, Rodman went to work as an airport laborer before an incredible nine-inch growth spurt convinced him to try basketball. He was a three-time NAIA All-American at S.E. Oklahoma State. Rodman played in two All-Star Games with Detroit, was twice named Defensive Player of the Year, and has led the league in rebounding five years in a row.

Strengths: No forward in history has dominated the glass like Rodman. His 18.7 RPG in 1991-92 was the highest average since Wilt Chamberlain snared 19.2 in 1971-72. "Worm" is also a stopper who can smother players at all five positions. He triggers the break with pinpoint outlet passes.

Weaknesses: Rodman has been a public-relations nightmare. His foul-ups include a bizarre weapons incident in Detroit, last year's head-butting of an official, and countless instances of absence or tardiness. He's a loose cannon, to say the least. Rodman has little offensive touch.

Analysis: Rodman's tattoo-covered body and colorful hairstyles don't even begin to describe how strange he is. Few teams in the NBA wanted to take on this problem child, but Chicago gambled in a trade with San Antonio and got the dominant rebounder it needed.

PLAYER SUMMARY	
Will	dominate the boards
Can't	blend in
Expect	controversy
Don't Expect	offense
Fantasy Value	$14-17
Card Value	25-60¢

COLLEGE STATISTICS

		G	FGP	FTP	RPG	PPG
82-83	CC	16	.616	.582	13.3	17.6
83-84	SOS	30	.618	.655	13.1	26.0
84-85	SOS	32	.648	.566	15.9	26.8
85-86	SOS	34	.645	.655	17.8	24.4
Totals		112	.635	.620	15.3	24.5

NBA REGULAR-SEASON STATISTICS

				FGs		3-PT FGs		FTs		Rebounds					
		G	MIN	FG	PCT	FG	PCT	FT	PCT	OFF	TOT	AST	STL	BLK	PTS	PPG
86-87	DET	77	1155	213	.545	0	.000	74	.587	163	332	56	38	48	500	6.5
87-88	DET	82	2147	398	.561	5	.294	152	.535	318	715	110	75	45	953	11.6
88-89	DET	82	2208	316	.595	6	.231	97	.626	327	772	99	55	76	735	9.0
89-90	DET	82	2377	288	.581	1	.111	142	.654	336	792	72	52	60	719	8.8
90-91	DET	82	2747	276	.493	6	.200	111	.631	361	1026	85	65	55	669	8.2
91-92	DET	82	3301	342	.539	32	.317	84	.600	523	1530	191	68	70	800	9.8
92-93	DET	62	2410	183	.427	15	.205	87	.534	367	1132	102	48	45	468	7.5
93-94	SA	79	2989	156	.534	5	.208	53	.520	453	1367	184	52	32	370	4.7
94-95	SA	49	1568	137	.571	0	.000	75	.676	274	823	97	31	23	349	7.1
95-96	CHI	64	2088	146	.480	3	.111	56	.528	356	952	160	36	27	351	5.5
Totals		741	22990	2455	.535	73	.235	931	.589	3478	9441	1156	520	481	5914	8.0

CARLOS ROGERS

Team: Toronto Raptors
Position: Forward/Center
Height: 6'11" **Weight:** 220
Birthdate: February 6, 1971
NBA Experience: 2 years
College: Arkansas-Little Rock;
Tennessee St.

Acquired: Traded from Warriors with
Victor Alexander and draft rights to
Dwayne Whitfield, Martin Lewis, and
Michael McDonald for B.J. Armstrong,
9/95

Background: After transferring from Arkansas-Little Rock to Tennessee State,
Rogers became a two-time Ohio Valley Player of the Year and the only collegian
in 1993-94 to finish in the top 15 nationally in scoring, rebounding, field-goal
accuracy, and blocked shots. Drafted 11th by Seattle and traded to Golden State,
he averaged 8.9 PPG as a rookie, then 7.7 PPG with Toronto.

Strengths: Rogers is blessed with great quickness and athletic ability. He gets
off the floor in a heartbeat, can be murder on the offensive boards, and blocks a
lot of shots. He has the potential to be a very good defensive player in the NBA.
Rogers runs the floor well and knows how to take the ball to the rim. He shoots
for a high percentage from the floor.

Weaknesses: Some contend Rogers is more athlete than basketball player. He
does not shoot the ball well at all, has no touch from the free-throw line, and
needs to develop a couple of reliable moves in the post. He is not as strong as
he needs to be to match up with the big, physical power forwards. Rogers is not a
steady ball-handler or passer, and his understanding of defense is unrefined.
He's known as a big talker.

Analysis: Rogers was sent from Golden State to Toronto in the deal that put B.J.
Armstrong in a Warrior uniform. All in all, Rogers's second season was not a lot
different from his first. He showed promise in transition, on the offensive glass,
and occasionally on defense. His free-throw shooting remained an
embarrassment and the rest of his offensive skills raw. A jump shot would help.

PLAYER SUMMARY	
Will ....run and jump	
Can't ....make two free throws	
Expect ....blocked shots	
Don't Expect ....10 PPG	
Fantasy Value $3-5	
Card Value ....12-20¢	

COLLEGE STATISTICS

		G	FGP	FTP	RPG	PPG
90-91	ALR	19	.508	.554	6.9	8.4
92-93	TSU	29	.621	.624	11.7	20.3
93-94	TSU	31	.614	.649	11.5	24.5
Totals		79	.603	.629	10.5	19.1

NBA REGULAR-SEASON STATISTICS

			FGs		3-PT FGs		FTs		Rebounds						
	G	MIN	FG	PCT	FG	PCT	FT	PCT	OFF	TOT	AST	STL	BLK	PTS	PPG
94-95 GS	49	1017	180	.529	2	.143	76	.521	108	278	37	22	52	438	8.9
95-96 TOR	56	1043	178	.517	3	.143	71	.546	80	170	35	25	48	430	7.7
Totals	105	2060	358	.523	5	.143	147	.533	188	448	72	47	100	868	8.3

RODNEY ROGERS

Team: Los Angeles Clippers
Position: Forward
Height: 6'7" **Weight:** 255
Birthdate: June 20, 1971
NBA Experience: 3 years

College: Wake Forest
Acquired: Traded from Nuggets with draft rights to Brent Barry for Randy Woods and draft rights to Antonio McDyess, 6/95

Background: Rogers earned second-team all-league honors as a freshman at Wake Forest and went on to become 1992-93 Player of the Year in the ACC, averaging 21.2 points and 7.4 rebounds per game. Rogers slipped to the ninth pick in the 1993 draft and did not make the NBA All-Rookie first or second team. After two years in Denver, he was traded to the Clippers and averaged 11.6 PPG in 1995-96.

Strengths: The muscular Rogers can handle himself against almost anyone in the post, yet he also has the ability to step outside and knock down 3-pointers. He creates matchup problems with inside-outside scoring skills. Rogers handles the ball well and has good quickness off the dribble. He is capable of playing tough defense against players who stand a few inches taller.

Weaknesses: Rogers does not attack the boards aggressively and has yet to develop into a consistent offensive force. While he can do a lot of things, he does not have a great feel for when to shoot, when to post up, and when to pass. He racks up too few assists and too many turnovers. Rogers fouls too frequently, makes free throws too infrequently, and defends too sporadically.

Analysis: Rogers played mostly small forward as a rookie, started at power forward in his second season in Denver, and was a starting small forward for most of his first season with the Clippers. His ever-changing role has slowed his development somewhat, as did an ankle injury that sidelined him for 15 games last year. Rogers came on late last season and looks to have a promising future.

PLAYER SUMMARY	
Will	play two positions
Can't	make free throws
Expect	inside-outside offense
Don't Expect	defensive finesse
Fantasy Value	$9-11
Card Value	15-25¢

COLLEGE STATISTICS

		G	FGP	FTP	RPG	PPG
90-91	WF	30	.570	.669	7.9	16.3
91-92	WF	29	.614	.683	8.5	20.5
92-93	WF	30	.555	.717	7.4	21.2
Totals		89	.579	.694	7.9	19.3

NBA REGULAR-SEASON STATISTICS

				FGs		3-PT FGs		FTs		Rebounds						
		G	MIN	FG	PCT	FG	PCT	FT	PCT	OFF	TOT	AST	STL	BLK	PTS	PPG
93-94	DEN	79	1406	239	.439	35	.380	127	.672	90	226	101	63	48	640	8.1
94-95	DEN	80	2142	375	.488	50	.338	179	.651	132	385	161	95	46	979	12.2
95-96	LAC	67	1950	306	.477	49	.320	113	.628	113	286	167	75	35	774	11.6
Totals		226	5498	920	.471	134	.341	419	.651	335	897	429	233	129	2393	10.6

SEAN ROOKS

Team: Los Angeles Lakers
Position: Center/Forward
Height: 6'10" **Weight:** 250
Birthdate: September 9, 1969

NBA Experience: 4 years
College: Arizona
Acquired: Signed as a free agent, 7/96

Background: After joining Brian Williams and Ed Stokes on the "Tucson Skyline," Rooks led Arizona in scoring and was second in rebounding as a senior. He was a first-team All-Pac-10 honoree. Rooks spent his first two NBA seasons with Dallas before trades to Minnesota and, last year, Atlanta. He was a 70-game starter for the Timberwolves in 1994-95 but was used off the bench last season. He will back up Shaq in L.A. this year.

Strengths: Rooks uses his wide body to score in the low post. He knows how to position himself against opposing centers to get his shot off. Rooks has a good idea of what to do with his back to the basket and can also knock down short jumpers. Rooks owns good hands and a decent feel for the game. He will block a few shots.

Weaknesses: Rooks has never achieved a level of consistency that would warrant a look as a regular starter. He does his best work against second-line players. He seems lost at times against the better centers in the league and goes into a shell. His rebounding and defense have not been selling points. Rooks does not get up and down the floor quickly and is not much of a passer or ball-handler.

Analysis: "Wookie," nicknamed after the *Star Wars* character, could help his cause considerably by developing a mean streak and taking it out on defense and the boards. Considering his size, his work in both areas remains subpar. He's a little slow and mechanical on offense, but he seems to get the job done. He's at least an adequate backup center.

PLAYER SUMMARY

Will ....get position
Can't ....lead the break
Expect...........................inside scoring
Don't Expect....consistency, defense
Fantasy Value.................................$1
Card Value ....7-10¢

COLLEGE STATISTICS

		G	FGP	FTP	RPG	PPG
88-89	ARIZ	32	.598	.615	2.8	5.6
89-90	ARIZ	31	.532	.708	4.9	12.7
90-91	ARIZ	35	.562	.658	5.7	11.9
91-92	ARIZ	31	.560	.651	6.9	16.3
Totals		129	.558	.664	5.0	11.6

NBA REGULAR-SEASON STATISTICS

				FGs		3-PT FGs		FTs		Rebounds						
		G	MIN	FG	PCT	FG	PCT	FT	PCT	OFF	TOT	AST	STL	BLK	PTS	PPG
92-93	DAL	72	2087	368	.493	0	.000	234	.602	196	536	95	38	81	970	13.5
93-94	DAL	47	1255	193	.491	0	.000	150	.714	84	259	49	21	44	536	11.4
94-95	MIN	80	2405	289	.470	0	.000	290	.761	165	486	97	29	71	868	10.9
95-96	MIN/ATL	65	1117	144	.505	1	.143	135	.668	81	255	47	23	42	424	6.5
Totals		264	6864	994	.487	1	.067	809	.684	526	1536	288	111	238	2798	10.6

JALEN ROSE

Team: Indiana Pacers
Position: Guard
Height: 6'8" **Weight:** 210
Birthdate: January 20, 1973
NBA Experience: 2 years

College: Michigan
Acquired: Traded from Nuggets with Reggie Williams and a 1996 first-round pick for Mark Jackson, Ricky Pierce, and a 1996 first-round pick, 6/96

Background: Rose became the second player in Michigan history to amass 1,500 points, 400 rebounds, 300 assists, and 100 steals. He played in two NCAA championship games during his three years and helped Michigan to a 13-3 record in tourney play. The third member of the Fab Five to be selected in the first round of the NBA draft (13th overall), Rose led Denver in assists in each of his first two seasons before the Pacers dealt for him in the off-season.

Strengths: Rose possesses great size for a point guard and is a dangerous post-up threat. He sees the floor, penetrates, can finish with either hand, and knows where and when to deliver the ball. He's a fine defensive rebounder who exudes confidence. Versatile and streetwise, Rose can also fill the shooting guard spot and is not a passive defender. He loves to play and longs to win.

Weaknesses: Rose's jump shot does not inspire fear in defenders. It is a crooked-looking release that does not find its mark often enough to warrant tight defense. He is at his best on the break and in the paint. Rose is a subpar free-throw shooter who does not always make the right decisions with the ball. Smaller, quicker point guards give him fits on defense; he is better off guarding two guards.

Analysis: Rose has started about half the time in each of his first two seasons, while spending the other half as a third guard. As his assist total indicates, Rose is a point guard first and everything else second. Brash and competitive, he might not fit the typical point guard mold, but his size and post-up ability give him an extra dimension. His scoring average is likely to soar.

PLAYER SUMMARY

Will ....post up
Can't ....shut down speedsters
Expect.............................court vision
Don't Expect..............sweet shooting
Fantasy Value $10-13
Card Value ....15-30¢

COLLEGE STATISTICS

		G	FGP	FTP	APG	PPG
91-92	MICH	34	.486	.756	4.0	17.6
92-93	MICH	36	.446	.720	3.9	15.4
93-94	MICH	32	.461	.734	3.9	19.9
Totals		102	.464	.738	3.9	17.5

NBA REGULAR-SEASON STATISTICS

			FGs		3-PT FGs		FTs		Rebounds						
	G	MIN	FG	PCT	FG	PCT	FT	PCT	OFF	TOT	AST	STL	BLK	PTS	PPG
94-95 DEN	81	1798	227	.454	36	.316	173	.739	57	217	389	65	22	663	8.2
95-96 DEN	80	2134	290	.480	32	.296	191	.690	46	260	495	53	39	803	10.0
Totals	161	3932	517	.468	68	.306	364	.712	103	477	884	118	61	1466	9.1

DONALD ROYAL

Team: Orlando Magic
Position: Forward
Height: 6'8" **Weight:** 210
Birthdate: May 2, 1966

NBA Experience: 6 years
College: Notre Dame
Acquired: Signed as a free agent, 8/92

Background: Royal averaged 15.8 PPG and 7.0 RPG during his senior year at Notre Dame, after which he was a third-round draft choice of Cleveland. He spent his first two pro seasons in the CBA and had his first NBA stint with Minnesota in 1989-90. He has since played in Israel, in San Antonio, and four years in Orlando. After starting in 1994-95, Royal's minutes took a plunge last season.

Strengths: Royal has made a living with the drive. The owner of a great first step, he is a slashing penetrator who knows no fear when taking the ball to the hole. He has spent a lot of time at the free-throw line and has worked hard on his jumper. Royal runs the floor, works hard, and plays tough defense against players at multiple positions.

Weaknesses: Royal is a predictable offensive player. Defenders can afford to back off, knowing to expect a drive. Sometimes they'll get burned anyway. Royal does not own a dangerous outside stroke, and the 3-pointer is out of his range. He is not a good ball-handler or passer, and his rebounding is nothing special.

Analysis: A pleasant surprise when he first came to the Magic, Royal has not been able to add a consistent jumper (or much else) to his game. That fact, along with the play of Dennis Scott, kept the hard-working Royal on the bench for most of the 1995-96 season. Royal would warrant a lot more than 15 minutes per game on a less talented team.

PLAYER SUMMARY	
Will	drive to the hoop
Can't	shoot 3-pointers
Expect	a quick first step
Don't Expect	offensive diversity
Fantasy Value	$1
Card Value	5-8¢

COLLEGE STATISTICS

		G	FGP	FTP	RPG	PPG
83-84	ND	31	.594	.622	2.3	3.4
84-85	ND	30	.497	.782	5.5	9.1
85-86	ND	28	.583	.766	4.9	10.6
86-87	ND	28	.576	.820	7.0	15.8
Totals		117	.560	.780	4.9	9.5

NBA REGULAR-SEASON STATISTICS

				FGs		3-PT FGs		FTs		Rebounds						
		G	MIN	FG	PCT	FG	PCT	FT	PCT	OFF	TOT	AST	STL	BLK	PTS	PPG
89-90	MIN	66	746	117	.459	0	.000	153	.777	69	137	43	32	8	387	5.9
91-92	SA	60	718	80	.449	0	.000	92	.692	65	124	34	25	7	252	4.2
92-93	ORL	77	1636	194	.496	0	.000	318	.815	116	295	80	36	25	706	9.2
93-94	ORL	74	1357	174	.501	0	.000	199	.740	94	248	61	50	16	547	7.4
94-95	ORL	70	1841	206	.475	0	.000	223	.746	83	279	198	45	16	635	9.1
95-96	ORL	64	963	106	.491	0	.000	125	.762	57	153	42	29	15	337	5.3
Totals		411	7261	877	.482	0	.000	1110	.764	484	1236	458	217	87	2864	7.0

CLIFFORD ROZIER

Team: Golden State Warriors
Position: Center/Forward
Height: 6'11" **Weight:** 255
Birthdate: October 31, 1972

NBA Experience: 2 years
College: North Carolina; Louisville
Acquired: First-round pick in 1994 draft (16th overall)

Background: One of the top high school talents in the nation out of Bradenton, Florida, Rozier played a nondescript freshman year at North Carolina before transferring to Louisville. He was voted Metro Conference Player of the Year in each of his two seasons with the Cardinals. A first-round choice of Golden State in 1994, he led the team in total rebounds as a rookie before seeing a dramatic decrease in playing time in 1995-96.

Strengths: Rozier is a potentially dominant rebounder and a physically strong inside player. He uses his strength to seal his man off the boards. Rozier was second among rookie rebounders during the 1994-95 season with 7.4 per game, and he averaged one every 4.2 minutes last season. Rozier is willing to throw his weight around, set picks, and get after bigger opponents.

Weaknesses: Though he shoots for a high percentage, Rozier is a very limited offensive player. A center in college, he lacks a face-up jumper and is one of the worst free-throw shooters you'll find. He does not own a workable set of post moves, either. Passing and ball-handling are not recommended. Rozier is not a threat to score, unless it's in transition or on a putback. He's too small to handle centers with great success.

Analysis: Rozier averaged 22.6 minutes as a rookie but just 12.3 last year. More than a dozen times he failed to get off the bench due to coach's decision. The play of rookie Joe Smith had something to do with that, but equally harmful has been Rozier's inability to occupy his man offensively. It's tough to play four-on-five. That's what Rozier's teams stand to face unless he finds a way to score.

PLAYER SUMMARY	
Will	rebound
Can't	drop jumpers
Expect	physical play
Don't Expect	much offense
Fantasy Value	$0
Card Value	8-12¢

COLLEGE STATISTICS

		G	FGP	FTP	RPG	PPG
90-91	NC	34	.471	.565	3.0	4.9
92-93	LOUI	31	.561	.568	10.9	15.7
93-94	LOUI	34	.618	.545	11.1	18.1
Totals		99	.573	.557	8.2	12.8

NBA REGULAR-SEASON STATISTICS

			FGs		3-PT FGs		FTs		Rebounds						
	G	MIN	FG	PCT	FG	PCT	FT	PCT	OFF	TOT	AST	STL	BLK	PTS	PPG
94-95 GS	66	1494	189	.485	2	.286	68	.447	200	486	45	35	39	448	6.8
95-96 GS	59	723	79	.585	0	.000	26	.473	71	171	22	19	30	184	3.1
Totals	125	2217	268	.510	2	.222	94	.454	271	657	67	54	69	632	5.1

TREVOR RUFFIN

Unrestricted Free Agent
Last Team: Philadelphia 76ers
Position: Guard
Height: 6'1" **Weight:** 185
Birthdate: September 26, 1970

NBA Experience: 2 years
College: Cuyahoga; Arizona Western;
Hawaii
Acquired: Signed as a free agent,
12/95

Background: Ruffin played his first two years of college ball at Cuyahoga Community College in Ohio and Arizona Western before transferring to Hawaii, where he was an All-Western Athletic Conference player as a senior. He led the Rainbows to their first-ever WAC tournament title in 1994. Undrafted, Ruffin played 49 games with Phoenix as a 1994-95 rookie. He chose not to sign with Vancouver after being taken in the 1995 expansion draft and averaged 12.8 PPG for the 76ers last season.

Strengths: Ruffin is a point guard with a scorer's mentality. He knows how to shake a defender and has to be respected from beyond the 3-point arc. He also hit a commendable 81.3 percent of his free throws last season. Ruffin is capable of creating for teammates, though he tends to look for his own offense first. He appreciates his NBA job, comes to work, and is capable of high-scoring efforts.

Weaknesses: Defense is not Ruffin's specialty. For one, he thinks like a scorer. He also pales in comparison to the NBA's pure point guards, yet is too small to guard the twos on the perimeter. Ruffin himself is not a pure point; Sixer forward Jerry Stackhouse piled up more assists than he did last season. Ruffin needs to wait for better shots and learn to create more for others.

Analysis: All things considered, Ruffin's 1995-96 season had to be considered a success. Some doubted whether he was NBA material, but he made 23 starts and finished fourth on his team in scoring. If he were three inches taller, he'd probably make 40 percent of his treys from the two spot. As it is, Ruffin needs to become a better playmaker.

PLAYER SUMMARY	
Will	get his shots
Can't	stop his man
Expect	a 3-point eye
Don't Expect	pure playmaking
Fantasy Value	$2-4
Card Value	12-20¢

COLLEGE STATISTICS

		G	FGP	FTP	RPG	PPG
92-93	HAW	27	.416	.679	2.6	12.7
93-94	HAW	30	.427	.743	3.2	20.8
Totals		57	.423	.726	2.9	17.0

NBA REGULAR-SEASON STATISTICS

			FGs		3-PT FGs		FTs		Rebounds						
	G	MIN	FG	PCT	FG	PCT	FT	PCT	OFF	TOT	AST	STL	BLK	PTS	PPG
94-95 PHO	49	319	84	.426	38	.384	27	.711	8	23	48	14	2	233	4.8
95-96 PHI	61	1551	263	.406	104	.366	148	.813	21	132	269	43	2	778	12.8
Totals	110	1870	347	.411	142	.371	175	.795	29	155	317	57	4	1011	9.2

BRYON RUSSELL

Team: Utah Jazz
Position: Forward
Height: 6'7" **Weight:** 225
Birthdate: December 31, 1970

NBA Experience: 3 years
College: Long Beach St.
Acquired: Second-round pick in 1993 draft (45th overall)

Background: Russell sat out a year of basketball at Long Beach State to become academically eligible, then steadily progressed the next three years while teaming with fellow 1993 second-round pick Lucious Harris. Russell led the 49ers in rebounding and blocked shots as a senior. His role with the Jazz has decreased in each of his three seasons. He averaged just 2.9 points per game in 1995-96.

Strengths: Russell is a quick player who brings energy to the floor and is willing to do the dirty work. He's tough and physical and is not afraid to wrestle with bigger players on defense. Russell has good instincts for the ball and comes up with his share of steals. He can guard both small forwards and power forwards. He is capable of making things happen off the drive.

Weaknesses: Russell is not a talented offensive player. His jump shot is the main reason he's spent more and more time on the bench every year. He will not rack up assists, he's prone to coughing up the ball, and his decisions leave a lot to be desired. His career field-goal percentage (44.8) tells all you need to know about his stroke. Russell is no better than average on the boards.

Analysis: The 1996-97 season shapes up as a big one for Russell. He needs to do something to stop a downward slide that left him with less than ten minutes of playing time per contest last season. The thing to do would be to develop an outside shot that defenders will respect. After watching him for three years, however, Jazz fans have to wonder if that's possible. Stay tuned.

PLAYER SUMMARY

Will...........................chase loose balls
Can't ....shoot straight
Expect ....defensive energy
Don't Expect ....double-teams
Fantasy Value.................................$0
Card Value ....7-10¢

COLLEGE STATISTICS

		G	FGP	FTP	RPG	PPG
90-91	LBS	28	.430	.652	5.8	7.9
91-92	LBS	26	.555	.656	7.4	13.9
92-93	LBS	32	.537	.727	6.7	13.2
Totals		86	.513	.683	6.6	11.7

NBA REGULAR-SEASON STATISTICS

				FGs		3-PT FGs		FTs		Rebounds						
		G	MIN	FG	PCT	FG	PCT	FT	PCT	OFF	TOT	AST	STL	BLK	PTS	PPG
93-94	UTA	67	1121	135	.484	2	.091	62	.614	61	181	54	68	19	334	5.0
94-95	UTA	63	860	104	.437	13	.295	62	.667	44	141	34	48	11	283	4.5
95-96	UTA	59	577	56	.394	14	.350	48	.716	28	90	29	29	8	174	2.9
Totals		189	2558	295	.448	29	.274	172	.659	133	412	117	145	38	791	4.2

ARVYDAS SABONIS

Team: Portland Trail Blazers
Position: Center
Height: 7'3" **Weight:** 292
Birthdate: December 19, 1964

NBA Experience: 1 year
College: None
Acquired: First-round pick in 1986 draft (24th overall)

Background: Sabonis led the Soviets to a gold medal at the 1988 Olympics and helped his native Lithuania to the bronze in 1992. Considered the premier big man in Europe for a decade, he led Real Madrid of Spain to the European club championship in 1995. Finally, nine years after Portland made him a first-round draft choice, Sabonis came to the NBA and enjoyed an impressive rookie season.

Strengths: Sabonis is blessed with a variety of skills that most men his size can only dream about. He is a brilliant passer who shoots with 3-point range and owns a soft touch around the basket. He was among the most accurate field-goal shooters in the league and one of the best rebounders among reserves. Sabonis takes up a lot of space and is a smart position defender. He has played in his share of big games.

Weaknesses: Sabonis did not play an NBA game before reaching the age of 30, and Achilles tendon surgery in his pre-NBA days has slowed him. He would have been better suited to handle the NBA grind five years ago, when he was thinner and more agile. Not surprisingly, Sabonis had trouble checking the quicker big men in the league. The shelf life of his legs remains a key issue.

Analysis: Coaches looking to teach the fundamentals of pivot play should use a videotape of Sabonis, the Lithuanian Olympic legend who knows how to play the game. He averaged 22.9 points and 13.1 rebounds per game in his final year in Spain, and his NBA numbers were not too shabby, either. As a starter late in the 1995-96 season, he contributed about 18 points and 11 boards per outing. He could have been an NBA star.

PLAYER SUMMARY	
Will	pass, score, rebound
Can't	get off the floor
Expect	great fundamentals
Don't Expect	a long NBA career
Fantasy Value	$17-20
Card Value	40-80¢

COLLEGE STATISTICS

—DID NOT PLAY—

NBA REGULAR-SEASON STATISTICS

			FGs		3-PT FGs		FTs		Rebounds						
	G	MIN	FG	PCT	FG	PCT	FT	PCT	OFF	TOT	AST	STL	BLK	PTS	PPG
95-96 POR	73	1735	394	.545	39	.375	231	.757	147	588	130	64	78	1058	14.5
Totals	73	1735	394	.545	39	.375	231	.757	147	588	130	64	78	1058	14.5

JOHN SALLEY

Team: Chicago Bulls
Position: Forward/Center
Height: 6'11" **Weight:** 255
Birthdate: May 16, 1964

NBA Experience: 10 years
College: Georgia Tech
Acquired: Signed as a free agent, 3/96

Background: "Spider" was Georgia Tech's all-time leader in blocked shots before being selected by the Pistons (along with Dennis Rodman) in the 1986 draft. He won two NBA championship rings with Detroit while earning a talented-but-inconsistent tag. Salley has since played bit parts in Miami, Toronto, and Chicago.

Strengths: Salley's value is his defense. He has good quickness to go along with his size and long arms. He can match up with centers and forwards and will soon block the 1,000th shot of his career. He runs the floor, passes fairly well, and can score with an occasional drive or jumper.

Weaknesses: Salley does not seem to enjoy the game itself as much as he enjoys making money and cracking jokes. He has never been very consistent, even in his best seasons. He does not own a powerful low-post game and has never averaged double figures in the scoring column. He no longer warrants big minutes.

Analysis: Salley is an aspiring comedian who has worked nightclub gigs. In a few years, his off-court bookings will be his only ones. Salley was not popular in Miami, and he was unable to earn more than 20 minutes per game with the expansion Raptors. He did provide Chicago's centers an occasional breather late last season.

PLAYER SUMMARY	
Will	block shots
Can't	earn steady minutes
Expect	public appearances
Don't Expect	impressive stats
Fantasy Value	$0
Card Value	5-8¢

COLLEGE STATISTICS

		G	FGP	FTP	RPG	PPG
82-83	GT	27	.502	.637	5.7	11.5
83-84	GT	29	.589	.674	5.8	11.8
84-85	GT	35	.627	.636	7.1	14.0
85-86	GT	34	.606	.594	6.7	13.1
Totals		125	.587	.633	6.4	12.7

NBA REGULAR-SEASON STATISTICS

		G	MIN	FGs FG	FGs PCT	3-PT FGs FG	3-PT FGs PCT	FTs FT	FTs PCT	Rebounds OFF	Rebounds TOT	AST	STL	BLK	PTS	PPG
86-87	DET	82	1463	163	.562	0	.000	105	.614	108	296	54	44	125	431	5.3
87-88	DET	82	2003	258	.566	0	.000	185	.709	166	402	113	53	137	701	8.5
88-89	DET	67	1458	166	.498	0	.000	135	.692	134	335	75	40	72	467	7.0
89-90	DET	82	1914	209	.512	1	.250	174	.713	154	439	67	51	153	593	7.2
90-91	DET	74	1649	179	.475	0	.000	186	.727	137	327	70	52	112	544	7.4
91-92	DET	72	1774	249	.512	0	.000	186	.715	106	296	116	49	110	684	9.5
92-93	MIA	51	1422	154	.502	0	.000	115	.799	113	313	83	32	70	423	8.3
93-94	MIA	76	1910	208	.477	2	.667	164	.729	132	407	135	56	78	582	7.7
94-95	MIA	76	1955	197	.499	0	.000	153	.739	110	336	123	47	85	547	7.2
95-96	TOR/CHI	42	673	63	.450	0	.000	59	.694	46	140	54	19	27	185	4.4
Totals		704	16221	1846	.509	3	.214	1462	.714	1206	3291	890	443	969	5157	7.3

DETLEF SCHREMPF

Team: Seattle SuperSonics
Position: Forward
Height: 6'10" **Weight:** 235
Birthdate: January 21, 1963
NBA Experience: 11 years

College: Washington
Acquired: Traded from Pacers for Derrick McKey and Gerald Paddio, 11/93

Background: A graduate of the University of Washington, Schrempf spent the first three-plus years of his NBA career in Dallas. He was traded to Indiana in 1989 and won the Sixth Man Award in 1991 and 1992. Another trade before the 1993-94 season sent him to Seattle, where he made a remarkable 51.4 percent of his 3-point attempts in 1994-95 and has been a standout starter.

Strengths: Complete, versatile, consistent. They all describe Schrempf, who provides a little bit of everything. He handles the ball, drives for dunks, posts up, shoots 3-pointers, rebounds, passes, and gives his all on defense. Few players in the league work harder than Schrempf, a two-time All-Star who hates losing.

Weaknesses: One of the few weaknesses in Schrempf's game has been his tendency to spend too much time pleading his case to the refs. He does not reject many shots and is not the quickest player in the league.

Analysis: Schrempf's numbers dipped somewhat in 1995-96, but consider his contributions to a contending team. His typical game includes better than 17 points, five rebounds, and four assists. A fractured left leg cost the dependable Schrempf more than a month before the All-Star break. The Sonics were not the same team without him.

PLAYER SUMMARY	
Will	give you his all
Can't	be left open
Expect	scoring, defense
Don't Expect	missed treys
Fantasy Value	$30-35
Card Value	10-20¢

COLLEGE STATISTICS

		G	FGP	FTP	RPG	PPG
81-82	WASH	28	.452	.553	2.0	3.3
82-83	WASH	31	.466	.717	6.8	10.6
83-84	WASH	31	.539	.736	7.4	16.8
84-85	WASH	32	.558	.714	8.0	15.8
Totals		122	.521	.708	6.2	11.9

NBA REGULAR-SEASON STATISTICS

				FGs		3-PT FGs		FTs		Rebounds						
		G	MIN	FG	PCT	FG	PCT	FT	PCT	OFF	TOT	AST	STL	BLK	PTS	PPG
85-86	DAL	64	969	142	.451	3	.429	110	.724	70	198	88	23	10	397	6.2
86-87	DAL	81	1711	265	.472	33	.478	193	.742	87	303	161	50	16	756	9.3
87-88	DAL	82	1587	246	.456	5	.156	201	.756	102	279	159	42	32	698	8.5
88-89	DAL/IND	69	1850	274	.474	7	.200	273	.780	126	395	179	53	19	828	12.0
89-90	IND	78	2573	424	.516	17	.354	402	.820	149	620	247	59	16	1267	16.2
90-91	IND	82	2632	432	.520	15	.375	441	.818	178	660	301	58	22	1320	16.1
91-92	IND	80	2605	496	.536	23	.324	365	.828	202	770	312	62	37	1380	17.3
92-93	IND	82	3098	517	.476	8	.154	525	.804	210	780	493	79	27	1567	19.1
93-94	SEA	81	2728	445	.493	22	.324	300	.769	144	454	275	73	9	1212	15.0
94-95	SEA	82	2886	521	.523	93	.514	437	.839	135	508	310	93	35	1572	19.2
95-96	SEA	63	2200	360	.486	73	.408	287	.776	73	328	276	56	8	1080	17.1
Totals		844	24839	4122	.497	299	.382	3534	.797	1476	5295	2801	648	231	12077	14.3

BYRON SCOTT

Unrestricted Free Agent
Last Team: Vancouver Grizzlies
Position: Guard
Height: 6'4" **Weight:** 202
Birthdate: March 28, 1961

NBA Experience: 13 years
College: Arizona St.
Acquired: Selected from Pacers in 1995 expansion draft

Background: In three years, Scott became Arizona State's career scoring leader. He worked his way into the Lakers' starting lineup as a rookie, broke Michael Cooper's team record for career 3-pointers, and helped the Lakers to three NBA championships in the 1980s. After ten Laker seasons, Scott spent two years with Indiana and spent last year with Vancouver.

Strengths: Scott is a classic spot-up shooter who is deadly when he gets his feet together. He has great range and has made countless clutch shots in his career. He can also get to the hoop, drill free throws, and provide veteran leadership.

Weaknesses: Scott has never been a defensive force, and he is not as quick as he once was. He is also no longer a primary scoring threat despite his 14,000 career points. Scott hit barely more than 40 percent from the floor last season.

Analysis: Scott kept one streak alive and saw another one end last season. His 10.2 PPG marked the 13th time in as many years he has averaged double figures in scoring. His streak of 12 consecutive trips to the playoffs, however, was bound to end with the Grizzlies.

PLAYER SUMMARY	
Will	lead by example
Can't	shut down his man
Expect	spot-up jumpers
Don't Expect	50-percent shooting
Fantasy Value	$0
Card Value	5-8¢

COLLEGE STATISTICS

		G	FGP	FTP	RPG	PPG
79-80	ASU	29	.500	.733	2.7	13.6
80-81	ASU	28	.505	.693	3.8	16.6
82-83	ASU	33	.513	.782	5.4	21.6
Totals		90	.507	.747	4.0	17.5

NBA REGULAR-SEASON STATISTICS

		G	MIN	FGs FG	FGs PCT	3-PT FGs FG	3-PT FGs PCT	FTs FT	FTs PCT	Rebounds OFF	Rebounds TOT	AST	STL	BLK	PTS	PPG
83-84	LAL	74	1637	334	.484	8	.235	112	.806	50	164	177	81	19	788	10.6
84-85	LAL	81	2305	541	.539	26	.433	187	.820	57	210	244	100	17	1295	16.0
85-86	LAL	76	2190	507	.513	22	.361	138	.784	55	189	164	85	15	1174	15.4
86-87	LAL	82	2729	554	.489	65	.436	224	.892	63	286	281	125	18	1754	21.7
87-88	LAL	81	3048	710	.527	62	.346	272	.858	76	333	335	155	27	1754	21.7
88-89	LAL	74	2605	588	.491	77	.399	195	.863	72	302	231	114	27	1448	19.6
89-90	LAL	77	2593	472	.470	93	.423	160	.766	51	242	274	77	31	1197	15.5
90-91	LAL	82	2630	501	.477	71	.324	118	.797	54	246	177	95	21	1191	14.5
91-92	LAL	82	2679	460	.458	54	.344	244	.838	74	310	226	105	28	1218	14.9
92-93	LAL	58	1677	296	.449	44	.326	156	.848	27	134	157	55	13	792	13.7
93-94	IND	67	1197	256	.467	27	.365	157	.805	19	110	133	62	9	696	10.4
94-95	IND	80	1528	265	.455	79	.389	193	.850	18	151	108	61	13	802	10.0
95-96	VAN	80	1894	271	.401	74	.335	203	.835	40	192	123	63	22	819	10.2
Totals		994	28712	5755	.484	702	.369	2359	.832	656	2869	2630	1178	260	14571	14.7

DENNIS SCOTT

Team: Orlando Magic
Position: Forward
Height: 6'8" **Weight:** 230
Birthdate: September 5, 1968

NBA Experience: 6 years
College: Georgia Tech
Acquired: First-round pick in 1990 draft (fourth overall)

Background: Scott led Georgia Tech to the NCAA Final Four as a senior. That year, he recorded the highest single-season point total in Atlantic Coast Conference history and was named ACC Player of the Year. He earned All-Rookie honors in 1990-91, but knee surgery and other injuries cut short his next two years. Scott was a sixth man before starting all 82 games for Orlando in 1995-96.

Strengths: Scott is one of the most dangerous long-range shooters in basketball. He set an NBA record with 267 3-pointers made last season and also established a single-game record with 11. He can spot up or create his shot off the dribble. Scott also handles the ball well, makes crisp passes, and comes up with better than one steal per game.

Weaknesses: Scott lives and dies with the 3-pointer, as more than half his shots originate behind the arc. When he's cold, his team suffers for it. He could stand to mix in a few more drives and post-ups. Scott does not boast great quickness, and he has not always kept in tip-top shape.

Analysis: Scott was one of the most improved players in the NBA in 1995-96. He reported to training camp in the best shape of his six-year career and, with the comfort of a new contract, gave the Magic an extra five points per game. His shooting stroke was the perfect complement to Shaquille O'Neal's inside presence. When he's hot, there's no stopping him.

PLAYER SUMMARY	
Will	dominate from deep
Can't	be left open
Expect	more 3-point records
Don't Expect	frequent drives
Fantasy Value	$12-15
Card Value	8-12¢

COLLEGE STATISTICS

		G	FGP	FTP	RPG	PPG
87-88	GT	32	.440	.655	5.0	15.5
88-89	GT	32	.443	.814	4.1	20.3
89-90	GT	35	.465	.793	6.6	27.7
Totals		99	.452	.777	5.3	21.4

NBA REGULAR-SEASON STATISTICS

				FGs		3-PT FGs		FTs		Rebounds						
		G	MIN	FG	PCT	FG	PCT	FT	PCT	OFF	TOT	AST	STL	BLK	PTS	PPG
90-91	ORL	82	2336	503	.425	125	.374	153	.750	62	235	134	62	25	1284	15.7
91-92	ORL	18	608	133	.402	29	.326	64	.901	14	66	35	20	9	359	19.9
92-93	ORL	54	1759	329	.431	108	.403	92	.786	38	186	136	57	18	858	15.9
93-94	ORL	82	2283	384	.405	155	.399	123	.774	54	218	216	81	32	1046	12.8
94-95	ORL	62	1499	283	.439	150	.426	86	.754	25	146	131	45	14	802	12.9
95-96	ORL	82	3041	491	.440	267	.425	182	.820	63	309	243	90	29	1431	17.5
Totals		380	11526	2123	.426	834	.405	700	.789	256	1160	895	355	127	5780	15.2

MALIK SEALY

Team: Los Angeles Clippers
Position: Forward
Height: 6'8" **Weight:** 190
Birthdate: February 1, 1970
NBA Experience: 4 years

College: St. John's
Acquired: Traded from Pacers with Pooh Richardson and draft rights to Eric Piatkowski for Mark Jackson and draft rights to Greg Minor, 6/94

Background: Sealy starred at Tolentine High in the Bronx. He led all Big East players in scoring as a senior (22.6 PPG) at hometown St. John's while earning his second straight spot on the all-conference first team. He finished his career as St. John's' all-time steals leader and was second to Chris Mullin in scoring. He played minimally with the Pacers for two years before a trade to the Clippers made him a starter.

Strengths: Sealy, who goes by the nickname "Silk," is a smooth offensive player who can drive past his man and finish with either hand. He is an energetic, versatile player. He plays both big guard and small forward, has great quickness, and is tougher than he appears. He thrives in a transition game and plays disruptive on-the-ball defense, even against the big guns.

Weaknesses: Give Sealy a cushion, because he won't burn you with his jump shot. He has not developed any consistency from the outside in four seasons of work, although his free-throw shooting has improved. Sealy is not adept at handling the ball against pressure, nor is he an accomplished playmaker. A hip injury two years ago and a fractured thumb last season have sidelined him.

Analysis: Sealy first gained NBA notoriety on a 1993 playoff trip to New York, when he lost his playbook and heard the scouting reports read over the radio. With the Clippers, he has emerged as a valuable player, especially for his defensive intensity. Consider that the Clippers were 4-17 without him last season. Sealy owns a family business that specializes in neckties and clothing he designs.

PLAYER SUMMARY

Will ....hustle on "D"
Can't ....avoid injury bug
Expect ....further improvement
Don't Expect..............sweet shooting
Fantasy Value $4-6
Card Value ....8-12¢

COLLEGE STATISTICS

		G	FGP	FTP	RPG	PPG
88-89	STJ	31	.489	.558	6.4	12.9
89-90	STJ	34	.525	.746	6.9	18.1
90-91	STJ	32	.492	.743	7.7	22.1
91-92	STJ	30	.472	.793	6.8	22.6
Totals		127	.494	.729	6.9	18.9

NBA REGULAR-SEASON STATISTICS

			FGs		3-PT FGs		FTs		Rebounds						
	G	MIN	FG	PCT	FG	PCT	FT	PCT	OFF	TOT	AST	STL	BLK	PTS	PPG
92-93 IND	58	672	136	.426	7	.226	51	.689	60	112	47	36	7	330	5.7
93-94 IND	43	623	111	.405	4	.250	59	.678	43	118	48	31	8	285	6.6
94-95 LAC	60	1604	291	.435	22	.301	174	.780	77	214	107	72	25	778	13.0
95-96 LAC	62	1601	272	.415	21	.210	147	.799	76	240	116	84	28	712	11.5
Totals	223	4500	810	.423	54	.245	431	.759	256	684	318	223	68	2105	9.4

RONY SEIKALY

Team: Golden State Warriors
Position: Center
Height: 6'11" **Weight:** 252
Birthdate: May 10, 1965
NBA Experience: 8 years

College: Syracuse
Acquired: Traded from Heat for Billy Owens and draft rights to Sasha Danilovic, 11/94

Background: A native of Greece, Seikaly was one of Syracuse's all-time great big men. He was inconsistent as a rookie in 1988-89 but won the NBA's Most Improved Player Award the next season. In six years with Miami, he averaged 15.4 PPG and 10.4 RPG, but various injuries have limited his contributions in two seasons since being traded to Golden State.

Strengths: Seikaly has been dominant on the boards at times. He once grabbed 34 rebounds in a game against Washington, more than the Bullets nabbed as a team. Seikaly has a polished low-post offensive game, with good footwork and effective moves. He can also provide a defensive presence.

Weaknesses: Passing is not high on Seikaly's priority list. He rarely gets credit for two assists in a game, and he frequently racks up more than five fouls and turnovers. He is not a great face-up shooter, nor has he been a big-time scorer. Seikaly's play has been up-and-down in the last two years, partly due to injuries.

Analysis: The Warriors have not gotten the consistent double-doubles they expected out of Seikaly since they traded his former college teammate, Billy Owens, for him. An ankle injury in 1994-95 and a torn tendon in his thumb in 1995-96 are among the assorted ailments that have slowed him. Seikaly has more than 5,000 career rebounds, but he is no longer a force in that or any other category.

PLAYER SUMMARY	
Will	have his nights
Can't	keep off injured list
Expect	rebounds
Don't Expect	assists
Fantasy Value	$13-16
Card Value	5-8¢

COLLEGE STATISTICS

		G	FGP	FTP	RPG	PPG
84-85	SYR	31	.542	.558	6.4	8.1
85-86	SYR	32	.547	.563	7.8	10.1
86-87	SYR	38	.568	.600	8.2	15.1
87-88	SYR	35	.566	.568	9.6	16.3
Totals		136	.560	.576	8.0	12.6

NBA REGULAR-SEASON STATISTICS

				FGs		3-PT FGs		FTs	Rebounds						
		G	MIN	FG	PCT	FG	PCT	FT	PCT	OFF	TOT	AST	STL	BLK	PTS	PPG
88-89	MIA	78	1962	333	.448	1	.250	181	.511	204	549	55	46	96	848	10.9
89-90	MIA	74	2409	486	.502	0	.000	256	.594	253	766	78	78	124	1228	16.6
90-91	MIA	64	2171	395	.481	2	.333	258	.619	207	709	95	51	86	1050	16.4
91-92	MIA	79	2800	463	.489	0	.000	370	.733	307	934	109	40	121	1296	16.4
92-93	MIA	72	2456	417	.480	1	.125	397	.735	259	846	100	38	83	1232	17.1
93-94	MIA	72	2410	392	.488	0	.000	304	.720	244	740	136	59	100	1088	15.1
94-95	GS	36	1035	162	.516	0	.000	111	.694	77	266	45	20	37	435	12.1
95-96	GS	64	1813	285	.502	2	.667	204	.723	166	499	71	40	69	776	12.1
Totals		539	17056	2933	.486	6	.222	2081	.669	1717	5309	689	372	716	7953	14.8

BRIAN SHAW

Team: Orlando Magic
Position: Guard
Height: 6'6" **Weight:** 194
Birthdate: March 22, 1966
NBA Experience: 7 years

College: St. Mary's (CA); Cal.-Santa Barbara
Acquired: Signed as a free agent, 9/94

Background: Shaw, the Pacific Coast Athletic Association Player of the Year as a senior at Cal.-Santa Barbara, was a second-team All-Rookie performer with the Celtics in 1988-89. He spent a season in Italy before returning to Boston and later playing two-plus years in Miami. He signed with Orlando before the 1994-95 season and has spent most of his two years there coming off the bench.

Strengths: Shaw's greatest asset might be his ability to defend players at either guard position. He brings good size to the backcourt and is an above-average rebounder among reserve guards. Shaw runs the offense and gets the ball to the right people. He has been Orlando's second-leading assist man for the last two years.

Weaknesses: Shaw is no shooter. He hits a 3-pointer from time to time, but he has not made even 42 percent of his field-goal attempts in any of the last five seasons. He struggles to convert on his drives into traffic and is better off giving it up. Shaw is not a consistent player, which is one more reason to bring him off the bench.

Analysis: Shaw has been one of the leading reserve assist men in the league since joining the Magic. Keep in mind, however, that he's been feeding to players like Anfernee Hardaway, Shaquille O'Neal, and Dennis Scott. Shaw does provide sturdy defense, but his shooting deficiencies are hard to hide.

PLAYER SUMMARY	
Will	play defense
Can't	shoot accurately
Expect	versatility
Don't Expect	starts
Fantasy Value	$1
Card Value	7-12¢

COLLEGE STATISTICS

		G	FGP	FTP	RPG	PPG
83-84	SM	14	.361	.737	0.9	2.9
84-85	SM	27	.402	.724	5.3	9.4
86-87	CSB	29	.434	.712	7.7	10.9
87-88	CSB	30	.466	.740	8.7	13.3
Totals		100	.434	.728	6.4	10.1

NBA REGULAR-SEASON STATISTICS

				FGs		3-PT FGs		FTs		Rebounds						
		G	MIN	FG	PCT	FG	PCT	FT	PCT	OFF	TOT	AST	STL	BLK	PTS	PPG
88-89	BOS	82	2301	297	.433	0	.000	109	.826	119	376	472	78	27	703	8.6
90-91	BOS	79	2772	442	.469	3	.111	204	.819	104	370	602	105	34	1091	13.8
91-92	BOS/MIA	63	1423	209	.407	5	.217	72	.791	50	204	250	57	22	495	7.9
92-93	MIA	68	1603	197	.393	43	.331	61	.782	70	257	235	48	19	498	7.3
93-94	MIA	77	2037	278	.417	73	.338	64	.719	104	350	385	71	21	693	9.0
94-95	ORL	78	1836	192	.389	48	.261	70	.737	52	241	406	73	18	502	6.4
95-96	ORL	75	1679	182	.374	41	.285	91	.798	58	224	336	58	11	496	6.6
Totals		522	13651	1797	.419	213	.289	671	.791	557	2022	2686	490	152	4478	8.6

LIONEL SIMMONS

Team: Sacramento Kings
Position: Forward
Height: 6'7" **Weight:** 210
Birthdate: November 14, 1968

NBA Experience: 6 years
College: La Salle
Acquired: First-round pick in 1990 draft (seventh overall)

Background: Simmons, who won the Wooden Award in 1990 as college basketball's Player of the Year, finished his career at La Salle third on the all-time NCAA scoring list. He was the first player in college history to amass more than 3,000 points and 1,100 rebounds. Simmons was runner-up for 1991 Rookie of the Year honors, but he has struggled for playing time in the last two of his six seasons.

Strengths: Simmons has been a player who can provide scoring, rebounding, passing, and leadership. He understands the game and has the ability to make those around him better. He works hard at both ends of the floor. He blocked 132 shots in his second season and has twice grabbed 600-plus rebounds in a year.

Weaknesses: Simmons did not have great athletic ability to begin with, and arthroscopic knee surgery two years ago did not help. In fact, he has not been the same player since. Shooting the ball has never been a strength, and Simmons continues to see his field-goal percentage dip. If he's not able to get past his man off the dribble, he is largely ineffective.

Analysis: Simmons surprised some when he averaged at least 15 points and seven rebounds per game over his first four years. He was living up to his lottery status before having repair work done to his right knee. Having lost both a step and his starting job, Simmons has not been a confident contributor, and it's hard to envision a dramatic turnaround.

PLAYER SUMMARY	
Will	look for teammates
Can't	regain his form
Expect	versatility
Don't Expect	a shooting star
Fantasy Value	$1
Card Value	8-15¢

COLLEGE STATISTICS

		G	FGP	FTP	RPG	PPG
86-87	LaS	33	.526	.763	9.8	20.3
87-88	LaS	34	.485	.757	11.4	23.3
88-89	LaS	32	.487	.711	11.4	28.4
89-90	LaS	32	.513	.661	11.1	26.5
Totals		131	.501	.722	10.9	24.6

NBA REGULAR-SEASON STATISTICS

		G	MIN	FGs FG	PCT	3-PT FGs FG	PCT	FTs FT	PCT	Rebounds OFF	TOT	AST	STL	BLK	PTS	PPG
90-91	SAC	79	2978	549	.422	3	.273	320	.736	193	697	315	113	85	1421	18.0
91-92	SAC	78	2895	527	.454	1	.200	281	.770	149	634	337	135	132	1336	17.1
92-93	SAC	69	2502	468	.444	1	.091	298	.819	156	495	312	95	38	1235	17.9
93-94	SAC	75	2702	436	.438	6	.353	251	.777	168	562	305	104	50	1129	15.1
94-95	SAC	58	1064	131	.420	6	.375	59	.702	61	196	89	28	23	327	5.6
95-96	SAC	54	810	86	.396	19	.373	55	.733	41	145	83	31	20	246	4.6
Totals		413	12951	2197	.436	36	.324	1264	.768	768	2729	1441	506	348	5694	13.8

DICKEY SIMPKINS

Team: Chicago Bulls
Position: Forward
Height: 6'10" **Weight:** 264
Birthdate: April 6, 1972

NBA Experience: 2 years
College: Providence
Acquired: First-round pick in 1994 draft (21st overall)

Background: A largely anonymous player at Providence, Simpkins vaulted himself into the first round of the 1994 draft with his showings at the Portsmouth Invitational and Phoenix Desert Classic. He fared much better in those camps than he did in college, where he averaged just 9.8 points and 6.3 rebounds per game. Chicago drafted him 21st overall but has used him sparingly in two seasons.

Strengths: Simpkins has good size, strength, and quickness to get after NBA forwards on defense, and he could develop into a player who can also battle centers. Drafted for his defensive potential, he gets in the passing lanes and knows how to seal a man off the boards. He can also contribute on the offensive glass. Simpkins runs the floor very well for a big man.

Weaknesses: Simpkins is quite limited offensively. He does not possess a great variety of moves in the post, and his jump shot is not a weapon. He does not have good range, and he is a poor free-throw shooter. He simply does not look comfortable with the ball. Simpkins is not a passing or ball-handling threat, and Chicago expected more of a shot-blocker than they wound up with. His offensive specialty to this point has been the "garbage bucket."

Analysis: Simpkins played only a little bit more during his second season than he did in his first. He did draw a dozen starting assignments last year, averaging 5.9 points and 4.1 rebounds per game in those outings. Even if he could earn significant playing time, Simpkins is not the type of player who will stuff the stat sheet. His future, if he can hang around, is as a defensive and rebounding specialist.

PLAYER SUMMARY

Will ....hit the boards
Can't ....pile up numbers
Expect ....defensive effort
Don't Expect ....much offense
Fantasy Value $0
Card Value ....5-8¢

COLLEGE STATISTICS

		G	FGP	FTP	RPG	PPG
90-91	PROV	32	.492	.609	6.6	7.8
91-92	PROV	30	.492	.703	5.8	9.0
92-93	PROV	33	.450	.596	6.5	10.6
93-94	PROV	30	.516	.686	6.3	11.8
Totals		125	.486	.646	6.3	9.8

NBA REGULAR-SEASON STATISTICS

			FGs		3-PT FGs		FTs		Rebounds						
		G	MIN	FG	PCT	FG	PCT	FT	PCT	OFF	TOT	AST	STL	BLK	PTS	PPG
94-95	CHI	59	586	78	.424	0	.000	50	.694	60	151	37	10	7	206	3.5
95-96	CHI	60	685	77	.481	11	.000	61	.629	66	156	38	9	8	216	3.6
Totals		119	1271	155	.451	11	.000	111	.657	126	307	75	19	15	422	3.5

CHARLES SMITH

Team: San Antonio Spurs
Position: Forward
Height: 6'10" **Weight:** 244
Birthdate: July 16, 1965
NBA Experience: 8 years

College: Pittsburgh
Acquired: Traded from Knicks with Monty Williams for J.R. Reid and Brad Lohaus, 2/96

Background: Smith, the Big East Player of the Year as a senior, left Pitt with the school's career records for points and blocked shots. He earned All-Rookie honors in 1988-89 with the Clippers, for whom he became a 20-point scorer and leading rebounder and shot-blocker. Smith was a disappointment in New York before last February's trade to San Antonio.

Strengths: Smith presents an effective combination of size, speed, and quickness. He has been a dominant scorer, rebounder, and shot-blocker at times during his career, and he still contributes in all three areas. He has spent a lot of time at each forward position and has polished his offensive moves in the post.

Weaknesses: Smith has undergone several knee surgeries in the past few years, and he is no longer the explosive athlete he once was. He remains capable of big games, but they have been few and far between. His inconsistent play at both ends of the court did not endear him to New York fans. Smith does not pass the ball well and is no longer a rebounding force.

Analysis: Smith's trade to San Antonio was a refreshing one. It gave him the chance to return to the power forward position at which he was one of the NBA's top frontcourt players with the Clippers from 1988-92. The Knicks had been using him primarily at the three spot. As long as his knees hold up, Smith will contribute.

PLAYER SUMMARY	
Will	score in the post
Can't	regain explosiveness
Expect	shot-blocking
Don't Expect	All-Star trips
Fantasy Value	$3-5
Card Value	7-10¢

COLLEGE STATISTICS

		G	FGP	FTP	RPG	PPG
84-85	PITT	29	.502	.706	8.0	15.0
85-86	PITT	29	.404	.762	8.1	15.9
86-87	PITT	33	.550	.735	8.5	17.0
87-88	PITT	31	.558	.764	7.7	18.9
Totals		122	.500	.753	8.1	16.8

NBA REGULAR-SEASON STATISTICS

			FGs		3-PT FGs		FTs		Rebounds						
	G	MIN	FG	PCT	FG	PCT	FT	PCT	OFF	TOT	AST	STL	BLK	PTS	PPG
88-89 LAC	71	2161	435	.495	0	.000	285	.725	173	465	103	68	89	1155	16.3
89-90 LAC	78	2732	595	.520	1	.083	454	.794	177	524	114	86	119	1645	21.1
90-91 LAC	74	2703	548	.469	0	.000	384	.793	216	608	134	81	145	1480	20.0
91-92 LAC	49	1310	251	.466	0	.000	212	.785	95	301	56	41	98	714	14.6
92-93 NY	81	2172	358	.469	0	.000	287	.782	170	432	142	48	96	1003	12.4
93-94 NY	43	1105	176	.443	8	.500	87	.719	66	165	50	26	45	447	10.4
94-95 NY	76	2150	352	.471	7	.226	255	.792	144	324	120	49	95	966	12.7
95-96 NY/SA	73	1716	244	.422	2	.133	119	.730	133	362	65	50	80	609	8.3
Totals	545	16049	2959	.476	18	.196	2083	.774	1174	3181	784	449	767	8019	14.7

JOE SMITH

Team: Golden State Warriors
Position: Forward
Height: 6'10" **Weight:** 225
Birthdate: July 26, 1975

NBA Experience: 1 year
College: Maryland
Acquired: First-round pick in 1995 draft (first overall)

Background: It took just two years for Smith to advance from an obscure high school player to the top pick in the NBA draft. During his brief tenure at Maryland, he garnered consensus national Freshman of the Year honors in 1993-94 and won the Naismith Award as the best player in the nation in 1994-95. Smith led all NBA rookies in rebounding last season (8.7 per game) and was third among first-year scorers (15.3 PPG).

Strengths: Smith is a multifaceted forward who enhances everything he does with hard work. A quick jumper, it did not take him long to become a rebounding force at the NBA level. He also ranked among league leaders in blocked shots and has an assortment of scoring moves in the post. Smith runs like the wind, handles the ball better than most forwards, and has a better jumper than most thought. Few players will outwork him.

Weaknesses: Smith, a college center, needs to add strength to become a durable power forward in the pros. The league's "horses" can push him around in the paint, although Smith's leaping ability has helped him negate some of his strength disadvantage. He also needs to improve his awareness of double-teams and make better passes. He battled foul trouble for much of his rookie season.

Analysis: Smith is a future star, and he's also a refreshing change of pace from the big-headed young millionaires that clutter the NBA. Joe's as unassuming as his name, having brought his mother to the Bay Area to live with him, cook his meals, and take care of him. An off-season brush with the law tarnished his image somewhat. On the hardwood, Smith needs little help. His scoring will soar when more plays are run for him.

PLAYER SUMMARY	
Will	score, rebound, block
Can't	manhandle centers
Expect	double-doubles
Don't Expect	a big ego
Fantasy Value	$20-25
Card Value	$1.50-3.00

COLLEGE STATISTICS

		G	FGP	FTP	RPG	PPG
93-94	MARY	30	.522	.734	10.7	19.4
94-95	MARY	34	.578	.741	10.6	20.8
Totals		64	.550	.737	10.7	20.1

NBA REGULAR-SEASON STATISTICS

			FGs		3-PT FGs		FTs		Rebounds						
	G	MIN	FG	PCT	FG	PCT	FT	PCT	OFF	TOT	AST	STL	BLK	PTS	PPG
95-96 GS	82	2821	469	.458	10	.357	303	.773	300	717	79	85	134	1251	15.3
Totals	82	2821	469	.458	10	.357	303	.773	300	717	79	85	134	1251	15.3

KENNY SMITH

Unrestricted Free Agent
Last Team: Houston Rockets
Position: Guard
Height: 6'3" **Weight:** 170
Birthdate: March 8, 1965

NBA Experience: 9 years
College: North Carolina
Acquired: Traded from Hawks with Roy Marble for Tim McCormick and John Lucas, 9/90

Background: Smith set all-time school records for assists and steals at North Carolina, where he was named All-Atlantic Coast Conference as a senior. He averaged double figures in scoring in his first three NBA seasons with Sacramento and Atlanta, but he did not truly shine until a 1990 trade brought him to Houston. He started at the point for championship teams in 1994 and 1995.

Strengths: Smith has been one of the NBA's better shooters, having once led all guards in field-goal percentage. He makes a high percentage of his 3-pointers and free throws and is capable of lining up at either guard spot. Smith is steady with the ball and provides veteran leadership.

Weaknesses: Smith's scoring average has declined in each of the past five seasons, and he has given way to others when games are on the line. His field-goal percentage last season was the worst of his career. Smith is not the most creative playmaker, and he does not specialize in defense.

Analysis: Smith has been an underrated player during much of his career. His talents were a perfect fit for the Rockets' back-to-back title teams. Smith runs the offense, gets the ball to the right people, and is capable of catching fire. His role was increasingly limited in the last two seasons.

PLAYER SUMMARY	
Will	run the offense
Can't	dazzle defenders
Expect	a 3-point threat
Don't Expect	great defense
Fantasy Value	$1-3
Card Value	5-10¢

COLLEGE STATISTICS

		G	FGP	FTP	APG	PPG
83-84	NC	23	.519	.800	5.0	9.1
84-85	NC	36	.518	.860	6.5	12.3
85-86	NC	34	.516	.808	6.2	12.0
86-87	NC	34	.502	.807	6.1	16.9
Totals		127	.512	.823	6.0	12.9

NBA REGULAR-SEASON STATISTICS

				FGs		3-PT FGs		FTs		Rebounds						
		G	MIN	FG	PCT	FG	PCT	FT	PCT	OFF	TOT	AST	STL	BLK	PTS	PPG
87-88	SAC	61	2170	331	.477	12	.308	167	.819	40	138	434	92	8	841	13.8
88-89	SAC	81	3145	547	.462	46	.359	263	.737	49	226	621	102	7	1403	17.3
89-90	SAC/ATL	79	2421	378	.466	26	.313	161	.821	18	157	445	79	6	943	11.9
90-91	HOU	78	2699	522	.520	49	.363	287	.844	36	163	554	106	11	1380	17.7
91-92	HOU	81	2735	432	.475	54	.394	219	.866	34	177	562	104	7	1137	14.0
92-93	HOU	82	2422	387	.520	96	.438	195	.878	28	160	446	80	7	1065	13.0
93-94	HOU	78	2209	341	.480	89	.405	135	.871	24	138	327	59	4	906	11.6
94-95	HOU	81	2030	287	.484	142	.429	126	.851	27	155	323	71	10	842	10.4
95-96	HOU	68	1617	201	.433	91	.382	87	.821	21	96	245	47	3	580	8.5
Totals		689	21448	3426	.482	605	.395	1640	.828	277	1410	3957	740	65	9097	13.2

MICHAEL SMITH

Team: Sacramento Kings
Position: Forward
Height: 6'8" **Weight:** 230
Birthdate: March 28, 1972

NBA Experience: 2 years
College: Providence
Acquired: Second-round pick in 1994 draft (35th overall)

Background: Smith attended the same Dunbar High in Baltimore that produced Reggie Lewis, David Wingate, and Muggsy Bogues. After sitting out his freshman year at Providence for academic reasons, he became the first player to ever lead the Big East in rebounding for three straight years. Smith was a second-round pick of Sacramento in 1994 but played all 82 games as a rookie. He has averaged almost six RPG in each of his two pro seasons.

Strengths: Rebounding, rebounding, and rebounding. Smith has averaged only slightly more than 20 minutes per game in his first two seasons, meaning he'd likely be a double-figure rebounder with a starter's minutes. He also runs the floor like a guard and plays physical defense. He can defend small forwards and power forwards. The unselfish Smith hustles and plays within his offensive limits.

Weaknesses: Smith's invisible offensive skills are the reason he has not earned more playing time. He poses almost no scoring threat, either in the post or on the perimeter. He makes Shaquille O'Neal look like a good free-throw shooter, and his 12-foot jumper is not much better. He needs a move. Smith is undersized for the big forward spot but is not equipped with the skills of a three.

Analysis: For a second-rounder, you have to consider Smith something of a steal. He is relentless in his attack of the backboards, and few young players understand the importance of defense like he does. It's a good thing Smith plays tough "D," because his offense would be substandard even in the CBA. Shoulder and ankle injuries nagged him last season, but overcoming those was nothing compared to the offensive work he has to do.

PLAYER SUMMARY	
Will	rebound, defend
Can't	hit two free throws
Expect	intensity, unselfishness
Don't Expect	a scoring threat
Fantasy Value	$1
Card Value	15-25¢

COLLEGE STATISTICS

		G	FGP	FTP	RPG	PPG
91-92	PROV	31	.495	.579	10.3	10.7
92-93	PROV	33	.514	.546	11.4	11.8
93-94	PROV	30	.605	.714	11.5	12.9
Totals		94	.539	.600	11.0	11.8

NBA REGULAR-SEASON STATISTICS

		G	MIN	FGs FG	FGs PCT	3-PT FGs FG	3-PT FGs PCT	FTs FT	FTs PCT	Rebounds OFF	Rebounds TOT	AST	STL	BLK	PTS	PPG
94-95	SAC	82	1736	220	.542	0	.000	127	.485	174	486	67	61	49	567	6.9
95-96	SAC	65	1384	144	.605	11	.000	68	.384	143	389	110	47	46	357	5.5
Totals		147	3120	364	.565	1	.333	195	.444	317	875	177	108	95	924	6.3

STEVE SMITH

Team: Atlanta Hawks
Position: Guard
Height: 6'8" **Weight:** 215
Birthdate: March 31, 1969
NBA Experience: 5 years

College: Michigan St.
Acquired: Traded from Heat with Grant Long and a future second-round pick for Kevin Willis and a future first-round pick, 11/94

Background: A Detroit product, Smith surpassed Scott Skiles as Michigan State's all-time leading scorer. He led the Big Ten in scoring as a junior and senior and set a conference record by hitting 45 straight free throws. Despite two knee surgeries while with Miami, Smith was chosen to play on Dream Team II. He led Atlanta in scoring with a career-high 18.1 PPG in 1995-96.

Strengths: Smith brings great size to the backcourt and is an outstanding post-up scorer. His size and ball-handling ability allow him to get his shot almost anytime he wants it, and he owns a dangerous long-range stroke. Smith can play point guard in addition to the two slot, and early in his career he drew comparisons to Magic Johnson. He hits his free throws.

Weaknesses: Smith is a below-average defensive player. He's slight in build and does not have great lateral quickness. Point guards give him fits. Smith has made less than a third of his 3-point shots over the last two seasons. His overall field-goal percentage has also slipped, a function of his inconsistency.

Analysis: Smith is a streaky player but a very talented one. When he's on his game, he rates among the best scoring guards in basketball. However, his change of teams, change of positions, and tender knees have contributed to an up-and-down tenure with the Hawks. If Smith can cut down the off nights, he'd make a strong case for All-Star recognition.

PLAYER SUMMARY

Will ....score from post, arc
Can't ....defend point guards
Expect ....16-plus PPG
Don't Expect................another Magic
Fantasy Value $12-15
Card Value ....8-12¢

COLLEGE STATISTICS

		G	FGP	FTP	APG	PPG
87-88	MSU	28	.466	.758	4.0	10.7
88-89	MSU	33	.478	.763	6.9	17.7
89-90	MSU	31	.526	.695	7.0	20.2
90-91	MSU	30	.474	.802	6.1	25.1
Totals		122	.487	.756	6.1	18.5

NBA REGULAR-SEASON STATISTICS

				FGs		3-PT FGs		FTs		Rebounds						
		G	MIN	FG	PCT	FG	PCT	FT	PCT	OFF	TOT	AST	STL	BLK	PTS	PPG
91-92	MIA	61	1806	297	.454	40	.320	95	.748	81	188	278	59	19	729	12.0
92-93	MIA	48	1610	279	.451	53	.402	155	.787	56	197	267	50	16	766	16.0
93-94	MIA	78	2776	491	.456	91	.347	273	.835	156	352	394	84	35	1346	17.3
94-95	MIA/ATL	80	2665	428	.426	137	.329	312	.841	104	276	274	62	33	1305	16.3
95-96	ATL	80	2856	494	.432	140	.331	318	.826	124	326	224	68	17	1446	18.1
Totals		347	11713	1989	.442	461	.339	1153	.819	521	1339	1437	323	120	5592	16.1

TONY SMITH

Unrestricted Free Agent
Last Team: Miami Heat
Position: Guard
Height: 6'4" **Weight:** 204
Birthdate: June 14, 1968

NBA Experience: 6 years
College: Marquette
Acquired: Traded from Suns for Terrence Rencher, 2/96

Background: As a senior, Smith set Marquette single-season records for points and scoring average, earning All-Midwestern Collegiate Conference honors. He climbed to second on the school's all-time assists list. Smith was a second-round draft pick who came off the Laker bench for most of his first five seasons. He played 34 games for the Suns last season and 25 more with the Heat.

Strengths: Smith has left behind his high-scoring college days to become a defensive specialist in the pros. He first proved himself as such against Michael Jordan in the 1991 NBA Finals. Smith has the strength, speed, and quickness to stick with his man. He has played both guard positions.

Weaknesses: Smith is not a great outside shooter and has not fared well from the 3-point arc or the free-throw line. He has scored eight PPG in just one pro season and has shot better than .450 only once as well. And Smith is not a natural point guard. He does not handle or pass the ball particularly well, nor is he a creative sort.

Analysis: Smith can play defense; there's no question about that. The rest of his game, however, is marginal at best. His jump shot is awkward and erratic, so he's not suited to start at the two spot. As a point guard, he's a third-stringer (if that). It appears Smith will have to settle for being a fourth or fifth guard who's in the game for defensive purposes alone.

PLAYER SUMMARY	
Will	stick with his man
Can't	score like in college
Expect	a defensive specialist
Don't Expect	a playmaker
Fantasy Value	$0
Card Value	7-10¢

COLLEGE STATISTICS

		G	FGP	FTP	APG	PPG
86-87	MARQ	29	.534	.753	2.1	8.1
87-88	MARQ	28	.523	.739	2.9	13.1
88-89	MARQ	28	.556	.730	5.6	14.2
89-90	MARQ	29	.495	.856	5.8	23.8
Totals		114	.521	.785	4.1	14.8

NBA REGULAR-SEASON STATISTICS

		G	MIN	FGs FG	FGs PCT	3-PT FGs FG	3-PT FGs PCT	FTs FT	FTs PCT	Rebounds OFF	Rebounds TOT	AST	STL	BLK	PTS	PPG
90-91	LAL	64	695	97	.441	0	.000	40	.702	24	71	135	28	12	234	3.7
91-92	LAL	63	820	113	.399	0	.000	49	.653	31	76	109	39	8	275	4.4
92-93	LAL	55	752	133	.484	2	.182	62	.756	46	87	63	50	7	330	6.0
93-94	LAL	73	1617	272	.441	16	.320	85	.714	106	195	148	59	14	645	8.8
94-95	LAL	61	1024	132	.427	32	.352	44	.698	43	107	102	46	7	340	5.6
95-96	PHO/MIA	59	938	116	.423	38	.328	28	.609	30	95	154	37	10	298	5.1
Totals		375	5846	863	.436	88	.308	308	.697	280	631	711	259	58	2122	5.7

RIK SMITS

Team: Indiana Pacers
Position: Center
Height: 7'4" **Weight:** 265
Birthdate: August 23, 1966

NBA Experience: 8 years
College: Marist
Acquired: First-round pick in 1988 draft (second overall)

Background: Smits, a two-time East Coast Athletic Conference Player of the Year at Marist, was the second overall pick in the 1988 draft. He was named to the NBA All-Rookie Team but led the league in disqualifications his first two years. Smits has since emerged as a high-scoring center and one of the league's most accurate field-goal shooters.

Strengths: Smits knows how to score. He has great touch on his low-post hook shots and a vast array of scoring moves. He also hits jumpers with range up to 18 feet. Get him the ball down low, and he'll get two points or get to the line. Smits is a good free-throw shooter. He has blocked 800-plus shots over eight seasons.

Weaknesses: Smits has always been below the norm on the boards. With his size, he should be pulling down nine or ten a night. He does not have a lot of spring and has been slowed by tendinitis in both knees, along with sore feet. Smits still commits too many fouls and is not a defensive force.

Analysis: The main issue with Smits is his health. When his legs are right, he is one of the best offensive centers in the game. He's not up there with the great ones because of his relatively skimpy contributions on the boards. When it comes to offense, however, Smits knows how to get it done.

PLAYER SUMMARY	
Will	fill the nets
Can't	shake injuries
Expect	offensive variety
Don't Expect	a rebounding machine
Fantasy Value	$17-20
Card Value	7-10¢

COLLEGE STATISTICS

		G	FGP	FTP	RPG	PPG
84-85	MAR	29	.567	.577	5.6	11.2
85-86	MAR	30	.622	.681	8.1	17.7
86-87	MAR	21	.609	.722	8.1	20.1
87-88	MAR	27	.623	.735	8.7	24.7
Totals		107	.609	.693	7.6	18.2

NBA REGULAR-SEASON STATISTICS

				FGs		3-PT FGs		FTs		Rebounds						
		G	MIN	FG	PCT	FG	PCT	FT	PCT	OFF	TOT	AST	STL	BLK	PTS	PPG
88-89	IND	82	2041	386	.517	0	.000	184	.722	185	500	70	37	151	956	11.7
89-90	IND	82	2404	515	.533	0	.000	241	.811	135	512	142	45	169	1271	15.5
90-91	IND	76	1690	342	.485	0	.000	144	.762	116	357	84	24	111	828	10.9
91-92	IND	74	1772	436	.510	0	.000	152	.788	124	417	116	29	100	1024	13.8
92-93	IND	81	2072	494	.486	0	.000	167	.732	126	432	121	27	75	1155	14.3
93-94	IND	78	2113	493	.534	0	.000	238	.793	135	483	156	49	82	1224	15.7
94-95	IND	78	2381	558	.526	0	.000	192	.753	192	601	111	40	79	1400	17.9
95-96	IND	63	1901	466	.521	1	.200	231	.788	119	433	110	21	45	1164	18.5
Totals		614	16374	3690	.515	1	.083	1641	.770	1132	3735	910	272	812	9022	14.7

FELTON SPENCER

Team: Orlando Magic
Position: Center
Height: 7'0" **Weight:** 265
Birthdate: January 5, 1968
NBA Experience: 6 years

College: Louisville
Acquired: Traded from Jazz for Brooks Thompson, Kenny Gattison, and a future first-round pick, 8/96

Background: Spencer ended his college career as Louisville's all-time leader in field-goal percentage and was third in the nation in that category in 1989-90. With Minnesota, he earned second-team NBA All-Rookie honors but has played his best ball since a trade to Utah three years ago. He came back from January 1995 Achilles tendon surgery and started 70 of 71 games in 1995-96. Utah dealt him to Orlando in the off-season.

Strengths: Spencer puts his heart and soul into his unglamorous job. He takes up a lot of space, does not back away from contact, and holds his defensive ground. Spencer has been productive on the boards and has worked hard on his low-post offense. He is a team player who doesn't try to perform above his head.

Weaknesses: Spencer is not a dangerous offensive player. His jumper is simply not reliable, even from short- to mid-range, and he is not a consistent scorer on the blocks. He remains one of the worst passing big men in basketball, scoring a "0" in the assist column in most of his games. He's slow on his feet, picks up a lot of fouls, and is prone to injuries.

Analysis: Spencer was a valuable complementary player with the Jazz. Knowing that Karl Malone is the main man inside, he was content to take up space, play defense, and do the dirty work required to free others for scoring chances. In that kind of role, Spencer does an admirable job. Just don't expect much offense out of him.

PLAYER SUMMARY	
Will	defend
Can't	spot open teammates
Expect	a role-player
Don't Expect	10 PPG
Fantasy Value	$1
Card Value	7-10¢

COLLEGE STATISTICS

		G	FGP	FTP	RPG	PPG
86-87	LOUI	31	.551	.492	2.7	3.8
87-88	LOUI	35	.592	.640	4.2	7.4
88-89	LOUI	33	.607	.733	5.1	8.2
89-90	LOUI	35	.681	.716	8.5	14.9
Totals		134	.628	.676	5.2	8.7

NBA REGULAR-SEASON STATISTICS

				FGs		3-PT FGs		FTs		Rebounds						
		G	MIN	FG	PCT	FG	PCT	FT	PCT	OFF	TOT	AST	STL	BLK	PTS	PPG
90-91	MIN	81	2099	195	.512	0	.000	182	.722	272	641	25	48	121	572	7.1
91-92	MIN	61	1481	141	.426	0	.000	123	.691	167	435	53	27	79	405	6.6
92-93	MIN	71	1296	105	.465	0	.000	83	.654	134	324	17	23	66	293	4.1
93-94	UTA	79	2210	256	.505	0	.000	165	.607	235	658	43	41	67	677	8.6
94-95	UTA	34	905	105	.488	0	.000	107	.793	90	260	17	12	32	317	9.3
95-96	UTA	71	1267	146	.520	0	.000	104	.689	100	306	11	20	54	396	5.6
Totals		397	9258	948	.488	0	.000	764	.685	998	2624	166	171	419	2660	6.7

LATRELL SPREWELL

Team: Golden State Warriors
Position: Guard
Height: 6'5" **Weight:** 190
Birthdate: September 8, 1970

NBA Experience: 4 years
College: Three Rivers; Alabama
Acquired: First-round pick in 1992 draft (24th overall)

Background: Though not recruited by a Division I school, Sprewell was a first-team All-SEC choice at Alabama and also made the All-Defensive team as a senior. Drafted 24th by Golden State, he made the All-Rookie second team and was an All-Star in each of the next two seasons. He again led the Warriors in scoring last season, but his average dipped under 20 PPG to 18.9.

Strengths: Sprewell was drafted for his defense, but he quickly became known for his high-energy play on both ends of the court. He has a quick first step to the bucket, and he can finish the drive with a dunk or pull up for a jumper. He also has 3-point range. Sprewell's long arms and anticipation have helped him be named to the NBA All-Defensive second team in the past. He's an athletic player.

Weaknesses: Sprewell is not the man you want bringing the ball up against pressure. His decision-making on offense also leaves a little to be desired. He annually coughs up more than 200 turnovers, about three per game, and he takes some poor shots. He has been in the doghouse for tardiness and unexcused absences.

Analysis: Sprewell, who did not play organized basketball until his senior year of high school, was a first-team All-NBA choice in his second season. In the two years since, he has not matched the high level of play that had him on the road to stardom. When performing at his best, Sprewell is a force both offensively and defensively. He needs to show more leadership and control.

PLAYER SUMMARY	
Will	get his points
Can't	regain all-NBA status
Expect	1.5 steals
Don't Expect	50-pct. shooting
Fantasy Value	$35-40
Card Value	15-30¢

COLLEGE STATISTICS

		G	FGP	FTP	RPG	PPG
90-91	ALAB	33	.511	.690	5.0	8.9
91-92	ALAB	35	.493	.771	5.2	17.8
Totals		68	.499	.740	5.1	13.5

NBA REGULAR-SEASON STATISTICS

		G	MIN	FGs FG	FGs PCT	3-PT FGs FG	3-PT FGs PCT	FTs FT	FTs PCT	Rebounds OFF	Rebounds TOT	AST	STL	BLK	PTS	PPG
92-93	GS	77	2741	449	.464	73	.369	211	.746	79	271	295	126	52	1182	15.4
93-94	GS	82	3533	613	.433	141	.361	353	.774	80	401	385	180	76	1720	21.0
94-95	GS	69	2771	490	.418	90	.276	350	.781	58	256	279	112	46	1420	20.6
95-96	GS	78	3064	515	.428	91	.323	352	.789	124	380	328	127	45	1473	18.9
Totals		306	12109	2067	.434	395	.330	1266	.775	341	1308	1287	545	219	5795	18.9

JERRY STACKHOUSE

Team: Philadelphia 76ers
Position: Guard/Forward
Height: 6'6" **Weight:** 218
Birthdate: November 5, 1974

NBA Experience: 1 year
College: North Carolina
Acquired: First-round pick in 1995 draft (third overall)

Background: Out of powerful Oak Hill Academy in Virginia, Stackhouse made an early impact at North Carolina. He earned MVP honors at the ACC Tournament as a freshman and got the 1994-95 national Player of the Year nod from *Sports Illustrated*. After leading the Tar Heels to a 56-13 ledger in his two seasons, Stackhouse was drafted third overall by Philadelphia in 1995 and led all rookie scorers at 19.2 PPG.

Strengths: Stackhouse has a remarkably complete game. He has the power and know-how to get to the basket and draw fouls, and he also has a better perimeter game than some anticipated. Strength, speed, and tenacity make him a potential big-time scorer and rebounder, and he was third among rookies in assists with 3.9 per game. He's capable of playing tough defense at both forward spots. Stackhouse blocks more than a shot per game.

Weaknesses: As expected, ball-handling is the weakest aspect of Stackhouse's vast repertoire. He committed 3.5 turnovers per game as a rookie, not handling double-teams particularly well and often trying to do too much. Consider, though, that he played on one of the worst teams in the league. Expect him to cut down on that total while hoisting his poor shooting percentage.

Analysis: Similar to a few other players who came out of North Carolina (yes, Michael Jordan among them), Stackhouse's scoring average will shoot up as he becomes an impact player in the pros. He struck for 27 points in his NBA debut and was Philly's main man from day one, playing mostly the four spot and some three. No, he's not another Jordan. He is, however, a rising star who needs only to cut down his turnovers to boast a complete game.

PLAYER SUMMARY

Will ....achieve stardom
Can't ....save 76ers immediately
Expect ....an All-Star regular
Don't Expect ....less than 20 PPG
Fantasy Value $20-25
Card Value $3.00-7.00

COLLEGE STATISTICS

		G	FGP	FTP	RPG	PPG
93-94	NC	35	.466	.732	5.0	12.2
94-95	NC	34	.517	.712	8.2	19.2
Totals		69	.496	.720	6.6	15.7

NBA REGULAR-SEASON STATISTICS

				FGs		3-PT FGs		FTs		Rebounds						
	G	MIN	FG	PCT	FG	PCT	FT	PCT	OFF	TOT	AST	STL	BLK	PTS	PPG
95-96 PHI	72	2701	452	.414	93	.318	387	.747	90	265	278	76	79	1384	19.2
Totals	72	2701	452	.414	93	.318	387	.747	90	265	278	76	79	1384	19.2

JOHN STARKS

Team: New York Knicks
Position: Guard
Height: 6'5" **Weight:** 185
Birthdate: August 10, 1965
NBA Experience: 7 years

College: Northern Oklahoma;
Oklahoma St.
Acquired: Signed as a free agent,
10/90

Background: Starks is a product of four colleges in four years, including Oklahoma State as a senior (1987-88). He signed on with Golden State as a free agent, but a back injury ended his rookie season prematurely. He became a CBA All-Star and played in the WBL before making the Knicks' roster in 1990. Starks has been one of New York's prominent players over the last five seasons.

Strengths: They don't come much more competitive than Starks, whose fiery style, long-distance shooting, and in-your-face defense can carry a team. He has made 360 3-pointers over the last two seasons, and he is also capable of burning defenders with quick drives. Starks is a skilled passer who does not back down from anyone.

Weaknesses: Starks has earned a reputation as a hothead with some highly publicized flagrant fouls. Ever since he fell in love with the 3-point shot a few years back, he no longer drives as frequently and his free-throw attempts have declined. Starks is a hot-and-cold shooter who sometimes hurts his team.

Analysis: Starks, who worked at a grocery store before gaining success in pro basketball, has seen his scoring average drop in each of the last two seasons. He cut down his 3-point attempts by better than 200 in 1995-96, which was a step in the right direction. When committed to the drive and playing his usual defense, Starks is a spark plug.

PLAYER SUMMARY

Will ....battle on defense
Can't ....avoid confrontations
Expect........................fiery leadership
Don't Expect..................shy shooting
Fantasy Value $5-7
Card Value ....7-12¢

COLLEGE STATISTICS

		G	FGP	FTP	RPG	PPG
84-85	NOU	14	.463	.774	2.4	11.1
87-88	OSU	30	.497	.838	4.7	15.4
Totals		44	.487	.820	4.0	14.0

NBA REGULAR-SEASON STATISTICS

				FGs		3-PT FGs		FTs		Rebounds						
		G	MIN	FG	PCT	FG	PCT	FT	PCT	OFF	TOT	AST	STL	BLK	PTS	PPG
88-89	GS	36	316	51	.408	10	.385	34	.654	15	41	27	23	3	146	4.1
90-91	NY	61	1173	180	.439	27	.290	79	.752	30	131	204	59	17	466	7.6
91-92	NY	82	2118	405	.449	94	.348	235	.778	45	191	276	103	18	1139	13.9
92-93	NY	80	2477	513	.428	108	.321	263	.795	54	204	404	91	12	1397	17.5
93-94	NY	59	2057	410	.420	113	.335	187	.754	37	185	348	95	6	1120	19.0
94-95	NY	80	2725	419	.395	217	.355	168	.737	34	219	411	92	4	1223	15.3
95-96	NY	81	2491	375	.443	143	.361	131	.753	31	237	315	103	11	1024	12.6
Totals		479	13357	2353	.426	712	.344	1097	.762	246	1208	1985	566	71	6515	13.6

BRYANT STITH

Team: Denver Nuggets
Position: Guard
Height: 6'5" **Weight:** 208
Birthdate: December 10, 1970

NBA Experience: 4 years
College: Virginia
Acquired: First-round pick in 1992 draft (13th overall)

Background: Without much fanfare, Stith was named All-ACC three consecutive seasons and led Virginia to the 1992 NIT championship as tournament MVP. He finished his career as the Cavaliers' all-time leader in scoring, minutes, and free throws made. Drafted 13th overall by Denver in 1992, Stith has missed only one game over the last three of his four professional seasons. He averaged 13.6 PPG in 1995-96, a career high.

Strengths: Stith is most valuable for his defense, his backcourt rebounding, and his intangibles. Leadership comes naturally, and he was named team captain in just his third year. He is an effective defensive player who combines anticipation and toughness. Stith can muscle for inside buckets, and he led the Nuggets in free-throw attempts last season. He hits well over 80 percent from the line.

Weaknesses: You'd never guess it from watching him drill free throws, but Stith is not a confident outside shooter. He hit less than 42 percent from the field last season, and he's not a dangerous long-range bomber, either. He's a below-average scorer for a starting two guard. Stith does not have great quickness and will not startle anyone with his ball-handling or passing.

Analysis: There is nothing flashy about Stith's game, and the Nuggets have tried alternatives to this former college forward at the two position. However, they keep coming back to the man who leads by example. The durable Stith started 77 of 82 games last season and compiled career highs in points, assists, and rebounds. Others are more talented, but few play harder or get as much out of their ability.

PLAYER SUMMARY	
Will	lead by example
Can't	dominate TV highlights
Expect	defense, rebounds
Don't Expect	many nights off
Fantasy Value	$8-10
Card Value	7-12¢

COLLEGE STATISTICS

		G	FGP	FTP	RPG	PPG
88-89	VIRG	33	.548	.769	6.5	15.5
89-90	VIRG	32	.481	.777	6.9	20.8
90-91	VIRG	33	.471	.791	6.2	19.8
91-92	VIRG	33	.452	.815	6.6	20.7
Totals		131	.483	.789	6.6	19.2

NBA REGULAR-SEASON STATISTICS

		G	MIN	FGs FG	FGs PCT	3-PT FGs FG	3-PT FGs PCT	FTs FT	FTs PCT	Rebounds OFF	Rebounds TOT	AST	STL	BLK	PTS	PPG
92-93	DEN	39	865	124	.446	0	.000	99	.832	39	124	49	24	5	347	8.9
93-94	DEN	82	2853	365	.450	2	.222	291	.829	119	349	199	116	16	1023	12.5
94-95	DEN	81	2329	312	.472	20	.294	267	.824	95	268	153	91	18	911	11.2
95-96	DEN	82	2810	379	.416	41	.277	320	.844	125	400	241	114	16	1119	13.6
Totals		284	8857	1180	.443	63	.275	977	.833	378	1141	642	345	55	3400	12.0

JOHN STOCKTON

Team: Utah Jazz
Position: Guard
Height: 6'1" **Weight:** 175
Birthdate: March 26, 1962

NBA Experience: 12 years
College: Gonzaga
Acquired: First-round pick in 1984 draft (16th overall)

Background: Stockton led the West Coast Athletic Conference in assists and steals for three years while at Gonzaga. He has shattered NBA assist records in 12 seasons with Utah. He owns the career lead with 11,310, and last year he led the league in assists for a record ninth time. An eight-time All-Star and two-time Olympian, Stockton also set the NBA career record for steals in 1995-96.

Strengths: Stockton can rightly be called the most accomplished playmaker in NBA history, and he remains a cut above the rest of the league. He is quick and masterful with the ball, with a sixth sense for spotting teammates in their favorite scoring spots. He is a great 3-point bomber and free-throw shooter as well as a defensive pest.

Weaknesses: Stockton does not have great size, but it has not held him back. He's not asked to rebound. He is not getting any faster.

Analysis: In less than 12 months, Stockton set all-time NBA standards for assists and steals. He then surpassed Bob Cousy's record of eight straight assist crowns. He also owns the longest current string of games started with 527. There are quicker and bigger point guards, to be sure, but none better.

PLAYER SUMMARY	
Will	make others better
Can't	control the boards
Expect	more assist titles
Don't Expect	missed starts
Fantasy Value	$35-40
Card Value	20-40¢

COLLEGE STATISTICS

		G	FGP	FTP	APG	PPG
80-81	GONZ	25	.578	.743	1.4	3.1
81-82	GONZ	27	.576	.676	5.0	11.2
82-83	GONZ	27	.518	.791	6.8	13.9
83-84	GONZ	28	.577	.692	7.2	20.9
Totals		107	.559	.719	5.2	12.5

NBA REGULAR-SEASON STATISTICS

		G	MIN	FGs FG	FGs PCT	3-PT FGs FG	3-PT FGs PCT	FTs FT	FTs PCT	Rebounds OFF	Rebounds TOT	AST	STL	BLK	PTS	PPG
84-85	UTA	82	1490	157	.471	2	.182	142	.736	26	105	415	109	11	458	5.6
85-86	UTA	82	1935	228	.489	2	.133	172	.839	33	179	610	157	10	630	7.7
86-87	UTA	82	1858	231	.499	7	.184	179	.782	32	151	670	177	14	648	7.9
87-88	UTA	82	2842	454	.574	24	.358	272	.840	54	237	1128	242	16	1204	14.7
88-89	UTA	82	3171	497	.538	16	.242	390	.863	83	248	1118	263	14	1400	17.1
89-90	UTA	78	2915	472	.514	47	.416	354	.819	57	206	1134	207	18	1345	17.2
90-91	UTA	82	3103	496	.507	58	.345	363	.836	46	237	1164	234	16	1413	17.2
91-92	UTA	82	3002	453	.482	83	.407	308	.842	68	270	1126	244	22	1297	15.8
92-93	UTA	82	2863	437	.486	72	.385	293	.798	64	237	987	199	21	1239	15.1
93-94	UTA	82	2969	458	.528	48	.322	272	.805	72	258	1031	199	22	1236	15.1
94-95	UTA	82	2867	429	.542	102	.449	246	.804	57	251	1011	194	22	1206	14.7
95-96	UTA	82	2915	440	.538	95	.422	234	.830	54	226	916	140	15	1209	14.7
Totals		980	31930	4752	.517	556	.378	3225	.821	646	2605	11310	2365	201	13285	13.6

DAMON STOUDAMIRE

Team: Toronto Raptors
Position: Guard
Height: 5'10" **Weight:** 171
Birthdate: September 3, 1973

NBA Experience: 1 year
College: Arizona
Acquired: First-round pick in 1995 draft (seventh overall)

Background: A three-time All-Pac-10 choice at Arizona, Stoudamire shared 1995 conference Player of the Year honors with UCLA's Ed O'Bannon. Stoudamire joined Gary Payton as the only players in Pac-10 history with 1,800 points, 600 assists, and 400 rebounds. The No. 7 draft choice, Stoudamire enjoyed a fabulous rookie year with Toronto in 1995-96. He led all first-year players in minutes (40.9 per game) and assists (9.3) and was second in scoring (19.0).

Strengths: Stoudamire doesn't think he's going to score tons of points; he knows he is. The left-handed water bug with lightning quickness and a killer crossover has a knack for scoring in traffic with off-balance shots and aggressive drives. He can also torch the nets from 3-point range. Stoudamire pushes a furious pace and gets his teammates involved. His quick hands and supreme confidence make him a defensive nuisance.

Weaknesses: Stoudamire is the definition of a scoring point, and the biggest question about him was whether he would be able to run an NBA team successfully. Most of those doubts were erased by his fifth-place standing among the 1995-96 assist leaders, but he also coughed up a whopping 3.8 turnovers per game. His shot selection is not always the best, and his size hurts him against the better post-up guards.

Analysis: Stoudamire reminds some of Isiah Thomas, the Raptors' general manager who said he took a chance on the diminutive Arizona guard because he felt Stoudamire could one day lead a club to a championship. Toronto has a long way to go, but Stoudamire is better than advertised. He has a tattoo of Mighty Mouse on his arm, and he plays the game like no one can stop him. Often times, no one can.

PLAYER SUMMARY	
Will	push the pace
Can't	avoid turnovers
Expect	20 PPG, 10 APG
Don't Expect	bench time
Fantasy Value	$20-25
Card Value	$2.00-5.00

COLLEGE STATISTICS

		G	FGP	FTP	APG	PPG
91-92	ARIZ	30	.455	.771	2.5	7.2
92-93	ARIZ	28	.438	.791	5.7	11.0
93-94	ARIZ	35	.448	.800	5.9	18.3
94-95	ARIZ	30	.476	.826	7.3	22.8
Totals		123	.457	.804	5.4	15.0

NBA REGULAR-SEASON STATISTICS

				FGs		3-PT FGs		FTs		Rebounds						
		G	MIN	FG	PCT	FG	PCT	FT	PCT	OFF	TOT	AST	STL	BLK	PTS	PPG
95-96	TOR	70	2865	481	.426	133	.395	236	.797	59	281	653	98	19	1331	19.0
Totals		70	2865	481	.426	133	.395	236	.797	59	281	653	98	19	1331	19.0

ROD STRICKLAND

Team: Washington Bullets
Position: Guard
Height: 6'3" **Weight:** 185
Birthdate: July 11, 1966
NBA Experience: 8 years

College: DePaul
Acquired: Traded from Trail Blazers with Harvey Grant for Rasheed Wallace and Mitchell Butler, 7/96

Background: Strickland left DePaul for the pros a year early, but not before he led the Blue Demons in scoring, assists, and steals as a junior and climbed among school career leaders in each category. He was a backup point guard with New York as a rookie before becoming a starter in San Antonio. The past two of his four seasons in Portland have been Strickland's statistical best. The Bullets dealt for him in the off-season.

Strengths: A quick first step and sure dribble allow Strickland to penetrate almost at will. He has an uncanny ability to finish among the seven-footers. He scores 18-plus PPG and has ranked fourth in the league in assists each of the last two seasons. Strickland also assists on the boards and makes steals.

Weaknesses: Strickland has been a better citizen after some off-court slipups earned him a reputation as a troublemaker in New York and San Antonio. He's not one of the easier players to get along with. Strickland is not a consistent shooter, and his defense is sporadic.

Analysis: Strickland is not often mentioned with the upper-echelon point guards, but he is right on the fringe. Few combine high-powered scoring and playmaking like he does. His last two seasons were worthy of All-Star consideration, but he is still awaiting an invitation. If he keeps up his current pace and steadies his stroke, it might arrive.

PLAYER SUMMARY	
Will	slice through traffic
Can't	stick to jump shots
Expect	18 PPG, 9 APG
Don't Expect	bashful drives
Fantasy Value	$45-50
Card Value	5-8¢

COLLEGE STATISTICS

		G	FGP	FTP	APG	PPG
85-86	DeP	31	.497	.675	5.1	14.1
86-87	DeP	30	.582	.606	6.5	16.3
87-88	DeP	26	.528	.606	7.8	20.0
Totals		87	.534	.626	6.4	16.6

NBA REGULAR-SEASON STATISTICS

				FGs		3-PT FGs		FTs		Rebounds						
		G	MIN	FG	PCT	FG	PCT	FT	PCT	OFF	TOT	AST	STL	BLK	PTS	PPG
88-89	NY	81	1358	265	.467	19	.322	172	.745	51	160	319	98	3	721	8.9
89-90	NY/SA	82	2140	343	.454	8	.267	174	.626	90	259	468	127	14	868	10.6
90-91	SA	58	2076	314	.482	11	.333	161	.763	57	219	463	117	11	800	13.8
91-92	SA	57	2053	300	.455	5	.333	182	.687	92	265	491	118	17	787	13.8
92-93	POR	78	2474	396	.485	4	.133	273	.717	120	337	559	131	24	1069	13.7
93-94	POR	82	2889	528	.483	2	.200	353	.749	122	370	740	147	24	1411	17.2
94-95	POR	64	2267	441	.466	46	.374	283	.745	73	317	562	123	9	1211	18.9
95-96	POR	67	2526	471	.460	38	.342	276	.652	89	297	640	97	16	1256	18.7
Totals		569	17783	3058	.470	133	.324	1874	.710	694	2224	4242	958	118	8123	14.3

DEREK STRONG

Team: Orlando Magic
Position: Forward
Height: 6'8" **Weight:** 250
Birthdate: February 9, 1968

NBA Experience: 5 years
College: Xavier
Acquired: Signed as a free agent, 8/96

Background: Strong played with Tyrone Hill as a collegian at Xavier (Ohio), where he averaged 9.9 rebounds per game as a senior. He was cut by Philadelphia after being drafted late in the second round. He played one game while on a ten-day contract with Washington in 1991-92 and was the CBA MVP in 1992-93. He has since served two years with the Bucks, one with the Celtics, and one with the Lakers. He joins the Magic for 1996-97.

Strengths: Strong lives up to his name on the boards. Though he is undersized for a power forward, he rebounds his position well and challenges his opponents on defense. He does not shy away from contact and has good athletic skills. Strong runs the floor, gets to the line, and is a good free-throw shooter.

Weaknesses: Strong has not learned to be as assertive on offense as he is on defense. He has respectable touch on his face-up jumper but no post moves to speak of. Strong is below the norm in the ball-handling and passing departments. His size puts him at a disadvantage against the bigger power forwards, and he is not quick enough to handle the high-scoring threes with great success.

Analysis: Strong's game is rough around the edges. While he is able to provide rebounding and tough defense off the bench, he has yet to average even seven PPG and has never shot better than 46 percent from the field. He saw very little action throughout the 1995-96 season. Strong then underwent surgery on his right foot in May.

PLAYER SUMMARY	
Will	rebound
Can't	light up the nets
Expect	aggressive defense
Don't Expect	Strong moves
Fantasy Value	$0
Card Value	7-10¢

COLLEGE STATISTICS

		G	FGP	FTP	RPG	PPG
87-88	XAV	30	.569	.718	7.1	10.6
88-89	XAV	33	.617	.817	8.0	15.3
89-90	XAV	33	.533	.839	9.9	14.2
Totals		96	.573	.802	8.4	13.4

NBA REGULAR-SEASON STATISTICS

				FGs		3-PT FGs		FTs	Rebounds					
		G	MIN	FG	PCT	FG	PCT	FT	PCT	OFF	TOT	AST	STL	BLK	PTS	PPG
91-92	WAS	1	12	0	.000	0	.000	3	.750	1	5	1	0	0	3	3.0
92-93	MIL	23	339	42	.457	4	.500	68	.800	40	115	14	11	1	156	6.8
93-94	MIL	67	1131	141	.413	3	.231	159	.772	109	281	48	38	14	444	6.6
94-95	BOS	70	1344	149	.453	2	.286	141	.820	136	375	44	24	13	441	6.3
95-96	LAL	63	746	72	.426	1	.111	69	.812	60	178	32	18	12	214	3.4
Totals		224	3572	404	.432	10	.270	440	.797	346	954	139	91	40	1258	5.6

BOB SURA

Team: Cleveland Cavaliers
Position: Guard
Height: 6'5" **Weight:** 200
Birthdate: March 25, 1973

NBA Experience: 1 year
College: Florida St.
Acquired: First-round pick in 1995 draft (17th overall)

Background: At Florida State, Sura was the first player in ACC history to compile 2,000 points, 700 rebounds, 400 assists, and 200 steals. As a freshman, he was the third wheel in a backcourt that included fellow NBA players Sam Cassell and Charlie Ward. Sura finished his career as FSU's all-time leading scorer and was drafted 17th overall by Cleveland. He saw action in 79 games as a rookie.

Strengths: Sura is an aggressive, competitive player with fine athletic skills. He's quick, he gets off his feet, and he is not afraid to put the ball on the floor and attack the basket. Sura could become a dangerous 3-point shooter. He passes well, has a good feel for the game, and rebounds better than most guards. Sura expends energy on defense and comes up with a good share of steals.

Weaknesses: Sura is not a consistent perimeter shooter. He converted 41.7 percent from the field as a college senior and 41.1 in his first pro season. If you cut off his drive, Sura becomes far less effective on the offensive end. He goes too fast for his own good at times. His rookie average of one turnover every ten minutes needs immediate attention. His scoring average is bound to climb.

Analysis: Sura enjoyed some fine games off the Cleveland bench during his first NBA season. Cavs coach Mike Fratello tried to ease him into the rotation as the season went on, and it did not take long for Sura to gain confidence. He was chosen to play in the Schick Rookie Game on All-Star Weekend. He needs to firm up his shooting stroke and take better care of the ball in order to advance to the next level.

PLAYER SUMMARY	
Will	attack the basket
Can't	shoot 50 percent
Expect	an aggressive style
Don't Expect	error-free games
Fantasy Value	$1-3
Card Value	20-30¢

COLLEGE STATISTICS

		G	FGP	FTP	RPG	PPG
91-92	FSU	31	.461	.627	3.5	12.3
92-93	FSU	34	.452	.638	6.1	19.9
93-94	FSU	27	.469	.654	7.9	21.2
94-95	FSU	27	.417	.687	6.9	18.6
Totals		119	.450	.652	6.0	17.9

NBA REGULAR-SEASON STATISTICS

				FGs		3-PT FGs		FTs		Rebounds						
		G	MIN	FG	PCT	FG	PCT	FT	PCT	OFF	TOT	AST	STL	BLK	PTS	PPG
95-96	CLE	79	1150	148	.411	27	.346	99	.702	34	135	233	56	21	422	5.3
Totals		79	1150	148	.411	27	.346	99	.702	34	135	233	56	21	422	5.3

ZAN TABAK

Team: Toronto Raptors
Position: Center
Height: 7'0" **Weight:** 245
Birthdate: June 15, 1970

NBA Experience: 2 years
College: None
Acquired: Selected from Rockets in
1995 expansion draft

Background: Tabak was under contract with a Yugoslavian pro team when he was selected by Houston in the second round of the 1991 draft. After averaging 15.1 points and 10.3 rebounds per game for Olympia Milano of the Italian League in 1993-94, he made his NBA debut in a 37-game season with Houston. His role doubled with Toronto in 1995-96.

Strengths: Size is the most obvious trait that endears Tabak to NBA teams. Few players are going to block his hook shots, which he converts with both hands from the low block. Tabak won't misfire often because he knows his range. The big guy is also a productive rebounder. He pulled down one board every four minutes or so last season. He's a decent passer who knows how to play team basketball.

Weaknesses: Tabak is not a good athlete. He has "hard" hands, and his scoring moves are slow and predictable for the most part. His range is very limited. Tabak is a dismal free-throw shooter, and he is not someone you want bouncing the basketball. His defense suffers for his lack of strength and quickness. Here's a stat worth noting: Tabak picked up more fouls (204) than defensive rebounds (203) last season.

Analysis: No. 51 draft choices don't come with guarantees, and such is the case with the seven-foot Croatian. He did not exactly earn a championship ring with Houston, but he got one. And Toronto had nothing to lose, so it gave Tabak 18 starts last season and watched him lead the team in field-goal accuracy (.543). Tabak is a project who belongs ninth or tenth in a team's rotation. His size guarantees him a continuing NBA career.

PLAYER SUMMARY	
Will	drop hook shots
Can't	avoid whistles
Expect	a learning process
Don't Expect	regular starts
Fantasy Value	$0
Card Value	15-25¢

COLLEGE STATISTICS

—DID NOT PLAY—

NBA REGULAR-SEASON STATISTICS

			FGs		3-PT FGs		FTs		Rebounds						
	G	MIN	FG	PCT	FG	PCT	FT	PCT	OFF	TOT	AST	STL	BLK	PTS	PPG
94-95 HOU	37	182	24	.453	0	.000	27	.614	23	57	4	2	7	75	2.0
95-96 TOR	67	1332	225	.543	0	.000	64	.561	117	320	62	24	31	514	7.7
Totals	104	1514	249	.533	0	.000	91	.576	140	377	66	26	38	589	5.7

KURT THOMAS

Team: Miami Heat
Position: Forward
Height: 6'9" **Weight:** 230
Birthdate: October 4, 1972

NBA Experience: 1 year
College: Texas Christian
Acquired: First-round pick in 1995 draft (tenth overall)

Background: In 1994-95, Thomas joined Hank Gathers and Xavier McDaniel as the only players to lead the NCAA Division I in scoring and rebounding in the same season. Thomas finished his career at Texas Christian with a record 166 blocks despite sitting out the 1992-93 season because of a broken leg. He was drafted tenth overall by Miami in 1995 and made 42 starts as a rookie, hitting 50.1 percent of his field-goal attempts.

Strengths: The consensus Southwest Conference Player of the Year as a senior, Thomas boasts great athletic skills. He's a quick leaper who gets off the floor and has the look of a strong rebounder and potential shot-blocker. He averaged 5.9 boards per game last season. Thomas also has a soft touch around the basket, some proficient moves in the post, and the ability to make the face-up jumper from 15 feet.

Weaknesses: Thomas is lacking in some of the finesse aspects of the game. He gets credit for an assist about once every two nights and commits far too many fouls. He was disqualified from seven games as a rookie. He gives up size to starting power forwards, yet he is not comfortable on the perimeter against the threes. His defense is raw. Thomas misses a lot of free throws, and his demeanor has been a turnoff to some.

Analysis: Thomas stepped into the Heat's starting power forward slot and played well after the team traded Kevin Willis last season. Thomas is no Willis when it comes to scoring and rebounding, but he has the potential to develop into a prominent board man and double-figure scorer who does some damage inside and out. He has a lot to learn about court awareness and defense.

PLAYER SUMMARY	
Will	get off the floor
Can't	keep from fouling
Expect	aggressive rebounding
Don't Expect	a full-time starter
Fantasy	$3-5
Card Value	20-40¢

COLLEGE STATISTICS

		G	FGP	FTP	RPG	PPG
90-91	TCU	28	.444	.500	0.5	1.9
91-92	TCU	21	.487	.667	5.4	7.1
93-94	TCU	27	.509	.645	9.7	20.7
94-95	TCU	27	.548	.714	14.6	28.9
Totals		103	.524	.682	7.6	14.7

NBA REGULAR-SEASON STATISTICS

				FGs		3-PT FGs		FTs		Rebounds						
		G	MIN	FG	PCT	FG	PCT	FT	PCT	OFF	TOT	AST	STL	BLK	PTS	PPG
95-96	MIA	74	1655	274	.501	0	.000	118	.663	122	439	46	47	36	666	9.0
Totals		74	1655	274	.501	0	.000	118	.663	122	439	46	47	36	666	9.0

OTIS THORPE

Team: Detroit Pistons
Position: Forward
Height: 6'10" **Weight:** 246
Birthdate: August 5, 1962
NBA Experience: 12 years

College: Providence
Acquired: Traded from Trail Blazers for Bill Curley and draft rights to Randolph Childress, 9/95

Background: Thorpe left Providence with the all-time Big East record for rebounds and was an all-conference selection as a senior. He started his NBA career with the Kings, spent six-plus years with Houston, and has played in Portland and Detroit over the last two seasons. Thorpe was a 1992 All-Star and has played all 82 games in nine of his 12 seasons.

Strengths: The durable Thorpe is annually one of the most accurate field-goal shooters in the league. He mops up on the offensive glass and uses his muscular frame to free himself in the post. Thorpe rebounds and plays tough defense. He handles the ball and runs the floor well for a big man.

Weaknesses: Thorpe does not offer much offense outside of a dozen feet. He gets his points because of hustle, not because of tremendous skills. He tied Elden Campbell for the NBA lead with 300 personal fouls in 1995-96.

Analysis: Thorpe is a team player who provides rebounding, relentless defense, and remarkable durability. He was the only Piston to start all 82 games last season, and he once played in 542 games in a row. Thorpe could finish his career with 15,000 points, 10,000 rebounds, and a .550 shooting percentage.

PLAYER SUMMARY	
Will	defend, rebound
Can't	avoid whistles
Expect	inside scoring
Don't Expect	shooting range
Fantasy Value	$10-13
Card Value	7-10¢

COLLEGE STATISTICS

		G	FGP	FTP	RPG	PPG
80-81	PROV	26	.515	.658	5.3	9.6
81-82	PROV	27	.541	.643	8.0	14.1
82-83	PROV	31	.636	.659	8.0	16.1
83-84	PROV	29	.580	.653	10.3	17.1
Totals		113	.575	.653	8.0	14.4

NBA REGULAR-SEASON STATISTICS

			FGs		3-PT FGs		FTs		Rebounds						
	G	MIN	FG	PCT	FG	PCT	FT	PCT	OFF	TOT	AST	STL	BLK	PTS	PPG
84-85 KC	82	1918	411	.600	0	.000	230	.620	187	556	111	34	37	1052	12.8
85-86 SAC	75	1675	289	.587	0	.000	164	.661	137	420	84	35	34	742	9.9
86-87 SAC	82	2956	567	.540	0	.000	413	.761	259	819	201	46	60	1547	18.9
87-88 SAC	82	3072	622	.507	0	.000	460	.755	279	837	266	62	56	1704	20.8
88-89 HOU	82	3135	521	.542	0	.000	328	.729	272	787	202	82	37	1370	16.7
89-90 HOU	82	2947	547	.548	0	.000	307	.688	258	734	261	66	24	1401	17.1
90-91 HOU	82	3039	549	.556	3	.429	334	.696	287	846	197	73	20	1435	17.5
91-92 HOU	82	3056	558	.592	0	.000	304	.657	285	862	250	52	37	1420	17.3
92-93 HOU	72	2357	385	.558	0	.000	153	.596	219	589	181	43	19	923	12.8
93-94 HOU	82	2909	449	.561	0	.000	251	.657	271	870	189	66	28	1149	14.0
94-95 HOU/POR	70	2096	385	.565	0	.000	167	.594	202	558	112	41	28	937	13.4
95-96 DET	82	2841	452	.530	0	.000	257	.710	211	688	158	53	39	1161	14.2
Totals	955	32001	5735	.553	3	.058	3368	.689	2867	8566	2212	653	419	14841	15.5

SEDALE THREATT

Unrestricted Free Agent
Last Team: Los Angeles Lakers
Position: Guard
Height: 6'2" **Weight:** 185
Birthdate: September 10, 1961

NBA Experience: 13 years
College: West Virginia Tech
Acquired: Traded from SuperSonics for 1994, 1995, and 1996 second-round picks, 10/91

Background: Threatt was an NAIA All-American at West Virginia Tech, where he finished his career as the school's all-time scoring leader. Originally a sixth-round draft pick of Philadelphia, he has played 13 seasons with the 76ers, Bulls, SuperSonics, and Lakers. He played in all 82 games last season.

Strengths: Threatt is a pure shooter. He can create his own shot off the dribble, is an 80-percent career free-throw shooter, and hit a personal-best 60 treys in 1995-96. Capable of playing both guard positions, he loves taking pressure shots. Threatt has more than 1,100 career steals.

Weaknesses: Threatt is not the dominant defender he once was, nor is he as potent on offense. Thirteen years in the NBA will claim some of your explosiveness. His shooting accuracy and scoring average are down.

Analysis: Threatt seems ideally suited to a third guard role at this stage of his career. He can come off the bench at either backcourt spot and still turns in strong stretches at both ends. And over the last two seasons, the Lakers were 9-1 when Threatt was called on to start.

PLAYER SUMMARY	
Will	...................work for shots
Can't	...............regain starting job
Expect	........................a third guard
Don't Expect	.................10 PPG
Fantasy Value	..................................$0
Card Value	...............................5-8¢

COLLEGE STATISTICS

		G	FGP	FTP	APG	PPG
79-80	WVT	28	.481	.714	3.9	17.8
80-81	WVT	31	.452	.712	5.7	17.7
81-82	WVT	34	.500	.729	5.9	22.2
82-83	WVT	27	.557	.732	6.7	25.5
Totals		120	.498	.724	5.5	20.7

NBA REGULAR-SEASON STATISTICS

				FGs		3-PT FGs		FTs		Rebounds						
		G	MIN	FG	PCT	FG	PCT	FT	PCT	OFF	TOT	AST	STL	BLK	PTS	PPG
83-84	PHI	45	464	62	.419	1	.125	23	.821	17	40	41	13	2	148	3.3
84-85	PHI	82	1304	188	.452	4	.182	66	.733	21	99	175	80	16	446	5.4
85-86	PHI	70	1754	310	.453	1	.042	75	.833	21	121	193	93	5	696	9.9
86-87	PHI/CHI	68	1446	239	.448	7	.219	95	.798	26	108	259	74	13	580	8.5
87-88	CHI/SEA	71	1055	216	.508	3	.111	57	.803	23	88	160	60	8	492	6.9
88-89	SEA	63	1220	235	.494	11	.367	63	.818	31	117	238	83	4	544	8.6
89-90	SEA	65	1481	303	.506	8	.250	130	.828	43	115	216	65	8	744	11.4
90-91	SEA	80	2066	433	.519	10	.286	137	.792	25	99	273	113	8	1013	12.7
91-92	LAL	82	3070	509	.489	20	.323	202	.831	43	253	593	168	16	1240	15.1
92-93	LAL	82	2893	522	.508	14	.264	177	.823	47	273	564	142	11	1235	15.1
93-94	LAL	81	2278	411	.482	5	.152	138	.890	28	153	344	110	19	965	11.9
94-95	LAL	59	1384	217	.497	36	.379	88	.793	21	124	248	54	12	558	9.5
95-96	LAL	82	1687	241	.458	60	.355	54	.761	20	95	269	68	11	596	7.3
Totals		930	22102	3886	.486	180	.289	1305	.816	366	1685	3573	1123	133	9257	10.0

WAYMAN TISDALE

Team: Phoenix Suns
Position: Forward/Center
Height: 6'9" **Weight:** 260
Birthdate: June 9, 1964

NBA Experience: 11 years
College: Oklahoma
Acquired: Signed as a free agent, 9/94

Background: Tisdale became the first player in college basketball history to be named first-team All-America in his first three seasons. He set 17 Oklahoma records and starred on the 1984 gold medal-winning U.S. Olympic team. Tisdale averaged 17.0 PPG over his first nine years with Indiana and Sacramento before spending the last two years as a Suns reserve.

Strengths: Tisdale is a steady mid-range jump-shooter and an accomplished low-post scorer who works for his points despite his relatively small size. He once averaged 22.3 PPG and is a 50-percent career shooter from the floor. He can play forward or center, and he's a class act off the floor.

Weaknesses: Tisdale has never been a great defensive player, and his rebounding contributions have declined drastically. His interests are mostly on the offensive end. He's neither a good dribbler nor an alert passer. Tisdale has never attempted a 3-point shot in 11 seasons.

Analysis: Tisdale is an accomplished bass player whose band, Fifth Quarter, cut an album in the summer of 1994. He also remains a pretty good scorer, with more than 12,000 points to his credit. He has never averaged less than 10 PPG in a season, although the day may be coming.

PLAYER SUMMARY

Will ....work free inside
Can't ....make a 3-pointer
Expect ....instant offense
Don't Expect ....assists
Fantasy Value $2-4
Card Value ....5-10¢

COLLEGE STATISTICS

		G	FGP	FTP	RPG	PPG
82-83	OKLA	33	.580	.635	10.3	24.5
83-84	OKLA	34	.577	.640	9.7	27.0
84-85	OKLA	37	.578	.703	10.2	25.2
Totals		104	.578	.661	10.1	25.6

NBA REGULAR-SEASON STATISTICS

				FGs		3-PT FGs		FTs		Rebounds						
		G	MIN	FG	PCT	FG	PCT	FT	PCT	OFF	TOT	AST	STL	BLK	PTS	PPG
85-86	IND	81	2277	516	.515	0	.000	160	.684	191	584	79	32	44	1192	14.7
86-87	IND	81	2159	458	.513	0	.000	258	.709	217	475	117	50	26	1174	14.5
87-88	IND	79	2378	511	.512	0	.000	246	.783	168	491	103	54	34	1268	16.1
88-89	IND/SAC	79	2434	532	.514	0	.000	317	.773	187	609	128	55	52	1381	17.5
89-90	SAC	79	2937	726	.525	0	.000	306	.783	185	595	108	54	54	1758	22.3
90-91	SAC	33	1116	262	.483	0	.000	136	.800	75	253	66	23	28	660	20.0
91-92	SAC	72	2521	522	.500	0	.000	151	.763	135	469	106	55	79	1195	16.6
92-93	SAC	76	2283	544	.509	0	.000	175	.758	127	500	108	52	47	1263	16.6
93-94	SAC	79	2557	552	.501	0	.000	215	.808	159	560	139	37	52	1319	16.7
94-95	PHO	65	1276	278	.484	0	.000	94	.770	83	247	45	29	27	650	10.0
95-96	PHO	63	1152	279	.495	0	.000	114	.765	55	214	58	15	36	672	10.7
Totals		787	23090	5180	.508	0	.000	2172	.762	1582	4997	1057	456	479	12532	15.9

GARY TRENT

Team: Portland Trail Blazers
Position: Forward
Height: 6'8" **Weight:** 250
Birthdate: September 22, 1974
NBA Experience: 1 year

College: Ohio
Acquired: Draft rights traded from Bucks with a 1996 first-round pick for draft rights to Shawn Respert, 6/95

Background: Dubbed "The Shaq of the MAC," Trent led the Mid-American Conference in scoring for three straight seasons and in rebounding twice. In just three years, he joined Ron Harper as the only MAC players with 2,000 points and 1,000 rebounds. Trent was drafted 11th by Portland and started 10 of his 69 games as a rookie in 1995-96. His .513 field-goal shooting put him among first-year leaders.

Strengths: Trent makes up for his short stature in the lane with great hands, brute strength, and excellent leaping ability. He uses an aggressive style to match players much taller, point for point and rebound for rebound. He knows how to position himself for boards. Trent runs well, and he shoots a high percentage from the field. He has the power to become a solid low-block defender. His work habits are where they need to be.

Weaknesses: Although he plays taller than his size, Trent can be exploited by the giants at his natural power forward position. He was a better defender than most expected, but he's susceptible to tough matchups. Trent is better with his back to the basket than facing the hoop. He has not shown signs of becoming a real shooting threat—as his troubles at the free-throw line (.553) indicate—or a ball-handler.

Analysis: Trent and Arvydas Sabonis gave the Blazers their highest-scoring rookie combination since Clifford Robinson and Drazen Petrovic seven years earlier. While Trent lacks the size and all-around ability of his Lithuanian teammate, he clearly has the more explosive body. Trent struggled at the outset, but he seems to grow more comfortable by the game. He has the potential to become a legitimate double-double performer.

PLAYER SUMMARY

Will ....use his strength
Can't ....drill free throws
Expect ....improved rebounding
Don't Expect..............perimeter skills
Fantasy Value $1
Card Value ....20-40¢

COLLEGE STATISTICS

		G	FGP	FTP	RPG	PPG
92-93	OHIO	27	.651	.696	9.3	19.0
93-94	OHIO	33	.576	.722	11.4	25.4
94-95	OHIO	33	.527	.642	12.8	22.9
Totals		93	.573	.687	11.3	22.7

NBA REGULAR-SEASON STATISTICS

			FGs		3-PT FGs		FTs		Rebounds						
	G	MIN	FG	PCT	FG	PCT	FT	PCT	OFF	TOT	AST	STL	BLK	PTS	PPG
95-96 POR	69	1219	220	.513	0	.000	78	.553	84	238	50	25	11	518	7.5
Totals	69	1219	220	.513	0	.000	78	.553	84	238	50	25	11	518	7.5

NICK VAN EXEL

Team: Los Angeles Lakers
Position: Guard
Height: 6'1" **Weight:** 183
Birthdate: November 27, 1971

NBA Experience: 3 years
College: Cincinnati
Acquired: Second-round pick in 1993 draft (37th overall)

Background: After spending his first two years at a junior college, Van Exel was the ringleader of a Cincinnati team that advanced to the Final Four in 1992 and the regional finals in 1993. He slipped to the second round of the 1993 draft but finished second among 1993-94 rookies in assists. Van Exel posted his best numbers last year, in his second of three pro seasons as the Lakers' starting point guard.

Strengths: Van Exel boasts supreme confidence and quickness that resonate throughout his game. He handles the ball, gets past his man, and finds teammates with sometimes spectacular passes. He can shoot the lights out from 3-point range and has made numerous clutch jumpers. Van Exel can play tenacious defense.

Weaknesses: Van Exel has a temper, as everyone found out last year when he shoved official Ron Garretson into a scorer's table during a game in Denver. It cost him seven games and a $25,000 fine. Van Exel has not been the type of leader who provides consistently strong play from one night to the next. He is prone to cold shooting spells and is not always focused on shutting down his man. He rubs some the wrong way.

Analysis: Van Exel, a second-round steal three years ago, has been a huge reason for the Lakers' recent revival. He gained notoriety for all the wrong reasons last season, and he is a streaky player in most areas. His high energy, playmaking, and scoring ability, however, will serve him well as he tries to attain stardom and lead the Lakers to a championship. He is one of the best young talents at his position.

PLAYER SUMMARY	
Will	run the show
Can't	afford more flare-ups
Expect	high energy
Don't Expect	a deliberate pace
Fantasy Value	$12-15
Card Value	25-40¢

COLLEGE STATISTICS

		G	FGP	FTP	APG	PPG
91-92	CINC	34	.446	.673	2.9	12.3
92-93	CINC	31	.386	.725	4.5	18.3
Totals		65	.409	.701	3.6	15.2

NBA REGULAR-SEASON STATISTICS

				FGs		3-PT FGs		FTs		Rebounds						
		G	MIN	FG	PCT	FG	PCT	FT	PCT	OFF	TOT	AST	STL	BLK	PTS	PPG
93-94	LAL	81	2700	413	.394	123	.338	150	.781	47	238	466	85	8	1099	13.6
94-95	LAL	80	2944	465	.420	183	.358	235	.783	27	223	660	97	6	1348	16.9
95-96	LAL	74	2513	396	.417	144	.357	163	.799	29	181	509	70	10	1099	14.9
Totals		235	8157	1274	.410	450	.352	548	.787	103	642	1635	252	24	3546	15.1

LOY VAUGHT

Team: Los Angeles Clippers
Position: Forward
Height: 6'9" **Weight:** 240
Birthdate: February 27, 1967

NBA Experience: 6 years
College: Michigan
Acquired: First-round pick in 1990 draft (13th overall)

Background: Vaught twice led the Big Ten in field-goal percentage and was the first Michigan player since Roy Tarpley to average double-figure points and rebounds. He led the league in rebounding as a senior. The six-year pro improved his scoring in each of his first five seasons and has taken his game to new heights over the past two years, leading the Clippers in scoring and rebounding.

Strengths: Vaught rarely misses from 15-20 feet out on the baseline. It's "his spot," and he manages to exploit it no matter how you defend him. Vaught approaches basketball in workmanlike fashion, and his 10.1 RPG ranked ninth in the NBA last season. He was also among the league leaders with his 52.5 field-goal percentage. The muscular Vaught has shown some leadership ability.

Weaknesses: Defense has long been considered the weak aspect of his game. He does not block many shots, and he too often resorts to fouling instead of staying in front of his man. His turnovers still outnumber his assists. He's not a good ball-handler, which might explain his hesitancy to mix in more drives.

Analysis: Vaught, who makes art gallery-caliber drawings, last year became the first Clipper since Michael Cage in 1987-88 to average a double-double. One of the most improved players in the NBA the year before, his scoring average slipped by about a point last season while his rebounding was up. The one thing he has not been able to do is rescue the hapless Clippers.

PLAYER SUMMARY	
Will	nail baseline jumpers
Can't	save his franchise
Expect	double-doubles
Don't Expect	ball-handling
Fantasy Value	$13-16
Card Value	5-8¢

COLLEGE STATISTICS

		G	FGP	FTP	RPG	PPG
86-87	MICH	32	.557	.500	3.9	4.6
87-88	MICH	34	.621	.724	4.4	10.5
88-89	MICH	37	.661	.778	8.0	12.6
89-90	MICH	31	.595	.804	11.2	15.5
Totals		134	.617	.752	6.8	10.8

NBA REGULAR-SEASON STATISTICS

				FGs		3-PT FGs		FTs		Rebounds						
		G	MIN	FG	PCT	FG	PCT	FT	PCT	OFF	TOT	AST	STL	BLK	PTS	PPG
90-91	LAC	73	1178	175	.487	0	.000	49	.662	124	349	40	20	23	399	5.5
91-92	LAC	79	1687	271	.492	4	.800	55	.797	160	512	71	37	31	601	7.6
92-93	LAC	79	1653	313	.508	1	.250	116	.748	164	492	54	55	39	743	9.4
93-94	LAC	75	2118	373	.537	0	.000	131	.720	218	656	74	76	22	877	11.7
94-95	LAC	80	2966	609	.514	7	.212	176	.710	261	772	139	104	29	1401	17.5
95-96	LAC	80	2966	571	.525	7	.368	149	.727	204	808	112	87	40	1298	16.2
Totals		466	12568	2312	.515	19	.279	676	.725	1131	3589	490	379	184	5319	11.4

RASHEED WALLACE

Team: Portland Trail Blazers
Position: Forward/Center
Height: 6'10" **Weight:** 245
Birthdate: September 17, 1974
NBA Experience: 1 year

College: North Carolina
Acquired: Traded from Bullets with Mitchell Butler for Rod Strickland and Harvey Grant, 7/96

Background: Wallace was heralded as the best prep big man to come out of Philadelphia since Wilt Chamberlain. He finished his two-year career at North Carolina as the leading field-goal marksman in ACC history, and he set a Tar Heels record with 93 blocks in 1994-95. Wallace was selected fourth overall by Washington in 1995, made 51 rookie starts, and averaged 10.1 PPG. He was sent to Portland in a July 1996 deal.

Strengths: Wallace is an exceptional athlete with the potential to emerge as a big-time scorer, rebounder, and shot-blocker. Bullets coach Jim Lynam has compared Wallace's surprising long-range stroke to that of Clifford Robinson, yet Wallace's best offense comes off dribble drives, in the post, and on the break. Wallace is a strong finisher. He has good instincts.

Weaknesses: Wallace is still maturing physically and could stand to add some muscle to his athletic frame. His emotional maturity has also been questioned, and he was whistled for 21 technical fouls as a rookie. He needs to improve his free-throw shooting, limit his turnovers, and become a more aware passer. Wallace has loads of defensive ability, but like most first-year players he was not consistently focused.

Analysis: Wallace became a starter earlier than expected when Bullets power forward Chris Webber went down with a shoulder injury just 15 games into the 1995-96 season. Wallace needed a little seasoning, and he got it in a hurry. In his 51 starts, he averaged 11.7 points and 5.5 rebounds per game while shooting .491 from the field. A broken thumb ended Wallace's rookie year a month prematurely, but there are great days ahead of him in Portland.

PLAYER SUMMARY

Will	finish the break
Can't	manhandle centers
Expect	big-time strides
Don't Expect	a stopper
Fantasy Value	$5-7
Card Value	60¢-$1.00

COLLEGE STATISTICS

		G	FGP	FTP	RPG	PPG
93-94	NC	35	.604	.604	6.6	9.5
94-95	NC	34	.654	.631	8.2	16.6
Totals		69	.635	.621	7.4	13.0

NBA REGULAR-SEASON STATISTICS

			FGs		3-PT FGs		FTs		Rebounds						
	G	MIN	FG	PCT	FG	PCT	FT	PCT	OFF	TOT	AST	STL	BLK	PTS	PPG
95-96 WAS	65	1788	275	.487	27	.329	78	.650	93	303	85	42	54	655	10.1
Totals	65	1788	275	.487	27	.329	78	.650	93	303	85	42	54	655	10.1

REX WALTERS

Team: Philadelphia 76ers
Position: Guard
Height: 6'4" **Weight:** 190
Birthdate: March 12, 1970
NBA Experience: 3 years

College: Northwestern; Kansas
Acquired: Traded from Nets with Sean Higgins and Derrick Coleman for Shawn Bradley, Tim Perry, and Greg Graham, 11/95

Background: Walters was ignored by Kansas University as a high school senior, but he transferred there after a strong sophomore campaign at Northwestern. He was a two-time All-Big Eight performer and played in the Final Four as a senior. Drafted 16th by New Jersey in 1993, Walters made 30 starts in his second season. He was sent to Philadelphia in the Shawn Bradley-Derrick Coleman deal in November 1995.

Strengths: Walters is a gym rat with great range. He made 38 percent of his 3-point bombs over his first two seasons before tailing off a bit last year. He is also a top-notch free-throw shooter. Walters is left-handed, which makes him tricky to guard, and he plays the game with fire. Few NBA types practice and play as hard as Walters, who has played both guard positions.

Weaknesses: After three years, just about everything falls into this category. Walters has not shot well enough to stay on the floor as a shooting guard, and he struggles even more at the point. He's a perimeter player, not a playmaker. He lacks the size, quickness, and athletic ability to provide good defense against either ones or twos. So far the fruits of his labor have been scarce.

Analysis: Walters has a limited supply of physical gifts. The Nets knew that when they drafted him. They hoped, however, that his work habits, wise decisions, and leadership would help Walters offset some of his deficiencies. No such luck. Walters, who has never missed a game because of injury, played in a career-low 44 games last season. It's not for a lack of effort.

PLAYER SUMMARY	
Will	give his all
Can't	overcome limitations
Expect	a 3-point threat
Don't Expect	playmaking
Fantasy Value	$0
Card Value	7-10¢

COLLEGE STATISTICS

		G	FGP	FTP	APG	PPG
88-89	NORT	24	.378	.917	1.4	2.1
89-90	NORT	28	.503	.794	4.5	17.6
91-92	KANS	32	.525	.827	3.9	16.0
92-93	KANS	36	.490	.873	4.3	15.3
Totals		120	.500	.837	3.6	13.4

NBA REGULAR-SEASON STATISTICS

		G	MIN	FGs FG	FGs PCT	3-PT FGs FG	3-PT FGs PCT	FTs FT	FTs PCT	Rebounds OFF	Rebounds TOT	AST	STL	BLK	PTS	PPG
93-94	NJ	48	386	60	.522	14	.500	28	.824	6	38	71	15	3	162	3.4
94-95	NJ	80	1435	206	.439	71	.362	40	.769	18	93	121	37	16	523	6.5
95-96	NJ/PHI	44	610	61	.412	22	.333	42	.808	13	55	106	25	4	186	4.2
Totals		172	2431	327	.447	107	.369	110	.797	37	186	298	77	23	871	5.1

CHARLIE WARD

Team: New York Knicks
Position: Guard
Height: 6'2" **Weight:** 190
Birthdate: October 12, 1970

NBA Experience: 2 years
College: Florida St.
Acquired: First-round pick in 1994 draft (26th overall)

Background: One of the most exciting college football players in recent years, Ward won the Heisman Trophy in 1993 after quarterbacking Florida State to a national championship. In basketball, he became the Seminoles' all-time steals leader despite playing just one full season. Ward was bypassed in the 1994 NFL draft but was selected by the NBA's Knicks late in the first round. He saw action in just ten games as a rookie before logging 62 last season.

Strengths: Only a handful of people have played two college sports at Ward's high level. He's a fabulous athlete with good speed and quickness, and his leadership ability was probably his greatest asset on the gridiron. Ward is a natural point guard who's able to drive through traffic and deliver the basketball where it needs to be. He can pressure the ball all night long and has a knack for steals.

Weaknesses: Ward's erratic jump shot is his biggest hurdle. He did not convert college shots at a respectable rate, and he needed just one more last season to eclipse the 40-percent barrier (he was .399). Ward is small by NBA standards, raising questions about his ability to hold up in halfcourt defense. He's a prime post-up target who has not battled starting guards with much success.

Analysis: Ward has great intangibles going for him. His take-charge attitude and natural leadership seem custom-made for the point guard position. Consider, too, that he has been a full-time basketball player for only two years of his life. Ward came off the bench and played some of his best basketball against the Bulls in the 1996 playoffs, giving Knick fans hope for a breakthrough in 1996-97.

PLAYER SUMMARY

Will ....pick your pocket
Can't ....play bruising "D"
Expect ....drives and dishes
Don't Expect ....a jump-shooter
Fantasy Value $1
Card Value ....12-20¢

COLLEGE STATISTICS

		G	FGP	FTP	APG	PPG
90-91	FSU	30	.455	.713	3.4	8.0
91-92	FSU	28	.497	.530	4.4	7.2
92-93	FSU	17	.462	.667	5.5	7.8
93-94	FSU	16	.365	.625	4.9	10.5
Totals		91	.441	.636	4.4	8.1

NBA REGULAR-SEASON STATISTICS

			FGs		3-PT FGs		FTs		Rebounds						
	G	MIN	FG	PCT	FG	PCT	FT	PCT	OFF	TOT	AST	STL	BLK	PTS	PPG
94-95 NY	10	44	4	.211	1	.100	7	.700	1	6	4	2	0	16	1.6
95-96 NY	62	787	87	.399	33	.333	37	.685	29	102	132	54	6	244	3.9
Totals	72	831	91	.384	34	.312	44	.688	30	108	136	56	6	260	3.6

CLARENCE WEATHERSPOON

Team: Philadelphia 76ers
Position: Forward
Height: 6'7" **Weight:** 240
Birthdate: September 8, 1970

NBA Experience: 4 years
College: Southern Mississippi
Acquired: First-round pick in 1992 draft (ninth overall)

Background: Weatherspoon attended Motley High in Crawford, Mississippi, the same school that produced NFL star Jerry Rice. "Spoon" finished his college career as Southern Mississippi's career leader in scoring, rebounding, and blocked shots. The No. 9 pick in 1992 was a second-team All-Rookie choice before averaging a double-double in 1993-94. His scoring average dipped from 18-plus to 16.7 PPG in 1995-96.

Strengths: Weatherspoon works for everything he gets. Some have compared him to Charles Barkley, and not without foundation. He has the same powerful build and leaping ability, and both are capable of holding their own in the paint with much taller players. Weatherspoon has a strong post-up game, he blocks shots, and he can dominate the boards. He also runs well and does not hold anything back.

Weaknesses: Sir Charles does several things that Spoon cannot. Clarence is not a reliable outside shooter, he does not handle the ball with ease, and he has trouble defending quicker forwards out on the wing. His high turnover total is partially due to his tendency to try to do too much on his own. Weatherspoon is not nearly as comfortable facing the basket as he is with his back to it.

Analysis: Weatherspoon gets the most out of his ability in most areas. He has played both forward positions, but he is better suited to the four spot where he can use his muscle to score inside and hit the boards with abandon. He has expressed frustration with the 76ers, who have yet to win more than 26 games in a season since his arrival. That's where Barkley has the big edge.

PLAYER SUMMARY	
Will	get off the floor
Can't	live on the perimeter
Expect	double-doubles
Don't Expect	a smooth stroke
Fantasy Value	$30-35
Card Value	7-12¢

COLLEGE STATISTICS

		G	FGP	FTP	RPG	PPG
88-89	SMU	27	.545	.590	10.7	14.7
89-90	SMU	32	.605	.691	11.6	17.8
90-91	SMU	29	.589	.745	12.2	17.8
91-92	SMU	29	.563	.675	10.5	22.3
Totals		117	.576	.677	11.3	18.7

NBA REGULAR-SEASON STATISTICS

			FGs		3-PT FGs		FTs		Rebounds						
	G	MIN	FG	PCT	FG	PCT	FT	PCT	OFF	TOT	AST	STL	BLK	PTS	PPG
92-93 PHI	82	2654	494	.469	1	.250	291	.713	179	589	147	85	67	1280	15.6
93-94 PHI	82	3147	602	.483	4	.235	298	.693	254	832	192	100	116	1506	18.4
94-95 PHI	76	2991	543	.439	4	.190	283	.751	144	526	215	115	67	1373	18.1
95-96 PHI	78	3096	491	.484	0	.000	318	.746	237	753	158	112	108	1300	16.7
Totals	318	11888	2130	.468	9	.205	1190	.725	814	2700	712	412	358	5459	17.2

SPUD WEBB

Unrestricted Free Agent
Last Team: Minnesota Timberwolves
Position: Guard
Height: 5'7" **Weight:** 133
Birthdate: July 13, 1963

NBA Experience: 11 years
College: Midland; North Carolina St.
Acquired: Traded from Hawks with
Andrew Lang for Christian Laettner
and Sean Rooks, 2/96

Background: After pacing North Carolina State in assists for two straight
seasons, Webb was drafted by Detroit in 1985 but signed with Atlanta before his
rookie year. He spent his first six years with the Hawks and was the league's top
free-throw shooter (.934) with Sacramento in 1994-95. He began last season
back in Atlanta before a trade to Minnesota.

Strengths: Almost everything Webb does starts with his quickness. He is
especially effective at creating an up-tempo game by racing the ball up-court, and
he is capable of taking the ball in traffic. He is close to automatic from the free-
throw line.

Weaknesses: Webb has never been one of the better distributors in the game,
despite his quick penetrating ability. For obvious reasons, he is always going to
be susceptible to being posted up and shot over by bigger players. He's not a
professional ball thief, either.

Analysis: A surprising winner of the NBA Slam Dunk Contest in his rookie year,
Webb has carved a long career out of playing larger than his size. He fashions
himself a starter, yet few teams have their sights set on a point guard who does
no better than 3-to-1 for an assist-to-turnover ratio.

PLAYER SUMMARY	
Will	penetrate
Can't	stop his man
Expect	free-throw swishes
Don't Expect	great playmaking
Fantasy Value	$0
Card Value	7-12¢

COLLEGE STATISTICS

		G	FGP	FTP	APG	PPG
81-82	MID	38	.515	.781	—	20.8
82-83	MID	35	.445	.774	—	14.6
83-84	NCST	33	.459	.761	6.0	9.8
84-85	NCST	33	.481	.761	5.3	11.1
Totals		139	.479	.773	5.7	14.3

NBA REGULAR-SEASON STATISTICS

			FGs		3-PT FGs		FTs		Rebounds						
	G	MIN	FG	PCT	FG	PCT	FT	PCT	OFF	TOT	AST	STL	BLK	PTS	PPG
85-86 ATL	79	1229	199	.483	2	.182	216	.785	27	123	337	82	5	616	7.8
86-87 ATL	33	532	71	.438	1	.167	80	.762	6	60	167	34	2	223	6.8
87-88 ATL	82	1347	191	.475	1	.053	107	.817	16	146	337	63	11	490	6.0
88-89 ATL	81	1219	133	.459	1	.045	52	.867	21	123	284	70	6	319	3.9
89-90 ATL	82	2184	294	.477	1	.053	162	.871	38	201	477	105	12	751	9.2
90-91 ATL	75	2197	359	.447	54	.321	231	.868	41	174	417	118	6	1003	13.4
91-92 SAC	77	2724	448	.445	73	.367	262	.859	30	223	547	125	24	1231	16.0
92-93 SAC	69	2335	342	.433	37	.274	279	.851	44	193	481	104	6	1000	14.5
93-94 SAC	79	2567	373	.460	55	.335	204	.813	44	222	528	93	23	1005	12.7
94-95 SAC	76	2458	302	.438	48	.331	225	.934	29	174	468	75	8	878	11.6
95-96 ATL/MIN	77	1462	186	.433	47	.364	125	.862	26	100	294	52	7	544	7.1
Totals	810	20254	2898	.452	320	.315	1944	.847	322	1739	4337	921	110	8060	10.0

CHRIS WEBBER

Team: Washington Bullets
Position: Forward
Height: 6'10" **Weight:** 250
Birthdate: March 1, 1973
NBA Experience: 3 years

College: Michigan
Acquired: Traded from Warriors for Tom Gugliotta and three future first-round picks, 11/94

Background: The cornerstone of Michigan's famed Fab Five class, Webber led the Wolverines to back-to-back appearances in the NCAA championship game. He was the first player to make the All-Final Four team as a freshman and sophomore. The top pick in the 1993 draft, he was traded from Orlando to Golden State on draft day and won Rookie of the Year honors. He was then traded to Washington, where a shoulder injury has limited him to 69 games over two seasons.

Strengths: Webber has been a dominant inside player at every level. His strength and quickness give him a great edge around the basket, and he runs the floor like a guard. Webber has soft but strong hands and uses them to dominate the offensive boards. He blocks a lot of shots, finds open men, leads the break, and scores 20-plus points.

Weaknesses: Webber is one of the worst free-throw shooters in basketball despite getting to the line some five times per contest. He has never made even 60 percent of his free throws in a season. His left shoulder is his biggest hurdle. He played with pain last season before surgery became necessary in February.

Analysis: Webber is one of the most talented forwards in basketball. He was destined to be an NBA star from the time he was a Detroit Country Day prep All-American. Unless his shoulder injuries hold him back (and he is expected to be 100 percent to start the 1996-97 season), there is no reason to think he will not make his first of several All-Star appearances this season.

PLAYER SUMMARY	
Will	come back strong
Can't	make two free throws
Expect	20-plus PPG
Don't Expect	All-Star absences
Fantasy Value	$65-70
Card Value	20-40¢

COLLEGE STATISTICS

		G	FGP	FTP	RPG	PPG
91-92	MICH	34	.556	.496	10.0	15.5
92-93	MICH	36	.619	.552	10.1	19.2
Totals		70	.589	.530	10.0	17.4

NBA REGULAR-SEASON STATISTICS

			FGs		3-PT FGs		FTs		Rebounds						
	G	MIN	FG	PCT	FG	PCT	FT	PCT	OFF	TOT	AST	STL	BLK	PTS	PPG
93-94 GS	76	2438	572	.552	0	.000	189	.532	305	694	272	93	164	1333	17.5
94-95 WAS	54	2067	464	.495	40	.276	117	.502	200	518	256	83	85	1085	20.1
95-96 WAS	15	558	150	.543	15	.441	41	.594	37	114	75	27	9	356	23.7
Totals	145	5063	1186	.527	55	.285	347	.528	542	1326	603	203	258	2774	19.1

BILL WENNINGTON

Team: Chicago Bulls
Position: Center
Height: 7'0" **Weight:** 277
Birthdate: April 26, 1963

NBA Experience: 9 years
College: St. John's
Acquired: Signed as a free agent, 9/93

Background: Wennington improved his scoring and rebounding numbers in each of his four years at St. John's, where he teamed with Walter Berry and Chris Mullin. The Montreal native spent his first five pro years in Dallas before a stint with Sacramento and in the Italian League. He has been a Chicago reserve for the past three seasons.

Strengths: Wennington has good size but has always had the ability to pull his man away from the basket. He is an accurate jump-shooter from medium range. He also makes his free throws, runs the floor well for a center, and is willing to fill whatever role he is given.

Weaknesses: For low-post play, Wennington is not your man. He is more comfortable facing the bucket, and he possesses neither the strength nor the know-how to wear down his man with strong defense. He's below average in many respects for a seven-footer, including rebounding and shot-blocking.

Analysis: Wennington has been part of a multiheaded center situation since coming to Chicago, and his value has come in his ability to provide a different look. After Luc Longley and his low-post threat checked out of the game, here came Wennington to pull his man outside. He'll never be a standout, but he doesn't need to be.

PLAYER SUMMARY

Will..............................face the basket
Can't.......................dominate the lane
Expect.......................reserve minutes
Don't Expect.............................power
Fantasy Value.................................$0
Card Value......................................5-8¢

COLLEGE STATISTICS

		G	FGP	FTP	RPG	PPG
81-82	STJ	30	.435	.676	4.2	3.2
82-83	STJ	33	.605	.698	4.4	5.5
83-84	STJ	26	.593	.675	5.7	11.7
84-85	STJ	35	.602	.816	6.4	12.5
Totals		124	.579	.738	5.2	8.2

NBA REGULAR-SEASON STATISTICS

		G	MIN	FGs FG	FGs PCT	3-PT FGs FG	3-PT FGs PCT	FTs FT	FTs PCT	Rebounds OFF	Rebounds TOT	AST	STL	BLK	PTS	PPG
85-86	DAL	56	562	72	.471	0	.000	45	.726	32	132	21	11	22	189	3.4
86-87	DAL	58	560	56	.424	0	.000	45	.750	53	129	24	13	10	157	2.7
87-88	DAL	30	125	25	.510	1	.500	12	.632	14	39	4	5	9	63	2.1
88-89	DAL	65	1074	119	.433	1	.111	61	.744	82	286	46	16	35	300	4.6
89-90	DAL	60	814	105	.449	0	.000	60	.800	64	198	41	20	21	270	4.5
90-91	SAC	77	1455	181	.436	1	.200	74	.787	101	340	69	46	59	437	5.7
93-94	CHI	76	1371	235	.488	0	.000	72	.818	117	353	70	43	29	542	7.1
94-95	CHI	73	956	156	.492	0	.000	51	.810	64	190	40	22	17	363	5.0
95-96	CHI	71	1065	169	.493	11	.000	37	.860	58	174	46	21	16	376	5.3
Totals		566	7982	1118	.466	4	.121	457	.780	585	1841	361	197	218	2697	4.8

DAVID WESLEY

Team: Boston Celtics
Position: Guard
Height: 6'0" **Weight:** 196
Birthdate: November 14, 1970

NBA Experience: 3 years
College: Temple J.C.; Baylor
Acquired: Signed as a free agent, 7/94

Background: Wesley was named the Southwest Conference's Player of the Year as a senior at Baylor after averaging 20.9 points, 4.7 assists, and 4.9 rebounds a game. Undrafted in 1992, he was cut by the Rockets and made the CBA All-Rookie Team. He spent his first NBA season as a backup with New Jersey in 1993-94, and he has started 89 of his 133 games in two years with Boston.

Strengths: Wesley is a point guard who blisters the nets from long range. He has converted better than 42 percent of his 3-pointers for two straight years with Boston, ranking 12th in the NBA in 1995-96. He presents a nice combination of quickness and surprising strength on defense, where he comes up with steals and plays with enthusiasm. He penetrates and keeps the ball moving.

Weaknesses: Wesley was primarily a shooting guard in college and the CBA, and the playmaking required of a starting NBA point guard is not second nature to him. He does not use the dribble drive as often or as effectively as coaches and teammates would like, and he is just becoming more comfortable from inside the arc. He does not always make the right call with the ball.

Analysis: Boston fully expected Wesley to play a backup role when they signed him two years ago. That he has been the starting point guard more often than not says two things: One, he is a better player than anyone thought. Two, the Celtics have done some backcourt juggling. Wesley came back from 1995 knee surgery to play in all 82 games last season, posting career highs in almost every statistical category.

PLAYER SUMMARY	
Will	make his 3s
Can't	rest on his laurels
Expect	defensive intensity
Don't Expect	big money
Fantasy Value	$13-16
Card Value	5-8¢

COLLEGE STATISTICS

		G	FGP	FTP	RPG	PPG
89-90	BAYL	18	.455	.836	2.2	11.6
90-91	BAYL	26	.424	.839	2.9	16.5
91-92	BAYL	28	.450	.817	4.9	20.9
Totals		72	.441	.828	3.5	17.0

NBA REGULAR-SEASON STATISTICS

				FGs		3-PT FGs		FTs		Rebounds						
		G	MIN	FG	PCT	FG	PCT	FT	PCT	OFF	TOT	AST	STL	BLK	PTS	PPG
93-94	NJ	60	542	64	.368	11	.234	44	.830	10	44	123	38	4	183	3.1
94-95	BOS	51	1380	128	.409	51	.429	71	.755	31	117	266	82	9	378	7.4
95-96	BOS	82	2104	338	.459	116	.426	217	.753	68	264	390	100	11	1009	12.3
Totals		193	4026	530	.433	178	.406	332	.763	109	425	779	220	24	1570	8.1

DOUG WEST

Team: Minnesota Timberwolves
Position: Guard/Forward
Height: 6'6" **Weight:** 220
Birthdate: May 27, 1967

NBA Experience: 7 years
College: Villanova
Acquired: Second-round pick in 1989 draft (38th overall)

Background: West was a four-year starter at Villanova, finishing his career third on the school's all-time scoring list. He was a Minnesota reserve in his first two NBA seasons before being promoted to the starting lineup in 1991-92. He led the Timberwolves in scoring with a career-high 19.3 PPG in 1992-93, but his average has declined in the three seasons since.

Strengths: West throws down some of the sweetest dunks in the league. An athletic player who has filled both the two and three slots, he can be deadly from 12-18 feet. West is also a reliable free-throw shooter. He has quick hands and feet and gets after his man on defense.

Weaknesses: West has been reluctant to drive, preferring the jumper instead. He's not as potent off the dribble as he is catching and shooting, and he's not a 3-point threat. He is not a gifted passer, and his ball-handling is below average for a guard. West is less adept at the small forward position when it comes to defense.

Analysis: West, who for the last two seasons has been the lone holdover from the original Timberwolves team, is in a rut that runs deeper than wins and losses. He has been frustrated with his ever-changing role, and his numbers have suffered for it. Perhaps a change is in order. His mix of shooting and defense could serve a lot of teams well.

PLAYER SUMMARY

Will .... hit mid-range jumpers
Can't .... reverse his slide
Expect .... above-average "D"
Don't Expect 3-pointers
Fantasy Value $1
Card Value .... 5-8¢

COLLEGE STATISTICS

		G	FGP	FTP	RPG	PPG
85-86	VILL	37	.515	.682	3.7	10.2
86-87	VILL	31	.479	.729	4.9	15.2
87-88	VILL	37	.497	.724	4.9	15.8
88-89	VILL	33	.463	.720	4.9	18.4
Totals		138	.486	.716	4.6	14.8

NBA REGULAR-SEASON STATISTICS

		G	MIN	FGs FG	FGs PCT	3-PT FGs FG	3-PT FGs PCT	FTs FT	FTs PCT	Rebounds OFF	Rebounds TOT	AST	STL	BLK	PTS	PPG
89-90	MIN	52	378	53	.393	3	.273	26	.813	24	70	18	10	6	135	2.6
90-91	MIN	75	824	118	.480	0	.000	58	.690	56	136	48	35	23	294	3.9
91-92	MIN	80	2540	463	.518	4	.174	186	.805	107	257	281	66	26	1116	13.9
92-93	MIN	80	3104	646	.517	2	.087	249	.841	89	247	235	85	21	1543	19.3
93-94	MIN	72	2182	434	.487	1	.125	187	.810	61	231	172	65	24	1056	14.7
94-95	MIN	71	2328	351	.461	11	.180	206	.837	60	227	185	65	24	919	12.9
95-96	MIN	73	1639	175	.445	1	.077	114	.792	48	161	119	30	17	465	6.4
Totals		503	12995	2240	.490	22	.157	1026	.812	445	1329	1058	356	141	5528	11.0

MARK WEST

Team: Cleveland Cavaliers
Position: Center
Height: 6'10" **Weight:** 246
Birthdate: November 5, 1960

NBA Experience: 13 years
College: Old Dominion
Acquired: Signed as a free agent, 8/96

Background: West ended his college career at Old Dominion as the third-leading shot-blocker in NCAA history. He played with Dallas, Milwaukee, and Cleveland in his first five years before landing with Phoenix for six-plus seasons and Detroit for the last two. West signed a free-agent deal with the Cavs in the off-season.

Strengths: West is a hard-working center who can still block shots and play tough interior defense. He rarely takes a bad shot and will finish his career among the all-time leaders in field-goal accuracy. He needs just ten rebounds to reach 5,000 for his career. He does not chase the spotlight.

Weaknesses: West has never been a reliable offensive threat. He has averaged double figures in scoring only once in his 13-year career. He can't dribble or pass, and he's a dismal free-throw shooter. He is no longer a stopper.

Analysis: Left knee surgery two years ago ended West's consecutive-games streak at 521, and it also robbed him of a very important step. West is still capable of swatting a few shots and providing smart defense, but age has played a role. He'll be 36 this season.

PLAYER SUMMARY

Will ....bang on defense
Can't ....dribble, pass, score
Expect ....a role-player
Don't Expect ....three more years
Fantasy Value $0
Card Value ....5-8¢

COLLEGE STATISTICS

		G	FGP	FTP	RPG	PPG
79-80	OD	30	.475	.370	7.1	4.8
80-81	OD	28	.527	.578	10.3	10.9
81-82	OD	30	.610	.531	10.0	15.7
82-83	OD	29	.569	.491	10.8	14.4
Totals		117	.559	.514	9.5	11.4

NBA REGULAR-SEASON STATISTICS

		G	MIN	FGs		3-PT FGs		FTs		Rebounds						
				FG	PCT	FG	PCT	FT	PCT	OFF	TOT	AST	STL	BLK	PTS	PPG
83-84	DAL	34	202	15	.357	0	.000	7	.318	19	46	13	1	15	37	1.1
84-85	MIL/CLE	66	888	106	.546	0	.000	43	.494	90	251	15	13	49	255	3.9
85-86	CLE	67	1172	113	.541	0	.000	54	.524	97	322	20	27	62	280	4.2
86-87	CLE	78	1333	209	.543	0	.000	89	.514	126	339	41	22	81	507	6.5
87-88	CLE/PHO	83	2098	316	.551	0	.000	170	.596	165	523	74	47	147	802	9.7
88-89	PHO	82	2019	243	.653	0	.000	108	.535	167	551	39	35	187	594	7.2
89-90	PHO	82	2399	331	.625	0	.000	199	.691	212	728	45	36	184	861	10.5
90-91	PHO	82	1957	247	.647	0	.000	135	.655	171	564	37	32	161	629	7.7
91-92	PHO	82	1436	196	.632	0	.000	109	.637	134	372	22	14	81	501	6.1
92-93	PHO	82	1558	175	.614	0	.000	86	.518	153	458	29	16	103	436	5.3
93-94	PHO	82	1236	162	.566	0	.000	58	.500	112	295	33	31	109	382	4.7
94-95	DET	67	1543	217	.556	0	.000	66	.478	160	408	18	27	102	500	7.5
95-96	DET	47	682	61	.484	0	.000	28	.622	49	133	6	6	37	150	3.2
Totals		934	18523	2391	.585	0	.000	1152	.575	1655	4990	392	307	1318	5934	6.4

GERALD WILKINS

Team: Orlando Magic
Position: Guard
Height: 6'7" **Weight:** 230
Birthdate: September 11, 1963
NBA Experience: 10 years

College: Moberly Area; Tennessee-Chattanooga
Acquired: Signed as a free agent, 7/96

Background: Dominique's little brother, Gerald enjoyed three outstanding collegiate seasons at Tennessee-Chattanooga. He spent his first seven pro years with the Knicks before Cleveland picked him up in 1992-93. He logged 80 or more games in eight of his first nine seasons before a ruptured Achilles tendon cost him the entire 1994-95 season. He returned with Vancouver in mid-1996, then signed a free-agent deal with the Magic for 1996-97.

Strengths: Wilkins can be an explosive player at both ends of the court. He has been a defensive stalwart because of his quickness, strength, leaping ability, and long arms. He also drives to the hoop with abandon. He was a much-improved 3-point shooter in his last full season of action.

Weaknesses: Streaky in all regards throughout his career, Wilkins will shoot the lights out one night and go 1-for-12 the next. Sound decisions have never been his trademark. He can be quite reckless. Wilkins will not convert a high percentage from the floor and is not a great passer. His health is a big concern.

Analysis: Like Dominique, Gerald Wilkins refused to let injuries end his career. After overcoming the Achilles tendon rupture, he underwent surgery in November 1995 to remove a herniated disc in his lower back. All told, Wilkins missed 133 regular-season games before returning for 28 last season.

PLAYER SUMMARY	
Will	attack the basket
Can't	match 'Nique's fame
Expect	tough defense
Don't Expect	a steady stroke
Fantasy Value	$1
Card Value	7-10¢

COLLEGE STATISTICS

		G	FGP	FTP	RPG	PPG
81-82	MA	39	.551	.770	5.9	18.5
82-83	TC	30	.483	.661	3.8	12.6
83-84	TC	23	.542	.695	4.0	17.3
84-85	TC	32	.519	.632	4.6	21.0
Totals		124	.526	.685	4.7	17.5

NBA REGULAR-SEASON STATISTICS

				FGs		3-PT FGs		FTs		Rebounds						
		G	MIN	FG	PCT	FG	PCT	FT	PCT	OFF	TOT	AST	STL	BLK	PTS	PPG
85-86	NY	81	2025	437	.468	7	.280	132	.557	92	208	161	68	9	1013	12.5
86-87	NY	80	2758	633	.486	26	.351	235	.701	120	294	354	88	18	1527	19.1
87-88	NY	81	2703	591	.446	39	.302	191	.786	106	270	326	90	22	1412	17.4
88-89	NY	81	2414	462	.451	51	.297	186	.756	95	244	274	115	22	1161	14.3
89-90	NY	82	2609	472	.457	39	.312	208	.803	133	371	330	95	21	1191	14.5
90-91	NY	68	2164	380	.473	9	.209	169	.820	78	207	275	82	23	938	13.8
91-92	NY	82	2344	431	.447	38	.352	116	.730	74	206	219	76	17	1016	12.4
92-93	CLE	80	2079	361	.453	16	.276	152	.840	74	214	183	78	18	890	11.1
93-94	CLE	82	2768	446	.457	84	.396	194	.776	106	303	255	105	38	1170	14.3
95-96	VAN	28	738	77	.376	14	.219	20	.870	22	65	68	22	2	188	6.7
Totals		745	22602	4290	.458	323	.320	1603	.749	900	2382	2445	819	190	10506	14.1

BRIAN WILLIAMS

Team: Los Angeles Clippers
Position: Forward/Center
Height: 6'11" **Weight:** 260
Birthdate: April 6, 1969

NBA Experience: 5 years
College: Maryland; Arizona
Acquired: Traded from Nuggets for Elmore Spencer, 9/95

Background: Williams, who played at three different high schools, had a terrific freshman season at Maryland but then transferred to Arizona. The Wildcats went 53-14 in his two seasons there. Drafted tenth by Orlando, he missed most of his second season because of a bout with clinical depression and a broken hand. He spent two years in Denver before exploding with the Clippers in 1995-96.

Strengths: Williams, who can play both center and power forward, has an abundance of physical gifts. He is quick, jumps well, runs the floor like a small forward, and knows how to score. He has a soft touch in the paint, with a hook shot that requires a double-team to stop. His 54.3 field-goal percentage was eighth in the league last season. He also rebounds and plays tough defense.

Weaknesses: The knock on Williams has been his horrible inconsistency, but a couple more seasons like the last one will silence his skeptics. He is not as comfortable facing the hoop as he is with his back to it, because the jump shot is not his primary scoring weapon. He picks up a lot of fouls and commits his share of turnovers.

Analysis: Williams earned his share of critics during his first four NBA seasons. Pegged by some as an All-Star talent, he never averaged more than 9.1 PPG until his stunning breakthrough last season. Consider that only two Western Conference centers posted a higher scoring average than Williams—Hakeem Olajuwon and David Robinson. He doubled many of his career highs.

PLAYER SUMMARY	
Will	score inside
Can't	afford to backslide
Expect	double-doubles
Don't Expect	much range
Fantasy Value	$14-17
Card Value	8-15¢

COLLEGE STATISTICS

		G	FGP	FTP	RPG	PPG
87-88	MARY	29	.600	.671	6.1	12.5
89-90	ARIZ	32	.553	.727	5.7	10.6
90-91	ARIZ	35	.619	.673	7.8	14.0
Totals		96	.594	.691	6.6	12.4

NBA REGULAR-SEASON STATISTICS

				FGs		3-PT FGs		FTs		Rebounds						
		G	MIN	FG	PCT	FG	PCT	FT	PCT	OFF	TOT	AST	STL	BLK	PTS	PPG
91-92	ORL	48	905	171	.528	0	.000	95	.669	115	272	33	41	53	437	9.1
92-93	ORL	21	240	40	.513	0	.000	16	.800	24	56	5	14	17	96	4.6
93-94	DEN	80	1507	251	.541	0	.000	137	.649	138	446	50	49	87	639	8.0
94-95	DEN	63	1261	196	.589	0	.000	106	.654	98	298	53	38	43	498	7.9
95-96	LAC	65	2157	416	.543	1	.167	196	.734	149	492	122	70	55	1029	15.8
Totals		277	6070	1074	.547	1	.100	550	.686	524	1564	263	212	255	2699	9.7

BUCK WILLIAMS

Team: New York Knicks
Position: Forward
Height: 6'8" **Weight:** 225
Birthdate: March 8, 1960

NBA Experience: 15 years
College: Maryland
Acquired: Signed as a free agent, 7/96

Background: Williams turned pro after his junior season at Maryland, was named 1982 NBA Rookie of the Year, and played in three All-Star Games as a Net. He won the field-goal percentage crown in 1990-91 and 1991-92 with Portland. Williams has played in 80-plus games in 12 of 15 seasons. He joins the Knicks for 1996-97.

Strengths: For rebounds and low-post defense, few players of his time have been as steady as Williams. He also hits open jumpers and hooks and never takes a bad shot. He has made at least 50 percent of his shots for 15 straight seasons.

Weaknesses: Williams is a below-average passer and ball-handler and a poor free-throw shooter. He does not score or dominate the boards like he used to, though he does contribute. His days as a starter are behind him.

Analysis: What better example for young forwards than Williams, one of the hardest-working men the game has known? He is one of eight players in NBA history with 16,000 points and 12,000 rebounds. The Hall of Fame could be his next milestone.

PLAYER SUMMARY

Will ....drill open jumpers
Can't ....turn back the clock
Expect ....a workaholic
Don't Expect ....82 starts
Fantasy Value $1
Card Value ....5-8¢

COLLEGE STATISTICS

		G	FGP	FTP	RPG	PPG
78-79	MARY	30	.583	.550	10.8	10.0
79-80	MARY	24	.606	.664	10.1	15.5
80-81	MARY	31	.647	.637	11.7	15.5
Totals		85	.615	.623	10.9	13.6

NBA REGULAR-SEASON STATISTICS

				FGs		3-PT FGs		FTs		Rebounds						
		G	MIN	FG	PCT	FG	PCT	FT	PCT	OFF	TOT	AST	STL	BLK	PTS	PPG
81-82	NJ	82	2825	513	.582	0	.000	242	.624	347	1005	107	84	84	1268	15.5
82-83	NJ	82	2961	536	.588	0	.000	324	.620	365	1027	125	91	110	1396	17.0
83-84	NJ	81	3003	495	.535	0	.000	284	.570	355	1000	130	81	125	1274	15.7
84-85	NJ	82	3182	577	.530	1	.250	336	.625	323	1005	167	63	110	1491	18.2
85-86	NJ	82	3070	500	.523	0	.000	301	.676	329	986	131	73	96	1301	15.9
86-87	NJ	82	2976	521	.557	0	.000	430	.731	322	1023	129	78	91	1472	18.0
87-88	NJ	70	2637	466	.560	1	1.000	346	.668	298	834	109	68	44	1279	18.3
88-89	NJ	74	2446	373	.531	0	.000	213	.666	249	696	78	61	36	959	13.0
89-90	POR	82	2801	413	.548	0	.000	288	.706	250	800	116	69	39	1114	13.6
90-91	POR	80	2582	358	.602	0	.000	217	.705	227	751	97	47	47	933	11.7
91-92	POR	80	2519	340	.604	0	.000	221	.754	260	704	75	62	41	901	11.3
92-93	POR	82	2498	270	.511	0	.000	138	.645	232	690	75	81	61	678	8.3
93-94	POR	81	2636	291	.555	0	.000	201	.679	315	843	80	58	47	783	9.7
94-95	POR	82	2422	309	.512	1	.500	138	.673	251	669	78	67	69	757	9.2
95-96	POR	70	1672	192	.500	2	.667	125	.668	159	404	42	40	47	511	7.3
Totals		1192	40230	6154	.550	5	.172	3804	.664	4282	12437	1572	1023	1047	16117	13.5

ERIC WILLIAMS

Team: Boston Celtics
Position: Forward
Height: 6'8" **Weight:** 220
Birthdate: July 17, 1972

NBA Experience: 1 year
College: Vincennes; Providence
Acquired: First-round pick in 1995 draft (14th overall)

Background: Williams played two seasons at Vincennes (Indiana) Junior College before going to Providence in 1993. In just two seasons, he scored more than 1,000 points and was a unanimous All-Big East first-team choice as a senior. His efforts in the pre-draft camps caught several sets of eyes, and Boston drafted him 14th overall in 1995. If that was a surprise to some, his 10.7-PPG rookie scoring average was even more of a shocker.

Strengths: Williams plays fearless basketball. He is a hard-nosed, aggressive forward who loves to take the ball to the basket. He led the Celtics in free-throw attempts last season with 298. He is also a dangerous transition player who jumps well and seldom seems to tire. He is an effective offensive rebounder, a promising defender, and an unselfish player with a fine feel for the game.

Weaknesses: Williams was neither the quickest nor the strongest small forward among the rookie class. He simply makes the most of what he has. Outside shooting is clearly his biggest trouble area. He made only 41 percent of his field goals as a college senior. His commitment to the drive begs a defender to give him space. He misses a lot of free throws and needs to crash the defensive board.

Analysis: Williams was not expected to make such a sudden impact at the NBA level, but the departure of Dominique Wilkins left Boston with a vacancy at small forward. Williams was one of the first Celtics off the bench for most of the season, showing no intimidation whatsoever in taking the ball at veterans who wanted to flatten him. He's an intense, scrappy player with a bright NBA future.

PLAYER SUMMARY	
Will	attack the basket
Can't	rely on his jumper
Expect	"hustle plays"
Don't Expect	20 PPG
Fantasy Value	$1-3
Card Value	20-40¢

COLLEGE STATISTICS

		G	FGP	FTP	RPG	PPG
93-94	PROV	30	.508	.660	5.0	15.7
94-95	PROV	30	.410	.687	6.7	17.7
Totals		60	.453	.673	5.9	16.7

NBA REGULAR-SEASON STATISTICS

				FGs		3-PT FGs		FTs		Rebounds						
		G	MIN	FG	PCT	FG	PCT	FT	PCT	OFF	TOT	AST	STL	BLK	PTS	PPG
95-96	BOS	64	1470	241	.441	3	.300	200	.671	92	217	70	56	11	685	10.7
Totals		64	1470	241	.441	3	.300	200	.671	92	217	70	56	11	685	10.7

JAYSON WILLIAMS

Team: New Jersey Nets
Position: Forward/Center
Height: 6'10" **Weight:** 245
Birthdate: February 22, 1968

NBA Experience: 6 years
College: St. John's
Acquired: Traded from 76ers for conditional draft picks, 10/92

Background: After guiding St. John's to an NIT title in 1989 as a junior (he was tourney MVP), Williams broke his foot halfway through his senior season. He was drafted by Phoenix but has spent his six seasons with Philadelphia and New Jersey after trades. After four disappointing seasons, he has begun to emerge as a prime-time rebounder for the Nets. He averaged 10.0 RPG in 1995-96.

Strengths: Williams loves to rebound and has made that part of the game his calling card. He can dominate the boards, as his 25-rebound game against Seattle last year shows. He has good leaping ability, a sculpted body, and plenty of desire. He scores on drives and putbacks, and his added strength helps him on defense. He plays the four and five spots.

Weaknesses: Don't look to Williams for offense. He has very little touch from the field and is especially woeful from the free-throw line. It's a mistake to have him on the floor late in a close game. Williams commits a truckload of fouls, very rarely gets an assist, and does not make great decisions with the ball.

Analysis: Williams is a new man. "There comes a point in every man's life when he has to grow up," he said. To that end, Williams toned down his social life, hired a personal trainer, and spent his 1995 summer running seven miles every morning and lifting twice a day. He was tenth in the league in rebounding last year, well ahead of any other reserve.

PLAYER SUMMARY	
Will	dominate the glass
Can't	shoot free throws
Expect	10-plus RPG
Don't Expect	sleek moves
Fantasy Value	$6-8
Card Value	7-10¢

COLLEGE STATISTICS

		G	FGP	FTP	RPG	PPG
87-88	STJ	28	.513	.600	5.1	9.9
88-89	STJ	31	.573	.702	7.9	19.5
89-90	STJ	13	.534	.613	7.8	14.6
Totals		72	.550	.652	6.8	14.9

NBA REGULAR-SEASON STATISTICS

				FGs		3-PT FGs		FTs		Rebounds						
		G	MIN	FG	PCT	FG	PCT	FT	PCT	OFF	TOT	AST	STL	BLK	PTS	PPG
90-91	PHI	52	508	72	.447	1	.500	37	.661	41	111	16	9	6	182	3.5
91-92	PHI	50	646	75	.364	0	.000	56	.636	62	145	12	20	20	206	4.1
92-93	NJ	12	139	21	.457	0	.000	7	.389	22	41	0	4	4	49	4.1
93-94	NJ	70	877	125	.427	0	.000	72	.605	109	263	26	17	36	322	4.6
94-95	NJ	75	982	149	.461	0	.000	65	.533	179	425	35	26	33	363	4.8
95-96	NJ	80	1858	279	.423	2	.286	161	.592	342	803	47	35	57	721	9.0
Totals		339	5010	721	.427	3	.214	398	.590	755	1788	136	111	156	1843	5.4

JOHN WILLIAMS

Team: Phoenix Suns
Position: Forward/Center
Height: 6'11" **Weight:** 245
Birthdate: August 9, 1962
NBA Experience: 10 years

College: Tulane
Acquired: Traded from Cavaliers for Dan Majerle, Antonio Lang, and a future first-round pick, 10/95

Background: Williams's involvement in an alleged point-fixing scandal at Tulane rocked the college basketball world in the mid-1980s. He paced the Green Wave in scoring for three years. Williams was an All-Rookie performer in his first of nine productive years in Cleveland. He was traded to Phoenix before last season and averaged a career-low 7.3 PPG.

Strengths: Williams is a standout defensive player who blocks shots and can handle either the center or power forward position. He goes hard to the basket, draws fouls, and is capable of nailing 15-foot jumpers. He also contributes on the boards. Williams knows the meaning of hard work.

Weaknesses: Williams almost never goes to his left because that hand is shaky. This fact is not lost on defenders. "Hot Rod" has seen a recent decline in his shooting percentage and scoring average. He has never been a great free-throw shooter.

Analysis: Williams took some heat for his seven-year, $26.5-million contract, but he has tried to earn every penny. He spent his last season with Cleveland as the starting center and played the same role for the Suns last year. He would rather return to forward, but he has lost a step and is now better suited for the middle. He's still a good bet to block 100 shots.

PLAYER SUMMARY	
Will	work on defense
Can't	use his left
Expect	100 blocks
Don't Expect	a quick step
Fantasy Value	$3-5
Card Value	7-12¢

COLLEGE STATISTICS

		G	FGP	FTP	RPG	PPG
81-82	TUL	28	.584	.662	7.2	14.8
82-83	TUL	31	.476	.703	5.4	12.4
83-84	TUL	28	.569	.761	7.9	19.4
84-85	TUL	28	.566	.774	7.8	17.8
Totals		115	.549	.731	7.0	16.0

NBA REGULAR-SEASON STATISTICS

				FGs		3-PT FGs		FTs		Rebounds						
		G	MIN	FG	PCT	FG	PCT	FT	PCT	OFF	TOT	AST	STL	BLK	PTS	PPG
86-87	CLE	80	2714	435	.485	0	.000	298	.745	222	629	154	58	167	1168	14.6
87-88	CLE	77	2106	316	.477	0	.000	211	.756	159	506	103	61	145	843	10.9
88-89	CLE	82	2125	356	.509	1	.250	235	.748	173	477	108	77	134	948	11.6
89-90	CLE	82	2776	528	.493	0	.000	325	.739	220	663	168	86	167	1381	16.8
90-91	CLE	43	1293	199	.463	0	.000	107	.652	111	290	100	36	69	505	11.7
91-92	CLE	80	2432	341	.503	0	.000	270	.752	228	607	196	60	182	952	11.9
92-93	CLE	67	2055	263	.470	0	.000	212	.716	127	415	152	48	105	738	11.0
93-94	CLE	76	2660	394	.478	0	.000	252	.728	207	575	193	78	130	1040	13.7
94-95	CLE	74	2641	366	.466	1	.200	196	.685	173	507	192	83	101	929	12.6
95-96	PHO	62	1652	180	.453	0	.000	95	.731	129	372	62	46	90	455	7.3
Totals		423	10966	1744	.454	53	.224	828	.726	673	2257	1182	529	251	4369	10.3

LORENZO WILLIAMS

Team: Washington Bullets
Position: Forward/Center
Height: 6'9" **Weight:** 220
Birthdate: July 15, 1969

NBA Experience: 4 years
College: Polk; Stetson
Acquired: Signed as a free agent, 7/96

Background: Williams played two seasons at Polk Community College in Florida before becoming the all-time Trans America Athletic Conference leader in blocked shots at Stetson. He was not drafted in 1991, so he played in the USBL, CBA, and Global Basketball Association before reaching the NBA. He played with three teams in each of his first two seasons, then was a two-year starter for Dallas before signing a free-agent deal with the Bullets last summer.

Strengths: Williams does three things well: He blocks shots, he rebounds, and he plays defense. Though undersized for a center, he has finished 12th in the league in shot-blocking in each of the last two seasons. His hard work and good timing also make him good for more than eight rebounds per contest. Happy to be starting in the NBA, Williams does not mind busting his tail on defense.

Weaknesses: Everything having to do with offense falls into this category. No one in the league is a worse free-throw shooter (.343 last season), and no starting center does less in the scoring column. Williams knows his shooting range is limited to putbacks, so that's about all he does. He commits fouls at a high rate while trying to overcome his size limitations.

Analysis: Williams played in his first 148 games as a Maverick before taking a Rik Smits elbow in the eye last season. It required surgery, ending a string of 106 consecutive starts. On offense, he was not missed a bit. There was no replacing him on the defensive end of the floor, however. A minor-leaguer no more, this diminutive center knows his role and fills it well.

PLAYER SUMMARY	
Will	stuff his man
Can't	make a free throw
Expect	defense, rebounds
Don't Expect	a trace of offense
Fantasy Value	$1
Card Value	5-8¢

COLLEGE STATISTICS

		G	FGP	FTP	RPG	PPG
89-90	STET	32	.520	.295	8.4	7.8
90-91	STET	31	.540	.667	10.1	9.2
Totals		63	.530	.484	9.2	8.5

NBA REGULAR-SEASON STATISTICS

			FGs		3-PT FGs		FTs		Rebounds						
	G	MIN	FG	PCT	FG	PCT	FT	PCT	OFF	TOT	AST	STL	BLK	PTS	PPG
92-93 CHA/ORL/BOS	27	179	17	.472	0	.000	2	.286	17	55	5	5	17	36	1.3
93-94 ORL/CHA/DAL	38	716	49	.445	0	.000	12	.429	95	217	25	18	46	110	2.9
94-95 DAL	82	2383	145	.477	0	.000	38	.376	291	690	124	52	148	328	4.0
95-96 DAL	65	1806	87	.407	0	.000	24	.343	234	521	85	48	122	198	3.0
Totals	212	5084	298	.449	0	.000	76	.369	637	1483	239	123	333	672	3.2

MICHEAL WILLIAMS

Team: Minnesota Timberwolves
Position: Guard
Height: 6'2" **Weight:** 175
Birthdate: July 23, 1966
NBA Experience: 8 years

College: Baylor
Acquired: Traded from Pacers with Chuck Person for Pooh Richardson and Sam Mitchell, 9/92

Background: Williams, a two-time all-league selection at Baylor, has played for a slew of pro teams. A member of Detroit's championship team in 1988-89, he spent the next season with Phoenix, Dallas, Charlotte, and the CBA's Rapid City Thrillers. He became one of the NBA's top thieves in Indiana. He led Minnesota in steals and assists for two years before a 1994 heel injury took him down.

Strengths: At 100 percent, Williams has blistering speed and quick hands. He is a scoring-minded point guard with a lightning-quick first step and an above-average pull-up jumper. He comes up with a lot of steals. He once made a league-record 97 consecutive free throws.

Weaknesses: Williams is not the defensive player his numbers say he is. He gets beaten routinely by his man and comes up with steals because he gambles. He is not a consistent shooter, nor is he a player consumed by the idea of making his teammates better. He falls short as a playmaker. The main concern is his health.

Analysis: Williams has played a grand total of ten games over the last two seasons. He tore the plantar fascia in his left heel one game into the 1994-95 season, and the same heel sent him back to the injured list nine games into last season. He might never regain his peak form, which once had Williams scoring 15-plus PPG.

PLAYER SUMMARY	
Will	beat his man
Can't	muscle his man
Expect	a scoring bent
Don't Expect	a star playmaker
Fantasy Value	$2-4
Card Value	5-8¢

COLLEGE STATISTICS

		G	FGP	FTP	APG	PPG
84-85	BAYL	28	.487	.793	2.4	14.6
85-86	BAYL	22	.462	.806	2.7	13.0
86-87	BAYL	31	.475	.714	5.1	17.2
87-88	BAYL	34	.505	.697	5.4	18.4
Totals		115	.485	.738	4.0	16.1

NBA REGULAR-SEASON STATISTICS

				FGs		3-PT FGs		FTs		Rebounds						
		G	MIN	FG	PCT	FG	PCT	FT	PCT	OFF	TOT	AST	STL	BLK	PTS	PPG
88-89	DET	49	358	47	.364	2	.222	31	.660	9	27	70	13	3	127	2.6
89-90	PHO/CHA	28	329	60	.504	0	.000	36	.783	12	32	81	22	1	156	5.6
90-91	IND	73	1706	261	.499	1	.143	290	.879	49	176	348	150	17	813	11.1
91-92	IND	79	2750	404	.490	8	.242	372	.871	73	282	647	233	22	1188	15.0
92-93	MIN	76	2661	353	.446	26	.243	419	.907	84	273	661	165	23	1151	15.1
93-94	MIN	71	2206	314	.457	10	.222	333	.839	67	221	512	118	24	971	13.7
94-95	MIN	1	28	1	.250	0	.000	4	.800	0	1	3	2	0	6	6.0
95-96	MIN	9	189	13	.325	1	.333	28	.848	3	23	31	5	3	55	6.1
Totals		386	10227	1453	.466	48	.232	1513	.866	297	1035	2353	708	93	4467	11.6

REGGIE WILLIAMS

Team: Indiana Pacers
Position: Forward/Guard
Height: 6'7" **Weight:** 195
Birthdate: March 5, 1964
NBA Experience: 9 years

College: Georgetown
Acquired: Traded from Nuggets with Jalen Rose and a 1996 first-round pick for Mark Jackson, Ricky Pierce, and a 1996 first-round pick, 6/96

Background: As a senior at Georgetown, Williams was an All-American and Big East Player of the Year. He was named NCAA Tournament MVP when the Hoyas won the national title in 1984. Drafted fourth, he was a letdown with the Clippers, Cleveland, and San Antonio before signing with Denver. He ranks among the Nuggets' top ten career scorers, but he was dealt to Indiana in the off-season.

Strengths: Williams is a slasher who thrives in transition and knows how to score. He can be a dangerous pull-up shooter, he has 3-point range, and he hits a high percentage of his free throws. He still has a quick first step. Williams has been an effective defender when he's focused.

Weaknesses: Halfcourt basketball is not for Williams. He is an erratic shooter, converting poor percentages from both inside and outside the 3-point arc, and he does not handle the ball well. His nine-year NBA career has been plagued by inconsistent play. Williams is far from a stopper.

Analysis: Williams began to shed his underachiever's label in his first few years with Denver, but it's clear he will never be seen as a No. 4 overall pick who lived up to his potential. He was sidelined the entire month of December last season with a stress fracture in his left fibula. He's likely to finish his career as a reserve.

PLAYER SUMMARY	
Will	get out on the break
Can't	maintain a high level
Expect	streak shooting
Don't Expect	stardom
Fantasy Value	$3-5
Card Value	5-8¢

COLLEGE STATISTICS

		G	FGP	FTP	RPG	PPG
83-84	GEOR	37	.433	.768	3.5	9.1
84-85	GEOR	35	.506	.755	5.7	11.9
85-86	GEOR	32	.528	.732	8.2	17.6
86-87	GEOR	34	.482	.804	8.6	23.6
Totals		138	.490	.768	6.4	15.3

NBA REGULAR-SEASON STATISTICS

			FGs		3-PT FGs		FTs		Rebounds						
	G	MIN	FG	PCT	FG	PCT	FT	PCT	OFF	TOT	AST	STL	BLK	PTS	PPG
87-88 LAC	35	857	152	.356	13	.224	48	.727	55	118	58	29	21	365	10.4
88-89 LAC	63	1303	260	.438	30	.288	92	.754	70	179	103	81	29	642	10.2
89-90 LAC/CLE/SA	47	743	131	.388	6	.162	52	.765	28	83	53	32	14	320	6.8
90-91 SA/DEN	73	1896	384	.449	57	.363	166	.843	133	306	133	113	41	991	13.6
91-92 DEN	81	2623	601	.471	56	.359	216	.803	145	405	295	148	76	1341	17.0
92-93 DEN	79	2722	535	.458	33	.270	238	.804	132	428	300	126	66	1341	17.0
93-94 DEN	82	2654	418	.412	64	.278	165	.733	98	392	300	117	66	1065	13.0
94-95 DEN	74	2198	388	.459	85	.320	132	.759	94	329	231	114	67	993	13.4
95-96 DEN	52	817	94	.370	20	.225	33	.846	25	122	74	34	21	241	4.6
Totals	586	15813	2963	.438	364	.299	1142	.784	780	2362	1482	794	403	7432	12.7

WALT WILLIAMS

Team: Toronto Raptors
Position: Guard/Forward
Height: 6'8" **Weight:** 230
Birthdate: April 16, 1970
NBA Experience: 4 years

College: Maryland
Acquired: Traded from Kings with Tyrone Corbin for Billy Owens and Kevin Gamble, 2/96

Background: Williams, the Washington, D.C.-area prep Player of the Year in 1988, broke Len Bias's Maryland record for points in a season. He averaged 26.8 points, 5.6 rebounds, 3.6 assists, and 2.1 steals per outing in his senior season. Drafted seventh in 1992, he was a second-team All-Rookie performer and received Most Improved Player votes in 1994-95. Williams was traded to Miami in 1995-96 and started all 73 games he played last year. He joins the Raptors for 1996-97.

Strengths: By two months into his rookie season, Williams had seen action at all five positions. He is a highly versatile talent who makes plays from any of three positions, generally the small forward and big guard spots. He is a dangerous 3-point shooter, yet he also has the ability to drive or post up. He can score points in bunches and is a keen passer. He blocks shots and makes steals.

Weaknesses: Williams's ever-changing role has not always worked to his advantage. Is he a shooter, should he drive and dish, or should he back smaller men into the lane? His defense has not been consistent. He picks up a lot of reaching fouls and does not always fight to hold his position. Williams is a below-average free-throw shooter who has been streaky in his play.

Analysis: "The Wizard" was asked to do a great deal for Sacramento, and he was never able to match his solid rookie numbers. Williams became a 3-point ace in 28 games with the Heat, making better than 45 percent from the arc (56 of 123) after hitting just 58 treys in 45 games with Sacramento last season.

PLAYER SUMMARY

Will ....change positions
Can't ....star on defense
Expect ....plays, treys
Don't Expect ....single digits
Fantasy Value $18-21
Card Value ....10-20¢

COLLEGE STATISTICS

		G	FGP	FTP	RPG	PPG
88-89	MARY	26	.441	.623	3.5	7.3
89-90	MARY	33	.483	.776	4.2	12.7
90-91	MARY	17	.449	.837	5.1	18.7
91-92	MARY	29	.472	.758	5.6	26.8
Totals		105	.466	.762	4.6	16.2

NBA REGULAR-SEASON STATISTICS

		G	MIN	FGs FG	FGs PCT	3-PT FGs FG	3-PT FGs PCT	FTs FT	FTs PCT	Rebounds OFF	Rebounds TOT	AST	STL	BLK	PTS	PPG
92-93	SAC	59	1673	358	.435	61	.319	224	.742	115	265	178	66	29	1001	17.0
93-94	SAC	57	1356	226	.390	38	.288	148	.635	71	235	132	52	23	638	11.2
94-95	SAC	77	2739	445	.446	103	.348	266	.731	100	345	316	123	63	1259	16.4
95-96	SAC/MIA	73	2169	359	.444	114	.389	163	.703	99	319	230	85	58	995	13.6
Totals		266	7937	1388	.433	316	.346	801	.708	385	1164	856	326	173	3893	14.6

CORLISS WILLIAMSON

Team: Sacramento Kings
Position: Forward
Height: 6'7" **Weight:** 245
Birthdate: December 4, 1973

NBA Experience: 1 year
College: Arkansas
Acquired: First-round pick in 1995 draft (13th overall)

Background: "Big Nasty" overpowered most of his opponents during his three seasons at Arkansas. Williamson led the Razorbacks to the 1994 national championship and averaged 20.2 points and 7.5 rebounds in 15 career NCAA Tournament games. Arkansas was 74-17 in games he played. The No. 13 draft choice in 1995, Williamson had some big rookie games but wound up averaging just 5.6 points in 11.5 minutes per game for Sacramento.

Strengths: Williamson is strong, has a great set of hands, and owns a soft touch around the basket. He plays the game with abandon and can handle himself against bigger players. He could become a force on the boards, and he has been particularly effective on the offensive glass. He attacks the rim and knows how to score inside. Williamson is a battler who wants to earn more minutes.

Weaknesses: For starters, Williamson is about three inches too short to handle the post-up scoring of the better power forwards in the league. A move to small forward is out of the question, because his ball-handling, passing, and shooting would not allow it. Williamson is an inside guy all the way. He has trouble matching up on defense, too. He's a poor free-throw shooter. Williamson will have to continue to work on his conditioning.

Analysis: Williamson began last season on the injured list after back surgery and did not join the active roster until mid-December. He had his moments, including a 26-point game, and he rebounded well enough at times to raise some hopes. The bottom line, however, is that Williams has much left to prove. He needs to overcome his lack of size with great desire and a commitment to getting in peak physical shape.

PLAYER SUMMARY	
Will	score on putbacks
Can't	play small forward
Expect	a physical style
Don't Expect	consistency
Fantasy Value	$1
Card Value	20-40¢

COLLEGE STATISTICS

		G	FGP	FTP	RPG	PPG
92-93	ARK	18	.574	.622	5.1	14.6
93-94	ARK	34	.626	.700	7.7	20.4
94-95	ARK	39	.550	.668	7.5	19.7
Totals		91	.583	.672	7.1	19.0

NBA REGULAR-SEASON STATISTICS

			FGs		3-PT FGs		FTs		Rebounds						
	G	MIN	FG	PCT	FG	PCT	FT	PCT	OFF	TOT	AST	STL	BLK	PTS	PPG
95-96 SAC	53	609	125	.466	0	.000	47	.560	56	114	23	11	9	297	5.6
Totals	53	609	125	.466	0	.000	47	.560	56	114	23	11	9	297	5.6

KEVIN WILLIS

Team: Houston Rockets
Position: Forward/Center
Height: 7'0" **Weight:** 240
Birthdate: September 6, 1962

NBA Experience: 11 years
College: Michigan St.
Acquired: Signed as a free agent, 8/96

Background: Willis led the Big Ten in rebounding and field-goal percentage as a junior at Michigan State, where he received all-conference mention as a senior. He played nine-plus years with Atlanta (he missed 1988-89 with a broken foot) and was a 1992 All-Star. Trades have since landed Willis in Miami and Golden State, and he signed a free-agent deal with the Rockets in July 1996.

Strengths: Willis has been one of the NBA's best rebounding forwards over the last several years, and he also provides low-post scoring. His jump hook is his best weapon, and he is also capable of drilling mid-range jumpers. He runs the floor well for a seven-footer.

Weaknesses: Willis rarely passes the ball, having dished out only 53 assists all last season. He is not a capable ball-handler or good free-throw shooter, either. Willis is a frequent liability on defense who no longer dominates the boards as he did a few years back.

Analysis: Willis has been a regular double-double contributor over much of his career after being pegged an underachiever early on. The years are catching up with him, however. He can still have an impact on a team's inside game. He has a chance to finish with 10,000 career boards.

PLAYER SUMMARY

Will .... score on hooks
Can't .... handle the ball
Expect .... double-doubles
Don't Expect .... passes
Fantasy Value $9-11
Card Value .... 5-8¢

COLLEGE STATISTICS

		G	FGP	FTP	RPG	PPG
81-82	MSU	27	.474	.567	4.2	6.0
82-83	MSU	27	.596	.514	9.6	13.3
83-84	MSU	25	.492	.661	7.7	11.0
Totals		79	.530	.579	7.1	10.1

NBA REGULAR-SEASON STATISTICS

		G	MIN	FGs FG	PCT	3-PT FGs FG	PCT	FTs FT	PCT	Rebounds OFF	TOT	AST	STL	BLK	PTS	PPG
84-85	ATL	82	1785	322	.467	2	.222	119	.657	177	522	36	31	49	765	9.3
85-86	ATL	82	2300	419	.517	0	.000	172	.654	243	704	45	66	44	1010	12.3
86-87	ATL	81	2626	538	.536	1	.250	227	.709	321	849	62	65	61	1304	16.1
87-88	ATL	75	2091	356	.518	0	.000	159	.649	235	547	28	68	42	871	11.6
89-90	ATL	81	2273	418	.519	2	.286	168	.683	253	645	57	63	47	1006	12.4
90-91	ATL	80	2373	444	.504	4	.400	159	.668	259	704	99	60	40	1051	13.1
91-92	ATL	81	2962	591	.483	6	.162	292	.804	418	1258	173	72	54	1480	18.3
92-93	ATL	80	2878	616	.506	7	.241	196	.653	335	1028	165	68	41	1435	17.9
93-94	ATL	80	2867	627	.499	9	.375	268	.713	335	963	150	79	38	1531	19.1
94-95	ATL/MIA	67	2390	473	.466	3	.200	205	.690	227	732	86	60	36	1154	17.2
95-96	MIA/GS	75	2135	325	.456	1	.111	143	.700	208	638	53	32	41	794	10.6
Totals		864	26680	5129	.498	35	.230	2108	.695	3011	8590	954	664	493	12401	14.4

DAVID WINGATE

Team: Seattle SuperSonics
Position: Guard/Forward
Height: 6'5" **Weight:** 185
Birthdate: December 15, 1963

NBA Experience: 10 years
College: Georgetown
Acquired: Traded from Hornets with Hersey Hawkins for Kendall Gill, 6/95

Background: Wingate was a member of the great Georgetown teams of the mid-1980s. He was drafted by Philadelphia and played his first three years with the 76ers. He has since served stints in San Antonio, Washington, Charlotte, and Seattle with varying amounts of work. His best statistical season was his lone year as a Bullet in 1991-92.

Strengths: Wingate has been a certified stopper for much of his career. He is still capable of staying in front of his man and getting after the ball. Wingate can also contribute with his ball-handling, passing, and rebounding. He made 15 of 34 3-point tries in 1995-96.

Weaknesses: For offense, look to someone other than Wingate. He has never averaged even nine PPG in his ten NBA seasons. Wingate had some problems off the court earlier in his career. San Antonio once put him on the suspended list. Knee trouble (he had surgery three years ago) has slowed him.

Analysis: Wingate has not been a spectacular player by any means, but his abilities on defense have made him a valuable reserve on most of his five teams. Unfortunately, Seattle was not among them. Wingate got off the bench in just 60 games (695 minutes) for the best team in the West. His knees will probably hold up for another season or two.

PLAYER SUMMARY	
Will	defend two positions
Can't	hold up as a starter
Expect	a role-playing reserve
Don't Expect	three more years
Fantasy Value	$0
Card Value	5-8¢

COLLEGE STATISTICS

		G	FGP	FTP	RPG	PPG
82-83	GEOR	32	.445	.702	3.0	12.0
83-84	GEOR	37	.435	.721	3.6	11.2
84-85	GEOR	38	.484	.689	3.6	12.4
85-86	GEOR	32	.497	.755	4.0	15.9
Totals		139	.467	.719	3.6	12.8

NBA REGULAR-SEASON STATISTICS

				FGs		3-PT FGs		FTs		Rebounds						
		G	MIN	FG	PCT	FG	PCT	FT	PCT	OFF	TOT	AST	STL	BLK	PTS	PPG
86-87	PHI	77	1612	259	.430	13	.250	149	.741	70	156	155	93	19	680	8.8
87-88	PHI	61	1419	218	.400	10	.250	99	.750	44	101	119	47	22	545	8.9
88-89	PHI	33	372	54	.470	2	.333	27	.794	12	37	73	9	2	137	4.2
89-90	SA	78	1856	220	.448	0	.000	87	.777	62	195	208	89	18	527	6.8
90-91	SA	25	563	53	.384	1	.111	29	.707	24	75	46	19	5	136	5.4
91-92	WAS	81	2127	266	.465	1	.056	105	.719	80	269	247	123	21	638	7.9
92-93	CHA	72	1471	180	.536	1	.167	79	.738	49	174	183	66	9	440	6.1
93-94	CHA	50	1005	136	.481	4	.333	34	.667	30	134	104	42	6	310	6.2
94-95	CHA	52	515	50	.410	4	.182	18	.750	11	60	56	19	6	122	2.3
95-96	SEA	60	695	88	.415	15	.441	32	.780	17	56	58	20	4	223	3.7
Totals		589	11635	1524	.446	51	.241	659	.741	399	1257	1249	527	112	3758	6.4

DONTONIO WINGFIELD

Team: Portland Trail Blazers
Position: Forward
Height: 6'8" **Weight:** 256
Birthdate: June 23, 1974

NBA Experience: 2 years
College: Cincinnati
Acquired: Signed as a free agent, 10/95

Background: Wingfield was a marquee recruit at Cincinnati and the top freshman scorer and rebounder in the Great Midwest Conference before bypassing his final three years to enter the NBA draft. A second-round choice, he played only 20 games for Seattle as a rookie. Toronto took him in the 1995 expansion draft, but he immediately became a free agent and signed with Portland. Wingfield played just 487 minutes in 1995-96.

Strengths: Wingfield is a versatile athlete who does a little bit of everything. He was a 40-percent 3-point shooter in college, yet he also averaged 9.0 RPG against some tough competition. He combines strength, speed, and leaping ability. Wingfield has NBA 3-point range, and he can also score inside. He has shot his handful of free throws well, and he hits the offensive boards.

Weaknesses: Wingfield, whose draft stock dropped with some teams because of several off-court incidents, has yet to prove he is ready to compete at the NBA level. In his limited minutes (he played just 81 as a rookie), he has shot well below 40 percent from the field. He has not made his outside shots and is too small to get by in the paint. He does not handle the ball well. Wingfield has been a defensive liability.

Analysis: Wingfield is no longer the youngest player in the league, as he was during his rookie season, but he still has a lot to learn. He needs to show a dedication to spending his off-season in the gym, working on his jump shot, his dribble, and his defense. He has done nothing to convince NBA followers he will be a standout player at this level. In his defense, however, he has not had enough chances to prove himself.

PLAYER SUMMARY	
Will	work inside and out
Can't	handle the ball
Expect	another chance
Don't Expect	20 minutes
Fantasy Value	$0
Card Value	7-12¢

COLLEGE STATISTICS

		G	FGP	FTP	RPG	PPG
93-94	CINC	29	.422	.669	9.0	16.0
Totals		29	.422	.669	9.0	16.0

NBA REGULAR-SEASON STATISTICS

				FGs		3-PT FGs		FTs		Rebounds						
		G	MIN	FG	PCT	FG	PCT	FT	PCT	OFF	TOT	AST	STL	BLK	PTS	PPG
94-95	SEA	20	81	18	.353	2	.167	8	.800	11	30	3	5	3	46	2.3
95-96	POR	44	487	60	.382	19	.302	26	.765	45	104	28	20	6	165	3.8
Totals		64	568	78	.375	21	.280	34	.773	56	134	31	25	9	211	3.3

JOE WOLF

Team: Orlando Magic
Position: Forward/Center
Height: 6'11" **Weight:** 257
Birthdate: December 17, 1964

NBA Experience: 8 years
College: North Carolina
Acquired: Signed as a free agent, 11/95

Background: Wolf averaged less than ten PPG during his four-year North Carolina career but was named All-Atlantic Coast Conference as a senior. The Clippers made him the 13th overall draft pick in 1987 and kept him for three years. Wolf has since seen action with Denver, Boston, Portland, Charlotte, and Orlando in addition to a brief stint in Spain. He has spent most of his career as a reserve.

Strengths: Wolf is a team player who does not mind doing the little things that help others fare better. He is a good passer for a big man, and he works hard on the defensive boards. Wolf is a decent shooter who is capable of pulling his man outside.

Weaknesses: Wolf is not strong enough to handle opposing big men for long stretches, and he lacks the quickness to defend on the perimeter. He is not one of the better athletes in the NBA. In fact, Wolf is marginal in most respects. He has to work for everything. Wolf commits a lot of fouls and is not a threat to block your shot.

Analysis: There's something about hard-working journeymen that fans find heroic. Whenever Wolf made a bucket or snared a rebound at home last year, Magic fans would give a wolf howl. "I've had to work for every contract," Wolf admitted last year. He played well when Shaquille O'Neal was injured but was not a regular contributor.

PLAYER SUMMARY	
Will	work for his pay
Can't	crack the rotation
Expect	mop-up minutes
Don't Expect	highlight reels
Fantasy Value	$0
Card Value	5-8¢

COLLEGE STATISTICS

		G	FGP	FTP	RPG	PPG
83-84	NC	30	.481	.758	2.8	3.4
84-85	NC	30	.566	.781	5.3	9.1
85-86	NC	34	.532	.712	6.6	10.0
86-87	NC	34	.571	.793	7.1	15.2
Totals		128	.551	.765	5.5	9.6

NBA REGULAR-SEASON STATISTICS

		G	MIN	FGs FG	FGs PCT	3-PT FGs FG	3-PT FGs PCT	FTs FT	FTs PCT	Rebounds OFF	Rebounds TOT	AST	STL	BLK	PTS	PPG
87-88	LAC	42	1137	136	.407	3	.200	45	.833	51	187	98	38	16	320	7.6
88-89	LAC	66	1450	170	.423	2	.143	44	.688	83	271	113	32	16	386	5.8
89-90	LAC	77	1325	155	.395	5	.200	63	.775	63	232	62	30	24	370	4.8
90-91	DEN	74	1593	234	.451	2	.133	69	.831	136	400	107	60	31	539	7.3
91-92	DEN	67	1160	100	.361	1	.091	53	.803	97	240	61	32	14	254	3.8
92-93	BOS/POR	23	165	20	.455	0	.000	13	.813	14	48	5	7	1	53	2.3
94-95	CHA	63	583	38	.469	2	.333	12	.750	34	129	37	9	6	90	1.4
95-96	CHA/ORL	64	1065	135	.513	0	.000	21	.724	49	187	63	15	5	291	4.5
Totals		476	8478	988	.427	15	.161	312	.782	527	1694	546	223	113	2303	4.8

DAVID WOOD

Unrestricted Free Agent
Last Team: Dallas Mavericks
Position: Forward
Height: 6'9" **Weight:** 230
Birthdate: November 30, 1964

NBA Experience: 6 years
College: Skagit Valley; Nevada-Reno
Acquired: Signed as a free agent, 1/96

Background: Wood was a center at Nevada-Reno, where he transferred after beginning his career in junior college. He played two games for Chicago in 1988-89 but served most of his first three years in the CBA and Europe. Wood has never played two full years with the same team. He was with the Warriors, Suns, and Mavericks last season after one year each in Houston, Spain, San Antonio, and Detroit.

Strengths: Wood wears his hard hat to work. He plays the game with heart and helps teammates look better. He hustles, takes charges, makes sound decisions, plays defense, rebounds, and is not afraid to mix it up. He's a 3-point threat when he gets a good look at the basket.

Weaknesses: Wood lacks the physical gifts like quickness, speed, and leaping ability. He plays defense with his head, not his feet. He gives up two steps to most of his opponents and unfortunately does not make up for it with strength. Wood offers precious little on offense. He does not create his own shot or shoot well on the move, he has a slow release, and he should not be dribbling the ball.

Analysis: Wood is a coach's player for his work ethic alone. He is not completely lacking in talent. He's not a bad outside shooter, he's a smart defensive player, and he knows how to block his man off the boards. He will never score 15 PPG as he did in Spain, but he has a knack for staying employed in the NBA.

PLAYER SUMMARY	
Will	bust his tail
Can't	unpack his bags
Expect	position defense
Don't Expect	6 PPG
Fantasy Value	$0
Card Value	5-8¢

COLLEGE STATISTICS

		G	FGP	FTP	RPG	PPG
83-84	SV	29	.546	.704	7.3	9.7
84-85	SV	26	.609	.719	11.6	18.2
86-87	NR	28	.511	.662	6.0	9.0
87-88	NR	30	.472	.726	9.4	12.1
Totals		113	.538	.709	8.5	12.1

NBA REGULAR-SEASON STATISTICS

		G	MIN	FGs FG	FGs PCT	3-PT FGs FG	3-PT FGs PCT	FTs FT	FTs PCT	Rebounds OFF	Rebounds TOT	AST	STL	BLK	PTS	PPG
88-89	CHI	2	2	0	.000	0	.000	0	.000	0	0	0	0	0	0	0.0
90-91	HOU	82	1421	148	.424	28	.311	108	.812	107	246	94	58	16	432	5.3
92-93	SA	64	598	52	.444	5	.238	46	.836	38	97	34	13	12	155	2.4
93-94	DET	78	1182	119	.459	22	.449	62	.756	104	239	51	39	19	322	4.1
94-95	GS	78	1336	153	.469	31	.341	91	.778	83	241	65	28	13	428	5.5
95-96	GS/PHO/DAL	62	772	75	.431	20	.323	38	.760	51	154	34	19	10	208	3.4
Totals		366	5311	547	.447	106	.339	345	.789	383	977	278	157	70	1545	4.2

HAYWOODE WORKMAN

Team: Indiana Pacers
Position: Guard
Height: 6'3" **Weight:** 180
Birthdate: January 23, 1966
NBA Experience: 5 years

College: Winston-Salem St.; Oral Roberts
Acquired: Signed as a free agent, 8/93

Background: A three-year starter after transferring to Oral Roberts, Workman posted averages of 17.9 points and 5.2 rebounds per game for the Monarchs. A second-round choice in 1989, he played just six games with Atlanta before making the CBA All-Rookie Team. After a year in Washington and two in the Italian League, Workman has spent the last three seasons with Indiana.

Strengths: Workman is aptly named. He knows his role involves playing tough defense, and most often he does it. He can defend point guards or shooting guards equally well, and his aggressive style results in a lot of steals. Workman keeps the ball moving on offense and shoots with 3-point range.

Weaknesses: Workman is neither a top-notch playmaker nor a strong finisher. Though he has tried to be a scorer, he does not do it well enough to keep the opposition on its toes. Workman is not a good shooter. He has converted less than 40 percent from the field in each of the last two seasons—a perfectly good explanation for his decline in minutes over those same two years.

Analysis: At times during his five NBA seasons, Workman has been a productive starter. He craves such a role and works very hard to impress his coaches. Unfortunately for Workman, a point guard is asked to provide a spark on offense as well as defense. When it comes to the former, he falls short. His willingness to play relentless defense should keep him in someone's rotation.

PLAYER SUMMARY

Will	dive for loose balls
Can't	lock up a starting job
Expect	good defense
Don't Expect	a specialist
Fantasy Value	$0
Card Value	5-8¢

COLLEGE STATISTICS

		G	FGP	FTP	RPG	PPG
84-85	WSS	25	.457	.589	3.0	10.3
86-87	OR	28	.365	.796	3.3	13.8
87-88	OR	29	.415	.755	6.0	19.4
88-89	OR	28	.483	.815	6.1	19.9
Totals		110	.430	.754	4.7	16.0

NBA REGULAR-SEASON STATISTICS

		G	MIN	FGs FG	FGs PCT	3-PT FGs FG	3-PT FGs PCT	FTs FT	FTs PCT	Rebounds OFF	Rebounds TOT	AST	STL	BLK	PTS	PPG
89-90	ATL	6	16	2	.667	0	.000	2	1.000	0	3	2	3	0	6	1.0
90-91	WAS	73	2034	234	.454	12	.240	101	.759	51	242	353	87	7	581	8.0
93-94	IND	65	1714	195	.424	18	.321	93	.802	32	204	404	85	4	501	7.7
94-95	IND	69	1028	101	.375	35	.357	55	.743	21	111	194	59	5	292	4.2
95-96	IND	77	1164	101	.390	23	.324	54	.740	27	124	213	65	4	279	3.6
Totals		290	5956	633	.420	88	.320	305	.766	131	684	1166	299	20	1659	5.7

SHARONE WRIGHT

Team: Toronto Raptors
Position: Forward/Center
Height: 6'11" **Weight:** 260
Birthdate: January 30, 1973
NBA Experience: 2 years

College: Clemson
Acquired: Traded from 76ers for Tony Massenburg, Ed Pinckney, and future considerations, 2/96

Background: Wright attended the same Southwest High School in Macon, Georgia, that produced Norm Nixon and Jeff Malone. Wright averaged a double-double in his last two seasons at Clemson and was among the nation's top shot-blockers as a sophomore. The 76ers drafted him sixth in 1994. He was a second-team All-Rookie pick with Philadelphia but was traded to Toronto last season.

Strengths: Wright has a strong body, and he is not afraid to use it against opponents. He can handle the center and power forward positions, and he works for his points inside. He is also driven to be a top rebounder, though he has a ways to go. Wright knows how to get to the free-throw line, he provides a physical presence in the middle, and he will swat his share of shots.

Weaknesses: Wright has work to do on both ends of the floor. He relies on power for his points. A polished low-post scorer he is not. You don't want him taking face-up jumpers, and his free-throw shooting is substandard. He has no clue about spotting open teammates, either. Wright does not have the quickness to be a stopper, but he needs to do a better job denying his man position.

Analysis: The 76ers probably gave up too early on Wright. No one would be too surprised to see him develop into a quality rebounder and inside scorer. He has averaged better than 11 PPG in each of his two seasons, and he improved to 16.5 PPG in 11 outings with Toronto before back spasms got the best of him. If Wright reports to camp in great shape, there's no reason 1996-97 can't be his breakthrough season.

PLAYER SUMMARY	
Will	get on the glass
Can't	pass the ball
Expect	a block per game
Don't Expect	great defense
Fantasy Value	$6-8
Card Value	10-15¢

COLLEGE STATISTICS

		G	FGP	FTP	RPG	PPG
91-92	CLEM	28	.498	.563	8.1	12.0
92-93	CLEM	30	.567	.669	10.5	15.0
93-94	CLEM	34	.525	.644	10.6	15.4
Totals		92	.531	.632	9.8	14.2

NBA REGULAR-SEASON STATISTICS

			FGs		3-PT FGs		FTs		Rebounds						
	G	MIN	FG	PCT	FG	PCT	FT	PCT	OFF	TOT	AST	STL	BLK	PTS	PPG
94-95 PHI	79	2044	361	.465	0	.000	182	.645	191	472	48	37	104	904	11.4
95-96 PHI/TOR	57	1434	248	.484	1	.333	167	.645	148	356	38	30	49	664	11.6
Totals	136	3478	609	.473	1	.091	349	.645	339	828	86	67	153	1568	11.5

GEORGE ZIDEK

Team: Charlotte Hornets
Position: Center
Height: 7'0" **Weight:** 272
Birthdate: August 2, 1973

NBA Experience: 1 year
College: UCLA
Acquired: First-round pick in 1995 draft (22nd overall)

Background: Zidek played with the Czech junior national team for three years, averaging 20 points and ten rebounds, before coming to UCLA. After averaging just 1.1 PPG as a freshman, he became a junior starter and helped the Bruins to the 1995 national title in his senior season. His work in the NCAA tournament helped make him a first-round draft choice of Charlotte. Zidek started 21 of 71 games for the Hornets in 1995-96.

Strengths: Though he struggled with it during his rookie season, Zidek does have a trusty, sweeping hook shot that he can make with either hand. He is a huge man who eats up space in both lanes and knows how to seal his man off the boards. His bulk also makes him a potential defensive specialist. He held NBA classmate Corliss Williamson to 12 points and four rebounds in the 1995 NCAA title game.

Weaknesses: Zidek is no athlete. He's slow afoot and will never make an impact with a running team. His lumbering style also hurts him on the defensive end, where foul trouble will be a big problem if he manages to gain more minutes. You won't find too many seven-footers who block fewer shots than the lead-footed Zidek. And passing? Not a chance. Zidek puts it up after the catch. He has no capacity to dribble.

Analysis: The son of the man considered Czechoslovakia's best player ever (Jiri Zidek, who was an assistant coach with the Czech national team), George had the modest rookie season he was expected to have. Although he had his moments, like his season-high 21 points in his second game, his biggest distinction so far is being the only first-round choice in NBA history whose last name starts with "Z."

PLAYER SUMMARY

Will	take up space
Can't	block shots
Expect	sweeping hooks
Don't Expect	quickness
Fantasy Value	$0
Card Value	15-30¢

COLLEGE STATISTICS

		G	FGP	FTP	RPG	PPG
91-92	UCLA	17	.381	.500	1.1	1.1
92-93	UCLA	26	.423	.760	1.7	2.4
93-94	UCLA	28	.517	.763	7.0	11.1
94-95	UCLA	33	.553	.731	5.4	10.6
Totals		104	.520	.744	4.2	7.1

NBA REGULAR-SEASON STATISTICS

			FGs		3-PT FGs		FTs		Rebounds						
	G	MIN	FG	PCT	FG	PCT	FT	PCT	OFF	TOT	AST	STL	BLK	PTS	PPG
95-96 CHA	71	888	105	.423	0	.000	71	.763	69	183	16	9	7	281	4.0
Totals	71	888	105	.423	0	.000	71	.763	69	183	16	9	7	281	4.0

1996 NBA Draft

	Player	College	Team
1)	Allen Iverson	Georgetown	Philadelphia
2)	Marcus Camby	Massachusetts	Toronto
3)	Shareef Abdul-Rahim	California	Vancouver
4)	Stephon Marbury	Georgia Tech	Milwaukee
5)	Ray Allen	Connecticut	Minnesota
6)	Antoine Walker	Kentucky	Boston
7)	Lorenzen Wright	Memphis	L.A. Clippers
8)	Kerry Kittles	Villanova	New Jersey
9)	Samaki Walker	Louisville	Dallas
10)	Erick Dampier	Mississippi State	Indiana
11)	Todd Fuller	North Carolina	Golden State
12)	Vitaly Potapenko	Wright State	Cleveland
13)	Kobe Bryant	(Lower Merion HS)	Charlotte
14)	Predrag Stojakovic	(Greece)	Sacramento
15)	Steve Nash	Santa Clara	Phoenix
16)	Tony Delk	Kentucky	Charlotte
17)	Jermaine O'Neal	(Eau Claire HS)	Portland
18)	John Wallace	Syracuse	New York
19)	Zydrunas Ilgauskas	(Lithuania)	Cleveland
20)	Dontae Jones	Mississippi State	New York
21)	Roy Rogers	Alabama	Phoenix
22)	George Zidek	UCLA	Vancouver
23)	Efthimios Rentzias	(Greece)	Denver
24)	Derek Fisher	Arkansas-Little Rock	L.A. Lakers
25)	Martin Muursepp	(Estonia)	Utah
26)	Jerome Williams	Georgetown	Detroit
27)	Brian Evans	Indiana	Orlando
28)	Priest Lauderdale	(Greece)	Atlanta
29)	Travis Knight	Connecticut	Chicago

	Player	College	Team
30)	Othella Harrington	Georgetown	Houston
31)	Mark Hendrickson	Washington State	Philadelphia
32)	Ryan Minor	Oklahoma	Philadelphia
33)	Moochie Norris	West Florida	Milwaukee
34)	Shawn Harvey	West Virginia State	Dallas
35)	Joseph Blair	Arizona	Seattle
36)	Doron Sheffer	Connecticut	L.A. Clippers
37)	Jeff McInnis	North Carolina	Denver
38)	Steve Hamer	Tennessee	Boston
39)	Russ Millard	Iowa	Phoenix
40)	Marcus Mann	Mississippi Valley State	Golden State
41)	Jason Sasser	Texas Tech	Golden State
42)	Randy Livingston	Louisiana State	Houston
43)	Ben Davis	Arizona	Phoenix
44)	Malik Rose	Drexel	Charlotte
45)	Joe Vogel	Colorado State	Seattle
46)	Marcus Brown	Murray State	Portland
47)	Ron Riley	Arizona State	Seattle
48)	Jamie Feick	Michigan	Philadelphia
49)	Amal McCaskill	Marquette	Orlando
50)	Terrell Bell	Georgia	Houston
51)	Chris Robinson	Western Kentucky	Vancouver
52)	Mark Pope	Kentucky	Indiana
53)	Jeff Norgaard	Wisconsin-Green Bay	Milwaukee
54)	Shandon Anderson	Georgia	Utah
55)	Ronnie Henderson	Louisiana State	Washington
56)	Reggie Geary	Arizona	Cleveland
57)	Drew Barry	Georgia Tech	Seattle
58)	Darnell Robinson	Arkansas	Dallas

SHAREEF ABDUR-RAHIM

Team: Vancouver Grizzlies
Position: Forward
Height: 6'10" **Weight:** 220
Birthdate: December 11, 1976
College: California
Acquired: First-round pick in 1996 draft (third overall)

PLAYER SUMMARY	
Will	play right away
Can't	bang with power forwards
Expect	a future All-Star
Don't Expect	much bench time
Fantasy $8-10	Card ...$3.00-6.00

Background: Abdur-Rahim was the Pac-10's leading scorer and the first freshman to be named Pac-10 Player of the Year. That the Marietta, Georgia, native chose California was a surprise, since he had been ticketed to join Stephon Marbury at Georgia Tech. Abdur-Rahim entered the draft after his freshman season.

Strengths: Capable at either small forward or power forward, Abdur-Rahim is comfortable facing the basket and running the court. He has excellent shooting range and a variety of moves in the low post. He said that he considers himself a point guard in a power forward's body.

Weaknesses: Lack of experience and a tendency to coast through games are Abdur-Rahim's only noticeable weaknesses. A finalizer, he had only 29 assists in 28 games last season.

Analysis: Abdur-Rahim agonized over his decision to leave school, then became the highest-drafted freshman ever. He figures to start his NBA career at power forward, perhaps moving to small forward in a few years if he improves his ball-handling. Scouts say he will have an easy adjustment to the NBA.

COLLEGE STATISTICS

	G	FGP	FTP	RPG	APG	PPG
95-96 CAL	28	.518	.683	8.4	1.0	21.1
Totals	28	.518	.683	8.4	1.0	21.1

RAY ALLEN

Team: Milwaukee Bucks
Position: Guard
Height: 6'5" **Weight:** 205
Birthdate: July 20, 1975
College: Connecticut
Acquired: Draft rights traded from Timberwolves with a future first-round pick for draft rights to Stephon Marbury, 6/96

PLAYER SUMMARY	
Will	fill it up from deep
Can't	miss as a pro
Expect	a rookie starter
Don't Expect	a power player
Fantasy $8-10	Card ...$1.25-2.50

Background: Allen was named Big East Player of the Year and UPI national Player of the Year in 1996. The fifth pick in the 1996 draft, Allen helped the Huskies into the Sweet 16 of the NCAA Tourney in each of his three seasons, and last season he made a school-record 115 3-pointers.

Strengths: Perhaps the best offensive player in the draft, Allen can score inside and out. He has good shooting range and is adept at slicing into the heart of the defense and drawing fouls. He's sensational in the open court. He is above average defensively and on the boards.

Weaknesses: Some scouts knock Allen's ball-handling, while others insist it is more than adequate. He also was criticized for never leading Connecticut to the Final Four.

Analysis: Like many players before him, Allen has been touted as the next Michael Jordan. He won't be that good, though he does shoot as well as Jordan did when he entered the NBA. Don't be surprised if, five years from now, Allen is considered the best player from the class of 1996.

COLLEGE STATISTICS

	G	FGP	FTP	RPG	APG	PPG
93-94 CONN	34	.510	.792	4.6	1.6	12.6
94-95 CONN	32	.489	.727	6.8	2.3	21.1
95-96 CONN	35	.472	.810	6.5	3.3	23.4
Totals	101	.490	.779	6.0	2.4	19.0

SHANDON ANDERSON

Team: Utah Jazz
Position: Forward/Guard
Height: 6'6" **Weight:** 205
Birthdate: December 31, 1973
College: Georgia
Acquired: Second-round pick in 1996 draft (54th overall)

PLAYER SUMMARY	
Will.............................hit the boards
Can't............................stick the trey
Expect ....a struggle to stick
Don't Expect......a finished product
Fantasy ....$0   Card ......10-20¢

Background: A wing player at Georgia, Anderson is the only player in school history to amass 1,500 points, 500 rebounds, and 300 assists. He tied for the SEC lead in steals (2.2 per game) in 1995-96. His brother, Willie Anderson, played with the New York Knicks last season.

Strengths: A superb athlete, Anderson displays good quickness, strength, leaping ability, and speed. He excels on the fastbreak and is good at slashing to the basket in the halfcourt. He defends aggressively.

Weaknesses: Anderson needs to fine-tune his jump shot, expand his range, and improve his ball-handling in order to make the jump to the pros.

Analysis: Anderson was invited to the Portsmouth Invitational and the Desert Classic and played well at both. Some scouts thought he would go higher in the draft, so Utah may have acquired a sleeper. Anderson is a better athlete than his brother, but not as good a ball-handler or jump-shooter. The Jazz don't have much room on their roster, but Anderson could surprise.

COLLEGE STATISTICS

	G	FGP	FTP	RPG	APG	PPG
92-93 GEOR	29	.493	.610	3.6	1.5	9.3
93-94 GEOR	30	.485	.660	5.6	3.8	13.8
94-95 GEOR	28	.473	.621	5.2	3.0	13.3
95-96 GEOR	31	.538	.657	5.5	2.7	14.9
Totals	118	.498	.640	5.0	2.7	12.9

DREW BARRY

Team: Seattle SuperSonics
Position: Guard
Height: 6'5" **Weight:** 191
Birthdate: February 17, 1973
College: Georgia Tech
Acquired: Second-round pick in 1996 draft (57th overall)

PLAYER SUMMARY	
Will......................................give it up
Can't.............................bang inside
Expect....................no-look passes
Don't Expect ....to see him soon
Fantasy ....$0   Card ......15-25¢

Background: One of the nation's top playmakers at Georgia Tech, Barry ranks eighth in ACC history with 724 assists (all accumulated while playing alongside NBA-caliber point guards Travis Best and Stephon Marbury). Barry ranks third on Tech's career list for 3-pointers (179) and fourth in steals (193).

Strengths: Barry has a good feel for the game and a good attitude. He has above-average shooting skills, 3-point range, and a sure stroke from the foul line. He passes the ball selflessly and is also quick defensively.

Weaknesses: Though listed at 6'5" and 191 pounds, Barry lacks the size to flourish at shooting guard in the NBA. He needs to upgrade his ball-handling and decrease his turnovers.

Analysis: Barry dropped in the draft after playing poorly at the Chicago camp, but he had a good senior year and could mature into a competent guard in the NBA, probably as a reserve who's capable of playing point or shooting guard. Seattle is not likely to have room for him on its roster in 1996-97.

COLLEGE STATISTICS

	G	FGP	FTP	RPG	APG	PPG
92-93 GT	30	.468	.805	3.4	5.5	7.3
93-94 GT	24	.421	.776	3.4	5.9	8.1
94-95 GT	27	.513	.753	4.9	6.7	13.4
95-96 GT	36	.406	.789	4.6	6.6	13.3
Totals	117	.447	.778	4.1	6.2	10.5

TERRELL BELL

Team: Houston Rockets
Position: Center
Height: 6'10" **Weight:** 240
Birthdate: December 15, 1973
College: Georgia
Acquired: Second-round pick in 1996 draft (50th overall)

PLAYER SUMMARY	
Will	swat shots
Can't	make shots
Expect	a string bean
Don't Expect	great statistics
Fantasy	$0 Card.....10-15¢

Background: Bell played a limited role at Georgia, coming to the school with raw skills after averaging just 14 points a game as a senior in high school. He started only two games in his first three college seasons, then ranked 19th nationally in blocked shots (2.7 per game) as a senior.

Strengths: Bell has only one NBA-level skill: shot-blocking. Scouts like the fact that he's still improving.

Weaknesses: Bell's skills leave a lot to be desired. His best shot is a dunk, and he's inept at passing and ball-handling. He never produced significant numbers in college, and he's a lousy free-throw shooter. He needs to bulk up and add muscle to compete against NBA big men.

Analysis: Bell will get a long look in training camp because pro teams like shot-blocking specialists. The Rockets may want to take a look at him for a year to see how much he improves. However, it would be a surprise if he played more than token minutes in 1996-97.

COLLEGE STATISTICS

	G	FGP	FTP	RPG	APG	PPG
92-93 GEOR	16	.467	.583	1.3	0.0	1.3
93-94 GEOR	27	.535	.429	3.8	0.1	3.5
94-95 GEOR	28	.520	.581	3.2	0.3	3.7
95-96 GEOR	31	.500	.587	6.3	0.7	6.3
Totals	102	.512	.550	4.0	0.3	4.1

JOSEPH BLAIR

Team: Seattle SuperSonics
Position: Forward
Height: 6'10" **Weight:** 251
Birthdate: June 12, 1974
College: Arizona
Acquired: Second-round pick in 1996 draft (35th overall)

PLAYER SUMMARY	
Will	push and shove
Can't	shoot free throws
Expect	an ordinary Joe
Don't Expect	a roster spot
Fantasy	$0 Card.....10-20¢

Background: Blair never was a go-to player at Arizona, averaging just over ten points a game in his career, but he is the school's all-time leader in field-goal percentage. He was limited to 14 games in his senior season because of an academic suspension. He improved his draft position by shedding 20 pounds and playing well at the pre-draft Desert Classic.

Strengths: Blair is a strong low-post player with a variety of power moves and a good hook shot. He gets his share of rebounds and plays with enthusiasm. He's willing to fit in and accept a limited role.

Weaknesses: Other than his moves around the basket, Blair is a poor offensive player, limited in his ability to handle the ball, pass it, or shoot it from more than ten feet away. He's a terrible free-throw shooter.

Analysis: It's doubtful Blair will find work in the NBA anytime soon. He isn't a good enough rebounder or defender, and his all-around game needs a lot of work. He also had the misfortune to be drafted by Seattle, a team that is loaded with frontcourt talent.

COLLEGE STATISTICS

	G	FGP	FTP	RPG	APG	PPG
92-93 ARIZ	28	.652	.596	3.8	0.4	7.1
93-94 ARIZ	34	.607	.435	7.2	0.6	10.1
94-95 ARIZ	28	.559	.465	7.0	0.9	12.0
95-96 ARIZ	14	.690	.400	8.9	2.1	14.7
Totals	104	.612	.462	6.5	0.8	10.4

MARCUS BROWN

Team: Portland Trail Blazers
Position: Guard
Height: 6'3" **Weight:** 185
Birthdate: April 3, 1974
College: Murray St.
Acquired: Second-round pick in 1996 draft (46th overall)

PLAYER SUMMARY	
Will	drill jumpers
Can't	run a team
Expect	a thoroughbred
Don't Expect	anything now
Fantasy	$0 Card	10-15¢

Background: Brown saw considerable action as a freshman at Murray State but wasn't one of the Racers' offensive mainstays. That changed the next three seasons, culminating with his ranking as the nation's No. 2 scorer in 1995-96. He was voted Ohio Valley Conference Player of the Year the past two seasons.

Strengths: An excellent athlete, Brown played shooting guard and small forward in college and looks to have the quickness to play point guard in the NBA. He shows steady aim on his jump shot, makes his free throws, and has 3-point range.

Weaknesses: While Brown has the tools to play the point, he hasn't demonstrated the playmaking acumen for the job.

Analysis: Brown could be one of the surprises of the draft. He fits in with the Portland Trail Blazers athletically and, if he can adjust to playing the point, he could hang around for awhile. It is more likely that he'll have to play in basketball's "minor leagues" for a year or two before taking his best shot at the NBA.

COLLEGE STATISTICS

		G	FGP	FTP	RPG	APG	PPG
92-93	MSU	30	.488	.789	2.8	1.1	2.8
93-94	MSU	29	.503	.839	3.8	2.7	18.1
94-95	MSU	30	.510	.896	4.9	2.1	22.4
95-96	MSU	29	.474	.841	4.8	4.1	26.4
Totals		118	.493	.849	4.1	2.5	18.9

KOBE BRYANT

Team: Los Angeles Lakers
Position: Guard
Height: 6'6" **Weight:** 200
Birthdate: August 23, 1978
College: None
Acquired: Draft rights traded from Hornets for Vlade Divac, 7/96

PLAYER SUMMARY	
Will	drive and dunk
Can't	start immediately
Expect	a cocky kid
Don't Expect	consistency
Fantasy	$0 Card	$2.00-4.00

Background: Kobe Bryant was widely hailed as the national prep Player of the Year in 1996. A year after Kevin Garnett went directly from high school to the NBA, Bryant followed in his footsteps. Just months after graduating from Lower Merion High School in Pennsylvania, Bryant, just 17 years old, was drafted 13th overall. His father, Joe "Jelly Bean" Bryant, played eight NBA seasons for the 76ers, Clippers, and Rockets.

Strengths: A quick, explosive athlete, Bryant is a good driver and finisher. He plays the game with a lot of enthusiasm. He has the skills to play shooting guard or move to the frontcourt against some of the less physical small forwards.

Weaknesses: Because he lacks experience against good players, Bryant will have a lot of work to do defensively. His shooting stroke isn't as good as it needs to be for him to excel as an NBA shooting guard.

Analysis: Bryant isn't ready to play in the NBA, but he has great potential. The Lakers have good players ahead of him, giving them the luxury of bringing him along slowly, and Lakers coach Del Harris is considered one of the best teachers in the league.

COLLEGE STATISTICS

—DID NOT PLAY—

DANTE CALABRIA

Team: Unsigned
Position: Guard
Height: 6'5" **Weight:** 198
Birthdate: November 8, 1973
College: North Carolina

PLAYER SUMMARY	
Will	bang the trey
Can't	scrape the rafters
Expect	steadiness
Don't Expect	anything soon
Fantasy	$0 Card ...... 10-15¢

Background: Calabria climbed steadily up the ladder at North Carolina, increasing his scoring average each season. He ranked fourth nationally in 3-point field-goal percentage as a junior (.496) while starting on a front line that also included current pros Jerry Stackhouse and Rasheed Wallace.

Strengths: A terrific shooter with 3-point range, Calabria can hurt opponents by spotting up for open jump shots. He's a careful ball-handler with a good assist-to-turnover ratio.

Weaknesses: While a steady player, Calabria lacks the all-around skills to make an impact in the NBA. He's not a particularly good athlete, with a vertical jump of less than 24 inches. He's a good free-throw shooter but doesn't penetrate well enough to draw a lot of fouls.

Analysis: Calabria was considered a marginal NBA prospect, capable of making a team as an off-the-bench shooting specialist. He wasn't drafted but will get a look in training camp unless he opts to play overseas. His college coach, Dean Smith, has a lot of friends in the NBA.

COLLEGE STATISTICS

		G	FGP	FTP	RPG	APG	PPG
92-93	NC	35	.462	.778	0.8	0.8	1.8
93-94	NC	35	.431	.724	2.9	2.4	8.1
94-95	NC	33	.506	.719	4.8	2.7	10.5
95-96	NC	32	.425	.709	4.3	4.2	12.7
Totals		135	.452	.719	3.2	2.5	8.1

MARCUS CAMBY

Team: Toronto Raptors
Position: Forward
Height: 6'11" **Weight:** 220
Birthdate: March 22, 1974
College: Massachusetts
Acquired: First-round pick in 1996 draft (second overall)

PLAYER SUMMARY	
Will	make an impact
Can't	muscle underneath
Expect	a good work ethic
Don't Expect	a bust
Fantasy	..$13-16 Card ...$2.00-4.00

Background: Steady improvement in three seasons at Massachusetts culminated with Camby's selection as the consensus national Player of the Year in 1995-96. He led the Minutemen to their first-ever appearance in the Final Four, ranked seventh nationally in blocked shots, and became just the fourth college player to surpass 300 career blocks.

Strengths: Quickness and timing make Camby an excellent shot-blocker. He has developed into a good shooter facing the basket and is a vastly improved free-throw shooter. He runs the floor easily.

Weaknesses: Considered a "tweener" by some, Camby lacks the bulk to excel at power forward in the NBA, and he needs to upgrade his ball-handling to make an impact at small forward. A fainting episode during his junior season is cause for some concern.

Analysis: Going to an expansion team will make it easier for Camby to put up good numbers his rookie season. Look for him to play at least 25 minutes a night and average close to 15 points a game while suffering growing pains at the hands of bigger, stronger NBA power forwards.

COLLEGE STATISTICS

		G	FGP	FTP	RPG	APG	PPG
93-94	MASS	29	.494	.596	6.4	1.2	10.2
94-95	MASS	30	.550	.643	6.2	1.2	13.9
95-96	MASS	33	.477	.700	8.2	1.8	20.5
Totals		92	.501	.661	7.0	1.4	15.1

ERICK DAMPIER

Team: Indiana Pacers
Position: Center
Height: 6'11" **Weight:** 265
Birthdate: July 14, 1974
College: Mississippi St.
Acquired: First-round pick in 1996 draft (tenth overall)

PLAYER SUMMARY	
Will	swat shots
Can't	make his free throws
Expect	a resolute worker
Don't Expect	3-pointers
Fantasy	$0 Card 20-35¢

Background: Dampier entered the NBA draft after his junior season at Mississippi State. He helped lead the Bulldogs to a composite record of 66-27 and three consecutive postseason appearances, culminating in a trip to the Final Four in 1996. He had 33 career double-doubles.

Strengths: An imposing physical presence, Dampier was the best true center in the draft. Defense is his strong suit. He blocks shots, moves people out from under the boards, and clogs the middle effectively. Most of his points result from hard work and tenacity. He runs the court well.

Weaknesses: Dampier's offensive game needs a lot of work. He lacks a go-to move in the low post, and his jump shot is inconsistent. He made barely half of his free-throw attempts during his college career.

Analysis: Dampier was the first center selected, and one of seven centers who went in the first round of the draft. He should be a starter eventually, but not in the next couple of years. (Indiana has Rik Smits.) His size and defensive acumen should guarantee Dampier a long NBA career.

COLLEGE STATISTICS

		G	FGP	FTP	RPG	APG	PPG
93-94	MSU	29	.589	.491	8.7	0.8	11.9
94-95	MSU	30	.640	.596	9.7	0.9	13.1
95-96	MSU	34	.551	.612	9.3	2.3	14.5
Totals		93	.587	.566	9.2	1.4	13.2

BEN DAVIS

Team: Phoenix Suns
Position: Forward
Height: 6'9" **Weight:** 240
Birthdate: December 26, 1972
College: Kansas; Hutchinson; Arizona
Acquired: Second-round pick in 1996 draft (43rd overall)

PLAYER SUMMARY	
Will	move the pile
Can't	pile up points
Expect	a quick exit
Don't Expect	anything now
Fantasy	$0 Card 10-20¢

Background: Davis had a checkered college career. He played one season at Kansas, finishing as the Jayhawks' second-leading rebounder, sat out the 1992-93 season as a transfer to Florida, was diverted to a junior college for one year, then landed at Arizona for two seasons. As a senior, he led the Pac-10 in rebounding (9.5 RPG) and double-doubles (17).

Strengths: Rebounding is Davis's greatest strength. He is strong enough to maintain position inside and has a nose for the ball.

Weaknesses: He measured a shade under 6'7" at the Chicago pre-draft camp, which won't cut it at power forward in the NBA. His perimeter game is raw, and he's a lousy passer. Scouts worry that Davis lacks discipline off the court.

Analysis: Davis has no chance to make it in the NBA anytime soon. He carries too much baggage, and his game isn't good enough. The Phoenix Suns know him as well as anybody, having seen most of his college games. Odds are, he will play in the CBA or overseas in 1996-97.

COLLEGE STATISTICS

		G	FGP	FTP	RPG	APG	PPG
91-92	KANS	32	.474	.522	4.5	0.5	6.6
93-94	HUTC	39	.587	.693	12.1	1.4	19.9
94-95	ARIZ	21	.538	.633	5.9	0.4	9.9
95-96	ARIZ	33	.546	.690	9.5	0.7	14.2
Totals		125	.553	.659	8.4	0.8	12.1

TONY DELK

Team: Charlotte Hornets
Position: Guard
Height: 6'1" **Weight:** 193
Birthdate: January 28, 1974
College: Kentucky
Acquired: First-round pick in 1996 draft
(16th overall)

PLAYER SUMMARY	
Will	stop and pop
Can't	run a team
Expect	a winner
Don't Expect	a starting role now
Fantasy	$0 Card ......15-25¢

Background: Delk had a marvelous career at Kentucky, finishing as the highest-scoring guard in school history and capping his run with MVP honors at the Final Four. He scored 20 points in the semifinals against Massachusetts, then had 24 points and seven rebounds in the championship game.

Strengths: Delk is a dead-eye shooter and a determined competitor who relishes pressure and taking the big shot. He has a strong, compact body and is durable.

Weaknesses: Experiments with Delk at point guard never worked at Kentucky, and he's too small to excel at shooting guard in the NBA. He doesn't handle the ball well, and he's more comfortable finishing plays than starting them.

Analysis: Charlotte drafted Delk and may try him at point guard, a position depleted by the loss of free-agent Kenny Anderson and injuries to Muggsy Bogues. Ideally, Delk would be a third guard, coming off the bench to ignite rallies with his jump shot. It's doubtful he'll make a big impact in 1996-97.

COLLEGE STATISTICS

	G	FGP	FTP	RPG	APG	PPG
92-93 KENT	30	.452	.727	1.9	0.7	4.6
93-94 KENT	34	.455	.639	4.5	1.7	16.6
94-95 KENT	33	.478	.674	3.3	2.0	16.7
95-96 KENT	36	.494	.800	4.2	1.8	17.8
Totals	133	.474	.709	3.5	1.6	14.2

BRIAN EVANS

Team: Orlando Magic
Position: Guard/Forward
Height: 6'8" **Weight:** 220
Birthdate: September 13, 1973
College: Indiana
Acquired: First-round pick in 1996 draft
(27th overall)

PLAYER SUMMARY	
Will	convert from downtown
Can't	muscle in the paint
Expect	a shooting specialist
Don't Expect	a starting role
Fantasy	$0 Card ......10-20¢

Background: As a senior at Indiana, Evans became the first Hoosier under coach Bob Knight to lead the Big Ten in scoring. He also led IU in rebounding, was second in assists, and was named Big Ten Player of the Year. He spent five years at Indiana, sitting out the 1991-92 season as a redshirt.

Strengths: One of the best shooters in the draft, Evans has great touch, impressive range, and good size. He can hurt teams with 3-pointers. He's a team-oriented player who has a good feel for the game and works hard defensively.

Weaknesses: Evans lacks the athletic skills of most NBA players and isn't particularly physical. Not especially good with his dribble, he needs help to get his shot off. His lack of aggressiveness can hurt him.

Analysis: Orlando could employ Evans as an off-the-bench sharp-shooter. He's not a good enough athlete to play guard in the NBA, but he's not strong or tough enough to play a starter's minutes at forward, either. He figures to be a reserve for the balance of his career.

COLLEGE STATISTICS

	G	FGP	FTP	RPG	APG	PPG
92-93 IND	35	.425	.685	3.9	1.3	5.3
93-94 IND	27	.448	.793	6.8	2.2	11.9
94-95 IND	31	.462	.783	6.7	3.3	17.4
95-96 IND	31	.447	.847	7.1	4.1	21.2
Totals	124	.449	.800	6.0	2.7	13.7

JAMIE FEICK

Team: Philadelphia 76ers
Position: Forward/Center
Height: 6′9″ **Weight:** 255
Birthdate: July 3, 1974
College: Michigan St.
Acquired: Second-round pick in 1996 draft (48th overall)

PLAYER SUMMARY	
Will	mix it up
Can't	fill it up
Expect	a Big Ten brawler
Don't Expect	a pro
Fantasy	$0 Card ..... 10-20¢

Background: Feick was a reserve his first two seasons at Michigan State before moving into the starting lineup as a junior. He ranked third in the Big Ten in rebounding that season, then led the conference in rebounding in 1995-96. He helped his draft status when he averaged 11 points and 16 rebounds at the Portsmouth Invitational.

Strengths: The prototypical banger, Feick is big, strong, and tough. He can hit the jumper if left alone, and he works hard for position in the low post. He has a good sense for the game and is a good passer. He was well coached at Michigan State, one of the leading producers of pro players in recent years.

Weaknesses: Feick needs a cushion to get his shot off and doesn't really have NBA-level skills. He lays bricks from the foul line.

Analysis: Drafted by Philadelphia, a team in the midst of a complete makeover, Feick didn't look good in the New York summer league and will be hard-pressed to make the team. A center in college, he will have to make the move to power forward. He looks like a long shot.

COLLEGE STATISTICS

		G	FGP	FTP	RPG	APG	PPG
92-93	MSU	14	.133	.250	1.4	0.1	0.4
93-94	MSU	32	.551	.488	3.3	0.7	3.0
94-95	MSU	28	.617	.581	10.0	1.0	9.9
95-96	MSU	32	.433	.617	9.5	2.3	10.1
Totals		106	.502	.577	6.7	1.2	6.6

DEREK FISHER

Team: Los Angeles Lakers
Position: Guard
Height: 6′1″ **Weight:** 200
Birthdate: August 9, 1974
College: Arkansas-Little Rock
Acquired: First-round pick in 1996 draft (24th overall)

PLAYER SUMMARY	
Will	draw and dish
Can't	shoot a high pct.
Expect	a dogged defender
Don't Expect	a rookie starter
Fantasy	$0 Card ...... 15-25¢

Background: Fisher attended prep powerhouse Parkview High School in Little Rock, Arkansas, then stayed in his hometown for college. He increased his rebounding and assist production in each of his four seasons at Arkansas-Little Rock and ranks second in school history in points, assists, and steals. He was named the Sun Belt Conference Player of the Year for 1995-96.

Strengths: Fisher is a well-built—albeit undersized—point guard who does a good job running the offense and creating scoring opportunities by penetrating and passing. He plays stout defense and rebounds well.

Weaknesses: While Fisher has no glaring weaknesses, he has no overwhelming strengths, either. He's just solid across the board. He's not as quick as the NBA's top point guards.

Analysis: With Magic Johnson and Sedale Threatt both gone, the Lakers moved to secure a backup point guard. Lakers GM Jerry West has a good track record with unheralded players. Fisher figures to make the team.

COLLEGE STATISTICS

		G	FGP	FTP	RPG	APG	PPG
92-93	ALR	27	.413	.772	3.3	3.4	7.2
93-94	ALR	28	.443	.774	3.9	3.6	10.1
94-95	ALR	27	.401	.722	5.0	4.6	17.7
95-96	ALR	30	.409	.744	5.2	5.1	14.6
Totals		112	.412	.747	4.4	4.2	12.4

TODD FULLER

Team: Golden State Warriors
Position: Center
Height: 6'11" **Weight:** 255
Birthdate: July 25, 1974
College: North Carolina St.
Acquired: First-round pick in 1996 draft
(11th overall)

```
              PLAYER SUMMARY
Will ...........................face and score
Can't .................contain the giants
Expect ...............an eventual starter
Don't Expect .............a lot of sizzle
Fantasy ............$1   Card ......25-50¢
```

Background: Fuller advanced steadily in his four years at North Carolina State, increasing his scoring each season and finally making first-team all-conference as a senior, when he led the ACC in scoring and was second in rebounding. Perhaps the smartest player in the draft, he had a 3.97 GPA.

Strengths: A workhorse and a strong offensive rebounder, Fuller averaged nearly 34 minutes and 3.5 offensive boards per game last season. He has a soft touch from 15 feet and in and shows steady aim from the foul line. He's a good low-post defender who doesn't shy from contact.

Weaknesses: While some scouts project Fuller as a center, others say he's not quite big enough for the job. He needs to improve his ball-handling and his defensive skills away from the basket.

Analysis: Fuller should become a solid NBA player, perhaps moving to power forward later in his career. Well-coached in college and in high school (by former NBA great Bobby Jones), Fuller should adapt quickly to the pro ranks.

COLLEGE STATISTICS

	G	FGP	FTP	RPG	APG	PPG
92-93 NCST	27	.457	.773	3.6	0.2	5.2
93-94 NCST	30	.488	.753	8.4	1.1	11.8
94-95 NCST	27	.519	.841	8.5	1.3	16.3
95-96 NCST	31	.506	.799	9.9	1.3	20.9
Totals	115	.498	.800	7.7	1.0	13.8

REGGIE GEARY

Team: Cleveland Cavaliers
Position: Guard
Height: 6'2" **Weight:** 187
Birthdate: August 31, 1973
College: Arizona
Acquired: Second-round pick in 1996
draft (56th overall)

```
              PLAYER SUMMARY
Will ...........................get in your face
Can't ...............................hit his shot
Expect ...........................floor burns
Don't Expect ...............lack of effort
Fantasy ............$0   Card ......10-20¢
```

Background: One of the nation's top defensive players in his four years at Arizona, Geary played alongside current NBA guards Damon Stoudamire and Khalid Reeves. He finished his career as the Wildcats' all-time steals leader. Geary stands third on Arizona's all-time assists list.

Strengths: Geary has a knack for getting big rebounds and key steals. He competes fiercely. He shows excellent quickness on defense and is capable of shutting down most opponents. His free-throw shooting improved greatly last season.

Weaknesses: His shooting needs a lot of work, although there's nothing wrong with his shot mechanically. That's his only significant weakness.

Analysis: Geary was named to the All-Tournament team at the pre-draft Desert Classic but slipped to the bottom of the second round. He was drafted by Cleveland but would be a better fit on a faster-paced team. His toughness and quickness could land him a spot on the roster but not a lot of playing time in 1996-97.

COLLEGE STATISTICS

	G	FGP	FTP	RPG	APG	PPG
92-93 ARIZ	28	.423	.458	1.9	3.4	4.2
93-94 ARIZ	35	.450	.600	3.7	3.5	7.4
94-95 ARIZ	31	.413	.432	3.1	3.6	6.2
95-96 ARIZ	33	.432	.733	3.6	7.0	9.8
Totals	127	.432	.589	3.1	4.4	7.0

ERIC GINGOLD
Team: Toronto Raptors
Position: Center
Height: 7'4" **Weight:** 295
Birthdate: December 26, 1973
College: Williams
Acquired: Signed as free agent, 7/96

```
            PLAYER SUMMARY
Will..............................score
Can't........................run and jump
Expect.......................a big project
Don't Expect...........big production
Fantasy ...........$0  Card .......7-10¢
```

Background: Gingold enrolled at Williams College in 1991 after playing just one year of high school ball. He played only token minutes in three seasons before transferring to West Virginia. However, he was injured in a car accident in 1994 and never played for the Mountaineers. He underwent 11 operations after the accident. Gingold caught the eye of pro scouts in private workouts before the draft.

Strengths: Gingold is a massive man who can score. He has a soft shooting touch and excellent footwork in the post. He lacks agility and stamina but has pushed himself into reasonable shape and gets up and down the court well enough.

Weaknesses: Lacking experience and polished basketball skills, Gingold is a long way from being a competent NBA player. He needs to expand his range and work on getting quicker.

Analysis: Gingold played with Toronto's team in the New York summer league and looked good. The Raptors may be willing to stash him on their bench for a year or two and hope for the best.

COLLEGE STATISTICS

	G	FGP	FTP	RPG	APG	PPG
91-92 WILL	8	.500	.250	1.1	0.0	0.6
92-93 WILL	13	.430	.500	1.0	0.1	1.2
93-94 WILL	9	.500	.000	1.6	0.3	1.1
Totals	30	.464	.384	1.2	0.1	1.0

STEVE HAMER
Team: Boston Celtics
Position: Center
Height: 7'0" **Weight:** 245
Birthdate: November 13, 1973
College: Tennessee
Acquired: Second-round pick in 1996 draft (38th overall)

```
            PLAYER SUMMARY
Will ...................................swat a few
Can't .......................post and score
Expect ......................a struggle to stick
Don't Expect ......................strength
Fantasy .............$0  Card ......10-15¢
```

Background: Relatively unsung at Tennessee, Hamer showed improvement in each of his four seasons while establishing the fourth-best field-goal percentage in school history. Hamer was named Tennessee's first team captain since 1979.

Strengths: He's seven feet tall and plays hard, but Hamer's game is underwhelming. He gets up and down the court okay and blocks a few shots. Scouts like the fact that he's still improving.

Weaknesses: Hamer lacks strength and any semblance of a low-post offensive game. His lack of strength hurts him defensively and as a rebounder, making it difficult for him to hold his position underneath. His free-throw shooting needs work, too.

Analysis: Hamer went to Boston, a team in need of competent big men, but he may not be good enough to stick. He played poorly in the New York summer league. He plays hard but doesn't accomplish enough to be an NBA player right now. He may find work in the CBA or overseas.

COLLEGE STATISTICS

	G	FGP	FTP	RPG	APG	PPG
92-93 TENN	26	.544	.635	4.6	0.3	7.0
93-94 TENN	24	.578	.802	5.8	0.8	13.9
94-95 TENN	25	.529	.641	8.8	0.6	15.0
95-96 TENN	29	.575	.615	9.4	1.0	18.2
Totals	104	.558	.661	7.2	0.7	13.6

OTHELLA HARRINGTON

Team: Houston Rockets
Position: Forward/Center
Height: 6'9" **Weight:** 235
Birthdate: January 31, 1974
College: Georgetown
Acquired: Second-round pick in 1996 draft (30th overall)

PLAYER SUMMARY	
Will	work his tail off
Can't	play the perimeter
Expect	a class act
Don't Expect	a finished product
Fantasy	$0 Card ...... 15-25¢

Background: Regarded as the nation's best high school player in 1992, Harrington was named Big East Rookie of the Year at Georgetown but failed in four years to become the superstar he was touted to be. He did have a rock-solid career, ranking in the Hoyas' all-time top five in points, rebounds, and blocked shots.

Strengths: Harrington always gives an honest effort. He gets out on the break and makes a beeline for the basket, getting a lot of easy buckets in the process. He boxes out for rebounds and has the strength to maintain his position. He plays a physical game and seems to relish contact.

Weaknesses: Harrington's game is limited, especially on offense, where he has trouble creating shots in the low post. He lacks the leaping ability to be a top-flight rebounder.

Analysis: Give Harrington credit for a great attitude despite some disappointing times at Georgetown. He should become a good pro, and with some hard work eventually could be a starting power forward. Don't expect much his first season.

COLLEGE STATISTICS

	G	FGP	FTP	RPG	APG	PPG
92-93 GEOR	33	.573	.746	8.8	1.0	16.8
93-94 GEOR	31	.551	.733	8.0	1.2	14.7
94-95 GEOR	31	.559	.706	6.0	0.8	12.2
95-96 GEOR	37	.559	.741	6.9	1.2	12.2
Totals	132	.561	.732	7.4	1.0	13.9

SHAWN HARVEY

Team: Dallas Mavericks
Position: Guard
Height: 6'4" **Weight:** 180
Birthdate: December 31, 1973
College: Essex County; West Virginia St.
Acquired: Second-round pick in 1996 draft (34th overall)

PLAYER SUMMARY	
Will	fill it up
Can't	draw and dish
Expect	3-point marksmanship
Don't Expect	a finished product
Fantasy	$0 Card ...... 10-15¢

Background: Harvey spent one year at a New York junior college, then three at West Virginia State, where he scored in double figures in 75 of his 78 games. He had three triple-doubles in his senior campaign, including one game with 40 points, 16 rebounds, and ten blocks. He was the leading scorer at the pre-draft Portsmouth Invitational.

Strengths: Harvey is a superb athlete who knows how to put the ball in the basket. He has a good body (though he could stand to add some weight), jumps well, and plays a physical style. He has 3-point shooting range and a sure stroke from the foul line.

Weaknesses: Harvey did as he pleased at a lower-division college and must prove he can adjust to better competition. His weaknesses won't become apparent until training camp.

Analysis: One of the sleepers of the draft, Harvey could prove to be an unpolished gem, or he could disappear. Dallas changed coaches during the off-season and got rid of a lot of players, clearing space for Harvey to make the team if he's good enough.

COLLEGE STATISTICS

	G	FGP	FTP	RPG	APG	PPG
91-92 ECC	27	.495	.752	9.1	3.0	22.4
93-94 WVS	26	.444	.743	5.5	2.6	23.1
94-95 WVS	26	.479	.798	6.7	4.2	25.3
95-96 WVS	26	.443	.742	9.8	4.6	27.5
Totals	105	.461	.759	7.8	3.6	24.6

RONNIE HENDERSON

Team: Washington Bullets
Position: Guard
Height: 6'4" Weight: 206
Birthdate: March 29, 1974
College: Louisiana St.
Acquired: Second-round pick in 1996 draft (55th overall)

PLAYER SUMMARY	
Will	fire from deep
Can't	resist temptation
Expect	a scorer
Don't Expect	stout defense
Fantasy	$0 Card 15-25¢

Background: Hailing from Jackson, Mississippi's Murrah High, the school that sent James Robinson, Lindsey Hunter, and Othella Harrington to the NBA, Henderson went to LSU touted as a can't-miss All-American. He put up huge numbers for the Tigers, leading the SEC in scoring as a sophomore and a junior. He scored 20 or more points 44 times in 77 career games and forfeited a year's eligibility to enter the draft.

Strengths: Henderson has an NBA body and a knack for putting the ball in the basket. His medium-range jump shot usually goes in, and he has the athleticism to penetrate and finish plays at the basket.

Weaknesses: He isn't as good a shooter as his scoring average suggests. His shot selection is poor, and he lacks a good feel for the game.

Analysis: Henderson suffered a knee injury that required minor surgery during the 1995-96 season, which concerned some scouts. He will have to beat out someone to make Washington's roster. That doesn't seem likely.

COLLEGE STATISTICS

		G	FGP	FTP	RPG	APG	PPG
93-94	LSU	27	.378	.711	3.6	1.1	15.9
94-95	LSU	27	.429	.734	5.3	2.2	23.3
95-96	LSU	23	.461	.685	4.7	1.4	21.8
Totals		77	.424	.713	4.5	1.6	20.3

MARK HENDRICKSON

Team: Philadelphia 76ers
Position: Forward
Height: 6'9" Weight: 220
Birthdate: June 23, 1974
College: Washington St.
Acquired: Second-round pick in 1996 draft (31st overall)

PLAYER SUMMARY	
Will	pound the boards
Can't	scrape the rafters
Expect	92-mph outlet passes
Don't Expect	eye-opening moves
Fantasy	$0 Card 15-25¢

Background: A two-time all-conference pick, Hendrickson finished his career as the Pac-10's active leader in double-doubles (43 in 108 games). In his final season, he ranked second in the league in rebounding and shooting percentage and fifth in scoring. Also a baseball pitcher, he was selected by the Texas Rangers in the 1996 draft.

Strengths: Hendrickson is an excellent athlete with an NBA-caliber body, good jumping ability, and speed on the fastbreak. He's strong enough to play power forward and is willing to mix it up physically. He has a nice shooting touch and is proficient as a dribbler and passer.

Weaknesses: Hendrickson has no overwhelming strengths, so it's doubtful he can become a shooting or defensive specialist in the NBA. Otherwise, he's average across the board.

Analysis: Hendrickson had the good fortune to be drafted by the 76ers, who are rebuilding and need a lot of new players. He figures to earn a roster spot, although playing time will be scarce.

COLLEGE STATISTICS

		G	FGP	FTP	RPG	APG	PPG
92-93	WSU	27	.556	.712	8.0	1.9	12.6
93-94	WSU	28	.485	.714	7.9	1.6	10.5
94-95	WSU	30	.667	.794	9.0	1.3	16.1
95-96	WSU	23	.572	.709	9.5	1.6	16.5
Totals		108	.567	.731	8.6	1.6	13.9

ZYDRUNAS ILGAUSKAS

Team: Cleveland Cavaliers
Position: Center
Height: 7'1" **Weight:** 238
Birthdate: June 5, 1975
College: None
Acquired: First-round pick in 1996 draft (20th overall)

PLAYER SUMMARY	
Will	shoot with touch
Can't	bump and grind
Expect	growing pains
Don't Expect	toughness
Fantasy	$0 Card ......20-35¢

Background: Ilgauskas applied for the 1995 draft, withdrew his name at the last instant, then sat out the 1995-96 season in Europe while undergoing rehabilitation for a broken foot. The previous season, he played 34 games for Atletas Basketball Club in his hometown of Kaunas, Lithuania, averaging 20.3 points, 12.8 rebounds, and 2.8 blocks per game.

Strengths: A highly skilled big man, Ilgauskas has good moves around the basket, a soft shooting touch, and good passing sense. His turnaround jump shot is particularly effective.

Weaknesses: Ilgauskas has been away from the game for a while because of his foot injury, and he let his body get soft during that time. He needs to slim down and get tougher. He lacks experience against good players, though he was Lithuania's backup center at the Olympics in Atlanta.

Analysis: Ilgauskas might have better skills than Vitaly Potapenko, the Cavs' first pick in the draft (12th overall), but he didn't play as well as Potapenko at the Chicago pre-draft camp. He might be a starter down the road, but it will take time because he's young and prefers a finesse game.

COLLEGE STATISTICS

—DID NOT PLAY—

ALLEN IVERSON

Team: Philadelphia 76ers
Position: Guard
Height: 6'0" **Weight:** 165
Birthdate: June 7, 1975
College: Georgetown
Acquired: First-round pick in 1996 draft (first overall)

PLAYER SUMMARY	
Will	excite the masses
Can't	miss as a pro
Expect	20 PPG
Don't Expect	a shrinking violet
Fantasy	..$15-18 Card ...$3.00-6.00

Background: During a three-year span, Iverson went from high school star to convicted felon to star at Georgetown to No. 1 pick in the NBA draft. He led the Big East in scoring his sophomore season and was named Big East Defensive Player of the Year in back-to-back seasons. He left college after two years.

Strengths: The quickest player in the 1996 draft, Iverson has the speed to keep pace with the NBA's fastest players. He's strong and durable, jumps out of the gym, and plays hard at both ends of the court. He's a good jump-shooter with range and is adept at getting to the basket.

Weaknesses: Iverson tends to shoot the ball whenever he gets it, which could sour his relationship with teammates, and he's cocky to a fault. His free-throw shooting needs work.

Analysis: Philadelphia needed a point guard and decided Iverson was a better choice than Stephon Marbury. One reason: Iverson will bring a more exciting style to the team and sell more tickets. He will put up big numbers as a rookie and should contend for NBA Rookie of the Year honors.

COLLEGE STATISTICS

	G	FGP	FTP	RPG	APG	PPG
94-95 GEOR	30	.390	.688	3.3	4.5	20.4
95-96 GEOR	37	.480	.678	3.8	4.7	25.0
Totals	67	.440	.683	3.6	4.6	23.0

DONTAE JONES

Team: New York Knicks
Position: Forward
Height: 6'7" **Weight:** 220
Birthdate: June 2, 1975
College: Northeast Mississippi;
Mississippi St.
Acquired: First-round pick in 1996 draft
(21st overall)

PLAYER SUMMARY	
Will	stir up the Garden
Can't	hunker down on "D"
Expect	a spectator this season
Don't Expect	a rookie inferno
Fantasy	$0 Card ...... 10-20¢

Background: Jones burst into national prominence in the 1995-96 season, his first at Mississippi State after two years at Northeast Mississippi Community College, helping lead State to its first-ever Final Four appearance. He was named MVP of the NCAA Southeast Regional. He forfeited his final year of eligibility to enter the draft.

Strengths: Scoring is Jones's strong suit. He hits the 15- to 20-foot jumper consistently and gets a lot of points on the fastbreak. He is a deft passer and has some tricky moves around the basket.

Weaknesses: Jones takes a lot of risks defensively and doesn't play as hard as scouts would like. There are concerns about his makeup and propensity for injuries.

Analysis: The Knicks claimed that Jones was the best athlete they tested before the draft, but they won't get much out of him in 1996-97 because of a foot injury that necessitated surgery and is expected to keep Jones out until January. He looks like a boom-or-bust draft pick, capable of rising to All-Star status or disappearing completely.

COLLEGE STATISTICS

		G	FGP	FTP	RPG	APG	PPG
93-94	NEM	29	.507	.602	11.2	1.2	25.2
94-95	NEM	32	.495	.641	13.3	2.4	28.7
95-96	MSU	33	.474	.744	6.8	1.9	14.7
Totals		94	.494	.644	10.4	1.9	22.7

KERRY KITTLES

Team: New Jersey Nets
Position: Guard
Height: 6'5" **Weight:** 179
Birthdate: June 12, 1974
College: Villanova
Acquired: First-round pick in 1996 draft
(eighth overall)

PLAYER SUMMARY	
Will	stroke it from deep
Can't	overpower people
Expect	a professional approach
Don't Expect	a point guard
Fantasy	$4-6 Card ...... 30-60¢

Background: Kittles was a four-year star at Villanova and helped restore the program to national prominence. He holds 15 school records, including most points, and in 1995-96 he became the first Villanova player in 25 years to be named first-team A.P. All-America. He was the first senior selected in the 1996 draft.

Strengths: A versatile offensive player, Kittles excels on the fastbreak and in the halfcourt. He has 3-point range and the ability to slash to the basket from the wing. Defensively, he's good both on and off the ball. He plays unselfishly and responds well to coaching.

Weaknesses: Kittles has been criticized for playing poorly in big games. He has a slight body and needs to get stronger, and his ballhandling must improve for him to see minutes at point guard.

Analysis: Kittles should develop into a topnotch pro, provided he demonstrates a little more mental toughness in big games. He may not start as a rookie, but he figures to play a lot and average in double figures.

COLLEGE STATISTICS

		G	FGP	FTP	RPG	APG	PPG
92-93	VILL	27	.482	.673	3.5	2.9	10.9
93-94	VILL	32	.452	.705	6.5	3.4	19.7
94-95	VILL	33	.524	.767	6.1	3.5	21.4
95-96	VILL	30	.455	.710	7.1	3.5	20.4
Totals		122	.478	.719	5.9	3.3	18.4

TRAVIS KNIGHT

Team: Los Angeles Lakers
Position: Center
Height: 7'0" **Weight:** 235
Birthdate: September 13, 1974
College: Connecticut
Acquired: Signed as a free agent, 7/96

PLAYER SUMMARY	
Will	play solid "D"
Can't	mash and maul
Expect	a soft touch
Don't Expect	bulk
Fantasy	$0 Card......25-50¢

Background: From a high school in Utah, Knight attended Connecticut, where he gradually grew into a prominent role, starting 65 of 67 games over his final two seasons. He ranks as the second-leading shot-blocker (179) and ninth most accurate shooter (.518) in school history. The Huskies logged a 104-26 record during his stay.

Strengths: A good athlete, Knight runs well and can play facing the basket. His shooting range extends to about 15 feet. He improved each year in college and does a lot of the little things that go unrecorded in box scores. He works hard defensively and is active on the press.

Weaknesses: The slender Knight will need to bulk up to make it in the NBA. His low-post offense needs a lot of work, and his free-throw accuracy leaves something to be desired.

Analysis: The last pick in the first round, Knight didn't last long with the Bulls, as they renounced his rights shortly after re-signing Michael Jordan. Knight will ride the Lakers' bench behind Shaq. Still improving, he could surprise some people down the road.

COLLEGE STATISTICS

	G	FGP	FTP	RPG	APG	PPG
92-93 CONN	24	.460	.407	2.5	0.4	2.9
93-94 CONN	33	.439	.500	2.9	0.7	2.5
94-95 CONN	35	.558	.651	8.2	1.2	9.1
95-96 CONN	34	.521	.694	9.3	2.1	9.1
Totals	124	.518	.622	6.0	1.1	6.1

PRIEST LAUDERDALE

Team: Atlanta Hawks
Position: Center
Height: 7'2" **Weight:** 340
Birthdate: August 31, 1973
College: Central St. (Ohio)
Acquired: First-round pick in 1996 draft (28th overall)

PLAYER SUMMARY	
Will	take up space
Can't	run and jump
Expect	tippy-toe dunks
Don't Expect	a skywalker
Fantasy	$0 Card......10-20¢

Background: Lauderdale dropped out of Carver High School and enrolled at a community college but left before the basketball season. He then played 13 games at Central State in 1993-94 before being ruled academically ineligible, then sat out a season. He averaged 16.1 points and shot 70.8 percent from the field in 23 games in Greece last season.

Strengths: The man is a monster, standing 7'2" (or more) and weighing anywhere from 340 to 400 pounds. He has excellent hands, a soft hook shot, and the bulk to clear space for himself in the low post. Scouts say he has vast potential.

Weaknesses: Lack of experience and lack of conditioning are two factors working against Lauderdale, who lost more than 50 pounds the year before he was drafted. He doesn't run well, and there are concerns about his work ethic.

Analysis: Lauderdale might be the biggest player in the NBA. With Dikembe Mutombo ahead of him, there won't be any pressure on Lauderdale to contribute as a rookie. Because of his size and skills, he figures to stick on the roster, but you won't see him unless it's garbage time. Eventually, he could be the next Gheorghe Muresan.

COLLEGE STATISTICS

	G	FGP	FTP	RPG	APG	PPG
93-94 CSU	13	.684	.404	10.2	1.2	20.1
Totals	13	.684	.404	10.2	1.2	20.1

RANDY LIVINGSTON

Team: Houston Rockets
Position: Guard
Height: 6'4" **Weight:** 209
Birthdate: April 2, 1975
College: Louisiana St.
Acquired: Second-round pick in 1996 draft (42nd overall)

```
            PLAYER SUMMARY
Will ....................distribute the ball
Can't .............................stay healthy
Expect ................................a gamer
Don't Expect.............a strong shot
Fantasy ...........$0   Card ......15-25¢
```

Background: The nation's hard-luck player the past three seasons, Livingston was limited to 29 games because of injuries, including a torn anterior cruciate ligament in his right knee in 1993 and a broken right kneecap in 1995. This all happened after he came to LSU as the nation's top-rated high school player and a surefire NBA lottery pick.

Strengths: Before his injuries, Livingston was a mercurial point guard who could penetrate, pass, score, and lead a team. He has good size and once had great quickness and athleticism. He plays smart and under control.

Weaknesses: Livingston's jump shot, which always has been the weakest part of his game, deserted him in 1995-96. Otherwise, his only weaknesses are related to injuries.

Analysis: Livingston gave up his final two years of eligibility to test the NBA draft waters. He passed his physical at the Chicago camp before the draft but reportedly had a pronounced limp. If he gets to 80-percent healthy by training camp, he could stick with Houston, a good team that might have the luxury of carrying Livingston for a year or maybe even two.

COLLEGE STATISTICS

		G	FGP	FTP	RPG	APG	PPG
94-95	LSU	16	.438	.677	4.0	9.4	14.0
95-96	LSU	13	.289	.790	2.3	5.3	6.1
Totals		29	.392	.720	3.2	7.6	10.5

MARCUS MANN

Team: Golden State Warriors
Position: Forward
Height: 6'8" **Weight:** 245
Birthdate: December 19, 1973
College: East Central; Miss. Valley St.
Acquired: Second-round pick in 1996 draft (40th overall)

```
            PLAYER SUMMARY
Will...............................run and gun
Can't......................bump and grind
Expect ...............a struggle to stick
Don't Expect ........to see him soon
Fantasy ...........$0   Card ......15-25¢
```

Background: Mann played two seasons at a junior college in Mississippi before enrolling at Mississippi Valley State, where he put up good numbers in the SWAC, a notorious run-and-gun league. He won the John B. McLendon Trophy, presented to the outstanding player attending a historically black college or university.

Strengths: Mann has good quickness in the post and a nice assortment of scoring moves. He delivers his turnaround jump shot with a quick release. He was a big-time rebounder at a small-time school.

Weaknesses: He hasn't played against good competition, and he's probably too small to be a power forward in the NBA. Mann will have to work extremely hard for rebounds. His free-throw shooting lacks consistency, and he's not much of a passer.

Analysis: Mann may be a classic case of a good player without an NBA position. His ability to score could land him a roster spot with Golden State, though the Warriors have a lot of veteran frontcourt players. More likely, Mann will head to the CBA.

COLLEGE STATISTICS

		G	FGP	FTP	RPG	APG	PPG
92-93	EC	30	.581	.636	12.0	1.8	20.3
93-94	EC	26	.630	.684	11.0	1.8	22.2
94-95	MVSU	27	.550	.596	11.7	0.9	16.7
95-96	MVSU	28	.618	.635	13.8	1.6	21.6
Totals		111	.595	.640	12.2	1.5	20.2

STEPHON MARBURY

Team: Minnesota Timberwolves
Position: Guard
Height: 6'2" **Weight:** 180
Birthdate: February 20, 1977
College: Georgia Tech
Acquired: Draft rights traded from Bucks with future considerations for draft rights to Ray Allen, 6/96

PLAYER SUMMARY	
Will	draw and dish
Can't	miss in the NBA
Expect	a future All-Star
Don't Expect	lack of effort
Fantasy	$12-15 Card ...$2.00-4.00

Background: A legend in Brooklyn before he entered high school, Marbury followed former New York City point guard phenom Kenny Anderson to Georgia Tech. In Atlanta, Marbury became one of just five freshmen in history to be named first-team All-ACC and the first freshman to lead Georgia Tech in scoring since Mark Price in 1983.

Strengths: Marbury is the prototypical point guard—adept at directing traffic, getting a team into its offense, and providing leadership. He's as quick as most of the point guards in the NBA. He can score when the need arises, and he plays solid defense.

Weaknesses: Marbury has no glaring weaknesses other than an extreme lack of experience. His college career consisted of only 36 games.

Analysis: Marbury was one of the few top collegiate players who actually wanted to play in Minnesota, so he should be a good match for the Timberwolves. Marbury counts Wolves forward Kevin Garnett among his good friends, an added bonus that could help make his transition to the pros easier. He'll have an outstanding career in the NBA.

COLLEGE STATISTICS

		G	FGP	FTP	RPG	APG	PPG
95-96	GT	36	.457	.738	3.1	4.5	18.9
Totals		36	.457	.738	3.1	4.5	18.9

WALTER McCARTY

Team: New York Knicks
Position: Forward
Height: 6'10" **Weight:** 230
Birthdate: February 1, 1974
College: Kentucky
Acquired: First-round pick in 1996 draft (19th overall)

PLAYER SUMMARY	
Will	run and jump
Can't	patrol the paint
Expect	a rangy small forward
Don't Expect	a rookie bust
Fantasy	$0 Card ......35-75¢

Background: A relatively overlooked player on Kentucky's national-championship squad, McCarty averaged just 25 minutes a game as a senior, yet ranked second on the team in rebounds. He played three seasons for the Wildcats, sitting out his freshman season because of NCAA academic requirements.

Strengths: A long, lean athlete, McCarty is a tremendous open-court player both offensively (running the break) and defensively (on the press). He has good size for a small forward—his probable position in the NBA—and good ball-handling skills. He competes fiercely and plays sound defense.

Weaknesses: Some teams were scared off by McCarty's slim body, and it's true he could stand to add some weight. He'll need to make some adjustments at small forward after playing mostly center at Kentucky.

Analysis: An excellent pick for New York, McCarty should have a good career in the NBA. He has the skills to develop into a well-rounded player at both forward positions. Look for him to get about 15 minutes a game in 1996-97.

COLLEGE STATISTICS

		G	FGP	FTP	RPG	APG	PPG
93-94	KENT	34	.471	.554	3.9	1.1	5.7
94-95	KENT	33	.510	.726	5.6	1.5	10.5
95-96	KENT	36	.543	.721	5.7	2.6	11.3
Totals		103	.515	.684	5.1	1.8	9.2

AMAL McCASKILL
Team: Orlando Magic
Position: Center
Height: 6'11" **Weight:** 235
Birthdate: October 28, 1973
College: Marquette
Acquired: Second-round pick in 1996 draft (49th overall)

PLAYER SUMMARY	
Will	bang the glass
Can't	draw and distribute
Expect	a rejector
Don't Expect	to see him soon
Fantasy	$0 Card .....10-20¢

Background: McCaskill took three years to become a major contributor at Marquette. He was a deep reserve in 1991-92, then sat out as a redshirt in 1992-93. As a senior, however, he ranked in the top five in Conference USA in rebounding, field-goal accuracy, and blocked shots.

Strengths: Like former Marquette center Jim McIlvaine, McCaskill is an excellent shot-blocker, but he's raw in other facets of the game. He rebounds well, and scouts like the fact that he improved each season in college.

Weaknesses: McCaskill needs to gain weight. His offense consists of only a turnaround, fadeaway jumper. He averaged less than one assist per game and got into foul trouble often.

Analysis: The ability to block shots has kept a lot of marginal players in the NBA. McCaskill has that skill, and Orlando, after losing Shaquille O'Neal, certainly could use another big body. However, McCaskill probably will play in the CBA or overseas for a couple years before making it in the NBA.

COLLEGE STATISTICS

		G	FGP	FTP	RPG	APG	PPG
91-92	MARQ	15	.360	.533	5.2	0.3	1.7
93-94	MARQ	33	.681	.635	3.3	0.5	5.2
94-95	MARQ	33	.511	.659	8.5	0.8	10.7
95-96	MARQ	30	.549	.649	8.9	1.3	10.3
Totals		111	.545	.644	6.3	0.8	7.8

JEFF McINNIS
Team: Denver Nuggets
Position: Guard
Height: 6'4" **Weight:** 190
Birthdate: October 22, 1974
College: North Carolina
Acquired: Second-round pick in 1996 draft (37th overall)

PLAYER SUMMARY	
Will	fire when ready
Can't	settle down
Expect	a solid body
Don't Expect	humility
Fantasy	$0 Card .....15-25¢

Background: McInnis passed up his senior season at North Carolina to enter the draft, but not before becoming one of only six Tar Heels with at least 1,000 points and 400 assists in a career. He made nearly 40 percent of his career 3-point attempts (138 of 348).

Strengths: McInnis has tremendous size, long arms, great quickness, and a good work ethic. He is a skilled player on both offense and defense with a decent jump shot. He has been well coached by Dean Smith.

Weaknesses: McInnis is cocky to a fault, rubbing some NBA teams the wrong way, and he shoots too much for a point guard. He needs to step up his defensive intensity and show that he can use his athleticism to guard people.

Analysis: McInnis left school thinking he might be a first-round pick, but questions about his attitude and commitment caused him to drop to the middle of the second round. Denver got him and—because the Nuggets are reshuffling—he has a chance to make the team. He won't play much, however.

COLLEGE STATISTICS

		G	FGP	FTP	RPG	APG	PPG
93-94	NC	35	.458	.638	1.7	2.4	5.6
94-95	NC	34	.491	.667	4.1	5.3	12.4
95-96	NC	31	.435	.800	2.6	5.5	16.5
Totals		100	.459	.719	2.8	4.4	11.3

RUSS MILLARD

Team: Phoenix Suns
Position: Forward
Height: 6'8" **Weight:** 240
Birthdate: March 1, 1973
College: Iowa
Acquired: Second-round pick in 1996 draft (39th overall)

PLAYER SUMMARY

Will ....get after it
Can't........................be a playmaker
Expect ....a few treys
Don't Expect.......All-Rookie choice
Fantasy ....$0 Card ......10-15¢

Background: Though he was only the fourth- or fifth-best player at Iowa in 1995-96, Millard drew the attention of NBA scouts at the Desert Classic, where he averaged 19.0 points per game. He spent five years at Iowa, sitting out a redshirt year in 1991-92. He played only 12 games as a junior because of illness and ineligibility.

Strengths: A tremendous leaper, Millard won the dunk competition at the Portsmouth Invitational. He has excellent offensive skills, showing both the ability to score inside and the dexterity to step outside and drill jump shots. He has good size and competitiveness and runs the floor easily.

Weaknesses: Millard isn't considered a go-to offensive player, and he's a poor passer, averaging one assist per game in college.

Analysis: Millard came from out of nowhere to land in the second round of the draft, and he could stick in the NBA. Phoenix, starting over with Cotton Fitzsimmons as coach, might be willing to see how he adjusts to the pro ranks. Don't look for him to get many minutes as a rookie.

COLLEGE STATISTICS

	G	FGP	FTP	RPG	APG	PPG
92-93 IOWA	17	.452	.674	3.8	0.5	5.2
93-94 IOWA	27	.507	.732	5.3	1.3	11.2
94-95 IOWA	12	.511	.588	3.3	0.9	5.2
95-96 IOWA	32	.609	.799	7.0	0.9	13.7
Totals	88	.547	.748	5.3	1.0	10.1

RYAN MINOR

Team: Philadelphia 76ers
Position: Forward/Guard
Height: 6'7" **Weight:** 220
Birthdate: January 5, 1974
College: Oklahoma
Acquired: Second-round pick in 1996 draft (32nd overall)

PLAYER SUMMARY

Will ....stop and pop
Can't....................race with the jets
Expect ....a streak shooter
Don't Expect..................Greg Minor
Fantasy ....$0 Card ......20-35¢

Background: A two-sport star in college, Minor played three seasons for the Oklahoma baseball team, helping it win the national championship in 1994. In basketball, he was All-Big Eight his junior and senior seasons and is the No. 6 scorer in school history.

Strengths: Minor is an outstanding shooter with a deadly stroke from 3-point range and the ability to create scoring chances with his dribble. He plays hard and rebounds aggressively. His free-throw shooting is first-rate.

Weaknesses: Questions were raised about Minor's adaptability when he complained about Oklahoma's offense. He played poorly at the pre-draft Desert Classic, where his shooting deserted him. He struggles to defend players on the perimeter.

Analysis: Minor signed a contract with the Baltimore Orioles but also attended Philadelphia's rookie camp and is expected to keep his options open for a while. If he can't recapture his shooting stroke, he will have to go with baseball whether he likes it or not.

COLLEGE STATISTICS

	G	FGP	FTP	RPG	APG	PPG
92-93 OKLA	31	.433	.667	2.7	1.0	4.7
93-94 OKLA	25	.498	.772	7.4	1.8	16.2
94-95 OKLA	32	.486	.823	8.4	2.1	23.6
95-96 OKLA	30	.417	.822	6.6	2.6	21.3
Totals	118	.460	.798	6.5	1.9	16.5

MARTIN MUURSEPP

Team: Miami Heat
Position: Forward
Height: 6'9" **Weight:** 235
Birthdate: September 26, 1974
College: None
Acquired: Draft rights traded from Jazz for a future first-round pick, 6/96

PLAYER SUMMARY	
Will	hit the 3
Can't	stroke the "J"
Expect	the unexpected
Don't Expect	name recognition
Fantasy	$0 Card	20-35¢

Background: Muursepp played last season for BC Kalev Talinn, a pro team in Estonia. The previous two seasons, he played for Maccabi Ramat Gan in Israel. He also played professionally in Sweden and represented the Soviet Union for two seasons on its national Under-22 team. He averaged 18.5 points a game in European Cup play in 1995-96.

Strengths: Though he was the most obscure first-round pick of any recent draft, Muursepp has skills that attracted Pat Riley to him. He shoots a high percentage, can make 3-pointers, and has good passing sense.

Weaknesses: Muursepp has never faced top-grade competition, so it's doubtful he'd be ready to make a sudden impact in the NBA. A propensity for playing soft also could hurt him.

Analysis: Miami acted on draft day to secure Muursepp, sending a future first-round pick to the Utah Jazz, who had selected him with the 25th pick in the draft. Muursepp has been compared to Toni Kukoc and Tom Chambers, meaning he's a finesse forward with a knack for scoring.

COLLEGE STATISTICS

—DID NOT PLAY—

STEVE NASH

Team: Phoenix Suns
Position: Guard
Height: 6'3" **Weight:** 195
Birthdate: February 7, 1974
College: Santa Clara
Acquired: First-round pick in 1996 draft (15th overall)

PLAYER SUMMARY	
Will	provide leadership
Can't	run with the jets
Expect	a clever playmaker
Don't Expect	a starting role now
Fantasy	$1 Card	20-35¢

Background: Born in South Africa, Nash grew up in Victoria, B.C. After being ignored by Pac-10 schools out of high school, he helped Santa Clara upset Arizona in the NCAA Tournament as a freshman. He is the Broncos' all-time leader in assists and free-throw accuracy.

Strengths: Scouts have called Nash the next John Stockton. Both players have extra-large hands, enabling them to manipulate the ball easily, and both are dead-eye shooters. Nash is smart defensively and excels against top-level competition. He converts his free-throw opportunities.

Weaknesses: Nash's lack of quickness will hurt him against some of the NBA's better point guards, and he won't be able to penetrate as much as he did in college. Otherwise, he has no significant weaknesses.

Analysis: After Allen Iverson and Stephon Marbury, Nash was the best point guard available in the draft. Phoenix is expected to groom him as the successor to Kevin Johnson. Nash has the makings of a solid NBA point guard.

COLLEGE STATISTICS

		G	FGP	FTP	RPG	APG	PPG
92-93	SC	31	.424	.825	2.5	2.2	8.1
93-94	SC	26	.414	.831	2.5	3.7	14.6
94-95	SC	27	.445	.879	3.8	6.4	20.9
95-96	SC	29	.431	.894	3.6	6.0	17.0
Totals		113	.429	.861	3.1	4.5	14.9

JEFF NORDGAARD

Team: Milwaukee Bucks
Position: Forward
Height: 6'7" **Weight:** 226
Birthdate: February 23, 1973
College: Wisconsin-Green Bay
Acquired: Second-round pick in 1996 draft (53rd overall)

PLAYER SUMMARY	
Will	scratch and claw
Can't	convert from deep
Expect	a struggle to stick
Don't Expect	a skywalker
Fantasy	$0 Card	10-20¢

Background: Nordgaard became a full-time starter as a sophomore and scored the winning basket in Wisconsin-Green Bay's upset of California in the NCAA Tournament. He added at least three points to his scoring average each season and ranked 15th nationally in scoring as a senior, when he was named the MCC Player of the Year.

Strengths: Nordgaard is a good shooter and a hard-nosed, durable competitor. He can play either small forward or shooting guard. He's smart, fundamentally sound, and plays well under pressure. He rebounds well and has good playmaking sense.

Weaknesses: He made only 13 3-pointers in his college career, so he needs to expand his range. Nordgaard lacks the athletic skills of most of the swingmen.

Analysis: Nordgaard made the All-Tournament team at the Portsmouth Invitational before being drafted by the Bucks. Nordgaard was a lot like Bucks coach Chris Ford in college: smart, tough, and a good shooter. Those attributes give him at least a fighting chance to make the team.

COLLEGE STATISTICS

	G	FGP	FTP	RPG	APG	PPG
92-93 WGB	27	.507	.464	2.9	1.1	6.1
93-94 WGB	34	.590	.768	6.4	2.1	15.6
94-95 WGB	30	.547	.788	7.5	2.3	18.6
95-96 WGB	29	.554	.710	6.3	2.3	22.6
Totals	120	.556	.741	5.8	2.0	15.9

MOOCHIE NORRIS

Team: Milwaukee Bucks
Position: Guard
Height: 6'1" **Weight:** 175
Birthdate: July 27, 1973
College: Odessa; Auburn; West Florida
Acquired: Second-round pick in 1996 draft (33rd overall)

PLAYER SUMMARY	
Will	stop and pop
Can't	bang inside
Expect	a future pro
Don't Expect	a slacker
Fantasy	$1 Card	25-50¢

Background: Norris played at three different colleges, beginning at perennial power Odessa (Texas) Junior College, then playing one year at Auburn, where he made third-team All-SEC. He left Auburn after being declared ineligible and landed at Division II West Florida, where he set a host of school records.

Strengths: A left-handed point guard with good quickness and scoring sense, Norris has tremendous potential if only he can demonstrate the ability to run a team. He has a good-looking jump shot, and scouts like his crossover move and the fact that he plays hard.

Weaknesses: His shot selection is questionable, and he is a streaky player, making less than 40 percent of his field-goal attempts in his one major-college season. Otherwise, he has no glaring weaknesses.

Analysis: Playing well at the Portsmouth Invitational earned Norris an invitation to the pre-draft Desert Classic, and he impressed scouts at both camps. He has a good chance to play in the NBA in 1996-97.

COLLEGE STATISTICS

	G	FGP	FTP	RPG	APG	PPG
92-93 ODES	32	.552	.708	2.8	7.0	14.3
93-94 ODES	27	.557	.692	3.9	7.9	14.9
94-95 AUB	29	.397	.699	4.0	4.9	12.5
95-96 WFU	16	.457	.761	5.8	8.9	23.6
Totals	104	.488	.715	3.9	7.0	15.4

JERMAINE O'NEAL

Team: Portland Trail Blazers
Position: Forward/Center
Height: 6'11" **Weight:** 226
Birthdate: October 13, 1978
College: None
Acquired: First-round pick in 1996 draft (17th overall)

PLAYER SUMMARY	
Will ....dunk with style
Can't ....hold the fort inside
Expect ....a long-term project
Don't Expect..............anything now
Fantasy ....$0　Card .....20-35¢

Background: O'Neal bypassed college to enter the draft after failing to achieve passing pre-college test scores. From Eau Claire High School in Columbia, South Carolina, he was a devastating shot-blocker at the prep level, averaging 5.2 swats per game in 1995-96, along with 22.4 points and 12.6 rebounds. *USA Today* named him to its high school All-America team.

Strengths: An agile, acrobatic leaper, O'Neal has the ability to score in close with either hand. He reacts quickly for rebounds and blocks, and he runs well.

Weaknesses: Physically as well as mentally immature, O'Neal has a long way to go before he can be competitive in the NBA. He's woefully weak for his size and will get tossed around underneath the basket. The rest of his game is raw.

Analysis: Portland general manager Bob Whitsitt was the man who drafted Shawn Kemp, another raw prospect who never played in college, and perhaps he sees similar potential in O'Neal. O'Neal won't come close to approaching Kemp's rookie numbers in 1996-97. He represents a big gamble that the rebuilding Trail Blazers were willing to take.

COLLEGE STATISTICS

—DID NOT PLAY—

MARK POPE

Team: Indiana Pacers
Position: Forward
Height: 6'10" **Weight:** 235
Birthdate: September 11, 1972
College: Washington; Kentucky
Acquired: Second-round pick in 1996 draft (52nd overall)

PLAYER SUMMARY	
Will ....push the pace
Can't......................keep up on "D"
Expect ....a solid citizen
Don't Expect.................much sizzle
Fantasy ....$0　Card .....10-15¢

Background: Pope began his college career at Washington, earning Pac-10 Freshman of the Year honors in 1991-92 and leading the conference in free-throw shooting the following season. When Washington fired coach Lynn Nance, Pope left for Kentucky. After sitting out a year, he moved into the Wildcats' rotation and helped them win the national championship in 1996.

Strengths: Pope is an unselfish, team-oriented player who is a fierce competitor. He can run and shoot, he has a nice jumper, and his size and long arms are assets. He has good all-around skills, and he defends aggressively. He's willing to accept any role.

Weaknesses: As much as scouts like Pope, he may not be good enough to compete in the NBA. He needs to get a little stronger without sacrificing any quickness.

Analysis: Kentucky coach Rick Pitino raved about Pope's work ethic, but work alone won't merit a spot in the NBA. He could stick with Indiana as the Pacers' 12th man, but it would be a surprise if he played more than token minutes in 1996-97.

COLLEGE STATISTICS

	G	FGP	FTP	RPG	APG	PPG
91-92 WASH	29	.579	.804	8.1	2.0	10.3
92-93 WASH	27	.527	.862	8.0	1.3	12.2
94-95 KENT	33	.514	.727	6.3	0.9	8.2
95-96 KENT	36	.482	.683	5.2	1.0	7.6
Totals	125	.526	.774	6.7	1.3	9.4

VITALY POTAPENKO

Team: Cleveland Cavaliers
Position: Forward/Center
Height: 6'10" **Weight:** 280
Birthdate: March 21, 1973
College: Wright St.
Acquired: First-round pick in 1996 draft (12th overall)

PLAYER SUMMARY	
Will	put his body on you
Can't	play the perimeter
Expect	a jump hook
Don't Expect	a jumping jack
Fantasy	$2-4 Card	15-25¢

Background: Potapenko attended Kiev State University in the Ukraine before coming to Wright State, where he made All-Midwestern Collegiate Conference both seasons before forfeiting his final year of eligibility to enter the draft. He improved his position with a strong showing at the Chicago pre-draft camp.

Strengths: A throwback to the old days when centers were enforcers, Potapenko is a low-post horse who throws his weight around and pounds the boards. His skills aren't great, but they're average across the board, and he has a great work ethic. He comes from an underrated college program and still has a lot of room for improvement.

Weaknesses: Potapenko needs to develop his offensive game and reduce his turnovers. He lacks the springs to be a shot-blocking threat.

Analysis: After dominating all comers in Chicago, Potapenko shot into the upper half of the first round. He could make a quick impression with the Cavaliers, who were badly undersized last season. He figures to have a long career as a key reserve and/or starter at either power forward or center.

COLLEGE STATISTICS

	G	FGP	FTP	RPG	APG	PPG
94-95 WSU	30	.602	.733	6.4	1.4	19.2
95-96 WSU	25	.612	.713	7.3	1.4	21.4
Totals	55	.607	.723	6.8	1.4	20.2

EFTHIMIOS RENTZIAS

Team: Denver Nuggets
Position: Center
Height: 6'11" **Weight:** 243
Birthdate: January 11, 1976
College: None
Acquired: First-round pick in 1996 draft (23rd overall)

PLAYER SUMMARY	
Will	score in many ways
Can't	scrape the rafters
Expect	a future stud
Don't Expect	anything now
Fantasy	$0 Card	15-25¢

Background: Rentzias entered the draft at age 20 after playing with the Greek national team since he was 16. He spent 1994 through 1996 in the Greek League, winning Rookie of the Year honors. In 1995, he was named MVP at the World Junior Championships, where Greece routed the United States en route to the championship.

Strengths: Rentzias is a fine young talent with great mobility and a good body considering his age. He's much more advanced offensively than defensively, with an assortment of low-post moves, a decent jump shot, and the ability to drive quickly from the wing. He has a good feel for the game and is experienced against good players.

Weaknesses: His defense needs work. Rentzias isn't much of a shot-blocker, and he isn't strong enough to deter most NBA centers. He had only 21 assists in 67 games in the Greek League.

Analysis: The Nuggets were fortunate that Rentzias fell to them with the 23rd pick in the draft, but they will have to wait for his services. He is under contract in Greece until at least January 1997, and he may opt to stay in Greece for two or three years before giving the NBA a try. He should be worth the wait.

COLLEGE STATISTICS

—DID NOT PLAY—

RON RILEY

Team: Detroit Pistons
Position: Guard
Height: 6'5" **Weight:** 205
Birthdate: December 27, 1973
College: Arizona St.
Acquired: Draft rights traded by SuperSonics for a future draft pick, 6/96

PLAYER SUMMARY	
Will	pull up from deep
Can't	share the wealth
Expect	a fighting chance
Don't Expect	a big contribution
Fantasy	$0 Card ..... 10-15¢

Background: Riley played four seasons at Arizona State, becoming the school's all-time leading scorer. He made 263 3-pointers in 116 games. In 1995, he led ASU to the Sweet 16 of the NCAA Tournament for the first time in 20 years.

Strengths: A durable athlete, Riley possesses a great body and decent jumping ability. He is a good shooter with soft touch and 3-point range. He has the quickness and long arms to be a strong defensive player.

Weaknesses: Scouts worry that Riley is a ball-hog: He shot the ball nearly every time he touched it at the Desert Classic (and didn't make many). His ball-handling needs work, and he needs better focus on defense.

Analysis: Riley might have been the luckiest player in the draft, going 47th overall to Seattle, then getting traded to Detroit, which lost shooting guard Allan Houston to free agency. Riley is a good enough athlete to match up with NBA players, but he will have to show more discipline to survive training camp.

COLLEGE STATISTICS

		G	FGP	FTP	RPG	APG	PPG
92-93	ASU	28	.355	.660	3.5	1.8	13.0
93-94	ASU	28	.363	.670	5.0	2.5	14.2
94-95	ASU	33	.439	.744	5.3	1.5	16.0
95-96	ASU	27	.389	.720	6.1	2.6	20.1
Totals		116	.389	.706	5.0	2.1	15.8

CHRIS ROBINSON

Team: Vancouver Grizzlies
Position: Guard
Height: 6'5" **Weight:** 205
Birthdate: April 2, 1974
College: Western Kentucky
Acquired: Second-round pick in 1996 draft (51st overall)

PLAYER SUMMARY	
Will	run and jump
Can't	nail the trifecta
Expect	a struggle to stick
Don't Expect	anything now
Fantasy	$0 Card ..... 10-15¢

Background: Robinson had an outstanding career at Western Kentucky, helping the Hilltoppers to a 26-6 record and the Sweet 16 of the NCAA Tournament as a frosh. He led the team in scoring the next three seasons and was named the Sun Belt Conference Player of the Year as a junior.

Strengths: Robinson has good skills and enough size and strength to compete in the NBA. A forward in college, he projects as a good rebounder at guard, his likely position in the pros. He comes from an underrated program and has been well coached.

Weaknesses: He needs to expand his guard skills (dribbling, passing, long-range shooting) to survive because he's too short to play forward in the NBA.

Analysis: Robinson didn't have a great senior year, though he did come on strong late in the season. His medical exam at the Chicago pre-draft camp raised concerns about his health. The Grizzlies are bringing a lot of players to camp, and Robinson figures to get lost in the shuffle.

COLLEGE STATISTICS

		G	FGP	FTP	RPG	APG	PPG
92-93	WKU	32	.509	.641	3.4	1.2	7.3
93-94	WKU	31	.478	.721	5.7	2.0	14.7
94-95	WKU	31	.453	.711	6.7	2.2	17.0
95-96	WKU	26	.455	.675	6.2	2.3	16.8
Totals		120	.468	.689	5.5	1.9	13.8

DARNELL ROBINSON

Team: Dallas Mavericks
Position: Center
Height: 6'11" **Weight:** 270
Birthdate: May 30, 1974
College: Arkansas
Acquired: Second-round pick in 1996 draft (58th overall)

PLAYER SUMMARY	
Will	look the part
Can't	play the part
Expect	a teaser
Don't Expect	a roster spot soon
Fantasy	$0 Card ......10-20¢

Background: Robinson had a bumpy career at Arkansas, missing games during his freshman and junior seasons because of injuries to his right foot. He started four times in the NCAA Tournament as the Razorbacks won the 1994 national championship. Robinson forfeited his final year of eligibility to enter the draft.

Strengths: Robinson boasts excellent size and strength and good athletic skills. He's active around the basket and has shooting range to about 15 feet.

Weaknesses: Robinson is not ready for the NBA. Even his shooting needs a lot of work, and he often settles for jump shots instead of working for position in the low post. He looked out of shape before the draft, and some think he may be injury prone.

Analysis: Ignoring the advice of many, Robinson came out of school early and became the last pick in the draft. Dallas took a flyer on him, but the Mavericks already have enough big bodies, giving Robinson virtually no chance to make the team. His game didn't improve much in college. Maybe he'll get better in the CBA.

COLLEGE STATISTICS

		G	FGP	FTP	RPG	APG	PPG
93-94	ARK	27	.457	.577	4.7	1.9	7.6
94-95	ARK	37	.411	.444	3.8	0.9	6.4
95-96	ARK	20	.457	.532	7.0	0.9	12.7
Totals		84	.440	.515	4.8	1.2	8.3

ROY ROGERS

Team: Vancouver Grizzlies
Position: Forward/Center
Height: 6'10" **Weight:** 238
Birthdate: August 19, 1975
College: Alabama
Acquired: First-round pick in 1996 draft (22nd overall)

PLAYER SUMMARY	
Will	motor on the break
Can't	knock down 3s
Expect	a rejector
Don't Expect	many assists
Fantasy	$1-3 Card ......25-50¢

Background: One of the nation's best defensive players in 1995-96, Rogers set an Alabama record with 156 blocked shots and tied an NCAA mark with 14 swats in one game. As a junior, he played on a front line that included 1995 first-round picks Antonio McDyess and Jason Caffey.

Strengths: Rogers is the prototypical Alabama big man who runs the court, blocks shots, hits short-range jump shots, and plays hard at both ends of the court. He is cat-quick and has a dandy jump hook. Shot-blocking is his greatest strength.

Weaknesses: Knee surgery in 1993 forced Rogers to miss games his first two seasons at Alabama, and lingering knee problems caused him to drop in the draft. He needs better upper-body strength and a more reliable stroke at the foul line.

Analysis: Rogers was exceptional in the Desert Classic before the draft. If he stays healthy, he could give Vancouver a lift off the bench and eventually find work as a starting power forward. He also could see a few minutes at center.

COLLEGE STATISTICS

		G	FGP	FTP	RPG	APG	PPG
92-93	ALAB	14	.516	.500	2.3	0.3	3.5
93-94	ALAB	23	.490	.682	2.7	0.1	3.0
94-95	ALAB	33	.505	.553	3.6	0.6	3.5
95-96	ALAB	32	.524	.622	9.3	0.9	13.5
Totals		102	.517	.610	5.0	0.5	6.4

MALIK ROSE

Team: Charlotte Hornets
Position: Forward
Height: 6'7" **Weight:** 250
Birthdate: November 23, 1974
College: Drexel
Acquired: Second-round pick in 1996 draft (44th overall)

PLAYER SUMMARY	
Will	post and score
Can't	stick the trey
Expect	an honest effort
Don't Expect	perimeter skills
Fantasy	$0 Card	20-35¢

Background: From Philadelphia's Overbrook High, the school that produced Wilt Chamberlain, Rose became a star at hometown Drexel, where he was the North Atlantic Conference Player of the Year his last two seasons. He ranked second in the nation in rebounding in 1995-96 and ranks second to Derrick Coleman on the NCAA's all-time modern rebounding list.

Strengths: Rose was a top-notch collegiate power forward with toughness and competitiveness. He has good moves in the post and a nose for rebounds. He is a much-improved free-throw shooter.

Weaknesses: Rose is undersized to play power forward in the NBA and lacks the shooting range and ball-handling skills to operate on the perimeter.

Analysis: In college, Rose got away with dominating in the paint, but he won't be able to do that in the NBA. Scouts like his work ethic but fear he is a player without a position. He has a chance to stick with Charlotte, but he won't play much. He will have problems on defense in the NBA.

COLLEGE STATISTICS

		G	FGP	FTP	RPG	APG	PPG
92-93	DREX	29	.502	.563	11.4	0.3	13.6
93-94	DREX	30	.520	.545	12.4	0.7	13.9
94-95	DREX	30	.563	.714	13.5	1.2	19.5
95-96	DREX	31	.595	.714	13.1	1.7	20.2
Totals		120	.549	.641	12.6	1.0	16.9

JASON SASSER

Team: Portland Trail Blazers
Position: Forward
Height: 6'7" **Weight:** 225
Birthdate: January 13, 1974
College: Texas Tech
Acquired: Draft rights traded from Kings for future considerations, 7/96

PLAYER SUMMARY	
Will	give his all
Can't	drain the trey
Expect	a slasher
Don't Expect	a big rookie splash
Fantasy	$0 Card	25-50¢

Background: Sasser moved into the starting lineup during his freshman season at Texas Tech and was the heart and soul of the program. He led the Red Raiders to a 30-2 record in 1995-96. Sasser scored 27 points as Tech beat North Carolina in the NCAA Tournament. Golden State chose him 41st in last year's draft but traded his rights to Portland.

Strengths: Sasser has been a winner at every level. Few players have a competitive fire to match his. He gets on the boards on every play, dives for loose balls, runs hard, and doesn't back down from a physical challenge. He thrives under pressure.

Weaknesses: His shooting and passing need a lot of work. He needs to hone his stroke from 15-18 feet. Some people question his leaping ability and overall athleticism.

Analysis: While he doesn't have great skills, Sasser is the kind of player scouts love to watch. If he makes enough jump shots in training camp, he could land a spot on Portland's roster.

COLLEGE STATISTICS

		G	FGP	FTP	RPG	APG	PPG
92-93	TT	30	.434	.629	5.1	1.6	10.6
93-94	TT	28	.482	.710	9.4	2.9	20.6
94-95	TT	30	.510	.793	7.8	2.9	20.1
95-96	TT	31	.458	.726	7.8	2.9	19.5
Totals		119	.474	.727	7.5	2.6	17.7

DORON SHEFFER

Team: Los Angeles Clippers
Position: Guard
Height: 6'5" **Weight:** 197
Birthdate: March 12, 1972
College: Connecticut
Acquired: Second-round pick in 1996 draft (36th overall)

PLAYER SUMMARY	
Will	distribute the rock
Can't	keep pace on "D"
Expect	pinpoint shooting
Don't Expect	a lot of points
Fantasy	$0 Card ...... 10-15¢

Background: Born in Israel, Sheffer came to America after playing for Galil Elyon and leading that team to the national championship in 1993. He then played three seasons at Connecticut. The Huskies went 89-13 with Sheffer and were Big East champions in each of his three seasons. He became the second player in school history with 1,200 points and 500 assists.

Strengths: Sheffer is an experienced, heady performer who knows how to complement good players and run a team. He has good size for a point guard and shows steady aim on his jump shot. He has 3-point range.

Weaknesses: Sheffer lacks quickness and is a step slow in the open court. His slow feet limit his ability to penetrate with his dribble and also make him a marginal defensive player when asked to contain fast point guards one-on-one.

Analysis: Scouts like Sheffer's ability and court savvy and say he has a chance to stick in the NBA despite his physical limitations. He signed with Maccabi Tel Aviv for 1996-97 but may one day land in the NBA.

COLLEGE STATISTICS

	G	FGP	FTP	RPG	APG	PPG
93-94 CONN	34	.505	.735	3.8	4.8	11.9
94-95 CONN	33	.401	.752	4.7	5.5	11.1
95-96 CONN	35	.430	.849	4.8	6.1	16.0
Totals	102	.443	.782	4.4	5.5	13.0

PREDRAG STOJAKOVIC

Team: Sacramento Kings
Position: Forward/Guard
Height: 6'9" **Weight:** 200
Birthdate: September 6, 1977
College: None
Acquired: First-round pick in 1996 draft (14th overall)

PLAYER SUMMARY	
Will	drain jump shots
Can't	miss as a pro
Expect	growing pains
Don't Expect	a grizzled veteran
Fantasy	$1 Card ...... 20-35¢

Background: A native of Belgrade, Yugoslavia, Stojakovic became a Greek citizen in 1993. He was drafted at age 18 after playing the 1994-95 and 1995-96 seasons for PAOK, a pro team in Greece. In 31 games last season, he averaged 16.9 points and 5.1 rebounds and made 39 percent of his 3-point attempts.

Strengths: Stojakovic has been compared to Detlef Schrempf, though he is much quicker than Schrempf and a better shooter. Scouts rated Stojakovic and Ray Allen as the best pure shooters in the draft. Stojakovic runs the court smoothly and handles the ball well. He's sound defensively.

Weaknesses: After playing at a slower pace in Europe, Stojakovic must adjust to the breakneck tempo of the NBA, as well as prove his durability over an 82-game haul (he has never played more than 44 games in a season).

Analysis: Stojakovic was prepared to withdraw from the draft unless he had assurances that he would be a top-15 pick. Sacramento selected him 14th, but the Kings may have to wait while he completes contractual obligations in Greece. If available, he should start the season as a backup small forward.

COLLEGE STATISTICS

—DID NOT PLAY—

JOE VOGEL

Team: Seattle SuperSonics
Position: Forward
Height: 6'11" **Weight:** 255
Birthdate: September 15, 1973
College: Colorado St.
Acquired: Second-round pick in 1996 draft (45th overall)

PLAYER SUMMARY	
Will	shoot with touch
Can't	make the team
Expect	an ordinary Joe
Don't Expect	a household name
Fantasy	$0 Card ...... 10-15¢

Background: Vogel was so obscure on draft day, he wasn't even included in the NBA's draft preview guide, which previewed 156 draft-eligible players. Injuries were a factor in his slow development, as he suffered a broken jaw, a broken foot, and a broken hand during his career. He impressed scouts at the 1996 WAC Tournament, but he wasn't invited to the pre-draft camps.

Strengths: Vogel displays soft touch on his jump shot and can knock down a 15-footer if left alone. He runs well and is a good post defender, having led the WAC in blocked shots. He has good hands and works hard on the boards.

Weaknesses: Vogel has been injury prone and has yet to produce much offensively. Some scouts don't think he has the physical tools and skill level to survive in the NBA.

Analysis: Vogel has almost no chance to earn a roster spot with Seattle, although the Sonics say they're convinced he has pro potential. His college coach compared him to Chris Dudley, though it's doubtful he's as good on the boards as Dudley.

COLLEGE STATISTICS

	G	FGP	FTP	RPG	APG	PPG
92-93 CSU	29	.442	.610	2.1	0.2	4.6
93-94 CSU	28	.446	.552	3.9	0.6	8.5
94-95 CSU	31	.450	.703	5.3	0.3	9.7
95-96 CSU	27	.489	.723	6.6	0.4	10.6
Totals	115	.459	.664	4.5	0.4	8.4

ANTOINE WALKER

Team: Boston Celtics
Position: Forward
Height: 6'8" **Weight:** 224
Birthdate: August 12, 1976
College: Kentucky
Acquired: First-round pick in 1996 draft (sixth overall)

PLAYER SUMMARY	
Will	run the floor
Can't	hammer inside
Expect	a thoroughbred
Don't Expect	a dead-eye shooter
Fantasy	$7-9 Card ...$2.00-4.00

Background: Walker led NCAA-champion Kentucky in rebounding and minutes last season and had 11 points, nine rebounds, and four assists in the title-game victory against Syracuse. A reserve as a freshman, he started 35 of 36 games as a sophomore before leaving Lexington to enter the NBA.

Strengths: Walker has sensational athletic tools and the potential to be an outstanding pro player. He handles the ball exceptionally well for his size, making him a threat to grab a rebound and go coast to coast. He's strong and tough defensively and has the quickness to disrupt opponents on the press.

Weaknesses: Walker's only glaring weakness is his outside shooting, which will have to get better for him to play small forward in the NBA. He played only two seasons of college ball and needs more experience.

Analysis: Boston traded Eric Montross to Dallas to move up in the draft and acquire Walker. He has a bright future in the NBA, most likely as a starting small forward. He is a good match for a team that likes to run, which the Celtics say they'll do more of in 1996-97.

COLLEGE STATISTICS

	G	FGP	FTP	RPG	APG	PPG
94-95 KENT	33	.419	.712	4.5	1.4	7.8
95-96 KENT	36	.463	.631	8.4	2.9	15.2
Totals	69	.449	.660	6.5	2.2	11.7

SAMAKI WALKER

Team: Dallas Mavericks
Position: Forward
Height: 6'9" **Weight:** 240
Birthdate: February 25, 1976
College: Louisville
Acquired: First-round pick in 1996 draft (ninth overall)

PLAYER SUMMARY	
Will	battle underneath
Can't	make the assist pass
Expect	continued improvement
Don't Expect	lack of effort
Fantasy	$0 Card	25-50¢

Background: Walker had a short career at Louisville, playing 29 games as a freshman and 21 as a sophomore, when he was sidelined for much of the season due to NCAA infractions. His 13.7 scoring average in 1994-95 was the second best ever for a Louisville freshman. As a freshman, Walker recorded the only triple-double in school history.

Strengths: Walker is a sensational athlete with a long wingspan, bounce in his legs, and above-average quickness. He's a scoring threat with his back to the basket, and he also has the agility to move outside for jump shots or quick drives. He rebounds well at both ends of the court.

Weaknesses: There were questions about Walker's ability to play at an NBA tempo, but these doubts were laid to rest in predraft workouts. His free-throw stroke and his passing both need work.

Analysis: Ready-made power forwards are hard to find, which is why scouts fell in love with Walker. He's not as quick as Marcus Camby, but he's a lot stronger and could make a quicker adjustment to the NBA. It won't be long before Walker finds a home in the Mavs' starting lineup.

COLLEGE STATISTICS

	G	FGP	FTP	RPG	APG	PPG
94-95 LOUI	29	.548	.537	7.2	1.3	13.7
95-96 LOUI	21	.599	.614	7.5	1.1	15.1
Totals	50	.570	.568	7.3	1.2	14.3

JOHN WALLACE

Team: New York Knicks
Position: Forward
Height: 6'8" **Weight:** 225
Birthdate: February 9, 1974
College: Syracuse
Acquired: First-round pick in 1996 draft (18th overall)

PLAYER SUMMARY	
Will	post up and score
Can't	defend the perimeter
Expect	a hard-nosed worker
Don't Expect	Derrick Coleman
Fantasy	$1-3 Card	$1.00-2.50

Background: Wallace considered leaving Syracuse after his junior season, but he stayed to lead the Orange to the NCAA championship game, where he scored 29 points in the loss. He finished as the third-leading scorer and rebounder in school history.

Strengths: Wallace is a top-flight athlete who runs well, jumps well, and has good hands. He rebounds strongly and works hard to get position offensively. He has expanded his shooting range to about 18 feet, and he's a deft post-up scorer.

Weaknesses: Wallace needs to improve his ball-handling and passing and show more determination on the defensive end of the court. Scouts question his makeup and worry that he didn't get proper fundamental training at Syracuse.

Analysis: Despite raves about his play at Syracuse, Wallace slipped in the draft because of concerns that he might be undersized for power forward and not skilled enough for small forward in the NBA. But his ability to score should guarantee him a spot in the league, probably as a reserve.

COLLEGE STATISTICS

	G	FGP	FTP	RPG	APG	PPG
92-93 SYR	29	.526	.718	7.6	1.3	11.1
93-94 SYR	30	.566	.761	9.0	1.7	15.0
94-95 SYR	30	.588	.679	8.2	2.6	16.8
95-96 SYR	38	.489	.763	8.7	2.4	22.2
Totals	127	.533	.738	8.4	2.0	16.7

JEROME WILLIAMS

Team: Detroit Pistons
Position: Forward
Height: 6'9" **Weight:** 206
Birthdate: May 10, 1973
College: Georgetown
Acquired: First-round pick in 1996 draft (26th overall)

PLAYER SUMMARY	
Will	guard his man
Can't	knock down 3s
Expect	a role-player
Don't Expect	lack of effort
Fantasy	$0 Card ...15-25¢

Background: Williams was third-team All-Big East in both of his seasons at Georgetown after attending Montgomery (MD) College for two years. He started all 68 games at Georgetown and registered 24 double-doubles. He improved his draft status with outstanding play at the Desert Classic, where he averaged 13.7 points, 8.0 rebounds, and 3.0 steals and won MVP honors.

Strengths: Williams is a tenacious competitor who plays hard-nosed defense and runs the court hard on every play. He has the quickness to cover opponents on the perimeter and the strength to work near the basket. He rebounds aggressively.

Weaknesses: Williams's shooting needs to improve. He made only three 3-pointers in college and shot poorly from the foul line. He needs to improve his low-post offense.

Analysis: Williams may have been the steal of the draft. He has superb potential and a work ethic that has led some scouts to call him a poor man's Dennis Rodman without the baggage. He figures to earn considerable playing time as a rookie—mostly at small forward but also grabbing some minutes at power forward. He'll be a solid pro.

COLLEGE STATISTICS

	G	FGP	FTP	RPG	APG	PPG
94-95 GEOR	31	.500	.629	10.0	1.5	10.9
95-96 GEOR	37	.588	.639	8.8	1.4	10.3
Totals	68	.544	.634	9.3	1.4	10.5

LORENZEN WRIGHT

Team: Los Angeles Clippers
Position: Forward
Height: 6'11" **Weight:** 225
Birthdate: November 4, 1975
College: Memphis
Acquired: First-round pick in 1996 draft (seventh overall)

PLAYER SUMMARY	
Will	work his tail off
Can't	knock down jumpers
Expect	a nose for the ball
Don't Expect	muscle
Fantasy	$1-3 Card ...25-50¢

Background: The Tennessee high school Player of the Year in 1994, Wright stayed home to attend Memphis University, where he made a sudden impact, scoring 20 or more points ten times in his freshman season. He had 31 double-doubles in his 64-game college career. He left school after his sophomore season.

Strengths: A fierce competitor and a tremendous athlete, Wright has great potential. He moves aggressively to the offensive boards and gets a lot of putbacks, and he has superb timing as a shot-blocker. He runs the court easily.

Weaknesses: Wright lacks the strength to win wrestling matches with NBA power forwards and needs to add about 20 pounds of muscle. His shooting, low-post moves, and passing need a lot of improvement.

Analysis: Wright and Marcus Camby are similar players, but many scouts think Wright has a stronger upside and would have been a top-three pick in the 1997 draft had he stayed in school. At the very least, Wright should develop into a solid 15-point, ten-rebound producer who gives an honest effort at both ends of the court.

COLLEGE STATISTICS

	G	FGP	FTP	RPG	APG	PPG
94-95 MEMP	34	.561	.626	10.1	1.5	14.8
95-96 MEMP	30	.542	.645	10.4	1.2	17.4
Totals	64	.551	.635	10.3	1.3	16.0

NBA Team Overviews

This section evaluates all 29 NBA teams, sectioning them off by their divisions. For each team, you'll find:

- the club's address
- arena information
- a listing of the team's owner, general manager (or equivalent thereof), and head coach
- the head coach's record (lifetime and with team)
- a review of the team's history
- a review of the team's 1995-96 season
- the club's 1996-97 roster
- a preview of the 1996-97 season

The team rosters include players who were drafted in June. The rosters list each player's 1995-96 statistics. Stats include games (G), rebounds per game (RPG), assists per game (APG), and points per game (PPG). The category "Exp." (experience) indicates the number of years the player has played in the NBA. An (∗) indicates the player was an unrestricted free agent as of late August.

Each 1996-97 season preview tips off with an "opening line," which looks at the players the team lost and those that are coming in. The preview then examines the team at each position, including guard, forward, center, and coaching. "Analysis" evaluates the team's strengths and weaknesses and puts it all into perspective. The preview ends with a prediction, stating where the club is likely to finish within its division.

BOSTON CELTICS

Home: FleetCenter
Capacity: 19,600
Year Built: 1995

Chairman of the Board: Paul E. Gaston
Director of Basketball Operations: M.L. Carr

Address:
FleetCenter
Boston, MA 02114

Head Coach: M.L. Carr
NBA: 33-49   Celtics: 33-49

Celtics History

The Celtics have won 16 world championships and must be listed among the greatest teams in sports history.

Beginning as a member of the old BAA in 1946-47, Boston joined the NBA at its inception. Red Auerbach took over as coach of the team in 1950-51 and began assembling the pieces of the Celtic machine. He started with guard Bob Cousy, added Bill Sharman, and in 1956 bagged the big one—Bill Russell.

Boston won its first championship in 1956-57, then claimed every title from 1958-59 through 1965-66, thoroughly dominating pro basketball. Russell, famous for his battles with Wilt Chamberlain, redefined post defense. His supporting cast included Sam and K.C. Jones, Tom Heinsohn, Frank Ramsey, and John Havlicek.

Auerbach moved to the front office in 1966, Russell took over as player/coach, and the Celtics won championships in 1968 and '69. Heinsohn assumed control of the bench in 1969 and won titles in 1974 and '76 with stars like Havlicek, center Dave Cowens, and guard Jo Jo White.

The Celtics' modern era dawned in 1979, when the team drafted forward Larry Bird. Behind Bird and frontcourt partners Robert Parish and Kevin McHale, Boston shared the 1980s' spotlight with the L.A. Lakers, taking world championships in 1981, '84, and '86. As those stars retired or moved on, Boston had no one to take their place. The tragic deaths of forward Len Bias (1985) and guard Reggie Lewis (1993), thought to be the team's next great players, doomed the Celts to mediocrity in recent years.

1995-96 Review

There is no truth to the rumor that the 1966 Celtic championship team challenged the '95-96 edition to a pick-up game and won by 20 points, but after watching the Celts bumble through a 33-49 season, one wonders whether a cast of old-time legends might have been more fun to watch. Boston had no stars of which to speak and was an appropriate tenant for the spanking-new FleetCenter, which lacks the character and championship history of its predecessor, venerable Boston Garden.

Boston was dreadful on defense, was outrebounded regularly, and was among one of the most foul-prone teams in the NBA. Other than that, things were just fine. Of course, not everything can be blamed on coach/GM M.L. Carr, who sculpted a team out of a collection of suspects. Had Reggie Lewis and Len Bias not suffered tragic deaths, the Celts might have been playing for championships. Instead, they were just playing for paychecks.

Despite injuries, forward Dino Radja (19.7 PPG, 9.8 RPG) again led the team on the court. Forward Rick Fox (14.0 PPG) provided some pop from the perimeter, and guard Dana Barros (13.0 PPG) was strong from beyond 3-point range.

The Celts got rid of point guard Sherman Douglas, but their situation at that position didn't improve much with a combination of Barros and David Wesley (12.3 PPG). Center Eric Montross (7.2 PPG, 5.8 RPG) continued to display his limitations, and the two-guard tandem of Todd Day (11.7 PPG) and Dee Brown (10.7 PPG) was second-rate. Rookie Eric Williams (10.7 PPG) displayed some promise at forward, but creaking Pervis Ellison looked ready for the last round-up.

Boston Celtics
1996-97 Season Preview

Opening Line: Nobody said rebuilding was going to be easy, and the Celts are proving that. Some off-season wheeling and dealing by M.L. Carr can't hide the fact that the Celtics remain a long way from contention. First-round pick Antoine Walker has great skills, but by trading up to get him, Boston left itself without a real center. The playoffs remain a long way off for a former postseason fixture, and an entire generation of new fans is in danger of never understanding the "Celtic Mystique."

Guard: This is a disaster area. Boston has about 12 guys, and none of them is truly an NBA starter. Dana Barros can shoot from long distance and push the ball, but he's too small. David Wesley would be a solid second-string point man, but he started 53 times last year. Todd Day is a shooting guard who can't. And Dee Brown's career has plummeted since his slam-dunk win way back when.

Forward: Walker needs to be introduced to the weight room, but there is no denying his substantial skills and versatility. He isn't a bad shooter and can pass the ball extremely well. He'll be a starter for a long time. Dino Radja is a solid four man, although he doesn't rebound quite enough and isn't a factor on defense. Rick Fox will lose time to Walker (unless Radja is pushed into the middle—a defensive nightmare) but could be a solid bench scorer. If Eric Williams shoots better, he could be a nice frontcourt component.

Center: Eric Montross wasn't exactly Bill Russell, but he was a center. By trading him away, the Celtics left themselves with either the too-soft Radja or rickety-kneed Pervis Ellison as their main center. The other options are bruiser Frank Brickowski, 38-year-old Alton Lister, and second-round draft pick Steve Hamer, a big but rough project.

Analysis: Walker is a nice starting point for Boston's turnaround, but the Celtics have miles to go. The backcourt is a mess, and the power positions are way too soft. It's only right that Carr coaches this team, since he put it together. The Celts might approach 40 wins, but anything more would be a miracle.

Prediction: Sixth place, Atlantic Division

1996-97 Roster

Player	Pos.	Ht.	Wt.	Exp.	College	G	RPG	APG	PPG
							—1995-96—		
Dana Barros	G	5'11"	175	7	Boston College	80	2.4	3.8	13.0
Frank Brickowski	F/C	6'9"	248	12	Penn St.	63	2.4	0.9	5.4
Dee Brown	G	6'2"	192	6	Jacksonville	65	2.1	2.2	10.7
*Junior Burrough	F	6'8"	252	1	Virginia	61	1.8	0.2	3.1
Todd Day	G/F	6'6"	185	4	Arkansas	79	2.8	1.4	11.7
*Pervis Ellison	F/C	6'10"	225	7	Louisville	69	6.5	0.9	5.3
Rick Fox	F/G	6'7"	250	5	North Carolina	81	5.6	4.6	14.0
Steve Hamer	C	7'0"	245	R	Tennessee	—	—	—	—
Alton Lister	F/C	7'0"	248	14	Arizona St.	64	4.4	0.3	2.2
Greg Minor	F/G	6'6"	210	2	Louisville	78	3.3	1.9	9.6
Dino Radja	F	6'11"	263	3	Croatia	53	9.8	1.6	19.7
Antoine Walker	F	6'8"	224	R	Kentucky	—	—	—	—
*David Wesley	G	6'0"	196	3	Baylor	82	3.2	4.8	12.3
Eric Williams	F	6'8"	220	1	Providence	64	3.4	1.1	10.7

MIAMI HEAT

Home: Miami Arena
Capacity: 15,200
Year Built: 1988

Owner: Micky Arison
V.P./Basketball Operations: Dave Wohl

Address:
Miami Arena
Miami, FL 33136

Head Coach: Pat Riley
NBA: 798-339   Heat: 42-40

Heat History

In its first three years of existence, Miami won 57 games—combined. But the Heat finally rose in 1991-92, becoming the first of the league's recent expansion teams to make the playoffs. In the ensuing seasons, however, Miami has been unable to replicate the success of its in-state rival, Orlando.

Miami was awarded a franchise in April 1987 and entered the league in 1988-89 under the direction of coach Ron Rothstein. The Heat stumbled to a 15-67 record in its inaugural campaign, relying on rookies Rony Seikaly and Kevin Edwards. The following year brought rookies Glen Rice and Sherman Douglas to the Heat, but only three more wins. The team struggled through another bad campaign in 1990-91. In May 1991, Rothstein resigned under pressure.

New coach Kevin Loughery arrived in 1991-92, and the Heat came alive. With the help of rookie guard Steve Smith, Seikaly in the middle, and an improved Rice, Miami snuck into the playoffs. Once there, however, they were quickly swept by the world-champion Chicago Bulls.

Despite its young nucleus, the team did not improve much due to injuries and the lack of a physical presence. Miami broke the .500 mark in 1993-94 but lost a nail-biting series to Atlanta in the first round of the playoffs. After a disappointing '94-95 campaign, Heat owner Micky Arison turned to Pat Riley. Riley made some huge changes, trading for center Alonzo Mourning, guard Tim Hardaway, and forward Walt Williams. The Heat were able to make it to the playoffs but were eliminated in the first round, again by the Chicago Bulls.

1995-96 Review

Despite all the hoopla over Pat Riley's move to south Florida, and despite all the personnel shuffling that went on, the 1995-96 Heat barely qualified for the playoffs and were easy first-round fodder for the Chicago Bulls. Miami won ten more games than it did in 1994-95 (42) and certainly played better defense, but the quick exit against Chicago proved the team still had a long way to go and proved Riley alone couldn't produce a title.

As could be expected, the Heat were among the most physical teams in the league, leading the NBA in total fouls and disqualifications. Riley established the club's personality early by engineering a blockbuster deal that sent Glen Rice and others to Charlotte for scowling defensive pivot specialist Alonzo Mourning. Riley didn't end the dealing there. By the end of the year, he had added Tim Hardaway and Chris Gatling from Golden State and Walt Williams and Tyrone Corbin from Sacramento, moves basically designed to free the roster of players he didn't want (Billy Owens, Kevin Willis).

Led by 'Zo, the Heat took quickly to Riley's aggressive style of play. They allowed only 95.0 PPG (fifth best in the league), but they countered that with a meager 96.5 PPG at the other end. Mourning (23.2 PPG, 10.4 RPG, 2.7 BPG) led the team in scoring but received criticism for not getting it done in the playoffs.

Hardaway (15.2 PPG) had a solid year, as did veteran Rex Chapman (14.0 PPG) when he wasn't injured. Rookies Sasha Danilovic (13.4 PPG) and Kurt Thomas (9.0 PPG, 5.9 RPG) showed promise, although Danilovic missed much of the year due to injury.

Miami Heat
1996-97 Season Preview

Opening Line: The first year of Pat Riley's tenure in south Florida was a tumultuous one, with plenty of player changes and growing pains. The off-season was even more chaotic. The Heat signed free-agent forward Juwan Howard but lost him due to salary-cap violations. Pat Riley lost big to the NBA, and the Heat will pay. Intimidating center Alonzo Mourning and point guard Tim Hardaway are good starting points, but without Howard and without a solid bench, the Heat are far from contention.

Guards: Hardaway played 28 games in Miami last year after coming over from Golden State and brings stability to the point. He'll try to regain his status as a 20-PPG, ten-APG man. Sasha Danilovic, who started 18 games last year before suffering an injury, has excellent shooting range and passing skills. Keith Askins can also fill it up from the outside and has good size (6'8"). Free-agent acquisition Dan Majerle brings outside pop and veteran leadership. Gary Grant will provide tough defense.

Forwards: Kurt Thomas, a rare rookie starter in Rileyland, has the potential to be a consistent double-double man at power forward, and he's athletic enough to slide over to the three spot. P.J. Brown is an excellent rebounder who will block at least a shot per game. Rookie Martin Muursepp scored consistently in Europe but didn't rebound all that well for someone 6'9".

Centers: Alonzo Mourning came over at the start of 1995-96 and gave Miami the kind of scowling countenance Riley wanted his team to have. Mourning's seven-year, $105-million deal will keep him blocking shots and bouncing people around the paint for a long time. Although he looked one-dimensional against the Bulls in the playoffs, Mourning is the perfect centerpiece for the tough, defensive-minded team that Riley loves.

Analysis: Just as the Knicks didn't grow into contenders right away, so, too, do the Heat need some time—even with the high-priced nucleus. The team's bench must be fortified. Howard would have made all the difference to this team, but Miami made more strides in one year under Riley than it did in its previous seven years of existence.

Prediction: Fourth place, Atlantic Division

1996-97 Roster

Player	Pos.	Ht.	Wt.	Exp.	College	G	RPG	APG	PPG
Keith Askins	G/F	6'8"	224	6	Alabama	75	4.3	1.6	6.1
P.J. Brown	F	6'11"	240	3	Louisiana Tech	81	6.9	2.0	11.3
Predrag Danilovic	G	6'6"	200	1	(Serbia)	19	2.4	2.5	13.4
Gary Grant	G	6'3"	185	8	Michigan	47	1.1	1.5	4.9
Tim Hardaway	G	6'0"	195	6	Texas-El Paso	80	2.9	8.0	15.2
*Voshon Lenard	G	6'4"	205	1	Minnesota	30	1.7	1.0	5.9
Dan Majerle	G/F	6'6"	220	8	Cent. Michigan	82	3.7	2.6	10.6
Alonzo Mourning	C	6'10"	261	4	Georgetown	70	10.4	2.3	23.2
Martin Muursepp	F	6'9"	235	R	(Estonia)	—	—	—	—
Kurt Thomas	F	6'9"	230	1	Texas Christian	74	5.9	0.6	9.0

NEW JERSEY NETS

Home: Continental Airlines Arena
Capacity: 20,039
Year Built: 1981

Chairman of the Board: Alan L. Aufzien
General Manager: John Nash

Address:
405 Murray Hill Pkwy.
East Rutherford, NJ 07073

Head Coach: John Calipari
NBA: 0-0   Nets: 0-0

Nets History

Basketball fans can choose from two images of the Nets. The first comes from the mid-1970s, back in the days of the ABA, when the club was still based on Long Island. Back then, the team featured skywalking forward Julius Erving, the man who carried the Nets to the 1976 league title. The second image is that from 1986 on, when the team enjoyed minimal success due to poor management and disinterested play.

The franchise was born in 1967 as the New Jersey Americans, a charter member of the ABA. The team moved to Long Island the next year, became the New York Nets, and acquired high-scoring Rick Barry for the 1970-71 season. The Nets made it to the ABA Finals the next year, but they lost Barry to the NBA. Erving came aboard in 1973-74 and led the team to the league title in 1975-76. When the Nets became one of four teams to merge with the NBA, they appeared to be in great shape.

Then the problems started. Erving had a contract dispute with owner Roy Boe, who sold him to Philadelphia. The Nets made the playoffs six of the next ten years but won only one series, beating Philadelphia in 1983-84. That team featured an impressive frontcourt of Buck Williams, Albert King, and Darryl Dawkins.

The years 1986-91 were dismal, as management made poor draft decisions. Though the Nets improved over the next three years, thanks to forward Derrick Coleman and guard Kenny Anderson, they fell quickly back into the Atlantic Division mire and ended up jettisoning both unhappy stars during a typically gruesome 1995-96 season.

1995-96 Review

There was no question that the Nets worked hard during the 1995-96 season to jettison their problems and try to lay the foundation for a future that would rely on hustling and willing—rather than supremely talented but recalcitrant—players. While the franchise might have looked good on paper, it was brutal to watch in action. By trading disgruntled free-agent-to-be Kenny Anderson to Charlotte and sending grouchy Derrick Coleman to the Sixers, the Nets got rid of the two players who failed to be the linchpins of a bright future.

New Jersey may have replicated its 30-52 record from the previous season, but it did so with a team free of malcontents that was actually fun to watch at times. The new attitude couldn't save coach Butch Beard, who was fired following the season. The highest-profile newcomer in the Meadowlands was 7'6" center Shawn Bradley (11.9 PPG, 8.1 RPG, 3.6 BPG), who failed to prosper in Philadelphia but showed signs of promise with the Nets. Beard abandoned efforts to cast Bradley as a true, back-to-the-basket pivotman and let him roam the baseline, where his athletic abilities took over.

Veteran forward Armon Gilliam (18.3 PPG, 9.1 RPG) was the team's steadiest performer but needed help. Point guard Chris Childs (12.8 PPG, 7.0 APG) was a solid point man, but he sued the team for breach of contract. First-round draft pick Ed O'Bannon (6.2 PPG) shot poorly and didn't seem quick enough for the pro game. Power forwards P.J. Brown and Jayson Williams were reliable, particularly on the backboards, but neither was much of a scorer.

New Jersey Nets
1996-97 Season Preview

Opening Line: John Calipari becomes the latest coach to jump from the college ranks to the NBA and hopes he can convince the Nets to "Refuse to Lose." Of course, given New Jersey's recent miseries, that slogan could quickly become "Refuse to Win." The Nets took a positive step foward by selecting Villanova guard Kerry Kittles with the eighth over-all pick in the '96 draft. More work needs to be done, however, before Calipari can enjoy the same kind of success in the Jersey swamps as he did at Massachusetts.

Guards: Kittles could give the Nets the kind of productive scorer they've lacked since the tragic death of Drazen Petrovic. Kittles has blinding speed, shoots well from the outside, and even plays defense. The loss of Chris Childs to the Knicks via free agency means Khalid Reeves must grow into the point guard spot quickly. Veteran Kendall Gill is a solid scorer close to the basket but hasn't had the best attitude throughout his career. Kevin Edwards's shot needs work. Vincent Askew, acquired over the off-season from Seattle, will help on defense.

Forwards: Jayson Williams doesn't shoot well, but he is a strong board man and lightens the mood in the locker room. Second-year man Ed O'Bannon struggled considerably with his shot last season and may lack NBA quickness. Free-agent pick-up David Benoit isn't the most reliable outside shooter, but he can approach double figures from the wing and on the break. The loss of Armon Gilliam and P.J. Brown may hurt here.

Centers: Shawn Bradley will never revolutionize the game, as the 76ers claimed when they selected him three years ago, but he can block a bunch of shots, get some rebounds, move well, and score 12-15 a game. Several NBA teams would take that right now. Backup Yinka Dare remains particularly raw and disappointing.

Analysis: Calipari doesn't have an empty cupboard, but he must reverse the Nets' history of front-office mistakes, on-court bumbling, and attitude problems. It's a big job that will take more than a year to complete. But the Nets aren't as far away from playoff contention as last year's 30 wins indicate. They rebound well and block plenty of shots. Those are good starting points.

Prediction: Fifth place, Atlantic Division

1996-97 Roster

Player	Pos.	Ht.	Wt.	Exp.	College	G	RPG	APG	PPG
Vincent Askew	G/F	6'6"	235	7	Memphis St.	69	3.2	2.4	8.5
David Benoit	F	6'8"	220	5	Alabama	81	4.7	1.0	8.2
Shawn Bradley	C	7'6"	248	3	Brigham Young	79	8.1	0.8	11.9
Yinka Dare	C	7'0"	265	2	G. Washington	58	3.1	0.0	2.8
Kevin Edwards	G	6'3"	210	8	DePaul	34	2.2	2.1	11.6
Kendall Gill	G	6'5"	210	6	Illinois	47	4.9	5.5	14.0
Kerry Kittles	G	6'5"	179	R	Villanova	—	—	—	—
Ed O'Bannon	F	6'8"	222	1	UCLA	64	2.6	1.0	6.2
Robert Pack	G	6'2"	190	5	Southern Cal.	31	4.3	7.8	18.1
Khalid Reeves	G	6'3"	201	2	Arizona	51	1.5	2.3	5.5
Jayson Williams	F	6'10"	245	6	St. John's	80	10.0	0.6	9.0

(Header spanning G RPG APG PPG: —1995-96—)

NEW YORK KNICKS

Home: Madison Square Garden
Capacity: 19,763
Year Built: 1968

Governor: Robert M. Gutkowski
V.P./General Manager: Ernie Grunfeld

Address:
Two Pennsylvania Plaza
New York, NY 10121

Head Coach: Jeff Van Gundy
NBA: 13-10   Knicks: 13-10

Knicks History

Despite playing in the nation's media capital, the Knicks have spent their existence in the shadows of other teams. For the franchise's first 40 years, New York chased the Celtics, while recent incarnations have labored to catch Chicago.

Soon after the franchise's inception as a BAA member, the Knicks made trips to the NBA Finals—in 1951, '52, and '53. Hall of Fame coach Joe Lapchick melded forward Carl Braun with Harry Gallatin, Dick McGuire, and Nat "Sweetwater" Clifton and reached the playoffs nine consecutive years (1947-55).

For the next ten years, the Knicks wandered through six coaches and made the playoffs only once. But fortunes changed quickly when Red Holzman took over in 1967-68. The Knicks built a powerhouse on the backs of center Willis Reed, forwards Bill Bradley and Dave DeBusschere, and guards Walt "Clyde" Frazier and Dick Barnett. In 1969-70, they defeated the Lakers in seven games for the title.

Jerry Lucas replaced Reed in the middle, and flashy Earl Monroe joined Frazier to form one of the game's best-ever backcourts. Together, they won the NBA championship in 1973.

Since then, the Knicks have seen only modest success. High-scoring Bernard King provided some thrills in the mid-1980s, and star center Patrick Ewing sparked the team to the Atlantic Division title in 1988-89. Pat Riley won three straight division titles in the 1990s but fell short in his quest for an NBA title, losing in the 1994 Finals to Houston. An aging nucleus led to Riley's decision to leave after 1995, as well as the subsequent firing of heralded replacement Don Nelson.

1995-96 Review

As the speed limit in the league's fast lane increased, the Knicks appeared too slow to keep up. Though New York's players rationalized that their playoff loss to Chicago could have been a win if this or that had gone right, the fact was that the 1995-96 Knicks incarnation was playing a different kind of game than the league's elite teams. It was enough to win 47 games and take a playoff series from Cleveland—and it was enough to scare the injury-depleted Bulls—but it was not enough to survive in the NBA's rarified air.

The season ended with several unanswered questions, including which team members would be back for 1996-97 and whether Jeff Van Gundy, the loyal Pat Riley assistant who had taken over as boss when Don Nelson was fired midway through his first year in Gotham, would be given a chance to prove himself full-time. (Van Gundy didn't wait long for an answer to this question, as his contract was renewed just one week after the Knicks were knocked out.)

Certain things remained constant. Center Patrick Ewing (22.5 PPG, 10.6 RPG) again led the Knicks in scoring, although his average was his lowest in eight years. Off guard John Starks (12.6 PPG) was alternately scintillating or maddening, depending on his mood and his accuracy. Anthony Mason (14.6 PPG, 9.3 RPG) thrived as a starter, and veteran Derek Harper (14.0 PPG) was again a rock at point guard. Charles Oakley (11.4 PPG, 8.7 RPG) missed nearly 30 games because of an injury, while reserves Hubert Davis and Willie Anderson provided some occasional punch off the bench.

New York Knicks
1996-97 Season Preview

Opening Line: New York set about reinventing itself after losing to the Bulls in the Eastern semis last year and certainly accomplished that goal. Now, we'll see if it acquired the proper new pieces. The Knicks have a new backcourt (Chris Childs and Allan Houston), a new small forward (Larry Johnson), and an almost entirely new collection of supporting players. The Knicks are more athletic, but it's up to coach Jeff Van Gundy, retained after a solid half-season in 1995-96, to fit everything together.

Guards: Childs emerged as a solid point man in New Jersey last year, although he must improve his shooting. With veteran Derek Harper gone, Charlie Ward gets the primary backup spot. He has demonstrated the ability to run the team despite his poor shooting. Houston is one of the top young off guards in the game and provides an immediate upgrade over moody John Starks, a streaky scorer who can either carry or kill a team.

Forwards: New York has about 50 of these guys. Charles Oakley battled foot troubles last year but is a first-rate scorer and rebounder at the four spot when healthy. Johnson's back doesn't allow him to bang the way he used to, but he was third in the NBA in minutes played last year and can still score inside and out. Syracuse's John Wallace heads the draft class and has talent, but he has already shown a petulant streak; Dontae Jones of Mississippi State could be a steal if his foot is healthy; and Walter McCarty is a big body who bangs and plays interior defense. Buck Williams will play defense and add class to the operation,

Centers: He's getting older and his numbers are slipping, but Patrick Ewing remains a formidable pivotman. He shoots well from the perimeter, handles the dirty work inside, and is still a double-figure board man. Ancient Herb Williams is a willing defender.

Analysis: These Knicks are definitely more athletic than last year's grind-it-out bunch, but the team is still a year or two away from real contention. Childs still needs to improve, and the young frontcourt guys must prove themselves worthy of playing in the NBA. Like everyone else in the Eastern Conference, New York is positioning itself to take over when Chicago slides back. This past off-season was a good first step.

Prediction: Second place, Atlantic Division

1996-97 Roster

Player	Pos.	Ht.	Wt.	Exp.	College	G	RPG	APG	PPG
							\multicolumn{3}{c}{—1995-96—}		
Chris Childs	G	6'3"	195	2	Boise St.	78	3.1	7.0	12.8
Patrick Ewing	C	7'0"	240	11	Georgetown	76	10.6	2.1	22.5
Allan Houston	G	6'6"	210	3	Tennessee	82	3.7	3.0	19.7
Larry Johnson	F	6'7"	250	5	UNLV	81	8.4	4.4	20.5
Dontae Jones	F	6'7"	220	R	Mississippi St.	—	—	—	—
Walter McCarty	F	6'10"	230	R	Kentucky	—	—	—	—
Charles Oakley	F	6'9"	245	11	Virginia Union	53	8.7	2.6	11.4
John Starks	G	6'5"	185	7	Oklahoma St.	81	2.9	3.9	12.6
John Wallace	F	6'8"	225	R	Syracuse	—	—	—	—
Charlie Ward	G	6'2"	190	2	Florida St.	62	1.6	2.1	3.9
Buck Williams	F	6'8"	225	15	Maryland	70	5.8	0.6	7.3
*Herb Williams	C/F	6'11"	260	15	Ohio St.	44	2.0	0.6	3.1

ORLANDO MAGIC

Home: Orlando Arena
Capacity: 15,998
Year Built: 1989

Chairman: Rich DeVos
V.P./Basketball Operations: John Gabriel

Address:
One Magic Place
Orlando, FL 32801

Head Coach: Brian Hill
NBA: 167-79   Magic: 167-79

Magic History

Magic fans have ridden a roller coaster of emotions during the team's seven-year existence. After a predictably dreadful 18-64 debut in 1989-90, the Magic improved to 31-51 in 1990-91. Injuries ruined the 1991-92 season, but center Shaquille O'Neal brought glittering new magic to Orlando in 1992-93 and an NBA Finals appearance two years later.

Orlando's inaugural season was noteworthy for style, as the Magic unveiled their classy pinstriped uniforms. Coach Matt Guokas blended expansion-draft acquisitions Reggie Theus, Sam Vincent, Otis Smith, and Scott Skiles with rookie Nick Anderson into a team that was exciting, though not very successful.

Things perked up in 1990-91. Orlando drafted sharp-shooter Dennis Scott, and Skiles developed into one of the league's top point guards. However, Skiles fizzled out in 1991-92 and Scott missed most of the year with an injury. With little other talent, Orlando finished the year as the East's worst team.

With the No. 1 pick in the 1992 draft, the Magic grabbed O'Neal, a mega-superstar who improved the club by 20 games in 1992-93. Orlando missed the 1993 playoffs by a tie-breaker but amazingly won the pre-draft lottery again. The team drafted Chris Webber, traded him for rookie Anfernee Hardaway, and dreamed of bright days ahead.

Orlando won 50 games in 1993-94 but was swept in the opening playoff round. The club added the final piece of the puzzle in 1994-95 (free agent power forward Horace Grant), finished with the best record in the conference, and advanced to the NBA Finals before losing to Houston.

1995-96 Review

It must have been difficult for Magic fans to realize that their team's visit to the NBA Finals in 1995 was merely the by-product of Michael Jordan's rustiness. Jordan returned to his true, amazing self in time for 1995-96, and the Bulls reasserted themselves as the dominant team in the East by sweeping Orlando in a conference final completely devoid of drama.

While the Bulls chased destiny, the Magic searched for solutions to their problems, the most glaring of which appeared to be a lack of team speed, poor focus, and the need for a true point guard. Even though Orlando won a franchise-record 60 games, it appeared to be an incomplete team on many levels. Its bench was too short, and its stars were too young.

Center Shaquille O'Neal (26.6 PPG, 11.0 RPG) again had big numbers, but his awful (48.7 percent) free-throw shooting and incomplete post repertoire hurt him against the league's best. Despite those flaws, Magic fans spent much of the off-season holding their collective breath to see whether free agent Shaq would sign with someone else.

Anfernee Hardaway (21.7 PPG) was again tremendous, although he was out of place at the point guard position. Horace Grant's season ended early, with an elbow injury in the Bulls series that expedited the Magic's demise against his old team.

Dennis Scott (17.5 PPG) continued to be one of the league's top long-range shooters, and Nick Anderson (14.7 PPG) was a reliable scorer but an erratic shooter. The bench troika of Donald Royal, Brian Shaw, and Anthony Bowie was adequate but hardly that of a championship-level team.

Orlando Magic
1996-97 Season Preview

Opening Line: The Magic suffered two huge losses during the 1996 postseason, absorbing a four-game sweep against Chicago in the Eastern finals and then watching franchise center Shaquille O'Neal bolt town for Los Angeles. The team enters this season as a perimeter-based club suddenly reliant on Felton Spencer for production in the middle.

Guards: Penny Hardaway's play against Chicago convinced the Magic brass that the multitalented 6'7" star is not a point man. He would be perfect in the two spot, where he can create things for himself and benefit from someone else's passing. Of course, that would relegate Nick Anderson to the bench, but Orlando could use some reliable scoring and rebounding in reserve. Brian Shaw is a weak shooter but a pretty good passer. Donald Royal and Anthony Bowie are at their best on defense and shooting short "Js."

Forwards: Dennis Scott remains the league's top long-distance shooter. No one can match his range or accuracy. His trouble comes on defense and in the open floor, where the same legs that provide power for the jumper slow him down. A postseason elbow injury notwithstanding, Horace Grant remains a stalwart at the four position. He plays hard, produces every night, and knows how to win. Joe Wolf is a competent scorer close to the basket, but provides little else. First-round pick Brian Evans is a tall (6'8") shooter.

Centers: New acquisition Felton Spencer is big and slow and—thankfully—will take over as starting center so that Jon Koncak won't have to. Spencer is no Shaq, but he's quite a sight better than Koncak would have been.

Analysis: This may sound crazy, but the Magic may be better off in the long run without O'Neal. There's no guarantee he'll ever concentrate on basketball enough to be a champion, and the Magic can use the truckload of money it will save to chase other free agents. Just remember, Chicago won it all last year with Luc Longley in the middle.

Prediction: First place, Atlantic Division

1996-97 Roster

Player	Pos.	Ht.	Wt.	Exp.	College	G	RPG	APG	PPG
							—1995-96—		
Nick Anderson	G/F	6'6"	220	7	Illinois	77	5.4	3.6	14.7
Darrell Armstrong	G	6'1"	180	2	Fayetteville	13	0.2	0.4	3.2
Anthony Bonner	F	6'8"	225	6	St. Louis	4	4.8	1.0	3.3
*Anthony Bowie	G	6'6"	200	7	Oklahoma	74	1.7	1.4	4.2
Brian Evans	F/G	6'8"	220	R	Indiana	—	—	—	—
Horace Grant	F	6'10"	235	9	Clemson	62	9.2	2.7	13.4
Anfernee Hardaway	G/F	6'7"	207	3	Memphis St.	82	4.3	7.1	21.7
Jon Koncak	C	7'0"	250	11	Southern Meth.	67	4.1	0.8	3.0
Amal McCaskill	C	6'11"	235	R	Marquette	—	—	—	—
Donald Royal	F	6'8"	210	6	Notre Dame	64	2.4	0.7	5.3
Dennis Scott	G/F	6'8"	230	6	Georgia Tech	82	3.8	3.0	17.5
Brian Shaw	G	6'6"	194	7	Cal.-Santa Barb.	75	3.0	4.5	6.6
Felton Spencer	C	7'0"	265	6	Louisville	71	4.3	0.2	5.6
Derek Strong	F	6'8"	250	5	Xavier	63	2.8	0.5	3.4
David Vaughn	F	6'9"	240	1	Memphis	33	2.4	0.2	1.9
Gerald Wilkins	G	6'7"	230	10	Tenn.-Chattan.	28	2.3	2.4	6.7
*Joe Wolf	F/C	6'11"	257	8	North Carolina	64	2.9	1.0	4.5

PHILADELPHIA 76ERS

Home: CoresStates Center
Capacity: 21,000
Year Built: 1996

Owner: Pat Croce
General Manager: Brad Greenberg

Address:
1 CoresStates Center
Philadelphia, PA 19148

Head Coach: Johnny Davis
NBA: 0-0   76ers: 0-0

Sixers History

The 76ers' history can be described as a roller coaster of highs and lows. The 1966-67 Sixers thrashed the league with a 68-13 record and a world title. On the other hand, the 1972-73 Sixers stumbled to the worst-ever mark of 9-73.

The Sixers began in 1949-50 as the Syracuse Nationals and reached the first NBA Finals series, losing in six games to Minneapolis. Hall of Fame center Dolph Schayes was the big gun on both that team and the 1953-54 squad that fell again in the NBA Finals, this time to the Lakers.

The team moved to Philadelphia in 1963-64 and acquired Wilt Chamberlain in a trade in early 1965. They moved onto a level with the dominating Boston Celtics and began to challenge them for league supremacy. In fact, the Nationals/Sixers have met the Celtics in 17 playoff series, winning seven. Philly beat Boston in the 1967 East finals en route to the NBA title.

The Sixers nosedived in the early 1970s, but the arrival of coach Gene Shue and ABA imports George McGinnis and Julius Erving signaled a renaissance. Philadelphia advanced to the NBA Finals in 1976-77 but lost to Portland. Similar excursions were made in 1979-80 and 1981-82, thanks to Erving, Bobby Jones, Maurice Cheeks, and Andrew Toney.

Moses Malone arrived for the 1982-83 season, and the Sixers blitzed to another NBA title. In 1984, Philly drafted super-forward Charles Barkley, who led the team to the 1989-90 Atlantic Division title. The team has struggled since trading Barkley in '92. The Sixers closed the 1995-96 season with the dubious distinction of having worsened their season record in six straight seasons, from 1990 through '96.

1995-96 Review

By the time the 1995-96 season was less than two months old, it was painfully obvious that the hasty repair job the Sixers had performed on their limping team was woefully inadequate. The experimental use of Vernon Maxwell was a flop. Wayward soul Richard Dumas was an inconsistent and unpredictable small forward. And center Shawn Bradley, who had appeared to make progress during the end of the 1994-95 campaign, regressed.

Philadelphia sunk to the worst non-expansion record in the league (18-64). Even with a mess that big, however, owner Harold Katz was able to peddle the franchise to local cable TV giant Comcast for a fat profit.

If rookie guard Jerry Stackhouse (19.2 PPG) hadn't decided to pick a fight during a late-season road game, he would have enjoyed a nearly perfect rookie season—aside from the team's losing. He gave the Sixers a legitimate wing scorer and a pillar around which future teams could be built. Bradley, however, was not impressive, and the Sixers dealt him to New Jersey for power forward Derrick Coleman, a deal that sent one headache away and brought another in return. Coleman played only 11 games with the Sixers before ankle problems ended his season. Maxwell (16.2 PPG) was out of place at the point and shot only 39 percent from the field.

Meanwhile, poor Clarence Weatherspoon (16.7 PPG, 9.7 RPG), one of the hardest-working players in the league, suffered through another losing season, his fourth in a row. Young guard Trevor Ruffin (12.8 PPG) showed promise, while high-priced forward Scott Williams played only 13 games due to injury.

Philadelphia 76ers
1996-97 Season Preview

Opening Line: The Sixers have a new ownership group (Comcast), a new president (Pat Croce), a new GM (Brad Greenberg), a new coach (Johnny Davis), a new arena (CoresStates Center), and a long way to go before they can be considered a playoff contender. But hope springs eternal, particularly when one considers the potential of first-overall draft pick Allen Iverson. The Sixers may not be near the postseason, but they will be more exciting and, more important, more focused than in recent years.

Guards: Iverson was a blur at Georgetown, capable of creating a variety of scoring opportunities for himself. In Philadelphia, he'll be asked to set up others, too. Backcourt mate Jerry Stackhouse enjoyed a big first year, leading all rookies in scoring, but he needs to improve his 3-point shooting and cut down on turnovers. Rex Walters has the potential to be a steady third guard, although his shooting must improve. Lucious Harris can bury the trey.

Forwards: If Derrick Coleman is happy (and that's a huge *if*), he can be one of the most talented power forwards in the league. Clarence Weatherspoon is a four in a three man's body, but nobody works harder than he does. Free-agent pickup Don MacLean is a one-dimensional jump shooter coming off an injury. Michael Cage rebounds and provides solid defense at the four and five spots. Oft-injured Scott Williams is a competent backup at power forward and can play some center. Ryan Minor leads a trio of second-round draft picks, although he may opt to play baseball instead. Mark Hendrickson has a nice shooting touch but needs strength. Jamie Feick has strength and little else.

Centers: Shawn Bradley wasn't a star, but he was better than what the Sixers have now. This area is a mess, but Cage will help out a bit here although it's not his natural spot. Williams is likely to contribute here as well.

Analysis: Iverson has plenty to learn. Coleman is a potential powder keg. And Stackhouse can't do it by himself. New president Pat Croce is as upbeat as one can get, but even he may be hard-pressed to find the silver lining in this cloud. At least the new arena will draw some interest, even if the team inside doesn't.

Prediction: Seventh place, Atlantic Division

1996-97 Roster

Player	Pos.	Ht.	Wt.	Exp.	College	G	RPG	APG	PPG
						|—1995-96—|			
Michael Cage	C/F	6'9"	248	12	San Diego St.	82	8.9	0.6	6.0
Derrick Coleman	F	6'10"	260	6	Syracuse	11	6.5	2.8	11.2
Jamie Feick	F/C	6'9"	255	R	Michigan St.	—	—	—	—
Lucious Harris	G	6'5"	205	3	Long Beach St.	61	2.0	1.3	7.9
Mark Hendrickson	F	6'9"	220	R	Washington St.	—	—	—	—
Allen Iverson	G	6'0"	165	R	Georgetown	—	—	—	—
Don MacLean	F	6'10"	225	4	UCLA	56	3.7	1.6	11.2
Ryan Minor	F/G	6'7"	220	R	Oklahoma	—	—	—	—
Jerry Stackhouse	G/F	6'6"	218	1	North Carolina	72	3.7	3.9	19.2
Rex Walters	G	6'4"	190	3	Kansas	44	1.3	2.4	4.2
C. Weatherspoon	F	6'7"	240	4	S. Mississippi	78	9.7	2.0	16.7
Scott Williams	C	6'10"	230	6	North Carolina	13	3.5	0.4	3.1

WASHINGTON BULLETS

Home: USAir Arena
Capacity: 18,756
Year Built: 1973

Chairman of the Board: Abe Pollin
V.P./General Manager: Wes Unseld

Address:
USAir Arena
Landover, MD 20785

Head Coach: Jim Lynam
NBA: 306-368   Bullets: 60-104

Bullets History

The Bullets' greatest years came in the 1970s, but the franchise rolled off the assembly line in 1961-62 as the Chicago Packers. In 1963, it blew the Windy City, moved to Baltimore, and adopted its current nickname.

In 1964-65, the Bullets advanced to the Western finals behind center Walt Bellamy and forward Bailey Howell. Prior to the 1968-69 season, Baltimore drafted huge Wes Unseld, who won the MVP Award in his first season. Unseld teamed with bruising Gus Johnson and slick Earl "The Pearl" Monroe to help the Bullets win the Eastern Division.

The Bullets made their first trip to the NBA Finals in 1970-71, but they were dispatched in four games by Milwaukee. They made it back in 1974-75, this time as Washington, but Golden State swept them. Dick Motta took over the Bullets in 1976-77 and led them to the Finals the following year. This time, Unseld, Elvin Hayes, Bob Dandridge, and company whipped Seattle in seven games. The Sonics got revenge in the Finals the next year, closing out the Bullets' big decade.

The 1980s featured some talented players (Jeff Ruland, Rick Mahorn, Greg Ballard, Jeff Malone) but few highlights. The Bullets won just one playoff series during the whole decade, and by its end they were a lottery team. Unseld took over as coach in 1987-88 but—outside of Bernard King and then Pervis Ellison—had little to work with. The club has been moribund throughout the 1990s, though it showed some sparks of life in 1995-96 under the guidance of coach Jim Lynam and behind the excellent play of forward Juwan Howard.

1995-96 Review

If the Bullets could have found a way to give Chris Webber a stainless steel shoulder, they might just have qualified for the playoffs for the first time since the Reagan administration. Washington staged a valiant, late-season drive for the postseason and ended up with 39 wins, their best effort since 1988-89. But the early-season loss of Webber (he played just 15 games) hurt the team's chances and consigned them to the lottery for the eighth straight season, despite the late drive.

You can't blame second-year forward Juwan Howard (22.1 PPG) for any of that. All Howard did was carry the Bullets all season and give the team an air of class and sportsmanship that has all but vanished from the game. He played hard every night and produced under every possible circumstance.

Center Gheorghe Muresan (14.5 PPG, 9.6 RPG), the league's Most Improved Player, continued developing into a pivot force, while Calbert Cheaney (15.1 PPG) finally showed glimpses of the wing scoring talent that led the Bullets to make him a first-round pick in 1993. Rookie Rasheed Wallace (10.1 PPG) was among the league leaders in technical fouls but proved he could be a productive frontcourt player once he gains some maturity.

The Bullets were hurt all year by trouble at the point guard spot. They traded for Mark Price before the season started, but foot problems limited him to just seven games. Injuries also limited Robert Pack to less than half a season, leaving overmatched Brent Price to lead the team. One of the season's more pleasant surprises was the play of Tim Legler, who led the NBA in 3-point shooting (.522).

Washington Bullets
1996-97 Season Preview

Opening Line: The Bullets made a valiant run at the NBA playoffs last year but return with a different team this season. Gone is forward Rasheed Wallace, and in are point guard Rod Strickland and Harvey Grant. Keeping Juwan Howard propels the Bullets into playoff contention, but the team's success will depend on Strickland's attitude and forward Chris Webber's health. Still, Washington is poised for a big jump.

Guards: Strickland is an excellent distributor and fine shooter, but a renowned trouble-maker who has sparred with all of his professional coaches. Calbert Cheaney showed signs of growing into the off guard role last year, but he needs to get better from the outside. Second-round pick Ronnie Henderson of LSU is athletic but a poor shot. Tim Legler, on the other hand, may just be the league's best pure shooter. Tracy Murray is a good sniper from the wing who surprised many with his production in Toronto last year.

Forwards: Howard has a rare blend of tremendous talent, a giant work ethic, and plenty of character. He may have played only two years, but he's worth the giant contract the Bullets signed him to. Webber can do it all from the power forward position if he stays healthy. Grant is a dependable scorer but hardly spectacular. Veteran Lorenzo Williams— an off-season free-agent acquisition—rarely scores, but he rebounds and is a willing banger.

Centers: Gheorghe Muresan is slow and deliberate, and all of a sudden everybody loves him. He shoots a ridiculously high percentage (.580) from the floor, grabs scads of rebounds, and blocks close to three shots a game. He'll never be an All-Star, but he could be an 18-10-5 man. Webber, Howard, and Williams all have experience in the pivot and give the Bullets loads of frontcourt options.

Analysis: This is a pretty good team, and it will get better if coach Jimmy Lynam can mix the new faces in with the holdovers and if everyone can avoid the injury bug. Strickland and Webber are the keys. Strickland needs to play ball and stop bellyaching, while Webber needs to have a pain-free season. If they're happy, the Bullets are in pretty good shape.

Prediction: Third place, Atlantic Division

1996-97 Roster

Player	Pos.	Ht.	Wt.	Exp.	College	G	RPG	APG	PPG
								—1995-96—	
Calbert Cheaney	F/G	6'7"	215	3	Indiana	70	3.4	2.2	15.1
Harvey Grant	F	6'9"	235	8	Oklahoma	76	4.8	1.5	9.3
Ronnie Henderson	G	6'4"	206	R	Louisiana St.	—	—	—	—
Juwan Howard	F	6'9"	250	2	Michigan	81	8.1	4.4	22.1
*Tim Legler	G	6'4"	200	6	La Salle	77	1.8	1.8	9.4
Gheorghe Muresan	C	7'7"	303	3	Cluj	76	9.6	0.7	14.5
Tracy Murray	F	6'7"	228	4	UCLA	82	4.3	1.6	16.2
Rod Strickland	G	6'3"	185	8	DePaul	67	4.4	9.6	18.7
Chris Webber	F	6'10"	250	3	Michigan	15	7.6	5.0	23.7
Chris Whitney	G	6'0"	170	3	Clemson	21	1.6	2.4	7.1
Lorenzo Williams	F/C	6'9"	220	4	Stetson	65	8.0	1.3	3.0

ATLANTA HAWKS

Home: The Omni
Capacity: 16,365
Year Built: 1972

Owner: Ted Turner
V.P./General Manager: Pete Babcock

Address:
One CNN Center, #405 South
Atlanta, GA 30303

Head Coach: Lenny Wilkens
NBA: 1014-993   Hawks: 145-101

Hawks History

Few teams have had as many different addresses as the Hawks. Before settling in Georgia, the franchise roamed the Midwest, calling Moline, Rock Island, Davenport, Milwaukee, and St. Louis home.

An original member of the NBA, the franchise was first known as the Tri-City (Moline, Rock Island, and Davenport) Blackhawks. Two years later, it moved to Milwaukee and shortened its nickname to its current form. Though active off the court, it wasn't until the team drafted Bob Pettit in 1954 that it started to show some life on it.

The Hawks moved to St. Louis in 1955, won consecutive Western Conference championships from 1957-61, and defeated Boston in 1958 for the franchise's lone NBA title. Pettit, Cliff Hagan, Ed Macauley, Charlie Share, and Slater Martin formed the nucleus of those teams. In the title win over Boston, Pettit played with his broken left wrist in a cast, and Share played with his busted jaw wired shut.

The 1960s featured talented players like Lou Hudson, Joe Caldwell, and Zelmo Beatty, but the Hawks could not get back to the Finals. The team moved to Atlanta for the 1968-69 season and staggered through the next decade as a .500 team.

Things started to change in 1982, when Atlanta drafted exciting forward Dominique Wilkins. The Hawks won the NBA Central Division title in 1986-87 and recorded a franchise-record 57 wins. The team hovered around .500 in the early 1990s before a 57-win season under new coach Lenny Wilkens in 1993-94. Subsequent editions have been solid but not anywhere near championship caliber.

1995-96 Review

The Hawks were dismissed from the second round of the 1996 playoffs by Orlando in just five games, but Atlanta's big-picture view of the entire season had to be a pleasant one. How else can one describe a season that included 46 wins and an improbable first-round postseason triumph over Indiana, all with a collection of talent that was hardly overwhelming?

One would be hard-pressed to find any greater evidence that Lenny Wilkens is a superb coaching talent. The Hawks thrived despite the lack of a true center and with a razor-thin bench. Believe it or not, the key to the season may have been the acquisition of forward Christian Laettner (16.4 PPG, 7.3 RPG), who came to the Hawks from Minnesota with Sean Rooks and hardly resembled the petulant player he was with the T'Wolves. Although he had to play out of position (center) most of the time, Laettner played well and unselfishly.

Off guard Steve Smith (18.1 PPG) continued to develop, although his shooting (43.2 percent, 33.1 percent from 3) was erratic. Point guard Mookie Blaylock (15.7 PPG, 5.9 APG, 2.6 SPG) was again one of the more underrated performers at his position, and Stacey Augmon (12.7 PPG) brought excellent athletic ability and defense to the small forward spot.

But the Hawks were thin up front, other than Laettner. Grant Long (13.1 PPG, 9.6 RPG) did his usual steady job at power forward, and Rooks contributed some heft after coming over from Minnesota, but that was about it. The rest of the bench was pedestrian. Rookie forward Alan Henderson displayed some promise, but veteran guard Craig Ehlo (8.5 PPG) showed signs of age.

Atlanta Hawks
1996-97 Season Preview

Opening Line: For all the kudos Lenny Wilkens received for squiring Dream Team III during the Atlanta Olympics, his best work in the past year came when he coaxed 46 wins out of the Hawks during the 1995-96 season. But thanks to the arrivals of power forward Christian Laettner (last year) and center Dikembe Mutombo (during the off-season), Wilkens may not have to do as much by himself this season.

Guard: Fans should hope that Mookie Blaylock's self-conversion from a great point man to a grenade-launcher was a one-year phenomenon. Blaylock is a superior defender and slick passer, but he shouldn't be shooting that much. That's Steve Smith's job. Smith is improving as an outside threat, has great size for an off guard, and isn't a bad passer. Free-agent acquisition Jon Barry will provide some outside pop. Depth, however, remains a problem for the Hawks.

Forward: The Hawks took a chance by acquiring Laettner from Minnesota late last season, since the former Duke All-American has had a renowned attitude problem. But Laettner is a solid inside scorer, an above-average rebounder, and a competitor. The small forward spot is quite thin since Atlanta sent Stacy Augmon to Detroit during the off-season. And Laettner had better behave—because steady power man Grant Long went to the Pistons as well. Second-year man Alan Henderson has the potential to be a solid baseline player, but he must shoot better, particularly from the foul line.

Center: It's a good thing the Hawks acquired Mutombo, because they spent their late-first-round draft pick on hulking 7'2", 340-pound Priest Lauderdale, a mechanical center who played just 13 collegiate games and spent last year in the Greek league. He is hardly the answer to the team's post problems. Mutombo is, however. He plays the kind of intimidating defense Wilkens loves, and even though he doesn't score much, Mutombo is a first-rate pivot and a big pickup for Atlanta.

Analysis: The acquisition of Mutombo means the Hawks will continue to win through defense, although a full year of Laettner and a developing Henderson could help the offensive side. Some NBA teams succeed in spite of their coaches. Atlanta succeeds because of its coach.

Prediction: Fourth place, Central Division

1996-97 Roster

| Player | Pos. | Ht. | Wt. | Exp. | College | —1995-96— | | |
						G	RPG	APG	PPG
Jon Barry	G	6'4"	194	4	Georgia Tech	68	0.9	1.3	3.8
Mookie Blaylock	G	6'1"	185	7	Oklahoma	81	4.1	5.9	15.7
Donnie Boyce	G	6'5"	196	1	Colorado	8	1.3	0.4	3.0
Alan Henderson	F	6'9"	235	1	Indiana	79	4.5	0.6	6.4
Christian Laettner	F	6'11"	245	4	Duke	74	7.3	2.7	16.4
Priest Lauderdale	C	7'2"	340	R	(Greece)	—	—	—	—
Dikembe Mutombo	C	7'2"	250	5	Georgetown	74	11.8	1.5	11.0
Ken Norman	F	6'8"	238	9	Illinois	34	3.9	1.9	8.9
Steve Smith	G	6'8"	215	5	Michigan St.	80	4.1	2.8	18.1

CHARLOTTE HORNETS

Home: Charlotte Coliseum
Capacity: 23,698
Year Built: 1988

Owner: George Shinn
V.P./Basketball Operations: Bob Bass

Address:
Hive Drive
Charlotte, NC 28217

Head Coach: Dave Cowens
NBA: 27-41   Hornets: 0-0

Hornets History

They've always loved college basketball down on Tobacco Road, so it was a natural for the NBA to tap into that market. Huge crowds have filled Charlotte Coliseum to back the Hornets since their inception. In the first three years, the level of play was below the high expectations of spoiled Carolina fans.

The 1988-89 Hornets may have looked sharp in their teal-and-blue pinstriped duds, but their 20-62 record wasn't as fashionable. Among the highlights of that first season was the play of veteran Kelly Tripucka and exciting guards Muggsy Bogues and Rex Chapman.

Charlotte took a step backward in 1989-90, winning only 19 games, and coach Dick Harter was replaced by Gene Littles. Rookie J.R. Reid, a star at North Carolina, was a crowd favorite, though at 6'9", he seemed too small for the center spot.

Littles boosted the team's production to 26 wins in 1990-91, as rookie guard Kendall Gill showed flashes of a brilliant future. In 1991-92, Allan Bristow took over as coach and the team added thunder-dunking rookie Larry Johnson.

With the addition of yet another stellar rookie—center Alonzo Mourning—Charlotte took a monster step in 1992-93, knocking off Boston in the first round of the playoffs. Injuries ruined the 1993-94 season, but the nucleus of Johnson, Mourning, Bogues, and sharp-shooters Hersey Hawkins and Dell Curry helped the team win 50 games in 1994-95. The following season, management began a rebuilding phase by sending Mourning to Miami when it became clear his contract demands were too high, and the Hornets failed to make the playoffs.

1995-96 Review

The Hornets may have launched a pre-emptive strike at center Alonzo Mourning and his expected gigantic contract demands by dealing him to Miami before 1995-96, but in doing so they turned their team into a perimeter-based unit with little character in the middle. The record dipped to 41-41, not good enough for the playoffs.

The Hornets won nine fewer games than in 1994-95 and all of a sudden appeared to be sliding away from the promise they showed earlier this decade, when the tandem of Mourning and Larry Johnson looked ready to propel Charlotte into the championship fray. The dismal season also led to the inevitable firing of coach Allan Bristow, who had been hanging on from year to year almost since being hired to lead the team.

Charlotte was capable of scoring points, but defense was another story. Opponents shot 48.9 percent from the field, second worst in the league, and took advantage of the overmatched pivot trio of Matt Geiger, George Zidek, and Robert Parish.

Johnson (20.5 PPG, 8.4 RPG), Glen Rice (21.6 PPG), and Kenny Anderson (15.2 PPG, 8.3 APG) led the way. Johnson played 81 games and appeared relatively free of the back problems that had hampered him the past two seasons. Rice, who came over from the Heat, continued to be one of the league's most lethal scorers, and Anderson, a New Jersey expatriate, ran the team well, although he continued to shoot poorly. Veteran Dell Curry again provided long-range production and moved into the starting lineup late in the year, but versatile forward Scott Burrell's promising career took another ugly turn when he suffered a serious knee injury.

Charlotte Hornets
1996-97 Season Preview

Opening Line: In just over three seasons, the Hornets have gone from a true contender to a mishmash of other people's castaways. Glen Rice arrived last year, and Vlade Divac and Anthony Mason showed up during the off-season. It could all fit together, but new coach Dave Cowens has plenty of work to do if he wants to put his kind of hustling, aggressive team on the court.

Guard: With Kenny Anderson gone, Charlotte is left with slim pickings at the point. Anthony Goldwire is still raw. Muggsy Bogues is talking about coming back after an injury-plagued 1995-96. The Hornets might be glad to see him, no matter how much of a defensive liability he has proved to be. They'd be even happier if Scott Burrell could play a full season after missing most of the last two with leg injuries. That would allow veteran bomber Dell Curry to come off the bench.

Forward: On paper, the Rice/Mason combo looks pretty good. But Rice is a confirmed gunner, and Mason didn't sound too enthused about coming to Charlotte. In fact, he seemed downright angry. If both play to their capabilities, Charlotte has an excellent scorer in Rice and a durable, energetic warrior in Mason. The reserve situation is bleak, although second-round pick Malik Rose could help on the backboards.

Center: Divac solves a big problem in the middle, because the triumvirate of Matt Geiger, George Zidek, and departed Robert Parish didn't get it done last year. Divac is mobile, shoots well, and will get close to ten RPG. He has grown considerably since entering the league and sits atop the second tier of NBA pivotmen. Brad Lohaus, who came from New York with Mason, is a seven-foot jump-shooter.

Analysis: Charlotte will be better this year, but it's wrong to expect anything more than a playoff cameo. Divac was a huge addition, and Cowens should do a good job getting the team ready to play hard every night. But until the point guard spot is settled, and until Rice and Mason co-exist on the perimeter, the Hornets won't contend.

Prediction: Sixth place, Central Division

1996-97 Roster

| Player | Pos. | Ht. | Wt. | Exp. | College | G | —1995-96— | | |
							RPG	APG	PPG
Rafael Addison	F/G	6'8"	250	5	Syracuse	53	1.7	0.6	3.2
Muggsy Bogues	G	5'3"	140	9	Wake Forest	6	1.2	3.2	2.3
Scott Burrell	F	6'7"	218	3	Connecticut	20	4.9	2.4	13.2
Dell Curry	G	6'5"	208	10	Virginia Tech	82	3.2	2.1	14.5
Tony Delk	G	6'1"	193	R	Kentucky	—	—	—	—
Vlade Divac	C	7'1"	250	7	Serbia	79	8.6	3.3	12.9
Matt Geiger	C	7'0"	260	4	Georgia Tech	77	8.4	0.8	11.2
Anthony Goldwire	G	6'2"	182	2	Houston	42	1.0	2.7	5.5
*Darrin Hancock	G/F	6'7"	205	2	Kansas	63	1.6	0.7	4.3
Brad Lohaus	F/C	6'11"	238	9	Iowa	55	1.2	0.8	3.6
Anthony Mason	F	6'7"	250	7	Tennessee St.	82	9.3	4.4	14.6
*Pete Myers	G/F	6'6"	192	8	Ark.-Little Rock	71	2.0	2.0	3.9
Glen Rice	G/F	6'8"	220	7	Michigan	79	4.8	2.9	21.6
Malik Rose	F	6'7"	250	R	Drexel	—	—	—	—
George Zidek	C	7'0"	272	1	UCLA	71	2.6	0.2	4.0

CHICAGO BULLS

Home: United Center
Capacity: 21,500
Year Built: 1994

Chairman: Jerry Reinsdorf
V.P./Basketball Operations: Jerry Krause

Address:
1901 W. Madison
Chicago, IL 60612

Head Coach: Phil Jackson
NBA: 414-160   Bulls: 414-160

Bulls History

The Bulls were defined in the early 1990s by the atmospheric antics of all-world Michael Jordan, whose 18-month hiatus from the game was a mere interruption of the team's dominance. But the team's 29-year history has not always been so spectacular. Until 1991, Chicago had never advanced to the NBA Finals.

The Bulls joined the league in 1966 as a lone expansion club and didn't enjoy success for their first four seasons. For the next five seasons, Chicago thrived with stars like Bob Love, Chet Walker, Jerry Sloan, and Norm Van Lier and even reached the Western Conference finals in 1974 and '75.

Chicago managed only two winning seasons during the next 12 and won just one playoff series, but the Bulls' fortunes changed radically in 1984 when they selected Jordan with the third pick in the draft.

By 1987, Jordan was the best player in the game, and he teamed with Scottie Pippen, John Paxson, and Horace Grant to lift the Bulls among the NBA elite. They lost to Detroit in the Eastern Conference finals in 1988-89 and 1989-90, but then knocked off the L.A. Lakers in the 1991 NBA Finals. In 1991-92, Chicago defeated Portland for its second world crown, then, in 1992-93, three-peated with a win over Phoenix. Chicago lost its invincibility when Jordan "retired" before the 1993-94 season to try a baseball career, but rebounded to win an NBA-record 72 games in '95-96, Jordan's first full season back after his failed experiment.

1995-96 Review

The Bulls staked their claim as one of the best teams in NBA history by rampaging to a league-record 72 wins during the regular season and then stomping all comers in the playoffs. The debates about whether Chicago was actually the best ever will continue for years, but there was no disputing the team's dominance during 1995-96. Fueled by Michael Jordan's first full season since leaving pro basketball for a flirtation with baseball, the Bulls became the most celebrated team in league history.

Jordan, Scottie Pippen, and Dennis Rodman gave the team three superstars and conferred rock-star status upon the Bulls. Though many wondered how well the volatile Rodman would blend in with the Bulls, the talented rebounder and defender caused little trouble—although his hair color and tattoos created a nightly personal spectacle.

Jordan, who had sparked some debate about whether he would perform at the same high level he did before "retiring," silenced critics with his eighth scoring title (30.4 PPG) and fourth league MVP Award. Pippen (19.4 PPG) was a force in his own right. Rodman (14.9 RPG) again led the league in rebounding and was a defensive force.

The rest of the Bulls filled their roles admirably. Toni Kukoc (13.1 PPG) wasn't too happy about being a sixth man, but he played hard every night. Luc Longley worked well as the pivot on a perimeter-based team and thrived in the postseason, while Ron Harper, a former skywalker, reinvented himself as a point guard grinder. Steve Kerr shot over 50 percent from 3-point range, and Bill Wennington was a baseline scoring specialist.

Chicago Bulls
1996-97 Season Preview

Opening Line: Yes, the Bulls have one more championship left in them. They may not win 70 regular-season games, but that doesn't define greatness: Rings do. And most of the NBA would be stunned if Chicago didn't add a fifth ring in 1996-97. As long as the Michael Jordan/Scottie Pippen axis is healthy, the Bulls are the best team in the league.

Guard: Jordan, the $30-million man, certainly answered all questions about whether he could come back strong after his ridiculous baseball experiment. He may not fly as high as he once did, but he's a smarter, more focused player. And that fadeaway jumper is a killer. Give Ron Harper credit for adapting to the point guard role and a supporting job after beginning his career as a fabulous scorer. Steve Kerr is an excellent shooter who spreads the defense out and can create more room for Jordan and Pippen.

Forward: Pippen remains one of the game's most exciting and complete players. With Dennis Rodman back for one more year, the Bulls can count on more rebounding, defense, mind games, and shenanigans. The guy is out there, but he does have three title rings and can be a big asset if focused. Toni Kukoc, the 1995-96 Sixth Man of the Year, has tremendous skills but needs to be more aggressive with his game. Sure, he'd love to start, but his contributions off the bench are vital.

Center: Luc Longley will never be confused with David Robinson, but he proved during the playoffs that he is a solid offensive weapon and a pretty fair rebounder. He isn't too quick, but he is big and isn't afraid to use his body. Backup Bill Wennington is a strong baseline shooter who will bang.

Analysis: With Jordan, all things are possible. But the key to this season may be Chicago's decision to give Phil Jackson a new contract. That will allow the Bulls to load up for one more run at the title and cement the franchise's lofty spot in NBA history.

Prediction: First place, Central Division

1996-97 Roster

						—1995-96—			
Player	Pos.	Ht.	Wt.	Exp.	College	G	RPG	APG	PPG
Randy Brown	G	6'2"	191	5	New Mexico St.	68	1.0	1.1	2.7
*Jud Buechler	F/G	6'6"	228	6	Arizona	74	1.5	0.8	3.8
Jason Caffey	F	6'8"	256	1	Alabama	57	1.9	0.4	3.2
*James Edwards	C	7'1"	252	19	Washington	28	1.4	0.4	3.5
Ron Harper	G	6'6"	216	10	Miami (OH)	80	2.7	2.6	7.4
Michael Jordan	G	6'6"	198	11	North Carolina	82	6.6	4.3	30.4
Steve Kerr	G	6'3"	181	8	Arizona	82	1.3	2.3	8.4
Travis Knight	C	7'0"	235	R	Connecticut	—	—	—	—
Toni Kukoc	F/G	6'10"	230	3	Croatia	81	4.0	3.5	13.1
Luc Longley	C	7'2"	292	5	New Mexico	62	5.1	1.9	9.1
Scottie Pippen	F	6'7"	228	9	Cent. Arkansas	77	6.4	5.9	19.4
Dennis Rodman	F	6'8"	220	10	S.E. Okla. St.	64	14.9	2.5	5.5
*John Salley	F/C	6'11"	255	10	Georgia Tech	42	3.3	1.3	4.4
Dickey Simpkins	F	6'10"	264	2	Providence	60	2.6	0.6	3.6
Bill Wennington	C	7'0"	277	9	St. John's	71	2.5	0.6	5.3

CLEVELAND CAVALIERS

Home: Gateway Arena
Capacity: 20,562
Year Built: 1994

Chairman of the Board: Gordon Gund
President: Wayne Embry

Address:
1 Center Court
Cleveland, OH 44115

Head Coach: Mike Fratello
NBA: 461-362   Cavaliers: 137-109

Cavaliers History

Since their debut in 1970, the Cavaliers have been one of the NBA's most disappointing teams, winning only one playoff series in their first 21 years. In their early years, the Cavs didn't have many marquee players—the result of some poor drafting and questionable trades during the 1970s. Things changed in the late 1980s thanks to smarter drafting and the stewardship of coach Lenny Wilkens.

Cleveland spent its first four seasons in the Central basement, but in 1975-76, coach Bill Fitch was rewarded for his patience with a division title, as well as the team's first playoff series win, a seven-game triumph over Washington in the Eastern Conference semis.

Center Jim Chones, forwards Campy Russell and Jim Brewer, and guard Bobby "Bingo" Smith were the main performers on that team, but the good times ended soon thereafter. Cleveland qualified for the playoffs the next two seasons but then made it back only once (1984-85) in the ensuing nine years.

In 1986, the Cavs began their renaissance by drafting center Brad Daugherty. Daugherty, guards Ron Harper and Mark Price, and forward Larry Nance led the Cavs to a 57-25 mark in 1988-89. Cleveland put it together again in 1991-92, going 57-25 and roaring to the conference finals, where they lost to Chicago in six games. After two more playoff losses to the Bulls, coach Mike Fratello began a rebuilding process, but the Cavs continued their early playoff exits.

1995-96 Review

It would appear as if coach Mike Fratello was worthy of a sorcerer's hat for coaxing 47 wins out of the Cavs during 1995-96. With Brad Daugherty missing yet another full season with a bad back and Mark Price having been shipped to Washington prior to the season, Cleveland hardly looked ready for playoff contention, much less an assault on 50 wins.

However, the Cavaliers again put together the league's best defense and managed a third-place finish in the Central Division by thoroughly disrupting their opponents' patterns and winning a lot of boring basketball games. At a time when the league was selling "Showtime" and high-flying excitement, the Cavs were sort of like the weird uncle nobody wanted to acknowledge. They averaged only 91.1 PPG but held rivals to a paltry 88.5.

The season ended abruptly with a first-round playoff loss to the Knicks, but it was rewarding, nonetheless. Terrell Brandon (19.3 PPG, 6.5 APG) proved himself a top-notch point guard. He and underrated Bobby Phills (14.6 PPG) comprised a steady backcourt that put significant pressure on opposing guards. Chris Mills (15.1 PPG) scored well inside and out, and Danny Ferry (13.3 PPG) went from perennial whipping boy to productive starter, proving nothing is impossible in professional sports.

Veteran Michael Cage (8.9 RPG) rebounded with a fervor while playing out of position in the middle, and Dan Majerle (10.6 PPG) continued to bomb away from 3-point range. Tyrone Hill, who was injured in a preseason auto accident, played only 44 games and didn't approach his previous form.

Cleveland Cavaliers
1996-97 Season Preview

Opening Line: The Cavaliers are one of the league's most interesting teams, if only because they succeed with extreme behavior. Coach Mike Fratello sold his troops on defense being the ticket, and Cleveland won 47 games last year. Now that the inside has been fortified somewhat with a pair of foreign pivots, the Cavs may be even more formidable.

Guards: Terrell Brandon is a quality NBA point man. He may not match the assist numbers of others in the league, but the Cavs aren't exactly stocked with prime dishing targets. Off guard Bobby Phills is adequate, but he would be best coming off the bench. Second-year man Bob Sura has the potential and athletic ability to become a good combo guard.

Forwards: If Tyrone Hill is completely recovered from the auto accident that robbed him of considerable effectiveness last season, the Cavs will be fine up front. Chris Mills has become a solid scorer, improving each year. If Cleveland played a faster style, he'd approach 20 points a game. Hill is a superb rebounder and strong inside scorer, and Danny Ferry might just have shed his punch-line status and blossomed into a productive third forward.

Centers: Veteran Mark West, a free-agent acquisition, plays good positional defense but does little else. The Cavs took Ukrainian Vitaly Potapenko from Wright State with the 12th pick in last year's draft and Lithuanian Zydrunas Ilgauskas with the 20th selection. Potapenko has solid skills, and if he can keep his weight down he could be a formidable post defender. Ilgauskas didn't play last year because of a lingering foot injury but is 7'1" and can do some damage close to the basket.

Analysis: Expect another year of scores in the 80s in Cleveland and a win total that approaches 50. Cleveland isn't ready yet to challenge for the top of the Eastern Conference, but Brandon's continued growth, an upgrade at the two spot, and the development of the pivots could position the Cavs for a run once Chicago slips.

Prediction: Second place, Central Division

1996-97 Roster

Player	Pos.	Ht.	Wt.	Exp.	College	G	RPG	APG	PPG
Terrell Brandon	G	5'11"	180	5	Oregon	75	3.3	6.5	19.3
Danny Ferry	F	6'10"	235	6	Duke	82	3.8	2.3	13.3
Reggie Geary	G	6'2"	187	R	Arizona	—	—	—	—
Tyrone Hill	F	6'9"	245	6	Xavier (OH)	44	5.5	0.8	7.8
Zydrunas Ilgauskas	C	7'1"	238	R	(Lithuania)	—	—	—	—
Antonio Lang	F	6'8"	238	2	Duke	41	1.3	0.3	2.8
Donny Marshall	F	6'7"	230	1	Connecticut	34	0.8	0.2	2.3
Chris Mills	F	6'6"	216	3	Arizona	80	5.5	2.4	15.1
Bobby Phills	G	6'5"	220	5	Southern	72	3.6	3.8	14.6
Vitaly Potapenko	F/C	6'10"	280	R	Wright St.	—	—	—	—
Bob Sura	G	6'5"	200	1	Florida St.	79	1.7	2.9	5.3
Mark West	C	6'10"	246	13	Old Dominion	47	2.8	0.1	3.2

DETROIT PISTONS

Home: The Palace
Capacity: 21,454
Year Built: 1988

Managing Partner: William Davidson
V.P./Player Personnel: Rick Sund

Address:
Two Championship Dr.
Auburn Hills, MI 48326

Head Coach: Doug Collins
NBA: 183-145   Pistons: 46-36

Pistons History

Any discussion of Pistons history is bound to be a little heavy on the "Bad Boy" years, which yielded back-to-back NBA titles in 1988-89 and 1989-90 after three fruitless decades.

The franchise was established in Fort Wayne, Indiana, in 1941 as a member of the old National Basketball League. It joined the BAA in 1948 and became a charter NBA club in 1949. The Fort Wayne Pistons, led by high-scoring George Yardley, advanced to the NBA Finals twice during the 1950s, losing to Syracuse in 1954-55 and Philadelphia in 1955-56.

The Pistons moved to Detroit in 1957 but began to falter, finishing below .500 for the next 13 seasons. Things got a little better in the mid-1970s. Detroit posted a 52-30 record in 1973-74, due largely to the play of guard Dave Bing and center Bob Lanier. But the Pistons were eliminated in the Western semis and had to wait another nine seasons for a strong team.

That came in 1983-84 when Chuck Daly took over as coach. Daly, building his team around point guard Isiah Thomas, won the Central Division title in 1987-88. Detroit advanced to the NBA Finals that season, losing to Los Angeles in seven games. Thomas, Bill Laimbeer, Dennis Rodman, and Joe Dumars were not denied the next two years, sweeping the Lakers in 1988-89 and whipping Portland in 1989-90 for the NBA title. Detroit fell from grace quickly, but new coach Doug Collins and superstar-in-the-making Grant Hill began the road back in 1995 with a 46-win season.

1995-96 Review

When Doug Collins took over as coach of the Pistons in 1995, he promised the team would be tougher and more competitive. Though everybody believed him, they didn't think it would happen right away. Detroit won 46 games, 18 more than it had in 1994-95, and made it into the playoffs with room to spare.

Even though Orlando dispatched the Pistons in three games, Collins had made his point. Detroit was an excellent defensive team, got the most out of a thin frontcourt on the backboards, and mixed veterans and youngsters into a consistent broth. The team had several flaws, but even the Bad Boys would have been proud of what the team accomplished after three years away from the postseason. The Pistons—a team that in 1993-94 looked ready to join the Sixers and Celtics on the scrap heap of former champions—enjoyed a renaissance last year.

The team's soul was clearly found in second-year forward Grant Hill (20.2 PPG, 9.8 RPG, 6.9 APG), whose all-around excellence brought him closer to the game's greats. Shooting guard Allan Houston (19.7 PPG) continued his maturation into a perimeter force and finished in the top ten in 3-point shooting. Graceful vet Joe Dumars split time at the point with Lindsey Hunter and continued to provide leadership, but Hunter was erratic and shot the ball poorly.

Otis Thorpe (14.2 PPG, 8.4 RPG) gave Collins the frontcourt strength and resolve the coach craved, but Terry Mills was soft and inconsistent. Rookie Don Reid and veteran Mark West didn't score much, but each used his sizable frame to help the Pistons' interior defensive presence.

Detroit Pistons
1996-97 Season Preview

Opening Line: Doug Collins wasn't kidding all those times he claimed he could still coach. He lifted the Pistons out of the lottery last year and into the playoffs with 46 regular-season victories. Now, he must hope Detroit can replace free-agent guard Allan Houston, who bolted for New York, and continue its progress toward becoming an Eastern Conference contender.

Guards: Losing Houston hurts, because he emerged from his rookie-year shooting funk to become one of the game's top shooting guards last year. A combination of veteran Joe Dumars, a classy performer who can't score like he used to, and point guard Lindsey Hunter spells big trouble. Hunter can't shoot, and he turns the ball over too often.

Forwards: Grant Hill's second season was as amazing as his first. He scored. He rebounded. He passed. He even led the team in steals. It is now time for him to start carrying the team to greater heights. He's ready. Veteran Otis Thorpe is an excellent rebounder and the kind of tough defender Collins loves. Terry Mills is not. The acquisitions of Stacey Augmon and Grant Long from Atlanta fortify this position and could even push Hill to guard on occasion. Second-year man Don Reid is a budding young enforcer who should set a good example for first-round draft choice Jerome Williams. Williams, the MVP of the Desert Classic pre-draft camp, has strength and athletic ability.

Centers: There's trouble here. Reid saw some minutes in the middle. Second-year man Theo Ratliff is a good shot-blocker who could become a solid backup center some day. That's not enough to get the Pistons into serious contention.

Analysis: Detroit is clearly heading down the right path, but there is work to be done, particularly at the point guard and center spots, which are arguably the game's two most important positions. Fans should have faith in Collins. He has the team playing solid defense and knocking some people around. The Bad Boys aren't back yet, but some of the old excitement is returning to the franchise.

Prediction: Fifth place, Central Division

1996-97 Roster

| Player | Pos. | Ht. | Wt. | Exp. | College | —1995-96— | | | |
						G	RPG	APG	PPG
Stacey Augmon	G/F	6'8"	205	5	UNLV	77	3.9	1.8	12.7
Michael Curry	G	6'5"	210	2	Georgia South.	46	1.8	0.6	4.6
Joe Dumars	G	6'3"	195	11	McNeese St.	67	2.1	4.0	11.8
Grant Hill	F	6'8"	225	2	Duke	80	9.8	6.9	20.2
Lindsey Hunter	G	6'2"	195	3	Jackson St.	80	2.4	2.4	8.5
Grant Long	F	6'9"	248	8	E. Michigan	82	9.6	2.2	13.1
Rick Mahorn	F	6'10"	260	15	Hampton Inst.	50	2.2	0.3	2.4
Terry Mills	F	6'10"	250	6	Michigan	82	4.3	1.2	9.4
Theo Ratliff	F/C	6'10"	225	1	Wyoming	75	4.0	0.2	4.5
Don Reid	F/C	6'8"	250	1	Georgetown	69	2.9	0.2	3.8
Ron Riley	G/F	6'5"	205	R	Arizona St.	—	—	—	—
Otis Thorpe	F	6'10"	246	12	Providence	82	8.4	1.9	14.2
Jerome Williams	F	6'9"	206	R	Georgetown	—	—	—	—

INDIANA PACERS

Home: Market Square Arena
Capacity: 16,530
Year Built: 1974

Owners: Melvin Simon, Herbert Simon
President: Don Walsh

Address:
300 E. Market St.
Indianapolis, IN 46204

Head Coach: Larry Brown
NBA: 585-437   Pacers: 151-95

Pacers History

If there could be such a thing as the "Boston Celtics of the ABA," it definitely would have been the Indiana Pacers. The Pacers won three ABA titles and finished second twice from 1968-69 through the 1974-75 season.

The old days were something in Indianapolis. Led by Mel Daniels, a 6'9" bull of a center, the early Pacers featured a lineup that was equal to many NBA teams. Guard Freddie Lewis and forward Roger Brown were deadly scorers, and power forward Bob Netolicky was a bruiser. The early-1970s additions of George McGinnis, Bill Keller, and Billy Knight made a potent rotation even stronger.

The same penchant for accumulating talented personnel did not carry over to Indiana's years in the NBA—until recently. The Pacers had only two winning seasons from 1976-77 through 1992-93. In the early '90s, the team scored a lot of points, thanks to long-range bombers Chuck Person and Reggie Miller and do-everything forward Detlef Schrempf, but it lacked the strong defense, team chemistry, and mental toughness necessary to excel in the playoffs.

New coach Larry Brown addressed all of those concerns, and the Pacers gutted out some tough wins in the 1994 and 1995 playoffs. Led by Miller and center Rik Smits, Indiana lost a seven-game war to New York in the '94 Eastern finals and reached the brink of the NBA Finals again in '95, only to lose in seven games to Orlando.

1995-96 Review

After coming within a game of the NBA Finals two straight seasons, the Pacers bowed out in the first round of the postseason against Atlanta. This completed a 52-30 season that featured injuries and some disappointing performances, leaving what had been considered to be an up-and-coming team in a state of flux. Throw in a little intrigue concerning the future of nomadic coach Larry Brown, and you had all the components of a soap opera.

The playoff loss wasn't completely unexpected, since star guard Reggie Miller (21.1 PPG) missed all but the finale of the five-game series with an eye injury. Without their main scorer and clutch performer, the Pacers were lost. But that doesn't absolve the team's other players of their sins. Nor does it help mend the relationship between Brown and Pacer GM Donnie Walsh, who went to bat for his coach during the season when the players complained about Brown's constant verbal abuse. The two close friends sparred over whether to break up the team's nucleus and also disagreed over how Brown handled rumors that he was interested in the Dallas Mavericks' vacant coaching job.

On the court, center Rik Smits (18.5 PPG, 6.9 RPG) was again steady, but he missed nearly 20 games due to injury. Dale Davis (10.3 PPG, 9.1 RPG) and Antonio Davis (8.8 PPG, 6.1 RPG) provided steady defense at power forward. Veteran Derrick McKey (11.7 PPG) was solid at the three spot, and Mark Jackson (10.0 PPG, 7.8 APG) ran the team well. Rookie point guard Travis Best showed signs of promise and gained more responsibility as the year went on.

Indiana Pacers
1996-97 Season Preview

Opening Line: Convinced this current incarnation of the team is incapable of winning the Eastern Conference, GM Donnie Walsh (with the blessing of coach Larry Brown) began cleaning house following the 1995-96 season. Plenty of new faces abound in Speedway City, with even more to come if the Pacers don't re-sign free-agent gunner Reggie Miller.

Guards: Miller is one of the game's premier long-distance shooters and lives for the spotlight of the playoffs. Without him, the offense would be stagnant, and center Rik Smits would find himself surrounded by scads of enemy defenders. In trading Mark Jackson to Denver, the Pacers either saw something in Jalen Rose the Nuggets didn't or else decided to give the ball to second-year point man Travis Best. Best is jet-quick, and although Rose has plenty of skills, he has yet to master the point guard position.

Forwards: Derrick McKey is steady and reliable, but not the most productive small forward around. Dale and Antonio Davis (no relation) provide plenty of power inside. Although neither is an accomplished scorer, each (particularly Dale) can board like a demon and play solid post defense. Veteran Reggie Williams, acquired from Denver, is a low-percentage shooter who can fill it up at times, something the Pacers lacked in recent seasons. Aging Eddie Johnson is another offensive-minded small forward.

Centers: Rik Smits retains his pivot primacy and will continue to be a valuable offensive performer who doesn't quite live up to his rebounding and shot-blocking potential. First-round pick Erick Dampier has a great NBA body and a desire to work, but he is mechanical and needs considerable time to blossom offensively.

Analysis: Until Indiana becomes a more capable offensive team, it will remain no better than one of the top four teams in the Eastern Conference. While that isn't so bad, it might not be enough to keep the long-wandering Brown happy and willing to stay in Indy.

Prediction: Third place, Central Division

1996-97 Roster

Player	Pos.	Ht.	Wt.	Exp.	College	G	RPG	APG	PPG
							1995-96		
Jerome Allen	G	6'4"	184	1	Pennsylvania	41	0.6	1.2	2.6
Travis Best	G	5'11"	182	1	Georgia Tech	59	0.7	1.6	3.7
*Adrian Caldwell	F/C	6'9"	265	4	Lamar	51	2.2	0.1	2.2
Erick Dampier	C	6'11"	265	R	Mississippi St.	—	—	—	—
Antonio Davis	F	6'9"	230	3	Texas-El Paso	82	6.1	0.5	8.8
Dale Davis	F	6'11"	230	5	Clemson	78	9.1	1.0	10.3
Duane Ferrell	F	6'7"	215	8	Georgia Tech	54	1.7	0.6	3.7
Scott Haskin	F	6'11"	250	2	Oregon St.	—	—	—	—
Fred Hoiberg	G	6'4"	203	1	Iowa St.	15	0.6	0.5	2.1
Eddie Johnson	F	6'7"	215	14	Illinois	62	2.5	1.1	7.7
Derrick McKey	F	6'10"	225	9	Alabama	75	4.8	3.5	11.7
*Reggie Miller	G	6'7"	185	9	UCLA	76	2.8	3.3	21.1
Mark Pope	F	6'10"	235	R	Kentucky	—	—	—	—
Jalen Rose	G	6'8"	210	2	Michigan	80	3.3	6.2	10.0
Rik Smits	C	7'4"	265	8	Marist	63	6.9	1.7	18.5
Reggie Williams	F/G	6'7"	195	9	Georgetown	52	2.3	1.4	4.6
Haywoode Workman	G	6'3"	180	5	Oral Roberts	77	1.6	2.8	3.6

MILWAUKEE BUCKS

Home: Bradley Center
Capacity: 18,633
Year Built: 1988

Owner: Herb Kohl
General Manager: Mike Dunleavy

Address:
1001 N. Fourth St.
Milwaukee, WI 53203

Head Coach: Chris Ford
NBA: 222-188   Bucks: 0-0

Bucks History

In their first 23 years of existence (through 1990-91), the Bucks missed out on postseason play only four times. But despite that gleaming record, the franchise's glory period is long past.

Milwaukee stumbled through its rookie season in 1968-69, but then won the coin toss with Phoenix for the rights to UCLA star Lew Alcindor and began a five-year run of success. In 1969-70, Milwaukee reached the Eastern finals, and the off-season arrival of guard Oscar Robertson was the final piece in coach Larry Costello's puzzle. In 1970-71, Alcindor, Robertson, Bob Dandridge, Greg Smith, and Jon McGlocklin led the Bucks to a 66-16 record and the NBA title.

Alcindor changed his name to Kareem Abdul-Jabbar, and in 1973-74 the Bucks made it back to the title series, losing in seven games to Boston. Jabbar was dealt to Los Angeles for four players following the 1974-75 season, and the Bucks floundered for the next four years, finishing over .500 just once.

Don Nelson took over as coach in 1976-77 and directed the team back into the playoffs on a regular basis. But although the nucleus of Sidney Moncrief, Junior Bridgeman, Marques Johnson, and Terry Cummings was strong enough to win 50-plus games each year from 1980-81 to 1986-87, the Bucks couldn't get back to the NBA Finals. The club had grown too old by the early 1990s and began a rebuilding program under Mike Dunleavy that failed to bear fruit.

1995-96 Review

It doesn't seem fair that after Mike Dunleavy spent four years assembling a questionable collection of talent he should be able to retain his player personnel title and hire somebody else to bear the brunt of his decisions on the court. The Bucks' 25-win season led owner Herb Kohl to relieve Dunleavy of his coaching duties, meaning somebody else will have the mission of trying to win next year with a team that has failed to make any significant strides during Dunleavy's term of power.

The 25 wins were the second-worst total in club history and consigned Milwaukee to the draft lottery for the fifth straight year. The Bucks scored only 95.6 PPG, sixth worst in the league, and could not combat the paltry output with a stout defensive effort, either. Opponents shot 48 percent from the field against Milwaukee and hammered them on the boards.

Milwaukee sunk quickly to the nether regions of the NBA's Central Division during 1995-96, despite continued inspired play by Vin Baker (21.1 PPG, 9.9 RPG), who continued to receive precious little acclaim for his excellent inside play. Though he couldn't have enjoyed another losing year, at least Baker got to play his customary power forward position, instead of laboring in the post.

His frontcourt mate, Glenn Robinson (20.2 PPG), continued to put up big scoring numbers but finished fourth in the league in turnovers. Early-season acquisition Benoit Benjamin underachieved in the middle, despite promises that he would give the Bucks a much-needed pivot presence. The backcourt of Sherman Douglas and Johnny Newman was pedestrian and failed to provide necessary leadership.

Milwaukee Bucks
1996-97 Season Preview

Opening Line: Mike Dunleavy is out as head coach but retains his GM position, and coaching vet Chris Ford moves back to the sidelines after a one-year hiatus. Also in is first-round draft choice Ray Allen, the kind of big scorer the Bucks have craved in the backcourt for years.

Guards: Allen is a multitalented off guard who shot almost 50 percent from 3-point range last year. He's dynamic on the break and gets his own shot as well. He isn't the most accomplished ball-handler or defender, but his outstanding physical skills don't rule out improvements in those areas. The point, however, remains a problem. Sherman Douglas isn't awful, but he isn't a first-line NBA floor leader, either. Second-round draft pick Moochie Norris has great speed. Shawn Respert must improve his shooting.

Forwards: Vin Baker remains one of the game's brightest young stars. He is unselfish, consistent, and willing to play either the power forward or center position. Glenn Robinson can hit the 3-pointer, rebound, and pass the ball on occasion. He isn't much of a defender, and his attitude has been questioned at times. Free-agent acquisition Armon Gilliam is anxious to get his hands on the ball. He's good for 18 points and ten rebounds just about every night. Veteran Johnny Newman can score either at small forward or guard. Marty Conlon works hard, but he doesn't have the most diverse skills around.

Centers: The Bucks made a good move renouncing the rights to Benoit Benjamin, who hasn't ever been accused of working hard or fulfilling his potential. In Andrew Lang, acquired from Minnesota during the off-season, Milwaukee gets a willing and able defender and a competent inside scorer. Gilliam will also see time in the middle.

Analysis: The arrival of Allen leaves the Bucks set at three positions, but there is still plenty of work to do. Milwaukee needs a point guard, a center, and several quality bench players. Ford will be happy to be back in the coaching game, but chances are he won't be smiling too much as the 1996-97 season wears on.

Prediction: Seventh place, Central Division

1996-97 Roster

| Player | Pos. | Ht. | Wt. | Exp. | College | —1995-96— | | |
						G	RPG	APG	PPG
Ray Allen	G	6'5"	205	R	Connecticut	—	—	—	—
Vin Baker	F	6'11"	250	3	Hartford	82	9.9	2.6	21.1
Marty Conlon	F	6'11"	245	5	Providence	74	2.4	0.9	5.3
*Terry Cummings	F	6'9"	250	14	DePaul	81	5.5	1.1	8.0
Sherman Douglas	G	6'1"	198	7	Syracuse	79	2.3	5.5	11.3
Kevin Duckworth	C	7'0"	290	10	E. Illinois	8	0.9	0.3	1.1
Armon Gilliam	F	6'10"	250	9	UNLV	78	9.1	1.8	18.3
*Randolph Keys	F	6'7"	210	5	Southern Miss.	69	1.8	0.9	3.4
Andrew Lang	C	6'11"	250	8	Arkansas	71	6.4	0.9	11.7
Johnny Newman	F/G	6'7"	205	10	Richmond	82	2.4	1.9	10.8
Jeff Nordgaard	F	6'7"	226	R	Wisc.-G.B.	—	—	—	—
Moochie Norris	G	6'1"	175	R	West Florida	—	—	—	—
*Mike Peplowski	C	6'10"	270	3	Michigan St.	7	0.6	0.1	1.0
Shawn Respert	G	6'2"	195	1	Michigan St.	62	1.2	1.1	4.9
Glenn Robinson	F	6'7"	240	2	Purdue	82	6.1	3.6	20.2

TORONTO RAPTORS

Home: SkyDome
Capacity: 23,000
Year Built: 1989

Address:
20 Bay St. #702
Toronto, ONT M5J 2N8

Chairman: David Peterson
Executive V.P./Basketball: Isiah Thomas

Head Coach: Darrell Walker
NBA: 0-0   Raptors: 0-0

1995-96 Season Review

If there was any question about whether Isiah Thomas was going to run the expansion Raptors with the same decisiveness and confidence with which he guided the Detroit Pistons to a pair of NBA titles, it was answered at the end of the 1995-96 season, when he canned coach Brendan Malone after just one year on the bench. It seemed Malone wanted to win games, while Thomas was interested in developing the team's young players, given the almost guaranteed dismal fate of any first-year franchise.

Though the Raptors played interesting basketball, won 21 games (six more than expansion partner Vancouver), and even defeated the Bulls, the franchise was fodder for the league. The NBA had even worked hard to make sure that would be the case by preventing both expansion teams from getting the top pick in the draft for a few years.

Rookie of the Year point guard Damon Stoudamire (19.0 PPG, 9.3 APG) established himself as a future star and injected excitement into the sagging Raptor offense (97.5 PPG). Forward Tracy Murray (16.2 PPG) and hefty center Oliver Miller (12.9 PPG, 7.4 RPG) gave the usual steady expansion performances, and midseason acquisition Sharone Wright (11.6 PPG, 6.2 RPG) looked like a future frontcourt contributor, despite missing several games due to injury.

1996-97 Season Preview

Opening Line: Year two of the Raptors' existence dawns with the team still a long way from contention but clearly moving in the right direction. First-round draft pick Marcus Camby teams with Damon Stoudamire to give new coach Darrell Walker two solid building blocks for the future.

Guards: Stoudamire was clearly the surprise of the '95 draft crop. He was an exciting playmaker and penetrator and a strong scorer from all over, although his shooting was at times erratic and somewhat ill-advised. Hubert Davis provides sound scoring, and Doug Christie has a live body and a poor shot. Walt Williams will contribute.

Forwards: Rebounding machine Popeye Jones is a physical presence at power forward. Expect Christie to get a look here as well, or maybe Carlos Rogers, a spindly, 6'11" player with a smooth offensive game close to the basket. Camby will be inserted at the four spot right away, bringing excellent shot-blocking skills and a fluid open-court game.

Centers: Even though Sharone Wright played forward in Philadelphia, he is best suited for the pivot position. Like Camby, he needs work in the weight room, because he's too thin. Wright is a big, soft guy with a lot of potential, but he needs to get meaner and tougher. Acie Earl, a huge disappointment with Boston who didn't do much to improve his reputation last year, will back Wright up. Camby will see time here, too.

Analysis: GM Isiah Thomas replaced Brendan Malone with Walker because Malone wanted to win games, not develop young players. That won't happen this year. Toronto is destined for another sub-25 win season, but it will at least be building for the future. Stoudamire and Camby are excellent starting points, but plenty of work remains.

Prediction: Eighth place, Central Division

See page 396 for the Toronto Raptors' 1996-97 roster.

DALLAS MAVERICKS

Home: Reunion Arena
Capacity: 17,502
Year Built: 1980

Owner: Donald Carter
General Manager: Jim Livingston

Address:
777 Sports St.
Dallas, TX 75207

Head Coach: Jim Cleamons
NBA: 0-0   Mavericks: 0-0

Mavericks History

Most NBA franchises start out bad and then get better. The Mavericks started out surprisingly well but then went down the tubes. Dallas entered the league in 1980 and soon made its mark. In the 1981 draft, the Mavs selected Mark Aguirre, Rolando Blackman, and Jay Vincent. After adding standout guards Dale Ellis and Derek Harper in the '83 draft, the Mavs won 43 games in 1983-84 and advanced to the West semifinals under coach Dick Motta.

Dallas won the Midwest in 1986-87, buoyed by the addition of mammoth center James Donaldson and rookie forward Roy Tarpley, but bowed out in the first round of the playoffs. Former Phoenix coach John MacLeod replaced Motta for the '87-88 season, and Dallas stretched eventual champion Los Angeles to seven games in the Western finals.

Things started to sour in 1988-89. Aguirre was traded in midseason to Detroit for the mercurial Adrian Dantley, and Tarpley played only 19 games due to alcohol-abuse problems. The Mavericks fell to 38-44 in 1988-89, and though they rebounded to 47-35 the next season, MacLeod was fired and Dallas lost in the first round of the 1990 playoffs.

The next four seasons were disastrous. The downfall was triggered by a lifetime ban on Tarpley, but injuries, bad trades, and dissension also crippled the Mavericks. High draft picks Jimmy Jackson, Jamal Mashburn, and Jason Kidd gave the Mavs hope, but despite 36 wins in 1994-95, contention was a long way off.

1995-96 Review

All of the goodwill generated by the Mavs' 1994-95 turnaround season disappeared during a campaign filled with dissension and wretched play. By season's end, the Mavericks had taken significant strides back to their bumbling days, costing coach Dick Motta his job and leading owner Donald Carter to sell the franchise to a group headed by Ross Perot. The Mavs played no defense, shot the ball poorly, and were actually lucky to win the 26 games they did.

Some of it could be blamed on injury, since machine-gunning forward Jamal Mashburn played only 18 games before undergoing knee surgery. But there's no guarantee that his presence would have ended the malaise that prevailed in '95-96. After all, he and shooting guard Jimmy Jackson began the year feuding. What makes anybody think that relationship would have improved throughout the rest of an arduous 82-game campaign?

Jackson's scoring average (19.6 PPG) fell a full six points from the previous year, even without Mashburn in the lineup. Jackson shot just 43.5 percent from the field and continued to prove he lacks the range to be a big-time shooting guard. Jason Kidd dished out plenty of assists (9.7 APG) and made plenty of highlight reels, but his 38.1-percent shooting showcased his one major flaw. Journeyman George McCloud (18.9 PPG) finally found a home at small forward, and Popeye Jones continued to rebound (10.8 RPG) with a fervor. But the inside triumvirate of Lorenzo Williams and rookies Loren Meyer and Cherokee Parks offered little on the offensive end and often less on defense.

Dallas Mavericks
1996-97 Season Preview

Opening Line: In the span of one season, the Mavs went from what appeared to be a promising team to one that was torn apart by personality conflicts. As new coach Jim Cleamons takes over, Dallas must deal with acrimony in the backcourt and find a way to integrate its new frontcourt pieces into the mix. Neither task will be easy.

Guards: Point guard Jason Kidd doesn't like two man Jimmy Jackson. That's not good. Both are extremely talented, although Kidd is a terrible free-throw shooter and Jackson needs to work on his long-range shooting. But they're young, and if Dallas can hold onto them and get them to behave, the Mavs are in great shape. George McCloud went from CBA All-Star to full-fledged NBA machine-gunner last year, attempting 678 3-pointers. He should calm down a little in 1996-97. Derek Harper provides veteran leadership and steady scoring. Rookie Shawn Harvey is a scorer who impressed scouts in pre-draft workouts.

Forwards: If Jamal Mashburn's knee is healthy, he'll battle McCloud and Jackson for available shots. Mashburn is a proven scorer who needs to rebound a bit more. Of course, rebounding is why Dallas drafted Samaki Walker of Louisville with the ninth pick and traded for plodding center Eric Montross. Walker has a great body and will have to take over Popeye Jones's rebounding job. Free-agent acquisition Chris Gatling can score extremely well near the basket, while Tony Dumas is a scorer with a wayward shot.

Centers: Montross will provide some beef in the middle and get his share of rebounds. Second-year man Loren Meyer is a project with the potential to be a solid, versatile scorer and a strong board man.

Analysis: Cleamons has a tricky task. He has to keep the stars happy while managing the potential frontcourt logjam. Dallas has assembled the beginnings of a worthy frontcourt component to match its solid perimeter. But harmony and chemistry should be the main goals for this year, with playoff contention a future concern.

Prediction: Fourth place, Midwest Division

1996-97 Roster

| Player | Pos. | Ht. | Wt. | Exp. | College | —1995-96— | | |
						G	RPG	APG	PPG
Terry Davis	F/C	6'10"	250	7	Virginia Union	28	4.2	0.8	4.9
Tony Dumas	G	6'5"	190	2	Missouri-K.C.	67	1.7	1.5	11.6
Chris Gatling	F/C	6'10"	230	5	Old Dominion	71	5.9	0.6	11.1
Derek Harper	G	6'4"	206	13	Illinois	82	2.5	4.3	14.0
Shawn Harvey	G	6'4"	180	R	W. Virginia St.	—	—	—	—
Jim Jackson	G	6'6"	215	4	Ohio St.	82	5.0	2.9	19.6
Jason Kidd	G	6'4"	208	2	California	81	6.8	9.7	16.6
Jimmy King	G	6'5"	210	1	Michigan	62	1.8	1.4	4.5
Jamal Mashburn	F	6'8"	250	3	Kentucky	18	5.4	2.8	23.4
George McCloud	G/F	6'8"	225	6	Florida St.	79	4.8	2.7	18.9
Loren Meyer	C	6'10"	260	1	Iowa St.	72	4.4	0.8	5.0
Eric Montross	C	7'0"	270	2	North Carolina	61	5.8	0.7	7.2
Darnell Robinson	C	6'11"	270	R	Arkansas	—	—	—	—
Samaki Walker	F	6'9"	240	R	Louisville	—	—	—	—

DENVER NUGGETS

Home: McNichols Sports Arena
Capacity: 17,171
Year Built: 1975

Owner: COMSAT Entertainment Group
President/GM: Bernie Bickerstaff

Address:
1635 Clay St.
Denver, CO 80204

Head Coach: Bernie Bickerstaff
NBA: 256-262   Nuggets: 55-59

Nuggets History

The Nuggets began life as a charter member of the old ABA—their original nickname was the Rockets—and evolved into a league power, even though they never won a title.

Early Rocket teams featured high-flying forward Spencer Haywood, who led Denver to the Western Conference finals in 1969-70, where it lost to Los Angeles. Haywood soon left, and the franchise's fortunes dimmed until 1974, when GM Carl Scheer and coach Larry Brown joined the club. Scheer immediately changed the team nickname to the Nuggets. Denver won 65 games in 1974-75 but lost in the Western finals to Indiana. The next season, the Nuggets acquired star guard David Thompson and made it to the league championship series.

The Nuggets were one of four ABA teams to merge with the NBA in 1976, and they won the Midwest Division in their first two seasons. Denver won Midwest titles in 1984-85 and 1987-88 under Doug Moe and made it to the Western finals in 1985, but they failed in their bid for the elusive NBA championship.

Following the 1989-90 season, Denver replaced Moe with Paul Westhead, whose running game produced the league's worst record in '90-91. Young stars like Dikembe Mutombo and Mahmoud Abdul-Rauf helped the team take a healthy step forward over the next three seasons. And though Denver upset Seattle in the 1994 playoffs, it remained far from true contention.

1995-96 Review

After two years of playoff participation, the Nuggets slid back some during a season more noteworthy for guard Mahmoud Abdul-Rauf's reluctance to stand for the national anthem and center Dikembe Mutombo's pending free agency than for anything the Nuggets did on the court.

Although Denver appeared to have a good collection of weapons, it lacked the necessary offensive pop, particularly up front. The Nuggets, who managed just 35 wins, also weren't particularly strong from 3-point range.

Abdul-Rauf, who created a stir when he claimed his Islamic beliefs prohibited him from standing during the national anthem, had a good year despite the controversy. Although he didn't shoot well and missed 25 games due to injury, he led the Nuggets in scoring (19.2 PPG). Jalen Rose continued to struggle with the finer points of the NBA point guard position.

Meanwhile, Mutombo had his usual excellent year on defense (4.5 BPG) and the backboards (11.8 RPG), but he scored only 11.0 PPG and spent the year dropping not-so-subtle hints that he might be leaving after the season. Rookie Antonio McDyess (13.4 PPG, 7.5 RPG) flashed much of the potential that made him the second pick in last year's draft.

Veteran guard Bryant Stith (13.6 PPG) continued his improvement, although he fizzled a little late in the year and remained unreliable from the perimeter, and Don MacLean (11.2 PPG), who came over in an early-season deal with Washington, shot the ball poorly. LaPhonso Ellis played in 45 games—good news considering the severity of 1994-95's knee injury—but he didn't approach his former level of play.

Denver Nuggets
1996-97 Season Preview

Opening Line: After slipping back into the lottery last year, the Nuggets embark on the 1996-97 season with a vastly changed character, partly by choice and partly due to the free-agency epidemic that hit the NBA during the off-season. Denver shipped out several components of last year's team in exchange for new faces and lost center Dikembe Mutombo to Atlanta. This looks to be a transition season without much hope for playoff contention.

Guards: The backcourt is almost entirely new. Mark Jackson, acquired with Ricky Pierce from Indiana for Jalen Rose and Reggie Williams, is a proven point man with good size and the ability to run a team well. Just don't expect too much speed or scoring from him. He'll team with Bryant Stith, who still needs work on his shooting. Dale Ellis is a machine-gunner off the bench, and Pierce, an aging 3-point shooter, will add more reserve fire-power. Sarunas Marciulionis (imported from Sacramento for Mahmoud Abdul-Rauf) brings a solid game and the ability to score well off the bench.

Forwards: Antonio McDyess had a great debut season and looks to be a potential star in the league. His offense remains unpolished, but he can rebound well and has a great NBA body for the power forward spot. LaPhonso Ellis should show some improvement, but he remains subpar after his serious knee injury two seasons ago. Dale Ellis, good for scoring but not defense or rebounding, will see time at small forward. Tom Hammonds is a strong man without much offense.

Centers: Ervin Johnson is tall enough but not strong enough. With Mutombo gone, the Nuggets need first-round draft choice Efthimios Rentzias (from Greece) to emerge quickly. Rentzias has a nice touch and can block some shots, but he won't provide the same defensive presence Mutombo did.

Analysis: Denver isn't done massaging its roster. Additions like Pierce and Marciulionis are clearly stopgap in nature. The Nuggets will need some time to climb back into the playoff picture, but at least they're trying.

Prediction: Fifth place, Midwest Division

1996-97 Roster

Player	Pos.	Ht.	Wt.	Exp.	College	—1995-96— G	RPG	APG	PPG
Dale Ellis	G/F	6'7"	215	13	Tennessee	81	3.9	1.7	14.9
LaPhonso Ellis	F	6'8"	240	4	Notre Dame	45	7.2	1.6	10.5
Tom Hammonds	F	6'9"	225	7	Georgia Tech	71	3.1	0.3	4.8
Mark Jackson	G	6'1"	192	9	St. John's	81	3.8	7.8	10.0
Ervin Johnson	C	6'11"	245	3	New Orleans	81	5.3	0.6	5.5
Sarunas Marciulionis	G	6'5"	215	6	(Lithuania)	53	1.5	2.2	10.8
Antonio McDyess	F	6'9"	220	1	Alabama	76	7.5	1.0	13.4
Jeff McInnis	G	6'4"	190	R	North Carolina	—	—	—	—
Ricky Pierce	G	6'4"	215	14	Rice	76	1.8	1.3	9.7
Efthimios Rentzias	C	6'11"	243	R	(Greece)	—	—	—	—
Bryant Stith	G	6'5"	208	4	Virginia	82	4.9	2.9	13.6

HOUSTON ROCKETS

Home: The Summit
Capacity: 16,311
Year Built: 1975

Owner: Les Alexander
V.P./Basketball Operations: Bob Weinhauer

Address:
10 Greenway Plaza
Houston, TX 77046

Head Coach: Rudy Tomjanovich
NBA: 224-134   Rockets: 224-134

Rockets History

Throughout their 28 seasons in San Diego and Houston, the Rockets have featured some of the NBA's finest big men. Their most recent pivot star, Hakeem Olajuwon, led the team to the league summit twice.

The tradition began during the team's second year when it drafted Elvin Hayes, the 1968-69 Rookie of the Year who led San Diego to the 1968-69 Western Conference semis, where it lost to Atlanta.

The Rockets moved to Houston in 1971, but Hayes was dealt to Baltimore the next season, and the team rebuilt around considerably shorter players such as 5'11" guard Calvin Murphy and forwards Mike Newlin and Rudy Tomjanovich.

Star center No. 2 came in 1976, when Moses Malone moved over from the defunct ABA. Houston won the Central Division crown in 1976-77 and advanced to the NBA Finals in 1980-81, losing in six games to Boston. In 1983, the Rockets drafted 7'4" Ralph Sampson from Virginia; one year later, they selected the dominating Olajuwon. In 1985-86, Houston made it back to the NBA Finals behind its "Twin Towers," only to lose to Boston in six.

Though the Rockets showed some spunk under Don Chaney in the late 1980s and early '90s, it wasn't until Rudy Tomjanovich took over as coach that the team soared. Houston won the Midwest Division title in 1992-93 and rode the inside power of Olajuwon and perimeter excellence of Robert Horry and Sam Cassell to an NBA title in 1993-94. Clyde Drexler spurred the team to another title in '94-95.

1995-96 Review

It wasn't going to last forever. Although the Rockets would have preferred their 1995-96 season to extend well into the playoffs, they exited in a second-round sweep courtesy of Seattle. They left with a 48-34 record for '95-96, a pair of championship rings, and status as one of the more unlikely mini-dynasties in NBA history.

Unlike the previous two seasons, when Houston was able to conjure up improbable postseason comebacks, the Rockets wilted when Seattle jumped out to a quick lead in their series. They tried to recapture their "Clutch City" magic, but it wasn't to be. Houston fans were left with plenty of injury-induced what-ifs to consider during the off-season.

Guards Clyde Drexler and Sam Cassell both missed more than 20 games due to injury, and Mario Elie was out for 37. Without those three, Houston was unable to unleash the inside-outside game that had carried it to the titles. Even center Hakeem Olajuwon (26.9 PPG, 10.9 RPG), who set the league's career record for blocked shots in 1995-96, missed ten games due to sore knees. Still, Houston managed to win 48 games and knock off favored Los Angeles in the first round of the playoffs.

When they played, Drexler (19.3 PPG), Cassell (14.5 PPG), and Elie (11.1 PPG) were a lethal perimeter trio and received support from surprising CBA alum Eldridge Recasner. Forward Robert Horry's production (12.0 PPG) increased slightly, but his shooting (41.0 FGP) was shaky. Veteran Kenny Smith shot well from 3-point range, as usual, while Chucky Brown and Mark Bryant provided some bulk on the boards and shot the ball well close to the hoop.

Houston Rockets
1996-97 Season Preview

Opening Line: Though the Rockets were unable to three-peat in 1995-96, they enter this season as one of the Western Conference's top teams. Any team with three perennial All-Stars—including Hakeem Olajuwon in the middle, Clyde Drexler at shooting guard, and Charles Barkley at forward—is certainly a force capable of doing some postseason damage. The point guard position lacks depth, however, and the Rockets need to avoid the injuries that plagued them last year to challenge for a spot in the Finals.

Guards: With Sam Cassell gone to Phoenix, free-agent pickup Brent Price gets the nod at the point position. A great outside shooter, the smallish Price is at best a role-player, though he may be forced into starting duty. Clyde Drexler missed 30 games last year but still played at his customary high level. Now entering his 14th year in the league, Drexler may not glide the way he used to, but he is a more accomplished all-around threat. CBA alumnus Sam Mack is an erratic shooter capable of providing an occasional scoring boost.

Forwards: Charles Barkley will liven up the frontcourt considerably. He is a consummate professional (despite the occasional temper tantrum) who will take control of the team and try to lead it back to postseason victory. Kevin Willis is likely to start at power forward. Veteran Mario Elie is mediocre offensively but remains a fine defensive player. He will provide support off the bench. With Robert Horry and Chucky Brown both gone to Phoenix, the Rockets may need second-round pick Othella Harrington of Georgetown to step up and become a solid player.

Centers: Olajuwon remains the game's best pivotman, no matter how many commercials Shaquille O'Neal has made. Olajuwon's ever-expanding arsenal of offensive moves continues to confound opponents, and his rebounding and shot-blocking are vital to the Houston equation. Second-round draft pick Terrell Bell of Georgia has a live body and a lot to learn.

Analysis: The Rockets know how to win big games, and they have Olajuwon and Barkley. Don't look for the team to dominate during the regular season, but woe is the opponent that draws Houston in the playoffs.

Prediction: Third place, Midwest Division

1996-97 Roster

Player	Pos.	Ht.	Wt.	Exp.	College	G	RPG	APG	PPG
Charles Barkley	F	6'6"	250	12	Auburn	71	11.6	3.7	23.2
Terrell Bell	C	6'10"	240	R	Georgia	—	—	—	—
Clyde Drexler	G	6'7"	222	13	Houston	52	7.2	5.8	19.3
Mario Elie	G/F	6'5"	210	6	American Inter.	45	3.4	3.1	11.1
Othella Harrington	F/C	6'9"	235	R	Georgetown	—	—	—	—
Charles Jones	C	6'9"	215	13	Albany St.	46	1.6	0.3	0.3
Randy Livingston	G	6'4"	209	R	Louisiana St.	—	—	—	—
Sam Mack	F	6'7"	220	2	Houston	31	3.2	2.5	10.8
Hakeem Olajuwon	C	7'0"	255	12	Houston	72	10.9	3.6	26.9
Brent Price	G	6'1"	185	3	Oklahoma	81	2.8	5.1	10.0
Kevin Willis	F/C	7'0"	240	11	Michigan St.	75	8.5	0.7	10.6

MINNESOTA TIMBERWOLVES

Home: Target Center
Capacity: 19,006
Year Built: 1990

Owner: Glen Taylor
V.P./Basketball Operations: Kevin McHale

Address:
600 First Ave. North
Minneapolis, MN 55403

Head Coach: Flip Saunders
NBA: 20-42   T'Wolves: 20-42

Timberwolves History

After seven years in the NBA, Minnesota finally finds itself moving slowly from the bottom of the league's ladder.

The Timberwolves debuted in 1989-90, with predictable results—22-60. The poor record did nothing to stem the enthusiasm of the Twin Cities faithful, who packed the Metrodome and established a season attendance record of more than one million patrons.

Among the early bright spots were forward Tony Campbell, a top scoring threat, and rookie playmaker Pooh Richardson. Under defense-minded coach Bill Musselman, the T'Wolves were one of the league's best at maintaining tempo and stopping opponents from scoring.

For 1990-91, Minnesota added 7'0" center Felton Spencer and forward Gerald Glass, and they moved into the brand-new Target Center in downtown Minneapolis. The team improved to 29-53, good for fifth in the Midwest Division. But despite the six-game improvement, Musselman was replaced by Jimmy Rodgers.

The change did nothing to help the team, as the 1991-92 T'Wolves finished with the league's worst record. After the season, Minnesota drafted Christian Laettner and landed standouts Chuck Person and Micheal Williams in a trade. Nevertheless, the 1992-93 club still lacked the talent to win 20 games. High-scoring rookie Isaiah Rider couldn't improve the Wolves in 1993-94. Under the stewardship of new GM Kevin McHale in 1995-96, Minnesota won 26 games and looked to rebuild around forward Kevin Garnett, who joined the NBA straight from high school.

1995-96 Review

On the surface, it was just another bleak year in the icy North. Minnesota won just 26 games, staggered through most of the year without much of an offense, and allowed many opponents to do whatever they wanted. Below the surface, however, there was some improvement. The 26 wins were the franchise's second-highest total, and it appeared the front office (specifically V.P. of Basketball Operations Kevin McHale) actually had a plan of action for making the T'Wolves competitive.

McHale was a busy man throughout 1995-96. By midseason, he had replaced head coach Bill Blair with GM Flip Saunders, an old pal from their days at the University of Minnesota. He then pulled off a blockbuster move, sending forward Christian Laettner, who had never liked Minnesota (and vice versa) to Atlanta. The deal didn't bring much in return, but it did clear cap space and help team morale considerably.

McHale even seemed to have a calming influence on volatile high-scoring guard Isaiah Rider (19.6 PPG), who suffered considerable embarrassment during a game with the Jazz, when his mother stormed onto the court and told him to quit complaining to the refs and take his ejection like a man. First-year player Kevin Garnett (10.4 PPG, 6.3 RPG) silenced those who criticized his move from high school to the pros with a strong second-half performance, while Tom Gugliotta (16.2 PPG, 8.8 RPG) performed well every night. Veteran forward Sam Mitchell (10.8 PPG) scored well off the dribble, while Terry Porter was a steady point man. Andrew Lang had some injury problems but was his usual solid self in the middle.

Minnesota Timberwolves
1996-97 Season Preview

Opening Line: Ever so slowly, the Timberwolves are accumulating quality young talent and moving forward. Credit unprecedented stability in the front office and a solid working relationship between talented GM Kevin McHale and coach Flip Saunders for the new direction. T'Wolves fans will embrace first-round draft pick Stephon Marbury, a gifted point guard who actually wanted to play in Minnesota. He'll team with second-year prodigy Kevin Garnett to form the nucleus of what could be a bright long-term outlook.

Guards: Marbury is a slick distributor, an accomplished scorer, and a classic floor general who could be great one day. Some consider him a "pure" point guard, but Marbury gets high marks for athletic ability and creating opportunities for himself. Veteran Terry Porter is a steady lead guard who can help Marbury get acclimated to the pros, while vet Doug West can score well from 18 feet and in. Second-year man Chris Carr was impressive in his debut with the Suns.

Forwards: McHale earned his first gold star when he traded disappointing Donyell Marshall to Golden State for Tom Gugliotta, a do-everything sort with a fabulous attitude and consistent production. McHale's second decoration came with the selection of Garnett, who showed vast potential and myriad skills just one year removed from high school. And all that talk about him being eaten alive by the NBA lifestyle didn't apply. "Da Kid" handled things well. He and Gugliotta comprise a solid tandem. Sam Mitchell is an instant-offense type off the bench. Cherokee Parks, acquired from Dallas, needs to improve his shooting if he wants minutes.

Centers: The Timberwolves sent Andrew Lang to Milwaukee in the off-season to complete the deal for Marbury, leaving them without a true center. Garnett has the height to play the position, but he isn't strong or heavy enough. Parks will contribute here as well. Look for Minnesota to acquire a free agent close to training camp, but don't expect him to be a stalwart.

Analysis: Don't get too excited about this team yet. There is still plenty of work to be done on the bench, and more heft is needed inside. Adding Marbury is a good move, just like picking Garnett was last year. Playoff contention, however, remains a long way off.

Prediction: Sixth place, Midwest Division

1996-97 Roster

Player	Pos.	Ht.	Wt.	Exp.	College	G	RPG	APG	PPG
							1995-96		
Chris Carr	G	6'6"	207	1	S. Illinois	60	1.7	0.7	4.0
Bill Curley	F	6'9"	245	1	Boston College	—	—	—	—
*Mark Davis	G/F	6'7"	210	1	Texas Tech	57	2.2	0.8	3.3
Kevin Garnett	F	6'11"	220	1	None	80	6.3	1.8	10.4
Tom Gugliotta	F	6'10"	240	4	N. Carolina St.	78	8.8	3.1	16.2
Stephon Marbury	G	6'2"	180	R	Georgia Tech	—	—	—	—
Sam Mitchell	F	6'7"	215	7	Mercer	78	4.3	0.9	10.8
Cherokee Parks	F/C	6'11"	275	1	Duke	64	3.4	0.5	3.9
Terry Porter	G	6'3"	195	11	Wisc.-Stev. Pt.	82	2.6	5.5	9.4
James Robinson	G	6'2"	180	3	Alabama	76	2.1	2.0	8.5
Doug West	G/F	6'6"	220	7	Villanova	73	2.2	1.6	6.4
*Micheal Williams	G	6'2"	175	8	Baylor	9	2.6	3.4	6.1

SAN ANTONIO SPURS

Home: Alamodome
Capacity: 20,662
Year Built: 1993

Chairman of the Board: Robert McDermott
V.P./Basketball Operations: Gregg Popovich

Address:
100 Montana St.
San Antonio, TX 78203

Head Coach: Bob Hill
NBA: 254-197   Spurs: 121-43

Spurs History

This Texas franchise was born as the Dallas Chaparrals in 1967 as a charter member of the ABA. The stay in Dallas was a haphazard one, featuring six coaches in six years, low attendance, and little playoff success.

Angelo Drossos moved the club to the home of the Alamo in 1973, and the team was renamed the Spurs. It was an exciting squad that fans embraced immediately. The Spurs had 50-plus-win seasons in 1974-75 and 1975-76 and moved into the NBA at full gallop.

Led by unstoppable guard George Gervin, mammoth center Artis Gilmore, and a talented supporting cast that included Johnny Moore, Larry Kenon, and James Silas, the Spurs won two Central and three Midwest Division championships in six years. Gervin was the NBA scoring champ four times. However, San Antonio was defeated in the conference finals three times.

Age ended the Spurs' run in the mid-1980s, but the team's fortunes rose again shortly after it drafted center David Robinson of Navy. After completing his military obligation, he joined the team two seasons later, in 1989-90, and quickly became one of the NBA's best centers. Robinson teamed with Terry Cummings and Sean Elliott to help San Antonio win the Midwest title in both 1989-90 and 1990-91. Despite fine records throughout the 1990s, the Spurs weren't able to reach the conference finals until 1995, when they lost to Houston.

1995-96 Review

The main question in San Antonio was whether the Spurs, free of the negative influence of Dennis Rodman, were too nice to succeed at the NBA's highest levels. Could the team, beginning with center David Robinson, be nasty enough to shake the reputation it had acquired during previous playoff flame-outs?

If the team's conference semifinal loss to Utah after 59 regular-season wins was any indication, the answer was no. It appeared Robinson had a legitimate beef with the officiating in the series, but he was again unable to carry the Spurs to the Finals. As usual, his regular-season numbers (25.0 PPG, 12.2 RPG) and behavior were excellent. Unfortunately, his playoff performance was a notch below that.

Of course, it wasn't entirely his fault. The Spurs were something of an imperfect team. Let's face it: When forward Charles Smith is acquired at midseason to improve the toughness of your front line, you have problems.

Robinson was joined atop the scorer's sheet most nights by forward Sean Elliott (20.0 PPG), while off guard Vinny Del Negro (14.5 PPG) continued his solid—but hardly upper-echelon—play. Point guard Avery Johnson (13.1 PPG, 9.6 APG) dazzled once again with his speed and defense, and Chuck Person (10.9 PPG) was always ready to hit the floor firing.

Will Perdue, acquired from the Bulls for Rodman, helped the Spurs inside, but he was not the kind of strongman the team needed. San Antonio may have been happy to see Rodman go, but there was no denying that the team advanced further in the 1994-95 playoffs with Dennis the Menace than it did in 1995-96 without him.

San Antonio Spurs
1996-97 Season Preview

Opening Line: It has become chic to bad-mouth David Robinson's fortitude and blame him for the Spurs' postseason problems, but San Antonio's critics should look at the big picture. The Spurs enter this season with the same troubles in the backcourt and at forward as they had last year. And those are the real reasons the team won't win a title.

Guards: Avery Johnson is a great penetrator, a whip-quick defender, and a strong assist man. But he made just three more 3-pointers than Robinson did last year. The guy just can't shoot from the outside. Off guard Vinny Del Negro is steady from 15 and in, but he's unreliable from long distance, too. And he isn't the fastest guy on defense. Vernon Maxwell will provide plenty of scoring if he can stay out of trouble. Doc Rivers retired in the off-season, so the Spurs hope second-year man Cory Alexander can evolve into the top backup for Johnson.

Forwards: Impugning Robinson's manhood without checking out the guys surrounding him is downright wrong. Sean Elliott scores plenty and gets a few rebounds every night, but don't count on him for any heavy lifting. And the Spurs actually acquired Charles Smith last year to strengthen their frontcourt after the Knicks got rid of him because he wasn't tough enough. At least Chuck Person isn't shy—about launching 65 percent of his shots from beyond the 3-point arc. "The Rifleman" is a big-time scorer off the bench who does one thing and does it well.

Centers: Robinson does it all every night. He is the league's most athletic pivotman, and just because he happens to be polite doesn't mean he isn't tough. Nice guys don't grab 1,000 rebounds in a season. Robinson is still maturing into the leadership role he needs to assume and will continue to produce big numbers until he's ready to hoist the team on his shoulders. Backup Will Perdue can play some power forward, but he's mainly a reliable scorer close to the basket and a pretty fair rebounder.

Analysis: The Spurs will come close to 60 victories, challenge for the Midwest Division title, and win a playoff series or two. And when San Antonio craps out in the postseason, let's look at the other guys, too.

Prediction: First place, Midwest Division

1996-97 Roster

| Player | Pos. | Ht. | Wt. | Exp. | College | —1995-96— | | |
						G	RPG	APG	PPG
Cory Alexander	G	6'1"	190	1	Virginia	60	0.7	2.0	2.8
Greg Anderson	F/C	6'10"	250	8	Houston	46	2.2	0.2	1.2
Vinny Del Negro	G	6'4"	200	6	N. Carolina St.	82	3.3	3.8	14.5
*Dell Demps	G	6'4"	210	2	Pacific	16	0.6	0.5	3.3
Sean Elliott	F	6'8"	220	7	Arizona	77	5.1	2.7	20.0
Carl Herrera	F	6'9"	225	5	Houston	44	1.8	0.4	1.9
Avery Johnson	G	5'11"	182	8	Southern	82	2.5	9.6	13.1
Vernon Maxwell	G	6'4"	190	8	Florida	75	3.1	4.4	16.2
Will Perdue	C	7'0"	240	8	Vanderbilt	80	6.1	0.4	5.2
Chuck Person	F	6'8"	235	10	Auburn	80	5.2	1.3	10.9
David Robinson	C	7'1"	250	7	Navy	82	12.2	3.0	25.0
Charles Smith	F	6'10"	244	8	Pittsburgh	73	5.0	0.9	8.3
Monty Williams	F	6'8"	225	2	Notre Dame	31	1.3	0.3	2.2

UTAH JAZZ

Home: Delta Center
Capacity: 19,911
Year Built: 1991

Owner: Larry H. Miller
General Manager: Tim Howells

Address:
301 W. South Temple
Salt Lake City, UT 84101

Head Coach: Jerry Sloan
NBA: 513-341   Jazz: 419-220

Jazz History

About the last city you'd expect to find a team named the Jazz would be in puritan Salt Lake City, Utah. However, the name comes with an easy explanation. When the franchise was born back in 1974, its hometown was New Orleans, a jazzy place if ever there was one. When the franchise moved west in 1979, it decided to hold on to the name.

The early days did have their moments. In the mid-1970s, Louisiana native "Pistol" Pete Maravich lit up the Bayou, scoring baskets in bushels and once torching the Knicks for 68 points. Maravich's knee went out in 1977-78 and, despite the emergence of all-world rebounder Leonard "Truck" Robinson, the Jazz limped along.

Coach Frank Layden was hired in 1981-82 and immediately became popular for his sense of humor and regular-guy charm. The Jazz captured the Midwest Division crown in 1983-84 and advanced to the conference semifinals, relying on league scoring leader Adrian Dantley, quick backcourt men Darrell Griffith and Ricky Green, and mammoth, 7'4" center Mark Eaton.

The Jazz selected power forward Karl Malone in the 1985 draft, and he was an immediate sensation, teaming with assist machine John Stockton to form a solid nucleus. Utah won the 1988-89 Midwest title under new coach Jerry Sloan before falling in the first round of the playoffs. Utah advanced to the Western finals in 1991-92 and 1993-94 but were beaten by Portland and Houston, respectively, and fizzled out of the '95 playoffs in the first round.

1995-96 Review

After bumbling to first-round playoff exits in two of the previous three seasons (including a particularly ugly one in 1995), the Jazz came within one game of reaching the Finals in '96, falling to Seattle in the Western Conference finals. Although no one in the Utah camp wanted to admit it, losing to the Sonics robbed the spectacular tandem of Karl Malone and John Stockton of perhaps their last chance to play for a league title and fueled speculation that age may prevent the two teammates from ever getting that close to the summit. Although neither retired after the season, both have played for a long time and are closer to the ends of their careers than the beginnings.

Malone (25.7 PPG, 9.8 RPG) was again one of the game's most reliable low-post options and continued to be the league's best at getting to the free-throw line. He proved throughout the playoffs that it is impossible to guard him one-on-one. Stockton (14.7 PPG, 11.2 APG) won yet another league assist title and continued to be the engine that drives the Jazz. He teamed with sharpshooting Jeff Hornacek (15.2 PPG) in a dynamic backcourt that was supplemented by the addition of Chris Morris (10.5 PPG).

David Benoit was again steady at the other forward spot, and Utah received strong play up front from Adam Keefe, Antoine Carr, and Bryon Russell. Felton Spencer returned from a torn Achilles tendon to handle the pivot spot and received adequate support from rookie Greg Ostertag and Greg Foster. Howard Eisley developed well at the point and appeared to have a bright future.

Utah Jazz
1996-97 Season Preview

Opening Line: The Western Conference's equivalent of Avis (they're No. 2, but they try harder) open another season under the Karl Malone/John Stockton marquee, hoping they can get its two big stars one shot at the Finals before their fabulous careers come to a halt. The usual cast of characters (give or take a few) returns to Salt Lake City for the '96-97 season, with the Jazz hoping to two-man-game their way to a conference title.

Guards: Stockton's game has fallen off in recent years, but he remains an assist machine and the perfect set-up man for Malone. Stockton is reliable from the outside, rarely makes the wrong pass, and is a lot tougher than you'd think. Backcourt mate Jeff Hornacek is an expert at pulling up from long range, but he would be better suited coming off the bench behind a more athletic scorer. That might be Chris Morris, if only he would fire better from 3-point land. Howard Eisley should be a steady point reserve.

Forwards: For all of Shawn Kemp's progress, Malone remains the game's preeminent power forward. No one gets to the line as much as he does, and he can be counted on for 25 points and ten rebounds just about every night. David Benoit is gone, but Adam Keefe improved considerably last year and is a valuable power player off the bench, while aging Antoine Carr works hard whether he's a power forward or pivot reserve. Second-round pick Shandon Anderson could provide some scoring pop.

Centers: With the departure of Felton Spencer, hulking second-year man Greg Ostertag will have to step up and watch Malone's back. Ostertag is big and slow. Greg Foster can move better than Ostertag but doesn't shoot as well.

Analysis: The Jazz are just good enough to reach the conference finals, but it's doubtful they can get over the hump and into the Finals. Malone and Stockton are great ones, but there doesn't appear to be enough around them to secure a championship. That's too bad, but plenty of stars have left the league without rings.

Prediction: Second place, Midwest Division

1996-97 Roster

Player	Pos.	Ht.	Wt.	Exp.	College	—1995-96—		
						G	RPG	APG	PPG
Shandon Anderson	F/G	6'6"	205	R	Georgia	—	—	—	—
Antoine Carr	F/C	6'9"	225	12	Wichita St.	80	2.5	0.9	7.3
Howard Eisley	G	6'3"	180	2	Boston College	65	1.2	2.2	4.4
Greg Foster	F/C	6'11"	240	6	Texas-El Paso	73	2.4	0.3	3.8
Kenny Gattison	F/C	6'8"	257	9	Old Dominion	25	4.6	0.6	9.2
Jeff Hornacek	G	6'4"	190	10	Iowa St.	82	2.5	4.1	15.2
*Adam Keefe	F	6'9"	241	4	Stanford	82	5.5	0.8	6.1
Karl Malone	F	6'9"	256	11	Louisiana Tech	82	9.8	4.2	25.7
Chris Morris	F	6'8"	220	8	Auburn	66	3.5	1.2	10.5
Greg Ostertag	C	7'2"	280	1	Kansas	57	3.1	0.1	3.6
*Bryon Russell	F	6'7"	225	3	Long Beach St.	59	1.5	0.5	2.9
John Stockton	G	6'1"	175	12	Gonzaga	82	2.8	11.2	14.7
Brooks Thompson	G	6'4"	193	2	Oklahoma St.	33	0.7	0.9	4.2
Jamie Watson	F	6'7"	190	2	South Carolina	16	1.7	1.5	3.0

VANCOUVER GRIZZLIES

Home: General Motors Place
Capacity: 20,004
Year Built: 1989

Co-chairman/CEO: Arthur Griffiths
President/General Manager: Stu Jackson

Address:
788 Beatty St. #201
Vancouver, BC V6B 2M1

Head Coach: Brian Winters
NBA: 15-67   Grizzlies: 15-67

1995-96 Review

So what if the Grizzlies won only 15 games (fewest in the NBA) and had a pair of prolonged losing streaks. The expansion franchise with the odd-looking uniforms was well-received on the Canadian left coast and earned cheers for its hustling—if not always successful—play. When you're referring to a first-year NBA team, what else can you ask for?

Like the Raptors, the Grizzlies had something of a revolving door policy on personnel. They made a big trade with Milwaukee early in the season, sending underachieving center Benoit Benjamin east in exchange for guard Eric Murdock (8.9 PPG, 4.5 APG) and center Eric Mobley, neither of whom made a big impact.

No player on the roster was dominant, although it was easy to predict a bright future for rookie center Bryant Reeves (13.3 PPG, 7.4 RPG), who became a fan favorite. Point guard Greg Anthony (14.0 PPG, 6.9 APG) finally got to run a team and did a fine job, although he didn't shoot the ball all that well. Veteran forward Blue Edwards (12.7 PPG) lived up to his steady reputation, while aging guard Byron Scott (10.2 PPG) fired at will from 3-point range. As can be expected, the rest of the roster was rather forgettable and demonstrated how far the Grizzlies must go before they can even think about contention.

1995-96 Season Preview

Opening Line: It may appear that the Grizzlies are a step behind their expansion counterparts, but don't concede the Battle of Canada just yet. A solid draft has built a potentially formidable frontcourt in Vancouver, and though lots of work remains, Vancouver is moving forward.

Guards: Greg Anthony is a competent point man who plays steady defense, but his poor shooting is a big liability. Free-agent acquisition Lee Mayberry continues to struggle with his shot. Anthony Peeler, acquired from the Lakers, will be a solid backup at the off guard position. The arrival of small forward Shareef Abdur-Rahim may push Blue Edwards to the shooting guard spot, because Lawrence Moten is too raw for it.

Forwards: Abdur-Rahim needs some strength and must improve his outside shot. That said, he's a great prospect. The Grizzlies' other first-round pick, Roy Rogers of Alabama, has a big body to block shots and help fortify the team's inside defense. George Lynch can rebound a little, but his shooting is also weak.

Centers: Bryant Reeves won't ever be one of the league's top pivotmen, but he will be steady, strong, and productive. That's what he was as a rookie, and he could be an even greater factor this season—provided he gets stronger and improves his ability to finish close to the basket. Eric Mobley is a large, one-dimensional pivot who operates well within five feet of the hoop.

Analysis: The expansion road is long, and the NBA likes it that way. Vancouver has upgraded itself and could even win 20 games. But the youngsters need time to develop, and the backcourt must be improved considerably before 30 wins are a possibility.

Prediction: Seventh place, Midwest Division

See page 396 for the Vancouver Grizzlies' 1996-97 roster.

GOLDEN STATE WARRIORS

Home: Oakland Coliseum Arena
Capacity: 15,025
Year Built: 1966

Chairman: Chris Cohan
General Manager: Dave Twardzik

Address:
Oakland Coliseum Arena
Oakland, CA 94621

Head Coach: Rick Adelman
NBA: 327-200   Golden State: 36-46

Warriors History

Present-day Warrior fans may find it difficult to identify with the team's East Coast roots. For 16 seasons, the Philadelphia Warriors enjoyed success in the old BAA and as a charter member of the NBA. Philadelphia won the first BAA championship in 1946-47 behind scoring machine Joe Fulks.

In '48, the Warriors lost to Baltimore in the BAA finals, but they defeated Fort Wayne in 1956. In 1959, Wilt Chamberlain joined the team and was an immediate sensation, winning the MVP Award in his rookie season. The team moved to San Francisco in 1962 and lost to Boston in the NBA Finals in 1963-64. The Warriors traded Chamberlain to the new Philadelphia 76ers in 1964-65, then lost to the Sixers in the NBA Finals two years later.

The Warriors changed their name to Golden State in 1971 and moved across the bay to Oakland, where the championship drought continued until 1974-75. That year, coach Al Attles incorporated a ten-man rotation around Rick Barry and took the Warriors to the NBA title.

Don Nelson took over as coach in 1988 and built a small lineup featuring Chris Mullin and Mitch Richmond. The Warriors made it to the Western semis in 1988-89. Point guard Tim Hardaway was added in '89 and helped Golden State advance to the 1991 Western semis. Injuries sabotaged the team's success in subsequent seasons, and a rebuilding program began in 1995 with the hiring of coach Rick Adelman.

1995-96 Review

Although the Warriors won only 36 games in 1995-96, they took the first steps in fixing what had been a fatally flawed team. The franchise had coaching problems and personality troubles. A midseason trade sent Tim Hardaway and Keith Gatling to Miami, ending the backcourt friction and helping ease the logjam of inadequate forwards/centers in the frontcourt.

New GM Dave Twardzik and coach Rick Adelman gave the Warriors a solid on-court presence. Golden State allowed its opponents 103.1 PPG, indicating that the transformation wasn't completed in a year, but the Warriors were moving in the right direction.

Once again, however, the team played largely without a pivotman. Although rookie forward Joe Smith (15.3 PPG, 8.7 RPG) provided a solid presence inside at both ends of the court, veteran Rony Seikaly (12.1 PPG, 7.8 RPG) was still a power forward trying to play center. Latrell Sprewell (18.9 PPG) remained prone to fits of crankiness at the off guard spot, but had to be pleased with the team's decision to get rid of Hardaway, his nemesis.

Meanwhile, lithe B.J. Armstrong (12.3 PPG, 4.9 APG) was his usual steady self at point guard. Chris Mullin (13.3 PPG) was able to play in only 55 games and continued to produce when he was on the floor, while veteran Jerome Kersey got 58 starts, despite a continued atrophying of his skills. Kevin Willis (10.6 PPG, 8.5 RPG)—acquired with guard Bimbo Coles (11.0 PPG) from Miami—rebounded well but wasn't close to the defensive presence his powerful 7'0" frame indicated he would be. Donyell Marshall and Clifford Rozier continued to disappoint.

Golden State Warriors
1996-97 Season Preview

Opening Line: After several years with a roster filled with excellent perimeter people and a suspect interior, Golden State is moving slowly toward becoming a real basketball team again. Year two of the Dave Twardzik/Rick Adelman era should feature a brush with the playoffs and the continued emergence of Joe Smith. True contention remains a ways off.

Guards: With cranky but multitalented Latrell Sprewell, life is good in the backcourt. Sprewell isn't the greatest pure shooter, but he can score in a lot of ways, pass the ball quite well, and is a demon on defense. The combination of B.J. Armstrong and Bimbo Coles in the backcourt hurts. Armstrong is a capable distributor and proven winner, and Coles is more of a point man than anything else. Free-agent acquisition Mark Price will add veteran leadership and sweet shooting, although his skills are not what they once were.

Forwards: Smith did nothing to make the Warriors regret picking him first overall. He scored well, rebounded even better, and blocked a few shots. He should be an All-Star before long. Chris Mullin is too injury-prone to be counted on for a full season at the three spot, but the Warriors have nothing else. Donyell Marshall still hasn't grasped the finer points of halfcourt basketball. Rookie Marcus Mann is a big body who will look good backing up Smith, but Clifford Rozier is a one-dimensional player who still doesn't get the pro game.

Centers: Golden State spent its first-round pick on the team's first legitimate center in more than a decade. North Carolina State's Todd Fuller is a good shooter and passer with plenty of potential. He'll work behind veteran Rony Seikaly at first but could allow Seikaly to play some power forward—his natural position.

Analysis: Don't expect more than about 40 wins. In an ironic twist, Golden State now has some holes on the perimeter, after years of concentrating exclusively on that part of the team. This rebuilding project will take time, but it's in good hands with Twardzik.

Prediction: Sixth place, Pacific Division

1996-97 Roster

Player	Pos.	Ht.	Wt.	Exp.	College	G	RPG	APG	PPG
							|—1995-96—|		
B.J. Armstrong	G	6'2"	185	7	Iowa	82	2.2	4.9	12.3
Bimbo Coles	G	6'2"	185	6	Virginia Tech	81	3.2	5.2	11.0
*Andrew DeClercq	F	6'10"	230	1	Florida	22	1.8	0.4	2.7
Todd Fuller	C	6'11"	255	R	N. Carolina St.	—	—	—	—
Marcus Mann	F	6'8"	245	R	Miss. Valley St.	—	—	—	—
Donyell Marshall	F	6'9"	230	2	Connecticut	62	3.4	0.8	5.5
Chris Mullin	F	6'7"	215	11	St. John's	55	2.9	3.5	13.3
Mark Price	G	6'0"	178	10	Georgia Tech	7	1.0	2.6	8.0
*Clifford Rozier	C/F	6'11"	235	2	Louisville	59	2.9	0.4	3.1
Rony Seikaly	C	6'11"	252	8	Syracuse	64	7.8	1.1	12.1
Joe Smith	F	6'10"	225	1	Maryland	82	8.7	1.0	15.3
Latrell Sprewell	G	6'5"	190	4	Alabama	78	4.9	4.2	18.9

LOS ANGELES CLIPPERS

Home: L.A. Memorial Sports Arena
Capacity: 16,021
Year Built: 1959

Owner: Donald T. Sterling
V.P./Basketball Operations: Elgin Baylor

Address:
3939 S. Figueroa St.
Los Angeles, CA 90037

Head Coach: Bill Fitch
NBA: 891-995   Clippers: 46-118

Clippers History

Despite brief success in the mid-1970s and playoff appearances in 1991-92 and 1992-93, the Clippers have been one of the league's weakest and most poorly managed teams.

Born the Buffalo Braves in 1970, the team flourished briefly under the direction of Jack Ramsay. The Braves crept above the .500 mark (42-40) in 1973-74, behind NBA scoring leader Bob McAdoo, slick playmaker Ernie DiGregorio, and sharp-shooting forward Jim McMillian. The Braves improved to 49-33 the next season with MVP McAdoo again leading the way. Washington bounced the Braves from the 1975 Eastern semifinals, but the Braves persevered and whipped Philadelphia in the first round of the 1976 playoffs before succumbing to Boston in the semis.

Thus ended the good times for Braves/Clippers fans. Prior to the 1978-79 season, Braves owner John Y. Brown traded the team to Irving Levin in return for control of the Celtics. Levin moved the club to San Diego, renamed it the Clippers, and watched it register an abysmal 17-65 mark in 1981-82. The Clippers moved north to L.A. for the 1984-85 season and were an immediate poor cousin to the flourishing Lakers.

Though they won 30-plus games in 1984-85 and 1985-86, the Clippers embarked on three straight miserable seasons, with the lowlight being a 12-70 mark in 1986-87. Despite amassing quality young talent, the Clippers failed to rise above mediocrity in the late '80s. After a two-year bout with respectability from 1991-93 that featured two first-round playoff losses, the Clippers sank back into the league dungeon.

1995-96 Review

Even though the 1995-96 season dissolved into a rather ugly 29-53 performance, there were actually signs of encouragement. Although Los Angeles wasn't anywhere near playoff contention, it wasn't nearly as bad as everybody figured it to be when the season started.

L.A. won 12 more games than it had the year before and actually demonstrated a little life. Sure, the Clips were overwhelmed on the backboards, didn't play much interior defense, and were among the worst free-throw shooting teams in the league, but those details obscured what was a brighter big picture for the first time in three seasons. For the first time in a while, the Clips had accumulated some young talent and didn't seem nearly as pathetic and mismanaged as earlier incarnations. Coach Bill Fitch, hardly known for his calm demeanor, actually exercised patience with the Clippers and was rewarded with periods of solid play.

Veteran forward Loy Vaught (16.2 PPG, 10.1 RPG) remained an NBA role model for his consistent hard work and absence of complaining. Brian Williams (15.8 PPG, 7.6 RPG) was steady in the middle but was often overmatched. Veteran Pooh Richardson (11.7 PPG) provided some stability at the point, but second-year man Lamond Murray stumbled at the small forward spot and didn't duplicate his solid rookie performance. Terry Dehere (12.4 PPG) was a valuable contributor off the bench, and first-round draft choice Brent Barry flashed signs of a sound all-around game. Rodney Rogers (11.6 PPG) had a good third year but didn't rebound as well as he should have, and Malik Sealy (11.5 PPG) was an adequate perimeter reserve.

Los Angeles Clippers
1996-97 Season Preview

Opening Line: Long-suffering Clipper fans shouldn't get too excited yet, but their heroes made some strides last season and are giving the indication that they might be turning into a real basketball team after a few years as an NBA sideshow. Of course, the curious selection of Lorenzen Wright with the seventh pick in the draft was a classic case of Clipper Logic: Your best player is a power forward? Why not draft another?

Guards: The Clipper backcourt may not be that well known, but it isn't so bad. Terry Dehere is showing signs of being a solid NBA scorer and a reliable passer, while veteran Pooh Richardson will run the team, hit too few of his shots, and take care of the ball. Second-year man Brent Barry has all the physical tools needed to be successful, plus a high basketball IQ. Eric Piatkowski likes to shoot and do little else.

Forwards: As always, Loy Vaught can be counted on for steady interior scoring and ten rebounds a game. But why did the Clips draft Memphis' Lorenzen Wright, a spindly, 6'11" fellow with a questionable shooting touch and no real chance of ever becoming a true NBA center? Rodney Rogers, Malik Sealy, and Lamond Murray comprise an imperfect small forward trio. Rogers is a little too small for his in-close game, Sealy is an inaccurate shooter, and Murray is struggling to fit into a half-court set. Bo Outlaw is a one-dimensional power player good for about ten minutes and three or four fouls a night.

Centers: Brian Williams played admirably in the middle for the Clips last year, but he is overmatched and would be the first to admit it. But L.A. needs him, because Stanley Roberts may never return to form after suffering a torn Achilles tendon.

Analysis: The Clippers are collecting players and should creep over the 30-win mark, but it's tough to divine what the team's strategy is. They remain a legitimate point guard and center away from real contention, and those are the two toughest pieces of the NBA puzzle to accumulate. Until the Clips can accomplish that, fans should be content with gradual improvement and small victory totals.

Prediction: Seventh place, Pacific Division

1996-97 Roster

Player	Pos.	Ht.	Wt.	Exp.	College	G	RPG	APG	PPG
Brent Barry	G	6'6"	185	1	Oregon St.	79	2.1	2.9	10.1
Terry Dehere	G	6'4"	190	3	Seton Hall	82	1.7	4.3	12.4
*Antonio Harvey	C/F	6'10"	246	3	Pfeiffer	55	3.6	0.3	3.7
Lamond Murray	F	6'7"	236	2	California	77	3.2	1.1	8.4
*Bo Outlaw	C/F	6'8"	210	3	Houston	80	2.5	0.6	3.6
Eric Piatkowski	G/F	6'7"	215	2	Nebraska	65	1.6	0.7	4.6
Pooh Richardson	G	6'1"	180	7	UCLA	63	2.5	5.4	11.7
Stanley Roberts	C	7'0"	290	4	Louisiana St.	51	3.2	0.8	7.0
Rodney Rogers	F	6'7"	255	3	Wake Forest	67	4.3	2.5	11.6
Malik Sealy	F	6'8"	190	4	St. John's	62	3.9	1.9	11.5
Loy Vaught	F	6'9"	240	6	Michigan	80	10.1	1.4	16.2
*Brian Williams	F/C	6'11"	260	5	Arizona	65	7.6	1.9	15.8
Lorenzen Wright	F/C	6'11"	225	R	Memphis	—	—	—	—

LOS ANGELES LAKERS

Home: The Great Western Forum
Capacity: 17,505
Year Built: 1967

Owner: Dr. Jerry Buss
V.P./Basketball Operations: Jerry West

Address:
3900 W. Manchester Blvd.
Inglewood, CA 90306

Head Coach: Del Harris
NBA: 433-404   Lakers: 101-63

Lakers History

No team has equaled the tradition and success of the Boston Celtics, but the Lakers have come close. During the franchise's 45 years of existence, it has put a dazzling array of talent onto NBA courts and won 11 world championships.

The Laker magic began in Minneapolis and was built around 6'10" center George Mikan, clearly the premier player of his day. He led the team to five titles from 1949 to 1954.

In 1960, the team moved to Los Angeles, but the early years in L.A. featured heartbreak, as the Lakers lost in the NBA Finals to the Celtics six times, despite the heroics of guard Jerry West and forward Elgin Baylor.

Even the arrival of Wilt Chamberlain in 1968-69 couldn't stop the string of runner-up finishes. The Lakers dropped the 1968-69 championship series to the Celtics and the 1969-70 series to the Knicks. Two years later, the Lakers went 69-13 (including a 33-game winning streak) and beat New York 4-1 in the Finals.

Kareem Abdul-Jabbar continued the tradition of Hall of Fame pivotmen when he was acquired from Milwaukee in 1975. But it wasn't until Magic Johnson was drafted in 1979 that the Lakers truly began to shine. The team won five titles in the 1980s and assumed the "Showtime" image that predominated its home city. Johnson's premature retirement in 1993 signaled the end of the era, and though he came back in 1996, the team still lost in the first round of the playoffs.

1995-96 Review

The excitement and promise spawned by Magic Johnson's return to the Lakers dissolved into a depressing close to the 1995-96 season. Johnson, who had energized the team and its fans by returning for the final 40 games, was unable to lift L.A. back to its glory days of the 1980s. By the time the year was over, Johnson had bumped an official (drawing a suspension), griped about playing time and how he was being used by coach Del Harris, and proved unable to help L.A. overcome Houston in the first round of the playoffs.

Not long after the postseason elimination, Johnson retired for the third time—this time, he claimed, for good—and left the Lakers to continue the rebuilding project. Though Johnson (14.6 PPG, 6.9 APG) provided a regular-season boost and helped the Lakers to 53 wins, he was unable to help some of the team's younger talents focus on the game and keep their emotions in control.

Guard Nick Van Exel (14.9 PPG, 6.9 APG) was suspended for seven games at the end of the year for shoving an official, and leading scorer Cedric Ceballos (21.2 PPG) took a leave of absence in midseason for no apparent reason. The rest of the Lakers merely tried to find spots in the Magic saga.

Elden Campbell (13.9 PPG, 7.6 RPG) went about his business quietly and had a productive, if not spectacular, year. Center Vlade Divac's numbers (12.9 PPG, 8.6 RPG) fell somewhat from his career year in 1994-95. Second-year man Eddie Jones (12.8 PPG) had early-season injury problems but continued to be one of the league's more promising young guards, particularly in the open court.

Los Angeles Lakers
1996-97 Season Preview

Opening Line: Now that Magic Johnson has decided to retire for what we all hope is the final time, the Lakers can get on with the business of finding a way back into title contention. If the new Magic Show couldn't do it, perhaps the arrival of Shaquille O'Neal in Tinseltown will.

Guards: The Lakers have a loose cannon in Nick Van Exel—a talented point man with a volcanic temper—and a somewhat reticent shooting guard in Eddie Jones, who has fabulous skills but defers too much. Journeyman Rumeal Robinson will provide some backup. Rookie Kobe Bryant comes directly from high school with plenty of potential but no true backcourt position. Of course, keeping recent history in mind, one has to wonder if Magic is truly gone for good.

Forwards: Cedric Ceballos's little self-imposed exile last year proved he was every bit as volatile as Van Exel, but oh, how the man can score. Ceballos is a slasher extraordinaire and one of the best closers on the break. Power forward Elden Campbell is an excellent shot-blocker, a good rebounder, and a competent interior scorer who has become more consistent in the past two years. Jerome Kersey is on his last legs.

Centers: The Lakers cleared room for O'Neal by sending Vlade Divac to Charlotte and now turn over the pivot position to a true NBA phenomenon with the hope he will blossom into more than just a regular-season star under the L.A. banner. O'Neal has great physical talents, but his offensive game is still somewhat rudimentary, his defensive positioning bad, and his foul shooting atrocious. Despite all that, his presence will help lift the Lakers to 60 regular-season wins and a high playoff seed.

Analysis: The fun is back at the Forum, and L.A. is again an NBA focal point, much to the delight of the league honchos. We'll soon see if O'Neal is a real leader and champion or merely a human multinational corporation with a basketball division.

Prediction: Second place, Pacific Division

1996-97 Roster

Player	Pos.	Ht.	Wt.	Exp.	College	G	—1995-96—RPG	APG	PPG
Corie Blount	F	6'10"	242	3	Cincinnati	57	3.0	0.7	3.2
Kobe Bryant	G	6'6"	200	R	None	—	—	—	—
Elden Campbell	F/C	6'11"	250	6	Clemson	82	7.6	2.2	13.9
Cedric Ceballos	F	6'7"	225	6	Cal. St. Fuller.	78	6.9	1.5	21.2
Derek Fisher	G	6'1"	200	R	Ark.-Little Rock	—	—	—	—
Eddie Jones	G/F	6'6"	190	2	Temple	70	3.3	3.5	12.8
Jerome Kersey	F	6'7"	225	12	Longwood	76	4.8	1.5	6.7
Travis Knight	C	7'0"	235	R	Connecticut	—	—	—	—
Shaquille O'Neal	C	7'1"	303	4	Louisiana St.	54	11.0	2.9	26.6
*Fred Roberts	F	6'10"	218	12	Brigham Young	33	1.4	0.8	3.7
Rumeal Robinson	G	6'2"	195	5	Michigan	43	1.8	3.3	5.7
Sean Rooks	C/F	6'10"	250	4	Arizona	65	3.9	0.7	6.5
Nick Van Exel	G	6'1"	183	3	Cincinnati	74	2.4	6.9	14.9

PHOENIX SUNS

Home: America West Arena
Capacity: 19,023
Year Built: 1992

Chief Executive Officer: Jerry Colangelo
V.P./Player Personnel: Dick Van Arsdale

Address:
201 E. Jefferson St.
Phoenix, AZ 85004

Head Coach: Cotton Fitzsimmons
NBA: 832-767   Suns: 341-200

Suns History

If there is one team in the NBA synonymous with the term "near miss," it is the Suns. Throughout its 27-year history, Phoenix has missed out on superstars and championships by the narrowest of margins.

The team's destiny was shaped by a coin toss following the 1968-69 season, when the Suns lost the draft rights to Lew Alcindor to the Milwaukee Bucks. A seven-year run of mediocrity ensued, with only one playoff appearance, despite exciting play by Connie Hawkins and Dick Van Arsdale.

The next close call came during the 1976 playoffs, when underdog Phoenix lost the NBA Finals to Boston, including a heart-stopping, triple-overtime loss in Game 5. In 1978-79, center Alvan Adams, forward Truck Robinson, and superb guard Paul Westphal formed a solid nucleus that again fell just short, losing to Seattle in a seven-game Western Conference finals.

The Suns enjoyed some success in the early 1980s and won the Pacific Division in 1980-81. They dropped off in the middle of the decade but picked it up again in the late 1980s. Tom Chambers, Kevin Johnson, and Dan Majerle led Phoenix to four straight 50-plus-win seasons. The addition of Charles Barkley pushed the Suns past the 60-win plateau in 1992-93, but they lost to Chicago in the NBA Finals. Injuries and trades broke apart the Phoenix nucleus soon thereafter, and the team headed into the late 1990s on the wane.

1995-96 Review

It was a sad last roundup in Barkleyville in 1995-96, as the Suns officially lost their status as serious title contenders. Little went right for what was once one of the most promising franchises in the NBA, and the Suns fell to 41-41, their worst record in eight years.

Coach Paul Westphal, a favorite of many players, was replaced in midseason by former bench jockey Cotton Fitzsimmons—an unfortunate turn of events that placed the blame for Phoenix's injury-induced poor start on Westphal. Most of Phoenix's top players missed at least ten games during the year, a condition that led to the Suns' slow start. By the time Phoenix dropped a first-round playoff series to San Antonio, it looked in need of a major overhaul.

One player who couldn't be held responsible for the collapse was forward Charles Barkley (23.2 PPG, 11.6 RPG), who enjoyed one of his best and most injury-free campaigns in recent years. But Barkley appeared to be close to the end of his career and his time in Phoenix, and rumors swirled during the latter part of the season about whether he would be traded.

Point guard Kevin Johnson (18.7 PPG, 9.2 APG) was again felled by injuries and played only 56 games. Danny Manning (13.4 PPG) made it to only 33, thanks to his cranky knee. And Hot Rod Williams, expected to be the team's center, missed 20 contests and was erratic when he did play. There were some bright spots, most notably the play of rookie Michael Finley (15.0 PPG), clearly one of the steals of the draft, and the steady performance of forward A.C. Green (7.5 PPG, 6.8 RPG).

Phoenix Suns
1996-97 Season Preview

Opening Line: Phoenix is a long way from the team that made it to the Finals in 1993. Charles Barkley is gone. Although Phoenix still has some recognizable names and has accumulated some quality young talent, the team is not near true contention. The Suns continue to build for the future.

Guards: When healthy, Kevin Johnson is a star, but he hasn't made it through a full season in years. Sam Cassell plays big in big games and handles the ball well, but he could use a shooting upgrade. Rookie Steve Nash has a great shot and feel for the game, but there are questions about his quickness. Wesley Person is a budding young scorer who needs just a bit more long-range accuracy to get up over the 15-PPG mark.

Forwards: Phoenix looked brilliant for taking small forward Michael Finley in last year's draft. He averaged 15.0 PPG and looked nothing like the guy who disappointed as a college senior. The Suns hope Danny Manning can work toward a full recovery of his knee and again bring his versatile game to the mix. Robert Horry spends too much of his time firing 3s but is a talented and versatile player. A.C. Green isn't as productive as he used to be, but he's out there banging and rebounding, no matter what.

Centers: If Hot Rod Williams is healthy, he'll be an athletic, undersized pivot who can block a few shots and score reasonably well along the baseline. Veteran Joe Kleine is stronger but slower and less polished on offense. Mark Bryant is a husky backup who scores well close to the hoop and can rebound.

Analysis: Phoenix is trying to reinvent itself slowly. Cotton Fitzsimmons has been charged with being a little sterner on the court than deposed coach Paul Westphal. The Suns had their shot and couldn't deliver. Now, they must regroup for another charge.

Prediction: Third place, Pacific Division

1996-97 Roster

Player	Pos.	Ht.	Wt.	Exp.	College	G	RPG	APG	PPG
Mario Bennett	F	6'10"	235	1	Arizona St.	19	2.6	0.3	4.5
Chucky Brown	F	6'8"	215	4	N. Carolina St.	82	5.4	1.1	8.6
Mark Bryant	F/C	6'9"	245	8	Seton Hall	71	4.9	0.7	8.6
Sam Cassell	G	6'3"	198	3	Florida St.	61	3.1	4.6	14.5
Ben Davis	F	6'9"	240	R	Arizona	—	—	—	—
Michael Finley	F	6'7"	215	1	Wisconsin	82	4.6	3.5	15.0
A.C. Green	F	6'9"	224	11	Oregon St.	82	6.8	0.9	7.5
Robert Horry	F	6'10"	220	4	Alabama	71	5.8	4.0	12.0
Kevin Johnson	G	6'1"	190	9	California	56	3.9	9.2	18.7
Joe Kleine	C	7'0"	271	11	Arkansas	56	2.4	0.8	2.9
Danny Manning	F	6'10"	234	8	Kansas	33	4.3	2.0	13.4
Russ Millard	F	6'8"	240	R	Iowa	—	—	—	—
Steve Nash	G	6'3"	195	R	Santa Clara	—	—	—	—
Elliot Perry	G	6'0"	160	4	Memphis	81	1.7	4.4	8.6
Wesley Person	G/F	6'6"	195	2	Auburn	82	3.9	1.7	12.7
*Terrence Rencher	G	6'3"	185	1	Texas	36	11.3	1.2	2.9
Wayman Tisdale	F	6'9"	260	11	Oklahoma	63	3.4	0.9	10.7
John Williams	F/C	6'11"	245	10	Tulane	62	6.0	1.0	7.3

PORTLAND TRAIL BLAZERS

Home: Rose Garden
Capacity: 20,300
Year Built: 1995

Chairman: Paul Allen
President: Bob Whitsitt

Address:
1 N. Center Ct. #200
Portland, OR 97227

Head Coach: P.J. Carlesimo
NBA: 88-76   Blazers: 88-76

Trail Blazers History

Few teams in sports are more popular than Portland, which has played to sellout crowds at the old Memorial Coliseum and the new Rose Garden for more than 20 consecutive years.

Portland was a typical expansion team in the early 1970s, losing far more often than it won, although it had some talent, like Geoff Petrie, Sidney Wicks, and future Blazers coach Rick Adelman.

Things began to change in 1974 when the Blazers drafted UCLA center Bill Walton. Two years later, Jack Ramsay became coach and led the team to its only NBA title, an upset win over Philadelphia in the 1977 Finals. Bob Gross, Maurice Lucas, Dave Twardzik, and Lionel Hollins joined Walton on the starting unit.

The Blazers appeared primed to repeat in 1977-78, but Walton injured his foot and Portland was eliminated by Seattle in the West semifinals. Walton never returned to form, and the Blazers fell behind Los Angeles and Seattle in the Pacific Division.

In the 1980s, management drafted star guards Clyde Drexler and Terry Porter, and in 1989 Portland traded for rebounding forward Buck Williams. The Blazers had world-championship talent, but they could not win the big one. Portland lost to Detroit in the 1990 NBA Finals and Chicago in the '92 title series. The Blazers fell quickly after that and made four straight first-round exits. Their current 14 consecutive playoff appearances is the longest active streak in the NBA.

1995-96 Review

Lost in the turmoil that surrounded the discontent of point guard Rod Strickland and the instability of coach P.J. Carlesimo was a Trail Blazers season that offered fans plenty of second-half excitement. After struggling early on with poor play and off-court distractions, the Blazers rebounded to win 44 games and then scare Utah in the first round of the playoffs.

But though Portland's first year in the spanking new Rose Garden was somewhat thrilling, it ended with a familiar thud. The Blazers exited the playoffs in the first round for the fourth straight year. The playoff appearance secured Carlesimo's job, but the quick finish didn't make Strickland (18.7 PPG, 9.6 APG) happy. He disappeared for a while in midseason, unhappy with his relationship with Carlesimo, and though he played brilliantly after returning, his days in Portland were numbered.

Forward Cliff Robinson (21.1 PPG, 5.7 RPG) again led the team in scoring, but he was unable to take on a star's burden during the postseason. One player who seemed to embrace attention was Arvydas Sabonis (14.5 PPG, 8.1 RPG), a 31-year-old who finished second in the NBA's Rookie of the Year balloting and who energized the Blazers with his excellent passing, shooting, and huge 7'3" presence.

Second-year man Aaron McKie (10.7 PPG) began to mature into the off guard position, and Harvey Grant was again a reliable offensive player. Rookie Gary Trent shot well from the field, and aging Buck Williams (5.8 RPG) remained a force on the boards but saw his minutes slip. Chris Dudley rebounded well and blocked shots in the pivot, but his offensive liabilities cost him his starting job to Sabonis.

Portland Trail Blazers
1996-97 Season Preview

Opening Line: The Blazers showed some spunk during last year's first-round playoff loss but enter 1996-97 in danger of losing their momentum, thanks to the departure of point guard Rod Strickland, who feuded with coach P.J. Carlesimo last year. The Blazers didn't do much to bolster the point guard position during the off-season, confounding experts and fans by selecting raw high-schooler Jermaine O'Neal with the 17th pick in the draft.

Guards: Portland wasted no time filling the troublemaker slot left open by Strickland's departure. Isaiah Rider is an excellent scorer and improving shooter. If he can only get his act together and stop acting like a child, he could be a tremendous addition to the backcourt. Kenny Anderson will run the show. Randolph Childress played the position in college but is really a gunner. Aaron McKie showed promise at the off guard spot last year but needs to improve his shooting range.

Forwards: Now that Clifford Robinson has proved he can score, he needs to stop launching so many 3-point shots and become a leader. He could be great if he played to win rather than just for points. The Blazers had better hope forward Rasheed Wallace (obtained from Washington in the Strickland deal) matures in a hurry. Wallace was among the league leaders in technical fouls last year, but if he acts like a grown-up, he could be a versatile frontcourt piece. Second-year man Gary Trent, who oozes potential and power, has a great future in the league. Dontonio Wingfield still has plenty to learn.

Centers: Despite playing on bum legs and surrendering stamina to age, Arvydas Sabonis was a revelation and enters the year as perhaps the league's best passing pivot. That means Chris Dudley comes off the bench to play defense, rebound, and miss foul shots. O'Neal begins a long apprenticeship with shot-blocking skills and little else.

Analysis: Portland is building a solid frontcourt but needs to fortify its guard line if it has any hopes of chasing the better Western Conference teams. Anderson and Rider have the skills but lack maturity. The Blazers will probably sneak into the playoffs, but don't expect them to last long.

Prediction: Fifth place, Pacific Division

1996-97 Roster

Player	Pos.	Ht.	Wt.	Exp.	College	G	RPG	APG	PPG
Kenny Anderson	G	6'1"	168	5	Georgia Tech	69	2.9	8.3	15.2
Marcus Brown	G	6'3"	185	R	Murray St.	—	—	—	—
Mitchell Butler	G/F	6'5"	210	3	UCLA	61	1.9	1.1	3.9
Randolph Childress	G	6'2"	188	1	Wake Forest	28	0.7	1.1	3.0
Chris Dudley	C	6'11"	240	9	Yale	80	9.0	0.5	5.1
Aaron McKie	G	6'5"	209	2	Temple	81	3.8	2.5	10.7
Jermaine O'Neal	F/C	6'11"	226	R	None	—	—	—	—
Isaiah Rider	G	6'5"	222	3	UNLV	75	4.1	2.8	19.6
Clifford Robinson	F	6'10"	225	7	Connecticut	78	5.7	2.4	21.1
Arvydas Sabonis	C	7'3"	292	1	(Lithuania)	73	8.1	1.8	14.5
Jason Sasser	F	6'7"	225	R	Texas Tech	—	—	—	—
Gary Trent	F	6'8"	250	1	Ohio	69	3.4	0.7	7.5
Rasheed Wallace	F/C	6'10"	245	1	North Carolina	65	4.7	1.3	10.1
*Dontonio Wingfield	F	6'8"	256	2	Cincinnati	44	2.4	0.6	3.8

SACRAMENTO KINGS

Home: ARCO Arena
Capacity: 17,317
Year Built: 1988

Managing General Partner: Jim Thomas
V.P./Basketball Operations: Geoff Petrie

Address:
One Sports Parkway
Sacramento, CA 95834

Head Coach: Garry St. Jean
NBA: 131-197   Kings: 131-197

Kings History

As the sun rises in the East and sets in the West, so has the Royals/Kings franchise. The Rochester (New York) Royals, a charter member of the NBA, won the franchise's only league title in 1950-51. Cross-country franchise moves, ending in Sacramento, have managed only marginal success.

That Rochester championship team featured a slick backcourt of Bob Davies, Bobby Wanzer, and Red Holzman, with Arnie Risen in the middle. Rochester advanced to the West finals in 1951-52, but lost to Minneapolis. The Royals made the playoffs only once from 1956 to '61, though they featured a potent forecourt of Maurice Stokes, Jack Twyman, and Clyde Lovellette.

The team moved to Cincinnati for the 1957-58 season and added exciting rookie Oscar Robertson in 1960. The Royals advanced to the Eastern finals in 1962-63 and 1963-64, thanks to Robertson, Twyman, and 1963-64 Rookie of the Year Jerry Lucas, but the success was short-lived. The team didn't have a winning season from 1966-67 to 1973-74 and moved again in 1972, splitting time between Kansas City and Omaha as the Kings.

In 1974-75, the team won 44 games and featured brilliant point guard Nate "Tiny" Archibald. The 1980-81 edition lost to Houston in the conference finals. The most recent move came in 1985, when the franchise landed in Sacramento. The Kings made the playoffs that season but failed to qualify in any of the next nine campaigns.

1995-96 Review

It was inevitable that the Kings' fast start wouldn't last, and that Sacramento would fade in the brutal reality of the NBA's long regular season. But it was great to be in first place for a while, and the blazing start showed everyone what the Kings might do once they grow up.

The Kings (39-43) did make it to the playoffs for the first time since 1986, and though they threw a scare into perennial first-round underachiever Seattle, the Kings faltered. That's not bad for a team that for the past decade had been able to RSVP to the draft lottery by February.

The Kings even received a nice bonus when underappreciated off guard Mitch Richmond (23.1 PPG) finally earned the respect he deserved and was named a member of the 1996 U.S. Olympic team. Richmond again led the Kings in scoring, but he could have used some help.

Second-year man Brian Grant (14.4 PPG, 7.0 RPG) continued his maturation into a quality NBA forward, but he wasn't exactly a top point producer. Neither was Billy Owens (13.0 PPG), who was acquired from Miami late in the year and continued to live up to his reputation as a skilled player with little ability to exert himself in key situations.

Rookie Tyus Edney (10.8 PPG, 6.1 APG) had a fine debut at the point, but he wore down as the season progressed. Veteran Olden Polynice (12.2 PPG, 9.4 RPG) rebounded and played defense, and Sarunas Marciulionis (10.8 PPG) was a steady perimeter performer off the bench. Several "name" players disappointed, such as Bobby Hurley, Lionel Simmons (4.6 PPG), and rookie Corliss Williamson (bad back).

Sacramento Kings
1996-97 Season Preview

Opening Line: The Kings finally made the playoffs last year but are in no way guaranteed a return trip this season. The team's young nucleus remains in place, and team officials hope talented first-round draft pick Predrag Stojakovic can escape his Greek League contract to play this year.

Guards: Mitch Richmond is a first-rate scorer and defender who keys the Kings offense. Second-year point guard Tyus Edney needs to get stronger, but he is a blur who flashed plenty of talent last year. He is a superior penetrator and good creator for teammates, but he must improve his outside shot. Mahmoud Abdul-Rauf, acquired from Denver for Sarunas Marciulionis, may not stand for the national anthem, but he can score and play some point guard and will fortify the backcourt. Bobby Hurley continues to struggle in the aftermath of his awful auto accident three years ago.

Forwards: Brian Grant is on the verge of becoming one of the league's top power forwards. He just needs a little more time and strength on the backboards. Billy Owens has multiple talents but has never found a home. He could be a good fit with the Kings. Michael Smith is a solid board man at the four spot, and Corliss Williamson enters his second year healthy and ready to produce at the three position. The 6'9" Stojakovic will provide perimeter pop if he can shake free from Greece. Veteran Lionel Simmons, however, a former bulwark of the Kings offense, has faded into the background.

Centers: Olden Polynice works hard, shoots well very close to the basket, and rebounds with a fervor. He just isn't a first-class NBA pivot. Backup Duane Causwell blocks shots and does little else.

Analysis: The Kings are slowly acquiring the components of a solid team, but guys like Edney, Grant, and Williamson still need time to develop. A playoff trip is possible, but Sacramento must avoid another late-season collapse like last year's.

Prediction: Fourth place, Pacific Division

1996-97 Roster

Player	Pos.	Ht.	Wt.	Exp.	College	—1995-96—		
						G	RPG	APG	PPG
Mahmoud Abdul-Rauf	G	6'1"	162	6	Louisiana St.	57	2.4	6.8	19.2
Duane Causwell	C	7'0"	240	6	Temple	73	3.4	0.3	3.4
Tyus Edney	G	5'10"	152	1	UCLA	80	2.5	6.1	10.8
*Kevin Gamble	G/F	6'6"	225	9	Iowa	65	1.7	1.5	5.9
Brian Grant	F	6'9"	254	2	Xavier	78	7.0	1.6	14.4
*Byron Houston	F	6'5"	250	4	Oklahoma St.	25	3.4	0.3	3.4
Bobby Hurley	G	6'0"	165	3	Duke	72	1.0	3.0	3.1
*Clint McDaniel	G	6'4"	180	1	Arkansas	12	0.8	0.6	2.5
Billy Owens	F/G	6'9"	225	5	Syracuse	62	6.6	3.3	13.0
Olden Polynice	C	7'0"	250	9	Virginia	81	9.4	0.7	12.2
Mitch Richmond	G	6'5"	215	8	Kansas St.	81	3.3	3.1	23.1
Lionel Simmons	F	6'7"	210	6	La Salle	54	2.7	1.5	4.6
Michael Smith	F	6'8"	230	2	Providence	65	6.0	1.7	5.5
Predrag Stojakovic	F/G	6'9"	200	R	(Greece)	—	—	—	—
Corliss Williamson	F	6'7"	245	1	Arkansas	53	2.2	0.4	5.6

SEATTLE SUPERSONICS

Home: The Key Arena
Capacity: 17,100
Year Built: 1995

Owner: Barry Ackerley
President/G.M.: Wally Walker

Address:
190 Queen Anne Ave. N. #200
Seattle, WA 98109

Head Coach: George Karl
NBA: 385-280   Sonics: 266-104

SuperSonics History

Prior to Seattle's resurgence in the 1990s, there was only one Sonic boom. It came in the late 1970s.

Seattle's 1977-78 team featured rookie center Jack Sikma, rebounding machine Paul Silas, and the guard triumvirate of Gus Johnson, Dennis Johnson, and "Downtown" Fred Brown. Though it fell in seven games to Washington in the NBA Finals that year, it prevailed over the Bullets the following season, winning the title in five games. That two-year period stands in stark contrast to the team's early years.

Born in 1967, the team failed to qualify for the playoffs for seven seasons and boasted few stars, other than powerful Bob Rule and highly talented but enigmatic Spencer Haywood. Seattle made it to the Western semifinals in 1974-75 and 1975-76, setting the stage for its runs to the Finals.

After a 56-26 season in 1979-80, the Sonics wallowed through a decade of mediocrity. The 1986-87 season was a stunner, however. Despite finishing with a losing record, the Sonics advanced to the Western finals, thanks to the high-scoring trio of Xavier McDaniel, Dale Ellis, and Tom Chambers. A new cast of characters emerged in the early 1990s, headed by Shawn Kemp and Gary Payton and coached by George Karl. They roared to the 1993 Western finals, losing to Phoenix in seven games, then suffered humbling first-round defeats the next two years.

1995-96 Review

Although the Sonics' 1995-96 season ended in the disappointment of a six-game Finals loss to Chicago, Seattle was able to silence all the critics who had deemed the team nothing more than a collection of immature choke artists. The Sonics established their supremacy in the Western Conference by winning 64 regular-season games and then whipping Sacramento, San Antonio, and Utah in the playoffs.

Even Seattle's Finals loss brought respect to the franchise. After spotting Michael Jordan and his pals a 3-0 lead, the Sonics charged back to earn two home wins and cause the Bulls to worry a little. Seattle was clearly a step below its conquerors, but it was worlds away from the team that had exited the previous two playoffs in humiliating first-round upsets.

The team was again led by the dynamic duo of point guard Gary Payton (19.3 PPG, 7.5 APG, 2.9 SPG) and forward Shawn Kemp (19.6 PPG, 11.4 RPG). Kemp was excellent during the regular season but even more impressive during the Finals, when he provided a consistent offensive threat. Payton was voted the league's top defender and keyed the Seattle attack, even though he was shackled somewhat by the Bulls.

Veteran forward Detlef Schrempf (17.1 PPG) again did a little bit of everything, and Hersey Hawkins (15.6 PPG) was a strong perimeter weapon. Sam Perkins (11.8 PPG) came off the bench bombing from the outside, while Nate McMillan and Vincent Askew were valuable defensive spark plugs. Ervin Johnson started most of the season at center, but he found himself caddying for tough guy Frank Brickowski during the Finals.

Seattle SuperSonics
1996-97 Season Preview

Opening Line: During last year's Finals series with the Bulls, Seattle grew up from a fraternity-league team to real contender. Now, the challenge is to sustain the status as Best in the West and find a way to overcome a solid defensive and halfcourt team like the Bulls in the playoffs. With point guard Gary Payton back, the Sonics can move ahead.

Guards: Payton is a fabulous defender and the epitome of the new scoring point guard hybrid that has taken over the NBA. He shoots well from the field (although his long-range stuff needs work) and still hands out a good number of assists. Veteran Hersey Hawkins brings quiet productivity to the Sonics, but his 3-point shooting could improve. Nate McMillan is a classy player and a fine athlete who plays great defense, rebounds well, and can pass. David Wingate plays solid defense, and second-year man Eric Snow showed some promise at the point last year. Craig Ehlo adds veteran leadership.

Forwards: Shawn Kemp emerged as a big-time star during the playoffs last year. Kemp is an expert at getting to the line, has improved his range, and is a bull on the boards. Detlef Schrempf continues to shine in all facets of the game, although he faltered somewhat in the playoffs. Second-round pick Joseph Blair of Arizona brings a wide body and an excellent shooting touch to Seattle.

Centers: Frank Brickowski and Ervin Johnson are gone. The Sonics don't really have a true pivot, but with their style of play, they don't really need one. Sam Perkins would rather slingshot 3-pointers toward the hoop. Jim McIlvaine proved to be a tremendous defensive force and a fair rebounder in Washington last year. He'll block a lot of shots.

Analysis: With Payton returning, the Sonics will again challenge for a spot in the Finals. But whether they can win it all depends on how well they learn to play halfcourt basketball. The pressing stuff works well during the regular season, but champions win when the tempo slows down.

Prediction: First place, Pacific Division

1996-97 Roster

| Player | Pos. | Ht. | Wt. | Exp. | College | —1995-96— | | |
						G	RPG	APG	PPG
Drew Barry	G	6'4"	191	R	Georgia Tech	—	—	—	—
Joseph Blair	F	6'10"	251	R	Arizona	—	—	—	—
Craig Ehlo	G/F	6'7"	205	13	Washington St.	79	3.2	1.7	8.5
Sherrell Ford	F	6'7"	210	1	Illinois-Chicago	28	0.9	0.2	3.2
Greg Graham	G	6'4"	182	3	Indiana	53	1.1	1.0	4.5
Hersey Hawkins	G	6'3"	190	8	Bradley	82	3.6	2.7	15.6
Shawn Kemp	F	6'10"	245	7	None	79	11.4	2.2	19.6
Jim McIlvaine	C	7'1"	260	2	Marquette	80	2.9	0.1	2.3
Nate McMillan	G/F	6'5"	200	10	N. Carolina St.	55	3.8	3.6	5.0
Gary Payton	G	6'4"	190	6	Oregon St.	81	4.2	7.5	19.3
Sam Perkins	F/C	6'9"	255	12	North Carolina	82	4.5	1.5	11.8
Steve Scheffler	C	6'9"	250	6	Purdue	35	0.9	0.1	1.7
Detlef Schrempf	F	6'10"	235	11	Washington	63	5.2	4.4	17.1
Eric Snow	G	6'3"	200	1	Michigan St.	43	1.0	1.7	2.7
Joe Vogel	F	6'11"	255	R	Colorado St.	—	—	—	—
David Wingate	G/F	6'5"	185	10	Georgetown	60	0.9	1.0	3.7

Toronto Raptors
1996-97 Roster

Player	Pos.	Ht.	Wt.	Exp.	College	G	RPG	APG	PPG
							—1995-96—		
Marcus Camby	F	6'11"	220	R	Massachusetts	—	—	—	—
Doug Christie	G/F	6'6"	205	4	Pepperdine	55	2.8	2.1	7.5
Hubert Davis	G	6'5"	183	4	North Carolina	74	1.7	1.4	10.7
Acie Earl	C/F	6'10"	240	3	Iowa	42	3.1	0.6	7.5
Vincenzo Esposito	G	6'3"	198	1	(Italy)	30	0.5	0.8	3.9
Popeye Jones	F	6'8"	255	3	Murray St.	68	10.8	1.9	11.3
Carlos Rogers	F	6'11"	220	2	Tennessee St.	56	3.0	0.6	7.7
Damon Stoudamire	G	5'10"	171	1	Arizona	70	4.0	9.3	19.0
Zan Tabak	C	7'0"	245	2	(Croatia)	67	4.8	0.9	7.7
B.J. Tyler	G	6'1"	185	2	Texas	—	—	—	—
Walt Williams	G/F	6'8"	230	4	Maryland	73	4.4	3.2	13.6
Sharone Wright	F/C	6'11"	260	2	Clemson	57	6.2	0.7	11.6

Vancouver Grizzlies
1996-97 Roster

Player	Pos.	Ht.	Wt.	Exp.	College	G	RPG	APG	PPG
							—1995-96—		
Shareef Abdur-Rahim	F	6'10"	220	R	California	—	—	—	—
Greg Anthony	G	6'1"	176	5	UNLV	69	2.5	6.9	14.0
*Tim Breaux	F	6'7"	215	2	Wyoming	54	1.1	0.4	3.0
Pete Chilcutt	F/C	6'11"	235	5	North Carolina	74	2.1	0.4	2.7
Blue Edwards	G/F	6'4"	229	7	East Carolina	82	4.2	2.6	12.7
Doug Edwards	F	6'7"	235	3	Florida St.	31	2.8	1.3	3.0
George Lynch	F	6'8"	223	3	North Carolina	76	2.8	0.7	3.8
*Rich Manning	C	6'11"	260	1	Washington	29	1.9	0.2	3.7
Lee Mayberry	G	6'1"	172	4	Arkansas	82	1.1	3.7	5.1
Eric Mobley	C	6'11"	257	2	Pittsburgh	39	3.6	0.6	4.8
Lawrence Moten	G	6'5"	186	1	Syracuse	44	1.4	1.1	6.6
Anthony Peeler	G	6'4"	212	4	Missouri	73	1.9	1.6	9.7
Bryant Reeves	C	7'0"	295	1	Oklahoma St.	77	7.4	1.4	13.3
Chris Robinson	G/F	6'5"	205	R	W. Kentucky	—	—	—	—
Roy Rogers	C	6'10"	238	R	Alabama	—	—	—	—

N B A Awards and Records

This section showcases the NBA's champions, award-winners, and record-setters—as well as a history of No. 1 draft picks. Here is a breakdown of what you'll find:

- World Champions
- Most Valuable Players
- Rookies of the Year
- NBA Finals MVPs
- Defensive Players of the Year
- Sixth Man Award winners
- Coaches of the Year
- All-NBA Teams
- All-Rookie Teams
- All-Defensive Teams
- All-Star Game results

- career leaders
- active career leaders
- regular-season records
- game records
- team records—season
- team records—game
- playoff records—career
- playoff records—game
- playoff records—team
- history of No. 1 draft picks

WORLD CHAMPIONS

	CHAMPION	FINALIST	RESULT		CHAMPION	FINALIST	RESULT
1946-47	Philadelphia	Chicago	4-1	1971-72	Los Angeles	New York	4-1
1947-48	Baltimore	Philadelphia	4-2	1972-73	New York	Los Angeles	4-1
1948-49	Minneapolis	Washington	4-2	1973-74	Boston	Milwaukee	4-3
1949-50	Minneapolis	Syracuse	4-2	1974-75	Golden State	Washington	4-0
1950-51	Rochester	New York	4-3	1975-76	Boston	Phoenix	4-2
1951-52	Minneapolis	New York	4-3	1976-77	Portland	Philadelphia	4-2
1952-53	Minneapolis	New York	4-1	1977-78	Washington	Seattle	4-3
1953-54	Minneapolis	Syracuse	4-3	1978-79	Seattle	Washington	4-1
1954-55	Syracuse	Fort Wayne	4-3	1979-80	Los Angeles	Philadelphia	4-2
1955-56	Philadelphia	Fort Wayne	4-1	1980-81	Boston	Houston	4-2
1956-57	Boston	St. Louis	4-3	1981-82	Los Angeles	Philadelphia	4-2
1957-58	St. Louis	Boston	4-2	1982-83	Philadelphia	Los Angeles	4-0
1958-59	Boston	Minneapolis	4-0	1983-84	Boston	Los Angeles	4-3
1959-60	Boston	St. Louis	4-3	1984-85	L.A. Lakers	Boston	4-2
1960-61	Boston	St. Louis	4-1	1985-86	Boston	Houston	4-2
1961-62	Boston	Los Angeles	4-3	1986-87	L.A. Lakers	Boston	4-2
1962-63	Boston	Los Angeles	4-2	1987-88	L.A. Lakers	Detroit	4-3
1963-64	Boston	San Francisco	4-1	1988-89	Detroit	L.A. Lakers	4-0
1964-65	Boston	Los Angeles	4-1	1989-90	Detroit	Portland	4-1
1965-66	Boston	Los Angeles	4-3	1990-91	Chicago	L.A. Lakers	4-1
1966-67	Philadelphia	San Francisco	4-2	1991-92	Chicago	Portland	4-2
1967-68	Boston	Los Angeles	4-2	1992-93	Chicago	Phoenix	4-2
1968-69	Boston	Los Angeles	4-3	1993-94	Houston	New York	4-3
1969-70	New York	Los Angeles	4-3	1994-95	Houston	Orlando	4-0
1970-71	Milwaukee	Baltimore	4-0	1995-96	Chicago	Seattle	4-2

MOST VALUABLE PLAYERS

	PLAYER	PPG		PLAYER	PPG
1955-56	Bob Pettit, St. Louis	25.7	1976-77	Kareem Abdul-Jabbar, L.A.	26.2
1956-57	Bob Cousy, Boston	20.6	1977-78	Bill Walton, Portland	18.9
1957-58	Bill Russell, Boston	16.6	1978-79	Moses Malone, Houston	24.8
1958-59	Bob Pettit, St. Louis	29.2	1979-80	Kareem Abdul-Jabbar, L.A.	24.8
1959-60	Wilt Chamberlain, Phil.	37.6	1980-81	Julius Erving, Philadelphia	24.6
1960-61	Bill Russell, Boston	16.9	1981-82	Moses Malone, Houston	31.1
1961-62	Bill Russell, Boston	18.9	1982-83	Moses Malone, Philadelphia	24.5
1962-63	Bill Russell, Boston	16.8	1983-84	Larry Bird, Boston	24.2
1963-64	Oscar Robertson, Cincinnati	31.4	1984-85	Larry Bird, Boston	28.7
1964-65	Bill Russell, Boston	14.1	1985-86	Larry Bird, Boston	25.8
1965-66	Wilt Chamberlain, Phil.	33.5	1986-87	Magic Johnson, L.A. Lakers	23.9
1966-67	Wilt Chamberlain, Phil.	24.1	1987-88	Michael Jordan, Chicago	35.0
1967-68	Wilt Chamberlain, Phil.	24.3	1988-89	Magic Johnson, L.A. Lakers	22.5
1968-69	Wes Unseld, Baltimore	13.8	1989-90	Magic Johnson, L.A. Lakers	22.3
1969-70	Willis Reed, New York	21.7	1990-91	Michael Jordan, Chicago	31.5
1970-71	Lew Alcindor, Milwaukee	31.7	1991-92	Michael Jordan, Chicago	30.1
1971-72	Kareem Abdul-Jabbar, Mil.	34.8	1992-93	Charles Barkley, Phoenix	25.6
1972-73	Dave Cowens, Boston	20.5	1993-94	Hakeem Olajuwon, Houston	27.3
1973-74	Kareem Abdul-Jabbar, Mil.	27.0	1994-95	David Robinson, San Antonio	27.6
1974-75	Bob McAdoo, Buffalo	34.5	1995-96	Michael Jordan, Chicago	30.4
1975-76	Kareem Abdul-Jabbar, L.A.	27.7			

ROOKIES OF THE YEAR

1952-53	Don Meineke, Fort Wayne		1974-75	Keith Wilkes, Golden State
1953-54	Ray Felix, Baltimore		1975-76	Alvan Adams, Phoenix
1954-55	Bob Pettit, Milwaukee		1976-77	Adrian Dantley, Buffalo
1955-56	Maurice Stokes, Rochester		1977-78	Walter Davis, Phoenix
1956-57	Tom Heinsohn, Boston		1978-79	Phil Ford, Kansas City
1957-58	Woody Sauldsberry, Philadelphia		1979-80	Larry Bird, Boston
1958-59	Elgin Baylor, Minneapolis		1980-81	Darrell Griffith, Utah
1959-60	Wilt Chamberlain, Philadelphia		1981-82	Buck Williams, New Jersey
1960-61	Oscar Robertson, Cincinnati		1982-83	Terry Cummings, San Diego
1961-62	Walt Bellamy, Chicago		1983-84	Ralph Sampson, Houston
1962-63	Terry Dischinger, Chicago		1984-85	Michael Jordan, Chicago
1963-64	Jerry Lucas, Cincinnati		1985-86	Patrick Ewing, New York
1964-65	Willis Reed, New York		1986-87	Chuck Person, Indiana
1965-66	Rick Barry, San Francisco		1987-88	Mark Jackson, New York
1966-67	Dave Bing, Detroit		1988-89	Mitch Richmond, Golden State
1967-68	Earl Monroe, Baltimore		1989-90	David Robinson, San Antonio
1968-69	Wes Unseld, Baltimore		1990-91	Derrick Coleman, New Jersey
1969-70	Lew Alcindor, Milwaukee		1991-92	Larry Johnson, Charlotte
1970-71	Dave Cowens, Boston		1992-93	Shaquille O'Neal, Orlando
	Geoff Petrie, Portland		1993-94	Chris Webber, Golden State
1971-72	Sidney Wicks, Portland		1994-95	Grant Hill, Detroit
1972-73	Bob McAdoo, Buffalo			Jason Kidd, Dallas
1973-74	Ernie DiGregorio, Buffalo		1995-96	Damon Stoudamire, Toronto

NBA FINALS MVPS

1969	Jerry West, Los Angeles	1983	Moses Malone, Philadelphia
1970	Willis Reed, New York	1984	Larry Bird, Boston
1971	Lew Alcindor, Milwaukee	1985	Kareem Abdul-Jabbar, L.A. Lakers
1972	Wilt Chamberlain, Los Angeles	1986	Larry Bird, Boston
1973	Willis Reed, New York	1987	Magic Johnson, L.A. Lakers
1974	John Havlicek, Boston	1988	James Worthy, L.A. Lakers
1975	Rick Barry, Golden State	1989	Joe Dumars, Detroit
1976	Jo Jo White, Boston	1990	Isiah Thomas, Detroit
1977	Bill Walton, Portland	1991	Michael Jordan, Chicago
1978	Wes Unseld, Washington	1992	Michael Jordan, Chicago
1979	Dennis Johnson, Seattle	1993	Michael Jordan, Chicago
1980	Magic Johnson, Los Angeles	1994	Hakeem Olajuwon, Houston
1981	Cedric Maxwell, Boston	1995	Hakeem Olajuwon, Houston
1982	Magic Johnson, Los Angeles	1996	Michael Jordan, Chicago

DEFENSIVE PLAYERS OF THE YEAR

1982-83	Sidney Moncrief, Milwaukee	1989-90	Dennis Rodman, Detroit
1983-84	Sidney Moncrief, Milwaukee	1990-91	Dennis Rodman, Detroit
1984-85	Mark Eaton, Utah	1991-92	David Robinson, San Antonio
1985-86	Alvin Robertson, San Antonio	1992-93	Hakeem Olajuwon, Houston
1986-87	Michael Cooper, L.A. Lakers	1993-94	Hakeem Olajuwon, Houston
1987-88	Michael Jordan, Chicago	1994-95	Dikembe Mutombo, Denver
1988-89	Mark Eaton, Utah	1995-96	Gary Payton, Seattle

SIXTH MAN AWARD WINNERS

1982-83	Bobby Jones, Philadelphia	1989-90	Ricky Pierce, Milwaukee
1983-84	Kevin McHale, Boston	1990-91	Detlef Schrempf, Indiana
1984-85	Kevin McHale, Boston	1991-92	Detlef Schrempf, Indiana
1985-86	Bill Walton, Boston	1992-93	Cliff Robinson, Portland
1986-87	Ricky Pierce, Milwaukee	1993-94	Dell Curry, Charlotte
1987-88	Roy Tarpley, Dallas	1994-95	Anthony Mason, New York
1988-89	Eddie Johnson, Phoenix	1995-96	Toni Kukoc, Chicago

COACHES OF THE YEAR

1962-63	Harry Gallatin, St. Louis	1979-80	Bill Fitch, Boston
1963-64	Alex Hannum, San Francisco	1980-81	Jack McKinney, Indiana
1964-65	Red Auerbach, Boston	1981-82	Gene Shue, Washington
1965-66	Dolph Schayes, Philadelphia	1982-83	Don Nelson, Milwaukee
1966-67	Johnny Kerr, Chicago	1983-84	Frank Layden, Utah
1967-68	Richie Guerin, St. Louis	1984-85	Don Nelson, Milwaukee
1968-69	Gene Shue, Baltimore	1985-86	Mike Fratello, Atlanta
1969-70	Red Holzman, New York	1986-87	Mike Schuler, Portland
1970-71	Dick Motta, Chicago	1987-88	Doug Moe, Denver
1971-72	Bill Sharman, Los Angeles	1988-89	Cotton Fitzsimmons, Phoenix
1972-73	Tom Heinsohn, Boston	1989-90	Pat Riley, L.A. Lakers
1973-74	Ray Scott, Detroit	1990-91	Don Chaney, Houston
1974-75	Phil Johnson, K.C.-Omaha	1991-92	Don Nelson, Golden State
1975-76	Bill Fitch, Cleveland	1992-93	Pat Riley, New York
1976-77	Tom Nissalke, Houston	1993-94	Lenny Wilkens, Atlanta
1977-78	Hubie Brown, Atlanta	1994-95	Del Harris, L.A. Lakers
1978-79	Cotton Fitzsimmons, Kansas City	1995-96	Phil Jackson, Chicago

ALL-NBA TEAMS

1946-47
Joe Fulks, PHI
Bob Feerick, WAS
Stan Miasek, DET
Bones McKinney, WAS
Max Zaslofsky, CHI

1947-48
Joe Fulks, PHI
Max Zaslofsky, CHI
Ed Sadowski, BOS
Howie Dallmar, PHI
Bob Feerick, WAS

1948-49
George Mikan, MIN
Joe Fulks, PHI
Bob Davies, ROC
Max Zaslofsky, CHI
Jim Pollard, MIN

1949-50
George Mikan, MIN
Jim Pollard, MIN
Alex Groza, IND
Bob Davies, ROC
Max Zaslofsky, CHI

1950-51
George Mikan, MIN
Alex Groza, IND
Ed Macauley, BOS
Bob Davies, ROC
Ralph Beard, IND

1951-52
George Mikan, MIN
Ed Macauley, BOS
Paul Arizin, PHI
Bob Cousy, BOS
Bob Davies, ROC
Dolph Schayes, SYR

1952-53
George Mikan, MIN
Bob Cousy, BOS
Neil Johnston, PHI
Ed Macauley, BOS
Dolph Schayes, SYR

1953-54
Bob Cousy, BOS
Neil Johnston, PHI

George Mikan, MIN
Dolph Schayes, SYR
Harry Gallatin, NY

1954-55
Neil Johnston, PHI
Bob Cousy, BOS
Dolph Schayes, SYR
Bob Pettit, MIL
Larry Foust, FTW

1955-56
Bob Pettit, STL
Paul Arizin, PHI
Neil Johnston, PHI
Bob Cousy, BOS
Bill Sharman, BOS

1956-57
Paul Arizin, PHI
Dolph Schayes, SYR
Bob Pettit, STL
Bob Cousy, BOS
Bill Sharman, BOS

1957-58
Dolph Schayes, SYR
George Yardley, DET
Bob Pettit, STL
Bob Cousy, BOS
Bill Sharman, BOS

1958-59
Bob Pettit, STL
Elgin Baylor, MIN
Bill Russell, BOS
Bob Cousy, BOS
Bill Sharman, BOS

1959-60
Bob Pettit, STL
Elgin Baylor, MIN
Wilt Chamberlain, PHI
Bob Cousy, BOS
Gene Shue, DET

1960-61
Elgin Baylor, LA
Bob Pettit, STL
Wilt Chamberlain, PHI
Bob Cousy, BOS
Oscar Robertson, CIN

1961-62
Bob Pettit, STL
Elgin Baylor, LA
Wilt Chamberlain, PHI
Jerry West, LA
Oscar Robertson, CIN

1962-63
Elgin Baylor, LA
Bob Pettit, STL
Bill Russell, BOS
Oscar Robertson, CIN
Jerry West, LA

1963-64
Bob Pettit, STL
Elgin Baylor, LA
Wilt Chamberlain, SF
Oscar Robertson, CIN
Jerry West, LA

1964-65
Elgin Baylor, LA
Jerry Lucas, CIN
Bill Russell, BOS
Oscar Robertson, CIN
Jerry West, LA

1965-66
Rick Barry, SF
Jerry Lucas, CIN
Wilt Chamberlain, PHI
Oscar Robertson, CIN
Jerry West, LA

1966-67
Rick Barry, SF
Elgin Baylor, LA
Wilt Chamberlain, PHI
Jerry West, LA
Oscar Robertson, CIN

1967-68
Elgin Baylor, LA
Jerry Lucas, CIN
Wilt Chamberlain, PHI
Dave Bing, DET
Oscar Robertson, CIN

1968-69
Billy Cunningham, PHI
Elgin Baylor, LA
Wes Unseld, BAL

Earl Monroe, BAL
Oscar Robertson, CIN

1969-70
Billy Cunningham, PHI
Connie Hawkins, PHO
Willis Reed, NY
Jerry West, LA
Walt Frazier, NY

1970-71
John Havlicek, BOS
Billy Cunningham, PHI
Lew Alcindor, MIL
Jerry West, LA
Dave Bing, DET

1971-72
John Havlicek, BOS
S. Haywood, SEA
K. Abdul-Jabbar, MIL
Jerry West, LA
Walt Frazier, NY

1972-73
John Havlicek, BOS
S. Haywood, SEA
K. Abdul-Jabbar, MIL
Nate Archibald, KCO
Jerry West, LA

1973-74
John Havlicek, BOS
Rick Barry, GS
K. Abdul-Jabbar, MIL
Walt Frazier, NY
Gail Goodrich, LA

1974-75
Rick Barry, GS
Elvin Hayes, WAS
Bob McAdoo, BUF
Nate Archibald, KCO
Walt Frazier, NY

1975-76
Rick Barry, GS
George McGinnis, PHI
K. Abdul-Jabbar, LA
Nate Archibald, KC
Pete Maravich, NO

1976-77
Elvin Hayes, WAS
D. Thompson, DEN
K. Abdul-Jabbar, LA
Pete Maravich, NO
Paul Westphal, PHO

1977-78
Truck Robinson, NO
Julius Erving, PHI
Bill Walton, POR
George Gervin, SA
D. Thompson, DEN

1978-79
M. Johnson, MIL
Elvin Hayes, WAS
Moses Malone, HOU
George Gervin, SA
Paul Westphal, PHO

1979-80
Julius Erving, PHI
Larry Bird, BOS
K. Abdul-Jabbar, LA
George Gervin, SA
Paul Westphal, PHO

1980-81
Julius Erving, PHI
Larry Bird, BOS
K. Abdul-Jabbar, LA
George Gervin, SA
Dennis Johnson, PHO

1981-82
Larry Bird, BOS
Julius Erving, PHI
Moses Malone, HOU
George Gervin, SA
Gus Williams, SEA

1982-83
Larry Bird, BOS
Julius Erving, PHI
Moses Malone, PHI
Magic Johnson, LA
Sidney Moncrief, MIL

1983-84
Larry Bird, BOS
Bernard King, NY
K. Abdul-Jabbar, LA
Magic Johnson, LA
Isiah Thomas, DET

1984-85
Larry Bird, BOS
Bernard King, NY
Moses Malone, PHI
Magic Johnson, LAL
Isiah Thomas, DET

1985-86
Larry Bird, BOS
D. Wilkins, ATL
K. Abdul-Jabbar, LAL
Magic Johnson, LAL
Isiah Thomas, DET

1986-87
Larry Bird, BOS
Kevin McHale, BOS
A. Olajuwon, HOU
Magic Johnson, LAL
Michael Jordan, CHI

1987-88
Larry Bird, BOS
Charles Barkley, PHI
A. Olajuwon, HOU
Michael Jordan, CHI
Magic Johnson, LAL

1988-89
Karl Malone, UTA
Charles Barkley, PHI
A. Olajuwon, HOU
Magic Johnson, LAL
Michael Jordan, CHI

1989-90
Karl Malone, UTA
Charles Barkley, PHI
Patrick Ewing, NY
Magic Johnson, LAL
Michael Jordan, CHI

1990-91
Karl Malone, UTA
Charles Barkley, PHI
David Robinson, SA
Michael Jordan, CHI
Magic Johnson, LAL

1991-92
Karl Malone, UTA
Chris Mullin, GS
David Robinson, SA
Michael Jordan, CHI
Clyde Drexler, POR

1992-93
Charles Barkley, PHO
Karl Malone, UTA
H. Olajuwon, HOU
Michael Jordan, CHI
Mark Price, CLE

1993-94
Scottie Pippen, CHI
Karl Malone, UTA
H. Olajuwon, HOU
John Stockton, UTA
Latrell Sprewell, GS

1994-95
Karl Malone, UTA
Scottie Pippen, CHI
David Robinson, SA
John Stockton, UTA
A. Hardaway, ORL

1995-96
Karl Malone, UTA
Scottie Pippen, CHI
David Robinson, SA
Michael Jordan, CHI
A. Hardaway, ORL

ALL-ROOKIE TEAMS

1962-63
Terry Dischinger, CHI
Chet Walker, SYR
Zelmo Beaty, STL
John Havlicek, BOS
D. DeBusschere, DET

1963-64
Jerry Lucas, CIN
Gus Johnson, BAL
Nate Thurmond, SF
Art Heyman, NY
Rod Thorn, BAL

1964-65
Willis Reed, NY
Jim Barnes, NY
Howard Komives, NY
Lucious Jackson, PHI
Wally Jones, BAL
Joe Caldwell, DET

1965-66
Rick Barry, SF
Billy Cunningham, PHI
T. Van Arsdale, DET
Dick Van Arsdale, NY
Fred Hetzel, SF

1966-67
Lou Hudson, STL
Jack Marin, BAL
Erwin Mueller, CHI
Cazzie Russell, NY
Dave Bing, DET

1967-68
Earl Monroe, BAL
Bob Rule, SEA
Walt Frazier, NY
Al Tucker, SEA
Phil Jackson, NY

1968-69
Wes Unseld, BAL
Elvin Hayes, SD
Bill Hewitt, LA
Art Harris, SEA
Gary Gregor, PHO

1969-70
Lew Alcindor, MIL
Bob Dandridge, MIL
Jo Jo White, BOS
Mike Davis, BAL
Dick Garrett, LA

1970-71
Geoff Petrie, POR
Dave Cowens, BOS
Pete Maravich, ATL
Calvin Murphy, SD
Bob Lanier, DET

1971-72
Elmore Smith, BUF
Sidney Wicks, POR
Austin Carr, CLE
Phil Chenier, BAL
Clifford Ray, CHI

1972-73
Bob McAdoo, BUF
Lloyd Neal, POR
Fred Boyd, PHI
Dwight Davis, CLE
Jim Price, LA

1973-74
Ernie DiGregorio, BUF
Ron Behagen, KCO
Mike Bantom, PHO
John Brown, ATL
N. Weatherspoon, CAP

1974-75
Keith Wilkes, GS
John Drew, ATL
Scott Wedman, KCO
Tom Burleson, SEA
Brian Winters, LA

1975-76
Alvan Adams, PHO
Gus Williams, GS
J. Meriweather, HOU
J. Shumate, PHO/BUF
Lionel Hollins, POR

1976-77
Adrian Dantley, BUF
Scott May, CHI
Mitch Kupchak, WAS
John Lucas, HOU
Ron Lee, PHO

1977-78
Walter Davis, PHO
M. Johnson, MIL
Bernard King, NJ
Jack Sikma, SEA
Norm Nixon, LA

1978-79
Phil Ford, KC
M.Thompson, POR
Ron Brewer, POR
Reggie Theus, CHI
Terry Tyler, DET

1979-80
Larry Bird, BOS
Magic Johnson, LA
Bill Cartwright, NY
Calvin Natt, POR
D. Greenwood, CHI

1980-81
Joe Barry Carroll, GS
Darrell Griffith, UTA
Larry Smith, GS
Kevin McHale, BOS
Kelvin Ransey, POR

1981-82
Kelly Tripucka, DET
Jay Vincent, DAL
Isiah Thomas, DET
Buck Williams, NJ
Jeff Ruland, WAS

1982-83
Terry Cummings, SD
Clark Kellogg, IND
D. Wilkins, ATL
James Worthy, LA
Quintin Dailey, CHI

1983-84
Ralph Sampson, HOU
S. Stipanovich, IND
Byron Scott, LA
Jeff Malone, WAS
Thurl Bailey, UTA
Darrell Walker, NY

1984-85
Michael Jordan, CHI
A. Olajuwon, HOU
Sam Bowie, POR
Charles Barkley, PHI
Sam Perkins, DAL

1985-86
Xavier McDaniel, SEA
Patrick Ewing, NY
Karl Malone, UTA
Joe Dumars, DET
Charles Oakley, CHI

1986-87
Brad Daugherty, CLE
Ron Harper, CLE
Chuck Person, IND
Roy Tarpley, DAL
John Williams, CLE

1987-88
Mark Jackson, NY
Armon Gilliam, PHO
Kenny Smith, SAC
Greg Anderson, SA
Derrick McKey, SEA

1988-89
Mitch Richmond, GS
Willie Anderson, SA
Hersey Hawkins, PHI
Rik Smits, IND
Charles Smith, LAC

1989-90
David Robinson, SA
Tim Hardaway, GS
Vlade Divac, LAL
S. Douglas, MIA
Pooh Richardson, MIN

1990-91
Derrick Coleman, NJ
Lionel Simmons, SAC
Dee Brown, BOS
Kendall Gill, CHA
Dennis Scott, ORL

1991-92
Larry Johnson, CHA
D. Mutombo, DEN
Billy Owens, GS
Steve Smith, MIA
Stacey Augmon, ATL

1992-93
Shaquille O'Neal, ORL
A. Mourning, CHA
C. Laettner, MIN
Tom Gugliotta, WAS
LaPhonso Ellis, DEN

1993-94
Chris Webber, GS
A. Hardaway, ORL
Vin Baker, MIL
Jamal Mashburn, DAL
Isaiah Rider, MIN

1994-95
Jason Kidd, DAL
Grant Hill, DET
Glenn Robinson, MIL
Eddie Jones, LAL
Brian Grant, SAC

1995-96
D. Stoudamire, TOR
Joe Smith, GS
Jerry Stackhouse, PHI
Antonio McDyess, DEN
Arvydas Sabonis, POR
Michael Finley, PHO

ALL-DEFENSIVE TEAMS

1968-69
D. DeBusschere, NY
Nate Thurmond, SF
Bill Russell, BOS
Walt Frazier, NY
Jerry Sloan, CHI

1969-70
D. DeBusschere, NY
Gus Johnson, BAL
Willis Reed, NY
Walt Frazier, NY
Jerry West, LA

1970-71
D. DeBusschere, NY
Gus Johnson, BAL
Nate Thurmond, SF
Walt Frazier, NY
Jerry West, LA

1971-72
D. DeBusschere, NY
John Havlicek, BOS
Wilt Chamberlain, LA
Jerry West, LA
Walt Frazier, NY
Jerry Sloan, CHI

1972-73
D. DeBusschere, NY
John Havlicek, BOS
Wilt Chamberlain, LA
Jerry West, LA
Walt Frazier, NY

1973-74
D. DeBusschere, NY
John Havlicek, BOS
K. Abdul-Jabbar, MIL
Norm Van Lier, CHI
Walt Frazier, NY
Jerry Sloan, CHI

1974-75
John Havlicek, BOS
Paul Silas, BOS
K. Abdul-Jabbar, MIL
Jerry Sloan, CHI
Walt Frazier, NY

1975-76
Paul Silas, BOS
John Havlicek, BOS
Dave Cowens, BOS
Norm Van Lier, CHI
Don Watts, SEA

1976-77
Bobby Jones, DEN
E.C. Coleman, NO
Bill Walton, POR
Don Buse, IND
Norm Van Lier, CHI

1977-78
Bobby Jones, DEN
Maurice Lucas, POR
Bill Walton, POR
Lionel Hollins, POR
Don Buse, PHO

1978-79
Bobby Jones, PHI
B. Dandridge, WAS
K. Abdul-Jabbar, LA
Dennis Johnson, SEA
Don Buse, PHO

1979-80
Bobby Jones, PHI
Dan Roundfield, ATL
K. Abdul-Jabbar, LA
Dennis Johnson, SEA
Don Buse, PHO
M.R. Richardson, NY

1980-81
Bobby Jones, PHI
Caldwell Jones, PHI
K. Abdul-Jabbar, LA
Dennis Johnson, PHO
M.R. Richardson, NY

1981-82
Bobby Jones, PHI
Dan Roundfield, ATL
Caldwell Jones, PHI
Michael Cooper, LA
Dennis Johnson, PHO

1982-83
Bobby Jones, PHI
Dan Roundfield, ATL
Moses Malone, PHI
Sidney Moncrief, MIL
Dennis Johnson, PHO
Maurice Cheeks, PHI

1983-84
Bobby Jones, PHI
Michael Cooper, LA
Tree Rollins, ATL
Maurice Cheeks, PHI
Sidney Moncrief, MIL

1984-85
Sidney Moncrief, MIL
Paul Pressey, MIL
Mark Eaton, UTA
Michael Cooper, LAL
Maurice Cheeks, PHI

1985-86
Paul Pressey, MIL
Kevin McHale, BOS
Mark Eaton, UTA
Sidney Moncrief, MIL
Maurice Cheeks, PHI

1986-87
Kevin McHale, BOS
Michael Cooper, LAL
A. Olajuwon, HOU
Alvin Robertson, SA
Dennis Johnson, BOS

1987-88
Kevin McHale, BOS
Rodney McCray, HOU
A. Olajuwon, HOU
Michael Cooper, LAL
Michael Jordan, CHI

1988-89
Dennis Rodman, DET
Larry Nance, CLE
Mark Eaton, UTA
Michael Jordan, CHI
Joe Dumars, DET

1989-90
Dennis Rodman, DET
Buck Williams, POR
A. Olajuwon, HOU
Michael Jordan, CHI
Joe Dumars, DET

1990-91
Dennis Rodman, DET
Buck Williams, POR
David Robinson, SA
Michael Jordan, CHI
Alvin Robertson, MIL

1991-92
Dennis Rodman, DET
Scottie Pippen, CHI
David Robinson, SA
Michael Jordan, CHI
Joe Dumars, DET

1992-93
Dennis Rodman, DET
Scottie Pippen, CHI
H. Olajuwon, HOU
Michael Jordan, CHI
Joe Dumars, DET

1993-94
Scottie Pippen, CHI
Charles Oakley, NY
H. Olajuwon, HOU
Gary Payton, SEA
Mookie Blaylock, ATL

1994-95
Scottie Pippen, CHI
Dennis Rodman, SA
David Robinson, SA
Gary Payton, SEA
Mookie Blaylock, ATL

1995-96
Scottie Pippen, CHI
Dennis Rodman, CHI
David Robinson, SA
Michael Jordan, CHI
Gary Payton, SEA

ALL-STAR GAMES

	RESULT	SITE	MVP
1950-51	East 111, West 94	Boston	Ed Macauley, Boston
1951-52	East 108, West 91	Boston	Paul Arizin, Philadelphia
1952-53	West 79, East 75	Fort Wayne	George Mikan, Minneapolis
1953-54	East 98, West 93 (OT)	New York	Bob Cousy, Boston
1954-55	East 100, West 91	New York	Bill Sharman, Boston
1955-56	West 108, East 94	Rochester	Bob Pettit, St. Louis
1956-57	East 109, West 97	Boston	Bob Cousy, Boston
1957-58	East 130, West 118	St. Louis	Bob Pettit, St. Louis
1958-59	West 124, East 108	Detroit	Elgin Baylor, Minnisota/ Bob Pettit, St. Louis
1959-60	East 125, West 115	Philadelphia	Wilt Chamberlain, Philadelphia
1960-61	West 153, East 131	Syracuse	Oscar Robertson, Cincinnati
1961-62	West 150, East 130	St. Louis	Bob Pettit, St. Louis
1962-63	East 115, West 108	Los Angeles	Bill Russell, Boston
1963-64	East 111, West 107	Boston	Oscar Robertson, Cincinnati
1964-65	East 124, West 123	St. Louis	Jerry Lucas, Cincinnati
1965-66	East 137, West 94	Cincinnati	Adrian Smith, Cincinnati
1966-67	West 135, East 120	San Francisco	Rick Barry, San Francisco
1967-68	East 144, West 124	New York	Hal Greer, Philadelphia
1968-69	East 123, West 112	Baltimore	Oscar Robertson, Cincinnati
1969-70	East 142, West 135	Philadelphia	Willis Reed, New York
1970-71	West 108, East 107	San Diego	Lenny Wilkens, Seattle
1971-72	West 112, East 110	Los Angeles	Jerry West, Los Angeles
1972-73	East 104, West 84	Chicago	Dave Cowens, Boston
1973-74	West 134, East 123	Seattle	Bob Lanier, Detroit
1974-75	East 108, West 102	Phoenix	Walt Frazier, New York
1975-76	East 123, West 109	Philadelphia	Dave Bing, Washington
1976-77	West 125, East 124	Milwaukee	Julius Erving, Philadelphia
1977-78	East 133, West 125	Atlanta	Randy Smith, Buffalo
1978-79	West 134, East 129	Detroit	David Thompson, Denver
1979-80	East 144, West 135 (OT)	Washington	George Gervin, San Antonio
1980-81	East 123, West 120	Cleveland	Nate Archibald, Boston
1981-82	East 120, West 118	E. Rutherford	Larry Bird, Boston
1982-83	East 132, West 123	Los Angeles	Julius Erving, Philadelphia
1983-84	East 154, West 145 (OT)	Denver	Isiah Thomas, Detroit
1984-85	West 140, East 129	Indianapolis	Ralph Sampson, Houston
1985-86	East 139, West 132	Dallas	Isiah Thomas, Detroit
1986-87	West 154, East 149 (OT)	Seattle	Tom Chambers, Seattle
1987-88	East 138, West 133	Chicago	Michael Jordan, Chicago
1988-89	West 143, East 134	Houston	Karl Malone, Utah
1989-90	East 130, West 113	Miami	Magic Johnson, L.A. Lakers
1990-91	East 116, West 114	Charlotte	Charles Barkley, Philadelphia
1991-92	West 153, East 113	Orlando	Magic Johnson, L.A. Lakers
1992-93	West 135, East 132 (OT)	Utah	Karl Malone, Utah/ John Stockton, Utah
1993-94	East 127, West 118	Minneapolis	Scottie Pippen, Chicago
1994-95	West 139, East 112	Phoenix	Mitch Richmond, Sacramento
1995-96	East 129, West 118	San Antonio	Michael Jordan, Chicago

CAREER LEADERS

(Players active at the close of 1995-96
are listed in **bold**)

POINTS

Kareem Abdul-Jabbar	38,387
Wilt Chamberlain	31,419
Moses Malone	27,409
Elvin Hayes	27,313
Oscar Robertson	26,710
John Havlicek	26,395
Alex English	25,613
Dominique Wilkins	25,389
Jerry West	25,192
Michael Jordan	**24,489**
Karl Malone	**23,343**
Adrian Dantley	23,177
Robert Parish	**23,173**
Elgin Baylor	23,149
Hakeem Olajuwon	**21,840**
Larry Bird	21,791
Hal Greer	21,586
Walt Bellamy	20,941
Bob Pettit	20,880
Charles Barkley	**20,740**

GAMES

Robert Parish	**1,568**
Kareem Abdul-Jabbar	1,560
Moses Malone	1,329
Elvin Hayes	1,303
John Havlicek	1,270
Paul Silas	1,254
Alex English	1,193
Buck Williams	**1,192**
James Edwards	**1,168**
Tree Rollins	1,155

MINUTES

Kareem Abdul-Jabbar	57,446
Elvin Hayes	50,000
Wilt Chamberlain	47,859
John Havlicek	46,471
Robert Parish	**45,298**
Moses Malone	45,071
Oscar Robertson	43,886
Bill Russell	40,726
Buck Williams	**40,230**
Hal Greer	39,788

SCORING AVERAGE

(Minimum 400 Games or 10,000 Points)

Michael Jordan	**32.0**
Wilt Chamberlain	30.1
Elgin Baylor	27.4
Jerry West	27.0
Bob Pettit	26.4
George Gervin	26.2
Karl Malone	**26.0**
Dominique Wilkins	25.8
Oscar Robertson	25.7
David Robinson	**25.6**

REBOUNDS

Wilt Chamberlain	23,924
Bill Russell	21,620
Kareem Abdul-Jabbar	17,440
Elvin Hayes	16,279
Moses Malone	16,212
Robert Parish	**14,635**
Nate Thurmond	14,464
Walt Bellamy	14,241
Wes Unseld	13,769
Jerry Lucas	12,942

ASSISTS

John Stockton	**11,310**
Magic Johnson	**10,141**
Oscar Robertson	9,887
Isiah Thomas	9,061
Maurice Cheeks	7,392
Lenny Wilkens	7,211
Bob Cousy	6,955
Guy Rodgers	6,917
Nate Archibald	6,476
John Lucas	6,454

STEALS

John Stockton	**2,365**
Maurice Cheeks	2,310
Alvin Robertson	**2,112**
Michael Jordan	**2,025**
Clyde Drexler	**1,962**
Isiah Thomas	1,861
Derek Harper	**1,749**
Magic Johnson	**1,724**
Hakeem Olajuwon	**1,694**
Lafayette Lever	1,666

BLOCKED SHOTS

Hakeem Olajuwon **3,190**
Kareem Abdul-Jabbar 3,189
Mark Eaton 3,064
Tree Rollins....................................2,542
Robert Parish.................................**2,342**
Patrick Ewing **2,327**
Manute Bol....................................2,086
George T. Johnson 2,082
Larry Nance 2,027
David Robinson **2,006**

PERSONAL FOULS

Kareem Abdul-Jabbar 4,657
Robert Parish **4,403**
Elvin Hayes...................................4,193
James Edwards.............................**4,042**
Buck Williams **3,970**
Jack Sikma 3,879
Hal Greer......................................3,855
Tom Chambers...............................3,726
Dolph Schayes...............................3,664
Bill Laimbeer 3,633

FIELD GOALS ATTEMPTED

Kareem Abdul-Jabbar 28,307
Elvin Hayes...................................24,272
John Havlicek 23,930
Wilt Chamberlain 23,497
Alex English 21,036
Dominique Wilkins 20,504
Elgin Baylor 20,171
Oscar Robertson.............................19,620
Moses Malone 19,225
Jerry West.....................................19,032

FIELD GOALS MADE

Kareem Abdul-Jabbar............................15,837
Wilt Chamberlain 12,681
Elvin Hayes...................................10,976
Alex English 10,659
John Havlicek 10,513
Robert Parish **9,544**
Dominique Wilkins 9,516
Oscar Robertson.............................9,508
Moses Malone 9,435
Michael Jordan.............................**9,161**

FIELD-GOAL PCT.
(Minimum 2,000 FGM)

Artis Gilmore .... .599
Mark West...................................**.585**
Shaquille O'Neal................................581
Steve Johnson .... .572
Darryl Dawkins.................................. .572

James Donaldson .... .571
Jeff Ruland......................................564
Kareem Abdul-Jabbar .... .559
Kevin McHale....................................554
Otis Thorpe..................................**.553**

FREE THROWS ATTEMPTED

Wilt Chamberlain 11,862
Moses Malone 11,090
Kareem Abdul-Jabbar.........................9,304
Oscar Robertson.............................9,185
Jerry West.....................................8,801
Adrian Dantley 8,351
Karl Malone.................................**8,293**
Dolph Schayes...............................8,273
Bob Pettit 8,119
Walt Bellamy..................................8,088

FREE THROWS MADE

Moses Malone 8,531
Oscar Robertson.............................7,694
Jerry West.....................................7,160
Dolph Schayes...............................6,979
Adrian Dantley 6,832
Kareem Abdul-Jabbar........................6,712
Bob Pettit 6,182
Wilt Chamberlain 6,057
Karl Malone.................................**5,984**
Elgin Baylor 5,763

FREE-THROW PCT.
(Minimum 1,200 FTM)

Mark Price.................................... **.907**
Rick Barry 900
Calvin Murphy 892
Scott Skiles 889
Larry Bird 886
Bill Sharman 883
Reggie Miller................................**.877**
Ricky Pierce.................................**.875**
Kiki Vandeweghe 872
Jeff Malone..................................**.871**

3-PT. FIELD GOALS ATTEMPTED

Dale Ellis......................................**3,147**
Reggie Miller **3,032**
Vernon Maxwell...............................**2,882**
Michael Adams.............................**2,857**
Chuck Person..................................**2,842**
Danny Ainge 2,651
Derek Harper...............................**2,569**
Dan Majerle.................................**2,379**
Glen Rice 2,235
Terry Porter **2,232**

3-PT. FIELD GOALS MADE

Dale Ellis	1,269
Reggie Miller	1,203
Chuck Person	1,046
Danny Ainge	1,002
Michael Adams	949
Vernon Maxwell	923
Derek Harper	908
Glen Rice	879
Dan Majerle	867
Terry Porter	844

3-PT. FIELD-GOAL PCT.
(Minimum 250 Made)

Steve Kerr	.480
Hubert Davis	.449
B.J. Armstrong	.446
Drazen Petrovic	.437
Dana Barros	.415
Tracy Murray	.413
Allan Houston	.410
Trent Tucker	.408
Mark Price	.408
Dennis Scott	.405

MOST VICTORIES, COACH

Lenny Wilkens	1,014
Red Auerbach	938
Dick Motta	918
Bill Fitch	891
Jack Ramsay	864
Don Nelson	851
Cotton Fitzsimmons	832
Pat Riley	798
Gene Shue	784
John MacLeod	707

ACTIVE CAREER LEADERS

(Includes players active at the close
of the 1995-96 season)

POINTS

Michael Jordan	24,489
Karl Malone	23,343
Robert Parish	23,173
Hakeem Olajuwon	21,840
Charles Barkley	20,740
Clyde Drexler	19,794
Patrick Ewing	19,788
Eddie Johnson	18,133
Terry Cummings	17,985
Magic Johnson	17,707

GAMES

Robert Parish	1,568
Buck Williams	1,192
James Edwards	1,168
Eddie Johnson	1,069
Herb Williams	1,048
Rick Mahorn	1,020
Derek Harper	1,013
Dan Schayes	1,000
Byron Scott	994
Terry Cummings	992

MINUTES

Robert Parish	45,298
Buck Williams	40,230
Hakeem Olajuwon	33,981
Karl Malone	33,801
Magic Johnson	33,245
Charles Barkley	32,932
Clyde Drexler	32,793
Derek Harper	32,695
Otis Thorpe	32,001
John Stockton	31,930

SCORING AVERAGE
(Minimum 400 Games or 10,000 Points)

Michael Jordan	32.0
Karl Malone	26.0
David Robinson	25.6
Hakeem Olajuwon	24.3
Patrick Ewing	23.7
Charles Barkley	23.5
Mitch Richmond	22.8
Chris Mullin	21.2
Clyde Drexler	20.7
Glen Rice	19.7

REBOUNDS

Robert Parish	14,635
Buck Williams	12,437
Hakeem Olajuwon	11,023
Charles Barkley	10,311
Karl Malone	9,733
Dennis Rodman	9,441
Patrick Ewing	8,679
Charles Oakley	8,590
Kevin Willis	8,590
Otis Thorpe	8,566

ASSISTS

John Stockton	11,310
Magic Johnson	10,141
Mark Jackson	5,890
Derek Harper	5,836
Kevin Johnson	5,789
Terry Porter	5,771
Muggsy Bogues	5,488
Clyde Drexler	5,389
Doc Rivers	4,889
Nate McMillan	4,698

STEALS

John Stockton	2,365
Alvin Robertson	2,112
Michael Jordan	2,025
Clyde Drexler	1,962
Derek Harper	1,749
Magic Johnson	1,724
Hakeem Olajuwon	1,694
Doc Rivers	1,563
Scottie Pippen	1,538
Nate McMillan	1,472

BLOCKED SHOTS

Hakeem Olajuwon	3,190
Robert Parish	2,342
Patrick Ewing	2,327
David Robinson	2,006
Herb Williams	1,589
Benoit Benjamin	1,576
Dikembe Mutombo	1,486
Alton Lister	1,458
Mark West	1,318
Charles Jones	1,124

PERSONAL FOULS

Robert Parish	4,403
James Edwards	4,042
Buck Williams	3,970
Hakeem Olajuwon	3,446
Rick Mahorn	3,320
Terry Cummings	3,300
Dan Schayes	3,215
Otis Thorpe	3,170
LaSalle Thompson	3,110
Alton Lister	3,072

FIELD GOALS ATTEMPTED

Michael Jordan	17,901
Robert Parish	17,780
Hakeem Olajuwon	16,800
Karl Malone	16,461
Clyde Drexler	15,715

Eddie Johnson	15,442
Terry Cummings	15,280
Patrick Ewing	15,136
Jeff Malone	14,674
Charles Barkley	13,445

FIELD GOALS MADE

Robert Parish	9,544
Michael Jordan	9,161
Hakeem Olajuwon	8,673
Karl Malone	8,646
Patrick Ewing	7,794
Clyde Drexler	7,486
Terry Cummings	7,428
Charles Barkley	7,393
Eddie Johnson	7,334
Jeff Malone	7,099

FIELD-GOAL PCT.
(Minimum 2,000 FGM)

Mark West	.585
Shaquille O'Neal	.581
Otis Thorpe	.553
Charles Barkley	.550
Buck Williams	.550
Robert Parish	.537
Dennis Rodman	.535
Horace Grant	.532
David Robinson	.526
Cedric Ceballos	.525

FREE THROWS ATTEMPTED

Karl Malone	8,293
Charles Barkley	7,454
Michael Jordan	6,818
Hakeem Olajuwon	6,297
Magic Johnson	5,850
Buck Williams	5,729
Robert Parish	5,663
Patrick Ewing	5,622
David Robinson	5,536
Clyde Drexler	5,348

FREE THROWS MADE

Karl Malone	5,984
Michael Jordan	5,753
Charles Barkley	5,502
Magic Johnson	4,960
Hakeem Olajuwon	4,478
Clyde Drexler	4,220
Patrick Ewing	4,183
David Robinson	4,134
Robert Parish	4,085
Buck Williams	3,804

FREE-THROW PCT.
(Minimum 1,200 FTM)

Mark Price	.907
Scott Skiles	.889
Reggie Miller	.877
Ricky Pierce	.875
Jeff Malone	.871
Hersey Hawkins	.867
Jeff Hornacek	.867
Micheal Williams	.866
Chris Mullin	.862
Michael Adams	.849

3-PT. FIELD GOALS ATTEMPTED

Dale Ellis	3,147
Reggie Miller	3,032
Vernon Maxwell	2,882
Michael Adams	2,857
Chuck Person	2,842
Derek Harper	2,569
Dan Majerle	2,379
Glen Rice	2,235
Terry Porter	2,232
Hersey Hawkins	2,085

3-PT. FIELD GOALS MADE

Dale Ellis	1,269
Reggie Miller	1,203
Chuck Person	1,046
Michael Adams	949
Vernon Maxwell	923

Derek Harper	.908
Glen Rice	.879
Dan Majerle	.867
Terry Porter	.844
Dennis Scott	.834

3-PT. FIELD-GOAL PCT.
(Minimum 250 Made)

Steve Kerr	.480
Hubert Davis	.449
B.J. Armstrong	.446
Dana Barros	.415
Tracy Murray	.413
Allan Houston	.410
Mark Price	.408
Dennis Scott	.405
Dale Ellis	.403
Hersey Hawkins	.399

MOST VICTORIES, COACH

Lenny Wilkens	968
Dick Motta	892
Bill Fitch	862
Pat Riley	756
Larry Brown	533
Jerry Sloan	458
Mike Fratello	414
Del Harris	380
Phil Jackson	342
George Karl	321

REGULAR-SEASON RECORDS

MINUTES
(First Kept in 1951-52)

3,882	Wilt Chamberlain, PHI	1961-62
3,836	Wilt Chamberlain, PHI	1967-68
3,806	Wilt Chamberlain, SF	1962-63
3,773	Wilt Chamberlain, PHI	1960-61
3,737	Wilt Chamberlain, PHI	1965-66
3,698	John Havlicek, BOS	1971-72
3,689	Wilt Chamberlain, SF	1963-64
3,682	Wilt Chamberlain, PHI	1966-67
3,681	Nate Archibald, KCO	1972-73
3,678	John Havlicek, BOS	1970-71

POINTS

4,029	Wilt Chamberlain, PHI	1961-62
3,586	Wilt Chamberlain, SF	1962-63
3,041	Michael Jordan, CHI	1986-87
3,033	Wilt Chamberlain, PHI	1960-61
2,948	Wilt Chamberlain, SF	1963-64

2,868	Michael Jordan, CHI	1987-88
2,831	Bob McAdoo, BUF	1974-75
2,822	Kareem Abdul-Jabbar, MIL	1971-72
2,775	Rick Barry, SF	1966-67
2,753	Michael Jordan, CHI	1989-90

SCORING AVERAGE
(Minimum 70 Games or 1,400 Points)

50.4	Wilt Chamberlain, PHI	1961-62
44.8	Wilt Chamberlain, SF	1962-63
38.4	Wilt Chamberlain, PHI	1960-61
37.6	Wilt Chamberlain, PHI	1959-60
37.1	Michael Jordan, CHI	1986-87
36.9	Wilt Chamberlain, SF	1963-64
35.6	Rick Barry, SF	1966-67
35.0	Michael Jordan, CHI	1987-88
34.8	Kareem Abdul-Jabbar, MIL	1971-72
34.7	Wilt Chamberlain, SF/PHI	1964-65

REBOUNDS
(First Kept in 1950-51)

2,149	Wilt Chamberlain, PHI	1960-61
2,052	Wilt Chamberlain, PHI	1961-62
1,957	Wilt Chamberlain, PHI	1966-67
1,952	Wilt Chamberlain, PHI	1967-68
1,946	Wilt Chamberlain, SF	1962-63
1,943	Wilt Chamberlain, PHI	1965-66
1,941	Wilt Chamberlain, PHI	1959-60
1,930	Bill Russell, BOS	1963-64
1,878	Bill Russell, BOS	1964-65
1,868	Bill Russell, BOS	1960-61

ASSISTS

1,164	John Stockton, UTA	1990-91
1,134	John Stockton, UTA	1989-90
1,128	John Stockton, UTA	1987-88
1,126	John Stockton, UTA	1991-92
1,123	Isiah Thomas, DET	1984-85
1,118	John Stockton, UTA	1988-89
1,099	Kevin Porter, DET	1978-79
1,031	John Stockton, UTA	1993-94
1,011	John Stockton, UTA	1994-95
991	Kevin Johnson, PHO	1988-89

STEALS
(First Kept in 1973-74)

301	Alvin Robertson, SA	1985-86
281	Don Buse, IND	1976-77
265	Micheal Richardson, NY	1979-80
263	John Stockton, UTA	1988-89
261	Slick Watts, SEA	1975-76
260	Alvin Robertson, SA	1986-87
259	Michael Jordan, CHI	1987-88
246	Alvin Robertson, MIL	1990-91
244	John Stockton, UTA	1991-92
243	Micheal Richardson, NJ	1984-85
243	Alvin Robertson, SA	1987-88

BLOCKED SHOTS
(First Kept in 1973-74)

456	Mark Eaton, UTA	1984-85
397	Manute Bol, WAS	1985-86
393	Elmore Smith, LA	1973-74
376	Akeem Olajuwon, HOU	1989-90
369	Mark Eaton, UTA	1985-86
351	Mark Eaton, UTA	1982-83
345	Manute Bol, GS	1988-89
343	Tree Rollins, ATL	1982-83
342	Hakeem Olajuwon, HOU	1992-93
338	Kareem Abdul-Jabbar, LA	1975-76

PERSONAL FOULS

386	Darryl Dawkins, NJ	1983-84
382	Darryl Dawkins, NJ	1982-83
372	Steve Johnson, KC	1981-82
367	Bill Robinzine, KC	1978-79
366	Bill Bridges, STL	1967-68
363	Lonnie Shelton, NY	1976-77
363	James Edwards, IND	1978-79
361	Kevin Kunnert, HOU	1976-77
358	Dan Roundfield, ATL	1978-79
358	Rick Mahorn, WAS	1983-84

DISQUALIFICATIONS
(First Kept in 1950-51)

26	Don Meineke, FTW	1952-53
25	Steve Johnson, KC	1981-82
23	Darryl Dawkins, NJ	1982-83
22	Walter Dukes, DET	1958-59
22	Darryl Dawkins, NJ	1983-84
21	Joe Meriweather, ATL	1976-77
20	Joe Fulks, PHI	1952-53
20	Vern Mikkelsen, MIN	1957-58
20	Walter Dukes, DET	1959-60
20	Walter Dukes, DET	1961-62
20	George Johnson, NJ	1977-78

FIELD GOALS ATTEMPTED

3,159	Wilt Chamberlain, PHI	1961-62
2,770	Wilt Chamberlain, SF	1962-63
2,457	Wilt Chamberlain, PHI	1960-61
2,311	Wilt Chamberlain, PHI	1959-60
2,298	Wilt Chamberlain, SF	1963-64
2,279	Michael Jordan, CHI	1986-87
2,273	Elgin Baylor, LA	1962-63
2,217	Rick Barry, GS	1974-75
2,215	Elvin Hayes, SD	1970-71
2,166	Elgin Baylor, LA	1960-61

FIELD GOALS MADE

1,597	Wilt Chamberlain, PHI	1961-62
1,463	Wilt Chamberlain, SF	1962-63
1,251	Wilt Chamberlain, PHI	1960-61
1,204	Wilt Chamberlain, SF	1963-64
1,159	Kareem Abdul-Jabbar, MIL	1971-72
1,098	Michael Jordan, CHI	1986-87
1,095	Bob McAdoo, BUF	1974-75
1,074	Wilt Chamberlain, PHI	1965-66
1,069	Michael Jordan, CHI	1987-88
1,065	Wilt Chamberlain, PHI	1959-60

FIELD-GOAL PCT.
(Minimum 300 FGM)

.727	Wilt Chamberlain, LA	1972-73
.683	Wilt Chamberlain, PHI	1966-67
.670	Artis Gilmore, CHI	1980-81
.652	Artis Gilmore, CHI	1981-82
.649	Wilt Chamberlain, LA	1971-72
.637	James Donaldson, LAC	1984-85

.633	Chris Gatling, GS	1994-95
.632	Steve Johnson, SA	1985-86
.626	Artis Gilmore, SA	1982-83
.625	Mark West, PHO	1989-90

FREE THROWS ATTEMPTED

1,363	Wilt Chamberlain, PHI	1961-62
1,113	Wilt Chamberlain, SF	1962-63
1,054	Wilt Chamberlain, PHI	1960-61
1,016	Wilt Chamberlain, SF	1963-64
991	Wilt Chamberlain, SF	1959-60
977	Jerry West, LA	1965-66
976	Wilt Chamberlain, PHI	1965-66
972	Michael Jordan, CHI	1986-87
951	Charles Barkley, PHI	1987-88
946	Adrian Dantley, UTA	1983-84

FREE THROWS MADE

840	Jerry West, LA	1965-66
835	Wilt Chamberlain, PHI	1961-62
833	Michael Jordan, CHI	1986-87
813	Adrian Dantley, UTA	1983-84
800	Oscar Robertson, CIN	1963-64
753	Rick Barry, SF	1966-67
742	Oscar Robertson, CIN	1965-66
737	Moses Malone, PHI	1984-85
736	Oscar Robertson, CIN	1966-67
723	Michael Jordan, CHI	1987-88

FREE-THROW PCT.
(Minimum 125 FTM)

.958	Calvin Murphy, HOU	1980-81
.956	M. Abdul-Rauf, DEN	1993-94
.948	Mark Price, CLE	1992-93
.947	Mark Price, CLE	1991-92
.947	Rick Barry, HOU	1978-79
.945	Ernie DiGregorio, BUF	1976-77
.935	Chris Jackson, DEN	1992-93
.935	Ricky Sobers, CHI	1980-81

.935	Rick Barry, HOU	1979-80
.934	Spud Webb, SAC	1994-95

3-PT. FIELD GOALS ATTEMPTED
(Rule went into effect in 1979-80)

678	George McCloud, DAL	1995-96
628	Dennis Scott, ORL	1995-96
623	Mookie Blaylock, ATL	1995-96
611	John Starks, NY	1994-95
564	Michael Adams, DEN	1990-91
555	Mookie Blaylock, ATL	1994-95
548	Dan Majerle, PHO	1994-95
515	Mitch Richmond, SAC	1995-96
511	Nick Van Exel, LAL	1994-95
510	Vernon Maxwell, HOU	1990-91

3-PT. FIELD GOALS MADE

267	Dennis Scott, ORL	1995-96
257	George McCloud, DAL	1995-96
231	Mookie Blaylock, ATL	1995-96
225	Mitch Richmond, SAC	1995-96
217	John Starks, NY	1994-95
199	Mookie Blaylock, ATL	1994-95
199	Dan Majerle, PHO	1994-95
197	Dana Barros, PHI	1994-95
195	Reggie Miller, IND	1994-95
192	Dan Majerle, PHO	1993-94

3-PT. FIELD-GOAL PCT.
(Minimum 50 Made; 1994-96: 82 Made)

.524	Steve Kerr, CHI	1994-95
.522	Tim Legler, WAS	1995-96
.515	Steve Kerr, CHI	1995-96
.514	Detlef Schrempf, SEA	1994-95
.507	Steve Kerr, CLE	1989-90
.491	Craig Hodges, MIL/PHO	1987-88
.486	Mark Price, CLE	1987-88
.481	Craig Hodges, CHI	1989-90
.478	Dale Ellis, SEA	1988-89
.476	Hubert Davis, NY	1995-96

GAME RECORDS

POINTS

- 100 ...Wilt Chamberlain, PHI vs. NY, March 2, 1962
- 78 .....Wilt Chamberlain, PHI vs. LA, Dec. 8, 1961 (3 OT)
- 73 .....Wilt Chamberlain, PHI vs. CHI, Jan. 13, 1962
- 73 .....Wilt Chamberlain, SF vs. NY, Nov. 6, 1962
- 73 .....David Thompson, DEN vs. DET, April 9, 1978
- 72 .....Wilt Chamberlain, SF vs. LA, Nov. 3, 1962
- 71 .....Elgin Baylor, LA vs. NY, Nov. 15, 1960

- 71 .....David Robinson, SA vs. LAC, Apr. 24, 1994
- 70 .....Wilt Chamberlain, SF vs. SYR, March 10, 1963
- 69 .....Michael Jordan, CHI vs. CLE, March 28, 1990 (OT)
- 68 .....Wilt Chamberlain, PHI vs. CHI, Dec. 16, 1967
- 68 .....Pete Maravich, NO vs. NY, Feb. 25, 1977

REBOUNDS

- 55 .....Wilt Chamberlain, PHI vs. BOS, Nov. 24, 1960
- 51 .....Bill Russell, BOS vs. SYR, Feb. 5, 1960

49 .....Bill Russell, BOS vs. PHI, Nov. 16, 1957
49 .....Bill Russell, BOS vs. DET, March 11, 1965
45 .....Wilt Chamberlain, PHI vs. SYR, Feb. 6, 1960
45 .....Wilt Chamberlain, PHI vs. LA, Jan. 21, 1961

ASSISTS

30 .....Scott Skiles, ORL vs. DEN, Dec. 30, 1990
29 .....Kevin Porter, NJ vs. HOU, Feb. 24, 1978
28 .....Bob Cousy, BOS vs. MIN, Feb. 27, 1959
28 .....Guy Rodgers, SF vs. STL, March 14, 1963
28 .....John Stockton, UTA vs. SA, Jan. 15, 1991

STEALS

11 .....Larry Kenon, SA vs. KC, Dec. 26, 1976
10 .....Jerry West, LA vs. SEA, Dec. 7, 1973
10 .....Larry Steele, POR vs. L.A., Nov. 16, 1974
10 .....Fred Brown, SEA vs. PHI, Dec. 3, 1976
10 .....Gus Williams, SEA vs. NJ, Feb. 22, 1978
10 .....Eddie Jordan, NJ vs. PHI, March 23, 1979
10 .....Johnny Moore, SA vs. IND, March 6, 1985
10 .....Fat Lever, DEN vs. IND, March 9, 1985
10 .....Clyde Drexler, POR vs. MIL, Jan. 10, 1986
10 .....Alvin Robertson, SA vs. PHO, Feb. 18, 1986
10 .....Alvin Robertson, SA vs. LAC, Nov. 22 1986
10 .....Ron Harper, CLE vs. PHI, March 10, 1987
10 .....Michael Jordan, CHI vs. NJ, Jan. 29, 1988
10 .....Alvin Robertson, SA vs. HOU, Jan. 11, 1989 (OT)
10 .....Alvin Robertson, MIL vs. UTA, Nov. 19, 1990
10 .....Kevin Johnson, PHO vs. WAS, Dec. 9, 1993

BLOCKED SHOTS

17 .....Elmore Smith, LA vs. POR, Oct. 28, 1973
15 .....Manute Bol, WAS vs. ATL, Jan. 25, 1986
15 .....Manute Bol, WAS vs. IND, Feb. 26, 1987
15 .....Shaquille O'Neal, ORL vs. NJ, Nov. 20, 1993

FIELD GOALS ATTEMPTED

63 .....Wilt Chamberlain, PHI vs. NY, March 2, 1962
62 .....Wilt Chamberlain, PHI vs. LA, Dec. 8, 1961 (3 OT)
60 .....Wilt Chamberlain, SF vs. CIN, Oct. 28, 1962 (OT)
58 .....Wilt Chamberlain, SF vs. PHI, Nov. 26, 1964

FIELD GOALS MADE

36 .....Wilt Chamberlain, PHI vs. NY, March 2, 1962

31 .....Wilt Chamberlain, PHI vs. LA, Dec. 8, 1961 (3 OT)
30 .....Wilt Chamberlain, PHI vs. CHI, Dec. 16, 1967
30 .....Rick Barry, GS vs. POR, March 26, 1974

FIELD-GOAL PCT.

(Minimum 15 Attempts)
1.000.Wilt Chamberlain, PHI vs. BAL, Feb. 24, 1967 (18/18)
1.000.Wilt Chamberlain, PHI vs. BAL, March 19, 1967 (16/16)
1.000.Wilt Chamberlain, PHI vs. LA, Jan. 20, 1967 (15/15)
.947 ..Wilt Chamberlain, SF vs. NY, Nov. 27, 1963 (18/19)
.941 ..Wilt Chamberlain, PHI vs. BAL, Nov. 25, 1966 (16/17)

FREE THROWS ATTEMPTED

34 .....Wilt Chamberlain, PHI vs. STL, Feb. 22, 1962
32 .....Wilt Chamberlain, PHI vs. NY, March 2, 1962
31 .....Adrian Dantley, UTA vs. DEN, Nov. 25, 1983
29 .....Lloyd Free, SD vs. ATL, Jan. 13, 1979
29 .....Adrian Dantley, UTA vs. DAL, Oct. 31, 1980
29 .....Adrian Dantley, UTA vs. HOU, Jan. 4, 1984

FREE THROWS MADE

28 .....Wilt Chamberlain, PHI vs. NY, March 2, 1962
28 .....Adrian Dantley, UTA vs. HOU, Jan. 4, 1984
27 .....Adrian Dantley, UTA vs. DEN, Nov. 25, 1983
26 .....Adrian Dantley, UTA vs. DAL, Oct. 31, 1980
26 .....Michael Jordan, CHI vs. NJ, Feb. 26, 1987

FREE-THROW PCT.

(Most with No Misses)
1.000..Dominique Wilkins, ATL vs. CHI, Dec. 8, 1992 (23/23)
1.000..Bob Pettit, STL vs. BOS, Nov. 22, 1961 (19/19)
1.000..Bill Cartwright, NY vs. KC, Nov. 17, 1981 (19/19)
1.000..Adrian Dantley, DET vs. CHI, Dec. 15, 1987 (19/19) (OT)

3-PT. FIELD GOALS ATTEMPTED
20.....Michael Adams, DEN vs. LAC, April 12, 1991
20.....George McCloud, DAL vs. NJ, March 5, 1996
19.....Dennis Scott, ORL vs. MIL, April 13, 1993
18.....Joe Dumars, DET vs. MIN, Nov. 8, 1994

3-PT. FIELD GOALS MADE
11.....Dennis Scott, ORL vs. ATL, April 18, 1996
10.....Brian Shaw, MIA vs. MIL, April 8, 1993
10.....Joe Dumars, DET vs. MIN, Nov. 8, 1994
10.....George McCloud, DAL vs. PHO, Dec. 16, 1995 (OT)

TEAM RECORDS—SEASON

HIGHEST WINNING PCT.
.878.....72-10 Chicago, 1995-96
.841.....69-13 Los Angeles, 1971-72
.840.....68-13 Philadelphia, 1966-67

LOWEST WINNING PCT.
.110..... 9-73 Philadelphia, 1972-73
.125..... 6-42 Providence, 1947-48
.134.....11-71 Dallas, 1992-93

HIGHEST WINNING PCT., HOME
.976.....40-1 Boston, 1985-86
.971.....33-1 Rochester, 1949-50
.969.....31-1 Syracuse, 1949-50

HIGHEST WINNING PCT., ROAD
.816.....31-7 Los Angeles, 1971-72
.805.....33-8 Chicago, 1995-96
.800.....32-8 Boston, 1972-73

CONSECUTIVE WINS
33........Los Angeles, Nov. 5, 1971-Jan. 7, 1972
20........Milwaukee, Feb. 6-March 8, 1971
20........Washington, March 13-Dec. 4, 1948
          (overlapping seasons)

CONSECUTIVE WINS
(Start of Season)
15........Washington, Nov. 3-Dec. 4, 1948
14........Boston, Oct. 22-Nov. 27, 1957
12........Seattle, Oct. 29-Nov. 19, 1982

CONSECUTIVE LOSSES
24........Cleveland, March 19-Nov. 5, 1982
          (overlapping seasons)
23........Vancouver, Feb. 16-April 2, 1996
21........Detroit, March 7-Oct. 22, 1980
          (overlapping seasons)

CONSECUTIVE WINS, HOME
44........Chicago, March 30, 1995-April 4, 1996
          (overlapping seasons)
40........Orlando, March 21, 1995-March 19, 1996
          (overlapping seasons)
38........Boston, Dec. 10, 1985-Nov. 28, 1986
          (overlapping seasons)

CONSECUTIVE WINS, ROAD
16........Los Angeles, Nov. 6, 1971-Jan. 7, 1972
15........Utah, Nov. 27, 1994-Jan. 26, 1995
13........Boston, Dec. 5, 1964-Jan. 20, 1965

HIGHEST SCORING AVERAGE
126.5...Denver, 1981-82
125.4...Philadelphia, 1961-62
125.2...Philadelphia, 1966-67

LOWEST SCORING AVERAGE
(Since 1954-55, first year of the 24-second clock)
87.4.....Milwaukee, 1954-55
89.8.....Vancouver, 1995-96
90.5.....Cleveland, 1994-95

FEWEST POINTS ALLOWED PER GAME
(Since 1954-55, first year of the 24-second clock)
88.5.....Cleveland, 1995-96
89.8.....Cleveland, 1994-95
89.9.....Syracuse, 1954-55

MOST POINTS ALLOWED PER GAME
130.8...Denver, 1990-91
126.0...Denver, 1981-82
125.1...Seattle, 1967-68

TEAM RECORDS—GAME

MOST POINTS
186 ......Detroit vs. Denver, Dec. 13, 1983
    (3 OT)
184 ......Denver vs. Detroit, Dec. 13, 1983
    (3 OT)
173 ......Boston vs. Minneapolis, Feb. 27, 1959
173 ......Phoenix vs. Denver, Nov. 10, 1990
171 ......San Antonio vs. Milwaukee, March 6,
    1982 (3 OT)
169 ......Philadelphia vs. New York, March 2,
    1962

FEWEST POINTS
(Since 1954-55, first year of the 24-second
    clock)
57 ....Milwaukee vs. Boston, Feb. 27, 1955
57 ....Philadelphia vs. Miami, Feb. 21, 1996
59 ....Sacramento vs. Charlotte, Jan. 10, 1991
61 ....New York vs. Detroit, April 12, 1992
61 ....Indiana vs. Cleveland, March 22, 1994

MOST POINTS, BOTH TEAMS
370 ...Detroit (186) vs. Denver (184), Dec. 13,
    1983 (3 OT)
337 ...San Antonio (171) vs. Milwaukee (166),
    March 6, 1982 (3 OT)
318 ...Denver (163) vs. San Antonio (155), Jan.
    11, 1984

316 ...Philadelphia (169) vs. New York (147),
    March 2, 1962
316 ...Cincinnati (165) vs. San Diego (151),
    March 12, 1970
316 ...Phoenix (173) vs. Denver (143), Nov. 10,
    1990

FEWEST POINTS, BOTH TEAMS
(Since 1954-55, first year of the 24-second
    clock)
119 ...Milwaukee (57) vs. Boston (62), Feb. 27,
    1955
123 ...Philadelphia (57) vs. Miami (66), Feb. 21,
    1996
133 ...New York (61) vs. Detroit (72), April 12,
    1992

LARGEST MARGIN OF VICTORY
68 .....Cleveland (148) vs. Miami (80), Dec. 17,
    1991
63 .....Los Angeles (162) vs. Golden State (99),
    March 19, 1972
62 .....Syracuse (162) vs. New York (100), Dec.
    25, 1960
59 .....Golden State (150) vs. Indiana (91),
    March 19, 1977
59 .....Milwaukee (143) vs. Detroit (84), Dec. 26,
    1978

PLAYOFF RECORDS—CAREER

POINTS
5,762 ...Kareem Abdul-Jabbar
4,717 ...Michael Jordan
4,457 ...Jerry West
3,897 ...Larry Bird
3,776 ...John Havlicek

SCORING AVERAGE
(Minimum 25 Games)
33.9 ....Michael Jordan
29.1 ....Jerry West
27.8 ....Hakeem Olajuwon
27.3 ....Karl Malone
27.0 ....Elgin Baylor

REBOUNDS
4,104 ...Bill Russell
3,913 ...Wilt Chamberlain
2,481 ...Kareem Abdul-Jabbar
1,777 ...Wes Unseld
1,761 ...Robert Parish

ASSISTS
2,346 ...Magic Johnson
1,175 ...John Stockton
1,062 ...Larry Bird
1,006 ...Dennis Johnson
  987 ...Isiah Thomas

STEALS
358 ...Magic Johnson
314 ...Michael Jordan
296 ...Maurice Cheeks
295 ...Maurice Cheeks
271 ...Scottie Pippen

BLOCKED SHOTS
476 ...Kareem Abdul-Jabbar
408 ...Hakeem Olajuwon
306 ...Robert Parish
281 ...Kevin McHale
244 ...Patrick Ewing

PLAYOFF RECORDS—GAME

POINTS
63.....Michael Jordan, CHI vs. BOS, April 20, 1986 (2 OT)
61.....Elgin Baylor, LA vs. BOS, April 14, 1962
56.....Wilt Chamberlain, PHI vs. SYR, March 22, 1962
56.....Michael Jordan, CHI vs. MIA, Apr. 29, 1992
56......Charles Barkley, PHO vs. GS, May 4, 1994

REBOUNDS
41.....Wilt Chamberlain, PHI vs. BOS, April 5, 1967
40.....Bill Russell, BOS vs. PHI, March 23, 1958
40.....Bill Russell, BOS vs. STL, March 29, 1960
40.....Bill Russell, BOS vs. LA, April 18, 1962 (OT)

ASSISTS
24......Magic Johnson, LA vs. PHO, May 15, 1984
24.....John Stockton, UTA vs. LAL, May 17, 1988

STEALS
8.......Rick Barry, GS vs. SEA, April 14, 1975
8.......Lionel Hollins, POR vs. LA, May 8, 1977
8.......Maurice Cheeks, PHI vs. NJ, April 11, 1979
8.......Craig Hodges, MIL vs. PHI, May 9, 1986
8.......Tim Hardaway, GS vs. LAL, May 8, 1991
8.......Tim Hardaway, GS vs. SEA, April 30, 1992
8.......Mookie Blaylock, ATL vs. IND, April 29, 1996

BLOCKED SHOTS
10.....Mark Eaton, UTA vs. HOU, April 26, 1985
10.....Akeem Olajuwon, HOU vs. LAL, April 29, 1990

PLAYOFF RECORDS—TEAM

CONSECUTIVE GAMES WON
13.....L.A. Lakers, 1988-89
12.....Detroit, 1989-90
9 .....Los Angeles, 1982
9 .....Chicago, 1992-93
9 .....Chicago, 1996

CONSECUTIVE GAMES LOST
11.....Baltimore, 1965-66 and 1969-70
11.....Denver, 1988-90 and 1994
10.....New Jersey, 1984-86 and 1992

CONSECUTIVE SERIES WON
18.....Boston, 1959-1967
13.....Chicago, 1991-94
11.....L.A. Lakers, 1987-89

MOST POINTS, GAME
157...Boston vs. New York, April 28, 1990
156...Milwaukee vs. Philadelphia, March 30, 1970
153...L.A. Lakers vs. Denver, May 22, 1985
153...Portland vs. Phoenix, May 11, 1992 (2 OT)

FEWEST POINTS, GAME
(Since 1954-55, first year of the 24-second clock)
64.....Portland vs. Utah, May 5, 1996

67.....Orlando vs. Chicago, May 25, 1996
68.....New York vs. Indiana, May 28, 1994

MOST POINTS, BOTH TEAMS, GAME
304...Portland (153) vs. Phoenix (151), May 11, 1992 (2 OT)
285...San Antonio (152) vs. Denver (133), April 26, 1983
285...Boston (157) vs. New York (128), April 28, 1990

FEWEST POINTS, BOTH TEAMS, GAME
145...Syracuse (71) vs. Ft. Wayne (74), March 24, 1956
153...Orlando (67) vs. Chicago (86), May 25, 1996
156...New York (68) vs. Indiana (88), May 28, 1994

LARGEST MARGIN OF VICTORY, GAME
58.....Minneapolis (133) vs. St. Louis (75), March 19, 1956
56.....Los Angeles (126) vs. Golden State (70), April 21, 1973
50.....Milwaukee (136) vs. San Francisco (86), April 4, 1971

NBA FIRST-ROUND PICKS
(Since 1974)

ATLANTA HAWKS
1997	Priest Lauderdale, Greece
1995	Alan Henderson, Indiana
1994	(no first-round pick)
1993	Doug Edwards, Florida St.
1992	Adam Keefe, Stanford
1991	Stacey Augmon, UNLV
	Anthony Avent, Seton Hall
1990	Rumeal Robinson, Michigan
1989	Roy Marble, Iowa
1988	(no first-round pick)
1987	Dallas Comegys, DePaul
1986	Billy Thompson, Louisville
1985	Jon Koncak, Southern Methodist
1984	Kevin Willis, Michigan St.
1983	(no first-round pick)
1982	Keith Edmonson, Purdue
1981	Al Wood, N. Carolina
1980	Don Collins, Washington St.
1979	(no first-round pick)
1978	Butch Lee, Marquette
	Jack Givens, Kentucky
1977	Tree Rollins, Clemson
1976	Armond Hill, Princeton
1975	David Thompson, N. Carolina St.
	Marvin Webster, Morgan St.
1974	Tom Henderson, Hawaii
	Mike Sojourner, Utah

BOSTON CELTICS
1996	Antoine Walker, Kentucky
1995	Eric Williams, Providence
1994	Eric Montross, N. Carolina
1993	Acie Earl, Iowa
1992	Jon Barry, Georgia Tech
1991	Rick Fox, N. Carolina
1990	Dee Brown, Jacksonville
1989	Michael Smith, Brigham Young
1988	Brian Shaw, Cal.-Santa Barbara
1987	Reggie Lewis, Northeastern
1986	Len Bias, Maryland
1985	Sam Vincent, Michigan St.
1984	Michael Young, Houston
1983	Greg Kite, Brigham Young
1982	Darren Tillis, Cleveland St.
1981	Charles Bradley, Wyoming
1980	Kevin McHale, Minnesota
1979	(no first-round pick)
1978	Larry Bird, Indiana St.
	Freeman Williams, Portland St.
1977	Cedric Maxwell, N.C.-Charlotte
1976	Norm Cook, Kansas
1975	Tom Boswell, S. Carolina
1974	Glenn McDonald, Long Beach St.

CHARLOTTE HORNETS
1996	Kobe Bryant, Lower Merion HS
	Tony Delk, Kentucky
1995	George Zidek, UCLA
1994	(no first-round pick)
1993	Greg Graham, Indiana
	Scott Burrell, Connecticut
1992	Alonzo Mourning, Georgetown
1991	Larry Johnson, UNLV
1990	Kendall Gill, Illinois
1989	J.R. Reid, N. Carolina
1988	Rex Chapman, Kentucky

CHICAGO BULLS
1996	Travis Knight, Connecticut
1995	Jason Caffey, Alabama
1994	Dickey Simpkins, Providence
1993	Corie Blount, Cincinnati
1992	Byron Houston, Oklahoma St.
1991	Mark Randall, Kansas
1990	(no first-round pick)
1989	Stacey King, Oklahoma
	B.J. Armstrong, Iowa
	Jeff Sanders, Georgia Southern
1988	Will Perdue, Vanderbilt
1987	Olden Polynice, Virginia
	Horace Grant, Clemson
1986	Brad Sellers, Ohio St.
1985	Keith Lee, Memphis St.
1984	Michael Jordan, N. Carolina
1983	Sidney Green, UNLV
1982	Quintin Dailey, San Francisco
1981	Orlando Woolridge, Notre Dame
1980	Kelvin Ransey, Ohio St.
1979	David Greenwood, UCLA
1978	Reggie Theus, UNLV
1977	Tate Armstrong, Duke
1976	Scott May, Indiana
1975	(no first-round pick)
1974	Maurice Lucas, Marquette
	Cliff Pondexter, Long Beach St.

CLEVELAND CAVALIERS
1996	Vitaly Potapenko, Wright St.
	Zydrunas Ilgauskas, Lithuania
1995	Bob Sura, Florida St.
1994	(no first-round pick)
1993	Chris Mills, Arizona
1992	(no first-round pick)
1991	Terrell Brandon, Oregon
1990	(no first-round pick)
1989	John Morton, Seton Hall
1988	Randolph Keys, Southern Miss.
1987	Kevin Johnson, California
1986	Brad Daugherty, N. Carolina
	Ron Harper, Miami (OH)

1985	Charles Oakley, Virginia Union
1984	Tim McCormick, Michigan
1983	Roy Hinson, Rutgers
	Stewart Granger, Villanova
1982	John Bagley, Boston College
1981	(no first-round pick)
1980	Chad Kinch, N.C.-Charlotte
1979	(no first-round pick)
1978	Mike Mitchell, Auburn
1977	(no first-round pick)
1976	Chuckie Williams, Kansas St.
1975	John Lambert, Southern Cal.
1974	Campy Russell, Michigan

DALLAS MAVERICKS

1996	Samaki Walker, Louisville
1995	Cherokee Parks, Duke
	Loren Meyer, Iowa St.
1994	Jason Kidd, California
	Tony Dumas, Missouri-K.C.
1993	Jamal Mashburn, Kentucky
1992	Jim Jackson, Ohio St.
1991	Doug Smith, Missouri
1990	(no first-round pick)
1989	Randy White, Louisiana Tech
1988	(no first-round pick)
1987	Jim Farmer, Alabama
1986	Roy Tarpley, Michigan
1985	Detlef Schrempf, Washington
	Bill Wennington, St. John's
	Uwe Blab, Indiana
1984	Sam Perkins, N. Carolina
	Terence Stansbury, Temple
1983	Dale Ellis, Tennessee
	Derek Harper, Illinois
1982	Bill Garnett, Wyoming
1981	Mark Aguirre, DePaul
	Rolando Blackman, Kansas St.
1980	Kiki Vandeweghe, UCLA

DENVER NUGGETS

1996	Efthimios Rentzias, Greece
1995	Brent Barry, Oregon St.
1994	Jalen Rose, Michigan
1993	Rodney Rogers, Wake Forest
1992	LaPhonso Ellis, Notre Dame
	Bryant Stith, Virginia
1991	Dikembe Mutombo, Georgetown
	Mark Macon, Temple
1990	Chris Jackson, Louisiana St.
1989	Todd Lichti, Stanford
1988	Jerome Lane, Pittsburgh
1987	(no first-round pick)
1986	Maurice Martin, St. Joseph's
	Mark Alarie, Duke
1985	Blair Rasmussen, Oregon
1984	(no first-round pick)
1983	Howard Carter, Louisiana St.
1982	Rob Williams, Houston

1981	(no first-round pick)
1980	James Ray, Jacksonville
	Carl Nicks, Indiana St.
1979	(no first-round pick)
1978	Rod Griffin, Wake Forest
	Mike Evans, Kansas St.
1977	Tom LaGarde, N. Carolina
	Anthony Roberts, Oral Roberts
1976	(no first-round pick)

DETROIT PISTONS

1996	Jerome Williams, Georgetown
1995	Theo Ratliff, Wyoming
	Randolph Childress, Wake Forest
1994	Grant Hill, Duke
1993	Lindsey Hunter, Jackson St.
	Allan Houston, Tennessee
1992	Don MacLean, UCLA
1991	(no first-round pick)
1990	Lance Blanks, Texas
1989	Kenny Battle, Illinois
1988	(no first-round pick)
1987	(no first-round pick)
1986	John Salley, Georgia Tech
1985	Joe Dumars, McNeese St.
1984	Tony Campbell, Ohio St.
1983	Antoine Carr, Wichita St.
1982	Cliff Levingston, Wichita St.
	Ricky Pierce, Rice
1981	Isiah Thomas, Indiana
	Kelly Tripucka, Notre Dame
1980	Larry Drew, Missouri
1979	Greg Kelser, Michigan St.
	Roy Hamilton, UCLA
	Phil Hubbard, Michigan
1978	(no first-round pick)
1977	(no first-round pick)
1976	Leon Douglas, Alabama
1975	(no first-round pick)
1974	Al Eberhard, Missouri

GOLDEN ST. WARRIORS

1996	Todd Fuller, N. Carolina St.
1995	Joe Smith, Maryland
1994	Clifford Rozier, Louisville
1993	Anfernee Hardaway, Memphis St.
1992	Latrell Sprewell, Alabama
1991	Chris Gatling, Old Dominion
	Victor Alexander, Iowa St.
	Shaun Vandiver, Colorado
1990	Tyrone Hill, Xavier
1989	Tim Hardaway, Texas-El Paso
1988	Mitch Richmond, Kansas St.
1987	Tellis Frank, Western Kentucky
1986	Chris Washburn, N. Carolina St.
1985	Chris Mullin, St. John's
1984	(no first-round pick)
1983	Russell Cross, Purdue

1982	Lester Conner, Oregon St.
1981	(no first-round pick)
1980	Joe Barry Carroll, Purdue
	Rickey Brown, Mississippi St.
1979	(no first-round pick)
1978	Purvis Short, Jackson St.
	Raymond Townsend, UCLA
1977	Rickey Green, Michigan
	Wesley Cox, Louisville
1976	Robert Parish, Centenary
	Sonny Parker, Texas A&M
1975	Joe Bryant, La Salle
1974	Jamaal Wilkes, UCLA

HOUSTON ROCKETS

1996	Othella Harrington, Georgetown
1995	(no first-round pick)
1994	(no first-round pick)
1993	Sam Cassell, Florida St.
1992	Robert Horry, Alabama
1991	John Turner, Phillips
1990	Alec Kessler, Georgia
1989	(no first-round pick)
1988	Derrick Chievous, Missouri
1987	(no first-round pick)
1986	Buck Johnson, Alabama
1985	Steve Harris, Tulsa
1984	Akeem Olajuwon, Houston
1983	Ralph Sampson, Virginia
	Rodney McCray, Louisville
1982	Terry Teagle, Baylor
1981	(no first-round pick)
1980	(no first-round pick)
1979	Lee Johnson, E. Texas St.
1978	(no first-round pick)
1977	(no first-round pick)
1976	John Lucas, Maryland
1975	Joe Meriweather, Southern Illinois
1974	Bobby Jones, N. Carolina

INDIANA PACERS

1996	Erick Dampier, Mississippi St.
1995	Travis Best, Georgia Tech
1994	Eric Piatkowski, Nebraska
1993	Scott Haskin, Oregon St.
1992	Malik Sealy, St. John's
1991	Dale Davis, Clemson
1990	(no first-round pick)
1989	George McCloud, Florida St.
1988	Rik Smits, Marist
1987	Reggie Miller, UCLA
1986	Chuck Person, Auburn
1985	Wayman Tisdale, Oklahoma
1984	Vern Fleming, Georgia
1983	Steve Stipanovich, Missouri
	Mitchell Wiggins, Florida St.
1982	Clark Kellogg, Ohio St.
1981	Herb Williams, Ohio St.
1980	(no first-round pick)
1979	Dudley Bradley, N. Carolina

1978	Rick Robey, Kentucky
1977	(no first-round pick)
1976	(no first-round pick)

LOS ANGELES CLIPPERS

1996	Lorenzen Wright, Memphis
1995	Antonio McDyess, Alabama
1994	Lamond Murray, California
	Greg Minor, Louisville
1993	Terry Dehere, Seton Hall
1992	Randy Woods, La Salle
	Elmore Spencer, UNLV
1991	LeRon Ellis, Syracuse
1990	Bo Kimble, Loyola Marymount
	Loy Vaught, Michigan
1989	Danny Ferry, Duke
1988	Danny Manning, Kansas
	Hersey Hawkins, Bradley
1987	Reggie Williams, Georgetown
	Joe Wolf, N. Carolina
	Ken Norman, Illinois
1986	(no first-round pick)
1985	Benoit Benjamin, Creighton
1984	Lancaster Gordon, Louisville
	Michael Cage, San Diego St.
1983	Byron Scott, Arizona St.
1982	Terry Cummings, DePaul
1981	Tom Chambers, Utah
1980	Michael Brooks, La Salle
1979	(no first-round pick)
1978	(no first-round pick)
1977	(no first-round pick)
1976	Adrian Dantley, Notre Dame
1975	(no first-round pick)
1974	Tom McMillen, Maryland

LOS ANGELES LAKERS

1996	Derek Fisher, Arkansas-Little Rock
1995	(no first-round pick)
1994	Eddie Jones, Temple
1993	George Lynch, North Carolina
1992	Anthony Peeler, Missouri
1991	(no first-round pick)
1990	Elden Campbell, Clemson
1989	Vlade Divac, Yugoslavia
1988	David Rivers, Notre Dame
1987	(no first-round pick)
1986	Ken Barlow, Notre Dame
1985	A.C. Green, Oregon St.
1984	Earl Jones, District of Columbia
1983	(no first-round pick)
1982	James Worthy, N. Carolina
1981	Mike McGee, Michigan
1980	(no first-round pick)
1979	Earvin Johnson, Michigan St.
	Brad Holland, UCLA
1978	(no first-round pick)
1977	Ken Carr, N. Carolina St.
	Brad Davis, Maryland
	Norm Nixon, Duquesne

1976	(no first-round pick)
1975	David Meyers, UCLA
	Junior Bridgeman, Louisville
1974	Brian Winters, S. Carolina

MIAMI HEAT

1996	(no first-round pick)
1995	Kurt Thomas, Texas Christian
1994	Khalid Reeves, Arizona
1993	(no first-round pick)
1992	Harold Miner, Southern Cal.
1991	Steve Smith, Michigan St.
1990	Willie Burton, Minnesota
	Dave Jamerson, Ohio
1989	Glen Rice, Michigan
1988	Rony Seikaly, Syracuse
	Kevin Edwards, DePaul

MILWAUKEE BUCKS

1996	Stephon Marbury, Georgia Tech
1995	Gary Trent, Ohio
1994	Glenn Robinson, Purdue
	Eric Mobley, Pittsburgh
1993	Vin Baker, Hartford
1992	Todd Day, Arkansas
	Lee Mayberry, Arkansas
1991	Kevin Brooks, S.W. Louisiana
1990	Terry Mills, Michigan
1989	(no first-round pick)
1988	Jeff Grayer, Iowa St.
1987	(no first-round pick)
1986	Scott Skiles, Michigan St.
1985	Jerry Reynolds, Louisiana St.
1984	Kenny Fields, UCLA
1983	Randy Breuer, Minnesota
1982	Paul Pressey, Tulsa
1981	Alton Lister, Arizona St.
1980	(no first-round pick)
1979	Sidney Moncrief, Arkansas
1978	George Johnson, St. John's
1977	Kent Benson, Indiana
	Marques Johnson, UCLA
	Ernie Grunfeld, Tennessee
1976	Quinn Buckner, Indiana
1975	(no first-round pick)
1974	Gary Brokaw, Notre Dame

MINNESOTA TIMBERWOLVES

1996	Ray Allen, Connecticut
1995	Kevin Garnett, Farragut Academy
1994	Donyell Marshall, Connecticut
1993	Isaiah (J.R.) Rider, UNLV
1992	Christian Laettner, Duke
1991	Luc Longley, New Mexico
1990	Felton Spencer, Louisville
	Gerald Glass, Mississippi
1989	Pooh Richardson, UCLA

NEW JERSEY NETS

| 1996 | Kerry Kittles, Villanova |
| 1995 | Ed O'Bannon, UCLA |

1994	Yinka Dare, G. Washington
1993	Rex Walters, Kansas
1992	(no first-round pick)
1991	Kenny Anderson, Georgia Tech
1990	Derrick Coleman, Syracuse
	Tate George, Connecticut
1989	Mookie Blaylock, Oklahoma
1988	Chris Morris, Auburn
1987	Dennis Hopson, Ohio St.
1986	Dwayne Washington, Syracuse
1985	(no first-round pick)
1984	Jeff Turner, Vanderbilt
1983	(no first-round pick)
1982	Sleepy Floyd, Georgetown
	Eddie Phillips, Alabama
1981	Buck Williams, Maryland
	Albert King, Maryland
	Ray Tolbert, Indiana
1980	Mike O'Koren, N. Carolina
	Mike Gminski, Duke
1979	Calvin Natt, N.E. Louisiana
	Cliff Robinson, Southern Cal.
1978	Winford Boynes, San Francisco
1977	Bernard King, Tennessee
1976	(no first-round pick)

NEW YORK KNICKS

1996	John Wallace, Syracuse
	Walter McCarty, Kentucky
	Dontae Jones, Mississippi St.
1995	(no first-round pick)
1994	Monty Williams, Notre Dame
	Charlie Ward, Florida St.
1993	(no first-round pick)
1992	Hubert Davis, North Carolina
1991	Greg Anthony, UNLV
1990	Jerrod Mustaf, Maryland
1989	(no first-round pick)
1988	Rod Strickland, DePaul
1987	Mark Jackson, St. John's
1986	Kenny Walker, Kentucky
1985	Patrick Ewing, Georgetown
1984	(no first-round pick)
1983	Darrell Walker, Arkansas
1982	Trent Tucker, Minnesota
1981	(no first-round pick)
1980	Mike Woodson, Indiana
1979	Bill Cartwright, San Francisco
	Larry Demic, Arizona
	Sly Williams, Rhode Island
1978	Micheal Ray Richardson, Montana
1977	Ray Williams, Minnesota
1976	(no first-round pick)
1975	Eugene Short, Jackson St.
1974	(no first-round pick)

ORLANDO MAGIC

1996	Brian Evans, Indiana
1995	David Vaughn, Memphis
1994	Brooks Thompson, Oklahoma St.

1993	Chris Webber, Michigan
	Geert Hammink, Louisiana St.
1992	Shaquille O'Neal, Louisiana St.
1991	Brian Williams, Arizona
	Stanley Roberts, Louisiana St.
1990	Dennis Scott, Georgia Tech
1989	Nick Anderson, Illinois

PHILADELPHIA 76ERS

1996	Allen Iverson, Georgetown
1995	Jerry Stackhouse, North Carolina
1994	Sharone Wright, Clemson
	B.J. Tyler, Texas
1993	Shawn Bradley, Brigham Young
1992	Clarence Weatherspoon, S. Miss.
1991	(no first-round pick)
1990	(no first-round pick)
1989	Kenny Payne, Louisville
1988	Charles Smith, Pittsburgh
1987	Chris Welp, Washington
1986	(no first-round pick)
1985	Terry Catledge, S. Alabama
1984	Charles Barkley, Auburn
	Leon Wood, Fullerton St.
	Tom Sewell, Lamar
1983	Leo Rautins, Syracuse
1982	Mark McNamara, California
1981	Franklin Edwards, Cleveland St.
1980	Andrew Toney, S.W. Louisiana
	Monti Davis, Tennessee St.
1979	Jim Spanarkel, Duke
1978	(no first-round pick)
1977	Glenn Mosley, Seton Hall
1976	Terry Furlow, Michigan St.
1975	Darryl Dawkins, Evans High School
1974	Marvin Barnes, Providence

PHOENIX SUNS

1996	Steve Nash, Santa Clara
1995	Michael Finley, Wisconsin
	Mario Bennett, Arizona St.
1994	Wesley Person, Auburn
1993	Malcolm Mackey, Georgia Tech
1992	Oliver Miller, Arkansas
1991	(no first-round pick)
1990	Jayson Williams, St. John's
1989	Anthony Cook, Arizona
1988	Tim Perry, Temple
	Dan Majerle, Central Michigan
1987	Armon Gilliam, UNLV
1986	William Bedford, Memphis St.
1985	Ed Pinckney, Villanova
1984	Jay Humphries, Colorado
1983	(no first-round pick)
1982	David Thirdkill, Bradley
1981	Larry Nance, Clemson
1980	(no first-round pick)
1979	Kyle Macy, Kentucky
1978	Marty Byrnes, Syracuse
1977	Walter Davis, N. Carolina
1976	Ron Lee, Oregon

1975	Alvan Adams, Oklahoma
	Ricky Sobers, UNLV
1974	John Shumate, Notre Dame

PORTLAND TRAIL BLAZERS

1996	Jermaine O'Neal, Eau Claire HS
1995	Shawn Respert, Michigan St.
1994	Aaron McKie, Temple
1993	James Robinson, Alabama
1992	Dave Johnson, Syracuse
1991	(no first-round pick)
1990	Alaa Abdelnaby, Duke
1989	Byron Irvin, Missouri
1988	Mark Bryant, Seton Hall
1987	Ronnie Murphy, Jacksonville
1986	Walter Berry, St. John's
	Arvidas Sabonis, Soviet Union
1985	Terry Porter, Wisc.-Stevens Point
1984	Sam Bowie, Kentucky
	Bernard Thompson, Fresno St.
1983	Clyde Drexler, Houston
1982	Lafayette Lever, Arizona St.
1981	Jeff Lamp, Virginia
	Darnell Valentine, Kansas
1980	Ronnie Lester, Iowa
1979	Jim Paxson, Dayton
1978	Mychal Thompson, Minnesota
	Ron Brewer, Arkansas
1977	Rich Laurel, Hofstra
1976	Wally Walker, Virginia
1975	Lionel Hollins, Arizona St.
1974	Bill Walton, UCLA

SACRAMENTO KINGS

1996	Predrag Stojakovic, Greece
1995	Corliss Williamson, Arkansas
1994	Brian Grant, Xavier
1993	Bobby Hurley, Duke
1992	Walt Williams, Maryland
1991	Billy Owens, Syracuse
	Pete Chilcutt, N. Carolina
1990	Lionel Simmons, La Salle
	Travis Mays, Texas
	Duane Causwell, Temple
	Anthony Bonner, St. Louis
1989	Pervis Ellison, Louisville
1988	Ricky Berry, San Jose St.
1987	Kenny Smith, N. Carolina
1986	Harold Pressley, Villanova
1985	Joe Kleine, Arkansas
1984	Otis Thorpe, Providence
1983	Ennis Whatley, Alabama
1982	LaSalle Thompson, Texas
	Brook Steppe, Georgia Tech
1981	Steve Johnson, Oregon St.
	Kevin Loder, Alabama St.
1980	Hawkeye Whitney, N. Carolina St.
1979	Reggie King, Alabama
1978	Phil Ford, N. Carolina
1977	Otis Birdsong, Houston

1976	Richard Washington, UCLA
1975	Bill Robinzine, DePaul
	Bob Bigelow, Pennsylvania
1974	Scott Wedman, Colorado

SAN ANTONIO SPURS
1996	(no first-round pick)
1995	Cory Alexander, Virginia
1994	Bill Curley, Boston College
1993	(no first-round pick)
1992	Tracy Murray, UCLA
1991	(no first-round pick)
1990	Dwayne Schintzius, Florida
1989	Sean Elliott, Arizona
1988	Willie Anderson, Georgia
1987	David Robinson, Navy
	Greg Anderson, Houston
1986	Johnny Dawkins, Duke
1985	Alfredrick Hughes, Loyola (IL)
1984	Alvin Robertson, Arkansas
1983	John Paxson, Notre Dame
1982	(no first-round pick)
1981	(no first-round pick)
1980	Reggie Johnson, Tennessee
1979	Wiley Peck, Mississippi St.
1978	Frankie Sanders, Southern
1977	(no first-round pick)
1976	(no first-round pick)

SEATTLE SUPERSONICS
1996	(no first-round pick)
1995	Sherell Ford, Illinois-Chicago
1994	Carlos Rogers, Tennessee St.
1993	Ervin Johnson, New Orleans
1992	Doug Christie, Pepperdine
1991	Rich King, Nebraska
1990	Gary Payton, Oregon St.
1989	Dana Barros, Boston College
	Shawn Kemp, Trinity J.C.
1988	Gary Grant, Michigan
1987	Scottie Pippen, Central Arkansas
	Derrick McKey, Alabama
1986	(no first-round pick)
1985	Xavier McDaniel, Wichita St.
1984	(no first-round pick)
1983	Jon Sundvold, Missouri
1982	(no first-round pick)
1981	Danny Vranes, Utah
1980	Bill Hanzlik, Notre Dame
1979	James Bailey, Rutgers
	Vinnie Johnson, Baylor
1978	(no first-round pick)
1977	Jack Sikma, Illinois Wesleyan
1976	Bob Wilkerson, Indiana
1975	Frank Oleynick, Seattle
1974	Tom Burleson, N. Carolina St.

TORONTO RAPTORS
| 1996 | Marcus Camby, Massachusetts |
| 1995 | Damon Stoudamire, Arizona |

UTAH JAZZ
1996	Martin Muursepp, Estonia
1995	Greg Ostertag, Kansas
1994	(no first-round pick)
1993	Luther Wright, Seton Hall
1992	(no first-round pick)
1991	Eric Murdock, Providence
1990	(no first-round pick)
1989	Blue Edwards, E. Carolina
1988	Eric Leckner, Wyoming
1987	Jose Ortiz, Oregon St.
1986	Dell Curry, Virginia Tech
1985	Karl Malone, Louisiana Tech
1984	John Stockton, Gonzaga
1983	Thurl Bailey, N. Carolina St.
1982	Dominique Wilkins, Georgia
1981	Danny Schayes, Syracuse
1980	Darrell Griffith, Louisville
	John Duren, Georgetown
1979	Larry Knight, Loyola (IL)
1978	James Hardy, San Francisco
1977	(no first-round pick)
1976	(no first-round pick)
1975	Rich Kelley, Stanford
1974	(no first-round pick)

VANCOUVER GRIZZLIES
1996	Shareef Abdul-Rahim, California
	Roy Rogers, Alabama
1995	Bryant Reeves, Oklahoma St.

WASHINGTON BULLETS
1996	(no first-round pick)
1995	Rasheed Wallace, North Carolina
1994	Juwan Howard, Michigan
1993	Calbert Cheaney, Indiana
1992	Tom Gugliotta, N. Carolina St.
1991	LaBradford Smith, Louisville
1990	(no first-round pick)
1989	Tom Hammonds, Georgia Tech
1988	Harvey Grant, Oklahoma
1987	Muggsy Bogues, Wake Forest
1986	John Williams, Louisiana St.
	Anthony Jones, UNLV
1985	Kenny Green, Wake Forest
1984	Melvin Turpin, Kentucky
1983	Jeff Malone, Mississippi St.
	Randy Wittman, Indiana
1982	(no first-round pick)
1981	Frank Johnson, Wake Forest
1980	Wes Matthews, Wisconsin
1979	(no first-round pick)
1978	Roger Phegley, Bradley
	Dave Corzine, DePaul
1977	Greg Ballard, Oregon
	Bo Ellis, Marquette
1976	Mitch Kupchak, N. Carolina
	Larry Wright, Grambling
1975	Kevin Grevey, Kentucky
1974	Len Elmore, Maryland

N B A Year-By-Year Results

This section lists the final standings of every NBA season since its inception in 1946-47. Actually, in its first three years of existence, the league was called the BAA (Basketball Association of America), but it is still considered part of NBA history.

This section also includes league leaders in every major category since 1946-47. In its first four years of existence, the league kept track of only four statistics—scoring, assists, field goal percentage, and free throw percentage. In 1950-51, it began keeping track of rebounds. In 1973-74, the league added blocked shots and steals to the stat sheets. In 1979-80, the 3-point shot arrived in the NBA.

Because most statistical categories are based on averages, the NBA has had to establish qualifying criteria (e.g., a player can only qualify for the scoring championship if he appears in at least 70 games). Through the years, the league has frequently changed its qualifying criteria. These are the standards that players have had to meet in order to qualify:

Scoring
• 1946-47 to 1968-69: Based on total points, not on an average.
• 1969-70 to 1973-74: Minimum 70 games.
• 1974-75 to present: Minimum 70 games or 1,400 points.

Rebounds
• 1950-51 to 1968-69: Based on total rebounds, not on an average.
• 1969-70 to 1973-74: Minimum 70 games.
• 1974-75 to present: Minimum 70 games or 800 rebounds.

Assists
• 1946-47 to 1968-69: Based on total assists, not on an average.
• 1969-70 to 1973-74: Minimum 70 games.
• 1974-75 to present: Minimum 70 games or 400 assists.

Steals
• 1973-74: Minimum 70 games.
• 1974-75 to present: Minimum 70 games or 125 steals.

Blocked Shots
• 1973-74: Minimum 70 games.
• 1974-75 to present: Minimum 70 games or 100 blocks.

Field-Goal Pct.
The NBA has changed the qualifications for field-goal percentage 14 times. Since 1974-75, a player has needed to make 300 field goals to qualify.

Free-Throw Pct.
Since its inception, the league has changed the qualifications for free-throw percentage 13 times. Since 1974-75, a player has needed to make 125 free throws in order to qualify.

3-Point Field-Goal Pct.
• 1979-80 to 1989-90: Minimum 25 3-point field goals made.
• 1990-91 to 1993-94: Minimum 50 3-point field goals made.
• 1994 to present: Minimum 82 3-point field goals made.

This section also contains results of every playoff series of every season. The last year of this section, 1995-96, has been expanded to include more statistical information.

1946-47 FINAL STANDINGS

Eastern Division

	W	L	PCT.	GB
Washington	49	11	.817	
Philadelphia	35	25	.583	14
New York	33	27	.550	16
Providence	28	32	.467	21
Toronto	22	38	.367	27
Boston	22	38	.367	27

Western Division

	W	L	PCT.	GB
Chicago	39	22	.639	
St. Louis	38	23	.623	1
Cleveland	30	30	.500	8.5
Detroit	20	40	.333	18.5
Pittsburgh	15	45	.250	23.5

POINTS	AVG.	NO.
J. Fulks, PHI	23.2	1389
B. Feerick, WAS	16.3	926
S. Miasek, DET	14.9	895
E. Sadowski, TOR/CLE	16.5	877
M. Zaslofsky, CHI	14.4	877
E. Calverley, PRO	14.3	845
C. Halbert, CHI	12.7	773
J. Logan, STL	12.6	770
L. Mogus, CLE/TOR	13.0	753
C. Gunther, PIT	14.1	734

ASSISTS	AVG.	NO.
E. Calverley, PRO	3.4	202
K. Sailors, CLE	2.3	134

O. Schectman, NY	2.0	109
H. Dallmar, PHI	1.7	104
M. Rottner, CHI	1.7	93

FIELD-GOAL PCT.

Bob Feerick, WAS	.401
Ed Sadowski, TOR/CLE	.369
Earl Shannon, PRO	.339
Coulby Gunther, PIT	.336

FREE-THROW PCT.

Fred Scolari, WAS	.811
Tony Kapper, PIT/BOS	.795
Stan Stutz, NY	.782
Bob Feerick, WAS	.762

QUARTERFINALS
Philadelphia 2, St. Louis 1
New York 2, Cleveland 1

SEMIFINALS
Chicago 4, Washington 2
Philadelphia 2, New York 0

BAA FINALS
Philadelphia 4, Chicago 1

1947-48 FINAL STANDINGS

Eastern Division

	W	L	PCT.	GB
Philadelphia	27	21	.563	
New York	26	22	.542	1
Boston	20	28	.417	7
Providence	6	42	.125	21

Western Division

	W	L	PCT.	GB
St. Louis	29	19	.604	
Baltimore	28	20	.583	1
Chicago	28	20	.583	1
Washington	28	20	.583	1

POINTS	AVG.	NO.
M. Zaslofsky, CHI	21.0	1007
J. Fulks, PHI	22.1	949
E. Sadowski, BOS	19.4	910
B. Feerick, WAS	16.1	775
S. Miasek, CHI	14.9	716
C. Braun, NY	14.3	671
J. Logan, STL	13.4	644
J. Palmer, NY	13.0	622
R. Rocha, STL	12.7	611
F. Scolari, WAS	12.5	589

ASSISTS	AVG.	NO.
H. Dallmar, PHI	2.5	120
E. Calverley, PRO	2.5	119
J. Seminoff, CHI	1.8	89

C. Gilmur, CHI	1.6	77
A. Phillip, CHI	2.3	74

FIELD-GOAL PCT.

Bob Feerick, WAS	.340
Ed Sadowski, BOS	.323
Carl Braun, NY	.323
Max Zaslofsky, CHI	.323
Chick Reiser, BAL	.322

FREE-THROW PCT.

Bob Feerick, WAS	.788
Max Zaslofsky, CHI	.784
Joe Fulks, PHI	.762
Buddy Jeannette, BAL	.758
Howie Dallmar, PHI	.744

QUARTERFINALS
Baltimore 2, New York 1
Chicago 2, Boston 1

SEMIFINALS
Philadelphia 4, St. Louis 3
Baltimore 2, Chicago 0

BAA FINALS
Baltimore 4, Philadelphia 2

1948-49 FINAL STANDINGS

Eastern Division

	W	L	PCT.	GB
Washington	38	22	.633	
New York	32	28	.533	6
Baltimore	29	31	.483	9
Philadelphia	28	32	.467	10
Boston	25	35	.417	13
Providence	12	48	.200	26

Western Division

	W	L	PCT.	GB
Rochester	45	15	.750	
Minneapolis	44	16	.733	1
Chicago	38	22	.633	7
St. Louis	29	31	.483	16
Fort Wayne	22	38	.367	23
Indianapolis	18	42	.300	27

POINTS

	AVG.	NO.
G. Mikan, MIN	28.3	1698
J. Fulks, PHI	26.0	1560
M. Zaslofsky, CHI	20.6	1197
A. Risen, ROC	16.6	995
E. Sadowski, PHI	15.3	920
B. Smawley, STL	15.5	914
B. Davies, ROC	15.1	904
K. Sailors, PRO	15.8	899
C. Braun, NY	14.2	810
J. Logan, STL	14.1	803

ASSISTS

	AVG.	NO.
B. Davies, ROC	5.4	321
A. Phillip, CHI	5.3	319

E. Calverley, PRO	4.3	251
G. Senesky, PHI	3.9	233

FIELD-GOAL PCT.

Arnie Risen, ROC	.423
George Mikan, MIN	.416
Ed Sadowski, PHI	.405
Jim Pollard, MIN	.396
Red Rocha, STL	.389

FREE-THROW PCT.

Bob Feerick, WAS	.859
Max Zaslofsky, CHI	.840
Bob Wanzer, ROC	.823
Herm Schaefer, MIN	.817

EAST SEMIFINALS
Washington 2, Philadelphia 0
New York 2, Baltimore 1

EAST FINALS
Washington 2, New York 1

WEST SEMIFINALS
Rochester 2, St. Louis 0
Minneapolis 2, Chicago 0

WEST FINALS
Minneapolis 2, Rochester 0

BAA FINALS
Minneapolis 4, Washington 2

1949-50 FINAL STANDINGS

Eastern Division

	W	L	GB
Syracuse	51	13	
New York	40	28	13
Washington	32	36	21
Philadelphia	26	42	27
Baltimore	25	43	28
Boston	22	46	31

Western Division

	W	L	GB
Indianapolis	39	25	
Anderson	37	27	2
Tri-Cities	29	35	10
Sheboygan	22	40	16
Waterloo	19	43	19
Denver	11	51	27

Central Division

	W	L	GB
Minneapolis	51	17	
Rochester	51	17	
Fort Wayne	40	28	11
Chicago	40	28	11
St. Louis	26	42	25

POINTS

	AVG.	NO.
G. Mikan, MIN	27.4	1865
A. Groza, IND	23.4	1496
F. Brian, AND	17.8	1138
M. Zaslofsky, CHI	16.4	1115
E. Macauley, STL	16.1	1081

ASSISTS

	AVG.	NO.
D. McGuire, NY	5.7	386
A. Phillip, CHI	5.8	377

FIELD-GOAL PCT.

Alex Groza, IND	.478
Dick Mehen, WAT	.420

FREE-THROW PCT.

Max Zaslofsky, CHI	.843
Chick Reiser, WAS	.835

EAST SEMIFINALS
Syracuse 2, Philadelphia 0
New York 2, Washington 0

EAST FINALS
Syracuse 2, New York 1

CENTRAL SEMIFINALS
Minneapolis 2, Chicago 0
Fort Wayne 2, Rochester 0

CENTRAL FINALS
Minneapolis 2, Fort Wayne 0

WEST SEMIFINALS
Indianapolis 2, Sheboygan 1
Anderson 2, Tri-Cities 1

WEST FINALS
Anderson 2, Indianapolis 1

NBA SEMIFINALS
Minneapolis 2, Anderson 0

NBA FINALS
Minneapolis 4, Syracuse 2

1950-51 FINAL STANDINGS

Eastern Division

	W	L	PCT.	GB
Philadelphia	40	26	.606	
Boston	39	30	.565	2.5
New York	36	30	.545	4
Syracuse	32	34	.485	8
Baltimore	24	42	.364	16
Washington	10	25	.286	14.5

Western Division

	W	L	PCT.	GB
Minneapolis	44	24	.647	
Rochester	41	27	.603	3
Fort Wayne	32	36	.471	12
Indianapolis	31	37	.456	13
Tri-Cities	25	43	.368	19

POINTS

	AVG.	NO.
G. Mikan, MIN	28.4	1932
A. Groza, IND	21.7	1429
E. Macauley, BOS	20.4	1384
J. Fulks, PHI	18.7	1236
F. Brian, TC	16.8	1144
P. Arizin, PHI	17.2	1121
D. Schayes, SYR	17.0	1121
B. Beard, IND	16.8	1111

REBOUNDS

	AVG.	NO.
D. Schayes, SYR	16.4	1080
G. Mikan, MIN	14.1	958
H. Gallatin, NY	12.1	800
A. Risen, ROC	12.0	795

ASSISTS

	AVG.	NO.
A. Phillip, PHI	6.3	414
D. McGuire, NY	6.3	400
G. Senesky, PHI	5.3	342
B. Cousy, BOS	4.9	341

FIELD-GOAL PCT.

Alex Groza, IND	.470
Ed Macauley, BOS	.466
George Mikan, MIN	.428

FREE-THROW PCT.

Joe Fulks, PHI	.855
Belus Smawley, SYR/BAL	.850
Bob Wanzer, ROC	.850

EAST SEMIFINALS
Syracuse 2, Philadelphia 0
New York 2, Boston 0

EAST FINALS
New York 3, Syracuse 2

WEST SEMIFINALS
Minneapolis 2, Indian. 1
Rochester 2, Fort Wayne 1

WEST FINALS
Rochester 3, Minneapolis 1

NBA FINALS
Rochester 4, New York 3

1951-52 FINAL STANDINGS

Eastern Division

	W	L	PCT.	GB
Syracuse	40	26	.606	
Boston	39	27	.591	1
New York	37	29	.561	3
Philadelphia	33	33	.500	7
Boston	20	46	.303	20

Western Division

	W	L	PCT.	GB
Rochester	41	25	.621	
Minneapolis	40	26	.606	1
Indianapolis	34	32	.515	7
Fort Wayne	29	37	.439	12
Milwaukee	17	49	.258	24

POINTS

	AVG.	NO.
P. Arizin, PHI	25.4	1674
G. Mikan, MIN	23.8	1523
B. Cousy, BOS	21.7	1433
E. Macauley, BOS	19.2	1264
B. Davies, ROC	16.2	1052
F. Brian, FTW	15.9	1051
L. Foust, FTW	15.9	1047
Bob Wanzer, ROC	15.7	1033

REBOUNDS

	AVG.	NO.
L. Foust, FTW	13.3	880
M. Hutchins, MIL	13.3	880
G. Mikan, MIN	13.5	866
A. Risen, ROC	12.7	841

ASSISTS

	AVG.	NO.
A. Phillip, PHI	8.2	539
B. Cousy, BOS	6.7	441
B. Davies, ROC	6.0	390
D. McGuire, NY	6.1	388

FIELD-GOAL PCT.

Paul Arizin, PHI	.448
Harry Gallatin, NY	.442
Ed Macauley, BOS	.432

FREE-THROW PCT.

Bob Wanzer, ROC	.904
Al Cervi, SYR	.883
Bill Sharman, BOS	.859

EAST SEMIFINALS
Syracuse 2, Phil. 1
New York 2, Boston 1

EAST FINALS
New York 3, Syracuse 1

WEST SEMIFINALS
Rochester 2, Fort Wayne 0
Minneapolis 2, Indian. 0

WEST FINALS
Minneapolis 3, Roch. 1

NBA FINALS
Minneapolis 4, New York 3

1952-53 FINAL STANDINGS

Eastern Division

	W	L	PCT.	GB
New York	47	23	.671	
Syracuse	47	24	.662	.5
Boston	46	25	.648	1.5
Baltimore	16	54	.229	31
Philadelphia	12	57	.174	34.5

Western Division

	W	L	PCT.	GB
Minneapolis	48	22	.686	
Rochester	44	26	.629	4
Fort Wayne	36	33	.522	11.5
Indianapolis	28	43	.394	20.5
Milwaukee	27	44	.380	21.5

POINTS

	AVG.	NO.
N. Johnston, PHI	22.3	1564
G. Mikan, MIN	20.6	1442
B. Cousy, BOS	19.8	1407
E. Macauley, BOS	20.3	1402
D. Schayes, SYR	17.8	1262
B. Sharman, BOS	16.2	1147
J. Nichols, MIL	15.8	1090
V. Mikkelsen, MIN	15.0	1047
B. Davies, ROC	15.6	1029

REBOUNDS

	AVG.	NO.
G. Mikan, MIN	14.4	1007
N. Johnston, PHI	13.9	979
D. Schayes, SYR	13.0	920
H. Gallatin, NY	13.1	916

ASSISTS

	AVG.	NO.
B. Cousy, BOS	7.7	547
A. Phillip, PHI/FTW	5.7	397
G. King, SYR	5.1	364
D. McGuire, NY	4.9	296

FIELD-GOAL PCT.

Neil Johnston, PHI	.45242
Ed Macauley, BOS	.45236
Harry Gallatin, NY	.444

FREE-THROW PCT.

Bill Sharman, BOS	.850
Fred Scolari, FTW	.844
Dolph Schayes, SYR	.827

EAST SEMIFINALS
New York 2, Baltimore 0
Boston 2, Syracuse 0

EAST FINALS
New York 3, Boston 1

WEST SEMIFINALS
Minneapolis 2, Indian. 0
Fort Wayne 2, Rochester 1

WEST FINALS
Minneapolis 3, Fort Wayne 2

NBA FINALS
Minneapolis 4, New York 1

1953-54 FINAL STANDINGS

Eastern Division

	W	L	PCT.	GB
New York	44	28	.611	
Boston	42	30	.583	2
Syracuse	42	30	.583	2
Philadelphia	29	43	.403	15
Baltimore	16	56	.222	28

Western Division

	W	L	PCT.	GB
Minneapolis	46	26	.639	
Rochester	44	28	.611	2
Fort Wayne	40	32	.556	6
Milwaukee	21	51	.292	25

POINTS

	AVG.	NO.
N. Johnston, PHI	24.4	1759
B. Cousy, BOS	19.2	1383
E. Macauley, BOS	18.9	1344
G. Mikan, MIN	18.1	1306
R. Felix, BAL	17.6	1269
D. Schayes, SYR	17.1	1228
B. Sharman, BOS	16.0	1155
L. Foust, FTW	15.1	1090
C. Braun, NY	14.8	1062

REBOUNDS

	AVG.	NO.
H. Gallatin, NY	15.3	1098
G. Mikan, MIN	14.3	1028
L. Foust, FTW	13.4	967
R. Felix, BAL	13.3	958

ASSISTS

	AVG.	NO.
B. Cousy, BOS	7.2	518
A. Phillip, FTW	6.3	449
P. Seymour, SYR	5.1	364
D. McGuire, NY	5.2	354

FIELD-GOAL PCT.

Ed Macauley, BOS	.486
Bill Sharman, BOS	.450
Neil Johnston, PHI	.449

FREE-THROW PCT.

Bill Sharman, BOS	.844
Dolph Schayes, SYR	.827
Carl Braun, NY	.825

EAST ROUND ROBIN
Syracuse 4, Boston 2, N.Y. 0

EAST FINALS
Syracuse 2, Boston 0

WEST ROUND ROBIN
Minneapolis 3, Rochester 2,
Fort Wayne 0

WEST FINALS
Minneapolis 2, Rochester 1

NBA FINALS
Minneapolis 4, Syracuse 3

1954-55 FINAL STANDINGS

Eastern Division

	W	L	PCT.	GB
Syracuse	43	29	.597	
New York	38	34	.528	5
Boston	36	36	.500	7
Philadelphia	33	39	.458	10

Western Division

	W	L	PCT.	GB
Fort Wayne	43	29	.597	
Minneapolis	40	32	.556	3
Rochester	29	43	.403	14
Milwaukee	26	46	.361	17

POINTS

	AVG.	NO.
N. Johnston, PHI	22.7	1631
P. Arizin, PHI	21.0	1512
B. Cousy, BOS	21.2	1504
B. Pettit, MIL	20.4	1466
F. Selvy, BAL/MIL	19.0	1348
D. Schayes, SYR	18.8	1333
V. Mikkelsen, MIN	18.4	1327
C. Lovellette, MIN	18.7	1311
B. Sharman, BOS	18.4	1253
E. Macauley, BOS	17.6	1248

REBOUNDS

	AVG.	NO.
N. Johnston, PHI	15.1	1085
H. Gallatin, NY	13.8	995
B. Pettit, MIL	13.8	994
D. Schayes, SYR	12.3	887

ASSISTS

	AVG.	NO.
B. Cousy, BOS	7.8	557
D. McGuire, NY	7.6	542
A. Phillip, FTW	7.7	491
P. Seymour, SYR	6.7	483

FIELD-GOAL PCT.

Larry Foust, FTW	.487
Jack Coleman, ROC	.462
Neil Johnston, PHI	.440
Ray Felix, NY	.438

FREE-THROW PCT.

Bill Sharman, BOS	.897
Frank Brian, FTW	.851
Dolph Schayes, SYR	.833

EAST SEMIFINALS
Boston 2, New York 1

EAST FINALS
Syracuse 3, Boston 1

WEST SEMIFINALS
Minneapolis 2, Rochester 1

WEST FINALS
Fort Wayne 3, Minn. 1

NBA FINALS
Syracuse 4, Fort Wayne 3

1955-56 FINAL STANDINGS

Eastern Division

	W	L	PCT.	GB
Philadelphia	45	27	.625	
Boston	39	33	.542	6
Syracuse	35	37	.486	10
New York	35	37	.486	10

Western Division

	W	L	PCT.	GB
Fort Wayne	37	35	.514	
Minneapolis	33	39	.458	4
St. Louis	33	39	.458	4
Rochester	31	41	.431	6

POINTS

	AVG.	NO.
B. Pettit, STL	25.7	1849
P. Arizin, PHI	24.2	1741
N. Johnston, PHI	22.1	1547
C. Lovellette, MIN	21.5	1526
D. Schayes, SYR	20.4	1472
B. Sharman, BOS	19.9	1434
B. Cousy, BOS	18.8	1356
E. Macauley, BOS	17.5	1240
G. Yardley, FTW	17.4	1233
L. Foust, FTW	16.2	1166

REBOUNDS

	AVG.	NO.
B. Pettit, STL	16.2	1164
M. Stokes, ROC	16.3	1094
C. Lovellette, MIN	14.0	992
D. Schayes, SYR	12.4	891

ASSISTS

	AVG.	NO.
B. Cousy, BOS	8.9	642
J. George, PHI	6.3	457
S. Martin, MIN	6.2	445
A. Phillip, FTW	5.9	410

FIELD-GOAL PCT.

Neil Johnston, PHI	.457
Paul Arizin, PHI	.448
Larry Foust, FTW	.447
Ken Sears, NY	.438

FREE-THROW PCT.

Bill Sharman, BOS	.867
Dolph Schayes, SYR	.858
Dick Schnittker, MIN	.856

EAST SEMIFINALS
Syracuse 2, Boston 1

EAST FINALS
Philadelphia 3, Syracuse 2

WEST SEMIFINALS
St. Louis 2, Minneapolis 1

WEST FINALS
Fort Wayne 3, St. Louis 2

NBA FINALS
Philadelphia 4, Fort Wayne 1

1956-57 FINAL STANDINGS

Eastern Division

	W	L	PCT.	GB
Boston	44	28	.611	
Syracuse	38	34	.528	6
Philadelphia	37	35	.514	7
New York	36	36	.500	8

Western Division

	W	L	PCT.	GB
St. Louis	34	38	.472	
Minneapolis	34	38	.472	
Fort Wayne	34	38	.472	
Rochester	31	41	.431	3

POINTS — AVG. NO.
P. Arizin, PHI 25.6 1817
B. Pettit, STL 24.7 1755
D. Schayes, SYR.....22.5 1617
N. Johnston, PHI 22.8 1575
G. Yardley, FTW.......21.5 1547
C. Lovellette, MIN ...20.8 1434
B. Sharman, BOS....21.1 1413
B. Cousy, BOS 20.6 1319
E. Macauley, STL....16.5 1187
D. Garmaker, MIN ...16.3 1177

REBOUNDS — AVG. NO.
M. Stokes, ROC 17.4 1256
B. Pettit, STL 14.6 1037
D. Schayes, SYR.....14.0 1008
B. Russell, BOS.......19.6 943

ASSISTS — AVG. NO.
B. Cousy, BOS.......... 7.5 478
J. McMahon, STL..... 5.1 367
M. Stokes, ROC 4.6 331
J. George, PHI 4.6 307

FIELD-GOAL PCT.
Neil Johnston, PHI............ .447
Charles Share, STL............ .439
Jack Twyman, ROC .... .439
Bob Houbregs, FTW.......... .432

FREE-THROW PCT.
Bill Sharman, BOS .... .905
Dolph Schayes, SYR........ .904
Dick Garmaker, MIN.......... .839

EAST SEMIFINALS
Syracuse 2, Philadelphia 0

EAST FINALS
Boston 3, Syracuse 0

WEST SEMIFINALS
Minneapolis 2, Fort Wayne 0

WEST FINALS
St. Louis 3, Minn. 0

NBA FINALS
Boston 4, St. Louis 3

1957-58 FINAL STANDINGS

Eastern Division

	W	L	PCT.	GB
Boston	49	23	.681	
Syracuse	41	31	.569	8
Philadelphia	37	35	.514	12
New York	35	37	.486	14

Western Division

	W	L	PCT.	GB
St. Louis	41	31	.569	
Detroit	33	39	.458	8
Cincinnati	33	39	.458	8
Minneapolis	19	53	.264	22

POINTS — AVG. NO.
G. Yardley, DET 27.8 2001
D. Schayes, SYR.....24.9 1791
B. Pettit, STL 24.6 1719
C. Lovellette, CIN ...23.4 1659
P. Arizin, PHI 20.7 1406
B. Sharman, BOS....22.3 1402
C. Hagan, STL..........19.9 1391
N. Johnston, PHI 19.5 1388
K. Sears, NY............18.6 1342
V. Mikkelsen, MIN ...17.3 1248

REBOUNDS — AVG. NO.
B. Russell, BOS.......22.7 1564
B. Pettit, STL 17.4 1216
M. Stokes, CIN 18.1 1142
D. Schayes, SYR.....14.2 1022

ASSISTS — AVG. NO.
B. Cousy, BOS......... 7.1 463
D. McGuire, DET...... 6.6 454
M. Stokes, CIN......... 6.4 403
C. Braun, NY............ 5.5 393

FIELD-GOAL PCT.
Jack Twyman, CIN .... .452
Cliff Hagan, STL................ .443
Bill Russell, BOS .... .442
Ray Felix, NY .... .442

FREE-THROW PCT.
Dolph Schayes, SYR........ .904
Bill Sharman, BOS .... .893
Bob Cousy, BOS .... .850

EAST SEMIFINALS
Philadelphia 2, Syracuse 1

EAST FINALS
Boston 4, Philadelphia 1

WEST SEMIFINALS
Detroit 2, Cincinnati 0

WEST FINALS
St. Louis 4, Detroit 1

NBA FINALS
St. Louis 4, Boston 2

1958-59 FINAL STANDINGS

Eastern Division

	W	L	PCT.	GB
Boston	52	20	.722	
New York	40	32	.556	12
Syracuse	35	37	.486	17
Philadelphia	32	40	.444	20

Western Division

	W	L	PCT.	GB
St. Louis	49	23	.681	
Minneapolis	33	39	.458	16
Detroit	28	44	.389	21
Cincinnati	19	53	.264	30

POINTS	AVG.	NO.
B. Pettit, STL	29.2	2105
J. Twyman, CIN	25.8	1857
P. Arizin, PHI	26.4	1851
E. Baylor, MIN	24.9	1742
C. Hagan, STL	23.7	1707
D. Schayes, SYR	21.3	1534
K. Sears, NY	21.0	1488
B. Sharman, BOS	20.4	1466
B. Cousy, BOS	20.0	1297
R. Guerin, NY	18.2	1291

REBOUNDS	AVG.	NO.
B. Russell, BOS	23.0	1612
B. Pettit, STL	16.4	1182
E. Baylor, MIN	15.0	1050
J. Kerr, SYR	14.0	1008

ASSISTS	AVG.	NO.
B. Cousy, BOS	8.6	557
D. McGuire, DET	6.2	443
L. Costello, SYR	5.4	379
R. Guerin, NY	5.1	364

FIELD-GOAL PCT.

Ken Sears, NY	.490
Bill Russell, BOS	.457
Cliff Hagan, STL	.456
Clyde Lovellette, STL	.454

FREE-THROW PCT.

Bill Sharman, BOS	.932
Dolph Schayes, SYR	.864
Ken Sears, NY	.861
Bob Cousy, BOS	.855

EAST SEMIFINALS
Syracuse 2, New York 0

EAST FINALS
Boston 4, Syracuse 3

WEST SEMIFINALS
Minneapolis 2, Detroit 1

WEST FINALS
Minneapolis 4, St. Louis 2

NBA FINALS
Boston 4, Minneapolis 0

1959-60 FINAL STANDINGS

Eastern Division

	W	L	PCT.	GB
Boston	59	16	.787	
Philadelphia	49	26	.653	10
Syracuse	45	30	.600	14
New York	27	48	.360	32

Western Division

	W	L	PCT.	GB
St. Louis	46	29	.613	
Detroit	30	45	.400	16
Minneapolis	25	50	.333	21
Cincinnati	19	56	.253	27

POINTS	AVG.	NO.
W. Chamberlain, PHI	37.6	2707
J. Twyman, CIN	31.2	2338
E. Baylor, MIN	29.6	2074
B. Pettit, STL	26.1	1882
C. Hagan, STL	24.8	1859
G. Shue, DET	22.8	1712
D. Schayes, SYR	22.5	1689
T. Heinsohn, BOS	21.7	1629
R. Guerin, NY	21.8	1615
P. Arizin, PHI	22.3	1606

REBOUNDS	AVG.	NO.
W. Chamberlain, PHI	27.0	1941
B. Russell, BOS	24.0	1778
B. Pettit, STL	17.0	1221
E. Baylor, MIN	16.4	1150

ASSISTS	AVG.	NO.
B. Cousy, BOS	9.5	715
G. Rodgers, PHI	7.1	482
R. Guerin, NY	6.3	468
L. Costello, SYR	6.3	449

FIELD-GOAL PCT.

Ken Sears, NY	.477
Hal Greer, SYR	.476
Clyde Lovellette, STL	.468
Bill Russell, BOS	.467

FREE-THROW PCT.

Dolph Schayes, SYR	.893
Gene Shue, DET	.872
Ken Sears, NY	.868
Bill Sharman, BOS	.866

EAST SEMIFINALS
Philadelphia 2, Syrac. 1

EAST FINALS
Boston 4, Philadelphia 2

WEST SEMIFINALS
Minneapolis 2, Detroit 0

WEST FINALS
St. Louis 4, Minneapolis 3

NBA FINALS
Boston 4, St. Louis 3

1960-61 FINAL STANDINGS

Eastern Division

	W	L	PCT.	GB
Boston	57	22	.722	
Philadelphia	46	33	.582	11
Syracuse	38	41	.481	19
New York	21	58	.266	36

Western Division

	W	L	PCT.	GB
St. Louis	51	28	.646	
Los Angeles	36	43	.456	15
Detroit	34	45	.430	17
Cincinnati	33	46	.418	18

POINTS	AVG.	NO.
W. Chamberlain, PHI..	38.4	3033
E. Baylor, LA	34.8	2538
O. Robertson, CIN	30.5	2165
B. Pettit, STL	27.9	2120
J. Twyman, CIN	25.3	1997
D. Schayes, SYR	23.6	1868
W. Naulls, NY	23.4	1846
P. Arizin, PHI	23.2	1832
B. Howell, DET	23.6	1815
G. Shue, DET	22.6	1765

REBOUNDS	AVG.	NO.
W. Chamberlain, PHI	27.2	2149
B. Russell, BOS	23.9	1868
B. Pettit, STL	20.3	1540
E. Baylor, LA	19.8	1447

ASSISTS	AVG.	NO.
O. Robertson, CIN	9.7	690
G. Rodgers, PHI	8.7	677
B. Cousy, BOS	7.7	587
G. Shue, DET	6.8	530

FIELD-GOAL PCT.	
W. Chamberlain, PHI	.509
Jack Twyman, CIN	.488
Larry Costello, SYR	.482
Oscar Robertson, CIN	.473

FREE-THROW PCT.	
Bill Sharman, BOS	.921
Dolph Schayes, SYR	.868
Gene Shue, DET	.856
Frank Ramsey, BOS	.833

EAST SEMIFINALS
Syracuse 3, Phil. 0

EAST FINALS
Boston 4, Syracuse 1

WEST SEMIFINALS
Los Angeles 3, Detroit 2

WEST FINALS
St. Louis 4, Los Angeles 3

NBA FINALS
Boston 4, St. Louis 1

1961-62 FINAL STANDINGS

Eastern Division

	W	L	PCT.	GB
Boston	60	20	.750	
Philadelphia	49	31	.613	11
Syracuse	41	39	.513	19
New York	29	51	.363	31

Western Division

	W	L	PCT.	GB
Los Angeles	54	26	.675	
Cincinnati	43	37	.538	11
Detroit	37	43	.463	17
St. Louis	29	51	.363	25
Chicago	18	62	.225	36

POINTS	AVG.	NO.
W. Chamberlain, PHI	50.4	4029
W. Bellamy, CHI	31.6	2495
O. Robertson, CIN	30.8	2432
B. Pettit, STL	31.1	2429
J. West, LA	30.8	2310
R. Guerin, NY	29.5	2303
W. Naulls, NY	25.0	1877
E. Baylor, LA	38.3	1836
J. Twyman, CIN	22.9	1831

REBOUNDS	AVG.	NO.
W. Chamberlain, PHI	25.7	2052
B. Russell, BOS	23.6	1790
W. Bellamy, CHI	19.0	1500
B. Pettit, STL	18.7	1459

ASSISTS	AVG.	NO.
O. Robertson, CIN	11.4	899
G. Rodgers, PHI	7.9	663
B. Cousy, BOS	7.8	584
R. Guerin, NY	6.9	539

FIELD-GOAL PCT.	
Walt Bellamy, CHI	.519
W. Chamberlain, PHI	.506
Jack Twyman, CIN	.479
Oscar Robertson, CIN	.478

FREE-THROW PCT.	
Dolph Schayes, SYR	.896
Willie Naulls, NY	.842
Larry Costello, SYR	.837

EAST SEMIFINALS
Philadelphia 3, Syrac. 2

EAST FINALS
Boston 4, Philadelphia 3

WEST SEMIFINALS
Detroit 3, Cincinnati 1

WEST FINALS
Los Angeles 4, Detroit 2

NBA FINALS
Boston 4, Los Angeles 3

1962-63 FINAL STANDINGS

Eastern Division

	W	L	PCT.	GB
Boston	58	22	.725	
Syracuse	48	32	.600	10
Cincinnati	42	38	.525	16
New York	21	59	.263	37

Western Division

	W	L	PCT.	GB
Los Angeles	53	27	.663	
St. Louis	48	32	.600	5
Detroit	34	46	.425	19
San Francisco	31	49	.388	22
Chicago	25	55	.313	28

POINTS	AVG.	NO.
W. Chamberlain, SF	44.8	3586
E. Baylor, LA	34.0	2719
O. Robertson, CIN	28.3	2264
B. Pettit, STL	28.4	2241
W. Bellamy, CHI	27.9	2233
B. Howell, DET	22.7	1793
R. Guerin, NY	21.5	1701
J. Twyman, CIN	19.8	1586
H. Greer, SYR	19.5	1562

REBOUNDS	AVG.	NO.
W. Chamberlain, SF	24.3	1946
B. Russell, BOS	23.0	1843
W. Bellamy, CHI	16.4	1309
B. Pettit, STL	15.1	1191

ASSISTS	AVG.	NO.
G. Rodgers, SF	10.4	825
O. Robertson, CIN	9.5	758
B. Cousy, BOS	6.8	515
S. Green, CHI	5.8	422

FIELD-GOAL PCT.

W. Chamberlain, SF	.528
Walt Bellamy, CHI	.527
Oscar Robertson, CIN	.518
Bailey Howell, DET	.516

FREE-THROW PCT.

Larry Costello, SYR	.881
Richie Guerin, NY	.848
Elgin Baylor, LA	.837

EAST SEMIFINALS
Cincinnati 3, Syracuse 2

EAST FINALS
Boston 4, Cincinnati 3

WEST SEMIFINALS
St. Louis 3, Detroit 1

WEST FINALS
Los Angeles 4, St. Louis 3

NBA FINALS
Boston 4, Los Angeles 2

1963-64 FINAL STANDINGS

Eastern Division

	W	L	PCT.	GB
Boston	59	21	.738	
Cincinnati	55	25	.688	4
Philadelphia	34	46	.425	25
New York	22	58	.275	37

Western Division

	W	L	PCT.	GB
San Francisco	48	32	.600	
St. Louis	46	34	.575	2
Los Angeles	42	38	.525	6
Baltimore	31	49	.388	17
Detroit	23	57	.288	25

POINTS	AVG.	NO.
W. Chamberlain, SF	36.9	2948
O. Robertson, CIN	31.4	2480
B. Pettit, STL	27.4	2190
W. Bellamy, BAL	27.0	2159
J. West, LA	28.7	2064
E. Baylor, LA	25.4	1983
H. Greer, PHI	23.3	1865
B. Howell, DET	21.6	1666
T. Dischinger, BAL	20.8	1662

REBOUNDS	AVG.	NO.
B. Russell, BOS	24.7	1930
W. Chamberlain, SF	22.3	1787
J. Lucas, CIN	17.4	1375
W. Bellamy, BAL	17.0	1361

ASSISTS	AVG.	NO.
O. Robertson, CIN	11.0	868
G. Rodgers, SF	7.0	556
K. Jones, BOS	5.1	407
J. West, LA	5.6	403

FIELD-GOAL PCT.

Jerry Lucas, CIN	.527
W. Chamberlain, SF	.524
Walt Bellamy, BAL	.513
Terry Dischinger, BAL	.496

FREE-THROW PCT.

Oscar Robertson, CIN	.853
Jerry West, LA	.832
Hal Greer, PHI	.829

EAST SEMIFINALS
Cincinnati 3, Philadelphia 2

EAST FINALS
Boston 4, Cincinnati 1

WEST SEMIFINALS
St. Louis 3, Los Angeles 2

WEST FINALS
San Francisco 4, St. L. 3

NBA FINALS
Boston 4, San Francisco 1

1964-65 FINAL STANDINGS

Eastern Division

	W	L	PCT.	GB
Boston	62	18	.715	
Cincinnati	48	32	.600	14
Philadelphia	40	40	.500	22
New York	31	49	.388	31

Western Division

	W	L	PCT.	GB
Los Angeles	49	31	.613	
St. Louis	45	35	.563	4
Baltimore	37	43	.463	12
Detroit	31	49	.388	18
San Francisco	17	63	.213	32

POINTS	AVG.	NO.
W. Chamber., SF/PHI	34.7	2534
J. West, LA	31.0	2292
O. Robertson, CIN	30.4	2279
S. Jones, BOS	25.9	2070
E. Baylor, LA	27.1	2009
W. Bellamy, BAL	24.8	1981
W. Reed, NY	19.5	1560
B. Howell, BAL	19.2	1534
T. Dischinger, DET	18.2	1456

REBOUNDS	AVG.	NO.
B. Russell, BOS	24.1	1878
W. Chamber., SF/PHI	22.9	1673
N. Thurmond, SF	18.1	1395
J. Lucas, CIN	20.0	1321

ASSISTS	AVG.	NO.
O. Robertson, CIN	11.5	861
G. Rodgers, SF	7.3	565
K. Jones, BOS	5.6	437
L. Wilkens, STL	5.5	431

FIELD-GOAL PCT.	
W. Chamberlain, SF/PHI	.510
Walt Bellamy, BAL	.509
Jerry Lucas, CIN	.498
Jerry West, LA	.497

FREE-THROW PCT.	
Larry Costello, PHI	.877
Oscar Robertson, CIN	.839
Howard Komives, NY	.835

EAST SEMIFINALS
Philadelphia 3, Cincinnati 1

EAST FINALS
Boston 4, Philadelphia 3

WEST SEMIFINALS
Baltimore 3, St. Louis 1

WEST FINALS
Los Angeles 4, Baltimore 2

NBA FINALS
Boston 4, Los Angeles 1

1965-66 FINAL STANDINGS

Eastern Division

	W	L	PCT.	GB
Philadelphia	55	25	.688	
Boston	54	26	.675	1
Cincinnati	45	35	.563	10
New York	30	50	.375	25

Western Division

	W	L	PCT.	GB
Los Angeles	45	35	.563	
Baltimore	38	42	.475	7
St. Louis	36	44	.450	9
San Francisco	35	45	.438	10
Detroit	22	58	.275	23

POINTS	AVG.	NO.
W. Chamberlain, PHI	33.5	2649
J. West, LA	31.3	2476
O. Robertson, CIN	31.3	2378
R. Barry, SF	25.7	2059
W. Bellamy, BAL/NY	22.8	1820
H. Greer, PHI	22.7	1819
D. Barnett, NY	23.1	1729
J. Lucas, CIN	21.5	1697
Z. Beaty, STL	20.7	1656

REBOUNDS	AVG.	NO.
W. Chamberlain, PHI	24.6	1943
B. Russell, BOS	22.8	1779
J. Lucas, CIN	21.1	1668
N. Thurmond, SF	18.0	1312

ASSISTS	AVG.	NO.
O. Robertson, CIN	11.1	847
G. Rodgers, SF	10.7	846
K. Jones, BOS	6.3	503
J. West, LA	6.1	480

FIELD-GOAL PCT.	
W. Chamberlain, PHI	.540
John Green, NY/BAL	.536
Walt Bellamy, BAL/NY	.506
Al Attles, SF	.503

FREE-THROW PCT.	
Larry Siegfried, BOS	.881
Rick Barry, SF	.862
Howard Komives, NY	.861

EAST SEMIFINALS
Boston 3, Cincinnati 2

EAST FINALS
Boston 4, Philadelphia 1

WEST SEMIFINALS
St. Louis 3, Baltimore 0

WEST FINALS
Los Angeles 4, St. Louis 3

NBA FINALS
Boston 4, Los Angeles 3

1966-67 FINAL STANDINGS

Eastern Division

	W	L	PCT.	GB
Philadelphia	68	13	.840	
Boston	60	21	.741	8
Cincinnati	39	42	.481	29
New York	36	45	.444	32
Baltimore	20	61	.247	48

Western Division

	W	L	PCT.	GB
San Francisco	44	37	.543	
St. Louis	39	42	.481	5
Los Angeles	36	45	.444	8
Chicago	33	48	.407	11
Detroit	30	51	.370	14

POINTS	AVG.	NO.
R. Barry, SF	35.6	2775
O. Robertson, CIN	30.5	2412
W. Chamberlain, PHI	24.1	1956
J. West, LA	28.7	1892
E. Baylor, LA	26.6	1862
H. Greer, PHI	22.1	1765
J. Havlicek, BOS	21.4	1733
W. Reed, NY	20.9	1628
B. Howell, BOS	20.0	1621

REBOUNDS	AVG.	NO.
W. Chamberlain, PHI	24.2	1957
B. Russell, BOS	21.0	1700
J. Lucas, CIN	19.1	1547
N. Thurmond, SF	21.3	1382

ASSISTS	AVG.	NO.
G. Rodgers, CHI	11.2	908
O. Robertson, CIN	10.7	845
W. Chamberlain, PHI	7.8	630
B. Russell, BOS	5.8	472

FIELD-GOAL PCT.	
W. Chamberlain, PHI	.683
Walt Bellamy, NY	.521
Bailey Howell, BOS	.512
Oscar Robertson, CIN	.493

FREE-THROW PCT.	
Adrian Smith, CIN	.903
Rick Barry, SF	.884
Jerry West, LA	.878

EAST SEMIFINALS
Philadelphia 3, Cincinnati 1
Boston 3, New York 1

EAST FINALS
Philadelphia 4, Boston 1

WEST SEMIFINALS
San Francisco 3, L.A. 0
St. Louis 3, Chicago 0

WEST FINALS
San Francisco 4, St. Louis 2

NBA FINALS
Philadelphia 4, S.F. 2

1967-68 FINAL STANDINGS

Eastern Division

	W	L	PCT.	GB
Philadelphia	62	20	.756	
Boston	54	28	.659	8
New York	43	39	.524	19
Detroit	40	42	.488	22
Cincinnati	39	43	.476	23
Baltimore	36	46	.439	26

Western Division

	W	L	PCT.	GB
St. Louis	56	26	.683	
Los Angeles	52	30	.634	4
San Francisco	43	39	.524	13
Chicago	29	53	.354	27
Seattle	23	59	.280	33
San Diego	15	67	.183	41

POINTS	AVG.	NO.
D. Bing, DET	27.1	2142
E. Baylor, LA	26.0	2002
W. Chamberlain, PHI	24.3	1992
E. Monroe, BAL	24.3	1991
H. Greer, PHI	24.1	1976
O. Robertson, CIN	29.2	1896
W. Hazzard, SEA	23.9	1894
J. Lucas, CIN	21.4	1760

REBOUNDS	AVG.	NO.
W. Chamberlain, PHI	23.8	1952
J. Lucas, CIN	19.0	1560
B. Russell, BOS	18.6	1451
C. Lee, SF	13.9	1141

ASSISTS	AVG.	NO.
W. Chamberlain, PHI	8.6	702
L. Wilkens, STL	8.3	679
O. Robertson, CIN	9.7	633
D. Bing, DET	6.4	509

FIELD-GOAL PCT.	
W. Chamberlain, PHI	.595
Walt Bellamy, NY	.541
Jerry Lucas, CIN	.519

FREE-THROW PCT.	
Oscar Robertson, CIN	.873
Larry Siegfried, BOS	.868
Dave Gambee, SD	.847

EAST SEMIFINALS
Philadelphia 4, New York 2
Boston 4, Detroit 2

EAST FINALS
Boston 4, Philadelphia 3

WEST SEMIFINALS
San Francisco 4, St. Louis 2
Los Angeles 4, Chicago 1

WEST FINALS
Los Angeles 4, S.F. 0

NBA FINALS
Boston 4, Los Angeles 2

1968-69 FINAL STANDINGS

Eastern Division

	W	L	PCT.	GB
Baltimore	57	25	.695	
Philadelphia	55	27	.671	2
New York	54	28	.659	3
Boston	48	34	.585	9
Cincinnati	41	41	.500	16
Detroit	32	50	.390	25
Milwaukee	27	55	.329	30

Western Division

	W	L	PCT.	GB
Los Angeles	55	27	.671	
Atlanta	48	34	.585	7
San Francisco	41	41	.500	14
San Diego	37	45	.451	18
Chicago	33	49	.402	22
Seattle	30	52	.366	25
Phoenix	16	66	.195	39

POINTS

	AVG.	NO.
E. Hayes, SD	28.4	2327
E. Monroe, BAL	25.8	2065
B. Cunningham, PHI	24.8	2034
B. Rule, SEA	24.0	1965
O. Robertson, CIN	24.7	1955
G. Goodrich, PHO	23.8	1931
H. Greer, PHI	23.1	1896
E. Baylor, LA	24.8	1881

REBOUNDS

	AVG.	NO.
W. Chamberlain, LA	21.1	1712
W. Unseld, BAL	18.2	1491
B. Russell, BOS	19.3	1484

ASSISTS

	AVG.	NO.
O. Robertson, CIN	9.8	772
L. Wilkens, SEA	8.2	674
W. Frazier, NY	7.9	635
G. Rodgers, MIL	6.9	561

FIELD-GOAL PCT.

W. Chamberlain, LA	.583
Jerry Lucas, CIN	.551
Willis Reed, NY	.521

FREE-THROW PCT.

Larry Siegfried, BOS	.864
Jeff Mullins, SF	.843
Jon McGlocklin, MIL	.842

EAST SEMIFINALS
New York 4, Baltimore 0
Boston 4, Philadelphia 1

EAST FINALS
Boston 4, New York 2

WEST SEMIFINALS
Los Angeles 4, San Fran. 2
Atlanta 4, San Diego 2

WEST FINALS
Los Angeles 4, Atlanta 2

NBA FINALS
Boston 4, Los Angeles 3

1969-70 FINAL STANDINGS

Eastern Division

	W	L	PCT.	GB
New York	60	22	.732	
Milwaukee	56	26	.683	4
Baltimore	50	32	.610	10
Philadelphia	42	40	.512	18
Cincinnati	36	46	.439	24
Boston	34	48	.415	26
Detroit	31	51	.378	29

Western Division

	W	L	PCT.	GB
Atlanta	48	34	.585	
Los Angeles	46	36	.561	2
Chicago	39	43	.476	9
Phoenix	39	43	.476	9
Seattle	36	46	.439	12
San Francisco	30	52	.366	18
San Diego	27	55	.329	21

SCORING

Jerry West, LA	31.2
Lew Alcindor, MIL	28.8
Elvin Hayes, SD	27.5
Billy Cunningham, PHI	26.1
Lou Hudson, ATL	25.4
Connie Hawkins, PHO	24.6
Bob Rule, SEA	24.6
John Havlicek, BOS	24.2

REBOUNDS

Elvin Hayes, SD	16.9
Wes Unseld, BAL	16.7
Lew Alcindor, MIL	14.5

ASSISTS

Len Wilkens, SEA	9.1
Walt Frazier, NY	8.2
Clem Haskins, CHI	7.6

FIELD-GOAL PCT.

Johnny Green, CIN	.559
Darrall Imhoff, PHI	.540
Lou Hudson, ATL	.531

FREE-THROW PCT.

Flynn Robinson, MIL	.898
Chet Walker, CHI	.850
Jeff Mullins, SF	.847

EAST SEMIFINALS
New York 4, Baltimore 3
Milwaukee 4, Philadelphia 1

EAST FINALS
New York 4, Milwaukee 1

WEST SEMIFINALS
Atlanta 4, Chicago 1
Los Angeles 4, Phoenix 3

WEST FINALS
Los Angeles 4, Atlanta 0

NBA FINALS
New York 4, Los Angeles 3

1970-71
FINAL STANDINGS

Eastern Conference
Atlantic Division

	W	L	PCT.	GB
New York	52	30	.634	
Philadelphia	47	35	.573	5
Boston	44	38	.537	8
Buffalo	22	60	.268	30

Central Division

	W	L	PCT.	GB
Baltimore	42	40	.512	
Atlanta	36	46	.439	6
Cincinnati	33	49	.402	9
Cleveland	15	67	.183	27

Western Conference
Midwest Division

	W	L	PCT.	GB
Milwaukee	66	16	.805	
Chicago	51	31	.622	15
Phoenix	48	34	.585	18
Detroit	45	37	.549	21

Pacific Division

	W	L	PCT.	GB
Los Angeles	48	34	.585	
San Francisco	41	41	.500	7
San Diego	40	42	.488	8
Seattle	38	44	.463	10
Portland	29	53	.354	19

SCORING
Lew Alcindor, MIL 31.7
John Havlicek, BOS 28.9
Elvin Hayes, SD 28.7
Dave Bing, DET 27.0
Lou Hudson, ATL 26.8
Bob Love, CHI....................25.2
Geoff Petrie, POR..............24.8
Pete Maravich, ATL 23.2
Billy Cunningham, PHI 23.0
Tom Van Arsdale, CIN 22.9
Chet Walker, CHI 22.0
Dick Van Arsdale, PHO......21.9
Walt Frazier, NY.................21.7
Earl Monroe, BAL...............21.4
Jo Jo White, BOS...............21.3
Archie Clark, PHI 21.3
Willis Reed, NY..................20.9
Connie Hawkins, PHO 20.9
Jeff Mullins, SF 20.8

REBOUNDS
W. Chamberlain, LA 18.2
Wes Unseld, BAL...............16.9
Elvin Hayes, SD 16.6
Lew Alcindor, MIL 16.0
Jerry Lucas, SF..................15.8
Bill Bridges, ATL 15.0
Dave Cowens, BOS...........15.0
Tom Boerwinkle, CHI 13.8
Nate Thurmond, SF 13.8
Willis Reed, NY..................13.7

ASSISTS
Norm Van Lier, CIN...........10.1
Len Wilkens, SEA............... 9.2
Oscar Robertson, MIL 8.2
John Havlicek, BOS 7.5
Walt Frazier, NY................. 6.7
Walt Hazzard, ATL 6.3
Ron Williams, SF............... 5.9
Nate Archibald, CIN.......... 5.5
Archie Clark, PHI.............. 5.4
Dave Bing, DET................. 5.0

FIELD-GOAL PCT.
Johnny Green, CIN............ .587
Lew Alcindor, MIL.............. .577
W. Chamberlain, LA .... .545
Jon McGlocklin, MIL.......... .535
Dick Snyder, SEA.............. .531
Greg Smith, MIL................ .512
Bob Dandridge, MIL .... .509
Wes Unseld, BAL .... .501
Jerry Lucas, SF .... .498

FREE-THROW PCT.
Chet Walker, CHI .... .859
Oscar Robertson, MIL ...... .850
Ron Williams, SF............... .844
Jeff Mullins, SF................. .844
Dick Snyder, SEA.............. .837
Stan McKenzie, POR .... .836
Jerry West, LA................... .832
Jimmy Walker, DET........... .831

EAST SEMIFINALS
New York 4, Atlanta 1
Baltimore 4, Philadelphia 3

EAST FINALS
New York 112, Baltimore 111
New York 107, Baltimore 88
Baltimore 114, New York 88
Baltimore 101, New York 80
New York 89, Baltimore 84
Baltimore 113, New York 96
Baltimore 93, New York 91

WEST SEMIFINALS
Milwaukee 4, San Francisco 1
Los Angeles 4, Chicago 3

WEST FINALS
Milwaukee 106, L.A. 85
Milwaukee 91, Los Angeles 73
Los Angeles 118, Milw. 107
Milwaukee 117, L.A. 94
Milwaukee 116, L.A. 98

NBA FINALS
Milwaukee 98, Baltimore 88
Milwaukee 102, Baltimore 83
Milwaukee 107, Baltimore 99
Milwaukee 118, Baltimore 106

1971-72
FINAL STANDINGS

Eastern Conference
Atlantic Division

	W	L	PCT.	GB
Boston	56	26	.683	
New York	48	34	.585	8
Philadelphia	30	52	.366	26
Buffalo	22	60	.268	34

Central Division

	W	L	PCT.	GB
Baltimore	38	44	.463	
Atlanta	36	46	.439	2
Cincinnati	30	52	.366	8
Cleveland	23	59	.280	15

Western Conference
Midwest Division

	W	L	PCT.	GB
Milwaukee	63	19	.768	
Chicago	57	25	.695	6
Phoenix	49	33	.598	14
Detroit	26	56	.317	37

Pacific Division

	W	L	PCT.	GB
Los Angeles	69	13	.841	
Golden State	51	31	.622	18
Seattle	47	35	.573	22
Houston	34	48	.415	35
Portland	18	64	.220	51

SCORING

K. Abdul-Jabbar, MIL	34.8
Nate Archibald, CIN	28.2
John Havlicek, BOS	27.5
Spencer Haywood, SEA	26.2
Gail Goodrich, LA	25.9
Bob Love, CHI	25.8
Jerry West, LA	25.8
Bob Lanier, DET	25.7
Archie Clark, BAL	25.2
Elvin Hayes, HOU	25.2
Lou Hudson, ATL	24.7
Sidney Wicks, POR	24.5
Billy Cunningham, PHI	23.3
Walt Frazier, NY	23.2
Jo Jo White, BOS	23.1
Jack Marin, BAL	22.3
Chet Walker, CHI	22.0
Jeff Mullins, GS	21.5
Nate Thurmond, GS	21.4
Cazzie Russell, GS	21.4

REBOUNDS

W. Chamberlain, LA	19.2
Wes Unseld, BAL	17.6
K. Abdul-Jabbar, MIL	16.6
Nate Thurmond, GS	16.1
Dave Cowens, BOS	15.2
Elmore Smith, BUF	15.2
Elvin Hayes, HOU	14.6
Clyde Lee, GS	14.5
Bob Lanier, DET	14.2

ASSISTS

Jerry West, LA	9.7
Len Wilkens, SEA	9.6
Nate Archibald, CIN	9.2
Archie Clark, BAL	8.0
John Havlicek, BOS	7.5
Norm Van Lier, CIN/CHI	6.9
Billy Cunningham, PHI	5.9
Jeff Mullins, GS	5.9
Walt Frazier, NY	5.8
Walt Hazzard, BUF	5.6

FIELD-GOAL PCT.

W. Chamberlain, LA	.649
K. Abdul-Jabbar, MIL	.574
Walt Bellamy, ATL	.545
Dick Snyder, SEA	.529
Jerry Lucas, NY	.512
Walt Frazier, NY	.512
Jon McGlocklin, MIL	.510
Chet Walker, CHI	.505
Lucius Allen, MIL	.505

FREE-THROW PCT.

Jack Marin, BAL	.894
Calvin Murphy, HOU	.890
Gail Goodrich, LA	.850
Chet Walker, CHI	.847
Dick Van Arsdale, PHO	.845
Stu Lantz, HOU	.838
John Havlicek, BOS	.834
Cazzie Russell, GS	.833

EAST SEMIFINALS
Boston 4, Atlanta 2
New York 4, Baltimore 2

EAST FINALS
New York 116, Boston 94
New York 106, Boston 105
Boston 115, New York 109
New York 116, Boston 98
New York 111, Boston 103

WEST SEMIFINALS
Los Angeles 4, Chicago 0
Milwaukee 4, Golden St. 1

WEST FINALS
Milwaukee 93, Los Angeles 72
Los Angeles 135, Milw. 134
Los Angeles 108, Milw. 105
Milwaukee 114, L.A. 88
Los Angeles 115, Milw. 90
Los Angeles 104, Milw. 100

NBA FINALS
New York 114, Los Angeles 92
Los Angeles 106, New York 92
Los Angeles 107, New York 96
Los Angeles 116, N.Y. 111 (OT)
Los Angeles 114, N.Y. 100

1972-73
FINAL STANDINGS

Eastern Conference
Atlantic Division

	W	L	PCT.	GB
Boston	68	14	.829	
New York	57	25	.695	11
Buffalo	21	61	.256	47
Philadelphia	9	73	.110	59

Central Division

	W	L	PCT.	GB
Baltimore	52	30	.634	
Atlanta	46	36	.561	6
Houston	33	49	.402	19
Cleveland	32	50	.390	20

Western Conference
Midwest Division

	W	L	PCT.	GB
Milwaukee	60	22	.732	
Chicago	51	31	.622	9
Detroit	40	42	.488	20
K.C.-Omaha	36	46	.439	24

Pacific Division

	W	L	PCT.	GB
Los Angeles	60	22	.732	
Golden State	47	35	.573	13
Phoenix	38	44	.463	22
Seattle	26	56	.317	34
Portland	21	61	.256	39

SCORING

Nate Archibald, KCO.........34.0
K. Abdul-Jabbar, MIL........30.2
Spencer Haywood, SEA ...29.2
Lou Hudson, ATL..............27.1
Pete Maravich, ATL..........26.1
Charlie Scott, PHO............25.3
Geoff Petrie, POR.............24.9
Gail Goodrich, LA..............23.9
Sidney Wicks, POR...........23.8
Bob Lanier, DET...............23.8
John Havlicek, BOS...........23.8
Bob Love, CHI...................23.1
Dave Bing, DET.................22.4
Rick Barry, GS...................22.3
Elvin Hayes, BAL...............21.2
Walt Frazier, NY................21.1
Austin Carr, CLE................20.5
Dave Cowens, BOS...........20.5
Len Wilkens, CLE..............20.5

REBOUNDS

W. Chamberlain, LA...........18.6
Nate Thurmond, GS...........17.1
Dave Cowens, BOS...........16.2
K. Abdul-Jabbar, MIL..........16.1
Wes Unseld, BAL...............15.9
Bob Lanier, DET................14.9
Elvin Hayes, BAL...............14.5
Walt Bellamy, ATL..............13.0
Paul Silas, BOS.................13.0
Spencer Haywood, SEA ...12.9

ASSISTS

Nate Archibald, KCO........11.4
Len Wilkens, CLE...............8.4
Dave Bing, DET..................7.8
Oscar Robertson, MIL.........7.5
Norm Van Lier, CHI.............7.1
Pete Maravich, ATL.............6.9
John Havlicek, BOS.............6.6
Herm Gilliam, ATL...............6.3
Charlie Scott, PHO..............6.1
Jo Jo White, BOS................6.1

FIELD-GOAL PCT.

W. Chamberlain, LA..........727
Matt Guokas, KCO............570
K. Abdul-Jabbar, MIL.........554
Curtis Rowe, DET..............519
Jim Fox, SEA....................515
Jerry Lucas, NY................513
Mike Riordan, BAL............510
Archie Clark, BAL..............507
Bob Kauffman, BUF..........505

FREE-THROW PCT.

Rick Barry, GS..................902
Calvin Murphy, HOU.........888
Mike Newlin, HOU.............886
Jimmy Walker, HOU..........884
Bill Bradley, NY................871
Cazzie Russell, GS...........864
Dick Snyder, SEA.............861
Dick Van Arsdale, PHO 859

EAST SEMIFINALS

Boston 4, Atlanta 2
New York 4, Baltimore 1

EAST FINALS

Boston 134, New York 108
New York 129, Boston 96
New York 98, Boston 91
New York 117, Bost. 110 (2OT)
Boston 98, New York 97
Boston 110, New York 100
New York 94, Boston 78

WEST SEMIFINALS

Los Angeles 4, Chicago 3
Golden St. 4, Milwaukee 2

WEST FINALS

Los Angeles 101, G.S. 99
Los Angeles 104, G.S. 93
Los Angeles 126, G.S. 70
Golden St. 117, L.A. 109
Los Angeles 128, G.S. 118

NBA FINALS

Los Angeles 115, N.Y. 112
New York 99, Los Angeles 95
New York 87, Los Angeles 83
New York 103, Los Angeles 98
New York 102, Los Angeles 93

1973-74
FINAL STANDINGS

Eastern Conference
Atlantic Division

	W	L	PCT.	GB
Boston	56	26	.683	
New York	49	33	.598	7
Buffalo	42	40	.512	14
Philadelphia	25	57	.305	31

Central Division

	W	L	PCT.	GB
Capital	47	35	.573	
Atlanta	35	47	.427	12
Houston	32	50	.390	15
Cleveland	29	53	.354	18

Western Conference
Midwest Division

	W	L	PCT.	GB
Milwaukee	59	23	.720	
Chicago	54	28	.659	5
Detroit	52	30	.634	7
K.C.-Omaha	33	49	.402	26

Pacific Division

	W	L	PCT.	GB
Los Angeles	47	35	.573	
Golden State	44	38	.537	3
Seattle	36	46	.439	11
Phoenix	30	52	.366	17
Portland	27	55	.329	20

SCORING
Bob McAdoo, BUF	30.6
Pete Maravich, ATL	27.7
K. Abdul-Jabbar, MIL	27.0
Gail Goodrich, LA	25.3
Rick Barry, GS	25.1
Rudy Tomjanovich, HOU	24.5
Geoff Petrie, POR	24.3
Spencer Haywood, SEA	23.5
John Havlicek, BOS	22.6
Bob Lanier, DET	22.5

REBOUNDS
Elvin Hayes, CAP	18.1
Dave Cowens, BOS	15.7
Bob McAdoo, BUF	15.1
K. Abdul-Jabbar, MIL	14.5
Happy Hairston, LA	13.5
Spencer Haywood, SEA	13.4
Sam Lacey, KCO	13.4
Bob Lanier, DET	13.3
Clifford Ray, CHI	12.2

ASSISTS
Ernie DiGregorio, BUF	8.2
Calvin Murphy, HOU	7.4
Len Wilkens, CLE	7.1
Walt Frazier, NY	6.9
Dave Bing, DET	6.9
Norm Van Lier, CHI	6.9
Oscar Robertson, MIL	6.4
Rick Barry, GS	6.1

STEALS
Larry Steele, POR	2.68
Steve Mix, PHI	2.59
Randy Smith, BUF	2.48
Jerry Sloan, CHI	2.38
Rick Barry, GS	2.11
Phil Chenier, CAP	2.04

BLOCKED SHOTS
Elmore Smith, LA	4.85
K. Abdul-Jabbar, MIL	3.49
Bob McAdoo, BUF	3.32
Bob Lanier, DET	3.04
Elvin Hayes, CAP	2.96
Garfield Heard, BUF	2.84

FIELD-GOAL PCT.
Bob McAdoo, BUF	.547
K. Abdul-Jabbar, MIL	.539
Rudy Tomjanovich, HOU	.536
Calvin Murphy, HOU	.522
Butch Beard, GS	.512
Clifford Ray, CHI	.511

FREE-THROW PCT.
Ernie DiGregorio, BUF	.902
Rick Barry, GS	.899
Jeff Mullins, GS	.875
Chet Walker, CHI	.875
Bill Bradley, NY	.874
Calvin Murphy, HOU	.868

EAST SEMIFINALS
Boston 4, Buffalo 2
New York 4, Capital 3

EAST FINALS
Boston 113, New York 88
Boston 111, New York 99
New York 103, Boston 100
Boston 98, New York 91
Boston 105, New York 94

WEST SEMIFINALS
Milwaukee 4, Los Angeles 1
Chicago 4, Detroit 3

WEST FINALS
Milwaukee 101, Chicago 85
Milwaukee 113, Chicago 111
Milwaukee 113, Chicago 90
Milwaukee 115, Chicago 99

NBA FINALS
Boston 98, Milwaukee 83
Milwaukee 105, Bos. 96 (OT)
Boston 95, Milwaukee 83
Milwaukee 97, Boston 89
Boston 96, Milwaukee 87
Milwaukee 102, Bos. 101 (2OT)
Boston 102, Milwaukee 87

1974-75
FINAL STANDINGS

Eastern Conference
Atlantic Division

	W	L	PCT.	GB
Boston	60	22	.732	
Buffalo	49	33	.598	11
New York	40	42	.488	20
Philadelphia	34	48	.415	26

Central Division

	W	L	PCT.	GB
Washington	60	22	.732	
Houston	41	41	.500	19
Cleveland	40	42	.488	20
Atlanta	31	61	.378	29
New Orleans	23	59	.280	37

Western Conference
Midwest Division

	W	L	PCT.	GB
Chicago	47	35	.573	
K.C.-Omaha	44	38	.537	3
Detroit	40	42	.488	7
Milwaukee	38	44	.463	9

Pacific Division

	W	L	PCT.	GB
Golden State	48	34	.585	
Seattle	43	39	.524	5
Portland	38	44	.463	10
Phoenix	32	50	.390	16
Los Angeles	30	52	.366	18

SCORING
Bob McAdoo, BUF 34.5
Rick Barry, GS 30.6
K. Abdul-Jabbar, MIL 30.0
Nate Archibald, KCO........26.5
Charlie Scott, PHO...........24.3
Bob Lanier, DET 24.0
Elvin Hayes, WAS.............23.0
Gail Goodrich, LA..............22.6
Spencer Haywood, SEA ...22.4
Fred Carter, PHI................21.9

REBOUNDS
Wes Unseld, WAS 14.8
Dave Cowens, BOS...........14.7
Sam Lacey, KCO 14.2
Bob McAdoo, BUF 14.1
K. Abdul-Jabbar, MIL 14.0
Happy Hairston, LA............12.8
Paul Silas, BOS 12.5
Elvin Hayes, WAS.............12.2
Bob Lanier, DET 12.0

ASSISTS
Kevin Porter, WAS 8.0
Dave Bing, DET................. 7.7
Nate Archibald, KCO 6.8
Randy Smith, BUF 6.5
Pete Maravich, NO 6.2
Rick Barry, GS................... 6.2
Slick Watts, SEA 6.1

STEALS
Rick Barry, GS 2.85
Walt Frazier, NY...............2.44
Larry Steele, POR............2.41
Slick Watts, SEA...............2.32
Fred Brown, SEA 2.31
Phil Chenier, WAS 2.29

BLOCKED SHOTS
K. Abdul-Jabbar, MIL 3.26
Elmore Smith, LA.............2.92
Nate Thurmond, CHI.........2.44
Elvin Hayes, WAS............2.28
Bob Lanier, DET 2.26
Bob McAdoo, BUF 2.12

FIELD-GOAL PCT.
Don Nelson, BOS .... .539
Butch Beard, GS .... .528
Rudy Tomjanovich, HOU... .525
K. Abdul-Jabbar, MIL......... .513
Bob McAdoo, BUF............ .512
Kevin Kunnert, HOU......... .512

FREE-THROW PCT.
Rick Barry, GS.................. .904
Calvin Murphy, HOU 883
Bill Bradley, NY .... .873
Nate Archibald, KCO .... .872
Jim Price, LA/MIL .... .871
John Havlicek, BOS .... .870

EAST FIRST ROUND
Houston 2, New York 1

EAST SEMIFINALS
Washington 4, Buffalo 3
Boston 4, Houston 1

EAST FINALS
Washington 4, Boston 2

WEST FIRST ROUND
Seattle 2, Detroit 1

WEST SEMIFINALS
Golden St. 4, Seattle 2
Chicago 4, K.C.-Omaha 2

WEST FINALS
Golden St. 4, Chicago 3

NBA FINALS
Golden St. 101, Washington 95
Golden St. 92, Washington 91
Golden St. 109, Wash. 101
Golden St. 96, Washington 95

1975-76
FINAL STANDINGS

Eastern Conference
Atlantic Division

	W	L	PCT.	GB
Boston	54	28	.659	
Buffalo	46	36	.561	8
Philadelphia	46	36	.561	8
New York	38	44	.463	16

Central Division

	W	L	PCT.	GB
Cleveland	49	33	.598	
Washington	48	34	.585	1
Houston	40	42	.488	9
New Orleans	38	44	.463	11
Atlanta	29	53	.354	20

Western Conference
Midwest Division

	W	L	PCT.	GB
Milwaukee	38	44	.463	
Detroit	36	46	.439	2
Kansas City	31	51	.378	7
Chicago	24	58	.293	14

Pacific Division

	W	L	PCT.	GB
Golden State	59	23	.720	
Seattle	43	39	.524	16
Phoenix	42	40	.512	17
Los Angeles	40	42	.488	19
Portland	37	45	.451	22

SCORING
Bob McAdoo, BUF 31.1
K. Abdul-Jabbar, LA.........27.7
Pete Maravich, NO.........25.9
Nate Archibald, KC 24.8
Fred Brown, SEA............23.1
George McGinnis, PHI 23.0
Randy Smith, BUF.........21.8
John Drew, ATL 21.6
Bob Dandridge, MIL.........21.5
Rick Barry, GS 21.0

REBOUNDS
K. Abdul-Jabbar, LA..........16.9
Dave Cowens, BOS.........16.0
Wes Unseld, WAS 13.3
Paul Silas, BOS 12.7
Sam Lacey, KC 12.6
George McGinnis, PHI 12.6
Bob McAdoo, BUF 12.4
Elmore Smith, MIL............11.4
Spencer Haywood, NY......11.3

ASSISTS
Slick Watts, SEA 8.1
Nate Archibald, KC............ 7.9
Calvin Murphy, HOU 7.3
Norm Van Lier, CHI........... 6.6
Rick Barry, GS.................. 6.1
Dave Bing, WAS................ 6.0
Randy Smith, BUF............ 5.9

STEALS
Slick Watts, SEA 3.18
George McGinnis, PHI 2.57
Paul Westphal, PHO 2.56
Rick Barry, GS 2.49
Chris Ford, DET...............2.17
Larry Steele, POR............2.10

BLOCKED SHOTS
K. Abdul-Jabbar, LA.........4.12
Elmore Smith, MIL............3.05
Elvin Hayes, WAS............2.53
Harvey Catchings, PHI.....2.19
George Johnson, GS 2.12
Bob McAdoo, BUF 2.05

FIELD-GOAL PCT.
Wes Unseld, WAS ..... .56085
John Shumate, BUF ..... .56081
Jim McMillian, BUF............ .536
Bob Lanier, DET............. .532
K. Abdul-Jabbar, LA .... .529
Elmore Smith, MIL............ .518

FREE-THROW PCT.
Rick Barry, GS................. .923
Calvin Murphy, HOU .... .907
Cazzie Russell, LA .... .892
Bill Bradley, NY............... .878
Fred Brown, SEA............. .869
Mike Newlin, HOU .... .865

EAST FIRST ROUND
Buffalo 2, Philadelphia 1

EAST SEMIFINALS
Boston 4, Buffalo 2
Cleveland 4, Washington 3

EAST FINALS
Boston 4, Cleveland 2

WEST FIRST ROUND
Detroit 2, Milwaukee 1

WEST SEMIFINALS
Golden St. 4, Detroit 2
Phoenix 4, Seattle 2

WEST FINALS
Phoenix 4, Golden St. 3

NBA FINALS
Boston 98, Phoenix 87
Boston 105, Phoenix 90
Phoenix 105, Boston 98
Phoenix 109, Boston 107
Boston 128, Phoe. 126 (3OT)
Boston 87, Phoenix 80

1976-77
FINAL STANDINGS

Eastern Conference
Atlantic Division

	W	L	PCT.	GB
Philadelphia	50	32	.610	
Boston	44	38	.537	6
N.Y. Knicks	40	42	.488	10
Buffalo	30	52	.366	20
N.Y. Nets	22	60	.288	28

Central Division

	W	L	PCT.	GB
Houston	49	33	.598	
Washington	48	34	.585	1
San Antonio	44	38	.537	5
Cleveland	43	39	.524	6
New Orleans	35	47	.427	14
Atlanta	31	51	.378	18

Western Conference
Midwest Division

	W	L	PCT.	GB
Denver	50	32	.610	
Detroit	44	38	.537	6
Chicago	44	38	.537	6
Kansas City	40	42	.488	10
Indiana	36	46	.439	14
Milwaukee	30	52	.366	20

Pacific Division

	W	L	PCT.	GB
Los Angeles	53	29	.646	
Portland	49	33	.598	4
Golden State	46	36	.561	7
Seattle	40	42	.488	13
Phoenix	34	48	.415	19

SCORING

Pete Maravich, NO	31.1
Billy Knight, IND	26.6
K. Abdul-Jabbar, LA	26.2
David Thompson, DEN	25.9
Bob McAdoo, BUF/NYK	25.8
Bob Lanier, DET	25.3
John Drew, ATL	24.2
Elvin Hayes, WAS	23.7
George Gervin, SA	23.1
Dan Issel, DEN	22.3

REBOUNDS

Bill Walton, POR	14.4
K. Abdul-Jabbar, LA	13.3
Moses Malone, BUF/HOU	13.1
Artis Gilmore, CHI	13.0
Bob McAdoo, BUF/NYK	12.9
Elvin Hayes, WAS	12.5
Swen Nater, MIL	12.0
George McGinnis, PHI	11.5

ASSISTS

Don Buse, IND	8.5
Slick Watts, SEA	8.0
Norm Van Lier, CHI	7.8
Kevin Porter, DET	7.3
Tom Henderson, ATL/WAS	6.9
Rick Barry, GS	6.0
Jo Jo White, BOS	6.0

STEALS

Don Buse, IND	3.47
Brian Taylor, KC	2.76
Slick Watts, SEA	2.71
Quinn Buckner, MIL	2.43
Mike Gale, SA	2.33
Bobby Jones, DEN	2.27

BLOCKED SHOTS

Bill Walton, POR	3.25
K. Abdul-Jabbar, LA	3.18
Elvin Hayes, WAS	2.68
Artis Gilmore, CHI	2.48
Caldwell Jones, PHI	2.44
George Johnson, GS/BUF	2.27

FIELD-GOAL PCT.

K. Abdul-Jabbar, LA	.579
Mitch Kupchak, WAS	.572
Bobby Jones, DEN	.570
George Gervin, SA	.544
Bob Lanier, DET	.534
Bob Gross, POR	.529

FREE-THROW PCT.

Ernie DiGregorio, BUF	.945
Rick Barry, GS	.916
Calvin Murphy, HOU	.886
Mike Newlin, HOU	.885
Fred Brown, SEA	.884

EAST FIRST ROUND

Washington 2, Cleveland 1
Boston 2, San Antonio 0

EAST SEMIFINALS

Philadelphia 4, Boston 3
Houston 4, Washington 2

EAST FINALS

Philadelphia 4, Houston 2

WEST FIRST ROUND

Portland 2, Chicago 1
Golden St. 2, Detroit 1

WEST SEMIFINALS

Los Angeles 4, Golden St. 3
Portland 4, Denver 2

WEST FINALS

Portland 4, Los Angeles 0

NBA FINALS

Philadelphia 107, Portland 101
Philadelphia 107, Portland 89
Portland 129, Philadelphia 107
Portland 130, Philadelphia 98
Portland 110, Philadelphia 104
Portland 109, Philadelphia 107

1977-78
FINAL STANDINGS

Eastern Conference
Atlantic Division

	W	L	PCT.	GB
Philadelphia	55	27	.671	
New York	43	39	.524	12
Boston	32	50	.390	23
Buffalo	27	55	.329	28
New Jersey	24	58	.293	31

Central Division

	W	L	PCT.	GB
San Antonio	52	30	.634	
Washington	44	38	.537	8
Cleveland	43	39	.524	9
Atlanta	41	41	.500	11
New Orleans	39	43	.476	13
Houston	28	54	.341	24

Western Conference
Midwest Division

	W	L	PCT.	GB
Denver	48	34	.585	
Milwaukee	44	38	.537	4
Chicago	40	42	.488	8
Detroit	38	44	.463	10
Indiana	31	51	.378	17
Kansas City	31	51	.378	17

Pacific Division

	W	L	PCT.	GB
Portland	58	24	.707	
Phoenix	49	33	.598	9
Seattle	47	35	.573	11
Los Angeles	45	37	.549	13
Golden State	43	39	.524	15

SCORING
George Gervin, SA 27.22
David Thompson, DEN 27.15
Bob McAdoo, NY 26.5
K. Abdul-Jabbar, LA 25.8
Calvin Murphy, HOU 25.6
Paul Westphal, PHO 25.2
Randy Smith, BUF 24.6
Bob Lanier, DET 24.5
Walter Davis, PHO............24.2
Bernard King, NJ 24.2

REBOUNDS
Truck Robinson, NO 15.7
Moses Malone, HOU..........15.0
Dave Cowens, BOS 14.0
Elvin Hayes, WAS.............13.3
Swen Nater, BUF 13.2
Artis Gilmore, CHI 13.1
K. Abdul-Jabbar, LA 12.9
Bob McAdoo, NY 12.8

ASSISTS
Kevin Porter, DET/NJ............10.2
John Lucas, HOU 9.4
Ricky Sobers, IND 7.4
Norm Nixon, LA 6.8
Norm Van Lier, CHI 6.8
Henry Bibby, PHI............... 5.7

STEALS
Ron Lee, PHO...................2.74
Gus Williams, SEA............2.34
Quinn Buckner, MIL 2.29
Mike Gale, SA...................2.27
Don Buse, PHO.................2.26
Foots Walker, CLE.............2.17

BLOCKED SHOTS
George Johnson, NJ 3.38
K. Abdul-Jabbar, LA..........2.98
Tree Rollins, ATL...............2.73
Bill Walton, POR...............2.52
Billy Paultz, SA..................2.43
Artis Gilmore, CHI 2.21

FIELD-GOAL PCT.
Bobby Jones, DEN .... .578
Darryl Dawkins, PHI .... .575
Artis Gilmore, CHI .... .559
K. Abdul-Jabbar, LA .... .550
Alex English, MIL............... .542

FREE-THROW PCT.
Rick Barry, GS.................. .924
Calvin Murphy, HOU .... .918
Fred Brown, SEA.............. .898
Mike Newlin, HOU .... .874
Scott Wedman, KC .... .870

EAST FIRST ROUND
Washington 2, Atlanta 0
New York 2, Cleveland 0

EAST SEMIFINALS
Philadelphia 4, New York 0
Washington 4, San Antonio 2

EAST FINALS
Washington 4, Philadelphia 2

WEST FIRST ROUND
Seattle 2, Los Angeles 1
Milwaukee 2, Phoenix 0

WEST SEMIFINALS
Seattle 4, Portland 2
Denver 4, Milwaukee 3

WEST FINALS
Seattle 4, Denver 2

NBA FINALS
Seattle 106, Washington 102
Washington 106, Seattle 98
Seattle 93, Washington 92
Washington 120, Seat. 116(OT)
Seattle 98, Washington 94
Washington 117, Seattle 82
Washington 105, Seattle 99

1978-79
FINAL STANDINGS

Eastern Conference
Atlantic Division

	W	L	PCT.	GB
Washington	54	28	.659	
Philadelphia	47	35	.573	7
New Jersey	37	45	.451	17
New York	31	51	.378	23
Boston	29	53	.354	25

Central Division

	W	L	PCT.	GB
San Antonio	48	34	.585	
Houston	47	35	.573	1
Atlanta	46	36	.561	2
Cleveland	30	52	.366	18
Detroit	30	52	.366	18
New Orleans	26	56	.317	22

Western Conference
Midwest Division

	W	L	PCT.	GB
Kansas City	48	34	.585	
Denver	47	35	.573	1
Indiana	38	44	.463	10
Milwaukee	38	44	.463	10
Chicago	31	51	.378	17

Pacific Division

	W	L	PCT.	GB
Seattle	52	30	.634	
Phoenix	50	32	.610	2
Los Angeles	47	35	.573	5
Portland	45	37	.549	7
San Diego	43	39	.524	9
Golden State	38	44	.463	14

SCORING
George Gervin, SA............29.6
Lloyd Free, SD.................28.8
Marques Johnson, MIL 25.6
Bob McAdoo, NY/BOS 24.8
Moses Malone, HOU 24.8
David Thompson, DEN 24.0
Paul Westphal, PHO 24.0
K. Abdul-Jabbar, LA 23.8
Artis Gilmore, CHI............23.7
Walter Davis, PHO............23.6

REBOUNDS
Moses Malone, HOU.........17.6
Rich Kelley, NO................12.8
K. Abdul-Jabbar, LA.........12.8
Artis Gilmore, CHI............12.7
Jack Sikma, SEA 12.4
Elvin Hayes, WAS.............12.1
Robert Parish, GS.............12.1

ASSISTS
Kevin Porter, DET 13.4
John Lucas, GS 9.3
Norm Nixon, LA...................9.0
Phil Ford, KC......................8.6
Paul Westphal, PHO 6.5
Rick Barry, HOU 6.3

STEALS
M.L. Carr, DET 2.46
Ed Jordan, NJ 2.45
Norm Nixon, LA................2.45
Foots Walker, CLE............2.36
Phil Ford, KC....................2.20
Randy Smith, SD 2.16

BLOCKED SHOTS
K. Abdul-Jabbar, LA..........3.95
George Johnson, NJ.........3.24
Tree Rollins, ATL..............3.14
Robert Parish, GS.............2.86
Terry Tyler, DET 2.45

FIELD-GOAL PCT.
Cedric Maxwell, BOS .... .584
K. Abdul-Jabbar, LA .... .577
Wes Unseld, WAS............. .577
Artis Gilmore, CHI .... .575
Swen Nater, SD................ .569

FREE-THROW PCT.
Rick Barry, HOU................ .947
Calvin Murphy, HOU......... .928
Fred Brown, SEA.............. .888
Robert Smith, DEN........... .883
Ricky Sobers, IND .... .882

EAST FIRST ROUND
Philadelphia 2, New Jersey 0
Atlanta 2, Houston 0

EAST SEMIFINALS
Washington 4, Atlanta 3
San Antonio 4, Philadelphia 3

EAST FINALS
Washington 4, San Antonio 3

WEST FIRST ROUND
Phoenix 2, Portland 1
Los Angeles 2, Denver 1

WEST SEMIFINALS
Seattle 4, Los Angeles 1
Phoenix 4, Kansas City 1

WEST FINALS
Seattle 4, Phoenix 3

NBA FINALS
Washington 99, Seattle 97
Seattle 92, Washington 82
Seattle 105, Washington 95
Seattle 114, Wash. 112 (OT)
Seattle 97, Washington 93

1979-80
FINAL STANDINGS

Eastern Conference
Atlantic Division

	W	L	PCT.	GB
Boston	61	21	.744	
Philadelphia	59	23	.720	2
Washington	39	43	.476	22
New York	39	43	.476	22
New Jersey	34	48	.415	27

Central Division

	W	L	PCT.	GB
Atlanta	50	32	.610	
Houston	41	41	.500	9
San Antonio	41	41	.500	9
Indiana	37	45	.451	13
Cleveland	37	45	.451	13
Detroit	16	66	.195	34

Western Conference
Midwest Division

	W	L	PCT.	GB
Milwaukee	49	33	.598	
Kansas City	47	35	.573	2
Denver	30	52	.366	19
Chicago	30	52	.366	19
Utah	24	58	.293	25

Pacific Division

	W	L	PCT.	GB
Los Angeles	60	22	.732	
Seattle	56	26	.683	4
Phoenix	55	27	.671	5
Portland	38	44	.463	22
San Diego	35	47	.427	25
Golden State	24	58	.293	36

SCORING
George Gervin, SA............33.1
Lloyd Free, SD.................30.2
Adrian Dantley, UTA..........28.0
Julius Erving, PHI.............26.9
Moses Malone, HOU.........25.8
K. Abdul-Jabbar, LA.........24.8
Dan Issel, DEN................23.8
Elvin Hayes, WAS............23.0
Otis Birdsong, KC............22.7
Mike Mitchell, CLE 22.2

REBOUNDS
Swen Nater, SD 15.0
Moses Malone, HOU.........14.5
Wes Unseld, WAS 13.3
Caldwell Jones, PHI..........11.9
Jack Sikma, SEA 11.1

ASSISTS
Micheal Richardson, NY ...10.1
Nate Archibald, BOS 8.4
Foots Walker, CLE 8.0
Norm Nixon, LA 7.8
John Lucas, GS................. 7.5

STEALS
Micheal Richardson, NY ...3.23
Ed Jordan, NJ 2.72

Dudley Bradley, IND 2.57
Gus Williams, SEA............2.44
Magic Johnson, LA 2.43

BLOCKED SHOTS
K. Abdul-Jabbar, LA.........3.41
George Johnson, NJ..........3.19
Tree Rollins, ATL 2.98
Terry Tyler, DET 2.68
Elvin Hayes, WAS.............2.33

FIELD-GOAL PCT.
Cedric Maxwell, BOS .... .609
K. Abdul-Jabbar, LA .... .604
Artis Gilmore, CHI .... .595
Adrian Dantley, UTA......... .576
Tom Boswell, DEN/UTA .... .564

FREE-THROW PCT.
Rick Barry, HOU............... .935
Calvin Murphy, HOU .... .897
Ron Boone, UTA .... .893
Paul Silas, SA.................. .887

3-PT. FIELD-GOAL PCT.
Fred Brown, SEA.............. .443
Chris Ford, BOS .... .427
Larry Bird, BOS .... .406
John Roche, DEN............. .380

EAST FIRST ROUND
Philadelphia 2, Washington 0
Houston 2, San Antonio 1

EAST SEMIFINALS
Boston 4, Houston 0
Philadelphia 4, Atlanta 1

EAST FINALS
Philadelphia 4, Boston 1

WEST FIRST ROUND
Seattle 2, Portland 1
Phoenix 2, Kansas City 1

WEST SEMIFINALS
Los Angeles 4, Phoenix 1
Seattle 4, Milwaukee 3

WEST FINALS
Los Angeles 4, Seattle 1

NBA FINALS
Los Angeles 109, Phil. 102
Philadelphia 107, L.A. 104
Los Angeles 111, Phil. 101
Philadelphia 105, L.A. 102
Los Angeles 108, Phil. 103
Los Angeles 123, Phil. 107

1980-81
FINAL STANDINGS

Eastern Conference
Atlantic Division

	W	L	PCT.	GB
Boston	62	20	.756	
Philadelphia	62	20	.756	
New York	50	32	.610	12
Washington	39	43	.476	23
New Jersey	24	58	.293	38

Central Division

	W	L	PCT.	GB
Milwaukee	60	22	.732	
Chicago	45	37	.549	15
Indiana	44	38	.537	16
Atlanta	31	51	.378	29
Cleveland	28	54	.341	32
Detroit	21	61	.256	39

Western Conference
Midwest Division

	W	L	PCT.	GB
San Antonio	52	30	.634	
Kansas City	40	42	.488	12
Houston	40	42	.488	12
Denver	37	45	.451	15
Utah	28	54	.341	24
Dallas	15	67	.183	37

Pacific Division

	W	L	PCT.	GB
Phoenix	57	25	.695	
Los Angeles	54	28	.659	3
Portland	45	37	.549	12
Golden State	39	43	.476	18
San Diego	36	46	.439	21
Seattle	34	48	.415	23

SCORING
Adrian Dantley, UTA 30.7
Moses Malone, HOU.........27.8
George Gervin, SA............27.1
K. Abdul-Jabbar, LA............26.2
David Thompson, DEN 25.5
Otis Birdsong, KC 24.6
Julius Erving, PHI.............24.6
Mike Mitchell, CLE 24.5
Lloyd Free, GS..................24.1
Alex English, DEN.............23.8

REBOUNDS
Moses Malone, HOU.........14.8
Swen Nater, SD 12.4
Larry Smith, GS 12.1
Larry Bird, BOS.................10.9
Jack Sikma, SEA 10.4

ASSISTS
Kevin Porter, WAS 9.1
Norm Nixon, LA 8.8
Phil Ford, KC 8.8
Micheal Richardson, NY 7.9
Nate Archibald, BOS 7.7

STEALS
Magic Johnson, LA 3.43
Micheal Richardson, NY ...2.94

Quinn Buckner, MIL 2.40
Maurice Cheeks, PHI 2.38
Ray Williams, NY 2.34

BLOCKED SHOTS
George Johnson, SA........3.39
Tree Rollins, ATL 2.93
K. Abdul-Jabbar, LA..........2.85
Robert Parish, BOS 2.61
Artis Gilmore, CHI 2.41

FIELD-GOAL PCT.
Artis Gilmore, CHI .... .670
Darryl Dawkins, PHI .... .607
Cedric Maxwell, BOS .... .588
Bernard King, GS .... .588
K. Abdul-Jabbar, LA .... .574

FREE-THROW PCT.
Calvin Murphy, HOU .... .958
Ricky Sobers, CHI .... .935
Mike Newlin, NJ .... .888
Jim Spanarkel, DAL........... .887

3-PT. FIELD-GOAL PCT.
Brian Taylor, SD .... .383
Freeman Williams, SD....... .340
Joe Hassett, DAL/GS.......... .340
Mike Bratz, CLE .... .337

EAST FIRST ROUND
Philadelphia 2, Indiana 0
Chicago 2, New York 0

EAST SEMIFINALS
Boston 4, Chicago 0
Philadelphia 4, Milwaukee 3

EAST FINALS
Boston 4, Philadelphia 3

WEST FIRST ROUND
Houston 2, Los Angeles 1
Kansas City 2, Portland 1

WEST SEMIFINALS
Kansas City 4, Phoenix 3
Houston 4, San Antonio 3

WEST FINALS
Houston 4, Kansas City 1

NBA FINALS
Boston 98, Houston 95
Houston 92, Boston 90
Boston 94, Houston 71
Houston 91, Boston 86
Boston 109, Houston 80
Boston 102, Houston 91

1981-82
FINAL STANDINGS

Eastern Conference
Atlantic Division

	W	L	PCT.	GB
Boston	63	19	.768	
Philadelphia	58	24	.707	5
New Jersey	44	38	.537	19
Washington	43	39	.524	20
New York	33	49	.402	30

Central Division

	W	L	PCT.	GB
Milwaukee	55	27	.671	
Atlanta	42	40	.512	13
Detroit	39	43	.476	16
Indiana	35	47	.427	20
Chicago	34	48	.415	21
Cleveland	15	67	.183	40

Western Conference
Midwest Division

	W	L	PCT.	GB
San Antonio	48	34	.585	
Denver	46	36	.561	2
Houston	46	36	.561	2
Kansas City	30	52	.366	18
Dallas	28	54	.341	20
Utah	25	57	.305	23

Pacific Division

	W	L	PCT.	GB
Los Angeles	57	25	.695	
Seattle	52	30	.634	5
Phoenix	46	36	.561	11
Golden State	45	37	.549	12
Portland	42	40	.512	15
San Diego	17	65	.207	40

SCORING
George Gervin, SA.............32.3
Moses Malone, HOU........31.1
Adrian Dantley, UTA.........30.3
Alex English, DEN............25.4
Julius Erving, PHI.............24.4
K. Abdul-Jabbar, LA.........23.9
Gus Williams, SEA............23.4
Bernard King, GS.............23.2
World B. Free, GS.............22.9
Larry Bird, BOS................22.9

REBOUNDS
Moses Malone, HOU........14.7
Jack Sikma, SEA 12.7
Buck Williams, NJ 12.3
Mychal Thompson, POR...11.7
Maurice Lucas, NY............11.3

ASSISTS
Johnny Moore, SA............. 9.6
Magic Johnson, LA............ 9.5
Maurice Cheeks, PHI 8.4
Nate Archibald, BOS 8.0
Norm Nixon, LA 8.0

STEALS
Magic Johnson, LA 2.67
Maurice Cheeks, PHI 2.65

Micheal Richardson, NY ...2.60
Quinn Buckner, MIL 2.49
Ray Williams, NJ 2.43

BLOCKED SHOTS
George Johnson, SA..........3.12
Tree Rollins, ATL 2.84
K. Abdul-Jabbar, LA..........2.72
Artis Gilmore, CHI 2.70
Robert Parish, BOS 2.40

FIELD-GOAL PCT.
Artis Gilmore, CHI .... .652
Steve Johnson, KC........... .613
Buck Williams, NJ............. .582
K. Abdul-Jabbar, LA .... .579
Calvin Natt, POR.............. .576

FREE-THROW PCT.
Kyle Macy, PHO .... .899
Charlie Criss, SD.............. .887
John Long, DET................ .865
George Gervin, SA .... .864

3-PT. FIELD-GOAL PCT.
Campy Russell, NY .... .439
Andrew Toney, PHI .... .424
Kyle Macy, PHO .... .390
Brian Winters, MIL............ .387

EAST FIRST ROUND
Philadelphia 2, Atlanta 0
Washington 2, New Jersey 0

EAST SEMIFINALS
Boston 4, Washington 1
Philadelphia 4, Milwaukee 2

EAST FINALS
Philadelphia 4, Boston 3

WEST FIRST ROUND
Seattle 2, Houston 1
Phoenix 2, Denver 1

WEST SEMIFINALS
Los Angeles 4, Phoenix 0
San Antonio 4, Seattle 1

WEST FINALS
Los Angeles 4, San Antonio 0

NBA FINALS
Los Angeles 124, Phil. 117
Philadelphia 110, L.A. 94
Los Angeles 129, Phil. 108
Los Angeles 111, Phil. 101
Philadelphia 135, L.A. 102
Los Angeles 114, Phil. 104

1982-83
FINAL STANDINGS

Eastern Conference
Atlantic Division

	W	L	PCT.	GB
Philadelphia	65	17	.793	
Boston	56	26	.683	9
New Jersey	49	33	.598	16
New York	44	38	.537	21
Washington	42	40	.512	23

Central Division

	W	L	PCT.	GB
Milwaukee	51	31	.622	
Atlanta	43	39	.524	8
Detroit	37	45	.451	14
Chicago	28	54	.341	23
Cleveland	23	59	.280	28
Indiana	20	62	.244	31

Western Conference
Midwest Division

	W	L	PCT.	GB
San Antonio	53	29	.646	
Denver	45	37	.549	8
Kansas City	45	37	.549	8
Dallas	38	44	.463	15
Utah	30	52	.366	23
Houston	14	68	.171	39

Pacific Division

	W	L	PCT.	GB
Los Angeles	58	24	.707	
Phoenix	53	29	.646	5
Seattle	48	34	.585	10
Portland	46	36	.561	12
Golden State	30	52	.366	28
San Diego	25	57	.305	33

SCORING
Alex English, DEN............28.4
Kiki Vandeweghe, DEN.....26.7
Kelly Tripucka, DET 26.5
George Gervin, SA............26.2
Moses Malone, PHI...........24.5
Mark Aguirre, DAL 24.4
Joe Barry Carroll, GS........24.1
World B. Free, GS/CLE........23.9
Reggie Theus, CHI 23.8
Terry Cummings, SD 23.7

REBOUNDS
Moses Malone, PHI...........15.3
Buck Williams, NJ 12.5
Bill Laimbeer, DET 12.1
Artis Gilmore, SA 12.0
Jack Sikma, SEA 11.4

ASSISTS
Magic Johnson, LA 10.5
Johnny Moore, SA.............. 9.8
Rickey Green, UTA 8.9
Larry Drew, KC.................. 8.1
Frank Johnson, WAS 8.1

STEALS
Micheal Richardson, GS/NJ ...2.84
Rickey Green, UTA 2.82

Johnny Moore, SA 2.52
Isiah Thomas, DET 2.46
Darwin Cook, NJ 2.37

BLOCKED SHOTS
Tree Rollins, ATL 4.29
Bill Walton, POR 3.61
Mark Eaton, UTA 3.40
Larry Nance, PHO.............2.65
Artis Gilmore, CHI 2.34

FIELD-GOAL PCT.
Artis Gilmore, SA..............626
Steve Johnson, KC............624
Darryl Dawkins, NJ............599
K. Abdul-Jabbar, LA 588
Buck Williams, NJ.............588

FREE-THROW PCT.
Calvin Murphy, HOU .... .920
Kiki Vandeweghe, DEN .... .875
Kyle Macy, PHO................ .872
George Gervin, SA .... .853

3-PT. FIELD-GOAL PCT.
Mike Dunleavy, SA............ .345
Isiah Thomas, DET............ .288
Darrell Griffith, UTA........... .288
Allen Leavell, HOU .... .240

EAST FIRST ROUND
Boston 2, Atlanta 1
New York 2, New Jersey 0

EAST SEMIFINALS
Philadelphia 4, New York 0
Milwaukee 4, Boston 0

EAST FINALS
Philadelphia 4, Milwaukee 1

WEST FIRST ROUND
Denver 2, Phoenix 1
Portland 2, Seattle 0

WEST SEMIFINALS
Los Angeles 4, Portland 1
San Antonio 4, Denver 1

WEST FINALS
Los Angeles 4, San Antonio 2

NBA FINALS
Philadelphia 113, L.A. 107
Philadelphia 103, L.A. 93
Philadelphia 111, L.A. 94
Philadelphia 115, L.A. 108

1983-84
FINAL STANDINGS

Eastern Conference
Atlantic Division

	W	L	PCT.	GB
Boston	62	20	.756	
Philadelphia	52	30	.634	10
New York	47	35	.573	15
New Jersey	45	37	.549	17
Washington	35	47	.427	27

Central Division

	W	L	PCT.	GB
Milwaukee	50	32	.610	
Detroit	49	33	.598	1
Atlanta	40	42	.488	10
Cleveland	28	54	.341	22
Chicago	27	55	.329	23
Indiana	26	56	.317	24

Western Conference
Midwest Division

	W	L	PCT.	GB
Utah	45	37	.549	
Dallas	43	39	.524	2
Denver	38	44	.463	7
Kansas City	38	44	.463	7
San Antonio	37	45	.451	8
Houston	29	53	.354	16

Pacific Division

	W	L	PCT.	GB
Los Angeles	54	28	.659	
Portland	48	34	.585	6
Seattle	42	40	.512	12
Phoenix	41	41	.500	13
Golden State	37	45	.451	17
San Diego	30	52	.366	24

SCORING
Adrian Dantley, UTA 30.6
Mark Aguirre, DAL 29.5
Kiki Vandeweghe, DEN....29.4
Alex English, DEN............26.4
Bernard King, NY 26.3
George Gervin, SA............25.9
Larry Bird, BOS................24.2
Mike Mitchell, SA 23.3
Terry Cummings, SD 22.9
Purvis Short, GS 22.8

REBOUNDS
Moses Malone, PHI...........13.4
Buck Williams, NJ 12.3
Jeff Ruland, WAS.............12.3
Bill Laimbeer, DET 12.2
Ralph Sampson, HOU 11.1

ASSISTS
Magic Johnson, LA 13.1
Norm Nixon, SD 11.1
Isiah Thomas, DET 11.1
John Lucas, SA................10.7
Johnny Moore, SA............. 9.6

STEALS
Rickey Green, UTA...........2.65
Isiah Thomas, DET 2.49

Gus Williams, SEA............2.36
Maurice Cheeks, PHI.........2.28
Magic Johnson, LA 2.24

BLOCKED SHOTS
Mark Eaton, UTA 4.28
Tree Rollins, ATL 3.60
Ralph Sampson, HOU 2.40
Larry Nance, PHO.............2.11
Artis Gilmore, SA 2.06

FIELD-GOAL PCT.
Artis Gilmore, SA 631
James Donaldson, SD...... .596
Mike McGee, LA................ .594
Darryl Dawkins, NJ............ .593
Calvin Natt, POR............... .583

FREE-THROW PCT.
Larry Bird, BOS .... .888
John Long, DET .... .884
Bill Laimbeer, DET .... .866
Walter Davis, PHO .... .863

3-PT. FIELD-GOAL PCT.
Darrell Griffith, UTA........... .361
Mike Evans, DEN.............. .360
Johnny Moore, SA............. .322
Michael Cooper, LA........... .314

EAST FIRST ROUND
Boston 3, Washington 1
Milwaukee 3, Atlanta 2
New Jersey 3 Philadelphia 2
New York 3, Detroit 2

EAST SEMIFINALS
Boston 4, New York 3
Milwaukee 4, New Jersey 2

EAST FINALS
Boston 4, Milwaukee 1

WEST FIRST ROUND
Los Angeles 3, Kansas City 0
Utah 3, Denver 2
Phoenix 3, Portland 2
Dallas 3, Seattle 2

WEST SEMIFINALS
Los Angeles 4, Dallas 1
Phoenix 4, Utah 2

WEST FINALS
Los Angeles 4, Phoenix 2

NBA FINALS
Los Angeles 115, Boston 109
Boston 124, L.A. 121 (OT)
Los Angeles 137, Boston 104
Boston 129, L.A. 125 (OT)
Boston 121, Los Angeles 103
Los Angeles 119, Boston 108
Boston 111, Los Angeles 102

1984-85
FINAL STANDINGS

Eastern Conference
Atlantic Division

	W	L	PCT.	GB
Boston	63	19	.768	
Philadelphia	58	24	.707	5
New Jersey	42	40	.512	21
Washington	40	42	.488	23
New York	24	58	.293	39

Central Division

	W	L	PCT.	GB
Milwaukee	59	23	.720	
Detroit	46	36	.561	13
Chicago	38	44	.463	21
Cleveland	36	46	.439	23
Atlanta	34	48	.415	25
Indiana	22	60	.268	37

Western Conference
Midwest Division

	W	L	PCT.	GB
Denver	52	30	.634	
Houston	48	34	.585	4
Dallas	44	38	.537	8
San Antonio	41	41	.500	11
Utah	41	41	.500	11
Kansas City	31	51	.378	21

Pacific Division

	W	L	PCT.	GB
L.A. Lakers	62	20	.756	
Portland	42	40	.512	20
Phoenix	36	46	.439	26
L.A. Clippers	31	51	.378	31
Seattle	31	51	.378	31
Golden State	22	60	.268	40

SCORING
Bernard King, NY 32.9
Larry Bird, BOS.................28.7
Michael Jordan, CHI 28.2
Purvis Short, GS 28.0
Alex English, DEN.............27.9
Dominique Wilkins, ATL....27.4
Adrian Dantley, UTA 26.6
Mark Aguirre, DAL 25.7
Moses Malone, PHI............24.6
Terry Cummings, MIL 23.6

REBOUNDS
Moses Malone, PHI............13.1
Bill Laimbeer, DET.............12.4
Buck Williams, NJ 12.3
Akeem Olajuwon, HOU......11.9
Mark Eaton, UTA 11.3

ASSISTS
Isiah Thomas, DET.............13.9
Magic Johnson, LAL...........12.6
Johnny Moore, SA..............10.0
Norm Nixon, LAC 8.8
John Bagley, CLE................ 8.6

STEALS
Micheal Richardson, NJ 2.96
Johnny Moore, SA 2.79

Lafayette Lever, DEN........2.46
Michael Jordan, CHI 2.39
Doc Rivers, ATL................2.36

BLOCKED SHOTS
Mark Eaton, UTA 5.56
Akeem Olajuwon, HOU......2.68
Sam Bowie, POR 2.67
Wayne Cooper, DEN 2.46
Tree Rollins, ATL 2.39

FIELD-GOAL PCT.
James Donaldson, LAC..... .637
Artis Gilmore, SA............... .623
Otis Thorpe, KC................. .600
K. Abdul-Jabbar, LAL .... .599
Larry Nance, PHO .... .587

FREE-THROW PCT.
Kyle Macy, PHO .... .907
Kiki Vandeweghe, POR.... .896
Brad Davis, DAL................. .888
Kelly Tripucka, DET........... .885

3-PT. FIELD-GOAL PCT.
Byron Scott, LAL .... .433
Larry Bird, BOS .... .427
Brad Davis, DAL................ .409
Trent Tucker, NY .... .403

EAST FIRST ROUND
Boston 3, Cleveland 1
Milwaukee 3, Chicago 1
Philadelphia 3, Washington 1
Detroit 3, New Jersey 0

EAST SEMIFINALS
Boston 4, Detroit 2
Philadelphia 4, Milwaukee 0

EAST FINALS
Boston 4, Philadelphia 1

WEST FIRST ROUND
L.A. Lakers 3, Phoenix 0
Denver 3, San Antonio 2
Utah 3, Houston 2
Portland 3, Dallas 1

WEST SEMIFINALS
L.A. Lakers 4, Portland 1
Denver 4, Utah 1

WEST FINALS
L.A. Lakers 4, Denver 1

NBA FINALS
Boston 148, L.A. Lakers 114
L.A. Lakers 109, Boston 102
L.A. Lakers 136, Boston 111
Boston 107, L.A. Lakers 105
L.A. Lakers 120, Boston 111
L.A. Lakers 111, Boston 100

1985-86
FINAL STANDINGS

Eastern Conference
Atlantic Division

	W	L	PCT.	GB
Boston	67	15	.817	
Philadelphia	54	28	.659	13
Washington	39	43	.476	28
New Jersey	39	43	.476	28
New York	23	59	.280	44

Central Division

	W	L	PCT.	GB
Milwaukee	57	25	.695	
Atlanta	50	32	.610	7
Detroit	46	36	.561	11
Chicago	30	52	.366	27
Cleveland	29	53	.354	28
Indiana	26	56	.317	31

Western Conference
Midwest Division

	W	L	PCT.	GB
Houston	51	31	.622	
Denver	47	35	.573	4
Dallas	44	38	.537	7
Utah	42	40	.512	9
Sacramento	37	45	.451	14
San Antonio	35	47	.427	16

Pacific Division

	W	L	PCT.	GB
L.A. Lakers	62	20	.756	
Portland	40	42	.488	22
L.A. Clippers	32	50	.390	30
Phoenix	32	50	.390	30
Seattle	31	51	.378	31
Golden State	30	52	.366	32

SCORING
Dominique Wilkins, ATL....30.3
Adrian Dantley, UTA 29.8
Alex English, DEN.............29.8
Larry Bird, BOS.................25.8
Purvis Short, GS................25.5
Kiki Vandeweghe, POR 24.8
Moses Malone, PHI...........23.8
Akeem Olajuwon, HOU.....23.5
Mike Mitchell, SA 23.4
World B. Free, CLE...........23.4

REBOUNDS
Bill Laimbeer, DET............13.1
Charles Barkley, PHI.........12.8
Buck Williams, NJ.............12.0
Moses Malone, PHI...........11.8
Ralph Sampson, HOU 11.1

ASSISTS
Magic Johnson, LAL 12.6
Isiah Thomas, DET 10.8
Reggie Theus, SAC............ 9.6
John Bagley, CLE............... 9.4
Maurice Cheeks, PHI 9.2

STEALS
Alvin Robertson, SA.........3.67
Micheal Richardson, NJ....2.66

Clyde Drexler, POR 2.63
Maurice Cheeks, PHI........2.52
Lafayette Lever, DEN........2.28

BLOCKED SHOTS
Manute Bol, WAS..............4.96
Mark Eaton, UTA 4.61
Akeem Olajuwon, HOU.....3.40
Wayne Cooper, DEN 2.91
Benoit Benjamin, LAC.......2.61

FIELD-GOAL PCT.
Steve Johnson, SA .... .632
Artis Gilmore, SA .... .618
Larry Nance, PHO............. .581
James Worthy, LAL............ .579
Kevin McHale, BOS .... .574

FREE-THROW PCT.
Larry Bird, BOS...............8963
Chris Mullin, GS 8957
Mike Gminski, NJ .... .893
Jim Paxson, POR............. .889

3-PT. FIELD-GOAL PCT.
Craig Hodges, MIL 4506
Trent Tucker, NY.............4505
Ernie Grunfeld, NY........... .426
Larry Bird, BOS................ .423

EAST FIRST ROUND
Boston 3, Chicago 0
Milwaukee 3, New Jersey 0
Philadelphia 3, Washington 2
Atlanta 3, Detroit 1

EAST SEMIFINALS
Boston 4, Atlanta 1
Milwaukee 4, Philadelphia 3

EAST FINALS
Boston 4, Milwaukee 0

WEST FIRST ROUND
L.A. Lakers 3, San Antonio 0
Houston 3, Sacramento 0
Denver 3, Portland 1
Dallas 3, Utah 1

WEST SEMIFINALS
L.A. Lakers 4, Dallas 2
Houston 4, Denver 2

WEST FINALS
Houston 4, L.A. Lakers 1

NBA FINALS
Boston 112, Houston 100
Boston 117, Houston 95
Houston 106, Boston 104
Houston 106, Boston 103
Boston 111, Houston 96
Boston 114, Houston 97

1986-87
FINAL STANDINGS

Eastern Conference
Atlantic Division

	W	L	PCT.	GB
Boston	59	23	.720	
Philadelphia	45	37	.549	14
Washington	42	40	.512	17
New Jersey	24	58	.293	35
New York	24	58	.293	35

Central Division

	W	L	PCT.	GB
Atlanta	57	25	.695	
Detroit	52	30	.634	5
Milwaukee	50	32	.610	7
Indiana	41	41	.500	16
Chicago	40	42	.488	17
Cleveland	31	51	.378	26

Western Conference
Midwest Division

	W	L	PCT.	GB
Dallas	55	27	.671	
Utah	44	38	.537	11
Houston	42	40	.512	13
Denver	37	45	.451	18
Sacramento	29	53	.354	26
San Antonio	28	54	.341	27

Pacific Division

	W	L	PCT.	GB
L.A. Lakers	65	17	.793	
Portland	49	33	.598	16
Golden State	42	40	.512	23
Seattle	39	43	.476	26
Phoenix	36	46	.439	29
L.A. Clippers	12	70	.146	53

SCORING
Michael Jordan, CHI 37.1
Dominique Wilkins, ATL....29.0
Alex English, DEN............28.6
Larry Bird, BOS.................28.1
Kiki Vandeweghe, POR 26.9
Kevin McHale, BOS 26.1
Mark Aguirre, DAL 25.7
Dale Ellis, SEA.................24.9
Moses Malone, WAS 24.1
Magic Johnson, LAL 23.9

REBOUNDS
Charles Barkley, PHI........14.6
Charles Oakley, CHI 13.1
Buck Williams, NJ 12.5
James Donaldson, DAL 11.9
Bill Laimbeer, DET............11.6

ASSISTS
Magic Johnson, LAL 12.2
Sleepy Floyd, GS...............10.3
Isiah Thomas, DET 10.0
Doc Rivers, ATL................10.0
Terry Porter, POR 8.9

STEALS
Alvin Robertson, SA..........3.21
Michael Jordan, CHI 2.88

Maurice Cheeks, PHI.......2.65
Ron Harper, CLE 2.55
Clyde Drexler, POR 2.49

BLOCKED SHOTS
Mark Eaton, UTA 4.06
Manute Bol, WAS.............3.68
Akeem Olajuwon, HOU....3.39
Benoit Benjamin, LAC.......2.60
Alton Lister, SEA..............2.40

FIELD-GOAL PCT.
Kevin McHale, BOS........... .604
Artis Gilmore, SA .... .597
Charles Barkley, PHI......... .594
James Donaldson, DAL.... .586
K. Abdul-Jabbar, LAL .... .564

FREE-THROW PCT.
Larry Bird, BOS .... .910
Danny Ainge, BOS .... .897
Bill Laimbeer, DET .... .894
Byron Scott, LAL .... .892

3-PT. FIELD-GOAL PCT.
Kiki Vandeweghe, POR.... .481
Detlef Schrempf, DAL....... .478
Danny Ainge, BOS .... .443
Byron Scott, LAL .... .436

EAST FIRST ROUND
Boston 3, Chicago 0
Atlanta 3, Indiana 1
Detroit 3, Washington 0
Milwaukee 3, Philadelphia 2

EAST SEMIFINALS
Boston 4, Milwaukee 3
Detroit 4, Atlanta 1

EAST FINALS
Boston 4, Detroit 3

WEST FIRST ROUND
L.A. Lakers 3, Denver 0
Seattle 3, Dallas 1
Houston 3, Portland 1
Golden St. 3, Utah 2

WEST SEMIFINALS
L.A. Lakers 4, Golden St. 1
Seattle 4, Houston 2

WEST FINALS
L.A. Lakers 4, Seattle 0

NBA FINALS
L.A. Lakers 126, Boston 113
L.A. Lakers 141, Boston 122
Boston 109, L.A. Lakers 103
L.A. Lakers 107, Boston 106
Boston 123, L.A. Lakers 108
L.A. Lakers 106, Boston 93

1987-88
FINAL STANDINGS

Eastern Conference
Atlantic Division

	W	L	PCT.	GB
Boston	57	25	.695	
Washington	38	44	.463	19
New York	38	44	.463	19
Philadelphia	36	46	.439	21
New Jersey	19	63	.232	38

Central Division

	W	L	PCT.	GB
Detroit	54	28	.659	
Atlanta	50	32	.610	4
Chicago	50	32	.610	4
Cleveland	42	40	.512	12
Milwaukee	42	40	.512	12
Indiana	38	44	.463	16

Western Conference
Midwest Division

	W	L	PCT.	GB
Denver	54	28	.659	
Dallas	53	29	.646	1
Utah	47	35	.573	7
Houston	46	36	.561	8
San Antonio	31	51	.378	23
Sacramento	24	58	.293	30

Pacific Division

	W	L	PCT.	GB
L.A. Lakers	62	20	.756	
Portland	53	29	.646	9
Seattle	44	38	.537	18
Phoenix	28	54	.341	34
Golden State	20	62	.244	42
L.A. Clippers	17	65	.207	45

SCORING
Michael Jordan, CHI	35.0
Dominique Wilkins, ATL	30.7
Larry Bird, BOS	29.9
Charles Barkley, PHI	28.3
Karl Malone, UTA	27.7
Clyde Drexler, POR	27.0
Dale Ellis, SEA	25.8
Mark Aguirre, DAL	25.1
Alex English, DEN	25.0
Akeem Olajuwon, HOU	22.8

REBOUNDS
Michael Cage, LAC	13.03
Charles Oakley, CHI	13.00
Akeem Olajuwon, HOU	12.1
Karl Malone, UTA	12.0
Buck Williams, NJ	11.9

ASSISTS
John Stockton, UTA	13.8
Magic Johnson, LAL	11.9
Mark Jackson, NY	10.6
Terry Porter, POR	10.1
Doc Rivers, ATL	9.3

STEALS
Michael Jordan, CHI	3.16
Alvin Robertson, SA	2.96

John Stockton, UTA	2.95
Lafayette Lever, DEN	2.72
Clyde Drexler, POR	2.51

BLOCKED SHOTS
Mark Eaton, UTA	3.71
Benoit Benjamin, LAC	3.41
Patrick Ewing, NY	2.99
Akeem Olajuwon, HOU	2.71
Manute Bol, WAS	2.70

FIELD-GOAL PCT.
Kevin McHale, BOS	.604
Robert Parish, BOS	.589
Charles Barkley, PHI	.587
John Stockton, UTA	.574
Walter Berry, SA	.563

FREE-THROW PCT.
Jack Sikma, MIL	.922
Larry Bird, BOS	.916
John Long, IND	.907
Mike Gminski, NJ/PHI	.906

3-PT. FIELD-GOAL PCT.
Craig Hodges, MIL/PHO	.491
Mark Price, CLE	.486
John Long, IND	.442
G. Henderson, NY/PHI	.423

EAST FIRST ROUND
Boston 3, New York 1
Detroit 3, Washington 2
Atlanta 3, Milwaukee 2
Chicago 3, Cleveland 2

EAST SEMIFINALS
Boston 4, Atlanta 3
Detroit 4, Chicago 1

EAST FINALS
Detroit 4, Boston 2

WEST FIRST ROUND
L.A. Lakers 3, San Antonio 0
Denver 3, Seattle 2
Utah 3, Portland 1
Dallas 3, Houston 1

WEST SEMIFINALS
L.A. Lakers 4, Utah 3
Dallas 4, Denver 2

WEST FINALS
L.A. Lakers 4, Dallas 3

NBA FINALS
Detroit 105, L.A. Lakers 93
L.A. Lakers 108, Detroit 96
L.A. Lakers 99, Detroit 86
Detroit 111, L.A. Lakers 86
Detroit 104, L.A. Lakers 94
L.A. Lakers 103, Detroit 102
L.A. Lakers 108, Detroit 105

1988-89 FINAL STANDINGS

Eastern Conference
Atlantic Division

	W	L	PCT.	GB
New York	52	30	.634	
Philadelphia	46	36	.561	6
Boston	42	40	.512	10
Washington	40	42	.488	12
New Jersey	26	56	.317	26
Charlotte	20	62	.244	32

Central Division

	W	L	PCT.	GB
Detroit	63	19	.768	
Cleveland	57	25	.695	6
Atlanta	52	30	.634	11
Milwaukee	49	33	.598	14
Chicago	47	35	.573	16
Indiana	28	54	.341	35

Western Conference
Midwest Division

	W	L	PCT.	GB
Utah	51	31	.622	
Houston	45	37	.549	6
Denver	44	38	.537	7
Dallas	38	44	.463	13
San Antonio	21	61	.256	30
Miami	15	67	.183	36

Pacific Division

	W	L	PCT.	GB
L.A. Lakers	57	25	.695	
Phoenix	55	27	.671	2
Seattle	47	35	.573	10
Golden State	43	39	.524	14
Portland	39	43	.476	18
Sacramento	27	55	.329	30
L.A. Clippers	21	61	.256	36

SCORING

Michael Jordan, CHI	32.5
Karl Malone, UTA	29.1
Dale Ellis, SEA	27.5
Clyde Drexler, POR	27.2
Chris Mullin, GS	26.5
Alex English, DEN	26.5
Dominique Wilkins, ATL	26.2
Charles Barkley, PHI	25.8
Tom Chambers, PHO	25.7
Akeem Olajuwon, HOU	24.8

REBOUNDS

Akeem Olajuwon, HOU	13.5
Charles Barkley, PHI	12.5
Robert Parish, BOS	12.5
Moses Malone, ATL	11.8
Karl Malone, UTA	10.7

ASSISTS

John Stockton, UTA	13.6
Magic Johnson, LAL	12.8
Kevin Johnson, PHO	12.2
Terry Porter, POR	9.5
Nate McMillan, SEA	9.3

STEALS

John Stockton, UTA	3.21
Alvin Robertson, SA	3.03

Michael Jordan, CHI	2.89
Lafayette Lever, DEN	2.75
Clyde Drexler, POR	2.73

BLOCKED SHOTS

Manute Bol, GS	4.31
Mark Eaton, UTA	3.84
Patrick Ewing, NY	3.51
Akeem Olajuwon, HOU	3.44
Larry Nance, CLE	2.82

FIELD-GOAL PCT.

Dennis Rodman, DET	.595
Charles Barkley, PHI	.579
Robert Parish, BOS	.570
Patrick Ewing, BOS	.567
James Worthy, LAL	.548

FREE-THROW PCT.

Magic Johnson, LAL	.911
Jack Sikma, MIL	.905
Scott Skiles, IND	.903
Mark Price, CLE	.901

3-PT. Field-Goal Pct.

Jon Sundvold, MIA	.522
Dale Ellis, SEA	.478
Mark Price, CLE	.441
Hersey Hawkins, PHI	.428

EAST FIRST ROUND
Detroit 3, Boston 0
New York 3, Philadelphia 0
Chicago 3, Cleveland 2
Milwaukee 3, Atlanta 2

EAST SEMIFINALS
Detroit 4, Milwaukee 0
Chicago 4, New York 2

EAST FINALS
Detroit 4, Chicago 2

WEST FIRST ROUND
L.A. Lakers 3, Portland 0
Golden St. 3, Utah 0
Phoenix 3, Denver 0
Seattle 3, Houston 1

WEST SEMIFINALS
L.A. Lakers 4, Seattle 0
Phoenix 4, Golden St. 1

WEST FINALS
L.A. Lakers 4, Phoenix 0

NBA FINALS
Detroit 109, L.A. Lakers 97
Detroit 108, L.A. Lakers 105
Detroit 114, L.A. Lakers 110
Detroit 105, L.A. Lakers 97

1989-90 FINAL STANDINGS

Eastern Conference
Atlantic Division

	W	L	PCT.	GB
Philadelphia	53	29	.646	
Boston	52	30	.634	1
New York	45	37	.549	8
Washington	31	51	.378	22
Miami	18	64	.220	35
New Jersey	17	65	.207	36

Central Division

	W	L	PCT.	GB
Detroit	59	23	.720	
Chicago	55	27	.671	4
Milwaukee	44	38	.537	15
Cleveland	42	40	.512	17
Indiana	42	40	.512	17
Atlanta	41	41	.500	18
Orlando	18	64	.220	41

Western Conference
Midwest Division

	W	L	PCT.	GB
San Antonio	56	26	.683	
Utah	55	27	.671	1
Dallas	47	35	.573	9
Denver	43	39	.524	13
Houston	41	41	.500	15
Minnesota	22	60	.268	34
Charlotte	19	63	.232	37

Pacific Division

	W	L	PCT.	GB
L.A. Lakers	63	19	.768	
Portland	59	23	.720	4
Phoenix	54	28	.659	9
Seattle	41	41	.500	22
Golden State	37	45	.451	26
L.A. Clippers	30	52	.366	33
Sacramento	23	59	.280	40

SCORING
Michael Jordan, CHI 33.6
Karl Malone, UTA..............31.0
Patrick Ewing, NY 28.6
Tom Chambers, PHO 27.2
Dominique Wilkins, ATL.....26.7
Charles Barkley, PHI..........25.2
Chris Mullin, GS 25.1
Reggie Miller, IND.............24.6
Akeem Olajuwon, HOU.....24.3
David Robinson, SA..........24.3

REBOUNDS
Akeem Olajuwon, HOU 14.0
David Robinson, SA..........12.0
Charles Barkley, PHI.........11.5
Karl Malone, UTA..............11.1
Patrick Ewing, NY 10.9

ASSISTS
John Stockton, UTA..........14.5
Magic Johnson, LAL 11.5
Kevin Johnson, PHO.........11.4
Muggsy Bogues, CHA.......10.7

STEALS
Michael Jordan, CHI 2.77
John Stockton, UTA...........2.65

Scottie Pippen, CHI...........2.57
Alvin Robertson, MIL.........2.56
Derek Harper, DAL 2.28

BLOCKED SHOTS
Akeem Olajuwon, HOU.....4.59
Patrick Ewing, NY 3.99
David Robinson, SA...........3.89
Manute Bol, GS.................3.17
Benoit Benjamin, LAC.......2.63

FIELD-GOAL PCT.
Mark West, PHO 625
Charles Barkley, PHI 600
Robert Parish, BOS...........580
Karl Malone, UTA 562

FREE-THROW PCT.
Larry Bird, BOS 930
Eddie Johnson, PHO..........917
Walter Davis, DEN 912
Joe Dumars, DET..............900

3-PT. FIELD-GOAL PCT.
Steve Kerr, CLE 507
Craig Hodges, CHI 481
Drazen Petrovic, POR 459
Jon Sundvold, MIA 440

EAST FIRST ROUND
Detroit 3, Indiana 0
Philadelphia 3, Cleveland 2
Chicago 3, Milwaukee 1
New York 3, Boston 2

EAST SEMIFINALS
Detroit 4, New York 1
Chicago 4, Philadelphia 1

EAST FINALS
Detroit 4, Chicago 3

WEST FIRST ROUND
L.A. Lakers 3, Houston 1
San Antonio 3, Denver 0
Portland 3, Dallas 0
Phoenix 3, Utah 2

WEST SEMIFINALS
Phoenix 4, L.A. Lakers 1
Portland 4, San Antonio 3

WEST FINALS
Portland 4, Phoenix 2

NBA FINALS
Detroit 105, Portland 99
Portland 106, Detroit 105 (OT)
Detroit 121, Portland 106
Detroit 112, Portland 109
Detroit 92, Portland 90

1990-91 FINAL STANDINGS

Eastern Conference
Atlantic Division

	W	L	PCT.	GB
Boston	56	26	.683	
Philadelphia	44	38	.537	12
New York	39	43	.476	17
Washington	30	52	.366	26
New Jersey	26	56	.317	30
Miami	24	58	.293	32

Central Division

	W	L	PCT.	GB
Chicago	61	21	.744	
Detroit	50	32	.610	11
Milwaukee	48	34	.585	13
Atlanta	43	39	.524	18
Indiana	41	41	.500	20
Cleveland	33	49	.402	28
Charlotte	26	56	.317	35

Western Conference
Midwest Division

	W	L	PCT.	GB
San Antonio	55	27	.671	
Utah	54	28	.659	1
Houston	52	30	.634	3
Orlando	31	51	.378	24
Minnesota	29	53	.354	26
Dallas	28	54	.341	27
Denver	20	62	.244	35

Pacific Division

	W	L	PCT.	GB
Portland	63	19	.768	
L.A. Lakers	58	24	.707	5
Phoenix	55	27	.671	8
Golden State	44	38	.537	19
Seattle	41	41	.500	22
L.A. Clippers	31	51	.378	32
Sacramento	25	57	.305	38

SCORING
Michael Jordan, CHI	31.5
Karl Malone, UTA	29.0
Bernard King, WAS	28.4
Charles Barkley, PHI	27.6
Patrick Ewing, NY	26.6
Michael Adams, DEN	26.5
Dominique Wilkins, ATL	25.9
Chris Mullin, GS	25.7
David Robinson, SA	25.6
Mitch Richmond, GS	23.9

REBOUNDS
David Robinson, SA	13.0
Dennis Rodman, DET	12.5
Charles Oakley, NY	12.1
Karl Malone, UTA	11.8
Patrick Ewing, NY	11.2

ASSISTS
John Stockton, UTA	14.2
Magic Johnson, LAL	12.5
Michael Adams, DEN	10.5
Kevin Johnson, PHO	10.1

STEALS
Alvin Robertson, MIL	3.04
John Stockton, UTA	2.85

Michael Jordan, CHI	2.72
Tim Hardaway, GS	2.61
Scottie Pippen, CHI	2.35

BLOCKED SHOTS
Hakeem Olajuwon, HOU	3.95
David Robinson, SA	3.90
Patrick Ewing, NY	3.19
Manute Bol, PHI	3.01
Chris Dudley, NJ	2.51

FIELD-GOAL PCT.
Buck Williams, POR	.602
Robert Parish, BOS	.598
Kevin Gamble, BOS	.587
Charles Barkley, PHI	.570

FREE-THROW PCT.
Reggie Miller, IND	.918
Jeff Malone, UTA	.917
Ricky Pierce, MIL/SEA	.913
Kelly Tripucka, CHA	.910

3-PT. FIELD-GOAL PCT.
Jim Les, SAC	.461
Trent Tucker, NY	.418
Jeff Hornacek, PHO	.418
Terry Porter, POR	.415

EAST FIRST ROUND
Chicago 3, New York 0
Boston 3, Indiana 2
Detroit 3, Atlanta 2
Philadelphia 3, Milwaukee 0

EAST SEMIFINALS
Chicago 4, Philadelphia 1
Detroit 4, Boston 2

EAST FINALS
Chicago 4, Detroit 0

WEST FIRST ROUND
Portland 3, Seattle 2
Golden St. 3, San Antonio 1
L.A. Lakers 3, Houston 0
Utah 3, Phoenix 1

WEST SEMIFINALS
Portland 4, Utah 1
L.A. Lakers 4, Golden St. 1

WEST FINALS
L.A. Lakers 4, Portland 2

NBA FINALS
L.A. Lakers 93, Chicago 91
Chicago 107, L.A. Lakers 86
Chicago 104, L.A. 96 (OT)
Chicago 97, L.A. Lakers 82
Chicago 108, L.A. Lakers 101

1991-92 FINAL STANDINGS

Eastern Conference
Atlantic Division

	W	L	PCT.	GB
Boston	51	31	.622	
New York	51	31	.622	
New Jersey	40	42	.488	11
Miami	38	44	.463	13
Philadelphia	35	47	.427	16
Washington	25	57	.305	26
Orlando	21	61	.256	30

Central Division

	W	L	PCT.	GB
Chicago	67	15	.817	
Cleveland	57	25	.695	10
Detroit	48	34	.585	19
Indiana	40	42	.488	27
Atlanta	38	44	.463	29
Charlotte	31	51	.378	36
Milwaukee	31	51	.378	36

Western Conference
Midwest Division

	W	L	PCT.	GB
Utah	55	27	.671	
San Antonio	47	35	.573	8
Houston	42	40	.512	13
Denver	24	58	.293	31
Dallas	22	60	.268	33
Minnesota	15	67	.183	40

Pacific Division

	W	L	PCT.	GB
Portland	57	25	.695	
Golden State	55	27	.671	2
Phoenix	53	29	.646	4
Seattle	47	35	.573	10
L.A. Clippers	45	37	.549	12
L.A. Lakers	43	39	.524	14
Sacramento	29	53	.347	28

SCORING
Michael Jordan, CHI 30.1
Karl Malone, UTA 28.0
Chris Mullin, GS...............25.6
Clyde Drexler, POR 25.0
Patrick Ewing, NY 24.0
Tim Hardaway, GS 23.4
David Robinson, SA 23.2
Charles Barkley, PHI 23.1
Mitch Richmond, SAC.......22.5
Glen Rice, MIA 22.3

REBOUNDS
Dennis Rodman, DET.......18.7
Kevin Willis, ATL...............15.5
Dikembe Mutombo, DEN ..12.3
David Robinson, SA 12.2
Hakeem Olajuwon, HOU ..12.1

ASSISTS
John Stockton, UTA 13.7
Kevin Johnson, PHO 10.7
Tim Hardaway, GS 10.0
Muggsy Bogues, CHA 9.1

STEALS
John Stockton, UTA 2.98
Micheal Williams, IND.......2.95

Alvin Robertson, MIL 2.56
Mookie Blaylock, NJ 2.36
David Robinson, SA 2.32

BLOCKED SHOTS
David Robinson, SA 4.49
Hakeem Olajuwon, HOU ..4.34
Larry Nance, CLE 3.00
Patrick Ewing, NY.............2.99
Dikembe Mutombo, DEN ..2.96

FIELD-GOAL PCT.
Buck Williams, POR......... .604
Otis Thorpe, HOU............. .592
Horace Grant, CHI........... .578
Brad Daugherty, CLE ...... .570

FREE-THROW PCT.
Mark Price, CLE .... .947
Larry Bird, BOS............... .926
Ricky Pierce, SEA............ .916
Rolando Blackman, DAL... .898

3-PT. FIELD-GOAL PCT.
Dana Barros, SEA .... .446
Drazen Petrovic, NJ......... .444
Jeff Hornacek, PHO......... .439
Mike Iuzzolino, DAL......... .434

EAST FIRST ROUND
Chicago 3, Miami 0
Boston 3, Indiana 1
Cleveland 3, New Jersey 1
New York 3, Detroit 2

EAST SEMIFINALS
Chicago 4, New York 3
Cleveland 4, Boston 3

EAST FINALS
Chicago 4, Cleveland 2

WEST FIRST ROUND
Portland 3, L.A. Lakers 1
Utah 3, L.A. Clippers 2
Seattle 3, Golden St. 1
Phoenix 3, San Antonio 0

WEST SEMIFINALS
Portland 4, Phoenix 1
Utah 4, Seattle 1

WEST FINALS
Portland 4, Utah 2

NBA FINALS
Chicago 122, Portland 89
Portland 115, Chi. 104 (OT)
Chicago 94, Portland 84
Portland 93, Chicago 88
Chicago 119, Portland 106
Chicago 97, Portland 93

1992-93 FINAL STANDINGS

Eastern Conference
Atlantic Division

	W	L	PCT.	GB
New York	60	22	.732	
Boston	48	34	.585	12
New Jersey	43	39	.524	17
Orlando	41	41	.500	19
Miami	36	46	.439	24
Philadelphia	26	56	.317	34
Washington	22	60	.268	38

Central Division

	W	L	PCT.	GB
Chicago	57	25	.695	
Cleveland	54	28	.659	3
Charlotte	44	38	.537	13
Atlanta	43	39	.524	14
Indiana	41	41	.500	16
Detroit	40	42	.488	17
Milwaukee	28	54	.341	29

Western Conference
Midwest Division

	W	L	PCT.	GB
Houston	55	27	.671	
San Antonio	49	33	.598	6
Utah	47	35	.573	8
Denver	36	46	.439	19
Minnesota	19	63	.232	36
Dallas	11	71	.134	44

Pacific Division

	W	L	PCT.	GB
Phoenix	62	20	.756	
Seattle	55	27	.671	7
Portland	51	31	.622	11
L.A. Clippers	41	41	.500	21
L.A. Lakers	39	43	.476	23
Golden State	34	48	.415	28
Sacramento	25	57	.305	37

SCORING
Michael Jordan, CHI 32.6
Dominique Wilkins, ATL....29.9
Karl Malone, UTA 27.0
Hakeem Olajuwon, HOU ..26.1
Charles Barkley, PHO.......25.6
Patrick Ewing, NY 24.2
Joe Dumars, DET 23.5
Shaquille O'Neal, ORL.......23.4
David Robinson, SA...........23.4
Danny Manning, LAC........22.8

REBOUNDS
Dennis Rodman, DET.......18.3
Shaquille O'Neal, ORL......13.9
Dikembe Mutombo, DEN..13.0
Hakeem Olajuwon, HOU ..13.0
Kevin Willis, ATL...............12.9

ASSISTS
John Stockton, UTA..........12.0
Tim Hardaway, GS 10.6
Scott Skiles, ORL................9.4
Mark Jackson, LAC 8.8

STEALS
Michael Jordan, CHI 2.83
Mookie Blaylock, ATL 2.54

John Stockton, UTA..........2.43
Nate McMillan, SEA.........2.37
Alvin Robertson, MIL/DET....2.25

BLOCKED SHOTS
Hakeem Olajuwon, HOU ..4.17
Shaquille O'Neal, ORL......3.53
Dikembe Mutombo, DEN ..3.50
Alonzo Mourning, CHA 3.47
David Robinson, SA..........3.22

FIELD-GOAL PCT.
Cedric Ceballos, PHO...... .576
Brad Daugherty, CLE ...... .571
Dale Davis, IND .... .568
Shaquille O'Neal, ORL .... .562

FREE-THROW PCT.
Mark Price, CLE .... .948
Chris Jackson, DEN .... .935
Eddie Johnson, SEA........ .911
Micheal Williams, MIN .... .907

3-PT. FIELD-GOAL PCT.
B.J. Armstrong, CHI .... .453
Chris Mullin, GS .... .451
Drazen Petrovic, NJ .... .449
Kenny Smith, HOU .... .438

EAST FIRST ROUND
New York 3, Indiana 1
Chicago 3, Atlanta 0
Cleveland 3, New Jersey 2
Charlotte 3, Boston 1

EAST SEMIFINALS
New York 4, Charlotte 1
Chicago 4, Cleveland 0

EAST FINALS
Chicago 4, New York 2

WEST FIRST ROUND
Phoenix 3, L.A. Lakers 2
Houston 3, L.A. Clippers 2
Seattle 3, Utah 2
San Antonio 3, Portland 1

WEST SEMIFINALS
Seattle 4, Houston 3
Phoenix 4, San Antonio 2

WEST FINALS
Phoenix 4, Seattle 3

NBA FINALS
Chicago 100, Phoenix 92
Chicago 111, Phoenix 108
Phoenix 129, Chic. 121 (3OT)
Chicago 111, Phoenix 105
Phoenix 108, Chicago 98
Chicago 99, Phoenix 98

1993-94 FINAL STANDINGS

Eastern Conference

Atlantic Division

	W	L	PCT.	GB
New York	57	25	.695	
Orlando	50	32	.610	7
New Jersey	45	37	.549	12
Miami	42	40	.512	15
Boston	32	50	.390	25
Philadelphia	25	57	.305	32
Washington	24	58	.234	33

Central Division

	W	L	PCT.	GB
Atlanta	57	25	.695	
Chicago	55	27	.671	2
Indiana	47	35	.573	10
Cleveland	47	35	.573	10
Charlotte	41	41	.500	16
Detroit	20	62	.244	37
Milwaukee	20	62	.244	37

Western Conference

Midwest Division

	W	L	PCT.	GB
Houston	58	24	.707	
San Antonio	55	27	.671	3
Utah	53	29	.646	5
Denver	42	40	.512	16
Minnesota	20	62	.244	38
Dallas	13	69	.159	45

Pacific Division

	W	L	PCT.	GB
Seattle	63	19	.768	
Phoenix	56	26	.683	7
Golden State	50	32	.610	13
Portland	47	35	.573	16
L.A. Lakers	33	49	.402	30
Sacramento	28	54	.341	35
L.A. Clippers	27	55	.329	36

SCORING

David Robinson, SA..........29.8
Shaquille O'Neal, ORL......29.3
Hakeem Olajuwon, HOU ..27.3
Dominique Wilkins, ATL/LAC 26.0
Karl Malone, UTA 25.2
Patrick Ewing, NY 24.5
Mitch Richmond, SAC 23.4
Scottie Pippen, CHI 22.0
Charles Barkley, PHO 21.6
Glen Rice, MIA.................21.1

REBOUNDS

Dennis Rodman, SA 17.3
Shaquille O'Neal, ORL....13.2
Kevin Willis, ATL 12.0
Hakeem Olajuwon, HOU ..11.9
Olden Polynice, DET/SAC ...11.9

ASSISTS

John Stockton, UTA..........12.6
Muggsy Bogues, CHA 10.1
Mookie Blaylock, ATL 9.7
Kenny Anderson, NJ 9.6

STEALS

Nate McMillan, SEA..........2.96
Scottie Pippen, CHI 2.93

Mookie Blaylock, ATL 2.62
John Stockton, UTA..........2.43
Eric Murdock, MIL 2.40

BLOCKED SHOTS

Hakeem Olajuwon, HOU ..3.71
David Robinson, SA..........3.31
Alonzo Mourning, CHA 3.13
Shawn Bradley, PHI.........3.00
Shaquille O'Neal, ORL......2.85

FIELD-GOAL PCT.

Shaquille O'Neal, ORL .... .599
Dikembe Mutombo, DEN .569
Otis Thorpe, HOU .... .561
Chris Webber, GS............ .552

FREE-THROW PCT.

M. Abdul-Rauf, DEN .... .956
Reggie Miller, IND............ .908
Ricky Pierce, SEA............ .896
Sedale Threatt, LAL .... .890

3-PT. FIELD-GOAL PCT.

Tracy Murray, POR.......... .459
B.J. Armstrong, CHI......... .444
Reggie Miller, IND............ .421
Steve Kerr, CHI............... .419

EAST FIRST ROUND

Atlanta 3, Miami 2
New York 3, New Jersey 1
Chicago 3, Cleveland 0
Indiana 3, Orlando 0

EAST SEMIFINALS

New York 4, Chicago 3
Indiana 4, Atlanta 2

EAST FINALS

New York 4, Indiana 3

WEST FIRST ROUND

Denver 3, Seattle 2
Houston 3, Portland 1
Phoenix 3, Golden St. 0
Utah 3, San Antonio 1

WEST SEMIFINALS

Houston 4, Phoenix 3
Utah 4, Denver 3

WEST FINALS

Houston 4, Utah 1

NBA FINALS

Houston 85, New York 78
New York 91, Houston 83
Houston 93, New York 89
New York 91, Houston 82
New York 91, Houston 84
Houston 86, New York 84
Houston 90, New York 84

1994-95 FINAL STANDINGS

Eastern Conference
Atlantic Division

	W	L	PCT.	GB
Orlando	57	25	.695	
New York	55	27	.671	2
Boston	35	47	.427	22
Miami	32	50	.390	25
New Jersey	30	52	.366	27
Philadelphia	24	58	.293	33
Washington	21	61	.256	36

Central Division

	W	L	PCT.	GB
Indiana	52	30	.634	
Charlotte	50	32	.610	2
Chicago	47	35	.573	5
Cleveland	43	39	.524	9
Atlanta	42	40	.512	10
Milwaukee	34	48	.415	18
Detroit	28	54	.341	24

Western Conference
Midwest Division

	W	L	PCT.	GB
San Antonio	62	20	.756	
Utah	60	22	.732	2
Houston	47	35	.573	15
Denver	41	41	.500	21
Dallas	36	46	.439	26
Minnesota	21	61	.256	41

Pacific Division

	W	L	PCT.	GB
Phoenix	59	23	.720	
Seattle	57	25	.695	2
L.A. Lakers	48	34	.585	11
Portland	44	38	.537	15
Sacramento	39	43	.476	20
Golden State	26	56	.317	33
L.A. Clippers	17	65	.207	42

SCORING
Shaquille O'Neal, ORL......29.3
Hakeem Olajuwon, HOU ..27.8
David Robinson, SA.........27.6
Karl Malone, UTA 26.7
Jamal Mashburn, DAL 24.1
Patrick Ewing, NY............23.9
Charles Barkley, PHO......23.0
Mitch Richmond, SAC......22.8
Glen Rice, MIA................22.3
Glenn Robinson, MIL 21.9

REBOUNDS
Dennis Rodman, SA 16.8
Dikembe Mutombo, DEN ..12.5
Shaquille O'Neal, ORL......11.4
Patrick Ewing, NY.............11.0
Tyrone Hill, CLE................10.9

ASSISTS
John Stockton, UTA..........12.3
Kenny Anderson, NJ..........9.4
Tim Hardaway, GS 9.3
Rod Strickland, POR..........8.8

STEALS
Scottie Pippen, CHI 2.94
Mookie Blaylock, ATL 2.50
Gary Payton, SEA.............2.49

John Stockton, UTA..........2.37
Nate McMillan, SEA..........2.06

BLOCKED SHOTS
Dikembe Mutombo, DEN ..3.91
Hakeem Olajuwon, HOU ..3.36
Shawn Bradley, PHI..........3.34
David Robinson, SA..........3.23
Alonzo Mourning, CHA 2.92

FIELD-GOAL PCT.
Chris Gatling, GS..............633
Shaquille O'Neal, ORL.....583
Horace Grant, ORL............567
Otis Thorpe, HOU/POR 565

FREE-THROW PCT.
Spud Webb, SAC..............934
Mark Price, CLE...............914
Dana Barros, PHI.............899
Reggie Miller, IND.............897

3-PT. FIELD-GOAL PCT.
Steve Kerr, CHI................524
Detlef Schrempf, SEA......514
Dana Barros, PHI.............464
Hubert Davis, NY 455

EAST FIRST ROUND
Orlando 3, Boston 1
Indiana 3, Atlanta 0
New York 3, Cleveland 1
Chicago 3, Charlotte 1

EAST SEMIFINALS
Indiana 4, New York 3
Orlando 4, Chicago 2

EAST FINALS
Orlando 4, Indiana 3

WEST FIRST ROUND
San Antonio 3, Denver 0
Phoenix 3, Portland 0
Houston 3, Utah 2
L.A. Lakers 3, Seattle 1

WEST SEMIFINALS
San Antonio 4, L.A. Lakers 2
Houston 4, Phoenix 3

WEST FINALS
Houston 4, San Antonio 2

NBA FINALS
Houston 120, Orlando 118 (OT)
Houston 117, Orlando 106
Houston 106, Orlando 103
Houston 113, Orlando 101

1995-96 FINAL STANDINGS

Eastern Conference
Atlantic Division

	W	L	PCT.	GB
Orlando	60	22	.732	
New York	47	35	.573	13
Miami	42	40	.512	18
Washington	39	43	.476	21
Boston	33	49	.402	27
New Jersey	30	52	.366	30
Philadelphia	18	64	.220	42

Central Division

	W	L	PCT.	GB
Chicago	72	10	.878	
Indiana	52	30	.634	20
Cleveland	47	35	.573	25
Atlanta	46	36	.561	26
Detroit	46	36	.561	26
Charlotte	41	41	.500	31
Milwaukee	25	57	.305	47
Toronto	21	61	.256	51

Western Conference
Midwest Division

	W	L	PCT.	GB
San Antonio	59	23	.720	
Utah	55	27	.671	4
Houston	48	34	.585	11
Denver	35	47	.427	24
Dallas	26	56	.317	33
Minnesota	26	56	.317	33
Vancouver	15	67	.183	44

Pacific Division

	W	L	PCT.	GB
Seattle	64	18	.780	
L.A. Lakers	53	29	.646	11
Portland	44	38	.537	20
Phoenix	41	41	.500	23
Sacramento	39	43	.476	25
Golden State	36	46	.439	28
L.A. Clippers	29	53	.354	35

SCORING
Michael Jordan, CHI 30.4
Hakeem Olajuwon, HOU ..26.9
Shaquille O'Neal, ORL......26.6
Karl Malone, UTA 25.7
David Robinson, SA.........25.0
Charles Barkley, PHO......23.2
Alonzo Mourning, MIA 23.2
Mitch Richmond, SAC......23.1
Patrick Ewing, NY 22.5
Juwan Howard, WAS........22.1
Anfernee Hardaway, ORL.21.7
Glen Rice, CHA 21.6
Cedric Ceballos, LAL 21.2
Reggie Miller, IND............21.1
Vin Baker, MIL 21.1
Clifford Robinson, POR 21.1
Larry Johnson, CHA 20.5

REBOUNDS
Dennis Rodman, CHI.......14.9
David Robinson, SA.........12.2
Dikembe Mutombo, DEN ..11.8
Charles Barkley, PHO.......11.6
Shawn Kemp, SEA 11.4
Hakeem Olajuwon, HOU ..10.9
Patrick Ewing, NY 10.6
Alonzo Mourning, MIA 10.4

ASSISTS
John Stockton, UTA..........11.2
Jason Kidd, DAL.................9.7
Avery Johnson, SA 9.6
Rod Strickland, POR...........9.6
Damon Stoudamire, TOR 9.3
Kevin Johnson, PHO 9.2
Kenny Anderson, NJ/CHA 8.3
Tim Hardaway, GS/MIA 8.0

STEALS
Gary Payton, SEA.............2.85
Mookie Blaylock, ATL 2.62
Michael Jordan, CHI 2.20
Jason Kidd, DAL................2.16
Alvin Robertson, TOR........2.16
Anfernee Hardaway, ORL.2.02
Eric Murdock, MIL/VAN.......1.85
Eddie Jones, LAL..............1.84

BLOCKED SHOTS
Dikembe Mutombo, DEN ..4.49
Shawn Bradley, PHI/NJ 3.65
David Robinson, SA...........3.30
Hakeem Olajuwon, HOU ..2.88
Alonzo Mourning, MIA 2.70
Elden Campbell, LAL........2.59
Patrick Ewing, NY 2.42

FIELD-GOAL PCT.
Gheorghe Muresan, WAS .584
Chris Gatling, GS/MIA.........575
Shaquille O'Neal, ORL......573
Anthony Mason, NY.........563
Shawn Kemp, SEA 561
Dale Davis, IND................558
Arvydas Sabonis, POR.....545

FREE-THROW PCT.
M. Abdul-Rauf, DEN 930
Jeff Hornacek, UTA 893
Terrell Brandon, CLE.........887
Dana Barros, BOS............884
Brent Price, WAS..............874
Hersey Hawkins, SEA.......873
Mitch Richmond, SAC........866
Reggie Miller, IND.............863

3-PT. FIELD-GOAL PCT.
Tim Legler, WAS...............522
Steve Kerr, CHI................515
Hubert Davis, NY 476
B.J. Armstrong, GS...........473
Jeff Hornacek, UTA 466
Brent Price, WAS..............462
Bobby Phills, CLE.............441
Terry Dehere, LAC............440

1996 PLAYOFFS

EAST FIRST ROUND
Chicago 102, Miami 85
Chicago 106, Miami 75
Chicago 112, Miami 91

Orlando 112, Detroit 92
Orlando 92, Detroit 77
Orlando 101, Detroit 98

Atlanta 92, Indiana 80
Indiana 102, Atlanta 94 (OT)
Atlanta 90, Indiana 83
Indiana 83, Atlanta 75
Atlanta 89, Indiana 87

New York 106, Cleveland 83
New York 84, Cleveland 80
New York 81, Cleveland 76

EAST SEMIFINALS
Chicago 91, New York 84
Chicago 91, New York 80
New York 102, Chicago 99 (OT)
Chicago 94, New York 91
Chicago 94, New York 81

Orlando 117, Atlanta 105
Orlando 120, Atlanta 94
Orlando 103, Atlanta 96
Atlanta 104, Orlando 99
Orlando 96, Atlanta 88

EAST FINALS
Chicago 121, Orlando 83
Chicago 93, Orlando 88
Chicago 86, Orlando 67
Chicago 106, Orlando 101

WEST FIRST ROUND
Seattle 97, Sacramento 85
Sacramento 90, Seattle 81
Seattle 96, Sacramento 89
Seattle 101, Sacramento 87

San Antonio 120, Phoenix 98
San Antonio 110, Phoenix 105
Phoenix 94, San Antonio 93
San Antonio 116, Phoenix 98

Utah 110, Portland 102
Utah 105, Portland 90
Portland 94, Utah 91 (OT)
Portland 98, Utah 90
Utah 102, Portland 64

Houston 87, L.A. Lakers 83
L.A. Lakers 104, Houston 94
Houston 104, L.A. Lakers 98
Houston 102, L.A. Lakers 94

WEST SEMIFINALS
Seattle 108, Houston 75
Seattle 105, Houston 101
Seattle 115, Houston 112
Seattle 114, Houston 107 (OT)

Utah 95, San Antonio 75
San Antonio 88, Utah 77
Utah 105, San Antonio 75
Utah 101, San Antonio 86
San Antonio 98, Utah 87
Utah 108, San Antonio 81

WEST FINALS
Seattle 102, Utah 72
Seattle 91, Utah 87
Utah 96, Seattle 76
Seattle 88, Utah 86
Utah 98, Seattle 95 (OT)
Utah 118, Seattle 83
Seattle 90, Utah 86

NBA FINALS
Chicago 107, Seattle 90
Chicago 92, Seattle 88
Chicago 108, Seattle 86
Seattle 107, Chicago 86
Seattle 89, Chicago 78
Chicago 87, Seattle 75

1995-96 OFFENSIVE TEAM STATISTICS

TEAM	FIELD GOALS			FREE THROWS			REBOUNDS			MISCELLANEOUS						SCORING	
	ATT	FGs	PCT	ATT	FTs	PCT	OFF	DEF	TOT	AST	PFs	DQ	STL	TO	BLK	PTS	AVG
Chicago	6892	3293	.478	2004	1495	.746	1247	2411	3658	2033	1807	10	745	1175	345	8625	105.2
Seattle	6401	3074	.480	2424	1843	.760	954	2449	3403	1999	1967	18	882	1441	393	8572	104.5
Orlando	6640	3203	.482	2232	1543	.691	966	2401	3367	2080	1709	19	663	1160	406	8571	104.5
Phoenix	6673	3159	.473	2472	1907	.771	1009	2501	3510	2001	1776	14	623	1207	331	8552	104.3
Boston	6942	3163	.456	2284	1630	.714	1050	2427	3477	1792	2041	14	653	1302	406	8495	103.6
San Antonio	6602	3148	.477	2261	1663	.736	937	2586	3523	2044	1820	6	645	1195	536	8477	103.4
L.A. Lakers	6706	3216	.480	2049	1529	.746	995	2303	3298	2080	1702	12	722	1163	516	8438	102.9
Charlotte	6618	3108	.470	2119	1631	.770	987	2256	3243	1907	1815	23	582	1241	277	8431	102.8
Dallas	7431	3124	.420	1975	1426	.722	1408	2379	3787	1913	1836	31	642	1270	342	8409	102.5
Washington	6618	3202	.484	2076	1511	.728	930	2327	3257	1815	1981	21	592	1327	506	8408	102.5
Utah	6417	3129	.488	2302	1769	.768	993	2373	3366	2139	2046	12	667	1215	418	8404	102.5
Houston	6638	3078	.464	2106	1611	.765	919	2455	3374	1982	1753	11	645	1245	476	8404	102.5
Golden State	6700	3056	.456	2340	1775	.759	1173	2285	3458	1889	1835	19	706	1343	470	8334	101.6
Sacramento	6494	2971	.457	2407	1759	.731	1114	2345	3459	1829	2131	29	643	1442	436	8163	99.5
L.A. Clippers	6618	3126	.472	1984	1392	.702	979	2190	3169	1672	2008	21	703	1355	411	8153	99.4
Portland	6688	3064	.458	2321	1537	.662	1160	2577	3737	1760	1859	20	594	1377	417	8145	99.3

(Continued on page 462)

(Continued from page 461)

1995-96 OFFENSIVE TEAM STATISTICS

TEAM	FIELD GOALS			FREE THROWS			REBOUNDS			MISCELLANEOUS						SCORING	
	ATT	FGs	PCT	ATT	FTs	PCT	OFF	DEF	TOT	AST	PFs	DQ	STL	TO	BLK	PTS	AVG
Indiana	6205	2979	.480	2416	1823	.755	1010	2262	3272	1917	2031	17	579	1335	323	8144	99.3
Atlanta	6665	2985	.448	2012	1523	.757	1182	2148	3330	1609	1714	18	771	1228	319	8059	98.3
Minnesota	6481	2974	.459	2314	1797	.777	985	2271	3256	1867	1994	15	650	1426	481	8024	97.9
Denver	6657	3001	.451	2173	1614	.743	1057	2487	3544	1851	1882	21	521	1265	597	8013	97.7
Toronto	6598	3084	.467	1953	1412	.723	1071	2213	3284	1927	1987	27	745	1544	493	7994	97.5
New York	6382	3003	.471	1954	1480	.757	829	2449	3278	1822	1864	17	645	1272	377	7971	97.2
Miami	6348	2902	.457	2187	1553	.710	999	2495	3494	1752	2158	32	574	1394	439	7909	96.5
Milwaukee	6490	3034	.467	1914	1412	.738	973	2164	3137	1755	1943	16	582	1295	307	7837	95.6
Detroit	6122	2810	.459	2206	1657	.751	884	2440	3324	1610	1953	16	506	1215	352	7822	95.4
Philadelphia	6418	2796	.436	2263	1662	.734	1031	2161	3192	1629	1777	16	643	1414	420	7746	94.5
New Jersey	6750	2881	.427	2244	1672	.745	1350	2503	3853	1752	1880	23	627	1375	571	7684	93.7
Cleveland	5998	2761	.460	1775	1355	.763	867	2055	2922	1818	1685	14	674	1073	340	7473	91.1
Vancouver	6483	2772	.428	1998	1446	.724	957	2170	3127	1706	1852	14	728	1347	333	7362	89.8

1995-96 DEFENSIVE TEAM STATISTICS

TEAM	FIELD GOALS			FREE THROWS			REBOUNDS			MISCELLANEOUS						SCORING		
	ATT	FGs	PCT	ATT	FTs	PCT	OFF	DEF	TOT	AST	PFs	DQ	STL	TO	BLK	PTS	AVG	DIF
Cleveland	5787	2674	.462	1844	1400	.759	874	2167	3041	1818	1667	9	504	1282	336	7261	88.5	+2.6
Detroit	6375	2827	.443	2039	1458	.715	964	2268	3232	1729	1887	19	556	1153	385	7617	92.9	+2.5
Chicago	6428	2880	.448	1985	1424	.717	981	2136	3117	1592	1856	25	595	1405	312	7621	92.9	+12.2
New York	6471	2859	.442	2191	1621	.740	995	2425	3420	1671	1762	11	653	1293	281	7781	94.9	+2.3
Miami	6303	2734	.434	2498	1878	.752	982	2315	3297	1645	2031	30	662	1288	403	7792	95.0	+1.4
Utah	6174	2747	.445	2422	1820	.751	936	2149	3085	1640	1983	25	584	1284	409	7864	95.9	+6.6
Indiana	6291	2841	.452	2302	1703	.740	1004	2051	3055	1726	2041	27	663	1259	420	7878	96.1	+3.2
Seattle	6553	2873	.438	2309	1654	.716	1074	2255	3329	1776	2010	29	758	1517	391	7933	96.7	+7.8
Portland	6677	2953	.442	2127	1574	.740	932	2316	3248	1807	1996	18	708	1192	409	7952	97.0	+2.4
Atlanta	6419	3044	.474	1865	1392	.746	1054	2292	3346	1841	1807	15	580	1405	338	7959	97.1	+1.2
San Antonio	6866	3017	.439	2034	1485	.730	1109	2473	3582	1849	1972	19	604	1257	428	7960	97.1	+6.3
New Jersey	6625	3006	.454	1994	1476	.740	1028	2355	3383	1876	1925	14	665	1270	516	8031	97.9	-4.2
L.A. Lakers	6806	3118	.458	1891	1395	.738	1146	2316	3462	2006	1806	14	588	1334	483	8073	98.5	+4.5
Orlando	6736	3060	.454	2037	1499	.736	1087	2365	3452	1869	1827	19	644	1238	324	8115	99.0	+5.6
Vancouver	6486	3080	.475	2129	1561	.733	1102	2550	3652	1988	1785	9	698	1423	474	8180	99.8	-10.0
Denver	6741	3091	.459	2105	1600	.760	934	2385	3319	1875	1899	18	617	1130	418	8235	100.4	-2.7
Houston	6910	3178	.460	2012	1423	.707	1126	2499	3625	1945	1847	14	670	1224	400	8261	100.7	+1.7
Milwaukee	6421	3084	.480	2193	1590	.725	998	2305	3303	1940	1752	12	648	1212	373	8272	100.9	-5.3
Washington	6650	3061	.460	2378	1822	.766	1105	2370	3475	1900	1891	16	696	1362	390	8321	101.5	+1.1
Sacramento	6461	2987	.462	2596	1950	.751	1056	2312	3368	1805	2006	21	767	1356	505	8385	102.3	-2.7
L.A. Clippers	6471	3090	.478	2444	1824	.746	1034	2362	3396	1658	1860	16	689	1357	401	8448	103.0	-3.6
Golden State	6753	3206	.475	2097	1564	.746	1114	2292	3406	2098	1959	23	698	1375	385	8453	103.1	-1.5
Minnesota	6586	3086	.469	2368	1761	.744	1036	2317	3353	1966	1940	17	725	1343	498	8463	103.2	-5.4
Charlotte	6651	3254	.489	1957	1440	.736	953	2358	3311	2049	1829	14	536	1215	368	8478	103.4	-0.6
Phoenix	6837	3217	.471	2083	1540	.739	1003	2382	3385	2088	2011	28	586	1191	420	8525	104.0	+0.3
Philadelphia	6796	3284	.483	1986	1472	.741	1164	2478	3642	2109	1912	17	723	1288	469	8566	104.5	-10.0
Toronto	6624	3146	.475	2416	1799	.745	1098	2274	3372	1990	1739	10	766	1326	482	8610	105.0	-7.5
Boston	6856	3296	.481	2366	1767	.747	1040	2590	3630	1916	1965	22	667	1314	489	8774	107.0	-3.4
Dallas	6921	3403	.492	2097	1535	.732	1087	2726	3813	1978	1841	15	702	1348	531	8811	107.5	-4.9

1996 NBA FINALS COMPOSITE BOX

Seattle	G	AVG MIN	FGs FG-ATT	PCT	3-PT FGs FG-ATT	PCT	FTs FT-ATT	PCT	REB	AST	STL	BLK	AVG PTS
Kemp	6	40.3	49-89	.551	0-1	.000	42-49	.857	60	13	8	12	23.3
Payton	6	45.7	40-90	.444	9-27	.333	19-26	.731	38	42	9	0	18.0
Schrempf	6	39.7	35-79	.443	7-18	.389	21-24	.875	30	15	3	1	16.3
Hawkins	6	38.3	25-55	.455	6-22	.273	24-26	.923	21	6	7	1	13.3
Perkins	6	31.7	23-61	.377	4-17	.235	17-21	.810	28	12	3	0	11.2
McMillan	4	12.8	3-7	.429	3-5	.600	2-2	1.00	11	6	2	0	2.8
Wingate	4	8.0	5-10	.500	1-2	.500	4-4	1.00	2	0	0	0	2.5
Askew	4	15.5	2-9	.222	1-5	.200	2-2	1.00	10	2	2	0	1.8
Johnson	3	6.7	2-6	.333	0-0	.000	0-0	.000	7	1	1	1	1.3
Brickowski	6	11.3	2-9	.222	1-5	.200	0-0	.000	12	3	1	1	0.8
Snow	6	1.5	0-2	.000	0-0	.000	0-0	.000	2	1	0	0	0.0
Scheffler	4	2.0	0-1	.000	0-0	.000	0-0	.000	2	0	0	0	0.0
Totals	6	48.0	186-418	.445	32-102	.314	131-154	.851	223	101	36	16	89.2

Chicago	G	AVG MIN	FGs FG-ATT	PCT	3-PT FGs FG-ATT	PCT	FTs FT-ATT	PCT	REB	AST	STL	BLK	AVG PTS
Jordan	6	42.0	51-123	.415	6-19	.316	56-67	.836	32	25	10	1	27.3
Pippen	6	41.3	34-99	.343	9-39	.231	17-24	.708	49	32	14	8	15.7
Kukoc	6	29.3	30-71	.423	10-32	.313	8-10	.800	29	21	5	2	13.0
Longley	6	28.3	27-47	.574	0-0	.000	16-22	.727	23	13	3	11	11.7
Rodman	6	37.5	17-35	.486	0-0	.000	11-19	.579	88	15	5	1	7.5
Harper	6	19.3	12-32	.375	4-13	.308	11-12	.917	13	10	4	2	6.5
Kerr	6	18.8	10-33	.303	4-22	.182	6-7	.857	5	5	1	0	5.0
Brown	6	8.2	6-12	.500	3-6	.500	2-4	.500	2	5	4	0	2.8
Wennington	6	7.0	8-12	.667	0-0	.000	1-2	.500	3	1	0	0	2.8
Buechler	6	5.5	2-9	.222	0-6	.000	0-2	.000	0	1	4	0	0.7
Salley	5	3.0	0-1	.000	0-0	.000	0-0	.000	1	2	0	0	0.0
Totals	6	48.0	197-474	.416	36-137	.263	128-169	.757	245	130	50	25	93.0

1995-96 MOST VALUABLE PLAYER VOTING

M. Jordan, CHI (109)	1,114	K. Malone, UTA (1)	85	M. Johnson, LAL	8
D. Robinson, SA	574	S. Kemp, SEA	73	A. Mourning, MIA	6
A. Hardaway, ORL (2)	360	G. Hill, DET	63	D. Rodman, CHI	4
H. Olajuwon, HOU (1)	238	S. O'Neal, ORL	63	T. Brandon, CLE	3
S. Pippen, CHI	226	J. Stockton, UTA	12	M. Richmond, SAC	3
G. Payton, SEA	98	C. Barkley, PHO	8		

* First-place votes in parentheses.

DEFENSIVE PLAYER OF THE YEAR

Gary Payton, SEA	56
Scottie Pippen, CHI	15
D. Mutombo, DEN	13
David Robinson, SA	9
H. Olajuwon, HOU	8
Michael Jordan, CHI	7
Dennis Rodman, CHI	4
Latrell Sprewell, GS	1
Bo Outlaw, LAC	1
Horace Grant, ORL	1

SIXTH MAN AWARD

Toni Kukoc, CHI	45
Arvydas Sabonis, POR	24
Jayson Williams, NJ	14
Sam Cassell, HOU	11
Magic Johnson, LAL	9
Chuck Person, SA	5
Chris Gatling, GS/MIA	2
Dell Curry, CHA	2
Steve Kerr, CHI	1

ROOKIE OF THE YEAR

Damon Stoudamire, TOR	76
Arvydas Sabonis, POR	17
Joe Smith, GS	15
Jerry Stackhouse, PHI	2
Michael Finley, PHO	2
Kevin Garnett, MIN	1

COACH OF THE YEAR

Phil Jackson, CHI	82
Mike Fratello, CLE	22
Doug Collins, DET	3
Bob Hill, SA	3
Rudy Tomjanovich, HOU	2
Lenny Wilkens, ATL	1

1996-97 NBA Schedule

Below is the NBA schedule for the 1996-97 season. All game times listed are local. TNT telecasts are denoted by a "•," TBS games by a "+," and NBC games by a "#." The symbol "@" indicates more games that NBC may telecast; the network will make its decision at a later date.

Fri, Nov 1
Chi at Bos, 7:00
Cle at NJ, 7:30
Mil at Phi, 7:30
Was at Orl, 7:30
Atl at Mia, 7:30
•NY at Tor, 8:00
Ind at Det, 7:30
SA at Min, 7:00
Sac at Hou, 7:30
Dal at Den, 7:00
Sea at Uta, 7:30
•Pho at LAK,
   7:30
LAC at GS, 7:30
Por at Van, 7:30

Sat, Nov 2
Cle at Was, 7:30
Tor at Cha, 7:30
Det at Atl, 7:30
Mia at Ind, 7:30
Phi at Chi, 7:30
Bos at Mil, 7:30
Sac at Dal, 7:30
Hou at Pho, 7:00
Uta at LAC, 7:30
Por at Sea, 7:00

Sun, Nov 3
Cha at NY, 6:00
Den at SA, 6:00
Min at LAK, 6:30
GS at Van, 6:00

Mon, Nov 4
Hou at Uta, 7:00
Atl at Por, 7:00

Tue, Nov 5
•LAK at NY, 8:00
Det at Phi, 7:30
Dal at Tor, 7:00
SA at Cle, 7:30
Van at Chi, 7:30
LAC at Den, 7:00
Min at Pho, 7:30
Por at GS, 7:30
Hou at Sac, 7:30
Atl at Sea, 7:00

Wed, Nov 6
Ind at Bos, 7:00
SA at Was, 7:30
+Chi at Mia, 8:00

LAK at Cha, 7:30
Dal at Det, 7:30
Van at Mil, 7:30

Thu, Nov 7
Orl at NJ (Tok),
   5:00 A.M.
Hou at Den, 7:00
Sea at Pho, 7:00
NY at GS, 7:30
Atl at Sac, 7:30
Min at Por, 7:00

Fri, Nov 8
Phi at Bos, 7:00
Cha at Was, 7:30
•NJ at Orl (Tok),
   10:30
Mil at Mia, 7:30
LAK at Tor, 7:00
Van at Cle, 7:30
•Chi at Det, 8:00
Sea at SA, 7:30
GS at Den, 7:00
NY at LAC, 7:30

Sat, Nov 9
Pho at Phi, 7:30
Mil at Cha, 7:30
Was at Ind, 7:30
Bos at Chi, 7:30
Mia at Dal, 7:30
Uta at Hou, 7:30
Por at Sac, 7:30

Sun, Nov 10
Den at Cle, 1:30
Min at LAC, 6:00
Atl at LAK, 6:30
SA at Por, 7:00
NY at Van, 6:00

Mon, Nov 11
Den at Tor, 7:00
Pho at Chi, 7:30
SA at Uta, 7:00
Sea at Sac, 7:30

Tue, Nov 12
Phi at NY, 7:30
Det at Was, 7:30
Cha at Mia, 7:30
Cle at Atl, 7:30
Pho at Mil, 7:30
Por at Min, 7:00
Ind at Dal, 7:30

•LAK at Hou, 7:00
GS at Sea, 7:00
LAC at Van, 7:00

Wed, Nov 13
Atl at Bos, 7:00
Was at NJ, 7:30
Phi at Tor, 7:30
Por at Cle, 7:30
Den at Det, 7:30
Mia at Chi, 7:30
LAK at SA, 7:30
Sac at Uta, 7:00

Thu, Nov 14
Tor at NY, 7:30
Cha at Orl, 7:30
Dal at Min, 7:00
Ind at Hou, 7:30
Sea at LAC, 7:30
Mil at GS, 7:30
Pho at Van, 7:00

Fri, Nov 15
Den at Bos, 7:00
Por at NJ, 7:30
Cle at Phi, 7:30
•Chi at Cha, 8:00
Mia at Atl, 7:30
Was at Det, 7:30
Ind at SA, 7:30
Van at Uta, 7:00
LAC at LAK, 7:30
Mil at Sac, 7:30

Sat, Nov 16
Min at NY, 1:00
Den at NJ, 8:00
Bos at Was, 7:30
Tor at Orl, 7:30
Phi at Mia, 7:30
Det at Cle, 7:30
Atl at Chi, 7:30
Uta at Dal, 7:30
GS at Hou, 7:30
Sac at Sea, 7:00

Sun, Nov 17
Por at Ind, 6:00
GS at SA, 6:00
LAK at Pho, 7:00
Mil at LAC, 6:00
Van at Sea, 6:00

Mon, Nov 18
Sac at Van, 7:00

Tue, Nov 19
•NY at Orl, 8:00
Sea at Tor, 7:00
Atl at Cle, 7:30
Dal at Mil, 7:30
Min at Hou, 7:30
Mia at Den, 7:00
LAK at GS, 7:30
Sac at Por, 7:00

Wed, Nov 20
Det at Bos, 7:00
Ind at Phi, 7:30
Sea at Was, 7:30
+NY at Cha, 8:00
LAC at SA, 7:30
+Chi at Pho, 8:30
Uta at LAK, 7:30
Mia at Van, 7:00

Thu, Nov 21
Min at Orl, 7:30
Cle at Tor, 7:00
NJ at Det, 7:30
Cha at Ind, 7:30
Atl at Mil, 7:30
LAC at Dal, 7:30
Pho at Hou, 7:30
Chi at Den, 7:00
GS at Uta, 7:00

Fri, Nov 22
Sea at Bos, 7:00
•Phi at Was, 8:00
SA at LAK, 7:30
Mia at Sac, 7:30

Sat, Nov 23
Dal at NJ, 7:30
NY at Phi, 7:30
Det at Cha, 7:30
Atl at Tor, 1:30
Orl at Ind, 7:30
Was at Mil, 7:30
LAC at Min, 7:00
Chi at Uta, 7:00
Hou at GS, 12:00
Den at Por, 7:00

Sun, Nov 24
Dal at Bos, 7:00
Sea at NY, 6:00
Sac at Cle, 1:30
Mia at Pho, 7:00
Hou at LAK, 6:30

SA at Van, 6:00
Mon, Nov 25
Min at Was, 7:30
Mil at Orl, 7:30
NJ at Uta, 7:00
Chi at LAC, 7:30
Tue, Nov 26
LAK at Phi, 7:30
Sea at Cha, 7:30
Van at Atl, 7:30
Sac at Tor, 7:00
SA at Dal, 7:30
•Por at Hou, 7:00
Pho at Den, 7:00
Mia at GS, 7:30
Wed, Nov 27
+LAK at Bos, 8:00
Atl at Orl, 7:30
Cha at Tor, 7:00
Van at Det, 7:30
Cle at Mil, 7:30
Sea at Min, 7:00
Por at SA, 7:30
Den at Uta, 7:00
NJ at Pho, 7:00
+Mia at LAC, 7:30
Thu, Nov 28
Sac at Ind, 7:30
NJ at GS, 7:30
Fri, Nov 29
Hou at Bos, 7:00
Orl at Phi, 7:30
Was at Atl, 7:30
•LAK at Det, 8:00
Van at Ind, 7:30
Chi at Dal, 7:30
Min at Den, 7:00
LAC at Uta, 7:00
GS at Por, 7:00
Pho at Sea, 7:00
Sat, Nov 30
Sac at NY, 1:00
Van at Phi, 7:30
Hou at Was, 7:30
Bos at Mia, 7:30
Orl at Cle, 7:30
Cha at Mil, 7:30
Tor at Min, 7:00
Chi at SA, 7:30
NJ at LAC, 7:30
Sun, Dec 1
Sac at Det, 7:00
Den at LAK, 6:30
Por at GS, 12:00
Uta at Sea, 5:00
Mon, Dec 2
Dal at Orl, 7:30
Hou at Tor, 7:00

Cha at Uta, 7:00
Tue, Dec 3
•Mia at NY, 8:00
Bos at Atl, 7:30
Tor at Cle, 7:30
Chi at Mil, 7:30
Sac at Min, 7:00
Cha at LAC, 7:30
Sea at LAK, 7:30
Den at GS, 7:30
Ind at Por, 7:00
Wed, Dec 4
NY at NJ, 7:30
Cle at Orl, 7:30
Dal at Mia, 7:30
Atl at Det, 7:30
Bos at Hou, 7:30
Phi at SA, 7:30
+LAK at Uta, 6:00
GS at Pho, 7:00
Ind at Van, 7:30
Thu, Dec 5
Was at Tor, 7:00
LAC at Chi, 7:30
Phi at Dal, 7:30
Por at Den, 7:00
Min at Sea, 7:00
Fri, Dec 6
NJ at Bos, 7:00
NY at Mia, 7:30
Cle at Det, 7:30
Van at SA, 7:30
Min at Uta, 7:00
•Orl at LAK, 7:30
Ind at GS, 7:30
•Pho at Sac, 5:00
Cha at Por, 7:00
Sat, Dec 7
LAC at NY, 7:30
Det at NJ, 8:00
Mil at Was, 7:30
Tor at Atl, 7:30
Mia at Chi, 7:30
Van at Dal, 7:30
Phi at Hou, 7:30
Uta at Den, 7:00
Cha at Sea, 7:00
Sun, Dec 8
Chi at Tor, 8:30
LAC at Cle, 6:00
Bos at Mil, 6:00
Ind at Pho, 7:00
Min at LAK, 6:30
SA at GS, 5:00
Orl at Sac, 6:00
Mon, Dec 9
Sea at Phi, 7:30
Cha at Van, 7:00

Tue, Dec 10
Was at NY, 7:30
Den at Atl, 7:30
GS at Tor, 7:00
Mia at Cle, 7:30
Det at Mil, 7:30
•Hou at Min, 7:00
Ind at Uta, 7:00
SA at Pho, 7:00
Dal at LAC, 7:30
LAK at Sac, 7:30
Orl at Por, 7:00
Wed, Dec 11
Tor at Bos, 7:00
Sea at NJ, 7:30
+Mia at Phi, 8:00
Cle at Was, 7:30
Den at Cha, 7:30
Min at Chi, 7:30
Ind at LAK, 7:30
Thu, Dec 12
GS at NY, 7:30
Sea at Mil, 7:30
Det at Hou, 7:30
Pho at Uta, 7:00
SA at LAC, 7:30
Dal at Sac, 7:30
Van at Por, 7:00
Fri, Dec 13
Chi at NJ, 7:30
Den at Was, 7:30
Phi at Cha, 7:30
•GS at Cle, 8:00
Bos at Ind, 7:30
Pho at Min, 7:00
Por at LAK, 7:30
Orl at Van, 7:00
Sat, Dec 14
Den at NY, 7:30
Tor at Mia, 1:00
Phi at Atl, 7:30
Cha at Chi, 7:30
NJ at Mil, 8:00
Cle at Min, 7:00
Dal at SA, 7:30
Orl at Uta, 7:00
Sac at LAC, 7:30
Hou at Sea, 7:00
Sun, Dec 15
Bos at Det, 7:00
Van at Pho, 7:00
Was at GS, 5:00
Hou at Por, 7:00
Mon, Dec 16
Mil at Bos, 7:00
Det at Tor, 7:00
Pho at LAC, 7:30
Was at Sac, 7:30

Tue, Dec 17
Uta at NY, 7:30
Tor at NJ, 7:30
Cha at Phi, 7:30
Ind at Mia, 7:30
•LAK at Chi, 7:00
Atl at Dal, 7:30
GS at Sea, 7:00
Hou at Van, 7:00
Wed, Dec 18
Ind at Orl, 7:30
NJ at Cle, 7:30
+NY at Det, 8:00
LAK at Mil, 7:30
Sac at Den, 7:00
Was at Pho, 7:00
Min at GS, 7:30
Sea at Por, 7:00
Thu, Dec 19
Uta at Mia, 7:30
Chi at Cha, 7:30
Mil at Tor, 7:00
SA at Hou, 7:30
Was at LAC, 7:30
Min at Sac, 7:30
Dal at Van, 7:00
Fri, Dec 20
NY at Phi, 7:30
•Uta at Orl, 8:00
NJ at Atl, 7:30
Tor at Cle, 7:30
Det at Ind, 7:30
Van at Den, 7:00
Dal at Por, 7:00
LAC at Sea, 7:00
Sat, Dec 21
Det at NY, 7:30
Bos at NJ, 7:30
Chi at Phi, 7:30
Atl at Cha, 7:30
Orl at Mil, 8:00
LAK at Min, 7:00
Mia at Hou, 7:30
Pho at SA, 7:30
Por at Sac, 7:30
Sun, Dec 22
Cha at Bos, 7:00
Uta at Cle, 1:30
Tor at Ind, 2:30
LAC at GS, 5:00
Dal at Sea, 5:00
Was at Van, 6:00
Mon, Dec 23
Atl at NY, 7:30
Cle at Orl, 7:30
NJ at Chi, 7:30
Uta at Min, 7:00
Mil at Hou, 7:30

Mia at SA, 7:30
Den at Pho, 7:00
LAC at Sac, 7:30
Was at Por, 7:00
Wed, Dec 25
#Det at Chi, 7:30
#LAK at Pho, 4:00
Thu, Dec 26
+Orl at Mia, 8:00
Chi at Atl, 7:30
NJ at Tor, 1:30
Ind at Det, 7:30
Hou at Mil, 7:30
NY at Min, 7:00
GS at Dal, 7:30
Phi at Den, 7:00
Por at Uta, 7:00
Van at Sac, 7:30
SA at Sea, 7:00
Fri, Dec 27
Ind at NJ, 7:30
Tor at Was, 7:30
Mia at Cha, 7:30
Mil at Cle, 7:30
Por at LAC, 7:30
Bos at LAK, 7:30
Sat, Dec 28
Orl at NY, 1:00
Atl at Was (Bal), 7:30
Cha at Det, 7:30
Cle at Chi, 7:30
Den at Min, 7:00
Sea at Dal, 7:30
GS at Hou, 7:30
Phi at Uta, 1:00
Bos at Sac, 7:30
Pho at Van, 7:00
Sun, Dec 29
NJ at Ind, 2:30
Mia at Mil, 6:00
Phi at LAK, 6:30
SA at Por, 7:00
Mon, Dec 30
NJ at NY, 7:30
Cha at Was, 7:30
Min at Cle, 7:30
Orl at Det, 7:30
Ind at Chi, 7:30
Sea at Hou, 7:30
Bos at Den, 7:00
Sac at Pho, 7:00
Uta at LAC, 7:30
SA at Van, 7:00
Thu, Jan 2
NY at Was, 7:30
Tor at Orl, 7:30
NJ at Mia, 7:30
Dal at Cha, 7:30

Pho at Cle, 7:30
Bos at Det, 7:30
Por at Hou, 7:30
Uta at SA, 7:30
LAK at Sac, 7:30
Phi at Sea, 7:00
Fri, Jan 3
Min at Bos, 7:00
Atl at NJ, 7:30
Pho at Ind, 7:30
•Orl at Chi, 7:00
SA at Den, 7:00
Sac at LAK, 7:30
Phi at GS, 7:30
Sea at Van, 7:00
Sat, Jan 4
Was at Cha, 7:30
NY at Atl, 7:30
Ind at Cle, 7:30
Tor at Det, 7:30
Min at Mil, 8:00
Por at Dal, 7:30
LAC at Hou, 7:30
Mia at Uta, 7:00
Sun, Jan 5
Pho at Bos, 7:30
Mil at NY, 6:00
LAC at SA, 6:00
Phi at Sac, 6:00
LAK at Van, 6:00
Mon, Jan 6
Uta at Chi, 7:30
Cha at GS, 7:30
LAK at Por, 7:00
Tue, Jan 7
Dal at NY, 7:30
SA at NJ, 7:30
Phi at Orl, 7:30
Pho at Atl, 7:30
LAC at Tor, 7:00
Mil at Det, 7:30
Cle at Ind, 7:30
Hou at Min, 7:00
Den at Sac, 7:30
•Mia at Sea, 5:00
Wed, Jan 8
SA at Bos, 7:00
Dal at Phi, 7:30
Pho at Was, 7:30
Hou at Cle, 7:30
Uta at Mil, 7:30
+Sea at Den, 6:00
Cha at LAK, 7:30
Van at GS, 7:30
Mia at Por, 7:00
Thu, Jan 9
Min at NJ, 7:30
Atl at Orl, 7:30

Uta at Tor, 7:00
GS at Van, 7:00
Fri, Jan 10
NY at Bos, 7:00
Hou at Phi, 7:30
LAC at Was, 7:30
•SA at Det, 8:00
Chi at Mil, 7:30
Ind at Den, 7:00
Cha at Pho, 7:00
Mia at LAK, 7:30
Sat, Jan 11
Bos at NY, 7:30
Tor at NJ, 7:30
SA at Atl, 7:30
Was at Cle, 7:30
Uta at Det, 7:30
Hou at Chi, 7:30
LAC at Min, 7:00
Den at Dal, 7:30
Ind at Sea, 7:00
Sac at Van, 7:00
Sun, Jan 12
Orl at Tor, 6:30
GS at Mil, 6:00
Cha at Sac, 6:00
Mon, Jan 13
Orl at NJ, 7:30
Uta at Phi, 7:30
Was at Mia, 7:30
Atl at Cle, 7:30
Pho at Dal, 7:30
Cha at Den, 7:00
Tue, Jan 14
GS at Bos, 7:00
Min at Atl, 7:30
Was at Chi, 7:30
•NY at Hou, 7:00
Den at Pho, 7:00
Van at LAK, 7:30
Ind at Sac, 7:30
Det at Por, 7:00
Wed, Jan 15
GS at Phi, 7:30
NJ at Cha, 7:30
Chi at Min, 7:00
+Orl at Dal, 7:00
NY at SA, 7:30
Ind at LAC, 7:30
Tor at Sea, 7:30
Det at Van, 7:00
Thu, Jan 16
Mia at Bos, 7:00
Orl at Atl, 7:30
Sac at Hou, 7:30
Cle at Den, 7:00
Pho at Uta, 7:00
Por at LAK, 7:30

Fri, Jan 17
NJ at Phi, 7:30
Mia at Was (Bal),
  7:30
GS at Ind, 7:30
Mil at Chi, 7:30
Hou at Dal, 7:30
Sac at SA, 7:30
Tor at Por, 7:00
Cle at Sea, 7:00
•Uta at Van, 6:00
Sat, Jan 18
Was at Bos, 7:00
Cha at NJ, 7:30
Mil at Atl, 7:30
GS at Min, 7:00
Dal at Den, 7:00
NY at Pho, 7:00
Det at LAK, 7:30
Sun, Jan 19
#Orl at Mia, 12:00
Phi at Ind, 2:30
#Chi at Hou, 1:30
Cle at LAC, 6:00
Uta at Por, 7:00
Tor at Van, 12:00
Mon, Jan 20
Was at NY, 1:00
Mil at Phi, 1:00
Cha at Atl, 1:00
SA at Min, 2:30
NJ at Den, 7:00
Cle at Uta, 7:00
Det at Pho, 7:00
Dal at LAK, 1:30
Van at Sea, 7:00
Tue, Jan 21
Was at Orl, 7:30
Atl at Mia, 7:30
Hou at Cha, 7:30
Min at Tor, 7:00
•NY at Chi, 7:00
Ind at Mil, 7:30
Dal at GS, 7:30
LAC at Por, 7:00
Wed, Jan 22
Phi at Bos, 7:30
NJ at SA, 7:30
Van at Den, 7:00
Uta at Pho, 7:30
+Det at Sac, 5:00
Por at Sea, 7:00
Thu, Jan 23
Mil at Orl, 7:30
Mia at Tor, 7:30
Chi at Cle, 7:30
NY at Ind, 7:30
NJ at Hou, 7:30

Sea at LAC, 7:30
Det at GS, 7:30
Min at Van, 7:00
Fri, Jan 24
Orl at Bos, 7:00
Sac at Phi, 7:30
•NY at Cha, 8:00
Was at Atl, 7:30
Dal at SA, 7:30
Por at Pho, 7:00
Den at LAC, 7:30
GS at LAK, 7:30
Sat, Jan 25
Sac at Was, 7:30
Bos at Atl, 7:30
Cha at Cle, 7:30
Phi at Det, 7:30
Mil at Ind, 2:30
Tor at Chi, 2:30
NJ at Dal, 7:30
Uta at Hou, 7:30
Min at Por, 7:00
Den at Van, 7:00
Sun, Jan 26
#Mia at NY, 12:30
SA at Mil, 1:30
#LAK at Sea, 12:00
Mon, Jan 27
Pho at Mia, 7:30
Van at GS, 7:30
Tue, Jan 28
Bos at NY, 7:30
Cle at NJ, 7:30
Orl at Was, 7:30
Por at Tor, 7:00
Cha at Ind, 7:30
•Det at Mil, 7:00
Sac at Min, 7:00
LAK at Dal, 7:30
Den at Uta, 7:00
Atl at LAC, 7:30
Chi at Van, 7:00
Wed, Jan 29
Tor at Phi, 7:30
Pho at Orl, 7:30
Bos at Mia, 7:30
Ind at Cha, 7:30
NY at Cle, 7:30
Por at Det, 7:30
+LAK at SA, 7:00
Sea at GS, 7:30
Thu, Jan 30
Pho at NJ, 7:30
Min at Dal, 7:30
Den at Hou, 7:30
Atl at Uta, 7:00
Van at LAC, 7:30
Chi at Sac, 7:30

Fri, Jan 31
Por at Bos, 7:00
Orl at Phi, 7:30
Mil at Cha, 7:30
•Hou at Ind, 8:00
Min at SA, 7:30
Chi at GS, 7:30
Was at Sea, 7:00
Atl at Van, 7:00
Sat, Feb 1
Det at NJ, 1:00
Pho at Tor, 3:00
Mia at Cle, 7:30
Phi at Mil, 8:00
Uta at Dal, 7:30
Sac at Den, 7:00
GS at LAC, 7:30
Sun, Feb 2
Van at Bos, 7:00
@Cha at NY, 1:00
@Hou at Orl, 1:00
Cle at Mia, 6:00
Pho at Det, 7:00
NJ at Ind, 2:30
Por at Min, 2:30
Atl at Den, 7:00
Was at LAK, 6:30
#Chi at Sea, 12:30
Mon, Feb 3
Bos at Tor, 7:00
Sac at SA, 7:30
Was at Uta, 7:00
Tue, Feb 4
•Hou at NY, 8:00
Van at NJ, 7:30
Ind at Orl, 7:30
Min at Cha, 7:30
Cle at Mil, 7:30
Sac at Dal, 7:30
LAK at LAC, 7:30
Atl at GS, 7:30
Chi at Por, 7:00
Wed, Feb 5
Mia at Bos, 7:00
SA at Phi, 7:30
Cle at Tor, 7:00
Was at Den, 7:00
Atl at Pho, 7:00
+Chi at LAK, 7:30
+Uta at Sea, 5:00
Thu, Feb 6
SA at NY, 7:30
Ind at NJ, 7:30
Bos at Orl, 7:30
Mil at Mia, 7:30
Sac at Cha, 7:30
Hou at Det, 7:30
Van at Min, 7:00

Sun, Feb 9
#All-Star Game (Cle), 6:00
Tue, Feb 11
NY at Was, 7:30
NJ at Orl, 7:30
•Det at Mia, 8:00
Phi at Cle, 7:30
Cha at Chi, 7:30
Tor at Mil, 7:30
SA at Dal, 7:30
Van at Hou, 7:30
Bos at LAC, 7:30
Uta at Sac, 7:30
Pho at Por, 7:00
Den at Sea, 7:00
Wed, Feb 12
NJ at Cha, 7:30
Tor at Atl, 7:30
+Orl at Det, 8:00
Cle at Ind, 7:30
LAK at Min, 7:00
Van at SA, 7:30
Bos at Pho, 7:00
Thu, Feb 13
Phi at NY, 7:30
Ind at Mia, 7:30
GS at Dal, 7:30
LAK at Den, 7:00
Por at Uta, 7:00
LAC at Sac, 7:30
Fri, Feb 14
NJ at Was (Bal), 7:30
Det at Cha, 7:30
•Chi at Atl, 8:00
Mil at Tor, 7:30
Orl at Min, 7:00
GS at SA, 7:30
LAC at Pho, 7:00
Hou at Sea, 7:00
Bos at Van, 7:00
Sat, Feb 15
Was at NJ, 7:30
Phi at Mia, 7:30
Den at Mil, 8:00
Atl at SA, 7:30
Dal at Uta, 7:00
Hou at Por, 7:00
Sun, Feb 16
Ind at NY, 12:30
Den at Phi, 7:00
Det at Tor, 12:30
#Orl at Chi, 4:30
Pho at Min, 2:30
#Sea at LAK, 12:00
GS at Sac, 6:00
Bos at Por, 7:00

Mon, Feb 17
Mil at Was, 1:00
Orl at Cha, 7:30
NJ at Cle, 5:00
Tor at Ind, 6:00
Atl at Hou, 7:30
Bos at Sea, 7:00
Dal at Van, 7:00
Tue, Feb 18
Pho at NY, 7:30
Mia at Phi, 7:30
Den at Chi, 7:30
•SA at Uta, 6:00
Dal at LAC, 7:30
Min at Sac, 7:30
Wed, Feb 19
+Por at Orl, 8:00
Pho at Cha, 7:30
Ind at Atl, 7:30
Was at Det, 7:30
Tor at SA, 7:30
Cle at LAK, 7:30
Bos at GS, 7:30
Min at Van, 7:00
Thu, Feb 20
Mia at NJ, 7:30
LAC at Phi, 7:30
Den at Ind, 7:30
Mil at Dal, 7:30
Tor at Hou, 7:30
Bos at Uta, 7:00
NY at Sac, 7:30
Fri, Feb 21
•Chi at Was, 8:00
Den at Orl, 7:30
Por at Mia, 7:30
LAC at Cha, 7:30
Hou at Atl, 7:30
NJ at Det, 7:30
GS at Min, 7:00
Mil at SA, 7:30
Cle at Pho, 7:30
Van at LAK, 7:30
NY at Sea, 7:00
Sat, Feb 22
Por at Phi, 7:30
Cha at Atl, 7:30
GS at Chi, 7:30
Tor at Dal, 7:30
Sun, Feb 23
@Bos at NJ, 1:00
@Det at Was, 1:00
Den at Mia, 6:00
Orl at Ind, 6:00
LAC at Mil, 1:00
@SA at Hou, 12:00
@Sea at Uta, 1:30
Dal at Pho, 7:00

@NY at LAK, 12:30
Cle at Van, 12:00

Mon, Feb 24
Det at Orl, 7:30
GS at Atl, 7:30
Por at Chi, 7:30
Cha at SA, 7:30

Tue, Feb 25
Sac at NJ, 7:30
Ind at Was, 7:30
Sea at Cle, 7:30
Cha at Dal, 7:30
•LAK at Hou, 7:00
Tor at Den, 7:00
NY at Uta, 7:00
Phi at LAC, 7:30

Wed, Feb 26
Sac at Bos, 7:00
Mia at Orl, 7:30
GS at Det, 7:30
+Sea at Ind, 8:00
Atl at Mil, 7:30
Min at SA, 7:30
Phi at Pho, 7:00
NY at Por, 7:00
LAC at Van, 7:00

Thu, Feb 27
LAK at Was, 7:30
Chi at Cle, 7:30
Min at Dal, 7:30
Cha at Hou, 7:30
Tor at Uta, 7:00

Fri, Feb 28
Det at Bos, 7:00
GS at NJ, 7:30
SA at Orl, 7:30
•Sea at Mia, 8:00
LAK at Atl, 7:30
Mil at Ind, 7:30
Sac at Chi, 7:30
NY at Den, 7:00
Tor at LAC, 7:30
Uta at Por, 7:00
Phi at Van, 7:00

Sat, Mar 1
GS at Was, 7:30
Bos at Cle, 7:30
Sac at Mil, 8:00
Dal at Hou, 7:30

Sun, Mar 2
Cle at NY, 7:30
@Sea at Orl, 3:30
@SA at Mia, 3:30
Atl at Det, 7:00
#LAK at Ind, 1:00
Cha at Min, 2:30
Pho at Dal, 7:00
LAC at Den, 7:00

Phi at Por, 7:00
Uta at Van, 12:00

Mon, Mar 3
Bos at Tor, 4:00
Mil at Chi, 7:30
Uta at GS, 7:30
NJ at Sac, 7:30

Tue, Mar 4
Mil at NY, 7:30
Was at Phi, 7:30
SA at Cha, 7:30
Cle at Atl, 7:30
Mia at Det, 7:30
Bos at Ind, 7:30
LAK at Dal, 7:30
Hou at LAC, 7:30
NJ at Por, 7:00
•Orl at Sea, 5:00

Wed, Mar 5
NY at Tor, 7:00
Ind at Cle, 7:30
+SA at Chi, 7:00
Det at Min, 7:00
Dal at Uta, 7:00
Por at Pho, 7:00
Hou at GS, 7:30
Den at Sac, 7:30

Thu, Mar 6
Atl at Phi, 7:30
Was at Mia, 7:30
Bos at Cha, 7:30
Orl at LAC, 7:30
NJ at Van, 7:00

Fri, Mar 7
NY at Bos, 7:00
Mia at Was, 7:30
Mil at Atl, 7:30
SA at Tor, 7:00
Ind at Chi, 7:30
Den at Min, 7:00
Det at Uta, 7:00
Sac at Pho, 7:00
Hou at LAK, 7:30
Orl at GS, 7:30
Dal at Por, 7:00
NJ at Sea, 7:30

Sat, Mar 8
Mil at Cle, 7:30
SA at Ind, 7:30
Det at LAC, 7:30

Sun, Mar 9
Atl at Bos, 12:30
#Chi at NY, 5:30
@Phi at Was, 3:00
Mia at Cha, 12:30
Van at Tor, 12:30
Uta at Min, 2:30
@Hou at Dal, 2:00

@Orl at Pho, 1:00
NJ at LAK, 6:30
Sac at GS, 7:30
@Sea at Por, 12:00

Mon, Mar 10
GS at LAC, 7:30

Tue, Mar 11
Chi at Bos, 7:00
Van at Cha, 7:30
Uta at Atl, 7:30
Mia at Mil, 7:30
Phi at Min, 7:00
NY at Dal, 7:30
•Hou at SA, 7:00
Orl at Den, 7:00
Tor at Pho, 7:30
Cle at Sac, 7:30
LAC at Por, 7:00
Det at Sea, 7:00

Wed, Mar 12
Uta at NJ, 7:30
Chi at Phi, 7:30
Van at Was, 7:30
Atl at Ind, 7:30
+Orl at Hou, 7:00
GS at LAK, 7:30

Thu, Mar 13
Sea at Min, 7:00
Bos at Dal, 7:30
Det at Den, 7:00
Pho at LAC, 7:30
Cle at GS, 7:30
Tor at Sac, 7:30

Fri, Mar 14
Chi at NJ, 7:30
Min at Phi, 7:30
Cha at Orl, 7:30
Van at Mia, 7:30
Sea at Atl, 7:30
Uta at Ind, 7:30
Was at Mil, 7:30
Bos at SA, 7:30
LAC at LAK, 7:30
Cle at Por, 7:00

Sat, Mar 15
Cha at Phi, 7:30
Uta at Was, 7:30
Atl at Chi, 7:30
SA at Den, 7:00
Dal at Pho, 7:00
Tor at GS, 12:00

Sun, Mar 16
@NJ at NY, 12:00
Van at Orl, 3:00
@Hou at Mia, 12:00
Sea at Det, 7:00
Ind at Mil, 1:30
Bos at Min, 2:30

Por at LAC, 6:00
Tor at LAK, 6:30
Dal at Sac, 6:00

Mon, Mar 17
Mil at Bos, 7:00
Uta at Cha, 7:30
Orl at Atl, 7:30
Det at Cle, 7:30
Was at SA, 7:30
LAK at Den, 7:00
Pho at GS, 7:30

Tue, Mar 18
Van at NY, 7:30
Hou at NJ, 7:30
Phi at Tor, 7:30
Min at Ind, 7:30
•Sea at Chi, 7:00
Was at Dal, 7:30
LAC at Pho, 7:00
Sac at Por, 7:00

Wed, Mar 19
Uta at Bos, 7:00
NY at Phi, 7:30
+GS at Mia, 8:00
Cle at Cha, 7:30
Ind at Atl, 7:30
Tor at Det, 7:30
Van at Min, 7:00
Sac at LAC, 7:30

Thu, Mar 20
GS at Orl, 7:30
LAK at Cle, 7:30
Por at Mil, 7:30
Was at Hou, 7:30
SA at Pho, 7:00,
Den at Sea, 7:00

Fri, Mar 21
Orl at Bos, 7:00
NJ at Phi, 7:30
LAK at Mia, 7:30
Dal at Atl, 7:30
Cha at Tor, 7:30
Min at Det, 7:30
Chi at Ind, 7:30
SA at Sac, 7:30
Den at Van, 7:00

Sat, Mar 22
Por at Was, 7:30
GS at Cha, 7:30
Det at Chi, 7:30
NY at Mil, 8:00
Cle at Dal, 7:30
Pho at Hou, 7:30
LAC at Uta, 7:00
Sac at Sea, 7:00

Sun, Mar 23
NJ at Bos, 3:00
Por at NY, 6:00

#LAK at Orl, 12:30
Atl at Tor, 3:00
Mia at Min, 2:30
Uta at Den, 7:00
SA at LAC, 6:00
Sea at Van, 6:00
Mon, Mar 24
LAK at NJ, 7:30
Tue, Mar 25
Sac at Orl, 7:30
Por at Atl, 7:30
Ind at Tor, 7:00
Dal at Chi, 7:30
Min at Hou, 7:30
•Cle at SA, 7:00
Mil at Pho, 7:00
Van at LAC, 7:30
Sea at GS, 7:30
Wed, Mar 26
+Det at NY, 8:00
Phi at NJ, 7:30
Bos at Was, 7:30
Sac at Mia, 7:30
Por at Cha, 7:30
Dal at Ind, 7:30
Min at Den, 7:00
Mil at LAK, 7:30
Pho at Sea, 7:00
Thu, Mar 27
LAC at Atl, 7:30
Chi at Tor, 7:00
Cle at Hou, 7:30
Orl at SA, 7:30
LAK at Van, 7:00
Fri, Mar 28
NY at NJ, 7:30
Bos at Phi, 7:30
Tor at Was, 7:30
Cle at Mia, 7:30
•Ind at Cha, 8:00
LAC at Det, 7:30
Mil at Uta, 7:00
GS at Pho, 7:00
Van at Por, 7:00
Min at Sea, 7:00
Sat, Mar 29
Dal at Was (Bal), 7:30
Sac at Atl, 7:30
NJ at Chi, 7:30
Den at Hou, 7:30
Uta at SA, 7:30
Sun, Mar 30
#NY at Orl, 12:30
Mia at Tor, 3:00
Dal at Cle, 6:00
Phi at Det, 7:00
LAC at Ind, 2:30
Mil at Den, 7:00

Sea at Pho, 7:00
Min at GS, 5:00
Tue, Apr 1
Phi at Orl, 7:30
LAC at Mia, 7:30
NY at Cle, 7:30
Was at Ind, 7:30
Bos at Chi, 7:30
Det at Dal, 7:30
Hou at Den, 7:00
GS at Por, 7:00
•LAK at Sea, 5:00
Mil at Van, 7:00
Wed, Apr 2
Cle at Bos, 7:00
Tor at Phi, 7:30
Atl at Cha, 7:30
NJ at Min, 7:00
+Det at SA, 7:00
Sac at Uta, 7:00
Hou at Pho, 7:00
Den at LAK, 7:30
Thu, Apr 3
Cha at NJ, 7:30
Chi at Was, 7:30
LAC at Orl, 7:30
Mia at Hou, 7:30
Dal at GS, 7:30
Mil at Sea, 7:00
Fri, Apr 4
LAC at Bos, 7:00
•Orl at NY, 8:00
Ind at Phi, 7:30
Det at Atl, 7:30
Cle at Chi, 7:30
Was at Min, 7:00
Pho at Den, 7:00
Van at Uta, 7:00
SA at LAK, 7:30
Hou at Sac, 7:30
Mil at Por, 7:00
Sat, Apr 5
Tor at Mia, 7:30
Phi at Cha, 7:30
NY at Atl, 7:30
SA at GS, 7:30
Pho at Por, 7:00
Dal at Sea, 12:30
Sun, Apr 6
Was at Bos, 1:00
LAC at NJ, 1:00
#Chi at Orl, 5:30
Ind at Min, 2:30
Dal at LAK, 6:30
Uta at GS, 6:00
Sea at Sac, 6:00
Hou at Van, 12:00
Mon, Apr 7

Cha at Cle, 7:30
Mia at Det, 7:30
Phi at Chi, 7:30
Por at Den, 7:00
Tue, Apr 8
•Cle at NY, 8:00
Mia at NJ, 7:30
Was at Tor, 7:00
Orl at Mil, 7:30
Por at Dal, 7:30
Den at SA, 7:30
Min at Pho, 7:00
Hou at LAC, 7:30
LAK at GS, 7:30
Van at Sac, 7:30
Wed, Apr 9
Atl at Phi, 7:30
Bos at Cha, 7:30
Chi at Ind, 7:30
+LAK at Uta, 6:00
Thu, Apr 10
Chi at NY, 7:30
Mil at NJ, 7:30
Det at Mia, 7:30
Orl at Tor, 7:00
Sea at Dal, 7:30
Van at Hou, 7:30
Por at SA, 7:30
Min at LAC, 7:30
Den at GS, 7:30
Pho at Sac, 7:30
Fri, Apr 11
Cle at Bos, 7:00
NJ at Was, 7:30
Cha at Det, 7:30
•Atl at Ind, 7:00
Phi at Mil, 7:30
Hou at Uta, 7:00
Pho at LAK, 7:30
GS at Sac, 7:30
Sat, Apr 12
Bos at Orl, 7:30
@NY at Mia, 3:30
Was at Cha, 7:30
Ind at Tor, 6:00
Phi at Cle, 7:30
Atl at Min, 7:00
Van at Dal, 7:30
@Sea at SA, 2:30
Den at LAC, 7:30
Sun, Apr 13
#Chi at Det, 1:00
NJ at Mil, 1:30
@Sea at Hou, 2:30
@Uta at LAK, 12:30
Pho at GS, 5:00
Mon, Apr 14
Was at Phi, 7:30

Det at Orl, 7:30
Min at Mia, 7:30
Cle at Cha, 7:30
NY at Ind, 7:30
Tor at Chi, 7:30
LAC at Dal, 7:30
GS at Den, 7:00
SA at Sac, 7:30
Tue, Apr 15
NJ at Atl, 7:30
Tor at Mil, 7:30
LAC at Hou, 7:30
•Uta at Pho, 5:00
SA at Sea, 7:00
Wed, Apr 16
Cha at Bos, 7:00
Atl at NY, 7:30
Phi at NJ, 7:30
Ind at Was, 7:30
+Chi at Mia, 8:00
Orl at Cle, 7:30
Mil at Det, 7:30
Dal at Min, 7:00
Den at Por, 7:00
Thu, Apr 17
Sea at Den, 7:00
GS at Uta, 7:00
Sac at LAK, 7:30
Por at Van, 7:00
Fri, Apr 18
Ind at NY, 7:30
Bos at Phi, 7:30
Orl at Was, 7:30
NJ at Mia, 7:30
Tor at Cha, 7:30
Cle at Det, 7:30
Mil at Min, 7:30
Dal at Hou, 7:30
•Pho at SA, 7:00
LAK at LAC, 7:30
Sat, Apr 19
Mia at Orl, 6:00
Phi at Atl, 6:00
#NY at Chi, 7:30
Den at Dal, 7:30
Min at Uta, 7:00
Van at Pho, 7:00
Sac at GS, 8:00
LAC at Sea, 7:00
Sun, Apr 20
Tor at Bos, 1:00
Atl at NJ, 6:00
@Was at Cle, 3:30
@Det at Ind, 2:30
Cha at Mil, 6:00
@Hou at SA, 2:30
Uta at Sac, 6:00
@LAK at Por, 12:30

BASKETBALL HALL OF FAME

This section honors the 103 players that are enshrined in the Naismith Memorial Basketball Hall of Fame in Springfield, Massachusetts. The section includes bios on each player in the Hall. At the end of each bio is a date in parentheses; this is the year the member was enshrined. A list of the coaches, contributors, referees, and teams enshrined in the Hall of Fame is on page 479.

Abbreviations include BAA (Basketball Association of America), NBL (National Basketball League), ABA (American Basketball Association), AAU (American Athletic Union), and NIT (National Invitational Tournament).

PLAYERS

KAREEM ABDUL-JABBAR
Center: The former Lew Alcindor led UCLA to an 88-2 record and three NCAA titles (1967-69). With his patented "sky hook," the 7'2" Jabbar won six NBA MVP Awards, was named to 19 All-Star teams, and won six NBA titles with Milwaukee and the L.A. Lakers. He holds NBA career records for scoring (38,387), seasons (20), games (1,560), minutes (57,446), blocked shots (3,189), and playoff scoring (5,762). (1995)

NATE ARCHIBALD
Guard: Small in stature at 6'1", "Tiny" Archibald was a giant on the court. After starring at Texas-El Paso, he began his pro career in Cincinnati in 1970-71. In 1972-73, he led the NBA in assists (11.4) and scoring (34.0). In 1980-81, he helped Boston win the NBA title. Archibald was league MVP in 1981. (1991)

PAUL ARIZIN
Forward: A star at Villanova, where he was college Player of the Year in 1950, the sharpshooting Arizin averaged better than 22 PPG over his ten-year NBA career in Philadelphia. Known for his deadly jump shot, Arizin led the league in scoring in 1952 and '57 and led the Warriors to the NBA title in 1956. He made ten All-Star Game appearances. (1977)

TOM BARLOW
Forward: When the Eastern League was popular, "Babe" Barlow was among the game's most exciting players. A pro at age 16, Babe enjoyed 20 seasons of roundball (from 1912-32). Barlow was known as much for his defensive skills as for his scoring. (1980)

RICK BARRY
Forward: One of the game's most accurate shooters, Barry starred at Miami of Florida and led the NCAA with 37.4 PPG in 1965. As a pro, he is the only player to lead both the ABA and NBA in scoring. His career NBA free-throw pct. was .900, a record that held until 1992-93. In 1975, he led Golden State to the NBA title. (1986)

ELGIN BAYLOR
Forward: Baylor was the most devastating, artistic forward of his era. After leading Seattle to the NCAA finals in 1958, Baylor debuted in the NBA in 1958-59. He averaged 24.9 PPG as a rookie with Minneapolis and won Rookie of the Year honors. Over his 14-year career, he averaged 27.4 PPG. (1976)

JOHNNY BECKMAN
Forward: From 1910 until the 1940s, Beckman was often called the Babe Ruth of basketball. A star in the Interstate, New York State, and Eastern Leagues, Beckman eventually joined the Original Celtics. As their captain, he led them to some of their greatest years. (1972)

WALT BELLAMY
Center: After playing for Indiana University, Bellamy became NBA Rookie of the Year with the 1962 Chicago Packers, averaging 31.6 PPG and 19.0 RPG. He played 14 NBA seasons with six different teams, averaging 20.1 PPG and 13.7 RPG. (1993)

SERGEI BELOV
Guard: Belov was a basketball magician who could score at will. The 6'3" guard led the Rus-

sian national team to four European and two world championships. He helped the Soviet national team to Olympic gold (1972). (1992)

DAVE BING

Guard: Born to score, Bing averaged 24.8 PPG in four years at Syracuse. The off guard was named NBA Rookie of the Year with Detroit in 1966-67 and won the scoring title the next year (27.1 PPG). Bing played in seven All-Star Games in his 12 NBA seasons. (1989)

CAROL BLAZEJOWSKI

Guard: Only Pete Maravich scored more points in college than Blazejowski. At 5'10", the "Blaze" totaled 3,199 points during her career (31.7 PPG) at New Jersey's Montclair State College. She was a three-time All-American. (1994)

BENNIE BORGMANN

Guard: Though only 5'8", Borgmann was one of the most popular touring pros on the East Coast in the early years. It wasn't unusual for Borgmann to score half of his team's points during any given game. He later coached both at the college and professional level. (1961)

BILL BRADLEY

Forward: "Dollar Bill" Bradley had a graceful, deadly shooting touch. A three-time All-American at Princeton and a Rhodes Scholar, he averaged 30 PPG and was the 1965 college Player of the Year. Bradley played ten seasons with the New York Knicks, amassing 9,217 points, 2,533 assists, and two NBA titles. He is currently a U.S. senator in New Jersey. (1982)

JOE BRENNAN

Forward: "Poison Joe" Brennan enjoyed a 17-year pro career, starting at age 19 when he joined the Brooklyn Visitation and led them to their greatest years. In 1950, the New York Basketball Old-Timers voted Brennan the second-greatest player of his era. (1974)

AL CERVI

Guard: An outstanding clutch performer, Cervi was an immediate star with the NBL's Buffalo Bisons. His pro career was interrupted by a five-year stint in World War II, but he resumed his career in 1945, playing for the Rochester Royals. In 1948, he became a player/coach for the Syracuse Nats. He was named Coach of the Year five times in the next eight seasons. (1984)

WILT CHAMBERLAIN

Center: At 7'1", Wilt "The Stilt" Chamberlain was an awesome, dominant figure on the court. After two All-America years at Kansas, Wilt spent a year with the Harlem Globetrotters before entering the NBA in 1959. In just his first year, he was named the NBA's MVP. During 14 years, he was the league MVP four times (1960, 1966-68). He still holds NBA records for career rebounds (23,924), season scoring average (50.4 in 1961-62), and most points in a game (100). He won world titles with Philadelphia (1967) and Los Angeles ('72). (1978)

CHARLES COOPER

Center: In his day, "Tarzan" Cooper was a giant among men. The 6'4", 214-pound Cooper was a consistent winner for 20 years of pro basketball. In 11 years with the New York Renaissance, his teams compiled a record of 1,303-203. He has been called the greatest center of his day. (1976)

KRESIMIR COSIC

Center: The rock in the middle for the Yugoslavian national team, Cosic played in four Olympics, leading his club to a silver medal in 1968 and a gold in 1980. Cosic won world championships in 1970 and '78. (1996)

BOB COUSY

Guard: At 6'1", Cousy made his name as the most sensational passer the game had ever known. After three All-America years at Holy Cross, "Mr. Basketball" joined the Boston Celtics in 1950. Eventually, he led them to six NBA titles, including five in a row (1959-63). He led the league in assists for eight straight years and played in 13 All-Star Games. (1970)

DAVE COWENS

Center: Cowens was a tough, physical player. "The Redhead" starred at Florida State, where he averaged 19 points and 17 rebounds per game. In ten seasons with the Celtics, he won two championships (1974 and '76) and was player/coach for a year. In his career, Cowens averaged 17.6 PPG and collected 10,444 rebounds. (1991)

BILLY CUNNINGHAM

Guard: A scrappy playmaker at North Carolina, Cunningham debuted with the 76ers in 1965. In 11 pro seasons, Cunningham made the All-NBA first team three times and was named ABA MVP in 1973. He became the 76ers' coach in 1978, bringing them a 454-196 record over eight seasons and winning the league title in 1983. (1985)

BOB DAVIES

Guard: Davies, the "first superstar of modern pro basketball," was a two-time All-American at Seton Hall. He turned pro in 1945 with Rochester. In ten BAA and NBA seasons, he was all-league seven times. He led the Royals to league titles in 1946, '47, and '51. (1969)

FORREST DeBERNARDI

Forward/Guard/Center: DeBernardi's career revolved around AAU tournaments. He was an AAU All-American in 1921, '22, and '23 and won four AAU titles. In 11 AAU tournaments, "De" was all-tournament seven times. (1961)

DAVE DeBUSSCHERE

Forward: DeBusschere was one of the game's great defensive forwards. After three All-America years at the University of Detroit, DeBusschere debuted with the Pistons in 1962. At age 24, he became the Pistons' player/coach. He was traded to the Knicks in 1969 and helped them to two championships (1970 and '73). (1982)

DUTCH DEHNERT

Guard: In the 1920s, Dehnert inadvertently invented pivot play when he routinely stationed himself at the foul line to relay passes back and forth to weaving Celtic teammates. He didn't play high school or college ball but honed his skills in Eastern pro leagues. (1968)

ANNE DONOVAN

Center: The 6'8" Donovan led Old Dominion to the 1980 AIAW title as a freshman. She was a three-time All-American, averaging 20.0 PPG and 14.5 RPG. Donovan helped the U.S. to the 1984 and 1988 Olympic gold medals. (1995)

PAUL ENDACOTT

Guard: "The greatest player ever coached" by Kansas' Phog Allen and Player of the Year in 1923, Endacott received the Sportsmen's World Award in basketball in 1969, because his "exemplary personal conduct has made him an outstanding inspiration for youth to emulate." (1971)

JULIUS ERVING

Forward: An extraordinary leaper, the spectacular Dr. J. had the ability to change directions in mid-air. The Massachusetts alum brought attention to the ABA, where he averaged 28.7 PPG and 12.1 RPG in five seasons. With the NBA's 76ers, he was named to 11 All-Star teams, averaged 22.0 PPG, and led his 1983 team to the world title. (1993)

BUD FOSTER

Guard: Harold "Bud" Foster, an All-American at Wisconsin in 1930, played briefly as a pro before embarking on a glorious 25-year career as a coach. He guided Wisconsin to three Big Ten titles and the NCAA title (1941). (1964)

WALT FRAZIER

Guard: A smooth guard known for sleek passing and laser-accurate shooting, "Clyde" Frazier played 13 seasons in the NBA. Frazier helped the Knicks to league titles in 1970 and 1973, played in seven All-Star Games, was a celebrated defensive wizard, and finished his career with an average of 18.9 PPG. (1986)

MARTY FRIEDMAN

Guard: Max "Marty" Friedman, one of the great defensive players of his era, was one of a pair of hoops stars known as the "Heavenly Twins" (his counterpart was Barney Sedran). Friedman played in six Eastern leagues and helped Carbondale win 35 straight games in 1915. He later was successful as a coach. (1971)

JOE FULKS

Forward: "Jumping Joe" Fulks was one of the first scoring superstars of the BAA and NBA. An ambidextrous jump-shot artist, Fulks shocked the BAA in 1946-47 by scoring 23.2 PPG for Philadelphia. Two years later, he averaged 26.0 PPG and was named *The Sporting News* Athlete of the Year for 1949. (1977)

LADDIE GALE

Forward: Lauren "Laddie" Gale's excellence on the court brought recognition to the basketball programs in the Pacific Northwest. Gale, an All-American at Oregon, led his school to the 1939 NCAA title. Gale played professionally and was also a successful coach. (1976)

HARRY GALLATIN

Center: A large center for his time (6'6"), Harry "The Horse" Gallatin was the centerpiece of the New York Knicks for nine years. In 1953-54, he led the NBA in rebounds (1,098). He later went on to a successful coaching career. (1991)

WILLIAM GATES
Guard: "Pop" Gates helped the New York Renaissance to 68 straight victories and a World Professional Championship. In his 12-year career, he played for many outstanding teams, including the Harlem Globetrotters, where he was a player/coach from 1950-55. (1988)

GEORGE GERVIN
Guard: A stone scorer, the "Iceman's" greatest years came with the San Antonio Spurs. Gervin led the NBA in scoring four times in five years, peaking at 33.1 PPG in 1979-80. He tallied 26,595 points in his pro career. (1996)

TOM GOLA
Forward: Gola combined outstanding scoring prowess with defensive wizardry. At La Salle in the mid-1950s, Gola was a four-year All-American, averaging 21 PPG and 20 RPG. He spent ten years as a pro with Philadelphia, San Francisco, and New York, scoring 7,871 points. He was often high in assists and rebounds. (1975)

GAIL GOODRICH
Guard: A two-time NCAA champ at UCLA (1964-65), the left-handed Goodrich was a brilliant long-range shooter in the NBA. Playing with the Lakers, Phoenix, and New Orleans, Goodrich topped 20 PPG six different seasons. He and Laker teammate Jerry West formed an unstoppable backcourt. (1996)

HAL GREER
Guard: Greer was the first black scholarship athlete to attend Marshall (1955-59). He played five years with the Syracuse Nationals before joining the powerful Philadelphia 76ers for another ten. He was named to ten All-Star teams and won a world title in 1967. (1981)

ROBERT GRUENIG
Center: A 6'8" center with a shooter's touch, "Ace" Gruenig was a brilliant AAU performer. From 1937-48, he was the annual choice as first-team all-tournament center. In 1943, he received the Los Angeles Sports Award Medallion as the nation's greatest player. (1963)

CLIFF HAGAN
Forward: Hagan was a two-time All-American who led Kentucky to an NCAA title in 1951 and a perfect 25-0 record in '54. During ten years in the NBA with the St. Louis Hawks, he scored 13,447 points, relying heavily on his amazingly accurate hook shot. He played in four All-Star Games and led the Hawks to the league title in 1958. He also spent three years in the ABA as player/coach for the Dallas Chaparrals. (1977)

VICTOR HANSON
Guard: Hanson starred at Syracuse in basketball, football, and baseball. He was a three-time All-American in hoops (1925-27), winning a national championship in 1926. He played pro ball with the Cleveland Rosenblums, as well as minor-league baseball. (1960)

LUSIA HARRIS
Center: The 6'3" Harris was one of women's basketball's early superstars. She left Delta State with 2,981 points (25.9 PPG) and 1,662 rebounds (14.4 RPG). She was a three-time All-American, won three national titles (1975-77), and played on the '76 Olympic team. (1992)

JOHN HAVLICEK
Forward: After leading Ohio State to three NCAA finals and one championship, "Hondo" Havlicek embarked on a 16-year NBA career with Boston. Havlicek began as the Celts' sixth man and was later named team captain. He scored 26,395 points, appeared in 13 All-Star Games, and was an eight-time member of the NBA All-Defensive Team. (1983)

CONNIE HAWKINS
Forward: Hawkins, similar in style to Julius Erving, left Iowa during his freshman year and played two years with the Harlem Globetrotters (1964-66). In the ABA's inaugural season, he was named league MVP after leading Pittsburgh to the title. Hawkins played seven NBA seasons with Phoenix, Los Angeles, and Atlanta, averaging 16.5 PPG and 7.9 RPG. (1992)

ELVIN HAYES
Forward: The 6'9" Hayes used strength, speed, and grace to achieve amazing results. At Houston, "The Big E." was the 1968 college Player of the Year. Hayes led the NBA in scoring as a rookie and played 16 years with San Diego, the Bullets, and Houston. He led the Bullets to the 1978 NBA title. He played exactly 50,000 NBA minutes—second most in league history—and scored 27,313 points. (1989)

TOMMY HEINSOHN
Forward: An All-American at Holy Cross, Heinsohn was the NBA Rookie of the Year for

Boston in 1957 and started for the champion Celtics for the next eight years. He was named to six All-Star teams and averaged 18.6 PPG over his career. In 1970, he took over as coach and led Boston to two NBA titles. (1985)

NAT HOLMAN
Guard: Holman, who gained fame as coach of the City College of New York Beavers, was also a player of note from 1916-33. He joined the Original Celtics in 1920 and stayed nine seasons, exploiting his skills as a passer, shooter, and strategist. In 1950, his Beavers won both the NIT and NCAA titles, which no team had ever done before. (1964)

BOB HOUBREGS
Center: Houbregs was an All-American with Washington in 1953. He held the second-highest scoring average in NCAA Tournament history (34.8 PPG) before being drafted by Milwaukee. He played five years in the NBA and later served as G.M. of the SuperSonics. (1986)

CHUCK HYATT
Forward: Hyatt starred at the University of Pittsburgh from 1927-30 and was a three-time All-American. He was the top scorer in the nation in 1930. The Panthers won national titles in 1928 and '30. He became a legend of the AAU circuit with the Phillips 66 Oilers. (1959)

DAN ISSEL
Forward: After averaging 25.8 PPG in college at Kentucky, Issel continued to smoke the nets in the ABA (six years, 25.6 PPG) and the NBA (nine years, all with Denver, 20.4 PPG). Though a solid rebounder, Issel will forever be known for his scoring. He became coach of the Nuggets in 1992-93. (1993)

HARRY JEANNETTE
Guard: "Buddy" Jeannette was basketball's top backcourt player from 1938-48. He was adept at passing, clutch shooting, and defense. He garnered four MVP Awards (NBL and ABL) and won five titles. He also coached for Georgetown and in the NBA (Baltimore). (1994)

WILLIAM JOHNSON
Center: "Skinny" Johnson was a dominant center for Kansas from 1930-33. He guided his squad to a 42-11 record and three Big Six championships. In 1975, he was named an All-Time Great in Oklahoma, his home state. (1976)

NEIL JOHNSTON
Center: After two years at Ohio State, the 6'8" Johnston tried his luck as a pitcher, signing a pro baseball contract. A sore arm turned him back to basketball, and he joined the Philadelphia Warriors in 1951. In eight seasons, he led the NBA in scoring and field-goal percentage three times, led in rebounding once, and helped the Warriors win the title in 1956. (1989)

K.C. JONES
Guard: After starring in college at San Francisco, Jones joined the Boston Celtics in 1958 and was a dependable guard on their great teams. As a coach, Jones won more than 500 NBA games, including 308 with the Celts. He was involved in 11 titles in Boston—eight as a player, one as an assistant coach, and two as head coach (1984 and '86). (1988)

SAM JONES
Guard: After playing brilliantly at tiny North Carolina College, Jones cracked the Celtics lineup in 1958 and became part of ten championship teams. He led the club in scoring three times and averaged 25.9 PPG in 1964-65. His patented jump shot off the glass was feared around the NBA. (1983)

EDWARD KRAUSE
Center: A star at Notre Dame in the early 1930s, Krause was a three-time All-American in two sports—basketball and football. At 6'3", 215 pounds, he was considered the first "agile" center. "Moose" later played professionally before returning to the college scene as a coach and athletic director. (1975)

BOB KURLAND
Center: The first of the truly great seven-foot centers, Kurland carved out one of the most impressive amateur careers ever. At Oklahoma State, he led his squad to NCAA titles in 1945 and '46, leading the nation in scoring the latter year. He later played six seasons of AAU ball and was an Olympian in 1948 and '52. (1961)

BOB LANIER
Center: A two-time All-American at St. Bonaventure, Lanier debuted with Detroit in 1970. The strong, no-nonsense center played in eight All-Star Games and tallied 19,248 points and 9,698 rebounds in his career. In each of Lanier's five seasons in Milwaukee, the Bucks won the Central Division title. (1992)

JOE LAPCHICK

Center: The son of immigrants, Lapchick began playing professional basketball at age 17. The 6'5" center played in several leagues and centered the Original Celtics from 1923-27. Later, he became a great coach, leading St. John's to four NIT titles. He also coached the New York Knicks for nine seasons. (1966)

NANCY LIEBERMAN

Guard: After winning Olympic silver at age 18, Lieberman won AIAW national titles and national Player of the Year awards in 1979 and 1980. In 1986, she became the first woman to play in a men's pro league (USBL). (1996)

CLYDE LOVELLETTE

Center: Lovellette was a winner wherever he played. As a college star at Kansas, he was a three-time All-American (1950-52). In 1952, he led the nation in scoring and guided the Jayhawks to the NCAA title. He played for the 1952 gold-medal Olympic team before starting an 11-year NBA career. He played with the champion Minneapolis Lakers in 1954 and later won titles with the 1963 and '64 Celtics. (1987)

JERRY LUCAS

Forward: A fine shooter, passer, and defensive ace, Lucas was a two-time college Player of the Year at Ohio State, where his team captured an NCAA title. He also helped the U.S. win the gold in the 1960 Olympics. In 1963-64 with Cincinnati, Lucas was the NBA's Rookie of the Year. He went on to play in seven All-Star Games and was part of the New York Knicks' 1973 championship team. He finished with 14,053 points and 12,942 rebounds. (1979)

HANK LUISETTI

Forward: Luisetti broke old standards by developing a one-handed shot. In three seasons at Stanford, Hank led his squad to successive Pacific Coast Conference titles. An All-American in 1937 and '38, Luisetti was the first college player ever to score 50 points in a game. He later starred on the AAU scene. (1959)

ED MACAULEY

Forward: "Easy Ed" Macauley was a four-time All-American at St. Louis (1946-49). In 1947, he led the nation with a .524 shooting percentage, and he was MVP of the NIT the following year. Macauley played ten NBA seasons, earning seven All-Star Game appearances. (1960)

PETE MARAVICH

Forward: Maravich, one of the greatest gunners in history, shattered many NCAA records, including highest career scoring average (44.2). He starred at Louisiana State, earning college Player of the Year honors in 1970. "Pistol Pete" played NBA ball with Atlanta, the Jazz, and Boston. In 658 NBA games, he averaged 24.2 PPG. In 1976-77, he led the league in scoring with a 31.1 average. (1986)

SLATER MARTIN

Guard: After three outstanding years at Texas, "Dugie" Martin joined the NBA, where, at 5'10", he was the league's first "small superstar." He played for four championship teams in Minneapolis before moving to St. Louis, where he won the 1958 title. In 11 seasons, he earned a reputation as a defensive genius. (1981)

BRANCH McCRACKEN

Forward: McCracken starred at Indiana University, winning the conference MVP Award in 1928. During his career, he scored nearly one-third of all points recorded by the Hoosiers. He also enjoyed success as a coach, winning four Big Ten and two NCAA titles at Indiana. (1960)

JACK McCRACKEN

Center: A two-time All-American at N.W. Missouri State (1931-32), McCracken was known for his outstanding passing and domination of the backboards. As a star of the AAU circuit, he was an eight-time All-American between 1932 and 1945 and won two AAU championships. (1962)

BOBBY McDERMOTT

Forward: McDermott turned pro as a teenager and played for 17 years. He was a seven-time NBL All-Star, won five straight MVP Awards, and led the league twice in scoring. He was a champion with Brooklyn, Fort Wayne, Chicago, and the Original Celtics. (1987)

DICK McGUIRE

Guard: McGuire, an All-American at St. John's, helped the New York Knicks to three straight NBA Finals (1951-53). Though he averaged just 8.0 PPG in 11 NBA seasons with New York and Detroit, McGuire made seven All-Star teams thanks to his point guard skills. (1993)

ANN MEYERS

Guard: Meyers, of UCLA, was women's basketball's first four-time All-American. She won

Olympic silver in 1976 and became the first and only woman to sign with an NBA club (Indiana in 1976), but did not make the team. (1993)

VERN MIKKELSEN
Forward: Out of tiny Hamline University, Mikkelsen became one of the NBA's first power forwards. He led Minneapolis to four NBA titles and played on six All-Star teams, averaging 14.4 PPG and 8.4 RPG over his career. (1995)

GEORGE MIKAN
Center: The game's first dominant big man, the 6'10" Mikan was a three-time NBA scoring leader. Previously, he was a three-time All-American at DePaul and two-time college Player of the Year (1945 and '46), leading the nation in scoring in both of those years. Mikan played on five NBA title teams. (1959)

CHERYL MILLER
Forward: The owner of a 105-point game in high school, Miller was a four-time high school and four-time college All-American. At Southern Cal., she won two NCAA titles (1983-84) and three Naismith Awards. (1995)

EARL MONROE
Guard: Earl "The Pearl" Monroe's slick ball-handling and dead-eye shooting made him a prolific scorer and crowd-pleaser. An All-American at Winston-Salem State, he was the NBA Rookie of the Year with Baltimore in 1968. He spent 13 years in the NBA and helped the New York Knicks win the 1973 league title. (1989)

CALVIN MURPHY
Guard: The 5'9" Murphy was a brilliant free-throw shooter, canning 78 straight with Houston in 1980-81. The mighty mite averaged 33.1 PPG as a three-time All-American at Niagara. He scored 17.9 per game in his 13 NBA seasons, all with the Rockets. (1993)

STRETCH MURPHY
Center: Murphy was one of the most feared big men of his time, as he helped Purdue to a Big Ten title in 1928. A two-time All-American, Murphy set a Big Ten scoring mark in 1929. In his senior year, 1930, he captained Purdue to an undefeated record. (1960)

PAT PAGE
Forward: An outstanding defensive player and a star in three sports, Page led his University of Chicago squad to Western Conference titles in 1907, 1909 (when they were undefeated), and 1910. In 1910, Page was named college Player of the Year. (1962)

BOB PETTIT
Forward: A three-time All-American at Louisiana State (1952-54), Pettit played ten NBA seasons with the St. Louis Hawks. He was named NBA MVP in 1956 and '59. He led the Hawks to the league title in 1958. He finished as the greatest scorer in league history with 20,880 points. (1970)

ANDY PHILLIP
Guard: One of the stars of the University of Illinois' "Whiz Kids," Phillip set Big Ten scoring marks in 1942 and '43 and once scored 40 points in a game. He later played in the BAA and NBA for more than a decade. (1961)

JIM POLLARD
Forward: Pollard led Stanford to an NCAA championship in 1942 and later starred in the AAU circuit, winning MVP honors in 1947 and '48. He joined the Minneapolis Lakers in 1949 and helped them to five league titles. (1977)

FRANK RAMSEY
Guard: A two-time All-American while playing at Kentucky (1952 and '54), Ramsey joined the Boston Celtics and revolutionized the game by "inventing" the sixth-man position. Ramsey won seven titles in nine NBA seasons. He was called "the most versatile player in the NBA" by his longtime coach, Red Auerbach. (1981)

WILLIS REED
Center: One of the most intense competitors of his time, Reed began as a two-time All-American at Grambling. In ten pro seasons with the New York Knicks, he won two NBA titles (1970 and '73) and played in seven All-Star Games. He averaged 18.7 PPG in his career. (1981)

OSCAR ROBERTSON
Guard: One of the greatest all-around players ever, "The Big O." starred at the University of Cincinnati, where he was a two-time college Player of the Year and a three-time scoring leader. As a pro for Cincinnati, he was league MVP in 1964. Later, he led the Milwaukee Bucks to the 1971 NBA title. He finished his career with 26,710 points (25.7 PPG) and set an NBA record with 9,887 assists. (1979)

JOHN ROOSMA

Forward: Roosma made his mark as a member of the U.S. Army squad. In his Army career, he scored more than 1,000 points. Roosma, whose Army team went 70-3 during his tenure, served in the military for 30 years. (1961)

BILL RUSSELL

Center: Russell reigns as one of the great winners and rebounders of all time. As a collegian, he was Player of the Year in 1956 for San Francisco and also led his school to two NCAA titles. He then led the U.S. to gold in the 1956 Olympic Games. As a pro, he helped the Celtics to eight straight NBA crowns (1959-66) and 11 in 13 years. He collected 21,620 rebounds, averaged 15.1 PPG, and was league MVP five times. As player/coach, he led the Celts to titles in 1968 and '69. (1974)

HONEY RUSSELL

Guard: A great defensive player, John "Honey" Russell played in virtually every pro league during his 28-year career. He led the Cleveland Rosenblums to five straight titles (1925-29) and later coached his alma mater, Seton Hall, to 44 straight wins. In 1946-47, he became the first coach of the NBA Boston Celtics. (1964)

DOLPH SCHAYES

Forward: Schayes played his college ball at New York University, where he was an All-American in 1948. In 15 seasons with the Syracuse Nationals, he chalked up 19,249 points (18.2 per game). From February 1952 to December 1961, he played in a record 765 straight games. Later, he guided the Philadelphia 76ers to a division title. (1972)

ERNEST SCHMIDT

Forward: Schmidt was known as "One Grand Schmidt" after scoring 1,000 career points in his Kansas State Teachers College days. He was a four-time conference All-Star in the early 1930s and was the greatest player ever to come out of the Missouri Valley. Later, he suited up for three seasons in the AAU. (1973)

JOHN SCHOMMER

Center: A star in basketball, football, baseball, and track, Schommer led the Chicago Maroon basketball squad to three straight Big Ten titles (1907-09) and was the conference scoring leader all three years. He also enjoyed a 47-year career as athletic director, coach, and teacher at Illinois Institute of Technology. In 1949, the Helms Foundation named him a center on its All-Time All-America Team. (1959)

BARNEY SEDRAN

Guard: At 5'4", Sedran proved that size truly wasn't everything. Despite being banished from high school basketball, Sedran starred at City College of New York and was his team's leading scorer three years in a row. Upon his graduation in 1911, he embarked on a 15-year pro career that included ten championships. He later coached for another 20 years. (1962)

JULIANA SEMENOVA

Center: The Soviet seven-footer dominated her opponents, winning two Olympic golds (1976 and 1980) and three world championship golds. Semenova never lost a game in 18 years of international competition. (1993)

BILL SHARMAN

Guard: After two All-America years at Southern California, the sharp-shooting Sharman enjoyed an 11-year stint in the NBA, where he played on four championship Boston Celtics teams in the 1950s and early 1960s. Sharman's secret weapon was free-throw shooting. After retiring with 12,665 points, he won titles as a coach in the ABA and NBA. (1975)

CHRISTIAN STEINMETZ

Guard: Steinmetz turned basketball into a recognized sport at the University of Wisconsin. As a senior in 1905, he set school scoring records (some of which would stand for the next 50 years), including most points in a game (50) and most points in a season (462). (1961)

DAVID THOMPSON

Guard: After leading North Carolina State to the 1974 NCAA title, Thompson starred with the Denver Nuggets in both the ABA and NBA. The high-flying Thompson exceeded 24 PPG five times, and his 73-point effort against Detroit in 1978 ranks third in NBA history. (1996)

JOHN THOMPSON

Guard: A star at Montana State, John "Cat" Thompson was selected to All-Rocky Mountain Conference teams four years in a row. In 1929, they were the Helms national champions and the Cat was named Player of the Year. Thompson eventually became a coach, where he remained for 14 years. (1962)

NATE THURMOND

Center: An All-American at Bowling Green, Thurmond was a defensive genius with strong shooting skills. In his 14-year NBA career, he averaged 15 points and 15 rebounds per game. In a 1974 game, he became the first to record a "quadruple-double." Playing for several NBA teams, Thurmond was named to seven All-Star teams. (1984)

JACK TWYMAN

Forward: An All-American at Cincinnati, Twyman joined the Rochester Royals in 1955-56. In 11 NBA seasons, he scored 15,840 points. A durable forward with precision shooting skills, Twyman played 823 games (including a stretch of 609 consecutively) and averaged 19.2 PPG. (1982)

WES UNSELD

Center: After an explosive career at Louisville, where he was an All-American in 1967 and '68, Unseld entered the NBA with an equally loud bang in 1968-69, when he was the NBA's MVP for the Baltimore Bullets. Unseld led the Bullets to an NBA title in 1978. In his career, he averaged 14 boards a game. He also served as coach of the Washington Bullets. (1987)

FUZZY VANDIVIER

Guard: Robert "Fuzzy" Vandivier became one of the greatest players in the history of Indiana basketball. He took his perennial-champion Franklin High School team directly to Franklin College in 1922 and helped establish a legendary squad. He is a member of the All-Time All-Star Five of Indiana. (1974)

ED WACHTER

Center: As a turn-of-the-century player, Wachter starred on nearly every team in the Eastern circuit. He was an annual scoring champion and a member of more title-winning clubs than anyone else of his time. Later, as a coach at Harvard, he founded the New England Basketball Association and struggled to gain national uniformity of rules and regulations. (1961)

BILL WALTON

Center: The big redhead carried UCLA to an 86-4 record and two NCAA titles (1972-73), earning college Player of the Year awards from 1972-74. Though he sat out four different NBA seasons because of injuries, he helped both Portland (1977) and Boston (1986) to NBA titles. Walton was named league MVP in 1977-78 with Portland. (1993)

BOBBY WANZER

Guard: An All-American at Seton Hall in 1946, Wanzer spent ten seasons with the Rochester Royals. He was the NBA's MVP in 1952-53 after helping the Royals win the 1951 NBA title. A great shooter, Wanzer led the league in free-throw accuracy (90 percent) in 1951-52. (1986)

JERRY WEST

Guard: One of the greatest high-pressure performers of all time, West earned his nickname "Mr. Clutch" during 14 seasons with the Los Angeles Lakers. A two-time All-American at West Virginia, West averaged 27.0 PPG in the NBA. He was also named to 14 All-Star teams and led L.A. to the 1972 NBA title. (1979)

NERA WHITE

Center: The 6'1" White was one of the most complete female players of all time. From 1955-69, she led Nashville Business College to ten AAU national titles. She was a ten-time AAU tournament MVP. In 1957-58, White led the U.S. to the world championship. (1992)

LENNY WILKENS

Guard: Wilkens enjoyed success at every level of the game. As an All-American at Providence College, he was the 1960 NIT MVP. Wilkens, a 6'1" guard, went on to play 15 seasons in the NBA, making nine All-Star appearances. He later coached Seattle, one of his former teams, to the 1979 NBA championship. As an NBA coach, he has won over 900 games. (1988)

JOHN WOODEN

Forward: Before becoming one of basketball's greatest coaches, Wooden was an outstanding player in his own right. A three-time All-American at Purdue (1930-32) and college Player of the Year (1932), he set a Big Ten scoring record in his senior year and led his team to the national title. (1960)

GEORGE YARDLEY

Forward: Yardley played just seven seasons in the NBA but appeared in six All-Star Games. His hallmark season came with Detroit in 1957-58, when he led the league in scoring (27.8 PPG) and became the first NBA player to reach 2,000 points in a season. (1996)

REMAINING MEMBERS OF THE BASKETBALL
HALL OF FAME

COACHES
Phog Allen (1959)
Harold Anderson (1984)
Red Auerbach (1968)
Sam Barry (1978)
Ernest Blood (1960)
Howard Cann (1967)
H. Clifford Carlson (1959)
Lou Carnesecca (1992)
Ben Carnevale (1969)
Everett Case (1981)
Denny Crum (1994)
Chuck Daly (1994)
Everett Dean (1966)
Ed Diddle (1971)
Bruce Drake (1972)
Clarence Gaines (1981)
Jack Gardner (1983)
Slats Gill (1967)
Aleksandr Gomelsky (1995)
Marv Harshman (1984)
Eddie Hickey (1978)
Howard Hobson (1965)
Red Holzman (1985)
Hank Iba (1968)
Doggie Julian (1967)
Frank Keaney (1960)
George Keogan (1961)
Bob Knight (1991)
John Kundla (1995)
Ward Lambert (1960)
Harry Litwack (1975)
Kenneth Loeffler (1964)
Dutch Lonborg (1972)
Arad McCutchan (1980)
Al McGuire (1992)
Frank McGuire (1976)
John McLendon (1978)
Walter Meanwell (1959)
Ray Meyer (1978)

Ralph Miller (1987)
Pete Newell (1978)
Jack Ramsay (1992)
Cesare Rubini (1994)
Adolph Rupp (1968)
Leonard Sachs (1961)
Everett Shelton (1979)
Dean Smith (1982)
Fred Taylor (1985)
Margaret Wade (1984)
Stanley Watts (1985)
John Wooden (1972)
Phil Woolpert (1992)

CONTRIBUTORS
Senda Abbott (1984)
Clair Bee (1967)
Walter Brown (1965)
John Bunn (1964)
Bob Douglas (1971)
Al Duer (1981)
Clifford Fagan (1983)
Harry Fisher (1973)
Larry Fleisher (1991)
Eddie Gottlieb (1971)
Luther Gulick (1959)
Lester Harrison (1979)
Ferenc Hepp (1980)
Edward Hickox (1959)
Tony Hinkle (1965)
Ned Irish (1964)
R. William Jones (1964)
J. Walter Kennedy (1980)
Emil Liston (1974)
Bill Mokray (1965)
Ralph Morgan (1959)
Frank Morgenweck (1962)
James Naismith (1959)
John O'Brien (1961)
Larry O'Brien (1991)

Harold Olsen (1959)
Maurice Podoloff (1973)
Henry Porter (1960)
William Reid (1963)
Elmer Ripley (1972)
Lynn St. John (1962)
Abe Saperstein (1970)
Arthur Schabinger (1961)
Amos Alonzo Stagg (1959)
Boris Stankovic (1991)
Edward Steitz (1983)
Chuck Taylor (1968)
Bertha Teague (1984)
Oswald Tower (1959)
Arthur Trester (1961)
Clifford Wells (1971)
Lou Wilke (1982)

REFEREES
Jim Enright (1978)
George Hepbron (1960)
George Hoyt (1961)
Pat Kennedy (1959)
Lloyd Leith (1982)
Red Mihalik (1985)
John Nucatola (1977)
Ernest Quigley (1961)
J. Dallas Shirley (1979)
Earl Strom (1995)
David Tobey (1961)
David Walsh (1961)

TEAMS
Buffalo Germans (1961)
First Team (1959)
New York Rens (1963)
Original Celtics (1959)

*Note: Year of election in
parentheses.*

100 Top College Stars & 64 Top College Teams

The following two sections evaluate the best players and teams in college basketball. Of the thousands of players in the college ranks, you'll read about the 100 that are expected to make the biggest impact in 1996-97. You'll also find season previews on the top 64 teams in the country.

Each player's scouting report begins with his vital stats, such as school, position, and height. Next comes a four-part evaluation of the player. "Background" reviews the player's career, starting with high school and continuing up through the 1995-96 season. "Strengths" examines his best assets, and "weaknesses" pinpoints his significant flaws. "Analysis" tries to put the player's whole game into perspective.

For a quick rundown on each player, you'll find a "player summary" box. You'll also get the player's career statistics. The stats include games (G), field-goal percentage (FGP), free-throw percentage (FTP), rebounds per game (RPG), assists per game (APG), and points per game (PPG).

Each of the 64 teams receives a one-page season preview. It begins with the basics, including 1995-96 overall record (this record includes NCAA or NIT games). It also lists the team's record in 1996 tournament play ("NCAAs: 2-1" means the team won two NCAA Tournament games and then lost the third). The coach's career Division I record is also listed.

Each season preview begins with an "opening line." The preview then rates the team at each position—guard, forward, and center. "Analysis" evaluates the team's strengths and weaknesses and puts it all into perspective.

Finally, each preview contains the team's 1996-97 roster, which includes the team's top 12 players. The roster lists each player's 1995-96 statistics. The stats include field-goal percentage (FGP), free-throw percentage (FTP), 3-point field goals/attempts (3-PT), rebounds per game (RPG), assists per game (APG), and points per game (PPG).

DANYA ABRAMS

School: Boston College
Year: Senior
Position: Forward/Center
Height: 6'7" **Weight:** 265
Birthdate: September 24, 1974
Hometown: Greenburgh, NY

PLAYER SUMMARY	
Will	play the body
Can't	shoot from deep
Expect	relentless rebounding
Don't Expect	him to back down

Background: Despite earning his state's distinction as Mr. Basketball in his senior year at the Hackley (NY) School, Abrams was something of an unknown entering college. Yet he immediately gained a starting spot in the Eagles lineup early in his freshman year and played a pivotal role in BC's charge to the East Regional final in 1994.

Strengths: In many ways Abrams was born to play in the rough-and-tumble Big East Conference. Never one to shy from contact, Abrams loves to work inside and is quite good at it. A nice pair of hands and soft touch around the goal make him a major scoring threat inside. He is also an improved free-throw shooter, a huge plus for a big man who operates on the interior.

Weaknesses: Fouls were a problem early in his career and still are on occasion. On the offensive end, Abrams is prone to turnovers and is not a good passer, which can inhibit BC's offensive balance.

Analysis: In a very understated manner, Abrams has enjoyed a stellar collegiate career. Barring injury, this sociology major should finish his career at Chestnut Hill as one of the school's top scorers.

COLLEGE STATISTICS

		G	FGP	FTP	RPG	APG	PPG
93-94	BC	34	.464	.585	7.1	0.7	10.4
94-95	BC	28	.514	.720	9.1	1.6	22.1
95-96	BC	30	.471	.705	9.6	1.5	19.6
Totals		92	.486	.682	8.5	1.2	17.0

RAYSHARD ALLEN

School: Tulane
Year: Senior
Position: Forward/Center
Height: 6'7" **Weight:** 245
Birthdate: October 9, 1975
Hometown: Marrero, LA

PLAYER SUMMARY	
Will	take smart shots
Can't	thread the needle
Expect	rebounding zest
Don't Expect	free throws

Background: This lifelong Louisianan was named a fifth-team All-American by *FutureStars* as a senior at John Ehret High School. In his college debut, Allen became one of two Tulane players to make the Metro Conference's All-Freshman team.

Strengths: Allen is most at home on the interior. He relishes the push and shove that is so much a part of the action in the post area and has the physical muscle to thrive there. His wide frame makes it almost impossible for him to be moved once he establishes position. Good hands make him an inviting target, and he has the shooting touch needed to capitalize on his chances.

Weaknesses: It would very much benefit Allen to improve his free-throw shooting. This man has been inconsistent from the stripe through his career. He also creates too many turnovers by failing to find the open man when he is double-teamed.

Analysis: A late-season plunge cost Tulane a spot in the NCAA Tournament, and like his mates, Allen is eager for redemption. He is a superior college player who can overpower less-muscular types in the painted area of the floor.

COLLEGE STATISTICS

		G	FGP	FTP	RPG	APG	PPG
93-94	TUL	29	.547	.611	5.1	0.7	8.8
94-95	TUL	32	.610	.564	7.8	1.1	16.4
95-96	TUL	31	.575	.636	6.8	1.7	13.0
Totals		92	.584	.605	6.6	1.2	12.9

CHAD AUSTIN

School: Purdue
Year: Junior
Position: Guard
Height: 6'2" **Weight:** 200
Birthdate: June 5, 1975
Hometown: Richmond, IN

PLAYER SUMMARY	
Will	hit long jumpers
Can't	be ignored
Expect	steady shooting
Don't Expect	weak defense

Background: The key to Austin's quick development at the collegiate level might have been his year in prep school at Maine Central Institute. It gave him a leg up when he returned to his native Indiana to attend Purdue. He made seven starts as a freshman and then emerged as one of the Big Ten's best players as a sophomore.

Strengths: When the Boilermakers need relief from deep, they look to Austin. A sharp shooting eye and a quick release make him a threat from beyond the 3-point line. As he has matured, his ball-handling has improved to the point where he can also dribble by opponents who pressure his shot. In addition, he's a dutiful defender.

Weaknesses: Austin is not a flashy player. He does things in an understated fashion that tends to hamper his recognition level. On the floor, he is only an average ball-handler and still relies a bit too much on others to create scoring chances for him.

Analysis: Keady thrives with underrated players like Austin. This guard's role has grown steadily in each of his first two seasons. Now he will be asked to be a leader. It's a task he can handle.

COLLEGE STATISTICS

	G	FGP	FTP	RPG	APG	PPG
94-95 PURD	32	.460	.660	2.0	2.0	5.7
95-96 PURD	32	.417	.733	2.9	2.3	12.8
Totals	64	.429	.710	2.4	2.2	9.2

TUNJI AWOJOBI

School: Boston University
Year: Senior
Position: Forward
Height: 6'7" **Weight:** 235
Birthdate: July 30, 1973
Hometown: Lagos, Nigeria

PLAYER SUMMARY	
Will	hustle relentlessly
Can't	launch 3s
Expect	high field-goal pct.
Don't Expect	much acclaim

Background: Born and raised in Nigeria, Awojobi transferred to Trinity High School in New Hampshire for his final year of prep school. With the departure of Drexel's Malik Rose, Awojobi became the preseason favorite to capture 1996-97 North Atlantic Conference Player of the Year honors.

Strengths: Awojobi is relentless on the backboards. He takes special delight in positioning himself underneath the goal so that he can come away with the carom. A powerful frame allows him to hold off foes in the post. Good hands make him a plus around the hole, and he rarely takes bad shots. His foot speed is remarkable for a big man.

Weaknesses: Awojobi's scoring range is limited. His jump shot lacks range, and his ball-handling is suspect. Although that isn't much of an issue in the NAC, it will become one if he attempts to compete at the next level.

Analysis: This is one of the most underrated players in college basketball. His work ethic alone is noteworthy. He is likely to be overlooked throughout the regular season, but don't be surprised if he pops up in the NCAA Tournament.

COLLEGE STATISTICS

	G	FGP	FTP	RPG	APG	PPG
93-94 BU	27	.556	.656	10.5	1.5	18.9
94-95 BU	31	.500	.683	11.8	1.4	19.8
95-96 BU	29	.582	.706	10.8	1.7	22.7
Totals	87	.544	.684	11.1	1.5	20.5

TOBY BAILEY

School: UCLA
Year: Junior
Position: Guard
Height: 6'5" **Weight:** 185
Birthdate: November 19, 1975
Hometown: Los Angeles, CA

PLAYER SUMMARY	
Will	leap high
Can't	take over a game
Expect	solid rebounding
Don't Expect	false modesty

Background: One of Southern California's top prep performers at Loyola High School, Bailey averaged 26.0 PPG as a senior. His coach there, Bill Thomason, labels him the best athlete he has ever coached. Bailey made 13 late-season starts as a freshman, the most memorable being his 26-point, nine-rebound effort in UCLA's 1995 title-game victory against Arkansas.

Strengths: Bailey is at his best off the basketball, roaming free to find the holes in a defense. At 6'5", he can see over most defenders, and he loves to take smaller guards inside, where he can post them up. He poses particular problems for foes on the offensive glass.

Weaknesses: The heroics of '95 probably raised expectations past appropriate levels for Bailey. He is not the kind of offensive star who can take over a game, and his perimeter shooting tends to run hot and cold. His faith in himself sometimes borders on the extreme.

Analysis: Some viewed Bailey's sophomore season as a letdown. Certainly he needs to be more consistent, but he has proved that he has the tools to be a superior college player. Some more experience should help.

COLLEGE STATISTICS

	G	FGP	FTP	RPG	APG	PPG
94-95 UCLA	33	.484	.564	4.8	1.9	10.5
95-96 UCLA	31	.458	.644	4.3	3.9	14.8
Totals	64	.469	.602	4.6	2.6	12.6

MICHAEL BIBBY

School: Arizona
Year: Freshman
Position: Guard
Height: 6'2" **Weight:** 200
Birthdate: May 13, 1978
Hometown: Phoenix, AZ

PLAYER SUMMARY	
Will	deliver the rock
Can't	terrorize defensively
Expect	instant success
Don't Expect	a backup's minutes

Background: The son of former NBA guard—and present USC coach—Henry Bibby, Michael grew up in the Phoenix area with his mother. During his junior season at Shadow Mountain High School, he established himself as one of the premier players in his age group. *FutureStars* rated him the top point guard prospect in the prep class of 1996.

Strengths: Arizona coach Lute Olson will rest easy when he places the ball into Bibby's hands. Though elusive, this youngster is different from most players his age in that he doesn't try to go too quickly. He can take people off the dribble and dish off to his teammates or step out to the 3-point line for long bombs.

Weaknesses: At the high school level, Bibby could afford to take time off at the defensive end. That's a luxury he will not be accorded in the Pac-10. The tools are there for him to be a superior defender, but he must add some savvy and muscle to augment that aspect of his game.

Analysis: This talent never let the recruiting process overheat. He surprised some by choosing Arizona ahead of UCLA or USC, but the move makes sense. In Tucson, he'll be close to home and have the opportunity to create his own place in school history.

CHAUNCEY BILLUPS

School: Colorado
Year: Sophomore
Position: Guard
Height: 6'3" **Weight:** 191
Birthdate: September 25, 1976
Hometown: Denver, CO

PLAYER SUMMARY	
Will	make free throws
Can't	do it all himself
Expect	a complete package
Don't Expect	blocked shots

Background: Billups averaged nearly 24 PPG during his four-year varsity career at George Washington High School. He helped the North team win the 1995 U.S. Olympic Festival. At Colorado, he was the Big Eight's Freshman of the Year and one of the nation's premier first-year players.

Strengths: Certain individuals find ways to create offense, and Billups is such a player. He is a combination guard by definition, meaning he can set up others or score himself. He can take it to the hole in transition—a huge plus, because he is an outstanding free-throw shooter. Few guards rebound as well as he does.

Weaknesses: Because Billups doesn't have much help at Colorado, teams pay an inordinate amount of attention to him, causing him to put up the occasional bad shot out of frustration. As a perimeter shooter, he tends to run hot and cold. He led the Buffaloes in minutes played, and fatigue caused him to coast at times on defense.

Analysis: Few freshmen did more for their units than this local product did. Were he at a bigger, more established program, Billups would be a household name by now. He may soon become one anyway.

COLLEGE STATISTICS

	G	FGP	FTP	RPG	APG	PPG
95-96 COLO	26	.413	.861	6.3	5.5	17.9
Totals	26	.413	.861	6.3	5.5	17.9

CALVIN BOOTH

School: Penn State
Year: Sophomore
Position: Center
Height: 6'11" **Weight:** 205
Birthdate: May 7, 1976
Hometown: Reynoldsburg, OH

PLAYER SUMMARY	
Will	deflect shots
Can't	rely on brute force
Expect	smoother offense
Don't Expect	great strength

Background: During Booth's senior season at Groveport-Madison (OH) High School, his team finished below .500, and Booth did not receive the kind of acclaim some of his classmates did. He then sat out as a freshman at Penn State, opting to work out in the weight room before emerging as the Big Ten's finest shot-blocker in '95-96.

Strengths: A new-age pivot, Booth runs the floor with grace. Long arms give him an enormous wingspan. His great sense of timing and strong legs make him a shot-blocking presence in the lane. Shooters have learned that it is unwise to challenge him directly.

Weaknesses: Although he has tried to add muscle, Booth remains long and lean. His lack of bulk creates problems for him against pivots with a lower center of gravity. Those types can pin him down low and keep him off the glass. Booth also needs to add a signature move on offense.

Analysis: This youngster was a revelation to the college hoops world in 1995-96. His interior defense was a major plus for new PSU coach Jerry Dunn. With a little more seasoning, Booth may remind fans of Detroit Piston Theo Ratliff.

COLLEGE STATISTICS

	G	FGP	FTP	RPG	APG	PPG
95-96 PSU	28	.549	.635	5.4	1.3	9.3
Totals	28	.549	.635	5.4	1.3	9.3

KEITH BOOTH

School: Maryland
Year: Senior
Position: Forward
Height: 6'6" **Weight:** 221
Birthdate: October 9, 1974
Hometown: Baltimore, MD

PLAYER SUMMARY	
Will	muscle inside
Can't	thread the needle
Expect	a heavier burden
Don't Expect	a lack of hustle

Background: As a junior at Dunbar High School, Booth led the school to a 29-0 record, earning No. 1 prep team ranking in *USA Today*. Following a senior year in which he earned a spot on the McDonald's All-America team, Booth signed with Maryland. He then stepped into a starting role, which he has occupied ever since.

Strengths: Contact in the lane does not slow Booth. He relishes the physical stuff underneath and won't shy away from a rebounding challenge. His quickness gives him an advantage, and he attacks tough defensive assignments with vigor.

Weaknesses: Perimeter offense is not in Booth's handbook. That means he must play power forward, and larger players can shoot over him and prevent him from getting his shot off near the goal. Booth also has to concentrate on making better passes to open players.

Analysis: Upon entering college, Booth was viewed as Maryland's key recruit. That fact takes on added meaning when you note that Joe Smith, now of Golden State, was in that same class. This is Booth's chance to prove he is a go-to man at the collegiate level.

COLLEGE STATISTICS

	G	FGP	FTP	RPG	APG	PPG
93-94 MARY	30	.454	.584	6.1	2.2	10.8
94-95 MARY	34	.455	.695	7.3	2.2	10.9
95-96 MARY	30	.442	.757	7.8	2.4	15.3
Totals	94	.450	.689	7.1	2.3	12.3

EARL BOYKINS

School: Eastern Michigan
Year: Junior
Position: Guard
Height: 5'7" **Weight:** 140
Birthdate: June 2, 1976
Hometown: Cleveland, OH

PLAYER SUMMARY	
Will	lead the team
Can't	do much on "D"
Expect	acrobatic shots
Don't Expect	foul trouble

Background: Despite being recognized as one of the top players in Ohio as a senior at Cleveland Central Catholic High School, Boykins was passed over by the Big Ten schools because of his size. Eastern Michigan elected to take a chance on him and has been richly rewarded.

Strengths: Boykins is the catalyst for the Eagles' offense. His short stature makes it difficult for foes to take the basketball from him, and he can use his great speed to go around them if they get too close. Among his favorite moves is one that takes him into the lane, where he is able to score or get fouled.

Weaknesses: At times Boykins becomes too enamored of his own scoring acumen. His teammates are then left to stand around and watch, which is never good in terms of developing a team offense. Boykins tries his best to be pesky on defense, but he is too attractive a target for opponents to resist in man-to-man situations.

Analysis: America got a taste of this man's gifts in the NCAA Tournament. Boykins led the charge as the Eagles defeated Duke and gave Connecticut a serious push in the Southeast Region. He's fun to watch.

COLLEGE STATISTICS

	G	FGP	FTP	RPG	APG	PPG
94-95 EMU	30	.413	.703	2.4	4.5	12.5
95-96 EMU	31	.432	.804	2.3	5.8	15.5
Totals	61	.438	.764	2.3	5.2	14.0

KENDRIC BROOKS
School: Fresno State
Year: Senior
Position: Forward/Guard
Height: 6'5" **Weight:** 210
Birthdate: September 30, 1973
Hometown: New Orleans, LA

PLAYER SUMMARY	
Will	score in bunches
Can't	excel as ball-handler
Expect	athletic maneuvers
Don't Expect	offensive patience

Background: This native of New Orleans made his reputation at the junior college level, playing at Hartnell (CA) College. As a sophomore, he was one of the top scorers in northern California. Soon after Jerry Tarkanian was named coach at Fresno State, Brooks signed on.

Strengths: Brooks found a perfect home in Fresno. His game fits nicely into Tarkanian's modus operandi. Athletically gifted, Brooks beats people down the floor and is a force filling the lane on the fastbreak. He possesses a solid face-up jumper and has worked hard to become a strong defender.

Weaknesses: Brooks must focus on keeping his man in front of him, and he must pay close attention to keeping opposing forwards off the glass. For all of his gifts, he is not a first-rate passer and rarely creates offense for his teammates.

Analysis: Tarkanian built up the UNLV program on the back of juco recruits. He lifted Fresno back into WAC contention in a similar fashion, with Brooks as the top attraction. Brooks's athletic gifts and willingness to learn have catapulted him into position to be one of the breakout stars in the West.

COLLEGE STATISTICS
		G	FGP	FTP	RPG	APG	PPG
95-96	FSU	33	.416	.744	3.8	1.3	19.4
Totals		33	.416	.744	3.8	1.3	19.4

GREG BUCKNER
School: Clemson
Year: Junior
Position: Guard
Height: 6'4" **Weight:** 200
Birthdate: September 16, 1976
Hometown: Hopkinsville, KY

PLAYER SUMMARY	
Will	clean the glass
Can't	drill 3s regularly
Expect	a complete package
Don't Expect	poor defense

Background: A graduate of University Heights Academy, Buckner signed a letter of intent to play at Providence in the fall of 1993. He sought and was granted a release from that letter when head coach Rick Barnes left the Friars to accept the top spot at Clemson. A year later, Buckner was named ACC Rookie of the Year.

Strengths: When the Tigers need a clutch basket, they turn to this man. Good size enables Buckner to take smaller guards into the paint, and he is an adroit finisher around the goal. He is also one of the ACC's finest defenders, thanks to good foot speed and sound fundamentals. Few backcourt players rebound as well as Buckner does.

Weaknesses: The range on Buckner's jumper does not extend beyond 15 feet, preventing him from becoming a major scoring force. Free-throw shooting is another area that could use attention.

Analysis: Buckner has all the equipment to become one of the best in the ACC. If he boosts his perimeter range, he'll slide into contention for All-America consideration. Some experts suspect that this unheralded swingman will one day continue the tradition of Clemson players in the pros.

COLLEGE STATISTICS
		G	FGP	FTP	RPG	APG	PPG
94-95	CLEM	28	.526	.513	5.9	2.1	12.0
95-96	CLEM	29	.472	.672	5.1	1.7	13.1
Totals		57	.499	.594	5.5	1.9	12.6

MARCUS BULLARD

School: Mississippi State
Year: Junior
Position: Guard
Height: 6'3" **Weight:** 200
Birthdate: November 19, 1974
Hometown: Long Beach, MS

PLAYER SUMMARY	
Will	arc rainbow shots
Can't	be careless with ball
Expect	competent playmaking
Don't Expect	dynamic moves

Background: A four-year starter at Long Beach (MS) High School, Bullard was named to the all-state first team as a senior. He set a school record with 60 points in one contest. As a sophomore at Mississippi State, he helped the Bulldogs to an appearance in the Final Four.

Strengths: While other point guards cannot be classified as pure shooters, Bullard can. He squares his body well, owns a soft touch, and is capable of entering zones in which he does not miss. A muscular sort, Bullard can also post up other guards and help on the boards. This hard worker gives an honest defensive effort as well.

Weaknesses: Experience is a necessity at the point, and Bullard's experience is limited thus far. In reality, he is an off guard attempting to handle some point guard responsibilities. When pressed, he will force passes, and the result is turnovers.

Analysis: MSU's guards were roundly criticized for their performance against Syracuse in the Final Four. Bullard and his sidekick Darryl Wilson threw the ball away often against a club that sat back in a two-three zone. One bad effort cannot obscure an otherwise superb season. Bullard will be back.

COLLEGE STATISTICS

		G	FGP	FTP	RPG	APG	PPG
94-95	MSU	30	.418	.667	2.2	1.8	5.4
95-96	MSU	34	.460	.654	3.9	5.1	12.1
Totals		64	.448	.659	3.1	3.5	9.0

LOUIS BULLOCK

School: Michigan
Year: Sophomore
Position: Guard
Height: 6'2" **Weight:** 165
Birthdate: May 20, 1977
Hometown: Temple Hills, MD

PLAYER SUMMARY	
Will	drop in 3s
Can't	depend on muscle
Expect	scoring binges
Don't Expect	post-up action

Background: As a high school senior, Bullock was voted Mr. Basketball in the Washington, D.C., area. *FutureStars* listed Bullock as the No. 18 player in the nation that year. As a freshman at Michigan, he quickly earned a starting nod and stepped forward as one of the Big Ten's finest freshmen.

Strengths: This secondary-education major is defined by his sweet shooting stroke. This touch is the weapon that allows him to be a viable option every time down the floor. Bullock's range extends beyond the 3-point line, and he can make shots under duress. He is also a first-rate free-throw shooter.

Weaknesses: At a measly 165 pounds, Bullock can be pushed around defensively. Michigan used him as a point guard but found he was more comfortable without having to direct the offense. Nonetheless, he will have to adjust to playing the point if he aspires to an NBA career. He also needs to look to drive to the basket more often.

Analysis: Although lacking the hype of the Fab Five, Bullock enjoyed a solid freshman season. His type of shooting skill has not been evidenced in Ann Arbor since Jimmy King's perimeter game eroded after his sophomore year. Hopefully, Bullock will be able to stay on track.

COLLEGE STATISTICS

		G	FGP	FTP	RPG	APG	PPG
95-96	MICH	32	.398	.845	3.0	1.7	13.5
Totals		32	.398	.845	3.0	1.7	13.5

TODD BURGAN
School: Syracuse
Year: Junior
Position: Guard/Forward
Height: 6'7" **Weight:** 225
Birthdate: December 4, 1974
Hometown: Detroit, MI

PLAYER SUMMARY	
Will	provide solid "D"
Can't	relax on defense
Expect	increased offense
Don't Expect	much rest

Background: Burgan was a first-team all-state pick as a high school senior. Next, he spent a year honing his game and academics at New Hampton (NH) Prep, where he averaged 24 points and nine rebounds a game. He saw limited action as a rookie at Syracuse, but then became an important ingredient as the Orangemen reached the national championship game last year.

Strengths: Burgan is a classic Syracuse player in many ways. His athleticism makes him an inviting target for alley-oop passes. He runs the floor very well and has enough quickness to go around defenders with the ball in his hands. He handles a variety of difficult defensive assignments with style.

Weaknesses: He is adept at taking the ball into the lane, but Burgan doesn't always finish what he starts. Indecisiveness has been a problem. It remains to be seen how good a man-to-man defender Burgan is, since the Orange usually rely on a two-three zone.

Analysis: Departed star John Wallace received a huge dose of credit for leading the Orange to within a game of the national title. He did not do it alone. Burgan was also a major plus, and now he will be asked to carry more of the scoring burden.

COLLEGE STATISTICS
	G	FGP	FTP	RPG	APG	PPG
94-95 SYR	27	.475	.656	2.2	0.5	4.0
95-96 SYR	38	.421	.623	6.8	2.3	12.1
Totals	65	.431	.628	4.9	1.6	8.7

JEFF CAPEL
School: Duke
Year: Senior
Position: Guard
Height: 6'4" **Weight:** 195
Birthdate: February 12, 1975
Hometown: Fayetteville, NC

PLAYER SUMMARY	
Will	hit pull-up "Js"
Can't	deliver consistently
Expect	drives to the hoop
Don't Expect	creative playmaking

Background: The son of Jeff Capel, Sr. (presently the coach at Old Dominion), Capel came by his basketball roots naturally. He was an all-state performer at South View (NC) High School and was a starter as the Blue Devils reached the NCAA championship game in 1994.

Strengths: Versatility is one of the most attractive features of Capel's game. He is capable of handling either guard spot and, in a pinch, can be used as a small forward. This explosive leaper is most effective driving hard to the goal. His 3-point shot can be a weapon when he is in a groove.

Weaknesses: Although he logged the most minutes of any Blue Devil last year, Capel really has not carved a niche for himself. As a point guard, he is methodical and lacks flair. It was thought that a move to off guard would free him up to score more, but his shooting from long range has been spotty.

Analysis: Playing with Grant Hill as a freshman, Capel appeared to have a bright future. Since then he has struggled to come into his own as an All-ACC-caliber player. Duke seniors, though, have a history of coming up big in the Mike Krzyzewski era.

COLLEGE STATISTICS
	G	FGP	FTP	RPG	APG	PPG
93-94 DUKE	34	.458	.656	2.7	3.2	8.6
94-95 DUKE	31	.446	.643	2.7	4.1	12.5
95-96 DUKE	31	.376	.763	3.9	3.7	16.6
Totals	96	.416	.700	3.1	3.6	12.4

GENO CARLISLE

School: Northwestern
Year: Junior
Position: Guard
Height: 6'2" **Weight:** 182
Birthdate: August 13, 1976
Hometown: Grand Rapids, MI

PLAYER SUMMARY	
Will	fly past defenders
Can't	wait to drive
Expect	all-out effort
Don't Expect	help from mates

Background: A product of Ottawa Hills High School in Michigan, Carlisle escaped the notice of most large Midwestern schools but moved directly into the starting lineup at Northwestern. An All-Big Ten selection as a sophomore, Carlisle is clearly one of the elite players you don't hear enough about.

Strengths: Elusiveness and ball-handling make Carlisle a tough target for foes to get a read on. A strong crossover dribble helps get him past defenders and into an area where he can create scoring chances for his teammates. In addition to his slashing tools, he also makes his jump shots.

Weaknesses: Lack of help from his teammates is what inhibits Carlisle most. Coach Ricky Byrdsong must have him on the floor at all times if the Wildcats are to be competitive in the Big Ten. That leads to fatigue for the slight Carlisle. It also forces him to pace himself at the defensive end.

Analysis: There aren't many more talented guards in the Big Ten than Carlisle. His scoring skills augment a solid sense of when to make plays and when to back off. He figures to remain a hidden gem as long as Northwestern struggles, and—sadly—there is no sign of an impending revival.

COLLEGE STATISTICS

	G	FGP	FTP	RPG	APG	PPG
94-95 NORT	26	.389	.756	2.8	3.9	11.7
95-96 NORT	27	.393	.773	2.6	2.7	19.7
Totals	53	.391	.766	2.7	3.3	15.8

VINCE CARTER

School: North Carolina
Year: Sophomore
Position: Guard/Forward
Height: 6'5" **Weight:** 210
Birthdate: January 26, 1977
Hometown: Ormond Beach, FL

PLAYER SUMMARY	
Will	make acrobatic moves
Can't	grow frustrated
Expect	more consistent scoring
Don't Expect	thundering picks

Background: Both Florida and Florida State spent a lot of time attempting to convince this star at Daytona Beach Mainland to attend college in his home state. Yet the *Basketball Times* 1995 prep Player of the Year chose North Carolina and quickly became a fixture in the Tar Heels' starting lineup.

Strengths: Possessing a sweet jumper, Carter can score from a variety of spots on the floor. His quickness permits him to create his own shots and take the ball to the basket when defenders play him too aggressively on the outside.

Weaknesses: As a prepster, Carter was used to a free-flowing game in which he got the most shots. He has struggled at times with UNC's more structured offensive roles. Too often there were occasions when he drifted into the background and was not a factor. He needs to maintain his concentration level at the defensive end at all times.

Analysis: It was a difficult first year for Carter in some respects. His statistics weren't bad, but he was not the offensive force many anticipated he would be. The trials of 1995-96 should pay dividends this year, though, because the talent to be an All-American is there.

COLLEGE STATISTICS

	G	FGP	FTP	RPG	APG	PPG
95-96 NC	31	.492	.689	3.8	1.3	7.5
Totals	31	.492	.689	3.8	1.3	7.5

KRIS CLACK

School: Texas
Year: Sophomore
Position: Guard
Height: 6'5" **Weight:** 195
Birthdate: July 6, 1977
Hometown: Austin, TX

PLAYER SUMMARY	
Will	fire in 3s
Can't	lose defensive focus
Expect	creative offense
Don't Expect	nifty passes

Background: This is the kind of athlete Texas coach Tom Penders had so much trouble luring to Austin in the late 1980s and early '90s. Like other Texans Shaquille O'Neal, LaBradford Smith, and Andrae Patterson, Clack was a McDonald's All-American. Unlike those stars, he decided to stay home for college.

Strengths: Long and lean, Clack is an efficient scorer. He blends smoothly into the offensive system at UT. His jumper is steadier than most, and its range goes past the 3-point line. Drives are also part of Clack's repertoire, and he can locate the open man when he encounters difficulty.

Weaknesses: Inconsistency can be a problem for youngsters, as it was at times for Clack in his freshman season. Trips to the weight room are a must for him if he is to bulk up and learn to play tough consistently. Attention to defensive detail is another area in which Clack needs to make gains.

Analysis: Many prepsters in the talent-rich Lone Star state are watching Clack as they assess their future. So far, both coach and player appear pleased. Clack logged heavy minutes as a rookie and looks to post some large scoring totals before his collegiate career concludes.

COLLEGE STATISTICS

	G	FGP	FTP	RPG	APG	PPG
95-96 TEX	31	.502	.534	6.6	1.6	9.4
Totals	31	.502	.534	6.6	1.6	9.4

MERL CODE

School: Clemson
Year: Senior
Position: Guard
Height: 6'2" **Weight:** 190
Birthdate: February 5, 1974
Hometown: Greenville, SC

PLAYER SUMMARY	
Will	create shots
Can't	cut on a dime
Expect	steady contributions
Don't Expect	gaudy statistics

Background: After completing his high school career at Greenville (SC) Southside, Code spent a year at Fork Union Prep. He opened his college career as Clemson's starting point guard and was named the Tigers' MVP as a sophomore. His 1995-96 campaign was cut short by knee surgery.

Strengths: Code does many things well. His ball-handling has improved every year at the collegiate level, and he possesses a smooth shooting touch. A strong free-throw shooter, Code has quick hands and understands how to play the passing lanes at the defensive end.

Weaknesses: Knee injuries like Code's are particularly problematic for guards. A lengthy rehab can rob an athlete of his quickness, which can be a major problem when his assignment is to check the likes of Harold Deane and Jeff Capel. Even at 100 percent, Code is not an explosive scorer.

Analysis: Clemson managed to reach the NCAA Tournament without Code, but coach Rick Barnes is eager to get him back in the lineup. This is not the kind of athlete who can take over. Rather, he is a sound performer with no serious flaws.

COLLEGE STATISTICS

	G	FGP	FTP	RPG	APG	PPG
93-94 CLEM	25	.333	.809	2.0	2.7	4.1
94-95 CLEM	28	.406	.814	3.8	4.0	11.8
95-96 CLEM	11	.442	.897	3.6	2.5	12.5
Totals	64	.401	.809	3.0	3.2	8.9

JASON COLLIER

School: Indiana
Year: Freshman
Position: Center
Height: 6'11" **Weight:** 235
Birthdate: September 8, 1977
Hometown: Springfield, OH

PLAYER SUMMARY	
Will ....earn important minutes
Can't.............................step outside
Expect...................early production
Don't Expect ....showy moves

Background: At Central Catholic High School in Ohio, Collier was one of the most sought-after big men in the nation. *Future-Stars* listed him as a second-team All-American. On the first day of the recruitment period last July, Bob Knight phoned and invited Collier to Bloomington. That head start gave the Hoosiers the edge they needed in the recruiting process.

Strengths: You will not find Collier drawing attention to himself by attempting to wander away from the basket. The most intriguing aspect of his game is his advanced ball-handling ability. He possesses a sweet shooting touch and a knack for finding the open man on the wing. His height makes him a presence in the lane.

Weaknesses: Knight is a stickler for man-to-man defensive skills, and Collier must make strides in that regard. He must get stronger so that he can grind with the powerful rebounders in the Big Ten. Also, he must prove he is tough enough mentally to handle Knight's periodic tests of his psyche.

Analysis: Indiana was the school Collier liked from the beginning. The discipline and tradition of the program suit him. A dearth of big men on the Indiana roster means he has a chance to make an immediate—and important—impact at IU.

JAMES COTTON

School: Long Beach State
Year: Junior
Position: Guard
Height: 6'5" **Weight:** 200
Birthdate: December 14, 1975
Hometown: San Pedro, CA

PLAYER SUMMARY	
Will ....deliver points
Can't.....................handle with style
Expect ....3-point action
Don't Expect..........front-page fame

Background: Cotton's bloodlines are strong. One cousin, Marcus Cotton, plays in the National Football League. Another, Mike Harkey, pitched for the Chicago Cubs. At Long Beach State, James was the Big West Conference's Freshman of the Year. An ankle injury cost him the 1994-95 season, but he responded by leading his league in scoring last year.

Strengths: Cotton has scored at every level. One plus for him is that he is able to operate at the two guard spot. At 6'5", this gives him a huge advantage. He can take smaller defenders into the lane or get good looks from long distance when shooting over them. His size creates defensive woes for his foes.

Weaknesses: There are still rough edges to Cotton's game. He is not a strong ballhandler, which leads to errors. While he is a decent rebounder for his size, Cotton needs to contribute a bit more effort in that area, especially at the defensive end.

Analysis: Athletes on the West Coast can get lost in the shuffle, particularly if they do not attend school in the powerful Pac-10. Pay heed to Cotton, though. This accomplished scorer has been a major factor in the 49ers' rise in the Big West.

COLLEGE STATISTICS

		G	FGP	FTP	RPG	APG	PPG
94-95	LBS	1	.300	.800	1.0	3.0	14.0
95-96	LBS	26	.433	.782	4.1	1.7	19.5
Totals		27	.430	.783	4.0	1.7	19.3

AUSTIN CROSHERE

School: Providence
Year: Senior
Position: Forward
Height: 6'9" **Weight:** 225
Birthdate: May 1, 1975
Hometown: Los Angeles, CA

PLAYER SUMMARY	
Will	convert 3s
Can't	block shots
Expect	strong FT shooting
Don't Expect	quickness

Background: Croshere landed at Providence upon graduating from Crossroads (CA) High School. As a freshman, he became a regular contributor and sometime-starter for Rick Barnes. When Barnes left for Clemson, Croshere struggled to adjust to new coach Pete Gillen. He became PC's go-to man as a junior.

Strengths: Croshere possesses very good ball skills for a big man. His jump shot is accurate, and he can sink it from beyond the 3-point line. If he elects to go around his man, he can draw a foul with a pump fake. He usually makes opponents pay the price for hacking him when he reaches the line.

Weaknesses: Defense is not the best part of his game. Croshere struggles with quicker forwards away from the basket. Usually he cannot duplicate their speed, and he isn't muscular enough to hold his ground with the giants inside.

Analysis: Croshere has blossomed nicely after some sophomore struggles in Gillen's debut. He is one of the best players in the Big East and is extremely good at what he does: scoring from medium range and assisting where he can on the glass.

COLLEGE STATISTICS

	G	FGP	FTP	RPG	APG	PPG
93-94 PROV	25	.400	.725	2.2	0.1	4.6
94-95 PROV	30	.459	.776	4.9	1.1	10.2
95-96 PROV	30	.421	.852	5.8	1.1	15.3
Totals	85	.431	.806	4.4	0.8	10.4

ACE CUSTIS

School: Virginia Tech
Year: Senior
Position: Forward
Height: 6'7" **Weight:** 217
Birthdate: May 24, 1974
Hometown: Eastville, VA

PLAYER SUMMARY	
Will	attack inside
Can't	forget his past
Expect	tireless efforts
Don't Expect	glamorous numbers

Background: A high school center, Custis arrived at Virginia Tech with a determined outlook after an auto accident nearly took his life. A knee injury prevented him from playing in 1992-93, but he's been on a roll ever since. In 1994-95, he earned first-team All-Metro Conference honors and helped the Hokies win the NIT.

Strengths: This is very much a self-made player. Effort is a given where Custis is concerned. He has learned how to play facing the basket and now offers a reliable medium-range jumper. At times he is unstoppable on the offensive glass.

Weaknesses: Custis isn't the kind of athlete who can create scoring opportunities merely by putting the basketball on the floor. His perimeter game is still not where it should be, and large power forwards can be a handful for him defensively.

Analysis: A neat nickname and a spot among America's best made Custis a household name in 1995-96. His task gets tougher in 1996-97, as most of his mates have completed their eligibility. However, Custis is the kind of leader a young team can rally around.

COLLEGE STATISTICS

	G	FGP	FTP	RPG	APG	PPG
93-94 VT	28	.523	.693	9.1	2.1	10.9
94-95 VT	35	.533	.669	10.5	2.5	15.8
95-96 VT	29	.507	.673	9.5	2.4	13.4
Totals	92	.522	.675	9.8	0.7	13.6

HAROLD DEANE

School: Virginia
Year: Senior
Position: Guard
Height: 6'1" **Weight:** 175
Birthdate: September 11, 1974
Hometown: Ettrick, VA

PLAYER SUMMARY	
Will	feed the scorers
Can't	grow frustrated
Expect	smooth ball-handling
Don't Expect	lack of FG attempts

Background: Fork Union Military Academy prepared Deane well for the rigors of college basketball. Forced into action when an injury sidelined starter Cory Alexander in 1993-94, this unheralded rookie emerged as a third-team Freshman All-America pick of *Basketball Times*. As a sophomore, he was a second-team All-ACC pick.

Strengths: A durable sort, Deane will not step away from a challenge. He creates scoring opportunities for his mates when slashing to the goal. He generally takes good care of the basketball and is a good rebounder for his position.

Weaknesses: Deane fancies himself to be an offensive weapon and too often tries to score first and create for his teammates second. He often does not react well to double-teams and forces shots that aren't there.

Analysis: At the start of 1995-96, Deane was considered second only to Kansas' Jacque Vaughn among point guards nationally. However, he and the Cavaliers endured a subpar season. There were too many instances of Deane attempting to do too much. If he learns to exhibit more control, he can reestablish himself.

COLLEGE STATISTICS

		G	FGP	FTP	RPG	APG	PPG
93-94	VIRG	31	.368	.706	3.5	2.8	12.3
94-95	VIRG	34	.392	.795	3.0	4.3	16.0
95-96	VIRG	27	.344	.808	4.4	3.7	16.7
Totals		92	.368	.774	3.6	3.6	14.9

MALIK DIXON

School: Arkansas-Little Rock
Year: Senior
Position: Guard
Height: 6'1" **Weight:** 180
Birthdate: September 7, 1975
Hometown: Chicago, IL

PLAYER SUMMARY	
Will	swish jumpers
Can't	direct the offense
Expect	plenty of points
Don't Expect	many open looks

Background: This product of Chicago endured two foot injuries that robbed him of all but eight games of his sophomore season at UALR. However, he rebounded nicely as a junior, leading the Trojans in scoring as the club won the regular-season Sun Belt Conference crown. He was voted first-team All-Sun Belt.

Strengths: Dixon gives Trojan coach Wimp Sanderson an essential element—steady perimeter shooting. He comes off screens and receives the ball well. A quick release enables him to make the shot even with a defender nearby. When he is not open, he is willing to make the extra pass.

Weaknesses: At 6'1", Dixon can encounter difficulty checking taller off guards. He is vulnerable to post-up situations and cannot be much of a factor on the backboards. If he is able to enhance his ball-handling, he might earn a look from the pros.

Analysis: This man was one-half of the Sun Belt's foremost backcourt combination. His partner, Derek Fisher, is gone, so defenses will now fix their gaze on Dixon. He is skilled enough to handle that assignment with style.

COLLEGE STATISTICS

		G	FGP	FTP	RPG	APG	PPG
93-94	ALR	28	.440	.738	2.8	3.0	10.3
94-95	ALR	8	.516	.675	3.1	2.5	22.1
95-96	ALR	30	.444	.824	3.5	2.5	17.8
Totals		66	.455	.773	3.2	2.7	15.1

TIM DUNCAN

School: Wake Forest
Year: Senior
Position: Center
Height: 6'10" **Weight:** 240
Birthdate: April 25, 1976
Hometown: St. Croix, Virgin Islands

PLAYER SUMMARY	
Will ....dominate down low
Can't.....................................open up
Expect ....workmanlike approach
Don't Expect.................loud boasts

Background: As a youth, Duncan focused much of his athletic energy on the swimming pool, where the 400-meter freestyle was his speciality. He didn't start playing organized basketball until the ninth grade. Duncan is now a two-time first-team All-American.

Strengths: Duncan has not picked up many of the bad habits today's players feature. For instance, he rarely gets in foul difficulty since he isn't fascinated with intimidation. Duncan makes all of the plays he should offensively. He is a huge shot-blocking presence and a strong rebounder.

Weaknesses: Duncan's offensive game remains somewhat raw. Though possessing a soft touch, he doesn't have the variety of post-up moves some of his rivals do. That will come in time, however. He is not the kind of firebrand some coaches prefer to have as their team leader.

Analysis: It's simple: Duncan is college basketball's premier player. Had he elected to declare for either of the last two NBA drafts, he would have been the No. 1 selection. By choosing to stay in school, this quiet leader made a strong statement.

COLLEGE STATISTICS

		G	FGP	FTP	RPG	APG	PPG
93-94	WF	33	.545	.745	9.6	0.9	9.8
94-95	WF	32	.591	.742	12.5	2.1	16.8
95-96	WF	32	.555	.687	12.3	2.9	19.1
Totals		97	.566	.718	11.5	2.0	15.2

DAN EARL

School: Penn State
Year: Senior
Position: Guard
Height: 6'4" **Weight:** 180
Birthdate: December 10, 1974
Hometown: Medford Lakes, NJ

PLAYER SUMMARY	
Will ....expertly direct attack
Can't............................fly by people
Expect...............minimal turnovers
Don't Expect .....flamboyant moves

Background: The son of a former player at Rutgers, Earl was the 1993 New Jersey Player of the Year. During his junior and senior seasons, Shawnee (NJ) High School posted a 59-3 record. In his frosh year at Penn State, Earl tied the school's freshman assists record (113). He gained All-Tournament raves when PSU reached the NIT Final Four in 1995.

Strengths: Earl might best be described as a minimalist: He stays within himself at all times and does not attempt an elaborate play when a simple one will do. Expert at locating the open man, Earl rarely makes an ill-advised pass. He scores just enough to keep defenders honest.

Weaknesses: Though a willing defender, Earl can be overmatched against speedy point guards. He simply has a hard time keeping pace with their quickness. He needs plenty of time to get his jump shot off at the offensive end.

Analysis: This is not an athlete for the dunk-and-jam set. However, Earl is effective in a very subtle manner. He understands how to get a team into its offense, and he delivers the ball to the right spot at the right time.

COLLEGE STATISTICS

		G	FGP	FTP	RPG	APG	PPG
93-94	PSU	27	.386	.652	2.5	4.2	8.4
94-95	PSU	32	.424	.835	2.3	5.7	9.3
95-96	PSU	28	.476	.681	2.6	5.4	11.7
Totals		87	.428	.722	2.5	5.1	9.8

DAMON FLINT

School: Cincinnati
Year: Senior
Position: Guard/Forward
Height: 6'5" **Weight:** 201
Birthdate: October 21, 1973
Hometown: Cincinnati, OH

PLAYER SUMMARY	
Will	peer over defenses
Can't	take care of ball
Expect	open-court efficiency
Don't Expect	rebounds

Background: This alumnus of Cincinnati's Woodward High School was the subject of an intense recruiting battle between the Bearcats and Ohio State. After signing with OSU, Flint ultimately was released from his letter because of NCAA violations. He was a sixth-team Freshman All-America pick of *The Sporting News*.

Strengths: Flint can utilize all of his skills in an open-court setting. At 6'5", he puts his lanky frame to good use against smaller guards. He presents problems for scoring guards more accustomed to shorter defenders. Flint is a very good ball-handler.

Weaknesses: Flint's shooting runs hot and cold. It is no coincidence that Mississippi State eliminated Cincinnati in the Southeast Regional final of the NCAA Tournament last season on an afternoon when Flint connected on only two of 14 from the field. Flint must be more consistent with his shot.

Analysis: Though he has not been the star his recruiting saga suggested he would be, Flint has been an important part of the puzzle at UC. His ball-handling, passing, and shooting give the Bearcats a dimension that few programs have at the wing spot.

COLLEGE STATISTICS

	G	FGP	FTP	RPG	APG	PPG
93-94 CINN	32	.375	.588	3.8	2.8	12.6
94-95 CINN	31	.398	.623	2.2	2.5	7.0
95-96 CINN	33	.433	.696	3.0	3.5	12.8
Totals	96	.401	.635	3.0	2.9	10.8

DANNY FORTSON

School: Cincinnati
Year: Junior
Position: Forward
Height: 6'7" **Weight:** 260
Birthdate: March 27, 1976
Hometown: Pittsburgh, PA

PLAYER SUMMARY	
Will	pound it inside
Can't	lift rainbow 3s
Expect	interior intimidation
Don't Expect	pinpoint passing

Background: This standout at Pittsburgh's Shaler High School had an unusual demand when picking a college: He wished to attend the school with the most difficult practice sessions. Fortson then picked rugged Cincinnati over Massachusetts—and coach Bob Huggins is glad he did. Fortson was a second-team All-America choice of *Basketball Times* as a sophomore.

Strengths: Fortson is an incredibly strong, muscular forward with an uncommon shooting touch. He likes to set up shop in the box by using his ample frame to establish position. Good hands allow him to grip most passes, and an array of moves usually results in a score or trip to the line.

Weaknesses: Fortson's physical play inside often results in foul trouble. He must be careful not to be overly aggressive when play heats up inside. Passing is not Fortson's trademark.

Analysis: A hard worker, Fortson accomplishes a great deal by sheer will. He is a relentless rebounder and one of the top interior point producers in the land. If he enjoys another good season at UC, look for him to move on to the NBA draft in 1997.

COLLEGE STATISTICS

	G	FGP	FTP	RPG	APG	PPG
94-95 CINN	34	.535	.684	7.6	1.1	15.1
95-96 CINN	33	.538	.753	9.6	1.4	20.1
Totals	67	.536	.725	8.6	1.2	17.6

ADONAL FOYLE

School: Colgate
Year: Junior
Position: Center
Height: 6'10" **Weight:** 255
Birthdate: March 9, 1975
Hometown: Hamilton, NY

PLAYER SUMMARY	
Will	reject shots
Can't	launch bombs
Expect	interior domination
Don't Expect	TV appearances

Background: Foyle grew up in the Grenadines and didn't play basketball in the U.S. until he was a sophomore in high school. As a junior, he moved to Hamilton, New York, where his legal guardians are professors at Colgate. That helped coach Jack Bruen convince the student with the 3.7 grade point average to spurn the likes of Duke and Syracuse.

Strengths: A solid frame and excellent athletic skills help make Foyle a menace inside. Excellent leaping ability and timing allow him to deflect shots (5.7 BPG last year, good for second in the nation). He combines these athletic tools with a rare work ethic, producing tremendous rebounding energy.

Weaknesses: By his own admission, Foyle is not as comfortable facing the basket as he is with his back to it. He must continue to work on his ball-handling and his passing from the high post. An enhanced medium-range jumper would also help.

Analysis: Don't look for Foyle to show up often in your living room—Colgate simply doesn't warrant that kind of coverage. Take note, though: This is an NBA lottery pick with a bright professional future.

COLLEGE STATISTICS

		G	FGP	FTP	RPG	APG	PPG
94-95	COLG	30	.559	.500	12.4	1.2	17.0
95-96	COLG	29	.517	.489	12.6	1.5	20.2
Totals		59	.536	.493	12.6	1.3	18.5

REGGIE FREEMAN

School: Texas
Year: Senior
Position: Guard
Height: 6'6" **Weight:** 200
Birthdate: May 17, 1975
Hometown: Bronx, NY

PLAYER SUMMARY	
Will	rack up numbers
Can't	attack defensively
Expect	vocal leadership
Don't Expect	high FG pct.

Background: Texas coach Tom Penders went back to familiar turf to bring Freeman to Austin. Penders coached at both Fordham and Columbia, both not far from Rice High School, where Freeman prepped. After frequently being overshadowed by Felipe Lopez at Rice, Freeman stepped forward as a star in the final season of Southwest Conference play in 1995-96.

Strengths: Under Penders, Texas has embraced a wide-open offensive philosophy that suits Freeman perfectly. Improved ball-handling allows him to use his athletic gifts to glide past defenders into the lane. This New Yorker is now a legitimate threat from 3-point territory, something that wasn't true when he came to Texas.

Weaknesses: Defense can be a hit-or-miss proposition for Freeman. Sometimes he is so focused on scoring that his concentration wavers at the other end. He needs to reduce the number of bad shots he takes.

Analysis: Texas is a scorer's haven, and Freeman is its most potent practitioner. His firepower and willingness to lead should make the Longhorns a presence in their first season of play in the Big 12.

COLLEGE STATISTICS

		G	FGP	FTP	RPG	APG	PPG
93-94	TEX	32	.420	.741	2.6	0.9	5.3
94-95	TEX	30	.440	.661	4.1	1.0	14.7
95-96	TEX	31	.376	.732	6.7	3.9	22.4
Totals		93	.403	.718	4.5	1.9	14.0

CHRIS GARNER

School: Memphis
Year: Senior
Position: Guard
Height: 5'10" **Weight:** 156
Birthdate: February 23, 1975
Hometown: Memphis, TN

PLAYER SUMMARY	
Will	disrupt offenses
Can't	connect from deep
Expect	presses to be broken
Don't Expect	long-range accuracy

Background: Memphis' roster is loaded with local products who stayed at home to play for Larry Finch. Garner is one of those, though he attracted less hype than teammate Cedric Henderson or predecessor Anfernee Hardaway. Garner has led the Tigers in assists in each of the past two seasons.

Strengths: Garner is a throwback, the kind of point guard who sets up his mates first and concerns himself with scoring last. A terrific dribbler, he makes it very difficult for opponents to press Memphis. Often he will defeat traps on his own. His quickness allows him to blow past defenders.

Weaknesses: Garner is a suspect long-range shooter. Teams are forever sagging inside and daring this product of Treadwell High School to beat them from deep. Generally he has not done so. His willingness to gamble defensively sometimes leaves him out of position.

Analysis: Aside from his assist totals, Garner's numbers are not overwhelming. He isn't much of a scorer, and his slight build keeps him away from the glass. But he makes the Tigers go and finds the open man at the offensive end.

COLLEGE STATISTICS

		G	FGP	FTP	RPG	APG	PPG
93-94	MEMP	28	.391	.650	2.8	4.4	6.4
94-95	MEMP	34	.421	.485	3.4	6.4	6.6
95-96	MEMP	30	.458	.565	3.5	5.7	7.6
Totals		92	.424	.541	3.2	5.6	6.9

KIWANE GARRIS

School: Illinois
Year: Senior
Position: Guard
Height: 6'2" **Weight:** 183
Birthdate: September 24, 1974
Hometown: Chicago, IL

PLAYER SUMMARY	
Will	handle the press
Can't	escape injuries
Expect	excellent FT shooting
Don't Expect	strong rebounding

Background: Garris lists former Illini guard Kendall Gill as one of the athletes he admires. It almost seems as though Garris has been in Champaign long enough to have played with Gill, who left in 1990. That's because the product of Westinghouse High School has been a fixture in the Illini lineup since the first game of his rookie season.

Strengths: Ex-head coach Lou Henson was most comfortable when Garris had the basketball in his hands. An elusive dribbler, Garris can take the defender off of the dribble. He is at his best slashing to the goal and offers a reliable perimeter jumper to keep opponents honest.

Weaknesses: Leg injuries slowed Garris in 1995-96. They robbed him of much of his speed, and that affected all aspects of his game. Defense was a particular problem, since he is not the kind of athlete who can rely on a big body to wear others down.

Analysis: When Garris was healthy in December, the Fighting Illini looked to be one of the top 25 teams in the nation. When he was injured in January, the club struggled. That fact underscores this player's importance to new coach Lon Kruger.

COLLEGE STATISTICS

		G	FGP	FTP	RPG	APG	PPG
93-94	ILL	28	.433	.803	3.5	3.8	15.9
94-95	ILL	31	.439	.831	2.8	3.8	15.9
95-96	ILL	25	.373	.862	3.4	3.9	15.4
Totals		84	.415	.829	3.2	3.8	15.8

PAT GARRITY

School: Notre Dame
Year: Junior
Position: Forward
Height: 6'9" **Weight:** 227
Birthdate: August 23, 1976
Hometown: Monument, CO

PLAYER SUMMARY	
Will	select good shots
Can't	find enough help
Expect	steady FT shooting
Don't Expect	electrifying slams

Background: A graduate of Lewis Palmer High School in Colorado, Garrity averaged 27 points and 12 rebounds per game as a senior. He picked Notre Dame and earned a starting berth as a freshman. His 361 points that year were the most by an Irish rookie since LaPhonso Ellis tallied 365 in 1988-89.

Strengths: In Notre Dame's first season of play in the rugged Big East Conference, Garrity was the school's only viable low-post threat. His soft shooting touch is augmented by a solid drop-step move that gets him around large defenders. He draws fouls and makes the foe pay with solid work at the free-throw line.

Weaknesses: Though he tries to overcome his lack of muscle with effort, Garrity struggles against some of the power players in the Big East. Stronger forwards are able to take him inside and do some damage. Despite his size, Garrity is not a shot-blocker, something the Irish could desperately use.

Analysis: Notre Dame has struggled in Garrity's two seasons, and that has conspired to keep him off the front page. He is not the glamorous leading-man type anyway. Garrity would be ideal as the second or third option on a Top 25 team.

COLLEGE STATISTICS

		G	FGP	FTP	RPG	APG	PPG
94-95	ND	27	.523	.766	5.1	1.3	13.4
95-96	ND	27	.476	.686	7.1	1.4	17.2
Totals		54	.500	.726	6.1	1.4	15.3

JEROD HAASE

School: Kansas
Year: Senior
Position: Guard
Height: 6'3" **Weight:** 185
Birthdate: April 1, 1974
Hometown: South Lake Tahoe, CA

PLAYER SUMMARY	
Will	put body on line
Can't	stay in one piece
Expect	streaky shooting
Don't Expect	a slacker

Background: The Nevada Class 3A Player of the Year as a senior at South Lake Tahoe High School, Haase enrolled at California as a freshman and played alongside Jason Kidd as the Golden Bears reached the NCAA Tournament's Sweet 16. Following that campaign, Haase transferred to Kansas, where he has been a two-year starter.

Strengths: When Haase is hitting from outside, the Jayhawks are brutal to defend. His range is nearly limitless, and he can sink jumpers with a hand in his face. Haase is all effort—a fact that makes him a nuisance as a defender. He will pressure the ball and use all of his 185 pounds to slow his foes.

Weaknesses: When Haase is cold, he becomes an offensive liability. He does not possess the kind of quickness that can take him past many guards. Turnovers are also an issue, as Haase sometimes tries too hard to make the perfect pass.

Analysis: While this is not the kind of player people leave the arena talking about, he is the kind of role-player every great team must have. Haase does the dirty work and more. He is gifted enough to damage the opponent with his tools as well as his effort.

COLLEGE STATISTICS

		G	FGP	FTP	RPG	APG	PPG
92-93	CAL	30	.389	.789	1.6	2.6	7.2
94-95	KANS	31	.436	.734	4.3	3.5	15.0
95-96	KANS	34	.356	.750	3.6	3.6	10.8
Totals		95	.398	.742	3.9	3.3	12.8

ZENDON HAMILTON

School: St. John's
Year: Junior
Position: Forward/Center
Height: 6'11" **Weight:** 225
Birthdate: April 27, 1973
Hometown: Floral Park, NY

PLAYER SUMMARY	
Will	finish the fastbreak
Can't	take much pounding
Expect	nifty plays around goal
Don't Expect	blocked shots

Background: In a bountiful crop of 1994 New York prep stars, Hamilton was rated behind only one—current teammate Felipe Lopez. Hamilton, a standout at Sewanhaka High School, was St. John's best player as a sophomore.

Strengths: This lean frontcourt star runs the court as well as anyone his size. Good hands enable Hamilton to receive the ball in the post or on the wing, and he knows how to finish a fastbreak. He possesses a smooth shooting touch to 12 feet and has developed into a good rebounder.

Weaknesses: Though 6'11", Hamilton is not really a center. He might not even be a power forward. His lithe frame simply does not stand up well to the kind of grinding that goes on against the likes of Danya Abrams and Jason Lawson. Hamilton also needs to become a better passer.

Analysis: Ironically, Hamilton's college career has been more impressive than his ballyhooed buddy Lopez's to this point. Unfortunately for the Red Storm, the club has missed the NCAA Tournament both years. New coach Fran Fraschilla was hired to see to it that the potential of both is maximized.

COLLEGE STATISTICS

		G	FGP	FTP	RPG	APG	PPG
94-95	STJ	28	.523	.617	5.0	0.6	11.4
95-96	STJ	27	.486	.797	10.3	0.8	20.8
Totals		55	.500	.729	7.6	0.7	15.7

MATT HARPRING

School: Georgia Tech
Year: Junior
Position: Forward
Height: 6'7" **Weight:** 226
Birthdate: May 31, 1976
Hometown: Dunwoody, GA

PLAYER SUMMARY	
Will	crash backboards
Can't	soar over guards
Expect	complete games
Don't Expect	much pine time

Background: Georgia's Player of the Year as a senior at Marist School, Harpring was a revelation as a rookie. Six games into his freshman season, Harpring was a starter scoring double figures. He bolstered that number as a sophomore, earning A.P. All-America honorable mention and helping Tech reach the NCAA Sweet 16.

Strengths: An excellent overall athlete, Harpring does a variety of things well. The experience he gained playing guard in high school helped make him an excellent ball-handler and passer. His face-up jumper is a reliable weapon that must be honored. He will also mix it up on the boards.

Weaknesses: Because of Tech's lack of power inside, Harpring is sometimes asked to play against big forwards or centers. Unfortunately, he really isn't muscular enough to handle those assignments. Shot-blocking is not a part of his game.

Analysis: This classy player was often overlooked due to the presence of the Yellow Jackets' guard tandem of Stephon Marbury and Drew Barry in 1995-96. Now that both are gone, this becomes Harpring's team. Look for him to step into the spotlight as one of the ACC's finest performers.

COLLEGE STATISTICS

		G	FGP	FTP	RPG	APG	PPG
94-95	GT	29	.484	736	6.2	2.3	12.1
95-96	GT	36	.510	.762	8.1	2.2	18.6
Totals		65	.501	.753	7.3	2.3	15.7

CEDRIC HENDERSON
School: Memphis
Year: Senior
Position: Forward
Height: 6'7" **Weight:** 215
Birthdate: March 11, 1975
Hometown: Memphis, TN

PLAYER SUMMARY	
Can	explode to goal
Can't	afford lack of focus
Expect	standout defense
Don't Expect	consistent shooting

Background: *Basketball Times* listed Henderson as the eighth-best "quick forward" in the class of 1993 when he was attending East High School. A McDonald's All-American, Henderson has been a fixture in the starting lineup since opening night of his freshman season.

Strengths: Observers marvel at Henderson's collection of athletic gifts. His skills are most vividly displayed in the open court, where he runs, jumps, and converts scoring chances. When he concentrates, those tools make him one of Conference USA's toughest defenders.

Weaknesses: Henderson is viewed by some as an underachiever because he is rarely consistent. Some of his worst performances have come against players and teams his skills suggest he should handle easily. He needs to focus more attention on fundamentals, such as long-range shooting.

Analysis: It's now or never for Henderson. Center Lorenzen Wright is gone, so Henderson will be Memphis' prime scoring option. Coach Larry Finch can no longer get by with sporadic moments of electricity from this man. He needs the whole package.

COLLEGE STATISTICS

	G	FGP	FTP	RPG	APG	PPG
93-94 MEMP	28	.465	.600	5.1	1.9	13.7
94-95 MEMP	34	.441	.583	5.1	1.4	12.9
95-96 MEMP	30	.492	.613	4.0	1.3	12.6
Totals	92	.463	.597	4.7	1.5	13.0

J.R. HENDERSON
School: UCLA
Year: Junior
Position: Forward
Height: 6'9" **Weight:** 215
Birthdate: October 30, 1976
Hometown: Bakersfield, CA

PLAYER SUMMARY	
Will	contribute where asked
Can't	make exotic passes
Expect	greater consistency
Don't Expect	multiple 3s

Background: The son of a former basketball standout at West Texas State (Milton Henderson), this youngster led East Bakersfield High School to the California State Division II title in 1994. As a freshman, Henderson became a key part of the rotation for a Bruin squad that won the NCAA championship.

Strengths: Although he is classified as a power forward, Henderson plays all three front-line positions. He appears most comfortable facing the basket, where a solid jumper makes him a scoring threat to 15 feet. His size makes him a factor on the boards, especially at the offensive end.

Weaknesses: Henderson does not have the body of a classic power forward. If he advances to the NBA, he will likely do so as a small forward. He is not much of a physical player and has a tendency to get lost in the Bruins' offense at times.

Analysis: There is no mistaking this man's athletic gifts or his ability to apply them in a variety of ways. Added maturity should help, though playing alongside All-America candidate Charles O'Bannon may keep him in the shadows for at least another season.

COLLEGE STATISTICS

	G	FGP	FTP	RPG	APG	PPG
94-95 UCLA	33	.547	.675	4.2	1.3	9.2
95-96 UCLA	29	.572	.678	7.0	1.9	14.4
Totals	62	.561	.677	5.5	1.6	11.7

OTIS HILL

School: Syracuse
Year: Senior
Position: Center
Height: 6'8" **Weight:** 255
Birthdate: March 31, 1974
Hometown: White Plains, NY

PLAYER SUMMARY	
Will	set crunching picks
Can't	shoot from deep
Expect	more minutes
Don't Expect	much finesse

Background: It shouldn't surprise anyone to learn that Hill played tight end for Pleasantville (NY) High School as well as center for the hoops team. This mammoth presence earned first-team all-state honors as a senior.

Strengths: Muscle is Hill's calling card. Establishing position in the low post is not a problem. Once he's in place, Hill has the kind of soft hands and touch needed to put points on the board. On defense, he anchors the middle of Syracuse's two-three zone. Rebounding is also one of his assets.

Weaknesses: The reason Hill's minutes have been limited is foul trouble—he fouled out nine times in 1995-96. He must do a better job of recognizing when to go for the shot block and when to ease off. Once the ball is fed to Hill in the post, it is rarely returned, as he struggles with the passing game.

Analysis: A mostly overlooked element in the Orange's March run to the NCAA championship game, Hill took a giant leap forward in 1995-96. He has the skills to become one of the East's top centers. If he avoids fouls, it can happen.

COLLEGE STATISTICS

		G	FGP	FTP	RPG	APG	PPG
93-94	SYR	30	.541	.585	5.6	1.2	7.9
94-95	SYR	30	.521	.662	4.4	0.7	6.5
95-96	SYR	38	.571	.681	5.4	0.6	12.7
Totals		98	.552	.653	5.2	0.8	9.3

JERALD HONEYCUTT

School: Tulane
Year: Senior
Position: Forward
Height: 6'9" **Weight:** 245
Birthdate: October 20, 1974
Hometown: Grambling, LA

PLAYER SUMMARY	
Will	slam home dunks
Can't	resist awkward shots
Expect	athletic achievement
Don't Expect	disciplined defense

Background: This McDonald's high school All-American was the object of an intense recruiting battle between Tulane and LSU. His enrollment at Tulane gave the program an instant boost. He was a first-team Conference USA selection last year and All-Southwest choice of *Basketball Times*.

Strengths: Honeycutt's tools would be imposing if he were 6'3". At 6'9", they elevate him into the class of special players. He is an intimidating sight on the break, filling the lane and converting passes into slam dunks. His medium-range jumper is effective, and he's tough on the offensive glass.

Weaknesses: His offensive tools sometimes captivate Honeycutt himself. There are periods when he is too content to loft jump shots. His 3-point shot is mediocre, yet he lifts it with the regularity of a marksman. He will have to pay much closer attention to defense at the next level.

Analysis: There has been plenty of highlight-reel material during Honeycutt's days at Tulane. But he has yet to elevate the program to the level that has been expected of him since he stepped onto campus.

COLLEGE STATISTICS

		G	FGP	FTP	RPG	APG	PPG
93-94	TUL	29	.403	.680	6.7	1.9	15.3
94-95	TUL	33	.446	.659	7.5	3.4	17.3
95-96	TUL	32	.402	.640	7.2	3.8	18.0
Totals		94	.417	.658	7.1	3.1	16.9

DEREK HOOD
School: Arkansas
Year: Sophomore
Position: Forward
Height: 6'8" **Weight:** 206
Birthdate: December 22, 1976
Hometown: Kansas City, MO

PLAYER SUMMARY	
Will	run the lanes
Can't	leap to the sky
Expect	consistent intensity
Don't Expect	him to back down

Background: An all-state and all-conference pick at Central High School in Kansas City, Hood played in the Magic Johnson Roundball Classic after his senior year. At Arkansas, he emerged as an instant force and a third-team Freshman All-America choice of *Basketball Times*.

Strengths: This gifted athlete loves to compete. He typifies the kind of intensity coach Nolan Richardson covets at Arkansas. Hood is at his best when the game is played in the open floor. At 6'8", he receives the ball well and can drill the pull-up jump shot. He is not afraid to mix it up defensively.

Weaknesses: There were times when it was hard to tell if Hood was on the floor last year. He was not as assertive as his skills suggest he should be. Also, he needs to reduce the number of forced shots and take better care of the basketball.

Analysis: Hood's decision to attend Arkansas was inspired. He fits into the Richardson system that features lots of pressure and scoring. After a season spent trying to fill Scotty Thurman's shoes, Hood should come into his own as a sophomore.

COLLEGE STATISTICS

	G	FGP	FTP	RPG	APG	PPG
95-96 ARK	33	.473	.439	6.1	1.1	7.5
Totals	33	.473	.439	6.1	1.1	7.5

AARON HUTCHINS
School: Marquette
Year: Junior
Position: Guard
Height: 5'10" **Weight:** 170
Birthdate: December 22, 1975
Hometown: Lima, OH

PLAYER SUMMARY	
Will	break a press
Can't	help on boards
Expect	long-range missiles
Don't Expect	intimidation

Background: As a prepster at Central Catholic (OH) High School, Hutchins led his team to a 75-5 record. He became the first Division III player to be named Ohio's Mr. Basketball when he took home the award in 1994. Hutchins assumed a starting berth for Marquette in 1995-96.

Strengths: Hutchins's 3-point accuracy earns him minutes. A quick release and smooth motion make him a threat from deep. These skills draw defenders' attention, creating openings for him to drive the lane. He's a good ball-handler who doesn't throw the ball away, and his 6.9 APG ranked among Division I leaders last year.

Weaknesses: Opponents try to take advantage of Hutchins's lack of height whenever possible. They want to try to wear him down in the belief that all the work he must do for the Eagles' offense will add up and take its toll late in a ballgame.

Analysis: Ohio has taken a rap in recent years for not producing the caliber of prep athletes it did in the past. Hutchins, though, is an exception. He is the motor in Marquette's offense that got it to the second round of the NCAA Tournament last year. This clutch performer will continue to thrive.

COLLEGE STATISTICS

	G	FGP	FTP	RPG	APG	PPG
94-95 MARQ	33	.410	.721	1.4	1.8	5.5
95-96 MARQ	31	.375	.849	3.8	6.9	14.0
Totals	64	.384	.802	2.6	4.3	9.6

MARC JACKSON

School: Temple
Year: Junior
Position: Center
Height: 6'10" **Weight:** 270
Birthdate: January 16, 1975
Hometown: Philadelphia, PA

PLAYER SUMMARY	
Will	use his bulk
Can't	fly down the floor
Expect	neat post moves
Don't Expect	gliding grace

Background: As a senior at Roman Catholic High School, Jackson was a part of one of Philadelphia's finest prep classes ever. It also featured Rasheed Wallace, Jason Lawson, Alvin Williams, and Tyrone Weeks. Jackson left the area to play at Virginia Commonwealth but returned to enroll at Temple after his freshman season.

Strengths: When Jackson receives the ball in the key, defenders have few options. He creates a seam for himself with his ample frame and has enough quickness to capitalize on it. His shooting touch near the basket is extraordinary for one so large.

Weaknesses: Temple's perimeter shooting was suspect in 1995-96—no less an authority than coach John Chaney said so—and that presents problems for Jackson. He struggles when he is double- and triple-teamed. He benefits on defense because Chaney's matchup zone relieves him of man-to-man responsibilities.

Analysis: The 1995-96 Temple Owls did not have much more going for them than Chaney's guile and Jackson's tools. That the club reached the second round of NCAA Tournament play and upended Kansas in the regular season speaks volumes about the value of each.

COLLEGE STATISTICS

		G	FGP	FTP	RPG	APG	PPG
95-96	TEMP	32	.477	.668	9.0	0.8	15.7
Totals		32	.477	.668	9.0	0.8	15.7

TIM JAMES

School: Miami (FL)
Year: Sophomore
Position: Forward
Height: 6'7" **Weight:** 190
Birthdate: December 25, 1976
Hometown: Miami, FL

PLAYER SUMMARY	
Will	leap high
Can't	distribute
Expect	an offensive burst
Don't Expect	hesitation

Background: This product of Miami's Northwestern High School was ranked among the top 25 prep players in America as a senior. He closed his career as the school's all-time leader in points (2,358), rebounds (1,170), and blocked shots (714). As a rookie, he was one of the better novices in the Big East Conference.

Strengths: An exceptional athlete, James beats most of his foes down the floor. This explosive leaper is capable of completing a play with an entertaining dunk. He does not hesitate to go to the boards, especially at the offensive end. His leaping ability gives him a great advantage.

Weaknesses: It's unfortunate for James that his vast athletic tools are under-utilized by the Hurricanes, who play a very methodical offense, limiting the number of open-court scoring chances that James could use to produce more points. Defensively, he sometimes suffers lapses that lead to scoring chances for his opponent.

Analysis: This business major was a hot commodity on the recruiting trail—and for good reason. As a freshman, he provided hints of what he may become—a dynamic offensive force with the gift for influencing shots at the other end of the floor.

COLLEGE STATISTICS

		G	FGP	FTP	RPG	APG	PPG
95-96	MIAM	28	.529	.541	5.4	0.4	10.1
Totals		28	.529	.541	5.4	0.4	10.1

ANTAWN JAMISON

School: North Carolina
Year: Sophomore
Position: Forward
Height: 6'8" **Weight:** 216
Birthdate: June 12, 1976
Hometown: Charlotte, NC

PLAYER SUMMARY	
Will	convert rebounds
Can't	shoot well from deep
Expect	defensive energy
Don't Expect	bad shots

Background: Originally an LSU fan, Jamison switched his allegiance to North Carolina when he moved into the state in 1990. He signed early with the Tar Heels and went on to earn a place in the prestigious McDonald's All-America game at the end of his senior year at Providence (NC) High School.

Strengths: Jamison's game is well-rounded. He runs the floor with grace and is a decent ball-handler for a power forward. His offensive skills are far more advanced than anyone expected. Included in his repertoire are short jumpers and quick moves from the low post.

Weaknesses: The only negative in Jamison's debut was that he seemed to fade as the campaign progressed. That was partly a tribute to him, as opponents began to make stopping him a defensive priority. Experience and conditioning should help correct that shortfall.

Analysis: Others drew more glory prior to college, but Jamison clearly established himself as one of the best in his class and a worthy heir to the likes of Rasheed Wallace and Jerry Stackhouse. This fundamentally sound youngster appears destined for a lengthy pro career.

COLLEGE STATISTICS

		G	FGP	FTP	RPG	APG	PPG
95-96	NC	32	.624	.526	9.7	1.0	15.1
Totals		32	.624	.526	9.7	1.0	15.1

KIRK KING

School: Connecticut
Year: Senior
Position: Forward
Height: 6'8" **Weight:** 235
Birthdate: December 24, 1975
Hometown: Baton Rouge, LA

PLAYER SUMMARY	
Will	take smart shots
Can't	arc 3-pointers
Expect	rebounds
Don't Expect	daring moves

Background: Connecticut coach Jim Calhoun has built his program into a national power on the strength of national recruiting. He plucked King, the Class A state Player of the Year, out of Louisiana. King made only one start during his first two seasons at UConn, but he emerged as a consistent offensive option in 1995-96.

Strengths: At one point during the season, King connected on 22 straight field goals, a statistic that proves he does not try to do things he cannot. A nice scoring touch around the goal is complemented by a powerful physique. King has become a more potent factor on the boards.

Weaknesses: A lack of self-confidence early in his career kept King from being the player the Huskies thought he was. He improved on that front but now must face the considerably harder job of being the go-to man. He can't slip back into his shell.

Analysis: King had the luxury of being a pleasant surprise for Calhoun. Now that four starters have departed, he must become a leader. His physical equipment and the progress he made last winter suggest he can fulfill that mission.

COLLEGE STATISTICS

		G	FGP	FTP	RPG	APG	PPG
93-94	CONN	32	.449	.267	2.4	0.3	1.5
94-95	CONN	33	.512	.708	2.7	0.2	3.2
95-96	CONN	35	.575	.689	6.3	1.0	9.9
Totals		100	.544	.643	3.2	0.5	5.0

BREVIN KNIGHT
School: Stanford
Year: Senior
Position: Guard
Height: 5'10" **Weight:** 173
Birthdate: November 8, 1975
Hometown: East Orange, NJ

PLAYER SUMMARY	
Will	slice through traffic
Can't	kill you from deep
Expect	assists
Don't Expect	slow reaction time

Background: This graduate of Seton Hall Prep has been named to the All-Pac-10 team in each of the past two seasons and led the Cardinal to consecutive NCAA Tournament appearances. Knight earned A.P. All-America honorable mention in 1995-96.

Strengths: Knight's game is predicated on his ability to handle the ball, but this might be the fastest man ever to play basketball at Stanford. His quickness makes him a defensive troublemaker, capable of disrupting an offense with steals. He also placed among Division I leaders in assists last year.

Weaknesses: Knight's glaring shortcoming is perimeter shooting. He is not a smooth shooter from long range and is prone to stretches in which he cannot find the bottom of the net.

Analysis: The Cardinal has reached the postseason every year since Knight came onboard. His combination of skills and his court presence—his coach Mike Montgomery refers to him as a "security blanket"—make Knight one of the West's top point guards.

COLLEGE STATISTICS

		G	FGP	FTP	RPG	APG	PPG
93-94	STAN	28	.354	.756	3.9	5.4	11.1
94-95	STAN	28	.455	.750	3.9	6.6	16.6
95-96	STAN	29	.433	.848	3.8	7.3	15.6
Totals		85	.419	.784	3.9	6.4	14.4

ALEXANDER KOUL
School: George Washington
Year: Junior
Position: Center
Height: 7'1" **Weight:** 296
Birthdate: April 25, 1975
Hometown: Borovoka, Belarus

PLAYER SUMMARY	
Will	take smart shots
Can't	pressure up the court
Expect	a defensive presence
Don't Expect	terrific foot speed

Background: GW fans got their first look at Koul in 1993 when the Belarus National Team came to the Smith Center for an exhibition. Koul outplayed Yinka Dare, the pivot he would replace a year later. He was the 1994-95 Atlantic 10 Rookie of the Year and a third-team All-East pick of *Eastern Basketball* in '95-96.

Strengths: In an era in which many collegians are reluctant to be classified as a center, Koul relishes the duties that come with that assignment. His soft shooting touch and passing ability demand a double-team in the low post. Koul's 63.7-percent field-goal shooting ranked fifth among collegiate leaders last season. He clogs the lane and isn't easily drawn off his feet by a fake.

Weaknesses: Koul's free-throw stroke could stand improvement in order to add points to his average. Despite his size, he is not a dominant shot-blocker. Koul fouled out of ten games as a freshman and must avoid the kind of silly reaches that can lead to cheap foul calls.

Analysis: Fans fretted about Dare's departure, but this man is a much better fit for Mike Jarvis. He is popular with his peers and more skilled offensively than Dare was.

COLLEGE STATISTICS

		G	FGP	FTP	RPG	APG	PPG
94-95	GW	32	.632	.584	6.6	0.5	12.8
95-96	GW	29	.642	.665	7.8	0.8	14.9
Totals		61	.637	.625	7.2	0.6	13.8

RAEF LaFRENTZ

School: Kansas
Year: Junior
Position: Forward
Height: 6'1" **Weight:** 220
Birthdate: May 29, 1976
Hometown: Monona, IA

PLAYER SUMMARY	
Will	drop in soft shots
Can't	overpower foes
Expect	steady shooting
Don't Expect	a lazy approach

Background: LaFrentz was billed as perhaps the greatest prep player in Iowa state history. The announcement of his college choice was broadcast live on an area radio station. He was the Big Eight's Freshman of the Year in 1994-95.

Strengths: This southpaw's trademark is his grace around the basket. LaFrentz's scoring touch is his greatest asset. His face-up jumper is extremely effective, and there aren't many collegians who can alter it. A willing worker, LaFrentz is a good rebounder as well.

Weaknesses: Slashing, quick forwards give LaFrentz fits defensively. He simply does not have the foot speed or quickness to match them. That LaFrentz is not a powerful presence at a position dominated by such creatures is somewhat of a concern.

Analysis: It is easy to get lost in a Kansas system that makes liberal use of nine or ten players a game. LaFrentz doesn't often log more than 30 minutes a night, which keeps his scoring numbers off the top shelf. Make no mistake, though: This is a gifted interior scorer and a major concern when opposing game plans are formulated.

COLLEGE STATISTICS

		G	FGP	FTP	RPG	APG	PPG
94-95	KANS	31	.534	.637	7.5	0.5	11.4
95-96	KANS	34	.543	.661	8.2	0.4	13.4
Totals		65	.539	.650	7.8	0.5	12.4

JASON LAWSON

School: Villanova
Year: Senior
Position: Center
Height: 6'11" **Weight:** 235
Birthdate: September 2, 1974
Hometown: Philadelphia, PA

PLAYER SUMMARY	
Will	jostle for position
Can't	step outside
Expect	strong moves to hoop
Don't Expect	placid play

Background: This Olney High School product spent most of his prep career as the "other" big man in Philadelphia: Rasheed Wallace was all the rage. Yet Lawson is a three-year starter for a program that spent most of 1995-96 ranked in the Top 10 nationally, and he is a viable candidate for Big East Player of the Year honors.

Strengths: Unlike many big men today, Lawson relishes post play. He is content to operate in the painted area, and he works hard for position. When he receives the ball, he has a nifty turnaround hook shot and spin move to get to the basket.

Weaknesses: Despite his impressive frame, Lawson is prone to some clumsy play. He is a limited passer and doesn't block as many shots as his height suggests he could. Foul trouble has been a constant problem throughout his career.

Analysis: Each year of his college career, Lawson has demonstrated progress. He has made himself into a quality collegiate center, and now he has the opportunity to make one more leap into the realm of premier player in an elite conference.

COLLEGE STATISTICS

		G	FGP	FTP	RPG	APG	PPG
93-94	VILL	32	.523	.583	6.6	1.2	10.1
94-95	VILL	33	.595	.730	6.7	1.5	12.9
95-96	VILL	32	.621	.693	6.8	1.2	12.3
Totals		97	.680	.670	6.7	1.3	11.7

PETE LISICKY
School: Penn State
Year: Junior
Position: Guard
Height: 6'4" **Weight:** 190
Birthdate: March 3, 1976
Hometown: Whitehall, PA

PLAYER SUMMARY	
Will	swish jumpers
Can't	get his own shot
Expect	accurate FTs
Don't Expect	flashy drives

Background: Two-time Lehigh Valley Player of the Year, Lisicky won the 3-point shooting contest at the Nike camp in July 1993. He left Whitehall High School as the school's all-time leading scorer, and he has established himself as one of the Big Ten's top bombers in his first two seasons at PSU.

Strengths: Lisicky's trademark is the long-range jumper. When he gets a clean look at the basket and has time to square his body, he is a deadly shooter. His range extends to 22 feet. As he has gained experience, he has better learned how to use screens to his advantage. His height can cause problems for smaller guards.

Weaknesses: Lisicky is not an inventive scorer. He is not the kind of whirlwind who can create his own shot. Picks are vital to his game; unfortunately, those become harder to navigate when teams pay special attention to you.

Analysis: This man had much to do with Penn State's second-place Big Ten finish. When Lisicky is in a groove, it appears as though he will never miss. His touch from deep gives the Nittany Lions the balance they require.

COLLEGE STATISTICS

		G	FGP	FTP	RPG	APG	PPG
94-95	PSU	32	.393	.831	2.0	1.6	9.7
95-96	PSU	27	.483	.778	2.8	2.4	13.3
Totals		59	.440	.818	2.4	2.0	11.3

FELIPE LOPEZ
School: St. John's
Year: Junior
Position: Guard/Forward
Height: 6'6" **Weight:** 190
Birthdate: December 19, 1974
Hometown: Bronx, NY

PLAYER SUMMARY	
Will	slash to the hoop
Can't	get used to hype
Expect	steadier work
Don't Expect	long-range accuracy

Background: Lopez is a hero in many ways to the Latin-American community of New York City. During his prep days at Rice High School, games were generally crowded to standing-room-only capacity. One of the main reasons Lopez chose to attend St. John's was its proximity to home.

Strengths: Lopez is a potent weapon when permitted to capitalize on his athletic skills. Superior quickness allows him to beat defenders off the dribble. He also possesses good court vision and can make the spectacular pass to an open mate. Unselfish to a fault, Lopez will pass up an open look if a partner is free closer to the goal.

Weaknesses: His first two seasons have exposed flaws in the game pundits fawned over just two years ago. For starters, Lopez is not a good perimeter shooter. This shortcoming is a boon for defenders who can lay off Lopez outside in order to stop his drives. He is not ready to run the offense.

Analysis: It's been a difficult career so far for the man dubbed the savior of Big East basketball. But he has the kind of gifts his new coach, Fran Fraschilla, can put to good use as he attempts to revive the program.

COLLEGE STATISTICS

		G	FGP	FTP	RPG	APG	PPG
94-95	STJ	28	.411	.753	5.7	2.8	17.8
95-96	STJ	27	.406	.683	6.2	1.9	16.2
Totals		55	.409	.721	6.0	2.3	17.0

MICHAEL MADDOX

School: Georgia Tech
Year: Junior
Position: Forward
Height: 6'8" **Weight:** 224
Birthdate: February 17, 1976
Hometown: Atlanta, GA

PLAYER SUMMARY	
Will	connect on some treys
Can't	forget interior tasks
Expect	improved consistency
Don't Expect	beautiful passes

Background: From his earliest days at Mays High School, Maddox was a prime target of the Tech coaching staff. He was a *USA Today* Top 25 selection his senior year. As a freshman, he made 12 starts and took on greater burdens as Tech won the regular-season Atlantic Coast Conference crown.

Strengths: Maddox doesn't really fit into the mold of a traditional forward. At times he appears more comfortable on the perimeter, shooting 3s over small forwards. On other occasions he seems better suited to bang inside. The skill to do both makes him unique.

Weaknesses: For the most part, Maddox is only an average defender. He can be beaten by quicker small forwards, and he doesn't always use his body to advantage against larger foes. His free-throw shooting needs work.

Analysis: A year ago, Maddox was the fourth option in a three-pronged attack. That will no longer be the case. Coach Bobby Cremins will demand much more this season, and this man has the necessary tools. If his face-up jumper is reliable, Maddox should post some imposing numbers.

COLLEGE STATISTICS

	G	FGP	FTP	RPG	APG	PPG
94-95 GT	30	.454	.574	4.5	1.2	9.1
95-96 GT	36	.498	.653	4.7	1.1	9.2
Totals	66	.477	.619	4.6	1.2	9.2

JELANI McCOY

School: UCLA
Year: Sophomore
Position: Center
Height: 6'10" **Weight:** 225
Birthdate: December 6, 1977
Hometown: San Diego, CA

PLAYER SUMMARY	
Will	deter drivers
Can't	hit from outside
Expect	defensive intimidation
Don't Expect	glittering passes

Background: A fine student, McCoy was named the 1995 All-California Inter-Scholastic Player of the Year for his 3.3 grade point average at St. Augustine High School. One of his life ambitions is to "become the next Ahmad Rashad." He was a first-team Freshman All-America choice of *Basketball Times*.

Strengths: Those who enter the lane do so at their own risk when McCoy is on the floor. A superb leaper, McCoy has the kind of timing that all great shot-blockers must possess. At 6'10", he is not the kind of pivot who will slow down a transition offense.

Weaknesses: McCoy is not nearly as comfortable in the half-court offensive set as he is at the other end of the floor. Although he has good hands and a sweet shooting touch, he needs to expand his moves in the paint. Also, he must do a better job of locating the open man when he is double-teamed inside.

Analysis: It was a strange season in Westwood, one which ended when Princeton unceremoniously shoved the Bruins out of the NCAA title chase. McCoy, though, was a bright spot. One day soon he will be a first-round NBA draft choice.

COLLEGE STATISTICS

	G	FGP	FTP	RPG	APG	PPG
95-96 UCLA	31	.676	.435	6.9	0.9	10.2
Totals	31	.676	.435	6.9	0.9	10.2

BJ McKIE

School: South Carolina
Year: Sophomore
Position: Guard
Height: 6'2" **Weight:** 185
Birthdate: September 9, 1977
Hometown: Irmo, SC

PLAYER SUMMARY	
Will	steal the rock
Can't	hit the long bomb
Expect	smart passes
Don't Expect	excessive turnovers

Background: One of Eddie Fogler's charges upon assuming command at South Carolina was to keep the in-state talent at home. McKie, an Irmo (SC) High School grad, is evidence that Fogler has begun to change the tide that had earlier worked against USC. McKie was named to the freshman All-America third team by *Basketball Times* last year.

Strengths: A strong ball-handler, McKie can play either guard position effectively. He has a solid medium-distance game and understands what he can and cannot do. He is especially adept at swiping the basketball from unsuspecting foes. His quickness afoot allows him to keep most foes in front of him.

Weaknesses: McKie's eagerness to force turnovers at the defensive end sometimes leaves him out of position. He will learn to pick his spots as he matures. Although a competent shooter, McKie is not a bomber. His points need to come in the context of the offense.

Analysis: South Carolina enjoyed a renaissance, advancing to the National Invitation Tournament and taking Alabama to the wire before falling. McKie's overall athleticism and playmaking ability label him a future star of the Southeastern Conference.

COLLEGE STATISTICS

	G	FGP	FTP	RPG	APG	PPG
95-96 SC	31	.467	.762	3.1	2.8	15.4
Totals	31	.467	.762	3.1	2.8	15.4

RON MERCER

School: Kentucky
Year: Sophomore
Position: Guard/Forward
Height: 6'7" **Weight:** 208
Birthdate: May 18, 1976
Hometown: Nashville, TN

PLAYER SUMMARY	
Will	play a larger role
Can't	step into background
Expect	smooth passes
Don't Expect	fiery quotes

Background: After spending his youth in Nashville, Mercer transferred to the famed Oak Hill Academy for his final prep season. He received the Ban/Naismith Award as the nation's top high school player in 1994-95.

Strengths: Few wing men offer as many perimeter skills as this youngster. A great first step makes him a handful for defenders. He possesses a smooth jump shot with tremendous range. Foes must be sure to locate this man or else be burned in the transition game.

Weaknesses: Like former college stars Danny Manning and Grant Hill, Mercer is something of a reluctant star. He defers to his older teammates, and there are times when coach Rick Pitino needs him to be more assertive.

Analysis: After spending much of the season in the shadows, Mercer finally displayed his true talent in the NCAA championship-game win over Syracuse, showing why everyone in the commonwealth was so excited when he signed with Kentucky. This gifted wing man is a throwback—he patiently waited his turn as a rookie and is now ready to assert himself.

COLLEGE STATISTICS

	G	FGP	FTP	RPG	APG	PPG
95-96 KENT	36	.457	.785	2.9	1.4	8.0
Totals	36	.457	.785	2.9	1.4	8.0

RICKY MOORE

School: Connecticut
Year: Sophomore
Position: Guard
Height: 6'1" **Weight:** 185
Birthdate: April 10, 1976
Hometown: Augusta, GA

PLAYER SUMMARY	
Will	fly high
Can't	help in paint
Expect	increased scoring
Don't Expect	leaky defense

Background: As a prepster in Georgia, Moore was rated as one of the top 25 seniors in the nation by *Basketball Times*. In addition, he was runner-up in the balloting for Mr. Basketball honors. He migrated to Connecticut for college and was the first guard off the bench in 1995-96.

Strengths: Moore's calling card is his excellent athletic ability. A strong ball-handler, he beats folks off the dribble and maintains composure when faced with full-court pressure. He displayed his perimeter scoring touch in the Huskies' Big East Tournament championship victory.

Weaknesses: Last year, while Moore enjoyed the luxury of being an apprentice, any production he gave UConn was a bonus. This year, he is expected to run the club in the absence of Ray Allen and Doron Sheffer. Moore will have to step it up and become a leader.

Analysis: It is no coincidence that when Moore was sidelined with an injury, the Huskies were eliminated in the NCAA Tournament. He provides a speedy scoring dimension that will be emphasized this year by coach Jim Calhoun.

COLLEGE STATISTICS

	G	FGP	FTP	RPG	APG	PPG
95-96 CONN	33	.500	.520	2.0	3.0	4.7
Totals	33	.500	.520	2.0	3.0	4.7

GREG NEWTON

School: Duke
Year: Senior
Position: Center
Height: 6'10" **Weight:** 220
Birthdate: September 7, 1974
Hometown: Niagara Falls, Ontario

PLAYER SUMMARY	
Will	take charges
Can't	intimidate inside
Expect	more scoring chances
Don't Expect	quick feet

Background: During the summer of 1992 Newton was rated the top power forward a the prestigious Nike camp. When he signed with Duke, he was likened to former Blue Devil star Christian Laettner, who grew up not far away from Newton's home. However Newton didn't become a starter until his junior year in Durham.

Strengths: Newton's skills with the basketball have always intrigued people. Soft hands and a nice touch around the goa make him a viable threat inside. A dedicated sort, Newton won't shy away from contact at the defensive end. As he has matured he has been less frequently out of position.

Weaknesses: Newton is fairly limited from an athletic standpoint. Leaping high is not an option for him, and quicker pivots are a nightmare for him. It isn't so much that he's slow afoot as it is that he lacks an explosive first step.

Analysis: Long ago, Duke fans came to terms with the fact that Newton is not Laettner. When viewed in that context, it is easier to appreciate him. As a junior he made great strides, and he should continue in that direction.

COLLEGE STATISTICS

	G	FGP	FTP	RPG	APG	PPG
93-94 DUKE	21	.364	.538	1.3	0.4	1.1
94-95 DUKE	25	.661	.472	3.4	0.2	4.0
95-96 DUKE	31	.568	.590	8.2	0.5	12.2
Totals	77	.572	.563	4.8	0.9	6.5

CHARLES O'BANNON

School: UCLA
Year: Senior
Position: Forward
Height: 6'7" **Weight:** 205
Birthdate: February 22, 1975
Hometown: Lakewood, CA

PLAYER SUMMARY	
Will ....make unselfish passes
Can't ....depend on long jumper
Expect.....................self-confidence
Don't Expect..................lack of flair

Background: During his senior season at Artesia High School, O'Bannon was the most coveted player in Southern California. He selected UCLA in part because his brother Ed was already established there. He was a first-team Freshman All-America selection by *Basketball Times* and was named All-Pac-10 in 1995-96.

Strengths: This left-hander is a smooth transition player. Whether he is exploding to the goal or pulling up for a short jumper, O'Bannon is a dangerous offensive weapon. On the backboards he is a spirited worker with good leaping ability. Those springs also make him a good shot-blocker.

Weaknesses: On a squad that cried out for steady leadership, O'Bannon did not offer much of it. He needs to take control of the team and provide guidance in addition to taking care of his own business. His perimeter shot remains suspect, which is a major issue if he hopes to have an NBA career.

Analysis: O'Bannon is one of the West Coast's most skilled wing players. He is capable of the spectacular but doesn't get carried away trying to overdo it. More veteran savvy will make him an All-American.

COLLEGE STATISTICS

		G	FGP	FTP	RPG	APG	PPG
93-94	UCLA	28	.514	.647	6.8	1.6	11.6
94-95	UCLA	33	.554	.739	6.1	3.3	13.6
95-96	UCLA	31	.527	.767	6.0	2.6	14.3
Totals		92	.533	.729	6.3	2.6	13.3

SAM OKEY

School: Wisconsin
Year: Sophomore
Position: Forward
Height: 6'7" **Weight:** 230
Birthdate: November 4, 1976
Hometown: Cassville, WI

PLAYER SUMMARY	
Will ....pound the boards
Can't.................wander defensively
Expect..................a complete game
Don't Expect..................lazy efforts

Background: No Wisconsin prepster in recent memory came to college with as much advance notice as Okey did. The consensus state Player of the Year and Wisconsin Mr. Basketball averaged 31.3 points, 14.2 rebounds, 5.3 assists, and 6.0 blocks per game as a senior at Cassville (WI) High School. He immediately became one of the best young players in the Midwest.

Strengths: Okey is sound in virtually every area. He owns a reliable face-up jumper and is willing to make the pass when the open shot is not available. His rough-and-tumble play inside helps make him a strong rebounder.

Weaknesses: There are still adjustments to be made in some facets of Okey's game. Instead of trying to force things inside, he should rely instead on patience, one of the cornerstones of coach Dick Bennett's game plan. Also, speedy forwards can be a nuisance for Okey defensively.

Analysis: So much hype was attached to this youngster that anything less than stardom seemed like a disappointment. In truth, Okey enjoyed a terrific freshman campaign. There are things he must yet learn, but he should become one of the Big Ten's elite.

COLLEGE STATISTICS

		G	FGP	FTP	RPG	APG	PPG
95-96	WISC	32	.440	.704	6.8	3.1	13.2
Totals		32	.440	704	6.8	3.1	13.2

EDGAR PADILLA

School: Massachusetts
Year: Senior
Position: Guard
Height: 6'2" **Weight:** 175
Birthdate: May 9, 1975
Hometown: Toa Alta, Puerto Rico

PLAYER SUMMARY	
Will	deal with pressure
Can't	help on offensive glass
Expect	smart passes
Don't Expect	flamboyant excess

Background: Padilla spent part of his high school years playing hoops in western Massachusetts. His last prep campaign was spent in his native Puerto Rico. In 1995-96, he quarterbacked the Minutemen to the Final Four of the NCAA Tournament and earned A.P. All-America honorable mention.

Strengths: Padilla is a fine ball-handler. He reads pressure well and does not try to make the spectacular pass when a simple one will do. On defense, he shifts his feet well and stays in front of the opponent. He does not run from the ball in crunch time.

Weaknesses: Perhaps because he is so focused on delivering the ball to its proper place, Padilla is not much of a scoring factor. When he does shoot from outside, he often rushes and appears less comfortable than he did when he came off the bench to drain the odd long bomb as an underclassman.

Analysis: There is no mistaking the monumental role this man played in the 35-2 record of UMass last season. He endured the demands of his coach and kept the Minutemen under control at all times. If Padilla relaxes and trusts his jumper, he will become one of the nation's premier guards.

COLLEGE STATISTICS

	G	FGP	FTP	RPG	APG	PPG
93-94 MASS	35	.413	.814	1.5	2.5	4.5
94-95 MASS	33	.409	.773	1.8	3.0	7.1
95-96 MASS	37	.416	.708	3.5	6.7	8.9
Totals	105	.413	.744	2.3	4.1	6.9

VICTOR PAGE

School: Georgetown
Year: Sophomore
Position: Guard
Height: 6'3" **Weight:** 205
Hometown: Washington, DC

PLAYER SUMMARY	
Will	play aggressive "D"
Can't	disappear
Expect	dribble drives
Don't Expect	passive nature

Background: Page's prep career at McKinley Tech in the District of Columbia was marked by prodigious scoring. He averaged 33.1 points per game as a senior in leading McKinley Tech to its first DCIAA championship. At Georgetown, he was a member of the Big East's All-Rookie team.

Strengths: Georgetown is a haven for dynamic, athletic wing types, and Page is a perfect fit. He loves to drive to the basket, and his quality long-range jumper creates the space needed to get there. On defense, Page is a competitor who gets in his opponent's face to harass him.

Weaknesses: Consistency was a problem for Page during his freshman campaign. There were times when he drifted out of the action. His offensive skills are too good to allow that to happen. His problem this year will be that defenses are going to be paying close attention now that defending Allen Iverson is not an issue.

Analysis: One of the East's brightest young guards, Page was a revelation at Georgetown. Unlike many of his teammates, Page is a serious long-range marksman. He'll have to cope with more double-teams, but this Hoya has a chance to ring up some impressive scoring totals.

COLLEGE STATISTICS

	G	FGP	FTP	RPG	APG	PPG
95-96 GEOR	37	.404	.667	3.2	1.6	12.5
Totals	37	.404	.667	3.2	1.6	12.5

ANTHONY PARKER

School: Bradley
Year: Senior
Position: Guard
Height: 6'5" **Weight:** 190
Birthdate: June 19, 1975
Hometown: Naperville, IL

PLAYER SUMMARY	
Will	stay under control
Can't	direct offense
Expect	deft shooting
Don't Expect	many open looks

Background: The son of a former Iowa Hawkeye, Parker immediately stamped himself a factor with a 20-point outing in his collegiate debut against Maine. He was named Missouri Valley Conference Player of the Year in 1995-96.

Strengths: Although any notoriety he has gained thus far is due to his ample offensive skills, it is interesting to note that Parker was voted to the MVC's All-Defensive team. Bradley prides itself on that aspect of the game, and as its star, Parker sets the tone with his willingness to go chest-to-chest with opposing guards.

Weaknesses: Ball-handling has never been Parker's strong suit. He is at his best alongside a true point guard who can feed him the basketball coming off screens. Though his scoring numbers are lofty, Parker is not a pure long-range shooter.

Analysis: Bradley has won 20 contests in each of Parker's three seasons. He is generally viewed as the school's best player since Hersey Hawkins. Parker's task gets tougher now as the Braves look to replace three key seniors, but Parker has the tools to keep Bradley in the MVC title picture.

COLLEGE STATISTICS

	G	FGP	FTP	RPG	APG	PPG
93-94 BRAD	31	.459	.700	4.4	2.5	11.1
94-95 BRAD	30	.425	.761	6.6	3.3	14.2
95-96 BRAD	30	.472	.797	6.5	3.5	18.9
Totals	91	.453	.758	5.8	3.1	14.7

ANDRAE PATTERSON

School: Indiana
Year: Junior
Position: Forward
Height: 6'8" **Weight:** 230
Birthdate: November 12, 1975
Hometown: Abilene, TX

PLAYER SUMMARY	
Will	get to the boards
Can't	hang on to the ball
Expect	a velvet shooting touch
Don't Expect	intimidating glares

Background: It was viewed as a major coup for Indiana when the Hoosiers attracted this elite Texan in 1994. A first-team *Parade* All-American, Patterson was named Mr. Basketball in the state of Texas as a senior. He has been a fixture in coach Bob Knight's starting lineup for most of his time as a Hoosier.

Strengths: Patterson provides a considerable package of offensive tools. Few big men are as comfortable stepping outside to make jumpers. When shooting well, Patterson can even make 3-pointers. He also does a good job near the goal and has improved as a rebounder.

Weaknesses: Patterson was a very raw defender when he came to Bloomington, and his gains since then have been incremental. He has been unpredictable at the offensive end: Some nights he appears to be headed to stardom, and other times he is hardly noticed. Turnovers have plagued him.

Analysis: When Alan Henderson graduated, Patterson loomed as the likely heir on the front line. Yet the Texan with the tools never seized the moment. He has another chance this year, though Knight won't wait forever.

COLLEGE STATISTICS

	G	FGP	FTP	RPG	APG	PPG
94-95 IND	28	.494	.689	3.9	0.8	7.3
95-96 IND	31	.461	.737	6.2	1.5	11.3
Totals	59	.473	.721	5.1	1.1	9.4

SCOONIE PENN

School: Boston College
Year: Sophomore
Position: Guard
Height: 5'10" **Weight:** 175
Birthdate: January 9, 1977
Hometown: Salem, MA

PLAYER SUMMARY	
Will	excite crowds
Can't	post up foes
Expect	long-range potency
Don't Expect	further anonymity

Background: In the wake of a fine prep career at Salem High School, Penn gave a hint of what was to come in his rookie year at BC with a superb performance in the summer of 1995. He was voted Most Valuable Player at the Boston Shootout and the National AAU Junior Tournament.

Strengths: Penn is not easy for opposing defenders to gauge because he is both an effective slasher and a good long-range shooter. An excellent ball-handler, he brings to the court outstanding vision and a willingness to surrender the basketball to the open man. He also displayed uncommon maturity as a freshman.

Weaknesses: At only 175 pounds, fatigue becomes a concern. Like many freshmen, Penn seemed to wear down in February. Coach Jim O'Brien will try to find him a bit more rest in '96-97. At times, Penn can force unwise shots.

Analysis: When touted recruit Chris Herren transferred in 1995 after playing only one game for the Eagles, observers wondered how O'Brien could hope to fill the void at point guard. Penn stepped in as a rookie and made everyone forget Herren. His tools make him one of the East's best young guards.

COLLEGE STATISTICS

		G	FGP	FTP	RPG	APG	PPG
95-96	BC	30	.438	.755	3.4	3.5	13.2
Totals		30	.438	.755	3.4	3.5	13.2

RICKY PERAL

School: Wake Forest
Year: Senior
Position: Forward
Height: 6'10" **Weight:** 230
Birthdate: February 13, 1974
Hometown: Valladolid, Spain

PLAYER SUMMARY	
Will	stroke long jumpers
Can't	bang with big boys
Expect	crisp fundamentals
Don't Expect	much hoopla

Background: A native of Spain, Peral grew up in Valladolid but went to high school in Madrid, a two-hour drive away. This dean's list student was forced to sit out his freshman year after an NCAA eligibility ruling. He's been a regular ever since.

Strengths: In many ways, Peral is the prototypical European big man. At 6'10", he is at home facing the basket. When he steps out beyond the line, the defense must go with him because he is deadly when left alone (48.3 percent from the arc last season). His height also helps make Peral a good passer from the high post, and good mobility makes him a competent defender.

Weaknesses: Contact is a problem for Peral. Opponents are convinced that the best way to disrupt Peral is to bump him. Peral encounters problems when he is forced to match up with big men.

Analysis: Two very solid seasons have established Peral as a quality collegian. His offensive productivity should grow in 1996-97 as Dave Odom looks for perimeter scoring options. If this smooth senior adds a bit of grit to his game, he is likely to move into the elite company of the ACC.

COLLEGE STATISTICS

		G	FGP	FTP	RPG	APG	PPG
94-95	WF	32	.518	.605	3.6	0.9	6.7
95-96	WF	32	.510	.755	4.3	1.4	9.4
Totals		64	.513	.688	4.0	1.1	8.0

PAUL PIERCE

School: Kansas
Year: Sophomore
Position: Forward
Height: 6'6" **Weight:** 220
Birthdate: October 13, 1977
Hometown: Los Angeles, CA

PLAYER SUMMARY	
Will	score in traffic
Can't	add a mean streak
Expect	fantastic finishes
Don't Expect	an attention hog

Background: Pierce was California's 1995 Gatorade Player of the Year as a senior at Inglewood High School, then became an immediate factor at Kansas. He was named a first-team Freshman All-American by *Basketball Times*.

Strengths: Tremendous athletic skills give Pierce an enormous advantage over most of his foes. His first step is among the best in the Midwest, and he is a superior finisher when he gets near the goal. The drive is not his only weapon, however, as he also possesses a reliable jump shot. Rebounding is yet another dimension he brings to the floor.

Weaknesses: Despite his talent, Pierce is something of a reluctant superstar. He tends to allow his elder mates to initiate the action even when he is probably better equipped to do so. He also needs to add muscle to his frame so that he doesn't fade late in the season as teams begin to focus on him.

Analysis: The advance notices on this youngster as he came out of high school indicated that he was headed to great heights, and nothing he displayed as a freshman detracted from that vision. Pierce has the tools, coaching, and style to emerge as one of the college game's great standouts in 1996-97.

COLLEGE STATISTICS

	G	FGP	FTP	RPG	APG	PPG
95-96 KANS	34	.419	.606	5.3	1.8	11.9
Totals	34	.419	.606	5.3	1.8	11.9

SCOT POLLARD

School: Kansas
Year: Senior
Position: Center
Height: 6'10" **Weight:** 250
Birthdate: February 12, 1975
Hometown: San Diego, CA

PLAYER SUMMARY	
Will	shoot with either hand
Can't	intimidate inside
Expect	silent production
Don't Expect	poor shots

Background: Although he hails from San Diego and played at Torrey Pines High School, Pollard spent his last prep season at Kamiakan High School in Washington. During his first two seasons at KU, Pollard was Greg Ostertag's understudy. He emerged as a full-time starter in 1995-96.

Strengths: Mobility helps set Pollard apart. There are few centers capable of beating him down the floor. This allows Pollard to establish position and contribute on the fastbreak. His ability to make a quality hook shot with either hand is a plus.

Weaknesses: Pollard is not a classic shot-blocker and, as such, isn't much of a defensive presence in the paint. This allows foes to come at him more than they otherwise might. He needs to do a better job of finding the open man when he receives the ball inside.

Analysis: Although virtually unknown outside the Big Eight, Pollard has enjoyed a very productive college career. He is a perfect fit for a system that emphasizes defense, teamwork, and an up-tempo attack. Pollard will find a spot in the NBA next year.

COLLEGE STATISTICS

	G	FGP	FTP	RPG	APG	PPG
93-94 KANS	35	.543	.685	4.9	0.4	7.5
94-95 KANS	31	.557	.654	6.2	0.5	10.2
95-96 KANS	34	.564	.636	7.4	0.3	10.1
Totals	100	.555	.656	6.2	0.4	9.2

NEIL REED

School: Indiana
Year: Junior
Position: Guard
Height: 6'2" **Weight:** 185
Birthdate: November 29, 1975
Hometown: Metairie, LA

PLAYER SUMMARY	
Will	find the open man
Can't	create his shot
Expect	more shots
Don't Expect	dramatic gestures

Background: The son of a coach, Reed signed with Indiana after a decorated prep career at East Jefferson (LA) High School. This marked a return to Bloomington, where Reed spent much of his youth before his family moved south when he was a sophomore. He has been an integral part of the guard corps at IU since his arrival.

Strengths: Intangible qualities help set Reed apart. His court vision is exceptional, and he takes extremely good care of the basketball. He reads and reacts to pressure very well. As a freshman, a shoulder injury inhibited his shooting. Off-season surgery restored his reliable jumper.

Weaknesses: There are some definite limitations on Reed's game. Quicker guards present problems for him at the defensive end, and he lacks the explosive speed to go past defenders with the basketball in his hands. He has a difficult time creating shots for himself.

Analysis: Indiana is in desperate need of scoring, and Reed will be asked to provide much of the punch. He'll have to rely on picks and gain confidence shooting with hands in his face, but he certainly has the tools needed to make that adjustment.

COLLEGE STATISTICS

		G	FGP	FTP	RPG	APG	PPG
94-95	IND	30	.383	.667	1.7	2.5	5.9
95-96	IND	31	.455	.802	2.4	4.4	10.5
Totals		61	.426	.745	2.0	3.5	8.2

KAREEM REID

School: Arkansas
Year: Sophomore
Position: Guard
Height: 5'11" **Weight:** 162
Birthdate: August 27, 1975
Hometown: New York, NY

PLAYER SUMMARY	
Will	attack on offense
Can't	impede foes' vision
Expect	penetration
Don't Expect	patience

Background: A coveted prepster, Reid first became familiar with Arkansas during his days at Bronx St. Raymonds High School when his school played in the King Cotton Classic in Pine Bluff. After graduating high school, Reid sat out a season as a part-time student at Arkansas. Last year, he was named *Basketball Times'* Newcomer of the Year in college basketball.

Strengths: The self-confident Reid had no problems assuming the reins for the Razorbacks as a rookie. It was his will that helped steer this collection of newcomers—only two holdovers from the '94 NCAA championship team remained—to a spot in last year's NCAA Sweet 16. His great speed with the basketball is his edge.

Weaknesses: As a prep standout, Reid often frustrated his teammates in All-Star games with his domination of the basketball. He needs the ball in his hands constantly, which sometimes means his teammates are not being utilized enough.

Analysis: Reid did what some of his critics said he could not—play under control—as a frosh, and the results were outstanding. His style is perfectly suited to that of coach Nolan Richardson, so theirs should remain a happy marriage.

COLLEGE STATISTICS

		G	FGP	FTP	RPG	APG	PPG
95-96	ARK	33	.395	.686	3.1	6.6	12.9
Totals		33	.395	.686	3.1	6.6	12.9

TERRANCE ROBERSON

School: Fresno State
Year: Sophomore
Position: Forward
Height: 6'8" **Weight:** 220
Birthdate: December 30, 1976
Hometown: Saginaw, MI

PLAYER SUMMARY	
Will	nail short jumpers
Can't	wait to begin
Expect	dynamic dunks
Don't Expect	outstanding defense

Background: At one point, Roberson was the most coveted player in the talent-rich state of Michigan. But he struggled with off-court problems at Buena Vista High School, which caused several schools, most notably Michigan and Michigan State, to back off recruiting him. He landed at Fresno State and sat out 1994-95 for academic reasons.

Strengths: Roberson's assortment of tools has always been enticing. He's got a soft shooting touch around the goal as well as the muscle needed to create space for himself inside. Offensive rebounding is a strength, and he's excellent in the open court.

Weaknesses: Roberson wasn't much of a defender in high school. Too often he relied on his leaping ability to make up for mistakes in positional defense. To play for coach Jerry Tarkanian, he needs to upgrade his effort and footwork.

Analysis: It is unlikely that Roberson ever would have landed at Fresno State had Tarkanian not been hired by his alma mater. But the veteran coach always has been a risk-taker, and he was pleased by Roberson's work ethic while he sat out last season. If Roberson has matured, he will provide an instant lift for Fresno.

MICHAEL ROBINSON

School: Purdue
Year: Freshman
Position: Forward/Guard
Height: 6'6" **Weight:** 200
Birthdate: December 31, 1976
Hometown: Peoria, IL

PLAYER SUMMARY	
Will	do his homework
Can't	be outworked
Expect	a sweet stroke
Don't Expect	him to accept losing

Background: When coveted prepster Robinson announced he was spurning home-state Illinois and nearby Bradley for Purdue, instant comparisons to former Boilermaker star Glenn "Big Dog" Robinson were drawn. Michael—who averaged 33 PPG as a senior at Peoria Richwoods High School and was a McDonald's All-American—was immediately dubbed "Little Dog."

Strengths: This Mr. Robinson is a student of the game. He studies hours of videotapes and toils diligently to apply the lessons learned to his game. That work ethic has helped him become a scoring demon. He uses a variety of pump fakes and dribbling skills to free himself up for scoring chances. Also, he moves well without the basketball.

Weaknesses: No less an authority than Robinson himself concedes he is not blessed with overpowering athletic gifts. He relies instead on subtlety, and there may be nights in the Big Ten where that is not enough, particularly early in his career. The comparisons to Glenn Robinson may grow onerous.

Analysis: Purdue must replenish its talent coffers, and this youngster is an important addition. He fills Gene Keady's need for a dynamic scoring force: a spot left empty since Glenn Robinson departed. If the faithful don't overwhelm him with expectations, he'll be a good one.

SHAWNTA ROGERS
School: George Washington
Year: Sophomore
Position: Guard
Height: 5'3" **Weight:** 155
Birthdate: January 5, 1976
Hometown: Baltimore, MD

PLAYER SUMMARY	
Will	swipe the ball
Can't	deter big guards
Expect	sweet passes
Don't Expect	dunk action

Background: As a senior at Baltimore Lake Clifton High School, Rogers received interest from mostly mid-major programs. Most of the larger schools were scared away by his height. He stated his intention to attend George Washington in the spring of 1995 but did not gain his eligibility to participate until the end of the first semester.

Strengths: The most oft-heard comparison of Rogers is to another Baltimore native: Muggsy Bogues. There are similarities between the two. Rogers is a terrific ball-handler and is nearly impossible to press. His speed allows him to penetrate easily, and he's got a keen eye for open teammates. He also rebounds well.

Weaknesses: There really is no way to hide Rogers's defensive shortcomings. Although he's a threat to steal the basketball, his inability to obstruct others' vision is a dilemma. Most guards can take him inside often. Fortunately for coach Mike Jarvis, that's less of a liability in college than it is in the pro game.

Analysis: The fact that he wasn't on GW's preseason roster last year kept him out of the spotlight early. But Rogers's impact on the Colonials was enormous. He figures to be one of the most entertaining players in all of college basketball this winter.

COLLEGE STATISTICS
	G	FGP	FTP	RPG	APG	PPG
95-96 GW	23	.379	.794	4.7	6.5	10.5
Totals	23	.379	.794	4.7	6.5	10.5

TONY RUTLAND
School: Wake Forest
Year: Junior
Position: Guard
Height: 6'2" **Weight:** 183
Birthdate: February 27, 1975
Hometown: Hampton, VA

PLAYER SUMMARY	
Will	not back down
Can't	be haunted by injury
Expect	steady ball-handling
Don't Expect	natural playmaking

Background: At Bethel High School in Virginia, Rutland combined with Allen Iverson to form an explosive backcourt. He was a reliable understudy to All-ACC guard Randolph Childress as a freshman at Wake Forest, then moved into the starting lineup in 1995-96.

Strengths: Rutland's value to the Demon Deacons was underscored when a knee injury sidelined him for the NCAA Tournament last year. A strong defender, he keeps his opponent in front of him. He is a double threat on offense, as he can penetrate or draw the defense to him with an accurate perimeter shot. Plus, he's a first-rate free-throw shooter.

Weaknesses: The knee injury Rutland suffered during the ACC Tournament is cause for concern. It clearly impacted his mobility, and there is no larger issue for a point guard. Hopefully, a summer of rehabilitation will bring him back up to speed.

Analysis: That Wake Forest reached the Final Eight without Childress speaks volumes about Rutland's contributions. He isn't flashy, but he makes all of the basic plays and his long-range accuracy keeps defenders from clogging the lane.

COLLEGE STATISTICS
		G	FGP	FTP	RPG	APG	PPG
94-95	WF	32	.325	.814	1.9	1.6	5.8
95-96	WF	31	.369	.756	2.7	3.9	11.9
Totals		63	.352	.779	2.3	2.7	8.8

MARK SANFORD
School: Washington
Year: Junior
Position: Forward
Height: 6'8" **Weight:** 200
Birthdate: February 7, 1976
Hometown: Dallas, TX

PLAYER SUMMARY	
Will	slash to goal
Can't	set up teammates
Expect	spectacular dunks
Don't Expect	much attention

Background: This native of Dallas transferred to San Diego's Lincoln Prep for his final year of prep eligibility. He chose Washington over California, Baylor, Tulsa, and Wichita State. In 1994-95, Sanford led all Pac-10 freshmen in scoring.

Strengths: This lithe forward is a first-rate athlete. He fills the lane exceptionally well on the fastbreak, and his ability to complete a play with a slam is his trademark. A quick first step takes him past most power forwards and gets him into traffic, where his leaping ability can take over.

Weaknesses: Although he is a scorer, Sanford cannot be categorized as a great shooter. His long-range accuracy is shaky, and he must learn to find the open man when cornered. Sometimes he gets so caught up in the chance for a breathtaking play that he loses control of the basketball.

Analysis: Obscured by more prominent names on the West Coast, Sanford is nonetheless a gifted performer. He gives the Huskies a flair they have lacked in this decade. Look for him to lead Washington back to the NCAA Tournament for the first time since the days of Christian Welp and Detlef Schrempf.

COLLEGE STATISTICS
	G	FGP	FTP	RPG	APG	PPG
94-95 WASH	26	.428	.603	5.7	1.0	14.5
95-96 WASH	28	.460	.652	6.1	1.1	16.5
Totals	54	.445	.632	5.9	1.1	15.6

SHEA SEALS
School: Tulsa
Year: Senior
Position: Guard/Forward
Height: 6'5" **Weight:** 200
Birthdate: August 26, 1975
Hometown: Tulsa, OK

PLAYER SUMMARY	
Will	drain free throws
Can't	take too many shots
Expect	multiple skills
Don't Expect	a high FG pct.

Background: Oklahoma's High School Player of the Year in 1993, Seals surprised some when he chose to stay in Tulsa. He was named a Freshman All-American by *Basketball Times* and *Basketball Weekly*. The Golden Hurricane has made it to the NCAA Tourney in each of his three seasons.

Strengths: Seals is Mr. Versatility for coach Steve Robinson. The McLain high school product will often back a smaller guard into the low post and go over him for a score. On other occasions, he will rely on quickness to slash to the goal. Few perimeter players rebound as well as Seals. He is not afraid to mix it up with taller players.

Weaknesses: This is not the most efficient offensive player in America. There are too many times when he forces off-balance shots. At the defensive end, Seals tends to roam for steals, allowing his man easy scoring opportunities.

Analysis: This sports management major is on course to finish his career as one of the best to ever play at Tulsa. He has been the constant as the Golden Hurricane has twice made advances to the Sweet 16 of the NCAA Tournament.

COLLEGE STATISTICS
	G	FGP	FTP	RPG	APG	PPG
93-94 TULS	28	.426	.748	6.5	3.5	16.8
94-95 TULS	32	.389	.793	6.9	4.0	18.8
95-96 TULS	30	.379	.652	5.7	2.2	17.1
Totals	90	.396	.728	6.4	3.2	17.6

JESS SETTLES
School: Iowa
Year: Senior
Position: Forward
Height: 6'7" **Weight:** 220
Birthdate: July 7, 1974
Hometown: Winfield, IA

PLAYER SUMMARY	
Will	find the open man
Can't	match foes' speed
Expect	smart play
Don't Expect	forced jumpers

Background: Settles took home the 1993 Iowa Mr. Basketball award. In 1993-94, he was tabbed Big Ten Freshman of the Year. A good student, Settles has made the Big Ten academic honor roll and was one of 42 players invited by USA Basketball to the national team trials in 1995.

Strengths: Settles is a multidimensional force. He can be especially dangerous at the top of the key, where he can locate a cutter for an easy score or perhaps drop in a face-up jumper. Most forwards find him difficult to check because of his ability to work inside or on the perimeter.

Weaknesses: Back woes have cut into Settles's effectiveness. They cost him seven games as a sophomore and appear to have impacted his mobility and stamina. Now some of his physical limitations—a lack of foot speed and leaping ability chief among them—are more easily exploited.

Analysis: One of Settles's trademarks prior to the back problems was a work ethic that saw him spend countless hours toiling on his game. The injuries make that a risk now, and Settles isn't making the progress he did earlier. There is still time, however.

COLLEGE STATISTICS
	G	FGP	FTP	RPG	APG	PPG
93-94 IOWA	27	.574	.789	7.5	2.3	15.3
94-95 IOWA	26	.469	.802	6.2	2.0	15.6
95-96 IOWA	32	.477	.741	7.5	3.1	15.1
Totals	85	.503	.777	7.1	2.5	15.3

MILES SIMON
School: Arizona
Year: Junior
Position: Guard
Height: 6'5" **Weight:** 199
Birthdate: November 21, 1975
Hometown: Fullerton, CA

PLAYER SUMMARY	
Will	make simple plays
Can't	be a presence inside
Expect	more points
Don't Expect	meek defense

Background: Simon played at Mater Dei High School, which has one of the most successful prep programs in California. He earned three letters in hoops and four in tennis. His dramatic shot from beyond halfcourt defeated Cincinnati in perhaps the most memorable single play of 1995-96.

Strengths: Mater Dei has a history of producing sound athletes, a description that fits Simon perfectly. He is usually in good defensive position and is quick enough to handle smaller guards. On offense, he is unafraid of taking the ball to the goal. He does it often and supplements that with a competent perimeter jump shot.

Weaknesses: Although strong in most facets of his game, Simon lacks the one quality that would set him apart from his peers. He has not shown the desire to take over a game and does not possess the explosive scoring moves to dominate.

Analysis: It is ironic that the play for which Simon is best remembered provided incredible drama, because he is generally the type of player who does his thing with subtlety. On most nights, appreciation of his skills comes after studying the stat sheet and seeing all of his little contributions.

COLLEGE STATISTICS
	G	FGP	FTP	RPG	APG	PPG
94-95 ARIZ	23	.482	.768	2.6	3.7	8.9
95-96 ARIZ	32	.446	.764	4.1	2.6	13.6
Totals	55	.457	.765	3.9	3.5	11.6

CURTIS STAPLES

School: Virginia
Year: Junior
Position: Guard
Height: 6'3" **Weight:** 181
Birthdate: July 14, 1976
Hometown: Roanoke, VA

PLAYER SUMMARY	
Will	square up for 3s
Can't	drive for scores
Expect	improved accuracy
Don't Expect	a lack of confidence

Background: Selected to both the McDonald's and *Parade* All-America teams as a senior at Oak Hill (VA) Academy, Staples was a coveted off guard prospect. He signed with Virginia and moved into the starting lineup midway through his freshman season. *The Sporting News* listed him among the nation's top 15 shooting guards entering 1995-96.

Strengths: There is no more dangerous long-distance dialer than this Virginian when he's in a groove. Staples brings a quick release and good mechanics to his shot. He reads screens well and knows how to catch and elevate in a hurry.

Weaknesses: Staples seemed to lose his touch as a sophomore. Bombs that drew nothing but net his rookie year clanged off the rim in '95-96. Part of the reason was that opposing teams paid more attention to him than they had as a freshman and step up. He needs to compensate for that and step up.

Analysis: Two years ago, longtime ACC observers marveled at the sweetness of this man's shot. Last year, though, it all unraveled. The best guess is that an off-season of hard work and newfound belief in himself will bring Staples back to top form.

COLLEGE STATISTICS

	G	FGP	FTP	RPG	APG	PPG
94-95 VIRG	34	.416	.755	3.0	0.8	11.9
95-96 VIRG	27	.374	.800	3.6	2.1	14.0
Totals	61	.394	.779	3.3	1.3	12.0

MAURICE TAYLOR

School: Michigan
Year: Junior
Position: Forward
Height: 6'9" **Weight:** 250
Birthdate: October 30, 1976
Hometown: Detroit, MI

PLAYER SUMMARY	
Will	help on the boards
Can't	take it to centers
Expect	self-congratulation
Don't Expect	solid fundamentals

Background: Although college coaches were aware of him, Taylor was something of a sleeper to the outside world at Henry Ford High School. He was overshadowed by city rivals and present teammates Willie Mitchell and Robert Traylor. To date, he has been a superior college player to both.

Strengths: Taylor has an abundant supply of natural gifts. His soft hands make him an inviting target inside, and he punishes smaller defenders in the post. He runs the floor exceptionally well and knows how to finish with a dunk. On defense he can come from the weak side to block shots.

Weaknesses: Taylor's immaturity is evidenced by the automobile accident last February in which five Wolverines and one recruit survived a scary wreck at 5:00 A.M. on the weekend of a big game. He speaks about making the improvements and sacrifices needed but in reality seems willing to rely solely on his athletic gifts.

Analysis: This is a crossroads year for Taylor. If he is content to merely coast, he will be a fairly successful college player. Should he elect to take a single-minded approach to making strides, he could step out as an All-American.

COLLEGE STATISTICS

	G	FGP	FTP	RPG	APG	PPG
94-95 MICH	30	.473	.602	5.0	1.0	12.5
95-96 MICH	32	.511	.592	7.0	1.3	14.0
Totals	62	.493	.596	6.0	1.2	13.3

KENNY THOMAS

School: New Mexico
Year: Sophomore
Position: Forward/Center
Height: 6'9" **Weight:** 250
Birthdate: July 25, 1977
Hometown: Albuquerque, NM

PLAYER SUMMARY	
Will	get to glass
Can't	avoid fouls
Expect	strong post moves
Don't Expect	poor shots

Background: After spending his formative years in El Paso, Texas, Thomas moved to Albuquerque, where he attended that city's high school for the last two years of his prep career. He was named the 1996 Western Athletic Conference Tournament MVP.

Strengths: Great size and skills give Thomas an edge in the WAC. At 250 pounds, he is a force near the basket, and his size makes him a shot-blocking presence on the defensive end as well. He expends maximum effort as a rebounder and is especially dangerous on the offensive glass. He's also a better passer than many other big men.

Weaknesses: The biggest problem coach Dave Bliss had was getting Thomas on the floor. NCAA bureaucrats sent him to the sidelines in the fall because he fell one half-credit short of high school requirements. An injunction overturned that ruling. When Thomas finally made it onto the floor, he had trouble staying there: He set a school record with 118 fouls—just under four a game.

Analysis: One of the nation's fine young big men, Thomas needs only to channel his aggressiveness to become a major star at the collegiate level. NBA scouts will be watching.

COLLEGE STATISTICS

		G	FGP	FTP	RPG	APG	PPG
95-96	NM	33	.578	.709	7.8	1.6	14.7
Totals		33	.578	.709	7.8	1.6	14.7

TIM THOMAS

School: Villanova
Year: Freshman
Position: Forward
Height: 6'10" **Weight:** 230
Birthdate: February 26, 1977
Hometown: Paterson, NJ

PLAYER SUMMARY	
Will	swish short jumpers
Can't	stand the pivot
Expect	explosive first step
Don't Expect	consistent intensity

Background: Thomas enters the Big East as perhaps the most touted member of the class of 1996. At Paterson Catholic High School, he was both a McDonald's and *Parade* All-American. Thomas was voted Most Valuable Player for the East team in Magic Johnson's postseason Roundball Classic All-Star Game.

Strengths: A combination of power and finesse made this youngster a much-desired recruiting commodity. At 6'10", he can drift outside to take aim at the goal with a solid 15-foot jumper, and he can punish a defense with putbacks off the offensive glass. Good springs make him a shot-blocking presence as well.

Weaknesses: Intensity was a problem for Thomas at the high school level. He had a tendency to relax, something he will not be able to do in the collegiate ranks. Thomas also wants no part of playing center; it's one of the reasons he chose the college he did. Villanova already has Jason Lawson.

Analysis: Perhaps the biggest name recruit to sign at Villanova in the 1990s, Thomas possesses all the tools for greatness. If he picks up his effort, there are no barriers to how high he can rise.

CARMELO TRAVIESO

School: Massachusetts
Year: Senior
Position: Guard
Height: 6'3" **Weight:** 180
Birthdate: May 9, 1975
Hometown: Boston, MA

PLAYER SUMMARY	
Will	make 3s
Can't	post up inside
Expect	hawking defense
Don't Expect	offensive rebounds

Background: Originally from Puerto Rico, Travieso moved to Boston at age 11. He attended Thayer Academy, leading his team to a 25-3 record as a senior. In his first two seasons at UMass he made only two starts, but he became a force in his junior year, helping UMass to the Final Four.

Strengths: Some of Travieso's best work comes away from the basketball. He does a superb job of shadowing the opponent's top-scoring perimeter player. Against Georgetown in the NCAA Tournament, he stifled Allen Iverson. He moves his feet well and is willing to get down and dirty. On offense he is a gifted long-range shooter.

Weaknesses: With pal Edgar Padilla running the offense, there isn't much need for Travieso to handle the ball. But if he is to have a chance in the NBA, Travieso will have to enhance that area of his game.

Analysis: Entering 1995-96, guards were considered to be the weak link of the UMass program. From the first game of the season, however, both Travieso and Padilla laid that notion to rest. Both are tough defenders, and Travieso's shot makes him one of the better backcourt players in the nation.

COLLEGE STATISTICS

		G	FGP	FTP	RPG	APG	PPG
93-94	MASS	28	.324	.833	0.5	0.3	2.3
94-95	MASS	32	.357	.478	2.3	1.0	5.3
95-96	MASS	37	.426	.636	3.2	2.1	12.6
Totals		97	.395	.613	2.1	1.2	7.2

WAYNE TURNER

School: Kentucky
Year: Sophomore
Position: Guard
Height: 6'2" **Weight:** 183
Birthdate: March 22, 1976
Hometown: Chestnut Hills, MA

PLAYER SUMMARY	
Will	rely on speed
Can't	drill from deep
Expect	entertaining playmaking
Don't Expect	awesome stats

Background: During his prep career, Turner was one of the most honored players in Massachusetts. His 2,563 career points landed him a spot on both the *Parade* and McDonald's All-America lists. He also sparked the Boston Amateur Basketball Club to the national AAU championship.

Strengths: With the basketball in his hands, Turner is a whirling dervish. Great speed is his best weapon, and he understands how to use it to his advantage. Defenders cannot get too near lest they be left in his dust. He is deadliest when leading the break because he is able to create a layup for himself or dish off to an open teammate.

Weaknesses: From the beginning, Turner seemed an odd fit for coach Rick Pitino's system because he is not adept at making goals from beyond the 3-point arc. That is a staple of Pitino's offense. For all of his quickness, Turner found it much more difficult to finish near the basket in college than he had at the prep level.

Analysis: Turner did not see any action in the NCAA Final, but that won't be the case in games next year. This enormous talent needs only to refine his skills and defense to suit Pitino before making his mark in Lexington. His opportunity has arrived.

COLLEGE STATISTICS

		G	FGP	FTP	RPG	APG	PPG
95-96	KENT	35	.533	.625	1.5	1.6	4.5
Totals		35	.533	.625	1.5	1.6	4.5

KEITH VAN HORN

School: Utah
Year: Senior
Position: Forward
Height: 6'9" **Weight:** 235
Birthdate: October 25, 1975
Hometown: Diamond Bar, CA

PLAYER SUMMARY	
Will	make free throws
Can't	attract attention
Expect	All-America votes
Don't Expect	lots of assists

Background: This Californian was an important cog in the Utah wheel from his first day of college practice. An instant starter, he was the WAC's Freshman of the Year in 1994 and Player of the Year in each of the past two seasons.

Strengths: There aren't many holes in Van Horn's game. He possesses a smooth jump shot with range extending to the 3-point arc. Unlike many stars, he rarely forces a shot. He is not afraid to mix it up underneath the basket.

Weaknesses: If there was a disappointment for Van Horn in 1995-96, it was his inability to play up to par in the postseason. He was felled by a nasty flu bug that robbed him of energy during the first and second round of tournament play. That is one of the reasons he chose to forego the NBA draft for another year.

Analysis: This is a legitimate candidate for 1996-97 national Player of the Year honors. He is as versatile and skilled a power forward as there is in the country, though he doesn't garner the publicity others do. Van Horn will be an understated but efficient achiever in the NBA.

COLLEGE STATISTICS

	G	FGP	FTP	RPG	APG	PPG
93-94 UTAH	25	.516	.775	8.3	0.8	18.3
94-95 UTAH	33	.545	.856	8.5	1.4	21.0
95-96 UTAH	32	.538	.851	8.8	1.0	21.7
Totals	90	.535	.833	8.6	1.1	20.4

JACQUE VAUGHN

School: Kansas
Year: Senior
Position: Guard
Height: 6'1" **Weight:** 195
Birthdate: February 11, 1975
Hometown: Pasadena, CA

PLAYER SUMMARY	
Will	see the court
Can't	shoot from deep
Expect	All-America honors
Don't Expect	turnovers

Background: Vaughn has been a star both on the floor and in the classroom. He was a McDonald's All-American at John Muir High School while finishing second in his class with a grade point average of 3.97. He set a freshman assist record at Kansas and is a two-time All-Big Eight first-team pick. He was selected to the 1995-96 A.P. All-America second team.

Strengths: Vaughn has few peers as a quarterback. Superior court vision allows him to locate the open man and pass the ball before the defense can react. His quickness makes him a constant threat to penetrate. He is also a sound defender.

Weaknesses: Perimeter shooting has long been Vaughn's Achilles' heel. It plagued him in high school and has improved only incrementally since. His release is slow, and defenders let him have the shot so that he won't penetrate.

Analysis: When experts rate the top guards in the nation, Vaughn's name is at the top of most lists. He pondered a move to the NBA at the close of his junior year but wisely elected to return for his senior season. As the leader of one of America's top units, he will be a player to watch this winter.

COLLEGE STATISTICS

	G	FGP	FTP	RPG	APG	PPG
93-94 KANS	35	.467	.670	2.5	5.2	7.8
94-95 KANS	31	.452	.687	3.7	7.7	9.7
95-96 KANS	34	.482	.695	3.1	6.6	10.9
Totals	100	.468	.685	3.1	6.4	9.4

DAMION WALKER

School: Texas Christian
Year: Sophomore
Position: Forward
Height: 6'8" **Weight:** 210
Birthdate: December 9, 1976
Hometown: Dallas, TX

PLAYER SUMMARY	
Will	rise for rebounds
Can't	make 3s
Expect	quality shots
Don't Expect	crisp passes

Background: Walker was a first-team all-state pick at Lincoln High School in Texas. He averaged 25 points and 13.5 rebounds per game. At TCU, his impact has been enormous. *Basketball Weekly* tabbed him a first-team Freshman All-American after he led all members of his class in scoring. The Southwest Conference named him Newcomer of the Year.

Strengths: Walker is difficult to stop when he gets the ball inside. A combination of athletic grace and power enables him to free himself, and he possesses a quality touch around the goal. He must be accounted for at all times on the backboards. He boxes out well and is a fine leaper.

Weaknesses: As the year went on and defenses began to target him, Walker struggled with his passing. He must learn to recognize where the double-team is coming from and who the open man is. Once that happens, the Horned Frog offense will flow more freely.

Analysis: TCU coach Billy Tubbs doesn't much care for defeat, so 1995-96's 12-16 campaign was hard for Tubbs to stomach. This youngster provided his only relief. Walker has established himself as one of the Southwest's premier performers.

COLLEGE STATISTICS

	G	FGP	FTP	RPG	APG	PPG
95-66 TCU	30	.503	.768	8.8	0.8	20.5
Totals	30	.503	.768	8.8	0.8	20.5

ERIC WASHINGTON

School: Alabama
Year: Senior
Position: Forward
Height: 6'4" **Weight:** 185
Birthdate: March 23, 1974
Hometown: Jackson, MS

PLAYER SUMMARY	
Will	light it up
Can't	handle tall forwards
Expect	abundant confidence
Don't Expect	wide notice

Background: This two-time all-state performer in his native Mississippi averaged 23.7 points and 13 rebounds per outing as a senior. After seeing spot duty as a freshman in Tuscaloosa, he improved his scoring dramatically as a sophomore and junior.

Strengths: Washington was in his element when he was encouraged to shoot more as a sophomore. Strong legs allow him to elevate well, and he possesses a nice stroke from deep. Teams must take care not to let him linger outside or they will lose him as he runs by screens.

Weaknesses: Matchup problems are a nightly concern for coach David Hobbs. In truth, Washington is a guard forced to play out of position. He lacks both size and strength in those battles. On offense, he is not a great passer and sometimes allows himself to get trapped in spots where the only outlet is a dangerous toss.

Analysis: The story at Alabama in 1995-96 centered largely on Roy Rogers's development inside. Yet Washington played a large part in helping the Crimson Tide reach the semifinals of the National Invitation Tournament in New York City.

COLLEGE STATISTICS

	G	FGP	FTP	RPG	APG	PPG
93-94 ALAB	17	.404	.727	1.0	0.7	3.5
94-95 ALAB	33	.459	.808	3.9	0.8	11.9
95-96 ALAB	32	.426	.790	6.9	1.0	18.6
Totals	82	.437	.792	4.5	0.9	12.8

BONZI WELLS

School: Ball State
Position: Guard
Year: Junior
Height: 6'5" **Weight:** 200
Birthdate: September 20, 1976
Hometown: Muncie, IN

PLAYER SUMMARY	
Will	score in bunches
Can't	ignore him defensively
Expect	a complete player
Don't Expect	national headlines

Background: Some have criticized the larger schools in the region for not recruiting him, but the truth is that Wells is a local boy who never wanted to leave home. That was good news for Ball State coach Ray McCallum, himself a local product. Wells was named Freshman of the Year in the Mid-American Conference in 1995.

Strengths: Pick your poison: Wells can beat you from inside or out. Perimeter players struggle to deal with him when he posts them up. At the defensive end, his quick hands make him one of the nation's top thieves (171 steals in two seasons). Wells also ranked among Division I leaders in scoring (25.4 PPG) last year.

Weaknesses: Turnovers have been a problem at times. Wells committed 106 last season, and that's too high for a guard who does not have the primary ball-handling responsibilities on his squad. His 3-point-shooting accuracy (33 percent) could stand some improvement as well.

Analysis: Wells reminds many veteran MAC watchers of a former swingman in the league, Ron Harper. Like Harper once was, Wells is a prolific scorer who toils in relative obscurity. That could change this year.

COLLEGE STATISTICS

		G	FGP	FTP	RPG	APG	PPG
94-95	BSU	30	.466	.617	6.1	2.8	15.8
95-96	BSU	28	.494	.708	8.8	2.9	25.4
Totals		58	.483	.671	7.4	2.8	20.4

TYSON WHEELER

School: Rhode Island
Year: Junior
Position: Guard
Height: 5'10" **Weight:** 155
Birthdate: October 8, 1975
Hometown: New London, CT

PLAYER SUMMARY	
Will	enter the lane
Can't	shut down foes
Expect	bursts of scoring
Don't Expect	post-up action

Background: Considered too small by many of the major programs in the East, Wheeler accepted a scholarship to Rhode Island. He was targeted as the backup to the more touted Sean Colson but won the job in fall practice and went on to achieve All-Rookie honors in the Atlantic 10.

Strengths: Speed and maneuverability help set Wheeler apart. He handles the ball well in congested areas and has the ability to blow past defenders who challenge him. His perimeter jumper must be respected, and he can locate the open man when cornered.

Weaknesses: Wheeler lacks the physical prowess to be a great defender, yet he has the ability to do more than he does. He needs to assert himself. His quickness should allow for more steals, but part of the dilemma is that he must conserve energy because so much is asked of him.

Analysis: Rhode Island coach Al Skinner has developed a knack for locating unknown high school players who are capable of fine college careers. Wheeler might be the best of the bunch. His offensive productivity lifted the Rams into the National Invitation Tournament last season.

COLLEGE STATISTICS

		G	FGP	FTP	RPG	APG	PPG
94-95	RI	27	.412	.677	2.7	5.0	13.2
95-96	RI	34	.406	.747	2.9	6.0	16.5
Totals		61	.408	.722	2.8	5.5	15.0

KENYA WILKINS

School: Oregon
Year: Senior
Position: Guard
Height: 5'10" **Weight:** 154
Birthdate: July 2, 1975
Hometown: Los Angeles, CA

PLAYER SUMMARY	
Will	steer the offense
Can't	defend the lane
Expect	pockets to be picked
Don't Expect	a high FG pct.

Background: Oregon coach Jerry Green sneaked a good one out from under the noses of UCLA and USC when he lured Wilkins to the Northwest. Wilkins started every game as a rookie and, after his sophomore year, won the prestigious Higdon Trophy as Oregon's top student-athlete.

Strengths: Wilkins must be accounted for in the open court. This quality ball-handler does not panic against pressure and loves to dish the ball off to his mates. Rarely does he force a pass that isn't there, and he keeps his turnovers to a minimum.

Weaknesses: Like many modern point guards, Wilkins's game is focused on the drive. The result is that his long-range shooting game is suspect. Despite efforts at improvement, Wilkins remains something of a liability with his jumper. He forces too many ill-advised shots without being set.

Analysis: After leading the Ducks into their first NCAA Tournament appearance in generations in 1994-95, Wilkins stepped back into the shadows to some extent last year. That was due mainly to an inexperienced cast surrounding him. As that group matures, Wilkins should continue to improve.

COLLEGE STATISTICS

	G	FGP	FTP	RPG	APG	PPG
93-94 OREG	27	.360	.709	3.3	5.3	11.5
94-95 OREG	28	.366	.735	3.2	6.1	12.1
95-96 OREG	29	.400	.846	3.4	5.9	13.7
Totals	84	.377	.765	3.3	5.8	12.5

ALVIN WILLIAMS

School: Villanova
Year: Senior
Position: Guard
Height: 6'4" **Weight:** 180
Birthdate: August 6, 1974
Hometown: Philadelphia, PA

PLAYER SUMMARY	
Will	feed the scorers
Can't	deflect shots
Expect	strong defense
Don't Expect	a high FG pct.

Background: When he signed a letter of intent at Villanova, Williams became the first Philadelphia prep player to sign with the school since 1973. The graduate of Germantown Academy was the first guard off the bench as a freshman and emerged as a full-time starter as a sophomore.

Strengths: At 6'4", Williams's height allows him to find open mates even under pressure. A good ball-handler, he is capable of playing either point guard or shooting guard. He loves to drive to the goal. He uses his size in the lane to create openings and find the open man.

Weaknesses: Opposing defenders will sometimes lay off Williams from long range because his perimeter jumper is a hit-or-miss proposition. This year he will be asked to score more points.

Analysis: In his debut as a regular, Williams was steadier than coach Steve Lappas could have envisioned. A hard-nosed kid, Williams provides a spirit and intensity that sets the tone for Villanova. This year, with Kerry Kittles departed for the NBA, Williams will get more scoring chances.

COLLEGE STATISTICS

	G	FGP	FTP	RPG	APG	PPG
93-94 VILL	31	.389	.698	2.8	2.8	7.9
94-95 VILL	33	.405	.744	3.5	4.8	7.1
95-96 VILL	33	.454	.710	3.5	5.4	11.0
Totals	97	.420	.715	3.3	4.4	8.6

CARLOS WILLIAMS

School: Alabama-Birmingham
Year: Senior
Position: Forward
Height: 6'6" **Weight:** 190
Birthdate: March 5, 1975
Hometown: Detroit, MI

PLAYER SUMMARY	
Will	rebound with vigor
Can't	shut down foes
Expect	offensive energy
Don't Expect	withering defense

Background: Williams was a star in Detroit's powerful public league. *FutureStars* rated him among the top 30 seniors in the prep class of 1993, and he participated in Magic Johnson's Roundball Classic at the close of that season. He led UAB in scoring in each of the past two seasons.

Strengths: Williams can put up the points from inside and out. A quick release on his shot gives him an edge, as does his foot speed. He does a lot of damage on the offensive glass, beating foes to the spot and connecting on tip-ins.

Weaknesses: Defense is not what Williams does best. His concentration at that end of the floor does not match his focus at the offensive end. He can stand to improve his passing skills too, particularly his ability to pass out of traps.

Analysis: In the last years of the Gene Bartow era, UAB stuck to a conservative offensive approach. In many ways, Williams was the only major weapon featured. New coach Murray Bartow should embrace a more liberal attack that will benefit Williams, a great offensive talent.

COLLEGE STATISTICS

	G	FGP	FTP	RPG	APG	PPG
94-95 UAB	14	.487	.672	7.0	1.3	17.0
95-96 UAB	30	.425	.709	8.4	1.7	20.2
Totals	44	.442	.698	8.0	1.6	19.2

GREG WILLIAMS

School: Florida
Year: Senior
Position: Guard
Height: 6'2" **Weight:** 183
Birthdate: March 12, 1974
Hometown: Fairfax, VA

PLAYER SUMMARY	
Will	toss crafty passes
Can't	rebound
Expect	penetrating drives
Don't Expect	3-pointers

Background: Nicknamed "Tiny" by former Gator teammate Craig Brown, Williams averaged 21.8 points per game as a senior in high school. He was the understudy to Dan Cross in his first year as a Gator, as Florida advanced to the Final Four in Charlotte.

Strengths: The ball is in good hands when Williams has it. Quickness with the basketball makes him a hard man to contain. His foot speed allows him to go by defenders and opens passing lanes for him to dish off. He is a viable threat from 3-point land. When on a roll, he can carry the Gators' offense.

Weaknesses: Williams's perimeter game tends to run hot and cold. He is not really an explosive scorer, so he needs to be careful about being too aggressive with his shot. He needs screens and openings to be a major point producer. On defense, he can be taken inside.

Analysis: Florida struggled through a disappointing campaign in 1995-96 and then lost Lon Kruger, the coach who took it to the Final Four, at season's end. New coach Billy Donovan will look to Williams to become the team's anchor as he attempts to lead UF back to the NCAA Tournament.

COLLEGE STATISTICS

	G	FGP	FTP	RPG	APG	PPG
93-94 FLOR	37	.286	.784	0.8	1.1	2.1
94-95 FLOR	30	.422	.779	2.7	4.0	8.4
95-96 FLOR	28	.368	.663	2.4	5.0	10.3
Totals	95	.376	.730	1.9	3.2	6.5

DEDRIC WILLOUGHBY

School: Iowa State
Year: Senior
Position: Guard/Forward
Height: 6'3" **Weight:** 180
Birthdate: May 27, 1974
Hometown: Harvey, LA

PLAYER SUMMARY	
Will	drop in 3s
Can't	avoid foul trouble
Expect	prolific point production
Don't Expect	much rest

Background: Willoughby originally signed with the University of New Orleans. He started four games in 1992 before suffering a knee injury. He returned to become one of the Sun Belt Conference's top freshmen in 1994. He transferred to Iowa State, where he was a first-team All-Big Eight pick in 1995-96.

Strengths: This pure shooter provides both range and variety with his shot. In respecting his perimeter jumper, opponents often open lanes to the goal that Willoughby is quick to take advantage of. He has learned how to come off of picks and free himself for shots.

Weaknesses: Willoughby is often asked to check forwards—a duty that does not play to his strength. He is not an outstanding man-to-man defender, an area he will have to address as he casts an eye in the direction of the NBA.

Analysis: ISU was one of the nation's best stories last year, and Willoughby was the main reason for that. Coach Tim Floyd and Willoughby share a long history—Willoughby followed Floyd to ISU—a fact that might translate to a run at All-America honors for this man in 1996-97.

COLLEGE STATISTICS

		G	FGP	FTP	RPG	APG	PPG
92-93	NO	5	.292	.556	2.6	2.4	2.6
93-94	NO	28	.432	.797	2.1	0.7	9.0
95-96	ISU	33	.415	.793	4.2	2.5	20.5
Totals		66	.415	.787	3.2	1.7	14.4

ANDRE WOOLRIDGE

School: Iowa
Year: Senior
Position: Guard
Height: 6'1" **Weight:** 190
Birthdate: November 11, 1973
Hometown: Omaha, NE

PLAYER SUMMARY	
Will	distribute in traffic
Can't	block anyone's vision
Expect	tenacious playmaking
Don't Expect	rebounding help

Background: Woolridge completed his prep career at Benson High School as Nebraska's top Class A prep scorer (1,911 points). He then signed with the state university and played one season for the Cornhuskers, making 30 starts. He transferred to Iowa at the end of the '92-93 season.

Strengths: This electric playmaker is hard to trap. He spots the open man and also understands how to run a half-court offense. Defenders find him difficult to contain because he has the quickness to beat them off the dribble and the touch to drain a perimeter jumper. He is at his best when the shot clock is winding down.

Weaknesses: The best Woolridge can hope to be at the defensive end is pesky. He lacks the size to confound opposing points, especially ones who are taller than he is. Sometimes Woolridge will wait too long on offense and will be forced to lift a bad jumper.

Analysis: One expert viewed Woolridge as the Big Ten's top performer in 1995-96. He plays with quickness, vision, and a belief in his own skill level. There aren't many better pure point guards.

COLLEGE STATISTICS

		G	FGP	FTP	RPG	APG	PPG
92-93	NEBR	30	.387	.615	1.7	2.0	4.9
94-95	IOWA	33	.478	.766	2.5	5.8	14.0
95-96	IOWA	32	.469	.735	3.2	6.0	13.5
Totals		95	.459	.728	2.5	4.7	10.8

DOMINICK YOUNG

School: Fresno State
Year: Senior
Position: Guard
Height: 5'10" **Weight:** 170
Birthdate: March 31, 1974
Hometown: Chicago, IL

PLAYER SUMMARY	
Will	add assists
Can't	ease up
Expect	competent ball-handling
Don't Expect	slow hands

Background: Young was selected to the All-Golden Gate Conference first team at Chabot College. He emerged as an immediate starter after transferring to Fresno and was named to the Western Athletic Conference's All-Newcomer team in 1994-95.

Strengths: Finding the open man has always been Young's forte. Like most good point guards, he is a strong ball-handler who can read opposing defenses. His quickness helps him beat defenders off the dribble. He can dish the ball off in traffic for scores. He also can connect on the long-range jumper.

Weaknesses: When you operate a high-speed offense like this one, turnovers are an issue. Young is sometimes so eager to make the great pass that he throws it away. He's never been afraid to take a shot, which can lead to some ill-advised launches.

Analysis: Young was one of the WAC's top point guards prior to Jerry Tarkanian's arrival, and the new coach helped him get even better. He was more under control in '94-95 and a better defender as well. This season, Young will be one of the sparks as Fresno attempts to take a step into the national Top 25.

COLLEGE STATISTICS

		G	FGP	FTP	RPG	APG	PPG
94-95	FSU	28	.462	.716	3.7	7.0	15.6
95-96	FSU	29	.407	.718	3.3	6.6	18.2
Totals		57	.432	.717	3.5	6.8	16.9

TIM YOUNG

School: Stanford
Year: Junior
Position: Center
Height: 7'1" **Weight:** 245
Birthdate: February 6, 1976
Hometown: Santa Cruz, CA

PLAYER SUMMARY	
Will	clog the middle
Can't	overdo his rehab
Expect	rebounding tenacity
Don't Expect	tons of assists

Background: Young spent countless hours working with former NBA center Mark McNamara, and the work paid off handsomely. Only the second seven-footer to play at Stanford, Young made an immediate impact as a rookie in 1994-95, earning Pac-10 All-Rookie honors. He missed most of the '95-96 campaign due to injury.

Strengths: A student of the game, Young is a very intelligent performer who understands his role. He can find the open man operating out of the high post. Great hands make him an inviting target inside. He is also quite agile and brings to the arena a sweet shooting stroke good to 15 feet.

Weaknesses: A long layoff like the one Young endured is dangerous for a big man. He must be careful not to add weight and may have a hard time scraping the rust off his game in 1996-97.

Analysis: Two years ago, Young was one of the most talked-about players in the Pac-10. His size and athletic gifts gave the Cardinal a legitimate threat in the middle for the first time since the days of Rich Kelley. Assuming he returns to the court fully healed, Young should continue his ascent to the top of the list of pure pivots.

COLLEGE STATISTICS

		G	FGP	FTP	RPG	APG	PPG
94-95	STAN	29	.500	.692	8.6	1.2	12.3
95-96	STAN	5	.421	.720	9.0	1.6	10.0
Totals		34	.490	.697	8.6	1.4	12.0

ALABAMA

Conference: Southeastern
1995-96: 19-13, T-2nd SEC West

1995-96 NIT: 3-2
Coach: David Hobbs (78-46)

Opening Line: The Crimson Tide redeemed what was, in some respects, a disappointing season prior to March with a strong run in the National Invitation Tournament. The year's most pleasant development was the play of Roy Rogers. He went from a reserve as a junior to one of the top players in the South as a senior.

Guard: From the time they signed, backcourt stars Brian Williams and Anton Reese were billed as the Tide's guards of tomorrow. Well, that day has arrived. Longtime starter Marvin Orange is gone, and Williams now takes command of the offense. He needs to concentrate on taking care of the basketball and not forcing shots. Reese, his sophomore classmate, is thin and needs to add some muscle in order to excel, but he's a natural scorer. Those two aren't alone, though, as combination guard Damon Bacote, a junior, will help out.

Forward: Senior Eric Washington is undersized at 6'4". Yet his athleticism and slashing ability make him a valued scorer at small forward. He could swing back to guard if needed. Alabama's most significant recruit is 6'8" Ricky Poole from Otero Junior College. He is a quick forward who is at his best slashing to the goal. Alfred Moss, 6'9", will be a player to watch. The freshman has good hands, runs the floor, and doesn't back away from contact.

Center: Senior Thalamus McGhee did not dominate inside as some expected he would after arriving from junior college. Although he's raw offensively, McGee's size can make him a rebounding menace.

Analysis: As Alabama discovered last winter, it's difficult to bank on freshmen in a league like the SEC. But the youngsters are older now and offer the prospect of improved guard play—long the soft spot in Tuscaloosa. A return to the NCAA Tournament is anticipated.

1996-97 ROSTER

	POS	HT	YR	FGP	FTP	3-PT	RPG	APG	PPG
Eric Washington	F	6'4"	Sr.	.426	.790	113/279	6.9	1.0	18.6
Brian Williams	G	6'1"	So.	.383	.802	36/110	2.7	2.6	10.4
Anton Reese	G	6'1"	So.	.377	.444	16/49	1.4	0.3	4.6
Thalamus McGhee	C	6'9"	Sr.	.388	.446	1/1	5.2	1.4	3.0
Damon Bacote	G	6'3"	Jr.	.294	.550	2/14	1.9	0.5	2.2
M.C. Mazique	F	6'10"	So.	.452	.417	1/4	2.1	0.3	1.8
Blake Thrasher	G	6'3"	So.	.250	.200	2/10	1.2	0.5	0.7
Demetrius Alexander	F	6'8"	Jr.	—	—	—	—	—	—
Jeremy Hays	F/C	6'9"	Fr.	—	—	—	—	—	—
Donnie Johnson	F	6'7"	Jr.	—	—	—	—	—	—
Alfred Moss	F	6'9"	Fr.	—	—	—	—	—	—
Ricky Poole	G/F	6'8"	Jr.	—	—	—	—	—	—

ALABAMA-BIRMINGHAM

Conference: Conference USA   **1995-96 NCAAs/NIT:** DNP
1995-96: 16-14, T-2nd C-USA Red   **Coach:** Murry Bartow (0-0)

Opening Line: Gene Bartow—the man responsible for building the program up from scratch and into an NCAA Tournament regular in the 1980s—retired from coaching at the end of the 1995-96 season. In his stead comes Murry Bartow, his son and longtime aide, to take command.

Guard: The backcourt showed signs last winter of emerging from the doldrums that plagued it in recent years. Sophomore Damon Cobb, 6'4", enjoyed a strong debut after sitting out the 1994-95 season. This shooting guard has the potential to score more, and Bartow may open up the offense so he can. Senior Chad Jones, while less of an offensive threat than Cobb, remains important to the Blazers for his athleticism and rebounding from the back line. Diminutive Cedric Dixon, 5'9", is the primary ball-handler, but he needs to be more consistent. Will Bailey, a 6'1" senior, also handles some point guard responsibilities.

Forward: Senior Carlos Williams is this squad's Mr. Everything. In fact, one of Bartow's biggest challenges is to find a way to create more offensive balance so that Williams is not required to carry such a hefty burden. A variety of freshmen will audition for the spot next to Williams up front: 6'7" Chris Albritton, 6'8" Earl Ike, and 6'6" Torrey Ward. Ike is a classic power forward, while Albritton and Ward are small forward types who could push Williams up to power forward.

Center: No one did much in the middle to distinguish himself last year. Travis Harper is gone, so the only alternatives are bulky 6'8" senior James Bristow and 6'7" senior Norman Williams. Neither figures to be much of an offensive factor. Ike might spend time in the middle.

Analysis: Bartow's first task is to make this group less reliant on Williams. If the freshmen and one or two veterans step up, UAB will be waiting for a phone call from a tournament committee next March.

1996-97 ROSTER

	POS	HT	YR	FGP	FTP	3-PT	RPG	APG	PPG
Carlos Williams	F	6'7"	Sr.	.425	.709	49/151	8.4	1.7	20.2
Cedric Dixon	G	5'9"	Jr.	.370	.650	45/148	3.0	3.1	11.2
Chad Jones	G	6'4"	Sr.	.405	.797	14/39	4.1	2.1	8.3
Damon Cobb	G	6'4"	So.	.307	.750	40/136	1.6	1.0	7.1
Norman Williams	F/C	6'7"	Sr.	.474	.478	0/1	5.7	0.5	4.2
James Bristow	F/C	6'8"	Sr.	.442	.444	1/4	3.8	0.2	3.9
Will Bailey	G	6'1"	Sr.	.418	.875	5/16	1.4	2.1	2.4
Chris Lee	F	6'8"	Sr.	.629	.375	2/5	1.8	0.3	2.1
Chris Albritton	F	6'7"	Fr.	—	—	—	—	—	—
Earl Ike	F/C	6'8"	Fr.	—	—	—	—	—	—
Felix Okam	C	6'9"	So.	—	—	—	—	—	—
Torrey Ward	G	6'3"	Fr.	—	—	—	—	—	—

ARIZONA

Conference: Pac-10
1995-96: 26-7, 2nd Pac-10

1995-96 NCAAs: 2-1
Coach: Lute Olson (507-194)

Opening Line: Despite the loss of star guard Damon Stoudamire to the NBA prior to last season and center Joseph Blair to academic woes in midseason, the Wildcats were able to bounce back from a 1994-95 campaign that concluded with a first-round NCAA Tournament loss to Miami of Ohio. The 'Cats finished second in the Pac-10 in 1995-96.

Guard: Reggie Geary was a dependable leader and excellent defender, but he could not match the skill of newcomer Michael Bibby. The son of USC coach Henry Bibby, this local product is rated as the top incoming point guard in the nation. He'll start from day one. Alongside him will be junior Miles Simon, 6'5", who needs to score more. Unfortunately, UA is short on depth at these positions.

Forward: Arizona's recruiting class was listed as one of the top ten in America, and forward is a spot where the Wildcats added many new faces. Three newcomers should see meaningful action. Stephen Jackson, 6'8", spent a year at Oak Hill Academy and ranked among the top 30 players in high school last winter. Eugene Edgerson, an athletic 6'8" wing, wasn't far behind. Holdover Michael Dickerson is a junior and could be invaluable for his experience.

Center: When Blair was sent to the sidelines, he left a void in the middle. Olson turned to power forward Ben Davis, who played well enough to lead the Wildcats into the NCAAs. Both are gone, though, and there are only untested types on hand. Bennett Davidson—a 6'8" junior college transfer—and 6'11" sophomore A.J. Bramlett are the likeliest alternatives.

Analysis: This the kind of program that doesn't have to panic when it suffers graduation losses. Although its numbers were depleted, the incoming talent is exciting. A growth period is inevitable, yet the 'Cats won't slip far from their perch.

1996-97 ROSTER

	POS	HT	YR	FGP	FTP	3-PT	RPG	APG	PPG
Miles Simon	G	6'5"	Jr.	.446	.764	45/139	4.0	4.1	13.2
Michael Dickerson	F	6'5"	Jr.	.438	.738	31/91	3.5	1.8	11.9
Jason Terry	G	6'2"	So.	.542	.593	15/26	0.7	1.1	3.1
A.J. Bramlett	F/C	6'11"	So.	.511	.357	0/0	1.9	0.3	1.9
Donnell Harris	F	6'11"	So.	.500	.400	0/0	1.1	0.2	1.1
Michael Bibby	G	6'2"	Fr.	—	—	—	—	—	—
Bennett Davidson	F	6'8"	Jr.	—	—	—	—	—	—
Eugene Edgerson	F	6'8"	Fr.	—	—	—	—	—	—
Stephen Jackson	F	6'8"	Fr.	—	—	—	—	—	—
Josh Pastner	G	6'0"	Fr.	—	—	—	—	—	—
Quynn Tebbs	G	6'3"	Fr.	—	—	—	—	—	—
Justin Wessel	F	6'8"	Fr.	—	—	—	—	—	—

ARKANSAS

Conference: Southeastern
1995-96: 20-13, 2nd SEC West

1995-96 NCAAs: 2-1
Coach: Nolan Richardson (391-132)

Opening Line: In what was coined a rebuilding year, the Razorbacks did not reach the Final Four last year for the first time in three seasons. Richardson was forced to incorporate nine newcomers into his team, and the Hogs struggled at points. Only a late rush in the SEC Tournament got Arkansas into the NCAA Tourney. But the squad proved its worthiness by advancing to the East Regional semifinal.

Guard: Freshmen Kareem Reid and Pat Bradley showed fine effort. Reid emerged as the team's floor leader and offensive catalyst. Lightly regarded Bradley developed into one of the SEC's top long-range marksmen. Talented wingman Jessie Pate was sidelined late in the year when questions were raised by the NCAA about courses he had taken in junior college. Pate is not expected back. Freshman Glendon Alexander, 6'5", could step into that hole.

Forward: The Razorbacks also lost a key forward prior to the start of the NCAA Tournament when 6'6" Sunday Adebayo fell under the NCAA's transcript eye. Richardson was thus forced to use a patchwork alignment opposite gifted 6'8" Derek Hood in the postseason. Hood is a lock to hold down one spot this year, but the power forward spot is up in the air.

Center: For three years, Arkansas relied upon the tag-team tandem of Darnell Robinson and Lee Wilson. But Robinson's early exit for the pros means that it is now up to Wilson in the middle. Wilson must come prepared to play every night, and he must avoid foul trouble because the Hogs are thin up front.

Analysis: Any time a team wins 20 games and moves into the Sweet 16 in a "rebuilding" year, you understand the program has arrived. The experience gained in 1995-96 should push the Razorbacks back into contention for an SEC title and a lofty seed in the NCAA Tournament.

1996-97 ROSTER

	POS	HT	YR	FGP	FTP	3-PT	RPG	APG	PPG
Kareem Reid	G	5'10"	So.	.395	.686	28/108	3.1	6.6	12.9
Pat Bradley	G	6'2"	So.	.418	.765	82/198	2.0	1.2	10.2
Derek Hood	F	6'8"	So.	.473	.439	0/0	6.1	1.1	7.5
Lee Wilson	C	6'11"	Sr.	.531	.617	0/0	4.4	0.7	6.3
Marlon Towns	G	6'4"	So.	.371	.595	24/78	1.6	1.9	6.0
Landis Williams	F	6'7"	Jr.	.506	.604	0/7	2.1	0.3	4.1
Nick Davis	F	6'9"	Jr.	.360	.750	3/16	2.7	0.4	3.4
Ali Thompson	F	6'5"	So.	.427	.710	0/6	1.9	0.7	3.1
Glendon Alexander	G	6'5"	Fr.	—	—	—	—	—	—
Steve Green	G	6'2"	Fr.	—	—	—	—	—	—
Tarik Wallace	G	6'2"	Jr.	—	—	—	—	—	—
Guy Whitney	G	6'5"	Jr.	—	—	—	—	—	—

BOSTON COLLEGE

Conference: Big East   **1995-96 NCAAs:** 1-1
1995-96: 19-11, 3rd Big East 6   **Coach:** Jim O'Brien (213-208)

Opening Line: Targeted for the bottom of the Big East Conference by most preseason pundits, the Eagles got off to a strong start last year and rarely faltered on their way back to the NCAA Tournament after a one-year absence. BC handed Indiana a 64-51 defeat in the opening round before dropping a 103-89 contest to Georgia Tech.

Guard: Few freshmen have made more of an impact on Chestnut Hill than James "Scoonie" Penn did. He led the Eagles in minutes played and assists. More important, he set the up-tempo tone for a team that had no one to do so in 1994-95. O'Brien usually paired Antonio Granger and Duane Woodward on the wings. Both are tall enough to handle small forwards at the defensive end and capable of draining open jumpers. Sophomore Andy Bedard logged significant minutes off the bench.

Forward: The power forward role is important at BC. Rebounding is essential, and 6'7" senior Keenan Jourdon makes a strong contribution in that area. Because fouls can be a problem for him, his understudy, 6'8" senior Bevan Thomas, sees a fair amount of action. Mickey Curley is prone to turnovers, but a nice touch around the goal makes him a valued role-player.

Center: Only one name matters here: Danya Abrams. His physical play gives the Eagles an important dimension in a league known for its rugged activity under the basket. Curley fills in when Abrams encounters foul difficulty or needs a short rest.

Analysis: One year ago, Boston College appeared to be a long distance away from respectability. However, with a healthy cast and Penn as the catalyst, the Eagles surprised many. There will be no more sneaking up on folks this year, but there is no reason this contingent should not be among the top of the Big East.

1996-97 ROSTER

	POS	HT	YR	FGP	FTP	3-PT	RPG	APG	PPG
Danya Abrams	F	6'7"	Sr.	.471	.705	9/28	9.6	1.5	19.6
Scoonie Penn	G	5'10"	So.	.438	.755	55/175	3.4	3.5	13.2
Antonio Granger	G/F	6'6"	Jr.	.442	.667	53/141	3.4	0.9	10.6
Duane Woodward	G	6'3"	Jr.	.433	.730	25/74	3.3	3.3	8.8
Keenan Jourdon	F	6'7"	Sr.	.532	.609	12/21	5.2	1.2	7.6
Bevan Thomas	F	6'8"	Sr.	.528	.655	15/38	4.3	0.8	6.9
Mickey Curley	F/C	6'9"	Jr.	.429	.814	0/0	3.5	0.5	5.4
Kostas Maglos	F	6'10"	So.	.565	.545	0/2	1.4	0.3	4.6
Andy Bedard	G	6'1"	So.	.430	.636	23/58	1.4	1.9	3.8
Brad Christianson	F	6'7"	Sr.	.360	.750	1/7	1.3	0.8	1.6
Damien Foster	G	6'7"	So.	—	—	—	—	—	—
Brian Keefe	G	6'4"	Jr.	—	—	—	—	—	—

CINCINNATI

Conference: Conference USA
1995-96: 28-5, 1st C-USA Blue

1995-96 NCAAs: 3-1
Coach: Bob Huggins (263-109)

Opening Line: Huggins's decision to stay in Cincy despite interest from the Miami Heat gave the Bearcats the fuel they needed to remain among the elite teams in the nation last year. Cincinnati took charge of C-USA in its debut campaign, winning the conference tournament title. A loss in the Southeast Regional final prevented Cincy from reaching its second Final Four of the Huggins era.

Guard: Keith LeGree gave the Bearcats a veteran leader at the point, but his deficiencies as a shooter often caught up with UC in big games. He's gone now, and because Huggins's staff was unable to land a big name to replace him, Damon Flint may find himself running the offense at times. Flint is better suited to playing off the ball. Darnell Burton offers prolific 3-point shooting, while Terrence Davis, D'Juan Baker, and freshman John Carson will fight for minutes.

Forward: The Bearcats' three-four combination could be a potential nightmare for the opposition. On one side is power forward Danny Fortson, the 6'7" low-post bull and preseason All-American. His running mate figures to be 6'7" Ruben Patterson, the top junior college prospect in America last winter. Throw in capable reserves such as 6'7" junior Bobby Brannen and 6'8" Kenyon Martin and this group rates as a clear strength.

Center: Gone is Art Long, the widebody who gave the 'Cats a presence in the lane. In his stead are two bangers. One, 6'9" Jackson Julson, served as Long's caddy in 1995-96. Prone to fouls, Julson must concentrate on setting picks, defending, and rebounding. Sophomore Ryan Fletcher didn't see much action in his first year, but that may change now.

Analysis: If the Bearcats' guards stand up to pressure—and they should—Cincinnati will have a potent package that could take it one step further than it went in 1996.

1996-97 ROSTER

	POS	HT	YR	FGP	FTP	3-PT	RPG	APG	PPG
Danny Fortson	F	6'7"	Jr.	.538	.753	0/1	8.6	1.2	17.6
Darnell Burton	G	6'2"	Sr.	.443	.671	89/215	2.6	1.9	14.0
Damon Flint	G/F	6'5"	Sr.	.433	.696	64/185	3.0	3.5	12.8
Jackson Julson	F/C	6'9"	Jr.	.534	.796	4/12	1.5	0.4	3.4
Rodrick Monroe	F	6'4"	Sr.	.530	.438	0/0	2.9	0.3	3.2
Terrence Davis	G	6'2"	Sr.	.512	.722	2/7	0.7	0.6	2.0
Bobby Brannen	F	6'7"	Jr.	.375	.550	0/1	2.7	0.5	1.8
Ryan Fletcher	F	6'8"	So.	.273	1.00	1/11	1.4	0.1	1.2
D'Juan Baker	G	6'5"	Jr.	—	—	—	—	—	—
John Carson	G	6'1"	Fr.	—	—	—	—	—	—
Kenyon Martin	F/C	6'8"	Fr.	—	—	—	—	—	—
Ruben Patterson	F	6'7"	Jr.	—	—	—	—	—	—

CLEMSON

Conference: Atlantic Coast
1995-96: 18-11, 6th ACC

1995-96 NCAAs: 0-1
Coach: Rick Barnes (161-110)

Opening Line: Barnes brought a specific plan to South Carolina when he accepted the head coaching position in 1994. In his first year, he guided an undermanned unit to a 15-13 finish and an appearance in the National Invitation Tournament. The Tigers went one better in 1995-96, sneaking into the NCAA's event. Best of all, not one Tiger on that team was a senior.

Guard: The Tigers' NCAA Tournament aspirations seemed to be in serious jeopardy when starting guard Merl Code went down in midseason with an injury. Yet Clemson survived, and now Code—one of the team's best players—is back. His presence is huge. His backcourt sidekick is 5'9" sophomore Terrell McIntyre, who brings confidence and ball-handling skill to the back line. Senior Bill Harder is the best of a thin reserve corps.

Forward: The Tigers' mainstay is small forward Greg Buckner. He originally signed with Providence and then followed Barnes here. A superior defender, his athleticism sets the tone for the Tigers. Sophomore Iker Iturbe missed the entire season with an injury but is healthy again and will see serious action. Sophomores Andrius Jurkunas and Tony Christie were both productive as freshmen.

Center: Two of the Tigers' most significant signees over the past two seasons may share time here. Sophomore Harold Jamison is a quality rebounder and doesn't shy away from contact. Freshman Woni Mohamed, 6'9", now gets his chance in the lane. If all else fails, Iturbe can return to the position he held down as a rookie.

Analysis: Clemson's basketball history is rather spotty. For instance, it has never won a game at North Carolina. All of that may be about to change. Barnes has accumulated a stockpile of young talent that should make the Tigers a major player in the ACC.

1996-97 ROSTER

	POS	HT	YR	FGP	FTP	3-PT	RPG	APG	PPG
Greg Buckner	F	6'4"	Jr.	.472	.672	1/25	5.1	1.7	13.1
Terrell McIntyre	G	5'9"	So.	.401	.792	43/123	2.8	3.1	12.7
Merl Code	G	6'2"	Sr.	.442	.897	19/46	3.6	2.5	12.5
Andrius Jurkunas	F	6'9"	So.	.420	.615	51/121	4.7	1.2	8.4
Tony Christie	F	6'7"	So.	.435	.556	20/75	2.7	1.4	8.0
Harold Jamison	F/C	6'8"	So.	.519	.615	0/0	5.9	1.0	7.6
Tom Wideman	C	6'10"	So.	.485	.562	0/0	5.2	1.1	5.8
Bill Harder	G	6'0"	Sr.	.333	.720	8/31	2.1	2.3	4.3
LeDarion Jones	F	6'6"	So.	.556	.250	0/3	1.4	0.3	2.6
Iker Iturbe	F/C	6'7"	So.	—	—	—	—	—	—
Woni Mohamed	C	6'9"	Fr.	—	—	—	—	—	—
Vincent Whitt	F/G	6'6"	Fr.	—	—	—	—	—	—

COLGATE

Conference: Patriot League
1995-96: 15-15, T-1st Patriot

1995-96 NCAAs: 0-1
Coach: Jack Bruen (94-108)

Opening Line: It is no coincidence that year two of Adonal Foyle's career produced the second NCAA Tournament berth in school history. The 6'10" pivot gives the Red Raiders a huge edge in their conference. Foyle also accounts for an overall record that is not overly impressive, however, because with him in the lineup, Bruen scheduled Colgate to take on the likes of Syracuse, Georgetown, Iowa, and Providence.

Guard: Jimmy Maloney, who graduated last season, was an integral part of the Red Raider attack. The burden now falls to candidates Ryan Clements, Chester Felts, and Chad Wiswall. The other guard spot belongs to Seth Schaeffer, a gifted long-range shooter. Schaeffer helps lighten the load for Foyle inside with his perimeter accuracy. He may be asked to handle some of the ball-handling if Bruen fails to find a pure point guard.

Forward: A couple of significant role-players have been lost to graduation. Mike Roberts and Malik Cupid weren't huge scorers, but they set picks and played good defense. One tested hand who does return is Rob Murray, 6'3", a senior not afraid of guarding taller players. Murray also offers a solid medium-range offensive game. Tim Bollin, a 6'9" senior, is the power forward. Although offensively limited, Bollin works the boards and can put a body on people at the defensive end.

Center: Foyle means everything to this team, and it's rare when he is off the court. Foyle twice has been voted Patriot League Player of the Year, and he more than holds his own in duels with centers at marquee schools.

Analysis: When Foyle chose to stay in Hamilton, some predicted there would be NCAA appearances for the Red Raiders as long as he was there. It's worked out that way so far, and there's no reason to think the trend won't continue.

1996-97 ROSTER

	POS	HT	YR	FGP	FTP	3-PT	RPG	APG	PPG
Adonal Foyle	C	6'10"	Jr.	.517	.489	0/3	12.6	1.5	20.2
Seth Schaeffer	G	6'3"	Jr.	.429	.823	84/208	3.2	1.5	13.1
Tim Bollin	F	6'9"	Sr.	.487	.774	0/0	4.6	0.9	6.6
Chad Wiswall	F/G	6'5"	So.	.367	1.00	6/13	0.8	0.1	2.2
Ben Wandtke	F	6'6"	So.	.462	.714	1/3	0.9	0.0	2.1
Chester Felts	G	6'2"	So.	1.00	1.00	0/0	1.5	0.5	2.0
Rob Murray	G/F	6'3"	Sr.	.324	.375	3/11	1.1	0.5	1.8
Russ Lynch	F	6'7"	Sr.	.565	.250	1/2	0.7	0.2	1.6
Mike Chemotti	G	6'3"	Fr.	—	—	—	—	—	—
Antonio Delgado	F/G	6'4"	So.	—	—	—	—	—	—
Pat Diamond	F	6'6"	Fr.	—	—	—	—	—	—
Jason Waysville	F	6'7"	Jr.	—	—	—	—	—	—

CONNECTICUT

Conference: Big East   **1995-96 NCAAs:** 2-1
1995-96: 32-3, 1st Big East 6   **Coach:** Jim Calhoun (472-236)

Opening Line: Only a loss to Georgetown prevented the Huskies from becoming the first team in Big East history to go through the league undefeated. This marked the third straight year in which UConn posted the best regular-season record in the Big East. Alas, the Huskies were brought up short by Mississippi State in the Southeast Regional semifinal of the NCAA Tournament.

Guard: For the past three seasons, Doron Sheffer, a veteran of the Israeli national team, was a security blanket for Calhoun. Sheffer could bring the ball up the floor against pressure and make open jumpers. Last year, Ricky Moore, 6'2", was groomed to assume that job full-time, and the results were promising. Look for 6'6" freshman Richard Hamilton, a McDonald's All-American, to make an immediate impact.

Forward: There exists a huge hole at small forward, where Ray Allen held court for the past two seasons. Rashamel Jones, a 6'5" sophomore, is the immediate heir. He is at his best in the transition game Calhoun plays, but he's not an accomplished jump-shooter. Michael LeBlanc, 6'7", is an energetic new arrival. Senior Kirk King is the only returning starter at power forward. Freshman Kevin Freeman, 6'6", and holdover Ruslan Inyatkin, 6'7", will play meaningful roles.

Center: Travis Knight is gone and so, for now, is the concept of a single starting center. This position will be occupied by several people, including King, 6'9" rookie Sam Funches, and 6'11" Jake Voskuhl. Only Voskuhl is a natural pivot, but his inexperience prevents him from handling 30-35 minutes a night.

Analysis: A brilliant regular season was capped by a postseason pratfall, something that has become a disturbing pattern in Storrs. Expectations will diminish without Allen, Sheffer, and Knight, but there is plenty of ability in place for a return to the NCAA Tournament.

1996-97 ROSTER

	POS	HT	YR	FGP	FTP	3-PT	RPG	APG	PPG
Kirk King	F	6'8"	Sr.	.575	.689	0/0	6.3	1.0	9.9
Rashamel Jones	G	6'5"	So.	.401	.629	21/97	1.9	0.9	5.6
Ricky Moore	G	6'2"	So.	.500	.520	10/34	2.0	3.0	4.7
Ruslan Inyatkin	F	6'7"	Jr.	.488	.609	1/2	1.0	0.1	2.0
Dion Carson	G	6'3"	Sr.	.404	.667	3/10	1.3	0.4	1.8
Antric Klaiber	F	6'10"	So.	.171	.438	1/4	1.7	0.2	0.8
Kevin Freeman	F	6'6"	Fr.	—	—	—	—	—	—
Sam Funches	F/C	6'9"	Fr.	—	—	—	—	—	—
Richard Hamilton	G/F	6'6"	Fr.	—	—	—	—	—	—
Michael LeBlanc	F	6'7"	Fr.	—	—	—	—	—	—
Jake Voskuhl	C	6'11"	Fr.	—	—	—	—	—	—
Souleymane Wane	C	6'11"	Fr.	—	—	—	—	—	—

DUKE

Conference: Atlantic Coast   **1995-96 NCAAs:** 0-1
1995-96: 18-13, T-4th ACC   **Coach:** Mike Krzyzewski (449-199)

Opening Line: An invigorated Krzyzewski, returning to the sidelines after missing much of 1994-95 due to the effects of back surgery, spurred the Blue Devils back into the NCAA Tournament after a one-year absence. This wasn't your typical Duke juggernaut, though, as shown when the Blue Devils fell to Eastern Michigan in the opening round.

Guard: As so many seniors have in the past for Krzyzewski, guard Chris Collins came alive in his farewell campaign. Now it's Jeff Capel's turn. His career has sagged since 1994, when he helped the Blue Devils to the NCAA Tournament final. If Capel can pick up where Collins left off, Duke will be in good shape. Trajan Langdon, a talented sophomore, will be welcomed back after missing all of 1995-96 with an injury. Point guard Steve Wojciechowski also returns.

Forward: The Blue Devils are intrigued by Roshown McLeod, the first transfer of the Krzyzewski era. A former prep standout, McLeod was excellent in practice last winter and, at 6'8", offers the kind of athletic rebounding Duke has been without of late. Ricky Price is another athletic type who needs only to gain confidence to assert himself as a fine player. Freshmen Mike Chappell, 6'8", Nate James, 6'6", and Chris Carrawell, 6'6", are prime additions who will factor into the playing rotation.

Center: Greg Newton finally began to deliver on some of his promise in 1995-96. The 6'10" center owns a good touch around the goal and will take charge defensively. Taymon Domzalski, 6'10", had his moments as a freshman and could end up seeing major minutes.

Analysis: Duke is not yet all the way back. It still lacks the ability to challenge people defensively as it once did. However, this team made strides last winter and promises to make several more this time around.

1996-97 ROSTER

	POS	HT	YR	FGP	FTP	3-PT	RPG	APG	PPG
Jeff Capel	G	6'4"	Sr.	.376	.763	73/221	3.9	3.7	16.6
Ricky Price	F	6'5"	Jr.	.439	.711	44/112	3.5	1.5	14.2
Greg Newton	C	6'10"	Sr.	.568	.590	0/0	8.2	0.5	12.2
Taymon Domzalski	C	6'10"	So.	.493	.818	0/0	5.0	0.2	6.5
Carmen Wallace	F	6'5"	Sr.	.430	.806	14/32	2.8	1.0	6.0
Steve Wojciechowski	G	5'11"	Jr.	.318	.762	19/68	2.1	2.7	3.4
Todd Singleton	F	6'4"	Jr.	.500	.833	0/0	0.1	0.1	0.8
Chris Carrawell	F	6'6"	Fr.	—	—	—	—	—	—
Mike Chappell	F	6'8"	Fr.	—	—	—	—	—	—
Nate James	F	6'6"	Fr.	—	—	—	—	—	—
Trajan Langdon	G	6'3"	So.	—	—	—	—	—	—
Roshown McLeod	F	6'8"	Jr.	—	—	—	—	—	—

EASTERN MICHIGAN

Conference: Mid-American
1995-96: 25-6, 1st MAC

1995-96 NCAAs: 1-1
Coach: Ben Braun (185-132)

Opening Line: EMU captured its third NCAA Tournament victory in Braun's ten years when the Eagles defeated Duke. Two days later, they gave Connecticut a strong push before going down in defeat. All of this came on the heels of MAC regular-season and tournament championships.

Guard: Earl Boykins is often mistaken for the ball boy. But this diminutive point guard (5'7") is a scorer whose fearless approach sets the tone for the Eagles. Now that his backcourt partner, leading scorer Brian Tolbert, has moved on, Boykins will look to create more offense for himself. Look for Derrick Dial to slide down from small forward to Tolbert's vacant spot. Dial did an admirable job while forced to play out of position last year. An excellent defender, he also has a knack for scoring key baskets. Junior Timi Berkovitch may see more action, too.

Forward: Torrey Mills served as Dial's understudy, and this jack-of-all-trades could move into the starting lineup. A solid defender who is capable of adding to his scoring average, he has a nice shooting touch. Opposite Mills will be returning starter James Head. Head signed with Iowa coming out of high school, and last year he did the dirty work of rebounding and shutting down the foe's top inside scorer. The junior now should receive a few offensive looks, too. Junior Jon Zajac is in reserve.

Center: Theron Wilson gave the Eagles a shot-blocking dimension that won't be duplicated by anyone on the present roster. Junior Mick Pennisi, a native of Australia, moves into the post with a nice offensive game. He is complemented by the athletic but raw Nkechi Ezugwu, 6'8".

Analysis: Few teams repeat in the balanced MAC. Yet the Eagles are strong enough to turn the trick if Dial, Head, and Mills step forward with more offense. Boykins will keep things exciting.

1996-97 ROSTER

	POS	HT	YR	FGP	FTP	3-PT	RPG	APG	PPG
Earl Boykins	G	5'7"	Jr.	.432	.804	23/75	2.3	5.8	15.5
Derrick Dial	G/F	6'4"	Jr.	.485	.700	47/127	5.7	2.0	13.7
James Head	G/F	6'7"	Jr.	.551	.463	6/25	6.4	1.2	6.6
Torrey Mills	G/F	6'6"	Sr.	.558	.623	4/12	2.5	1.0	5.7
Jon Zajac	F	6'7"	Jr.	.468	.528	1/7	3.1	0.7	3.7
Nkechi Ezugwu	C/F	6'8"	Jr.	.530	.397	0/0	3.5	0.1	3.6
Timi Berkovitch	G	6'4"	Jr.	.417	.750	16/40	0.7	0.7	2.4
Mick Pennisi	F/C	6'9"	Jr.	.424	.545	3/6	1.2	0.2	1.3
Todd Beeten	G	6'2"	So.	.143	.765	0/1	0.1	0.4	0.9
Charlie Eibeler	G	6'4"	Jr.	.174	.500	3/14	0.2	0.1	0.8
Dionte Blevins	G/F	6'3"	Fr.	—	—	—	—	—	—
Cory Tarrent	G	6'4"	Fr.	—	—	—	—	—	—

FLORIDA STATE

Conference: Atlantic Coast   **1995-96 NCAAs/NIT:** DNP
1995-96: 13-14, 8th ACC   **Coach:** Pat Kennedy (306-179)

Opening Line: Little went right for the Seminoles in 1995-96. An early-season blowout loss to Connecticut in Tallahassee seemed to set the tone for an entire season. Coach Kennedy was suspended for a game by his athletic director for poor on-court conduct, and FSU was shut out of the postseason for a third consecutive season.

Guard: While Kennedy has a plethora of talented guards, he has none that can be accurately described as a playmaker. Junior LaMarr Greer offers good court vision and post-up ability but struggles to defend quicker points. James Collins is an explosive scorer with a pro future. However, he is no distributor of the basketball. It may be left to a freshman, 6'5" Devonaire Deas, to take command.

Forward: Randell Jackson and Corey Louis were high school All-Americans who arrived with impressive clip files. Neither has dominated as many thought they would, and consistency has been hard to come by. Now a junior, Louis brings a world of tools to the table. He must put forth effort each night. Jackson, 6'11", is not muscular enough to thrive at power forward or center but not agile enough to check small forwards. His potential, though, is awesome. He just needs to bulk up a bit. Sophomore Geoff Brower earns time due to his affinity for helping out with the nasty chores.

Center: Powerful Kirk Luchman is slow afoot and a limited defender. Yet his willingness to rough it up inside makes him a valued commodity because neither Jackson nor Louis is a power player.

Analysis: Kennedy is undeniably on the hot seat. Without a return to the NCAA Tournament, his job could well be in jeopardy. Fortunately for him, there is a passel of unrefined talent that needs only to be focused on improvement to make that leap into the field of 64.

1996-97 ROSTER

	POS	HT	YR	FGP	FTP	3-PT	RPG	APG	PPG
James Collins	G	6'4"	Sr.	.417	.675	69/199	4.5	3.2	18.3
Randell Jackson	F	6'11"	So.	.500	.632	4/14	5.3	0.5	9.5
LaMarr Greer	G	6'5"	Jr.	.448	.639	18/62	3.4	4.9	9.4
Corey Louis	F	6'9"	Jr.	.424	.627	0/0	6.5	0.5	9.3
Kirk Luchman	F/C	6'10"	Sr.	.626	.688	0/0	6.4	0.8	9.2
Geoff Brower	G	6'4"	So.	.436	.706	27/71	1.7	1.2	6.7
Kelvin McClendon	G	6'5"	Sr.	.321	.467	2/6	2.1	0.3	3.0
Gentry Sparks	F	6'8"	Jr.	.475	.579	3/7	1.9	0.4	2.6
Devonaire Deas	G	6'5"	Fr.	—	—	—	—	—	—
Ron Hale	F	6'8"	Fr.	—	—	—	—	—	—
Kerry Thompson	G	6'1"	Jr.	—	—	—	—	—	—
Ronald Thompson	F	6'8"	Fr.	—	—	—	—	—	—

FRESNO STATE

Conference: Western Athletic   **1995-96 NIT:** 2-1
1995-96: 22-11, 3rd WAC   **Coach:** Jerry Tarkanian (625-122)

Opening Line: It did not take long for Tarkanian, the coach with the greatest winning percentage in college basketball history, to make his mark at his alma mater. The Bulldogs rebounded from a shellacking in the preseason National Invitation Tournament to become one of the top teams in the WAC. This was achieved with two key recruits—Terrance Roberson and Chris Herren—on the sidelines. Both are back, and Fresno looms as a Top 25 team.

Guard: Dominick Young, 5'10", and James Gray—both seniors this year—combined to form a potent backcourt last year, but one of them is destined to be displaced in the starting lineup. That's because Herren, a one-time McDonald's All-American who began his collegiate career at Boston College, is now eligible. He is a sharp passer and terrific long-range shooter. The only questions about him center on his maturity level and willingness to work.

Forward: Here's where Roberson would have been such a boost. The athletic wingman can operate on either the interior or the perimeter, and his tools are perfect for the up-tempo system favored by Tarkanian. If he steers clear of the kind of travails that marked his prep career in Michigan, he'll offer a huge boost. Also in the mix is accomplished 6'5" senior Kendric Brooks and 6'5" junior Darnell McCulloch. McCulloch is more of an interior presence, while Brooks is a big-time scorer who slashes to the goal and pours in 3s.

Center: Darrnaryl Stamps transferred, leaving the job to Rahsaan Smith and Khary Stanley, both 6'10". They each have size but don't mesh well into this style of play.

Analysis: Tarkanian made it clear when he went back to Fresno that he didn't go there to lose. He won't. This team is potent, and there are more reinforcements in the wings for 1997-98.

1996-97 ROSTER

	POS	HT	YR	FGP	FTP	3-PT	RPG	APG	PPG
Kendric Brooks	G/F	6'5"	Sr.	.416	.744	96/243	3.8	1.3	19.4
Dominick Young	G	5'10"	Sr.	.407	.718	120/316	3.3	6.6	18.2
Darnell McCulloch	F	6'5"	Jr.	.580	.591	2/28	6.9	1.0	11.3
Rahsaan Smith	C	6'10"	Sr.	.563	.376	0/0	7.2	0.4	10.5
James Gray	G	6'3"	Sr.	.436	.724	21/71	2.9	4.3	9.2
Khary Stanley	C	6'10"	Sr.	.500	.627	0/1	4.5	0.3	5.7
Gerrit Terdenge	F	6'10"	So.	.463	.765	6/16	2.2	0.7	2.7
Larry Abney	F	6'8"	So.	—	—	—	—	—	—
Daymond Forney	F	6'8"	Jr.	—	—	—	—	—	—
Chris Herren	G	6'3"	So.	—	—	—	—	—	—
Demetrius Porter	G	5'10"	Fr.	—	—	—	—	—	—
Terrance Roberson	F	6'7"	So.	—	—	—	—	—	—

GEORGETOWN

Conference: Big East   **1995-96 NCAAs:** 3-1
1995-96: 29-8, 1st Big East 7   **Coach:** John Thompson (553-208)

Opening Line: Riding the coattails of superstar guard Allen Iverson, Georgetown charged to the 1996 Big East Tournament final, where it fell when Connecticut's Ray Allen made a jumper with time running out. The Hoyas then advanced to the East Regional final for a showdown with Massachusetts. The Minutemen stifled Iverson and won 86-62. Iverson then gave up his final two seasons of eligibly to enter the NBA draft.

Guard: Thompson realizes it's impossible to replace Iverson. The entire offense was funneled through Iverson, and no one will have that kind of freedom in 1996-97. Joseph Touomou, 6'2", is likely to inherit Iverson's starting spot. Touomou has few of the offensive tools his predecessor possessed besides the defensive tenacity that is a Hoya trademark. Victor Page will be asked to provide more offense. Freshman Ed Sheffey, 6'0", is a playmaker who will see plenty of action at the point. Junior Jerry Nichols is a shooter, which means he can gain minutes.

Forward: Boubacar Aw, a 6'8" junior, provides defensive pressure and rebounding. A summer of workouts may have enhanced his limited offensive tools. Freshman Shamel Jones was a Top 100 prospect whose offensive tools are very promising. Rheese Gibson, 6'8", is another rookie, though a bit more raw than Jones. Seniors Godwin Owinje and Cheikh "Ya-Ya" Dia will see time as defensive specialists.

Center: Jahidi White came to Georgetown accompanied by lofty expectations but has not cracked the starting lineup until now. Weight has been an issue. White's size belies a soft shooting touch and quick feet. A key is keeping him out of foul trouble.

Analysis: You don't lose a talent like Iverson and not take a step down. The Hoyas won't be quite the powerhouse they were in 1995-96, but they won't fall too far out of contention.

1996-97 ROSTER

	POS	HT	YR	FGP	FTP	3-PT	RPG	APG	PPG
Victor Page	G	6'3"	So.	.404	.667	40/120	3.2	1.7	12.5
Jahidi White	F/C	6'9"	Jr.	.560	.483	0/0	3.7	0.1	4.9
Jerry Nichols	G	6'5"	Jr.	.379	.367	36/98	1.9	0.9	4.6
Boubacar Aw	F	6'8"	Jr.	.507	.417	0/0	3.0	1.1	4.5
Chiekh Dia	F/C	6'10"	Sr.	.533	.611	0/0	3.9	0.6	2.9
Daymond Jackson	G/F	6'4"	So.	.458	.360	1/8	1.8	0.6	2.5
Joseph Touomou	G	6'2"	So.	.341	.316	18/57	1.1	1.4	2.5
Godwin Owinje	F	6'8"	Sr.	.282	.538	1/11	1.9	0.2	1.2
Rheese Gibson	F	6'8"	Fr.	—	—	—	—	—	—
Shamel Jones	F/C	6'8"	Fr.	—	—	—	—	—	—
Shernard Long	G/F	6'4"	Fr.	—	—	—	—	—	—
Ed Sheffey	G	6'0"	Fr.	—	—	—	—	—	—

GEORGE WASHINGTON

Conference: Atlantic 10
1995-96: 21-8, T-1st A-10 West

1995-96 NCAAs: 0-1
Coach: Mike Jarvis (214-118)

Opening Line: The Colonials were all but discounted when Yinka Dare left school prematurely in 1994, yet they have prospered quite nicely in his absence. After a near miss in 1995, GW left no room for doubt in 1996. It was the only Atlantic 10 squad to defeat Massachusetts in the regular season, and only some shaky last-minute free-throw shooting kept it from downing Iowa in the NCAA Tournament.

Guard: It didn't take long for Shawnta Rogers to make an impact at GW. Though a mere 5'3", he was exactly the kind of orchestrator Jarvis sought. Full-court pressure is no longer a headache for the Colonials, and Rogers is a surprisingly good rebounder for a guy his size. It will be difficult to make up for the loss of Vaughn Jones's experience at the other guard spot. Moving into that gap is J.J. Brade, a 6'5" sophomore.

Forward: Kwame Evans was a three-year starter this young group depended on at crunch time. Sophomore Seco Camara, 6'5", is an athlete with a pleasant upside. He gets first crack at the small forward job. Junior Darin Green is also in the picture. The other forward post belongs to sophomore Yegor Mescheriakov, a native of Belarus. Excellent ball skills and an eye for the open man make him a valuable weapon.

Center: Junior Alexander Koul is a terrific post player with good hands and a soft touch. Much of the offense goes through him. When Koul needs a break, Jarvis looks to Ferdinand Williams, a 6'10" senior not afraid to foul.

Analysis: Playing in the shadow of UMass isn't easy. However, Jarvis and company have made the best of it. This is a national program in its own right. A couple of NCAA Tourney wins by GW would remind America that the Atlantic 10 is a lot more than just Massachusetts.

1996-97 ROSTER

	POS	HT	YR	FGP	FTP	3-PT	RPG	APG	PPG
Alexander Koul	C	7'1"	Jr.	.642	.665	0/0	7.8	0.8	14.9
Shawnta Rogers	G	5'3"	So.	.379	.794	28/78	4.7	6.5	10.5
Yegor Mescheriakov	F	6'8"	So.	.482	.742	7/19	4.6	1.3	9.7
J.J. Brade	G	6'5"	So.	.572	.617	0/0	3.4	1.9	8.0
Darin Green	F	6'5"	Jr.	.432	.735	12/33	2.2	0.9	5.0
Ferdinand Williams	C	6'10"	Sr.	.154	.577	0/0	1.5	0.1	0.8
Andrei Krivonos	G	6'3"	So.	.267	.800	3/8	0.5	0.2	0.6
Seco Camara	F	6'5"	So.	.118	.000	1/8	0.9	0.2	0.3
Francisco de Miranda	F	6'9"	Fr.	—	—	—	—	—	—
Patrick Ngongba	F	6'7"	Fr.	—	—	—	—	—	—
Jackson Payne	G	6'4"	Fr.	—	—	—	—	—	—
Kinte Smith	G	6'3"	Fr.	—	—	—	—	—	—

GEORGIA

Conference: Southeastern   **1995-96 NCAAs:** 2-1
1995-96: 21-10, 2nd SEC East   **Coach:** Tubby Smith (100-53)

Opening Line: Smith's magic touch followed him from Tulsa to his new post in Athens. For the third consecutive season, Smith guided a club to the regional semifinals of the NCAA Tournament. It was Georgia's deepest run since its 1983 trip to the Final Four. The only negative is that the squad was loaded with seniors, including all five starters.

Guard: Although they didn't start, sophomores Orlando "G.G." Smith (son of the coach), Ray Harrison, and Michael Chadwick gained critical experience in the NCAA Tournament. Smith spelled Katu Davis and proved an able quarterback for the offense. This year, he will be asked to score more often. Harrison, 6'3", is an athletic guard who can get into the lane or score from deep. Chadwick brings good height (6'4") and versatility to the backcourt. Freshman David Taylor rounds out the troops.

Forward: Gone are Shandon Anderson and Carlos Strong, two keys to last year's success. Smith went looking for immediate help at those two spots and wound up with three gifted junior college transfers: 6'9" Lorenzo Hall, 6'7" Devin Baker, and 6'7" Derrick Dukes. Those three have an edge on Badi Oliver, a 6'8" freshman. Sophomore Jon Nordin also gets a chance to show what he's got.

Center: Several Southern programs made a strong push for 7'1" Robb Dryden of Jacksonville, Florida. Though raw, Dryden possesses an enormous upside. In the beginning, he'll be asked to contribute where he can, specifically on the boards and near the basket. Juco transfer Eric DeYoung is also in this derby.

Analysis: Year two may prove to be a much greater test of Smith's mettle than year one. He is an excellent coach, however, and the newcomers are gifted. It is simply a matter of molding them into an effective unit without taking too many hits in the loss column.

1996-97 ROSTER

	POS	HT	YR	FGP	FTP	3-PT	RPG	APG	PPG
Ray Harrison	G	6'3"	So.	.430	.741	27/81	2.1	1.9	6.3
Michael Chadwick	G	6'4"	So.	.433	.409	14/45	1.7	0.5	3.5
G.G. Smith	G	5'11"	So.	.329	.526	18/61	0.8	0.9	3.0
Jon Nordin	F	6'8"	So.	.453	.714	1/5	1.9	0.2	2.8
Devin Baker	F	6'7"	Jr.	—	—	—	—	—	—
Eric DeYoung	C	7'0"	Jr.	—	—	—	—	—	—
Robb Dryden	C	7'1"	Fr.	—	—	—	—	—	—
Derrick Dukes	F	6'7"	Jr.	—	—	—	—	—	—
Lorenzo Hall	F/C	6'9"	Jr.	—	—	—	—	—	—
Adrian Jones	G	6'5"	Fr.	—	—	—	—	—	—
Badi Oliver	F	6'8"	Fr.	—	—	—	—	—	—
David Taylor	G	6'4"	Fr.	—	—	—	—	—	—

GEORGIA TECH

Conference: Atlantic Coast
1995-96: 24-12, 1st ACC

1995-96 NCAAs: 2-1
Coach: Bobby Cremins (398-242)

Opening Line: Last year was a season of renewal for the Yellow Jackets. Despite a sluggish November and December, Georgia Tech claimed its first-ever regular-season Atlantic Coast Conference crown. This put Tech back into the NCAA Tournament after a two-year hiatus. The Jackets advanced to the regional semifinals before falling.

Guard: Even though the program listed Stephon Marbury as a freshman, Cremins knew better. He spent most of his recruiting hours in search of a point guard because the consensus was that Marbury was destined to play only one year of college basketball. When that became a reality, Cremins signed 5'11" Kevin Morris. A gifted setup man, Morris will need more seasoning than Marbury did. Also gone is Drew Barry, the other backcourt starter. Sophomore Gary Saunders, a smooth shooter, is in line to step into that hole.

Forward: This is where Tech's strength lies. Juniors Matt Harpring and Michael Maddox form a terrific pair of college forwards. If Maddox gains the consistency Harpring has already demonstrated, the duo can achieve great things. Freshman Jon Babul, a Top 100 prospect, should be able to crack Cremins's tight playing rotation as the first big front-line player off the bench.

Center: Slender Eddie Elisma finally came into his own last winter. He upgraded his shaky free-throw shooting, made the occasional basket, and grew more comfortable in the warfare in the low post. This isn't his ideal position, but he is more than capable of manning it. Cremins likes 6'10" freshman Pablo Machado, though he figures to be brought along slowly.

Analysis: Marbury gave Georgia Tech the lift it needed. Now that he's gone, it's up to the front line to carry the load. Another ACC title is certainly in reach. Much depends on rookie Morris.

1996-97 ROSTER

	POS	HT	YR	FGP	FTP	3-PT	RPG	APG	PPG
Matt Harpring	F	6'7"	Jr.	.510	.762	66/154	8.1	2.2	18.6
Michael Maddox	F	6'8"	Jr.	.498	.653	29/68	4.7	1.1	9.2
Eddie Elisma	F	6'9"	Sr.	.639	.583	0/0	7.3	1.3	8.8
Gary Saunders	G	6'5"	So.	.441	.698	28/80	1.7	1.1	6.6
Bryan Brennan	G	6'4"	Jr.	.231	.500	1/4	0.2	0.0	0.6
Ajani Williams	F	6'7"	So.	.333	.000	0/0	0.5	0.3	0.5
Ryan Murphy	G	6'3"	Jr.	.333	.000	1/1	0.2	0.5	0.3
Ashley Kelly	F	6'6"	So.	.000	.000	0/0	0.3	0.0	0.0
Jon Babul	F	6'7"	Fr.	—	—	—	—	—	—
Jason Floyd	G/F	6'6"	Fr.	—	—	—	—	—	—
Pablo Machado	C/F	6'10"	Fr.	—	—	—	—	—	—
Kevin Morris	G	5'11"	Fr.	—	—	—	—	—	—

ILLINOIS

Conference: Big Ten
1995-96: 18-13, 9th Big Ten

1995-96 NIT: 0-1
Coach: Lon Kruger (237-185)

Opening Line: When the Fighting Illini defeated Duke at Cameron Indoor Stadium in December (the first non-conference team to do that in more than ten years), it appeared they were on their way to a strong season. However, an injury to star guard Kiwane Garris stymied Illinois, and the club never did climb above .500 in a subpar Big Ten. Coach Lou Henson retired at season's end, and Kruger was hired away from Florida.

Guard: If it seems like Garris has been in Champaign for a while, it's because he has. A starter from his first day on campus, Garris is the rare floor leader who is a threat from long range as well as on drives. Off guard Richard Keene has moved on, and the onus now falls on Bryant Notree, who must increase his production. The junior spent much of his time at small forward, but his size and tools give him the inside track to operate alongside Garris. Junior Kevin Turner is first off the bench.

Forward: Senior Jerry Hester and junior Jerry Gee simply must produce. Both were touted prepsters who have been tormented by inconsistency as collegians. Hester, 6'6", needs to upgrade his perimeter shooting. Gee has to be more of a physical presence on the glass than he's been to date. Freshmen Victor Chukwudebe, 6'7", and Fess Hawkins, 6'9", will push those two if they don't pick up the pace.

Center: Henson never enjoyed the luxury of a classic pivot. He instead relied on undersized athletic types. Chris Gandy, a 6'9" senior, fits that description. Lacking bulk, Gandy sometimes gets pushed around in the rugged Big Ten.

Analysis: This isn't an overwhelming supply of talent, but Kruger is an expert teacher and has sufficient ammunition to get the Illini back into the NCAA Tournament. His real test comes on the recruiting trails.

1996-97 ROSTER

	POS	HT	YR	FGP	FTP	3-PT	RPG	APG	PPG
Kiwane Garris	G	6'2"	Sr.	.373	.862	38/117	3.4	3.9	15.4
Jerry Hester	F	6'6"	Sr.	.455	.708	38/98	4.0	1.3	11.0
Bryant Notree	G	6'5"	Jr.	.515	.559	17/47	6.1	1.0	10.5
Jerry Gee	F	6'8"	Jr.	.509	.461	0/0	6.1	0.5	8.5
Chris Gandy	F/C	6'9"	Sr.	.469	.673	4/14	4.1	0.5	6.1
Matt Heldman	G	6'0"	Jr.	.417	.886	30/78	0.9	1.4	5.6
Kevin Turner	G	6'2"	Jr.	.361	.455	25/89	1.6	1.7	5.5
Brian Johnson	F	6'6"	Jr.	.500	.750	0/2	1.2	0.9	1.5
Herb Caldwell	F	6'8"	Sr.	.500	.700	0/0	0.6	0.1	0.9
Halim Abdullah	G	5'9"	Jr.	—	—	—	—	—	—
Victor Chukwudebe	F	6'7"	Fr.	—	—	—	—	—	—
Fess Hawkins	F/C	6'9"	Fr.	—	—	—	—	—	—

INDIANA

Conference: Big Ten   **1995-96 NCAAs:** 0-1
1995-96: 19-12, T-2nd Big Ten   **Coach:** Bob Knight (678-247)

Opening Line: Three seasons have passed since the Hoosiers last won a Big Ten title. In 1995-96, Indiana's offensive options were essentially limited to forward Brian Evans. Evans is gone, but a solid recruiting class along with some prominent holdovers should make the Hoosiers part of the Big Ten chase.

Guard: Juniors Neil Reed and Charlie Miller were viewed as impact recruits but have demonstrated their gifts only sporadically thus far. Miller must become a more reliable ball-handler and long-range shooting threat. Reed, a fine 3-point marksman, has to take better care of the basketball. Newcomer Mike Lewis, 6'3", can lend a hand. Sherron Wilkerson was dropped from the club when he was involved in an off-court incident with a former girlfriend. The decision—though laudable—created a hole in IU's lineup.

Forward: Coming up with someone to draw the kind of defensive attention Evans did will be difficult. The most reliable weapon the Hoosiers possess is Andrae Patterson, a 6'8" junior who has had his ups and downs. Dependable scoring is a must for him this time, however. Senior Haris Mujezinovic, 6'9", brings some scoring tools and a willingness to toil near the basket. It is imperative that he reduce his fouls, though. Miller will see plenty of time at small forward.

Center: Jason Collier, 7'0", was Indiana's primary recruiting target for good reason. He is being counted upon to step into the lineup immediately. Already he is more skilled than his predecessor, Todd Lindeman. Junior Richard Mandeville is available if Collier falters.

Analysis: Two consecutive first-round losses in the NCAA Tournament have the Hoosier faithful vexed. This year's squad appears to have the equipment to give Indiana another crack at the field of 64, but it is not the kind of unit that looms as a national title contender.

1996-97 ROSTER

	POS	HT	YR	FGP	FTP	3-PT	RPG	APG	PPG
Andrae Patterson	F	6'8"	Jr.	.486	.712	17/42	6.2	1.7	12.4
Neil Reed	G	6'2"	Jr.	.444	.778	34/78	2.8	4.8	10.8
Charlie Miller	F/G	6'7"	Jr.	.435	.692	8/32	4.9	2.3	9.0
Haris Mujezinovic	F/C	6'9"	Sr.	.589	.583	0/0	2.9	0.3	5.2
Richard Mandeville	C	7'0"	Jr.	.385	.833	2/5	2.3	0.5	2.2
Robbie Eggers	F	6'10"	Jr.	.476	.500	4/11	1.7	0.4	1.6
Chris Rowles	G	6'1"	Jr.	.357	.583	0/1	1.4	1.1	1.3
Jason Collier	C	7'0"	Fr.	—	—	—	—	—	—
A.J. Guyton	G	6'0"	Fr.	—	—	—	—	—	—
Luke Jimenez	G	6'3"	Fr.	—	—	—	—	—	—
Michael Lewis	G	6'3"	Fr.	—	—	—	—	—	—
Larry Richardson	F	6'8"	Fr.	—	—	—	—	—	—

IOWA STATE

Conference: Big 12   **1995-96 NCAAs:** 1-1
1995-96: 24-9, 2nd Big Eight   **Coach:** Tim Floyd (209-103)

Opening Line: After ISU lost the likes of seniors Fred Hoiberg, Loren Meyer, and Julius Michalik at the close of 1994-95, few anticipated that the Cyclones would be able to reach .500 last year. Yet this team responded with a school-record 24 wins and upset Kansas to win the Big Eight Conference championship.

Guard: The only significant holdover from the 1994-95 team, Jacy Holloway stepped forward with a strong season. As the point guard, Holloway focuses on driving the offense. He's not a scorer, but Floyd doesn't ask him to be. DeAndre Harris, a 6'0" junior college transfer, is expected to spell Holloway and provide a bit more offense from the point guard position. Off guard Kenny Pratt was among Big Eight leaders in scoring and steals last season.

Forward: The main attraction for the Cyclones is 6'3" senior Dedric Willoughby. The entire offense is funneled through this athletic wingman. Floyd believes he has found some help for Willoughby in 6'5" freshman Stevie Johnson. Johnson, who has a 38-inch vertical leap, was billed as the best recruit to sign with ISU since Jeff Grayer did so a decade ago. Senior Shawn Bankhead, 6'6", will see meaningful action at the power forward post. Brad Johnson, a 3-point specialist, may also play a role.

Center: Kelvin Cato, 6'11", became a reliable option in the middle last year. His major chore is rebounding, which he does well. Most of his offense comes off putbacks. Sophomore Tyler Peterson is the top backup.

Analysis: Floyd squeezed the maximum out of this team last year. Sound defense and a good dose of Willoughby provided the foundation for all that happened. A strong recruiting class should offer more athleticism, making ISU into a contender in the newly configured Big 12.

1996-97 ROSTER

	POS	HT	YR	FGP	FTP	3-PT	RPG	APG	PPG
Dedric Willoughby	G/F	6'3"	Sr.	.415	.793	88/261	4.2	2.5	20.5
Kenny Pratt	G/F	6'4"	Sr.	.466	.626	2/12	6.5	2.1	15.3
Kelvin Cato	C	6'11"	Sr.	.503	.640	0/0	7.7	0.6	9.6
Shawn Bankhead	F	6'6"	Sr.	.438	.699	0/1	3.0	1.2	7.7
Jacy Holloway	G	6'0"	Sr.	.344	.727	24/76	2.6	4.5	4.6
Klay Edwards	F	6'6"	So.	.576	.580	0/0	4.2	0.5	4.1
Tony Rampton	C	6'11"	So.	.295	.500	0/0	2.3	0.3	1.9
Tyler Peterson	C	7'0"	So.	.500	.857	0/0	0.8	0.0	1.5
DeAndre Harris	G	6'0"	Jr.	—	—	—	—	—	—
Brad Johnson	F	6'6"	Jr.	—	—	—	—	—	—
Stevie Johnson	F	6'5"	Fr.	—	—	—	—	—	—
Paul Shirley	F	6'8"	Fr.	—	—	—	—	—	—

KANSAS

Conference: Big 12   **1995-96 NCAAs:** 3-1
1995-96: 29-5, 1st Big Eight   **Coach:** Roy Williams (213-56)

Opening Line: Only a slip in the NCAA West Regional final against Syracuse last season prevented the Jayhawks from reaching the Final Four for the third time in Williams's eight years as a head coach. The 1995-96 season marked the seventh consecutive time Kansas won more than 25 games. It enters the new season as a consensus pick to be in Indianapolis for the Final Four next spring.

Guard: Few tandems offer the kind of skills seniors Jacque Vaughn and Jerod Haase do. Each plays hard and complements the other. Vaughn is the orchestrator, while Haase is the 3-point marksman who can ring up points in a hurry. Junior Billy Thomas is a reliable role-player off the bench, and 6'5" sophomore Ryan Robertson also doesn't hurt the club when he is on the floor.

Forward: Sophomore Paul Pierce is overshadowed by Vaughn, but Pierce is the Jayhawks' most dynamic performer. A bit more assertiveness at the offensive end would benefit him. At power forward, Raef LaFrentz brings a nifty touch around the goal and willingness to scrap on the boards. In reserve, Roy Williams can turn to energetic rebounder B.J. Williams or 6'9" T.J. Pugh.

Center: Scot Pollard is truly a top center. His numbers aren't overwhelming, but he can score with either hand and has a nice jump hook. Pugh is on hand to provide a solid ten minutes or so of relief per night.

Analysis: For all of the success KU has enjoyed under Williams, this could be the first time it enters the season as a consensus pick to win the national championship. Certainly all of the ingredients are in place. If the outside shooting improves and Pierce becomes the star his skills suggest he can be, this unit can claim the trophy.

1996-97 ROSTER

	POS	HT	YR	FGP	FTP	3-PT	RPG	APG	PPG
Raef LaFrentz	F	6'11"	Jr.	.543	.661	2/7	8.2	0.4	13.4
Paul Pierce	F	6'6"	So.	.419	.606	35/115	5.3	1.8	11.9
Jacque Vaughn	G	6'1"	Sr.	.482	.695	39/92	3.1	6.6	10.9
Jerod Haase	G	6'3"	Sr.	.356	.750	55/188	3.6	3.6	10.8
Scot Pollard	C	6'10"	Sr.	.564	.636	0/0	7.4	0.3	10.1
B.J. Williams	F	6'8"	Sr.	.485	.673	0/0	3.9	0.4	4.8
Billy Thomas	G/F	6'4"	Jr.	.358	.714	42/125	1.5	0.6	4.7
Ryan Robertson	G	6'5"	So.	.488	.770	19/42	1.3	0.9	4.3
T.J. Pugh	F	6'9"	So.	.461	.492	4/9	2.3	0.2	3.4
Steve Ransom	F	6'5"	Sr.	.300	.700	0/1	0.4	0.1	0.7
Nicky Bradford	G/F	6'5"	Fr.	—	—	—	—	—	—
Travis Williams	C	7'0"	So.	—	—	—	—	—	—

KENTUCKY

Conference: Southeastern
1995-96: 34-2, 1st SEC East

1995-96 NCAAs: 6-0
Coach: Rick Pitino (317-119)

Opening Line: Pegged as the preseason No. 1 team in the land by every major wire service and publication, the Wildcats delivered a national championship in April. Kentucky lost only twice along the way—to Massachusetts at the Great Eight in Auburn Hills, Michigan, and to Mississippi State in the finals of the SEC Tournament. Both of those clubs also reached the Final Four.

Guard: If the Wildcats had a go-to man in their championship year, it was Tony Delk. His clutch shooting won't be easily duplicated. Senior Anthony Epps, who keeps mistakes to a minimum, gets the starting nod at point guard. Sophomore Wayne Turner, 6'2", is a man to watch. He is a terrific ball-handler with outstanding speed. Senior Jeff Sheppard plays at a fevered pitch and can rain down 3s when hot.

Forward: No question, the early exit of Antoine Walker was both unexpected and unwanted. This was to have been the marquee name on the Wildcat roster this winter. Yet it isn't as if the 'Cats are devoid of talent. Ron Mercer, 6'7", is a star in waiting at small forward. Derek Anderson will work there and in the backcourt, and he was a star earlier in his career at Ohio State. Senior Jared Prickett returns from a medical redshirt to contribute at power forward, and freshman Jamaal Magloire could be a future star.

Center: Three untested youngsters figure to share this spot. Sophomores Nazr Mohammed and Oliver Simmons saw little action as freshmen, stuck behind Walter McCarty and Mark Pope. Mohammed has more size, but Simmons has more skill.

Analysis: The loss of Walker was a blow, but it also provides a release valve of sorts—now Kentucky doesn't figure to be an overwhelming pick to repeat. Make no mistake, however; there's ample equipment in place to make a repeat a reality.

1996-97 ROSTER

	POS	HT	YR	FGP	FTP	3-PT	RPG	APG	PPG
Derek Anderson	G/F	6'4"	Sr.	.509	.784	23/59	3.4	2.4	9.4
Ron Mercer	G/F	6'7"	So.	.457	.785	23/69	2.9	1.4	8.0
Anthony Epps	G	6'2"	Sr.	.429	.817	43/105	3.1	4.9	6.7
Jeff Sheppard	G	6'3"	Sr.	.520	.621	22/44	2.1	1.9	5.5
Wayne Turner	G	6'2"	So.	.533	.625	1/4	1.5	1.6	4.5
Jared Prickett	F	6'9"	Sr.	.500	.714	0/1	1.6	0.6	3.4
Allen Edwards	G	6'5"	Jr.	.463	.739	7/23	1.1	1.2	3.3
Nazr Mohammed	C	6'10"	So.	.448	.458	0/0	1.5	0.2	2.3
Oliver Simmons	F/C	6'8"	So.	.481	.556	1/1	1.1	0.1	1.8
Cameron Mills	G	6'3"	Jr.	.400	1.00	0/1	0.3	0.1	0.9
Jamaal Magloire	C	6'10"	Fr.	—	—	—	—	—	—

LOUISVILLE

Conference: Conference USA
1995-96: 22-12, 2nd C-USA White

1995-96 NCAAs: 2-1
Coach: Denny Crum (587-224)

Opening Line: Crum said he was as pleased with his 1995-96 team as any he had coached. Indeed, Louisville got by without most of its front line for most of the year. Jason Osborne and Alex Sanders never played a minute due to academic woes, and center Samaki Walker missed half the season due to an NCAA investigation. Yet Louisville persevered and nearly defeated Wake Forest in the Midwest Regional semifinal of the NCAA Tourney.

Guard: Louisville lost some important players but not the most significant performer—DeJuan Wheat. This 6'0" senior is the man who makes it all go for the Cardinals. His excellent perimeter skills make him a huge riddle for the opposition. His sidekick, Tick Rogers, is gone, but returning after missing most of last year is swingman Eric Johnson, who started 21 games in 1994-95.

Forward: Swingman Alvin Sims is the kind of gritty worker coaches yearn for. He contributes rebounds, tough defense, and important baskets. Damion Dantzler, 6'7", is a bit thin to play power forward and not an accomplished enough shooter for small forward, yet he does plenty of little things. Sanders could be a powerful presence at the four spot. Freshmen Jeff McKinley and Nate Johnson are promising small forwards.

Center: Beau Zach Smith was viewed as nothing more than a mop-up man for Samaki Walker prior to 1995-96. Yet when Walker was out, it was Smith who kept the Cardinals on track. He is not a great scorer, nor is he very quick. But he has a knack for getting to the right spot at the right time.

Analysis: Crum is convinced that the Cards could have made a run at a national title in 1995-96 had off-court matters not intervened. This year's group is not quite ready for that assignment, but a 25-win campaign is within reach.

1996-97 ROSTER

	POS	HT	YR	FGP	FTP	3-PT	RPG	APG	PPG
DeJuan Wheat	G	6'0"	Sr.	.451	.731	78/222	3.4	3.9	17.7
Alvin Sims	G/F	6'4"	Sr.	.520	.590	18/56	5.0	2.6	11.9
Eric Johnson	F/G	6'3"	So.	.636	.500	2/5	3.0	0.0	8.5
Damion Dantzler	F	6'7"	Jr.	.461	.598	17/69	5.0	1.1	7.6
B.J. Flynn	G	6'2"	Sr.	.493	.739	6/18	1.2	1.4	4.4
Beau Zach Smith	C	6'8"	Sr.	.505	.656	0/0	3.0	0.6	3.3
Charlie Taylor	G	5'9"	So.	.344	.619	1/11	0.9	1.4	2.1
Jerry Johnson	G	6'3"	Fr.	—	—	—	—	—	—
Nate Johnson	F	6'6"	Fr.	—	—	—	—	—	—
Jeff McKinley	G/F	6'5"	Fr.	—	—	—	—	—	—
Alex Sanders	F/C	6'7"	So.	—	—	—	—	—	—
Tony Williams	F/G	6'7"	Fr.	—	—	—	—	—	—

MARQUETTE

Conference: Conference USA
1995-96: 23-8, 2nd C-USA Blue

1995-96 NCAAs: 1-1
Coach: Mike Deane (210-97)

Opening Line: A trip to the finals of the NIT in 1995 gave Marquette a strong push heading into 1995-96. The Eagles were close on the heels of Cincinnati in Conference USA during the regular season and nearly upended the Bearcats in the final game of the league tournament. Arkansas eliminated the Eagles from the NCAA Tournament in the second round.

Guard: The tandem of Aaron Hutchins, a 5'10" junior, and Anthony Pieper, a 6'3" senior, receives little hype beyond the Milwaukee city limits. Yet these two are invaluable to Deane. Both are capable of knocking down the long-range 3 and don't need to be in the open court to score. Newcomer Marcus West, 5'10", will back up Hutchins. Meanwhile, 6'1" John Cliff and 6'5" Bart Miller can earn spots in the rotation with solid practice work.

Forward: This is where Deane must do some repair work. Two workhorses, Amal McCaskill and Roney Eford, are gone. This duo was part of the foundation of success laid by former coach Kevin O'Neill. Picking up the slack are seniors Chris Crawford, a double-digit scorer last year, and Faisal Abraham. Freshman John Polonowski, 6'8", will earn some minutes.

Center: Junior Abel Joseph isn't a true center, but he may have to be stationed there if sophomore Jarrod Lovette, 6'10", isn't ready for full-time duty. Junior Richard Shaw, 6'11", is another possibility. Deane would prefer to use one of the latter two in the post so he can keep Joseph at forward, but that may not be possible.

Analysis: Not many are familiar with the individual components of the Marquette puzzle. More than most teams, the Marquette squad is a unit. That helps defray the loss of key figures like Eford and McCaskill. Of Conference USA rivals, only Cincinnati brings more weapons to the arena on game night than the Eagles do.

1996-97 ROSTER

	POS	HT	YR	FGP	FTP	3-PT	RPG	APG	PPG
Aaron Hutchins	G	5'10"	Jr.	.375	.849	71/192	3.8	6.9	14.0
Anthony Pieper	G	6'3"	Sr.	.414	.831	62/162	3.2	1.9	11.6
Chris Crawford	F	6'9"	Sr.	.421	.716	29/84	4.1	0.9	11.2
Faisal Abraham	F	6'7"	Sr.	.579	.561	0/0	5.0	0.3	4.7
Richard Shaw	F/C	6'11"	Jr.	.477	.568	0/1	2.3	0.3	2.9
Mike Bargen	G/F	6'7"	So.	.382	.455	7/24	1.0	0.6	1.8
Jarrod Lovette	C	6'10"	So.	.370	.611	0/1	1.6	0.2	1.6
John Cliff	G	6'1"	Fr.	—	—	—	—	—	—
Abel Joseph	F	6'9"	Jr.	—	—	—	—	—	—
Bart Miller	G/F	6'5"	Fr.	—	—	—	—	—	—
John Polonowski	F	6'8"	Fr.	—	—	—	—	—	—
Marcus West	G	5'10"	Jr.	—	—	—	—	—	—

MARYLAND

Conference: Atlantic Coast
1995-96: 17-13, T-4th ACC

1995-96 NCAAs: 0-1
Coach: Gary Williams (329-218)

Opening Line: The brief career of center Joe Smith turned out to be a good news/bad news proposition for Williams. Obviously, it was a boon to have the No. 1 pick in the 1995 NBA draft for two seasons. But Smith's departure robbed Williams of the key piece of the puzzle in 1995-96—the year targeted to be the pinnacle of his rebuilding job. Without Smith, the Terrapins always seemed a man short.

Guard: Duane Simpkins and Johnny Rhodes were the cornerstones of Williams's original rebuilding blueprint; however, the Terps' offense ran more smoothly when 6'0" sophomore Terrell Stokes was at the helm than when Simpkins directed the show. The loss of Rhodes will be harder to digest. Sarunas Jasikevicius, 6'4", did not see consistent action in his first two seasons. That changes now.

Forward: The Terps are set here. One spot belongs to 6'6" Keith Booth, the power forward in a small forward's body. If Booth can add scoring skills to supplement his defense and grit, Williams will have the team leader he needs. Sophomore Laron Profit is an athletic wingman who thrives in the open court. Brian Watkins, 6'9", transfers in from Notre Dame to give Maryland another proven scorer.

Center: Obinna Ekezie's game is replete with rough edges. Yet his 6'9" frame is powerful, and he owns a soft touch around the goal. Plus, he's a fast learner. Rodney Elliott, a 6'8" junior, is ready to fill in here or at power forward.

Analysis: There was considerable moaning when Maryland was spurned in its efforts to land a marquee recruit. That does not figure to be a mortal blow, however. The chemistry here should be better than it was a season ago, and there are enough weapons for this squad to make a push for postseason play.

1996-97 ROSTER

	POS	HT	YR	FGP	FTP	3-PT	RPG	APG	PPG
Keith Booth	F	6'6"	Sr.	.442	.757	7/34	7.8	2.4	15.3
Laron Profit	F/G	6'5"	So.	.482	.756	12/33	2.7	1.2	5.7
Rodney Elliott	F/C	6'8"	Jr.	.500	.692	8/24	3.1	0.4	4.9
Obinna Ekezie	F/C	6'9"	So.	.472	.550	0/0	3.7	0.3	4.5
Sarunas Jasikevicius	G	6'4"	Jr.	.427	.500	20/44	1.2	1.2	3.9
Terrell Stokes	G	6'0"	So.	.470	.635	5/11	1.3	2.8	3.3
Norman Fields	G	6'0"	So.	.286	.000	0/2	0.4	0.1	0.5
Matt Raydo	G	5'10"	Sr.	.250	.500	0/2	0.0	0.4	0.5
Matt Kovarik	G	6'4"	Jr.	.000	.500	0/0	0.4	0.6	0.4
Kelly Hite	G	6'2"	Fr.	—	—	—	—	—	—
Mike Mardesich	C	7'0"	Fr.	—	—	—	—	—	—
Brian Watkins	F	6'9"	So.	—	—	—	—	—	—

MASSACHUSETTS

Conference: Atlantic 10   **1995-96 NCAAs:** 4-1
1995-96: 35-2, 1st A-10 East   **Coach:** James Flint (0-0)

Opening Line: Only Kentucky has more wins over the last five seasons than the Minutemen. Sparked by consensus national Player of the Year Marcus Camby, UMass did not lose its first game until George Washington downed it on February 24. The Minutemen spent eight weeks as the No. 1 team in the country. At season's end, Camby departed for the NBA along with ex-coach John Calipari.

Guard: Entering 1995-96, this area was labeled a weakness. Yet Edgar Padilla and Carmelo Travieso stepped up to make it a strength. Now, these two battle-tested seniors are the backbone of this program. They should get more rest this year, as Charlton Clarke, 6'3", appears ready to bounce back from an injury-riddled freshman campaign. Clarke can play either guard spot. Monty Mack, a 6'3" freshman, also can expect to see spot duty.

Forward: The departed Dana Dingle and Donta Bright were quiet individuals often lost in Camby's shadow. But the work of both men was vital and won't be easily replaced. Moving into a more prominent role is 6'7" senior forward Tyrone Weeks. A physical rebounder, Weeks is an improved defender and owns a decent scoring touch. Mike Babul, a 6'6" freshman, can stroke the long jumper and will take a charge. Another rookie, 6'5" Winston Smith, looms as Weeks's understudy.

Center: Inus Norville saw limited minutes in support of Camby. Now the 6'8" junior is in position to take charge of the center spot. A bit more confidence in himself would be a big boost. Keep an eye on 6'10" sophomore Lari Ketner. The Philadelphian sat out 1995-96, but the coaches are intrigued by his athletic gifts.

Analysis: Camby's exit was not unexpected, so the Minutemen are prepared for life after their All-American. More balance and reliance on defense and intensity will keep this program among the nation's best.

1996-97 ROSTER

	POS	HT	YR	FGP	FTP	3-PT	RPG	APG	PPG
Carmelo Travieso	G	6'2"	Sr.	.426	.636	104/258	3.2	2.1	12.6
Edgar Padilla	G	6'2"	Sr.	.416	.708	41/120	3.5	6.7	8.9
Tyrone Weeks	F	6'7"	Sr.	.464	.700	0/0	5.2	0.4	5.8
Inus Norville	F	6'8"	Jr.	.508	.564	1/3	2.1	0.0	2.4
Charlton Clarke	G	6'3"	So.	.324	.429	1/16	0.5	0.7	1.4
Ross Burns	G	6'3"	So.	.500	.500	0/1	0.1	0.2	0.4
Mike Babul	F	6'6"	Fr.	—	—	—	—	—	—
Ajmal Basit	C	6'9"	Fr.	—	—	—	—	—	—
Lari Ketner	C	6'10"	So.	—	—	—	—	—	—
Chris Kirkland	F	6'6"	Fr.	—	—	—	—	—	—
Monty Mack	G	6'3"	Fr.	—	—	—	—	—	—
Winston Smith	F	6'5"	Fr.	—	—	—	—	—	—

MEMPHIS

Conference: Conference USA
1995-96: 22-8, 1st C-USA White

1995-96 NCAAs: 0-1
Coach: Larry Finch (204-115)

Opening Line: A season that began with much promise—the Tigers were ranked as high as No. 3 in the country in early January—ended with a thud when Memphis fell to upstart Drexel in the opening round of the NCAA Tournament. Finch endured widespread criticism, and the blow became worse when center Lorenzen Wright left for the NBA.

Guard: Mingo Johnson completed his eligibility, and his firepower alongside Chris Garner will be missed. Attempting to step into that void is John Gales, a 6'1" senior whose opportunities were limited in his first year with the program in 1995-96. Two years ago, Gales averaged 20.9 PPG for Motlow State Community College.

Forward: One frontcourt spot is set in stone, while the other remains up for grabs. Senior Cedric Henderson is the anchor. No Tiger has more experience than this man, and he must be consistent in his effort so the inexperienced players on the club have a lead to follow. The unexpected transfer of small forward Dorian Davis means Henderson will see even more action. In the mix to establish themselves at power forward are 6'10" senior Chad Allen and 6'4" sophomore Damonn Fuller. Allen possesses the most offensive tools of the two, and Fuller the most determination.

Center: This is where it gets tricky for Finch. In the other vacated spots, he can turn to experienced players or valued prospects as replacements. No such luck in the lane. The top option is Allen, and at less than 200 pounds, he gets sand kicked in his face on a regular basis. Newcomer Michael Brittian will get a look.

Analysis: It was a harsh spring in Memphis for the Tigers. First came the NCAA loss and then Wright's exit. There's talent present, though not enough to keep Memphis in the Top 25.

1996-97 ROSTER

	POS	HT	YR	FGP	FTP	3-PT	RPG	APG	PPG
Cedric Henderson	F	6'6"	Sr.	.492	.613	30/77	4.0	1.3	12.6
Chris Garner	G	5'10"	Sr.	.458	.565	18/49	3.5	5.7	7.6
Chad Allen	F/C	6'10"	Sr.	.510	.667	0/0	3.6	0.5	5.0
John Gales	G	6'1"	Sr.	.296	.450	14/56	1.0	0.6	2.7
Larry Finch	G	5'9"	So.	.267	.500	4/11	0.6	0.2	1.4
Cody Hopson	G/F	6'5"	Sr.	.160	.667	1/12	1.1	0.3	0.9
Damonn Fuller	F	6'4"	So.	.000	.333	0/0	0.4	0.0	0.3
Harry Allen	G	6'3"	Jr.	—	—	—	—	—	—
Michael Brittian	C	6'9"	Jr.	—	—	—	—	—	—
Keldrick Bradford	F	6'4"	Jr.	—	—	—	—	—	—
Demond Lyles	G	5'11"	Jr.	—	—	—	—	—	—
Josh Steinthal	G	6'4"	Fr.	—	—	—	—	—	—

MIAMI OF FLORIDA

Conference: Big East
1995-96: 15-13, 4th Big East 7

1995-96 NCAAs/NIT: DNP
Coach: Leonard Hamilton (120-169)

Opening Line: The road has not been kind to the Hurricanes during Hamilton's six seasons. It was a problem again in 1995-96 as Miami recorded only two triumphs away from home—at Florida Atlantic and at Notre Dame. Meanwhile, the Hurricanes won 12 of 16 played in Miami Arena and nearly upset Villanova there.

Guard: Kevin Norris directs the offense, and he's a competent distributor. However, he is not much of a scoring threat, and teams know to sag off him because he's not a good long-range shooter. Senior guard Clifton Clark is an athletic defender who also struggles to score from deep. Senior Steve Frazier offers a lift off the bench, although he isn't the force he was prior to injuries. Lucas Barnes, a 6'6" freshman, could be the scoring answer at off guard. Vernon Jennings, a combination guard from Maine Central Institute, will also be in the mix.

Forward: Tim James did not make a start for the Hurricanes last year but was the team's second-leading scorer. This versatile sophomore has the equipment to be a force. Jermaine Walker, a 6'7" freshman, also offers all kinds of athletic skills. Senior Alex Fraser is the incumbent at power forward, and he relies upon rebounding and defensive intensity. Freshman Mario Bland, 6'7", is another option.

Center: Steve Rich completed his eligibility just as he seemed to be coming into his own. Hamilton may have to slide Fraser into this spot. There are a glut of forwards on this roster, but only raw seven-footer Will Davis qualifies as a natural pivot.

Analysis: Hamilton's 1996 recruiting class was listed among the best in America. He is stockpiling a collection of gifted athletes. If he is willing to turn them loose—and not rely on a plodding offense—this could be a fun team to watch.

1996-97 ROSTER

	POS	HT	YR	FGP	FTP	3-PT	RPG	APG	PPG
Tim James	F	6'7"	So.	.529	.541	2/6	5.4	0.4	10.1
Steve Frazier	G	6'2"	Sr.	.351	.681	27/80	3.3	2.0	7.0
Alex Fraser	F	6'8"	Sr.	.486	.545	0/1	3.9	0.6	6.1
Clifton Clark	G/F	6'4"	Sr.	.409	.631	5/20	2.7	1.1	6.0
Kevin Norris	G	5'9"	Jr.	.327	.721	23/65	1.0	4.0	5.9
Torey McCormick	G	6'3"	Sr.	.316	.938	14/47	1.0	1.0	2.6
Will Davis	C	7'0"	Sr.	.414	.550	0/0	1.3	0.1	2.1
Nick Donovan	F	6'11"	So.	.357	.400	0/1	1.0	0.0	1.8
Lucas Barnes	G/F	6'6"	Fr.	—	—	—	—	—	—
Mario Bland	F	6'7"	Fr.	—	—	—	—	—	—
Vernon Jennings	G/F	6'3"	Fr.	—	—	—	—	—	—
Jermaine Walker	F	6'7"	Fr.	—	—	—	—	—	—

MICHIGAN

Conference: Big Ten
1995-96: 20-12, T-5th Big Ten

1995-96 NCAAs: 0-1
Coach: Steve Fisher (160-71)

Opening Line: Finally rid of the last vestiges of the Fab Five era, Michigan hoped to begin anew last season. In some respects, it did. However, the Wolverines did not win a Big Ten title for the tenth straight year, and they were bounced from the NCAA Tournament in the opening round for the second consecutive year.

Guard: The point guard spot has been a problem. Junior Travis Conlan, 6'5", is a competent defender, but teams love to pressure him. Fisher signed Brandun Hughes, 6'0", from junior college to run the point. If the Wolverines were that sold on Hughes, however, why did they pursue Michigan prepster Mateen Cleaves with such ardor? Louis Bullock's shooting is of critical importance at the other guard position.

Forward: The transfer of Willie Mitchell and Makhtar Ndiaye leaves the Wolverines with some holes. Much weight rests on the shoulders of Jerod Ward, a 6'9" junior who was rated as the No. 1 prep player in America three years ago. His first two seasons have been a major letdown. Maurice Taylor, 6'9", is a powerful rebounder who needs only to apply discipline to his work habits. Sophomore Albert White is a dynamic athlete who will see plenty of action.

Center: Maceo Baston is something of an odd fit. This thin youngster is a fine shot-blocker, but his lack of muscle is a problem inside. Robert Traylor, 6'8", could be a superior pivot if he loses some of his bulk. As it is now, he can't go longer than 20 minutes a night due to poor conditioning.

Analysis: Michigan has seen its share of defections and underachievement in the years since Chris Webber, Jalen Rose, Juwan Howard, and the rest left the scene. This team is talented enough to reclaim the spotlight, but it may not be disciplined enough to do so.

1996-97 ROSTER

	POS	HT	YR	FGP	FTP	3-PT	RPG	APG	PPG
Maurice Taylor	F/C	6'9"	Jr.	.511	.592	1/4	7.0	1.3	14.0
Louis Bullock	G	6'2"	So.	.398	.845	70/182	3.0	1.7	13.5
Maceo Baston	F/C	6'9"	Jr.	.682	.678	0/1	6.6	0.6	11.7
Robert Traylor	C	6'8"	So.	.554	.548	0/0	5.9	0.5	9.0
Albert White	F/G	6'6"	So.	.398	.713	11/49	4.7	1.2	9.0
Jerod Ward	F/G	6'9"	Jr.	.317	.455	5/30	4.8	1.0	7.2
Travis Conlan	G	6'5"	Jr.	.326	.608	23/74	2.9	4.8	4.5
Ron Oliver	G	6'0"	So.	.200	.556	0/3	0.3	0.1	0.4
Ryan DeKuiper	G/F	6'3"	Sr.	.500	.500	1/2	0.4	0.1	0.6
Brandun Hughes	G	6'0"	Jr.	—	—	—	—	—	—
Erik Szyndlar	F	6'6"	So.	—	—	—	—	—	—
Peter Vignier	C	6'11"	Fr.	—	—	—	—	—	—

MISSISSIPPI STATE

Conference: Southeastern
1995-96: 26-8, 1st SEC West

1995-96 NCAAs: 4-1
Coach: Richard Williams (164-130)

Opening Line: After several years of unheralded success, Mississippi State caught America's attention in 1995-96. First, it stunned No. 1-ranked Kentucky in the final of the SEC Tournament. Next, it downed both Connecticut and Cincinnati to capture the Southeast Regional portion of the NCAA Tournament and reach its first Final Four.

Guard: The Bulldog guards played one of their poorest games of the season at the most inopportune moment of the year—against Syracuse at the Final Four. Against a simple two-three zone, MSU committed numerous turnovers. Part of the problem is that 6'3" Marcus Bullard is as much a scorer as he is a point guard. However, Bullard is gritty and should improve. Partner Darryl Wilson, the top 3-point threat on the roster, is gone. The burden falls on freshmen T.J. Billups and Derrick Jones. Sophomore Bart Hyche, 5'11", backs up Bullard at the point.

Forward: Dontae Jones gave MSU a lift for one year but then left for the NBA. Terry Lawyer, 6'8", is expected to step into Jones's shoes. He is quick and can make medium-range jumpers. Junior Whit Hughes, 6'5", is a grinder with a reputation for solid defense and hustle. Sophomore Tyrone Washington has a chance to use his 250 pounds and good height to take over the power forward position.

Center: Freshman Quentin Smith is a decorated prepster with good hands and foot movement. With Eric Dampier gone to the pros, there's no time for a smooth transition. Smith, as well as Washington, will have to be force-fed.

Analysis: Of the 1996 Final Four participants, MSU is probably the least equipped on paper to return to that event. The subtraction of its top three players is a large blow, but there is ability here. How fast it develops will dictate what kind of tumble the Bulldogs take.

1996-97 ROSTER

	POS	HT	YR	FGP	FTP	3-PT	RPG	APG	PPG
Marcus Bullard	G	6'3"	Jr.	.460	.654	70/172	3.9	5.1	12.1
Bart Hyche	G	5'11"	So.	.447	.840	18/42	1.0	0.9	3.5
Whit Hughes	F	6'5"	Jr.	.385	.782	2/17	2.5	1.5	2.5
Tyrone Washington	C/F	6'10"	So.	.404	.600	0/0	2.1	0.1	1.9
McKie Edmonson	G	6'0"	Jr.	.500	1.00	2/5	0.1	0.1	1.6
T.J. Billups	G	6'4"	Fr.	—	—	—	—	—	—
Derrick Jones	G	6'4"	Fr.	—	—	—	—	—	—
Terry Lawyer	F	6'8"	Fr.	—	—	—	—	—	—
Trey Moore	G	6'4"	Jr.	—	—	—	—	—	—
Early Smith	C/F	6'8"	Fr.	—	—	—	—	—	—
Quentin Smith	F/C	6'9"	Fr.	—	—	—	—	—	—
Horatio Webster	F	6'7"	Jr.	—	—	—	—	—	—

MISSOURI

Conference: Big 12
1995-96: 18-15, 6th Big Eight

1995-96 NIT: 1-1
Coach: Norm Stewart (678-334)

Opening Line: It is difficult to characterize 1995-96 as anything less than a disappointment for Missouri. The Tigers were ranked No. 15 in the nation in *Basketball Times'* preseason poll but never achieved that kind of stature. In the end, Mizzou had to settle for the NIT.

Guard: This is an area of concern. Julian Winfield, one of the few who played up to expectations in 1995-96, completed his eligibility. His potential heir, 6'2" Kendrick Moore, transferred. That leaves the Tiger backcourt in the hands of 6'1" senior Jason Sutherland, an aggressive sort who makes free throws; 6'4" senior Corey Tate, a versatile defender and scorer; and Danny Allouche, a sophomore with 3-point shooting skills and plenty of international experience. Stewart needs his guards to take better shots and do more to find the open man inside.

Forward: Kelly Thames was not the same player he was prior to tearing an anterior cruciate ligament in his knee before the 1994-95 season. Upon returning to the lineup, a more muscular but rusty Thames did not find the success he had when he was the Big Eight's Freshman of the Year in 1993-94. It's not hard to envision Thames back at full speed this year, though. Opposite Thames is Derek Grimm, a perimeter shooting threat at 6'10". Grimm isn't very gritty, though, and can be taken advantage of on defense.

Center: The touted Haley twins, Simeon and Sammie, have moved on. Stepping into the center spot will be untested sophomore Monte Hardge, a powerful 6'11" pivot, and freshman Tate Decker, also 6'11". Hardge was a decorated prepster who looks to have a solid future.

Analysis: The determination to erase the bad taste left by a disappointing 1995-96 season should fuel the Tigers in the new Big 12. Thames's progress is important, as he's the team's sole impact player.

1996-97 ROSTER

	POS	HT	YR	FGP	FTP	3-PT	RPG	APG	PPG
Jason Sutherland	G	6'1"	Sr.	.478	.877	69/148	2.0	1.6	14.0
Kelly Thames	F	6'8"	Jr.	.457	.773	3/14	5.3	2.3	12.7
Derek Grimm	F	6'10"	Sr.	.439	.885	41/104	5.1	2.9	8.7
Corey Tate	G/F	6'4"	Sr.	.540	.642	0/8	3.3	1.5	5.5
Danny Allouche	G	6'5"	So.	.355	.813	11/37	1.8	0.8	4.3
L. Dee Murdock	F	6'9"	So.	.543	.581	0/2	1.7	0.2	3.4
Monte Hardge	C	6'11"	So.	.439	.417	0/0	2.1	0.2	2.5
Dustin Reeve	F	6'10"	Sr.	1.00	.000	0/0	1.5	0.0	1.0
Tate Decker	F/C	6'11"	Fr.	—	—	—	—	—	—
Jeff Hafer	G	6'5"	Fr.	—	—	—	—	—	—
Tyron Lee	F/G	6'6"	Jr.	—	—	—	—	—	—
Didi Ray	G	5'10"	Jr.	—	—	—	—	—	—

NEVADA-LAS VEGAS

Conference: Western Athletic
1995-96: 10-16, 9th Big West

1995-96 NCAAs/NIT: DNP
Coach: Bill Bayno (10-16)

Opening Line: Since UNLV won its first-ever national championship in 1990, it has been a miserable decade for the Runnin' Rebels. They underwent NCAA inquiries, the ugly ouster of Jerry Tarkanian, the ill-fated Rollie Massimino era, and a decline to a spot in the bottom of the Big West. For the first time in five years, though, the momentum appears to have turned upward due to the great recruiting strides of second-year coach Bill Bayno.

Guard: This is one area that will look familiar to those who watched UNLV last year. Chancellor Davis, an ultra-quick penetrator, again gets the call at point guard. Though only 5'8", he brings the kind of speed Bayno wants in his up-tempo attack. Senior Jermaine Smith will see action at both guard spots. A good passer, he will try to pick it up on the scoring end. Senior Damian Smith and sophomore Ben Sanders are also in the picture at off guard.

Forward: The new faces figure to have an impact on the front line. Perhaps the most gifted newcomer is 6'10" Issiah Epps from Maine Central Institute. Epps was coveted by major programs and is an instant starter. His face-up skills allow him to play either forward spot. Donovan Stewart, a 6'5" freshman from Cheshire Academy in Connecticut, will also see time. Seniors Tony Lane and Warren Rosegreen are dependable veterans.

Center: Another recruiting prize is 6'11" Keon Clark, a junior college transfer. He is penciled in as the starter at center. Though not as potent a scoring weapon as Epps, he is a strong rebounder and willing defender. Holdover Eric Lee is around if Clark struggles.

Analysis: It may take some time to develop chemistry here, especially in a new conference. Still, few teams in America have upgraded their personnel as noticeably as UNLV has.

1996-97 ROSTER

	POS	HT	YR	FGP	FTP	3-PT	RPG	APG	PPG
Jermaine Smith	G	6'1"	Sr.	.407	.821	50/121	2.7	1.9	13.2
Warren Rosegreen	F	6'5"	Sr.	.542	.494	0/0	9.5	0.7	11.5
Tony Lane	F	6'7"	Sr.	.605	.546	0/0	5.1	0.6	10.9
Damian Smith	G	6'3"	Sr.	.316	.000	7/22	1.3	1.3	7.8
Eric Lee	C	6'10"	So.	.500	1.00	0/0	6.5	0.0	6.0
Chancellor Davis	G	5'8"	Sr.	.388	.731	12/38	2.0	3.4	5.0
Eddie Corbett	F/C	6'8"	Sr.	.500	.477	0/0	1.7	0.1	2.9
Ben Sanders	G	6'4"	So.	.600	.310	0/3	1.5	1.0	2.5
Kevin James	G	5'11"	Sr.	.305	.522	7/26	1.6	3.0	2.1
Keon Clark	C	6'11"	Jr.	—	—	—	—	—	—
Issiah Epps	C	6'10"	Fr.	—	—	—	—	—	—
Donovan Stewart	G	6'5"	Fr.	—	—	—	—	—	—

NEW MEXICO

Conference: Western Athletic
1995-96: 28-5, 2nd WAC

1995-96 NCAAs: 1-1
Coach: Dave Bliss (391-246)

Opening Line: A dip to the .500 level in 1994-95 was reversed in grand style last year as the Lobos returned to the NCAA Tournament. Yet the history books won't reflect the considerable hand-wringing that took place to get there. Most of the trouble centered on the eligibility of prize freshman Kenny Thomas. It took a court order to get Thomas on the hardwood.

Guard: Neither Charles Smith nor David Gibson is a marquee name. However, both are efficient, solid veterans. At 6'4", Smith is one of the WAC's finest guards. He hits the pull-up jumper and beats men with the dribble. Gibson is not a scorer. His job is to set up others, and he appeared to grow more comfortable in that role as the season progressed. Combination guard Kavossy Franklin relieves both men and can provide quick scores. Royce Olney can hit the 3.

Forward: Clayton Shields is a two-year starter who prefers the perimeter to crashing the boards inside. The arrival of Thomas allowed him to spend more time away from the shadow of the basket. Senior Greg Schornstein, 6'7", is a valued role-player. Schornstein manages to score garbage points off putbacks and other broken plays. Thomas may see more action at power forward now that the Lobos have several natural pivots on the roster.

Center: Thomas was awesome once the injunction permitted him to play (a controversy arose when the NCAA Clearinghouse ruled him ineligible). Yet he could give way in the middle to Ben Baum, a 6'11" transfer from Oklahoma State. Junior Chris Paddock, 7'0", is also available, and 7'1" Daniel Santiago could be a factor as well.

Analysis: Only one role-player was lost off the NCAA Tournament team, and Baum can pick up that slack. This unit is a threat to play on the 1997 NCAA Tournament's second weekend.

1996-97 ROSTER

	POS	HT	YR	FGP	FTP	3-PT	RPG	APG	PPG
Charles Smith	G	6'4"	Sr.	.460	.811	69/188	4.6	3.1	19.5
Kenny Thomas	F/C	6'9"	So.	.578	.709	0/3	7.8	1.6	14.7
Clayton Shields	F	6'8"	Jr.	.480	.655	67/164	6.5	1.5	14.5
Royce Olney	G	6'2"	Jr.	.483	.804	38/87	2.2	2.4	8.0
Greg Schornstein	F	6'7"	Sr.	.474	.645	35/83	3.8	2.5	7.6
David Gibson	G	6'2"	Jr.	.490	.585	4/29	3.1	3.6	6.3
Daniel Santiago	C	7'1"	Jr.	.706	.729	0/0	1.5	0.1	3.2
Kavossy Franklin	G	6'2"	Sr.	.273	.588	6/17	1.5	1.0	2.4
Chris Paddock	C	7'0"	Jr.	.444	.000	0/0	0.4	0.0	1.1
Ben Baum	F/C	6'11"	Jr.	—	—	—	—	—	—
Damion Jenkins	G	5'10"	Fr.	—	—	—	—	—	—
Lamont Long	G	6'4"	Fr.	—	—	—	—	—	—

NORTH CAROLINA

Conference: Atlantic Coast　　　**1995-96 NCAAs:** 1-1
1995-96: 21-11, 3rd ACC　　　**Coach:** Dean Smith (851-247)

Opening Line: The early departure of Jerry Stackhouse and Rasheed Wallace to the NBA left the Tar Heels short of depth for the first time in recent memory. Smith was forced to play more zone than ever and couldn't substitute as freely as he might have liked. Yet the Tar Heels again won 20 games, reached the NCAA Tournament, and recruited well.

Guard: Jeff McInnis followed his former classmates and pals, Stackhouse and Wallace, to the NBA. Junior Shammond Williams, 6'2", will be eased into the point guard slot. He was effective as the third guard last year and is ready for more responsibility. Also in the picture is 6'1" Ed Cota. This youngster did not receive much notoriety, but he can play. Super-talented Vince Carter, 6'5", slides back to the off guard spot after spending most of 1995-96 out of position at small forward.

Forward: Antawn Jamison and Ademola Okulaja each made a sizable contribution last year. Okulaja is intriguing. He did not play high school ball, and Smith was tipped off to his presence in Germany by former UNC forward Henrik Rodl. A terrific athlete, Okulaja gave tantalizing hints of what he may become. Another option here may be 6'9" Vasco Evtimov, a big freshman with small forward skills.

Center: A big part of why Carolina used a zone defense was its center, 7'2" Serge Zwikker. This mechanical big man is often overmatched in man-to-man situations. A solution might be former Michigan Wolverine Makhtar Ndiaye. The 6'9" junior is unpolished offensively yet is much quicker than Zwikker.

Analysis: North Carolina still hasn't recovered all the way from the early exit of its prep class of 1993. The worst is over, though, and the Tar Heels are probably one year away from returning to the ranks of legitimate national title contenders.

1996-97 ROSTER

	POS	HT	YR	FGP	FTP	3-PT	RPG	APG	PPG
Antawn Jamison	F	6'8"	So.	.624	.526	0/1	9.7	1.0	15.1
Serge Zwikker	C	7'2"	Sr.	.517	.617	0/0	6.2	0.7	9.5
Shammond Williams	G	6'2"	Jr.	.452	.768	46/116	2.6	2.0	8.3
Vince Carter	G/F	6'5"	So.	.492	.689	19/55	3.8	1.3	7.5
Ademola Okulaja	F	6'8"	So.	.525	.742	20/41	5.2	2.2	6.2
Charlie McNairy	F	6'6"	Sr.	.700	.733	0/0	0.5	0.3	1.7
Ryan Sullivan	G	6'3"	So.	1.00	.000	3/3	0.4	0.2	1.0
Michael Brooker	G/F	6'6"	Fr.	—	—	—	—	—	—
Ed Cota	G	6'1"	Fr.	—	—	—	—	—	—
Vasco Evtimov	F	6'9"	Fr.	—	—	—	—	—	—
Makhtar Ndiaye	C/F	6'9"	Jr.	—	—	—	—	—	—
Terrence Newby	G	6'2"	Fr.	—	—	—	—	—	—

NORTH CAROLINA-CHARLOTTE

Conference: Conference USA   **1995-96 NCAAs/NIT:** DNP
1995-96: 14-15, 3rd C-USA White   **Coach:** Melvin Watkins (0-0)

Opening Line: Jeff Mullins endured only two losing seasons in his ten years at the helm of the 49er basketball program—his first and his last. Last year, UNC-Charlotte struggled as it coped with the loss of forward linchpin Jarvis Lang and an extremely tough schedule. UNC-Charlotte lost to seven teams that were rated in the Top 25. Watkins, a longtime aide to Mullins, replaced his former boss, who stepped down at season's end.

Guard: Mullins relied on two point guards last year, but Watkins probably will have to use just one—senior Roderick Howard. The 5'10" guard is an effective scorer who needs to play under control and direct the offense. Andre Davis is a weapon at the off guard position who missed all of last season due to academic issues. If available, he helps. Shanderic Downs is a senior with good size who needs to shoot more consistently.

Forward: Although he did not compile the kind of numbers Lang did, Bobby Kummer is another forward who won't easily be replaced. He offered all of the intangibles that coaches cherish—heart, passing, and smarts. Sophomore Tremaine Gardiner joins freshman Ellious Swanigan in the duel for minutes at small forward. The power forward spot belongs to athletic banger DeMarco Johnson. The 6'8" junior was a second-team All-Conference USA pick.

Center: Alexander Kuehl arrived from Palm Beach Community College with some fanfare. Athletically gifted, the 7'2" giant has the tools to make himself an effective pivot. He must learn to recognize the open man and avoid silly fouls.

Analysis: The biggest void here will be the character Mullins offered this program. He was its anchor for the past decade. However, Watkins has the kind of athletes required to get the 49ers back over .500 and into the postseason picture again.

1996-97 ROSTER

	POS	HT	YR	FGP	FTP	3-PT	RPG	APG	PPG
DeMarco Johnson	F	6'8"	Jr.	.499	.665	5/24	8.8	1.1	18.1
Shanderic Downs	G	6'5"	Sr.	.392	.535	45/143	3.9	2.4	10.7
Roderick Howard	G	5'10"	Sr.	.394	.903	48/131	1.3	1.5	10.5
Alexander Kuehl	C	7'2"	Sr.	.432	.578	0/0	5.1	0.5	6.0
Andre Davis	G	6'1"	Sr.	.372	.654	12/47	2.0	1.0	5.8
Tremaine Gardiner	F	6'6"	So.	.455	.667	6/15	2.5	0.3	3.1
Dimingus Bundy	G	6'5"	Jr.	—	—	—	—	—	—
Sean Colson	G	6'0"	Jr.	—	—	—	—	—	—
Versile Shaw	F	6'7"	Jr.	—	—	—	—	—	—
Kedric Smith	G	5'11"	So.	—	—	—	—	—	—
Ellious Swanigan	F	6'7"	Fr.	—	—	—	—	—	—
Galen Young	G/F	6'6"	Jr.	—	—	—	—	—	—

OKLAHOMA

Conference: Big 12
1995-96: 17-13, 3rd Big Eight

1995-96 NCAAs: 0-1
Coach: Kelvin Sampson (216-170)

Opening Line: The Sooners saw every kind of gimmick zone imaginable last year, as teams attempted to slow All-Big Eight performer Ryan Minor. Minor struggled with the multiple defenses at times, but all of the preoccupation with OU's star created openings for others. The Sooners capitalized often enough to sneak into the NCAA Tournament field, where they were quickly dispatched for the second consecutive season.

Guard: The off guard spot belongs to Nate Erdmann. This 6'5" senior played for Sampson at Washington State and is a terrific athlete. Plus, he can drill the 3-point shot. John Ontjes helped keep the Sooners in a smooth offensive rhythm, and his loss was felt more last year than most might have anticipated. With Tyrone Foster transferring unexpectedly last summer, point guard will again be a concern. Freshman Tim Heskett and holdovers Robert Allison and Michael Cotton will put their cards on the table.

Forward: It's quite possible Erdmann will see time here as Sampson attempts to replace Minor. That will allow the Sooners to better defend the perimeter. Otherwise, OU will have to go with a big lineup, featuring the likes of Eduardo Najera, 6'8". Najera is more of a power forward, but Sampson can use 6'9" Renzi Stone, a coveted freshman, at that spot. Junior Evan Wiley, 6'11", also will see action.

Center: When Sampson signed Bobby Joe Evans two seasons ago, it was viewed as a major coup. Evans is the kind of low-post threat the Sooners haven't had since Stacey King left campus in the late 1980s. Evans made some youthful mistakes last year, but his talent is very promising.

Analysis: The Sooners have received some heat for the consecutive pratfalls in the NCAA Tournament. This team is good enough to give them a shot at redemption in March.

1996-97 ROSTER

	POS	HT	YR	FGP	FTP	3-PT	RPG	APG	PPG
Nate Erdmann	G	6'5"	Sr.	.502	.716	36/99	5.6	2.6	12.8
Bobby Joe Evans	C	6'9"	So.	.454	.655	2/6	3.7	0.4	5.7
Evan Wiley	F/C	6'11"	Jr.	.418	.449	0/0	3.8	0.3	3.8
Michael Cotton	G	6'5"	So.	.286	.636	2/10	1.3	0.6	2.2
Robert Allison	G	6'5"	Jr.	.143	.750	1/10	1.0	0.3	2.0
Corey Brewer	G	6'2"	Jr.	—	—	—	—	—	—
Tony Heard	G	6'0"	Fr.	—	—	—	—	—	—
Tim Heskett	G	6'2"	Fr.	—	—	—	—	—	—
Daryl Kelsey	G	6'2"	Jr.	—	—	—	—	—	—
Lou Moore	F	6'7"	Jr.	—	—	—	—	—	—
Eduardo Najera	F	6'8"	Fr.	—	—	—	—	—	—
Renzi Stone	F	6'9"	Fr.	—	—	—	—	—	—

OKLAHOMA STATE

Conference: Big 12
1995-96: 17-10, T-4th Big Eight

1995-96 NCAAs/NIT: DNP
Coach: Eddie Sutton (570-219)

Opening Line: The Cowboys suffered through Final Four fallout in 1995-96. One season after participating in the NCAA's favorite weekend, they missed the entire affair. The club never recovered from the departure of center Bryant "Big Country" Reeves. Sutton hopes a collection of gifted newcomers can change that.

Guard: It was hoped that Chianti Roberts would emerge as a star last year. It didn't happen. The 6'6" senior relies on his athleticism too often, resulting in forced shots and turnovers. His biggest plus is that he can play four positions, and it's likely he will as Sutton attempts to integrate five freshmen into the rotation. Freshman Joe Adkins is a highly touted point guard. He will attempt to replace Andre Owens. Meanwhile, Estell Laster could emerge as a starter at off guard and push Roberts to the frontcourt. Sophomore Adrian Peterson is the team's leading returning scorer.

Forward: Desmond Mason is a prize freshman forward. The rangy athlete fits in well and can make jump shots. If Roberts is needed in the backcourt, Mason might step into the frontcourt. Jason Skaer, a contributor on the Final Four squad, offers rebounding and 3-pointers. Power foward Maurice Robinson, 6'7", 272 pounds, creates room inside, although he is not very polished offensively.

Center: Jerome Lambert was supposed to be an able replacement for Reeves. Yet he never appeared comfortable, and now his eligibility is complete. This is the biggest hole for Sutton to fill. Two 6'10" freshmen, Alex Webber and Scott Robisch, will get a chance to see what they can do.

Analysis: Last season's flop appears to be more of an aberration than anything else. A fresh crop of talent should place OSU back near the top of the Big 12.

1996-97 ROSTER

	POS	HT	YR	FGP	FTP	3-PT	RPG	APG	PPG
Adrian Peterson	G	6'4"	So.	.420	.757	38/96	2.7	1.6	11.3
Chianti Roberts	G/F	6'6"	Sr.	.509	.452	4/21	5.4	1.9	11.1
Maurice Robinson	F/C	6'7"	Sr.	.575	.478	0/0	3.2	0.6	9.1
Jason Skaer	F	6'7"	Jr.	.398	.600	32/88	6.0	1.3	8.8
Marlon Dorsey	G	6'4"	Sr.	.395	.750	22/61	2.1	1.7	5.1
Chad Alexander	G	6'3"	Jr.	.438	1.00	23/52	1.3	0.7	4.0
R.W. McQuarters	G	5'11"	So.	.524	.308	3/6	0.8	1.4	2.4
Joe Adkins	G	6'2"	Fr.	—	—	—	—	—	—
Estell Laster	G	6'2"	Fr.	—	—	—	—	—	—
Desmond Mason	F	6'6"	Fr.	—	—	—	—	—	—
Brett Robisch	F/C	6'11"	Jr.	—	—	—	—	—	—
Scott Robisch	F/C	6'10"	Fr.	—	—	—	—	—	—
Reggie Tate	G	6'4"	Fr.	—	—	—	—	—	—
Alex Webber	F	6'10"	Fr.	—	—	—	—	—	—

OREGON

Conference: Pac-10
1995-96: 16-13, T-5th Pac-10

1995-96 NCAAs/NIT: DNP
Coach: Jerry Green (205-167)

Opening Line: Oregon ended a 34-year drought in 1994-95 with an NCAA Tournament appearance. The challenge in 1995-96 was to find a way to stay on top with four starters from that unit absent. Although they did not earn a postseason invitation in 1995-96, the Ducks remained competitive with a young lineup. Now, that experience should help thrust Oregon back into the postseason picture.

Guard: Kenya Wilkins is Oregon's catalyst. The point guard provides smart direction and doesn't turn the ball over. Wilkins's backcourt partner is Terik Brown, the 6'1" son of former Seattle SuperSonic star Fred "Downtown" Brown. Brown was selected to the Pac-10 All-Freshman team last winter. Junior Jamar Curry rarely takes a bad shot and is also a key. Athletic long-range shooter Donte Quinine will contribute here as well.

Forward: Senior Jamal Lawrence established himself as one of the Pac-10's better 3-point shooters last year. This swingman also needs to be aware of his duties on the glass. Power forward Kyle Milling began his career at Cal.-Santa Barbara before transferring to Eugene. The 6'9" senior is a strong rebounder and interior presence who was voted to the Pac-10's All-Newcomer team. Sophomore A.D. Smith was ranked as the top prep player in Oregon two years ago.

Center: Like Milling, Rob Ramaker came to Eugene from Cal.-Santa Barbara. And like his sidekick, Ramaker made a major impact on the Ducks. The 230-pound pivot was steady in the lane and effective on the backboards. Seven-footer Michael Carson provides experience.

Analysis: As signaled by a fine 1995-96 season, this program is no one-year wonder. Green has assembled an athletic cast that thrives in an open-court setting. This team is deeper than most, which permits Green to keep the tempo at a high pitch. The Ducks could sneak up on America again in 1996-97.

1996-97 ROSTER

	POS	HT	YR	FGP	FTP	3-PT	RPG	APG	PPG
Jamal Lawrence	G/F	6'2"	Sr.	.416	.690	80/201	3.0	1.6	13.7
Kenya Wilkins	G	5'10"	Sr.	.400	.846	32/89	3.4	5.9	13.7
Kyle Milling	F/C	6'9"	Sr.	.515	.716	0/1	7.6	1.2	12.2
Jamar Curry	G	6'3"	Jr.	.510	.567	10/37	4.0	1.7	10.6
Terik Brown	G	6'1"	So.	.354	.711	61/177	1.9	0.9	8.6
Rob Ramaker	F/C	6'10"	Sr.	.519	.338	9/26	6.8	1.6	6.0
Michael Carson	C	7'0"	Jr.	.493	.463	0/0	3.4	0.3	3.4
A.D. Smith	F	6'8"	So.	.492	.591	4/6	2.2	0.3	3.2
Andre Larry	F	6'9"	So.	.370	.476	3/12	1.3	0.1	2.5
Donte Quinine	G/F	6'6"	So.	.313	.714	9/31	0.9	0.2	2.3
Henry Madden	F	6'6"	Jr.	—	—	—	—	—	—
Tyron Manlove	G	6'4"	Fr.	—	—	—	—	—	—

PENN STATE

Conference: Big Ten
1995-96: 21-7, T-2nd Big Ten

1995-96 NCAAs: 0-1
Coach: Jerry Dunn (21-7)

Opening Line: Last September, Bruce Parkhill turned the reins over to his untested assistant, Jerry Dunn. The new coach proved himself quite capable, leading the Nittany Lions into the national Top 10 in January. Penn State chased Purdue to the wire in the Big Ten race before falling short of the school's first-ever men's basketball title. A loss to Arkansas in the first round of the NCAA Tournament ended the Lions' season.

Guard: This is what you would call an economical backcourt. Neither Dan Earl nor Pete Lisicky will overwhelm foes with their speed or leaping ability. But this duo keeps mistakes to a minimum and connects on long-range jumpers that draw the defense away from the goal. Dunn will have to force-feed freshmen Titus Ivory and Greg Stevenson because experienced depth is lacking.

Forward: The departure of Glenn Sekunda and Matt Gaudio leaves the Nittany Lions without two starters. Gaudio in particular will be tough to replace. Stepping into Sekunda's shoes is Rahsaan Carlton, a starter who missed the 1994-95 season with an injury. Carlton is more of a slasher than Sekunda was, but he can handle this assignment. Burly rebounder Phil Williams is on call at power forward. Sophomore Jarrett Stephens, 6'7", is ready to spell Williams.

Center: Calvin Booth was a revelation in the lane for the Lions as a rookie. As he matures, he should emerge as a quality scoring threat. He offers a terrific shot-blocking dimension on defense that camouflages some of the athletic shortcomings among the perimeter people.

Analysis: It was a long way from Penn State's entrance into the Big Ten to this stage. The next challenge is adding another 20-win season to the ledger. There is plenty of reason to expect just that. As long as PSU is not complacent, it is in position to chase a Big Ten title.

1996-97 ROSTER

	POS	HT	YR	FGP	FTP	3-PT	RPG	APG	PPG
Pete Lisicky	G	6'4"	Jr.	.483	.778	89/189	2.8	2.4	13.3
Dan Earl	G	6'4"	Sr.	.476	.681	48/115	2.6	5.4	11.7
Calvin Booth	C	6'11"	So.	.549	.635	0/1	5.4	1.3	9.3
Phil Williams	F/C	6'8"	Sr.	.415	.569	0/0	5.1	0.4	3.5
Jarrett Stephens	F	6'7"	So.	.516	.667	0/2	2.0	0.3	3.3
Jeremy Metzger	C	6'10"	Sr.	.400	.514	0/0	2.1	0.3	1.9
Aaron Jack	F	6'8"	Fr.	.250	.750	0/1	2.5	0.0	1.8
Ryan Bailey	G	6'3"	Fr.	—	—	—	—	—	—
Rahsaan Carlton	F	6'6"	Sr.	—	—	—	—	—	—
Titus Ivory	G	6'4"	Fr.	—	—	—	—	—	—
Carl Jackson	F/C	6'9"	Fr.	—	—	—	—	—	—
Greg Stevenson	G/F	6'5"	Fr.	—	—	—	—	—	—

PRINCETON

Conference: Ivy League   **1995-96 NCAAs:** 1-1
1995-96: 22-7, 1st Ivy   **Coach:** Bill Carmody (0-0)

Opening Line: Pete Carril called it a career after 29 years as head coach and did it in style. The Tigers defeated archrival Pennsylvania in a one-game playoff to reach the NCAA Tournament. Then they stunned defending national champion UCLA in the first round on a backdoor layup with less than five seconds remaining. Mississippi State eliminated Princeton two days later.

Guard: Sydney Johnson is the anchor in the backcourt. He's generally on the floor for at least 35 minutes a night and is the club's clear leader. His sidekick is Mitch Henderson. At 6'2", Henderson is a sound perimeter shooter. He also might be the team's best all-around athlete. Sophomore Brian Earl is a gifted quarterback who should see more action this year. A newcomer of note is 6'3" freshman guard J.R. Gillern, a long-range shooter.

Forward: Given Princeton's depth at guard, it is likely that Johnson will see plenty of minutes at one forward spot despite the fact he's listed as a guard. The other forward position belongs to 6'4" Jamie Mastaglio, an ace free-throw shooter. Junior Darren Hite will play an important role as a rebounder and defender of power forwards. Backup center Jesse Rosenfeld will also see time here.

Center: Steve Goodrich has started every game the Tigers have played since he came to Princeton two years ago. This fundamentally sound pivot isn't a leaper, but he finds the open man from the high post and can hit medium-range jumpers.

Analysis: New coach Carmody promises a few new wrinkles. Fastbreak opportunities will be exploited more than they have been in the past, and there might even be a little defensive pressure away from the basket. Yet he won't tinker too much because this is a roster that is still best suited to sling rocks at Goliath through the use of patient offense and the 3-pointer.

1996-97 ROSTER

	POS	HT	YR	FGP	FTP	3-PT	RPG	APG	PPG
Steve Goodrich	F/C	6'7"	Jr.	.608	.724	16/39	3.8	1.8	11.6
Brian Earl	G	6'2"	So.	.468	.712	55/135	1.9	1.6	9.2
Mitch Henderson	G	6'2"	Jr.	.409	.631	35/109	1.9	1.7	8.9
Sydney Johnson	G	6'3"	Sr.	.431	.738	39/122	4.4	3.0	8.7
Jamie Mastaglio	G/F	6'4"	Jr.	.487	.824	9/28	2.0	0.5	4.7
Gabe Lewullis	F	6'5"	So.	.388	.609	15/52	2.0	1.1	4.4
Jesse Rosenfeld	F/C	6'9"	Sr.	.540	.606	1/1	2.1	0.6	2.8
Darren Hite	F	6'3"	Jr.	.444	1.00	0/1	0.3	0.1	1.1
J.R. Gillern	F	6'3"	Fr.	—	—	—	—	—	—
John McCann	F	6'6"	Fr.	—	—	—	—	—	—
Mason Rocca	F	6'7"	Fr.	—	—	—	—	—	—
Nathan Walton	F	6'7"	Fr.	—	—	—	—	—	—

PROVIDENCE

Conference: Big East   **1995-96 NIT:** 1-1
1995-96: 18-12, 3rd Big East 7   **Coach:** Pete Gillen (237-100)

Opening Line: Following an exciting 84-77 win at home over Georgetown, it appeared that the Friars had played their way into the NCAA Tournament. A defeat in Providence's next outing, though, took the club off the NCAA bubble and into the NIT. This marked the second straight near miss for the Friars.

Guard: No one knew quite what to call him at first. In high school, he had been known as Shammgod Wells. Upon his arrival in college, the 6'0" youngster announced he preferred to be known by his given name: God Shammgod. Whatever he's called, Wells gets the job done. An expert ball-handler, he only needs to enhance his perimeter shooting. Juco transfer Kevin Simpson stunned the coaching staff when he declared himself available for the NBA draft. Veteran Jason Murdock may have to pick up the slack.

Forward: Senior Austin Croshere brings excellent shooting and big scoring numbers to the table. Derrick Brown was brought in from junior college to provide offense from the wing, and he delivered. Brown shoots a solid percentage by taking it strong to the goal. Abdul Brown is a strong rebounder with decent footwork near the basket. He may split time in the pivot. Sophomore Jamel Thomas's role will grow as he matures.

Center: The only thing limiting Ruben Garces to 22 minutes a game last winter was fouls. He was disqualified five times and accumulated 99 fouls in 671 minutes. That Garces pulled down almost eight rebounds a game in those limited minutes is encouraging.

Analysis: Providence hasn't turned into the overnight success some expected when Gillen arrived. Misfortune, several recruiting setbacks, and some tough road losses have conspired to keep the Friars out of the NCAA Tournament. This year, though, all of the ingredients are in place.

1996-97 ROSTER

	POS	HT	YR	FGP	FTP	3-PT	RPG	APG	PPG
Austin Croshere	F	6'9"	Sr.	.421	.852	47/141	5.8	1.1	15.3
Derrick Brown	F	6'6"	Sr.	.482	.754	26/86	6.8	1.6	14.8
God Shammgod	G	6'0"	So.	.336	.690	19/91	1.7	6.5	9.6
Jamel Thomas	F	6'6"	So.	.453	.621	24/64	4.6	1.5	9.3
Ruben Garces	C	6'9"	Sr.	.492	.400	0/0	7.5	0.7	7.1
Jason Murdock	G	6'3"	Sr.	.336	.766	8/37	1.9	0.9	4.3
Llewellyn Cole	F	6'7"	So.	.459	.613	1/1	1.0	0.1	1.5
Richard Cordella	F	6'4"	So.	.500	.000	0/1	0.2	0.0	0.4
Abdul Brown	F/C	6'9"	Jr.	—	—	—	—	—	—
Kendrick Moore	G	6'2"	Jr.	—	—	—	—	—	—
Koli Pointer	F	6'8"	Fr.	—	—	—	—	—	—
Corey Wright	G	5'8"	So.	—	—	—	—	—	—

PURDUE

Conference: Big Ten   **1995-96 NCAAs:** 1-1
1995-96: 26-6, 1st Big Ten   **Coach:** Gene Keady (386-167)

Opening Line: Despite being targeted for the middle of the pack, the Boilermakers became the first Big Ten team since Ohio State in the early 1960s to
record three consecutive outright league titles. The Boilermakers survived
humbling pre-league losses to Memphis and Villanova to emerge as the
conference's premier unit. Keady was selected Coach of the Year by the United
States Basketball Writers Association and the Associated Press.

Guard: Neither Porter Roberts nor Todd Foster made any All-America rosters.
However, each understood what Keady expected from his guards. Prize freshmen Jaraan Cornell and Mosi Barnes bring more individual skill to the table than
the departed veterans, but they will endure growing pains. Helping to bridge the
gap is junior stalwart Chad Austin, one of the Big Ten's top guards.

Forward: Herb Dove was much like Roberts and Foster: solid if not spectacular.
His heir is 6'6" prep All-American Mike Robinson, a potent offensive weapon with
an enormous upside. Look for him to play an extensive role. Power forward will
likely fall into the hands of 6'9" sophomore Luther Clay. Clay's path to minutes
was blocked by old hands Brandon Brantley and Justin Jennings last year. Two
6'8" newcomers, Gary McQuay and Brian Cardinal, are also in the mix.

Center: Junior Brad Miller had to share time last year, but at 6'11" he is good
enough to become a consistent force. More of the offense will be funneled
through him this year.

Analysis: Although some may count the Boilermakers out of the Big Ten title
hunt because they are young, it would be wise to realize that the assembled
youngsters possess more individual skill than their predecessors, and also that
the Big Ten will again be weak. Beware the Boilermakers.

1996-97 ROSTER

	POS	HT	YR	FGP	FTP	3-PT	RPG	APG	PPG
Chad Austin	G	6'2"	Jr.	.417	.733	53/140	2.9	2.3	12.8
Brad Miller	C	6'11"	Jr.	.518	.738	1/6	4.9	1.4	9.6
Luther Clay	F	6'9"	So.	.463	.476	0/1	1.6	0.2	2.5
David Lesmond	F	6'8"	Jr.	.389	.500	9/21	0.9	0.4	1.8
Alan Eldridge	G	6'1"	So.	.448	.545	7/16	0.6	0.7	1.3
Matt ten Dam	C	7'2"	Jr.	.400	.500	0/0	0.6	0.1	0.8
Mosi Barnes	G	6'0"	Fr.	—	—	—	—	—	—
Brian Cardinal	F	6'8"	Fr.	—	—	—	—	—	—
B.J. Carretta	G	6'3"	Fr.	—	—	—	—	—	—
Jaraan Cornell	G	6'3"	Fr.	—	—	—	—	—	—
Gary McQuay	F	6'8"	Fr.	—	—	—	—	—	—
Michael Robinson	F	6'6"	Fr.	—	—	—	—	—	—

RHODE ISLAND

Conference: Atlantic 10   **1995-96 NIT:** 2-1
1995-96: 20-14, 4th A-10 East   **Coach:** Al Skinner (118-116)

Opening Line: The Rams rang up 20 losses two seasons ago, but in the process a young core unit grew up. The result was a 20-win campaign last winter. URI even eliminated vaunted Virginia Tech in the first round of the Atlantic 10 Tournament.

Guard: A catalyst, 5'10" junior Tyson Wheeler is one of the best guards you've never heard of. His aggressive point guard play sets the tone for the entire team. His partner is 6'4" junior Cuttino Mobley. Mobley, who played only two games last year, is a legitimate scoring threat whose height allows him to post up smaller guards. Chad Thomas is another double-digit scorer.

Forward: The revelation here last year was Antonio Reynolds. The 6'7" forward is a superior athlete who finished fifth in A-10 rebounding. As he develops, he will become more of a scorer, too. Another 6'7" forward plays a much different style than Reynolds. That's Josh King, a junior. King loves to step outside for 3-point opportunities and is dangerous from there. Ibn-Hashim Bakari and David Arigbabu provide solid depth.

Center: During the first two seasons of his career, 7'0" senior Michael Andersen shared the middle with David Bialski. In 1995-96, Andersen proved he could handle the spot on his own. He is a competent rebounder with a decent touch around the goal.

Analysis: Few teams toil in more anonymity than the Rams do. To the north they are obscured by Providence, to the west lies the shadow of Massachusetts, and to the south are the Connecticut Huskies. However, Skinner has pieced together a strong club, one that figures to make an NCAA Tournament push and might even create a headache or two for the Minutemen in the Atlantic 10's East division.

1996-97 ROSTER

	POS	HT	YR	FGP	FTP	3-PT	RPG	APG	PPG
Tyson Wheeler	G	5'10"	Jr.	.406	.747	79/213	2.9	6.0	16.5
Antonio Reynolds	F	6'7"	So.	.466	.632	0/2	8.7	1.6	12.1
Cuttino Mobley	G	6'4"	Jr.	.643	.500	5/7	0.0	2.5	12.0
Chad Thomas	G	6'3"	Sr.	.484	.667	29/92	4.9	2.5	11.5
Joshua King	F	6'7"	Jr.	.367	.800	54/155	4.5	1.1	9.2
Michael Andersen	C	7'0"	Sr.	.482	.610	0/0	6.0	0.8	8.9
Preston Murphy	G	6'1"	So.	.422	.732	45/110	2.8	1.9	7.9
David Arigbabu	F	6'8"	So.	.445	.582	0/2	3.7	0.6	6.3
Ibn-Hashim Bakari	F	6'9"	Sr.	.398	.714	7/31	1.7	0.7	3.5
John Bennett	F	6'8"	Jr.	.500	.750	0/0	0.5	0.0	1.2
Brock Erickson	G	6'1"	Jr.	.333	.667	0/1	0.1	0.1	0.6
Matt Selmer	C	6'10"	Jr.	—	—	—	—	—	—

ST. JOHN'S

Conference: Big East   **1995-96 NCAAs/NIT:** DNP
1995-96: 11-16, 5th Big East 6   **Coach:** Fran Fraschilla (85-35)

Opening Line: Year two of the Felipe Lopez era was supposed to have delivered the Red Storm back into the NCAA Tournament. When it didn't happen, coach Brian Mahoney was asked to leave. Stepping into the post is Fran Fraschilla, the architect of Manhattan College's 1995 NCAA Tournament success.

Guard: If there has been one single failing at St. John's in the 1990s, it is the lack of a quality point guard. There hasn't been an exceptional one on the Jamaica campus since Mark Jackson left in 1987. Tarik Turner gets a clean slate after two disappointing seasons. He must take better care of the basketball. Other possibilities are 5'10" Collin Charles and 6'5" Lavor Postell, both freshmen. Lopez is set at the other guard spot and may even assume some of the ball-distribution chores if needed.

Forward: Rebounding and interior toughness have been a problem for the Red Storm of late, but the return of 6'6", 225-pound Charles Minlend will provide a lift. He was a medical redshirt in 1995-96. In his absence, 6'7" Tyrone Grant displayed grit and seems well suited to Fraschilla's demanding style. Fred Lyson is another forward who should see plenty of action on the wing.

Center: Because he's 6'11", Zendon Hamilton is listed as the center. However, he is a unique player who really can't be labeled a pivot. Finesse is a staple of his game, though he has made gains as a rebounder. Senior Tom Bayne gets one more chance to prove he can contribute.

Analysis: This program is in need of energy. Fortunately, energy is something Fraschilla will supply. His emphasis of defense and effort should push the Red Storm back into the postseason tournament picture. Hamilton and Lopez are star-caliber players. With some heady point guard play and better long-range shooting, it can move up.

1996-97 ROSTER

	POS	HT	YR	FGP	FTP	3-PT	RPG	APG	PPG
Zendon Hamilton	C	6'11"	Jr.	.486	.797	0/4	10.3	0.7	20.8
Felipe Lopez	G	6'6"	Jr.	.406	.683	26/100	6.2	1.9	16.2
Tyrone Grant	F	6'7"	So.	.579	.608	0/0	7.1	1.7	7.8
Fred Lyson	F/G	6'7"	Sr.	.383	.714	34/89	1.4	1.0	5.3
Tarik Turner	G	6'5"	Jr.	.352	.553	10/35	1.8	2.3	4.0
Charles Minlend	F	6'6"	Sr.	.352	.550	0/0	3.2	0.6	2.5
Tom Bayne	C	6'10"	Sr.	.500	.750	0/0	1.5	0.1	1.7
Ed Brown	F	6'8"	So.	.375	.833	0/0	0.9	0.1	1.3
Collin Charles	G	5'10"	Fr.	—	—	—	—	—	—
Chudney Gray	G	6'2"	Fr.	—	—	—	—	—	—
Mike Menniefield	F	6'8"	Sr.	—	—	—	—	—	—
Lavor Postell	G	6'5"	Fr.	—	—	—	—	—	—

ST. LOUIS

Conference: Conference USA
1995-96: 16-14, 3rd C-USA Blue

1995-96 NIT: 0-1
Coach: Charlie Spoonhour (271-126)

Opening Line: After a period of relative darkness, the Billiken program has come alive under Charlie Spoonhour. In 1992-93, Spoonhour's first season after stepping in from Southwest Missouri State, St. Louis finished below .500. In the three seasons since, the Billikens have been in the postseason each time.

Guard: There was some question of how the Billikens' offense would fare with three fresh faces last year. Spoonhour made it work. He slowed the offense down, focused on defense, and had his perimeter players launching 3s. One huge plus was the development of point guard Jamall Walker, 6'0", now a sophomore. He delivers the ball to the shooters and also can make 3s himself. Corey Frazier launches the long ball but must improve his accuracy. Carlos McCauley, C-USA's top percentage 3-point shooter, completed his eligibility.

Forward: Sophomore Virgel Cobbin is a guard playing the forward spot. At 6'4", though, he competes defensively and is an exceptional 3-point shooter. Cobbin is often paired with power forward Jeff Harris. The senior, only 6'5", uses his bulk to create rebounding room. He also can set a solid screen.

Center: As usual, the Billikens are a bit undersized at this spot. Junior Tyrone Caswell, 6'7", finally appears to have shaken off the effects of a shoulder injury that hampered him in junior college. He is unafraid of contact. Ryan Luechtefeld has smooth skills but little muscle, while Paul Nondas is more of a finesse forward than he is a pivot, despite his height (6'9").

Analysis: Spoonhour is one of the best at maximizing what he's got. The Billikens just don't have sufficient size to derail this league's top teams. But these guys don't lose games they shouldn't and figure to be in the hunt for one of the last at-large bids to the NCAA Tournament.

1996-97 ROSTER

	POS	HT	YR	FGP	FTP	3-PT	RPG	APG	PPG
Jeff Harris	F	6'5"	Sr.	.446	.745	2/4	7.9	1.2	13.6
Virgel Cobbin	G/F	6'4"	So.	.418	.763	57/135	2.8	0.8	9.2
Corey Frazier	G	6'1"	Jr.	.302	.737	42/137	3.0	2.4	8.5
Jamall Walker	G	6'0"	So.	.351	.730	26/72	1.6	2.1	4.8
Tyrone Caswell	F/C	6'7"	Jr.	.552	.628	0/1	2.2	0.2	3.5
Ryan Luechtefeld	F/C	6'8"	So.	.241	.708	6/34	1.8	0.8	2.0
Paul Nondas	F/C	6'9"	Sr.	.478	.750	2/4	1.4	0.1	1.9
Sekeue Barentine	F/C	6'8"	Sr.	.200	.750	0/0	1.1	0.2	0.5
Jeramy Biles	G	5'10"	Fr.	—	—	—	—	—	—
Rasheed Malik	F	6'6"	Jr.	—	—	—	—	—	—
Troy Robertson	G/F	6'4"	Fr.	—	—	—	—	—	—
Larry Simmons	F	6'7"	Fr.	—	—	—	—	—	—

SETON HALL

Conference: Big East
1995-96: 12-16, 5th Big East 7

1995-96 NCAAs/NIT: DNP
Coach: George Blaney (422-346)

Opening Line: Although not picked as a preseason favorite in the powerful Big East, the Pirates appeared poised for a solid campaign on the eve of 1995-96. A veteran cast seemed to ensure production. Alas, only senior Adrian Griffin enjoyed a big year, and the Pirates were a minor disappointment. Spotty shooting was a major woe.

Guard: Pirate fans breathed a sigh of relief when gifted 5'10" point guard Shaheen Holloway officially signed a letter of intent. This McDonald's All-American will make an instant impact. The ball will be in his hands constantly. Junior Levell Sanders mans the other backcourt post. He needs to take better care of the basketball. Freshman Rimantas Kaukenas averaged 35 points a game as a high school senior.

Forward: After a strong freshman season, 6'7" Donnell Williams regressed last year, making only two starts and shooting only 34 percent from the floor. It would help if he were less enamored with his perimeter jumper and more willing to get it to the goal. Senior Bayonne Taty, 6'10", is a weak free-throw shooter but an able defender. Sophomores Duane Jordan and Roy Leath have a chance to expand their limited roles in Griffin's absence.

Center: Jacky Kaba, only in his junior year, is slowly developing into a quality pivot. A large frame allows him to move people around inside, and he's got some touch around the goal. Passing is a problem, though—he recorded only ten assists in 615 minutes of action last year.

Analysis: For all of the fuss made when the Hall did not sign a plethora of prospects from New Jersey, the Pirates actually should be in good shape to surprise a few folks in 1996-97. Down the road, though, the Pirates may wish they had signed more of those recruits to help Holloway.

1996-97 ROSTER

	POS	HT	YR	FGP	FTP	3-PT	RPG	APG	PPG
Levell Sanders	G	6'2"	Jr.	.399	.681	40/113	3.8	2.9	12.3
Bayonne Taty	F	6'10"	Sr.	.517	.447	0/0	4.8	0.4	7.9
Donnell Williams	F	6'7"	Jr.	.335	.714	20/91	3.5	1.2	7.5
Jacky Kaba	C	6'10"	Jr.	.452	.573	0/0	5.0	0.4	7.3
Kelland Payton	C	6'10"	So.	.433	.550	0/0	1.3	0.0	1.8
Duane Jordan	F	6'6"	So.	.386	.394	0/0	1.7	0.2	1.6
Roy Leath	F	6'7"	So.	.208	.750	2/9	1.5	0.1	1.4
Shaheen Holloway	G	5'10"	Fr.	—	—	—	—	—	—
Rimantas Kaukenas	G	6'4"	Fr.	—	—	—	—	—	—
Jalil Roberts	G	6'4"	Jr.	—	—	—	—	—	—

SOUTH CAROLINA

Conference: Southeastern
1995-96: 19-12, 3rd SEC East

1995-96 NIT: 2-1
Coach: Eddie Fogler (180-128)

Opening Line: Prior to the start of 1995-96, coach Fogler announced that the Gamecocks had completed the rebuilding phase of this program and were embarking upon the competitive phase of matters. He proved to be a prophet. After winning only 19 games in his first two seasons, Fogler's club came within one possession of reaching the Final Four of the NIT.

Guard: BJ McKie was supposed to make a difference in the USC backcourt, and he did just that. A good 3-point shooter and ball-handler, McKie can run the offense or play off the basketball. Manning the other guard slot is 6'2" junior Melvin Watson, a quick slasher and good passer. Watson also brings physical strength to the floor. When those two stalwarts need a break or when Fogler goes with a three-guard lineup, senior Larry Davis gets the call. This North Carolina transfer provides an offensive lift when he enters the game.

Forward: There is some retooling to be done here since both Malik Russell and William Unseld have completed their eligibility. Junior Ryan Stack, 6'11", is a finesse player with shooting range that extends to the 3-point arc. More time in the weight room will help him on the interior. Other options include sophomore Arthur Carlisle, 6'5", and freshman Herbert Lee Davis, 6'5". Each is an athletic swing type who will try to ease the pain of Russell's exit.

Center: One-time Ohio State Buckeye Nate Wilbourne won't make anyone forget that USC didn't land touted prepster Jermaine O'Neal. However, he has good hands and an eye for passing. Sophomore Leonard "Bud" Johnson brings a physical presence in relief or when he steps in at forward.

Analysis: Landing O'Neal would have taken this program up a notch. As it is, though, the experience of 1995-96 should be enough to lift this program back into the NCAA Tournament.

1996-97 ROSTER

	POS	HT	YR	FGP	FTP	3-PT	RPG	APG	PPG
Larry Davis	G	6'3"	Sr.	.450	.774	78/220	4.7	1.8	18.0
BJ McKie	G	6'2"	So.	.467	.762	43/123	3.1	2.8	15.4
Melvin Watson	G	6'2"	Jr.	.450	.740	28/83	4.0	4.5	12.2
Nate Wilbourne	C	6'11"	Sr.	.496	.647	11/38	5.4	0.8	10.6
Bud Johnson	F/C	6'10"	So.	.545	.566	0/0	5.5	0.2	5.5
Ryan Stack	F/C	6'11"	Jr.	.506	.773	7/20	2.7	0.5	4.2
William Gallman	F	6'7"	So.	.506	.568	0/0	2.1	0.0	3.5
Arthur Carlisle	F	6'5"	So.	.414	.800	6/20	0.5	0.3	2.2
George Formanek	C	6'11"	Sr.	.231	.500	0/1	1.1	0.1	0.5
Hagan Rouse	G	6'3"	Fr.	.000	.000	0/0	0.0	0.0	0.0
Herbert Lee Davis	G/F	6'5"	Fr.	—	—	—	—	—	—
Antonio Grant	F	6'5"	Fr.	—	—	—	—	—	—

STANFORD

Conference: Pac-10
1995-96: 20-9, 3rd Pac-10

1995-96 NCAAs: 1-1
Coach: Mike Montgomery (336-197)

Opening Line: Despite losing center Tim Young to injury for virtually the entire 1995-96 season, Stanford posted its fourth 20-win season in Mike Montgomery's ten years as coach in Palo Alto. The Cardinal downed Bradley in their NCAA Tournament opener and pushed UMass for 30 minutes before fading down the stretch.

Guard: For three years, the tandem of Dion Cross and Brevin Knight was one of the West's premier duos. This double-play act was broken up when Cross graduated. Knight, the point guard, will look to set up sophomores Kris Weems and Arthur Lee. Both saw limited duty as rookies and now have an opportunity to see more substantial action. Freshman David Moseley, 6'4", also is in the picture.

Forward: The Cardinal suffered damaging losses here, too. Forwards Darren Allaway and Andy Poppink weren't generally newsmakers, yet each contributed the kind of grunt work good teams must generate to succeed. Power forward Mark Seaton, 6'9", learned valuable lessons in 1995-96, gaining a spot on the Pac-10's All-Freshman team. Peter Van Elswyk, a 6'9" transfer from South Carolina, is eligible and looms large in the playing rotation. Rebounding is his forte.

Center: Thanks to Seaton, the Cardinal survived without Young in the middle. However, they are delighted to again have the services of the seven-footer. He is an athletic low-post threat who gives Stanford a huge lift over most of its rivals.

Analysis: In a very understated manner, Stanford has emerged as a West Coast menace. It doesn't have the resources to match UCLA and Arizona on a regular basis, but it takes a back seat to few other programs west of the Mississippi River. Unfortunately, the Bruins and Wildcats happen to play in the Pac-10, too, so the Cardinal will have to settle for another NCAA Tournament bid.

1996-97 ROSTER

	POS	HT	YR	FGP	FTP	3-PT	RPG	APG	PPG
Brevin Knight	G	5'10"	Sr.	.433	.848	18/61	3.8	7.3	15.5
Tim Young	C	7'1"	Jr.	.421	.720	0/0	9.0	1.6	10.0
Mark Seaton	F	6'9"	So.	.605	.642	0/0	3.2	0.2	4.8
Peter Sauer	F	6'8"	So.	.494	.643	7/19	3.3	0.2	4.1
Kris Weems	G	6'3"	So.	.400	.778	14/38	0.7	0.5	3.0
Arthur Lee	G	6'0"	So.	.326	.625	3/17	2.5	0.8	2.2
Rich Jackson	F	6'6"	Sr.	.326	.625	3/17	2.5	1.1	2.1
Mark Madsen	F	6'9"	Fr.	—	—	—	—	—	—
Andy McClelland	C	6'10"	Jr.	—	—	—	—	—	—
Ryan Mendez	F/G	6'7"	Fr.	—	—	—	—	—	—
David Moseley	G	6'4"	Fr.	—	—	—	—	—	—
Peter Van Elswyk	F	6'9"	Jr.	—	—	—	—	—	—

SYRACUSE

Conference: Big East   **1995-96 NCAAs:** 5-1
1995-96: 29-9, 2nd Big East 7   **Coach:** Jim Boeheim (483-159)

Opening Line: Although they disliked the label, the Orangemen were clearly the Cinderella of the 1996 NCAA Tournament. They capped a solid season with a heart-pounding run to the finish line. Included were victories over Georgia, Kansas, and Mississippi State. John Wallace emerged as the dominant individual player in the Tournament.

Guard: When Michael Lloyd departed school in the summer of 1995, there was great dread in central New York. Without him, there was no point guard. Into that gap stepped three-year reserve Lazarus Sims, who provided a steady hand. Sims too has departed, and there is again a void. Coach Boeheim hopes it will be filled by 6'2" Jason Hart, a freshman who was rated as the ninth-best point guard prospect in the land by *Basketball Weekly*. Ramel Lloyd, a 6'4" freshman from New York, is another blue-chipper. The well-built youngster knows how to score.

Forward: This is where it gets tough for Boeheim. There is no natural successor to Wallace. Todd Burgan, second in minutes played on the club, will see action here and in the backcourt. He might even have to shoulder some ball-distribution responsibility in relief of freshman Hart. Jason Cipolla, a 6'7" senior, is another gifted wing player. More perimeter shots will be available for him this year, and he has the touch to convert them. Marius Janulis will also see meaningful action.

Center: The knock on Otis Hill is that he is too foul-prone to remain on the floor. Sidekick J.B. Reafsnyder is gone, so Hill must learn to back away at times. A push could come from 6'9" Derrick Thomas, a muscular athlete from Tulsa who also may figure prominently in the rotation at power forward.

Analysis: Boeheim attracts a lot of criticism, yet he annually produces 20-win squads. This season should be no different. Another Final Four, though, seems unrealistic.

1996-97 ROSTER

	POS	HT	YR	FGP	FTP	3-PT	RPG	APG	PPG
Otis Hill	C	6'8"	Sr.	.571	.681	0/1	5.4	0.6	12.7
Todd Burgan	G/F	6'7"	Jr.	.421	.623	49/144	6.8	2.3	12.1
Jason Cipolla	G/F	6'7"	Sr.	.383	.667	40/129	1.9	1.4	7.7
Marius Janulis	G/F	6'5"	Jr.	.452	.846	42/101	2.1	1.4	6.1
Elvir Ovcina	C/F	6'11"	Fr.	.435	.500	0/3	2.0	0.2	2.7
Donovan McNabb	G	6'2"	So.	.167	1.00	0/2	0.6	0.2	1.0
Jason Hart	G	6'2"	Fr.	—	—	—	—	—	—
LaSean Howard	F/G	6'6"	Fr.	—	—	—	—	—	—
Ramel Lloyd	G	6'4"	Fr.	—	—	—	—	—	—
Derrick Thomas	C/F	6'9"	Fr.	—	—	—	—	—	—
Walton Winfred	F	6'9"	Fr.	—	—	—	—	—	—

TEMPLE

Conference: Atlantic 10
1995-96: 20-13, 2nd A-10 East
1995-96 NCAAs: 1-1
Coach: John Chaney (315-129)

Opening Line: Coach John Chaney lamented his club's lack of offensive proficiency, but the Owls still managed to create a fair share of headaches for opposing coaches in 1995-96. A highlight came in December, when Temple upset Kansas 74-66 in overtime. Another highlight for the Owls was having center Marc Jackson named to the A-10's all-conference first team.

Guard: Johnny Miller would like to forget much about his sophomore season. A shoulder injury hampered his shooting motion, causing this quality marksman to struggle from long range. A healthy Miller provides this club a huge lift. Freshman Malik Moore, 6'2", is slated to be his backup. Two other freshmen, 6'3" Juan Sanchez and 6'0" Larry Allaway, are among those set to vie for the off guard berth previously held by Levan Alston.

Forward: Lynard Stewart is a gifted all-around player. He must improve his perimeter game and dribble moves to provide a consistent scoring option. Keep an eye on 6'8" freshman Julian Dunkley, too. He's very athletic and brings a wide collection of tools to the arena. Huey Futch, a 6'7" senior, will provide defense and some of the intangibles that Chaney covets.

Center: Perhaps Temple's only reliable scoring weapon in 1995-96, Marc Jackson carried the Owls at times. Chaney hopes to bring him more help this year. Jackson is a classic low-post presence with muscle and enough dexterity to release his soft shot.

Analysis: Since the departure of Eddie Jones and Aaron McKie, Temple has survived largely on its matchup zone and Chaney's guile. The emergence of Jackson, coupled with a solid recruiting class, should re-energize this program. This unit might sneak back into the Top 25 poll and could be a matchup nightmare for more glamorous schools in the early stages of the NCAA Tournament.

1996-97 ROSTER

	POS	HT	YR	FGP	FTP	3-PT	RPG	APG	PPG
Marc Jackson	F/C	6'10"	Jr.	.477	.668	2/4	9.0	0.8	15.7
Johnny Miller	G	6'1"	Jr.	.291	.520	31/138	2.1	1.7	9.9
Lynard Stewart	F	6'7"	Jr.	.332	.646	30/108	3.8	1.6	7.2
Huey Futch	F	6'7"	Sr.	.357	.689	38/135	3.5	1.1	7.1
Larry Allaway	G	6'0"	Fr.	—	—	—	—	—	—
Lamont Barnes	C	6'9"	Fr.	—	—	—	—	—	—
Julian Dunkley	F	6'8"	Fr.	—	—	—	—	—	—
Malik Moore	G	6'2"	Fr.	—	—	—	—	—	—
Juan Sanchez	G	6'3"	Fr.	—	—	—	—	—	—
Kenton Sanders	G/F	6'6"	Fr.	—	—	—	—	—	—
Quincy Wadley	G	6'4"	Fr.	—	—	—	—	—	—
Marvin Webster	C	6'10"	Fr.	—	—	—	—	—	—

TENNESSEE

Conference: Southeastern
1995-96: 14-15, T-5th SEC East

1995-96 NIT: 0-1
Coach: Kevin O'Neill (129-104)

Opening Line: In his second season since arriving from Marquette, Kevin O'Neill lifted the Volunteers back to respectability. But O'Neill's biggest gains came on the recruiting trail. Tennessee landed seven newcomers, including blue-chipper Charles Hathaway. Its class was ranked fourth nationally by *FutureStars* magazine.

Guard: O'Neill inherited a club that was not terribly athletic. Through recruiting, he has changed that. DaShay Jones, 6'2", was brought in from Vincennes Junior College to direct the offense. He's a probable starter. Another newcomer, 6'5" freshman Cornelius Jackson, is a gifted perimeter scorer. He joins sophomores Brandon Wharton—the team's leading returning scorer—and Aaron Green in the scrap for action.

Forward: Damon Johnson completed his career, so there's time to be had here. Marques Maybin, 6'4", is a versatile sort who plays three positions. Also looking to carve a niche for himself is 6'9" Isiah Victor, who might be athletic enough to play small forward. He was a Top 50 prospect on most lists. Power forward C.J. Black is a 240-pounder with a knack for rebounding. All three will push the incumbents hard.

Center: Some services rated the 6'10" Hathaway as high as No. 6 in the nation. No doubt, he's the most touted signee here since Wade Houston brought his son Allan to campus when he replaced Don DeVoe as head coach in 1989. Hathaway averaged 21 points and 13 rebounds as a high school senior. Pencil him into the low post as the starter.

Analysis: O'Neill's reputation is that of a relentless recruiter, and he certainly lived up to the billing with this group. This young team can't hope to challenge Kentucky just yet, but there should be plenty of tape for the highlight video.

1996-97 ROSTER

	POS	HT	YR	FGP	FTP	3-PT	RPG	APG	PPG
Brandon Wharton	G	6'3"	So.	.376	.748	56/141	3.5	2.8	12.6
Aaron Green	G	6'2"	So.	.407	.674	46/117	0.9	1.3	6.8
Maurice Robertson	F	6'5"	So.	.379	.882	3/9	2.4	0.6	3.6
Rashard Lee	F	6'6"	So.	.333	.542	10/32	2.2	0.9	2.5
Torrey Harris	F	6'10"	So.	.394	.412	0/0	2.3	0.1	1.2
Antonio Harris	G	6'3"	So.	.500	.000	2/4	0.1	0.2	0.7
C.J. Black	F	6'8"	Fr.	—	—	—	—	—	—
Charles Hathaway	C	6'10"	Fr.	—	—	—	—	—	—
Cornelius Jackson	G	6'5"	Fr.	—	—	—	—	—	—
DaShay Jones	G	6'2"	Jr.	—	—	—	—	—	—
Marques Maybin	G/F	6'4"	Fr.	—	—	—	—	—	—
Isiah Victor	F	6'9"	Fr.	—	—	—	—	—	—

TEXAS

Conference: Big 12
1995-96: 21-10, 3rd Southwest

1995-96 NCAAs: 1-1
Coach: Tom Penders (392-272)

Opening Line: In the final go-around of the Southwest Conference, Texas found itself in the shadow of Texas Tech until the NCAA Tournament. That's when the Longhorns defeated Michigan and pushed Wake Forest to the wire. Texas loses only two role-playing seniors off that team and appears primed for a smashing debut in the newly configured Big 12 Conference.

Guard: Names like Travis Mays, Lance Blanks, B.J. Tyler, and Terrence Rencher have kept the energy at a high pitch, and there are two worthy successors to that legacy on the present roster. Senior Reggie Freeman, 6'6", emerged as the club's offensive leader last year, and 6'5" sophomore Kris Clack demonstrated he is a potent scorer, too. Both can drive to the goal or pull up for jumpers, and neither is afraid of taking the tough shot. Junior Brandy Perryman is the designated long bomber off the bench, while 6'4" sophomore DeJuan Vazquez delivers steady ball-handling and the odd basket.

Forward: In truth, Freeman is actually the small forward. Penders favors a three-guard rotation that presents some defensive headaches. Two newcomers will join holdover Carlton Dixon in the forward rotation: 6'7" Gabe Muoneke, a freshman, and 6'8" junior college transfer Ira Clark. All three thrive in the transition game played in Austin.

Center: The only real hole to fill is here, where the affable if limited Sonny Alvarado held court. His backup, 6'9" Dennis Jordan, gets the nod in his absence. Jordan is not much of a scorer and can be prone to fouls. Senior Sheldon Quarles looks like the backup.

Analysis: Of the four longtime members of the Southwest Conference moving to the old Big Eight, Texas is the best equipped to contend immediately. This is a Top 25-caliber team, and only Kansas appears out of its reach in the new league.

1996-97 ROSTER

	POS	HT	YR	FGP	FTP	3-PT	RPG	APG	PPG
Reggie Freeman	G	6'6"	Sr.	.376	.732	87/270	6.7	3.9	22.4
Kris Clack	G	6'5"	So.	.502	.534	14/39	8.2	3.1	12.6
Brandy Perryman	G	6'2"	Jr.	.363	.883	65/194	1.7	2.7	9.3
DeJuan Vazquez	G	6'4"	So.	.384	.417	21/67	2.5	1.6	5.9
Carlton Dixon	F	6'5"	Jr.	.500	.653	0/4	2.9	0.5	5.8
Titus Warmsley	G	5'10"	So.	.266	.630	10/46	0.6	0.6	2.8
Dennis Jordan	C	6'9"	Sr.	.508	.400	0/1	2.7	0.3	2.3
Sheldon Quarles	F/C	6'10"	Sr.	.368	.609	0/2	2.1	0.1	2.3
Al Coleman	G	6'1"	Sr.	.143	.571	1/6	0.2	0.3	0.5
Ira Clark	F/C	6'8"	Jr.	—	—	—	—	—	—
Anthony Goode	G	6'1"	Fr.	—	—	—	—	—	—
Gabe Muoneke	F	6'7"	Fr.	—	—	—	—	—	—

TEXAS CHRISTIAN

Conference: Western Athletic
1995-96: 15-15, 4th Southwest

1995-96 NCAAs/NIT: DNP
Coach: Billy Tubbs (470-226)

Opening Line: When Tubbs arrived in Ft. Worth two years ago, he promised to turn up the tempo. He has done just that: The Horned Frogs averaged 84 PPG last year. Unfortunately, they surrendered 85 PPG, which helps explain the .500 record. But this was a young team, featuring a freshman All-American in Damion Walker, that should improve as it enters the expanded WAC.

Guard: Jeff Jacobs, a 6'1" senior, logged the most action in the backcourt, averaging 31 minutes per night. In Tubbs's frenetic system, that's a lot. Jacobs is a good passer who will give up the basketball, and Tubbs encourages him to take the 3-point shot. He is not a penetrator. Senior Anthony Burks made 20 starts last winter, and he must concentrate on taking better shots. He made only one of every three attempts from the field. TCU's small guards are an easy target for foes at the defensive end. Senior Sharif Butler adds offense from the bench.

Forward: Versatile James Penny can swing to guard but will likely settle in at small forward. The team's second-leading scorer, he is an adequate 3-point shooter who can also drive to the basket. He is an excellent rebounder for his size. Walker, meanwhile, averaged 20.5 PPG and is the team's go-to man. In addition, he is a terrific rebounder and doesn't launch bad shots.

Center: Byron Waits held the fort here last year, but the burly pivot is gone—as are reserves Chris Richards and Saiplee Tuialli. Junior Dennis Davis, 6'10", is more suited to power forward, but he'll likely get the call here. Davis struggles with fouls. When he stays on the floor, he is a rebounding force.

Analysis: Tubbs has been absent from postseason play for two consecutive years. In all likelihood, the streak should end here. Walker could challenge for the national scoring title.

1996-97 ROSTER

	POS	HT	YR	FGP	FTP	3-PT	RPG	APG	PPG
Damion Walker	F/C	6'7"	So.	.503	.768	0/1	8.8	0.8	20.5
Jeff Jacobs	G	6'1"	Sr.	.362	.722	57/167	3.3	5.0	11.1
James Penny	F	6'6"	Jr.	.421	.615	33/91	5.8	1.7	11.1
Anthony Burks	G	6'0"	Sr.	.325	.752	32/116	2.2	4.1	9.2
Sharif Butler	G	6'4"	Sr.	.356	.545	29/106	2.6	1.4	7.5
Dennis Davis	F/C	6'10"	Jr.	.474	.667	0/0	5.1	0.3	5.2
Luke Allan	G	6'5"	So.	.421	.700	7/18	1.9	1.2	2.4
Scott Barrett	F	6'8"	Fr.	—	—	—	—	—	—
Prince Fowler	G	5'11"	So.	—	—	—	—	—	—
Malcolm Johnson	G	6'4"	Jr.	—	—	—	—	—	—
Mike Jones	G	6'3"	Jr.	—	—	—	—	—	—

TEXAS TECH

Conference: Big 12
1995-96: 30-2, 1st Southwest

1995-96 NCAAs: 2-1
Coach: James Dickey (100-49)

Opening Line: The Red Raiders closed out the Southwest Conference in style. They earned an undisputed regular-season championship and captured the postseason conference tournament as well. They helped redeem some of the SWC's tarnished hoops image with a convincing win over North Carolina and a strong game against Georgetown in the NCAA Tournament. Tech forward Darvin Ham provided one of the Tournament's most memorable moments when his dunk broke the backboard against the Tar Heels.

Guard: Five seniors started for Tech last winter, so there is not a lot of experience returning. Archie Myers, a 6'3" juco transfer, figures to earn a good chunk of playing time. He can handle the basketball or drive to the hole. Alongside him should be 6'4" junior Cory Carr. Carr displayed flashes of brilliance in his first two years but always had to look over his shoulder to see when he would be coming out of the contest. Now is his chance. Sophomore Stanley Bonewitz and junior Brock Barnes also can earn spots in the rotation.

Forward: Neither Jason Sasser nor Ham will be easily replaced. Junior Tony Battie, a 6'11" power forward, was asked only to provide defense and rebounding in the past. Now he must record double figures in scoring, too. Gracen Averil, 6'5", and Da'Mon Roberts, 6'7", were both accomplished scorers in junior college. They will compete with 6'5" freshman Richard Evans at small forward.

Center: Gionet Cooper, a 6'8" senior, is a solid role-player. He will occupy the post until Ross Carmichael, a touted 6'10" freshman, is ready for full-time duty. Carmichael is one of the players around whom Dickey hopes to rebuild.

Analysis: Duplicating 1995-96 is out of the question. Dickey must hope he can blend his holdovers quickly so that his Red Raiders don't sink to the depths of the Big 12.

1996-97 ROSTER

	POS	HT	YR	FGP	FTP	3-PT	RPG	APG	PPG
Cory Carr	G	6'4"	Jr.	.440	.761	92/235	3.8	1.5	16.1
Tony Battie	F/C	6'11"	Jr.	.516	.632	4/14	8.9	1.1	9.7
Stanley Bonewitz	G	6'3"	So.	.452	.722	29/74	1.0	2.1	4.3
Gionet Cooper	F/C	6'8"	Sr.	.536	.615	0/0	4.1	0.5	3.9
Deuce Jones	G	6'1"	Sr.	.424	.600	4/17	0.9	1.3	2.0
Da'Mon Roberts	F	6'7"	Sr.	.548	.556	0/0	1.5	0.3	1.8
Brock Barnes	G	6'5"	Jr.	.222	.833	3/15	0.7	0.2	1.1
Gracen Averil	G/F	6'5"	Jr.	.000	.000	0/0	0.0	0.0	0.0
Ross Carmichael	F/C	6'10"	Fr.	—	—	—	—	—	—
Richard Evans	G/F	6'5"	Fr.	—	—	—	—	—	—
Archie Myers	G	6'3"	Jr.	—	—	—	—	—	—
Cliff Owens	F	6'8"	Fr.	—	—	—	—	—	—

TULANE

Conference: Conference USA   **1995-96 NIT:** 3-1
1995-96: 22-10, 1st C-USA Red   **Coach:** Perry Clark (126-86)

Opening Line: A late-season slump probably cost the Green Wave an NCAA Tournament berth. The most damaging defeat may have been the blowout loss to Louisville in the second round of the Conference USA Tournament. Tulane rallied in the NIT, advancing to the Final Four before stumbling against Nebraska. Clark was linked with several openings at other schools over the summer, but none panned out.

Guard: This has been the weak link in Tulane's armor over the past three seasons. Spotty play from the backcourt has kept this program from taking the next step up the ladder. Turnovers have been a particular problem. Holdover Chris Cameron, 6'4", is ticketed for a heavy workload at one guard spot. He needs to become more reliable with his jumper. Sophomore Derrick Moore can distribute the basketball and is a threat to force a turnover. Senior Patrick Lewis's specialty is the 3-point shot.

Forward: The bookends have been in place here for three seasons: Jerald Honeycutt and Rayshard Allen. Now seniors, they must take charge off the floor as well as on it. Instant offense is supplied by 6'6" Correy Childs. Childs loves to attack the basket and knows how to convert once he gets there. Freshman Sterling Davis, 6'6", and sophomore Keith Harris will battle for what minutes are left.

Center: Junior Lawrence Nelson, 6'10", was labeled a project when he was recruited, but he has slowly made strides. He blocks shots and has a good feel for the basketball. What he lacks is muscle. Freshman Morris Jordan is his understudy, but don't be surprised to see Allen in the middle at crunch time.

Analysis: There really was no excuse for this club's late-season fade. The Green Wave possess all the tools to reach the field of 64, yet their guards must improve for them to last past the first weekend.

1996-97 ROSTER

	POS	HT	YR	FGP	FTP	3-PT	RPG	APG	PPG
Jerald Honeycutt	F	6'9"	Sr.	.402	.640	45/154	7.2	3.8	18.0
Rayshard Allen	F	6'7"	Sr.	.575	.636	0/5	6.8	1.7	13.0
Chris Cameron	G	6'4"	Sr.	.502	.596	20/66	5.1	1.6	9.5
Patrick Lewis	G	6'2"	Sr.	.397	.756	54/151	1.9	2.4	8.1
Correy Childs	F	6'6"	Sr.	.524	.500	1/4	3.0	1.7	6.1
Lawrence Nelson	C	6'10"	Jr.	.544	.392	0/0	3.5	0.6	5.3
Derrick Moore	G	6'1"	So.	.409	.692	11/25	2.1	1.2	2.7
Dan Smith	G	6'0"	Jr.	.000	1.00	0/0	0.3	0.6	0.3
Sterling Davis	G/F	6'6"	Fr.	—	—	—	—	—	—
Keith Harris	F	6'7"	So.	—	—	—	—	—	—
Morris Jordan	F	6'9"	Fr.	—	—	—	—	—	—
Billy Wells	G	6'2"	Fr.	—	—	—	—	—	—

TULSA

Conference: Western Athletic
1995-96: 22-8, 3rd Missouri Valley

1995-96 NCAAs: 0-1
Coach: Steve Robinson (22-8)

Opening Line: Some feared the Golden Hurricane would collapse when coach Tubby Smith left after fashioning back-to-back trips to the NCAA Tournament. It didn't happen. Steve Robinson, a former aide to Kansas coach Roy Williams, kept the momentum alive. Indeed, Tulsa was in position to defeat Louisville in the final minutes in the opening round of the NCAA Tournament.

Guard: One spot is locked up. It belongs to Shea Seals, the All-America candidate who might be the best player to attend Tulsa in the modern era. The point guard position is up for grabs, and two newcomers will have a chance to make their presence felt. One, 6'5" Adrian Crawford, looks like he might be ready to assume minutes as a freshman. Eric Coley, 6'5", is probably further away. Junior Rod Thompson saw action as a freshman and may have an inside line.

Forward: Several experienced hands completed their eligibility last spring, including Craig Hernadi and Ray Poindexter. But sophomore Michael Ruffin emerged as a future star. At 6'8", he is destined for heavy minutes. A smooth shot and the ability to play either facing the basket or posting up make him an intriguing prospect. Redshirt freshmen Zac Bennett and John Cornwell have a chance to contribute now.

Center: Rafael Maldonado and J.R. Rollo formed a strong tandem in the middle for the past three seasons. Rollo is gone, and Maldonado might not be equipped to handle the post full-time. Cornwell could see more time in the middle, and Ruffin might play here as well.

Analysis: Some valuable experience has been lost in the past two years, but the Golden Hurricane still have the ingredient that matters—Seals. Some strong role-players will help, too. Adjusting to the long road trips in the WAC won't be easy, but Tulsa appears strong enough to cope.

1996-97 ROSTER

	POS	HT	YR	FGP	FTP	3-PT	RPG	APG	PPG
Shea Seals	G/F	6'5"	Sr.	.379	.652	59/201	5.7	2.2	17.1
Michael Ruffin	F	6'8"	So.	.534	.463	0/1	7.7	0.7	7.1
Rod Thompson	G	6'0"	Jr.	.413	.844	18/46	2.6	2.8	6.7
Rafael Maldonado	C	6'11"	Sr.	.477	.558	0/0	2.6	0.6	3.7
Jonnie Gendron	G	6'3"	So.	.427	.733	14/30	1.5	0.7	3.3
Jamie Gillin	G	6'2"	Jr.	.500	.000	2/6	0.4	0.3	1.7
Jason Williams	G	6'1"	So.	.405	.750	4/6	0.6	0.8	1.5
Zac Bennett	F	6'9"	Fr.	—	—	—	—	—	—
Eric Coley	F	6'5"	Fr.	—	—	—	—	—	—
John Cornwell	F	6'9"	Fr.	—	—	—	—	—	—
Adrian Crawford	G	6'5"	Fr.	—	—	—	—	—	—
J.R. Cunningham	F/C	6'9"	Jr.	—	—	—	—	—	—

UCLA

Conference: Pac-10   **1995-96 NCAAs:** 0-1
1995-96: 23-8, 1st Pac-10   **Coach:** Jim Harrick (358-160)

Opening Line: One year after capturing its first national championship since the John Wooden era ended in 1975, UCLA fell into an old pattern, stumbling in the first round of the NCAA Tournament. Princeton pulled off the stunning upset, 43-41. That loss spoiled an otherwise successful season that included a Pac-10 championship.

Guard: The injury woes of lead guard Cameron Dollar contributed to the early knockout. Dollar played much of last season at less than 100 percent, and his renewed health this year will be an immediate plus. The 5'11" senior runs the show and understands where and when to feed the ball to the likes of running mate Toby Bailey, a 6'5" junior. One of the problems Dollar's absence underscored, though, was a lack of depth, especially of competent ball-handlers.

Forward: The regular starters are 6'9" J.R. Henderson and 6'5" Charles O'Bannon. These two terrific athletes are skilled scorers who need only a touch more consistency to be grouped with the best of the West. Kris Johnson scored a dozen points a game last season. He'll also swing to the backcourt, leaving the Bruins thin on the front line.

Center: In his debut, Jelani McCoy demonstrated that he is a force in the lane. He is a shot-blocking menace at the defensive end, which permits the Bruins' perimeter people to be more adventurous in applying pressure. With the unexpected departure of Ike Nwanko, Harrick is left without a backup in the middle.

Analysis: The loss to Princeton could haunt this program for a while. At the very least, it has muted the good vibrations produced by the '95 championship. The Bruins must respond again in the postseason so that critics don't renew their attacks on coach Harrick's credentials. A key issue is depth, and the early recruiting didn't produce any apparent solutions to that problem.

1996-97 ROSTER

	POS	HT	YR	FGP	FTP	3-PT	RPG	APG	PPG
Toby Bailey	G	6'5"	Jr.	.458	.644	62/157	4.3	3.4	14.8
J.R. Henderson	F	6'9"	Jr.	.572	.678	1/3	7.0	1.9	14.4
Charles O'Bannon	F	6'5"	Sr.	.527	.767	23/62	6.0	2.6	14.3
Kris Johnson	G/F	6'4"	Jr.	.569	.764	8/23	4.4	1.7	12.5
Jelani McCoy	C	6'10"	So.	.676	.435	0/0	6.9	0.9	10.2
Cameron Dollar	G	5'11"	Sr.	.372	.653	6/23	2.8	4.5	4.1
Bob Myers	F	6'7"	Sr.	.667	.654	0/0	1.6	0.2	2.7
Brandon Loyd	G	5'10"	So.	.286	.875	4/15	0.1	0.3	1.4
Harold Sylvester	G	5'10"	Jr.	.167	.000	1/3	0.2	0.2	0.3
Rico Hines	G	6'4"	Fr.	—	—	—	—	—	—

UTAH

Conference: Western Athletic
1995-96: 27-7, 1st WAC

1995-96 NCAAs: 2-1
Coach: Rick Majerus (250-103)

Opening Line: Only two of *Basketball Times'* first-team All-Americans returned to college for 1996-97, and the Utes have one of them—Keith Van Horn, the multidimensional senior forward. Van Horn pondered a declaration for the NBA draft but felt that there was unfinished business in Salt Lake City.

Guard: This is an area of concern for Majerus now that both Mark Rydalch and Brandon Jessie are gone. The loss of Jessie is huge: He was the club's most potent offensive weapon this side of Van Horn. His scoring punch kept teams from cornering Van Horn. Two Top 100 freshmen are among those looking to pick up the slack. Jeff Johnsen and David Jackson are sound players with scoring potential. Majerus can depend upon 5'11" senior Terry Preston to efficiently direct traffic, while senior Ben Caton will provide dependable 3-point shooting.

Forward: One spot here belongs to Van Horn, who will log upwards of 35 minutes a night. Majerus will call on a variety of players to work with Van Horn at forward. One is 6'9" Will Carlton, a sophomore who understands his role: to help out on defense, take the occasional charge, and rebound when needed. The coach will also look to 6'11" Ben Melmeth, a natural center. Melmeth struggles defensively with power forwards but is a quality contributor.

Center: Michael Doleac is a strong low-post presence who cleans the boards and plays with a lot of heart. Melmeth will also spend time at center, as will freshman Nate Althoff, a seven-footer.

Analysis: Utah has dominated the WAC in this decade, and Van Horn's decision to stay takes them to yet another level. Majerus is one of the nation's top coaches—don't let the self-deprecating humor fool you—and in Van Horn he has a legitimate superstar.

1996-97 ROSTER

	POS	HT	YR	FGP	FTP	3-PT	RPG	APG	PPG
Keith Van Horn	F	6'9"	Sr.	.538	.851	54/132	8.8	1.0	21.4
Ben Caton	G	6'3"	Sr.	.490	.859	39/98	1.8	2.3	8.8
Michael Doleac	F/C	6'11"	Jr.	.463	.793	0/1	7.7	0.8	8.6
Ben Melmeth	F/C	6'11"	Jr.	.421	.717	0/0	4.8	1.9	4.3
Will Carlton	F	6'9"	So.	.632	.667	0/1	1.8	1.1	3.1
Drew Hansen	F/G	6'5"	Jr.	.462	.778	11/34	1.8	0.7	2.7
Terry Preston	G	5'11"	Sr.	.367	.615	8/32	0.9	1.4	1.7
Kelly Leonard	G	6'5"	Sr.	.250	.400	0/0	0.5	0.5	0.8
Nate Althoff	C	7'0"	Fr.	—	—	—	—	—	—
David Jackson	G	6'4"	Fr.	—	—	—	—	—	—
Jeff Johnsen	G/F	6'5"	Fr.	—	—	—	—	—	—
Ashante Johnson	F	6'8"	So.	—	—	—	—	—	—
Jordie McTavish	G	6'0"	Fr.	—	—	—	—	—	—

VILLANOVA

Conference: Big East
1995-96: 26-7, 2nd Big East 6

1995-96 NCAAs: 1-1
Coach: Steve Lappas (135-108)

Opening Line: Led by All-American Kerry Kittles, the Wildcats spent the entire 1995-96 season ranked in the Associated Press Top 10. Matters unraveled a bit when Kittles was hit with a three-game NCAA suspension for improper use of a telephone credit card in late February. The 'Cats never seemed to regain their momentum, falling to Georgetown in the Big East Tournament semifinal and to Louisville (68-64) in the second round of the NCAA Tournament.

Guard: Kittles's unprecedented four-year run on the Main Line is over, and that is the largest problem. Senior Alvin Williams, 6'5", can increase his scoring. His penetrating skills will be a key of the motion offense. Gobbling up the majority of Kittles's minutes will be sophomores Howard Brown and John Celestand. Brown is an explosive athlete, while Celestand's great gift is his quickness. Freshman Brian Lynch, 6'6", could see action here too, especially if the sophomores falter.

Forward: What could have been a weakness became a strength when 6'9" Tim Thomas signed on with the 'Cats. This freshman was the most coveted prospect in America this side of NBA-bound Kobe Bryant. Thomas can step outside for medium-range jumpers and is quick enough to guard smaller players. Another freshman, 6'10" Malik Allen, will spell holdover Chuck Kornegay, 6'9", but Kornegay's penchant for silly mistakes may earn Allen some time. Senior Zeffy Penn brings defense and enthusiasm.

Center: The post belongs to 6'11" Jason Lawson, a candidate for All-America honors. Lawson's backup is 7'1" Rafal Bigus. The sophomore displayed flashes of potential in his debut.

Analysis: When the exit of a star like Kittles doesn't knock a squad from the preseason Top 10—and it won't at Villanova—it's clear that program is a prominent force nationally. Much of the focus this year will center on Thomas.

1996-97 ROSTER

	POS	HT	YR	FGP	FTP	3-PT	RPG	APG	PPG
Jason Lawson	C	6'11"	Sr.	.621	.693	0/1	6.8	1.2	12.3
Alvin Williams	G	6'5"	Sr.	.454	.710	35/101	3.5	5.4	11.0
Chuck Kornegay	F	6'9"	Sr.	.467	.603	0/0	4.8	1.7	6.3
Zeffy Penn	F	6'6"	Sr.	.488	.767	3/11	3.1	0.9	4.7
Howard Brown	G	6'5"	So.	.358	.588	16/56	2.0	1.0	3.6
John Celestand	G	6'3"	So.	.376	.692	10/39	1.2	1.5	3.3
Rafal Bigus	C	7'1"	So.	.532	.462	0/0	2.2	0.4	2.8
Brian Noone	G	6'1"	Jr.	.500	.000	3/5	0.1	0.0	1.1
Malik Allen	F	6'10"	Fr.	—	—	—	—	—	—
T.J. Caouette	F	6'7"	Fr.	—	—	—	—	—	—
Brian Lynch	G	6'6"	Fr.	—	—	—	—	—	—
Tim Thomas	F	6'9"	Fr.	—	—	—	—	—	—

VIRGINIA

Conference: Atlantic Coast   **1995-96 NCAAs/NIT:** DNP
1995-96: 12-15, 7th ACC   **Coach:** Jeff Jones (117-72)

Opening Line: The Cavaliers tied for the 1995 ACC regular-season title before falling upon hard times in 1995-96. Poor play from the touted guard combination of Harold Deane and Curtis Staples, combined with a weak front line, doomed the Cavs in the ACC. A dose of experience, sound recruiting, and some promising rookies should put Virginia back into the postseason picture.

Guard: Neither Deane nor Staples was among the best guards in the ACC, let alone the country. Both shot poorly, which seemed to affect the entirety of their games. Another problem is that both are relatively small, allowing opposing guards clear passing lanes. Deane must remain under control, and Staples needs to reclaim the sweet shooting stroke he displayed in his debut campaign. Courtney Alexander, a 6'6" sophomore, is an exceptional athlete with a superb first step.

Forward: Jamal Robinson's career at UVA has been wildly erratic. This is his final chance to prove his worth. He will receive a strong push from 6'5" freshman Willie Dersch, a smooth-shooting New Yorker, and transfer Monte Marcaccini, a 6'5" sophomore transfer. Marcaccini averaged 9.9 points per game for Pepperdine two years ago and has international experience with the junior national team. The power forward spot belongs to 6'8" Norman Nolan, an aggressive rebounder with decent shooting skills.

Center: Both Chris Alexander and Chase Metheney are gone, but help has arrived. Kris Hunter, a 6'10" freshman from Tallahassee, could move in next to Nolan. This rookie was courted by a collection of ACC and Big East powers.

Analysis: The Cavs' plunge below .500 won't last long. It will be a major upset if they are not included when the postseason invitations are handed out next March.

1996-97 ROSTER

	POS	HT	YR	FGP	FTP	3-PT	RPG	APG	PPG
Harold Deane	G	6'2"	Sr.	.344	.808	64/186	4.4	3.7	16.7
Curtis Staples	G	6'3"	Jr.	.374	.800	82/249	3.6	2.1	14.0
Courtney Alexander	G/F	6'6"	So.	.487	.768	18/35	4.5	1.3	13.9
Norman Nolan	F	6'8"	Jr.	.453	.552	0/0	7.0	0.8	9.5
Jamal Robinson	G/F	6'7"	Sr.	.456	.614	7/29	5.3	2.5	7.5
Michael Curtis	G	6'3"	Jr.	.333	.000	1/2	0.2	0.1	0.4
Martin Walton	F	6'9"	Sr.	.250	.286	0/0	1.3	0.0	0.3
Willie Dersch	G/F	6'5"	Fr.	—	—	—	—	—	—
Colin Ducharme	F	6'8"	Fr.	—	—	—	—	—	—
Kris Hunter	C	6'10"	Fr.	—	—	—	—	—	—
Monte Marcaccini	G/F	6'5"	So.	—	—	—	—	—	—
Craig McAndrew	F	6'10"	Fr.	—	—	—	—	—	—

VIRGINIA TECH

Conference: Atlantic 10
1995-96: 23-6, 1st A-10 West

1995-96 NCAAs: 1-1
Coach: Bill Foster (407-278)

Opening Line: The 1995 NIT champions returned every key component for the 1995-96 campaign and used that power to move into the Associated Press Top 25 for the first time in a decade. The Hokies climbed as high as No. 9 in February before a loss to Massachusetts at Cassell Coliseum.

Guard: The Hokies' reliable duo of Damon Watlington and Shawn Good is gone. Yet coach Foster is fortunate to have seasoned hands to step into their places in the lineup. Troy Manns, a 6'1" senior, was a two-year starter at George Mason before transferring here. He'll have a greater opportunity to demonstrate his explosive scoring skills now. Twins David and Jim Jackson, both 6'5" seniors, are veterans with tons of experience. Both are fundamentally sound and gifted shooters. Myron Guillory, 6'1", enjoyed some big moments in the run to the NIT crown in '95.

Forward: Jim Jackson could easily wind up as the starter at small forward. The senior would be paired with another seasoned player, All-America candidate Ace Custis. Custis is a strong enough rebounder that the Hokies may be able to get away with using a perimeter athlete like Jim Jackson at forward. Youngsters Shawn Browne and Andre Ray were buried by the Hokies' depth last year. Now is there opportunity to prove they belong.

Center: Senior Keefe Matthews shared time in the post with Travis Jackson last season. Jackson has moved on, so Foster is counting on Matthews as his main pivot. Sophomore Alvaro Tor, 6'9", might surface as his chief substitute.

Analysis: Topping 1995-96 is a tall order for the Hokies. However, this is a well-coached team with an All-America contender and a collection of gifted role-players. Plus, Cassell Coliseum offers a tremendous home-court advantage. VTU might falter a bit, but it won't fall far from its perch of a season ago.

1996-97 ROSTER

	POS	HT	YR	FGP	FTP	3-PT	RPG	APG	PPG
Ace Custis	F	6'7"	Sr.	.507	.673	6/21	9.5	2.4	13.4
Troy Manns	G	6'1"	Sr.	.413	.685	14/37	1.7	2.6	4.7
Jim Jackson	G/F	6'5"	Sr.	.432	.627	10/30	2.3	1.0	4.6
Keefe Matthews	C/F	6'8"	Sr.	.441	.424	0/1	1.8	0.3	3.4
David Jackson	G/F	6'5"	Sr.	.423	.700	11/31	1.3	0.4	3.1
Myron Guillory	G	6'1"	Jr.	.412	.625	4/16	0.5	0.6	1.5
Shawn Browne	F	6'6"	Jr.	.375	.500	0/0	0.3	0.0	1.0
Alvaro Tor	C/F	6'9"	So.	.333	.000	0/0	0.9	0.0	0.5
Brendan Dunlop	G	6'2"	Fr.	—	—	—	—	—	—
Andre Ray	F	6'4"	Fr.	—	—	—	—	—	—
Jesus Rodriguez	F	6'8"	Fr.	—	—	—	—	—	—
Russ Wheeler	F	6'8"	Fr.	—	—	—	—	—	—

WAKE FOREST

Conference: Atlantic Coast   **1995-96 NCAAs:** 3-1
1995-96: 26-6, 2nd ACC   **Coach:** Dave Odom (180-114)

Opening Line: After waiting 33 years to win an ACC championship, the Demon Deacons won two consecutive titles (1995 and 1996). The repeat was accomplished without Randolph Childress, the heart of the 1995 team. And even though center Tim Duncan was bothered by the flu in the NCAA Tournament, Wake Forest advanced to the Midwest Regional final before bowing out against eventual national champion Kentucky.

Guard: A major problem in the postseason was a knee injury that hampered 6'2" Tony Rutland. Rutland makes the offense go and should be back up to speed in 1996-97. Ace bomber Rusty LaRue has graduated. Attempting to pick up the slack is 6'1" junior Jerry Braswell. Steve Goolsby is a fine shooter whose chances will multiply this season.

Forward: Both starting forwards, 6'10" Ricky Peral and 6'8" Sean Allen, are back in the fold. Peral operates on the perimeter, where his smooth release makes him a deadly 3-point threat. Allen runs interference for Duncan, setting screens, rebounding, and checking some of the tougher interior athletes. The athletic William Stringfellow has the tools to be a strong rebounder off the bench.

Center: When Duncan stated he would spurn the NBA dollars again for another year of college, the delight in Winston-Salem was obvious. This is the nation's top player, a gifted big man devoid of many of the bad habits of his contemporaries. Now, Odom has signed an heir apparent in 7'1" McDonald's All-American Loren Woods. Woods is not unlike Duncan was entering college in that he is raw offensively but has plenty of room for development.

Analysis: One more year of Duncan means at least one more year in the national spotlight. If the guard play is solid—and that depends largely on Rutland's recovery—Wake Forest can make a legitimate push for the Final Four.

1996-97 ROSTER

	POS	HT	YR	FGP	FTP	3-PT	RPG	APG	PPG
Tim Duncan	C	6'10"	Sr.	.555	.687	7/23	12.3	2.9	19.1
Tony Rutland	G	6'2"	Jr.	.369	.756	75/187	2.7	3.9	11.9
Ricky Peral	F	6'10"	Sr.	.510	.755	51/100	4.3	1.4	9.4
Jerry Braswell	G	6'1"	Jr.	.435	.709	27/69	2.1	1.6	7.2
Sean Allen	F	6'8"	Sr.	.455	.681	0/2	4.4	1.0	5.0
Steven Goolsby	G/F	6'4"	Jr.	.450	.609	33/72	1.7	0.6	4.6
William Stringfellow	F	6'8"	So.	.458	.533	0/1	2.1	0.2	1.5
Joseph Amonett	G/F	6'5"	Jr.	.143	.571	1/12	0.3	0.1	0.8
Marc Scott	G	6'2"	Sr.	.167	.000	0/3	0.1	0.1	0.2
Rodney West	F/C	6'10"	Fr.	—	—	—	—	—	—
Loren Woods	C	7'1"	Fr.	—	—	—	—	—	—

WASHINGTON

Conference: Pac-10
1995-96: 16-12, T-5th Pac-10

1995-96 NIT: 0-1
Coach: Bob Bender (90-109)

Opening Line: In just his third season in Seattle, Bob Bender captured Pac-10 Coach of the Year honors last year. The Huskies reached postseason play for the first time since 1987. At year's end, forward Mark Sanford announced he was making himself available for the NBA draft, then changed his mind and undeclared.

Guard: Two key operatives, Bryant Boston and Jason Hamilton, used up their final year of eligibility in 1995-96. Bender now must incorporate a solid recruiting class with several veterans. Senior Jamie Booker, 6'3", is destined to play a large role. Junior Chris Thompson, 6'1", is a point guard with good vision. Sophomore Donald Watts and junior college transfer Jan Wooten are also in the picture.

Forward: Sanford, a terrific athlete, specializes in taking it to the hole. He needs to improve his outside shooting to open up the middle for Washington. Freshman Thalo Green received nice reviews from prep scouts and could make an impact. The Huskies know they can count on Jason Hartman, 6'6", a fine wing shooter. The junior finished third in the Pac-10 in 3-point shooting percentage.

Center: A redshirt season in 1994-95 offered 7'0" center Todd MacCulloch the chance to adapt to college life. The native of Winnipeg, Manitoba, then emerged as one of the league's top freshmen. His 270-pound frame and good height make him a huge interior threat in post-up situations. As his shot selection improves, he should be even better.

Analysis: With Sanford back in the mix, the Huskies wear the look of an NCAA Tournament contender. Look for MacCulloch—who was often mistaken for Bryant "Big Country" Reeves while working as a volunteer at the 1995 Final Four—to become a focal point of the offense.

1996-97 ROSTER

	POS	HT	YR	FGP	FTP	3-PT	RPG	APG	PPG
Mark Sanford	F	6'8"	Jr.	.460	.652	32/102	6.1	1.1	16.5
Todd MacCulloch	C	7'0"	So.	.675	.644	0/0	4.8	0.1	8.8
Jason Hartman	F	6'6"	Jr.	.388	.767	29/70	3.3	0.9	7.1
Jamie Booker	G	6'3"	Sr.	.384	.630	17/54	4.3	4.0	6.6
Patrick Femerling	C	7'1"	So.	.492	.553	0/0	2.7	0.5	3.0
Donald Watts	G	6'3"	So.	.222	.628	5/27	1.6	1.4	3.0
Chris Thompson	G	6'1"	Jr.	.400	.750	0/4	0.4	0.2	1.8
Thalo Green	F	6'7"	Fr.	—	—	—	—	—	—
Deon Luton	G	6'3"	Fr.	—	—	—	—	—	—
Chris Walcott	F	6'7"	Fr.	—	—	—	—	—	—
Quincy Wilder	G	6'2"	Fr.	—	—	—	—	—	—
Jan Wooten	G	5'11"	Jr.	—	—	—	—	—	—

WASHINGTON STATE

Conference: Pac-10   **1995-96 NIT:** 1-1
1995-96: 17-12, 7th Pac-10   **Coach:** Kevin Eastman (94-77)

Opening Line: A broken hand that felled four-year starting forward Mark Hendrickson probably kept the Cougars out of the NCAA Tournament. Hendrickson's absence resulted in a midseason swoon, leaving WSU short of a bid to the big dance. Now the Cougars have to learn how to live without Hendrickson for good.

Guard: Last year, WSU had one of the Pac-10's finest backcourt duos in Isaac Fontaine and Dominic Ellison. Fontaine is an athletic swingman and an important leader for this club. His complete game is the most potent weapon in WSU's arsenal. Ellison won't be easily replaced. Kareem Jackson, who set a school assist record at Sacramento City College but was injured last season, will get a shot at point guard. Senior Chris Scott is a fine rebounder off the bench.

Forward: Junior Carlos Daniel came into his own in 1995-96 and is now being counted on to pick up the slack from the exit of Hendrickson. Long arms and an aggressive attitude make him a defensive nuisance, and he has a few scoring moves, too. Tavares Mack runs the floor well and has a nose for the basketball around the basket. Freshman Chris Crosby presents matchup problems at 6'7" because he can put the ball on the floor or draw defenders away from the goal with an odd-looking but effective jumper.

Center: In truth, the Cougars don't really have a center. Eastman favors the use of three guards and two forwards most of the time. Justin Mott, a 6'10" freshman, could change that. He won't be much of a scoring threat early, but Eastman will be delighted if he contributes as a rebounder.

Analysis: Eastman has kept the momentum built by Kelvin Sampson alive. A healthier campaign than the one they endured last year would give the Cougars a chance to move into the top half of the Pac-10.

1996-97 ROSTER

	POS	HT	YR	FGP	FTP	3-PT	RPG	APG	PPG
Isaac Fontaine	G	6'3"	Sr.	.462	.822	66/136	5.6	2.7	18.1
Carlos Daniel	F	6'7"	Jr.	.534	.701	0/0	5.9	1.1	9.5
Tavares Mack	F	6'9"	Sr.	.576	.576	0/0	4.5	0.3	7.4
Chris Scott	G	6'2"	Sr.	.300	.588	4/29	2.0	0.9	2.2
Cameron Johnson	F	6'7"	Sr.	.379	.667	0/0	1.7	0.4	1.8
Kareem Jackson	G	6'2"	Sr.	.258	.286	5/12	1.4	1.3	1.0
Will Hutchens	G	6'3"	So.	.250	.000	0/2	0.6	0.4	0.4
Beau Archibald	G	6'7"	Fr.	—	—	—	—	—	—
Chris Crosby	F	6'7"	Fr.	—	—	—	—	—	—
Rodrigo de la Fuente	G	6'7"	Jr.	—	—	—	—	—	—
Justin Mott	C	6'10"	Fr.	—	—	—	—	—	—
Blake Pengelly	G	5'10"	Fr.	—	—	—	—	—	—

College Basketball Review

The final section in the book reviews the 1995-96 college basketball season and lists important historical information.

First, you'll find the final 1995-96 standings of 32 conferences in Division I. Their conference records include regular-season conference games only. Their overall records include all postseason tournament games, including conference tournaments, the NCAA, and the NIT. The standings indicate the teams that made the NCAA Tournament (*) and those that won their conference tournaments (#).

The recap of the 1995-96 season also includes the following:

- final A.P. poll and A.P. All-Americans
- Division I statistical leaders
- NCAA Tournament game-by-game results
- NCAA finals box score
- NIT results
- final A.P. women's poll
- women's NCAA tourney results

Finally, you'll find Division I historical information, including the following:

- national champions (1901-96)
- Final Four results (1939-96)
- Division I career leaders
- Division I season records
- Division I game records
- winningest Division I teams

The NCAA Tournament didn't begin until 1939. Prior to that, there were no official national champions. However, the Helms Foundation selected national champs retroactively for the years 1901-38. These are the teams that are listed in the national champions chart.

DIVISION I FINAL STANDINGS, 1995-96

American West

	Conference			Overall		
	W	L	Pct.	W	L	Pct.
Cal. Poly-SLO	5	1	.833	16	13	.552
#Southern Utah	3	3	.500	15	13	.536
Cal. St.-Northr.	2	4	.333	7	20	.259
Cal. St.-Sacra.	2	4	.333	7	20	.259

Atlantic Coast

	Conference			Overall		
	W	L	Pct.	W	L	Pct.
*Georgia Tech	13	3	.813	24	12	.667
*#Wake Forest	12	4	.750	26	6	.813
*North Carolina	10	6	.625	21	11	.656
*Duke	8	8	.500	18	13	.581
*Maryland	8	8	.500	17	13	.567
*Clemson	7	9	.438	18	11	.621
Virginia	6	10	.375	12	15	.444
Florida St.	5	11	.313	13	14	.481
N. Carolina St.	3	13	.188	15	16	.484

Atlantic 10
Eastern Division

	Conference			Overall		
	W	L	Pct.	W	L	Pct.
*#Massachusetts	15	1	.938	35	2	.946
*Temple	12	4	.750	20	13	.606
St. Joseph's	9	7	.563	19	13	.594
Rhode Island	8	8	.500	20	14	.588
St. Bonaventure	4	12	.250	10	18	.357
Fordham	2	14	.125	4	23	.148

Western Division

	Conference			Overall		
	W	L	Pct.	W	L	Pct.
*Virginia Tech	13	3	.813	23	6	.793
*G. Washington	13	3	.813	21	8	.724
Xavier (OH)	8	8	.500	13	15	.464
Dayton	6	10	.375	15	14	.517
La Salle	3	13	.188	6	24	.200
Duquesne	3	13	.188	9	18	.333

Big East
BE7 Division

	Conference			Overall		
	W	L	Pct.	W	L	Pct.
*Georgetown	13	5	.722	29	8	.784
*Syracuse	12	6	.667	29	9	.763
Providence	9	9	.500	18	12	.600
Miami (FL)	8	10	.444	15	13	.536
Seton Hall	7	11	.389	12	16	.429
Rutgers	6	12	.333	9	18	.333
Pittsburgh	5	13	.278	10	17	.370

BE6 Division

	Conference			Overall		
	W	L	Pct.	W	L	Pct.
*#Connecticut	17	1	.944	32	3	.914
*Villanova	14	4	.778	26	7	.788
*Boston College	10	8	.556	19	11	.633
West Virginia	7	11	.389	12	15	.444
St. John's	5	13	.278	11	16	.407
Notre Dame	4	14	.222	9	18	.333

Big Eight

	Conference			Overall		
	W	L	Pct.	W	L	Pct.
*Kansas	12	2	.857	29	5	.853
*#Iowa St.	9	5	.643	24	9	.727
*Oklahoma	8	6	.571	17	13	.567
Oklahoma St.	7	7	.500	17	10	.630
*Kansas St.	7	7	.500	17	12	.586
Missouri	6	8	.429	18	15	.545
Nebraska	4	10	.286	21	14	.600
Colorado	3	11	.214	9	18	.333

Big Sky

	Conference			Overall		
	W	L	Pct.	W	L	Pct.
*#Montana St.	11	3	.786	21	9	.700
Weber St.	10	4	.714	20	10	.667
Montana	10	4	.714	20	8	.714
Boise St.	10	4	.714	15	13	.536
Idaho St.	7	7	.500	11	15	.423
Idaho	5	9	.357	12	16	.429
Northern Arizona	3	11	.214	6	20	.231
E. Washington	0	14	.000	3	23	.115

Big South

	Conference			Overall		
	W	L	Pct.	W	L	Pct.
*#N.C.-Greens.	11	3	.786	20	10	.667
N.C.-Asheville	9	5	.643	18	10	.643
Liberty	9	5	.643	17	12	.586
Charleston So.	9	5	.643	15	13	.536
Radford	8	6	.571	14	13	.519
Winthrop	6	8	.429	7	19	.269
Md.-Balt. County	3	11	.214	5	22	.185
Coastal Carolina	1	13	.071	5	21	.192

Big Ten

	Conference			Overall		
	W	L	Pct.	W	L	Pct.
*Purdue	15	3	.833	26	6	.813
*Penn St.	12	6	.667	21	7	.750
*Indiana	12	6	.667	19	12	.613
*Iowa	11	7	.611	23	9	.719
*Michigan	10	8	.556	20	12	.625
Minnesota	10	8	.556	19	13	.594
Michigan St.	9	9	.500	16	16	.500
Wisconsin	8	10	.444	17	15	.531
Illinois	7	11	.389	18	13	.581
Ohio St.	3	18	.143	10	17	.370
Northwestern	2	16	.111	7	20	.259

Big West

	Conference			Overall		
	W	L	Pct.	W	L	Pct.
Long Beach St.	12	6	.667	17	11	.607
Cal.-Irvine	11	7	.611	15	12	.556
Pacific	11	7	.611	15	12	.556
Utah St.	10	8	.556	18	15	.545
Nevada	9	9	.500	16	13	.552
*#San Jose St.	9	9	.500	13	17	.433
New Mexico St.	8	10	.444	11	15	.423
Cal.-Santa Barb.	8	10	.444	11	15	.423
UNLV	7	11	.389	10	16	.385
Cal.-Fullerton	5	13	.278	6	20	.231

Colonial Athletic

	Conference			Overall	
	W	L	Pct.	W	L	Pct.
*#Virginia Comm.	14	2	.875	24	9	.727
Old Dominion	12	4	.750	18	13	.581
N.C.-Wilmington	9	7	.563	13	16	.448
East Carolina	8	8	.500	17	11	.607
American	8	8	.500	12	15	.444
George Mason	6	10	.375	11	16	.407
William & Mary	6	10	.375	10	16	.385
James Madison	6	10	.375	10	20	.333
Richmond	3	13	.188	8	20	.286

Conference USA
Red Division

	Conference			Overall	
	W	L	Pct.	W	L	Pct.
Tulane	9	5	.643	22	10	.688
Alabama-Birm.	6	8	.429	16	14	.533
S. Mississippi	6	8	.429	12	15	.444
South. Florida	2	12	.143	12	16	.429

White Division

	Conference			Overall	
	W	L	Pct.	W	L	Pct.
*Memphis	11	3	.786	22	8	.733
*Louisville	10	4	.714	22	12	.647
N.C.-Charlotte	6	8	.429	14	15	.483

Blue Division

	Conference			Overall	
	W	L	Pct.	W	L	Pct.
*#Cincinnati	11	3	.786	28	5	.848
*Marquette	10	4	.714	23	8	.742
St. Louis	4	10	.286	16	14	.533
DePaul	2	12	.143	11	18	.379

Ivy League

	Conference			Overall	
	W	L	Pct.	W	L	Pct.
*Princeton	13	2	.867	22	7	.759
Pennsylvania	12	3	.800	17	10	.630
Dartmouth	9	5	.643	16	10	.615
Harvard	7	7	.500	15	11	.577
Brown	5	9	.357	10	16	.385
Cornell	5	9	.357	10	16	.385
Yale	3	11	.214	8	18	.308
Columbia	3	11	.214	7	19	.269

Metro Atlantic Athletic

	Conference			Overall	
	W	L	Pct.	W	L	Pct.
Iona	10	4	.714	21	8	.724
Fairfield	10	4	.714	20	10	.667
Manhattan	9	5	.643	17	12	.586
Loyola (MD)	8	6	.571	12	15	.444
*#Canisius	7	7	.500	19	11	.633
Niagara	6	8	.429	13	15	.464
St. Peter's	5	9	.357	15	12	.556
Siena	1	13	.071	5	22	.185

Mid-American

	Conference			Overall	
	W	L	Pct.	W	L	Pct.
*#E. Michigan	14	4	.778	25	6	.806
W. Illinois	13	5	.722	15	12	.556
Miami (OH)	12	6	.667	16	14	.724
Ohio	11	7	.611	16	12	.533
Ball St.	11	7	.611	16	12	.571
Bowling Green	9	9	.500	14	13	.519
Toledo	9	9	.500	18	14	.563
Kent	8	10	.444	14	13	.519
Central Michigan	3	15	.167	6	20	.231
Akron	0	18	.000	3	23	.115

Mid-Continent

	Conference			Overall	
	W	L	Pct.	W	L	Pct.
*#Valparaiso	13	5	.722	21	11	.656
Western Illinois	12	6	.667	17	12	.586
N.E. Illinois	10	8	.556	14	13	.519
Buffalo	10	8	.556	13	14	.481
Missouri-K.C.	10	8	.556	12	15	.444
Central Conn. St	9	9	.500	13	15	.464
Eastern Illinois	9	9	.500	13	15	.464
Troy St.	8	10	.444	11	16	.407
Youngstown St.	7	11	.389	12	15	.444
Chicago St.	2	16	.111	2	25	.074

Mid-Eastern Athletic

	Conference			Overall	
	W	L	Pct.	W	L	Pct.
*#S. Carolina St.	14	2	.875	22	8	.733
Coppin St.	14	2	.875	19	10	.655
Bethune-Cookman	8	8	.500	12	15	.444
Delaware St.	8	8	.500	11	17	.393
N. Carolina A&T	7	9	.438	10	17	.370
Md.-East Shore	6	10	.375	11	16	.407
Howard	6	10	.375	7	20	.259
Morgan St.	6	10	.375	7	20	.259
Florida A&M	3	13	.188	8	19	.296
Hampton	—	—	—	9	17	.346

Midwestern Collegiate

	Conference			Overall	
	W	L	Pct.	W	L	Pct.
*Wis.-Green Bay	16	0	1.000	25	4	.923
Butler	12	4	.750	19	8	.731
*#Northern Illinois	10	6	.625	20	10	.667
Wright St.	8	8	.500	14	13	.519
Detroit	8	8	.500	18	11	.621
Wis.-Milwaukee	5	11	.313	9	18	.333
Illinois-Chicago	5	11	.313	10	18	.357
Loyola (IL)	5	11	.313	8	19	.296
Cleveland St.	3	13	.188	5	21	.192

Missouri Valley

	Conference			Overall	
	W	L	Pct.	W	L	Pct.
*Bradley	15	3	.833	22	8	.733
Illinois St.	13	5	.722	22	12	.647
*#Tulsa	12	6	.667	22	8	.733
S.W. Missou. St.	11	7	.611	16	12	.571
Creighton	9	9	.500	14	15	.483
Evansville	9	9	.500	13	14	.481
Northern Iowa	8	10	.444	14	13	.519
Drake	8	10	.444	12	15	.444
Indiana St.	6	12	.333	10	16	.385
Southern Illinois	4	14	.222	11	18	.379
Wichita St.	4	14	.222	8	21	.276

North Atlantic Conference

	Conference			Overall		
	W	L	Pct.	W	L	Pct.
*#Drexel	17	1	.944	27	4	.871
Boston U.	13	5	.722	18	11	.621
Maine	11	7	.611	15	13	.536
Delaware	11	7	.611	15	12	.556
Towson St.	11	7	.611	16	12	.571
Vermont	10	8	.555	12	15	.444
Hofstra	5	13	.278	9	18	.333
New Hampshire	5	13	.278	6	21	.222
Hartford	5	13	.278	5	22	.214
Northeastern	2	16	.111	4	24	.143

Northeast Conference

	Conference			Overall		
	W	L	Pct.	W	L	Pct.
Mount St. Mary's	16	2	.889	21	8	.724
Marist	14	4	.778	22	7	.808
*#Monmouth (NJ)	14	4	.778	20	10	.654
Rider	12	6	.667	19	11	.630
St. Francis (PA)	11	7	.611	13	13	.500
Wagner	7	11	.389	10	17	.385
Fairleigh Dickin.	6	12	.333	7	20	.259
Long Island	5	13	.278	9	19	.321
St. Francis (NY)	3	15	.167	9	18	.333
Robert Morris	2	16	.111	5	23	.179

Ohio Valley Conference

	Conference			Overall		
	W	L	Pct.	W	L	Pct.
Murray St.	12	4	.750	19	10	.655
Tennessee St.	11	5	.687	15	13	.536
*#Austin Peay	10	6	.625	19	11	.633
Middle Tenn. St.	9	7	.563	15	12	.556
Tenn.-Martin	9	7	.563	13	14	.481
Eastern Kentucky	7	9	.437	13	14	.481
Tennessee Tech	7	9	.437	13	15	.464
S.E. Missouri St.	5	11	.313	8	19	.296
Morehead St.	2	14	.125	7	20	.259

Pacific-10 Conference

	Conference			Overall		
	W	L	Pct.	W	L	Pct.
*UCLA	16	2	.889	23	8	.742
*Arizona	13	5	.722	26	7	.788
*Stanford	12	6	.667	20	9	.690
*California	11	7	.611	17	11	.607
Washington	9	9	.500	16	12	.571
Oregon	9	9	.500	13	13	.552
Washington St.	8	10	.444	17	12	.586
Arizona St.	6	12	.333	11	16	.407
Southern Cal.	4	14	.222	11	19	.367
Oregon St.	2	16	.111	4	23	.148

Patriot League Conference

	Conference			Overall		
	W	L	Pct.	W	L	Pct.
Navy	9	3	.750	15	12	.556
*#Colgate	9	3	.750	15	15	.500
Bucknell	8	4	.667	17	11	.607
Holy Cross	8	4	.667	16	13	.552
Lafayette	4	8	.333	7	20	.259
Army	2	10	.167	7	20	.259
Lehigh	2	10	.167	4	23	.148

Southeastern

Eastern Division

	Conference			Overall		
	W	L	Pct.	W	L	Pct.
*Kentucky	16	0	1.000	34	2	.944
*Georgia	9	7	.563	21	10	.677
South Carolina	8	8	.500	19	12	.613
Vanderbilt	7	9	.438	18	14	.563
Florida	6	10	.375	12	16	.429
Tennessee	6	10	.375	14	15	.483

Western Division

	Conference			Overall		
	W	L	Pct.	W	L	Pct.
*#Mississippi St.	10	6	.625	26	8	.765
*Arkansas	9	7	.563	20	13	.606
Alabama	9	7	.563	19	13	.594
Mississippi	6	10	.375	12	15	.444
Auburn	6	10	.375	19	13	.594
LSU	4	12	.250	12	17	.414

Southern

North Division

	Conference			Overall		
	W	L	Pct.	W	L	Pct.
Davidson	14	0	1.000	25	5	.833
Virginia Military	10	4	.714	18	10	.643
Marshall	8	6	.571	17	11	.607
E. Tenn. St.	3	11	.214	7	20	.259
Appalachian St.	3	11	.214	8	20	.286

South Division

	Conference			Overall		
	W	L	Pct.	W	L	Pct.
*#W. Carolina	10	4	.714	17	13	.567
Tenn.-Chatta.	9	5	.643	15	12	.556
Furman	6	8	.429	10	17	.370
Citadel	5	9	.357	10	16	.385
Georgia Southern	2	12	.143	3	23	.115

Southland Conference

	Conference			Overall		
	W	L	Pct.	W	L	Pct.
*#N.E. Louisiana	13	5	.722	16	14	.533
North Texas	12	6	.667	15	13	.536
Texas-San Ant.	12	6	.667	14	14	.500
Stephen Austin	11	7	.611	17	11	.607
McNeese St.	11	7	.611	15	12	.556
Sam Houston St.	9	9	.500	11	16	.407
S.W. Texas St.	7	11	.389	11	15	.423
Texas-Arlington	7	11	.389	11	15	.423
Nicholls St.	5	13	.278	5	21	.192
Northwestern St.	3	15	.167	5	21	.192

Southwest Conference

	Conference			Overall		
	W	L	Pct.	W	L	Pct.
*#Texas Tech	14	0	1.000	30	2	.938
Houston	11	3	.786	17	10	.630
*Texas	10	4	.714	21	10	.677
Texas Christian	6	8	.429	15	15	.500
Rice	5	9	.357	14	14	.500
Baylor	4	10	.286	9	18	.333
SMU	3	11	.214	8	20	.286
Texas A&M	3	11	.214	11	16	.407

Southwestern Athletic

	Conference			Overall		
	W	L	Pct.	W	L	Pct.
*#Missi. Valley St.	11	3	.786	22	7	.759
Jackson St.	11	3	.786	16	13	.552
Southern-B.R.	9	5	.643	17	11	.607
Texas Southern	7	7	.429	11	15	.423
Alcorn St.	7	7	.500	10	15	.400
Grambling	6	8	.429	12	16	.429
Alabama St.	6	8	.429	9	18	.333
Prairie View	0	14	.000	4	23	.148

Sun Belt

	Conference			Overall		
	W	L	Pct.	W	L	Pct.
Arkan.-Little Rock	14	4	.778	23	7	.767
*#New Orleans	14	4	.778	21	9	.700
Jacksonville	10	8	.556	15	13	.536
West. Kentucky	10	8	.556	13	14	.481
S.W. Louisiana	9	9	.500	16	12	.571
Lamar	7	11	.389	12	15	.444
South Alabama	7	11	.389	12	15	.444
Arkansas St.	7	11	.389	9	18	.333
Louisiana Tech	6	12	.333	11	17	.393
Texas-Pan Am.	6	12	.333	9	19	.321

Trans America Athletic

East Division

	Conference			Overall		
	W	L	Pct.	W	L	Pct.
Charleston (SC)	15	1	.938	25	4	.862
Campbell	11	5	.688	17	11	.607
*#Central Florida	6	10	.375	11	19	.367
Stetson	6	10	.375	10	17	.370
Florida Int'l	6	11	.353	13	15	.464
Florida Atlantic	5	11	.313	9	18	.333

Final A.P. Poll, 1995-96

	W-L	Points
1. Massachusetts (53)	31-1	1,587
2. Kentucky (2)	28-2	1,513
3. Connecticut (8)	30-2	1,499
4. Georgetown	26-7	1,259
4. Kansas	26-4	1,259
4. Purdue	25-5	1,259
7. Cincinnati	25-4	1,248
8. Texas Tech (1)	28-1	1,231
9. Wake Forest	23-5	1,118
10. Villanova	25-6	995
11. Arizona	24-6	857
12. Utah	25-6	793
13. Georgia Tech	22-11	693
14. UCLA	23-7	688
15. Syracuse	24-8	675
16. Memphis	22-7	527
17. Iowa St.	23-8	516
18. Penn St.	21-6	497
19. Mississippi St.	22-7	496
20. Marquette	22-7	492
21. Iowa	22-8	445
22. Virginia Tech	22-5	324
23. New Mexico	27-4	211
24. Louisville	20-11	157
25. North Carolina	20-10	151

West Division

	Conference			Overall		
	W	L	Pct.	W	L	Pct.
Samford	11	5	.687	16	11	.593
S.E. Louisiana	11	5	.687	15	12	.556
Centenary (LA)	8	8	.500	11	16	.407
Mercer	8	9	.471	15	14	.517
Georgia St.	6	10	.375	10	16	.385
Jacksonville St.	4	12	.250	10	17	.370

West Coast

	Conference			Overall		
	W	L	Pct.	W	L	Pct.
*Santa Clara	10	4	.714	20	9	.690
Gonzaga	10	4	.714	21	9	.700
Loyola Marymount	8	6	.571	18	11	.621
San Francisco	8	6	.571	15	12	.556
*#Portland	7	7	.500	19	11	.633
San Diego	6	8	.429	14	14	.500
St. Mary's (CA)	5	9	.357	12	15	.444
Pepperdine	2	12	.143	10	18	.357

Western Athletic

	Conference			Overall		
	W	L	Pct.	W	L	Pct.
*Utah	15	3	.833	27	7	.794
*#New Mexico	14	4	.778	28	5	.848
Fresno St.	13	5	.722	22	11	.667
Colorado St.	11	7	.611	18	12	.600
Brigham Young	9	9	.500	15	13	.536
San Diego St.	8	10	.444	15	14	.517
Wyoming	8	10	.444	14	15	.483
Hawaii	7	11	.359	10	18	.357
Texas-El Paso	4	14	.222	13	15	.464
Air Force	1	17	.056	5	23	.179

Independents

	Overall		
	W	L	Pct.
Oral Roberts	18	9	.667
Wofford	4	22	.154

* Selected to the NCAA Tournament.
# Won postseason conference tournament.

A.P. ALL-AMERICA TEAMS

First Team
*Marcus Camby, Massachusetts
Ray Allen, Connecticut
Allen Iverson, Georgetown
Tim Duncan, Wake Forest
Kerry Kittles, Villanova

Second Team
Keith Van Horn, Utah
Tony Delk, Kentucky
Danny Fortson, Cincinnati
Jacque Vaughn, Kansas
John Wallace, Syracuse

* Winner of the Wooden Award, Naismith Award, and Rupp Trophy as national Player of the Year.

Poll taken prior to the NCAA Tournament and the NIT. Won-loss records reflect performances at the time the polls were taken. First-place votes in parentheses.

DIVISION I LEADERS, 1995-96

SCORING

Kevin Granger, Texas Southern	27.0
Marcus Brown, Murray St.	26.4
Bubba Wells, Austin Peay	26.3
JaFonde Williams, Hampton Institute	25.7
Bonzi Wells, Ball St.	25.4
Anquell McCollum, Western Carolina	25.0
Allen Iverson, Georgetown	25.0
Eddie Benton, Vermont	24.5
Matt Alosa, New Hampshire	24.0
Ray Allen, Connecticut	23.4
Michael Hart, Tennessee-Martin	22.8
Tunji Awojobi, Boston University	22.7
Darren McLinton, James Madison	22.7
Reggie Elliott, Mercer	22.6
Jeff Norgaard, Wisconsin-Green Bay	22.6
Reggie Freeman, Texas	22.4
Anthony Harris, Hawaii	22.4
Jason Daisy, Northern Iowa	22.3
Chris McGuthrie, Mt. St. Mary's	22.3
John Wallace, Syracuse	22.2
Curtis McCants, George Mason	22.0
Sam Bowie, Southeastern Louisiana	21.9
Craig Thames, Toledo	21.8
Ronnie Henderson, LSU	21.8
Marcus Mann, Mississippi Valley St.	21.7

REBOUNDS

Marcus Mann, Mississippi Valley St.	13.6
Malik Rose, Drexel	13.2
Adonal Foyle, Colgate	12.6
Tim Duncan, Wake Forest	12.3
Scott Farley, Mercer	12.0
Chris Ensminger, Valparaiso	11.5
Alan Tomidy, Marist	11.4
Quadre Lollis, Montana St.	11.3
Thaddeous DeLaney, Charleston (SC)	11.3
Kyle Snowden, Harvard	11.1

ASSISTS

Raimonds Miglinieks, California-Irvine	8.5
Curtis McCants, George Mason	8.3
Dan Pogue, Campbell	8.0
Pointer Williams, McNeese St.	7.4
Lazarus Sims, Syracuse	7.4
Brevin Knight, Stanford	7.3
Phillip Turner, California-Santa Barbara	7.3
Reggie Geary, Arizona	7.0
David Fizdale, San Diego	7.0
Aaron Hutchins, Marquette	6.9

STEALS

Pointer Williams, McNeese St.	4.4
Johnny Rhodes, Maryland	3.7
Roderick Taylor, Jackson St.	3.7
Rasul Salahuddin, Long Beach St.	3.6
Andrell Hoard, N.E. Illinois	3.6
Ben Larson, Cal. Poly SLO	3.4
Allen Iverson, Georgetown	3.4
Bonzi Wells, Ball St.	3.1
Jerry McCullough, Pittsburgh	3.0

BLOCKED SHOTS

Keith Closs, Central Connecticut St.	6.4
Adonal Foyle, Colgate	5.7
Roy Rogers, Alabama	4.9
Jerome James, Florida A&M	4.4
Alan Tomidy, Marist	3.9
Peter Aluma, Liberty	3.9
Marcus Camby, Massachusetts	3.9
Tim Duncan, Wake Forest	3.8
Calvin Booth, Penn St.	3.6
Lorenzo Coleman, Tennessee Tech	3.4

FIELD-GOAL PCT.

Quadre Lollis, Montana St.	67.5
Daniel Watts, Nevada	65.6
Lincoln Abrams, Centenary (LA)	65.4
Alexander Koul, George Washington	64.2
Terquin Mott, Coppin St.	63.8
Antawn Jamison, North Carolina	62.4
Stanley Caldwell, Tennessee St.	61.8
Greg Smith, Delaware	61.3
Marcus Mann, Mississippi Valley St.	60.5
Curtis Fincher, Eastern Kentucky	60.4

FREE-THROW PCT.

Mike Dillard, Sam Houston St.	92.6
Dion Cross, Stanford	92.0
Roderick Howard, North Carolina-Charlotte	90.3
Geoff Billet, Rutgers	90.0
Derek Grimm, Missouri	88.5
Marcus Wilson, Evansville	88.2
Nod Carter, Middle Tennessee St.	88.1
Alhamisi Simms, Maryland-Baltimore County	88.1
Jason Alexander, Stetson	87.9
Jason Sutherland, Missouri	87.7

3-PT. FIELD-GOAL PCT.

Joe Stafford, Western Carolina	52.7
Ricky Peral, Wake Forest	51.0
Justyn Tebbs, Weber St.	50.0
Aaron Brown, Central Michigan	49.0
Isaac Fontaine, Washington St.	48.5
Mike DeRocckis, Drexel	47.8
Mike Frensley, St. Peter's	47.2
Pete Lisicky, Penn St.	47.1
Jimmy DeGraffenried, Weber St.	47.0
Justin Jones, Utah St.	46.7
Shane Miller, Fairfield	46.7

SCORING OFFENSE, TEAM

Troy St.	94.5
Kentucky	91.4
Marshall	91.4
George Mason	90.5
Southern-B.R.	90.0
Mississippi Valley St.	85.7
Southeastern Louisiana	85.0
Davidson	84.3
Virginia Military	84.2
Weber St.	84.1

NCAA MEN'S TOURNAMENT 1996

EAST

1. Massachusetts 92
16. Central Florida 70
> Massachusetts 79

8. Bradley 58
9. Stanford 66
> Stanford 74

> Massachusetts 86

5. Penn St. 60
12. Arkansas 86
> Arkansas 65

> Arkansas 63

4. Marquette 68
13. Monmouth 40
> Marquette 56

> North Carolina 73

6. North Carolina 83
11. New Orleans 62
> North Carolina 73

> Massachusetts 79

3. Texas 92
14. N. Illinois 73
> Texas Tech 92

> Texas Tech 90

7. New Mexico 69
10. Kansas St. 48
> New Mexico 62

> Georgetown 62

2. Georgetown 93
15. Miss. Valley St. 56
> Georgetown 73

> Georgetown 98

> Massachusetts 74

MIDWEST

1. Kentucky 110
16. San Jose St. 72
> Kentucky 84

8. Wisconsin-GB 48
9. Virginia Tech 61
> Virginia Tech 60

> Kentucky 101

5. Iowa St. 74
12. California 64
> Iowa St. 67

> Kentucky 83

4. Utah 72
13. Canisius 43
> Utah 73

> Utah 70

6. Louisville 82 (OT)
11. Tulsa 80
> Louisville 68

> Louisville 59

3. Villanova 92
14. Portland 58
> Villanova 64

> Wake Forest 60

7. Michigan 76
10. Texas 80
> Texas 62

> Wake Forest 63

2. Wake Forest 62
15. N.E. Louisiana 50
> Wake Forest 65

> Kentucky 81

> Kentucky 76
> Syracuse 67

SOUTHEAST

1. Connecticut 68
16. Colgate 59
> Connecticut 95

8. Duke 60
9. E. Michigan 75
> E. Michigan 81

> Connecticut 55

5. Mississippi St. 58
12. Virginia Comm. 51
> Mississippi St. 63

> Mississippi St. 73

4. UCLA 41
13. Princeton 43
> Princeton 41

> Mississippi St. 60

6. Indiana 51
11. Boston College 64
> Boston College 89

> Georgia Tech 70

3. Georgia Tech 90
14. Austin Peay 79
> Georgia Tech 103

> Cincinnati 63

7. Temple 61
10. Oklahoma 43
> Temple 65

> Cincinnati 87

2. Cincinnati 66
15. N.C.-Greensboro 61
> Cincinnati 78

> Mississippi St. 69

WEST

1. Purdue 73
16. W. Carolina 71
> Purdue 69

8. Georgia 81
9. Clemson 74
> Georgia 76

> Georgia 81

5. Memphis 63
12. Drexel 75
> Drexel 58

> Syracuse 69

4. Syracuse 88
13. Montana St. 55
> Syracuse 69

> Syracuse 83

6. Iowa 81
11. G. Washington 79
> Iowa 73

> Arizona 87

3. Arizona 90
14. Valparaiso 51
> Arizona 87

> Arizona 80

7. Maryland 79
10. Santa Clara 91
> Santa Clara 51

> Kansas 83

2. Kansas 92
15. S. Carolina St. 54
> Kansas 76

> Syracuse 60

> Syracuse 77

1996 NCAA FINALS BOX SCORE

Kentucky 76, Syracuse 67

Syracuse	MIN	FG-A	FT-A	REB	AST	PF	PTS
Burgan	39	7-10	2-5	2-8	1	5	19
Wallace	38	11-19	5-5	3-10	1	5	29
Hill	28	3-9	1-1	2-10	1	2	7
Sims	38	2-5	1-2	1-2	7	2	6
Cipolla	35	3-8	0-0	0-1	2	1	6
Reafsnyder	13	0-1	0-0	0-4	0	0	0
Janulis	8	0-0	0-0	0-2	0	2	0
Nelson	1	0-0	0-0	0-0	0	0	0
Totals	200	26-52	9-13	8-37	12	17	67

FGP—.500. FTP—.692. 3-PT FGP—6-15, .400
(Burgan 3-5, Wallace 2-3, Sims 1-4, Cipolla 0-3).

Kentucky	MIN	FG-A	FT-A	REB	AST	PF	PTS
Anderson	16	4-8	1-1	3-4	1	2	11
Walker	32	4-12	3-6	4-9	4	2	11
McCarty	19	2-6	0-0	5-7	3	3	4
Delk	37	8-20	1-2	1-7	2	2	24
Epps	35	0-6	0-0	1-4	7	1	0
Pope	27	1-6	2-2	1-3	2	3	4
Mercer	24	8-12	1-1	1-2	2	3	20
Sheppard	7	1-2	0-1	1-2	0	3	2
Edwards	3	0-1	0-0	0-0	1	0	0
Totals	200	28-73	8-13	17-38	22	19	76

FGP—.384. FTP—.615. 3-PT FGP—12-27, .444 (Delk
7-12, Mercer 3-4, Anderson 2-3, Walker 0-1,
Sheppard 0-1, Pope 0-2, Epps 0-3).

Halftime—Kentucky 42, Syracuse 33.
Attendance—19,229 (The Meadowlands).

1996 NIT RESULTS

First Round
Rhode Island 82, Marist 77
College of Charleston 55, Tennessee 49
South Carolina 100, Davidson 73
Michigan St. 64, Washington 50
Minnesota 68, St. Louis 52
Missouri 89, Murray St. 85
Illinois St. 73, Mount St. Mary's, 49
Wisconsin 55, Manhattan 42
Tulane 87, Auburn 73, OT
Vanderbilt 86, Arkansas-Little Rock 80
Alabama 72, Illinois 69
Fresno St. 58, Miami, Ohio 57
St. Joseph's 82, Iona 78
Nebraska 91, Colorado St. 83
Washington St. 92, Gonzaga 73
Providence 91, Fairfield 79

Second Round
South Carolina 80, Vanderbilt 70
Tulane 84, Minnesota 65
Illinois St. 77, Wisconsin 62
Alabama 72, Missouri 49
St. Joseph's 82, Providence 62
Nebraska 82, Washington St. 73
Fresno St. 80, Michigan St. 70
Rhode Island 62, College of Charleston 58, OT

Quarterfinals
Alabama 68, South Carolina 67
Tulane 83, Illinois St. 72
St. Joseph's 76, Rhode Island 59
Nebraska 83, Fresno St. 71

Semifinals
St. Joseph's 74, Alabama 69
Nebraska 90, Tulane 78

Finals
Nebraska 60, St. Joseph's 56

FINAL A.P. WOMEN'S POLL, 1995-96

	W-L	Points
1. Louisiana Tech (35)	28-1	994
2. Connecticut (2)	30-3	945
3. Stanford (1)	25-2	912
4. Tennessee	26-4	882
5. Georgia (1)	23-4	854
6. Old Dominion	27-2	780
7. Iowa	25-3	742
8. Penn St.	25-6	716
9. Texas Tech	24-4	651
10. Alabama	22-7	617
11. Virginia	23-6	540
12. Vanderbilt	20-7	538
13. Duke	25-6	500
14. Clemson	22-7	470
15. Purdue	20-10	451
16. Florida	21-8	416
17. Colorado	25-8	319
18. Wisconsin	20-7	290
19. Auburn	20-8	284
20. Kansas	20-9	207
21. Notre Dame	22-7	172
22. Oregon St.	19-8	161
23. North Carolina St.	19-9	140
24. Mississippi	18-10	123
25. Texas A&M	20-11	51

Poll taken prior to the NCAA Tournament. Won-loss
records reflect performances at the time the poll was
taken. First-place votes in parentheses.

NCAA WOMEN'S TOURNAMENT
1996

EAST

1. Tennessee 97
16. Radford 56

Tennessee 97

8. Memphis 75
9. Ohio St. 97

Ohio St. 65

Tennessee 92

5. Texas 73
12. S.W. Missouri 55

Texas 70

Kansas 71

4. Kansas 72
13. Mid. Tenn. 57

Kansas 77

6. G. Washington 83
11. Maine 67

G. Washington 43

Tennessee 52

3. Virginia 100
14. Manhattan 55

Virginia 62

Virginia 72

7. Mississippi 53
10. Toledo 65

Toledo 66

Virginia 46

2. Old Dominion 63
15. Holy Cross 66

Old Dominion 72

Old Dominion 60

Tennessee 88 (OT)

MIDEAST

1. Connecticut 94
16. Howard 63

Connecticut 88

8. Massachusetts 57
9. Mich. St. 60 (OT)

Michigan St. 68

Connecticut 72

5. Florida 61
12. San Francisco 68

San Francisco 64

San Francisco 44

4. Duke 85
13. J. Madison 53

Duke 60

Connecticut 67

6. Wisconsin 74
11. Oregon 60

Wisconsin 82

Vanderbilt 74

3. Vanderbilt 100
14. Harvard 83

Vanderbilt 96

Vanderbilt 57

7. DePaul 96
10. SMU 82

DePaul 71

Iowa 63

2. Iowa 72
15. Butler 67

Iowa 72

Connecticut 83

**Tennessee 83
Georgia 65**

WEST

1. Stanford 82
16. Grambling 43

Stanford 94

8. Colorado St. 66
9. Nebraska 62

Colorado St. 63

Stanford 78 (OT)

5. N.C. State 77
12. Montana 66

N.C. State 68

Stanford 71

4. Alabama 95
13. Appalachian St. 56

Alabama 76

Alabama 88

6. Auburn 73
11. Hawaii 53

Auburn 68

Auburn 75

3. Colorado 83
14. Tulane 75

Colorado 61

Auburn 57

7. Texas A&M 68
10. Kent 72

Kent 59

Penn St. 69

2. Penn St. 94
15. Young. St. 74

Penn St. 86

Stanford 76

MIDWEST

1. Louisiana Tech 98
16. Central Florida 41

Louisiana Tech 84

8. Utah 66
9. S. Mississippi 74

S. Mississippi 46

Louisiana Tech 66

5. Purdue 60
12. Notre Dame 73

Notre Dame 67

Louisiana Tech 76

4. Texas Tech 78
13. Portland 61

Texas Tech 82

Texas Tech 55

6. Oregon 65
11. S.F. Austin 67

S.F. Austin 93 (OT)

S.F. Austin 64

3. Clemson 79
14. Austin Peay 52

Clemson 88

Georgia 90

7. Oklahoma St. 90
10. Rhode Island 82

Oklahoma St. 55

Georgia 78

2. Georgia 98
15. St. Francis 66

Georgia 83

Georgia 86

NATIONAL CHAMPIONS

YEAR	CHAMPION	RECORD	COACH	YEAR	CHAMPION	RECORD	COACH
1901	Yale	10-4	No coach	1949	Kentucky	32-2	Adolph Rupp
1902	Minnesota	11-0	Louis Cooke	1950	CCNY	24-5	Not Holman
1903	Yale	15-1	W.H. Murphy	1951	Kentucky	32-2	Adolph Rupp
1904	Columbia	17-1	No coach	1952	Kansas	28-3	Phog Allen
1905	Columbia	19-1	No coach	1953	Indiana	23-3	Branch McCracken
1906	Dartmouth	16-2	No coach	1954	La Salle	26-4	Ken Loeffler
1907	Chicago	22-2	Joseph Raycroft	1955	San Francisco	28-1	Phil Woolpert
1908	Chicago	21-2	Joseph Raycroft	1956	San Francisco	29-0	Phil Woolpert
1909	Chicago	12-0	Joseph Raycroft	1957	North Carolina	32-0	Frank McGuire
1910	Columbia	11-1	Harry Fisher	1958	Kentucky	23-6	Adolph Rupp
1911	St. John's	14-0	Claude Allen	1959	California	25-4	Pete Newell
1912	Wisconsin	15-0	Doc Meanwell	1960	Ohio St.	25-3	Fred Taylor
1913	Navy	9-0	Louis Wenzell	1961	Cincinnati	27-3	Edwin Jucker
1914	Wisconsin	15-0	Doc Meanwell	1962	Cincinnati	29-2	Edwin Jucker
1915	Illinois	16-0	Ralph Jones	1963	Loyola (IL)	29-2	George Ireland
1916	Wisconsin	20-1	Doc Meanwell	1964	UCLA	30-0	John Wooden
1917	Washington St.	25-1	Doc Bohler	1965	UCLA	28-2	John Wooden
1918	Syracuse	16-1	Edmund Dollard	1966	Texas Western	28-1	Don Haskins
1919	Minnesota	13-0	Louis Cooke	1967	UCLA	30-0	John Wooden
1920	Pennsylvania	22-1	Lon Jourdet	1968	UCLA	29-1	John Wooden
1921	Pennsylvania	21-2	Edward McNichol	1969	UCLA	29-1	John Wooden
1922	Kansas	16-2	Phog Allen	1970	UCLA	28-2	John Wooden
1923	Kansas	17-1	Phog Allen	1971	UCLA	29-1	John Wooden
1924	North Carolina	25-0	Bo Shepard	1972	UCLA	30-0	John Wooden
1925	Princeton	21-2	Al Wittmer	1973	UCLA	30-0	John Wooden
1926	Syracuse	19-1	Lew Andreas	1974	N. Carol. St.	30-1	Norm Sloan
1927	Notre Dame	19-1	George Keogan	1975	UCLA	28-3	John Wooden
1928	Pittsburgh	21-0	Doc Carlson	1976	Indiana	32-0	Bobby Knight
1929	Montana St.	36-2	Shubert Dyche	1977	Marquette	25-7	Al McGuire
1930	Pittsburgh	23-2	Doc Carlson	1978	Kentucky	30-2	Joe B. Hall
1931	Northwestern	16-1	Dutch Lonborg	1979	Michigan St.	26-6	Jud Heathcote
1932	Purdue	17-1	Piggy Lambert	1980	Louisville	33-3	Denny Crum
1933	Kentucky	20-3	Adolph Rupp	1981	Indiana	26-9	Bobby Knight
1934	Wyoming	26-3	Dutch Witte	1982	North Carolina	32-2	Dean Smith
1935	New York	18-1	Howard Cann	1983	N. Carol. St.	28-8	Jim Valvano
1936	Notre Dame	22-2-1	George Keogan	1984	Georgetown	34-3	John Thompson
1937	Stanford	25-2	John Bunn	1985	Villanova	25-10	Rollie Massimino
1938	Temple	23-2	James Usilton	1986	Louisville	32-7	Denny Crum
1939	Oregon	29-5	Howard Hobson	1987	Indiana	30-4	Bobby Knight
1940	Indiana	20-3	Branch McCracken	1988	Kansas	27-11	Larry Brown
1941	Wisconsin	20-3	Bud Foster	1989	Michigan	30-7	Steve Fisher
1942	Stanford	28-4	Everett Dean	1990	UNLV	35-5	Jerry Tarkanian
1943	Wyoming	31-2	Everett Shelton	1991	Duke	32-7	Mike Krzyzewski
1944	Utah	22-4	Vadal Peterson	1992	Duke	34-2	Mike Krzyzewski
1945	Oklahoma A&M	27-4	Hank Iba	1993	North Carolina	34-4	Dean Smith
1946	Oklahoma A&M	31-2	Hank Iba	1994	Arkansas	31-3	Nolan Richardson
1947	Holy Cross	27-3	Doggie Julian	1995	UCLA	31-2	Jim Harrick
1948	Kentucky	36-3	Adolph Rupp	1996	Kentucky	33-2	Rick Pitino

FINAL FOUR RESULTS

YEAR	CHAMPION	FINALS OPP.	SCORE	RUNNER-UP	RUNNER-UP
1939	Oregon	Ohio St.	46-33	Oklahoma	Villanova
1940	Indiana	Kansas	60-42	Duquesne	Southern Cal.
1941	Wisconsin	Washington St.	39-34	Arkansas	Pittsburgh
1942	Stanford	Dartmouth	53-38	Colorado	Kentucky
1943	Wyoming	Georgetown	46-34	DePaul	Texas
1944	Utah	Dartmouth	42-40 (OT)	Iowa St.	Ohio St.
1945	Oklahoma A&M	New York	49-45	Arkansas	Ohio St.
1946	Oklahoma A&M	North Carolina	43-40	Ohio St.	California
1947	Holy Cross	Oklahoma	58-47	Texas	CCNY
1948	Kentucky	Baylor	58-42	Holy Cross	Kansas St.
1949	Kentucky	Oklahoma A&M	46-36	Illinois	Oregon St.
1950	CCNY	Bradley	71-68	N. Carol. St.	Baylor
1951	Kentucky	Kansas St.	68-58	Illinois	Oklahoma A&M
1952	Kansas	St. John's	80-63	Illinois	Santa Clara
1953	Indiana	Kansas	69-68	Washington	Louisiana St.
1954	La Salle	Bradley	92-76	Penn St.	Southern Cal.
1955	San Francisco	La Salle	77-63	Colorado	Iowa
1956	San Francisco	Iowa	83-71	Temple	SMU
1957	North Carolina	Kansas	54-53 (3 OT)	San Francisco	Michigan St.
1958	Kentucky	Seattle	84-72	Temple	Kansas St.
1959	California	West Virginia	71-70	Cincinnati	Louisville
1960	Ohio St.	California	75-55	Cincinnati	New York
1961	Cincinnati	Ohio St.	70-65 (OT)	St. Joe's (PA)	Utah
1962	Cincinnati	Ohio St.	71-59	Wake Forest	UCLA
1963	Loyola (IL)	Cincinnati	60-58 (OT)	Duke	Oregon St.
1964	UCLA	Duke	98-83	Michigan	Kansas St.
1965	UCLA	Michigan	91-80	Princeton	Wichita St.
1966	Texas Western	Kentucky	72-65	Duke	Utah
1967	UCLA	Dayton	79-64	Houston	North Carolina
1968	UCLA	North Carolina	78-55	Ohio St.	Houston
1969	UCLA	Purdue	92-72	Drake	North Carolina
1970	UCLA	Jacksonville	80-69	New Mexico St.	St. Bonaventure
1971	UCLA	Villanova	68-62	W. Kentucky	Kansas
1972	UCLA	Florida St.	81-76	North Carolina	Louisville
1973	UCLA	Memphis St.	87-66	Indiana	Providence
1974	N. Carol. St.	Marquette	76-64	UCLA	Kansas
1975	UCLA	Kentucky	92-85	Louisville	Syracuse
1976	Indiana	Michigan	86-68	UCLA	Rutgers
1977	Marquette	North Carolina	67-59	UNLV	N.C.-Charlotte
1978	Kentucky	Duke	94-88	Arkansas	Notre Dame
1979	Michigan St.	Indiana St.	75-64	DePaul	Pennsylvania
1980	Louisville	UCLA	59-54	Purdue	Iowa
1981	Indiana	North Carolina	63-50	Virginia	Louisiana St.
1982	North Carolina	Georgetown	63-62	Houston	Louisville
1983	N. Carol. St.	Houston	54-52	Georgia	Louisville
1984	Georgetown	Houston	84-75	Kentucky	Virginia
1985	Villanova	Georgetown	66-64	Memphis St.	St. John's
1986	Louisville	Duke	72-69	Kansas	Louisiana St.
1987	Indiana	Syracuse	74-73	Providence	UNLV
1988	Kansas	Oklahoma	83-79	Arizona	Duke
1989	Michigan	Seton Hall	80-79 (OT)	Duke	Illinois
1990	UNLV	Duke	103-73	Arkansas	Georgia Tech
1991	Duke	Kansas	72-65	North Carolina	UNLV
1992	Duke	Michigan	71-51	Indiana	Cincinnati
1993	North Carolina	Michigan	77-71	Kansas	Kentucky
1994	Arkansas	Duke	76-72	Arizona	Florida
1995	UCLA	Arkansas	89-78	Oklahoma St.	North Carolina
1996	Kentucky	Syracuse	76-67	Massachusetts	Mississippi St.

DIVISION I CAREER LEADERS

POINTS

3,667	Pete Maravich, Louisiana St.
3,249	Freeman Williams, Portland St.
3,217	Lionel Simmons, La Salle
3,165	Alphonso Ford, Miss. Valley St.
3,066	Harry Kelly, Texas Southern
3,008	Hersey Hawkins, Bradley
2,973	Oscar Robertson, Cincinnati
2,951	Danny Manning, Kansas
2,914	Alfredrick Hughes, Loyola (IL)
2,884	Elvin Hayes, Houston

SCORING AVERAGE

44.2	Pete Maravich, Louisiana St.
34.6	Austin Carr, Notre Dame
33.8	Oscar Robertson, Cincinnati
33.1	Calvin Murphy, Niagara
32.7	Dwight Lamar, S.W. Louisiana
32.5	Frank Selvy, Furman
32.3	Rick Mount, Purdue
32.1	Darrell Floyd, Furman
32.0	Nick Werkman, Seton Hall
31.5	Willie Humes, Idaho St.

REBOUNDS

2,201	Tom Gola, La Salle
2,030	Joe Holup, George Washington
1,916	Charlie Slack, Marshall
1,884	Ed Conlin, Fordham
1,802	Dickie Hemric, Wake Forest
1,751	Paul Silas, Creighton
1,716	Art Quimby, Connecticut
1,688	Jerry Harper, Alabama
1,679	Jeff Cohen, William & Mary
1,675	Steve Hamilton, Morehead St.

ASSISTS

1,076	Bobby Hurley, Duke
1,038	Chris Corchiani, N. Carolina St.
983	Keith Jennings, E. Tennessee St.
960	Sherman Douglas, Syracuse
956	Tony Miller, Marquette
950	Greg Anthony, Portland & UNLV
939	Gary Payton, Oregon St.
902	Orlando Smart, San Francisco
894	Andre LaFleur, Northeastern
884	Jim Les, Bradley

STEALS

376	Eric Murdock, Providence
344	Gerald Walker, San Francisco
344	Johnny Rhodes, Maryland
341	Michael Anderson, Drexel
341	Kenny Robertson, Cleveland St.
334	Keith Jennings, E. Tennessee St.
329	Greg Anthony, Portland & UNLV
328	Chris Corchiani, N. Carolina St.
321	Gary Payton, Oregon St.
314	Mark Woods, Wright St.
314	Pointer Williams, Tulane/McNeese St.

BLOCKED SHOTS

453	Alonzo Mourning, Georgetown
425	Theo Ratliff, Wyoming
419	Rodney Blake, St. Joseph's (PA)
412	Shaquille O'Neal, Louisiana St.
409	Kevin Roberson, Vermont
399	Jim McIlvaine, Marquette
392	Tim Perry, Temple
379	Tim Duncan, Wake Forest
374	Pervis Ellison, Louisville
365	Acie Earl, Iowa
354	Dikembe Mutombo, Georgetown

FIELD-GOAL PCT.

69.0	Ricky Nedd, Appalachian St.
68.5	Steve Scheffler, Purdue
67.8	Steve Johnson, Oregon St.
66.8	Murray Brown, Florida St.
66.5	Lee Campbell, S.W. Missouri St.
66.4	Warren Kidd, Middle Tenn. St.
66.2	Joe Senser, West Chester
65.6	Kevin Magee, California-Irvine
65.4	Orlando Phillips, Pepperdine
65.1	Bill Walton, UCLA

FREE-THROW PCT.

90.9	Greg Starrick, Kentucky & S. Illinois
90.1	Jack Moore, Nebraska
90.0	Steve Henson, Kansas St.
89.8	Steve Alford, Indiana
89.8	Bob Lloyd, Rutgers
89.5	Jim Barton, Dartmouth
89.2	Tommy Boyer, Arkansas
88.8	Rob Robbins, New Mexico
88.5	Sean Miller, Pittsburgh
88.5	Ron Perry, Holy Cross

3-PT FIELD-GOAL PCT.

49.7	Tony Bennett, Wisc.-Green Bay
49.3	Keith Jennings, E. Tennessee St.
47.5	Kirk Manns, Michigan St.
47.2	Tim Locum, Wisconsin
46.6	David Olson, Eastern Illinois
46.0	Sean Jackson, Ohio & Princeton
46.0	Barry Booker, Vanderbilt
45.9	Kevin Booth, Mt. St. Mary's
45.9	Dave Calloway, Monmouth
45.8	Tony Ross, San Diego St.

MOST VICTORIES, COACH

876	Adolph Rupp
830	Dean Smith
767	Hank Iba
759	Ed Diddle
746	Phog Allen
724	Ray Meyer
665	Don Haskins
664	John Wooden
660	Norm Stewart
659	Bob Knight